a DICTIONARY of the Avant-Gardes

Other Works by Richard Kostelanetz

Books Authored

The Theatre of Mixed Means (l968)
Master Minds (l969)
Visual Language (1970)
In the Beginning (1971)
The End of Intelligent Writing (1974)
I Articulations/Short Fictions (l974)
Recyclings, Volume One (1974)
Openings & Closings (1975)
Portraits from Memory (1975)
Constructs (1975)
Numbers: Poems & Stories (1975)
Modulations/Extrapolate/Come Here (1975)
Illuminations (1977)
One Night Stood (1977)
Wordsand (1978)
Constructs Two (1978)
"The End" Appendix/"The End" Essentials (l979)
Twenties in the Sixties (l979)
And So Forth (1979)
More Short Fictions (1980)
Metamorphosis in the Arts (1980)
The Old Poetries and the New (l98l)
Reincarnations (1981)
Autobiographies (l98l)
Arenas/Fields/Pitches/Turfs (l982)
Epiphanies (1983)
American Imaginations (1983)
Recyclings (1984)
Autobiographien New York Berlin (1986)
The Old Fictions and the New (1987)
Prose Pieces/Aftertexts (1987)
The Grants-Fix (1987)
Conversing with Cage (1988)
On Innovative Music(ian)s (1989)
Unfinished Business: An Intellectual Nonhistory (1990)
The New Poetries and Some Old (1991)
Politics in the African-American Novel (1991)
Solos, Duets, Trios, & Choruses (1991)
On Innovative Art(ist)s (1992)
Wordworks: Poems New & Selected (1993)
Twenty-Five Years After (1993)
On Innovative Performance(s) (1994)
Minimal Fictions (1994)
Fillmore East: Recollections of Rock Theater (1995)
Crimes of Culture (1995)
Radio Writings (1995)
An ABC of Contemporary Reading (1995)
John Cage (ex)plain(ed) (1996)
Thirty Years of Critical Engagements with John Cage (1996)
Vocal Shorts: Collected Performance Texts (1998)
3-Element Stories (1998)
Political Essays (1999)
30 Years of Visable Writing (1999)

Books Edited

On Contemporary Literature (l964, l969)
Twelve from the Sixties (l967)
The Young American Writers (l967)
Beyond Left & Right: Radical Thought for Our Times (l968)
Possibilities of Poetry (l970)
Imaged Words & Worded Images (l970)
Moholy-Nagy (l970, 1991)
John Cage (1970, 1991)
Social Speculations (l97l)
Human Alternatives (l97l)
Future's Fictions (l97l)
Seeing through Shuck (l972)
In Youth (l972)
Breakthrough Fictioneers (l973)
The Edge of Adaptation (l973)
Essaying Essays (l975)
Language & Structure (l975)
Younger Critics in North America (l976)
Esthetics Contemporary (l978, 1989)
Assembling Assembling (l978)
Visual Literature Criticism (l979)
Text-Sound Texts (l980)
The Yale Gertrude Stein (l980)
Scenarios (l980)
Aural Literature Criticism (l98l)
The Literature of SoHo (1981)
American Writing Today (l98l, 1991)
The Avant-Garde Tradition in Literature (l982)
Gertrude Stein Advanced (1989)
Merce Cunningham (1992, 1998)
John Cage: Writer (1993, 2000)
Writings About John Cage (1993)
Nicolas Slonimsky: The First 100 Years (1994)
A Portable Baker's Biographical Dictionary of Musicians (1995)
A B. B. King Companion (1997)
Writings on Glass (1997, 1999)
A Frank Zappa Companion (1997)
AnOther E. E. Cummings (1998)

Books Co-authored & Edited

The New American Arts (1965)

Books Co-compiled & Introduced

Assembling (Twelve vols, 1970-1981)

Performance Scripts

Epiphanies (1980)
Seductions (1986)
Lovings (1991)

Limited Editions: Books and Prints

Numbers One (1974)
Word Prints (1975)
Tabula Rasa (1978)
Inexistences (1978)
Constructs Three (1991)
Intermix (1991)
Constructs Four (1991)
Fifty Untitled Constructivist Fictions (1991)
Constructs Five (1991)
Flipping (1991)
Constructs Six (1991)
Two Intervals (1991)
Parallel Intervals (1991)

Audiotapes

Experimental Prose (1976)
Openings & Closings (1976)
Foreshortenings & Other Stories (1977)
Praying to the Lord (1977, 1981)
Asdescent/Anacatabasis (1978)
Invocations (1981)
Seductions (1981)
The Gospels/Die Evangelien (1982)
Relationships (1983)
The Eight Nights of Hanukkah (1983)
Two German Hörspiel (1983)
New York City (1984)
A Special Time (1985)
Le Bateau Ivre/The Drunken Boat (1986)
Resume (1988)
Onomatopoeia (1988)
Carnival of the Animals (1988)
Americas' Game (1988)
Kaddish (1990)
Epiphanies (1982)
More or Less (1988)

Extended Radio Features

Audio Art (1978)
Text-Sound in North America (1981)
Hörspiel USA: Radio Comedy (1983)
Glenn Gould as a Radio Artist (1983)
Audio Writing (1984)
Audio Comedy Made in America Today (1986)
New York City Radio (1987)
Orson Welles as an Audio Artist (1988)
Norman Corwin: Pioniere der US-Radiokunst (1991)

Videotapes

Three Prose Pieces (1975)
Openings & Closings (1975)
Declaration of Independence (1979)
Epiphanies (1980)
Partitions (1986)
Video Writing (1987)
Home Movies Reconsidered (1987)
Two Erotic Videotapes (1988)
Americas' Game (1988)
Invocations (1988)
The Gospels Abridged (1988)
Kinetic Writing (1989)
Video Strings (1989)
Onomatopoeia (1990)
String Two (1990)
Kaddish (1990)

Films Produced & Directed

Epiphanies (in German, 1983; in English, 1981)

Films Co-produced & Directed

Constructivist Fictions (1978)
Ein Verlorenes Berlin (1983)
Ett Forlorat Berlin (1984)
A Berlin Lost (1985)
Berlin Perdu (1986)
El Berlin Perdido (1987)
Berlin Sche-Einena Jother (1988)

Holograms

On Holography (1978)
Antitheses (1985)
Hidden Meanings (1989)

Retrospective Exhibitions

Wordsand (1978)

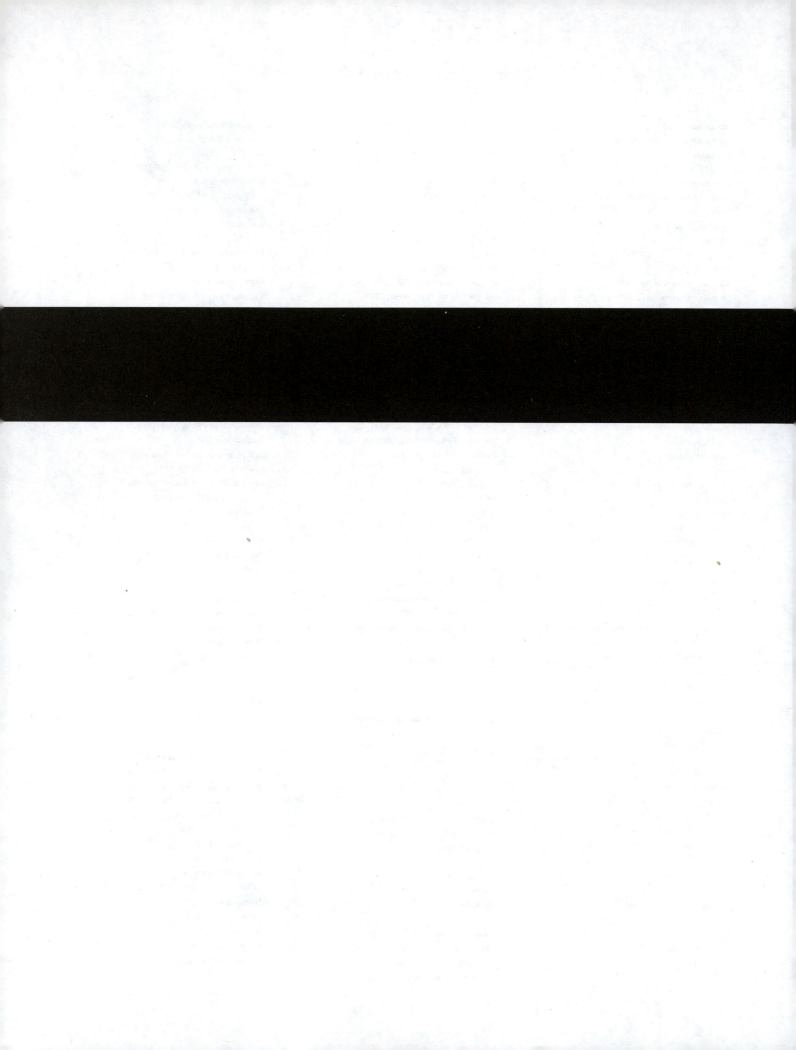

a DICTIONARY of the Avant-Gardes

SECOND EDITION

BY RICHARD KOSTELANETZ

WITH CONTRIBUTIONS FROM H. R. BRITTAIN, RICHARD CARLIN, MARK DANIEL COHEN, JOHN ROBERT COLOMBO, TONY COULTER, CHARLES DORIA, MICHAL ULRIKE DORDA, BOB GRUMMAN, ROBERT HALLER, BROCK HELANDER, GEOF HUTH, GERALD JANECEK, KATY MATHESON, GLORIA S. AND FRED W. MCDARRAH, MICHAEL PETERS, DOUGLAS PUCHOWSKI, JOHN ROCCO, IGOR SATANOVSKY, NICOLAS SLONIMSKY, FRED TRUCK

SENIOR EDITOR, RESEARCHER, AND BIBLIOGRAPHER:
DOUGLAS PUCHOWSKI

ASSISTANT EDITOR: GREGORY BRENDER

ROUTLEDGE
NEW YORK & LONDON

The avant-garde was something constituted from moment to moment by artists—a relative few in each moment—going toward what seemed the improbable. It was only after the avant-garde, as we now recognize it, had been under way for some fifty years that the notion of it seemed to begin to correspond to a fixed entity with stable attributes.

—**Clement Greenberg, "Counter-Avant-Garde" (1971)**

In the case of Duchamp, the antagonism he arouses is an element of his role, and even, if one wishes, of his greatness and profundity.

—**Harold Rosenberg, *Art on the Edge* (1975)**

To write a history of the avant-garde is already to contain it: obviously within a narrative structure and thus inevitably within a certain ideological regime, a certain formation of (pre)judgments. Every history is to some extent an attempt to determine (to comprehend and to control) the avant-garde's currency, its demise, or its survival today.

—**Paul Mann, *The Theory-Death of the Avant-Garde* (1991)**

For a very long time everybody refuses and then almost without a pause almost everybody accepts. In the history of the refused in the arts and literature the rapidity of the change is always startling. When the acceptance comes, by that acceptance the thing created becomes a classic. It is a natural phenomenon, a rather extraordinary natural phenomenon that a thing accepted becomes a classic. And what is the characteristic quality of a classic? The characteristic quality of a classic is that it is beautiful. . . . Of course it is beautiful but first all beauty in it is denied and then all the beauty of it is accepted. If every one were not so indolent they would realize that beauty is beauty even when it is irritating and stimulating not only when it is accepted and classic.

—Gertrude Stein, "Composition as Explanation" (1926)

The situation of [Arnold] Schoenberg is typical—he was never in fashion and now he's become old-fashioned.

—Milton Babbitt, *Words about Music* (1987)

The viability of a genre like the viability of a family is based on survival, and the indispensable property of a surviving family is a continuing ability to take in new members who bring fresh genetic material into the old reservoir. So the viability of a genre may depend fairly heavily on an avant-garde activity that has often been seen as threatening its very existence, but is more accurately seen as opening its present to its past and to its future.

—David Antin, "The Stranger at the Door" (1988)

FOR NICOLAS SLONIMSKY

(1894–1995)

Cher maître

Published in 2001 by
Routledge
29 West 35th Street
New York, NY 10001

Published in Great Britain by
Routledge
11 New Fetter Lane
London EC4P 4EE

Routledge is an imprint of the Taylor & Francis Group.

Originally published in 2000 by Schirmer Books, an imprint of the Gale Group.
Reprinted by arrangement with the Gale Group.

Printed in the United States of America on acid free paper.

10 9 8 7 6 5 4 3 2 1

Library of Congress Cataloging-in-Publication Data

Kostelanetz, Richard.
A dictionary of the avant-gardes / by Richard Kostelanetz with contributions from H.R. Brittain . . . [et al.].
p. cm.
Originally published: New York: Schirmer Books, 2000. 2nd ed.
Includes bibliographical references and indexes.
ISBN 0-415-93764-7 (pbk.)
1. Arts, Modern—20th century—Dictionaries. 2. Avant-garde (Aesthetics)—History—20th century—Dictionaries. 3. Artists—Biography—Dictionaries. I. Brittain, H. R. II. Title.

NX456 .K67 20001
700'.411—dc21

2001019929

DESIGN: TOMEK LAMPRECHT STUDIO

Contents

Carl Andre. *Lever*, 1966. Courtesy National Gallery of Canada, Ottawa.

PREFACE

It takes approximately twenty years to make an artistic curiosity out of a modernistic monstrosity, and another twenty to elevate it to a masterpiece.

—Nicolas Slonimsky, *Lexicon of Musical Invective* (1953)

MY PRINCIPAL REASON FOR HAVING DONE AND NOW REDOING a book of this title would be to defend the continuing relevance of the epithet *avant-garde*, which frequently appears in my own critical writing. A second reason is that I enjoy reading cultural dictionaries myself and own a goodly number of them; but as my library lacks any volume resembling a dictionary of avant-gardes, the first reader for any book emblazoned with that title would be myself. A third reason is that I've come to think there is only one art, called Art, and thus that dance, literature, etc., are merely categorical conveniences, designed to make the history and the material of Art more accessible to students and other beginners.

My basic measures of avant-garde work are esthetic innovation and initial unacceptability. Add to this my own taste for art that is extreme, unique, distinct, coherent, witty, technological, and esthetically resonant. (An artist's courage in the choice of subject, such as scatology, say, or child abuse, is not avant-garde if the artist's esthetic is traditional. Nor is the first play by a three-handed dwarf avant-garde by virtue of the peculiarities of its author.) It follows that the most consequential artists, in any medium, are those who make genuine discoveries about the possibilities of art.

Though one often hears about "the death of the avant-garde," usually from publicists with cemeteries to defend, it is not the purpose of this book to engage in an argument I take to be irrelevant at best. Though most entries here feature contemporary avant-garde activities, major historical precursors, some of whom worked two centuries ago, are acknowledged as well. Though the epithet avant-garde is applicable to other cultural domains, they are not covered here. (My editor proposed including the basketball player Daryl Dawkins for inventing "the slam dunk," which is, I suppose, a monumental choreographic innovation, though not commonly regarded as such.)

Proclaiming the avant-garde's death is no less disreputable than the claim, from another corner, of one or another group to represent "*the* avant-garde" to the exclusion of all others. The plural avant-garde*s* in the title is appropriate, as this book contains entries on individuals or developments representing opposed positions, if not contrary esthetics. As I warn in the entry on Pluralism, beware of anyone or any group declaring itself the sole avant-garde, especially if they exclude or ignore people doing work that is roughly similar or closely related. Be even more wary if they try to sell you anything, intellectual as well as physical. Suspect it to be a road map directing all traffic to a dead end.

Trained elaborately in cultural history, I think I can discern the future from the past and thus direction in cultural produce. Because I don't often read newsprint, I can claim resistance to, if not an ignorance of, transient fashions of many kinds. One additional principle behind my writing about the avant-garde in one art is an authority gained from familiarity with avant-garde work in other arts.

This book is admittedly biased, not only in judgments but in selections, because it is impossible to write about the avant-gardes, with any integrity and excellence, without seeming opinionated. (If you don't like opinions, well, you're welcome to read the telephone book.) Because this book was written not just to be consulted but to be read from beginning to end, it eschews abbreviations that interrupt attention and minimizes dependency on cross-references. I would have liked to do more entries on avant-garde artists new to the 1990s, who are true heroes at a time when the idea of an esthetic vanguard has been subjected to all sorts of Philistine attack, and apologize now particularly to those individuals, whoever you are, whose names will be featured in future editions.

Just as most of the first edition of this book was written in several months, so it was rewritten in a comparatively short time. Both then and now I have typically drawn largely upon my memory and sometimes upon earlier reviews and notes that were generally made when I first experienced something important. In writing critically about art (or in editing anthologies or even returning to restaurants), I have learned to trust my memory to separate the strongest work from everything else. One reason for my faith in memory is that it does not lie to me, which is to say that no matter my personal feelings toward an artist, no matter what reviewers might have said about his or her work, no matter what other factors might try to influence me, one working principle remains: If I cannot remember an artist's work distinctly or I cannot from memory alone characterize it, it probably was not strong enough.

It follows that only art already lodged in my head will appear in my critical writing. (One of my favorite ways of testing the true quality of any well-known artist's work is to ask myself, as well as others, whether any specific work[s] can be identified from memory. Thanks mostly to professional hustling, many artists' names are more familiar than their works.) Quite simply, what my memory chose to remember for me became the basis for this *Dictionary*. In the back of my mind was the image of the great Erich Auerbach, a German scholar living in Istanbul during World War II, writing his grandly conceived *Mimesis* (1946) without footnotes, because useful libraries were far away.

Another assumption is that what distinguishes major artists from minor is a vision of singular possibilities for their art and/or for themselves as creative people.

Because I resist doing anything professional, even a dictionary entry, that anyone else can do better, I recruited colleagues to write as many entries as possible, adding a bibliography proportionate to the length of their entry. These colleagues' names appear after the entries (which are otherwise mine); it is not for nothing that their names also accompany mine on the title page. For the late Nicolas Slonimsky, I drew upon texts already published, thanks to our common publisher. I regret that one recruit who promised to write about avant-garde film could not deliver. Within the entries, names and sometimes words set in small caps receive fuller treatment in an alphabetically placed entry. Other names are alphabetically indexed in the back of the book.

My model arts lexicographer, who deserves the dedication of this new edition as well as its predecessor, was Nicolas Slonimsky, who, incidentally, preferred the epithet "Lectionary" to "Dictionary" because the former term refers to reading, the second to speaking. (The first edition of this book appeared before his centenary, 28 April 1994.) My model for the writing of concise remarks is Ambrose Bierce, an

American author too opinionated to be "great," but whose best writing (see the entry on him) nonetheless survives changes in fashion.

This *Dictionary* differs from others in the arts in emphasizing esthetic characterization over, say, a recital of institutional positions held, teachers or students had, or awards won. My implicit rules for writing entries were that they should be at least one hundred words long and that each should portray a person or concept distinctive from all others. More than once I discarded a draft, including some about personal friends, because the results would look suspiciously deficient for failing either of these two requirements. (I considered appending their names here, if only to honor them, but fear that such acknowledgment might have an opposite effect.) Obviously, a book with avant-garde in the title ignores those individuals who have spent their lives trying to be acceptable to one or another orthodoxy (including an earlier avant-garde).

I would be disingenuous if I did not thank previous compilers of basic arts information—all of them—without whom, to be frank, the following pages would have been inconceivable. I quote them frequently, perhaps more frequently than other dictionary authors, out of respect. Another source frequently used, I must confess, was earlier writings by myself. I am also grateful to Richard Carlin for his continuing support in encapsulating a lifetime of enthusiasms and reviewers and readers enthusiastic about the previous edition, as well as my sometime intern, Douglas Puchowski, who assisted the publisher in compiling expanded documentation and collecting illustrations. All of us thank helpful librarians, beginning with those at the Museum of Modern Art, and our excellent student copyeditor and proofreader, Gregory Brender.

Because this book covers several arts, documentation is meant to be more useful than consistent or pseudo-definitive. Following Slonimsky's example, Puchowski and I tried to include complete birthdates and death dates, down to months and days whenever possible, acknowledging that sometimes so much detail was unavailable (particularly about individuals not yet customarily included in such compendia). In the case of Michael Kirby, for example, we asked several people for his complete dates of birth and death: his first ex-wife, his principal academic colleague, the younger admirer who ran Kirby's memorial service, and several keepers of such information; but none knew. Since he didn't receive an obituary in the *New York Times*, it couldn't be a source; and neither he nor his twin brother had children. So we gave up (until an online search of the Social Security Death Index revealed the truth!), as we did with many others not already acknowledged in encyclopedias that customarily include complete birthdates. We gave up likewise with Kenneth King who asked that we put "(unknown)" in lieu of a birthdate, taking a guess on the year while refusing to do what Slonimsky probably would have done: unearthing a birth certificate. To preserve an illusion of pristine research, we could have removed entries whose documentation was incomplete—by and large people whose loss would not be noticed—but instead decided that the inclusion of unfamiliar names was a more important value.

Usually the order of multiple bibliographical entries is based upon the alphabet or chronology; sometimes, the criteria of critical judgment require that certain titles belong at the top of lists. Since the number of works produced by a visual artist usually exceeds the number of novels produced by a writer, lists of the former are necessarily more selective. Puchowski and I listed exhibition catalogs and monographs, because they customarily contain reproductions of a visual artist's major works. (For writers, there is no comparable form.) We've tried to distinguish exhibition catalogs from critical books, though remembering too well that some titles beginning as the former survive as the latter. Especially with literary figures, we've tried to separate biographies from book-length criticism, though likewise understanding that some books serve two functions. In general, we aimed to be clear and informative in the admittedly incomplete documentation, thus always fearing obscurity and confusion more than mistakes, of which there are no doubt many.

We have listed select Websites that we feel (a) will survive long enough so that by the time you look them up, they'll still be there; (b) offer links to other Websites so you can begin searching for more information; (c) are unusual or provocative; (d) and—whenever possible—are prepared by or represent accurately the work of the person to whom they are dedicated. Websites come and go, so you may have to resort to using a good search engine—such as Yahoo or Excite—to find what you're looking for. Our listing of a website is not an endorsement, but an indication of what is available.

A book with so much detail about contemporary figures will surely contain misspellings and other minor errors of fact, especially in the documentation, as well as unintentional omissions. If only to prepare for the possibility of a third edition, the author welcomes corrections and suggestions, by mail, please, if they are to go into a single repository, to P. O. Box 444, Prince St., New York, New York 10012-0008. To be helpful again, we have tried, whenever possible, to add addresses of smaller publishers and record companies, hoping that they survive for the life of this book. If anyone has disappeared, please let me know. No kidding.

Richard Kostelanetz

INTRODUCTION

The avant-garde consists of those who feel sufficiently at ease with the past not to have to compete with it or duplicate it.

—Dick Higgins, "Does Avant-Garde Mean Anything?" (1970)

The avant-garde cannot easily become an academy, because avant-garde artists usually sustain the quality which made them avant-garde artists in the first place. The styles they develop will become academic in other hands.

—Darby Bannard, "Sensibility of the Sixties" (1967)

THE TERM "AVANT-GARDE" REFERS TO THOSE OUT FRONT, forging a path previously unknown, a road that others will take. Initially coined to characterize the shock troops of an army, the epithet passed over into art. Used precisely, avant-garde should refer, first, to rare work that on its first appearance satisfies three discriminatory criteria:

It transcends current esthetic conventions in crucial respects, establishing discernible distance between itself and the mass of recent practices;

it will necessarily take considerable time to find its maximum audience;

and it will probably inspire future, comparably advanced endeavors.

Only a small minority working within any art can ever be avant-garde; for once the majority has caught up to something new, whether as creators or as an audience, those doing something genuinely innovative will, by definition, have established a beachhead someplace beyond. Problems notwithstanding, avant-garde remains a critically useful category.

As a temporal term, avant-garde characterizes art that is "ahead of its time"—that is beginning something—while "decadent" art, by contrast, stands at the end of a prosperous development. "Academic" refers to art that is conceived according to rules that are learned in a classroom; it is temporally post-decadent. Whereas decadent art is created in expectation of an immediate sale, academic artists expect approval from their social superiors, whether they be teachers or higher-ranking colleagues. Both academic art and decadent art are essentially opportunistic, created to realize immediate success, even at the cost of surely disappearing from that corpus of art that survives merely by being remembered. Both decadent art and academic art realize their maximal audience upon initial publication.

One secondary characteristic of avant-garde art is that, in the course of entering new terrain, it violates entrenched rules—it seems to descend from "false premises" or "heretical assumptions"; it makes current "esthetics" seem irrelevant. For instance, Suzanne Langer's theory of symbolism, so prominent in the 1940s and even the 1950s, hardly explains the new art of the past four decades. Relevant though Langer's esthetics were to the arts of Aaron Copland and Martha Graham, among their contemporaries, theories of symbolism offered little insight into, say, the music of John Cage or Milton Babbitt, the choreography of Merce Cunningham, or the poetry of John Ashbery, where what you see or hear is generally most, if not all, of what there is. This sense of irrelevance is less a criticism of Langer's theories, which sixty years ago seemed so persuasively encompassing, than a measure of drastic artistic difference between work prominent then and what followed.

One reason why avant-garde works should be initially hard to comprehend is not that they are intrinsically inscrutable or hermetic but that they defy, or challenge as they defy, the perceptual procedures of artistically educated people. They forbid easy access or easy acceptance, as an audience perceives them as inexplicably different, if not forbiddingly revolutionary. In order to begin to comprehend such art, people must work and think in unfamiliar ways. Nonetheless, if an audience learns to accept innovative work, this will stretch its perceptual capabilities, affording kinds of esthetic experience previously unknown. Edgard Varèse's revolutionary *Ionisation* (1931), for instance, taught a generation of listeners about the possible coherence and beauty in what they had previously perceived as noise.

It follows that avant-garde art usually offends people, especially serious artists, before it persuades, and offends them not in terms of content, but as Art. They assert that Varèse's noise (or Cage's, or Babbitt's) is unacceptable as music. That explains why avant-garde art strikes most of us as esthetically "wrong" before we acknowledge it as possibly "right"; it "fails" before we recognize that it works. (Art that offends by its content challenges only as journalism or gossip, rather than as Art, and is thus likely to disappear as quickly as other journalism or gossip.)

Those most antagonized by the avant-garde are not the general populace, which does not care, but the guardians of culture, who do, whether they be cultural bureaucrats, established artists, or their epigones, because they feel, as they sometimes admit, "threatened."

Though vanguard activity may dominate discussion among sophisticated professionals, it never dominates the general making of art. Most work created in any time, in every art, honors long-passed models. Even today, in the United States, most of the fiction written and published and reviewed has, in form, scarcely progressed beyond early twentieth-century standards; most poetry today is similarly decadent.

The "past" that the avant-garde aims to surpass is not the tradition of art but the currently decadent fashions, for in Harold Rosenberg's words, "Avant-garde art is haunted by fashion." Because avant-gardes in art are customarily portrayed as succeeding one another, the art world is equated with the world of fashion, in which styles also succeed one another. However, in both origins and function, the two are quite different. Fashion relates to the sociology of lucrative taste; avant-garde, to the history of art. In practice, avant-garde activity has a dialectical relationship with fashion, for the emerging remunerative fashions can usually be characterized as a synthesis of advanced art (whose purposes are antithetical to those of fashion) with more familiar stuff. When fashion appears to echo advanced art, a closer look reveals the governing model as art actually of a period recently past.

The term "avant-garde" can also refer to individuals creating such path-forging art; but even by this criterion, the work itself, rather than the artist's intentions, is the ultimate measure of the epithet's applicability to an individual. Thus, an artist or writer is avant-garde only at certain crucial points in his or her creative career, and only those few works that were innovative at their debut comprise the history of modern avant-garde art. The phrase avant-garde may also refer to artistic groups, if and only if most of their members are (or were) crucially contributing to authentically exploratory activity.

The term is sometimes equated with cultural antagonism, for it is assumed that the "avant-garde" leads artists in their perennial war against the Philistines.

However, this Philistine antagonism is a secondary characteristic, as artists' social position and attitudes descend from the fate of their creative efforts, rather than the reverse. Any artist who sets out just to mock the Philistines is not likely to do anything original.

Certain conservative critics have recently asserted that "the avant-garde no longer exists," because, as they see it, the suburban public laps up all new art. However, it is critically both false and ignorant to use a secondary characteristic in lieu of a primary definition. Avant-garde is an art-historical term, not a sociological category. The conservative charge is factually wrong as well, as nearly all avant-gardes in art are ignored by the middle-class public (and its agents in the culture industries), precisely because innovative work is commonly perceived as "peculiar," if not "unacceptable," not only by the mass public but by those producers who make a business of selling culture in large quantities. Indeed, the pervasiveness of those perceptions of oddity is, of course, a patent measure of a work's being art-historically ahead of its time. Those who deny the persistence of the avant-garde are comparable to those who deny the existence of poverty, each by its fakery implicitly rationalizing retrograde attitudes and perhaps the retention of tenuous privileges.

Because the avant-garde claims to be prophetic, the ultimate judge of current claims can only be a future cultural public. For now, future-sensitive critics should proceed under the assumption that they might, just might, be wrong.

Sources: Kirby, Michael. *The Art of Time*. New York: Dutton, 1969; Kostelanetz, Richard, ed. *Esthetics Contemporary*. 2d ed. Buffalo, NY: Prometheus, 1989; Krantz, Stewart. *Science and Technology in the Arts*. New York: Van Nostrand Reinhold, 1974; Mann, Paul. *The Theory-Death of the Avant-Garde*. Bloomington: Indiana University Press, 1991; McLuhan, Marshall. *Understanding Media*. New York: McGraw-Hill, 1964; Moholy-Nagy, L. *Vision in Motion*. Chicago, IL: Paul Theobald, 1947; Motherwell, Robert, ed. *The Dada Painters and Poets*. New York: Wittenborn, 1951; Peckham, Morse. *Man's Rage for Chaos*. Philadelphia: Chilton, 1965.

ABISH, Walter

(24 December 1931).

Born in Vienna, raised in Shanghai's Jewish community during World War II, Abish worked in city planning before he began publishing. The distinguishing mark of his novel *Alphabetical Africa* (1974) is its severe compositional discipline. The first chapter has only words beginning with the letter A ("Ages ago, Alex, Allen and Alva arrived at Antibes," etc.). For the second chapter, he additionally uses words beginning with the letter B. Only by the Z chapter, which is in the middle of the book, does the full alphabet become available, then to contract again to a conclusion composed exclusively of words beginning with the letter A. As JEROME KLINKOWITZ has sensitively written, "Like breathing in and then breathing out, the reader has experienced the expansion and contraction, the life and death of a work of fiction." The next two Abish books are collections of stories, some of them more experimental than others. Each pair of paragraphs in "In So Many Words" is preceded by a numeral announcing how many words are in the following paragraph; while the second paragraph in each pair, set in roman type, tells a dry story, the first paragraph contains all of its successor's words set in italics in alphabetical order. In short, Abish displays a fascination with numbers reminiscent of RAYMOND QUENEAU, though lacking the latter's extravagant wit and audacity. It was Abish's good fortune, or misfortune, to write *How German Is It* (1980), a far more accessible novel that won him a Guggenheim fellowship, a CAPS grant, and later a lush MacArthur fellowship, in addition to a contract from a slick publisher not known for publishing avant-garde writers. The result was *Eclipse Fever* (1993), a fiction more conventional than its predecessors, which nonetheless had minimal impact.

Writings: *Duel Site*. New York: Tibor de Nagy, 1970; *Alphabetical Africa*. New York: New Directions, 1974; *Minds Meet*. New York: New Directions, 1975; *In the Future Perfect*. New York: New Directions, 1977; *How German Is It*. New York: New Directions, 1980; *99: The New Meaning*. Providence, RI: Burning Deck Press, 1990. *Eclipse Fever.* New York: Knopf, 1993.

Criticism: Arias-Misson, Alain. "The Puzzle of Walter Abish," *Sub-Stance* 27, Madison, WI: 1980; Baker, Kenneth. "Restrictive Fiction," *New Directions* 35, New York: 1977; Caramello, Charles. "On the Guideless Guidebooks of Postmodernism," *Sun & Moon*, nos. 9 and 10, 1980; Klinkowitz, Jerome. "Walter Abish: An Interview," *Fiction International* Nos. 4–5, 1975; ——. *The Life of Fiction*. Urbana: University of Illinois Press: 1977.

ABSTRACT EXPRESSIONISM

(c. 1958).

If only because it emphasizes esthetic qualities, this term has come to be the most acceptable epithet for the innovative painting that became prominent in New York in the late 1940s (and was thus sometimes called the "NEW YORK SCHOOL"). Drawing not only from SURREALISM but from JAZZ-BASED ideas of improvisatory gestural expression, these artists laid paint on the canvas in ways that reflected physical attack, whether in the extended dripped lines of Jackson Pollock or in the broad strokes of Franz Kline. "Action painting," another epithet once popular for this style of painting, was coined by the critic Harold Rosenberg, who theorized that these abstractions represented the artist's mental state at the moment(s) of composition. One esthetic characteristic of such painting was "all-over" composition, which is to say that the activity was just as strong near the edges of the canvas as in the center, purportedly in contrast to the more hierarchical focusing typical of traditional art. Willem de Kooning's work is customarily placed within this term, even though his best paintings acknowledge figuration and focusing; so are Burnett Newman and Ad Reinhardt, perhaps because they were roughly the same age as the others (and thus belonged to the "New York School"), even though their art proceeds from nonexpressionist premises.

a

Anthology: Ross, Clifford, ed. *Abstract Expressionism: Creators and Critics*. New York: Abrams, 1990.

Exhibition Catalogs: Arnason, H. H., ed. *American Abstract Expressionists and Imagists*. New York: Guggenheim Museum, 1961; Geldzahler, Henry, et al., with Harold Rosenberg, Robert Rosenblum, Clement Greenberg, William Rubin & Michael Fried. *New York Painting and Sculpture: 1940–1970*. New York; Metropolitan Museum, 1970; Tuchman, Maurice, ed. *The New York School: Abstract Expressionism in the 40s and 50s*. Los Angeles: Los Angeles County Museum of Art, 1971; Hobbs, Robert C., and Gail Levin. *Abstract Expressionism: The Formative Years*. New York: Whitney Museum, 1978; Marter, Joan. *Women and Abstract Expressionism*. New York: Sidney Mishkin Gallery at Baruch College, 1997.

Interpretation: De Kooning, Elaine. *Spirit of Abstract Expression: Selected Writings*. New York: George Braziller, 1994; Foster, Stephen C. *The Critics of Abstract Expressionism*. Ann Arbor: UMI Research, 1981; Greenberg, Clement. *The Collected Essays and Criticism*. Ed. John O'Brien. Chicago: University of Chicago Press, 1986–93; Guilbaut, Serge. *How New York Stole the Idea of Modern Art*. Chicago: University of Chicago Press, 1983; Kingsley, April. *The Turning Point*. New York: Simon & Schuster, 1992; Polcari, Stephen. *Abstract Expressionism and the Modern Experience*. New York: Cambridge University Press, 1991; Rosenberg, Harold. "The American Action Painters" (1952). In *The Tradition of the New*. New York: Horizon, 1959; ——. *De-Definition of Art* (1973). Chicago: University of Chicago Press, 1983; Sandler, Irving. *The Triumph of American Painting*. New York: Praeger, 1970.

Documentation: Goodall, Donald B. *Partial Bibliography of American Abstract-Expressive Painting, 1943–1958*. Los Angeles: University of Southern California Press, 1958.

ABSTRACT MUSIC

(1950s).

Abstraction in music implies a separation of sonic structures from representational images, whether pictorial or psychological. Abstract music is the antonym of all musical styles that are concrete or naturalistic; abstract works are usually short, athematic, and rhythmically asymmetric. Intellectual fantasy, rather than sensual excitation, is the generating impulse of abstract music; its titles are derived from constructivistic and scientific concepts: Structures, Projections, Extensions, Frequencies, Sound. The German composer Boris Blacher has developed a successful form of abstract opera in which concrete action takes place in a swarm of discrete sonic particles, disjected words in several languages, and isolated melodic fragments. Abstract expressionism, a term applied to nonobjective painting, is sometimes used to describe musical works of abstract quality with expressionistic connotations. A subsidiary genre of abstract music is Aleatory Music, in which the process of musical cerebration is replaced by a random interplay of sounds and rhythms.

—Nicolas Slonimsky

Recording: Blacher, Boris. *Abstrakte Oper No. 1*, Frankfurt Radio, 1953.

ABSTRACTION

(c. 5000 B.C.).

This term defines artwork, whether visual, aural, or verbal, that neither represents nor symbolizes anything in the mundane world; but, because pure abstraction is primarily an ideal, it also refers to work that at least approaches the absence of identifiable representation. Although some commentators make a case for abstraction as a new development in the history of visual art, such a generalization necessarily depends upon ignorance of Islamic art that obeys the proscription against graven images. (Those arguing for the uniqueness of modern abstraction dismiss such Islamic art as "decorative.") It must have been avant-garde at its beginnings, precisely because the most instinctive impulse of even the newborn visual artist is representation. Within modern Abstract Art are two divergent traditions, one emphasizing structure and the other favoring expression; examples of both of these traditions appear not only in painting and sculpture but also in music and literature. One reason for the oft-heard piety that "painting is more advanced than poetry" is that abstraction became more acceptable among visual artists than among poets in our century.

Exhibition Catalogs: *Cubism and Abstract Art*. Ed. Alfred H. Barr. New York: MOMA, 1936; *The World of Abstract Art*. New York: American Abstract Artists, 1957; *Paths of Abstract Art*. Ed. E. B. Henning. Cleveland, OH: Cleveland Museum of Art, 1960; *Geometical Abstraction in America*. Ed. John Gordon. New York: Whitney Museum, 1962; *Abstraction: Towards a New Art*. London: Tate, 1980.

Interpretation: Capon, Robin. *Introducing Abstract Painting*. London: Batsford Books, 1973; Hess, Thomas B. *Abstract Painting: Background and American Phase*. New York: Viking, 1951; Haffman, Wener et al. *Abstract Art since 1945*. London: Thames & Hudson, 1971; Osborne, Harold. *Abstraction and Artifice in Twentieth-Century Art*. New York: Oxford University Press, 1979; Seuphor, Michel. *A Dictionary of Abstract Painting: Preceded by a History of Abstract Painting*. New York: Paris Book Centre, 1957; ——. *Abstract Painting from Kandinsky to the Present*. New York: Abrams, 1962; Worringer, Wilhelm. *Abstraction and Empathy* (1953). Trans., Michael Bullock. Chicago: Ivan R. Dee, 1997.

ABSURD, THEATRE OF THE

(c.1961).

The term comes from Martin Esslin's brilliant 1961 book of the same title. In the plays of SAMUEL BECKETT and EUGÈNE IONESCO, and to a lesser extent others, Esslin found nonsensical and ridiculous events that have sufficient metaphysical resonance to suggest the ultimate absurdity, or meaninglessness, of human existence. Reflecting philosophical Existentialism, absurd writing represents an advance on the literature incidentally composed by the existentialist philosophers. If the latter sought a serious surface, the absurdists favored dark comedy. The innovation was to *demonstrate* the theme of absurdity, in contrast to an earlier theater, identified with Jean-Paul Sartre (1905–1980) and Albert Camus (1913–1960), where characters debate it. At the end of Ionesco's *The Chairs*, a particularly neat model of the convention, a hired lecturer addresses a nonexistent audience in an indecipherable tongue. This is the absurd surface. Because the lecturer's message is supposed to represent the final wisdom of a ninety-five-year-old couple, the meaningless message becomes an effective symbol for the metaphysical void. In a more familiar example from Samuel Beckett, two men wait for a mysterious Godot, who obviously is not coming. On the strictly theatrical influence of absurd theater, the *Cambridge Guide to Literature in English* (1988) says: "The carrying of logic *ad absurdum*, the dissolution of language, the bizarre relationship of stage properties to dramatic situation, the diminution of sense by repetition or unexplained intensification, the rejection of narrative continuity, and the refusal to allow character or even scenery to be self-defining have become acceptable stage conventions." (Thanks for the summary.) A quarter-century ago, I found a similar absurdist style in certain early-1960s American fiction by JOHN BARTH, Joseph Heller (1922), and THOMAS PYNCHON, among others. What seemed awesomely original and percipient in 1960s theater and fiction, now strikes most viewers as dated.

a

Writing: Beckett, Samuel. *En attendant Godot* (1952). Trans. by the author as *Waiting for Godot*. New York: Grove, 1954; *Fin de Partie, suivi de Acte Sans Paroles* (1957). Trans. by the author as *Endgame*, followed by *Act Without Words*. New York: Grove, 1958; *Krapp's Last Tape and Other Dramatic Pieces*. New York; Grove, 1960; *Happy Days*. New York: Grove, 1961; Ionesco, Eugène. *Plays*. 7 vols. London & New York: John Calder-Grove Press, 1960.

Interpretation: Esslin, Martin. *The Theatre of the Absurd* (1961). Rev. ed. Garden City, NY: Doubleday Anchor, 1969; Kostelanetz, Richard. "The American Absurd Novel" (1965). In *The Old Fictions and the New*. Jefferson, NC: McFarland, 1987; Cohn, Ruby, ed. *Casebook on Waiting for Godot*. New York: Grove, 1967.

ACADEMIC CRITICS

When professors discuss avant-garde art, particularly literature, they tend to focus upon the more conservative, more accessible dimensions of an artist's work, in part to make their criticism more digestible to their students and colleagues, rather than pursuing radical implications to their critical extremes. Thus, it becomes opportune for even an advocate of the more experimental GERTRUDE STEIN to confine discussion to *Three Lives* (drafted around 1904) and/or *The Autobiography of Alice B. Toklas* (1933); an academic discussion of MERCE CUNNINGHAM, say, will feature his connections to ballet rather than his departures from it; VELIMIR KHLEBNIKOV is portrayed as the epitome of RUSSIAN FUTURISM instead of his more radical colleague ALEKSEI KRUCHONYKH. Academics tend as well to reveal incomplete familiarity with new developments (especially if these would be unknown to their fellow professors).

The now-forgotten books that Wallace Fowlie published twenty to thirty years ago epitomize such deficiencies; J. H. Matthews wrote comparable books two decades ago; Marjorie Perloff (1930), Henry Sayre (1949), and Johanna Drucker (1952), among others, have published similar volumes more recently. One rule evident in these books is simply: When a professor writes three words about an avant-garde subject, one of them is likely to be superficial and a second to reveal ignorance, even if the writing comes accompanied, as it usually is, by encomia from other academics. (If you think about the time and effort spent to get these blurbs, you begin to understand why such books disappoint.)

Among the full-time academics who have written intelligent books on avant-garde art at one time or another, count Sally Banes on dance, GERALD JANECEK in two books on Russian literature, Roger Shattuck only in *The Banquet Years* (1958), MICHAEL KIRBY in *The Art of Time* (1969), Mark Ensign Cory on German radio, John Tytell in *Naked Angels* (1976), Jack Burnham on sculpture, HUGH KENNER on BUCKMINSTER FULLER, L. MOHOLY-NAGY (though he actually worked as an art-college administrator while writing *Vision in Motion*), Jo-Anna Isaak in *The Ruin of Representation* (1986), and the classicist Donald Sutherland writing in 1951 on Gertrude Stein. It is lamentable, alas, that there are not many more titles on this selective list, professors remaining academic, while genuinely innovative art measures itself as avant-garde by maintaining a healthy distance from any academy.

Books: Banes, Sally. *Terpsichore in Sneakers* (1980). 2nd ed. Middletown: Wesleyan University Press, 1987;

Democracy's Body: The Judson Dance Theater 1962–64 (1983). Durham: Duke University, 1993; Burnham, Jack. *Beyond Modern Sculpture*. New York: Braziller, 1968; *The Great Western Salt Works*. New York: Braziller, 1974; Cory, Mark Ensign. *The Emergence of an Acoustical Art Form*. Lincoln: University of Nebraska Studies, 1974; Shattuck, Roger. *The Banquet Years*. New York: Harper, 1958; Tytell, John. *Naked Angels*. New York: McGraw-Hill, 1976.

ACCONCI, Vito

(25 January 1939).

He began as a poet and translator; and though Acconci subsequently had a distinguished career as a visual artist, mounting exhibitions and producing videotapes as well as presenting live performances and INSTALLATIONS, his poetry remains his most innovative work. One 350-line poem was distributed one line per page over 350 separate sheets of paper, which were then bound into 350 copies of Acconci's otherwise uniform magazine, *0 to 9*. His definitive work is *Book Four* (1968), which he self-published in photocopies. As literature on the cusp of CONCEPTUAL ART, it contains a series of self-reflexive texts, beginning with a page that reads at its upper left: "(It stopped back.) ," and then at its lower right: "(This page is not part/of the four books/and is at the top)," with the page entirely blank in between. *Book Four* concludes with a GERTRUDE STEINIAN text in which separate sentences, in sum suggesting a narrative, are each preceded by the numeral "1."

Of Acconci's performance pieces, I remember best one in which he invited you into a kind of confessional booth and told you an authentic secret; another in which he sat at the bottom of a stairwell, blindfolded, with a metal pipe in his hand, defending the space in front of him with a genuine violence; a third, *Seedbed* (1972), in which he purportedly masturbated under a sloping wood floor, letting spectators hear the sound of his effort. Recalling that Acconci attended New York City's most rigorous Jesuit high school, I think he has been making a Catholic art concerned with abnegation and spiritual athleticism.

Besides performance pieces and writings, Acconci also made a series of films and videotapes.

Writings: *Book Four*. Self Published, New York: 1968.

Films/Videos: *Three Frame Studies*, 1969, Super 8 film, 10:58 min., b&w and color, silent; *Applications*, 1970, Super 8 film, 19:32 min., color, silent; *Open-Close*, 1970, Super 8 film, 6:40 min., color, silent; *Openings*, 1970, Super 8 film, 14 min., b&w, silent; *Rubbings*, 1970, Super 8 film, 5:06 min., color, silent; *See Through*, 1970, Super 8 film, 5 min., color, silent; *Three Adaptation Studies*, 1970, Super 8 film, 8:05 min., b&w, silent; *Three Relationship Studies*, 1970, Super 8 film, 12:30 min., b&w and color, silent; *Two Cover Studies*, 1970, Super 8 film, 7:46 min., color, silent; *Two Takes*, 1970, Super 8 film, 9:40 min., b&w, silent; *Association Area*, 1971, 62 min., b&w, sound; *Centers*, 1971, 22:28 min., b&w, sound; *Claim Excerpts*, 1971, 62:11 min., b&w, sound; *Contacts*, 1971, 29:47 min., b&w, sound; *Filler*, 1971, 29:16 min., b&w, sound; *Focal Point*, 1971, 32:47 min., b&w, sound; *Pryings*, 1971, 17:10 min., b&w, sound; *Pull*, 1971, 32:37 min., b&w, sound; *Two Track*, 1971, 28:35 min., b&w, sound; *Waterways: 4 Saliva Studies*, 1971, 22:27 min., b&w, sound; *Conversions*, 1971, Super 8 film, three parts, 65:30 min., b&w, silent; *Pick-ups*, 1971, Super 8 film, 16:50 min., color, silent; *Watch*, 1971, Super 8 film, 9 min., b&w, silent; *Zone*, 1971, Super 8 film, 15:37 min., color, silent; *Remote Control*, 1971, two channels, 62:30 min., b&w, sound; *Face to Face*, 1972, Super 8 film, 15 min., color, silent; *Hand to Hand*, 1972, Super 8 film, 12 min., color, silent; *Face-Off*, 1973, 32:57 min., b&w, sound; *Full Circle*, 1973, 30 min., b&w, sound; *Home Movies*, 1973, 32:19 min., b&w, sound; *Recording Studio From Air Time*, 1973, 36:49 min., b&w, sound; *Stages*, 1973, 32:30 min., b&w, sound; *Theme Song*, 1973, 33:15 min., b&w, sound; *Undertone*, 1973, 34:12 min., b&w, sound; *Walk-Over*, 1973, 30 min., b&w, sound; *My Word*, 1973–74, Super 8 film, 91:30 min., color, silent; *Command Performance*, 1974, 56:40 min., b&w, sound; *Face of the Earth*, 1974, 22:18 min., color, sound; *Open*

Book, 1974, 10:09 min., color, sound; *Shoot*, 1974, 10:18 min., color, sound; *Turn-On*, 1974, 21:52 min., color, sound; *The Red Tapes*, 1976, 141:27 min., b&w, sound; *Election Tape '84*, 1984, 12:34, color, sound.

Exhibition Catalogs: *Leap/Think/Rethink/Fall*. Dayton: Wright State University Press, 1977; *Assembled Works of Art Using Photography as a Construction Element*. Dayton: Wright State University Press, 1990; Kirshner, Judith Russi. *Vito Acconci*. Chicago, IL: Museum of Contemporary Art, 1980.

Websites: http://www.stroom.nl/eng/archief/enexpoacconci.html (includes description of two of Acconci's installations); http://www.eai.org (biography and film list).

Video-Interview: *Willoughby Sharp Videoviews Vito Acconci*. 1973, 62:07 min., b&w.

Interpretation: Diacono, Mario. *Vito Acconci* (in Italian, with illustrations in English and a bibliography). New York: Out of London, 1975; Linker, Kate. *Vito Acconci*. New York: Rizzoli, 1993; Meyer, Ursula. *Conceptual Art*. New York: Dutton, 1972.

ACTION PAINTING

See **ABSTRACT EXPRESSIONISM; ROSENBERG, Harold**.

ACKER, Kathy

(18 April 1947–30 November 1997).

She was a prolific, brilliant writer who had two subjects: previous literature that she would exploit for her own novels, sometimes appropriating whole chunks without acknowledgment, and unfettered female erotic experience. C. Carr in the *Village Voice* speaks of "female narrators who seem interchangeable from book to book, different names tagged to the sound of one voice raging—obscene, cynical, bewildered, and demanding to fuck." I've noticed that women tend to be more enthusiastic about her books than men, perhaps as a successor to Anaïs Nin (1903–77), who pioneered the representation of female eroticism. Perhaps because her prose was more accessible than distinguished—and called more postmodern than modern—Acker was one of the few smallpress writers to be received by commercial publishers without compromising her radical sensibility.

Novels: *The Childlike Life of the Black Tarantula: Some Lives of Murderesses*. New York: Vanishing Rotating Triangle, 1975; *Great Expectations*. San Francisco: Re/Search, 1982; *Blood and Guts in High School*. New York: Grove, 1984; *Don Quixote: Which Was a Dream*. New York: Grove, 1986; *Empire of the Senseless*. New York: Grove, 1988; *Portrait of an Eye: Three Novels*. New York: Pantheon, 1992; *My Mother: Demonology*. New York: Pantheon, 1993.

Website: http://acker.thehub.com.au/

ACTIONISM

(early 1960s, aka Vienna Actionism).

This term historically referred to four Viennese artists who gave highly provocative performances based on bodies—not only their own but those of other people and of animals. Perhaps most refined in the hands of Hermann Nitsch (1938) and his "Orgien Mysterien Theater," presentations typically included recently butchered animals and a good deal of blood (or pseudo-blood), all with an extremism that should be intellectually appealing, were the results not often viscerally disgusting (before such in-your-face moves became more popular in the 1990s, at least in America). Reflecting their collective exacerbated sensibility, Otto Mühl (1925) has written:

> I acted like a murderer against sheet metal, wood, against all possible useful objects of our civilization. I smashed everthing. I smashed it into junk art. My tools were no longer the paintbrush, they were the pick-axe and the hatchet, but even this wasn't enough for me. I invented the material action. This gave me the possibility of coming out with my aggressions much more directly and intensively. I worked with women and men. I showered and smeared them with food. I literally buried them in consumer products.

Willfully provocative, the Actionists, as they were called, were egregiously misrepresented in the American cultural press and so rarely returned there. The others involved were Günter Brus (1938) and Rudolf Schwarzkogler (1940–69). The former gave up live performance after being hounded out of his native country by the Austrian police, instead producing drawings that reflected, more than anyone else, the influence of WILLIAM BLAKE. The last was particularly notorious for willfully inserting blades into his body and, alas, dying young. If they came more often to America, this entry would probably be richer. Their celebrity in Europe notwithstanding, literature in English about the Vienna Actionists is remarkably scarce.

Interpretation: Mühl, Otto. In *Contemporary Artists*. Ed. Muriel Emanuel, et al., eds. New York: St. Martin's, 1983.

ADLER, Larry

(10 December 1914; b. Lawrence A.).

It is said that as a young teenager in Baltimore he won a contest by playing a Beethoven Minuet on the harmonica, a hand-held popular musical instrument also called a "mouth organ." Adler subsequently decided to make it his instrument for playing classical music, including arrangements of solo sonatas by J. S. Bach, that invariably sound fresh, especially on first hearing. In this respect, he foreshadowed later interpretations of Bach for vernacular and new instruments, presaging WALTER CARLOS'S Switched-On Bach (1968) for MOOG synthesizer, among others. Thanks to his virtuosity and musical intelligence, many modern composers have produced works expressly for Adler, including Malcolm Arnold, Paul Hindemith, Darius Milhaud, and Ralph Vaughan-Williams. Exiled from America during 1950s McCarthyism, Adler became a European celebrity, somewhat to America's embarrassment. Ahead of the times in other ways, Adler also recorded in 1932 a song, "Smoking Reefer," that is explicitly about marijuana.

Recordings: *Larry Adler in the 30's*. Asv Living Era, 1995; *The Great Larry Adler*. Pearl Flapper, 1996; *Harmonica Virtuoso*. Legacy, 1997; *Rhapsody in Blue*. Empress/Empire, 1998.

ADORNO, Theodor

(11 November 1903–7 August 1969; b. T. Wiesengrund).

Essentially a philosopher, sometimes classified as a social theorist, he has also written books about music that are admired by some and loathed by many. They are filled with sentences that are hard to decipher and thoughts that, even if understood, seem to go nowhere. Often Adorno is simply wrong, as when he opens a paragraph with the declaration that "Stravinsky also asserts his right to an extreme position in the modern music movement," because Stravinsky spent most of his career separating his work from extremism. Plentiful references to both Karl Marx and Sigmund Freud contribute to an illusion of critical weight. As Adorno writes in pretentious, jargonious [*sic*] language that is meant to impress with its cumbersome sentences and high-faluting diction, rather than communicate from one person to another, his books on music in particular are valued by people who don't know much about the subject. It could be said that their principal implicit theme is the intimidating power of Teutonic language and perhaps the intellectual privileges (aka indulgences) available to those who wield it. Some people have a taste for this kind of criticism, just as others have a taste for S&M. Adorno reportedly advised the German author Thomas Mann, likewise an exile in America during World War II, on the musical intelligence in the latter's novel *Doctor Faustus* (1947), which may or may not account for that book's musical irrelevance. (In truth, I wrote this entry only because my publisher insisted that this *Dictionary* should acknowledge Adorno.)

Writings: Adorno, Theodor. *Die Philosophie der neuen Musik* (1949). Trans. Anne G. Mitchell & Wesley V. Blomster as *The Philosophy of New Music*. New York:

Continuum, 1973; *Negative Dialectics*. Trans. E. B. Ashton. New York: Seabury, 1973; *Introduction to the Sociology of Music*. Trans. E.B. Ashton. New York: Seabury, 1976; *Quasi una Fantasia: Essays on Modern Music* (1963). London: Verso, 1992; *Aesthetic Theory*. Ed. Gretel Adorno and Rolf Tiedemann. Trans. C. Lenhardt. London: Routledge & Kegan Paul, 1984.

Website: http://www.columbia.edu/~anr5/adorno.html

AGAM, Yaacov

(11 May 1928, b. Jacob Gipstein).

An Israeli, the son of a rabbi, Agam moved to Paris as a very young man, creating the epitome of Jewish rationalist art that, thanks to his artistry, realizes irrational ends. Respecting the biblical commandment proscribing graven images, Agam works with simple geometric illusions, such as an undulated surface whose imagery changes as the viewer moves from side to side. Even though nothing physical changes, this movement creates the illusion of KINETIC ART. Agam has also made transformable sculptures composed of modular elements that can be varied by spectators—that exist, indeed, only through audience interaction. The French historian Frank Popper speaks of "inventions, ranging from the single print to the holograph by way of multigraphs, polymorph graphics, interspaceographs, environmental graphics, primographics, and video graphics. Agam's other achievements include constructions with artificial light, water-fire sculptures, monumental mixed media works such as the fountain at the Défence complex near Paris." Agam is one of those artists whose simplicity is deceptive—easily dismissed by some while respected by others for the profound thought behind it.

Books: *The Agam Passover Haggadah*. Trans. Moshe Kohn. Hewlett, NY: Geffen, 1993; *Art and Judaism: A Conversation between Yaakov Agam and Bernard Mandlebaum*. New York: BLD Ltd., 1981.

Films: Agam, Yaakov & Mambush, I. *Recherches et Inventions*, 1956; *Le Désert Chante, Microsalon*, 1957.

Sculpture: *Sculpture Tente*, n.d.; *Maaloth 18*, 1971; *Mille Portes (A Thousand Doors)*, 1972.

Works: *Relief Transformable*, 1956; *Fusion 1*, 1956–66; *Tactile Sonore*, 1963; *8 + 1 en mouvement*, 1968–9; *Couple*, 1970; *Puissance 9 (To the 9th power)*, 1971; *Neon Chandalier*, 1971–2; *Beating Heart in Nature*, 1971; *All Directions*, 1972.

Website: http://www.israeliart.com/contemp/agam.htm

Exhibition Catalogs: *Yaakov Agam*. New York: Marlborough-Gerson Gallery, 1966; *Yaakov Agam: Transformable Transformables*. New York: Galerie Denise René, 1971; *Homage to Yaakov Agam*, with essays by Frank Popper, Eugene Ionesco et. al. New York: Lèon Amiel/Guggenheim, 1980.

Interpretation: Metken, Günter. *Yaakov Agam*. London: Thames and Hudson, 1977; Popper, Frank. *Origins and Development of Kinetic Art*. Greenwich, CT: New York Graphic Society, 1968; ——. *Agam*. New York: Abrams, 1973, 1983; Reichardt, Jasia. *Yaakov Agam*. London: 1966.

ALBERS, Josef

(19 March 1888–26 March 1976).

A student and then an instructor at the BAUHAUS, Albers emigrated to America soon after that legendary German school was closed by the Nazi authorities, teaching first in North Carolina at BLACK MOUNTAIN COLLEGE until 1949, and then at Yale University until his retirement. Intentionally restricting his imagery to rectangles within rectangles, which he considered scrupulously neutral shapes, Albers created paintings and drawings based primarily upon the relationships of shapes and of colors. His series "Homage to the Square" reportedly includes hundreds of paintings that are not only distinctly his, but they also suggest alternative directions, as only the best teacher's art can. The fact that little need be said about his art should not diminish any estimate of his achievement.

Visual Art: *Zeichnungen: Drawings*. New York: 1956.

Writings: Albers, Josef. *Despite Straight Lines*. New Haven: Yale University Press, 1961; *The Interaction of*

Color. 2 vols. New Haven: Yale University Press, 1963.

Exhibition Catalogs: Hamilton, George Heard. *Joseph Albers*. New Haven: Yale University Art Gallery, 1956; *JA*. New York: MoMA, 1964; *JA: The American Years*. Washington: Washington Gallery of Modern Art, 1965; Hunter, Sam, ed. *JA: Paintings and Graphics 1917–1970*. Princeton: The Art Museum, Princeton University, 1971; Miller, Jo. *JA: Prints 1915–1970*. New York: Brooklyn Museum, 1973; *JA: A Retrospective*. New York; Guggenheim Museum-Harry N. Abrams, 1988; *JA: A National Touring Exhibition*. London: The Centre, 1994.

Website: http://sheldon.unl.edu/HTML/ARTIST/Albers_J/AA.html

Interpretation: Bayer, Herbert & Gropius, Walter & Ilse. *Bauhaus 1919–1928*. New York: MoMA, 1938; Gomringer, Eugen. *Joseph Albers*. New York: Wittenborn, 1968; Bucher, François. *Josef Alberts: Despite Straight Lines: An Analysis of His Graphic Constructions*. Cambridge: MIT, 1977; Feeney, Kelly. *Joseph Albers: Works on Paper*. Alexandria, VA: Art Services International, 1991.

ALBERT-BIROT, Pierre

(22 April 1876–25 July 1967).

An inventive writer, frequently acknowledging GUILLAUME APOLLINAIRE (though the latter was four years younger), Albert-Birot produced texts that were experimental in all sorts of ways. He edited the magazine *SIC* (1916–19), its title an acronym for *Sons Idées Couleurs* (Sounds Ideas Colors). In its pages appeared figures associated with ITALIAN FUTURISM, SURREALISM, and DADA, along with chapters of his novel *Grabinoulor* (1919). Barbara Wright, who specializes in translating avant-garde French texts into English, describes

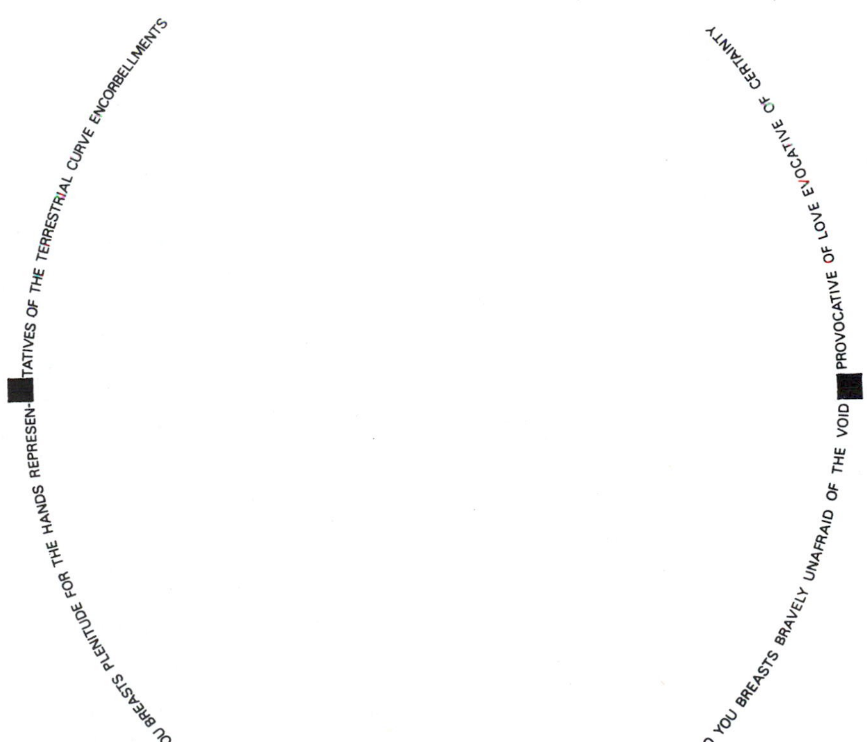

Pierre Albert-Birot. From *Grabinoulor*. Copyright © 1987. Reprinted with permission of Dalkey Archive Press.

Albert-Birot's principal activities as "poems of every conceivable kind: sound poems, typographical poems, simultaneous poems, poster-poems, square, rectangular, chess-board poems. And even straightforward poems. Plays. Novels." Albert-Birot should be remembered, if for nothing else, for this classic aphorism: "If anything can be said in prose, then poetry should be saved for saying nothing." That's a gloriously liberating idea; too bad nobody known to me had thought of it before and few have observed it since.

Writings: Albert-Birot, Pierre. *The First Book of Grabinoulor* (1924). Trans. Barbara Wright. Elmwood Park, IL: Dalkey Archive, 1987; Poésie 1916–1924. Paris: Gallimard, 1964; *Les mémoires d'Adam* .Paris: Editions Balzac, 1943; *Les Amusements Naturels*. Paris: Denoël, 1945; *Silex, Poèmes des cavernes*. Bonaguil, France: Éditions du Cercle culturel et artisanal, 1966; *Cent Nouvelles gouttes de poésie*. Bonaguil: Cercle culturel et artisanal, 1967; *Long Cours*. Montmartre: Rougerie, 1974; *Le train bleu*. Paris: G. Chambelland, 1979; *Poésie 1927–37*. Montmartre: Rougerie, 1981; *Poésie 1931–38*. Montmartre: Rougerie, 1982; *Poésie 1938–39*. Montmartre: Rougerie, 1983; *Poésie 1916–24*. Montmartre: Rougerie, 1992.

Interpretation: Kelly, Debra. *Pierre Albert-Birot: A Poetics in Movement; a Poetics of Movement*. Rutherford, NJ: Fairleigh Dickinson University Press, 1997; Seaman, David W. "Albert-Birot." In *Concrete Poetry in France*. Ann Arbor: UMI Research, 1981.

ALEATORY MUSIC

(1950s).

The word aleatory is derived from the Latin "alea," that is, a die. (Julius Caesar exclaimed after crossing the Rubicon, "Alea jacta est.") Aleatory music in the literal sense is not a new invention. "Dice music" was a popular parlor game in the eighteenth century. A celebrated example is *Musikaisches Warfespiel*, attributed to Mozart. In the second half of the twentieth century, composers of the avant-garde introduced true aleatory methods. A pioneer work was *Music of Changes* by John Cage, derived from chance operations found in the ancient Chinese book of oracles *I Ching*, in which random numbers are obtained by throwing sticks. By drawing an arbitrary table of correspondences between numbers and musical parameters (pitch, note-value, rests) it is possible to derive a number of desirable melorhythmic curves. Human or animal phenomena may also serve as primary data. Configurations of fly specks on paper, pigeon droppings on a park bench, the parabolic curve of an expectoration directed towards a spittoon, dissection of birds as practiced in ancient Rome, etc. are all excellent materials for aleatory music. At a HAPPENING in an American midwestern university, the anal discharge of a pig, which was administered a clyster, was used as an aleatory datum. Mauricio Kagel has made use of partially exposed photographic film for aleatory composition. The composer-engineer Iannis Xenakis organizes aleatory music in STOCHASTIC terms, which possess the teleological quality absent in pure aleatory pursuits.

—Nicolas Slonimsky

Recordings: Cage, John. *Music of Changes*. Wergo 60099-50.

ALEXEIEFF, Alexander

(5 August 1901–1982; b. Alexandre A.).

Born in Kazan, Russia, he studied painting, designed ballet costumes, executed wood engravings and lithographs, in addition to developing very personal styles of etching and book illustration. Awed by Fernand Léger's *Ballet Méchanique*, which he first saw in 1933, Alexeieff turned to cinema. His innovation was a "pin-board" technique that depended upon a large board covered with pins the size of small nails, each of which could be raised or lowered, usually by hand. When lit from the side, the different heights of the pins produced shadows of different lengths, forming pictures both abstract and representational. Alexeieff's later work was produced in collaboration with Claire Parker, an American whom he married in 1941. Striking and respected though this pin-board technique is, few others tried it.

Films: *La Belle au bois dormant*, 1935; *En Passant*, 1943; *Séve de la terre*, 1955; *Le Nez*, 1963.

Interpretation: Russett, Robert, & Cecile Starr, "Alexander Alexeieff and Claire Parker." In *Experimental Animation*. New York: Van Nostrand Reinhold, 1976.

ALLEN, Roberta

(6 October 1945).

Whereas many avant-garde writers were influenced by CONCEPTUAL ART, Allen actually did it, before she began publishing. She exhibited pieces concerned with the ambiguity of direction, position, and placement, particularly favoring arrows that pointed in contrary directions, so "that the meaning of a sign is not inherent in the sign," as she once told me. Her prose writings are spare, almost minimal, held together by the thoughts of a female narrator adrift in the world. In *The Daughter* (1992), episodes from childhood alternate with recollections of traveling in Latin America.

Writings: *Everything in the World There Is to Know*. Aachen, Germany: Ottenhausen, 1981; *The Daughter*. Brooklyn, NY: Semiotext(e), 1992; *Certain People: & Other Stories*. Coffeehouse Press, 1997.

Exhibition Catalogs: *Ascending/Descending Arrows: A Floor Installation*. München: Die Gallery, 1981.

ALTERNATIVE SPACES

(1970s).

This has been the preferred American epithet for galleries that exhibit art and present performances without the expectation of a profit. They were founded in the wake of largesse made available by the National Endowment for the Arts and its imitators in the states, initially to serve artists who found commercial channels closed. Perhaps the largest and most famous, PS 1 in Astoria, New York, took over a vacated public school (thus the "PS") that was among the largest in New York City. While its former auditoriums and gymnasiums were used for exhibitions and performances, the sometime classrooms housed smaller shows or became studios mostly for artists from abroad. (I had in 1979 an exhibition of my Book Art in a groundfloor corner space that must have been a principal's office, because it housed a machine for making bells ring throughout the building.) In one of its top-floor classrooms, PS 1 also has JAMES TURRELL's *Meeting*, whose roof can be opened to exhibit the changing sky. Thousands of arists from around the world, avant-garde and otherwise, have benefited from the existence of such alternative spaces.

Exhibition Catalogs: *Rooms P.S. 1*. New York: Institute for Art and Urban Resources, 1977.

AMATO, Micaela

(29 July 1945, b. Michelle Amateau).

Beginning as a painter skilled at producing diaphanous textures, particularly on glass, Amato made abstractions through the 1970s. The change in her work came in the wake of her father's death in 1979. She chose to change her name from its French orthography back to a version reflecting her origins as a Sephardic or Spanish Jew. After all, her father came not from France, as "Amateau" suggested, or, like most American Jews, from Central Europe, but from Rhodes, the island (at different times Italian and Greek) off the coast of Asia Minor. Moreover, he worked as the proprietor of a *botanica*, a shop selling herbs and oils largely to Mediterranean peoples. As a minority within a minority, Sephardic Jews developed even in America a culture different from the predominant Ashkenazim. "I grew up," Amato once wrote memorably, "with hyperbole and parables, and a sense of the magical—*cante hondo*/flamenco, Italian opera, salted fish, loukum, honey, pastachio, and Turkish coffee." Her art since the 1980s has reflected this Mediterranean Jewish culture in its sensuousness, its light, its colors, and even its iconography. One of several works titled *Cante Hondo* (1997), slightly less than two feet square, has a wood relief incorporating spirals painted brightly in oil and neon light; another with the same title is eight feet high, incorporating a mirror and plate glass along with neon. *Tijuana Tavolettas* is the name of a traveling retrospective that, in different forms, stopped at American universities in the late 1990s.

a

Works: *I Am So Vast, I Eat My Own Placenta*, neon text, plate glass, paint, transparent acetate photos, and welded steel brackets, 1994; *What Web Is This, Of Will Be, Is*, transparent acetate photos and wireglass, on paper, 1995.

Paintings: *Memory Trace I*, 1994; *Memory Trace II*, 1994; *Cuando sale la luna, nadie come naranjas*, 1994; *Miro the Xueta*, 1996; *Velasquez the Marrano*, 1996; *Tijuana Tavolettas: "Cante Hondo,"* 1997.

Exhibition Catalogs: Lippard, Lucy R. Introduction to *Tijuana Tavolettas.* Easton, PA: Morris R. Williams Center for the Arts/Lafayette College, 1998.

AMBIENT MUSIC

(c. 1920).

Ambient or background music was first suggested as a possible art form by ERIK SATIE. His described his concept of "furniture music" (*musique d'ameublement*) as "new music [to be] played during intermission at theatrical events or at a concert, designed to create a certain ambience." In the 1930s, the Muzak Company was founded to transmit, by radio, soothing background music that would be appropriate for offices and factories. These selections were psychologically tested either to encourage more productivity or to ease stressful situations (e.g., the ever-present Muzak heard while sitting in the dentist's chair). A common nickname for this type of overly pleasant background music is Elevator Music.

In the postwar years, American composer JOHN CAGE reintroduced Satie's notion of music to be played as a background accompaniment to other activities. This idea has been most actively espoused by composer/producer BRIAN ENO who took the term "ambient music" from Cage. Eno's background music is supposed to be both "interesting as well as ignorable," in the words of critic Stuart Isacoff. The most famous example of Eno's ambient work is *Music for Airports*, which, ironically, has been used as Muzak in several major airports.

Another development in background music briefly flourished in the late '50s and early '60s, mostly in the hands of eccentric sound composer Esquivel. His creations, now known as "space-age bachelor pad music," combined electronic sounds with futuristic background music. This music was designed to be played in the homes of forward-looking young men, anticipating the advances of the space age. As pure kitsch, this music was briefly revived in the late '90s.

—Richard Carlin

Works: Satie, Erik. *Furniture Music (Musique d'ameublement)*. Presented in the Galéries Barbezanges, Paris, March 8, 1920; Cage, John. *4'33"*. New York: C.F. Peters, 1952; Eno, Brian. *Music for Airports* (Ambient 001, 1979); Esquivel and others. *Cocktail Mix: The Bachelor's Guide to the Galaxy* (Rhino 72237, c. 1995).

Interpretation: Isacoff, Stuart. "Environmental Music." In *The New Grove Dictionary of American Music*. New York: Grove's Dictionaries, 1986; Rockwell, John. "Environmental Composers and Ambient Music." In *All-American Music* (1983). New York: Da Capo, 1997; Lanza, Joseph. *Elevator Music*. New York: St. Martin's Press, 1994.

AMERICAN ACADEMY OF ARTS AND LETTERS (1904) NATIONAL INSTITUTE OF ARTS AND LETTERS (1898–1993)

These are self-replicating clubs, chartered by acts of Congress no less, of living artists, composers, and writers that, notwithstanding their monikers, include among their members remarkably few of the Americans mentioned in this book. (The former AAAL was until 1993 an inner circle of fifty drawn from the latter NIAL.) The AAAL's literature department can be characterized as less advanced than its music division, while that devoted to visual arts is, by common consent, the most backward of all. When I first observed its membership, around 1965, I thought that every major writer born before 1910 (and thus fifty-five at the time) belonged; now, over three decades later, that qualitative generalization covers only authors born before 1911 (NORMAN CORWIN being the oldest flagrant omission). Consider this other comparative measure: It would now be very easy to make a list of visual artists not belonging, who are collectively better than current members; fairly easy to make a stronger list of writers (and harder, if not impossible, to make a competitive list of composers). In 1961, the painter AD REINHARDT, who had a sure instinct for professional fakery, noted that in the Manhattan telephone directory that year were seven "National Institutes," consecutively:

National Institute for Architectural Education
National Institute for Disaster Mobilization
National Institute for Straight Thinking
National Institute for the Blind
National Institute of Arts and Letters
National Institute of Credit
National Institute of Diaper Services

Anybody want to make anything of that?

Yes, the NIAL, wholly on its own volition, situated the putative top drawer of American arts between credit advisors and the blind and just a step away from diaper providers.

What AAAL represents culturally is a European model for collecting retrograde (and thus fundamentally un-American) kinds of talents. What it displays provincially is a weakness for middling writers appearing frequently in slick commercial magazines such as *The New Yorker*, thus reflecting a general and continuing decline of standards within the self-appointed guardians. (Only a few decades ago, it was generally assumed that no writer could do optimal work contributing to a magazine, with all its constraints on subject, length, and style.) The distinguished Harvard professor Harry Levin (1912), himself a member of the NIAL, called it, in a memorable phrase, "one of those professional societies which exist primarily for mutual admiration." Because this is the United States, rather than Europe, the retrograde Academy's influence on the development and even the direction of native culture is, thankfully, negligible. That last fact perhaps accounts for why no book-length history of it exists.

Bibliography: Levin, Harry. *Memories of the Moderns*. New York: New Directions, 1980; Reinhardt, Ad. In ARTnews, LX/2 (April 1961). Auchincloss, Louis, et al. (eds.). *A Century of Arts and Letters*. New York: Columbia University Press, 1998.

AMIRKHANIAN, Charles

(19 January 1945).

A pioneering American sound poet, educated in music as well as literature, Amirkhanian began his compositional career in the wake of STEVE REICH'S *It's Gonna Rain* (1965) by using looped audiotape and several tape recorders to create *If In Is* (1971), which he characterizes as "an eleven-minute tape based on strong rhythmic patterns created through the repetition of three words ('mini,' 'bullpup,' 'banjo'). " In *Seatbelt, Seatbelt* (1973), his strongest work in this form (and, in my judgment, one of the best American TEXT-SOUND pieces), the title word is repeated in various ways, by an increasing number of voices, until the chorus suddenly switches to "chung chung quack quack bone" in unison, and then to "cryptic cryptic quack quack," before dividing into two groups, one pair saying the first sequence, the second pair the second sequence. The remainder of this fifteen-minute piece has other propulsive variations within a severely limited verbal palette. Amirkhanian has since produced other kinds of audio art, which I have heard but scarcely remember—indicating to me that it is not as strong as his earlier work. A native Californian, whose critical taste is prejudicially disposed to West Coast culture, he was long an executive at the Pacifica radio station in Berkeley.

Works: *Words*, 1969; *Oratora konkurso rezulto: Auturo de la Jaro,* 1970; *If In Is*,1971; *Spoffy Nene*, 1971; *Just,* 1972; *Heavy Aspirations* 1973; *Seatbelt, Seatbelt,* 1973; *MUGIC* ,1973; *Muchrooms*,1974; *Beemsterboer*, 1975; *Mahogany Ballpark*, 1976; *Dutiful Duck*, 1977; *Mental Radio*, 1985; *Politics as Usual,* 1988; *Walking Tune*,1986–87.

Recordings: *Lexical Music*. Berkeley, CA: 1750 Arch, 1979; *Walking Tune*. Boulder, CO: Starkland (P.O. Box 2190, 80306), 1992; with Noah Creshevsky. *Auxesis-Electroacoustic Music—Amirkhanian, Creshevsky*. Baton Rouge, LA: Centaur (8867 Highland Rd. #206, 70808), 1995.

Interpretation: Cahill, Sarah. "Charles Amirkhanian." *Ear Magazine* (July, 1989); Kostelanetz, Richard. *The Old Poetries and the New*. Ann Arbor, MI: University of Michigan, 1981; Kresh, Paul. "An Art between Speech & Music." *New York Times*, April 3, 1983.

ANALOG-TO-DIGITAL CONVERSION

(1980s).

Whereas film captures the image of an object, standard audiotape and videotape record continuous wave forms as magnetic impulses that, when played back through a transducer (or audio/video player), reproduce the original recorded sound or image. The epithet "DIGITAL" refers to the conversion of analog impulses into a binary form that can be stored *digitally* in a computer or on a computer disc. The only way to turn such digital information into sound or image would be through an opposite process—digital-to-analog conversion. By this last method it becomes possible for codes created wholly within a computer to be generated and understood as sound.

Bibliography: Holmes, Thomas B. *Electronic and Experimental Music*. New York: Scribner's, 1985.

AND, Miekal

(25 December 1957).

A longtime cultural anarchist who early in his career converted his name from his pedestrian birth-name to what it is now, And is the creator of 20 years' worth of visual poetry, audio-art, performance ritual, and hypermedia for the Macintosh. He is also the co-founder (with Liz Was, aka Lyx Ish, in 1981) of Xexoxial Editions (formerly Xerox Sutra) and, since 1985, editor of *Xerolage*, a single-artist-per-issue magazine devoted to unpredictable mixes of concrete, xerox collage and visual poetry. And has since 1991 overflowed into Dreamtime Village, a plant-based experimental cultural wilderness he oversees in the boondocks of West Lima, Wisconsin. He is probably the leading theorist of noise in the U.S., and an absolutely manic collector and publisher of neologies of every degree of sanity.

—Bob Grumman

Bibliography: *Knowledge Swirling Man Tell Slow Stories*. Madison, WI: Xexoxial, 1985; *no moon dante*. Madison, WI: Xexoxial (now at Rt. 1, Box 131, LaFarge, WI 54639), 1987; *The Quotes of Rotar Storch*. Port Charlotte, FL: Runaway Spoon, 1989.

ANDERSON, Beth

(3 January 1950).

Although scarcely a prolific speech composer, Anderson has created some masterpieces in that special vein. Drawing upon her Kentucky upbringing, she introduced tobacco auctioneering rhythm to the simple phrase, "If I were a poet, what would I say," to produce audio art that transcends both the phrase and any recall of that folk model. As a music composer, Anderson has worked with instruments and tape, for pieces both short and long, including *The Fat Opera* (1991). After collaborating on the publication of *Ear* (intermittently in San Francisco, 1973), she came to New York. There she founded and for many years published the new music magazine, *Ear-New York* (1975–1991), although that fact was not acknowledged in later issues of that journal.

Works/Writings: *Queen Christina* (an opera), 1973; *Soap Tuning* (theatre), 1976; *Zen Piece* (theatre), 1976; "If I Were a Poet" in *Text-Sound Texts,* ed. Richard Kostelanetz. New York: Morrow, 1980; *Nirvana Manor* (musical), 1981; "Kentucky Poem" *Ear Magazine* vol. 2 #5/6, 1976; *The Fat Opera,* 1991.

Website: http://www.users. interport.net/~Beand

ANDERSON, Laurie

(5 June 1947).

Anderson has been sporadically popular since the early '80s, following the surprise hit of her eight-minute audio montage "O Superman." Working in New York since 1973, Anderson had been exposed to the musical experiments of Brian Eno and Philip Glass in evolving her stage shows that included spoken word (often electronically distorted), tape loops, synthesized sounds, mime, film, and light shows. Her best-known work in this mode was the seven-hour production *The United States* (1984), the audio portion of which was released as a five-volume set by rock label Warner Brothers in the wake of her pop hit. By the mid-'90s, however, she had disappeared from the pop scene as well as from more progressive venues. Anderson's work fails to meet the claims made for it, whether as visual art, music, writing, or performance, for it has from its beginnings been invariably more slick than avant-garde and more acceptable than challenging.

Recordings: *United States*. New York: Warner Brothers 25192-1, 1984.

Books: *United States*. New York: Harper & Row, 1984; *Stories from the Nerve Bible: A Twenty-Year Retrospective*. New York; Harper Perennial, 1994; In *The Guests Go into Supper*. Ed. Melody Summer. San Francisco, CA: Burning Books, 1986.

Exhibition Catalog: Kardon, Janet. *Laurie Anderson, Works from 1969 to 1983*. Philadelphia: Institute of Contemporary Art, 1983.

Interview: Duckworth, William. *Talking Music*. New York: Schirmer, 1995.

Interpretation: Rockwell, John. "Laurie Anderson." In *All-American Music* (1983). New York; Da Capo, 1997; White, Robin. "Laurie Anderson" 1980. In *Art Talk in the Early 80s (1988*), ed. Jeanne Siegel. New York: Da Capo, n.d.

Website: http://www.cc.gatech.edu/~jimmyd/laurie-anderson/

ANDRE, Carl

(16 September 1935).

Andre, more than anyone else, persuasively established the idea of a situational sculpture in which materials, sometimes purchased or found (rather than fabricated), are imported into a particular space (usually where "art" is the currency of admission). Because these sculptures exist only in that situation, only for the duration of their display there, the parts can be separated and retrieved at the exhibition's end, if not later organized into a totally different work—what Andre calls "clastic" art. As these works may be taken apart (or gathered up) and recomposed, they look intentionally unfinished and impermanent (thus denying the classic piety that "sculptural art" must necessarily be a finished product); they also look as though someone else could easily duplicate them with commonly available materials. Therefore Andre's sculpture *Lever* (1966) assumes an untraditional horizontal form,

Carl Andre. *Lever*, 1966. Courtesy National Gallery of Canada, Ottawa.

consisting of 137 pieces of separate but visibly identical (and thus interchangeable) firebricks laid side to side in a single line thirty feet across the floor. An adept aphorist ("Art is what we do; culture is what is done to us"), Andre has also written comparably innovative, nonsyntactical literary texts that, although they are exhibited from time to time (and even reprinted in the catalogues accompanying exhibitions), have yet to be collected into a book.

Writings: *7 Books of Poetry: Passport, Shape and Structure, A Theory of Poetry, 100 Sonnets, American Drill, 3 Operas, Lyrics and Odes*. New York: 1969; "Sensibility of the 60's" in *Art in America*. New York: Jan/Feb. 1967; *12 Dialogues, 1962–1963/Carl Andre, Hollis Frampton*. With Frampton's photographs of early Andre work. Ed. Benjamin H. D. Buchloh. Halifax & New York: Nova Scotia College of Art & Design/New York University, 1981; *Stillanovel*. Produced Rosemarie Castoro. London & New York: Anthony D'Offay & Paula Cooper, 1992.

Exhibition Catalogs: Develing , Enno. *Carl Andre*. The Hague: Haags Gemeentemuseum, 1969; Waldman, Diane. *Carl Andre*. New York: Guggenheim Museum, 1970; Fuchs, R. H. *Carl Andre: Wood*. Eindhoven: Stedlijk Van Abbemuseum, 1978.

Anthology: *Carl Andre Works in Belgium*. Gent, Belgium: Imschoot Uitgevers, 1993.

Biography: Katz, Robert. *Naked by the Window: The Fatal Marriage of Carl Andre and Ana Mendieta*. New York: Atlantic Monthly, 1990.

Interpretation: Müller, Gregoire. *The New Avant Garde*. New York: 1972.

Catalogue Raisonné: Sartorius, Rita. *Carl Andre*. Den Haag: Haags Gemeentemuseum, 1987.

ANGER, Kenneth

(3 February 1930).

A child of the Los Angeles film world, Anger began precociously with a trilogy of SURREALISTIC and disjointed films that were juvenile in both content and, seemingly, inspiration, the antithesis of slick Hollywood films: *Fireworks* (1947), *Eaux d'Artifice* (1953), and *Inauguration of the Pleasure Dome* (1954, recut 1966). Perhaps the best of them is the first, which portrays a young man's homoerotic dreams. (It reportedly got Anger a letter from JEAN COCTEAU, inviting him to come to Europe, where he lived for most of the 1950s. Returning to New York in 1962, he lived initially near Coney Island, where he reportedly learned about socially marginal America.)

Only with *Scorpio Rising* (1964) did Anger emerge as a mature innovative filmmaker. The subject is motorcyclists, and this film emphasizes their insane love of their machines, their attempts to imitate film heroes such as James Dean, and their rowdy, implicitly homoerotic parties. In the third section of the film, against the motorcyclists are juxtaposed some blue-tinted scenes from a black-and-white version of the Christ story. This last contrast is reinforced by the shrewd use on the soundtrack of rock 'n' roll music that has the distinct virtue of being at once both resonant and ironic. As Anger's cutting from one kind of scene to another becomes quicker, *Scorpio Rising* becomes hysterically funny. The film somewhat resembles POP painting in its use of very familiar quotations, as well as its author's ambivalent attitude toward popular materials—in the artful mixing of high culture with low. Also an author, Anger published the classic exposés of individual turpitude (as distinct from corporate sin) in Hollywood, *Hollywood Babylon* (1965) and *Hollywood Babylon II* (1984).

Works: *Hollywood Babylon*. Phoenix, AZ: Associated Professional Services, 1965; *Hollywood Babylon II*. New York: Dutton, 1984.

Videos: *Fireworks* (1947). New York: Mystic Fire, 1987; *Inauguration of the Pleasure Dome*. New York: Mystic Fire, 1987; *Lucifer Rising*. New York: Mystic Fire, 1987; *The Mighty Civic*. New York: Mystic Fire, 1987.

ANIMATED FILM

(c. 1900).

It is my considered idiosyncratic opinon that animation in film has always constituted an avant-garde. Since film extended from photography, where anything resembling animation has always been scarce, animation has from its beginnings necessarily reflected discoveries about properties that made film different from photography. Whereas representational films were shot scene by scene, most animation was produced frame by frame. Movement on screen comes not from moving the camera or the actors but from changes made on a drawing board by hand.

Throughout the history of film production, animation has always been a sorry sister. It is said that the producer in charge of cartoons at WARNER BROTHERS, where some of the best animation was achieved, arrived at screenings with the epithet, "Roll the trash." And the censors at the time didn't examine animated shorts as closely as feature films, allowing, say, the eroticism of the Fleischers' Betty Boop to go into movie houses, where such sensuous moves by human beings in feature-length films would be forbidden. Few critics at the time acknowledged the WARNER toons, which didn't earn much critical writing until the 1970s. Only in 1985 did the Museum of Modern Art mount a retrospective, curated by Steve Schneider, of Warner work. The only animated film ever to command much critical respect at its premiere was Walt Disney's feature-length *Fantasia* (1941), which is indeed a masterpiece.

Curiously, the development of animated film created a precondition for video, which at its truest is not a representational medium, like most film, but something else, containing as it does the potential to generate its own imagery and to process electronically (and thus easily) prerecorded pictures.

Though I've read many histories of animated film, I don't consider any of them to be critically smart. Nonetheless, I recommend the thick Giannalberto Bendazzi Cartoons for its international information. Otherwise, animation remains film's sorry sister. The anthology *Frames* (1978), assembled by George Griffin, himself a distinguished animator, presents a page or two of credible sample images from American animators. I reprint all their names, not because they are familiar but because, two decades later, they aren't, though many probably should be: Jane Aaron, Martin Abrahams, Karen Aqua, Mary Beams, Lisze Bechtold, Adam Beckett, Gary Beydler, David Blum, Lowell Bodger, Barbara Bottner, Robert Breer, Ken Brown, Carter Burwell, John Canemaker, Vincent Collins, Lisa Crafts, Sally Cruikshank, Larry Cuba, Jody Culkin, Howard Danelowitz, Carmen D'Avino, Loring Doyle, Irra Duga, Eric Durst, Tony Eastman, David Ehrlich, Jules Engel, Victor Faccinto, Roberta Friedman, Paul Glabicki, Andrea Romez, James Gore, Linda Heller, Louis Hock, Al Jarnow, Flip Johson, Linda Klosky, Ken Kobland, Candy Kugel, Maria Lassing, Kathleen Laughlin, Carolina Leaf, Fran-

a

cis Lee, Jerry Lieberman, Anthony McCall, Frank & Carolina Mouris, Eli Noyes, Pat O'Neill, Sara Petty, Dennis Pies, Suzan Pitt, Richard Protovin, Kathy Rose, Peter Rose, Susan Rubin, Robert Russett, Steve Segal, Maureen Selwood, Janet Shapero, Jim Shook, Jody Silver, Lillian & J.P. Somersaulter, Robert Swarthe, Mary Dzilagyi, Anita Thacher, STAN VANDERBEEK, Peter Wallach, and James Whitney. Consider this an indication of how avant-garde nearly all animation must be, even in America.

Histories: Lutz, E. G. *Animated Cartoons: How They Are Made, Their Origin, and Development*. New York: Scribner's, 1920; Stephenson, Ralph. *Animation in the Cinema*. London: A. Zwemmer, 1967 (reprinted as *The Animated Film*. London/New York: Tantivy & Barnes, 1973); Maltin, Leonard. *The Disney Films* (1973). Abridged & updated ed. New York: Popular Library, 1978; ——. *Of Mice and Magic: A History of American Animated Cartoons*. New York: New American Library, 1980; Schneider, Steve. *That's All Folks!*. New York: Holt, 1988; Bendazzi, Giannalberto. *Cartoons: One Hundred Years of Cinema Animation*. Trans. Ana Taraboletti-Segre. Bloomington: Indiana University Press, 1994; Kanfer, Stefan. *Serious Business: The Art and Commerce of Animation in America*. New York: Scribner's, 1997; Solomon, Charles. *Enchanted Drawings: The History of Animation*. New York: Knopf, 1989.

Anthologies: Griffin, George. *Frames*. New York: Metropolitan Graphics (349 West Fourth St., 10014), 1978; Russett, Robert, and Cecile Starr. *Experimental Animation*. New York: Van Nostrand Reinhold, 1976; Peary, Danny, and Gerald Peary. *The American Animated Cartoon: A Critical Anthology*. New York: Dutton, 1980.

Website: http://www.frizbee.demon.co.uk/anim.html.

ANTHEIL, George

(8 July 1900–12 February 1959).

Residing in Europe in the middle 1920s, Antheil became the epitome of the outrageous avant-garde American composer, producing piano pieces with such aggressive titles as *Sonata Sauvage*, *Mechanisms*, and *Airplane Sonata*. Returning to America for a one-person Carnegie Hall concert in 1927, he composed a *Ballet mécanique* (having already produced a score for a Ferdinand Léger film of the same title) with airplane propellers, several pianos, and many drums. (In a 1989 complete re-creation of this historic concert, I thought it by far the strongest work on the program.) His opera *Transatlantic* (1928–29) was the first American opera to receive its premiere in Europe, in Frankfurt in 1930. (Not until 1998 was it produced in his native country, with five performances by the Minnesota Opera, where K. Robert Schwarz saw it, producing an appreciation of its "delirious intricacy . . . in text, staging, and music" for *Opera News*.)

George Antheil at the piano, c. 1935. CORBIS/Bettmann.

Lionized by some literati, Antheil helped EZRA POUND to complete his opera *Le Testament de Villon* (1926), and in return became the subject of Ezra Pound's booklet *Antheil and the Treatise on Harmony* (1927). Back in America in the early 1930s, Antheil produced less distinguished music before moving to Hollywood, where he wrote undistinguished film scores and a syndicated newspaper column titled "Boy Meets Girl" offering advice to the romantically distraught. He collaborated with the film actress Hedy Lamarr (1913–) in inventing (and even patenting) a radio-directed torpedo. No longer an avant-garde composer by his forties, he published a memoir with the audacious title *Bad Boy of Music* (1945).

Compositions: *Airplane Sonata*, Sonata No. 2, 1921; *Sonata Sauvage*, Sonata No. 1, 1922; *Jazz Sonata,* Sonata No. 4, 1922; *Sonata Number Five*, 1923; *Woman Sonata*, Sonata No. 6, 1923; *Death of Machines*, Sonata No. 3, 1923; *Ballet mécanique*, 1926; *La femme 100 têtes*, 1933; *Transatlantic*. opera, 1928–29; *Helen Retires*. opera, 1934.

Books: *Every Man His Own Detective*. New York: Stackpole, 1937; *The Shape of the War to Come*. New York, Toronto: Longmans, 1940; *Bad Boy of Music* (1945). Los Angeles: Samuel French, 1990.

Recordings: *Ballet mécanique & A Jazz Symphony* (1923–25), New Palais Royale Orch. & Percussion Ensemble; Quartet No. 1 for strings (1924), Mendelssohn String Quartet; Sonata No. 2 for Violin & Piano (1923), Castleman/Hodgkinson Violin-Piano Duo (MusicMasters 01612-67094). Pound, Ezra. *Le Testament de Villon* (1926). Conducted by Reinbert de Leeuw. Breukelen, Holland: Philips 1980.

Website: http://www.schirmer.com/composers/antheil_bio.html

Interpretation: Ford, Hugh. "George Antheil." In *Four Lives in Paris*. San Francisco: North Point, 1987; Schafer, R. Murray, ed. *Ezra Pound and Music: The Complete Criticism*. New York: New Directions, 1977. (This includes Anthiel's review, "Why the Poet Quit the Muses," on Pound's music.); Schwarz, K. Robert, "Bad Boy Makes Good," *Opera News* (28 March 1998); Whitesitt, Linda. *The Life and Music of George Antheil, 1900–1959*. Ann Arbor: UMI Research, 1983.

ANTIN, David

(1 February 1932).

Beginning as an independent New York poet and art critic, Antin became a Southern Californian and state-university academic. A handful of his essays are illuminating and persuasive—especially one on the unprecedented character of video and another on American poetry between the wars; others are unintelligible in ways more typical of, and available to, professors than lay writers. His early poems, collected in the marvelously titled *Code of Flag Behavior* (1968), reveal an arbitrary Expressionism that becomes more pronounced in the "talk poems" he developed in the 1970s. Essentially improvisations that exploit his intimidating facility with complex sentences (in the tradition of the art historian Meyer Schapiro, who declaimed them more gracefully), these solo gabfests customarily begin as philosophical investigations before sinking invariably into anecdotes that have only tenuous connections to their initial concerns. Antin's works are sometimes transcribed to appear in print, their eccentric spacing and lack of punctuation purportedly reflective of his speech.

Writings: *Definitions*. New York: Caterpillar Press, 1967; *Autobiography*. New York: Something Else Press, 1967; *Code of Flag Behavior*. Los Angeles: Black Sparrow Press, 1968; *Meditations*. Los Angeles: Black Sparrow Press, 1971; *Talking*. New York: Kulchur, 1972; "Modernism and Postmodernism: Approaching the Present in American Poetry," *Boundary 2* (1972). Reprinted in *The Avant-Garde Tradition in Literature*, ed. Richard Kostelanetz. Buffalo, New York: Prometheus, 1982; *After the War* (A Long Novel with Few Words). Los Angeles: Black Sparrow Press, 1973; *Talking at the Boundaries*. New York: New Directions, 1976; *Tuning*. New York: New Directions, 1984; *What It Means to Be Avant-Garde*. New York: New Directions, 1993.

Interpretation: Alpert, Barry. "John Cage, Bucky Fuller, and David Antin" *Boundary 2* (1972); Fredman, Stephen. *The Poet's Prose*. Cambridge: Cambridge University Press, 1983; Paul, Sherman. *So To Speak: Rereading David Antin*. London: Binnacle, 1982; Perloff, Marjorie. *The Poetics of Indeterminacy*. Princeton: Princeton University Press, 1982.

ANTIN, Eleanor

(27 February 1935).

In the early 1970s, Eleanor Antin mailed to selected correspondents, one every fortnight, a series of black-and-white photographic postcards showing fifty pairs of tall black boots in various settings. Especially in sequence, the herd of boots assumes a life of its own, the photographs becoming an epistolary narrative that, after a quarter-century, finally became a book. She also made videotapes, installations, and even a book based upon her assuming the persona of a Russian ballerina several decades ago. For a brief while, such stunts were called "post-conceptual art," the prefix "post" being no more substantial here than it is for "postmodernism" perhaps because, in both cases, the prefix functions to rationalize reaction and/or decline.

Visual Art: *California Lives*. New York: Gain Ground Gallery, 1970; *100 Boots*. San Diego, CA: Privately published, 1970. (Exhibited at Museum of Modern Art, NY, 1973); *I Dreamed I Was a Ballerina*. Los Angeles: Orlando Gallery, 1973; *Eleanor Antin, R.N.* Los Angeles: The Clocktower, 1976; *Before the Revolution*. Exhibited at Ronald Feldman Fine Arts Gallery, NY and published in Santa Barbara, CA, 1979.

Eleanor Antin. *100 Boots on the Job*. Signal Hill, California, 15 February 1972, 12:15 PM (mailed 11 September, 1972). Courtesy: Ronald Feldman Fine Arts, New York.

Books: *Being Antinova*. Los Angeles: Astro Artz, 1983. *100 Boots*. Philadelphia, PA: The Running Press, 1999.

Exhibition Catalogs: *The Angel of Mercy*. La Jolla, CA: La Jolla Museum of Contemporary Art, 1977; Gumpert, Lynn, and Ned Rifkin. *Persona: Eleanor Antin . . . Marital Westburg*. New York: New Museum, 1981; *EA: Ghosts*. Winston-Salem, NC: Southeastern Center for Contemporary Arts, 1996; Fox, Howard N. *EA*. Los Angeles: LA County Museum of Art, 1999.

Interpretation: Loefler, Carl & Darlene Tong, eds. *Performance Anthology: Source Book for a Decade of California Performance Art*. San Francisco: Contemporary Arts Press, 1980; Nemser, Cindy. *Art Talk: Conversations with 12 Women Artists*. New York: Scribner's, 1975.

ANTONAKOS, Stephen

(1 November 1926).

Born in Greece, he came to the United States as a child and studied art. Around 1960, he discovered *neon*, which has been his principal medium since. Whereas DAN FLAVIN used the other medium of *fluorescent* light for its peculiar kind of glow, what Antonakos loved in neon was its colors. First he added neon tubes to his assemblages; then he let the lamps stand by themselves. Later he had them fill an entire room, realizing an environment wholly with light. In 1973, he made the radical move of placing ten large neon works outdoors around the architecture of the Ft. Worth Museum, making the entire building into a prop for a giant light sculpture.

Though neon has always been popular in commercial signage, Antonakos appropriated it for modern art by

Eleanor Antin, *100 Boots Out of a Job*. Terminal Island, California, 15 February 1972, 4:45 PM (mailed 25 September 1972). Courtesy: Ronald Feldman Fine Arts, New York.

using it abstractly, typically for curved lines apparently suspended in space. Most of his works in recent years have been for public spaces, where they customarily appear without his name attached: on the south side of West 42nd Street between 9th and 10th Avenues in Manhattan; in the Exchange Place PATH station in Jersey City; in the Pershing Square station in Los Angeles; and the Providence Convention Center in Rhode Island. Typically, they are visible from greater distances than most public art. In the 1980s, Antonakos began producing sacred reliefs that benefit from placing neon lamps behind a rectangular, mostly monotonal painting.

Installations: *Incomplete Neon Circle*, Federal Building, Dayton, OH: 1978; *Incomplete Red Neon Square Exterior Corner*, Fine Arts Center, Amherst, University of Massachusetts, 1979; *Incomplete Square*, Denver, 1982; *Neon for Charles Street Station*, Baltimore, 1983; *Neon for Nevers, France Atheneum*, University of Dijon, 1984; *Neon for York College*, Jamaica, NY, 1986; *Neon for La Jolla Museum of Contemporary Art*, La Jolla, CA, 1986.

Exhibition Catalogs: Spector, Naomi. *Stephen Antonakos: Six Corner Neons*. Albany, NY: Gallery Association of New York State, 1973; *Neons and Drawings*. Waltham, MA: Brandeis University, 1986. *Stephen Antonakos*. New York: Kouros, 1989; *The Chapel of the Saints*. Ed. Haris Kambouridis. Rhodes, Greece: Municipal Art Gallery, 1993; *Stephen Antonakos: Inner Light*. Northampton, MA: Smith College Museum of Art, 1997.

Interpretation: Sandler, Irving. *Stephen Antonakos: The Enlightenment of Art*. New York: Hudson Hills, 1999.

APOLLINAIRE, Guillaume

(26 August 1880–9 November 1918; b. Wilhelm Apollinaris de Kostrowitzky).

Born of a Polish mother who brought her fatherless sons to Monaco, where they received a French education, Kostrowitzky, known even in his adult years as "Kostro," took a French name for a mercurial literary career that included art criticism, plays, fiction, pornography, and poetry. An early avant-garde text was the *poème simultané*, "Zone" (in *Alcools*, 1913), in which events in several places are portrayed in adjacent lines, as though the writer were a bird rapidly moving from place to place. To foster perceptions that are not linear but spatial, Apollinaire adopted the simple innovation of eschewing punctuation. His second innovation, presaging literary MINIMALISM was the one-line poem, "Chantre" (or "Singer"), which William Meredith (1919) translates as "And the single string of the trumpets marine." Apollinaire's third major innovation was VISUAL POEMS that he called "calligrammes," in which words are typeset or handwritten to make expressive shapes, which he dubbed "visual lyricism." For "Il pleut" (or "It rains"), the letters stream down the page, in appropriately uneven lines; "The Little Car" has several shapes reflective of automotive travel; "Mandolin Carnation and Bamboo" incorporates three roughly representational forms on the same page. Some of these handwritten poems have lines extending at various angles, words with letters in various sizes, musical staves, or diagonal typesetting, all to the end of enhancing language. Not only do such poems display a freedom in the use of materials, but Apollinaire apparently made it a point of principle not to repeat any image. Another, perhaps lesser, innovation he called "conversation poems" ("Les Fenêtres" and "Lundi Rue Christine"), because they were assembled from morsels overheard (and in their spatial leaping resemble "Zone").

Apollinaire's best-remembered play, *Les Mamelles de Tirésias* (*The Breasts of Tiresias*, 1918, but written many years before), is a satire on sex and genius that Martin Esslin rates as a distinguished precursor to the THEATRE OF THE ABSURD. Apollinaire's strongest piece of criticism is the essay "L'Esprit nouveau et les poètes" ("The New Spirit and the Poets," 1918), which is no less valid today than it

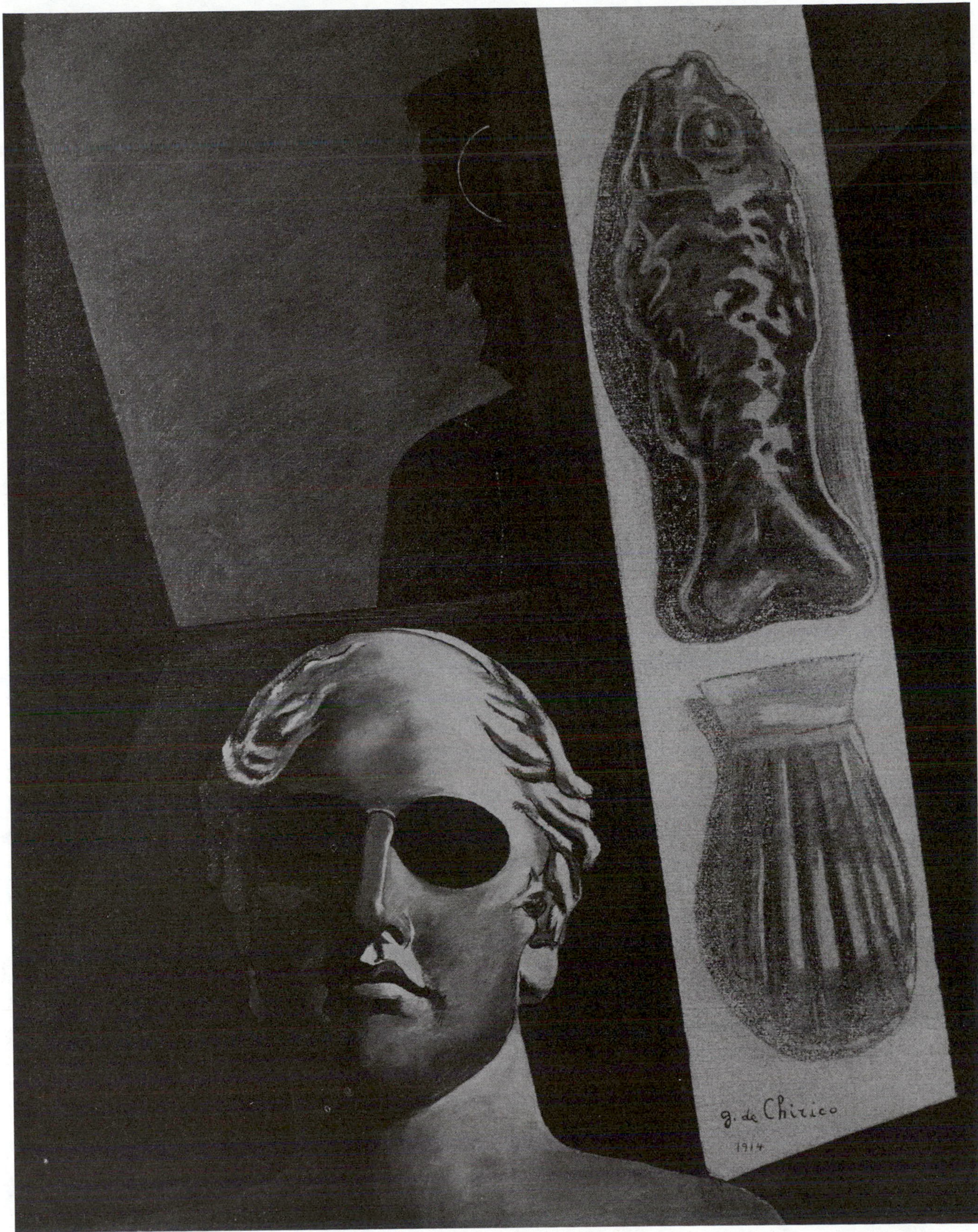

Girogio de Chirco, *Portrait of Guillaume Apollinaire*. CORBIS/Archive Iconografica, S.A. © Foundation Girogio de Chirico/Licensed by VAGA, New York, NY.

was when written, because of its emphasis upon surprise as an avant-garde esthetic value. It should not be forgotten that, in the cultural milieus of Paris at the beginning of the century, Apollinaire performed invaluable service in bringing together advanced artists and writers and helping them understand one another. As Roger Shattuck elegantly puts it, "He wrote on all subjects, in all forms, and for all purposes. For him there was no separation of art and action; they were identical."

Writings: *Les Onze Mille Verges* (1907). Trans. anon., as *The Debauched Hodspodar*. Los Angeles: Holloway, 1967; *L'Hérésiarque et Cie* (1910). Trans. Remy Inglis Hall. New York: Doubleday, 1965; *Les Peintres Cubistes: Méditations Esthétiques* (1913). Trans. Lionel Abel. New York: Wittenborn, 1949; *Alcools: Poems 1898–1913* (1913). Trans. William Meredith; intro. and notes Francis Steegmuller. Garden City, New York: Doubleday, 1964; *Calligrammes* (1918). Trans. Anne Hyde Greet. Berkeley: University of California Press, 1980; *The Poet Assassinated* (1916). Trans. Ron Padgett. New York: Holt, Rinehart & Winston, 1968.

Anthologies: Shattuck, Roger, ed. *Apollinaire*. New York: New Directions, 1949; Breunig, Leroy *Apollinaire on Art: Essays and Reviews 1902–1918*. Trans. Susan Suleiman. New York: Viking, 1972.

Exhibition Catalog: *Guillaume Apollinaire*. Paris: Bibliothèque Nationale, 1969.

Website: www.wiu.edu/Apollinaire ("official" site, in French).

Biography: Steegmuller, Francis. *Apollinaire: Poet among the Painters*. New York: Farrar, Straus, 1963.

Interpretation: Adéma, Pierre Marcel. *Guillaume Apollinaire*. Paris: La Table Ronde, 1968; Bates, Scott. *Guillaume Apollinaire* (1967). New York: Twayne, 1989; Bohn, Willard. *Apollinaire and the Faceless Man*. Rutherford, NJ: Fairleigh Dickinson University, 1991; Carmody, Francis J. *The Evolution of Apollinaire's Poetics, 1901–1914*. Berkeley: 1963; Shattuck, Roger. *The Banquet Years*. New York: Harper & Bros., 1958; Themerson, Stefan. *Apollinaire's Lyrical Ideograms*. London: Gabberbocchus, 1968.

APPIA, Adolphe

(1 September 1862–29 February 1928).

A Swiss theater designer who in 1891 had published a pamphlet about *Staging the Wagnerian Ring*, Appia a few years later wrote *Die Musik und die Inzenierung*, in which he advocated a theater of atmosphere succeeding a theater based on appearances, which is to say nineteenth-century realism. "We need not try to represent a forest," he wrote. "What we must give the spectator is man in the atmosphere of a forest." In James Roose-Evans' summary: "It was Appia who first demonstrated the necessity of visualizing the mood and the atmosphere of a play; the importance of suggestion completed in the imagination of the spectator; the effectiveness of an actor stabbed by a spotlight in a great dim space; the significance of a 'space-stage'; and the more abstract forms of scenic art. He foresaw not only the possibility of spot-lighting but also of projected scenery."

Dismissed at first, Appia persisted, staging scenes from *Carmen* and *Manfred* privately in Paris in 1903, then *Orpheus and Euridice* in 1903, *Tristan und Isolde* at La Scala in Milan in 1923, and finally *Das Rheingold*, *Die Walküre*, and *Prometheus* in Basle in 1924–25. Needless to say, a century ago Appia scarcely imagined subsequent developments not only in illumination but projection.

Books: *The Work of Living Art: A Theory of the Theatre*. Ed. & trans. Barbara Hewitt. Coral Gables, FL: University of Miami Press, 1960; *Music and the Art of the Theatre*. Coral Gables, FL: University of Miami Press, 1962; *Staging Wagnerian Drama* (1891). Trans. & intro. Peter Loeffler. Boston: Birkhaüser, 1982; *Texts on Theatre*. Trans. Richard C. Beacham. London & New York: Routledge, 1993.

Interpretation: Beacham, Richard C. *Adolphe Appia: Artist and Visionary of the Modern Theatre*. Philadelphia: Harwood Academic, 1994; Roose-Evans, James.

Experimental Theatre (1970). New York: Avon, 1971; Volbach, Walter R. *Adolphe Appia: Prophet of the Modern Theater*. Middletown: Wesleyan University Press, 1968.

ARAKAWA

(6 July 1936. b. Shusaku A.).

It is easier to describe Arakawa's paintings than to say what they mean. His paintings tend to be large, usually containing sketchily rendered images, devoid of colors other than black, gray, and white. Often there are letters produced with large stencils, as well as handwriting with roman letters. The simple names for these paintings are customarily devoid of symbolic suggestion. The parts are sufficiently distant from one another, as well as from the painting's title, to suggest mysteries that are not easily penetrated, and indeed they aren't. Arthur Danto (1924), a sometime Columbia University philosophy professor, has reportedly identified Arakawa as "the most philosophical of living artists." Arakawa has also collaborated with his wife, MADELINE GINS , in producing a visual-verbal book, *The Mechanism of Meaning,* that has gone through three radically different editions (1971, 1979, 1988) and is sometimes identified as the epitome of CONCEPTUAL ART. This is no less penetrable than Arakawa's visual art, finally posing the question, rarely raised, of how much unintelligibility is acceptable in contemporary art. It is not for nothing that few articles about Arakawa's work are long and that even shorter appreciations come to drastically different conclusions. The voluminous catalog of a 1997 retrospective that reveals that he ceased painting at the end of the 1980s to concentrate on architecture (mostly conceptual) also includes two-page spreads of stills from films (1969, 1971) that, mysteriously, are not acknowledged in the concluding documentation.

Writings: with Madeline H. Gins. *The Mechanism of Meaning*. 3d ed. New York: Abbeville, 1988; *For Example (A Critique of Never).* Milan: 1974; *To Not To Die.* Paris: Editions de las Différence, 1987; *Architecture: Sites of Reversible Destiny*. London: Academy Editions, 1994.

Films: *Why Not? (A Serenade of Eschatological Ecology)*, 1969; *For Example (A Critique of Never)*, 1971.

Exhibition Catalogs: *Arakawa: Print Works 1965–1983*. Kitakyushu, Japan: Kitakyushu Municipal Museum of Art, 1983; *Arakawa/Gins: Reversible Destiny*. New York: Guggenheim Museum, 1997.

Interpretation: Danto, Arthur. "Gins and Arakawa: Building Sensoriums" *The Nation* (October 15, 1990); Rotzler, Willy. *Constructive Concepts: A History of Constructive Art from Cubism to the Present*. New York: Rizzoli, 1989.

ARCHIGRAM

(1961–1974).

"Archigram" was the name of the architectural newsletter documenting the designs and theories of Warren Chalk, Peter Cook, Dennis Crompton, David Greene, Ron Herron, and Michael Webb. These British architectural visionaries of the 1960s are remembered for reshaping architecture with outlandish designs influenced by consumer culture and entertainment. Synthesizing science fiction, futuristic comic books, and amusement park aesthetics, *Archigram* challenged architecture's rigidity with bravado, effectively epitomizing CONCEPTUAL ARCHITECTURE. Although the group's fantastically innovative forms were never realized, the designs and titles for *Archigram* constructs such as "A Walking City," "Plug-In City," and "Instant City" are in themselves examples of the group's inventiveness and social concerns. "A Walking City" is a take on New York City's future, wherein the city consists of several colossal, insect-like structures with retractable legs that dwarf the background of New York City's skyline, gently mocking what some consider the ultimate architectural achievement of the twentieth Century: the skyscraper.

With sufficient illustrations that may one day rival the prescience of Leonardo's proposed inventions, *Archigram* was able to illuminate and even liberate architecture's potential with utopian optimism, however naïve. And despite the demands of an architecture with material limits, *Archigram* avoided compromise, promoted liberation, and protested all limitations with a bold advertising cum marketing campaign that is still applicable to the ongoing hyper-urbanization of modern cities and American cities in particular.

—Michael Peters

Anthology: *Archigram*. Ed. Peter Cook. New York: Praeger, 1973.

Interpretation: Crompton, Dennis, & Pamela Johnston. *A Guide to Archigram*. London: Academy, 1994.

Exhibition Catalog: *Concerning Archigram 1961–74*. Ed. Dennis Crompton. London: Archigram Archives, 1998.

ARCHIPENKO, Alexander

(30 May, 1880–25 February, 1964).

Archipenko can be credited with being the first artist who worked principally in sculpture to absorb successfully the lessons of Analytic Cubism from painting and introduce them into his three-dimensional work. Although Pablo Picasso's own *Head of a Woman* (1909–10) is the earliest execution of sculptural Cubism, it was a group of sculptors, including Archipenko, Jacques Lipchitz, Raymond Duchamp-Villon, and Henri Laurens, who consistently worked out the formal problems of applying Cubism to their art. Archipenko's *Seated Mother* (1911) probably predates the efforts of the rest. It was a modest and tentative attempt compared to later works: a female figure, who seems totemic in her passive and stiffly upright posture, sits with her legs folded, her figure cut across and divided up by curving planes that slip around and under each other. The basic purpose of Cubism, the simultaneous presentation of multiple perspectives, was not and could not be physically achieved in sculpture. But the efforts of Archipenko and the rest did contribute to the expansion of sculptural form. Though Archipenko extended his influence through the schools he ran in France, Germany, and eventually, the United States, the sculptures he created throughout the rest of his long career were largely unimpressive.

—Mark Daniel Cohen

Works: *Seated Mother*, 1911; *Medrano I*, 1912; *Madonna of the Rocks*, 1912; *Boxers*, 1913; *The Last Moment of the City of Pompeii*, 1925; *Hand*, 1928; *Iron Figure*, 1951; *King Solomon*, 1963.

Biography: Archipenko, Alexander. *Archipenko, Fifty Creative Years, 1908–1958*. New York: TEKHNE, 1960.

Exhibition Catalogs: Apollinaire, Guillaume. *Alexandre Archipenko: Der Sturm*. Berlin: Der Sturm, 1913; *Alexander Archipenko: Bronzes*. New York: Perls Gallery, 1959; *Archipenko at Pace*. New York: Pace Gallery, 1973; *Archipenko, Polychrome Sculpture*. New York: Zabriskie Gallery & Chicago: Arts Club of Chicago, 1976; *Alexander Archipenko, The Late Experimental Years*. New York: Zabriskie Gallery, 1979; Karshan, Donald H. *Archipenko: The Early Works, 1910–1921: The Erich Goeritz Collection at The Tel Aviv Museum*. Tel Aviv, Israel: The Tel Aviv Museum, 1981.

Catalog Raisonné: Karshan, Donald H. *Archipenko: The Sculpture and Graphic Art, including a print catalogue raisonné*. Tübingen, Germany: Wasmuth, 1974.

ARDITTI QUARTET

(1974).

In nearly every instrumental genre there are individuals who make a specialty of performing avant-garde works as no one else can. What David Tudor was to the traditional piano, Paul Zukofsky (1943) was to the solo violin, Loretta Goldberg (1945) has become to electric keyboards, and Margaret Leng Tan (1944) is becoming to the grand piano, Irvine Arditti's string quartet has become to its literature.

His group's typical feat is to perform the complete string quartets of ELLIOTT CARTER, MAURICIO KAGEL, or GYÖRGY LIGETI in a single evening or on a single set of discs. They did so well with JOHN CAGE'S early quartets that he wrote some new ones for them. In their taste for high modernist music, the London-based Ardittis, as they are commonly called, contrast with the San Francisco-based Kronos Quartet, who have made a specialty of adapting pop songs to their instruments and of playing flashier, more accessible music.

Recordings: *Carter: Works for String Quartet, Vols. 1 & 2*. Etcetera, 1992; *Arditti String Quartet 1974–1994*. Montaigne, 1994; *Xenakis 1: musique de chambre 1955–1990*. Montaigne, 1994; *Györgi Ligeti Edition Vol. 1 String Quartets & Duets*. Sony, 1997; *Complete String Quartets of John Cage*. 2 vols. New York: Mode (17, 27), 1989 & 1992; Goldberg, Loretta. *Soundbridge*. N.p.: Opus One (CD 152), n.d. (c.1991).

ARIAS-MISSON, Alain

(11 December 1936).

A truly "mid-Atlantic" literary artist, a Harvard-educated classicist who works as a dexterous simultaneous interpreter, Arias-Misson has published literature and produced performances in both America and Europe. His first novel, *Confessions of a Murderer, Rapist, Fascist, Bomber, Thief* (1974), engages contemporary history in an imaginative way, as a series of fictionalized glosses on reproduced newspaper clippings, becoming, in sum, a coherent portrait of the gratuitous violence in our time. What is stylistically special about the novel is the exploitation of both the language and photographs of journalism. Arias-Misson has also produced, more in Europe than here, "public poems," which are language-based provocative performances, the words customarily appearing as signs rather than speech.

Works: *Confessions of a Murderer, Rapist, Fascist, Bomber, Thief; or A Year in the Life of an Ordinary American*. Chicago: Chicago Review, 1974; *The Public Poem Book*. CalaoneBaone, Italy: Factotumbook, 1978; *The Visio-Verbal Sins of a Literary Saint*. Verona, Italy: Rara, 1993; *The Mind Crime of August Saint*. Normal, IL: FC 2, 1993.

Exhibition Catalog: Dachy, Marc. *Alain Arias-Misson: opere dal 1974 al 1996*. Prato, Italy: Dopurtutto Centro Culturale, 1996.

ARMA, Paulo *see* WEISSHAUS, I.

ARMAJANI, Siah

(10 July 1939)

An Iranian who emigrated to America in the 1960s, Armajani moved from creating eccentric sculpture to building elegant and highly original pedestrian bridges. Beginning with models that were included in museum sculptural exhibitions, he was eventually invited to execute commissions. Perhaps the most successful, the 375-foot Irene Hixon Whitney Bridge (1988), arches over several lanes of highway, connecting the sculpture garden of the Walker Art Center to central Minneapolis. A slim structure with a curved arc that becomes inverted in the middle, the bridge incorporates words from American writers as various as Herman Melville and JOHN ASHBERY and colors reflective of American intellectual history. ("The yellow is from Monticello," Armajani once told an interviewer. "Jefferson called it the color of wheat, of the harvest.") These marvelous structures rank as architecture to some, but not to others.

Exhibition Catalogs: Princenthal, Nancy. *Siah Armajani: Elements*. New York: Max Protech Gallery, 1991; *SA: Contributions Anarchistes 1962–1994. Nice: Villon Arson, 1994.*

Interpretation: Crowe, Ann Glen. "Siah Armajani." In *Contemporary Masterworks,* ed. Colin Naylor. Chicago: St. James's Press, 1991.

ARMAN

(17 November 1928; b. Armand Fernandez).

As one of the self-proclaimed "New Realists" in Paris at the beginning of the 1960s, Arman used authentic objects, generally in abundance—overwhelming abundance. Simple though the idea of making a sculpture of only one kind of thing was, he produced, with audacity and witty style, accumulations of, for example, dollar bills, bullets, musical instruments, old cameras, watch parts, and kitchen utensils. Sometimes these accumulations are welded together; other times they lie free in a glass case. If metacollage consists of elements with something in common, these would be meta-assemblages. "He is always bending the object to his entirely personal and purely arbitrary will," writes the critic Henry Martin (1942), "as though to tell us that will is what we are most truly made of." Though the process of making his assemblages reflects mad and messy inspiration, Arman's results are always neat and picturesque.

Works: *Accumulations,* c.1957; *Home Sweet Home*, 1960; *Dustbins*, c. 1960; *Fullness*, 1960; *Chopin's Waterloo*, 1962; *Combustions*, 1963; *Renault Accumulations*, 1967–69; *Venus of the Shaving Brushes*, 1969; *Long Term Parking*, 1982–83.

Exhibition Catalog: *Arman Selected Works 1958–1974*. La Jolla, CA: La Jolla Museum of Contemporary Art, 1974.

Interpretation: Martin, Henry. *Arman*. New York: Abrams, 1973; Van der Marck, Jan. *Arman*. New York: Abbeville, 1984.

Catalogs Raisonnés: Otmezguine, Jane. *Arman etampes: catalogue raisonnée*. Paris: Marval, 1990; Durand-Ruel, Denise. *Arman Catalog Raisonné II*. Paris: Editions de la Différence, 1991.

ARMITAGE, Merle

(12 February 1893–March 1975).

By most measures the most distinctive book designer of his generation, Armitage used, in Dick Higgins's summary, "color and printed end leaves in most books, few rules or 'spinich' (characteristic of Bauhaus and Art Deco design), large page folios, minimalist title spreads with very large type size, unusual mixtures of typefaces, and, in his later books, recurring visual motifs, such as a Navaho rug in a book on Stravinsky." Armitage also authored and edited many volumes about modern art and modern dance, in addition to working as a promoter, publicist, and presenter of concerts, for which he customarily designed memorable brochures. Among his numerous books were anthologies of criticism about Igor Stravinsky, Martha Graham, Arnold Schoenberg, and George Gershwin (1898–1937). Though many of these volumes were reissued in their times, few are in print now. In 1957, the UCLA Library mounted an exhibition of Armitage's books. He worked briefly as an art director of slick magazines and in titling design for Hollywood studios. Armitage reportedly declared, "I write in order to have something to design." *Accent on Life* (1965) is Armitage's autobiography.

Works: *Edward Weston*. New York: E. Weyhe, 1932; *Picasso: Two Statements*. Los Angeles: Merl Armitage, 1936; *Accent on America*, New York: E. Weyhe, 1944; *Notes on Modern Printing*, New York: Wm. E. Rudge's Sons, 1945; *The Sculpture of Frances Rich*, Manzanita Press, 1974; *Dance Memorabilia*, ed. by Edwin Corle. New York: Duell, Sloan & Pearce, 1947; *Operations Santa Fe: Atchison, Topeka & Santa Fe Railway System*, ed. by Edwin Corle. New York: Duell, Sloan & Pearce, 1948.

Edited and Designed Anthologies: *Martha Graham: The Early Years* (1937). New York: Da Capo, 1978; *Schoenberg* (1937). Westport, CT: Greenwood Press, 1977; *George Gershwin* (1937). New York: Da Capo, 1995.

Works Edited and Designed by: Schmitz, Elie Robert. *The Piano Works of Claude Débussy* (1950). New York: Da Capo, 1984.

Biography: Purcell, Robert M. *Merle Armitage Was Here!: A Retrospective of a 20th Century Renaissance Man*. Morongo Valley, CA: Sagebrush Press, 1981; Ritchie,

Ward, *Merle Armitage: His Loves and His Many Lives*. Laguna Beach, CA: Laguna Verde Imprints, 1982.

Exhibition Catalogs: *Designed Book*. Ed. Ramiel McGhee. New York: E. Weyhe, 1938; *An Exhibition of the Books . . . by Merle Armitage*. Detroit: The Library, 1942.

ARMORY SHOW

(17 February–15 March 1913).

Officially called "The International Exhibition of Modern Art" and installed at the 69th Regiment Armory in New York, this was the single most influential exhibition of avant-garde painting ever in America. With over 1,600 objects, it was really two exhibitions within a single space. The American section, which contained roughly three-quarters of the items, was an unbiased comprehensive survey of current American activity. In the European section, however, were canvases by Impressionists, Georges Seurat, the Symbolists Odilon Redon and Puvis de Chavannes, Paul Cézanne, Vincent Van Gogh (eighteen items), Pierre Gauguin, Henri Matisse (forty items), while Pablo Picasso and Georges Braque, for two, were slighted. The edge of new European art was represented by Francis Picabia and Marcel Duchamp whose "Nude Descending a Staircase, No. 2" (1913) inspired outraged reviews in the press (a newspaper critic dubbed it "Explosion in a Shingle Factory"). Of the 174 works sold, the preponderance of 123 were made by European artists. The general unsophistication of the American public notwithstanding, nearly a half million people saw the Armory Show in New York, ten thousand visitors arriving on the final day, and at its later venues in Chicago and Boston—many of them remembering it for decades afterwards.

Marcel Duchamp, *Nude Descending a Staircase, No. 2*. Philadelphia Museum of Art: The Louise and Walter Arensberg Collection.

Bibliography: Association of American Painters and Sculptors. *For and Against: Anthology of Commentary on the Armory Show of 1913*. Ed. Frederick J. Gregg. New York: Privately pub., 1913; Brown, Milton W. *The Story of the Armory Show*. New York: Abbeville, 1988; Kuhn, Walt. *The Story of the Armory Show*. New York: Assoc. of American Painters and Sculptors, 1938; Schapiro, Meyer. "The Armory Show." In *Modern Art*. New York: Braziller, 1978.

Exhibition Catalogs: *Catalogue of International Exhibition of Modern Art, at the Armory of the Sixty-Ninth Infantry*. New York: Association of American Painters and Sculptors, 1913; *The Armory Show: 50th Anniversary Exhibition*. Utica, NY: Munson-Williams-Proctor, 1963.

ARMSTRONG, Louis

(4 August 1901–6 July 1971).

A precocious horn player from an indigent family, he was gigging in black bands around his native New Orleans as a teenager. By 1922 he went to Chicago to play in Oliver's Creole Jazz Band, a prominent group, making his first recordings with them in 1923. Quick to exploit the possibilities of records for disseminating his music, initially to black audiences, eventually to a larger multicultural audience, he made countless recordings with innumerable assortments of other musicians. By 1925, still in Chicago, he organized his own groups—initially the Hot Five, later the Hot Seven, etc.

Armstrong's first musical innovations were rhythmic. As the cultural critic Albert Murray put it, Armstrong became "the intimate beneficiary of ragtime and stride, the shift from the popularity of the 3/4 waltz beat of the operetta to the 4/4 of the fox trot, the one-step, the two-step, the drag, the stomp, the Afro-U.S. emphasis on percussion and on syncopation, the break, stop time, and so on." On a different sense of time, initially learned in black New Orleans, Armstrong founded an African-American modern music, incidentally becoming more influential than Bix Beiderbecke, an Iowa-born German–American cornetist, who epitomized a Caucasian style of horn-based jazz. (Whereas Beiderbecke died from disease exacerbated by excessive alcohol, and certain later jazz stars succumbed early to heroin, Armstrong's principal recreation/distraction was reportedly marijuana.) On the strength of his art, coupled with his persistence, Armstrong successfully imported African–American street culture into all of America's living rooms. Given the strength of racial prejudice, not to mention the practice of segregation, during the first half of the twentieth century, this was no easy feat—forging a cultural path that other African-American musicians have since successfully pursued.

Once Armstrong's reputation as a trumpeter was securely established, he became a successful singer, in a gravelly style uniquely his, even producing best-selling disks in which his trumpet took a back seat to his voice. Well-managed and generous with his time, he played in the largest and most prestigious venues around the world and appeared regularly in films and on radio and then television, working steadily until his death. The best encomium comes from Murray: "He took jazz from the level of popular entertainment and into the realm of a fine art that requires a level of consummate professional musicianship unexcelled anywhere in the world."

Recordings: *Let's Do It: The Best of the Verve Years* (PGD/Verve, 1995); *Essential Louis Armstrong* (Laserlight, 1995); *The Complete RCA Victor Recordings* (BMG, 1997); *Happy Fifties* (Ambassador, 1997); *An American Icon* (Uni/Hip-O), 1998.

Writings: *Swing that Music* (1936). New York: Da Capo, 1993; *Satchmo: My Life in New Orleans* (1954). New York: Da Capo, 1988.

Biography: Bergreen, Laurence. *Louis Armstrong*. New York: Broadway, 1997; Storb, Ilse. *Louis Armstrong: The Definitive Biography.* New York: Peter Lang, 1999.

Website: http://www.satchmo.net/

Interpretation: Bennett, Joshua. *The Louis Armstrong Companion*. New York: Schirmer Books, 1998; Murray, Albert. *The Blue Devils of Nada*. New York: Pantheon, 1996.

ARMSTRONG, Sara Garden

(5 April 1943).

In a series called *Airplayers,* begun in 1982, Armstrong made a series of progressively more complex kinetic sculptures that depend upon mechanically blown air for their movements. Notwithstanding surfaces reminiscent of Eva Hesse, these become in their breathing somewhat anthropomorphic, especially when several are exhibited in a single space, and their shadows create landscapes on the surrounding walls. The sounds initially come from the blowers switching on and off. By *Airplayer XIII* (1991), Armstrong had added two computers to control both variously and randomly the emission of lights and sounds.

Armstrong also produced extremely inventive book-art, likewise titled *Airplayers* (1990), that is filled with page-turning surprises, including, in addition to illustrations of her sculptures, such unusual materials as transparent sheets, silkscreened plastic vinyl, sandblasted lenses, and an LCD (liquid-crystal display).

Works: *Airplayers*. New York: Willis, Locker, & Owens, 1990; *Fragile Connections*. New York: Privately published, 1992.

Exhibition Catalogs: Trechsel, Gail Andres. *Sara Garden Armstrong: Given A Space*. Birmingham, AL: Birmingham Museum of Art, 1981; *Sound Sculpture Installation*. New York: Sou Yun Yi, 1988.

ARNESON, Robert

(4 September 1930–2 November 1992).

Arneson is the only innovative artist other than PETER VOULKOS to make ceramics his chosen medium. Unlike Voulkos, who took his inspiration from the ABSTRACT EXPRESSIONIST ferment that surrounded him and sought to enter the rarefied realm of high artistic aspiration, Arneson was more down to earth, so to speak, in his work with clay. He aimed satirical barbs at pomposity and self-importance, particularly his own. Arneson's many ceramic self-portraits combine references to art history, such as Chinese bowls and Roman columns, with comic renditions of his face, genitalia, hands, and feet. He portrays himself as a very ordinary human being trying to poke his head, and other parts, out of the great tradition. An idiosyncratic artist who mocked artistic ambition, Arneson managed through his self-deprecating humor to stand alone.

—Mark Daniel Cohen

Works: *Self-Portrait of the Artist Losing His Marbles*, 1965; *Smorg: Bob, the Cook*, 1971; *Assassination of a Famous Nut Artist*, 1972; *Classical Exposure*, 1972; *Captain Ace*, 1978; *This Head Is Mine*, 1981; *Chemo I*, 1992; *Chemo II*, 1992.

Exhibition Catalogs: Fineberg, Jonathan. *Robert Arneson: Self-Reflections*. San Francisco: San Francisco Museum of Modern Art, 1977; McTwigan, Michael. *Heroes and Clowns: Robert Arneson*. New York: Allan Frumkin Gallery, 1979; Kuspit, Donald. *Robert Arneson*. San Francisco: Fuller Goldeen Gallery, 1985; Benezra, Neal David. *Robert Arneson, A Retrospective*. Des Moines, IA: Des Moines Art Center, 1985; *Robert Arneson: From the Jackson Pollock Series*. Hartford, CT: Wadsworth Atheneum, 1990; *Robert Arneson: The Last Works*. San Francisco: John Berggruen Gallery, 1993.

ARP, Jean

(16 September 1887–7 June 1966; aka Hans A.).

Born a German citizen in Strasbourg, Arp moved easily between France and Germany (and between two first names), between the French and German languages, and between visual art and poetry. In the first respect, he made abstract reliefs dependent upon cutouts and highly distinctive sculptures utilizing curvilinear shapes. He worked with automatic composition, chance, and collaborations. He appropriated the epithet "concrete art," even though his biomorphic forms were quite different from the geometries of THEO VAN DOESBURG, who originated the term, and MAX BILL, who popularized it. Arp spoke of wanting "to attain the transcendent, the eternal which lies above and beyond the human." *Papiers déchirés* he composed by tearing up paper whose pieces fell randomly onto the floor in an analogue to the "automatic writing" of SURREALISM. He wrote, "I continued the development of glued works by structuring them spontaneously, automatically. I called this working 'according to the law of chance.' The 'law of chance,' which incorporates all laws and is as inscrutable to us as is the abyss from which all life comes, can only be experienced by surrendering completely to the unconscious." So profoundly did Arp believe in the implications of his method, he added, "I claimed that, whoever follows this law, will create pure life."

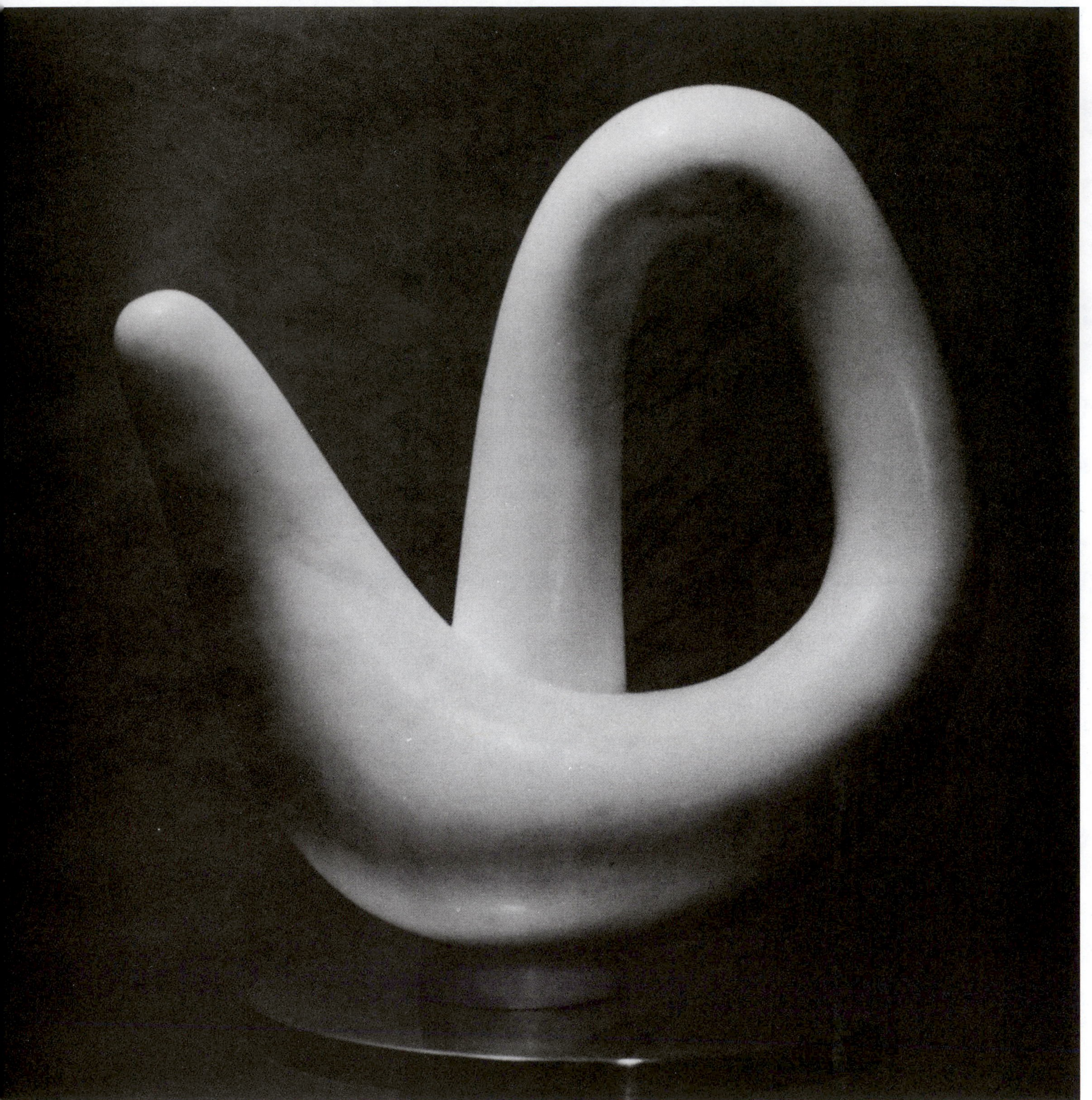

Jean Arp, *White Form*. CORBIS/Burstein Collection/© 2000 Artists Rights Society (ARS), New York/VG Bild-Kunst, Bonn.

One quality peculiar to Arp's work is the integration of contraries, which is to say that his art seems to belong to Surrealism as well as to DADA, to CONSTRUCTIVISM as well as to EXPRESSIONISM. His poems are commonly praised for their "lyrical innocence," especially by more conservative critics. One quality common to his visual art and his poetry is simplicity of shape and color.

Arp also published criticism that included *Die Kunstismen* (Isms of Art, 1925), written in collaboration with EL LISSITZKY, in which the two participants correctly identified all the avant-garde movements dating back to 1914. Oddly, this percipient text is not reprinted in the standard English-language anthology of Arp's writings. Not unlike other Dadaists, he evaded conscription into World War I with a certain theatrical style. As Matthew Josephson tells it, the German consul in Zurich gave Arp "a form to fill in, listing about thirty questions starting with his birth. He wrote down the day, month, and year—1889 [*sic*]—on the first line, repeated this for all the rest of the questions, then drew a line at the bottom of the page, and added it all up to the grand total of something like 56,610!" I've always wondered whether his reputation gained or lost from his having a surname that sounded like the English word for Art and thus prompted such striking epithets as Arp's Art.

Selected Works: *Untitled*, 1915; *Collage with Squares Arranged According to the Laws of Chance*, 1916–17; *Lunar Frog*, 1925; *Calligraphy of Navals*, 1928.

Writings: *On My Way*. New York: Wittenborn, 1948; *Arp on Arp: Poems, Essays, Memories.* (1966). Ed. Marcel Jean. Trans. Joachim Neugroschel. New York: Viking, 1972; *Three Painter Poets: Arp/Schwitters/Klee*. Trans. Harriet Watts. Harmondsworth, England: Penguin, 1974; and El Lissitzky. (1925). *Die Kunstismen/Les ismes de l'art/The Isms of Art*. Baden, Switzerland: Lars Muller (CH-5401), 1990.

Exhibition Catalogs: Soby, James Thrall. *Arp*. New York: Museum of Modern Art, 1958; *Exhibition of Sculpture in Marble, Bronze, and Wood Relief from 1923–1963*. New York: Sidney Janis Gallery, 1963; *Hommage à Jean Arp*. Paris: Galerie Denise René, 1974; *Jean Hans Arp: Sculpture, Relief, Drawing*. New York: New Art Center Gallery, 1962.

Interpretation: Giedion-Welcker, Carola. *Jean Arp*. New York: Abrams, 1957; Josephson, Matthew. *Life among the Surrealists*. New York: Holt, 1962; Last, H. W. *Hans Arp: The Poet of Dadaism*. London: Oswald Wolf, 1969; Read, Herbert. *The Art of Jean Arp*. New York: Abrams, 1968; Trier, Eduard. *Jean Arp: Sculpture, His Last Ten Years*. New York: Abrams, 1968.

THE ART STRIKE

(1990–1993).

One of the most famous examples of artistic PRAECISIO was the Art Strike (1990–1993), when on at least three continents artists agreed "to stop making, distributing, selling, exhibiting or discussing their work." Stewart Home (1962), the major architect and proponent of the strike, saw art as "a symptom of the disease capitalism" and the strike as a means of undermining capitalism by "intensifying the class war." The strikers, however, were always quick to point out that the Art Strike was a bad idea and that it would fail to accomplish what it set out to do. The importance of the strike, finally, existed in the mere conception of the strike rather than in the execution of it, and as such it was designed as one large conceptual art piece: performance art without the performance. The Art Strike was meant to allow time to reconceptualize art, to get people to stop viewing it as a superior form of knowledge, to return to reality (after having spent decades escaping reality through art); it was a time to stop understanding art as a special activity.

A number of reactions to the Art Strike appeared as it progressed. The first might have been the Forced Art Participation (FAP), which had a goal of forcing people to take part in art. The proprietors of Xexoxial Endarchy, an indefatigable multimedia art establishment, called for an Art

Glut (1990–2000). U.S. artist Mark Bloch (1956) suggested a Word Strike (1991–94), during which artists were supposed to follow the motto "Don't say 'art' unless you mean 'money.'" After the end of the Art Strike, art returned to normal, as if nothing had happened.

—Geof Huth

Bibliography: Home, Stewart. *Neoist Manifestos/The Art Strike Papers*. Stirling, Scotland: A.K. (P.O. Box 4682, San Francisco, CA 94140-0682), 1991; "Assessing the Art Strike, 1990–1993," *Yawn: Critique of Culture*, 38 (March 1993).

a

ARTAUD, Antonin

(4 September 1896–4 March 1948).

Artaud is the author of a theoretical book so extraordinary, *Le Théâtre et son double* (1938; *The Theatre and Its Double,* 1958), that it lends authority to everything else he ever did: books of plays, his movie appearances, even his persistent madness. Influenced particularly by Balinese dancers he saw in Paris in the early 1930s, Artaud imagined a Western theater that would neglect realism and narrative for kinetic images, rituals, and even magic. Such theater could surround the audience, even enticing it to participate. Thus, under the banner of "theatre of cruelty," he forecast not only Peter Brook's (1925) more radical performances and the LIVING THEATER, but HAPPENINGS and subsequent PERFORMANCE ART. Though Artaud aspired to create consequential avant-garde art and sometimes did inspired performances of his own texts, it is as a theorist and an artistic "personality" that he is mostly remembered.

Writings: *The Theatre and Its Double* (1938). Trans. M. C. Richards. New York: Grove, 1958; *Selected Writings*. Ed. Susan Sontag. Berkeley: University of California Press, 1988.

Website: http://www.hydra.umn.edu/artaud/

Exhibition Catalog: Houstian, Christina. *Antonin Artaud: Works on Paper*. New York: MoMA, 1996.

Interpretation: Mauriac, Claude. "Antonin Artaud," *The New Literature* (1958). Trans. Samuel I. Stone. New York: Braziller, 1959.

ART POVERA, L'ART CONTEMPORAIN, ART INFORMEL, ART BRUT, ART AUTRE, SUPERREALISM, NEW ESTHETIC, ART OF THE REAL, TRANSAVANTGARDE, NEO-GEO, UNEXPRESSIONISM, etc.

These terms are grouped together because they were used at one time or another to merchandise a new group of artists; although some of the individual artists promoted under these banners might have survived, the terms did not, mostly because they (and others with a similarly short life span) were coined out of the intelligence of advertising and promotion rather than art criticism and art history. (What is surprising is that most of the critics adopting such opportunistic epithets survived their decline and disappearance, perhaps indicating how the business of criticism differs from the life of art.)

Bibliography: To list one or another book over many others would make unnecessarily invidious comparisons.

ARTISTS' BOOKS

This term arose in the 1970s to encapsulate anything bookish made by individuals established in the visual-arts world or who had gone to art school. Like most art terms based on biography, rather than the intrinsic properties of the art, it was a marketing device, designed to sell works to an audience respectful of "artists"; because of the biographical base, the term forbade qualitative distinctions, "better" artists not necessarily producing superior books. Artistically considered, alternative book forms should be called *book-art*; the produce, *book-art books* (to further distinguish them from "art books," which are illustrated books, customarily in a large format, about visual art). Some of us have favored this esthetic definition over the autobiographical, without success so far.

Among the major practitioners of book-art are Sol Le Witt, Tom Phillips, Dieter Rot, Paul Zelevansky, and Sara Garden Armstrong.

Interpretation: Lyons, Joan, ed. *Artists' Books*. Layton, UT: Peregrine Smith, 1985; Mœglin-Delcroix, Anne. *Esthétique du livre d'artiste*. Paris: Jean Michel Place, 1997.

Exhibition Catalog: *Artists' Books*. Philadelphia: Moore College of Art, 1973.

ASHBERY, John

(28 July 1927).

Because Ashbery has by the 1990s become the epitome of the "Major American Poet," it is easy to forget that he began as a fairly experimental writer. His long poem "Europe" (1960) is a classic of acoherent diffuseness, which is to say that the poet drew words from a variety of sources, barely connecting them. (Acoherence in literature is comparable to atonality in music.) When this poem appeared in Ashbery's second book, *The Tennis Court Oath* (1962), the critic John Simon (1925), a sure barometer of conservative prejudices, wrote, "It never deviates into—nothing so square as sense!—sensibility, sensuality, or sentences." None of Ashbery's many later poems equal "Europe" for esthetic deviance in my opinion (acknowledging that others might disagree with me). Ashbery also coedited two moderately avant-garde English-language literary journals published in France, *Locus Solus* (1960–62), named after a book by Raymond Roussel, on whom Ashbery wrote his M.A. thesis, and *Art and Literature* (1964–1968).

After he received three prominent literary prizes for *Self-Portrait in a Convex Mirror* (1975), Ashbery's professional life changed precipitately. He received university positions and praise from academic critics, becoming the principal example in the argument that nothing, but nothing, will elevate the reputation of a sometime experimental writer as successfully as a "major prize." He became, enviably, perhaps the only American poet whose books appear nearly biannually from commercial houses, establishing a bibliography nearly as long as that of a poet much loved by smaller publishers. Oddly, perhaps because his effects are so subtle, those acknowledging his influence rarely write as well.

Poetry: *Turandot and Other Poems*. New York: Tibor de Nagy, 1953; *Some Trees*. New Haven: Yale University Press, 1956; *The Poems*. New York: Tiber Press, 1960; *The Tennis Court Oath*. Middletown: Wesleyan University Press, 1962; *Rivers and Mountains*. New York: Holt, Rinehart, 1966; *Selected Poems*. London: Jonathan Cape, 1967; *Three Madrigals*. New York: Poet's Press, 1968; *Sunrise in Suburbia*. New York: Phoenix Book Shop, 1968; *Fragment*. Los Angeles: Black Sparrow Press, 1969; *Evening in the Country*. San Francisco: Spanish Main, 1970; *The Vermont Notebook*. Los Angeles: Black Sparrow Press, 1975; *Self-Portrait in a Convex Mirror*. New York: Viking, 1975; *Houseboat Days*. New York: Viking Press, 1977; *As We Know*. New York: Viking Press, 1979; *Shadow Train*. New York: Viking, 1981; *A Wave*. New York: Viking, 1984; *April Galleons*. New York: Viking, 1987; *Flow Chart*. New York: Knopf, 1991; *Hotel Lautreamont*. New York; Knopf, 1992; *And the Stars Were Shining*. New York; Farrar, Straus, 1994; *The Mooring of Staring Out: The First Five Books of Poetry*. Hopewell, NJ: Ecco, 1997.

Fiction: with James Schuyler. *A Nest of Ninnies* (1969). Calais, VT: Z Press, 1975.

Plays: *Three Plays*. Calais, VT: Z Press, 1975.

Art Criticism: *Reported Sightings: Art Chronicles 1957–1987*. Ed. David Bergman. Cambridge, MA: Harvard University Press, 1991.

Biography: None yet, curiously.

Interpretation: Kostelanetz, Richard. "John Ashbery" (1976). In *The Old Poetries and the New*. Ann Arbor: University of Michigan, 1981; Shapiro, David. *John*

Ashbery: An Introduction to the Poetry. New York: Columbia University Press, 1979; Lehman, David. ed. *John Ashbery*. Ithaca, New York: Cornell University Press, 1979; Schultz, Susan M., ed. *The Tribe of John Ashbery and Contemporary Poetry*. Tuscaloosa: University of Alabama Press, 1995.

Bibliography: Kermani, David K. *John Ashbery: A Comprehensive Bibliography*. New York: Garland, 1976.

a

ASHER, Michael

(15 July 1943).

Asher's field of concern has been the exposure of the institutional environments and social power structures that determine the nature of what is accepted as art. His method is to rearrange the elements in existing exhibition spaces to emphasize the conventions under which they are displayed. His two Chicago projects in 1979 are the most effective examples of his method. At the Art Institute of Chicago, he moved a statue of George Washington by Jean-Antoine Houdon from the top of a staircase to the room below, suggesting the transformation of a 1917 sculpture into a contemporary installation by the merest gesture. At the Museum of Contemporary Art, Asher removed aluminum panels from the exterior of the building and installed them inside, implying their alteration into artworks.

More critiques of art than works of art, his efforts have an advantage over BRUCE NAUMAN's critical inversions of the circumstances by which art is viewed. Nauman's assaults on the viewer amount to nothing more than assaults on the viewer. Asher's projects suggest a coherent idea: that we struggle to see and interpret a work of art wherever the exhibiting institution tells us it is to be found; and without such institutional aegis, we might not see art at all.

—Mark Daniel Cohen

Works: *The Appearing/Disappearing Image/Object*, 1969; *Anti-Illusion: Procedures/Materials*, 1969.

Installations: Stedelijk Van Abbemuseum, Eindhoven, Netherlands, 1973; *Los Angeles in the Seventies*, Fort Worth Art Museum, Fort Worth, TX, 1979; Gallery A 402, California Institute of the Arts, Valencia, CA, 1973; Art Institute of Chicago, Chicago, IL, 1979; Museum of Contemporary Art, Chicago, IL, 1979.

Writings: with Buchloh, Benjamin H. D. *Writings 1973–1983 On Works 1969–1979*. Halifax, NS: Press of the Nova Scotia College of Art and Design; Los Angeles: Museum of Contemporary Art, 1983.

Exhibition Catalogs: *Michael Asher: University Art Museum, November–December, 1983*. Berkeley: University Art Museum, University of California, 1983; *MA: The Renaissance Society, University of Chicago, January 21–March 4, 1990*. Chicago: The Renaissance Society, 1990; Foray, Jean-Michel and Duruel, Catherine. *MA: Centre Georges Pompidou, Musée Nationale d'Art Moderne, Galeries Contemporaines, 10 Juillet–15 Septembre 1991*. Paris: Editions du Centre Pompidou, 1991; *MA: Kunsthalle Bern*. Bern, Switzerland: Kunsthalle, 1995.

ASHLEY, Robert

(28 March 1930).

Ashley's specialty has been a theatrical music that draws upon speech that he customarily performs in oddly flat and barely intelligible ways, as though he were talking to himself. In an early example, *Wolfman* (1964), he declaims against a noisy tape collage, both raised to an offensively high volume. Kyle Gann writes, "In another, equally provocative nightclub-ambiance piece, *Purposeful Lady Slow Afternoon* (1968), a woman hesitantly, without using any explicit words, describes being forced to give oral sex, over a disarmingly innocent accompaniment of bells." For later subjects, Ashley usually draws upon American myth. In *Perfect Lives* (1983), he both scored and wrote a seven-part opera designed for the scale of television; versions also exist on two audiocassettes and three compact discs (and parts were adapted for live performance). Ashley's book of that same title is also radically different from any other book about an opera, indicatively lacking any photographs or musical scores. *Atalanta* (1985) is a more conventional opera that, given its middle-American content, sounds odd in Italian. Yet later Ashley operas were created expressly for the small screen over the large stage, the composer reportedly declaring, not unsympathetically, "I don't believe that this recent fashion of American composers trying to imitate state opera from Europe means anything." Given his laudable purposes, one wishes his work were stronger.

Works: *Heat*, 1961; *Public Opinion Descends upon the Demonstrators*, 1962; *Boxing*, 1964; *Wolfman*, 1964; *Purposeful Lady Slow Afternoon*, 1968; *Illusion Models*, 1970; *Night Sport*, 1973.

Recordings: *Perfect Lives*. New York: Lovely Music, 1983.

Books: *Perfect Lives*. New York & San Francisco: Archer Fields-Burning Books, 1991.

Interpretation: DeLio, Thomas. *Circumscribing the Open Universe: Essays on Cage, Feldman, Wolff, Ashley, and Lucier*. Washington, DC: University Press of America, 1984; Osterreich, Norbert. "Music with Roots in the Aether," *Perspectives of New Music* (1977); Rockwell, John. "Post-Cageian Experimentation and New Kinds of Collaboration: Robert Ashley," *All-American Music: Composition in the Late Twentieth Century* (1983). New York: Da Capo, 1997.

ASSEMBLAGE

(1950s–1970s).

This term was purportedly coined in the early 1950s by the French artist Jean Dubuffet (1901–1985) initially for lithographs made from paper COLLAGES and then for small sculptures made from papier-mâché, scraps of wood, sponge, and other debris. The word was popularized by a 1961 exhibition at New York's Museum of Modern Art, whose catalog spoke of works that "are predominantly *assembled* rather than painted, drawn, modeled, or carved." On display were by-then classic collages along with sculptures by LOUISE NEVELSON, RICHARD STANKIEWICZ (1922–1983), JOSEPH CORNELL, and EDWARD KIENHOLZ, whose contribution was really a tableau (which differs from sculpture in having a theatrical frontside, forbidding close access). By now, the epithet "assemblage" functions best as a definition for three-dimensional collage.

Exhibition Catalog: Seitz, William C. *The Art of Assemblage*. New York: MoMA, 1961.

Interpretation: Kaprow, Allan. *Assemblage, Environments & Happenings*. New York: Abrams, 1966.

ASSEMBLING

(1968).

This has become the generic name for a book/periodical in which contributors submit copies of whatever they want to include and their paper is collated and bound into finished books. Meant to service alternative work, such media made the contributors responsible for design and typesetting, eliminating "editorial" objections and interference. The name is taken from *Assembling* (1970–83), which was founded by Henry James Korn (1945), later a museum director, and RICHARD KOSTELANETZ, who also prepared a retrospective catalog for an exhibition in an alternative space. Scarcely the first, *Assembling* had a long life, second only to *Art/Life* (1981), published monthly by Joe Cardella, and was consistently the thickest, serving the largest constituency of writer/artist self-printers. Assemblings continue to appear around the world. Appreciative of true freedom of publication, a Hungarian named Géza Perneczky has become the principal historian of this radical movement. It could be said that the sum of self-prepared artists' home pages on the INTERNET represent an Assembling.

Books: *Art/life*. Ed. Joe Cardella (P.O. Box 23020, Ventura, CA 93002).

Exhibition Catalogs: Kostelanetz, Richard, ed. *Assembling Assembling*. New York: Assembling (P.O. Box 444, Prince St., New York, NY 10012-0008), 1978;

Perkins, Stephen. *Assembling Magazines: International Networking Collaborations*. Iowa City, IA: Subspace, 1996.

History: Perneczky, Géza. *The Magazine Network: The Trends of Alternative Art in the Light of Their Periodicals 1968–1988* (1991). Trans (into English) Tibor Szendrei. Köln: Soft Geometry, 1993.

ATONALITY

(1908).

This term became current in the 1910s among Viennese musicians who felt they were avoiding the traditional relationships that defined both major and minor scales. The technique of atonal writing depended upon the unconstrained use of all notes, as though they had equal weight, regardless of previous "harmonious" relationships, thereby creating music that seems to float above any foundation. Arnold Schoenberg, for instance, refused to use a key signature in his work from the 1910s, preferring, in Nicolas Slonimsky's phrases, to let "the melody flow freely unconstrained by the rigid laws of modulation, cadence, sequence, and other time-honored devices of tonal writing." (Slonimsky adds that Schoenberg himself, predisposed to Viennese precision in language, preferred the term "atonicality," because his music lacked not tones but tonics and dominants, the traditional touchstones of Western harmony.)

Once the principle of atonality was understood, the question arose whether there hadn't been precursors. Paul Griffiths (1947), among the more sophisticated music reviewers currently writing in English, says that "atonal means of order may be distinguished as far back as Mozart: one *locus classicus* is the Commendatore's grim statement in the penultimate scene of *Don Giovanni* (1787), where in seven bars he touches eleven of the twelve notes. Still more striking is the opening of Liszt's *Faust Symphony* (1853–57), where the unharmonized theme stikes the twelve different notes within the first thirteen." Griffith continues, "One may say there is here the threat of atonality, but the threat does not begin to be carried out until dissonant harmonies are sustained over a longer period, as they are in several of Liszt's late piano pieces (1880–86)." My own opinion is that those predecessors' practices were too slight to represent a radical position (that would, say, warrant an entry in a book like this).

In a dialectical interpretation of modern musical tonality, atonality becomes the antithesis that is resolved with the discovery of Serial Music as a new, alternative structure for the strict ordering of pitches. In fact, after 1923, neither Arnold Schoenberg nor Anton Webern returned to nonserial atonality, having completed the dialectical synthesis. (I have coined the epithet *acoherence* as a literary analog, initially to characterize the early poetry of John Ashbery, who is musically sophisticated, but now as a definition for all writing that eschews traditional grammatical and semantic structures.) Though much recent music could be defined as atonal, the term is no longer used, or useful.

Interpretation: Forte, Allan. *The Structure of Atonal Music*. New Haven, CT: Yale University Press, 1973; Griffith, Paul. *The Thames and Hudson Encyclopedia of 20th-Century Music*. London: Thames & Hudson, 1986; Perle, George. *Serial Composition and Atonality* (1962). 6th ed. Berkeley, CA: University of California, 1991; Rahn, John. *Basic Atonal Theory*. New York: Schirmer Books, 1980.

ATTIE, Dotty

(20 March 1938).

Taking the comic-book form of sequential panels, Attie has made an unusually allusive art that echoes classical painting, particularly Jean Auguste Dominique Ingres (1780–1867), and Victorian literature, particularly Anthony Trollope (1815–82), in addition to comic books. Her square, bordered panels tend to have either picture or text, in either case propelling a narrative; and beneath the

Dotty Attie. *Justine Remembered*, 27 September–15 October 1983. Courtesy A.I.R. Gallery, New York.

innocuous surface are hints of menace and nightmare. The pictures are usually drawn from details in masterpiece paintings (thus making her work comparable to music compositions that draw phrases from the classics). "Often as not," writes the curator Howard Fox, "her stories involve the nobility of another century, usually in polite company at formal social occasions. This innocent facade seems to mask an underlying corruption."

Exhibition Catalogs: *Pierre and Lady Holland*. New York: A.I.R. Gallery, 1976; *Dotty Attie: Wadsworth Atheneum*. Hartford, CT: Wadsworth Atheneum, 1980; *Attie: Paintings and Drawings*. Pittsburgh, PA: Pittsburgh Center for the Arts, 1989.

AUDIO ART

(1980s).

This term arose to define esthetic experience based on sound, as distinct from music on one side and language on the other. It can exist in live performance, whether on radio or on stage, as well as on audiotape. Typical pieces of audio art are about the sound of something—say, the sound of seduction, the sound of the language of prayer, the sound of particular cities, or sounds of nature. Among the major practitioners are John Cage (particularly in his early *Williams Mix* (1953), Sorrel (Doris) Hays (especially in her *Southern Voices,* 1981), Jackson Mac Low, Makoto Shinohara (1931, especially in *City Visit* [1971]), Frits Wieland (especially in *Orient Express),* and Noah Creshevsky.

Bibliography: Lander, Dan, and Micah Lexier, eds. *Audio by Artists*. Toronto: Art Metropole, 1990.

AUDIOVIDEOTAPES

(c. 1980).

This is my coinage for video art in which the image accompanies highly articulate sound, usually because the soundtrack is composed before the image and/or the videoartist also works in audio art or music composition. The master here is Reynold Weidenaar, who indeed took degrees in music composition before turning to video, whose best videotapes incorporate his own music compositions. This procedure of sound preceding image is scarcely new. Some classic cartoons were produced this way—it's hard to imagine how Walt Disney's *Fantasia* could have been made otherwise. Likewise the excerpts that comprise *Opera Imaginaire*, an anthology of imaginative French television programs, mostly based on familiar recorded arias, which were subsequently released on commercial videotape. Orson Welles, who made classic radio programs before he produced films, reportedly recorded the soundtrack of his films before he shot any footage, finding sound a surer guide to visual-verbal narrative art.

Videotapes: Weidenaar, Reynold. *Love of Line, of Light, and Shadow: The Brooklyn Bridge*, 1982; Welles, Orson. *Citizen Kane,* 1940.

Interpretation: Kostelanetz, Richard. "Orson Welles as Acoustic Filmmaker." In *Special Sounds: The Art of Radio in North America* (forthcoming).

AUSTIN, Larry

(12 September 1930).

A professor who founded the extravagantly designed periodical *Source: Music of the Avant-Garde* (1967–74), which printed variously alternative scores and interviews, as well as including ten-inch records of previously suppressed music, Austin has worked adventurously with Electronic Music, live electronic performance, and theatrical conceptions. I remember best *The Magicians* (1968), which was performed on Halloween on a stage bathed in black light, with two screens that apparently swiveled with the breeze. The performers included several children performing elementary tasks, singing songs that resounded through an amplification system that treated soft, high notes gently. Austin spoke of this piece as a "time object. I wanted to take music out of the context of a dramatic flow of consequential events and to lose, as much as possible, the sense of time." More recently, Austin has used computers not only to make music but to create interactive situations for live ensembles.

Works: *Piano Variations*, 1960; *Collage*, for Several Instruments, 1963; *Quartet 3*, electronic music on tape, 1972; *Prelude and Postlude to Plastic Surgery*, for Keyboards, Film, and Tape, 1971; *Phoenix*, Computer Music on Tape, 1974; *Maroon Bells*, for Voice, Piano, and Tape, 1976; *Beachcomber*, for 4 Musicians and Tape, 1983; *Montage: Theme and Variations I*, for Violin and Computer Music on Tape, 1985; *Accidents 2*, sound projections for Piano and Computer Music, 1992.

Publications: *Source: Music of the Avant-Garde* (thirteen vols.). Davis, CA: Composer/Performer Federal, 1967–1974.

AVERY, Tex

(26 February 1907–27 August 1980; b. Frederick B. A.).

After directing some "Oswald the Rabbit" cartoons for Walter Lantz at Universal in the mid-'30s, he became a principal creator of Bugs Bunny (1940, in *A Wild Hare*), who subsequently appears in over 150 films as an anarchistic protagonist who survives all adversity (as, needless to say, a descendant of preternaturally wise rabbits in American folklore and literature). What distinguished the best Avery cartoons from Walt Disney's, say, are such qualities as quicker pace, a sharper edge, continous detailed movement, greater violence (though no injury is permanent), unsupervised activities (typically devoid of parents), improbable situations (when some other studies were cultivating realism), and a nightmare from which a protagonist cannot escape. No other animator produced so many classics. One of my favorites is *Billy Boy* (1953), which portrays an insatiably voracious goat that eats up everything around him until he is rocketed to the moon, which he devours as well. The film is a linear narrative wholly devoid of digression, epiphany, or climax. Avery also nurtured the talents of Chuck Jones (1912), I. M. Freleng (1905–1995, aka Fritz F.), and other Warner Brothers animators prior to his quitting them in 1940. Among Avery's other creations were Chilly Willy the Penguin, Lucky Ducky, and Droopy the sorrowful-looking Dog. Among the masterpieces starring the last is *Droopy's Double Trouble* (1951), in which Droopy has an identical twin, Drippy, who terrorizes a canine lummox named Spike who can't distinguish between the two. Avery's Bugs Bunny cartoons are widely available on videotape.

Works: *A Wild Hare*, 1941; *Henpecked Hoboes*, 1941; *Dumb-Hounded*, 1943; *Happy-Go-Nutty*, 1944; *The Shooting of Dan MacGoo*, 1945; *King-Sized Canary*, 1947; *Slaphappy Lion*, 1947; *Lucky Ducky*, 1948; *Bad Luck Blackie*, 1949; *The Cat that Hated People*, 1949; *The Car of Tomorrow*, 1952; *Flea Circus*, 1953; *Deputy Droopy*, 1954.

Interpretation: Adamson, Joe. *Tex Avery: King of Cartoons* (1975). New York: Da Capo, 1985.

AYLER, Albert

(13 July 1936–25 November 1970).

More than any other, Ayler realized the highly abrasive, EXPRESSIONISTIC music that seemed to become the avant-garde edge for the younger jazz cognoscenti in the 1960s. He performed on the tenor saxophone, often in collaboration with his brother Donald, a trumpeter; among the records that epitomize his style is *Bells* (ESP, 1965), which captures a live concert at New York's Town Hall on 1 May 1965. I have played this single-sided record for people who think themselves enthusiasts for everything "way out," only to watch them wince. Ayler's body was found in New York's East River; the cause of his death has never been explained.

Works: *Albert Ayler* (with "Bells," recorded in 1965). Therwil, Switzerland: Hat Hut, 1990; *Witches & Devils*. *Freedom*, 1964; *Vibrations, Arista Freedom 1000*, 1975; *Spiritual Unity*. Albert Ayler Trio, New York: ESP 1002, 1965.

Website: http://www.gslis.utexas.edu/~jeffs/ayler.html (bio of the artist in several parts).

BAADER, Johannes

(22 June 1876–15 January 1955).

An architect by training, Baader became the ironic *Oberdada* in the brief life of Berlin DADA, proclaiming himself "President of the League of Intertelluric Superdadaist Nations." As a dense collagist, he filched posters off the streets and mixed fragments of them with newspaper articles and miscellaneous numbers and letters. In 1919 and 1920, he exhibited two different versions of his *Handbuch des Oberdadaismus* (Manual of Superdadaism, abbreviated to HADO), which presages later book-art created mostly for gallery exhibitions. In the center of the 1919 Dada Fair, Baader constructed an early ASSEMBLAGE, the *Plasto-Dio-Dada-Drama,* which, in a departure, included "instructions for gazing at it": "Monumental Dadaist architecture on five floors with three gardens, a tunnel, two lifts, and a door shaped like a top hat. The ground floor or level is the fate predetermined before birth and has nothing to do with the story. Description of the floor: 1) The Preparation of the Oberdada. 2) The Metaphysical Ordeal. 3) Initiation. 4) The World War. 5) The World Revolution." Baader also exhibited a plan for a zoo without bars that was actually realized in a different form.

Exhibition Catalog: Scholz, Dieter, et al. (eds.). *Ich Segne Hölle*. Siegen, Germany: Universitäte\-Gesamthachschule Siegen, 1995.

Interpretation: Dachy, Marc. *The Dada Movement*. New York: Rizzoli, 1990.

BABBITT, Milton

(10 May 1916).

Credit ARNOLD SCHOENBERG with inventing an entirely new language for music—a revolutionary reordering of tonal possibilities—but credit Milton Babbitt with extending the SERIAL idea to musical dimensions other than pitch—duration (including rhythm), register, dynamics (attack), and timbre. The result of this logical extension of Schoenberg's ideas was a twelve-tone music of unprecedented structural complexity, in which every note contributed to several kinds of serial relationships. From this principle of simultaneous development, Babbitt developed a revolutionary esthetic that equated excellence with "the multiplicity of function of every event" (the variety of serial relationships each note developed). "I want a piece of music to be literally as much as possible," he once said, and his favorite words of praise are "profoundly organized" and "structurally intricate." Recorded examples of this phase of Babbitt's career include *Du* (1951), a song cycle, and *Composition for Four Instruments* (1948).

Because his music was too difficult for nearly all performers, he began in the mid-1950s to use an early music SYNTHESIZER that was constructed, with Babbitt as a consultant, by RCA. It offered the twofold possibility of achieving precisely all of the complicated effects he desired and of fixing on audiotape a "performance" for all time. From this encounter came such serial compositions as *Ensembles for Synthesizer* (1964) and *Philomel* (1964), in which even the listener unfamiliar with serial music theory can hear a complexity of articulation and an absence of repetition.

It is fair to say that success came to Babbitt in the 1960s, in his late forties, when he became a chaired professor of music at Princeton University. Of the numerous commissions he has subsequently received, I would particularly recommend *Phonemena* (1974, from "phonemes," not "phenomena"), which typically exists in two versions—one for soprano and tape, the second for soprano and piano. He is probably one of few individuals mentioned in this book to receive a MacArthur "genius" grant. Perhaps this success reflects his talents as a standup speaker who is at once witty and provocative, intimidating and engaging.

Writings: "Twelve-Tone Rythmic Structure and the Electronic Medium," *Perspectives of New Music* (Fall 1962); "The Composer as Specialist." In *Esthetics Contemporary* (1978), ed. Richard Kostelanetz. 2d ed. Buffalo, New York: Prometheus, 1989.

Compositions: *3 Compositions* for Piano, 1947; *Composition* for Four Instruments, 1948; *Du*, song cycle for Soprano and Piano, 1951; *Partitions*,1957; *Vision and Prayer* for soprano and tape, 1964; *Philomel* for Soprano and Tape, 1964; *Post-Partitions*, 1966; *Sextets* for Violin and Piano, 1966; *Phonemena* for Soprano and Tape, 1975; *The Head of the Bed* for Soprano and Four Instruments, 1982; *None but the Lonely Flute* for Flute, 1991; *Septet, But Equal* for Three Clarinets, String Trio, and Piano, 1992.

Website: http://www.schirmer.com/composers/babbitt_bio.html

Conversations: Dembski, Stephen, and Joseph N. Straus, eds. *Milton Babbitt: Words About Music*. Madison: University of Wisconsin Press, 1987; Biggs, Hays, & Susan Orgel. eds. *Musically Incorrect: Conversations about Music at the End of the 20th Century*. New York: C. F. Peters, 1998.

Interpretation: Mead, Andrew Washburn. *An Introduction to the Music of Milton Babbitt*. Princeton: Princeton University Press, 1993.

BACH, P.D.Q.

(1959).

This entry belongs under P. D. Q. Bach (1807–1742), because a "dummy" by this name produces far more innovative music than his ventriloquist, Peter Schickele (July 17, 1935). Perhaps the greatest and most fertile comic composer in musical history, P. D. Q. Bach excels at mixing cultural periods, beginning with his titles: *Concerto for Horn and Hardart* (referring to a chain of automats in New York City), *Iphigenia in Brooklyn, Hansel and Gretel and Ted and Alice,* and *The Safe Sextette*. "P. D. Q." does not quote classical compositions as much as write melodies of similar structure and texture but with a contemporary sense of harmony and musical literacy. The innovation is pseudo-classical music that reflects the influence of modernists such as STRAVINSKY and incidentally resembles conceptually certain fictions by JORGE LUIS BORGES. Especially in concert tours, P. D. Q. Bach's work is customarily introduced by a disheveled figure called "Professor Peter Schickele" who claims scholarly expertise on "P. D. Q." Because "P. D. Q."'s subjects-for-disruption have included not only the Bach family but Mozart, Copland, and Schickele's Juilliard classmate PHILIP GLASS, it could be said that "P. D. Q." has produced a kind of DADA music funnier than that of, say, SATIE and SLONIMSKY.

Recordings: *Addicted to P. D. Q. Bach & Prof. Peter Schickele* (Vanguard CSRV 375); *An Evening with P. D. Q. Bach* (Vanguard VBD 79195); *Black Forest Bluegrass* (Vanguard CV 79427); *An Hysteric Return* (Vanguard VBD 79223); *The Intimate P.D.Q. Bach* (Vanguard CV 79335); *Liebeslieder Polkas* (Vanguard CV 79438); *A Little Nightmare Music* (Telarc CD 80376); *Music for an Awful Lot of Winds & Percussion*. (Telarc CD 80307); *Oedipus Tex & Other Choral Calamities* (Telarc CD 80239); *P.D.Q.*

Bach on the Air (Vanguard VDB 79268); *Portrait of P.D.Q. Bach* (Vanguard CV 79399); *1712 Overture & Other Musical Assaults* (Telarc CD 80210); *The Wurst of P.D.Q. Bach* (Vanguard CVSD2-719/20).

Biography: Schickele, Peter. *The Definitive Biography of P.D.Q. Bach*. New York: Random House, 1976.

Website: http://www.sit.wisc.edu/~drsillars/pdq/

Critical Studies: Kostelanetz, Richard. "Peter Schickele (1989)." In *On Innovative Music(ian)s*. New York: Limelight, 1989.

b

BALL, Hugo

(22 February 1886–14 September 1927).

A cofounder of DADA who ended his short life as a Catholic writer, the mercurial Ball, born in Switzerland, began by rejecting German EXPRESSIONISM as fundamentally violent. He reportedly coined the term "Dada," which he picked randomly from the dictionary, meaning "hobby horse," among other definitions. Ball is best remembered for early sound poetry, which he called "Klanggedicht (1916)," that made equal sense in every language. One poem begins: "gadji beri bimba/ glandridi laula lonni cadori/ gadjama him geri glassala," which sounds just as fresh today as it did then. "Introduce symmetries and rhythms instead of principles. Contradict the existing world orders," he wrote in his diary in 1916. "What we are celebrating is at once a buffoonery and a requiem mass," acknowledging a sacred dimension that distinguished him from his Dada colleagues.

Writings: *Flight Out of Time*. Ed. John Elderfield (1974). Berkeley: University of California Press, 1996.

Biography: Steinke, Gerhardt. *The Life and Works of Hugo Ball*. The Hague: Mouton, 1967.

Interpretation: Pichon, Brigitte, and Karl Riha, eds. *Dada Zurich: A Clown's Game from Nothing*. New York: G. K. Hall, 1996; Mann, Philip. *Hugo Ball: An Intellectual Biography*. London: Institute for Germanic Studies, University of London, 1987; White, Ermute Wenzel. *The Magic Bishop: Hugo Ball, Dada Poet*. Columbia, SC: Camden House, 1998.

BARLOW, Clarence

(1945; aka Klarenz B.).

Though born and educated in Calcutta, where he took his first degrees in science, Barlow resided for many years in Cologne, becoming one of the major avant-garde composers in the German-speaking world. His strengths are the use of computers in composition (since 1971), tonality and metricism based on number theory, pastiches that draw upon his musical literacy, and language creations that depend upon his personal fluency in various tongues. The cofounder of GIMIK (Initiative Music and Informatics Cologne), he produced an acoustic portrait of his birthplace for the "Metropolis" series of Westdeutscher Rundfunk. He was recently the artistic director of the Institut voor Sonologie (1967) in The Hague, The Netherlands.

Recordings: *Çogluotobüsiletmesi*. Mainz, Germany: Wergo (60098), 1982.

BARNES, Djuna

(12 January 1892–18 June 1982).

Though she did other things in her life, including journalism, illustration, short fiction, poetry, and a play, Barnes is best remembered for *Nightwood* (1936), an extraordinary novel that T.S. ELIOT testified, in his preface to the first edition, had "a quality of doom and horror very nearly related to that of Elizabethan tragedy." Barnes's style combines Elizabethan English with turn-of-the-century avant-garde prose, giving *Nightwood* the quality of elegant nightmare.

Books: *Nightwood*. London: Faber, 1936; *Ryder* (1928). Elmwood Park, IL: Dalkey Archive, 1990; *Ladies Almanack* (1928). Elmwood Park, IL: Dalkey Archive, 1992; *Collected Stories*. Ed. Phillip Herring. Los Angeles: Sun & Moon, 1996.

Drama: *The Antiphono* (1958). New York: Farrar, Strauss, 1983.

Biography: Field, Andrew. *Djuna: The Formidable Miss Barnes*. Austin: University of Texas Press, 1985.

Memoir: O'Neal, Hank. *Life is Painful, Nasty & Short [etc.]: An Intimate Memoir*. New York: Paragon House, 1990.

Website: http://lalaland.simplenet.com/ctmimages/d/djb/index.html

Interpretation: Frank, Joseph. *The Widening Gyre: Crisis and Mastery in Modern Literature*. New Brunswick: Rutgers University Press, 1963; Scott, James B. *Djuna Barnes*. Boston: Twayne, 1976.

BARNETT, Peter H.

(23 July 1945).

A retired philosophy professor married to an art curator, Barnett also produces conceptually original and profound book-art. His interest is visually portraying philosophical questions. The first and most accessible of his books consists of unanswerable questions, all handwritten in capital letters: "Can critical activity take place where there is not yet theory?" Four statements of this sort appear in the four quadrants of square pages; but to complicate the reading experience, Barnett has cut away outside quadrants from many pages, so that a question in the lower righthand corner becomes a continuous counterpoint to the questions on previous pages from which the lower right hand corner has been cut away.

The structure of *Time Trap* (1980) depends upon a string that runs through the middle of all the book's pages, its ends tied to make a loose circle. I own a handmade dummy copy of his third book, *Reciprocal Encoding-Decoding Construction,* which measures fourteen inches square, bound on both sides, with die-cut pages that must be turned if the book is to be understood (which means, as one measure of its mediumistic integrity, that it cannot be conveniently exhibited in an art gallery). Unlike Barnett's two previous books, this work can be reproduced only by hand. Because each of these three books is far more complicated than its predecessor (much in the tradition of JAMES JOYCE), it is not surprising that the fourth, *Thinking without Surfaces* (1987), was done on and for a computer disc.

Works: *Time Trap*. Brooklyn: Assembling (P.O. Box 444, Prince St., New York, NY 10012-0008), 1980; *Can you tell me how what you are doing now is to do something philosophical?* Brooklyn, New York: Assembling. 1980; *Reciprocal encoding-decoding construction F/2*. New York: Privately published, 1981; *Questioning Time*. Lewiston, New York: Edwin Mellen, 1995; *Picking Up Stones or Folly Love*. New York: Privately published, 1998.

BAROWITZ, Elliott

(22 August 1936).

Essentially a political artist, Barowitz frequently incorporates not reproductions but reproductions of reproductions (and sometimes later-generation copies) along with texts often drawn from newspapers. As the overly copied images lose their slickness, they become more painterly. One result is the exploitation of visual technologies unavailable before, now at the service of truly contemporary commentary. In work drawing imagery from the *New York Times* along with its familiar logo, he added pointed handwritten commentary.

In the late 1990s, Barowitz was copying his favorite modern masters with gouache on canvas, appropriating imagery without simulating texture, in increasingly more populous visual fields. One work from 1996–97, for instance, includes its title on the edges of the rectangular canvas: "MODERNIST FORMALISM/AND THE WORK OF/CLEMENT GREENBERG/THE ART CRITIC." Within this verbal frame Barowitz paints rough copies of works by JACKSON POLLOCK and FRANZ KLINE, in addition to inserting into the center a photocopy of a photograph of Greenberg himself. Elsewhere in the field are copies and photocopies of other painters admired by Greenberg. A companion panel deals with Harold Rosenberg. Given Barowitz's commitments, it is scarcely surprising that he was also for several years the editor of an important newsprint journal called successively *Art&Artists* and *Artworkers News*.

Exhibition Catalog: *In the New York Times*. Köln: Arting, 1995.

b

BARRON, Susan

(15 May 1947).

After premedical studies, Barron began working as a photographer, realizing supremely fine-textured smallscale prints, mostly of fields, trees, and lakes. Selecting from a decade of this work, she produced *Another Song* (1981) in an edition of only fifty-three copies, each with thirty-nine original prints. Extending her art into other materials, she created a true magnum opus, *Labyrinth of Time* (1987), a one-of-a-kind eleven-volume "book," 152 feet when laid out, that spectacularly updates the tradition of the unique illuminated manuscript. In its large pages are photographs, drawings, etchings, collages (many of which involve words in several languages, some of which are music). Nicolas Barker, the Keeper of Rare Books and Manuscripts at the British Library, finds it "a true labyrinth, a passage that leads you on . . . something to wander through, astounded by an illusion here, captivated by a message there, like one of the dioramas that so delighted our forefathers. The change from one medium to another, the differences in scale (large to small letters, vast and minute pictures) all engage and lure mind and eye into the maze." Its immensity notwithstanding, *Labyrinth of Time* traveled from the Newberry Library in Chicago in 1995 to the Philadelphia Museum of Art in 1996 and London's Victoria and Albert Museum in 1997. Barron has also produced more modest book-art.

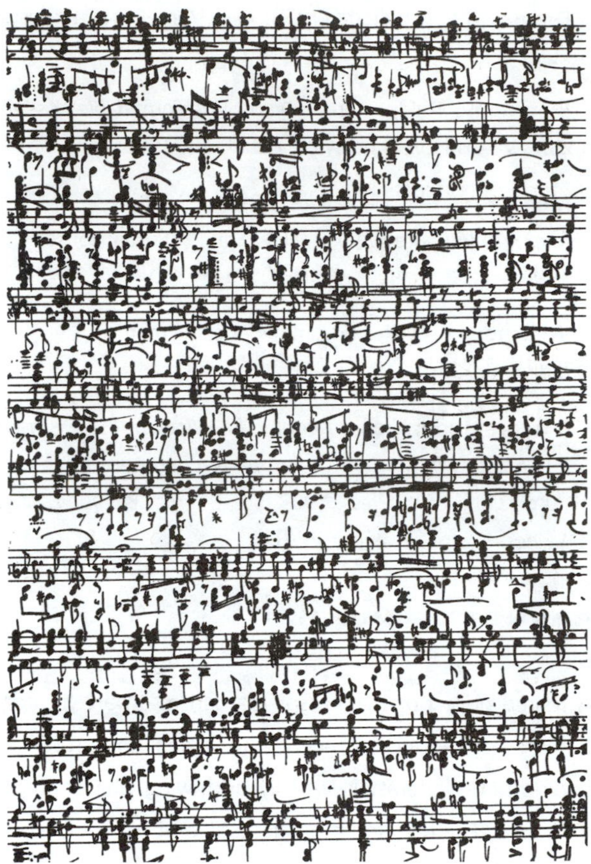

Susan Barron, *Musical Composition (Untitled)*, Ground for Vol. IX *Labyrinth of Time* (11 volume work). Actual size 11 X 8". Courtesy the artist.

Books: *Another Song*. New York: Callaway Editions, 1981.

Interpretation: Cage, John. "Another Song." In *X*. Middletown: Wesleyan University Press, 1982.

BARTH, John

(27 May 1930).

Through the late 1960s, in his own late thirties, John Barth was testing the extremes of literature. "Frame Tale," the opening story in his 1968 collection *Lost in the Funhouse*, appears in the form of a Möbius strip that, to be read appropriately, must be cut out of the book and its ends pasted together with a single twist, so that it will forever read: ". . . once upon a time there was a story that began. . . . " Another story reprinted in this book, "Menelaiad," adds interior quotations until several sets appear around every new quotation. My anthology *Breakthrough Fictioneers* (1973) includes a marvelous visual fiction, subtitled "A stereophonic narrative for authorial voice," which is not reprinted in any of Barth's books. Around this time I saw Barth give a literary recital in which, standing between two loudspeakers, he spoke live in a trio between two prerecorded tapes of his own voice, his performance invigorating the otherwise decadent art of the literary recital. In both practice and later theory, Professor Barth retreated, alas, from advanced positions for more opportune and acceptable kinds of fiction and literary performance.

Fiction: *The Floating Opera*. New York: Appleton Century Crofts, 1956; *The End of the Road*. New York: Doubleday, 1958; *The Sot-Weed Factor*. New York: Doubleday, 1960; *Giles Goat-Boy*. New York: Doubleday, 1966; *Lost in the Funhouse*: Fiction for Print, Tape, Live Voice. Garden City, NY: Doubleday, 1968; *Chimera*. New York: Random House 1973; *Letters*. New York: Putnam 1979.

Essays: *The Friday Book*. New York: Putnam's, 1984; *The Literature of Exhaustion and the Literature of Replenishment*. Northridge, CA: Lord John Press, 1982; *Further Fridays*. Boston: Little, Brown, 1995.

Website: http://members.aol.com/dabug/barth/barth.htm

Interpretation: Fogel, Stan & Slethaug, Gordon. *Understanding John Barth.* Columbia, SC: University of South Carolina Press, 1990; Harris, Charles B. *Passionate Virtuosity: The Fiction of Barth*. Urbana: University of Illinois Press, 1983; Joseph, Gerhard. *John Barth*. Minneapolis: University of Minnesota Press, 1970; Klinkowitz, Jerome. "John Barth." In Richard Kostelanetz, ed. *American Writing Today*. Troy, New York: Whitston, 1991; Stark, John. *The Literature of Exhaustion: Borges, Nabokov, and Barth*. Durham: Duke University Press, 1974.

BARZUN, Henri-Martin

(1907–1972).

In an essay on "The Aesthetics of Dramatic Poetry" (1912–1914), published in his own periodical *Poème et Drame*, Barzun presented his theory of "*simultanéisme*" which the historian Marc Dachy describes as "a program for adapting the musical technique of polyphony to literary creation. He composed odes that later took the form of 'dramas' consisting of poems (dramatism) and songs alternating three groups of four voices each. As the attempt to express reality under all its aspects, not in succession but simultaneously, it can be seen as an extension of the Cubist rendering of objects and figures from several angles at once." The idea was not Barzun's alone, as Dachy reprints a collaborative simultaneous poem ("The Admiral's in Search of a House to Rent," [1916] composed by "R. HUELSENBECK, Tr. TZARA, M. JANCO"). In 1967, Barzun, by then long a resident of America, sent me an inscribed copy of *Orpheus: Choric Education*, which was subtitled "A Record of Labors and Achievements 1920–1945" and filled with reminiscences and encomia, as well as manifestos and sample texts. An informative article on him in English was written by his son Jacques B. (1907), a noted American cultural historian.

Intrepretation: Barzun, Jacques. "Some Notes on Créteil and French Poetry." *New Directions 9* (1946); Dachy, Marc. *The Dada Movement, 1915–1923*. New York: Rizzoli, 1990.

BASINSKI, Michael

(19 November 1950).

Somewhere in Basinski's often infraverbally post-Joycean chapbook, *SleVep*, he writes of "A Vvind/ O/ el ear wooRds/ of the mead/ ing." A wind, oh? A window? A Vivid owl? Vowel? woods? words? worlds? woo-roads? And what kind of participle might a mead become? This kind of multi-connotative, microherent meta-garble is typical of his many poetries (visual, performance, sound alone and mixed, among them). But Basinski is also a Bukowski scholar, and a champion of the poetry of plain technique but enlargement of subject matter that Bukowski's followers sometimes achieve—as well as a librarian/curator at the poetry/rare books collection at SUNY, Buffalo, where he has had much to do with making its collection of avant garde poetry and zines among the best in the world.

—Bob Grumman

Writings: *Red Rain Too*. Port Charlotte, FL: Runaway Spoon, 1992; *Cynttan*. Buffalo, NY: Meow, 1993; *SleVep*. Buffalo, NY: Tailspin, 1995; *Idyl*. Charlottesville, VA: Juxta Press (977 Seminole Trail, #331, 22901), 1996; *Nome*. Buffalo: Buffalo Vortex, 1997.

b

BASS, Saul

(8 May 1920–April 1996).

Initially another graphic designer among many, whose most enduring emblem was a globe logo for AT&T, he contributed to the history of film by introducing animated opening and closing credits to replace rote listings that were customarily produced by shooting a succession of cards or, at times, a moving drum. Bass's titles ideally complimented the opening images in suggesting the unique quality of a film. In *The Seven-Year Itch* (1955), for instance, the colors and layout were reminiscent of Piet Mondrian, while the letter T in *Itch* scratched itself. So stunning were some of his credits that critics in the 1950s sometimes proclaimed them better than the following footage. Among the feature films to incorporate his way with kinetic words were *Carmen Jones*, *The Big Knife*, *The Seven Year Itch*, all in 1955; *Saint Joan*, *Johnny Concho*, *Around the World in 80 Days*, and, especially, *The Man with the Golden Arm*, all in 1956. They appeared later in *West Side Story* (1961), *It's a Mad Mad Mad Mad World* (1963), *Goodfellas* (1990), and *Cape Fear* (1991). Bass's example inspired other producers to hire other animators, such as Alexandre Alexeieff, to produce titles. As a filmmaker, Bass also directed and produced TV commercials, animated shorts, and live documentaries.

Documentaries: *The Searching Eye*, 1963; *From Here to There*, 1964; *Why Man Creates*, 1968 (Academy Award). [A sequence of stills appears in the entry on Bass in *Art without Boundaries*. Ed. Gerald Woods, et al. New York: Praeger, 1972.]; *Phase IV*, 1974.

BAUDELAIRE, Charles

(9 April 1821–31 August 1867).

French poet and critic, commonly credited with initiating literary modernism. The poems collected in *Les Fleurs du Mal (Flowers of Evil,* 1857) include "Correspondences" in which Baudelaire expresses the theory, basic to Symbolism, that the different sensations of sound, color, and perfume become synesthetically associated with one another, creating images that, instead of being descriptive, are evocative or suggestive, thereby enabling the poet to portray deeper levels of psychological experience. As a person of letters, Baudelaire also produced translations of Edgar Allan Poe (giving the American decadent more influence in France than he had at the time at home), and brilliant art criticism.

Writings: *Mirror on Art*. Trans. Jonathan Mayne. Garden City, NY: Doubleday Anchor, 1956; *The Painter of Modern Life and Other Essays*. Ed. & trans. Jonathan Mayne, London: Phaidon, 1970; New York:Da Capo, 1986; *Complete Poems*. Trans. Walter Martin. London: Paul & Co., 1998; *Flowers of Evil*. Trans. F. Duke. Charlottesville: University of Virginia Press, 1961. Trans. Marthiel & Jackson Mathews. Rev. Ed. New York: New Directions, 1962. Trans. Wallace Fowlie. New York: Bantam, 1964; *Selected Verse*. Trans. F. Scarfe. Baltimore: Penguin, 1961; *Twenty Prose Poems*. Trans. Michael Hamburger. London: Cage, 1968; *Baudelaire as Literary Critic: Selected Essays*. Trans. Lois Boe Hyslop and Francis E. Hyslop. University Park: Penn State University Press, 1964.

Biography: Starkie, Enid. *Baudelaire*. New York: New Directions, 1958; Turnell, Martin. *Baudelaire*. London:

Hamilton, 1953; Wagner, Geoffrey. *The Wings of Madness: A Biographical Novel of Charles Baudelaire*. London: Robert Hale, 1978; Peyre, Henri, ed. *Baudelaire*. Englewood Cliffs, NJ: Prentice–Hall, 1962.

BAUDRILLARD, Jean

(1929).

This confession no doubt reflects serious defects in my otherwise elaborate education and literacy, but my Anglo-American head has difficulty reading "Frogthink," which is my epithet for English written like an inadequate translation from the French that supposedly gains profundity from the inadequacy of the translation and/or the text's initial opacity. So I find Baudrillard no more edifying than Roland Barthes, Louis Althusser, Luce Irigary, JACQUES DERRIDA, and other French thinkers customarily characterized (and merchandised) as progressive, even though their rhetorical strategies stink of old-fashioned, class-aggrandizing elitism. What can be understood in Baudrillard seems no more than familiar radical platitudes about evil capitalism—the sort of remarks that can be profound only to people who have not encountered them before, which is to say undergraduates and undereducated postgraduates. My skepticism of adult English-speakers who revere these guys equals that reserved for those who claim they "understand" the IRS guidelines. If you don't believe me, read (or try to read) them yourselves, and don't be surprised if your mind wanders or you fall asleep.

Writings: *The Mirror of Production*. St. Louis, MO: Telos, 1975; *For a Critique of the Political Economy of the Sign*. St. Louis, MO: Telos, 1981; *Forget Foucault*. New York: Autonomedia, 1987; *America*. Trans. Chris Turner. New York: Verso, 1988; *Seduction*. Trans. Brian Singer. New York: St. Martin's, 1990; *Cool Memories 1980–85*. Trans. Chris Turner. New York: Verso, 1990; *The Transparency of Evil: Essays on Extreme Phenomena*. Trans. James Benedict. New York: Verso, 1993; *The System of Objects*. New York: Verso, 1996.

Anthology: *Jean Baudrillard: Selected Writings*. Ed. Mark Poster. Stanford: Stanford University Press, 1988.

Web Site:

http://www.ctheory.com/apataphysics_of_year.html (Essay by Baudrillard)

BAUHAUS

(1919–1933).

In its short lifetime, the Bauhaus was the most advanced school for architecture and applied arts. Not surprisingly, it became more influential after its premature death by Nazi decree, if not the epitome of avant-garde esthetics well into the 1950s. Its teachers included Walter Gropius (1883–1969), LUDWIG MIES VAN DER ROHE, OSKAR SCHLEMMER, Herbert Bayer (1900), and L. MOHOLY-NAGY, who disseminated its ideas in subsequent teaching and writings. Among the central Bauhaus principles were the adaptation of technology to artistic uses, the refusal to distinguish between fine and applied art, and the teaching of all the arts collectively on the persuasive assumption that literacy in only one form or only one communications medium signifies functional illiteracy before the diversity of contemporary information. The Bauhaus's so-called foundation course became a general introduction to materials, from which the individual student could then ideally concentrate on the medium of his or her choice. This last purpose accounts for why the original Bauhaus in Weimar (1919–25) had no course officially in architecture; that was added, purportedly for practical reasons, after its move to Dessau (1925). The Bauhaus books, edited and designed by Moholy-Nagy, became the first series of extended illustrated essays on architectural high modernism. Though Bauhaus ideas encouraged solid and economical construction over esthetic excellence, the result of Bauhaus influence has been new kinds of formalism: in design, artificial streamlining; in architecture, the slick, glass-walled boxes that have become depressingly abundant on the American

Bauhaus Modern Art College in Dessau, Arnhalt, Germany, c. 1930. CORBIS/Austrian Archives.

urban landscape. Similarly, an initially anti-academic educational program, emphasizing individual enthusiasm and choice over particular results, generated its own academic pieties of stylistic correctness (geometric patterns in textiles, say, rather than representational images). In both architecture and design education, then, a limited interpretation of the Bauhaus esthetic placed an emphasis upon certain end products, rather than upon educational processes that might produce entirely different results.

Exhibition Catalogs: Bayer, Herbert, and Walter & Ilse Gropius. *Bauhaus 1919–1928*. New York: Museum of Modern Art, 1938; Herzogenrath, Wulf. *50 Years Bauhaus*. London: Royal Academy of Arts, 1968; *Concepts of the Bauhaus*. Cambridge, MA: Busch-Reisinger Museum, 1971.

Anthologies: Droste, Magdalena. *Bauhaus 1919–1933*. Köln: Taschen, 1996; Whitford, Frank, ed. *The Bauhaus: Masters & Students by Themselves*. New York: Overlook, 1993.

Interpretation: Dearstyne, Howard, and David Spaeth, eds. *Inside the Bauhaus*. New York: Rizzoli, 1986; Fiedler, Jeannine, ed. *Photography at the Bauhaus*. Cambridge: MIT Press, 1990; Fransciscono, Marcel. *Walter Gropius & the Creation of the Bauhaus in Weimar*. Urbana: University of Illinois Press, 1971; Gropius, Walter. *The New Architecture and Bauhaus*. Cambridge: MIT Press, 1965; Hirschfield-Mack, Ludwig. *The Bauhaus: An Introductory Survey*. Chicago: Theobald, 1947; Itten, Johannes. *Design and Form: The Basic Course at the Bauhaus*. New York: Reinhold, 1964; Kentgens-Craig, Margaret. *The Bauhaus and America*. Cambridge: MIT Press, 1999; Naumann,

Eckhard, ed. *Bauhaus and Bauhaus People*. New York: Van Nostrand Reinhold, 1970; Naylor, Gillian. *The Bauhaus*. New York: Dutton, 1968; ——. *The Bauhaus Reassessed: Sources & Design Theory*. London: Herbert Press, 1985; Roters, Eberhard. *Painters of the Bauhaus*. New York: Praeger, 1969; Rowland, Anna. *Bauhaus Source Book*. New York: Van Nostrand Reinhold, 1990; Scheidig, Walther. *Crafts of the Weimar Bauhaus, 1919–24*. London: Studio-Vista, 1967; Whitford, Frank. *Bauhaus: World of Art*. London: Thames & Hudson, 1984; Wingler, Hans Maria. *The Bauhaus* (1962, 1968). Cambridge: MIT Press, 1969.

Website: http://www.cs.umb.edu/~alilley/bauhaus.html

BAUSCH, Pina

(27 July 1940).

Born in Germany, Bausch trained at the (Kurt Jooss [1901–1979]) Folkwang School in Essen before studying at the Juilliard School of Dance in New York, where she worked with, among others, the EXPRESSIONISTIC ballet choreographer Anthony Tudor (1908–1987). Becoming director of the city-subsidized Wuppertal Dance Theater company in 1973, Bausch evolved a *Tanz Theater* ("dance theater") that is a rich and complex amalgam of movement, text, music, and stunning visual effects. In *Nelken* (*Carnations,* 1982), the stage is filled with flowers; for *Arien* (*Arias,* 1979), it is a pool of water. Although most of Bausch's performers are trained dancers, their movements rarely display virtuosic skills, instead reflecting dance techniques in their stylized interactions, mimed incidents, and gestural repetitions.

—Katy Matheson

Choreography: *Fritz* (1974); *Iphigenie auf Tauris*, 1974; *Zwei Krawatten*, 1974; *Ich bring dich um die Ecke . . . /Adagio - Fünf Lieder von Gustav Mahler*, 1974; *Orpheus und Eurydike*, 1975; *Frühlingsopfer* (*Wind von West / Der zweite Frühling / Le Sacre du Printemps*), 1975; *Die sieben Todsünden*, 1976; *Blaubart - Beim Anhören einer Tonbandaufnahme von Béla Bartóks Oper "Herzogs Blaubarts Burg*," 1977; *Komm tanz mit mir*, 1977; *Renate wandert aus*, 1977; *Er nimmt sie an der Hand und führt sie in das Schloss, die anderen folgen,* 1978; *Café Müller,* 1978; *Kontakthof*, 1978; *Arien,* 1979; *Keuschheitslegende*, 1979; 1980; *Bandoneon,* 1980; *Walzer,* 1982; *Nelken,* 1982; *Auf dem Gebirge hat man ein Geschrei gehört,* 1984; *Two Cigarettes in the Dark,* 1985; *Viktor*, 1986; *Ahnen,* 1987; *Die Klage der Kaiserin (Kinofilm),* 1989; *Palermo, Palermo*, 1989; *Tanzabend II (Madrid),* 1991; *Das Stück mit dem Schiff,* 1993; *Ein Trauerspiel,* 1994; *Danzón,* 1995; *Nur Du*, 1996; *Der Fensterputzer*, 1997; *Masurca Fogo,* 1998.

Interpretation: Servos, Norbert. *Pina Bausch—Wuppertal Dance Theater*. Köln: Ballett-Bühnen-Verlag, 1984.

Website: http://www.pinabausch.de (In German)

BEACH, Sylvia

(14 March 1887– 6 October 1962).

In a letter dated the same day he saw the first published copy of his *ULYSSES* (2 February 1922), JAMES JOYCE acknowledged a debt: "I cannot let today pass without thanking you for all the trouble and worry you have given yourself about my book during the last year." He was thanking Sylvia Beach, an expatriate American and the owner of Shakespeare and Company, a Paris bookshop. Beach had published *Ulysses* under the imprint of her bookstore and thus provided for the birth of one of the key texts of high MODERNISM.

Before she became, in the words of the Joycean scholar Shari Benstock, "the patron saint of literary experimentalism," Sylvia Beach sold books. Located at 12, rue de l'Odeón, Shakespeare and Co. was a cultural and literary outpost for American and English expatriates in Paris. Many writers such as Joyce, Ernest Hemingway, H. D., Sherwood Anderson, and Katherine Anne Porter used the store as a meeting place and source for books and literary gossip. Across the street was the bookshop of Adrienne Monnier, Beach's long-time companion and her French

b

Sylvia Beach and James Joyce standing in the doorway of Beach's bookstore, Shakespeare and Company, c. 1925. CORBIS/Bettmann.

counterpart in the selling and promotion of avant-garde literature.

Before Beach offered in 1921 to print *Ulysses*, Joyce had been faced with the daunting task of trying to publish a book that had been declared obscene even before he had finished writing it. A conventional English-language publisher was out of the question. The bookseller Beach took on the herculean task of the seeing the book into print. She hired a French printer named Maurice Darantière to set the first edition of the novel. Darantière provided two important qualities of a printer for Joyce: he had limited knowledge of English, and thus was not liable to react to the text as some earlier typesetters and readers had. And, even more important, he provided Joyce with numerous page proofs that the writer used to add and change text almost up to the moment of publication. However, a consequence of this printing arrangement also created a legion of errors in the first edition. Debate over the "correct" text of the novel still rages and there are currently two different editions of the novel on the market.

Beach's service to *Ulysses* did not end with her having the notoriously "dirty" book printed; she also enabled Joyce to profit from the book by engineering an aggressive subscription drive for the first edition. This assistance provided for Joyce over the next decade as Beach acted as his informal literary agent and manager. Under her auspices the French critic and defender of the avant-garde Valery Larbaud was given early chapters of the novel. Larbaud almost immediately arranged for the first foreign language translation. He also gave the first public lecture on the new novel across the street in Monnier's bookshop.

Beach published two more important Joyce works: *Poems Penyeach* in 1927 and, continuing her help in the critical reception of Joyce's work, a symposium with the audacious title of *Our Exagmination Round His Factification for Incamination of Work in Progress* in 1929. In 1932 Beach was forced to give up the world rights to *Ulysses* because of financial difficulties. She closed her bookshop in 1941, soon after she refused to sell a valuable personal copy of *Finnegans Wake* to a Nazi officer.

—John Rocco

References and Resources: Arnold, Bruce. *The Scandal of "Ulysses."* New York: St. Martin's Press, 1991; Beach, Sylvia. *Shakespeare and Company*. New York: Harcourt, Brace, 1959; ———, ed and intro. *Our Exagmination Round His Factification for Incamination of Work in Progress*. Paris: Shakespeare and Company, 1929; Benstock, Shari. *Women of the Left Bank: Paris, 1900–1940*. Austin: University of Texas Press, 1986; Ellmann, Richard. *James Joyce* (1959). Rev. Ed. New York: Oxford University Press, 1982; Fitch, Noel Riley. *Sylvia Beach and the Lost Generation: A History of Literary Paris in the Twenties and Thirties*. New York: Norton, 1983; Hemingway, Ernest. *A Moveable Feast*. New York: Charles Scribner's Sons, 1964; Joyce, James. *James Joyce's Letters to Sylvia Beach, 1921–1940*. Ed. Melissa Banta and Oscar A. Silverman. Bloomington: Indiana University Press, 1987; Scott, Bonnie Kime. *Joyce and Feminism*. Bloomington: Indiana University Press, 1984.

Website:
http://libserv3.princeton.edu/rbsc2/portfolio/sb/index.html (images from the Sylvia Beach archives at Princeton University).

BEATLES, THE

(1962–1969).

The story of this immensely popular singing group of the sixties need not be retold; their avant-garde innovations as revolutionaries in popular song were many. They took the basic elements of '50s rock and roll and R&B and recast them, including varied influences from such unrelated styles as country, pre-rock pop, and classical and avant-garde music. They stretched the limits of both the subject matter and length of the standard 45-rpm single, creating miniature soundscapes that were self-contained musical units (for example, consider the matched pair of memoir-recordings, "Strawberry Fields Forever" and "Penny

Lane"). They renounced touring at a time when most groups made their livings on the road. They experimented with multitracking, tape looping, backwards recording, and other "effects" that had previously only been heard in the realm of MUSIQUE CONCRÈTE. They created the "concept album" with their 1967 release, *Sergeant Pepper's Lonely Hearts Club Band*, forever after elevating the album from a mere collection of hit singles to a coherent "artwork."

As fashion revolutionaries, they introduced long hair for men, and also popularized various styles of dress through their careers. They were also among the first pop groups to mold a specific image—the four adorable mop tops—and then, half-way through their careers, seriously challenge it by radically altering their appearances (remember the shock when the first pictures of the bearded Beatles were shown?). In their native England, where lower-class accents such as their native Liverpudlian speech were considered déclassé, they insisted on maintaining their natural speech, introducing local slang expressions (from song lyrics such as "Yeah! Yeah! Yeah!" to off-the-cuff slang such as "gear" and "fab") into the international language.

b

And, they influenced countless others to switch from folk and other musical forms to electrified rock, including, but not limited to BOB DYLAN, the Byrds, Buffalo Springfield, The Rolling Stones (at least changing them from a blues-oriented cover band to creators of original songs), and many, many more.

—Richard Carlin

Original British albums: *Please Please Me* (1963); *With the Beatles* (1963); *A Hard Day's Night* (1964); *Beatles for Sale* (1964); *Help*! (1965); *Rubber Soul* (1965); *Revolver* (1966); *Sergeant Pepper's Lonely Hearts Club Band* (1967); *Magical Mystery Tour* (1968); *The Beatles* (1968); *Yellow Submarine* (1969); *Abbey Road* (1969); *Let It Be* (1970).

Films: *A Hard Day's Night* (1964); *Help!* (1965); *Yellow Submarine* (1968); *Let It Be* (1970).

Video History: *The Beatles' Anthology*. London: Apple Corps, 1996.

Biographies: Davies, Hunter, *The Beatles* (1968). 2d rev. ed. New York: Norton, 1996; Norman, Philip. *Shout! The True Story of the Beatles*. New York: Simon & Schuster, 1981; Brown, Peter, and Steven Gaines. *The Love You Make: An Insider's Story of the Beatles*. New York: McGraw-Hill, 1983.

Chronology: Lewison, Mark, *Complete Beatles' Chronicle*. New York: Harmony, 1992.

Sessionography: Lewison, Mark. *Complete Beatles' Recording Sessions: The Abbey Road Years*. New York: Harmony, 1988, 1990.

Website: http://www.getback.org/ (one of many; this offers links to other sites).

Interpretation: Mellers, Wilfred. *Twilight of the Gods: The Beatles in Retrospect.* London: Faber & Faber, 1973; MacDonald, Ian. *Revolution in the Head: The Beatles Records in the Sixties,* London: Fourth Estate/New York: Holt, 1994; Hertsgaard, Mark. *A Day in the Life: The Music and Artistry of the Beatles*. New York: Delacorte Press, 1995; Riley, Tim. *Tell Me Why*. New York: Vintage, 1988; Dowlding, William J. *Beatlesongs*. New York: Simon & Schuster, 1992.

BEBOP

(c. 1945).

Perhaps the first musical form named after its characteristic sound (an onomatopoeia), Bebop was the brainchild of a group of second-generation JAZZ musicians who disliked the brash commercialism and easy accessibility of big-band jazz. Saxophonist CHARLIE PARKER and trumpeter Dizzy Gillespie (1917–1993) evolved a technique for improvising over standard chord progressions to create entirely new and unexpected melodies. In this manner they produced "new" compositions out of old standards, allowing the rhythm instruments (piano, bass, and drums) to play their old parts. Working in smaller ensembles, these Bebop musicians invented a new kind of "chamber jazz" that became popular around the world in the 1950s. They demonstrated a freer interplay among ensemble members, with a generally lighter and more subtle approach to rhythm than was heard in big-band or raucous Dixieland groups, typically emphasizing staccato and legato, especially when played together (also in the word bebop, when spoken). Finally, Bebop musicians displayed a greater intellectualism than their jazz predecessors, believing that jazz was a true art form, and not merely a popular fad.

—with Richard Carlin

Recordings: *The Bebop Era* (various artists). Sony Music, 1987; *Bebop and Bird*. 2 vols. Wea/Atlantic/Rhino, 1988; *Classic Bebop: Vol.1* (various artists). MVP, 1997.

Bibliographies: Davis, Francis. *Bebop and Nothingness*. New York: Schirmer, 1996; DeVeaux, Scott. *The Birth of Bebop*. Berkeley: University of California Press, 1999; Goldberg, Joe. *Jazz Masters of the '50s* (1965). New York: Da Capo, 1979; Owens, Thomas. *Bebop: The Music and its Players*. New York: Oxford University Press, 1996; Williams, Martin. ed. *The Art of Jazz: Ragtime to Bebop*. New York: Da Capo, 1988.

BECK, Stephen

(1950).

In 1976, I saw extraordinary video works that were so unfashionable that I did not see, or even hear of, them again for fifteen years. One Beck piece *Video Weavings* (1974), has hypnotic, metamorphosing geometric shapes that change color rapidly. The syntax of change consisted mostly of pulsations, in and out, but the speeds of change are quick and the colors are ethereal. Beck had synthesized imagery directly onto videotape, in live time (rather than distorting images previously recorded with a camera), thanks to a Direct (i.e., cameraless) Video Synthesizer that he, as a B.S. in Electrical Engineering and Computer Science (EECS), had invented in 1969.

"I had developed various styles—geometrics, metamorphosis, soft edge, etc.," he wrote in the mid-1970s. "It was very much an invention spawned by inner necessity, as Kandinsky put it." (Beck was also early in putting color bars at the beginning of the tape, asking viewers to "tune" their monitors before playing the tape, much as musicians tune their instruments before performing a score.) In 1972, for *Illuminated Music,* Beck also synthesized imagery in live time over a San Francisco TV station—a feat rarely, if ever, repeated in this age of pretaped transmission. In addition to making live concerts with his video synthesizer, Beck collaborated with the filmmaker Jordan Belson (1926) on one of the first film/video collaborations, *Cycles* (1974), which was available in both media.

If only because Beck's tapes were made without a camera (and all the nuisances that accompany the shooting of videotape, not to mention film), they suggest the possibility of producing video much as one writes books—mostly by oneself. Beck has recently been involved in creating and designing electronic toys and games, as well as varieties of computer-assisted "virtual reality," which he thinks (as do I) may or may not be an artistic medium.

Works: *Video Weavings* 1974; & Belson, Jordan. *Cycles* 1974.

Collections on videotape: *Illuminated Music*. Berkeley, CA: Electronic Video Creations (c/o Lapis, 1100 Marina Village Pkwy., Alameda, CA, 94501), 1984.

Writings: "Image Processing and Video Synthesis." In *Eigenwelt der Apparatemelt/Pioneers of Electronic Art*. Linz, Austria, and Santa Fe, NM: Ars Electronica and the Vasulkas (Rt. 6, Box 100, 87501), 1992.

BECKETT, Samuel

(13 April 1906–22 December 1989).

Working against the grain of his upbringing, Beckett was an Irishman whose first successful works were written in

French. A disciple of JAMES JOYCE, whose succession of books increasingly came to epitomize esthetic abundance, Beckett instead explored lessness or, to be precise, lessness as moreness, or, to be more precise, the possibilities of moreness with lessness; for Beckett's fundamental effort has been language so spare it would render the surrounding silence resonant. At the end of one play, a character declares, "Yes, let's go," only to stand still silently. The quietude in such early plays as *Waiting for Godot* is by now universally familiar, but Beckett's later plays are yet more spare, often consisting of monologues punctuated by literary silences so uniquely resonant we call them Beckettian.

b

There has been a parallel, if less familiar, evolution in his fiction—away from the repetitious, limited vocabulary (which now curiously seems more Steinian than Joycean) through *L'Innommable* (1955, translated as *The Unnamable* [1958]), which many regard as his greatest novel, to such nonsyntactic flows as this from *Comment c'est* (1961): "in me that were without when the panting stops scraps of an ancient voice in me not mine." With images of pointless activities, personal alienation, and historical meaninglessness, this passage illustrates the Beckettian knacks of being at once abstract and very concrete, at once lightly comic and deadly serious. Beckett transcended being a one-note author by using various forms to realize his themes—extended prose, short prose, live theater, radio plays, and ballets—appearing with sufficient time between them to make each work a cultural event. It should not be forgotten that back in 1929 Beckett wrote an essay about *FINNEGANS WAKE* that ranks among the classics of genuinely avant-garde criticism. Not unlike Joyce, Beckett is perhaps best read in parts, rather than as a whole. He has translated all his works into English, at times with collaborators.

Fiction: *Murphy* (1938). New York: Grove, 1970; *Molloy* (1951). Trans. Patrick Bowles & Samuel Beckett. New York: Grove, 1955; *Malone meurt/Malone Dies* (1951). Trans S. Beckett (1956). New York: Grove, 1956; *L'Innommable/The Unnamable* (1953). Trans. S. Beckett. New York: Grove, 1958; *Watt*. Paris: Olympia, 1953; *How It Is*. New York: Grove, 1961; *Stories and Texts for Nothing*. New York: Grove, 1967; *Company*. New York: Grove, 1980.

Scripts: *En attendant Godot/Waiting for Godot* (1952). Trans. S. Beckett (1956). New York: Grove, 1997; *Fin de partie/Endgame* (1957). Trans. S. Beckett (1958). New York: Grove, 1970; *Film: Complete Scenario, Illustrations, Production Shots*. New York: Grove, 1969; *The Lost Ones*. New York: Grove, 1972; *Collected Shorter Plays of Samuel Beckett*. London: Faber & Faber, 1984; *The Complete Dramatic Works*. London & Boston: Faber, 1986.

Poetry: *Collected Poems in English*. New York: Grove, 1989; *Complete Poems 1930–1978*. London: Calder, 1991.

Critical Prose: *Proust with Three Dialogues with Georges Duthuit*. London: Calder 1931, 1949.

Anthologies: *Three Novels: Molloy, The Unnamable, & Malone Dies*. New York: Grove, 1959; *Cascando and Other Short Dramatic Pieces*. New York: Grove, 1978. (This slim volume also contains *Words and Music*, *Eh Joe*, *Play*, *Come and Go*, *Film*.); *I Can't Go On, I'll Go On: A Selection from Samuel Beckett's Work*. Ed. and intro. Richard W. Seaver. New York: Grove, 1976. (This single volume contains not only *Waiting for Godot* and the first part of *Comment c'est* but also Beckett's essay "Dante. . . Bruno. Vito. . Joyce." [1929]); *The Complete Short Prose 1929–1989*. Ed. S. E. Gontarski. New York: Grove, 1995.

Website: http://humanitas.ucsb.edu/projects/beckett/society.html

Biographies: Hayman, Ronald. *Samuel Beckett*. London: Heinemann, 1968. Bair, Dierdre. *Samuel Beckett* (1978). New York: Harcourt Brace, 1980; Knowlson, James. *Damned to Fame* (1996). New York: Touchstone Books, 1997.

Interpretation: Brater, Enoch. *Beyond Minimalism: Beckett's Late Style in the Theater*. New York: Oxford University Press, 1987; ——. *Why Beckett*? New York: Thames & Hudson, 1989; Coe, Richard N. *Beckett*. Edinburgh: Oliver & Boyd, 1964; Cohn, Ruby. *Samuel Beckett: The Comic Gamut*. New Brunswick: Rutgers University Press, 1962; Elam, Keir. "Dead Heads: Damnation-Narration in the 'Dramaticules'" in *The Cambridge Companion to Samuel Beckett*. Ed. John Pilling. Cambridge & New York: Cambridge University Press, 1994; Esslin, Martin. *The Theatre of the Absurd* (1961). Rev. ed. Garden City, NY: Doubleday Anchor, 1969; "Samuel Beckett." In *The Novelist as Philosopher*, ed. John Cruickshank. New York: Oxford University Press, 1962; Federman, Raymond. *Samuel Beckett's Early Fiction*. Berkeley, CA: University of California, 1965; Gontarski, S.E. *The Intent of Undoing in Samuel Beckett's Dramatic Texts*. Bloomington: Indiana University, 1985; ———, ed.*The Beckett Studies Reader*. Gainesville, FL: University of Florida, 1993; Gordon, Lois.*The World of Samuel Beckett: 1906–1946*. New Haven, CT: Yale University, 1996; Kalb, Jonathan. *Beckett in Performance*. Cambridge & New York: Cambridge University, 1989; Kenner, Hugh. *Samuel Beckett: A Critical Story*. New York: Grove, 1961; *The Stoic Comedians: Flaubert, Joyce, and Beckett*. Berkeley: University of California, 1975; Ricks, Christopher. *Beckett's Dying Words*. Oxford & New York: Oxford University Press, 1995.

BEIDERBECKE, Bix

(10 March 1903–6 August 1931; b. Leon Bismarck B.). The son of Iowa German immigrants who were amateur musicians, he began to play music as a small child and developed an interest in ragtime and jazz that were beginning to receive national dissemination through records and radio, not to mention traveling musicians. Playing his cornet (a kind of trumpet) in improvising bands composed mostly of white people (the Original Dixieland Jazz Band, The Wolverines), Beiderbecke gravitated to New York where, collaborating with saxophonist Frankie Trumbauer, he created the epitome of white jazz—a happy improvisatory music utterly lacking in "soul" but still musically impressive, if not contagious. At his most innovative, Beiderbecke pioneered individuality in ensemble playing and mixed classical influences with improvisation, establishing a "third stream" long before that epithet was coined. Every year on his birthday, a university radio station in New York plays Beiderbecke around the clock, annually recovering a kind of music that got lost, if not buried, in America's competitive music marketplace. As one older black musician explained during one of those progams, the horn style represented by Louis Armstrong "defeated" Beiderbecke's, partly because the latter died young from alcohol-induced pneumonia.

So powerful was this image of the jazzman's short, self-destructive life in the decade following his death that novels based on it appeared, most notably Dorothy Baker's *Young Man with a Horn* (1938). The composer Richard Sudhalter, who coauthored a biography of Bix, recently published a thick book, *Lost Chords* (1998), obviously featuring Bix, about forgotten American jazz produced by white people.

Recordings: *Bix Beiderbecke Vol 1: Singin' the Blues*. Sony, 1990; *Bix Beiderbecke Vol.2: At the Jazz Band Ball*. Sony, 1990; *The Genius of Bix Beiderbecke*. Pearl Flapper, 1993; *Indispensable Bix Beiderbecke 1924–1930*. BMG/RCA 1995.

Biography: Berton, Ralph. *Remembering Bix: A Memoir of the Jazz Age*. New York: Harper & Row, 1974; Sudhalter, Richard M., and Philip R. Evans. *Bix: Man and Legend*. New Rochelle, NY: Arlington House, 1974.

Website: http://www.qconline.com/bix/

Interpretation: Avakian, George. "Bix Beiderbecke." In *The Art of Jazz*, ed. Martin T. Williams. New York: Oxford University Press, 1959; Sudhalter, Richard M. *Lost Chords*. New York: Oxford University Press, 1998.

BEINING, Guy R.

(26 September 1938).

A major post-T. S. ELIOT/CHARLES OLSON word- and field-jumbler early in his creative life, most signally in his long series, *Stoma* (to this day incompletely published), Beining turned painter, as well, in his forties. The result has been an outburst of master-collages that combine texts (his own and found or appropriated), photographs (ranging from porn to high science), and his own inimitable, often figure-based doodles, in which Pollockian splash-strokes unexpectedly achieve a Matisse-like elegance, with hints of JOSEPH BEUYS and MARCEL DUCHAMP prominently in the background. In most of these pieces, varied fragments jar against and/or flow from one another (e.g., on the first page of his 1994 *Unwrapping Spheres of Cloud & Skulls* where the list, "clodde/ clott/ kloz/ ie./ block/ clud/ rock/ hillock/ clod/ clot/ klut/ ie./ lump," flanks a photograph of a stairway up to a circular opening into a sky from which an over-sized man—probably Beining—looks down, and a photograph of some kind of modernistic dark-glassed container of candles). Such works seem to be Beining's present specialty.

—Bob Grumman

Bibliography: *Stoma 1322*. Toronto: Curvd H&Z (#2 - 856 Somerset W., Ottawa, Canada, K1R 6R7),1984; *Piecemeal I through VIII*. Port Charlotte, FL: Runaway Spoon, 1989; *Stoma: Selected Poems*. Huntington, WV: Aegina Press (59 Oak Lane, Spring Valley, 25704), 1990; *Carved Erosion*. Seattle: Elbow (Box 21671, 98111-3671), 1995; *too far to hear*. Morris, MN: Standing Stones (7 Circle Pines, 56267), 1997.

BELGUM, Erik

(16 August 1961).

Among the best of the younger writers of fiction, let alone experimental fiction, Belgum draws upon a background in avant-garde music and a familiarity with advanced word processors to produce highly innovative texts that in their original form exploit laser printer typography to enhance their style. Such books should be reproduced directly from typescript, just as TYPEWRITER LITERATURE was. I find in his fugitive texts a recurring interest in aberrant speech. Belgum, who lives near Minneapolis, also produces AUDIO ART, for which there is presently as much of a future in the U.S. as for, say, the best contemporary geometric painting.

Works: *The Man Who Could Talk*. Minneapolis, MN: Privately published (27375 Redwing Ave., Shafer, MN 55074), 1991; *Star Fiction*. St. Paul, MN: Detour Press, 1996; *Human Death Not Meant To Be Part of The Sport*. Morris, MN: Standing Stone, 1997.

Recordings: *Bad Marriage Mantra*. Shafer, MN: Voys, 1997; with Lyon, Eric. *Retirement Fund: A Chamber Opera*. Shafer, MN: Voys, nd; with Lyon, Eric. *Retirement Fund II (The Audit)*. (nd).

Interpretation: Raskin, Keith. "True or False? YES," *Collages & Bricolages* #11, 1998.

BELL, Larry

(6 December 1939).

A decade younger than ROBERT IRWIN, whose ideas were particularly influential in Southern California, Bell has specialized in glass and plastic sculptures that unusually affect light. After making framed cubes containing mirrored and coated glass, he used new technological processes to make panels that were at different times transparent, translucent, and even opaque. These were sometimes placed on a transparent base to allow light to pass through all parts of the work. Especially when exhibited together, these panels could be a strong presence in museum exhibitions such as "Spaces" at the Museum of Modern Art in 1970.

Book Art: *Larry Bell/Guy de Cointet*. Venice, CA: Sure Company, 1975.

Exhibition Catalogs: *Larry Bell, Robert Irwin, Doug Wheeler*. London: Tate, 1970; *Larry Bell*. Pasadena, CA: Pasadena Art Museum, 1972; *Larry Bell: Works from New Mexico*. Lyons, France: Musée d'Art Contemporain, 1989.

Critical Studies: Baker, Kenny. "The Grip of the Iceberg" *Boston Phoenix* (February 8, 1977); Henry, Gerrit. "Larry Bell and Eric Orr" *Art News* (May, 1979).

Documentaries: Hunt, John (director). *A Video Portrait: Larry Bell*. 1976.

BENCHLEY, Robert

(15 September 1889–21 November 1945).

Beginning as a Harvard boy who worked for slick magazines and newspapers, Benchley became the epitome of the cultivated essayist, first as the drama editor of the original *Life* and then as a theater critic for *The New Yorker*. Improbable though it seems now, he was invited to make several cheaply produced short films in which, standing before a camera that he addresses as he would a friend, he ineptly lectures on banal subjects he obviously knows nothing about: *The Sex Life of the Polyp* (1928), *The Trouble with Husbands* (1940), *How to Take a Vacation* (1941), and *How to Sleep* (1935, which won an Academy Award for best short comedy, wonder of wonders). The result is subtle irony, camp of a sort not often seen today, even on television. His example, along with those of The Three Stooges (1934–1959) films and Bugs Bunny cartoons, reminds us that, after the advent of sound, much of the most advanced Hollywood-produced work appeared in low-budget short films that are rarely acknowledged by film historians. Once Hollywood ceased producing shorts, independent filmmakers had a near total monopoly on innovative cinema.

Robert Benchley giving a speech. CORBIS/Bettmann.

Films: *The Sex Life of the Polyp*, 1928; *The Treasurer's Report*, 1928; *Stewed Fried and Boiled*, 1929; *Your Technology and Mine*, 1933; *How to Sleep*, 1935; *How to Behave*, 1936; *How to Vote*, 1936; *How to Become a Detective*, 1936; *The Romance of Digestion*, 1937; *A Night at the Movies*, 1937; *How to Figure Income Tax*, 1938; *Music Made Simple*, 1938; *The Courtship of a Newt*, 1938; *Mental Poise*, 1938; *How to Eat*, 1939; *See Your Doctor*, 1939; *That Inferior Feeling*, 1940; *Home Movies*, 1940; *The Trouble with Husbands*, 1940; *How to Take a Vacation*, 1941; *Crime Control*, 1941; *The Forgotten Man*, 1941; *Nothing but Nerves*, 1942; *Keeping in Shape*, 1941; *My Tomato*, 1943; *No News Is Good News*, 1943; *Boogie Woogie*, 1945.

Books: *Of All Things*. New York: Holt, 1921; *Love Conquers All*. New York: Holt, 1922; *Pluck and Luck*. New York: Holt, 1925; *The Early Worm*. New York: Holt, 1927; *The Treasurer's Report*, New York: Harper Bros., 1930; *No Poems*, New York: Harper Bros., 1932; *From Bed to Worse*. New York: Harper Bros., 1934; *My Ten Years in a Quandary*. New York: Harper Bros., 1936; *After 1903—What?* New York: Harper Bros., 1938; *Inside Benchley*. New York: Harper Bros., 1942; *Benchley Beside Himself*. New York: Harper Bros., 1943.

Anthologies: *The Best of Robert Benchley*. New York: Wings, 1983. Ketchell, Charles (ed.). *Benchley at the Theatre*. Ipswich, MA: Ipswich Press, 1985.

Website: http://www.levity.com/corduroy/benchley.htm

Interpretation: Maltin, Leonard. *Selected Short Subjects* (1972). New York: Da Capo, n.d.; Redding, Robert. *Starring Robert Benchley: "Those Magnificent Movie Shorts."* Albuquerque, NM: University of New Mexico Press, 1983.

Biography: Altman, Billy. *Laughter's Gentle Soul: The Life of Robert Benchley*. New York: Norton, 1996.

b

BENJAMIN, Walter

(15 July 1892–25 September 1940).

A brilliantly insightful German philosopher and arts critic, Benjamin became, well after his premature death, a hero to radical intellectuals around the world. He figures in this book by authoring "The Work of Art in the Age of Mechanical Reproduction" (1936), which remains one of the most insightful essays on the modernist difference. "For the first time in world history, mechanical reproduction emancipates the work of art from its parasitical dependence upon ritual. To an ever greater degree the work of art reproduced becomes the work of art designed for reproducibility," he wrote. "But the instant the criterion of authenticity ceases to be applicable to artistic production, the total function of art is reversed. Instead of being based on ritual, it begins to be based on another practice—politics." Most students of high MODERNISM, including me, would give their eyeteeth to have written sentences like these.

Leaving his native Berlin for Paris in 1933, Benjamin befriended the Surrealists and began a comprehensive study of Charles Baudelaire in nineteenth-century Paris that was published posthumously. When the Nazis invaded France, Benjamin fled to the Spanish frontier. Denied entry because of his Marxist past, he committed suicide.

Writings: "The Work of Art in the Age of Mechanical Reproduction" (1936). In *Illuminations* (1969). Trans. Harry Zohn. New York: Schocken, 1985; *Charles Baudelaire: A Lyric Poet in the Era of High Capitalism*. Trans. Harry Zohn. London: New Left, 1973; *One-Way Street and Other Writings*. Ed. Susan Sontag. Trans. Edmund Jephcott & Kingsley Shorter. London: New Left, 1979; *Reflections: Essays, Aphorisms, Autobiographical Writings*. Ed. Peter Demetz,. New York: Schocken, 1986; *Selected Writings 1927–1934*. Ed. Michael Jennings. Cambridge, MA: Harvard University Press, 1999.

Interpretation: Alter, Robert. *Necessary Angels: Tradition and Modernity in Kafka, Benjamin, and Scholem*. Cambridge, MA: Harvard University Press, 1990; Buck-Morss, Susan. *The Dialectics of Seeing: Walter Benjamin and the Arcades Project*. Cambridge, MA: MIT Press, 1993; Frisby, David. *Fragments of Modernity: Theories of Modernity in the Work of Simmel, Kracauer, and Benjamin*. Cambridge, MA: MIT Press, 1986; Jennings, Michael W. *Dialectical Images: Walter Benjamin's Theory of Literary Criticism*. Ithaca, New York: Cornell University Press, 1987.

BENNETT, John M.

(12 October 1942).

While working as a university librarian initially specializing in Latin Americana, Bennett has produced a variety of experimental poems. Many of these reflect the arbitrariness of SURREALISM; some are done in absentee collaboration with others. Most of these have been scattered in many chapbooks that, while each may have its point, diffuse Bennett's impact. Among their titles, in sum perhaps reflective of his particular imagination, are *Lice, Jerks, Burning Dog, Parts, Nose Death, Nips Poems, Milk, Fenestration, Meat Watch, Meat Dip,* and *Tempid*. Under the banner of Luna Bisonte (Moon Bison) Prods, Bennett has also issued printed labels and audiotapes of his own authorship, in addition to publishing *Lost and Found Times* (1975–), which has probably been the most persistently experimental literary magazine to survive for more than a decade in America. This longevity reflects, along with his collaborations with many colleagues, Bennett's genuine professional generosity, which becomes the principal theme of *Loose Watch* (1998), the anthology compiled from its pages. *Johnee's Box* is a cased retrospective of his "visual and sound-text poetry." Do not confuse him with John Bennett (1938), no middle initial, who is a provocative small-press writer living in the state of Washington.

Writings: *Found Objects*. New York: New Rivers, 1973; *Parts*. Columbus, OH: Luna Bisonte (137 Leland Ave., Columbus, OH 43214), 1974; *White Screens*. New York: New Rivers, 1976; *Do Not Cough: Select Labels*. Columbus, OH: Luna Bisonte, 1976; *Meat Watch*. Columbus, OH: Luna Bisonte, 1977; *Puking Horse*. Columbus, OH: Luna Bisonte, 1980; *Motel Moods*. Columbus, OH: Luna Bisonte, 1980; *Burning Dog*. Columbus, OH: Luna Bisonte, 1983; *Swelling*. Pt. Charlotte, FL: Runaway Spoon, 1988; *Johnee's Box*. Cincinnati, OH: Volatile (P.O. Box 32740, 45201), 1991; *Reversion: Piles of That*. Columbus, OH: Luna Bisonte, 1994; *Spinal Speech*. Port Charlotte, FL: Runaway Spoon, 1995.

Recording: *Live Chains: Poetry Performances* Columbus, OH: Luna Bisonte, 1990.

Critical Studies: Trawick, Leonard M. "John Bennett's Poetry of Beauty and Disgust." *The Gamut* 16 (Fall 1985).

Anthology: Bennett, John M., et al., ed. *Loose Watch: A Lost and Found Times Anthology*. London: Invisible (BM Invisible, SC1N 3XX), 1998.

BERIO, Luciano

(24 October 1925).

An Italian composer working in various media with various materials, Berio often combines spoken texts, sung texts, acoustic and electronic instruments, taped sounds, lighting effects, and theatrical movements, including dance. He regards all types of sound—from speech to noise to so-called "musical" sound—as forming a single continuum and thus himself as not so much a "composer" of works as an assembler, putting together different elements to create a total esthetic experience. The division between musical concert, spoken word, and theatrical event is an artificial one, he believes, and in his compositions he has worked toward synthesizing these elements, citing as his principal predecessor not a musician but the author JAMES JOYCE, who also tried to combine language and music. He has explored graphic notation, producing scores that resemble expressionist drawings, and for various reasons has probably received more nasty reviews that most of his comparably deviant contemporaries. Some of his strongest early pieces, such as *In Circles* (1960), to a text by E.E. CUMMINGS, were composed for his wife at that time, the American singer Cathy Berberian (1925–83), who was regarded as among the supreme interpreters of avant-garde music. Berio's best-known work is his *Sinfonia,* composed for the New York Philharmonic's 125th anniversary in 1968 and revised in 1969, typically incorporating recognizable quotations from Gustav Mahler (1860–1911), Richard Strauss (1864–1949), and Maurice Ravel (1875–1937) as the musical analogy of FOUND ART made before the arrival of computer-aided SAMPLING.

Works: *Chamber Music*,to poems by James Joyce, for voice, clarinet, cello, and harp, 1952; *5 Variazioni* for Piano, 1952; *Sequenze I* for flute & fourteen instruments, 1957; *II* for Harp, 1963; *III* for female voice, 1966; *IV* for piano, 1967; *V* for trombone solo, 1966; *VII* for oboe, 1969; *VIII* for violin, 1975–77; *IX* for percussion, 1978–79; *IX A* for clarinet,1980; *IX B* for alto saxophone, 1981; *X* for trumpet, 1984; *Thema (Omaggio à Joyce)*, 1958; *Epifanie for female voices, with orch*., 1959–63; *In Circles*, to a text by e. e. cummings, 1960; *Sincronie* for string quartet, 1964; *Laborintus II*, for voices, instruments, and tape, 1965; *Sinfonia for Eight Voices and Orchestra*,1968–69; *Air* for soprano and orchestra, 1969; *Diario Imaginario*, 1975; *Lied*, for clarinet, 1983.

Interpretation: Dalmonte, R, & Varga, Brown. *Luciano Berio: Two Interviews*. London: Marion Boyars, 1985; Osmond-Smith, David. *Playing on Words: A Guide to Berio's Sinfonia*. London: Royal Musical Assn., 1985; *Berio*. New York: Oxford University Press, 1991.

BERNARD, Kenneth

(7 May 1930).

An ultimate fringe writer, Bernard's work might have remained unknown, were his plays not picked up in the late 1960s by John Vaccaro's Play-House of the Ridiculous, which developed apart from CHARLES LUDLAM'S theater with a similar name. Remembering the Ridiculous's commitment to extremes of language and content, Bernard writes this about himself: "His decimation of plot and character, his mixture of dictions, his addiction to both low and high cultures, his palimpsest reference and quotation, all combined with large and deadly themes obviously appealed to the apocalyptic, parodic mania-despair of the Play-House." One additional departure, apparently too strong for Vaccaro, who refused to produce it, is *How We Danced While We Burned* (1973), requiring that the theater itself be made into a cabaret that resembles a German beer hall. It becomes clear that the emcee is the commandant of a death camp and that the performers are inmates. When they step off the interior stage, the audience's attention is drawn to a sign above a heavy metal door reading, ominously, "EXIT." The suggestion, almost too much to bear, is that each actor has made his or her last performance. As Bernard's plays were less frequently produced in the 1980s, he turned to fictions, most of them very short, that have what he calls "first-person narrations that contain inward-spiraling ironies."

Plays: *The Moke-Eater* produced in New York: 1968; *The Lovers* published in *Trace*. London: May, 1969; *Nightclub* produced in New York: 1970; *The Monkeys of the Organ Grinder* produced in New York: 1970; *Mary Jane* produced in New York: 1973; *The Night Club and Other Plays* (includes all previously listed plays). New York: Winter House, 1971; *Two Plays: How We Danced While We Burned* produced in Yellow Springs OH: 1974; published with *La Justice or The Cock That Crew*. Santa Maria, CA: Asylum Arts, 1990; *Play with an Ending: or, Columbus Discovers the World* produced in New York: 1984; *Curse of Fool: Three Plays*. Santa Maria, CA: Asylum Arts, 1992; *The Que Parle: Play & Poems*. Paradise, CA: Asylum Arts (5847 Sawmill Rd, 95969), 1999.

Short Stories: *From the Distinct File*. Normal, IL: Fiction Collective, 1992.

Anthology: *Clown at Wall: A Kenneth Bernard Reader*. New York: Confrontation, 1979.

Critical Studies: Brecht, Stephen. *The Original Theatre of New York*. Frankfurt am Main: Suhrlamp, 1978; Cohn, Ruby. *Contemporary American Dramatists 1960–1980*. New York: Grove Press, 1982.

BERNE, Stanley

(8 June 1923), and **Arlene ZEKOWSKI** (13 May 1922).

Berne and Zekowski are tied together not only because they have been married for nearly fifty years but also because they customarily publish their books in tandem and reflect a common esthetic, which begins with the conviction that the conventional sentence is esthetically outmoded. Usually classified as "fiction," their books are typically difficult, in the tradition of GERTRUDE STEIN at her most opaque. They are innovative stylists remembered not for their "content" but for their original ways of structuring language. They aptly characterize themselves as "pure researchers in literature." Their original banner was "neo-narrative," which advocates transcending, according to the critic Welsh Everman, "the traditional literary elements of character, theme, plot, chronology, even storiness and grammar, in favor of a flow of language." Like Stein before them, they have experimented with not one alternative style but several; their individual works, though different, are complementary. While Zekowski sometimes favors severely truncated sentences, Berne's sentences are often long and elegant. DICK HIGGINS thinks Berne "is more romantic and less inclined to linguistic experiment, while [Zekowski] is less focused on grammar and has a more classical thrust." Their names are rarely mentioned in literary histories and they are not listed in *Contemporary Novelists,* even though they have been publishing for decades. Now that their principal publisher has disappeared, their special books are available only from themselves (P.O. Box 4595, Santa Fe, NM 87502-4595).

Writings: *By Stanley Berne: A First Book of the Neo-Narrative*. Stonington, CT: Métier, 1954; *Every Person's Little Book of P=L=U=T=O=N=I=U=M*. Santa Fe, NM: Rising Tide (P.O. Box 6136, 87502-6163), 1992; *The Dialogues*. New York: Métier-Wittenborn, 1962; *The Multiple Modern Gods and Other Stories*. New York: Wittenborn, 1964; *The Unconscious Victorious and Other Stories*. New York: Wittenborn, 1969; *The New Rubaiyat of Stanley Berne: Volume One*. Portales, NM: American–Canadian, 1973; *Future Language*. New York: Horizon, 1976; *The Great American Empire*. New York: Horizon, 1982; *Alphabet Soup: An Orderly Collection of Disorderly Thought*. Santa Fe, NM: Danrus (320 Sandoval, 87501), 1995; *TO HELL WITH OPTIMISM*. Santa Fe, NM: Rising Tide Press, 1996.

By Arlene Zekowski: Thursday's Season. Paris: Parnasse, 1950; *Concretions*. New York: Métier-Wittenborn, 1962; *Abraxas*. New York: Wittenborn, 1964; *Seasons of the Mind*. New York: Wittenborn, 1969; *The Age of Iron and Other Interludes: Volume One*. Portales, NM: American–Canadian, 1973; *Image Breaking Images: A New Mythology of Language*. New York: Horizon, 1976; *Histories and Dynasties*. New York: Horizon, 1982; *Against the Disappearance of Literature*. Troy, NY: Whitston, 1999.

By both: Cardinals and Saints. Croton-on-Hudson, New York: Métier, 1958.

BERNERS, Lord

(18 September 1883–19 April 1950; b. Sir Gerald Hugh Tyrwhitt-Wilson, Baronet).

A minor POLYARTIST, he was a self-taught composer who wrote ballet music for DIAGHILEV and an opera with GERTRUDE STEIN. In his compositions, which are rarely played, Nicolas Slonimsky finds "humor and originality, . . . a subtle gift for parody." He wrote a number of memorably witty short poems of three quatrains accounting for why he preferred "red noses" to red roses. Berners also published six novels, including *Far from the Madding War*, in which he portrayed himself as Lord Fitzcricket, in addition to stylish autobiographies that are reprinted long after his death. Unashamedly eccentric and financially secure, Berners also exhibited oil paintings in 1931 and 1936.

Compositions: *3 Little Funeral Marches*, piano, 1914; *Fragments psychologiques*, piano, 1915; *Valses bourgeoises*, piano duet, 1915; *Fantasie Espagnole* for 2 pianos, 1921; *Le Carrosse du Saint-Sacrement*, opera, 1924; *The Triumph of Neptune*, ballet, 1926; *Luna Park*, ballet, 1930; *A Wedding Bouquet*, ballet, 1937.

Collected Music: *Collected Music for Solo Piano*. New York: Chester Music, 1982; *Collected Vocal Works*. New York: Chester Music, 1982.

Novels: *The Camel*. London: Constable, 1936; *The Girls of Radcliff Hall*. London: Constable, 1937; *Far from the Madding War*. London: Constable, 1941; *The Romance of a Nose*. London: Constable, 1942.

Fiction: *Collected Tales & Fantasies*. Chappaqua, New York: Helen Marx/Turtle Point, 1999.

Autobiographies: *First Childhood*. New York: Farrar & Reinhart, 1934 ; *A Distant Prospect*. London: Constable, 1945.

Biography: Amory, Mark. *Lord Berners: The Last Eccentric*. London: Chatto & Windus, 1998.

BERNSTEIN, Charles

(4 April 1950).

The most conspicuous of the LANGUAGE-CENTERED POETS who gained a precarious prominence in the 1990s, Bernstein is initially a personable publicist, very much in the tradition of F.T. MARINETTI, whom Bernstein resembles in his modes of operation and general impact. Trained at Harvard in philosophy and thus rhetorically skilled, Bernstein's writing is derived from early CLARK COOLIDGE and middle GERTRUDE STEIN. Though his experiments in poetry are various, there is not enough consistent character, even in the kinds of experimental intelligence, for many (if any) poems published under his name to be immediately recognizable as his, which is to say that they lack signature. The second, perhaps related problem is that few, if any, are individually memorable. Ask even his admirers which poems they like best, and you will find them unable to identify anything. Thus, Bernstein's career raises the radical question of whether a purportedly major experimental poet can be someone whose *poems*, apart from his or her theories, lack signature and are not remembered. (You can understand why he and his supporters might want to argue "yes.") Nearly all the essays in his book *Content's Dream* (1986) are about himself and his close colleagues. If only to mock the historicism of T. S. ELIOT and EZRA POUND, say, Bernstein discusses no poet earlier than W. C. WILLIAMS, analyzing his work only in relation to the group gathered around his inventively titled, photocopied magazine *L=A=N=G=U=A=G=E*. The fact that Bernstein was selected to replace Robert Creeley (1926, whose historical memory is likewise short) in the poetry chair at SUNY-Buffalo perhaps reflects a revolution less in poetry than in academic standards for poets' acceptability.

Writings: *Asylums*. New York: Asylum's Press, 1975; *Parsing*. New York: Asylum's Press, 1976; *Controlling Interests*. New York: Roof, 1980; *Stigma*. Barrytown, New York: Station Hill, 1981; *Content's Dream*. Los Angeles: Sun & Moon, 1986; *The Sophist*. Los Angeles: Sun & Moon, 1987; *Poems of Nude Formalism*. Los Angeles: Sun & Moon, 1989; *Poetics*. Cambridge: Harvard University Press, 1992; *My Way: Speeches and Poems*. Chicago: University of Chicago Press, 1999.

Anthologies: ed. *The Politics of Poetic Form: Poetry and Public Policy*. New York: Roof Books, 1990; with Bruce Andrews, eds. *The L-A-N-G-U-A-G-E Book*. Carbondale, IL: Southern Illinois Printing Press, 1989.

Interpretation: Hartley, George. *Textual Politics and the Language Poets*. Bloomington: Indiana University Press, 1989; Perloff, Marjorie. "L=A=N=G=U=A=G=E Poetry in the Eighties," *American Poetry Review* May/June 1984.

BERRY, CHUCK

(b. 18 October 1926 b. Charles B.).

Berry was one of the creators of rock 'n' roll and one of rock's greatest composer/performers. Certainly the single

Chuck Berry performing in Portsmouth, Virginia on 30 August 1959. CORBIS/Bettmann.

most influential black artist in the history of rock 'n' roll, Chuck Berry is arguably the most important figure, regardless of race, in rock history. As the first major rock artist to compose virtually all of his own material, Berry provided songs that were aggressive, exuberant, and wry, and reflected the romance between rock 'n' roll and the youth culture and its concerns (school, cars, girls, and dancing). He is often cited as rock's first folk poet. With his engaging lyrics, enticing music, and uncommonly clear diction, Berry became the first black artist to achieve mass popularity with the young white audience. Moreover, his innovative use of boogie-woogie and shuffle rhythms, his alternating chord changes on rhythm guitar and his distinctive off-time double-note lead guitar playing set the early standard for rock guitar and helped popularize the electric guitar. Despite his personal penchant for the blues, Chuck Berry's primary influence came through his uptempo rock songs. The Beatles, the Rolling Stones, and most other British groups recorded his songs during their early careers, and The Beach Boys' "Surfin' U.S.A." is an obvious reworking of "Sweet Little Sixteen." Bob Dylan's first rock hit, "Subterranean Homesick Blues," bears a remarkable resemblance to Berry's "Too Much Monkey Business." Virtually every rock group performing today has at least one Chuck Berry song in its repertoire.

—Brock Helander

Discography: *After School Sessions*, Chess, 1426, 1957; *One Dozen Berrys*, Chess, 1432, 1958; *Chuck Berry Is on Top*, Chess, 1435, 1959; *Rockin' at the Hops*, Chess, 1448, 1960; *New Juke Box Hits*, Chess, 1456, 1960; *Chuck Berry Twist*, Chess, 1465, 1962; *Chuck Berry on Stage*, Chess, 1480, 1963; *St. Louis To Liverpool*, Chess, 1488, 1964; *Two Great Guitars* (with Bo Diddley), Checker, 2991, 1964; *Chuck Berry in London*, Chess, 1495, 1965; *Fresh Berrys*, Chess, 1498, 1965; *In Memphis*, Mercury, 61123, 1967; *Live at the Fillmore*, Mercury, 61138, 1967; *From St. Louie to Frisco*, Mercury, 61176, 1968; *Concerto In B. Goode*, Mercury, 61223, 1970; *St. Louie to Frisco to Memphis*, Mercury, (2)6501, 1972; *Back Home*, Chess, 1550, 1970; *San Francisco Dues*, Chess, 50008, 1971; *The London Chuck Berry Sessions*, Chess, 50001, 1972; *Bio*, Chess, 50043, 1973; *Chuck Berry*, Chess, 60032, 1975; *Rockit*, Atco, 38-118, 1979; *Live On Stage* (recorded 1983 in the United Kingdom), Magnum Archives, 16, 1995; *Hail! Hail! Rock 'n' Roll* (music from soundtrack), MCA, 6217, 1988; *The Chess Box*, 80001, 1988.

Autobiography: *The Autobiography*. New York: Harmony Books, 1987.

Documentary Film: *Hail! Hail! Rock 'n' Roll*, 1987.

Website: http://shell.ihug.co.nz/~mauricef/frames9.htm

Interpretation: De Witt, Howard A. *Chuck Berry: Rock 'n' Roll Music*. Fremont, CA: Horizon, 1981; Reese, Krista. *Chuck Berry: Mr. Rock n' Roll*. London, New York: Proteus Publishing Co., 1982; Helander, Brock. The Rockin' '50s. New York: Schirmer Books, 1998; Koda, Cub. "Chuck Berry: And the Joint Was Rockin'." (Discography by Neal Umphred); *Goldmine*. December 13, 1991. Vol. 17, No. 25.

BERRY, Jake

(16 June 1959).

Berry is the poet of the unhampered subconscious, moving (as many avant-gardists have) from the distorted reality of the surrealists to a distorted method of communication. Working in collage, sound, and especially the written word, Jake Berry veers between two worlds of discourse: a faux bureaucratese or academese (seen in works like *Unnon Theories*) to a full-bore, all-out verbal (and sometimes verbo-visual) assault upon the senses in works like his *Brambu Drezi*. Here's a snippet from the first, which begins innocently enough: "At first one denies the gradual opposition because it emulates a hypnotic simulation in the obverse. Affluent constraint in conjunction with the idea can cripple resilience before temporal immunity can be applied." Is this a medical text? an oration on economics? The stance is right but the words don't quite make it. We are thrown back and forth between ways of seeing, never resting on a thought long enough to finish it. This is abstract art, where the trick is to let your mind experience what it cannot fathom: the abstract image, that idea that can be written or spoken but not quite read or thought, but still it exists. The mind always forces us to conceive of something, even in the face of confusion. But the abstractness of *Unnon Theories* pales in the shadow of *Brambu Drezi*, a ritualistic work full of verbal transsense (beyond sense, but not mere entertaining nonsense), chants, word, and image that produce text that looks and sounds something like this: "mahseetah/in bombay's riotous/dagon countenanced/king leer's foolhearty/round-table screw plotting . . . ."

b

A step before and beyond FINNEGANS WAKE and ABRAHAM LINCOLN GILLESPIE, Jake Berry writes a thought that he cannot quite catch, to disturb and enthrall the reader/viewer/listener patient enough to sit still. As with most artists working in the avant-garde micropress, Berry is also a publisher, producing both the e-zine named *The Experioddicist* and the 9th St. Laboratories electronic chapbook series.

—Geof Huth

Books: *Brambu Drezi: Book One*. Port Charlotte, FL: Runaway Spoon, 1993; *Unnon Theories*. Seattle: Bomb Shelter Props (P.O. Box 12268, 98102), 1989.

BEUYS, Joseph

(12 May 1921–23 January 1986).

Beuys was a German artist and art college professor who customarily made his sculptures out of found material, such as bricks or bits of felt. Often, his "sculptures" were assembled and disassembled on the spot, as part of the work itself, by the viewers, giving the exhibition of his art some qualities of a theatrical event. He hit New York in 1974 with a gallery show in which he lived in a cage with a coyote for several days. Beuys also exhibited his drawings, which, the *Oxford Companion to 20th Century Art* succinctly says, "do not for the most part invite assessment by current or traditional standards." The most extraordinary innovation of Beuys's career was getting his image, usually wearing a broad-brimmed hat in a frontal photo, to register far more memorably than his work. "Dressed like an old-fashioned rural worker, his gaze beaming intently from under the brim of his fedora," the American art critic Carter Ratcliff wrote, "Beuys personified a Europe that advances optimistically while maintaining contact with a myth of its pastoral origins." Beuys became much like a car salesman or some other huckster who puts his face in his promotions in lieu of any ostensible product—in Beuys's case art of dubious worth (or else the seductive face wouldn't have been necessary, natch). Some people were impressed by this radical transvaluation of esthetic merchandising; others, including me, were not. Nonetheless, Beuys got a lot of publicity for his claims of experiencing a miracle in World War II, as though that would give a saintly authority to his subsequent work; but all that was affected, as far as any larger public was concerned, was distribution of pictures of his face.

Books: *The Essential Joseph Beuys*. Ed. Alain Borer & Lothar Schrimer. Cambridge, MA: MIT Press, 1997; with Durini, Lucrezia Dedomizio. *The Felt Hat: Joseph Beuys a Life Told*. Milan: Charta, 1997; *Energy Plan for the Western Man: Writings by and Interviews with the Art: Joseph Beuys in America*. Ed. Carin Kuoni. New York: Four Walls Eight Windows, 1990.

Website: http://www.fh-furtwangen.de/~schoenfe/3-3.html

Exhibition Catalogs: Tisdall, Caroline. *Joseph Beuys*. New York: Guggenheim Museum, 1979.

Catalog Raisonné: *Joseph Beuys: Multiples and Prints 1965–1980*. Eds. Jörg Schellman & Bernd Kluser. New York: New York University Press, 1980.

Interpretation: Ratcliff, Carter. "Ways to Be." In *Breakthroughs*. New York: Rizzoli, 1991; Moffitt, John F.

Occultism in Avant-Garde Art: The Case of Joseph Beuys. Ann Arbor: UMI Research Press, 1988.

BIEDERMAN, Charles

(23 August 1906).

Initially a geometric painter who also made abstract reliefs, in the early 1940s Biederman assimilated Alfred Korzybski's theories about the general structure of language. Moving to Red Wing, Minnesota, he produced a series of self-published books, beginning with his masterwork *Art as the Evolution of Visual Knowledge* (1948), that rank among the most ambitious writing projects ever undertaken by an American visual artist. His themes were that representational art hampers human invention (especially after the development of the camera) and that his kind of CONSTRUCTIVISM, which he called Constructionism, should avoid an illusion, including virtual space. Not wishing to deny the possibility of three dimensions, Biederman favored reliefs that are commonly regarded as "bridging" painting and sculpture. One charm of his writings is the assurance with which he proceeds.

Writings: *Art as the Evolution of Visual Knowledge*. Red Wing, MN: Charles Biederman, 1948; *The New Cezanne*. Red Wing, MN: Charles Biederman, 1952; *Search for New Arts*. Red Wing, MN: Charles Biederman, 1979; *Art-Science-Reality*. Red Wing, MN: Charles Biederman, 1988.

Exhibition Catalog: *Charles Biederman: The Structurist Relief 1935–1964*. Minneapolis, MN: Walker Art Center, 1965; *Charles Biederman*. London: Hayward Gallery, 1969; Charles *Biederman: A Retrospective*. Minneapolis, MN: Minneapolis Institute of Arts, 1976.

Interpretation: Hill, Anthony, ed. *DATA: Directions in Art, Theory and Aesthetics*. London: Faber, 1968.

BIERCE, Ambrose

(24 June 1842–1914).

A courageous independent author, of an adventurous character more possible in the United States than in Europe, Bierce belongs to the avant-garde tradition less for his fiction, which was no less conventional when it was written than it is today, than for his aphorisms, which are distinctly original precisely for their dictionary-like form and their critical intelligence. Indeed, this tart inversion of both the lexicographical and aphoristic tradition gives his concise paragraphs a distinctly modernist signature. Only a twentieth-century aphorist could have written: "Faith, n. Belief without evidence in what is told by one who speaks without knowledge, of things without parallel"; or "Politics is the conduct of public affairs for private advantage." To sense how unacceptable Bierce the American aphorist has been, consider that the W. H. Auden-Louis Kronenberger edited *Book of Aphorisms* (1962) has only one line from Bierce, compared to over thirty-five from Sir Francis Bacon and forty-nine from George Santayana; and that there is nothing by Bierce in *The Concise Oxford Dictionary of Quotations* (1964). Begun in a weekly newspaper in 1881, his "The Cynic's Word Book," as it was originally called, finally appeared under a less appropriate, if more fanciful, name. An overage war reporter, he disappeared in Mexico in 1913.

Writings: *The Collected Writings of Ambrose Bierce*. New York: Citadel Press, 1946; *The Devil's Dictionary* (1906, 1911). New York: Dover, 1958; *The Enlarged Devil's Dictionary*. Ed. E. J. Hopkin. Garden City, New York: Doubleday, 1967; *Fantastic Fables*. New York: Dover, 1970.

Biographies: Morris, Roy, Jr. *Ambrose Bierce: Alone in Bad Company*. New York: Crown, 1995; O'Connor, Richard. *Ambrose Bierce*. Boston: Little Brown, 1967.

Website: gopher://wiretap.area.com/00/Library/Classic/devils.txt (text of the *Devil's Dictionary* online).

Interpretation: Davidson, Cathy N., ed. *Critical Essays on Ambrose Bierce*. Boston: G. K. Hall, 1982.

BILL, Max

(22 December 1908–9 December 1994).

One of the few Swiss artists with an international avant-garde reputation, Bill is a severe geometricist predisposed

Max Bill, *Form*. Metalwork sculpture. CORBIS/Burstein collection./© 2000 Artists Rights Society (ARS), New York/Pro Litteris, Zürich.

to mathematical formulas, in his words, "arisen by virtue of their original means and laws—without external support from natural appearances." His is a pure art without ostensible relation to the natural world. In 1936, he adopted the term "Concrete Art," which had been coined by THEO VAN DOESBURG only a few years before, as superior to ABSTRACT ART, and this epithet was subsequently adopted by other Swiss artists such as Richard Lohse (1902) and Karl Gerstner (1930). As a painter, Bill favored complicated geometries, and as a sculptor, austere materials with smooth surfaces, which are sometimes large enough to become monuments. Bill also organized major exhibitions of Abstract Art, beginning with that of his hero GEORGES VANTONGERLOO. Long a teacher, in the early 1950s Bill was appointed chief of the Hochschule für Gestaltung in Ulm, which became the European center for his kind of CONSTRUCTIVISM.

Exhibition Catalogs: *Max Bill*. Ed. Eugen Gomringer. Teufen: Arthur Niggli, 1958; *Max Bill, Oeuvres 1928–1969*. Paris: Centre National d'Art Contemporain,

1969; *Max Bill*. Ed. Max Bill & James. H. Wood. Buffalo, NY: Buffalo Fine Arts Academy, 1974; *Max Bill, Retrospektive: Skulpturen, Gemälde, Graphik 1928–1987*. Frankfurt, Germany: Kunsthalle, 1987; *Max Bill*. Zürich, Switzerland: Gimpel & Hanover, 1963.

Interpretation: Hill, Anthony, ed. *DATA: Directions in Art, Theory and Aestheics*. London: Faber, 1968; Staber, Margit. *Max Bill*. London: Marlborough Fine Art, 1974.

BILLINGS, William

(7 October 1746–26 September 1800).

A tanner by trade, Billings compensated for a lack of formal education by closely studying the music manuals popular in his time until he could create compositions scarcely less eccentric now than they were then. His song "Jargon," which is filled with dissonances perhaps humorous, is prefaced by a "manifesto" to the Goddess of Discord. He invented a "fuguing piece" composed of independent vocal lines that enter one after another and sometimes echo one another. His sometimes humorous pieces ended in a different key from that used at the beginning. Even today, it is hard to believe that such music was composed in eighteenth-century America. It is scarcely surprising Billings' few prose statements forecast avant-garde manifestos: "I don't think myself confin'd to any Rules for composition, laid down by any that went before me, neither should I think (were I to pretend to lay down Rules) that any who came after me were any ways obliged to adhere to them. . . . I think it is best for every Composer to be his own Carver." Though some of his hymns became popular ("Chester," "The Rose of Sharon"), Billings died poor, America being no more supportive of its avant-garde then than now; yet his music is continually being "rediscovered." I include Billings here partly to deflect the false academic question of "When did the avant-garde start?" If an eighteenth-century composer of such initially unacceptable originality is denied the honorific "avant-garde," then consider for him the silly epithet "proto-avant-garde."

Works: *The Singing Master's Assistant*, 1778; *Music in Miniature*, 1779; *The Continental Harmony* (1794). Ed. Hans Nathan. Cambridge: Harvard University Press, 1961.

Interpretation: McKay, David, and Richard Crawford. *William Billings of Boston: Eighteenth-Century Composer*. Princeton, NJ: Princeton University Press, 1975.

BIRKHOFF, George D.

(21 March 1884–12 November 1944).

While a Harvard professor (and the only tenured one included in this book, so different was Harvard then from now), Birkhoff proposed in his *Aesthetic Measure* (1933) the formula M = O/C, where, "within each class of aesthetic objects," M equals esthetic measure, O is order, and C is complexity. However, one problem with this "quantitative index of [art objects'] comparative aesthetic effectiveness" is that it offers no empirical methods for specifying exact degrees of each factor in the equation. A second problem is its predisposition to measuring unity in variety, which is at best only one of several dimensions of artistic value. Such deductive theorizing, in contrast to the inductive generalizations more appropriate to science, prompted Thomas Munro, a sympathetic observer, to comment in 1946 that quantitative esthetics so far "has dealt less with works of art than with preferences for various arbitrary, simplified linear shapes, color combinations, and tone-combinations." Wait until the next century, maybe.

Writings: *Aesthetic Measure*. Cambridge: Harvard University Press, 1933; *Dynamical Systems: A Renewal of Mechanism Centennial of George D. Birkhoff*. eds. S. Diner, D. Fargue, G. Luchak World Scientific, 1987.

Interpretation: Eysenck, H.J. *Sense and Nonsense in Psychology*. Baltimore, MD: Penguin, 1958.

BISSETT, Bill

(23 November 1939).

A Canadian poet, Bissett resembles W. Bliem Kern and Norman Henry Pritchard II in his eccentric orthography and

b

in performing visually idiosyncratic texts that often depend upon repeating a single phrase, such as "Awake in the Red Desert," which is also the title of a 1968 collection. However, whereas a repeated phrase becomes something else in Kern and Pritchard, in Bissett it remains audibly the same. In opening one of his chapbooks he accurately outlines his way of working:

Spelling—mainly phonetic

Syntax—mainly expressive or musical rather than grammatic

Visual form—apprehension of th spirit shape of the pome rather than stanzaic nd rectangular

Major theme—search fr harmony within th communal self thru sharing (dig Robin Hood), end to war thereby—good luck

Characteristic stylistic device—elipse

Regarding his orthography, Caroline Bayard has written: "You invariably becomes yu; most terminal endings in *le* such as *single,* become *ul* (*singul*); *ought is* transcribed as *at; thought* and *brought* as *that* and *brat*. All past participles are contracted into *d's,* such as *sd* for *said* or *mood* for *moved*. Long diphthongs such as the [i:] of *beautiful* are recorded as *beeutiful*. Phonetic representation is obviously what Bissett is striving for."

Self-educated, extremely prolific and self-indulgent, Bissett is an iconoclastic free spirit. Someday, someone other than himself will collect the gems from a mountain of distinctive work. Not unlike other visual poets, he has also exhibited paintings.

Writings: *Th jinx ship nd othr trips: pomes-drawings-collage*. Vancouver: Very Stone House, 1966; *we sleep inside each other all*. Toronto: Ganglia Press, 1966; *Awake in the Red Desert!* Vancouver: Talonbooks, 1968; *S th Story I to*. Vancouver: Blewointmentpress, 1970; *space travl*. Vancouver: AIR, 1974; *Selected Poems: Beyond Even Faithful Legends* (1980). Vancouver: Talonbooks, 1993; *Seagull on Yonge Street*. Vancouver: Talonbooks, 1983; *Cander Gees Mate for Life*. Vancouver: Talonbooks, 1985; *Animal Uproar*. Vancouver: Talonbooks, 1988; *Hard 2 beleev*. Vancouver: Talonbooks, 1990; *The Last Photo Uv th Human Soul*. Vancouver: Talonbooks, 1993; *The Influenza of Logic*. Vancouver: Talonbooks, 1996; *Loving Without Being Vulnrabul*. Toronto: Stoddart, 1997; ed. *The Last Blew Ointment Anthology 1963–1983*.Toronto: Nightwood, 1985–86.

Exhibition Catalog: Watson, Scott. *Fires in the Tempul*. Vancouver: Vancouver Art Gallery 1984.

Interpretation: Bayard, Caroline. *The New Poetics in Canada and Quebec*. Toronto, Canada: University of Toronto, 1989; Nichol, bp. "The Typography of bill bissett." In *we sleep inside each other all*. Toronto: Ganglia Press, 1966.

BLACK MOUNTAIN COLLEGE

(1933–1957).

Even though it never had more than 100 students at any time in its regular sessions, it was, by the measure of producing avant-garde professionals, the most successful art school ever in America—an American Bauhaus, although, unlike the original Bauhaus it did not produce any major styles identifiable with it. One way in which Black Mountain College transcended its prototype was in incorporating music into the curriculum. Among its distinguished alumni are the painters Robert Rauschenberg and Kenneth Noland (1924), the poets Robert Creeley (1926) and Jonathan Williams, the filmmakers Arthur Penn (1922) and Stan Vanderbeek, and the sculptors John Chamberlain and Kenneth Snelson. The reasons for its success appear to have been that the teachers were active professionals (including at various times John Cage, Merce Cunningham, Buckminster Fuller, Josef Albers, Paul Goodman [1911–72], Franz Kline, and Alfred Kazin [1914–99]), it taught all the arts (rather than just visual art or just music), and the school was small in size. It closed in 1957, the same year that Jackson Pollock crashed, both deaths ending an era. Though American arts educators are forever trying and even claiming to re-create Black Mountain, the mold must have been broken.

Bibliography: Harris, Mary Emma. *The Arts at Black Mountain College*. Cambridge, MA: MIT Press, 1986; Duberman, Martin. *Black Mountain College*. New York: Dutton, 1972; Lane, Melvin. ed. *Black Mountain College: Sprouted Seeds: An Anthology of Personal Accounts*. Knoxville: University of Tennessee Press, 1991.

BLAKE, William

(28 November 1757–12 August 1827).

Blake was by many measures the most original British poet, who not only self-published his major illuminated books, but drew upon his training as an engraver to print and hand-color them. He had to self-publish, because no one else could have reproduced his mixtures of picture and script with any fidelity. The next time you hear some wise guy say that only "loser poets" self-publish or self-print (which becomes more possible in this age of photocopying), always cite the counterexample of Blake. It is hard for us to understand now how unacceptable Blake once was. S. Foster Damon (1893–1971), who was my great teacher at college, told me that when he was a graduate student at Harvard after World War I, students typically responded to the mention of Blake's name with "Oh, he was crazy," swiftly terminating all discussion of his work. In response, Damon wrote the first major book on Blake's work in America (in 1924), showing its ultimate consistencies by a systematic study of Blake's idiosyncratic mythology.

William Blake, *Ancient of Days*, 1796. CORBIS/Leonard de Salva.

More than 150 years after his death (and a half-century after Damon's first Blake book), this British artist's work remains incompletely observed. In his preface to *The Illuminated Blake* (1974), David V. Erdman writes that, even after years of lecturing on Blake's "pictorial language," he was shocked to make further discoveries: "that there were numerous animal and human forms of punctuation that I had not noticed at all! Nor was their presence or absence unimportant in the drama of the work, not to mention the choreography." Precisely because Blake's hand-written words and pictures were physically separate (and he neither found shape in words alone nor considered fragmenting language), he is not a progenitor of VISUAL POETRY, PATTERN POETRY, or CONCRETE POETRY, as they are understood here. Rather, successors to his example include KENNETH PATCHEN and, curiously, photographers such as DUANE MICHALS, among many others, who handwrite highly personal captions to their work. Don't be surprised by Blake's influence on photographers, most of whom are, of necessity, likewise self-printers, at least in beginning the distribution of their work.

Books: *The Marriage of Heaven and Hell*. London: William Blake, 1793; *Visions of the Daughters of Albion*.

London: William Blake, 1793; *Jerusalem: The Emanation of the Giant Albion*. London: William Blake, 1804; *Milton A Poem in 2 Books*. London: William Blake, 1804.

Anthologies: *The Illuminated Blake*. Ed. David V. Erdman. Garden City, NY: Doubleday Anchor, 1974; *The Complete Poetry and Prose of William Blake*. Rev. Ed. David V. Erdman. New York: Doubleday, 1988; *Selected Works*. Ed. David Stevens, Cambridge, England: Cambridge University Press, 1995.

Website: http://jefferson.village.virginia.edu/blake/ (Online archive of poems and images)

Interpretation: Damon, S. Foster. *The Blake Dictionary*. Providence: Brown University Press, 1965; Frye, Northrop. *Fearful Symmetry: A Study of William Blake*. Princeton: Princeton University Press, 1947; ———, ed. *Blake: A Collection of Critical Essays*. Englewood Cliffs, NJ: Prentice-Hall, 1966; Schorer, Mark. *William Blake: The Politics of Vision*. New York: Holt, 1946.

BLANC, Mel

(30 May 1908–10 July 1989; b. Melvin Jerome Blank).

Beginning as a musician, Blanc became in the heyday of American radio comedy "the man of a thousand voices," because he could do imitations, at once credible and ironic, of nearly anything that made a distinctive sound. He could imitate animals; he could reproduce innumerable national accents; for *The Jack Benny Show* he mimicked the sound of a sputtering car—a stunt for which I know no precedent. For cartoons such as TEX AVERY'S Bugs Bunny series, Blanc made animals speak English with nuances that reflected their animal nature. In many cartoons, he spoke all the voices, giving each character a sound unique to him, her, or it. Perhaps the surest measure of his extraordinary talents is that, even after his death, there has been no one quite like him, though many opportunities remain for anyone with such verbal dexterity to display his or her stuff.

Autobiography: Blanc, Mel, and Philip Bashe. *That's Not All, Folks!* New York: Warner, 1988.

Interpretation: Perry, Danny, and Gerald. ed. *The American Animated Cartoon*. New York: E. P. Dutton, 1980.

BLANCO, Juan

(29 June 1920).

By common consent, the most distinguished Cuban composer of his generation, Blanco is best respected for music that is channeled to many loudspeakers distributed over a space. Little about him appears in English print. Visiting Puerto Rico in 1990, I heard of a tape work designed to be played through speakers distributed throughout a hospital, among other radical departures in the presentation of contemporary music. John Vinton's *Dictionary of Contemporary Music* describes these works by Blanco: "*Contrapunto espacial I* for organ with 3 wind groups, 4 percussion groups distributed throughout the space to make triangular and rhomboidal floor patterns (1965–1966); *Poema especial No. 3*, 'Viet-Nam,' sound-light composition for 4 tape tracks distributed live to 37 loudspeakers (c. 1968–); *Contrapunto especial II*, 'Erotofonías,' for 60 strings divided into 20 groups, 5 percussion groups, guitar, alto saxophone, 3 tape tracks derived from recitations of the Song of Solomon (1968); *Contrapunto espacial IV*, 'Boomerang,' for 10 actors, 5 instrumental groups, tape (1970);" and so on. My attempts to get more recent information from Cuban cultural agencies here were not successful.

Works: Blanco, Juan. *Texturas*, for Orchestra and Tape, 1964; *Contrapunto espacial*, four sets, 1965–1970; *Vietnam*, 1968.

Interpretation: "Juan Blanco." In *Dictionary of Contemporary Music*, ed. John Vinton. New York: Dutton, 1974.

BLAST

(1914–1915).

Edited by WYNDHAM LEWIS, this was commonly regarded as the most advanced English-language magazine of its time.

When its two issues were republished in America in 1981, *Blast* still looked advanced, if only for typographical deviance greater than that developed, say, at the Bauhaus in the 1920s. MARSHALL MCLUHAN paid homage to both the spirit and design of *Blast* with his *Counterblast* (1969, designed by Harley Parker), a manifesto of Canadian cultural independence. With its large page size (twelve inches by nine and one half inches), "bright puce colour" cover, crudely uneven large typefaces, and extra space between paragraphs and graphic "designs," as they were called in the table of contents, *Blast* represented British VORTICISM in both form and content. Never before had so much abstract visual art been presented in a British magazine. Among the contributors to the second number were GAUDIER-BRZESKA, T. S. ELIOT (with his first British publication), EZRA POUND, Ford Madox Ford (1873–1939, under the name F.M. Hueffer), and the editor, Wyndham Lewis, who also contributed illustrations. The principal criticism made in retrospect is that Lewis's contributions made everyone else's seem less radical, as perhaps they were. Lewis later edited another magazine that had three issues, *The Enemy* (1927–29), while Black Sparrow Press, in the course of reissuing facsimiles of the two Blasts in the early 1980s, produced *Blast 3* (1986), which contains, among other things, previously unpublished letters from Lewis to Pound and a once-suppressed extended essay on Lewis by the British poet Roy Campbell (1902–57).

Primary: Lewis, Wyndham. *Blast* (1915). 2 vols. Santa Barbara, CA: Black Sparrow, 1981, 1982; Cooney, Seamus, et al., eds. *Blast 3*. Santa Barbara, CA: Black Sparrow, 1984.

Secondary: Hanna, Susan J., "Blast" In *British Literary Magazines: The Modern Age, 1914–1984*. Ed. Alvin Sullivan. Westport, CT: Greenwood, 1986; McLuhan, Marshall. *Counterblast*. New York: Harcourt, Brace, 1969.

BLUM, Eberhard

(14 February 1940).

An accomplished flutist specializing in contemporary music, raised in East Germany, long resident in (West) Berlin, Blum has also become the most adept performer at reciting infamously difficult modern texts, such as KURT SCHWITTERS'S *The Ursonate*, Erust Jandl's German translation of JOHN CAGE'S *45' for Speaker*, and RICHARD KOSTELANETZ'S *Stringsieben* (1981), among others. It is not just a matter of other performers not approaching his level; few can even begin to recite these pieces.

Recordings: Blum, Eberhard. *62 Mesostics re Merce Cunningham*. Therwil, Switzerland: Hat Hut 1991; *Kurt Schmitters Ursonate*. Therwil, Switzerland: Hat Hut 1992.

Catalog: *Eberhard Blum: Recordings on CD, 1990–1996*. Berlin: Eberhard Blum, 1997.

Interpretation: Dick, Robert. *The Other Flute*. New York: Oxford University Press, 1975.

BODIN, Lars-Gunnar

(15 July 1935).

As a Swede atuned to the international avant-garde from his professional beginnings, Bodin wrote experimental poetry, produced MIXED-MEANS THEATER, and interviewed JOHN CAGE at length before focusing upon electro-acoustic composition. His tapes have appeared on radio, discs, and in mixed-media presentations that include song, dance, and even visual art. I find in some of his later works a narrative quality that suggests acoustic fiction, which is to say a story composed entirely of a sequence of sounds. For many years the chief of EMS, the Stockholm Institute of Electro-Acoustic Music, he recently received a state stipend that will keep him an independent artist for the rest of his life.

Works: *Semikolon*, 1965; *Fikonsnackarna*, 1966; *from one point to any other point*, 1968; *Anima* for Soprano, Flute, and Tape, 1984; *Retrospective Episodes*, 1986; *Diskus*, for Wind Quartet and Tape, 1987.

Recordings: Bodin, Lars-Gunnar. *En Fance*. Phono Suecia, 1995; *Cybo II* (1967), *Enbart för Kerstin* (1979), *For Jon III, Part I (They extricated their extremities)* (1982), *On Speaking Terms II: Poem no 4*. (1986), *On Speaking Terms II: Poem no 5* (1986). On *The Pioneers: Five Text-Sound Artists*. Stockholm: Phono Suecia, 1992; *Semicolon*; *Seance 4*. In *Bits and Pieces-EMS 30 Years*. Stockholm: Caprice, 1994.

BODY ART see TATTOOING.

b

BOGGS, DOCK

(7 February 1878–February 1971, b. Moran Lee B.). Boggs was a sometime banjo player and coal miner who recorded a handful of 78s in 1927 and 1928 and then was "rediscovered" during the folk revival of the 1960s. Boggs's most successful recording of his early career was "Country Blues," a piece that combined the "high, lonesome" sound of Appalachian vocal music with the bluesy inflections of African–American music. His stark, two-finger style banjo accompaniment perfectly suited his hard-edged voice, and the song became a classic among mountain music fans. However, after his marriage, Boggs pretty much abandoned banjo playing and his career, not taking up the instrument again until the mid-1950s when he retired from coal mining.

Legendary eccentric documentarian HARRY SMITH included one of Boggs's early recordings on his *Anthology of American Folk Music* (1952; reissued 1997), which had a great impact on the folk revival. Inspired by this set, folklorist/musician Mike Seeger (1935) went in search of Boggs, rediscovering him in Norton, Virginia, by consulting the local phone directory. Boggs was soon touring the folk circuit, performing many of his older songs and ones that he had not previously recorded. However, ill health led him to cease performing in the late sixties, and he died in 1971.

Boggs's stature in the musical world received an unexpected boost when rock and culture critic Greil Marcus promoted him to the pantheon of such great American originals as Ralph Waldo Emerson and BOB DYLAN in his 1997 book, *Invisible Republic*.

—Richard Carlin

Recordings: *Complete Original Recordings*, Revenant; *Complete Folkways Recordings*, Smithsonian-Folkways (also includes an excellent essay on Boggs's music and life).

Interpretation: Marcus, Greil. *Invisible Republic: Bob Dylan and the Making of the Basement Tapes*. New York: Holt, 1997.

BÖHM, Hartmut

(19 April 1938).

The principle of this German artist's work is geometric images whose differences point to infinity. He works with systematic directionality in squares and lines, both in two dimensions and three. For instance, in the striped relief, *Streifenrelief 10* (1972/76), the vertical bars become increasingly protuberant in a progression that, if extended beyond the frame, would go to infinity. In a series of floor sculptures, *Progression gegen Unendlich* (Progression toward Infinity) (1974), the opening figure resembles the letter L. In succeeding sculptures, the vertical line folds diagonally down and sideways until the ends barely touch, implicitly suggesting (but not realizing) the conclusion of infinite flatness. The Viennese critic Dieter Bogner attributes to Böhm "the desire to reveal the relations between the elements as carriers of content." Since the theme of infinity is implicit and ephemeral, his work could be characterized as CONCEPTUAL.

Works: *Quadratrelief 198*, 1972/75; *Quadratrelief 27*, 1966/68; *Progression 1*, 1981; *Raumstrukur 5*, 1970; *Integration 23*, 1982; *Progression Toward the Infinite with 30°*, 1985; *Progression Toward the Infinite with 18°—Vertical Parameters 1*, 1986; *Progression Toward the Infinite with 15°/18°/22.5°/30°/45°—Vertical Parameters II*, 1987.

Exhibition Catalogs: *Arbeiten von 1959 – 1986*. Hagen, Germany: Kart Ernst Osthaus Museum, 1986; *Hartmut Böhm*. Essay "Progression Toward the Infinite" by Dieter Bogner. Hagen, Germany: Wilhelm-Hack Museum, 1990.

Hartmut Böhm. *Progression gegen Unendlich mit 10°, III* 1985/86. Courtesy the artist.

b

BOLDEN, BUDDY

(6 September 1877–4 November 1931; b. Charles Joseph B.).

Shadowy, legendary figure in the history of early jazz, perhaps more important as a legend than as an actual musician. Cornet-player Bolden never recorded, so the style and sound of his playing is unknown; however, contemporary observers, including LOUIS ARMSTRONG, praised him for his magnificent tone and incredible volume. It was said that when Bolden played in an outdoor setting, his cornet could be heard for miles around. This would have been an obvious advantage to a street musician.

In a surviving photograph, Bolden's band appears to have been a cross between a dance-oriented ensemble and a brass band. The frontline instruments are all brass, but the accompaniment is upright bass and guitar. Jazz theorists speculate that the band's repertoire included late Victorian social dances and pop songs as well as early "ragtime" and syncopated dance music.

Bolden's career was cut short by end of the first decade of the century. He was a heavy drinker, and his behavior also became erratic. Suffering apparently from a mental disorder, he was institutionalized in 1907 where he would remain until his death in 1931.

As a missing link, and as a romantic myth of an artist who died too young, Bolden stands as an important figure, at least in the mythic history of jazz.

—Richard Carlin

Biography: Marquis, Donald. *In Search of Buddy Bolden: The First Man of Jazz*. Baton Rouge, LA: Louisiana State University Press, 1978.

Fictional Biography: Ondaatje, Michael. *Coming Through Slaughter*. New York: Norton, 1976.

BONSET, I.K.

See **VAN DOESBURG, Theo.**

BONTECOU, Lee

(15 January 1931).

In his richly insightful essay on "The Aesthetics of the Avant-Garde" (1969), MICHAEL KIRBY notes, "It should not be surprising that even the artists who are involved with the avant-garde do not agree among themselves about the artistic worth of particular pieces. (I can think of only two artists whose work as a whole has achieved an even approximately unanimous acceptance, for however brief a time, among my many friends and acquaintances who are artists.)" Though he did not identify them, it was clear to me, reading that essay at the time, that one example was CLAES OLDENBURG around 1966; the other, he had to tell me, was Lee Bontecou around 1960. Bontecou had made fairly large wall-mounted sculptures, with cloth swatches leading from the bottom edges to a large dark hole in the middle. The image echoed jet-engine exhausts, with an added hint of soft female sexuality; it was radically original for sculpture. What else she has done, or what she has done since, I do not know, because it is rarely seen. She remains an example of an artist whose work was avant-garde for a brief moment in the time of modernist art.

Exhibition Catalog: Ratcliff, Carter. *Lee Bontecou*. Chicago: Museum of Contemporary Art, 1972.

Interpretation: Kirby, Michael. "The Aesthetics of the Avant-Garde." In *Esthetics Contemporary,* ed. Richard Kostelanetz. 2d ed. Buffalo, NY: Prometheus, 1989; Picard, Lil. "Lee Bontecou" *Kunstwerk,* Summer Baden-Baden, West Germany: 1971.

BOOK-ART.

See **ARTIST'S BOOKS**

BORETZ, Benjamin.

See **RANDALL, J. K.**

BORGES, Jorge Luis

(24 August 1899–14 June 1986).

A prolific Argentinian writer who was by turns both decidedly avant-garde and self-consciously conventional, Borges was educated in Europe (and buried in Geneva) and always read English in the original. He is best treasured for a group of short stories that he called *Ficciones* (1944; rev. 1961). Written in forms typical of expositions (e.g., a critical article, a librarian's report, a footnoted scholarly essay, a writer's obituary), these fictions portray as they exemplify the primacy of the imagination. One is about a man who discovers in his edition of an encyclopedia an imaginary country previously unknown to him or anyone else. The classic Borges is "Pierre Menard, Author of Don Quixote," which appears to be a sober, straightforward obituary of a writer whose" admirable ambition was to produce [out of his own head] pages which would coincide—word for word and line for line—with those of Miguel de Cervantes." In one of the shrewdest passages, the narrator shows how the same words that might have been obscure in the sixteenth century become in the twentieth century a meditation on William James. What begins as a complicated joke raises critical questions about authenticity, professional integrity, interpretation, and much else. Like the book it resembles, *Pale Fire* (1962) by his exact contemporary VLADIMIR NABOKOV, *Ficciones* broaches subtleties that many readers miss.

Writings: *Ficciones* (1944). New York: Grove, 1962; *El Aleph* (1949). Buenos Aires: Emecé Editions 1962; *Labyrinths: Selected Stories & Other Writings* (1962). 2d ed. New York: New Directions, 1964.

Anthologies: *Antología Personal*. Buenos Aires: Editorial Sur, 1961. Trans. as *A Personal Anthology*. New York: Grove, 1967; *A Reader*. Eds. Emir Rodriguez Monegal and Alastair Reid. New York: Knopf, 1981; *Collected Fiction*. Trans. Andrew Hurley. New York: Viking Press, 1998; *The Gold of the Tigers: Selected Later Poems* New York: Dutton 1977.

Biography: Woodall, James. *Borges: A Life*. New York: Basic Books, 1997.

Website: http://web.nwe.ufl.edu/~mcasal/borges.html (in Spanish)

Interpretation: Alazraki, Jaime ed. *Critical Essays on Jorge Luis Borges*. Boston: G. K.Hall, 1987; Balderston, Daniel. *Out of Context: Historical Reference and the Representation of Reality in Borges*. Durham: Duke University Press, 1993; Murillo, L.A. "The Labyrinths of Jorge Borges, An Introduction to the Stories of *El Aleph*," *Modern Language Quarterly* Vol. 20 No. 3, 1959; "Borges on Literature," *Américas* December, 1961; Wheelock, Carter. *The Mythmaker: A Study of Motif and Symbol in the Short Stories of Jorge Luis Borges*. Austin: University of Texas Press, 1969.

BORKHUIS, Charles

(10 November 1943).

A downtown New York playwright and poet, Borkhuis is also the author of several extraordinary skeletal stories that suggest within a few lines spaced apart a large narrative. Consider this from his chapbook *Dinner with Franz* (1998):

each story ends
with an ostensible acquittal

followed by another arrest
with new paragraphs and chapters
to be written until a new
acquittal is obtained
followed by a new arrest . . . .

Note that each line constitutes a significant element in the narrative and that the conclusion of three periods, rather than four, indicates that the narrative is incomplete, perhaps even suggesting a return to its beginning. With the title of his collection echoing Kafka, Borkhuis has extended the psychological tale into new literary territory. Otherwise, his plays have been produced across the United States, and he edited *Theater/Ex*, a publication focusing on experimental theater and performance.

Books: *Dinner with Franz*. New York: Poetry New York (P.O. Box 3184, Church St. Station, 10008), 1998; *Hypnogogic Sonnets*. New York: Red Dust, 1992; *Month of Shadows*. New York: Spuyten Duyvil, 1999; *Alpha Ruins*. Lewisburg, PA: Bucknell University Press, 1999.

BORY, Jean-François

(2 May 1938).

By the late 1960s, Bory had established himself as the master of visual fiction, which is to say images—in his case

b

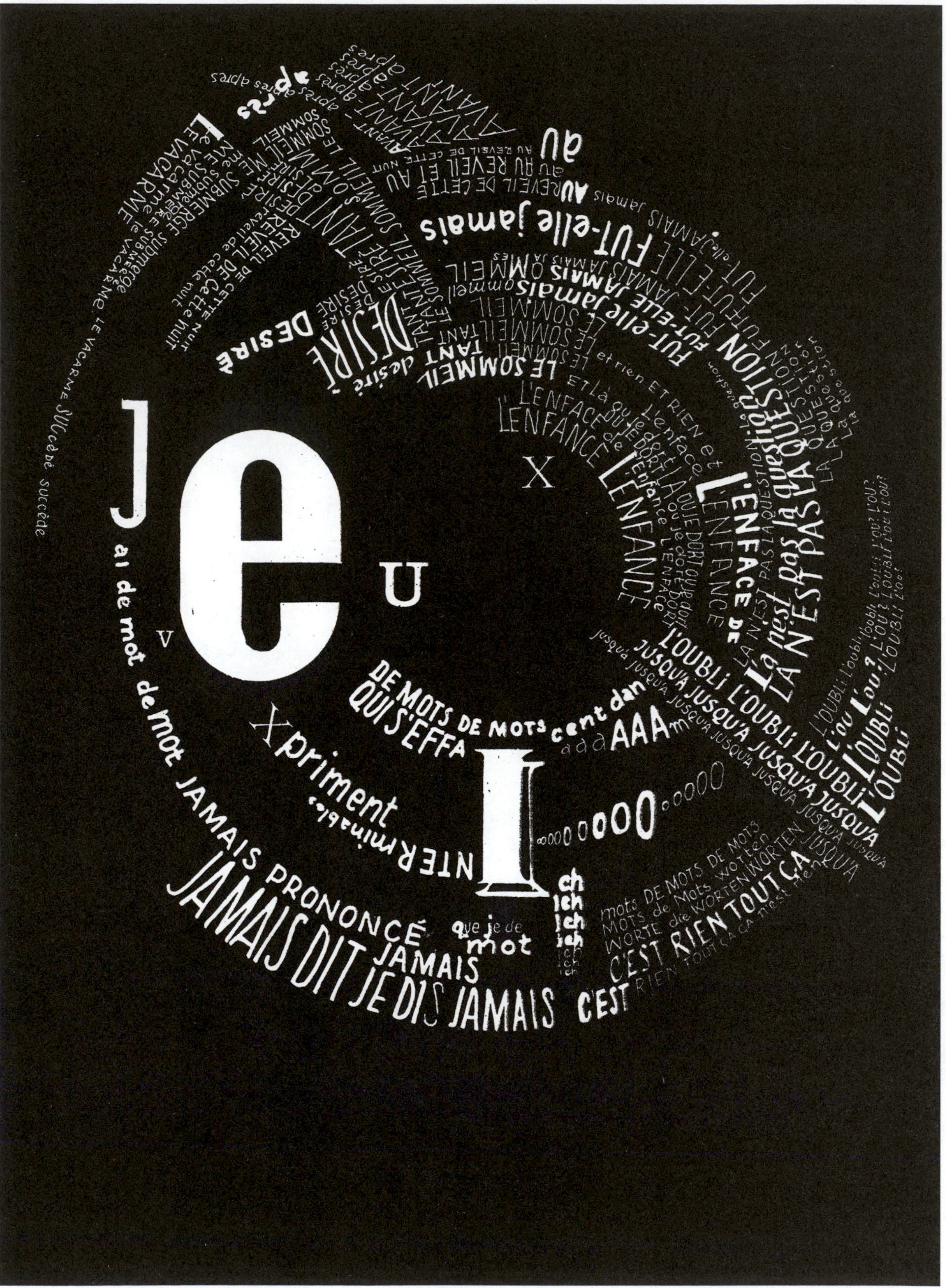

Jean-François Bory. From *Album*. Courtesy the artist.

customarily including words—that suggest narrative through the transitions from page to page. He made the rectangular page, rather than the sentence or the paragraph, the basic unit of fictional exposition. In "Spot" (1967), for instance, the same image of miscellaneous letters is progressively magnified over seven right-hand pages until the page is all but entirely blackened by just a portion of the middle letter. This inundating image becomes an ironic inversion of the otherwise progressive process of magnification (in a form similar to EUGÈNE IONESCO's ironically linear *The New Tenant*, in which the room fills up with so many objects that the new occupant is smothered). "Spot," like later Bory visual fictions, is neat and clean (and thus graphic) rather than handmade (or painterly).

In his classic collection, *Post-Scriptum* (1970), is longer visual fiction, a novella if you will, "Saga," in which the phrase *On y Pa,* or "One Gets By," is superimposed over background photographs. Its twenty-eight pages portray a descent into a mysterious realm, where images are forbidding and unclear, and vaguely perceptible letters are scrambled. The reader then encounters surreal maps, where places are renamed as parts of speech, only to emerge at the conclusion with an image identical to that at the beginning. When I first read "Saga," I wrote, "Within less than thirty pages, in sum, is all the material and linear experience of a silent movie or, perhaps, a novel." Decades later, I am no less impressed. Bory also coedited with the French poet Julien Blane (1942) the seminal periodical *Approches* (1966–1969). More recently, he has exhibited word-based objects.

Writings: *Post-Scriptum*. Paris, France: Eric Losfeld, 1970; *Made in Machine*. Brescia, Italy: 1970; *Logorinthe*. Rome: 1970; ed. *Once Again*. New York: New Directions, 1968.

Recording: with Patrick Muller. *La Fabrication du Crépuscule*. Paris, France: trAce, 1998.

Interpretation: Dupey, S. "Jean-François Bory," *Art Press* [Paris], September: 1973.

Exhibition Catalog: *Jean-François Bory*. Ventabren, France: La Commune de Vertabren, 1998.

BOULEZ, Pierre

(26 March 1925).

Why is he here? As a composer, Boulez incorporated avant-garde developments into more familiar structures, always rationalizing what might otherwise be perceived as steps backward with claims to independence and individuality, pretending that his conservative opportunism should be regarded as avant-garde. NICOLAS SLONIMSKY writes, "He specifically disassociated himself from any particular modern school of music." As a musical director, beginning with *Domaine Musical* in Paris in 1953 and later with the New York Philharmonic (1971–1978) and the BBC Symphony Orchestra, Boulez tends to include avant-garde works without favoring them. That perhaps accounts for why his interpretations of them tend to be neither excellent nor eccentric. In 1974, the French government appointed him chief of the Institut de Recherche & Coordination Acoustique/Musique, called IRCAM (commonly pronounced "ear-com"), which purportedly does something incomparably futuristic, although those results publicly released seem less than expected or promised. Boulez's unending assumption of seats of power forces dependent colleagues to be respectful; but once he is deposed, don't be surprised to see his reputation fall and his work be forgotten.

Selected Compositions: *3 Sonatas for piano: No. 1* (1946), *No. 2* (1946–48), *No. 3* (1955–57); *La Marteau sans Maître* for alto, alto flute, guitar, vibraphone, xylorimba, percussion, and viola, 1953–55; rev. 1957; *Pli selon pli (Don, Improvisation sur Mallarmé I–III, Tombeau),* for soprano and orchestra, 1957–90. *cummings ist her dichter* for 16 solo voices and 24 instruments, 1970; ev. 1986.

Recordings: *Boulez: Piano Sonatas 1–3* (Astree, 1994); *Boulez Conducts Boulez* (Deutsche Grammophon, 1996). As conductor of works by others, too numerous to list.

Books: *Notes of an Apprenticeship*. Trans. Herbert Weinstock. New York: Knopf, 1968; *Conversations with Celestin Deliege*. London: Eulenberg, 1976; Nattiez Jean Jacques, & Samuels, Robert. ed. *The Boulez-Cage Correspondence*. New York: Cambridge University Press, 1993.

Biography: Peyser, Joan. *Pierre Boulez: Composer, Conductor, Enigma*. New York: Schirmer, 1976.

Website: www.ircam.fr (in French).

Interpretation: Born, Georgina. *Rationalizing Music: IRCAM, Boulez, and the Institutionalization of the Avant-Garde*. Berkeley: University of California Press, 1995.

b

BOURGEOIS, Louise

(25 December 1911).

Bourgeois has had a remarkably long artistic career. Over the course of it, she has practiced drawing, painting, and, finally, sculpture, to which she has exclusively devoted her efforts since the late 1940s. A mercurial artist, Bourgeois is the very model of an independent creator. She has been responsible for developing an impressive breadth of new sculptural forms and styles devised to express her personal concerns. Her imagery has ranged from the purely abstract to the overtly sexual; her materials from the traditional marble, bronze, and wood to rubber, fabric, and found objects; her themes from oblique and richly suggestive symbolism, the meaning of which is impossible to nail down, to politically blatant and doctrinaire statements. Her most influential and best-known work is the savage *Destruction of the Father* (1974), a large and cavernous environment filled with globules that line the floor and ceiling, suggesting either the absorption of the masculine into the womb-like image of the feminine, or the mastication of everything organic in the jaws of the masculine. Ultimately, her single and unchanging subject is psychological complexity, and the varied and contradictory interpretations many of her works permit serve only to heighten their effectiveness and impact. Bourgeois's continually changing manner defies art historical analysis and testifies to the indomitable nature of the individual imagination, free of the currents of stylistic innovation that surround her. She is an artist *sui generis*, entirely self-determined, and to many, the woman herself may be her own most significant creation.

—Mark Daniel Cohen

Works: *The Blind Leading the Blind*, 1947–49; *Sleeping Figure II*, 1950; *The Fingers*, 1960; *Germinal*, 1967; *Fillette*, 1968; *Destruction of the Father*, 1974; *Eyes*, 1982; *Blind Man's Buff*, 1984; *Nature Study*, 1986; *No Exit*, 1988; *Cell (Eyes and Mirrors)*, 1989–93; *Arch of Hysteria*, 1993; *Spiders*, 1995.

Exhibition Catalogs: Wye, Deborah. *Louise Bourgeois*. New York: MoMA, 1982; Kotik, Charlotta, Sultan, Terrie, and Leigh, Christian. *Louise Bourgeois: The Locus of Memory, Works 1982–1993*. New York: Brooklyn Museum & Abrams, 1994; Bourgeois, Louise Rinder, Lawrence. *Louise Bourgeois, Drawings & Observations*. Berkeley: University Art Museum and Pacific Film Archive, University of California, 1995; Bernadac, Marie-Lauren. *Louise Bourgeois*. Trans. Deke Dusinberre. Paris: Flammarion, 1996. Inman, Lucy Daniels, Paschal, Huston, and Waterfall, Ann. *Sacred and Fatal: The Art of Louise Bourgeois: North Carolina Museum of Art, March 8–May 31, 1998*. Raleigh: North Carolina Museum of Art, 1998; Clair, Jean. *Five Notes on the Work of Louise Bourgeois*. New York: Cheim & Read, 1998.

Catalog Raisonné: Wye, Deborah and Smith, Carol Hynning. *The Prints of Louise Bourgeois*. New York: MoMA, distributed by H. N. Abrams, 1994.

Interpretation: Kuspit, Donald, B. *Bourgeois*. New York: Vintage Books, 1988; Gardner, Paul. *Louise Bourgeois*. New York: Universe, 1994; Crone, Rainer. *Louise Bourgeois: The Secret of the Cells*. Munich & New York: Prestel, 1998.

BRAKHAGE, Stan

(14 January 1933).

He has ranked since the 1950s among the foremost American independent filmmakers, producing an abundance of films of various lengths and of differing quality, all in a style uniquely his. The best definition of this style appears in a book by a Canadian filmmaker nearly a generation younger, R. Bruce Elder. Rather than steal, I quote:

> His films typically employ intense, expressionistic camera movements, frequent use of extremely close camera positions, rapid cutting between shots having contrasting attributes, and complex rhythmic structures created by the conjoint effect of the cutting and the camera movement and the movement of shots' object matter. The style forged from these devices tends to rivet the spectator's attention to the screen. Brakhage's works are so rapidly passed and have so much intensity that viewers must give their entire attention to the task of grasping what occurs in the very instant of its happening.

True as this is as description, Elder also identifies an implication for the audience: "Spectators of a Brakhage film are fascinated spectators, absorbed completely in the given moment; they occupy a realm without any temporal extension, for in it everything exists in a timeless present." Given the alternative nature of his work, Brakhage has been particularly effective at the filmmaker's version of a poetry reading, where he travels with his films, presenting them as a legendarily brilliant talker to generally sympathetic audiences.

Selected Films: *Anticipation of the Night*, 1958; *Prelude: Dog Star Man*, 1961. New York: Mystic Fire Video, 1987; *Dog Star Man*, 1962–64; *Songs 1–7*, 1964/80; *8–14*, 1966/80; *16–22*, 1966/80; *23rd Psalm*, two parts, 1966/78; *Scenes from Childhood*, 4 Sections, 1967–70; *Sincerity*, 5 reels, 1973, 1978, 1979, 1980; *Tortured Dust*, 1984.

Books: *Metaphors of Vision*. New York: Film Culture, 1963; *Brakhage Scrapbook: Collected Writings 1964–1980*. Ed. Robert Haller. New Paltz, NY: Documentext-Treacle, 1982.

Interpretation: Elder, R. Bruce. *Image and Identity*. Waterloo, Ontario: Wilfrid Laurier University Press, 1989; ——. *The Films of Stan Brakhage in the American Tradition of Ezra Pound, Gertrude Stein, and Charles Olson*. Waterloo, Ontario: Wilfrid Laurier University Press, 1998; Sitney, P. Adams. *Visionary Film: The American Avant-Garde 1943–1978*. New York: Oxford University Press, 1974.

BRANCA, Glenn

(1949).

After desultory efforts in playwriting, Branca joined another aspiring theater colleague, Jeffrey Lohn (1947) in forming a "punk rock" band, Theoretical Girls (1977–79). Later influenced by Krzysztof Penderecki's use of tone clusters produced by a single instrument massed in large numbers, he brought together six electric guitars, imperfectly tuned, to play together at a loud level. In the cacophony he discovered overtones that were previously unavailable. Exploiting a good idea, he wrote whole "symphonies" initially for massed electric guitars. Kyle Gann's *American Music in the Twentieth Century* (1977) includes a close musicological analysis of Branca's *Symphony No. 10* (1994), whose two movements are called respectively "The Final Problem" and "The Horror." At one point, Gann notes, "Similar textures continue throughout the movement, interspersed with passages of cluster chords moving in parallel, crescendoing (if possible) to a triumphant cadence that dies away in a long, feedback-laced delay," implicitly demonstrating, to no surprise really, that even such radical music is susceptible to mature critical analysis. Not unlike David Moss, Branca makes raucous art whose implicit themes include the end of the world. If you can stand the noise, the result is impressive, especially in live performance. Given the expense of producing his concerts, it is not surprising that he works mostly in Europe.

Recordings: *Selections from the Symphonies*, Atavistic 1997; *Songs 1977–79*, Atavistic 1996; *Symphony No.1 (Tonal Plexus)*, Roir 1998; *Symphony No.2 (The Peak of the Sacred)*, Atavistic 1992; *Symphony No.3*, Atavistic 1993; *The World Upside Down*, Atavistic 1994; Symphony

No. 9 for chorus & Orch, "L'Ève future" (Point Music 446505-2).

Interview: Duckworth, William. *Talking Music*. New York: Schirmer, 1995.

Interpretation: Gann, Kyle. *American Music in the Twentieth Century*. New York: Schirmer, 1977.

BRANCUSI, Constantin

(9 February 1876–16 March 1957).

Apprenticed to a cabinetmaker, Brancusi studied art, first in Bucharest and then in Munich, finally reaching Paris in 1904. Though his initial work reflected first the influence of Auguste Rodin (1840–1917), and he then created faces resembling those in Amadeo Modigliani's (1884–1920) work, Brancusi finally concentrated on abstract sculpture, which he thought captured the "essence" of things beneath surface characteristics. After 1910, Brancusi made it a point of principle to carve everything himself, rather than employing craftsmen, and to work without prior clay models. A proto-MINIMALIST, Brancusi favored simple abstract shapes, one barely different from another, sometimes duplicating in polished bronze what he had previously done in wood, or vice versa. He thought of his sculptures as beings—his thin verticals, for instance, as birds, thicker horizontals as fishes. "I live in a desert," he once declared, "alone with my animals." His most ambitious image was the *Endless Column*, whose first version, 23 feet high, was carved in wood in 1920; in Romania in 1937, he made a cast iron *Endless Column* nearly 100 feet tall. Brancusi struck his contemporaries as being in touch

Constantin Brancusi, *Head.* CORBIS/Adam Woolfitt./© 2000 Artists Rights Society (ARS), New York/ADGAP, Paris.

with spiritual currents not available to normal people. In spite of his penchant for replicating his work, his work and career have come to represent a standard of integrity.

Works: *Endless Column*, 1938; *Table of Silence*, 1938; *Gate of the Kiss*, 1938.

Exhibition Catalog: Geist, Sidney. *Constantin Brancusi: A Retrospective Exhibition*. New York: Guggenheim Museum, 1969.

Interpretation: Paleolog, V. G. *C. Brancusi*. Bucharest, Romania: Standard Graphica, 1947; Brezianu, Barbu. *Brancusi in Romania*. Bucharest: Editura Academiei Republicii Socialist România, 1976; Geist, Sidney. *Brancusi: A Study of the Sculpture*. New York: Grossman, 1968; Giedion-Welcker, Carola. *Constantin Brancusi, 1876–1957*. New York: Braziller, 1959; Lewis, David. *Brancusi*. New York: Wittenborn, 1957; Van Doesburg, Theo. "Constantin Brancusi" *De Stijl* 79–84 (1927).

BRANNEN, Jonathan

(1 November 1950).

Early in his career, Jonathan Brannen was affiliated with the small press, Konglomerati, which produced many remarkable works, including his own *Approaching the Border*. Although there are many facets to Brannen's work (he's a fiction writer, a textual poet, a visual poet, and an aural poet), the hallmark of his oeuvre is its careful beauty. From his few one-word poems like "laugnage" and "pigeoneon" through his short prose poems to his long "found fiction" *Sunset Beach*, Brannen carefully constructs a vision that is rare in the avant-garde: one that respects people's sense of esthetics even as it works to expand and disrupt that comfortable esthetic. Brannen is also a master of the typewriter poem and has produced many "texts" with such judicious and scrupulous overtyping and collaging that they appear to have not only shape, but also shadow and depth and movement—sometimes reminiscent of Joàn Miro or Paul Klee and at other times reminding us of tapestries or quilts. Brannen has exhibited his visual literature in Australia, Mexico, Japan, France, and the United States. A Southerner by birth and subsequence, he currently resides in Morris, Minnesota, where he edits Standing Stones Press.

—Geof Huth

Books: *Approaching the Border*. Gulfport, FL: Konglomerati Press, 1982; *Sunset Beach*. Pt. Charlotte, FL: Runaway Sppon, 1991; *Nothing Doing Never Again*. Pullman, WA: Score (1015 NW Clifford St., 99164-3203), 1995; Brannen, Jonathan. *No Place to Fall*. San Francisco: Sink, 1999.

BRAXTON, Anthony

(4 June 1945).

I'd love to do a coherent introduction on this African–American whose music straddles both jazz and classical worlds, who studied philosophy as well as music, who has received a MacArthur "Genius" Award; but, in truth, it resists my taste for classification. Bits and pieces of his work are impressive, beginning with his prose writings (until they fall into jargon, mysticism, or incomprehensibility) and his visually imaginative scores. Initially an alto saxophonist, he also perfoms on the other saxophones, along with the contrabass clarinet, and various percussion instruments, sometimes within a single concert. As far as I can tell, his music at various times includes not only improvisation (with Braxton himself a virtuoso on saxophone) by himself or with musicians descending from both classical and jazz, but open forms in the tradition of EARLE BROWN, scored compositions (*For Four Orchestras* [1978]), minimalist music, and moves that defy description, all with an ambition (if not pretention) that resembles KARLHEINZ STOCKHAUSEN'S. He was hailed at the beginning of his career, around 1970s, by critics who identified him as a likely successor to John Coltrane, only to drop him by 1980. By the time the next edition of this *Dictionary* is written, I'll either understand his art better or not at all.

Texts: *Composition Notes E*. Hanover, NH: Frog Peak Music, 1988; *The Tri-Axium Writings*. Hanover, NH: Frog Peak Music, n.d.

Recordings: *Composition No. 107* for saxophones, piano, percussion & computer music (1982) (selections) (Centaur CC 2110); *Compositions Nos. 136, 140, 62 & 116,* for flute/saxophone & piano, rec. live at 1989 Vancouver Jazz Festival (Music & Arts cd 611); *Solo Piano (Standards) 1995* (Box Set), No More Records, 1996; *Four Compositions* (quartet), Black Saint, 1983; *Twelve Compositions*, Music & Arts, 1995; *Six Compositions* (quartet), Black Saint, 1994.

Website: http://www.wesleyan.edu/music/braxton/

Interpretation: Ford, Alun. *Anthony Braxton: Creative Music Continuums*. Exeter, England: Stride (11 Sylvan Rd., EX4 6EW), 1998; Heffley, Mike. *The Music of Anthony Braxton*. New York: Excelsior Music, 1995; Lock, Graham. *Forces in Motion: The Music and Thoughts of Anthony Braxton*. New York: Da Capo, 1988; Radano, Ronald M. *New Musical Figurations: Anthony Braxton's Cultural Critique*. Chicago: University of Chicago Press, 1993.

THE BREAD AND PUPPET THEATER

(1962).

Formed by Peter Schumann (1934), a German refugee then living in lower Manhattan, the company took its name from the dark homemade bread that they shared with audiences after each performance and from the use of stick puppets. The spectacle-styled pieces are usually narrated by someone who controls the sound, while the puppets, usually quite large, often require several people to manipulate them. I have seen them work in churches as well as outdoors, with and for both adults and children, often recruiting performers on the spot during tours. The historian Theodore Shank reports that by 1981 Schumann "had created well over a hundred productions." Many of the works are political parables that incorporate mythical figures and biblical images. Typical titles include *The Twelve Stations of the Cross* (1972), *Christmas Story* (1967, 1974), and A Monument for *Ishi—An Anti-Bicentennial Pageant* (1975). Even the principals of Cirque de Soleil have acknowledged its influence.

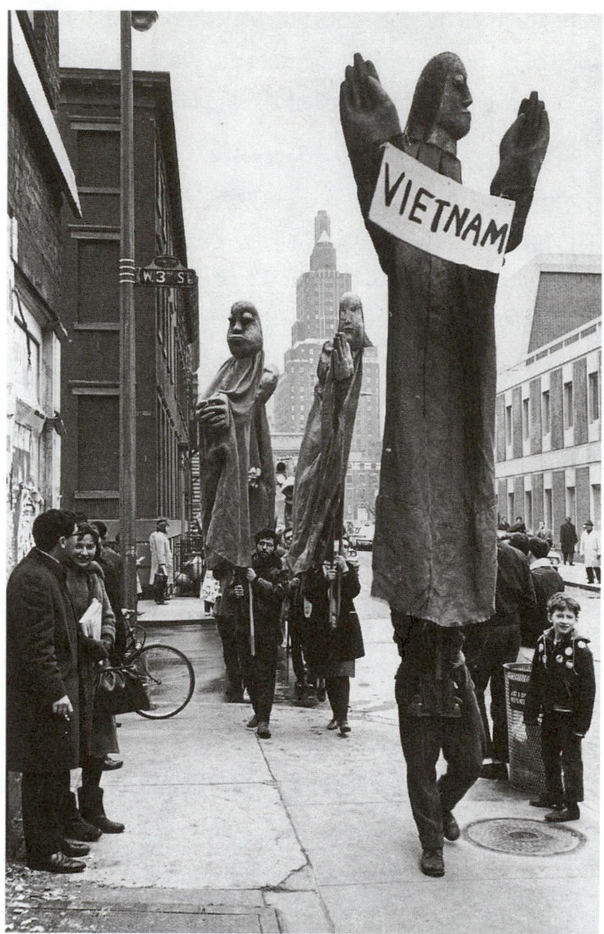

Bread and Puppet Theater performing for an antiwar demonstration, 9 March 1965. Photograph © Fred W. McDarrah.

Bibiliography: *Landscape and Desire: Bread and Puppet Pageants in 1990s*. Text by John Bell; photographs by Ronald Simon. Glover, VT: Bread and Puppet Press (USA 05839), 1997; Brecht, Stefan. *The Bread and Puppet Theater*. 2 vols. New York: Methuen, 1988; Shank, Theodore. *American Alternative Theatre*. New York: Grove, 1982.

Website: http://www.pbpub.com/bread&puppet/bread.htm

BRECHT, George

(7 March 1926).

Trained in science, he worked initially as a quality-control supervisor and research chemist before becoming an artist. Having studied with JOHN CAGE at the New School in 1958 and 1959, he participated in FLUXUS activities organized by GEORGE MACIUNAS. Brecht's first innovation was a particular kind of minimal text, some of which were headlined "events." Examples read in their entirety:

> INSTRUCTION * Turn on a radio./ At the first sound, turn it off.

> THREE DANCES: 1. Saliva//2. Pause./ Urination./ Pause.//3. Perspiration.

> TWO APPROXIMATIONS
>
> (
>
> obituary
>
>)

The Book of the Tumbler in Fire (1978) is a self-retrospective of works from 1962. Brecht also coedited an unprecedented anthology composed wholly of paradoxes. The critic Henry Martin (1942) writes: "The internal logic of George Brecht's work is entirely impossible to describe, since his problem as an artist is always and only to work towards an intuitive grasp of the problems of knowledge and awareness that are central to his own individual being in the universe." As an American living in Germany, this Brecht is more truly avant-garde than another writer with the same surname, more commercial in his orientation, who lived for a while in America.

Books: *Chance Images*. New York: Something Else, 1966; with Filliou, Robert. *Games at the Cedillas or the Cedillas Takes Off*. New York: Something Else, 1967; *The Book of the Tumbler in Fire.* Intro. by Henry Martin. Milan, Italy: Multiplitha, 1978; Hughes, Patrick, and George Brecht, eds. *Vicious Circles and Infinity* (1975). New York: Penguin, 1979.

Exhibition Catalog: Marter, Joan, ed. *Off Limits: Rutgers University and the Avant-Garde, 1957–1963*. Newark, NJ: The Newark Museum & Rutgers University Press, 1999.

Interpretation: Higgins, Dick. *Postface*. New York: Something Else, 1964; Kaprow, Allen. *Assemblage, Environments and Happenings*. New York: Abrams, 1966.

BRETON, André

(19 February 1896–28 September 1966).

Initially part of Paris DADA, Breton broke with TRISTAN TZARA and became the founder and self-styled "pope" of SURREALISM. Primarily a novelist and theoretical critic, he was a physically imposing figure whose critical specialty was manifestos that formulated and reformulated the Surrealist esthetic. As a literary radical, he preached the virtues of "automatic writing" (purportedly without conscious control) and of the "exquisite corpse," which was his term for collaboration, both of which he thought were psychologically enriching. He edited collections that are still useful, including *Anthologie de l'humour noir* (1940), which finds Surrealist precursors in Jonathan Swift, G. C. Lichtenberg, Charles Fourier, Thomas de Quincey, Edgar Allan Poe, and LEWIS CARROLL, among others, creating the image of an underground, proto-Surrealist tradition dating back several centuries. Authoritarian in temper, Breton convened his followers daily at certain Parisian cafés. Exiled in the U.S. during World War II, he refused to learn English and, after the war ended, returned to France. His claims to earlier Parisian authority were undermined by the new postwar fashion called existentialism. Breton's negative example perhaps accounts for why the notion of a self-conscious artists' group has never had much currency in the United States in general and in New York in particular. Breton's creative writings, once so prominent, are now forgotten—his novels no less than his poetry.

Writings: *The Magnetic Fields*, 1919; *Conversations: The Autobiography of Surrealism*. Trans and intro. Mark

Polizzotti. New York: Paragon House, 1993; *Manifestos of Surrealism*. Ann Arbor: University of Michigan Press, 1969; *Nadja* (1928). New York: Grove, 1960.

Anthologies: *Anthologie de l'Humour noir*. Paris: Jean-Jacques Pauvert, 1966; *Selected Poems*. Trans. Kenneth White. London: Cape, 1969; *What Is Surrealism?: Selected Writings*. Ed. Franklin Rosemont. New York: Monad, 1978

Biography: Balakian, Anna. *André Breton*. New York: Oxford Unviersity Press, 1971; Polizzotti, Mark. *Revolution of the Mind: The Life of André Breton*. New York: Farrar, Straus, 1995.

Interpretation: Carrouges, Michel. *André Breton and the Basic Concepts of Surrealism* (1950). Trans. Maura Prendergast. Tuscaloosa: University of Alabama Press, 1974; Caws, Mary Ann. *Surrealism and the Literary Imagination: A Study of Breton and Bachelard*. The Hague: Mouton, 1966; *André Breton*. New York: Twayne, 1970; *The Poetry of Dada and Surrealism*. Princeton: Princeton University Press, 1970.

BROWN, Bob

(14 June 1886–7 August 1959; b. Robert Carlton B.).

Brown is another one of those early twentieth-century avant-garde writers whose reputations were lost in the insufficient assimilation of extreme modernism. (Whenever you hear anyone say that "all avant-garde art has been accepted," point to individuals like Brown, among too many others.) After a peripatetic career as a stock-market speculator, a magazine publisher in South America, and the inventor of a proto-microfilm reader (according to Hugh Ford's *Four Lives in Paris* [1987]), Brown became both a "straight" poet and a visual poet. Perhaps because his work in the former vein resembles the informal poetry popularized by the "New York School" in the late 1960s, I would think that anyone reading it today would find the later work fresher. In addition to publishing his own poetry, he edited *Readies for Bob Brown's Machine* (1931), an anthology that included the more experimental works of many of his contemporaries. He also coauthored several cooking books with his sister.

Writings: *Globe Gliding*. Cagnes-sur-Mer: Roving Eye Press, 1930; *The Readies*, Cagnes-sur-Mer: Roving Eye Press, 1931; *Words*. Paris: Hours Press, 1931; *Nomadness*. New York: Dodd, Mead, 1931; *You Gotta Live*. Londone: D. Harmsworth, 1932; *1450/1950*. New York: Jargon-Corinth, 1959.

Edited Works: *Readies for Bob Brown's Machine*. Cagnes-sur-Mer: Roving Eye Press, 1931; *Gems: A Censored Anthology*. Cagnes-sur-Mer: Roving Eye Press, 1931.

BROWN, Earle

(26 December 1926).

Echoing both John Cage and Alexander Calder, Earle Brown developed in the early 1950s graphic notation that encouraged both aleatory and improvisatory techniques. *Folio* (1952–53) is actually six compositions in which the performer is instructed to vary the duration, pitch, and rhythm. *25 Pages* (1953) is designed to be played by as many as twenty-five pianists, reading the music pages in any desired order and playing the notes upside down or right-side up. Brown's *Available Forms I* (1961) and *Available Forms II* (1962), respectively for chamber ensemble and full orchestra, contain pages of eccentric (but fixed) notation, or "available forms," which may be sounded in any order, repeated, and combined in varying tempi, all at the spontaneous discretion of the performers. Nicolas Slonimsky finds Brown's music represents "a mobile assembly of plastic elements in open-ended or closed forms. As a result, his usages range from astute asceticism and constrained constructivism to soaring sonorism and lush lyricism." Perhaps because he favors conventional modernist musical instrumentation, Brown's music sometimes sounds serial, notwithstanding differences in compositional philosophies.

Compositions: *Fugue* for piano, 1949; *Home Burial* for piano, 1949; *Passacaglia* for piano, 1950; *Strata* for 2 pianos, 1950; String Quartet, 1950; *3 Pieces* for piano, 1951; *Perspectives* for piano, 1952; *December*, 1952; *Music* for violin, cello, and piano, 1952; *Folio* for unspecified instruments, 1952–53; *Music for "Tender Buttons"* for speaker, flute, horn, and harp 1953; *Octet I*, 1953; *25 Pages* for 1 to 25 pianos, 1953; *4 Systems* for unspecified instruments, 1954; *Holograph I* for flute, piano, and percussion, 1959; *Available Forms I* for 18 musicians, 1961; *II* for large orchestra and 2 conductors, 1962; *Calder Piece* for four percussion and mobile, 1963–66; *Times Five* for flute, trombone, harp, violin, cello, and 4-track tape, 1963; *Corroboree* for three or two pianos, 1964; *9 Rarebits* for 1 or 2 harpsichords, 1965; *Sign Sounds* for 18 instruments, 1972; *Cross Section and Color Fields* for orchestra, 1975; *Sounder Rounds* for orchestra, 1982; *Tracer* for flute, oboe, bassoon violin, cello, double bass, and 4-track tape, 1984.

Recordings: *Centering: The Music of Earle Brown*. Newport Classics, 1998.

BROWN, Trisha

(25 November 1936).

One of several distinguished dancers associated with the JUDSON DANCE THEATER, Brown has made the wit and intelligence of her inquiries the core of her esthetic. Her early works included "equipment pieces" that explored the possibilities of body movements with a variety of supports, such as ropes enabling dancers to "walk" up a vertical wall. For her "accumulation pieces," Brown developed various strategies for gathering movement material. She frequently incorporates improvisational structures into her works. In recent years, her work has depended more upon virtuoso dance techniques, rather than ordinary movements. She has collaborated with ROBERT RAUSCHENBERG and DONALD JUDD, among others.

—Katy Matheson

Selected Works: *Trillium*, 1962; *Lightfall*, 1963; *Planes*, 1968; *Man Walking Down the Side of a Building*, 1970; *Walking on the Wall*, 1971; *Spiral*, 1974; *Locus*, 1975; *Glacial Decoy*, 1979; *Opal Loop*, 1980; *Son of Gone Fishin'*, 1981: *Set and Reset*, 1983; *If You Couldn't See Me*, 1994.

Interpretation: Banes, Sally. *Terpsichore in Sneakers* (1980). 2d ed. Middletown: Wesleyan University Press, 1987; "Trisha Brown." In *Contemporary Dance*, ed. Anne Livet. New York: Abbeville, 1978.

BRUCE, Neely

(21 January 1944; b. Frank N. B.).

He was one of seven harpsichordists in the original performance of JOHN CAGE'S *HPSCHD* and the sole pianist on WILLIAM DUCKWORTH'S *The Time Curved Preludes*. He has also composed dozens of songs (some of them to texts of the more experimental American poets), a four-act opera about the American Revolution, and an eccentrically eclectic oratorio, *The Plague* (1983), which incorporates a variety of familiar musical styles, both high and low, classical and contemporary, in a way that might be classified as "postmodernist" were not the final result, at least in the British group Electric Phoenix's recording, so peculiar. With typical wit, Bruce speaks of his "eclecticism which is occasionally so extreme as to be virtually incomprehensible."

Works: *The Plague* (1983), performed by Electric Phoenix. New York: Mode (#20), 1991.

Website: http://www.wesleyan.edu/course/faculty/bruceneelyx.htm

BRYANT, Allan

(12 July 1931).

I include him here not because I know his music but because I don't and should. A Princeton-educated American who has worked mostly in Europe, at times in collaboration with MEV, he also made, according to Slonimsky, *"Quadruple Play* for Amplified Rubber Bands utilizing Contact microphones and coordinated with an Audio-controlled Lighting System (1966); *Impulses* for a Variety of Percussion, Concussion, and Discussion Sounds (1967); *X-es Sex,* an intersexual happening with Boots and Balloons (1967); also political works, e.g., *Liberate Isang Yun* (1967), for a Multimilliondecibel Electronic Sound calculated to reach the ears of the South Korean abductors of the dissident Korean Composer," all of which I would have loved to have seen and heard. Such compositional ideas deserve inclusion here if only for their conceptual quality.

Recordings: *Space Guitars*. New York: CRI (#366), 1977.

b

BRYARS, Gavin

(16 January 1943).

Bryars has been a mysterious figure, a Briton known only for a few compositions, most of which depend upon the possibilities for repetition offered by audiotape. *Jesus' Blood Never Failed Me Yet* (1971) draws upon a London tramp's *a cappella* singing of an old English hymn, which is looped to repeat itself and then gradually accompanied by strings and other instruments. When the only recording of it was long out of print in the 1980s, it became a favorite of American radio stations that like to surprise their audiences and of avant-garde music buffs who like to shock their friends. *The Sinking of the Titanic* (1969) repeats in slightly different ways, for well over an hour, tunes reportedly played by the ship's drowning orchestra. *Media* (1982) is an opera produced in collaboration with the theater artist Robert Wilson. Bryars also founded the Portsmouth Sinfonia whose sublimely comic recordings were produced by Brian Eno.

Recordings: *Three Viennese Dances* for string quartet, french horn, and percussion, with the Arditti Quartet, et al. (ECM 829484-1); *Vita Nova, Glorious Hill, Four Elements, Sub Rosa,* with The Hilliard Ensemble; Gavin Bryers Ensemble; David James, countertenor. München: ECM, 1994; *After the Requiem* (1990), *The Old Tower of Löbenicht* (1987), *Alaric I or II* (1989), *Allegrasco* (1983), with A. Balanescu, G. Bryars, Bill Frisell, et al. (ECM 78118-21533-2); *Allegrasco, Alaric, Three Elegies*. Media 7, 1998; ——— et al. *Portsmouth Sinfonia*. New York: Columbia (KC 33049), 1974.

Web Site: http://www.december.org/bryars.htm

BUCKLEY, Lord

(5 April 1906–13 November 1960; b. Richard Myrle B.).

Though Buckley's monologues are known to me only from recordings made in the 1950s, I'm prepared to rank him the strongest and most original practitioner of that great American standup art. He becomes, therefore, the precursor of, among others, Lenny Bruce (1925–66), Richard Pryor (1940), George Carlin (1938), and Joan Rivers (1937), who are all good and sophisticated in different ways. Buckley was a Caucasian of unknown American origins who feigned British manners and yet specialized in rendering a familiar story in the jive (African-American) lingo of his time. Take, for instance, this passage from "The Naz," which retells the life story of the man from Nazareth:

> But, I'm gonna' part a Cat on you, who was the Sweetest, Grooviest, Strongest, Wailinest, Swinginest, Jumpinest, most far out Cat that ever Stomped on this Sweet Freen Sphere, and they called this here Cat, THE NAZ, that was the Cat's name.
>
> He was a carpenter kitty. Now the Naz was the kind of a Cat that came on so cool and so wild and so groovy and so WITH IT, that when he laid it down *WHAM!* It stayed there! Naturally, all the rest of the Cats say:
>
> "Dig what this Cat is puttin' down! Man! Look at that Cat Blow!"

Because Buckley introduced slang that has since become more familiar, his monologues sound contemporary to a degree that those of, say, Will Rogers (1879–1935) do not. Even today, long after his death, not much is known, or believed, about Buckley's life.

Books: *Hiparama of the Classics*. San Francisco, CA: City Lights, 1980.

Recordings: *Lord Buckley: Friends, Romans and Countrymen*, RCA; *Euphoria*, Vaya; *In Concert*, World Pacific; *Buckley's Best*, World Pacific; *Blowing His Mind*, World Pacific (reissued Demon Verbals); *Bad Rapping of the Marquis de Sade*, World Pacific (reissued Demon Verbals); *A Most Immaculately Hip Aristocrat*, Straight (reissued Enigma); *The Best of Lord Buckley*, [n.p.] Elektra 1969; *Lord Buckley Live* (audiocassette). Boston: Shambala, 1991; *His Royal Hipness*. Santa Monica, CA: Discovery (First Media, 2052 Broadway, Santa Monica, CA 90404), 1992.

Website:
http://www.industrialhaiku.com/Lord_Buckley_Online.html

BUÑUEL, Luis

(22 February 1900–29 July 1983).

Filmmaker who successfully translated SURREALISTIC imagery onto the screen. Working originally in conjunction with the artist SALVADOR DALI, Buñuel created the classic *Un Chien andalou* (*The Andalusian Dog*, 1928), incorporating Freudian imagery such as the putting out of an eye (from the Oedipal myth) and ants crawling out of the center of a hand. In his later career, Buñuel achieved fame as a social critic in his biting satires of middle-class life, such as *The Discrete Charm of the Bourgeoise* (1972) and *The Phantom of Liberty* (1974). In these later films, he continued to use dreamlike narratives, discontinuous story lines, and "shocking" imagery, making him the only practitioner on a large scale of a Surrealist cinema.

Salvador Dali, *Portrait of Luis Buñuel*, 1924. CORBIS/Archivo Iconogrfico, S.A./© 2000 Artists Rights Society (ARS), New York.

Films: *L'Age d'or/The Golden Age*, 1930; *Los Olvidados/The Young and the Damned*, 1950; *Robinson Crusoe/The Adventures of Robinson Crusoe*, 1952; *El/This Strange Passion*, 1952; *The Criminal Life of Archibaldo de la Cruz*, 1955; *Nazarin*, 1959; *Viridiana*, 1961; *El Angel Exterminador/The Exterminating Angel*, 1962; *Simon del Desierto/Simon of the Desert*, 1965; *La Voie lactée/The Milky Way*, 1969; *Le Charme discret de la bourgeoisie/The Discrete Charm of the Bourgeoise,* 1972; *The Phantom of Liberty,* 1974; *Cet Obscur Objet du désire/That Obscure Object of Desire*, 1977; With Salvador Dali. *Un Chien andalou* (*The Andalusian Dog*), 1928.

Writings: *My Last Sigh*. New York: Knopf, 1983.

Interpretation: Buache, Freddy. *The Cinema of Luis Buñuel*. New York: A. S. Barnes, 1973; Mellen, Joan. ed. *The World of Luis Buñuel: Essays in Criticism*. New York: Oxford University Press, 1978; Stauffacher, Frank, ed. *Art in Cinema: A Symposium on the Avant Garde Film* (1947). New York: Arno, 1968.

BURCHFIELD, Charles

(9 April 1893–10 January 1967).

Burchfield's place in the story of innovative American art is due not to any formal innovations he devised but to the distinctiveness of the temperament he infused into his watercolor paintings. A quality of romantic mysticism runs

Charles Burchfield, *Sunday Morning at 6 AM*, 1917. Watercolor. CORBIS/Burstein collection.

through the principal works of Burchfield. He viewed nature as a source of wonders, fears, and miracles. Beginning in the mid-teens of the century, after undergoing a psychological crisis, influenced by Japanese prints and story book illustrators, such as Arthur Rackham and Edmund Dulac, he developed a style of rendering nature scenes that was flat, decorative, and calligraphic. In his early paintings, nature was a fairy land: fields, country roads, and lines of trees were distorted, such that flowers towered out of all proportion and the wind rode visibly through the night sky, looking like a phantom. Burchfield employed, somewhat crudely, techniques of abstraction, which were already being developed by WASSILY KANDINSKY and ARTHUR DOVE (*), to render optically the peals of church bells and the sounds of insects as roughly defined geometric forms inserted into his compositions. In the 1930s, Burchfield turned to regional realism, producing very little work of serious interest. But in 1943, he returned to his first preoccupation with nature as an animistic force and a source of religious experience. All in all, he produced intriguing works, but not a single major painting, and it may be wondered whether the depression and obsessive fears he suffered in his youth helped him to make art, or if he was practicing a form of self-therapy that merely resembled art.

—Mark Daniel Cohen

Works: *Ghost Plants*, 1916; *Church Bells Ringing, Rainy Winter Night*, 1917; *Sunday Morning at 6 AM*, 1917; *The Night Wind*, 1918; *Haunted Evening*, 1919; *November Evening*, 1931–34; *Winter Bouquet*, 1933; *An April Mood*, 1946–55; *Hot September Wind*, 1953; *Charles Burchfield's Journals: The Poetry of Place*. Ed. J. Benjamin Townsend. Albany, NY: SUNY, 1993.

Biography: Baur, John I. H. *The Inlander: Life and Work of Charles Burchfield, 1893–1967*. Newark: University of Delaware & New York: Cornwall Books, 1984.

Exhibition Catalogs: Barr, Alfred Hamilton. *Charles Burchfield: Early Water Colors, April 11–April 26, 1930, Museum of Modern Art, New York*. New York: MoMA, 1930; Baur, John I. H. *Charles Burchfield*. New York: Whitney Museum of American Art, 1956; *Charles Burchfield: Watercolors and Drawings, 1915–1966: October 15–November 1, 1975*. New York: Kennedy Galleries, 1975; Baigell, Matthew. *Charles Burchfield*. New York: Watson-Guptill, 1976. *The Early Works of Charles E. Burchfield*. Columbus, OH: Columbus Museum of Art, 1987; Weekly, Nancy. *Charles E. Burchfield: The Sacred Woods*. Buffalo, NY: Burchfield Art Center & Albany, New York: SUNY, 1993.

Catalog Raisonné: Munsun-Williams-Proctor Institute. *Charles Burchfield: Catalogue of Paintings in Public and Private Collections*. Utica, New York: Munsun-Williams-Proctor Institute, Museum of Art, 1970.

BURDEN, Chris

(11 April 1946).

In the early 1970s, Burden commanded respectful attention for a series of one-person performance pieces that customarily involved genuine personal risk: He imprisoned himself in a university locker for five days; he crawled on broken glass; he stuck pins into his stomach; he asked a friend to shoot him in the arm; he lay under a tarpaulin on a Los Angeles street; he had himself chained to the floor between bare electrical wires and buckets of water that, if knocked over, might have electrocuted him; and so on. For *Transfixed* (1974), Burden had himself "crucified" on the back end of a Volkswagen with nails driven through his hands. He subsequently created fuel-efficient, one-person land transports and sculptural pieces with many parts, some of which incorporated political thrusts unpopular in the art world, such as *The Reason for the Neutron Bomb* (1979), in which 50,000 nickels, each with a match on top, symbolize the number of Soviet tanks on Eastern European borders.

Exhibition Catalog: *Chris Burden: A Twenty-year Survey*. Newport Beach, CA: Newport Harbor Art Museum, 1988.

Interpretation: Cooper, Dennis. "Chris Burden," in *Artforum International* (March, 1988); Levin, Kim. "Chris Burden: America's Darker Moments," *Grand Street* (Spring, 1995).

BURGESS, Anthony

(25 February 1917–22 November, 1993; b. John A. B. Wilson).

A prolific writer, he authored a large number of ordinary books in addition to a few extraordinary ones. *A Clockwork Orange* (1962) portrays a future in which unruly teenagers insert Russian words into basically English sentences, or more accurately meld new language with old idiom. On the opening page, the narrator Alex remembers, "We sat in the Korova Milkbar making up our rassoodocks what to do with the evening, a flip dark chill winter bastard though dry. The Korova Milkbar was a milk-plus besto, and you may, O my brothers, have forgotten what these mestos were like, things changing so skorry these days . . . ." Through such original language Burgess realized an image of a violent future. A complete man of letters, he was also a prolific reviewer and even an editor. In this last category, his most remarkable achievement is *A Shorter Finnegans Wake* (1967), which manages to extract choice passages from Joyce's essentially nonlinear novel (whose theme of familial conflict is continuously present) to make a shorter Joycean book that is considerably more accessible than the original. Modesty in crediting notwithstanding, this is an extraordinary feat that no one else could have done. Also a trained composer, Burgess produced works for conventional instruments that are rarely played or recorded, either because of or in spite of his literary reputation.

Selected Books: *A Clockwork Orange*. New York: Norton, 1962; *Re Joyce* (1965). Rev. ed. New York: Norton, 1982; ——, ed. *A Shorter Finnegans Wake*. New York: Viking, 1967.

Website: http://www.levity.com/corduroy/burgess.htm

Interpretation: *Critical Essays on Anthony Burgess*. Boston: Hall, 1986; Mathews, Richard. *The Clockwork Universe of Anthony Burgess*. San Bernadino, CA: Borgo Press, 1978.

BURGESS, Gelett

(30 January 1866–18 September 1951).

Burgess suffered from the most heinous effects of Andy Warhol's fifteen minutes of fame; he is remembered more for a single four-line verse, "The Purple Cow," written in 1895 ("I never saw a purple cow . . . ") than for anything else he ever did. Burgess left his mark on the lexicon of English with such coinages as "blurb," "bromide," and "goop." He even developed a little book of 100 such coinages, and his use of them represents the next step after Lewis Carroll's "Jabberwocky" toward a fully realized language for new creative expression: "No more tintiddling slobs, like fidgelticks,/ Rizgidgeting your speech, shall lallify;/ But your jujasm, like vorgid gollohix,/ Shall all your waxy meem golobrify!"

Early in his career, Burgess edited a few literary magazines, including *Le Petit Journal des refusées*, printed on discontinued samples of wallpaper. Although primarily a writer, Burgess also enjoyed building things, including nonsense machines. When in 1910 he showed thirty of his watercolors under the title "Experiments in Symbolistic Psychology," critics debated (to no apparent resolution) whether the works were serious art or satirical deflations. The truth of the matter should not be important to us.

—Geof Huth

Books: *The Purple Cow*. San Francisco: W. Doxey, 1899; *Are You A Bromide?* New York: B. W. Huebsch, 1906; *The Goop Encyclopedia*. New York: Frederick A. Stokes Co., 1916; *The Romance of the Commonplace*. Indianapolis: Bobbs-Merrill, 1916.

Anthology: *Burgess Unabridged: A New Dictionary of Words You Have Always Needed* (1914). Hamden, CT: Archon, 1986.

BURKE, Kenneth

(5 May 1897–11 November 1993).

A protean writer who worked steadily in several literary forms from his youth into his mid-nineties, Burke long ago produced theoretical treatises that were so "ahead of their time" that they are still in print, continually rediscovered by each new self-conscious group of American critics. He is now as much a hero to Marxists as he was to the text-oriented "New Critics" so prominent in the 1940s and 1950s, and what Burke had to say is not lost on "Deconstructionists" either. The persistence of his influence is amazing, given how thick and digressive, and often abstruse and abstract, his books are. Burke was also a fiction writer and, not surprisingly, an experimental poet whose more unusual works include VISUAL POEMS, called "Flowerishes," and a conceptual poem, "Project for a Poem on [F.D.] Roosevelt," which is really a suggestive prose outline that succeeds, poetically, on its own terms. Consider the opening of the third section (stanza):

> New approach. Picture of democracy as it works in business structure. Many conflicts among business interests. Not only conflicts between the hirers, and internecine conflicts among the hired. How tariff may protect one hirer-hired group at the expense of another. How industrial centers as a whole can profit *for a time* at the expense of agrarian areas. How crooked promoters actually stimulate the speed-up of money (and hence the distribution of goods among all) until the false basis of their promises is disclosed. How wastage serves to promote the common good.

Though I have read Burke many times and written on him more than once, I'm sure that a subsequent commentator on avant-garde literature will find innovation(s) I've missed.

Books: *Counter-Statement* (1931). Rev ed. Berkeley: University of California Press, 1968; *The Philosophy of Literary Form* (1941). Berkeley: University of California Press, 1973; *Collected Poems*. Berkeley: University of California Press, 1968; *The Complete White Oxen's Collected Short Fiction*. Berkeley: University of California Press, 1968; *Attitudes Toward History* (1937). Berkeley: University of California Press, 1984; *A Grammar of Motives* (1945). Berkeley: University of California Press, 1969; *A Rhetoric of Motives* (1950). Berkeley: University of California Press, 1969; *Language as Symbolic Action: Essays on Life, Literature, and Method* (1966). Berkeley: University of California Press, 1986.

Anthologies: *Perspectives by Incongruity*. Ed. Stanley Edgar Hyman and Barbara Karmiller. Bloomington: Indiana University Press, 1965; *Terms for Order*. Ed. Stanley Edgar Hyman and Barbara Karmiller. Bloomington: Indiana University Press, 1965.

Biography: Selzer, Jack. *Kenneth Burke in Greenwich Village: Conversing with the Moderns, 1915–1931*. Madison: University of Wisconsin Press, 1996.

Website: http://www.cudenver.edu/~mryder/itc/burke.html (links to all things Burkean on the web).

Interpretation: Hyman, Stanley Edgar. *The Armed Vision*. New York: Knopf, 1948; Frank, Armin Paul. *Kenneth Burke*. New York: Twayne, 1969; Henderson, Grieg E. *Kenneth Burke: Literature and Language as Symbolic Action*. Athens: University of Georgia Press, 1988; Kostelanetz, Richard. "Kenneth Burke at 92." In *The New Poetries and Some Old*. Carbondale: Southern Illinois University Press, 1991; Rueckert, William H. *Kenneth Burke and the Drama of Human Relations*. Minneapolis: University of Minnesota Press, 1963; ——. *Encounters with Kenneth Burke*. Urbana: University of Illinois Press, 1994; ——. *Critical Responses to Kenneth Burke*. Minneapolis: University of Minnesota Press, 1969; Simons, Herbert & Melia, Trevor. ed. *The Legacy of Kenneth Burke*. Madison: University of Wisconsin Press, 1989.

BURROUGHS, William S.

(5 February 1914–2 August 1997).

An American original, the Harvard-educated scion of a family memorialized on a brand of adding machines, Burroughs came late to literature, beginning with an undistinguished memoir, *Junkie* (1953, published under the pseudonym of William Lee). Inspired by his friendship with Allen Ginsberg, he dabbled in formal experiments, some of them in collaboration with others, including the mixing of passages drawn from different sources, not only in adjacent paragraphs but in the horizontal lines of the page. Some of this experimentation dominates shorter pieces, collected in several books, beginning with *The Exterminator* (1960, with Brion Gysin); it informs *Naked Lunch* (1959) as well, an hallucinatory nightmare that remains his masterpiece. Most of Burroughs's other books are indubitably prosaic in style and structure. Some readers admire his rendering of narcotic experiences, including withdrawal; others, his dark vision; yet others, his homosexual fantasies; all of which have little to do with what makes some of his writing avant-garde.

Books: *Naked Lunch* (1959). New York: Grove, 1992; *Junkie* (1953, as "William Lee"). New York: Penguin, 1977; *The Burroughs File*. San Francisco: City Lights, 1984; and Allen Ginsberg. *The Yage Letters*. San Francisco: City Lights, 1960; and Brion Gysin. *The Exterminator*. San Francisco: Auerhahn Press, 1960; and Brion Gysin. *The Third Mind*. New York: Seaver, 1978.

Biography: Morgan, Ted. *Literary Outlaw: The Life and Times of William S. Burroughs*. New York: Holt, 1988.

Website: http://www.hyperreal.org/wsb/

Critical Studies: Goodman, Michael Barry. *Contemporary Literary Censorship: The Case History of Burroughs' Naked Lunch*. Metuchen, NJ: Scarecrow, 1981; Lyndenberg, Robin. *Word Cultures: Radical Theory and Practice in William W. Burroughs' Fiction*. Urbana: University of Illinois Press, 1987; Mottram, Eric. *William Burroughs: The Algebra of Need*. London: Boyars, 1977; Skerl, Jennie and Lydenberg, Robin, eds. *William S. Burroughs at the Front: Critical Reception 1959–1989*. Carbondale: Southern Illinois University Press, 1991; Tytell, John. *Naked Angels: Kerouac, Ginsberg, Burroughs*. New York: McGraw-Hill, 1976.

Bibliography: Goodman, Michael. *William S. Burroughs: An Annotated Bibliography*. New York: Garland, 1975; Maynard, Joe, and Barry Miles. *William S. Burroughs: A Bibliography 1953–1973*. Charlottesville: University of Virginia Press, 1978.

BURSTNORM POETRY

(1994).

Term coined by taxonomaniac Bob Grumman as an attempt objectively—outside of time, place, politics, philosophy, religion, ethnicity, person or persons of origin—to classify nontraditional poetry—that is, usually but not necessarily "avant garde/otherstream/out-rider/underground/otherground/experimental/alternative/cutting-edge" poetry. Grumman uses it to distinguish such poetry from what he calls "songmode" and "plaintext" poetry, the first being traditional metric and/or rhymed poetry, the second now-traditional free verse. The norms burst are (1) expressive decorum, or the rule that poetry should be verbal only; (2) logic, in particular, narrative and/or sensory logic; and (3) linguistic propriety, in spelling as well as grammar, both the strict grammar of prose, and the looser grammar of traditional verse (which permits, for instance, inversions—e.g. noun followed, in English, by adjective instead of the reverse).

According to Grumman's taxonomy, poetry that uses more than the one expressive modality for words, as Visual Poetry uses graphics, mathematical poetry math, sound poetry more-than-verbal-sound, and so forth, is "Pluraesthetic Poetry," or poetry that is aesthetically expressive in more than one way. Poetry breaking normal logic is "Idiological Poetry"—and is further divided into surrealistic (sensorily illogical) and jump-cut (narratively disjunctive) poetry. The third variety of burstnorm poetry for Grumman is "Xenolinguistic Poetry." It divides into "Infra-Verbal Poetry," which is orthographically eccentric, and "Sprung-Grammar Poetry," which meddles (significantly) with syntax and inflection. Roughly speaking, Xenolinguistic Poetry is a synonym for Language-Centered Poetry—except that it refers only to what such poetry does verbally, not to the political and other baggage the latter term, and similar terms like "Language Poetry" and "Langpo," have accumulated.

There are, needless to say, subdivisions of these terms, and some poems can be appropriately described by more than one term (in which case Grumman would call them "compound burstnorm poems"). The term, "burstnorm" is also applicable to other forms of literature besides poetry, and to painting, sculpture, music and the other arts, nonrepresentational painting being a prime example of an art that burst a norm (that the norm it burst is no longer much in evidence is irrelevant).

—Bob Grumman

References: "Notes Toward a Taxonomy of Literature." At *Comprepoetica*.

Website: http://www.geocities.com/SoHo/Cafe/1492/index.html

BURY, Pol

(26 April 1922).

Whereas most kinetic sculptures incorporate quick movements, this Belgian sculptor makes work that moves slowly, very slowly, so slowly that the movement can't be observed by the continuous eye, but measured if one turns away before returning. *The Staircase* (1965) has several circular, slanted platforms on a vertical core over six feet high. On each of these platforms are several tiny balls that slowly, ever so slowly, roll down the inclines; but instead of falling off, they roll back up. The French critic Frank Popper describes earlier work by Bury as being "mobile planes" made of masonite. In contrast to those kinetic sculptors who expose their work's mechanisms, Bury hides his, thus becoming a magician whose tricks remain unknown to even the most inquisitive spectator. His "cinematizations," as he calls them, come from cutting concentric circles out of photographs of familiar objects (the Eiffel Tower, the Mona Lisa) and then realigning internal shapes to create images of slow movement. Beginning as a painter who exhibited with the SURREALISTS until 1945, Bury abandoned painting completely in 1953 and remains among the few ex-Surrealists to do substantial innovative work.

Works: *Mobile Planes*, 1953; *Multiplanes*, 1957; *Luminous Punctuations*, 1959–1961; *Erectile Punctuations*, 1959–1961; *112 Cylinders in 12 Apertures*, 1966.

Exhibition Catalogs: *Twice Pol Bury Moving Sculptures.* New York: Lefebre Gal.,1966; *Ashton, Dore. Pol Bury*. Paris: Maeght, 1970; *Pol Bury*, with an introduction by Eugène Ionesco, a biographical sketch by André Balthazar, an interview with Bury, and excerpts from his writings. Berkeley, CA: University Art Museum, 1970; *Pol Bury Sculptures 1959–1985 Cinétisations 1962–1988*. Paris: Galerie 1900–2000, 1988.

Interpretation: Popper, Frank. *Origins and Development of Kinetic Art.* London, England: Studio Vista, 1968.

BUSONI, Ferruccio

(1 April 1866–27 July 1924).

After studies in his native Italy and Austria, Busoni lived from 1894 mostly in Berlin. Traveling widely as both a pianist and a conductor of his own music, he aimed initially as a synthesis of traditional musical techniques with new developments in the early twentieth century under the banner "Young Classicism" (preceding the Stravinsky-based "neo-classicism" of the 1930s and 40s, which claimed a similar synthesis). With his seven Elegies (1907) for piano solo, Busoni broached ATONALITY, which culminated in his *Sonatina No. 2* (1912). In this period he wrote "Sketch of a New Aesthetic of Music" (1911), a brilliant essay that was reprinted into the 1960s, because its radical biases seemed ever fresh. Interested in alternative relationships between music and drama, Busoni worked for years on an opera, *Doktor Faust* (1925), that was completed by a pupil after Busoni's death. He also made classic arrangements for piano of J. S. Bach compositions initially for other instruments.

Compositions: *Suite campestre*, 1878; *Solo dramatique* for clarinet and piano, 1879; *24 Préludes*, 1881; *Danza notturna*, 1882; *Introduction and Scherzo* for piano and orchestra, 1882–84; *5 Études*, 1882–88; *Sigune*, 1885–88; *4 Bagatelles* for violin and piano, 1888; *Concert Fantasy* for piano and orchestra, 1888–89; *Konzertstück* for piano and orchestra, 1889–90; *Turandot*, incidental music, 1905; *Die Brautwahl*, 1906–11; *Fantasia contrappuntistica* after J.S. Bach, for piano, 1910; 3d verson, 1912; *Nocturne symphonique*, 1912–13; *Indianische Fantasie* for piano and orchestra, 1913–14; *Arlecchino*, 1914–16; *Albumleaf* for flute or muted violin and piano, 1916; *Turandot*, 1916–17; *Doktor Faust*, 1916–23; *Lied des Méphistophèlés* for baritone and small orchestra after Goethe, 1918; *Divertimento* for flute and orchestra, 1920; *Tanzwalzer*, 1920; *Prélude et étude en arpèges*, 1923; *Schlecter Trost* for baritone and orchestra, 1924.

Recordings: *Doctor Faust*. Bavarian Radio Orch. & Chorus (DGG); *Oeuvres pour piano*, Solstice, 1998; *String Quartets*, CPO, 1995; *String Quartets Op.19, Op. 26*, Centaur, 1995; *Chamber Music*, Italy: Dynamic, 1996; *The Essence of Busoni*, Altarus, 1996.

Writings: "Sketch for a New Aesthetic of Music" (1911). In *Three Classics in the Aesthetic of Music*. New York: Dover, 1962.

Biography: Dent, Edward J. *Ferruccio Busoni: A Biography*. Oxford, England: Clarendon, 1966.

Website: http://www.comune.empoli.fi.it/empoli/busoni.html (in Italian).

Interpretation: Sitsky, Larry. *Busoni and the Piano: The Works, The Writings, and the Recordings*. Westport, CT: Greenwood, 1986.

BUTE, Mary Ellen

(1906–1983).

Originally a painter from Texas, Bute assisted the pioneering light artist THOMAS WILFRED, and collaborated with LEON THEREMIN on the possibility of sound-light synchronization; she also worked with the musicologist-mathematician JOSEPH SCHILLINGER, all before making her own animated abstract films. Her earliest works, based upon mathematical formulas, display, in Lewis Jacobs's words, "ever-changing lights and shadows, growing lines and forms, deepening colors and tones, the tumbling, racing impressions evoked by the musical accompaniment." Bute's later animations were created to music, photographed under various speeds and lights. In the 1950s, she choreographed images with an electronically controlled beam of light, using an oscilloscope. "Beautiful Lissajous curves (curves resulting from the combination of two harmonic motions, named for French scientist Jules A. Lissajous, 1822–80), can be put through a choreography that inspires—and startles—the imagination," she wrote in 1954. "The resulting beauty and movement contains intimations of occurrences in the sub-atomic world that hitherto have been accessible to the human mind merely as mathematical possibilities." The two "abstronic films," as she called them, were based respectively on the Hoe Down music of Aaron Copland and Ranch House Party by Don Gills. She also produced with human actors a feature-length version of James Joyce's *Finnegans Wake* (1965). The first misfortune was that she didn't survive into the era of computer animation. The second is that, for unfortunate estate-mismanagement reasons, none of Bute's films were at last report publicly available.

Films: *Rhythm in Light*, 1934; *Synchrony No. 2*, 1936; *Evening Sun*, 1937; *Spook Sport*, 1939; *Escape*, 1940; *Tarantella*, 1941; *Polka Graph*, 1952; *Mood Contrasts*, 1953; *Abstronics*, 1954; *The Boy Who Saw Through*, 1956; *Passages from Finnegans Wake*, 1965.

Writings: "Abstronics." In Russett, Robert, and Cecile Starr. *Experimental Animation.* New York: Van Nostrand Reinhold, 1976.

Interpretation: Rabinovitz, Lauren. "Mary Ellen Bute." In *Lovers of Cinema: The First American Film Avant-Garde*,

1919–1945, ed. Jan-Christopher Horak. Madison: University of Wisconsin Press, 1995.

BUTOH

(1959).

Though this Japanese dance-theater originated in 1959, cofounded by TATSUMI HIJIKATA and KAZUO OHNO, only in the 1980s did Western audiences become familiar with it. Although the term "Butoh" incorporates different approaches, a typical performance might include nearly nude, grimacing dancers in white body paint who are striking grotesque poses or contorting in slow motion, summoning up images of nature, crisis, and ancestral spirits. Some, but not all, of the Butoh performances incorporate improvisation. The stark, dangerous aspect of Butoh was evident in Sankai Juku's *Jomon Sho* (*Hommage to Pre-History*, 1982), in which several performers, nearly nude and covered with white powder, hung upside down at perilous heights. (The risk was real; in 1985, in Seattle, one performer fell to his death.) Although drastically different from such reigning forms as traditional Japanese dance and mainstream Euro-American modern dance, Butoh reflects some of their influence (e.g., the slow motion esthetic of the Japanese stage and the angst of German EXPRESSIONISTIC dance). Other performers and companies central to the development of Butoh include Yoko Ashikawa (1947) and the company Hakutobo (founded in 1974), Akali Maro and the company Dal Rakuda Kan (founded in 1972), Ushio Amagatsu and the company Sankai Juku (founded in 1975), Natsu Nakajima (1943) and the company Muteki-sha (founded in 1969), and Min Tinaka (1945).

—Katy Matheson

Butoh Dancers, c. 1990. CORBIS/Earl Kowall.

Books: Viala, Jean, and Nourit Masson-Sekine. *Butoh: Shades of Darkness.* Tokyo: Shufonotomu, 1988; *Butch: Dance of the Dark Soul.* New York: Aperture, 1987; Fraleigh, Sandra. *Dancing into Darkness: Butoh, Zen, and Japan*. Pitttsburgh: University of Pittsburgh Press, 1999; *The Drama Review,* T110 (Summer 1986).

Documentary Film: Blackwood, Michael. *Butoh: Body on the Edge of Cry*. New York: Michael Blackwood Productions, 1990.

b

BUTOR, Michel

(14 September 1926).

First connected to the "NOUVEAU ROMAN" school that emerged in France in the late 1950s, Butor has remained the most experimental of that bunch, working in various innovative ways, including extended criticism. Beginning in the 1960s, after securing a modest fame, he explored alternative structures and typographical possibilities, particularly in *Mobile* (1963), a detailed but elliptical portrait of America as seen not from the road but from the air, as though the author were a helicopter landing here and there. Advancing the art of travel writing, Butor composed a mosaic of impressions, along with quotations from historic memoirs (especially François René de Chateaubriand's eighteenth-century *America*). Later works exemplifying his historical-geographic imagination include *6 810 000 1itres d'eau par second (étude stéréophonique)* (1965; *Niagara: A Stereophonic Novel* [1969]) and *Boomerang* (1978; *Letters from the Antipodes* [n.d.]). As a literary artist, Butor has tried to replace two-dimensional linear history with a three-dimensional spatial one.

Books: *Change of Heart* (1957). Trans. Jean Stewart. New York: Simon & Schuster, 1959; *Passing Time* (1957). Trans. Jean Stewart. New York: Simon & Schuster, 1960; *Degrees* (1960). New York: Simon & Schuster, 1961; *Mobile* (1962). Trans. Richard Howard. New York: Simon & Schuster, 1963; *Inventory: Essays*. Ed. & trans. Richard Howard. New York: Simon & Schuster, 1968; *Niagara: A Stereophonic Novel* (1965). Trans. Elinor A. Miller. Chicago: Regnery, 1969; *Letters from the Antipodes* (A selection from *Boomerang*, 1978). Trans. Michael Spencer. Athens: Ohio University Press, 1981; *The Spirit of Mediterranean Places* (1958). Trans. Lydia Davis. Marlboro, VT: Marlboro, 1986; *Portrait of the Artist as a Young Ape*. Normal, IL: Dalkey Archive, 1995.

Interpretation: Lydon, Mary. *Perpetuum Mobile: A Study of the Aesthetics of Michel Butor*. Edmonton, Alberta: University of Alberta Press, 1980; Mercier, Vivian. *A Reader's Guide to the New Novel from Queneau to Pinget*. New York: Farrar, Straus, 1971; Roudier, Léon S. *Michel Butor*. New York: Columbia University, 1965; Waelti-Walters, Jennifer. *Michel Butor: A Study of his View of the World and a Panorama of his Work 1954–1974*. Victoria, BC: Sono Nis, 1977.

BYRUM, John

(1952).

An experimental poet and publisher, Byrum works with nonsyntactic streams of unrelated words and, more successfully, with VISUAL POEMS that present one word in larger type, its letters distributed over the page, juxtaposed against other words, mostly in smaller type. "They exist as matrices rather than as linear constructions," He writes about this last innovation. "Each is a multiplex of con- and divergent apparitions, a polyvocality at play in the languaged fields." Byrum also likes rectangular arrays whose letters spell one set of words horizontally, another set vertically—in the tradition of "magic squares." The most illuminating criticism of Byrum's poetry comes from BOB GRUMMAN, naturally.

Works: *Meant*. [Mentor, OH:] 1 2 3 4 5 6 7 8 9, 1987.
———, and Craig Hill, ed. *CORE: A Symposium on Contemporary Visual Poetry*. Mentor, OH and Mill Valley, CA: Genatorscore, 1993

CABARET VOLTAIRE

(1916).

This was the favored name of the first venue for Zurich Dada. Essentially a room in the back of the Meierei restaurant on Marktgasse, an alleyway a few yards from the entrance to the Spiegelgasse in Zurich's Niederdorf (reddish light) section, it contained a small stage, a piano, and enough tables and chairs to seat fifty people, which is to say it was ideal for small pieces for a small audience. Operating only for five months from February through early July 1916, Cabaret Voltaire housed the epochal presentations of TRISTAN TZARA, EMMY HENNINGS, and HUGO BALL, among others. Members of the audience frequently became performers. Once the cabaret closed, Cabaret Voltaire also became the name of a one-shot anthology (May 1916) and a Zurich art gallery, not to mention later publications in other countries, so honorific had the name become.

Bibliography: Ball, Hugo. ed. *Cabaret Voltaire.* Zurich:[n.p.] 1916; Lewer, Debbie. "From the Cabaret Voltaire to the Kaufleutensaal." In *Dada Zurich: A Clown's Game from Nothing*. Ed. Brigitte Pichon and Karl Riha. New York: G. K. Hall, 1997.

CAGE, John

(5 September 1912–12 August 1992).

Cage was one of the few individuals of whom it can be said, without dispute, that had he not existed, the development of more than one art would have been different. The truest POLYARTIST, Cage produced distinguished work in music, theater, literature, and visual art. As a de facto esthetician, he had a discernible influence upon the creation of music, several areas of performance, the visual arts, and, to a lesser extent, literature and social thought. His principal theme, applicable to all arts, was the denial of false authority by expanding the range of acceptable and thus employable materials, beginning with nonpitched "noises," which he thought should be heard as music "whether we're in or out of the concert hall."

Though some consider Cage an avatar of "chance," I think of him as an extremely fecund inventor who, once he disregarded previous conventions, was able to realize a wealth of indubitably original constraints. The famous "PREPARED PIANO," which prevented the emergence of familiar keyboard sounds, was merely the beginning of a career that included scrupulously alternative kinds of musical scoring, idiosyncratically structured theatrical events, and unique literary forms. Perhaps because Cage never doubled back, never dismissing his earlier works as wrong, his art remained "far-out," challenging, and generally unacceptable to the end. In the last months of his life, he completed a ninety-minute film whose visual content was a white screen violated by various shades and shapes of gray.

So much of an icon has he become that many forget that, four decades ago, when I first began following Cage's activities, no one, but no one, received so many persistently

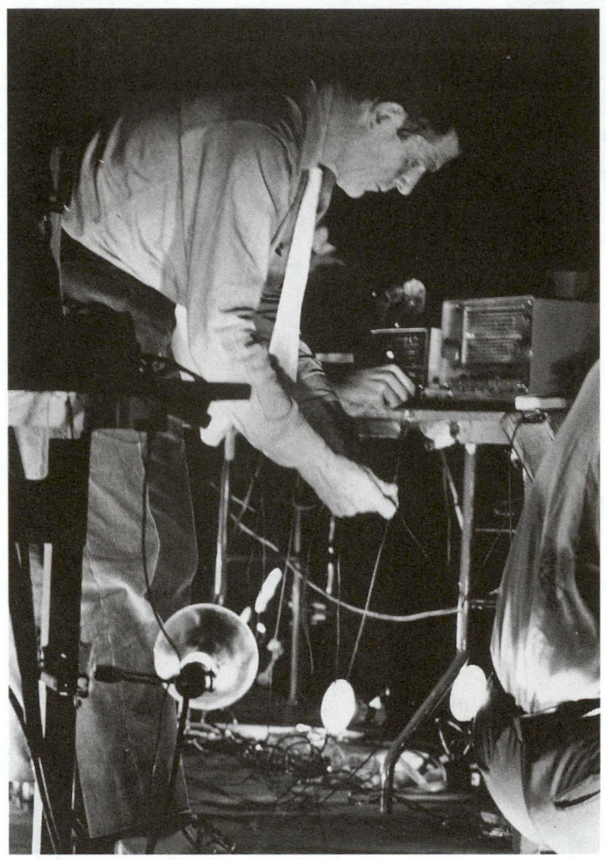

John Cage at Evenings of Art and Engineering at the Armory, Lexington Avenue, in performance of *Variations VII*, 15 October 1966. Copyright © Fred W. McDarrah.

negative comments, not just in print but in collegial conversations. When invited to give the 1988–89 Charles Eliot Norton lectures at Harvard, perhaps the most prestigious appointment of its kind, he delivered statements so barely connected that few professors returned after Cage's initial lecture! As an anarchist from his professional beginnings, he worked, as much through example as assertion, to eliminate authority and hierarchy, even in his life, never accepting a position that might give him cultural power (as distinct from influence), never composing any work that requires an authoritarian conductor or even a lead instrumentalist who stands before a backup group. When Cage accepted the Norton position that gave him a title elevating him above the rest of us humans, I asked him what it was like being a Harvard professor. "Not much different from not being a Harvard professor," he replied, true to his politics.

Not unlike other avant-garde artists, Cage made works, in his case in various media, that are much more or much less than art used to be. Though the MINIMAL pieces should not be slighted, in my considered opinion the greatest Cage works are his MAXIMAL compositions: *Sonatas and Interludes for Prepared Piano* (1946–48) is his longest and most exhaustive exploration of his first musical invention. *Williams Mix* (1953) is a tape collage composed of thousands of bits, intricately fused onto six tapes that should be played simultaneously, so that the result is an abundance of sounds within only several minutes. In *HPSCHD* (1969), Cage filled a 15,000-seat basketball arena with a multitude of sounds and sights, and *EUROPERA* (1987) draws upon nineteenth-century European opera for musical parts, costumes, and scenarios that are then distributed at random to performers in a professional opera company. Given my bias toward abundance, my favorite Cage visual art is the sequence of Plexiglas plates that became *Not Wanting to Say Anything about Marcel* (1969); my favorite Cage text, the Harvard lectures that became the long poem *I–VI* (1990).

In his notorious "silent piece," the superficially much, much less *4'33"* (1952), he became an avatar of CONCEPTUAL ART. By having the distinguished pianist DAVID TUDOR make no sound in a concert otherwise devoted to contemporary piano music, Cage framed four minutes and thirty-three seconds of a pianist's silence to suggest that the inadvertent sounds within the auditorium constitute the "musical" experience and, by extension, that all sounds, whether intentional or not, can be considered music. (One strain of conceptual art consists of demonstrations or statements that convey radical esthetic implications.) Since the content of *4'33"* and its successors is miscellaneous sounds, it is more accurate to characterize it as a *noise piece*.

Cage also revolutionized musical scoring (eventually collecting an anthology of *Notations* [1969] that mostly reflects his influence), introducing graphic notations and prose instructions in place of horizontal musical staves. The most extraordinary of his own scores is the two-volume *Song Books (Solos for Voice, 3–92)* (1970), which contains, in part through length and number, an incomparable wealth of alternative performance instructions. He was also among the rare artists whose statements about his own work were often more true and insightful than his critics' writings.

Select Compositions: *The Perilous Night* for prepared piano, 1944; *Root of an Unfocus* for prepared piano, 1944; *Sonatas and Interludes*, 1946–48; *Williams Mix* for magnetic tape, 1952; *Winter Music*, 1956–57; *Fontana Mix*, 1958; *Indeterminacy*, 1959; *HPSCHD*, 1979; *Roaratorio*, 1979; *Europera 1&2*, 1987.

Selected Recordings: Cage, John & Tudor, David. *Indeterminacy* (1959). Washington, DC: Smithsonian Folkways, 1992; *25-Year Retrospective Concert of the Music of John Cage*. Wergo, 1994.

Select Visual Art: *Not Wanting to Say Anything about Marcel*, 1969; *Changes and Disappearances*, 1979–82; *On the Surface*, 1980–82; *Fire*, 1985; *Ryoku*, 1985; *Eninka*, 1986; *Deka*, 1987; *Variations*, 1987; *Where There Is Where There*, 1987; *New River Watercolors*, 1988; *Global Village 1–36* & *Global Village 37–48*, 1989; *Without Horizon*, 1992; *Variations III*, 1992.

Writings: *Silence* (1961). Middletown: Wesleyan University Press, 1973; *A Year From Monday*. Middletown CT: Wesleyan University Press, 1967; *M: Writings '67–'73*. Middletown, CT: Wesleyan University Press, 1973; *Empty Words*. Middletown, CT: Wesleyan University Press, 1979; *Writings through Finnegans Wake*. Barrytown, NY: Printed Editions, 1978; *Themes and Variations*. Barrytown, NY: Station Hill, 1982; *X: Writings,'79–'82*. Middletown, CT: Wesleyan University Press, 1984; *I–VI*. Cambridge, MA: Harvard University Press, 1989; *Composition in Retrospect*. Cambridge, MA: Exact Change, 1993.

Anthologies: *John Cage: Writer*. Ed. Kostelanetz, Richard. New York: Cooper Square, 2000.

Interviews: Charles, Daniel. *For the Birds* (1976). London: Calder & Boyars, 1981; Kostelanetz, Richard. *Conversing with Cage*. New York: Limelight, 1987. [The Italian edition, *John Cage: Lettera a Uno Sconosciuto* (Edizioni Socrates, 1996), has elaborate documentation of Cage's works in several media, as well as secondary literature, not available in the original.]

Biography: Revill, David. *The Roaring Silence*. New York: Holt, 1992.

Exhibition Catalog: Brown, Kathan, et al. *John Cage: Etchings 1978–1982*. Oakland, CA: Crown Point, n.d; Kass, Ray. *New River Watercolors*. Richmond, VA: Virginia Museum of Fine Arts, 1988; *Rolyholyover*. Los Angeles: Museum of Contemporary Art, 1993.

Website: http://www.realtime.net/~jzitt/Cage/

Interpretation: Etrog, Sorel. *Dream Chamber: Joyce and the Dada Circus*. Ed. Robert O'Driscoll. Toronto: Black Brick, 1982; Fleming, Richard, & William Duckworth, eds. *John Cage at Seventy-Five*. Lewisburg, PA: Bucknell University, 1989; Gena, Peter, and Jonathan Brent, eds. *A John Cage Reader in Celebration of his 70th Birthday*. New York: C. F. Peters, 1982; Griffiths, Paul. *Cage*. New York: Oxford University Press, 1980; Kostelanetz, Richard. *Conversing with Cage*. New York: Limelight, 1988; ——. *Thirty Years of Critical Engagements with John Cage*. New York: Archae, 1996; ——. *John Cage (Ex)plain(ed)* (1996). New York: Archae, 1999; ——. "The Keystone of the Cagean Canon (1989)" "HPSCHD: Environmental Abundance (1969) "John Cage, 75, Writes First, 'Great American' Opera (1988)"; and others. In *On Innovative Music(ian)s*. New York: Limelight, 1989; ——, ed. *Writings about John Cage* (1993). Ann Arbor: University of Michigan, 1996; ——, ed. *John Cage* (1970). 2nd ed. New York: Da Capo, 1991; Perloff, Marjorie, and Charles Junkerman, eds. *John Cage: Composed in America*. Chicago: University of Chicago Press, 1994; Pritchett, James W. *The Music of John Cage*. New York: Cambridge University, 1993.

CALDER, Alexander

(22 July 1899–11 November 1976).

The son and grandson of sculptors, but also an alumnus of the Stevens Institute of Technology, Calder was a great inventor who recognized that the early modern avant-garde idea of KINETIC ART could be realized without motors. His innovation was art that moved through the balancing and counterbalancing of weights within the piece itself. His colleague MARCEL DUCHAMP dubbed them mobiles. Initially Calder used simple wooden shapes, most of them painted, which are delicately suspended from wooden dowels. He later used metals of various kinds, in various shapes and sizes. Whereas individual images in the 1930s reflected the geometries of PIET MONDRIAN, those from later times echo the abstract-organic forms of Joán Miró (1893–1983).

C

In lieu of physical space typical of previous sculpture, a mobile creates *virtual* space, which is to say that it assumes a lot more space than it physically occupies (and thus becomes an implicit precursor of other virtual art). Of all Calder's many enthusiasts, none is more curious, or perceptive, than the French writer Jean-Paul Sartre, who wrote: "A mobile does not suggest anything; it captures genuine living movements and shapes them. Mobiles have no meaning, make you think of nothing but themselves. They are, that is all; they are absolutes. There is more of the unpredictable about them than in any other human creation."

These Calder sculptures can be divided into those that hang from supports and those that rest on the ground. Having become known for "mobiles," he had to give another name to his stationary sculptures, "stabiles," which seems an ironic joke on himself. Generally larger than mobiles, these fulfilled commissions for outdoor sites. The largest, the 60-foot high *Teodelapio*, was installed at a road junction in Spoleto, Italy, in 1962.

Prior to his discovery of mobile, Calder was known to his Parisian colleagues for his miniature puppet-circus, with figures and animals made from wire and string. Sounding extraordinary in descriptions, it is remembered only in photographs.

Though Calder's unwillingness or inability to talk about art made him seem unserious, the physical truth is that he produced approximately 15,000 pieces, which is to say nearly one a day for fifty years. He was a sort of automatic artist. In a documentary film about Calder, someone notes that, though he may have drunk too much alcohol, his hands never stopped making objects.

Selected Works: *Circus*, 1926–32; *A Universe*, 1934; *Lobster Trap and Fish Tail*, 1939; *Towers*, c.1950s; *Gongs*, c.1950s; *125*, 1957; *Big Red*, 1959; *Teodelapio*, 1962; *Man*, 1967; *Flamingo*, 1973.

Writings:. *An Autobiography with Pictures*. New York: Pantheon, 1966; Prather, Marla. *Alexander Calder 1898–1976*. New Haven: Yale University Press, 1998.

Exhibition Catalogs: Sweeney, James Johnson. *Mobiles by Calder*. Chicago: Arts Club, 1935; *AC*. New York: MoMA, 1951; *AC*. London: Arts Council of G. B., 1962; Sartre, Jean-Paul. *AC: Mobiles, Stabiles, Constellations*. Paris: Louis Carré Gallerie, 1946; *AC*. New York: MoMA, 1951; *AC*. Amsterdam: Stedelijk, 1959; *AC: A Retrospective Exhibition*. New York: Guggenheim, 1964; *A Salute to AC*. New York: MoMA, 1969; *Calder's Universe*. New York: MoMA, 1977; *Calder: A Retrospective*. Köln: Gallerie Linsen, 1987; *AC: Selected Works 1932–1972*. New York: O'Hara Gallery, 1994.

Website: http://www.calder.infogate.de/

Interpretaton: Arnason, H. H., and P. E. Guerrero. *Calder*. Princeton, NJ: Van Nostrand, 1966; Giedion-Welcker, Carola. *Contemporary Sculpture*. New York: Wittenborn, 1960; Lipman, Jean, and Aspinwall, Margaret. *Alexander Calder and His Magic Mobiles*. New York: Hudson Hills, 1981; Marder, Joan M. *Alexander Calder*. New York: Cambridge University, 1992.

Alexander Calder, *Stabile*. Yale University Campus. CORBIS/Lee Snider.

C

CALDIERO, A.F.

(23 September 1949; b. Alissandru F. C.).

Sicilian-born, New York-reared Caldiero has created distinguished sound poetry and performance, as well as visual art, most of it as elaborate expositions of spiritual themes that draw upon his European background. "The sacred and the secular have been at the very core of my formative years," he writes. "For me this twin presence is a pivot between sideshow and temple, between entertainer or jester and priest. In the process of making and presenting a work, this precarious position is the opening by which I can hope to glimpse the Real." He moved to Utah around 1980 and has since been exhibiting and performing mostly in and around Salt Lake City. *OR, Book o' Lights* ranks among the most imaginative and ambitious visual-verbal books of the 1990s.

Books: *Book of Lights.* Privately published, 1992; *Various Atmospheres*. Salt Lake City, UT: Signature (564 W. 400 N., 84116-3411), 1998.

Exhibition Catalog: *Performing the Book: A. F. Caldiero's "The Food That Fits the Hunger"* with an essay by Scott Abbott and photos by Jim Taylor. Salt Lake City, UT: Salt Lake Art Center, 1995.

CALDWELL, Sarah

(6 March 1924).

As a pioneering woman conductor, especially of opera, Caldwell has had an uneven career. In 1946, at the Tanglewood summer school, where ambitious students could make a mark, she staged Ralph Vaughan Williams's *Riders to the Sea*, establishing a capability that wasn't immediately developed. Founder of the Boston Opera Group in 1958, which became in 1965 the Opera Company of Boston, she is best remembered for conducting the American stage premieres of such important modern operas as Arnold Schoenberg's *Moses und Aron* (in 1966), Sergei Prokofiev's *War and Peace* (in 1974), Luigi Nono's *Intolleranza*, Roger Sessions's *Montezuma* (in 1976), and Michael Tippett's *The Ice Break* (in 1979), which represented opportunities to her precisely because conservative opera impresarios have avoided them. Caldwell also became the first woman to conduct at New York's Metropolitan Opera, albeit not a modern piece but Giuseppi Verdi's *La Traviata* in 1976.

Recordings: (as conductor) *Donizetti: Don Pasquale*. EMI/EMI Classics 1996.

Biography: Kufrins, Joan. *Uncommon Women*. Piscataway, NJ: New Century, 1981.

Video Documentary: *Camera Three: Sarah Caldwell and the Opera Company of Boston*. Dir. Thomas Knott. New York: CBS TV, 1973.

CALLAHAN, Michael

See **USCO.**

CAMINI, Aldo

See **VAN DOESBURG, Theo.**

CANADA COUNCIL

(1958).

A culturally superior counterpart to our own National Endowment for the Arts, this makes the NEA look amateur, perhaps because of the Canadian recognition that the best work and avant-garde art especially must be supported if a country's culture is to survive. Should you not believe me, just compare its publicly available annual reports to those of the NEA.

Address: Canada Council, P.O.Box/Case postale 1047, Ottawa, Canada K1P 5VI.

CANTSIN, Monty

(c. 1978).

Originally, Monty Cantsin was a real person, but Monty Cantsin wasn't his name. For years, Istvan Kantor was associated directly with Monty Cantsin: The two men were the same person. At that time, somewhere around 1978, Istvan Kantor and his friends living in Montreal began developing the concept of Neoism (a kind of neo-futurism that ironically looked to newness as an esthetic good). Neoism was focused on performance art, musical performance, and video/film as major outlets of expression. Their main esthetic goal was to make people—often unintentional audience members—uncomfortable: a major goal in much avant-garde performance for the twentieth century. But the concept of Monty Cantsin began to grow. Rather than just being Kantor, Cantsin became a persona that Kantor would give to the audience, allowing them to become Cantsin, originally manifested as a pop performer. Eventually, the concept of Monty Cantsin became so broad that most Neoists and allied cultural workers took on the guise of Monty Cantsin. During the late 1980s and early 1990s there were over a score of Cantsins in at least eight countries. And each of these versions of Monty Cantsin ("a name chosen/invented by Monty Cantsin to refer to an international star who can be anyone") began to produce multifarious versions of *Smile Magazine* ("a name chosen/invented by Monty Cantsin to refer to an international magazine with multiple origins"). In the hands of artists like tENTATIVELY, a cONVENIENCE (the most famous of the pseudonyms of one Monty Cantsin), these magazines were interesting pieces of MAIL ART; in the hands of others, they were leftist rants.

—Geof Huth

Bibliography: Home, Stewart. *The Assault on Culture: Utopian Currents from Lettrisme to Class War*. Stirling, Scotland: A. K. Press, 1991; *Smile Magazine: Deaf Education System Card*. Baltimore: privately printed, c. 1989; *Smile: Transparent Monty Cantsin*. Baltimore: privately printed, ca. 1989. [A zippered two-liter soda bottle with an assembling of "portraits" of Monty Cantsin on transparent materials.]

CAPTAIN BEEFHEART

(15 January 1941, b. Don Vliet).

Born Don Vliet (later changed to Don Van Vliet), he is without doubt one of rock music's most unique and profound figures. His paradoxical achievement was to create a music which had deep roots in raw, unadulterated blues—he is certainly one of the most "authentic" white blues singer ever—but which was at the same time extremely innovative and avant-garde.

The details of Beefheart's life history are rather nebulous. He claims to have dropped out of school permanently after one day and then devoted himself to art—particularly sculpture—until turning to music in his teens. In 1964 Beefheart formed the Magic Band, which began as a fairly straightforward blues-based rock group, but quickly began to mutate. Beefheart's decidedly uncommercial inclinations led to problems with successive record labels, until, in 1969, he was signed by Frank Zappa to Zappa's new Warner Brother's subsidiary, Straight/Bizarre.

For the first time, with Zappa as producer, Beefheart had complete freedom to realize his ambitions, and the two albums he recorded in, respectively, 1969 and 1970—*Trout Mask Replica* and *Lick My Decals Off Baby*—still hold up three decades later as two of the greatest and most challenging rock records ever. His lyrics on these two albums are quite striking; surrealistic wordplay somewhat in the manner of a bluesified Dylan Thomas, they make a much stronger claim to be considered "poetry" than most other rock lyrics. For example, "Pena," from the double LP *Trout Mask Replica*, begins:

Pena,

Her little head clinking
Like uh barrel of red velvet balls
Full past noise
Treats filled 'er eyes
Turning them yellow like enamel coated tacks.

Beefheart's music on both these discs is dense and abrasive, and struck many listeners at the time as formless—in reality it is anything but. With amazing invention and in defiance of conventional musical logic, Beefheart and his fellow band members combined musical parts in wildly different time signatures, keys, and tunings; this was not improvisation, as many have mistakenly assumed, but very carefully conceived composition.

So dedicated were the members of the Magic Band that they endured real deprivation and hardship during these years, living on virtually no money, practicing endlessly, and putting up with Beefheart's capricious and dictatorial temperment. Eventually, however, the strains became too much, and in 1974 the remaining musicians left en masse. Shaken by this, and disappointed by the generally hostile or confused reactions to his records so far, Beefheart now embarked on a misconceived (and clearly ambivalent) attempt to make his music more mainstream. This proved to be both a commercial and an artistic failure.

After a partial return to form, on a trio of adventurous albums released between 1978 and 1982, Beefheart in 1986 permanently retired from recording and performance. The stated reason was to be able to pursue a career as a painter, but one suspects that the serious health problems which have increasingly incapacitated him played a part in his decision. In any case, Beefheart went on to make far more money as a painter than he ever did as a musician.

—Tony Coulter

Recordings: *The Legendary A&M Sessions* (1965–66). A&M SP 12510, 1985; *Safe As Milk*. Buddha BDM 5001, 1967; *Strictly Personal*. Blue Thumb S-1, 1968; *May Be Hungry, But I Sure Ain't Weird* (1967–68). Sequel NEX CD 215-11, 1992; *Trout Mask Replica*. Straight STS 1053, 1969; *Lick My Decals Off, Baby*. Straight RS 6420, 1970; *Mirror Man* (1967–68). Buddha BDS–5077, 1971; *Spotlight Kid*. Reprise MS 2050, 1972; *Clear Spot*. Reprise MS–2115, 1972; *Unconditionally Guaranteed*. Mercury SRM–1–709, 1974; *Bluejeans and Moonbeams*. Mercury SRM–1–1018, 1974; *Shiny Beast (Bat Chain Puller)*. Warner Bros. BSK–3256, 1978; *Doc At the Radar Station*. Virgin VA–13148, 1980; *Ice Cream for Crow*. Epic/Virgin ARE–38274, 1982.

Autobiography: *Skeleton Breath, Scorpion Blush*. Bern, Switzerland: Gachnang & Springer, 1987.

Website: www.beefheart.com

Interpretation: Muir, John. *The Lives and Times of Captain Beefheart*. 2d revised ed. Manchester, England: Babylon Press, 1980; Webb, C. D. *Captain Beefheart: The Man and His Music*. 2d revised ed. Cornwall, England: Kawabata Press, 1989.

CARDEW, Cornelius

(7 May 1936–13 December 1981).

In that vacuum that is avant-garde culture in Great Britain, Cardew filled a big balloon, less through his own originality than for his association with advanced developments elsewhere in the world. The son of a noted potter, he sang in the chorus at Canterbury Cathedral from 1943 to 1950 and studied, from 1953 to 1957, at London's Royal Academy of Music (granting its alumni a lifetime professional imprimateur unknown elsewhere), before assisting KARLHEINZ STOCKHAUSEN and writing music, mostly for piano, in the SERIAL tradition. Coming under the contrary influence of JOHN CAGE in the 1960s, Cardew then preached and practiced graphic scores and indeterminacy, cofounding AMM, an improvisatory group that resembled the Americans in MEV. By the 1970s, he was writing, mostly for nonmusicians, which he called a Scratch Orchestra, defined as "a large number of enthusiasts pooling their resources (not primarily musical) and assembling for action." Several Cardew compositions from this period acknowledged the influence of Mao Zedong, prompting Cardew to renounce his bourgeois past, and, need we say, the influence of Stockhausen, though Cardew still won attention, especially in England, as a former R.A.M. golden boy. He died in a traffic accident.

Compositions: *Volo Solo* for any handy musical instrument, 1965; *The Great Learning*, c.1968; *3 Winter Potatoes* for piano and various assorted concrete sounds, as well as for newspapers, balloons, noise, and people working, 1968; *The East is Red* for violin and piano, 1972; *The Old and the New* for soprano, chorus, and orchestra, 1973.

Recordings: *Piano Music*, B&L Records, 1991.

Writings: *Scratch Music*. London: Latimer, 1972; *Stockhausen Serves Imperialism*. London: Latimer, 1974.

CARLOS, Wendy

(14 November 1939, b. Walter C.).

Educated first in physics and then in music composition, Carlos released *Switched-on Bach* in 1968, which was the first recording of "Electronic Music" to sell a million copies. Working with an early monophonic Moog synthesizer, Carlos laid individual lines of notes on a multitrack tape recorder. He then adjusted the levels of the various tracks (or lines) in creating (literally mixing them down onto) a two-track, stereophonic tape. It was painstaking and pioneering work, unlike anything anyone had done (or thought about doing) in Electronic Music before; but one benefit, especially in comparing Carlos's interpretation of J. S. Bach's *Brandenburg* concerti to traditional instrumental recordings, was revealing contrapuntal lines that were previously muffled. Carlos subsequently produced other albums, some likewise original interpretations of classical warhorses, others of his own music (e.g., the soundtrack to Stanley Kubrick's *A Clockwork Orange*), none of which were quite so innovative or successful. Born Walter Carlos, he became Wendy C. in the mid-seventies, discussing this voluntary gender reassignment at length in a memorable *Playboy* interview (May 1979).

Compositions: *Noah*, opera 1964–64; *Timesteps*, for synthesizer, 1970; *Sonic Seasons*, for synthesizer and tape, 1971; *Pompous Circumstances*, for synthesizer and orchestra, 1974–75; *Variations on Dies irae*, for orchestra, 1980; *The Shining*, 1978–80; *TRON*, 1981–82.

Recordings: *Switched-on Bach*. New York: Columbia, 1968 (reissued in 25th anniversary edition by Telarc 80323); *The Well-Tempered Synthesizer*. New York: Columbia, 1969; *A Clockwork Orange* (1971). East Side Digital 81362; *Wendy Carlos/By Request*. New York: Columbia, 1975; *Switched-on Brandenburgs: The Complete Concertos*. New York: Columbia, 1980; *Carnival of the Animals*, w/ "Weird Al" Yankovic. New York: CBS, 1988.; *Sonic Seasonings and Land of the Midnight Sun* (1976/1982). East Side Digital ESD 81372; *Tales of Heaven and Hell*. East Side Digital, 1998, ESD 81352.

Website: http://www.wendycarlos.com/; also www.noside.com.esd (for East Side Digital recordings).

Interpretation: Darter, Tom, compiler. *The Art of Electronic Music*. New York: Morrow, 1984.

CARLSON, Chester

(8 February 1906–19 September 1968).

As a teenager, Carlson worked for a printer and even acquired a printing press. Taking a degree in physics from Cal Tech, he joined the Bell Telephone Laboratories, which was for decades a hothouse for significant modern invention (communications satellites, transistors, information theory, etc.). Taking a law degree, Carlson later ran the patent department of another, smaller electronics firm. In his spare time, in the late 1930s, he developed a *dry* method of direct image production that moved technically beyond *wet* processes of photography. By 1944 Carlson consigned the development of this invention to the Battelle Memorial Institute, which in turn sold the invention to the Haloid Company, which later called itself Xerox.

Artists in the 1960s exploited Xerox copying for its imperfections, typically making copies of copies until marks indigenous to the copying process obliterated an original image. The introduction of color copying increased the possibilities. By the 1990s, copies on both black & white and color were so clear and clean they were superficially indistinguishable from the originals. This technical advance meant that Xerography could replace offset technology in the production of books and other "printed" materials.

For a while the Xerox company insisted in that "word" be spelled with a capital letter, even when used as a verb; but once competitors developed equally accurate technology, the preferred epithet became "photocopy." From the historical point of view, Carlson's principal error was not naming the process after himself.

C

Interpretation: Brand, Rien van den. *Uitvinder, filsoof en filantroop Chester Floyd Carlson: grondlegger van een revolutionair reproductiesysteem, de xerografie van XEROX.* Verney, Netherlands: R. van den Brand, 1993; Jacobson, Gary. *Xerox.* New York: Macmillan, 1986; Hiltzik, Michael A. *Dealers of Lightning*. New York: HarperBusiness, 1999.

CARROLL, Lewis

(27 January 1832–14 January 1898; b. Charles Lutwidge Dodgson).

A university lecturer in mathematics who was also an ordained minister, Carroll wrote *Alice's Adventures in Wonderland* (1865), the first children's book to have enough cultural resonance to interest sophisticated adult readers as well. Martin Gardner, among others, has interpreted the book as portraying more than three dimensions and similarly sophisticated themes. *Through the Looking Glass and What Alice Found There* (1872) continues the story, with a greater sense of what adults might appreciate. *The Hunting of the Snark* (1876) is a highly metrical nonsense poem, written well before similar efforts by Kenneth Koch, among others. After you've read Carroll, whose complete literary works fit into a single volume, check out the editions intelligently annotated by Martin Gardner.

Writings: *The Works*. London: Paul Hamlyn, 1965; *Mathematical Recreations of Lewis Carroll*. New York: Dover, 1958; *The Complete Illustrated Works of Lewis Carroll*. Ed. Edward Guiliano. New York: Avenel, 1982; *The Complete Sylvie and Bruno*. San Francisco: Mercury House, 1995; *The Annotated Alice* (1960). Ed. Martin Gardner. New York; Wings Books, 1998.

Anthologies: Almansi, Guide, ed. *Lewis Carroll: Photos and Letters to His Child Friends*. Trans. William Weaver. New York: Rizzoli, 1976; Cohen, Morton N., ed. *The Selected Letters of Lewis Carroll*. New York: Oxford University Press, 1978; ——. *Lewis Carroll: Interviews and Recollections*. Iowa City, IA: University of Iowa, 1989.

Biographies: Cohen, Morton. *Lewis Carroll: A Biography*. New York: Knopf, 1995; Gattégno, Jean. *Lewis Carroll: Fragments of a Looking-Glass*. New York: Crowell, 1976.

Website: www.lewiscarroll.org

CARTER, Elliott

(11 December 1908).

Educated in English literature before he turned to music composition, Carter was, until his forties, one of many Americans working in "neoclassicism," which was in the 1930s and 1940s an encompassing term for tonal music that acknowledged traditional forms (purportedly in reaction to nineteenth-century romantic Expressionism). With his first *Piano Sonata*, he began to explore overtones (sounds inadvertently produced by notes in combination) and also the ways in which these overtones create their own semblance of melodies. Carter's *Sonata for Cello and Piano* (1948) incorporates a musical idea that he would subsequently develop: the individuality of each instrument prevents them from blending together completely. This idea was developed in a series of string quartets that rank among the strongest in contemporary music (1952, 1959,

1971, 1988–89, 1995). Carter required that the performers sit farther apart than customary. Carter also introduced an innovative technique, since called "metrical modulation," which depends upon continual changes of speed. That is to say, his rhythms are neither regular nor syncopated but continually rearticulated until the sense of perpetual rhythmic change becomes itself a major theme of the piece. He recalled in 1969, with characteristically multicultural reference, that

> rhythmic means [had] begun to seem a very limited routine in most contemporary and older Western music. I had taken up again an interest in Indian *talas*, the Arabic *durub*, the "tempi" of Balinese gamelans (especially the accelerating *Gangsar* and *Rangkep*), and studied the newer recordings of African music, that of the Watusi in particular. At the same time, the music of the early *quattrocento*, of Scriabin, Ives, and the techiques described in [Henry] Cowell's *New Musical Resources* also furnished me with many ideas. The result was a way of evolving rhythms and rhythmic continuities, sometimes called "metrical modulation."

Such music realizes a textual intensity that reflects the complexity of SERIAL MUSIC without literally following Schoenbergian rules. Indeed, precisely because Carter's best music must be reheard even to begin to be understood, it could be said that he composes not for the live concert hall but for reproductive media, at first records, then cassette tapes, and now compact discs, which enable listeners to rehear an initially evasive work as often as they wish. Of his other pieces, the most monumental is *A Symphony of Three Orchestras* (1977), in which Carter is continually dividing and redividing the instruments into smaller groups more typical of chamber ensembles. Incidentally, this interest in rearticulating pace prompted the art critic John Russell for one to suggest that Carter has "speculated about the nature of time and memory as persistently as anyone since Marcel Proust and Edmund Husserl." Though Carter has continued composing into his nineties, his latest monumental birthday was recognized with more fanfare, not to mention premieres, in England than in the United States, for reasons that are perhaps indicative of larger cultural discrepancies. Not unlike other composers of his generation, Carter could also be a discriminating critic, eventually collecting his best essays and talks into a single book, where the strongest single line mocks American orchestras for commissioning in the 1960s not "good, effective yet technically advanced scores [that] would be helpful in maintaining high performance standards in an orchestra . . . but new works that make an immediate effect with a minimum of effort and time." Three decades later, that's still true.

Select Compositions: *Prelude, Fanfare, and Polka*, for small orchestra, 1938; *Canonic Suite*, for 4 saxophones, 1939; *Pastoral*, for English horn or viola or clarinet and piano, 1940; *The Defense of Corinth*, for speaker, men's voices, and piano 4-hands, 1941; Three Poems of Robert Frost, for mezzo-soprano or baritone and piano, 1941; *Elegy*, for cello and piano, 1943; *Holiday Overture*, 1944; rev. 1961; *Musicians Wrestle Everywhere*, for mixed voices and strings ad libitum, 1945; *Piano Sonata*, 1945–46; *Warble for Lilac Time after Walt Whitman*, for soprano and instruments, 1943; *Sonata for Cello and Piano*, 1948; *8 Etudes and a Fantasy*, for flute, oboe, clarinet, and bassoon, 1949–50; *String Quartets* No. 1, 1950–51; No. 2, 1959; No. 3, 1971; No. 4, 1985–86; No. 5, 1995; Double Concerto, for harpsichord, piano, and 2 chamber orchestras, 1961; *Elegy*, for strings, 1952; *Variations*, for orchestra, 1954–55; *A Mirror on Which to Dwell*, for soprano and 9 players to a cycle of 6 poems by Elizabeth Bishop, 1975; *A Symphony of Three Orchestras*, 1976; *Syringa Cantata*, for soprano and small ensemble, to John Ashbery text, 1978; *In Sleep, in Thunder*, song cycle for tenor and 14 players to poems by Robert Lowell, 1981; *Esprit rude/esprit doux*, for flute and clarinet, 1984; *Penthode*, for 5 instrumental quartets, 1984–85; *3 Occasions* (1. *A Celebration of Some 100 x 150 Notes*. 2. *Remembrance*. 3; *Anniversary*), 1986–89; *Adagio Tenebroso*, 1994; *Figment*, for cello, 1994.

Recordings: *The Four String Quartets*, Juilliard String Quartet. New York: Sony Classical, 1991; *Music of Carter*, w/ various performers. New York: Bridge (9044); *Syringa; In Sleep, in Thunder; Mirror* & *Three Poems*, with Speculum Musicæ. New York: Bridge (9014); *American Masters: The Music of Elliott Carter*. Composers Records, 1993.

Books: *Collected Essays and Lectures, 1937–1995*. Ed. Jonathan W. Bernard. Rochester, New York: University of Rochester Press, 1997.

Festscrift: *Elliott Carter: A 70th Birthday Tribute*. London: AMP, 1978.

Website: http://www.schirmer.com/composers/carter_bio.html

Interpretation: Edwards, Allen. *Flawed Words and Stubborn Sounds: A Conversation with Elliott Carter*. New York: Norton, 1971; Harvey, D. *The Later Music of Elliott Carter: A Study in Music Theory and Analysis*. New York: Garland, 1989; Kostelanetz, Richard. "Elliott Carter (1968)." In *On Innovative Music(ian)s*. New York: Limelight, 1989; Schiff, David. *The Music of Elliott Carter* (1983). 2d ed. Foreword by Elliott Carter. Ithaca, New York: Cornell University, 1998.

CASSAVETES, John

(9 December 1929–3 February 1989).

Before he became a prominent Hollywood actor and sometime director, Cassavetes independently directed an innovative feature-length film in which he didn't appear. Shot on 16 mm film, reportedly for less than $50,000, *Shadows* (1960) is an extraordinarily intimate portrait of a love affair between a white teenager and a fair-skinned black girl—decades before interracial romance ever became a popular subject. Filming in situ in New York City, Cassavetes directed his cameramen to move around, getting close to things and people, again well before such moves became popular. Some of the most memorable scenes were filmed in rooms with low ceilings. At the time, I remember comparing the scene of the protagonists in bed to a more formal treatment of a similar sequence in Alain Resnais's *Hiroshima Mon Amour*, which was made around the same time. Indicatively, when Cassavetes' female protagonist walks down 42nd Street between Seventh and Eighth Avenue, the lights flicker not up in the sky but right behind her ears. A scene in which guys pick up three girls has an air of authenticity precisely because of the clumsiness of both the actors and the camera. The footage shot in the New York City subway gains from showing the place's real ceiling. Perhaps Cassavetes' real achievement was making the camera more responsible than the actors for defining his characters. Even in Hollywood, he did not forget his independence, frequently blaming studios for their insufficiencies, financing his own films, using hand-held cameras, allowing his releases to appear erratic and perhaps unfinished, etc.

Films on video: *Shadows* (1960), Orion Home Video, 1996; *A Child is Waiting* (1962), MGM/UA Studios, 1990; *Faces* (1968), Fox Lorber/Orion Home Video, 1996; *The Killing of A Chinese Bookie*. Touchstone Video, 1995.

Bibliography: Carney, Ray. *The Films of John Cassavetes*. New York: Cambridge University Press, 1994.

Website:
http://astro.ocis.temple.edu/~pth/cassavetes/index.html

CASTILLEJO, Jose Luis

(c. 1930).

Among the most extreme books ever to have come my way are *The Book of Eighteen Letters* (1972), *El Libro de las Dieciocho Letras* (1972), and *The Book of i's* (1969), all of them well-produced hardbacks. The first and the second are essentially similar, differing only in their title and dedication pages, which are in English in the first and in Spanish for the second. Both are dedicated to Walter Marchetti, a principal of the Spanish group Zaj. Each page consists of fifteen lines of type that runs continuously from margin to margin, with thirty letters in each line. The lines on each page are composed of only two letters, mixed so that no letter appears more than twice in succession. Therefore, the book's closing line reads: "k g k g k g k g k k g k g k g k g g k g k g k g k g g k g k."

Accompanying the book is a separate sheet with Castillejo's English-language manifesto entitled "Modern Writing," which declares, not unreasonably, that "words, syllables, stories, sounds, psychology, music, etc. are no longer needed in writing; advanced writing can do without intermediary elements," which certainly don't appear in *Eighteen Letters*. "The freedom achieved by writing (as a 'medium') may perhaps become," he continues, "an inspiration (a 'metaphor') of what could be achieved elsewhere (in the 'reality'), independently and without imitation." This statement gives a political dimension to books authored by a man who was at the time working in Bonn (Germany) for Generalissimo Franco's embassy.

The Book of i's likewise has pages almost nine inches high and five and three-quarter inches wide. On most of them, centered, is a lowercase "i," in sum five-eighths inches high, its dot very visible. Many of the book's pages, sometimes five in succession, are completely blank. On the verso of the title page appears "Copyright 1969." In this book was enclosed another separately printed manifesto, likewise in clear English, that opens: "My books are to mark the beginning of a true writing."

An earlier "book," *La Caída del Avión en el terreno baldío* (1967), is a box of loose cardboard sheets, eight and one-half inch by eleven inch, with poems, sentences, quotes from avant-garde sages, letters, and other curiosities, mostly in Spanish, imaginatively arranged. In sum, these volumes constitute such an impressive avant-garde debut that I regret to report that nothing further from Castillejo has come my way, not even any news, for over two decades now. I don't even know where he is.

Writings: *La Caída del Avión en el terreno baldío*. Madrid: Zaj, 1967; *La Politica*. N.p.: Zaj, 1968; *The Book of I's*. N.p.: n.p., 1969; *The Book of Eighteen Letters*. Madrid: L. Perez, 1972.

CBGBs

(c. 1974).

This Lower East Side New York City club, actually named CBGB & OMFUG (Country bluegrass gospel blues and other music for urban gourmandizers), was founded by eccentric owner Hilly Krystal. PUNK ROCK actually was first presented in New York at DOWNTOWN venues like Max's Kansas City. However, the bar/club most closely associated with the early U.S. punk movement remains CBGBs. Many bands got their start or played there early in their careers, including Blondie, the B-52s, the Ramones, and hundreds of lesser bands. The club has continued to operate through the nineties, although now more as a nostalgic venue than as a cutting-edge place to hear tomorrow's top-pop acts. Next door, CBGB 313 Gallery has been opened to celebrate the bar's punk heritage.

—Richard Carlin

Documentary: Bayley, Roberta, et al. *Blank Generation Revisited: The Early Days of Punk Rock*. NY: Schirmer Books, 1997.

Interpretation: Heylin, Clinton. *From the Velvets to the Voidoids: A Pre-Punk History for a Post-Punk World*. New York: Penguin, 1993; Henry, Tricia. *Break All Rules: Punk Rock and the Making of A Style*. Ann Arbor: UMI Press, 1989.

CELENDER, Don

(11 November 1930).

Celender's characteristic exhibitions have been horizontal eye-level mountings of the responses to cunning questionnaires that he has sent to circumscribed groups of people. Sometimes these responses are also bound into eight and one-half inch by eleven inch books published by

C

his New York gallery. To get serious answers, he depends upon the pseudoauthority of academic stationery to inform recipients that he is indeed a chaired professor with a Ph.D. The most successful is still *Museum Piece* (1975), for which museums around the world were asked to send, for "a research project dealing with museum architecture," a photograph of "your loading dock, or receiving area." The request was open and yet unprecedented enough to prompt officials of each museum to respond in a revealing manner. One wrote that his museum had no "loading dock" because its collection was permanent; another asks Celender for funds to hire someone to photograph its dock. (No fool he, Celender wanted only their letter.) The reply from the National Museum of Korea might seem tasteless if Celender had not reproduced the accompanying letterhead and signature as well: "We removed new building in 1972. But this museum has not any receiving area. The loading dock is imperfection. Anyway inveloped photos are loading dock from outside to inside. Dock is basement."

Celender constructs shrewd response-devices that encourage people (and institutions) to display themselves merely by providing answers that they think are "normal" to them; but by assembling their separate responses into a single context, he not only makes FOUND ART that is uniquely identifiable with his name, but also allows his respondents to contrast and augment one another in a burgeoning irony that is marvelously funny—a rare quality in the visual-arts world.

Books: *Political Art Movement Religious Art Movement Affluent Art Movement Academic Art Movement Corporate Art Movement Cultural Art Movement Mass Media Art Movement Organizational Art Movement*. N. p.: N. p., 1972; *Opinions of Working People Concerning the Arts*. New York: O. K. Harris (383 West Broadway, 10012), 1975; *Museum Piece*. New York: O. K. Harris, 1975; *Observation and Scholarship: Examination for Art Historians, Museum Directors, Artists, Dealers, and Collectors* [n.p.], 1975; *Destiny of a Name*. New York: O. K. Harris, 1979; *Observations, Protestations and Lamentations of Museum Guards Throughout the World*. 2 vols. New York: O. K. Harris, 1978; *National Architects Preference Survey*. New York: O. K. Harris, 1979; *Vermeer Paints a Picture*. New York: O. K. Harris, 1981; *Reincarnation Study*. [n.p.] 1982.

CÉLINE, Louis-Ferdinand

(27 May 1894–1 July 1961; b. L-F. Auguste Destouches). Céline was a notable French writer and, by all reports, a humane doctor, in spite of his disagreeable Fascist politics and bursts of inexcusable anti-Semitism. Seriously wounded in the head during World War I, he suffered for the rest of his life from vertigo, chronic migraine, partial paralysis of his right arm, and a constant buzz in his ears. Out of this deranged mentality, he concocted a literary style of unprecedented splenetic frustration and despair, comic in its excesses, whose truest subject is not society but the contents of his damaged head:

> My great rival is music, it sticks in the bottom of my ears and rots . . . it never stops scolding. . . it dazes me with blasts of the trombone, it keeps on day and night. I've got every noise in nature, from the flute to Niagara Falls . . . . Wherever I go, I've got drums with me and an avalanche of trombones . . . for weeks on end I play the triangle . . . . On the bugle I can't be beat. I still have my own private birdhouse complete with three thousand five hundred and seven birds that will never calm down. I am the organs of the Universe.

As his later translator Ralph Manheim (1907–92) points out, the slight innovation of three dots, "which so infuriated academic critics at the time . . . mark the incompleteness, the abruptness, the sudden shifts of direction characteristic of everyday speech." Those who can read his Parisian slang, itself new to literature in his times, testify that Céline's prose is even more extraordinary in the original.

"Fiction": *Death on the Installment Plan* (1933). Trans. Ralph Manheim. New York: New Directions, 1966; *Voyage au bout de la nuit/Journey to the End of Night* (1934). Trans. John H. P. Marks. New York: New Directions, 1983; *D'un château l'autre/Castle to Castle* (1957). Trans. Ralph Manheim. Normal, IL: Dalkey Archive, 1997; *Rigodon/Rigadoon* (1969). Trans. Ralph Mannheim. Normal, IL: Dalkey Archive, 1997; *North* (1980). Normal, IL: Dalkey Archive, 1997.

Biography: Ostrovsky, Erika. *Voyeur Voyant: A Portrait of Louis-Ferdinand Céline*. New York: Random House, 1971; McCarthy, Patrick. *Céline: A Critical Biography*. London: Allen Lane, 1975.

Interpretation: Buckley, William K. ed. *Critical Essays on Louis-Ferdinand Céline*. New York: G. K. Hall, 1989; Hayman, David. *Louis-Ferdinand Céline*. New York: Columbia University Press, 1965; Hindus, Milton. *The Crippled Giant: A Bizarre Adventure in Contemporary Letters*. New York: Boar's Head, 1950; Ostrovsky, Erika. *Céline and His Vision*. New York: New York University Press, 1967; Thiher, Allen. *Céline: The Novel as Delirium*. New Brunswick: Rutgers University Press, 1972.

CENDRARS, Blaise

(1 September 1887–21 January 1961; b. Frederic-Louis Sauser).

Born in Switzerland of a Scottish mother, Cendrars wrote in French and lived a mercurial cosmopolitan life. Creating the persona of himself as a man of action, he concocted a propulsive, rhythmically abrupt literary style that informed both his poetry and his prose. To put it differently, self-possessed and up-to-date, he made much, in style as well as content, of the mania of being so self-possessed and up-to-date. "I have deciphered all the confused texts of the wheels and I have assembled the scattered elements of a most violent beauty/That I control/And which compels me," he writes in *La Prose du Transsibérien*.

Writings: *Selected Writings*. Ed. Walter Albert. New York: New Directions, 1966; *Complete Poems*, Trans. Ron Padgett. Berkeley: University of California Press, 1992; *Modernities and Other Writings*. Ed. Monique Chefdor. Lincoln: University of Nebraska Press, 1992.

Interpretation: Miller, Henry. *The Books in My Life*. New York: New Directions, 1952; Bochner, Jay. *Blaise Cendrars: Discovery and Re-creation*. Toronto: University of Toronto Press, 1978.

CHAIKIN, Joseph (1935)

See **OPEN THEATER.**

CHAMBERLAIN, John

(16 April 1927).

Taking from David Smith a taste for industrial materials and a competence in welding, Chamberlain made sculptures composed initially of iron pipes and then of crushed automobile parts, usually preserving their original industrial colors. Even with materials as culturally resonant as cars, he finds formal qualities rather than social comment, the compositional syntax of his sculpture reflecting de Kooning's interpretation of Cubism. Though Chamberlain later worked with other materials, including urethane and fiber glass, and then galvanized steel and aluminum, nothing else he ever did was quite as stunning and innovative as his "junk sculpture."

Works: *Cord*, 1957; *Manitou*, 1959; *Zaar*, 1959; *White Thumb*, 1960–61; *Mr. Press*, 1961; *Miss Lucy Pink*, 1962; *Dolores James*, 1962; *Shan*, 1967; *Tonalea*, 1970; *Na-An-Tee*, 1970; *Untitled*, 1973; *Golden Smell*, 1973; *Rooster Starfoot*, 1976; *White Thumb Four*, 1978; *Three-Cornered Desire*, 1979; *The Line Up*, 1982; *Bent Tynes*, 1983; *The Arch of Lumps (A Tribute to An Act of Unclarity, The Vietnam War)*, 1983; *American Tableu*, 1984.

Exhibition Catalogs: Waldman, Diane. *John Chamberlain*. New York: Guggenheim Museum, 1971; *Sculpture: John Chamberlain: 1970s and 1980s*. Eds. Walter Hopps & Robert Greeley. Houston: Menil Collection, 1987; *John Chamberlain: New Sculpture*. New York: Pace Gallery, 1991; *John Chamberlain: Current*

Works and Fond Memories: Sculpture and Photographs 1967–1995. Amsterdam: Stedelijk, 1996; *John Chamberlain's Fauve Landscapes*. New York: Pace Wildenstein, 1998.

Catalog Raisonée: Sylvester, Julie. *John Chamberlain: A Catalogue Raisonée of the Sculpture 1954–1985*. New York: Hudson Hills, 1986.

CHAMPION, Cleury

(23 November 1972; b. Charles C.).

A poet-publisher residing in Tucson, Arizona, Champion is mentioned here to illustrate my belief that the idea of the avant-garde survives, even among artist/writers born in the 1970s. Champion has published his visual poems and asyntactical poems, as well as chapbooks by others, under the imprint "eXpeRimeNtaL pReSs" and in his now-defunct periodical *eXpeRimeNtal (basEmeNt)* (3740 N. Romero Rd., A-191, Tucson, AZ 85705). Long may he thrive, well into the 21st century.

Website: www.azstarnet.com/~imagicra/terminal.htm.

CHATHAM, Rhys

(19 September 1952).

Impressive as a very young man, Rhys became in his late teens the first musical director at the New York multi-art performance space called the Kitchen, initially from 1971 to 1973 and then again from 1977 to 1980, while working parttime with other musicians on plumbing in SoHo loft renovations (including mine). Deviating from standard DOWNTOWN taste at the time, Chatham programmed some experimental rock, incidentally forecasting a direction his own music would take. His *Guitar Trio* (1977) developed the overtones of a single pitch. His most notorious pieces are written for massive ensembles of electric guitars: *An Angel Moves Too Fast to See* (1989), *Warehouse of Saints, Songs for Spies* (1991), and *Music for Tauromaquia* (1992–93), producing a sea of sounds reflecting the texture and sonorities of each instrument. With some humor, Chatham claims that music from a brace of electric guitars should be classified as "rock," that from a gang of saxophonists as "jazz," and that from strings as "classical." In part because the resulting sounds depend upon seeing their origins, Chatham's music is invariably more successful in live concerts than on discs. So closely does his music resemble GLENN BRANCA'S that there is a continuing debate, hot only to a few, over who did what first. A New Yorker by birth, Chatham has recently been living in France.

Recordings: *Die Donnergötter*. Berlin, Germany: Dossier ST 7538 (Köloniestr. 25A, D-1000/65), 1987; *Septile*. N Tone, 1998; *Factor X*. Moors Music (includes *For Brass* [1982], *Guitar Ring* [1982], *The Out of Tune Guitar* [1982], and *Cadenza* [1981]).

Website: http://perso.wandoo.fr/rhys.chatham/

CHAZAL, Malcolm de

(12 September 1902–1 October 1981).

Born French on the island of Mauritius in the Indian Ocean, Chazal studied engineering at Louisiana State University before returning home to work in the sugar industry and then with the department of telecommunications, retiring early. Meanwhile, he wrote several volumes of aphoristic prose, most of them initially published in his native Mauritius or nearby Madagascar, then sometimes later reprinted in Paris. Chazal's idiosyncratic, often fanciful sentences tend to be more whimsical than, say, AMBROSE BIERCE'S or OSCAR WILDE'S and yet not as patently fictional as GOMEZ DE LA SERNA'S. In the words of his American translator, "They are also science fictions, extensions of present knowledge, visionary statements, verbal accounts of a sensory investigation of man and nature, mostly visual but frequently deriving from the other senses." Whereas most concise statements are designed to terminate discussion, those by Chazal typically tend to provoke further comments.

> The final test of beauty is that it remain beautiful in ugly surroundings. Whenever the frame affects the beauty of a painting, it is always a sign that to some extent the painting deserves its frame.
>
> Two is civility, three is mediocrity, ten is vulgarity, and then the mob takes over, the more the uglier. The day we all become aristocrats will mean the end of aristocracy.
>
> All in all, the laws represent a minority plot against the best interests of the majority, which is why there are always more policemen patrolling the other side of the railroad tracks than the center of town.
>
> Crows are comforting to those who are physically dissatisfied with themselves.
>
> Shifting into reverse while making love can kill you.
>
> Monkeys are superior to me in this: when a monkey looks into a monkey, he sees a monkey.
>
> I am the owner of my shoulders, the tenant of my hips.
>
> She gave herself, he took her; the third party was time, who made cuckolds of them both.

To compare him with another writer of French aphorisms (E. M. Cioran, likewise born outside of France—in his case in Rumania) is to realize Chazal's superiority. Parisian critics gave him considerable attention in the late 1940s, only to drop him. Irving Weiss, himself a distinguished critic and poet, has translated him into English for over thirty years now.

Books: *Lavie filtrée*. Paris: Gallimard, 1949; *Sens unique*. Port Louis: Les Editions le chien de plomb, 1974; *Sens magique*. Paris: Lachenal & Ritter, 1983; *L'homme et la connaissance*. Paris: J.J. Pauvert, 1974; *Poèmes*. Paris: J. J. Pauvert, 1968; *Apparadoxes*. Port Louis, Ile Maurice: Impr. Almadinah, 1958; *Sens-plastique/Plastic Sense* (1948). Trans. Irving Weiss. New York: Herder & Herder, 1971. 2d enlarged ed. New York: Sun, 1979.

CHICHERIN, Aleksei Nikolaevich

(February 1889–20 October 1960).

Initially Futurist in his orientation, Chicherin became the founder and theoretician of Russian Literary Constructivism in the early 1920s, attempting to apply the principles of Constructivism (practical application of avant-garde achievements in the visual arts to design and architecture) within the literary sphere. The main principle was "maximal concentration of function on units of the construction" ("We Know," 1922). His most significant works are *Fluks* (1922), in which he introduced a system of phonetic transcription and diacritical marks to convey the precise features of idiolect, and his contributions to the important Constructivist collection *Change of All* (1924). His works in *Change of All* initially employ a transcription like those in *Fluks*, which are designed to ensure the accurate performance of a compact text, but step by step the recitational cues become more elaborate, resembling musical notation, while the text becomes briefer. In the final stages of this development, verbal elements give way entirely to geometric figures that can be interpreted symbolically. Chicherin's booklet *Kan-Fun* (1926) elaborates on his theories of Constructivist functionalism. However, a split developed between Chicherin and his less radical, more practical colleagues in Literary Constructivism, who expelled him from their association in 1924. He spent the latter part of his life quietly working as a book designer.

—Gerald Janecek

Interpretation: Janecek, Gerald. "A. N. Chicherin, Constructivist Poet." *Russian Literature, XXV* (1989).

CHILDS, Lucinda

(26 June 1940).

Noted throughout her career for her cool but dramatic performing presence, Childs contributed to the innovative spirit of the Judson Dance Theater. In *Carnation* (1964), she made surprising use of props, such as a colander that she placed on her head like a weird hat and foam hair curlers and sponges that she both stuffed into her mouth and attached to her colander-hat. Her later choreography reflects Minimalism. Childs collaborated with Philip Glass and Robert

WILSON on the classic original production of Glass's opera, *Einstein on the Beach*, in 1976. In the evening-length *Dance* (1979, in a collaboration of choreography with music by Glass and film and decor by SOL LEWITT, eight dancers seem to be in perpetual motion as they sweep through the space. In technically based but minimally ranged movements that seem highly repetitious but are full of subtle changes, their carriage is elegant, their legs extend and point (but do not lift high), and they move buoyantly (but close to the ground, eschewing, say, spectacular leaps).

—Katy Matheson

C

Works: *Pastime*,1963; *Three Pieces*,1963; *Minus Auditorium Equipment and Furnishings*,1963; *Egg Deal*,1963; *Cancellation Sample*,1964; *Carnation*, 1964; *Street Dance*, 1964; *Model*, 1964; *Geranium*, 1965; *Museum Piece*, 1965; *Screen*, 1965; *Agriculture*, 1965; *Vehicle*, 1966; *Untitled Trio*, 1968, revised 1973; *Particular Reel/Checkered Drift/Calico Mingling*, 1973; *Duplicate Suite/Reclining Rondo/Congeries on Edges for 20 Obliques*, 1975; *Radial Courses/Mix Detail/Transverse Exchanges*, 1976; *Cross Words/Figure Eights*, 1976; *Plaza/Melody Excerpt/Interior Drama*, 1977; *Katema*, 1978; *Dance*, 1979; *Mad Rush*, 1981; *Relative Calm*, 1981; *Formal Abandon* (Pts I and II), 1982; *Available Light*, 1983; *Formal Abandon* (Pt III), 1983; *Cascade*, 1984; *Outline*, 1984; *Premiere Orage*, 1984; *Field Dances*, 1984; *Portraits in Reflection*, 1986; *Clarion*, 1986; *Hungarian Rock*, 1986; *Calyx*, 1987; *Lichtknall*, 1987; *Mayday*, 1989; *Perfect Stranger*, 1990; *Four Elements*, 1990; *Rhythm Plus*, 1991; *Oophaa Naama,* 1992; *Concerto*, 1993; *One and One*, 1993; *Impromptu*, 1993; *Chamber Symphony*, 1994; *Trilogies*, 1994; *Histoire*, 1995; *Solstice*, 1995; *Kenger*, 1995; *From the White Edge of Phrygia*, 1995.

Interpretation: Kreemer, Connie. "Lucinda Childs." In *Further Steps: Fifteen Choreographers on Modern Dance*. New York: Harper & Row, 1987.

CHION, Michel

(16 January 1947).

French composer Michel Chion specializes in electroacoustic music that is lively, sensual, and cinematic, as well as open to the whole world of music and sounds. His works often incorporate elements from traditional forms—sonatas, requiems, masses, waltzes, mambos—but these are transformed in the context of his sound-based art, which is ultimately associational in structure. Indeed, his primary concern has been associations between sound and image, sound and memory. He has written, for example, a book about the use of sound (as distinct from music) in film; on a more personal level, several of his compositions are intended as evocations of childhood.

Beginning in 1970, Chion worked for the ORTF (French Radio and Television Organization), where he was assistant to Pierre Schaeffer. Between 1971 and 1976 he worked at the INA-GRM (Institut National de l'Audiovisuel-Groupe du Recherches Musicales), with which he has been frequently associated ever since. In the mid-1970s, he began a close association with the composer and video artist Robert Cahen; Chion has since produced a series of films and videos, generally incorporating his own music, including the 150-minute *Messe de Terre* (1996). Between 1981 and 1986 Chion worked as a film critic for the Parisian critical journal *Cahiers du cinéma*, and he has published book-length studies of Jacques Tati and David Lynch. His many theoretical writings deal not only with associations between the visual and the auditory, but also with the connections between language and sound: in *Le promeneur écoutant* (1993) he attempts a systematic classification of sound units, analogous to the basic elements of verbal language.

With the exception of some of his books and essays on cinema, Chion's writings remain untranslated, and his films and videos are very rarely shown outside of France—I, for one, have never seen any. His music, however, has been fairly well served, with seven CDs available currently. On the strength of these works alone, Chion has been revealed as a major artistic force, whose dreamlike yet structurally fascinating works are innovative, challenging, and beautiful at the same time.

—Tony Coulter

Discography: *Requiem*. Paris: INA-GRM, 1978; *La Ronde*. Paris: INA-GRM, 1983; *La Tentation de Sainte-Antoine*. Paris: INA-GRM, 1991; *Credo Mambo*. Fontaine, France: Metamkine, 1992; *Requiem*. Montreal: empreintes DIGITALes, 1993 [different mix from LP above]; *Préludes à la vie*. Montreal: empreintes DIGITALes, 1995; *Gloria*. Fontaine, France: Metamkine, 1995; *On n'arrête pas le regret*. Paris: INA-GRM/Musidisc, 1996; *L'Opéra concret: musiques concrètes 1971–1997*. Paris: INA-GRM, 1998.

Selected Bibliography: In French: *Les musiques électroacoustiques* (with Guy Reibel). Paris: INA-GRM/Edisud, 1976; *Pierre Henry*. Paris: Fayard/Sacem, 1979; *La voix au cinéma*. Paris:Cahiers du Cinéma/Editions de l'étoile, 1982; *Guide des objets sonores*. Paris: INA-GRM/Buchet-Chastel, 1983; *Jacques Tati*. Paris: Cahiers du Cinéma, 1987; L'Audio-vision. Nathan-Université, 1990; *David Lynch*. Paris: Cahiers du Cinéma, 1992; *Musiques, médias et technologies*. Paris: Flammarion, 1994; *La musique au cinéma*. Paris: Fayard, 1995; *Le son*. Nathan-Université, 1995. In English: *The Voice in Cinema*. Ed. and trans. Claudia Gorbman. New York: Columbia University Press, 1999; *David Lynch*. Trans. Robery Julian. London: BFI, 1995; *Films of Jacques Tati*. Trans. Monique Vinas, et al. New York: Guernica, 1997; *Audio-vision*. Ed. and trans. Claudia Gorbman. New York: Columbia University Press, 1994.

Interpretation: Marchetti, Lionel. *La musique concrète de Michel Chion*. Rives, France: Metamkine, 1998.

CHOPIN, Henri

(18 June 1922).

A Frenchman who emigrated to England in 1968, this Chopin published for several years the periodical *Ou*, which included a record, of mostly TEXT-SOUND, along with printed texts. His own compositions display hysterical articulations and overlapping speech-sounds, thanks to elementary MULTITRACKING; they are, by common consent, unforgettable. His 1979 book-length history of sound poetry suffers from an egocentrism that makes it no more reliable as criticism than as history (see Claudia Reeder's review in the anthology *Aural Literature Criticism* [1981]). Nonetheless, *Poèsie sonore internationale* comes with two audiocassettes containing works by MICHEL SEUPHOR, FRANÇOIS DUFRÊNE, BRION GYSIN, STEN HANSON, and BERNARD HEIDSIECK, among others, whose audio realizations are unavailable elsewhere.

Recordings: *Audiopoems 1956–1980 Henri Chopin*. Köln: Hundertmark, 1983.

Books: *Poèsie sonore internationale*. Paris, France: Jean-Michel Place, 1979; *The Cosmological Lobster: A Poetic Novel*. London: Gaberbocchus, 1976; *Typewriter Poems, Henri Chopin*. Berlin & Köln: Hundertmark 1982; *Mil 1000 mille dates*. Antwerpen, Belgium: G. Schraenen, 1990.

Interpretation: Reeder, Claudia. "Henri Chopin: The French Connection." In Richard Kostelanetz, ed. *Aural Literature Criticism*. New York: Archae, 1981.

CHRISTO

(13 June 1935; b. C. Jarachev).

Born in Bulgaria, Christo emigrated first to Paris, where he took a wife, Jeanne-Claude, whose collaborative enterprise is envied by other artists and their spouses, and then to New York. His original sculptural idea, in the late 1950s, involved wrapping familiar objects in cloth, initially, I suppose, to give them esthetic value by destroying their original identity. He began with small objects before wrapping a wheelchair, a motorcycle, and then a small car. Instead of moving onto other ideas, Christo escalated his wrapping idea to monumental and, at times, comic proportions, encasing at various times an exhibition space in Berne, Switzerland, a section of Australian coast, islands in Miami's Biscayne Bay, the Museum of Contemporary Art in Chicago, and the Reichstag in Berlin. He also built a fence running twenty-four miles long in California in 1976. Christo's installation of hundreds of oversize umbrellas in Southern California and Japan (1991) became notorious, particularly after several umbrellas toppled during storms, endangering local populations. Though some of his projects are unrealized, including one long in progress for New York City's Central Park, Christo's proposals, pre-

Christo. *Reichstag Building Covered,* July 1995. CORBIS/Manfred Volmer.

sented in drawings, benefit from arriving in the wake of CONCEPTUAL ART. Recent works are customarily credited to "Christo and Jeanne-Claude."

Selected Works: *Wrapped Women*, Paris, 1962; *Wrapped Road Sign*, New York, 1963; *Dolly*, New York, 1964; *5,600 Cubic Meter Package*, Kassel, Germany, 1968; *Wrapped Painting*, 1968; *Wrapped Coast*, Little Bay, Australia, 1969; *Museum of Contemporary Art*, Chicago, 1969; *Wrapped Monument to Leonardo*, 1970; *Valley Curtain*, Rifle Gap, Colorado, 1972; *Wrapped Book*, 1973; *Wrapped Roman Wall*, Porta Pinciana, Rome, 1974; *The Pont Neuf Wrapped*, Paris, 1975–85; *Wrapped Monument to Vittorio Emmanuele*, Project for Piazzo del Duomo, Milan, Italy, 1975; *The Pont Neuf Wrapped*, Paris, 1975–85; *Running Fence*, California, 1977; *Wrapped Armchair*, 1977; *Wrapped Tree Project*, 1979; *Surrounded Islands*, Biscayne Bay, Miami, FL, 1980–83; *The Umbrellas*, project for Japan and California, 1984–1991; *Verhullter-Wrapped Reichstag*, Berlin, Germany, June 1995; *Wrapped Trees, The Fondation Beyeler, Berower Park, Riehen, Switzerland*, 1997–98; *Over the River*, Project for Arkansas River, Colorado, in progress; *The Wall* (36,000 oil barrels), Oberhausen, Germany, in progress.

Exhibition Catalogs: Schellman, Jörg, Benecke, Joséphine. *Christo Prints and Objects, 1963–1987: A Catalogue Raisonné*. New York: Abbeville, 1988; *Christo: Projects Not Realised and Works in Progress*. London: Annely Juda, 1991; *Christo and Jeanne Claude: Wrapped Reichstag, Berlin 1971–1995*. Köln: Taschen, 1996; *Christo and Jeanne Claude*. Basel, Switzerland: Gall. Beyeler, 1998.

Documentaries: *The Wrapped Coast*. Michael Blackwood, 1969; *Christo's Valley Curtain*. Maysles Brothers and Ellen Giffard, 1972; *The Running Fence*. Maysles Brothers and Charlotte Zwerin, 1977; *Wrapped Walkways*. Michael Blackwood, 1978; *The Pont Neuf*. Maysles Brothers, 1990.

Website: www.beakman.com/christo

Interpretation: Bourdon, David. *Christo*. New York: Abrams, 1971; Spies, Werner, and Wolfgang Volz. *The Running Fence Project*. New York: Abrams, 1977; Vaizey, Marina. *Christo*. New York: Rizzoli, 1990; Baal-Teshuva, Jacob, & Wolfgang Volz. *Christo and Jeanne-Claude*. Köln: Taschen, 1996; Volz, Wolfgang. *Christo the Pont Neuf, Wrapped Paris 1975–85*. New York: Abrams, 1990.

For more bibliographic information, see http://users.deltanet.com/~plockton/christo_bibliography.html.

CHRYSSA

(31 December 1933; b. C. Vardea Mavromichali).

Born in Athens, Chryssa studied in Paris and San Francisco before embarking in 1956 on a precocious exhibition career with works using letter forms for their design possibilities rather than any specific communication. Initially preceding Andy Warhol in the repetitive use of popular imagery, she turned to dark Plexiglas boxes filled with neon lamps programmed to turn themselves on and off. Inspired by New York's Times Square, whose vulgarity she found poetic, she adopted neon lamps for making *Times Square Sky* (1962) and *Gates to Times Square* (1964–66). The latter work is ten feet tall, built of steel, aluminum, and Plexiglas, in the shape of a three-dimensional triangle, supporting stacked rows of metal letters amid flowing curves of neon script, likewise enclosed in grey Plexiglas boxes. In works she calls "ruminates" she reflects her birthplace, Athens, which to my recollection has more neon light than any other city.

Works: *Times Square Sky*, 1962; *Gates to Times Square* 1964–66.

Exhibition Catalogs: *Chryssa: Selected Works 1955–1967*. New York: Pace Gallery, 1968; *Chryssa: Urban Icons*. Intro. Douglas C. Schultz, Buffalo, New York: Albright-Knox, 1983.

Website: http://ul.net/~artopos/artists/chryssa/chryssa-bio-en.html

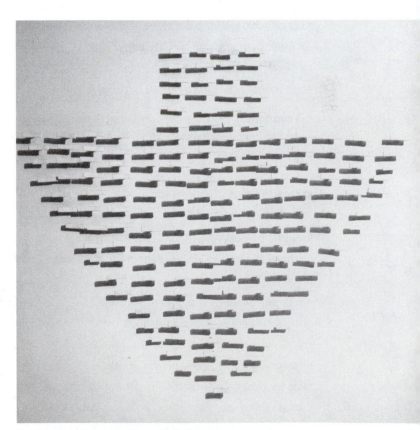

Chryssa, *Arrow: Homage to Times Square*, 1958. Painted cast aluminum. CORBIS/State of New York.

Interpretation: Restany, Pierre. *Chryssa*. New York: Abrams, 1977; *Chryssa: Cityscapes*. New York: Thames & Hudson, 1990.

CINEMASCOPE

(c. 1925).

Invented by the French physicist Dr. Henri Chrétien (1879–1956), this is the name for a film projection system that produces a far wider image than that of conventional film. Thirty-five-millimeter film is shot with an anamorphic lens that squeezes the wider image into the standard film ratios, and then, to be seen properly, this compressed image must be projected through a compensating lens that extends it horizontally. CinemaScope was first used commercially for *The Robe* (1953) and contributes, in my opinion, to the excellence and character of such films as David Lean's *Lawrence of Arabia* (1962) and Stanley Kubrick's *2001*. When shown on television or videotapes, such films generally are visually compromised, their sides lost from view, unless reproduced in the so-called "letter-box" format with their tops and bottoms blackened.

Videotapes: Lean, David. *Lawrence of Arabia* (1962). Revised print, letterbox format. Burbank, CA: RCA/Columbia Pictures Home Video, 1989.

CINERAMA

(c. 1938).

Invented by Fred Waller (1886–1954), this is the name for a three-screen projection system whose images are recorded by three synchronized cameras. The synchronized films were then projected with their seams aligned onto a curvilinear screen that filled the audience's horizontal vision. *This Is Cinerama* (1952) was one of the great moviegoing experiences of my youth, establishing my taste for physically expanded film. The success of that film prompted the use of CinemaScope, which offered the economic advantage of requiring only one projector at the esthetic cost of a flatter, less extended image; but every time I remember any multiple projection, I wish that I could see *This Is Cinerama* again. It is unfortunate that it is no longer available, some of its esthetic terrain superseded by more recent developments such as IMAX.

Interpretation: Belton, John. *Widescreen Cinema*. Cambridge: Harvard University Press, 1992.

ĈIURLIONIS, Mikalojus

(4 October 1875–10 April 1911).

A trained Lithuanian composer who worked in Warsaw as a choral conductor from 1902 to 1909 and whose Symbolist music resembles that of his contemporary Alexander Scriabin, Ĉiurlionis developed theories of "tonal ground formation" that presaged serialmusic. A proto-polyartist, he later became a painter of cosmic, Symbolist landscapes, often in series, with such musical titles as *Sonata of the Stars* and *Prelude and Fugue. Sea Sonata* (1908–09), for instance, has panels with titles such as "Allegro," "Andante," and "Finale." The third number (1914) of the St. Petersburg magazine *Apollon*, as well as a 1961 issue of the Brooklyn journal *Lituanus* (Vol. 7, no. 2), were entirely devoted to the composer-painter who, like Kandinsky, explored analogies between the two arts. One principal scholar on Ĉiurlionis has been Vytautas Landsbergis (1932), who, after editing his letters, writing monographs, and introducing his visual art, became president of Lithuania in 1990. Ĉiurlionis died young of tuberculosis.

Recordings: *Ĉiurlionis: Symphonic Poems*. Marco Polo (8.223323), 1993; *Ĉiurlionis: Piano Works*, Vol 1. Marco Polo (8.223549), 1994; *Ĉiurlionis: Piano Works*, Vol 2. Marco Polo (8.223550), 1994.

Interpretation: Landsbergis, Vytautas. *Pasaulio sutvrimas* (Creation of the World, with text in several languages). Vilnius, Lithuania: Vaga, 1971; *Sonatos ir fugos* (Sonatas and Fugues, with text in several languages). Vilnius, Lithuania: Vaga, 1971; Gostautas, Stasys. *Ĉiurlionis: Painter and Composer*. Vilnius, Lithuania: Vaga, 1994.

CLAYMATION

(c. 1974).

Generally credited to animator Will Vinton, claymation has been around since the early '30s, but came of age in the mid-'70s with Vinton's artfully crafted short films and television commercial. The children's TV show *Gumby* of the early '60s was perhaps the first popularization of claymation, although the Gumby figure moved crudely. As a satire of the adventures of the clay figure and his friends, *Saturday Night Live* introduced the "Mr. Bill Show" in the mid-'70s. In this, the clay figure is barely animated at all, with the ever-present hand clearly shown manipulating (and occasionally squashing) the figure. Vinton's innovation was to make claymation reasonably smooth and lifelike by introducing a computer-controlled camera and modeling movements on live action figures. The result was a fresh and highly human animation with vast appeal. Vinton's first short film was completed in 1975, but his real success came in 1986 with the introduction of a series of television commercials for the "California Raisins." These dancing figures, who strutted to the tune of Marvin Gaye's "I Heard It through the Grapevine," became widely popular, and children's action figures and other Raisinabilia were soon marketed throughout the land. In order to achieve this realistic movement, "each clay-sculpted figure must be oh-so-slightly adjusted and filmed 24 times [per frame]," in the words of Richard Harrington. Vinton's commercial success has allowed him to build a studio with a staff of over 100 people, with many tiny "sound stages" in operation constantly. A six-second shot can take a day-and-a-half to film, and a minute of film may involve as many as 1,400 changes to characters and background. In order to further promote his creation, Vinton has sponsored a touring "Festival of Claymation" throughout the country. Vinton's other creations include the Noid character in Pizza Hut commercials (also late '80s); and *Celebrity Death Match*, an MTV series featuring professional wrestling matchups between Hollywood stars, and Eddie Murphy's animated series, *The PJs*, both of which premiered in 1998. Like some other radical artforms, claymation has been primarily celebrated in the popular press, and has not yet received much academic attention.

—Richard Carlin

Articles: Van Biema, David and Kelly, Jack. "Filmmaker Will Vinton and His Feats of Clay are Giving Animation a New Raisin D'Etre." *People Weekly* (March 9, 1987), p. 76; Barrier, Michael. "The Clay's the Thing." *Nation's Business*, 76 (12), p. 57; Darlin, Damon and Joshua Levine. "Introducing Mr. Resistor." *Forbes* 153 (5), p. 98; Harrington, Richard. "Magical Feats of Clay." *Washington Post* (April 8, 1987), p. C4; Hamilton, Joan. "You've Come A Long Way, Gumby." *Business Week* (December 8, 1986), p. 74.

CLOSE, Chuck

(5 July 1940).

Continuing the most familiar tradition of human portraiture, Close has created innovative paintings that depend upon making faces large, say nine by seven feet, and thus capturing a wealth of facial detail. Initially working in black and white before turning to color, he nonetheless kept his method of subjecting a photograph to a grid of varying light and dark areas that were then transferred to canvas. Especially in prints, watercolors, and pastels, Close customarily reveals his alternative processes by leaving the grid visible. Sometimes his blurred images resemble computer printouts, increasing the impression of impersonality. Though working with sizes conducive to heroic sentiment, Close still presents individuals objectively. Severely crippled by a spinal-artery collapse in his late forties, he has recently been making gridportraits with brighter colors and with less realistic images.

Writings: and John Guare. *Chuck Close: Life and Work 1988–1995*. New York: Thames & Hudson, 1995.

Exhibition Catalogs: Westerbeck, Colin. *Chuck Close*. Chicago: Art Institute of Chicago, 1989; *Chuck Close:*

Editions: A Catalog Raisonné and Exhibition. Youngstown, OH: The Butler Institute of American Art, 1989; *A Print Project by Chuck Close*. New York: MOMA 1993; *Chuck Close: Recent Paintings*. Essay by John Yau. New York: Pace Wildenstein, 1995.

Bibliography: Greenberg, Jan and Jordan, Sandra. *Chuck Close, Up Close*. New York: D. K. Ink 1998; Lyon, Lisa, and Robert Storr. *Chuck Close*. New York: Rizzoli, 1987.

Webpage: http://www.artincontext.com/listings/pages/artist/u/0o2vmf9u/menu.htm

C

COBBING, Bob

(30 July 1920).

A sometime civil servant, farmer, teacher, and manager of a London literary bookshop, Cobbing has for many years been the principal mover and shaker in British experimental literature, first as a prolific poet, then as a strong performer, especially of his sound poems, but also as the founder of the chapbook-publishing Writers Forum (since 1963) and coeditor of the occasional periodical *Kroklok* (1971), which was at its beginnings among the most avant-garde literary magazines in England. If only for his organizational work with the Poetry Society, the National Poetry Centre, and the Association of Little Presses, Cobbing has been a model literary citizen.

Not unlike other strong poets who survive apart from career-managing publishers and agents, he has published scores of books and chapbooks, in addition to audiotapes. His texts-for-print include linear poems, sound poems, self-obliterating texts, classic CONCRETE POETRY (which he accurately defines as "an emphasis on the physical substance of language"), pseudo-alphabets, pseudo-words, and much, much else. Perhaps the best one-volume introduction to his work is *bill jubobe* (1976), which the poet selected in collaboration with a colleague. Cobbing has also performed improvisations with other sound poets and instrumentalists. To gauge the scope of his work, consider this statement from 1975: "At present I am working on single-voice poems; multi-voiced poems; poems based on words; poems not using words or even letters; poems for electronic treatment on tape; poems for 'voice as instrument and instruments as speaking voices'; poems as scores for dance or drama, invitations to act out an event in space, sound, and choreography." In his prolific eclecticism, Cobbing very much resembles his American contemporary JACKSON MAC LOW.

Writings: With John Rowan. *The Massacre of the Innocents*. London: Writers Forum, 1963; *Sound Poems: An ABC of Sound*. London: Writers Forum, 1965; *Whississippi*. London: Writers Forum, 1969; *Etcetera*. Cardiff, Wales: Vertigo Publications, 1970; *Bill Jubobe: Selected Texts 1942–1975*. Toronto: Coach House, 1976; *Towards the City*. London: Writers Forum, 1977; *Cygnet Ring: collected poems 1*. London: Tapocketa, 1977; *A B C/Wan Do Tree: collected poems 2*. London: El Uel Uel U, 1978; *A Peal in Air: collected poems 3*. Toronto: AnonbeyondgrOnkoontaktewild Press, 1978; *Vowels and Consequences: collected poems 7*. Newcastle-upon-Tyne, England: Galloping Dog, 1985; *Lame, Limping, Mangled, Marred and Mutilated: collected poems 9*. London: David Barton, 1986; *Processual: collected poems 10*. London: New River Project, 1987; *Improvisation Is a Dirty Word: collected poems 12*. Heptonstall, Yorkshire: Magenta, 1990.

Interpretation: Mayer, Peter, ed. *Bob Cobbling and Writers Forum*. Sunderland, England: Ceolfrith Press, 1974; Woods, Gerald, et al. *Art Without Boundaries*. New York: Praeger, 1972.

COCTEAU, Jean

(5 July 1889–11 October 1963).

Cocteau was one of those figures who flirt with the avant-garde without ever joining it, perhaps because he was too self-conscious of his early celebrity to be courageously radical, mostly because he simply lacked originality while aspiring to be fashionable. He once told FRANCIS PICABIA,

"You are the extreme left, I am the extreme right." As a slick POLYARTIST, Cocteau wrote plays and directed films, in addition to exhibiting drawings that, in LUCY R. LIPPARD'S phrases, "remained firmly Picassoid, dry, coquettish, over-refined, and elegant." In his pretentious compromises, as well as his position in French culture, Cocteau very much resembles the composer PIERRE BOULEZ.

Writings: *The Art of the Cinema* (1952). London: Marion Boyars, 1994; *The Journals of Jean Cocteau*. Ed. Wallace Fowlie. London: Museum, 1956; *The Infernal Machine and Other Plays*. New York: New Directions, 1964.

Sculpture: *Blue Satyr (Left Profile)*. 1958.

Films: *Le Sang d'un Poète/The Book of a Poet*, 1930; *Le Belle et la Bête/Beauty and the Beast*, 1946; *Les Parents Terribles/The Storm Within*, 1948; *Le Testament d'Orphée/The Testament of Orpheus*, 1960.

Exhibition Catalogs: *La Chapelle Saint Pierre, Villefranche sur Mer*. Monaco: Rocher, 1957; *La Salle des Mariages, Hotel de Ville Menton*. Monaco: Rocher, 1958.

Biography: Brown, Frederick. *An Impersonation of Angels: A Biography of Jean Cocteau*. New York: Viking, 1968; Crosland, Margaret. *Jean Cocteau: A Biography*. New York: Knopf, 1956; Steegmuller, Francis. *Cocteau: A Biography*. Boston, MA: Atlantic Monthly, 1970.

Webpage: http://www.scf.usc.edu/~pkon/Cocteau.html

Interpretation: Oxenhandler, Neal. *Scandal & Parade: The Theatre of Jean Cocteau*. New Brunswick, NJ: Rutgers University, 1957.

COINTET, Guy de

(1940–1983).

After working as a visual artist's assistant, Cointet exhibited, usually in a Los Angeles gallery, drawings whose imagery consists only of sans-serif capital letters and numbers. Many of these drawings of superficially disconnected signs were actually codes that, though he was French, could be "translated" into English. When collecting some of them into books, Cointet usually incorporated a semantically clear English sentence into a text that was otherwise unintelligible. For instance, one page in *A Few Drawings* (1975) opens: "IN A FRENZY OF CURIOSITY THE HAPPY MOTHER TRIES HARD TO SEE: 107 325/ 290 344 58726 956 325/418 932 69408 571 823. . . ." One of his earlier books has, even for its title, just signs resembling parentheses, tilted at various angles to become an uncompromised pseudo-language, punctuated only by occasional staves of music. Sometimes he would hire professional actors to perform his texts. Though a skeptic might say such work "is easy to do," I've not seen anyone do anything similar since. Cointet died young of a mysterious illness.

Writings: *TSNX C24VA7ME: A PLAY BY DR HUN*. Venice, CA: Sure Co. (76 Market Street), 1974; *A Few Drawings*. N.p.: n. p., 1975; *Espahor ledet ko uluner!*. N.p. (Los Angeles?): n. p. (self?), n.d. (c. 1976).

Exhibition Catalog: *Guy de Cointet: Wadsworth Atheneum, mid-April to mid-June*. Hartford, CT: Wadsworth Atheneum, 1978.

Bibliography: *Larry Bell & Guy de Cointet*. Venice, CA: Sure Co., 1975.

COLEMAN, Ornette

(9 March 1930).

Born in Texas, self-taught as a musician, Coleman around 1960 caused a stir in the world of JAZZ music comparable to that of IGOR STRAVINSKY in classical music decades before. Coleman's innovation was instrumental independence, which is to say that the soloist performs independently of any preassigned harmonic scheme, and that everyone in his group performs with scant acknowledgment of the percussionist's beat. Called "FREE JAZZ," Coleman's improvisations, mostly on the alto saxophone, gained a strong following in New York in the sixties and Europe in the seventies. In addition to performing on the violin and trumpet, he has composed extended works for classical ensembles.

Recordings: *The Shape of Jazz to Come*. New York: Atlantic (SD 1317), 1959; *Change of the Century*. New York: Atlantic, 1959; *Free Jazz*. New York: Atlantic, 1960; *The Great London Concert* New York: Arista Freedom, 1975; *Forms and Sounds* for Woodwind Quintet & *Saints and Soldiers: Space Flight* for String Quartet, with Philadelphia Woodwind Quintet & Philadelphia Chamber Symphony String Quartet (Bluebird 65610-2 RB).

Biography: Spellman, A. B. *Four Lives in the Bebop Business* (1966). New York: Limelight, 1985; Litweiler, John. *Ornette Coleman: A Harmolodic Life* (1992). New York: Da Capo, 1994.

Webpage: http://www.harmolodic.com/

Interpretation: Rockwell, John. "Ornette Coleman." In *All-American Music* (1983). New York: Da Capo, 1997.

COLLAGE

(c. 1910).

The earliest fine-art examples of collage depended upon the incorporation of real objects, such as bits of newspaper or other mass-produced images, into the picture's field, the objects at once contributing to the image and yet suggesting another dimension of experience. One visual theme was perceiving the difference between pasted object and material surface. Initiated by CUBISTS, the principle was extended by FUTURISTS, DADAISTS, and SURREALISTS, always in ways typical of each. Collage was, by many measures, the most popular innovation of early twentieth-century art. Later collages depended upon using separate images for ironic juxtapositions; others functioned to expand the imagery available to art. The collage principle influenced work in other arts, including sculpture, where ASSEMBLAGE is three-dimensional collage; PHOTOMONTAGE; music, where the post-World War II development of audiotape facilitated the mixing of dissimilar sounds; and VIDEO, even though that last art did not arise until the late 1960s. Max Ernst's *La femme 100 fetes* (1932) is a book-length narrative composed of collages. The Czech artist JI_Í KOLÀ_ (whose last name is pronounced to sound like "collage") has extended the compositional principle, often in ironic ways, to works he calls "crumplage," "rollage," "intercollage," "prollage," "chiasmage," and "anti-collage." Another innovation in this tradition is the composer MAURICIO KAGEL'S "Metacollage," where all the materials for his mix come from a single source (e.g., Beethoven's music, for example, or nineteenth-century German culture). I believe that collage, as an easily adopted innovation, had become dead by the 1960s, which is to say that, although collages continue to appear, none of them, especially in visual art, are strikingly original or excellent. (A contrary interpretation of collage sees it as not early modernist, as I do, but proto-postmodernist: "Unlike the works of modernism proper, it is an assault on the integrity of the work of art in that it brings foreign materials into the space previously reserved for painting on the canvas. Since these materials include such things as newspaper clippings, collage thus forges a line between 'high' art and mass culture." This comes from *The Columbia Dictionary of Modern Literary and Cultural Criticism* [1995], which is self-consciously up-to-date.)

Exhibition Catalog: *Collage International: From Picasso to the Present*. Houston, TX: Museum of Contemporary Arts, 1958.

Interpretation: Janis, Harriet, and Rudi Blesh. *Collage*. Philadelphia: Chilton, 1967. Laiberté, Norman, and Alex Mogelon. *Collage, Montage, Assemblage: History and Contemporary Techniques*. New York: Van Nostrand Reinhold, 1971; Weschler, Herta. *Collage*. Trans. Robert E. Wolf. New York: Abrams, 1971; Wolfram, Eddie. *History of Collage*. New York: Macmillan, 1975; Hoffman, Katherine, ed. *Collage: Critical Views*. Ann Arbor: UMI Research, 1989; Poggi, Christine. *Cubism, Futurism, and* *the Invention of Collage*. New Haven: Yale University Press, 1993; Childers, Joseph, and Gary Hentzi, eds. *The Columbia Dictionary of Modern Literary and Cultural Criticism*. New York: Columbia University Press, 1995.

COLOMBO, John Robert

(24 March 1936).

Very much an odd man both out and in Canadian literature, a prolific writer and editor whose achievements are so numerous they are foolishly taken for granted, Colombo has worked with a variety of unusual poetic strategies. His first books were FOUND POETRY, each dependent upon making art from esoteric texts found in his unusually wide reading; his term at the time was "redeemed prose." The Canadian critic Douglas Barbour writes that Colombo's *The Great Cities of Antiquity* (1979) "is a collection of found poems in a dizzying variety of modes, based on entries in the famous eleventh edition of the *Encyclopedia Britannica*. Written in 1969, it is possibly Colombo's most extreme collage, a veritable textbook on the many formal experiments of modern and post-modern poetry." Of the poems written out of Colombo's own head, consider "Secret Wants" in *Neo Poems* (1971).

A full-time booksmith, writing and editing well over 120 volumes for publishers both large and small (no false snob he), Colombo has also collaborated on literary translations from several languages and edited several important anthologies of poetry and of science fiction, including *New Directions in Canadian Poetry* (1970, perhaps the only English language anthology of avant-garde poetries aimed at high-school students). In addition, he compiled such pioneering culturally patriotic compendia as *Colombo's Canadian Quotations* (1994), *Colombo's Canadian References* (1976), *Colombo's Book of Canada* (1978), and *The Dictionary of Canadian Quotations* (1991), which all have the distinction of being books that nobody else could create, even if they tried.

Colombo's single most marvelous book is likewise unique—*Self-Schrift* (1999), which contains, as he puts it, "commentaries—anecdotes, insights, appreciations, criticisms, ideas, and theories—about the 136 books that he has written, compiled, or translated over the years." Why invite others, the book implies, when you can honor yourself? Contagiously readable, at once proud and modest, it will become, I suspect, a model for similarly professional autobiographies by authors fortunate enough to be prolific.

Poetry: *Neo Poems*. Vancouver: Sono Nis, 1970; *Translations from the English: Found Poems*. Toronto: Peter Martin Associates, 1974; *The Great Cities of Antiquity* Toronto: Hounslow Press, 1979; *Selected Poems*. Windsor, Ont: Black Moss, 1982; *Off-Earth*. Toronto: Hounslow, 1987; *Selected Poems*. Windsor, Ont: Black Moss, 1982; *Selected Translations*. Windsor, Ont: Black Moss, 1982; *Luna Park: One Thousand Poems*. Toronto: Hounslow, 1994.

Prose: *Canadian Literary Landmarks*. Toronto: Hounslow, 1981; *Great Moments in Canadian History*. Toronto: Hounslow, 1984; *Mysterious Canada: Strange Sights, Extraordinary Events, and Peculiar Places*. Toronto: Doubleday, 1988.

Translations: *From Zero to One*. With Robert Zend. Vancouver: Sono Nis, 1973; *Under the Eaves of a Forgotten Village: Sixty Poems from Contemporary Bulgaria*. With Nikola Roussanoff. Toronto: Hounslow, 1975; *Such Times: Selected Poems*. With Waclaw Iwaniuk. Toronto: Hounslow, 1981; *Beyond Labels*. With Robert Zend. Toronto: Hounslow, 1982; *Symmetries*. With Petronela Negosanu. Toronto: Hounslow, 1982.

Anthologies: Colombo, John Robert, ed. *Rubato: New Poems by Young Canadian Poets*. Toronto: Purple Partridge, 1958; *New Directions in Canadian Poetry*. Toronto: Holt, 1971; *Poems of the Inuit*. Ottawa: Oberon, 1981; *Songs of the Indians*. 2 vols. Ottawa: Oberon, 1983; *Songs of the Great Land*. Ottawa: Oberon, 1989.

Compendia: *Colombo's Canadian Quotations*. Edmonton: Hurtig, 1974; *Colombo's Canadian References* (1976). New

York: Oxford University Press, 1977; *Colombo's Book of Canada*. Edmonton: Hurtig, 1978; *Dictionary of Canadian Quotations*. Toronto: Stoddart, 1991.

Autobiography: *Self-Schrift*. Toronto: Colombo & Company (42 Dell Park Avenue, M6B 2T6), 1999.

COLON, Fleury

(9 September 1905–21 May 1964).

This enigmatic French architect carried reductionist architectural doctrines to new heights by isolating the decorative finial, or épi, that usually adorns the top of a gable, canopy, or pinnacle in French architecture, thus making the finial his ultimate form. Educated at L'École d'Architecture (Paris), Colon was one of many gifted graduates employed in the construction of the Maginot Line. Eager for exciting architectural challenges in postwar Paris, Colon was drawn to Isidore Isou's Lettriste ideology wherein art, according to Isou, has two characteristic phases: amplic (expansion) and "chiseling" (deconstruction). Colon saw Isou's doctrine as further justification of his own theory to dismiss traditional structure and to focus solely on the finial. But the ideological tryst was shortlived. In a fierce café debate, Colon accused Isou of expanding his ego and nothing else. Isou's followers retaliated by

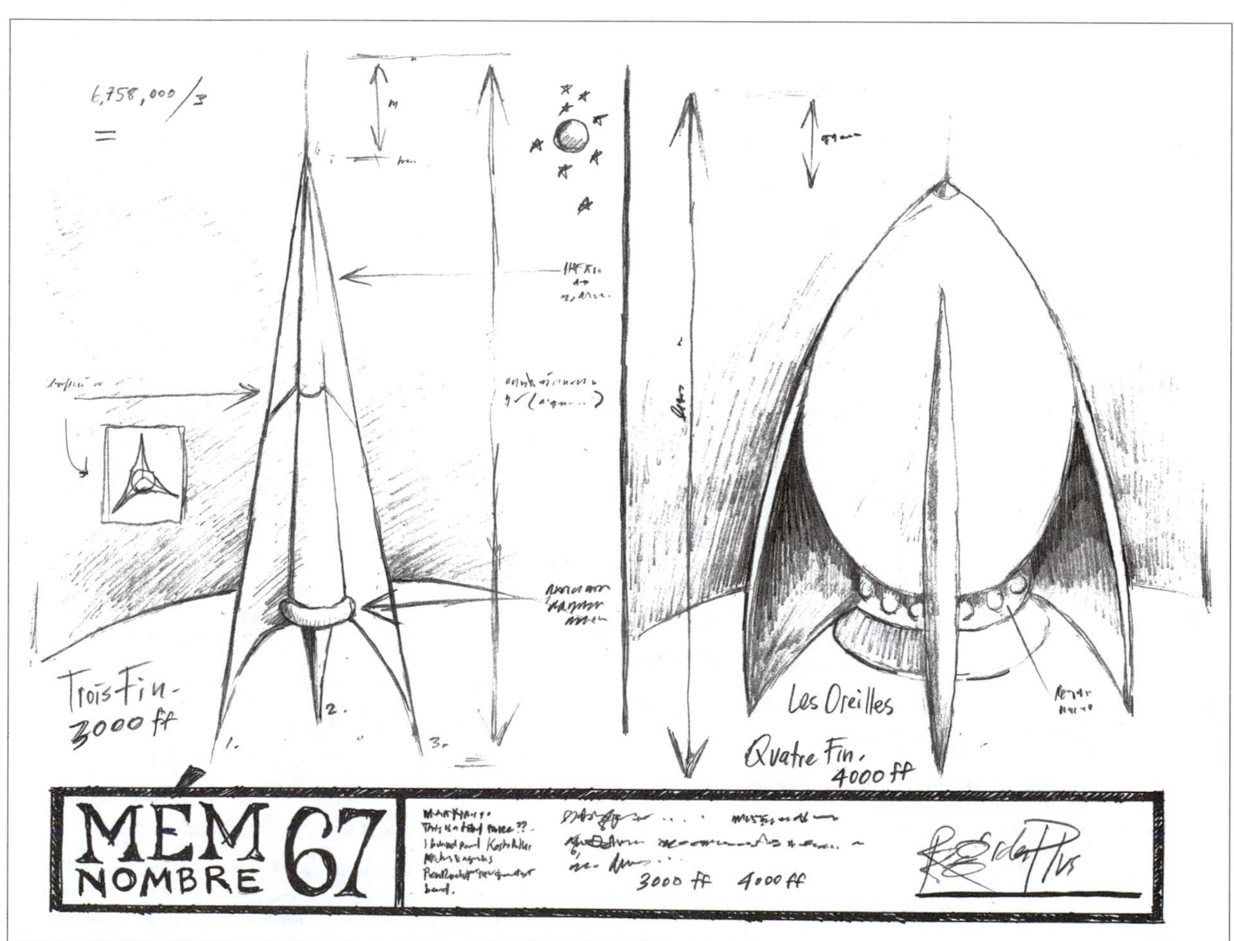

Fleury Colon, *Plan for MEM, Nombre 67*. Courtesy L'Archive de Colon, Montreal.

accusing Colon of "intention to collaborate" with the Vichy Government, citing his failed proposal to design train station shelters shaped like finials.

Bruised by the politics of LETTRISM, the architect manqué relocated to Montreal in 1950 and changed his name to Regarder Plus (To Look Further). Colon acquired financiers, and established an artistic commune in the wilderness northwest of Montreal, wherein his application of the finial was finally realized. Although similar in some regards to R. BUCKMINSTER FULLER's Dymaxion Deployment Unit, Colon's Max Épi Maison (MÉM) was finial-shaped, stood 25 feet high, and was made of pewter. This commune consisted of 16 of these spire-like MÉMs standing in a teepee-like cluster on the edge of a meadow. Amidst the dense Canadian forest and without the artificial light of the city, Colon became enamored with the stars and turned MÉM 3, his studio, into an observatory complete with telescope. Convinced he could see Sputnik in orbit above the tops of the pines, Colon hurled himself into the most peculiar of his finial-related obsessions: Aeronautics. Blueprints and sketches for hundreds of finial-shaped missiles and rockets adorned the inside of his studio/observatory. Colon wrote volumes of letters petitioning the Canadian Space & Aeronautics Commission (CSAC) with the hope of gaining funding for the finial's aerodynamic possibilities. Small finial-fuselage test models were built from scraps of pewter while Colon anxiously awaited access to CSAC's wind tunnels. But his pleas for assistance met with bureaucratic indifference. The letters slowed to a trickle.

Colon cloistered himself inside his MÉM developing a morose dementia for the night sky. It was clear, even to the commune, that Colon's cause was failing. Death can be impressive, even to the avant-garde, and Colon's demise was no less ironic. Alarmed commune members looked on as the aging architect, with the intention of cleaning his telescope lens, scaled the MÉM Observatory using a new system of ropes and pulleys. A pulley snapped, and Colon fell, impaling himself on a small doghouse shaped like a finial.

—Michael Peters

Writings: *The Finial Automaton; The Collected Writings of Fleury Colon and Regarder Plus* (1936–1964). Ed. Jean-Jacques Cory. Nice, France: La Banque d'Écrits, 1968; *Le Petit Épi; Un Manifeste Fétu*, with sketches, notes, blueprints, & related ephemera (1942–48). Ed. Maurice Fragonette. Paris, France: Faux-Semblant Livres, 1971; *Regarder Plus: The CSAC Letters*. Ed. Thomas Knowlton, with sketches, blueprints, and photos. Toronto: Red Leaf Editions, 1974.

Plans: Fleury Colon, *Finial-Fuselage 3000–4000 Series #67* (preliminary sketches), 1961.

Interpretation: C. Miasma. *Theory and Design; The History of the Finial*. Montreal: Worthington Publishing Collective, 1978

COLOR-FIELD PAINTING

(c. 1950).

The idea is to use color apart from drawing, apart from shape, and apart from shading, until it acquires a purely visual status. However, in contrast to monochromic painting, most color-field work involves at least two colors, which prompt surprising retinal responses, such as ambiguous figure-ground reversals, usually along the sharply delineated border between the colors. The last fact prompted the epithet "hard-edge abstraction," which is also used to describe this style of painting. One master is Ellsworth Kelly (1923), who was also among the first to paint on nonrectangular canvases. Since many post-World War II color-field painters had worked in camouflage during the War, the military must have taught them strategic tricks about color relationships that afterwards were turned to esthetic uses. In my living room is a Suzan Frecon (1941) painting, in which a deeply repainted black rectangle sits in the center of a very white larger canvas. Stand at least fourteen feet away from this work and stare at it intently, and you will observe that the black rectangle starts to shimmer. (And the shimmering won't stop!)

Exhibition Catalog: *Ellsworth Kelly.* New York: Whitney Museum, 1982; *Ellsworth Kelly Prints 1949–1989.* New York: Susan Sheehan Gallery, 1990; *Suzan Frecon.* Berkeley: University Art Museum, 1989.

COMBINATORIALITY

(1950s).

In general topology the concept of combinatoriality applies to the functional congruence of geometrical figures of the same order of continuity. Thus a square can be brought into topological congruence with a circle because all the points of the former are in an enumerable correspondence of the other. On the other hand, the geometry of the figure 8 cannot be made congruent with a square or a circle without cutting. The American composer and theorist MILTON BABBITT extended the term combinatoriality to serial techniques. The parameter of continuity in dodecaphonic writing is the order of succession of the 12 thematic notes in their four forms, basic, retrograde, inversion, and inverted retrograde, all of which are combinatorially congruent. Furthermore, the tone-row can be functionally divided into two potentially congruent groups of six notes each, or three groups of four notes each, or four groups of three notes each, with each such group becoming a generating serial nucleus possessing a degree of subsidiary combinatoriality. Extending the concept of combinatoriality to other parameters of SERIAL MUSIC, a state of total Serialism is attained, in which not only the actual notes of a series, but also meter, rhythm, intervallic configurations, dynamics, and instrumental timbres are organized in sets and subsets. The subsets in turn are organized as combinatorial derivations, possessing their own order of continuity and congruence. Of these, the most fruitful is the principle of rotation, in which each successive set is obtained by the transposition of the first note of the series to the end of a derived set. Thus the first set, 1, 2, 3, . . . 12, appears after rotation as subset 2, 3, 4, 5, . . . 12, 1, or as 3, 4, 5, 6, . . . 12, 1, 2, etc. Inversion, retrograde and inverted retrograde can be subjected to a similar type of rotation. The additive Fibonacci series, in which each number equals the sum of the two preceding numbers, as in 1, 1, 2, 3, 5, 8, 13, 21, is another fertile resource for the formation of sets, subsets, and other derivations. The Fibonacci numbers can be used for building non-dodecaphonic tone-rows, in which case the numbers will indicate the distance from the central tone in semitones, modulo 12, so that 13 becomes functionally identical with 1, 21 with 9, etc. The numerical field of combinatoriality is circumscribed by 12 different notes. But experiments have been conducted, notably by ERNST KRENEK, with artificial scales of 13 equal degrees, obtained with the aid of electronic instruments. Potential uses of combinatoriality operating with sets of more than 12 notes in an octave are limitless.

—Nicolas Slonimsky

Writings: Babbitt, Milton."The Composer as Specialist." In *Esthetics Contemporary* (1978), ed. Richard Kostelanetz. 2d ed. Buffalo, NY: Prometheus, 1989; Dembski, Stephen, and Joseph N. Straus, eds. *Milton Babbitt: Words About Music.* Madison: University of Wisconsin Press, 1987.

COMBINE

See **RAUSCHENBERG, Robert.**

COMPUTER

(c. 1945).

Information is entered, by one of many possible channels, into a machine that converts it into digital impulses that can then be manipulated in a variety of ways. Such information may be words, as many of us enter these on word processors; it may also be pictures or sounds. In music, computers now enable composers to create on their cathode-ray tubes (aka CRTs) works that can be transformed, thanks to digital-to-analog conversion, into audiotape that may be played back through conveniently available transducers. In literary composition, computers had less influence until the 1980s, with the development first of the affordable "personal computer" that could sit on your desk next to, or in place of, the typewriter, and then of multipath HYPERTEXTS that are best "read" not sequentially in print but by clicking various options on a cathode-ray tube.

In visual art, the influence of the computer has been more problematic, in part because it works so much better with abstraction than representation. Look at the catalogue of the first institutional computer-art exhibition, *Cybernetic Serendipity*, organized in 1968 by Jasia Reichardt for the Institute of Contemporary Arts in London, and you'll be struck by the lack of interesting art. This exhibition partially accounts for the anonymous author of the entry on computer art in *The Oxford Companion to Twentieth-Century Art* (1981) declaring, partly out of ignorance, "By the mid 1970s no visual art of significant quality had been produced with the aid of computers." By the 1980s, exhibitions were filled with computer graphics different in content but lacking individual style, all in contrast to the distinguished computer-assisted art of MANFRED MOHR, who begins with algorithms. My own opinion, evident occasionally in this book, is that computers have been most successful in film (particularly by STAN VANDERBEEK) and then video animation (particularly by STEPHEN BECK), but the latter happens to be the best artistic use to which I put them.

Interpretation: Goodman, Cynthia. *Digital Visions: Computers and Art*. New York: Abrams, 1987; Hillis, Daniel. *The Pattern on the Stone: The Simple Ideas That Make Computers Work*. New York: Basic Books, 1998; Lovejoy, Margot. "The Computer as a Dynamic Imaging Tool," *Postmodern Currents*. Ann Arbor: UMI Research, 1990; Sumner, Lloyd. *Computer Art and Human Response*. Charlottesville, VA: Paul B. Victorius (1413 W. Main St.), 1968.

Exhibition Catalog: Reichardt, Jasia, ed. *Cybernetic Serendipity*. London, England: I.C.A., 1968.

COMPUTER POETRY

(1960s?).

This term is used so loosely that it is almost useless, but computer poetry is any poetry that depends on the computer for its construction or presentation, and usually for both. The earliest examples consisted of "poems" devised of randomly generated or randomly ordered words. The output that spilled forth was nonsense, nonsense made interesting by two facts: that it was generated without the direct intervention of a human mind and that it veered unexpectedly towards sense as the reader attempted to distill order from the chaos. I know of none of these poems (which sometimes were mere Proteus poems) that an artist produced. These were programmer's games: yards of scrolls furling forth from TRS-80 computers onto the floor of Radio Shack, more a sideshow than a performance. Occasionally, people use the term "computer poetry" to define visual poems written with the aid of the computer (just as the term "typewriter poem" describes a type of poetry that depends on the typography of the Olivetti, or the Selectric II, or the Smith-Corona for its particular presence). These poems could consist of visual collage, shaped text, overwriting, and a faux palimpsest for their visual and semiotic sense. Other computer poetry includes visual kinetic poems programmed for the cathode ray tube. Poets have fashioned these poems using such varied tools as BASIC and HTML to produce everything from simple growing, twisting, and contracting words that shuffled across or huddled upon the screen to complex, hyperhuman bursts of visual text, reminiscent of CONLON NANCARROW's music for the piano roll. With the advent of the Internet as a canvas and a lingua franca for the writing of these poems, the work produced has become more varied, more colorful, and more intermediary, combining movement, word, color, and even sound into mini-movies of cybertext, a new cinematic poetry for a new age.

—Geof Huth

Webpage: Dartmouth Computer Poetry Homepage: http://www.cs.dartmouth.edu/~brd/alfred/ (where a new poem is generated every two minutes by "Alfred, the Mail Agent," whenever the server is running, producing approximately 150,000 poems each year; none of these poems is saved unless a viewer decides to save one, so this millionth monkey may have already written a masterpiece without anyone ever knowing it).

Books: Nichol, bp. *First Screening: Computer Poems by bpNichol*. Toronto: Underwhich Editions, 1984.

C

CONCEPTUAL ARCHITECTURE

(forever).

This is my coinage for architectural proposals that were never realized, and were in some cases never intended to be realized, but have in a format other than architecture sufficient clarity and originality to be exhibited. The classic modernist example is Vladimir Tatlin's *Monument to the Third International* (1920), which had considerable influence on subsequent architecture, even though it was never more substantial than a sculpture. A more recent example of Conceptual Architecture was Buckminster Fuller's proposal to put a geodesic dome over an entire city. Alison Sky and Michelle Stone compiled a marvelous anthology of comparable plans drawn from American history. In 1976, an ambitious architect, since more successful, Peter Eisenman (1932), organized an exhibition whose catalog became the book *Idea as Model* (1981). In the introduction, he suggested that an architectural model "could be something other than a narrative record of a project or a building [because models] could well have an artistic or conceptual existence of their own, one which was relatively independent of the project that they represented."

The critical question posed by the publication or exhibition of such work is whether the proposal can have an esthetic status comparable to its realization, and thus whether a comprehensive critical appraisal of, say, an architect's work should include those images that were never realized along with those that were. If, like myself, you affirm the former position, then you must consider extending the principle to other cultural areas. If only to raise the possibility of doing so, I self-published a 140-page book *Unfinished Business* (1991), collecting my grant applications, anthology outlines, and proposals for both full-length books and extended media compositions, all of which went unrealized for reasons beyond my control, implicitly raising the question whether such "unfinished business" belongs to my intellectual record.

Bibliography: Eisenman, Peter, et al. *Idea as Model*. New York: Rizzoli, 1981; Sky, Alison, and Michelle Stone. *Unbuilt America*. New York: McGraw-Hill, 1976; Vostell, Wolf, and Dick Higgins, eds. *Fantastic Architecture*. New York: Something Else, 1970; Kostelanetz, Richard. *Unfinished Business: An Intellectual Nonhistory*. New York: Archae Editions, 1991.

CONCEPTUAL ART

(c. 1960).

The radical idea is that a statement, which need not be in words, can generate an esthetic experience, if properly interpreted. The classic forerunner, conceived nearly a decade before the epithet was coined, is John Cage's oft-called "silent" piece, *4'33"* (1952), in which, in a concert situation, pianist David Tudor plays no notes for the required duration of four minutes and thirty-three seconds. By framing the performance situation, Cage suggested that all the miscellaneous noises heard in that space during that duration constitute " music." It logically follows that any unintended noise, even apart from the 4'33" enclosure, could provide esthetic experience (and thus that what has commonly been called Cage's "silent piece" is really a *noise piece*).

Much depends upon a resonant context. The sometime economist Henry Flynt (1940) is commonly credited with originating the radical notion of statement-alone-art in his 1961 essay "Concept Art," which he defined as "first of all an art of which the material is concepts, as the material of e.g. music is sound."

Self-conscious conceptual art, which arrived in the late 1960s, customarily took such forms as written instructions, esthetically undistinguished photographs, scale models, maps, or documentary videotapes, all of which are theoretically intended to suggest esthetic experiences that could not be evoked in any other way. YOKO ONO specialized in performance instructions that could not be realized, such as, simply, "Fly." A later, charming example was CLAES OLDENBURG'S "inverted monument" for New York City, for which he hired professional grave diggers to excavate and then fill in a large rectangular hole behind New York's Metropolitan Museum (rather than, say, at a garbage dump, which would be contextually less resonant). Even as late as 1996, Hanne Darboven (1941, Germany) explored the nature of time in Kulturgeschichte 1880–1983, an exibition of 1,589 panels uniform in size and format that document those years with photographs, numbers, texts, and historic postcards.

Among the pioneering practitioners were Douglas Huebler (1924), JOSEPH KOSUTH, Lawrence Weiner (1940), John Baldessari (1931), the German–American HANS HAACKE, the German Hanne Darboven (1941), and Frenchman Daniel Buren (1938). In SOL LE WITT'S classic phrase, "In conceptual art, the idea, or concept, is the most important aspect of the work."

Interpretation: Battock, Gregory, ed. *Idea Art*. New York: Dutton, 1973; Flynt, Henry. *Blueprint for a Higher Civilization*. Milan, Italy: Multhipla, 1975; Godfrey, Tony. *Conceptual Art*. London: Phaidon, 1998; Lippard, Lucy R. *Six Years: The Dematerializaton of the Art Object from 1966 to 1972*. New York: Praeger, 1972; Meyer, Ursula. *Conceptual Art*. New York: Dutton, 1972; Morgan, Robert C. *Conceptual Art: An American Perspective*. Jefferson, NC: McFarland, 1994; *Art into Ideas: Essays on Conceptual Art*. New York: Cambridge University, 1996; Piper, Adrian. *Out of Order, Out of Sight*. Cambridge: MIT Press, 1999; Vries, Gerd de, ed. *Über Kunst/On Art*. Köln, Germany: DuMont, 1974.

CONCRETE POETRY

(1950s).

Concrete Poetry aims to reduce language to its concrete essentials, free not only of semantic but of syntactical necessities. It is often confused with SOUND POETRY and VISUAL POETRY (which are, respectively, the enhancement of language primarily in terms of acoustic qualities and the enhancement of language primarily through image), but is really something else. The true Concrete Poem is simply letters or disconnected words scattered abstractly across the page or a succession of aurally nonrepresentational (and linguistically incomprehensible) sounds. The rationale comes from KURT SCHWITTERS' 1924 manifesto "Consistent Poetry":

> Not the word but the letter is the original material of poetry. Word is 1.) Composition of Letters. 2.) Sound. 3.) Denotation (Meaning). 4.) Carrier of associations of ideas.

In his or her use of language, the poet is generally reductive; the choice of methods for enhancing language could be expansive. Unfortunately, the earliest anthologies of Concrete Poetry did more to obscure than clarify the issue of its differences, particularly by including poems that were primarily visual or acoustic. Among the truest practitioners of Concrete Poetry are IAN HAMILTON FINLAY, DOM SYLVESTER HOUÉDARD, Haroldo and Augusto de Campos (1929, 1931), Decio Pignatari (1927), Max Bense (1910),

Pierre Garnier (1928), Paul de Vree (1909–84), Heinz Gappmayr (1925), and EUGEN GOMRINGER. What had first seemed puzzling to readers, not to mention critics, has since inspired a growing scholarly literature.

Anthologies: Bory, Jean-François, ed. *Once Again*. New York: New Directions, 1968; Solt, Mary Ellen, ed. *Concrete Poetry: A World View.* Bloomington: Indiana University Press, 1970; Wildman, Eugene, ed. *Anthology of Concretism*. Chicago: Swallow, 1967; Williams, Emmett, ed. *An Anthology of Concrete Poetry*. New York: Something Else, 1967.

Exhibition Catalog: *Sound Texts? Concrete Poetry Visual Texts*. Amsterdam: Stediljk, 1969.

Interpretation: Cobbing, Bob, and Peter Mayer, eds. *Concerning Concrete Poetry*. London: Writers Forum, 1978; Schwitters, Kurt. "Consistent Poetry," in *Poems Performance Pieces Proses Plays Poetics: Kurt Schwitters*. Ed. & trans. Jerome Rothenberg & Pierre Joris. Philadelphia: Temple University Press, 1993; Seaman, David W. *Concrete Poetry in France*. Ann Arbor: UMI Research, 1981; Webster, Michael. *Reading Visual Poetry After Futurism*. New York: P. Lang, 1995; Gumpel, Liselotte. *"Concrete" Poetry from East and West Germany*. New Haven: Yale University Press, 1976.

Webpage: http://cadre.sjsu.edu/switch/sound/articles/wendt/ng1.htm (History of the movement with examples).

Bibliography: McCullough, Kathleen. *Concrete Poetry: An Annotated International Bibliography*. Troy, NY: Whitston, 1989; Sackner, Marvin & Ruth, eds. *The Ruth & Marvin Sackner Archive of Concrete and Visual Poetry 1984*. Miami Beach, FL: Privately published, 1986.

CONCRETISM

See **FOUND ART.**

CONRAD, Tony

(1940).

His film *The Flicker* (1966) has such classic simplicity you wonder why no one thought of doing it before—a film consisting entirely of black frames and white frames, alternating in various patterns and frequencies, causing the eye to see nonexistent colors and even images. The structure appears to be that black frames, comparatively sparse at the beginning, become more frequent in the middle, only to become sparse again. The sometime critic Sheldon Renan speaks of "forty-seven different patterns of black and white combinations." Conrad himself has written about making almost 600 splices in 4,000 frames of footage. As the experience of continuous sharp reversals produces peculiar effects on the viewer's sensibility, the implicit point is that even the most minimal abstract film can be very moving, if not emotionally, then at least viscerally. Meanwhile, the soundtrack's buzzing noise that resembles an airplane motor becomes faster and faster, while fluctuating slightly in volume throughout. No summary can duplicate the experience of actually seeing *The Flicker.*

Conrad is also a musician who has performed solo, mostly on a violin, in addition to collaborating since the 1960s with John Cale and La Monte Young, among other avatars of minimal/modular music. More recently, he told an interviewer in 1998, "I've been working with public access, organizing independent collectives to produce alternative video; producing homework-help lines for kids in the city; and developing information systems that can link urban kids to their schools." He has long been teaching at SUNY-Buffalo.

Films: *The Flicker*, 1966; *Raw Film*, 1973; *Deep Fried*, 1973; *Fade*, 1976.

Recordings: *Early Minimalism: Volume One*. San Francisco: Table of Elements, 1997 (4 CD set); *Slapping Pythagoras*. San Francisco: Table of the Elements, 1996; with Faust. *Outside the Dream Syndicate* (1972). San Francisco: Table of Elements, 1993.

Writings: "On 'The Flicker.'" In Robert Russett & Cecile Starr. *Experimental Animation*. New York: Van Nostrand, 1976.

Interpretation: Renan, Sheldon. *An Introduction to the American Underground Film. New York:* Dutton, 1967.

CONSTRUCTIVISM

(c. late 1910s).

In the decade after World War I, this term was, like FUTURISM, adopted by two groups, one in Russia, the other in Western Europe, whose aims were sufficiently different to distinguish between them. Coming in the wake of the Bolshevik Revolution, most Soviet Constructivists were ABSTRACT artists participating in social change with applied projects that nonetheless reflected their esthetic heritage. Thus, the historical exhibition *Art into Life* (1990) included large-scale graphics, environments, photomontage, stage designs, and architectural proposals, along with paintings and sculptures. The key figure in this exhibition was ALEKSANDR RODCHENKO, whose environmental *The Workers Club* (1925) included unusual chairs and reading tables. Also in this exhibition was VLADIMIR TATLIN'S *Letatlin* (1932), which is the model for a flying machine; EL LISSITZKY; and various works by GUSTAV KLUCIS, a Latvian slighted in previous surveys. (This exhibition did not include Antoine Pevsner [1886–1962] and NAUM GABO, brothers who objected to utilitarian art, or the mercurial KAZIMIR MALEVICH, who was, strictly speaking, not a Constructivist.) Rejecting traditional artistic practice as reflecting bourgeois individualism, they explored factory production. Once cultural policy tightened in Russia, culminating in the purges of the 1930s, Russian Constructivism disintegrated. Klucis died in a World War II concentration camp and Tatlin died a decade later of food poisoning, in relative obscurity.

European Constructivism, sometimes called International Constructivism, favored conscious and deliberate compositions that were supposedly reflective of recently discovered universal and objective esthetic principles. Thus, its artists made scrupulously nonrepresentational Abstract structures that differed from the other avant gardes of the earlier twentieth century in favoring simplicity, clarity, and precision. Among the principal participants at the beginning were THEO VAN DOESBURG, PIET MONDRIAN and HANS RICHTER; the principal magazines were *DE STIJL* and Richter's *G*. Among the later International Constructivists were MICHEL SEUPHOR, GEORGES VANTONGERLOO, JOAQUIN TORRES-GARCIA, CHARLES BIEDERMAN, and MOHOLY-NAGY. The last of these artists introduced Constructivist ideas to the BAUHAUS, where he taught from 1923 to 1928; and as the publisher of the pioneering Bauhaus books, Moholy-Nagy issued a collection of Mondrian's essays in 1925 and Malevich's *The Non-Objective World* in 1927. When Naum Gabo moved to England, he collaborated with the painter Ben Nicholson (1894–1982) and the young architect J. L. Martin in editing *Circle* (1937), an impressive anthology subtitled *International Survey of Constructive Art*. Constructivism came to America with art-school teachers such as Moholy-Nagy and JOSEF ALBERS, the former in Chicago after 1938, the latter first at BLACK MOUNTAIN COLLEGE from the middle 1930s to the late 1940s and then at Yale until he retired. Constructivism survives in certain kinds of Minimal geometric sculpture; in the mobiles of GEORGE RICKEY, who incidentally wrote an excellent history of the movement; in certain strains of COLOR-FIELD painting; in the Constructivist fictions of RICHARD KOSTELANETZ; and in the magazine *The Structurist* (1958), which the American–Canadian artist Eli Bornstein (1922) edits out of the University of Saskatchewan.

Exhibition Catalogs: *Geometric Abstraction in America*. New York: Whitney Museum, 1962; *Constructivism in Poland 1923–1936*. Lódz, Poland: Museum of Fine Arts, 1973; *Russian Constructivism Revisited*. Newcastle-upon-Tyne, England: Hatton Gallery, University of Newcastle-upon-Tyne, 1973; Barron, Stephanie, and Maurice Tuchman, eds. *The Avant-Garde in Russia, 1910–1930: New Perspectives*. Los Angeles: L.A. Country Museum of Art, 1980; *Eli Bornstein: Selected Works/Oeuvres Choisies, 1957–1982*. Saskatoon, Canada: Mendel Art Gallery, 1982; Andrews, Richard, and Milena Kalinova, eds. *Art Into Life: Russian Constructivism, 1914–32*. New York: Rizzoli, 1990.

Interpretation: Rickey, George. *Constructivism: Origins and Evolution*. New York: Braziller, 1967; Nash, J. M. *Cubism, Futurism, and Constructivism*. London: Thames & Hudson, 1974; Hill, Anthony, ed. *DATA: Directions in Art, Theory and Aesthetics*. London: Faber, 1968; Lodder, Christina. *Russian Constructivism*. New Haven: Yale University Press, 1983; Bann, Steven. ed. *The Tradition of Constructivism* (1974). New York: Da Capo, 1990; Marquardt Virginia M. & Roman, Gail H. eds. *The Avant-Garde Frontier: Russia Meets the West 1910–1930*. Gainesville, FL: University Press of Florida, 1992.

Book Art: Kostelanetz, Richard. *Constructs*. Several volumes. New York: Archae, 1975–91.

C

COOLIDGE, Clark

(26 February 1939).

Very much a progenitor of "LANGUAGE-CENTERED" POETRY, Coolidge began, in *Flag Flutter* & *U.S. Electric* (1966), with forays into POST-ASHBERYIAN poetic structuring in which he attempted to realize semblances of literary coherence without using such traditional organizing devices as meter, metaphor, exposition, symbolism, consistent allusion, or declarative statements. His most avant-garde poetry appears in *Space* (1970), including an untitled poem beginning "by an I" that contains individually isolated words no more than two letters long, scattered across the space of the page, which then appeared to be Coolidge's primary compositional unit. These words are nonetheless related to one another—not only in terms of diction and corresponding length (both visually and verbally) but also in spatial proximity. *Suite V* (1972), published as a chapbook, is yet more outrageously spare, containing only pairs of three-letter words in their plural forms, with one four-letter word at the top of the page and the other at the bottom of otherwise blank pages.

Coolidge has published many other books in the past three decades, all of them with smaller presses (as one measure of his continuing integrity), but none of them is quite as avant-garde or as consequential as his opening moves. One of the thicker collections, *Solution Passage: Poems 1978–81* (1986), contains implicit elaborations of Noam Chomsky's "colorless green ideas sleep furiously," which is to say phrases that seem syntactically acceptable without making immediate semantic sense. In the late 1960s, Coolidge also worked as the drummer for Serpent Power, one of the more culturally sophisticated rock groups, which was headed by the San Francisco poet David Meltzer (1937).

Writings: *Flag Flutter and U.S. Electric*. New York: Lines, 1966; *(Poems)*. New York: Lines, 1967; *Ing*. New York: Angel Hair, 1969; *Space*. New York: Harper & Row, 1970; *Moroccan Variations*. Bolinas, CA: Big Sky, 1971; *Suite V*. New York: Adventures in Poetry, 1972; *The Maintains*. San Francisco: This Press, 1974; *Polaroid*. New York: Boke, 1975; *Quartz Hearts*. San Francisco: This Press, 1978; *Own Face*. Lenox, MA: Angel Hair, 1978; *American Ones*. Bolinas, CA: Tombouctou, 1981; *The Crystal Text*. Great Barrington, MA: Figures, 1986; *Solution Passage: Poems 1978–81*. Los Angeles, CA: Sun & Moon, 1986; *At Egypt*. Great Barrington, MA: Figures, 1988; *Sound as Thought: Poems 1982–1984*. Los Angeles: Sun & Moon, 1990; *The Book of During*. Great Barrington, MA: Figures, 1991; *Own Face*. Los Angeles: Sun & Moon, 1993; *The ROVA Improvisations*. Los Angeles: Sun & Moon, 1994; *The Time We Are Both/City in Regard*. Los Angeles: Sun & Moon, 1999.

COPLAND, Aaron

(14 November 1900–2 December 1990).

A two-sided composer, he produced a few works that were moderately avant-garde and many works that weren't. These more avant-garde efforts appear, almost as surprises, at various times in his career. One is a Concerto for Piano and Orchestra (1927) that incorporated jazz elements into a score for the Boston Symphony. A second is *Vitebsk: Study on a Jewish Theme* (1928) for piano trio. A third is the *Piano Variations* (1930), which has in its dissonance a seven-note theme that is repeated in ways suggesting SERIAL MUSIC, which appears fully formed in Copland's *Piano Quartet* (1950). Another is his *Piano Fantasy* (1952–57). Those committed to strict Serial Music consider Copland's *Connotations* (1962) for orchestra to signal his conversion, but he later strayed from that church. Perhaps a few other pieces belong in the select canon of radical works.

Otherwise, Copland produced many compositions that made his name familiar around the world, most of them sounding much like one another in the repeated use of certain strategies, such as open chords and modest syncopation. My own sense of his career is that Copland's composition became thinner whenever he got involved with theater or film, even though the results of these involvements include some of his more attractive scores—*Rodeo* (1942), *Appalachian Spring* (1944), *The Red Pony* (1948), and the ever-popular *Lincoln Portrait* (1942), which has a narration so performer-proof that hot politicians can read it without embarrassment.

Copland was also a masterful arts politician particularly skilled at getting all the rewards for himself (including his name on a school of music founded at the City University of New York in his lifetime) but also apportioning widely the spoils that came to him and especially in giving advice to potential sponsors. As early as 1928, he joined ROGER SESSIONS, then a young composer slightly older and likewise Brooklyn-born, in sponsoring three years of presentations that were known and long remembered as the Copland-Sessions Concerts because of their influence. As a result, just as several younger composers acknowledged Sessions among their teachers, so many more American composers of this next generation readily identified "Aaron" as their "best friend" among the older titans. These last achievements of his extraordinary career shouldn't be ignored, hopefully to be covered in the biography that hasn't yet been written.

Selected Other Compositions: *Billy the Kid*, ballet, 1938; Suite for orchestra from ballet, 1941; *Rodeo*, ballet, 1942; *The Tender Land*, opera, 1954; *12 Poems of Emily Dickinson*, 1949–50; *Nonet* for 3 violins, 3 violas, and 3 cellos, 1960; *Music for a Great City*, symphonic suite, 1954; *Inscale*, 1967; *Threnody I: Igor Stravinsky, In Memoriam*, for flute and string trio, 1971.

Books: *What To Listen for in Music* (1939). Rev. ed. New York: McGraw-Hill, 1957; *Our New Music* (1941). 2d ed., rev. and enlarged as *The New Music, 1900–1960*. New York: Norton, 1968; *Music and Imagination*. Cambridge: Harvard University Press, 1952; *Copland on Music*. Garden City, NY: Doubleday, 1960.

Biography: Pollack, Howard. *Aaron Copland: The Life and Work of an Uncommon Man*. New York: Holt, 1999.

Autobiography: *Aaron Copland*. With Vivian Perlis. Vol. 1. New York: St. Martin's Press, 1984; vol. 2. New York: St. Martin's Press, 1989.

Website: http://voodoo.acomp.usf.edu/copland.html

Interpretation: Berger, Arthur. *Aaron Copland* (1953). New York: Da Capo, 1990; Butterworth, Neil. *The Music of Aaron Copland*. New York: Universe, 1985.

COPY CULTURE

(c. 1980s).

One important aspect of our culture is the numerous technological opportunities, chiefly XEROGRAPHY, that allow *individuals* to produce and reproduce "publications" cheaply. Because xerography allows the quick and simple reproduction of images, it encourages distribution to others. The most important concept in copy culture is that an individual, without the prerequisite of massive amounts of capital, can copy and distribute art, literature, or political ranting without resorting to a "publisher" as an intermediary. The advantages of this system of personal dissemination are present not only in xerography, but also in audiotape, videotape, computer disks and, to a lesser degree, microfiche. Precisely because such methods of reproduction are more accessible to the individual, they make possible the unfettered distribution of even the most avant-garde, or culturally unacceptable, arts and thoughts.

—Geof Huth

Bibliography: Lovejoy, Margot. "The Copier: Authorship and Originality," *Postmodern Currents*. Ann Arbor: UMI Research, 1990.

CORNELL, Joseph

(24 December 1903–29 December 1972).

An American original, without formal art education, Cornell made small boxes with cutaway fronts—a form closer to reliefs and a theatrical proscenium than sculpture proper in demanding a view from the frontal perpendicular perspective—and meticulously filled these boxes with many objects not usually found together in either art or life. "Their imagery includes mementos of the theater and the dance, the world of nature and that of the heavens," writes the historian Matthew Baigell. "Cornell's boxes also often contain nineteenth century memorabilia (especially those made during the 1940s, of ballerinas)." Miniaturized tableaus, rather than true sculptures, these boxes combine the dreaminess of SURREALISM with the formal austerity of CONSTRUCTIVISM and the free use of materials typical of DADA. Each enclosure seems, not unlike a JACKSON POLLOCK painting, to represent in objective form a particu-

Joseph Cornell, *Suzy's Sun (for Judy Tyler)*, 1957. CORBIS/North Carolina Museum.

lar state of mind in a moment of time, as well as an immense but circumscribed world of theatrical activity. Cornell often produced works in series, exploring themes through variations. Though others have made excellent tableaus, no one else ever did boxed sculpture so well.

Exhibition Catalog: Tyler, Parker. *Exhibition of Objects by Joseph Cornell*. New York: Julian Levy Gallery, 1939; *JC*. Pasadena, CA: Pasadena Art Museum, 1966; Waldman, Diane. *JC*. New York: Guggenheim, 1967; Richebourg, Betsy, et al. *JC Collages 1931–72. New York: Leo Castelli,* 1978; *JC: Box Constructions and Collages.* New York: C&M Arts, 1995.

Biography: Solomon, Deborah. *Utopia Parkway: The Life and Work of Joseph Cornell*. New York: Farrar Straus, 1997.

Interpretation: Ashton, Dore. *A Joseph Cornell Album* (1974). New York: Da Capo, 1989.

CORRIGAN, Donald

(4 November 1943).

One of the most audacious CONCEPTUAL ARTISTS, for professional courage the equal of ELAINE STURTEVANT, Corrigan exhibited charts of power in the art world, particularly in his hometown. In his *Tree of Modern Art in Washington, DC* (1972), a detailed drawing measuring twenty-three by eighteen inches, Corrigan graphs relationships and sympathies among the commercial galleries on one side and the nonprofit institutions on the other in a brilliant and accurate way, adding art critics, art schools, and constellations of avowedly independent individuals, by his documentation making the invisible visible, which is what visual art has always done. Rarely permitted to exhibit, Corrigan gave up visual art by the 1980s; he was recently working, like Herman Melville and CLEMENT GREENBERG before him, for the U.S. Customs Service.

Works: *Tree of Modern Art in Washington, DC*, 1972 (also reproduced in Kostelanetz, Richard, ed. *Essaying Essays* [1975]. New York: Archae, 1981).

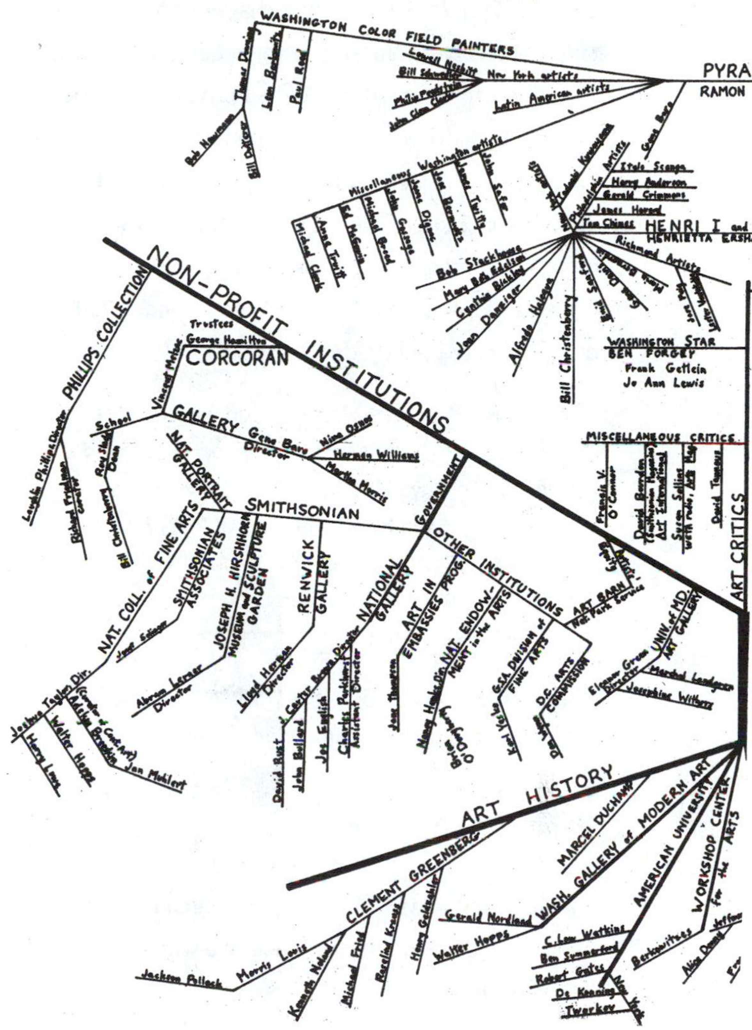

Don Corrigan. Detail of *Tree of Modern Art in Washington, D.C.* Courtesy the artist.

CORTÀZAR, Julio

(26 August 1914–12 February 1984).

An Argentine who lived mostly in Paris, whose books were initially published everywhere besides his two home countries, Cortàzar made formal alternatives a recurring subject. He prefaces *Rayuela* (1963; *Hopscotch*, 1966) with the advice that it "consists of many books, but two books above all. The first can be read in a normal fashion, and it ends with Chapter 56." He then suggests an alternative route, beginning with chapter 73 and continuing with "1-2-116-3-84-4-71-5-81-74 . . ." that not only includes certain chapters twice but directs the reader as far as chapter 155. The American edition did surprisingly well, perhaps because the cover of its 1967 paperback edition promised "life/love/sex." Although other books of his have appeared in English, I've yet to find any translations of the more experimental short pieces in *La Vuelta al dia en ochenta mundos* (1967) and *Ultimo Round* (1969), both of which were published in Mexico.

C

Writings: *Hopscotch*. Trans. Gregory Rabassa. New York: Pantheon, 1966; *La Vuelta al dia in ochenta mundos*. 2 vols. Mexico City: Siglo XXI, 1967; *Ultimo Round*. 2 vols. Mexico City: Siglo XXI, 1969; *62: A Model Kit*. New York: Pantheon, 1972; *A Manual for Manuel*. New York: Pantheon, 1978; *Blow Up and Other Stories*. New York: Random House, 1985.

Interpretation: Boldy, Steven. *The Novels of Cortàzar*. Cambridge, England: Cambridge University Press, 1980.

COWELL, Henry

(11 March 1897–10 December 1965).

If Aaron Copland was the great mainstream arts politician of his time, distributing patronage to a wide variety of otherwise neglected composers who would remain personally indebted to him, Cowell was the great radical mover and shaker, helping establish the reputations of a large number of American composers, beginning with Charles Ives, in the course of a productive compositional career.

As a teenager, Cowell wrote and performed piano pieces that incorporated what he called tone-clusters, which are produced by striking groups of adjoining notes simultaneously, customarily not with one's fingers but with a fist, a palm, or even a whole forearm. Within the composition, the clusters become huge blocks of sound moving up and down the keyboard, sometimes becoming atonal clouds that complement the melodic lines. In the early 1920s, while still in his own mid-twenties, Cowell directly attacked the strings of a grand piano—plucking, striking, sweeping, and dampening them as though they were on a harp; sometimes stroking them with a china darning egg. His classic *Aeolian Harp* (1923) requires that one hand works the piano keyboard, holding down keys, while the other "plays" the strings until the sound of the depressed keys decays. In the 1930s, he collaborated with Leon Theremin in constructing a keyboard percussion instrument that he called the "rhythmicon," a precursor of modern drum machines, to create music with overlapping rhythmic patterns.

As a prolific composer, Cowell worked with a variety of ideas, some of them more radical than others, beginning with alternative ways of striking the piano. Some pieces from the 1930s have parts of varying lengths that he said performers may assemble to their tastes, even excluding or repeating sections. Others permitted improvisation in certain sections. Later pieces drew upon Americana and modal folk tunes. Late in his career, Cowell discovered Asian musics and their instruments, less for quotations than for sonorities and rhythms unavailable in the West. Typical pieces from this period combine an Asian soloist with a Western orchestra. Some mellifluous works composed just before his death reflect Persian music.

As a musical theorist, Cowell wrote between 1916–19 the manuscript later released as *New Musical Resources* (not published until 1930), whose theme was expanding the musical palette. He edited and partially authored *American Composers on American Music: A Symposium* (1933), which was the first survey of native achievement. With his wife Sidney Robertson Cowell (1903-97), he published the first book on *Charles Ives and His Music* (1955), which remains a model of its introductory kind. Cowell was often the first to write extended articles on emerging American composers; so that nearly every advanced composer's bibliography, from Carl Ruggles to John Cage, includes a reference to Cowell. As an advocate of American composition, he founded in 1927 *New Music Quarterly*, not only to publish their works but to record them. Among the composers issued under the New Music imprint were Ives, Ruggles, and VIRGIL THOMSON (1896–1989); it even included distinguished Europeans such as ARNOLD SCHOENBERG and ANTON WEBERN.

As a generous teacher, Cowell directed musical activities intermittently at New York's underpaying New School from 1928 to 1963 and also taught at Columbia from 1951 to 1965; he gave private lessons to John Cage, Lou Harrison (1917), and George Gershwin (1898–1937). Sent to San Quentin prison on a trumped-up homosexual charge in 1937, he spent four years giving music lessons to his fellow inmates and organizing a band. Once released, he married the musicologist Sidney Robertson and, as a devoted lover, incidentally composed 85 short pieces for her to celebrate various anniversaries.

As both a teacher and a publicist, Cowell anticipated current opinion in insisting that Americans pay greater attention to "music of the world's peoples," as he called it, directing the recording of world music for Folkways in the early 1950s.

Selected Compositions: *Adventures in Harmony*, 1910; *6 Ings: Floating Frisking Fleeting Scooting Wafting Seething*, 1916; *Aeolian Harp*, 1923; Ensemble for Strings, 1954; Twenty Symphonies: No. 1, 1916—17; No. 2, *Anthropos*, 1938; No. 3, *Gaelic Sympony*, 1942; No. 4, *Short Symphony*, 1946; No 5, 1948; No. 6, 1950—55; No. 7, 1952; No. 8, *Choral* for chorus & orchestra; No 9, 1953; No. 10, for chamber orchestra, 1953; No. 11, *The 7 Rituals of Music*, 1953; No. 12, 1955—56; No. 13, *Madras Symphony* for small orchestra & 3 Indian instruments, 1957–58; No. 14 (1960–61); No. 15, *Thesis*, 1961; No. 16, *Icelandic Symphony*, 1962; No. 17, 1962–63; No. 18, 1964; No. 19, 1965; No. 20, 1965; *Persian Set for 12 instruments*, 1956–57.

Recordings: *Piano Music: Twenty Pieces Played by the Composer* (1963). Washington, DC: Smithsonian/Folkways, 1993. [This disc concludes with a tape of Cowell describing each of the selections.]; *American Masters: Henry Cowell*. Composers Recordings, 1997. *Songs of Henry Cowell*. Albany Records, 1998; Hays, Sorrel Doris. *The Piano Music of Henry Cowell* (1977). Frederick, MD.: Town Hall (THCD-48), 1997.

Compositions Catalog: Lichtenwanger, William. *The Music of Henry Cowell: A Descriptive Catalog*. Brooklyn, NY: ISAM, 1986.

Writings: *Charles Ives and His Music*. New York: Oxford University Press, 1955; *New Musical Resources* (1930). New York: Something Else, 1969; ——, ed. *American Composers on American Music: A Symposium* (1933). New York: Ungar, 1962.

Bibliography: Manion, M. L. *Writings About Henry Cowell: An Annotated Bibliography*. Brooklyn, NY: ISAM, 1982.

Interpretation: Mead, Rita. *Henry Cowell's New Music 1925–1936*. Ann Arbor: UMI Research, 1981.

CRAGG, Tony

(1949).

Cragg emerged in the late 1970s as the most interesting of a group of young sculptors who sought to reorient British sculpture away from landscape and onto the urban environment, rejecting the influence of the Earth Artists who preceded them. Cragg's earliest significant works are assemblies of found and used manufactured objects, distributed in carefully arranged patterns on gallery floors and walls. In *New Stones, Newton's Tones* (1978), he laid on the floor such items as small shovels, combs, cigarette lighters, spoons, and broken plates. The items were arranged in a rectangle and painted in solid colors that made a rainbow running from one end of the pattern to the other. At the time, his works were viewed as attempts to flout traditional sculptural practices, particularly the conventions of direct carving and the welding of metals, but such titles as *New Stones, Newton's Tones* indicated, or should have, that his concerns were more intellectually intriguing. Cragg in that period was something of an archeologist of contemporary culture, conveying the idea that the very science upon which our industrial civilization is based, and the simple geometric conceptions that underlie that science, have become obsolete and are already part of the past. Simple linear geometry is virtually useless in the post-Newtonian science that is now directing the development of technology. (Cragg worked as a scientist before he became an artist.)

More interesting, more direct, and more individual are Cragg's later works, in which he attempts to employ directly more complex forms of geometry. In such works as *Envelope* (1998), a single molded shape overlays the forms of simple geometry upon more mathematically complex ones, such as toruses. (A torus is a smoothly curving shape whose surface folds in on itself to create a tube that runs through the entire form and emerges on the other side. One very simple example is a donut.) Cragg's work shares with the recent work of Richard Serra this interest in advanced geometry.

—Mark Daniel Cohen

Works: *New Stones, Newton's Tones*, 1978; *Oval*, 1982; *Spectrum*, 1983; *Eroded Landscape*, 1987; *Spill*, 1987; *Matruschka*, 1989; *Envelope*, 1998.

Exhibition Catalogs: Barnes, Lucinda, Knode, Marilu, Francis, Mark, McEvilley, Thomas, and Schjeldahl, Peter. *Tony Cragg: Sculpture 1975–1990*. Newport Beach, CA: Newport Harbor Art Museum & New York: Thames and Hudson, 1991; Weber, John S. *Material Identity: Sculpture between Nature and Culture, April 20-June 27, 1993*. Portland, OR: Portland Art Museum, 1993; *Sculptures on the Page: Tony Cragg*. Leeds, England: Henry Moore Institute, 1996; Bond, Anthony and Hopper, Robert. *Tony Cragg*. Sydney, Australia: Art Gallery of New South Wales, 1997.

Interpretation: Celant, Germano. *Tony Cragg*. New York: Thames and Hudson, 1996.

CRAIG, Gordon

(16 January 1872–29 July 1966).

The illegimate son of the great British actress Ellen Terry, purportedly by the architect Edward William Godwin, Craig began as an actor. In addition to producing visual art, particularly wood-engraving, Craig worked in fringe English theaters at the beginning of the century, designing several productions that were regarded as challenges to the conventions of Victorian theater. Disappointed with his native country, he moved to the European continent where he developed a vision of an alternative theater less in actual productions than in books and articles, drawings and woodcuts, models and engravings. Many of his essays appeared in a periodical he founded and edited intermittently between 1908 and 1929, *The Mask*, and in his book *On the Art of Theatre* (1911). A series of etchings, *Scene* (1923), advocates a great flexible performing area in which a great variety of things can happen. Craig imagined a theater that would engage spectators through movement alone, probably without a plot or verbal text, but through the programmed movement of sound, light, and people in motion.

Not unlike other theatrical visionaries, he thought the actor to be the most recalcitrant link in a retrograde chain, and so proposed in his classic 1907 essay that "in his place comes the inanimate figure—the Uber-marionette we may call him." Craig continued, "The Uber-marionette will not compete with life—rather will go beyond it. Its ideal will not be the flesh and blood but rather the body in trance—it will aim to clothe itself with a death-life beauty while exhaling a living spirit." Raising the ante yet more, as any good polemicist should, Craig concluded:

> I pray earnestly for the return of the image—the Uber-marionette to the theatre; and when he comes again and is but seen, he will be loved so well that once more will it be possible for the people to return to their ancient joy in ceremonies—once more will Cre-

ation be celebrated—homage rendered to existence—
and divine and happy intercession made to Death.

Wow! Writing like this could be influential, even as it was resisted and dismissed. Craig lived another fifty years, producing books about his mother and other British theatricists, in addition to an autobiography, *Index to the Story of My Days* (1957); so that his evocative prose about theater remained more influential than any productions.

Books: *Towards a New Theatre*. London: Dent, 1913; *On the Art of the Theatre*. Boston: Small, Maynard & Co., 1925; *The Theater Advancing* (1919). New York: B. Blom, 1963; *Books and Theatres* (1925). Freeport, NY: Books for Libraries, 1967; *Index to the Story of My Days*. NY: Viking, 1957.

Anthology: *Craig on Theatre*. Ed. J. Michael Watson. London: Methuen, 1983.

Biography: Craig, Edward. *Gordon Craig: The Story of His Life*. New York: Knopf, 1968.

Exhibition Catalog: Rood, Arnold. *Edward Gordon Craig: Artist of the Theatre, 1872–1966*. New York: New York Public Library, 1971.

Interpretation: Innes, Chris. *Edward Gordon Craig: A Vision of the Theatre*. Amsterdam: Harwood, 1998; Marker, Frederick. *Edward Gordon Craig and the Pretenders*. Carbondale: S. Illinois University Press, 1981; Eynat-Confino, Irene. *Beyond the Mask: Gordon Graig, Movement, and the Actor*. Carbondale: S. Illinois University Press, 1987.

CRAWFORD SEEGER, Ruth

(3 July 1901–18 November 1953).

The wife of the pioneering musicologist Charles Seeger, the mother of the folksingers Peggy S. (1935) and Mike S. (1933) and stepmother to the more legendary Pete S. (1919), she composed several advanced chamber works of a quality that has become more appreciated over time. The most famous is her *String Quartet* (1931), whose slow movement, according to Nicolas Slonimsky, "anticipates the 'static' harmonies and 'phase shifts' prominent in minimal music." The pianist-composer Sorrel Hays praises Crawford's 1920s piano preludes for "structural spareness divorced from nineteenth-century harmonies and climactic structures." An early, busy short masterpiece is *Study in Mixed Accents* (1930) for solo piano. After her family's move to Washington, D.C., in 1935, Crawford's music succumbed to the political fashions of the time and her family's folkloristic interests. She reportedly transcribed several thousand American folk songs from recordings at the Library of Congress and made exquisite piano accompaniments for hundreds of them. Some of the latter appear in two children's songbooks.

Works: *5 Preludes,* 1924–25; *Adventures of Tom Thumb*, for narrator and piano. 1925; *4 Preludes,* 1927–28; Suite for small orchestra,1926; Suite for five winds and piano,1927; *Suite No. 2* for strings and piano, 1929; *Piano Study in Mixed Accents*, 1930; *Four Diaphonic Suites*, for various instruments, 1930; *String Quartet*, 1931; *Rissolty, Rossolty*, 1939.

Recordings: *Animal Folk Songs for Children.* Folkways Records, 1968; *American Masters: Ruth Crawford*. With *Study in Mixed Accents* & Sonata for Violin and Piano. New York: CRI, 1993; *Ruth Crawford Seeger: Portrait.* Deutsche Grammophon, 1998.

Interpretation: Gaume, Matilda. *Ruth Crawford Seeger: Memoirs, Memories, Music*. Metuchen, NJ: Scarecrow Press, 1986; Straus, Joseph N. *The Music of Ruth Crawford Seeger*. New York: Cambridge University Press, 1995; Tick, Judith. *Ruth Crawford Seeger: A Composer's Search for American Music*. New York: Oxford University Press, 1997.

CRESHEVSKY, Noah

(31 January 1945).

Trained in music composition at the Eastman School of Music and Juilliard, Creshevsky became by the 1980s an audiotape artist using familiar devices of processing and editing in distinguished ways. *In Other Words* (1976) enhances the distinctive speaking voice of JOHN CAGE. His *Highway* (1978), which is *MUSIQUE CONCRÈTE* of and about familiar Americana, becomes an acoustic trip through the aural equivalent of POP ART. His ten-minute *Strategic Defense Initiative* (1986), its title alluding to President Reagan's "Star Wars" proposal, draws upon the soundtrack of Bruce Lee movies to satirize sadism. Another Creshevsky departure involves giving instrumentalists a score composed not of traditional musical notes but only of words. More recently, he has been using electronic sampling to incorporate fragments of classical music into his own work.

Recordings: *Man and Superman*, with *Variations* (1987), *Electric String Quartet* (1988), *Memento Mori* (1989), *Electric Partita* (1990), *Talea* (1991). Baton Rouge, LA: Centaur (8867 Highland Rd. #206, 70808), 1992; *Auxesis—Electroacoustic Music*, with Charles Amirkhanian, with the former's *Borrowed Time, Private Lives, Coup d'état*. Baton Rouge, LA: Centaur, 1995.

C

CRESTON, Bill

(6 March 1932).

Initially a painter, he was among the first aspiring filmmakers to recognize that the technology of black and white video, introduced in the late 1960s, was a less expensive medium for producing moving images. Creston was early in teaching video around New York City and was, he thinks, among the first to keep a video journal (whose tape, alas, did not survive subsequent decades as well as handwritten pages). In the mid-1970s, he turned to another new medium, Super-8 sound color film, which was a gauge much cheaper than the 16 millimeter stock used by most independent filmmakers (or the 35mm. used in Hollywood), while it offered color at a time when, remember, videotape capable of recording in color was far more expensive than the standard black-and-white. "I chose Super-8 becase it was possible to make complete color sound films entirely on my own. The price of all the equipment, mostly used, was so low that I could purchase all of it myself from the receipts of taxi-driving in the City." Although this alternative film medium never became popular, it did have credibility—at least as measured by screenings at major museums and occasional festivals around the world.

Early into less expensive new media, Creston also pioneered another low-cost contemporary form. In 1969, as he recalls:

> I made a piece called *Construction Site*, which was meant to blend so well into the real world as to become a part of it, and not be noticed as anything special, obtrusive as it might be. I bought lumber, traffic-marking-yellow paint, special blinking lights, and other materials. I built a fake construction site, including an obviously fake hole, installing it on 6th Avenue between 22nd and 23rd Streets, in front of a vacant store. It was up for weeks, and several times protected by the police, who supplemented my materials with barricades.

Reflecting 1960s ideals of meshing art with life and of making art available to a public larger than well-heeled collectors, *Construction Site* also echoed Creston's films in a fascination with New York City street life.

Films: *Open 7 Days a Week, 24 Hours a Day*. New York: Bill Creston (463 West St., A-628, New York, NY 10014-2035), 1976; *Six Short Films*. New York: Bill Creston, 1976; *Ola: A Film by Her Father*. New York: Bill Creston, 1977; *I Saw Where You Was Last Night*. New York: Bill Creston, 1984; *Garbage, Etc*. New York: Bill Creston, 1991; *Lunch Hour*. New York: Bill Creston, 1996; *Duets*. New York: Bill Creston, 1996.

Videotapes: *Bert Lahr*. New York: Bill Creston, 1969; *Video Journal (and European Journal)*. New York: Bill Creston, 1970–75; *Newsdealer*. New York: Bill Creston, 1972; *Urinals*. New York: Bill Creston, 1974.

CROSBY, Harry

(4 June 1898–10 December 1929).

Commonly regarded as the epitome of the self-destructive 1920s poet (and vulgarly exploited for that myth in a Geoffrey Wolff biography), Crosby also wrote some "mad" inspired prose, and at least one great VISUAL POEM that will ensure his literary immortality, "Photoheliograph (for Lady A.)":

black black black black black
black black black black black
black black black black black
black black black black black
black black SUN black black
black black black black black
black black black black black
black black black black black
black black black black black
black black black black black

Another similarly simple-minded gem, "Pharmacie du Soleil," simply lists its chemical components: "calcium iron hydrogen sodium nickel magnesium cobalt," etc.

Prolific once he quit his day-job at a bank, Crosby self-published between 1924 and 1939 several handsomely produced books, mostly under his Black Sun imprint (founded in 1928), which also published original works by Kay Boyle, Archibald MacLeish, and EUGENE JOLAS.

Another memorable Crosby text is his "Short Introduction to the Word," which is, inadvertently perhaps, one of the great satirical manifestos of literary modernism. Consider the concluding paragraphs:

> 4) I believe that certain physical changes in the brain result in a given word—this word having the distinguished characteristic of unreality being born neither as a result of connotation nor of conscious endeavor: Starlash.
>
> 5) There is the automatic word as for instance with me the word Sorceress; when the word goes on even while my attention is focused on entirely different subjects just as in swimming my arms and legs go on automatically even when my attention is focused on subjects entirely different from swimming such as witchcraft for instance or the Sorceress.

Richly indulgent as well as indulgently rich (as the nephew of J. Pierpont Morgan), Crosby drank to excess, gambled away much of his inheritance, and frequently drugged himself, in addition to squandering his genuine innovative literary talent and supportive taste for innovative literature. A few months after the stock market collapse, he shot another man's new wife and then himself in a New York City studio apartment he used for assignations. The tragedy of his life is featured in Malcolm Cowley's popular memoir of the literary 1920s, *Exile's Return* (1934), though, in fact, the two men scarcely knew each other, so mythical did Crosby become and, even later, continue to be.

Works: *Shadows of the Sun*. Paris: Black Sun, 1928; *Transit of Venus* (1928). 2d ed. Paris: Black Sun, 1929; *Mad Queen*. Paris: Black Sun, 1929; *Sleeping Together*. Paris: Black Sun, 1929; *Collected Poems of Harry Crosby*. 4 vols. Paris: Black Sun, 1931; *Shadows of the Sun: The Diaries*. Ed. Edward Germain. Santa Barbara, CA: Black Sparrow, 1977.

Interpretation: Cowley, Malcolm. *Exile's Return* (1934). New York: Viking, 1956.

Websites: http://www.pagan.net/~tomhb/banger/crosby/ and http://www.sirius.com/~ademas/fire/index.html

(Both offer poems and other information).

Biography: Wolff, Geoffrey. *Black Sun: The Brief Transit and Violent Eclipse of Harry Crosby*. New York: Random House, 1976.

CROSS, Doris

(10 December 1906–11 January 1994).

A widely-exhibited painter, visual poet, sculptor, filmmaker, and lithographer who studied with Hans Hoffman,

Cross was one of the earliest artists to "treat" books: i.e., to subject books' texts to paint or other means that emphasize, change, obscure, or delete parts of them in order to render them anew, often as lyric poetry (enhanced and/or commented on by the shapes and colors used in the re-rendering). Her one great inspiration in bookart was to treat the columns of a dictionary (the 1913 edition of *Webster's Secondary School Dictionary*), playing the language of intuitively playful semi- or non-representational visual images against the attempt at systematic rational clarity that a dictionary represents, and the multi-connotative poetry of the texts she "found" against rigorously denotative *definition*. Thus, she isolated the phrase "the infinitive with" above the phrase "as in prayer," in a column whose heading reads "MAY" . . . next to a column with a sparrow engraved in it whose heading is "MEANING." Elsewhere she achieved a wonderful tension by playing a "REVERENCE" column (which contained "musing; daydream/vision/reversing") against a "REVOLVER" column, at the bottom of which is part of a diagram of a handgun's trigger mechanism. Cross's "col.umns," as she called them, remain regrettably incompletely studied, published, and celebrated, three main signs of their excellence.

—Bob Grumman

Books: *Col.umns*. San Francisco: Trike (277 23rd Avenue, 94121), 1982.

CROWDER, Al

(1904–1981).

Crowder was a radio personality who invented the imaginary company Orville K. Snav and Associates and its line of BunaBs. Each BunaB was actually an example of primitive CONCEPTUAL ART. Conceived as a form of humor (which is the most conceptual art can hope for), these BunaBs were generally small pieces of machinery that Crowder/Snav distributed with arcane and ridiculous instructions and warranties. The most famous BunaB (produced in an edition of 40,000) was two pieces of wire taped together and stored in an empty clarinet reed case. The customer who returned its registration card would be greeted with a long, rambling letter explaining the difficulties of Orville K. Snav's life at that particular time. Two other BunaBs were interesting examples of PRAECISIO: # 3, "The Man's Between Shave Lotion," which was an empty plastic bottle whose contents were to be reconstituted by adding water; and # 5, a completely blank record, designed to be listened to while watching television.

—Geof Huth

Bibliography: Dickson, Paul. *Family Words: The Dictionary for People Who Don't Know a Frone from a Brinkle*. Reading, MA: Addison-Wesley, 1988.

CRUMB, R.

(30 August 1943, b. Robert C.).

Probably the most famous of the underground comics artists of the 1960s, Crumb was instrumental in expanding the possibilities for the comic book form. Before him and his compatriots, comic books had superheroes and fuzzy animal stories, but little else. What Crumb added to comic books was not only graphic sex (often undertaken by fuzzy animals) and freedom of expression, but also a disdain for narrative flow. Crumb was more willing than anyone else to experiment with narrative—to tell the modern disjointed story. Some of his stories lacked protagonists or stable settings, and although such tricks might have been common in the NOUVEAU ROMAN, they were never common in American comic book art. Crumb is best remembered for his character Fritz the Cat and his slogan (with its familiar big-footed incarnation) "Keep on Truckin'." Remarkably, Crumb lost two lawsuits: one in which he tried to obtain compensation for the use of Fritz the Cat in the eponymous X-rated cartoon and a similar suit concerning the once-ubiquitous "Keep on Truckin'"

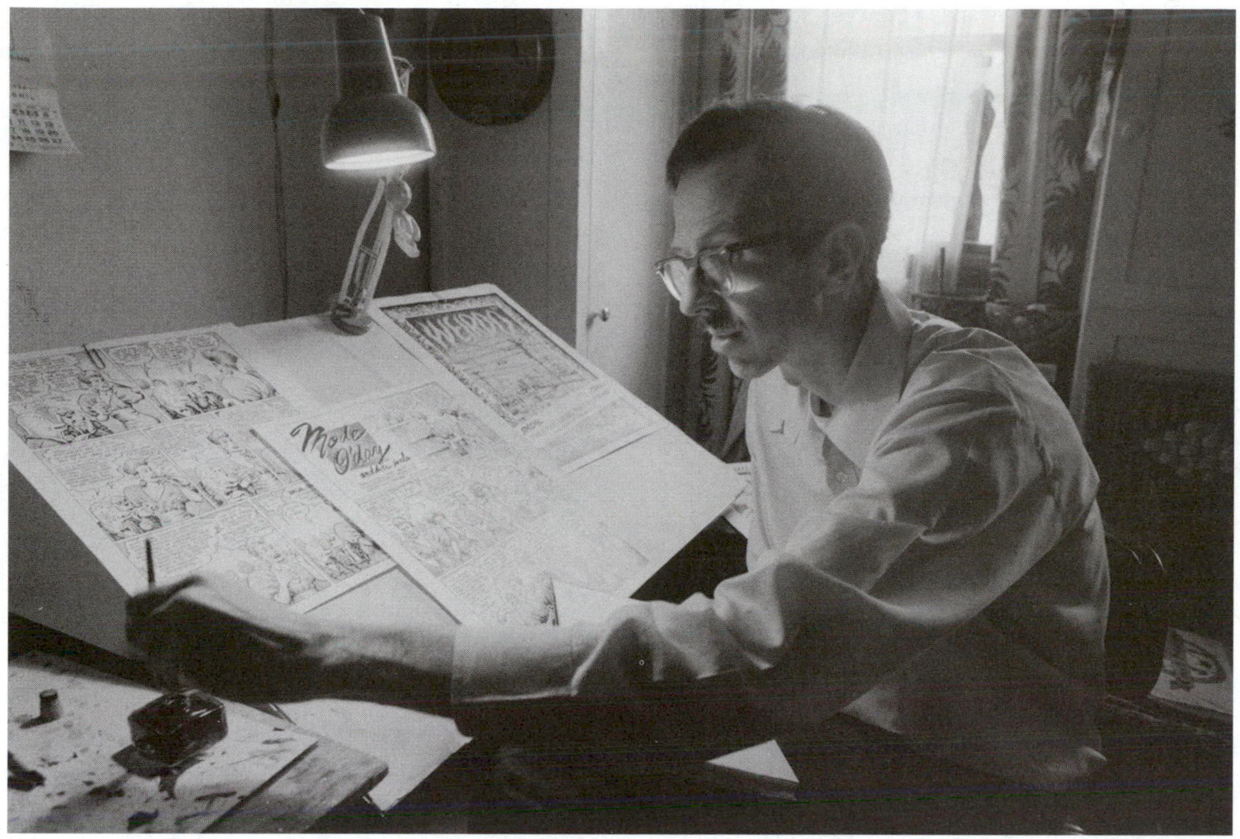

R. Crumb at work in his studio, 9 April 1985. CORBIS/Roger Ressmeyer.

logo. A quirky and powerful portrait of Crumb and his family emerges from Terry Zwigoff's intimate documentary film *Crumb* (1995).

—Geof Huth

Anthology: *The R. Crumb Coffee Table Art Book*. Boston: Little, Brown, 1997; *Crumb's Head Comix*. New York: Simon & Schuster, 1988; *The Complete Crumb*. 11 vols. Seattle, WA: Fantagraphics (7563 Lake City Way, NE, 98115), 1995; *The New Comics: Interiews from the Pages of Comics Journal*. Ed. Gary Groth and Robert Fiore. New York: Berkeley, 1988.

Website: http://w1.870.telia.com/~u87004729/ (Among others; this one has links).

Documentary: Terry Zwigoff, *Crumb*, 1995.

CUBISM

(c. 1907–1921).

Cubism was the creation of the painters Georges Braque (1882–1963) and Pablo Picasso, working separately in Paris around 1907. Art historians customarily divide its development into two periods: Analytic Cubism (1907–12) and Synthetic Cubism (1912–21). The signature of Cubism is the rendering of solid objects—whether they be musical instruments, household objects, or human forms—as overlapping "cubes" or planes, giving the illusion of portraying simultaneously several different perspectives and, by extension, different moments in time. Regarding the radical implications of such reinterpretation of pictorial representations, the art historian Robert Rosenblum (1927) wrote:

> For the traditional distinction between solid form and the space around it, Cubism substituted a radically new fusion of mass and void. In place of earlier perspective systems that determined the precise location of discrete objects in illusory depth, Cubism offered an unstable structure of dismembered planes in indeterminate spatial positions. Instead of assuming that the work of art was an illusion of a reality that lay behind it, Cubism proposed that the work of art was itself a reality that represented the very process by which nature is transformed into art.

C

The rigorous analytic phase epitomized a more austere Cubism, as painters eschewed traditional subject matter and a full palette in the course of dissecting light, line, and plane, incidentally draining much earlier emotional content from painting. Thus, a typical Cubist still life from this period might consist of several intersecting planes portrayed in various neutral, nearly monochromatic tones (often different shades of brown).

Synthetic Cubism, by contrast, introduced objects found in the real world, such as newspaper clippings, wallpaper, ticket stubs, or matchbooks, which were attached to the canvas. Rosenblum comments on an example, "Perhaps the greatest heresy introduced in this collage concerns Western painting's convention that the artist achieve his illusion of reality with paint or pencil alone." Cubist painters introduced an additional visual irony by simulating these objects, thus introducing *trompe l'oeil* effects by creating false woodgrains or wallpaper patterns, making it appear as if fragments of these objects were part of the canvas. A fuller palette and more sensuous texture were other hallmarks of Synthetic Cubism.

The Cubist movement was perhaps as important as an intellectual revolt against "pretty" art as for its actual products. Many Cubist paintings inspired heated debate not only among art critics but among the general public as well. Perhaps the most famous single example was MARCEL DUCHAMP'S *Nude Descending a Staircase*, No. 2 (1912), which was the star of the ARMORY SHOW NEW YORK, although it could be said that Duchamp departed from Cubism as quickly as he entered it. The power of Cubism is evident not only in such immediate successors as FUTURISM and VORTICISM, especially in WYNDHAM LEWIS'S illustrations for Shakespeare's *Timon of Athens* (1913 or 1914), but also in the careers of such older artists as PIET MONDRIAN and KAZIMIR MALEVICH, and then, more than a generation later, in the best work of WILLEM DE KOONING, among other major modern painters.

Bibliography: Rosenblum, Robert. *Cubism and Twentieth-Century Art* (1961). New York: Abrams, 1977; Gamwell, L.W. *Cubist Criticism, 1907–1925*. Ann Arbor, 1980.

Exhibition Catalog: Barr, Alfred H. Jr. *Cubism and Abstract Art*. New York: MOMA, 1936; Repr. Cambridge, MA: Belknap Press of Harvard University Press, 1986; *The Essential Cubism, 1907–1920*. London: Tate, 1983.

CUBO-FUTURISM

(c. 1909).

This term arose in Russia to distinguish native work from EUROPEAN CUBISM. Whereas the work of Natalia Goncharova (1882–1962) and Mikhail Larionov (1882–1964) favored a POST-PICASSO modernist primitivism based upon Russian peasant art, the brothers Burliuk (Vladimir [1886–1916] and David [1882–1967]) preferred more urban subjects. The innately mercurial KAZIMIR MALEVICH used this epithet for works he submitted for exhibitions in 1912 and 1913. Vladimir Markov's *Russian Futurism* (1968) devotes an entire chapter to Cubo-Futurism in poetry.

Bibliography: Barooshian, Vahan D. *Russian Cubo-Futurism*. The Hague: Mouton, 1974; Gray, Camilla. *The Russian Experiment in Art*. London, England: Thames & Hudson, 1962; Markov, Vladimir. *Russian Futurism*. Berkeley: University of California Press, 1968; Compton, Susan P. *The World Backwards: Russian Futurist Books 1912–1916*. London; Museum, 1978.

CULTURAL WORKER

(1980s).

At least by the 1980s, the left-wing political sphere of the Western avant-garde took on this term to represent the usual meaning of Artist. A cultural worker, therefore, is a laborer, just like any member of the proletariat, but one who works to develop "cultural" materials (poems, films, plays, novels, sculptures, paintings), rather than, say, Chevrolets. The interesting fact about self-proclaimed "cultural workers" as artists is that their interests were often less artistic than political. As a matter of fact, the term was most prominent during 1989–93, during the period of the greatest discussion of the ART STRIKE. And the goal of this strike was to get artists not to produce art. This term has been common in the writings of the neoist MONTY CANTSIN, KAREN ELIOT, and others involved in the ART STRIKE.

—Geof Huth

Bibliography:. Home, Stewart. *Neoist Manifestos/The Art Strike Papers*. Stirling, Scotland: A.K., 1991.

CUMMINGS, E.E.

(14 October 1894–3 September 1962).

The avant-garde Cummings is not the author of lyrics reprinted in nearly every anthology of American verse or of a name entirely in lowercase letters, but of several more inventive, less familiar poems. Appreciation of this alternative Cummings should begin with such poetic wit as "Gay-Pay-Oo" for the Soviet secret police (G.P.U.); his use of prefixes and suffixes to modify a root word in various subtle ways (so that "unalive" is not synonymous with dead); his evocative typography (as in a familiar poem about grasshoppers, or "t,a,p,s," or "SpRiN,K,LiNG"); and his integration of the erotic with the experimental. He wrote poems that cohere more in terms of sound than syntax or semantics: "bingbongwhom chewchoo/laugh dingle nails personally/bin" loamhome picpac /obviously scratches tomorrowlobs." He wrote abstract poetry long before most of the LANGUAGE-CENTERED gang were born, the opening poem of *1 X 1* (1944) beginning: "nonsum blob a /cold to /skylessness /sticking fire Amy are you /are birds our all/and one gone/away the they." "No Thanks" (1935) is an extraordinary poem beginning "bright" that contains only eleven discrete words, all six letters or less in length; they are successfully broken apart and nonsyntactically combined to form fifteen lines of forty-four words—all three-letter words appearing thrice, all four-letter words four times, etc. With such rigorous structures Cummings presaged several major developments in contemporary avant-garde poetry. Though some of these innovations were not included in earlier selections and collections of Cummings's poetry, thankfully they all appear in the latest edition of his *Complete Poems* (1991), which incidentally demonstrates that these more experimental poems were written throughout his career, rather than, say, being bunched within a short period. They are featured in *AnOther E. E. Cummings* (1998), which also includes examples of his highly experimental plays, perhaps the first film scenario written in America by a noted poet (1926), elliptical narratives, theater criticism that emphasizes performance over drama, and the opening chapter of a text known only as [*No Title*] (1930), whose prose broaches abstraction. Consider these concluding lines from its opening chapter:

> while generating a heat so terrific as to evaporate the largest river of the kingdom—which,completely disappearing in less than eleven seconds,revealed a gilt-edged submarine of the UR type,containing(among other things)the entire royal family(including the king, who still held his hat in his hand) in the act of escaping,disguised as cheeses.

(A reviewer of *AnOther E.E.C.* noted that the book places Cummings "not among Pound and Eliot, with whom he has little in common, but rather with Russian Futurists and

Dadaists; with Latin American and German concrete poets; [etc.]", all of which I wish I had said before him, because this reassignment is true.) No appreciation of the avant-garde Cummings would be complete without acknowledging his *Eimi* (1933, often out-of-print), a prose memoir of his disillusioning 1931 trip to the Soviet Union, as audacious in style as it is in content, along with the brilliant retrospective summary of this book that he prepared for a reprint in the late 1950s.

C

Cummings also produced a considerable amount of visual art, which has never been fully exhibited (even though his oeuvre reportedly includes over 2,000 paintings and over 10,000 sheets of drawings). In short, don't forget the avant-garde Cummings behind the familiar versifier.

Writings: Cummings, E.E. *Eimi* (1933). 2d ed. New York: Grove, 1958; *The Complete Poems, 1904–62*. New York: Norton, 1991; *100 Selected by E.E. Cummings*. New York: Grove, 1989; *AnOther E.E. Cummings*. Ed. Richard Kostelanetz. New York: Liveright, 1998.

Visual Art: *CIOPW*. New York: Covici-Friede, 1930.

Collected Correspondence: *Selected Letters of E. E. Cummings*. Ed. F. W. Dupee and George Stade. New York: Harcourt, Brace, 1969; *Pound/Cummings*. Ed. Barry Ahearn. Ann Arbor: University of Michigan Press, 1996.

Biography: Norman, Charles. *E. E. Cummings: The Magic Maker*. New York: Duell, Sloan, Pearce, 1964. Kennedy, Richard S. *Dreams in the Mirror*. New York: Liveright, 1980.

Website: http://members.tripod.com/~DWipf/cummings.html ("Unofficial" links page).

Interpretation: Kostelanetz, Richard. "E.E. Cummings" (1980). In *The Old Poetries and the New*. Ann Arbor: University of Michigan Press, 1981; Cohen, Milton A. *Poet and Painter: The Aesthetics of E.E. Cummings*. Detroit: Wayne State University Press, 1987; Fairley, Irene R. *E.E. Cummings & Ungrammar*. Searingtown, NY: Windmill, 1975; Rotella, Guy, ed. *Critical Essays on E.E. Cummings*. Boston: G.K. Hall, 1984.

CUNNINGHAM, Merce

(16 April 1919).

After years off the edge of American dance, Cunningham became, beginning in the late 1960s, the principal figure in advanced American choreography, remaining, even today, its most influential individual, as much by example as by becoming a monument whose activity still intimidates his successors. Originally part of MARTHA GRAHAM'S dance company, he presented in 1944, in collaboration with JOHN CAGE, his first New York recital of self-composed solos. Rejected by dance aficionados who were devoted to prior masters, Cunningham earned his initial following among professionals in other arts.

The initial reason for the dance world's neglect was that Cunningham had drastically reworked many dimensions of dance-making: not only the articulation of performance time, but the use of theatrical space; not only the movements of dancers' bodies, but their relationship to one another on the stage. For instance, if most ballet and even modern dance had a front and a back, Cunningham's works are designed to be seen from all sides; and though theatrical custom has forced him to mount most of his performances on a proscenium stage (one that has a front and thus a back), his pieces have also been successfully performed in gymnasiums and museums.

Time in Cunningham's work is nonclimactic, which means that a piece begins not with a fanfare but a movement, and it ends not with a flourish but simply when the performers stop. Because he eschews the traditional structure of theme and variation, the dominant events within a work seem to proceed at an irregular, unpredictable pace; their temporal form is, metaphorically, lumpy. "It's human time," he explains, "which can't be too slow or too fast, but includes various time possibilities. I like to change tempos."

Cunningham's dances generally lack a specific subject or story, even though interpretation-hungry spectators

Merce Cunningham in *Theatre Piece* at the Phoenix Theatre, with music by Morton Feldman and John Cage, 16 February 1960. Copyright © Fred W. McDarrah.

sometimes identify particular subjects and/or semblances of narrative (and more than one Cunningham dancer has suspected the existence of secret stories). It follows that his dancers eschew dramatic characterizations for nonparticularized roles, which is to say that Cunningham dancers always play themselves and no one else. Just as he defied tradition by allowing parts of a dancer's body to function disjunctively and nonsynchronously, so the distribution of Cunningham's performers customarily lacks a center—important events occur all over the performing area, even in the corners. The result is organized disorganization, so to speak, that initially seems chaotic only if strict forms of ordering are expected.

The titles of Cunningham's works tend to be abstract (*Aeon* [1961], *Winterbranch* [1964]), or situational (*Rain-Forest* [1968], *Summerspace* [1958], *Place* [1966]), or formally descriptive (*Story* [1963], *Scramble* [1967], *Walkaround Time* [1968]). As his dancers' gestures have been ends in themselves, rather than vehicles of emotional representation or narrative progression, Cunningham freed himself to explore the possibilities of human movement. In this respect, he has been incomparably inventive and remarkably prolific. To put it differently, once he decided that the old rules need not be followed, he was free to produce many dances filled with unfamiliar moves and innovative choreographic relationships.

Because Cunningham's activities are not symbolic of human activities or emotions, they are meant to be appreciated as ends in themselves. His dance thus demands not empathy from the spectator but, as Cage once explained, "your faculty of kinesthetic sympathy. It is this faculty we employ when, seeing the flight of birds, we ourselves, by identification, fly up, glide and soar." What seems at first inscrutable about Cunningham's choreography is quite comprehensible, providing one does not strive too hard to find underlying "significances." What you see is most of what there is.

Another departure comes with his use of music. Whereas most choreographers draw their inspirations from particular scores, Cunningham composes all but a few of his pieces without music; his dancers count to themselves for their cues. What music is heard in his work is customarily composed apart from the dance, as are the decor and costumes, and thus not mixed with the dance until the final rehearsals. The music tends to be harshly atonal and rhythmically irrelevant, as Cunningham has for his accompaniments long favored John Cage and those composers gathered around him.

Cunningham's choreographies are generally many-sided, nonlinear, nonexpressionistic, spatially noncentered, temporally nonclimactic, and compositionally assembled. The decor and sound are supplementary, rather than complementary; and the dancers are highly individualized. Though Cunningham's art is avant-garde, his sensibility is classical, which is to say precise, CONSTRUCTIVIST, and severe. He reveals the scope of his choreographic intelligence through his profound knowledge of dance and dancers, coupled with his seemingly limitless capacity for invention.

Selected Dances: *Root of an Unfocus*, 1944; *Four Walls*, 1944; *The Seasons*, 1947; *Sixteen Dances* for Soloist and Company of Three, 1951; *Solo Suite in Space & Time*, 1953; *Minutiae*, 1954; *Suite for Five*, 1956–58; *Summerspace*, 1958; *Antic Meet*, 1958; *Rune*, 1959; *Crises*, 1960; *Aeon*, 1961; *Story*, 1963; *Field Dances*, 1963; *Museum Event*, Nos.1, 2, & 3, 1964; *Winterbranch*, 1964; *Variations V*, 1965; *How to Pass, Kick, Fall, and Run*, 1965; *Place*, 1966; *Scramble*, 1967; *Walkaround Time*, 1968; *Rainforest*, 1968; *Canfield*, 1969; *Objects*, 1970; *Second Hand*, 1970; *Land Rover*, 1972; *Un Jour ou Deux*, 1973; *Sound Dance*, 1974–75; *Rebus*, 1975; *Torse*, 1976; *Travelogue*, 1977; *Road Runner*, 1979; *Gallopade*, 1981; *Quartet*, 1981; *Pictures*, 1984; *Doubles*, 1984; *Phrase*, 1984; *Native Green*, 1985; *Arcade*, 1985; *Grange Eve*, 1986; *Fabrications*, 1987; *Shards*, 1987; *Carousal*, 1987; *Doubles*, 1989; *Neighbors*, 1991; *Beach Birds*, 1991; *Loose Strife*, 1991; *Change of Address*, 1992; *Enter*, 1992; *Touchbase*, 1992; *Doubletoss*, 1993; *Breakers*, 1993; *CRWDSPCR*, 1993; *Ocean*, 1994; *Windows*, 1995; *Ground Level Overlay*, 1995; *Rando*, 1996.

Films and Videos: *Story*, 1964; *Variations*, 1966; *Westbeth*, 1974; *Blue Studio*, 1975; *Squaregame Video*, 1976; *Fractions I*, 1977; *Grant for Television*, 1977; *Torse*, 1978; *Locale*, 1979; *Channels/Inserts*, 1981; *Points in Space*, 1986; *Cage/Cunningham*, 1991; *CRWDSPCR*, 1996.

Books: with Frances Starr. *Changes*. New York: Something Else, 1968.

Recording: *Music for Merce*, with works by John Cage, Morton Feldman, Alexei Haieff, Lou Harrison. Eos Ensemble cond. Jonathan Sheffer. New York: BMG Catalyst, 1997.

Website: www.Merce.org

Interpretation: Kostelanetz, Richard, ed. *Merce Cunningham: Dancing in Space and Time* (1992). New York: Da Capo, 1998; Klosty, James. *Merce Cunningham* (1975). 2d ed. New York: Limelight, 1986; Lesschaeve, Jacqueline. *The Dancer and the Dance (1980)*. New York: Marion Boyars, 1985; Vaughan, David. *Merce Cunningham*. New York: Aperture, 1997.

CURRAN, Alvin

(13 December 1938).

An intelligent musician, educated at Brown and Yale universities, Curran usually works with electronic instruments in live performance, mostly in collaboration with others, initially with the ensemble MUSICA ELETTRONICA VIVA (MEV), which he organized while residing in Rome in the late 1960s. He typically mixes natural sounds with improvised music. His strongest work is *Crystal Psalms* (1988), which was commissioned by several European radio stations for live broadcast on the fiftieth anniversary of *Kristallnacht*. Incorporating the lamentations of Jewish cantors along with the repeated sound of glass breaking and live choruses, the piece vividly and inventively evokes the night when Jewish synagogues were destroyed all over Nazi Europe.

Compositions: *Music for Every Occasion*, Fifty Monodic Pieces for Any Use, 1967–77; *Songs and Views from the Magnetic Garden* for Voice Flugelhorn, Synthesizer and Tape, 1973–75; *Light Flowers, Dark Flowers*, for Piano, Ocarina, Synthesizer, and Tape, 1974–77; *The Works*, for Voice, Piano, Synthesizer, and Tape, 1977–1980; *The Crossing*, for 4 Sopranos, Chorus, 7 Instruments, and Tape. 1978; *Natural History*, for Tape, 1984; *Maritime Rites Satellite Music*—10 radio concerts for the Sounds of the Eastern U.S. Seaboard and Soloists, 1984–85; *Electric Rags I*, for Piano and Computer-controlled Synthesizers, 1985; *For Four or More*, for Amplified String Quartet and Computer-controlled Synthesizers, 1986; *7 Articles*, for 10 Instruments, 1989.

Recordings: *Crystal Psalms: Live from 6 European Countries* (1988). San Francisco: New Albion, 1993; *Schtyx*. New York: CRI, 1994; *Animal Behavior*. New York: Tzadik, 1995.

CYBERNETICS

(c. 1945).

This word was Norbert Wiener's coinage for self-steering mechanisms, which is to say those entities that, like human beings, respond intelligently to considerations of their own output. For example, if you step (output) on a hot coal (input), you'll probably pull back your foot and won't step on hot coals again. The idea was to make robots capable of this human trait. Necessarily incorporating the new disciplines of information theory, control systems, automatons, artificial intelligence, computer-simulated activities, and information processing, cybernetics had great influence, particularly in the 1960s.

A good example of cybernetic art would be the responsive mechanism, such as James Seawright's *Scanner* (1966), which is a large, plastic-ribbed, ball-shaped cage some six feet in diameter that is suspended from the ceiling. From the ball's lowest point extends a thin metal arm that contains photocells. A strobe light is projected upwards out of the piece's vertical core and then reflected by mirrors at its top, both down the plastic ribs and into the field around the sculpture. The photocells respond to decided changes in the room's lighting (natural as well as artificial, depending upon the hour) by halting the arm, which then swings in either direction (depending upon whether the alternating current is positive or negative at the precise moment of contact). The turning of the arm inevitably gives the photocells a different perspective on the field, causing another decisive change in the light that prompts the system to halt again and electronically reconsider the direction of its movement. In sum, then, this self-considering activity makes Scanner a genuine example of a cybernetic machine whose output (the movement of the arm) causes it to reconsider its input (the field of light) and to continually adjust itself. Within its normal operations are the cybernetic processes of response, information-processing, selection, and self-control.

Cynthia Goodman describes NICOLAS SCHÖFFER'S earlier "Cysp" series (the term being an abbreviation of cybernetics and spatiodynamics), which were CONSTRUCTIVIST structures that performed like robots. "They were mounted on four rollers that gave them the capability to move. Photoelectric cells, microphones, and rotating blades powered by small motors were connected to their scaffold-like structures. Controlled by an electronic brain developed by Philips [the Dutch electronics business], a Cysp responded to variations in color intensity, light, and sound." Goodman, who is the principal American critic/curator of this turf, praises a robot (1984–87) modeled after ANDY WARHOL that was constructed by a former Walt Disney animator to be a surrogate for Warhol on lecture tours. "An appropriate tribute to a man who so often claimed he wanted to be a machine, the computer-controlled robot is endowed with preprogrammed speech and fifty-four separate body movements that supposedly will be barely distinguishable from Warhol's."

Bibliography: Goodman, Cynthia. *Digital Visions*. New York: Abrams, 1987; Reichardt, Jasia. *Cybernetics, Art, and Ideas*. Greenwich, CT: New York Graphic Society, 1971; Seawright, James. "Phenomenal Art." (1970). In *Esthetics Contemporary*, ed. Richard Kostelanetz. 2d ed. Buffalo, New York: Prometheus, 1989.

C

CYBERPOETRY

(1990s).

The most common name for a brand of visual poetry that expresses itself over the Internet, rather than on the page, on film, or across the air, cyberpoetry has come into its own only as of the mid-1990s. Examples existed before that time, but without the development of HTML, the regularization of the Internet, and the mass ingress of people to the Internet, little occurred. These new kinetic poems have more potential than their decades of predecessors beginning with the kinetic semiobjects of the 1960s. Today's cyberpoet can work with color and movement just as easily as earlier poets worked with shapes and words. Some of the current crop of cyberpoetry stuns the viewer with its naturalness, their ease of presentation; these cyberpoems seem less forced than the crude beginnings of visual computer poetry in the mid-1980s. No real master of the form has yet appeared, but soon that should occur.

—Geof Huth

Web Site: Wr-eye-tings Scratchpad: http://www.burning-press.org/wreyeting/index.html (this site exhibits a quantity of cyberpoetry).

CYBERSPACE

(1984).

This term exploits the acceptance of the epithet Cybernetics without acknowledging its meaning, referring to something else instead. In *The Columbia Dictionary of Modern Literary and Cultural Criticism* (1995), a book self-consciously swimming in early 1990s currents, has the following definition that is quoted partly out of respect for modish authority:

> Cyberspace is a virtual world being developed through the interface of the human mind and computer technology. It is an electronically defined world in which a human can experience an environment completely outside the one that he or she physically occupies. The term was coined by the science-fiction writer William Gibson in his novel *Neuromancer*, although his imaginative rendition of the concept is a good deal ahead of the technology presently available and more dystopian than most writing on the subject.

In other words, this seems to be a pseudo-synonym for VIRTUAL REALITY, which, surprise, doesn't rate an entry in the *Columbia Dictionary*. Acceptance of Cyberspace has generated secondary epithets such as cybercafes (that sell computer time along with coffee) and cybermalls (which encourage shopping on the Internet), not to mention cyberjunkies (who are addicted to the Internet).

Bibliography: Benedikt, Michael, ed. *Cyberspace: First Steps*. Cambridge: MIT Press, 1991; Gibson, William. *Neuromancer*. New York: Ace, 1984; O'Donnell, James Joseph. *Avatars of the Word from Papyrus to Cyberspace*. Harvard University Press, 1998.

DAAD BERLINER KUNSTLERPROGRAMM

(The Berlin Artists' Program; 1963–).

Whereas most of the grant-giving programs in the arts have no shame about mostly supporting people whose work is conventional, who are safely established professionally, the first distinction of this artists' program, to translate, was to invite to Berlin, customarily for several months at a stretch, the world's avant-garde, including many of the artists and writers featured in this book—among them, MICHEL BUTOR (in 1964), GYÖRGY LIGETI (1969), DICK HIGGINS (1969, 1981), TOM JOHNSON (1983), YVONNE RAINER (1976), DAN GRAHAM (1976), ON KAWARA (1976), STEPHEN ANTONAKOS (1980), and DIAMANDA GALÀS (1987). Because the DAAD Artists' Program was part of the effort to bolster the culture of West Berlin as a vulnerable island inside East Germany, it wanted its beneficiaries to contribute to West Berlin culture. Founded by the Ford Foundation in 1963, perhaps with a dash of surreptitious U.S. government money, it was turned over to German control in 1966.

Had it not invited strong artists and encouraged them to work in Berlin, the DAAD program would have jeopardized its funding. (Few cultural benefactors known to me operate under as much reality-corrective.) So, instead of simply giving the recipient a place to live along with a stipend, as most "residency" programs do, DAAD administrators invited the program's guests to cultural events around town and introduced them to cultural officials who could mount exhibitions by the guest-artists, perform their music, commission radio programs, finance films, and much, much else. The American composer ROGER SESSIONS came in 1964 to oversee the first production anywhere of the opera *Montezuma* (1964) that he had begun decades before. George Rickey came to install a sculpture and returned annually to Berlin for many years after. A few guests stayed in Berlin, in part because their native countries were politically inhospitable: ARVO PÄRT (1981), the Chilean writer Antonio Avaria (1978), and the Korean composer Isang Yun (1964).

I know about the DAAD program, because I was a guest in 1981–83, and while in Berlin I wrote severely minimal fictions, coproduced one film and began another, and composed electroacoustic art for the radio stations, among other things I couldn't do back home. One way I can personally measure DAAD's decidedly avant-garde bias is that I have received grants for many things (scholarship, films, criticism, radio, visual art), but the Berliner Kunstlerprogramm was the only institution ever to reward me as a Schriftsteller, or writer, which is what most colleagues think I mostly do, albeit in unusual ways. Unfortunately, once the Berlin Wall went down and Germany was unified, the rationale for bolstering Berlin's isolated culture disintegrated. The Kunstlerprogramm has continued, albeit with fewer funds and, alas, less impact. It is lamentable that cultural officials in other major cities aren't so needy, or so smart.

Bibliography: *25 Jahre Berliner Künstlerprogramm: Blickwechsel*. Ed. Stefanie Endlich and Rainer Höynck. Berlin: Argon, 1988.

DADA

(c. 1916).

Dada and SURREALISM are popularly regarded as nearly synonymous movements, or as precursor and successor in the step-by-step history of modern art. Although their memberships overlapped and both espoused two major esthetic positions in common—the irrelevance of nineteenth-century forms of comprehension and the rejection of established modes of artistic rendering—they differed from each other in one crucial respect. Whereas Surrealism was the art of representing subconscious psychological terrains, Dada artists dealt primarily with the external world: the character of the commonly perceived environment; patterns of intellectual and artistic coherence; and standard definitions of meaning and significance. Therefore, while Surrealistic art presents the experience of hallucinations, Dada favors the distortion, usually ludicrous, of familiar contexts, and the portrayal of worldly absurdity. Surrealists ANDRÉ BRETON and SALVADOR DALI purportedly cast their interior fantasies in objective forms and, unlike the Dadaists, acknowledged the theories of Sigmund Freud. Dada master MARCEL DUCHAMP, by contrast, drew his models from the mundane environment (often *finding* his actual material there) and thereby confronted "Art" with "non-art," implicitly questioning all absolutist esthetics and creating impersonal objects that relate not to the psychic life of his audience but to their perception of the world around them. Finally, whereas Surrealism was serious, Dada established a radical esthetic that regarded laughter as a laudable response (so that any subsequent art incorporating humor was glibly classified as neo-Dada).

The masters of Dada used a variety of esthetic designs on behalf of their purposes. One consisted of infusing distortion and mundane gesture into a conventional form: painting a mustache on Leonardo's *Mona Lisa*, speaking gibberish at a poetry reading, fragmenting an image or narrative beyond the point of comprehension, introducing a urinal into an exhibition of sculpture, etc. At its best, this dash of nonsense revealed the ridiculous irrelevance of certain social or artistic hierarchies and conventions, as well as initiating such anticonventions for subsequent modern art as the artistic validity of all manufactured objects. This rejection of established forms of order complemented an anarchistic political bias. Whereas Surrealism is concise and imagistic, like poetry, Dada is more diffuse, like fiction.

Dada historically began in Zurich in 1915–16 when young artists, very much distressed by the burgeoning world war, engaged in esthetic actions, collectively and individually, that seemed socially subversive and politically revolutionary. The origin of the name Dada has been endlessly debated, some saying it comes from the French word for a "hobbyhorse," while others regard it as taken from the Slavonic words for "yes, yes." Within two years, similar developments occurred in New York and Berlin, particularly but also in Hanover, Cologne, and Paris. Zurich Dada was predominantly literary and theatrical. RICHARD HUELSENBECK brought to Berlin a Dada more predisposed to art exhibitions and political satire. Hanover Dada was mostly the invention of KURT SCHWITTERS; Cologne Dada depended upon MAX ERNST. Paris Dada initially consisted mostly of young writers briefly enamored with TRISTAN TZARA; most of them eventually became, like Tzara, Surrealists. New York Dada has a more complicated history, including as it does immigrants such as Marcel Duchamp and FRANCIS PICABIA, along with natives, all of whom gathered regularly at the West 67th Street apartment of the art patron Walter Conrad Arensberg (1878–1954). So pervasive were Dada ideas that they persisted even among those who publicly converted to Surrealism, who sometimes insisted that they were Dadaists at heart. So strong was the Dada esthetic that a Dada magazine appeared in the mid-1920s in the European boonies of the Soviet republic of Georgia (I remember the Slavic scholar John Bowlt [1943] sharing this information with a professional audience, all of us as ignorant of Georgian as he). So strong was Dada politics that even today we sympathize with the 1918 demand for "the introduction of progressive unemployment through comprehensive mechanization of every field of activity."

Anthologies: Motherwell, Robert. *The Dada Painters and Poets* (1948). 2d ed. Cambridge: Belknap, 1989; Lippard, Lucy. ed. *Dadas on Art*. Englewood Cliffs, NJ: Prentice–Hall, 1971.

Website: www.jough.com/dada

Interpretation: Ades, Dawn. *Dada and Surrealism*. London: Thames & Hudson, 1974; Coutts-Smith, Kenneth. *Dada*. London: Studio Vista, 1970; Dachy, Marc. *The Dada Movement*. New York: Rizzoli, 1990; Foster, Stephen, and Rudolf Kuenzli, eds. *Dada Spectrum: The Dialectics of Revolt*. Madison, WI: Coda Press, 1979; Foster, Steven C., ed. *Dada Dimensions*. Ann Arbor: UMI Research, 1985; Gale, Matthew. *Dada and Surrealism*. New York: Phaidon Press, 1998; Greenberg, Allen Carl. *Artists and Revolution: Dada and The Bauhaus, 1917–25*. Ann Arbor: UMI Research, 1979; Kuenzli, Rudolf E., ed. *New York Dada*. New York: Willis Locker & Owens, 1986; Naumann, Francis M. *New York Dada*. New York: Abrams, 1994; Pinchon, Brigitte, and Karl Riha, eds. *Dada Zurich: A Clown's Game from Nothing*. New York: G. K. Hall, 1977; Richter, Hans. *Dada: Art and Anti-Art* (c. 1966). London: Thames & Hudson, 1997; Rubin, William S. *Dada and Surrealist Art*. New York: Abrams, n.d. (c. 1968); Tashjian, Dickran. *Skyscraper Primitives: Dada and the American Avant-Garde, 1910–1925*. Middletown: Wesleyan University Press, 1975.

Exhibition Catalogs: Barr, Alfred H., Jr., ed. *Fantastic Art: Dada, Surrealism*. New York: MOMA, 1936; Rubin, William S. *Dada, Surrealism, and Their Heritage*. New York: MOMA, 1968; Schwarz, Arturo. *New York Dada: Duchamp, Man Ray, Picabia*. Münich: Städtische Galerie im Lenbachhaus, 1973; Ades, Dawn. *Dada and Surrealism Revisited*. London: Arts Council of Great Britain, 1978; *Dada and New York*. New York: Whitney Museum, 1979; Neff, Terry Ann R. *In the Mind's Eye: Dada and Surrealism*. Chicago: Museum of Contemporary Art, 1984; Naumann, Francis M., with Beth Venn. *Making Mischief: Dada Invades New York*. New York: Whitney Museum, 1996; Newland, Joseph N., ed. *No! Contemporary American DADA*. Seattle: Henry Art Gallery of the University of Washington, 1985.

DALI, Salvador

(11 May 1904–23 January 1989).

A painter and filmmaker, Dali is best remembered for meticulously rendered SURREALIST paintings that portray a dreamlike world with images of melting watches and half-open drawers suggesting erotic resonances. Such paintings influenced subsequent realists, sometimes called Magic Realists, who adopted the Surrealist interest in dream imagery while primarily portraying the real world. Dali also collaborated with LUIS BUÑUEL on two classic avant-garde films, *Un Chien andalou* (1928) and *L 'Age d'or* (1931), which feature Surrealist imagery and allusions to both classical mythology and Freudian symbolism. Such classic/contemporary juxtapositions of often violent images greatly influenced later filmmakers, both avant-garde and mainstream.

From roughly 1940 onwards, Dali and his wife Gaia, a true coconspirator, spent too much of their time in ceaseless self-promotion, making his face (with its outrageously wide-open eyes and pointed, pencil-thin mustache) as famous in its day as ANDY WARHOL'S or JOSEPH BEUYS'S visages would become years later, in all cases the face becoming a stronger professional signature, or afterimage, than any other of their creations. In this sense, Dali's persona was his most successful invention, a Surreal figure come to life. Among other affronts to the ideals of pro-

Salvador Dali, *Virgin of Guadalupe*, 1959. CORBIS/Francis G. Meyer/© 2000 Artists Rights Society (ARS), New York.

fessional integrity, Dali produced numerous signed editions that were printed *after* he autographed them. He authored books whose pages, as well as their titles, reflect his commitment to relentless self-promotion: *The Secret Life of Salvador Dali* (1961) and *Diary of a Genius* (1966). Books debunking him have since appeared, to no surprise.

Selected Works: *Senicitas*, 1926–27; *Dismal Sport*, 1929; *Great Masturbator*, 1929; *Persistence of Memory*, 1931; *Sleep*, 1936; *Soft Construction with Boiled Beans: Premonition of Civil War*, 1936; *Autumn Canabalism*, 1936; *The Enigma of Hitler*, 1937; *Metamorphosis of Narcissus*, 1937; *Atavism of Twilight*, 1937; *Endless Enigma*, 1938; *Madonna of Port Light*, 1949; *Exploding Raphaelesque Head*, 1951; *Corpuscular Madonna*, 1952; *Sacrament of the Last Supper*, 1955; *Dream of Christopher Columbus*, 1958–59; *Portraits of My Dead Brother*, 1963; *The Chair*, 1975.

Films: with Luis Buñuel. *Un Chien andalou*, 1928; *L 'Age d'or*, 1931.

Anthologies: Descharnes, Robert, & Néret, Gilles. *Salvadore Dali: The Paintings*. 2 vols. Köln: Taschen, 1994; *Salvadore Dali and Mixed Media Prints 1924–1980*. Eds. Ralph Michler and Lutz W. Löpsinger. Munich: Prestel, 1994.

Autobiography:*The Secret Life of Salvador Dali* (1942). New York: Dover, 1993; *Diary of a Genius* (1966). London, England: Hutchinson, 1990; *Dali*. New York: Abrams, 1968.

Biographies: Gibson, Ian. *The Shameful Life of Salvador Dali*. New York: Norton, 1998; Edgerton-Smith, Meredith. *The Persistence of Memory: A Biography of Dali*. New York: Random House, 1992; Cowles, Edgar. *The Case of Salvador Dali*. Boston: Little Brown, 1959.

Website: http://www.nol.net/~nil/dali.html (offers many images to download).

Exhibition Catalog: *Paintings, Drawings, Prints: Salvador Dali*. New York: MOMA, 1946.

Interpretation: Descharnes, Robert. *The World of Salvador Dali*. London: Macmillan, 1979; Gomez de la Serna, Ramon, et al. *Dali* (1977). Edison, NJ: Wellfleet-Book Sales, 1996; Morse, Albert Reynolds. *Dali: A Study of His Life and Work*. Greenwich, CT: New York Graphic Society, 1958; Nadeau, Maurice.*The History of Surrealism*. Trans. Richard Howard. New York: Macmillan, 1965.

DAMON, S. Foster

(22 February 1893–25 December 1971; b. Samuel F. D.). An intellectual pioneer, he is known to literary history for having published the first sympathetic critical book on WILLIAM BLAKE in America (1924) and for early extended critical essays on JAMES JOYCE. Music historians remember him for his pioneering 1936 collection of 100 American popular songs.

Damon is better remembered nowadays for his crucial influence on avant-garde people. VIRGIL THOMSON testifies that Damon introduced him to ERIK SATIE and GERTRUDE STEIN, in addition to publishing the song scores from which Thomson frequently drew American tunes for his own compositions. In 1952 E. E. CUMMINGS recalled that four decades before Damon "opened my eyes and ears not merely to Domenico Theocopuli [commonly known as 'El Greco'] and William Blake, but to all ultra (at that moment) modern music and poetry and painting." The impresario and critic LINCOLN KIRSTEIN wrote in his autobiography:

> I had as my freshman advisor S. Foster Damon, who had just published the first important American explication of William Blake's symbols and story. To Harvard's everlasting shame, he was denied tenure and was let go to Brown. Providence was then considered provincial exile, and it was this proprietary attitude of Harvard's Department of English that *Hound and Horn* [the literary magazine Kirstein founded] sought to contest.

Even in his absence, Damon had influence.

Were Damon not already enough of a hidden presence behind advanced arts in America, I recall that, of all the teachers I had, first in college, and then in graduate school here and abroad, he had the greatest impact in shaping the polyartistic, avant-garde intelligence behind this book, though, I should add, he was 67 years old when I first met him. A few years later, he published his *summa summarum* on Blake in the form of an alphabetical dictionary.

Books: *William Blake: His Philosophy and Symbols* (1924). Gloucester, MA: Peter Smith, 1958; *Amy Lowell: A Chronicle*. Boston: Hougton Mifflin, 1935; *Old American Songs*. Providence: Brown University Library, 1936; *A Blake Dictionary: The Idea and Symbols of William Blake* (1965). 2d ed., with a new index by Morris Eaves. Boston: Shambhala, 1979.

d

Interpretation: Cummings, E. E. *Six Nonlectures*. Cambridge: Harvard University Press, 1953; Kirstein, Lincoln. *By With To & From*. New York: Farrar, Straus, 1991; Rosenfeld, Alvin, ed. *Willliam Blake: Essays for S. Foster Damon*. Providence: Brown University Press, 1969; Thomson, Virgil. *Virgil Thomson*. New York: Knopf, 1967.

DAVIS, R. G.

See **SAN FRANCISCO MIME TROUPE**

DAVIS, Lydia

(15 July 1947).

Noted initially for translations of such French philosophical and literary behemoths as Jean-Paul Sartre, Michel Foucault, Georges Simenon, Maurice Blanchot, Michel Leiris, and MARCEL PROUST, Lydia Davis should be, one might expect, the author of bloated, tautologically epic fiction. Though the influences of her translations are evident, Davis, to the contrary, has subtly reinvented short fiction. Her short story "Foucault and Pencil" begins:

> Sat down to read Foucault with pencil in hand. Knocked over glass of water onto waiting-room floor. Put down Foucault and pencil, mopped up water, refilled glass. Sat down to read Foucault with pencil in hand. Stopped to write note in notebook. Took up Foucault with pencil in hand. Counselor beckoned from doorway. Put away Foucault and pencil as well as notebook and pen. Sat with counselor discussing situation fraught with conflict.

Implying internal narratives that implode with residual philosophies, Davis possesses a wry, tragicomedic sense of narrative that is downplayed by her neutrality and textual economy. It is hard to laugh at first, but her stories linger, as the humor, along with philosophical meat, congeals on the skeletal frame of her words. The dryness bears a slight theoretical resemblance to ALAIN ROBBE-GRILLET's *Snapshots* or *Jealousy*, and likewise, the NOUVEAU ROMAN's attempt to free the object from anthropomorphic adjectives and metaphors, but the resemblance is purely theoretical. Lydia Davis is never that verbose. Even in 12-point type, Davis's fiction is usually only a half-page to three pages long, and *End of the Story* (1995), her only novel to date, is replete with numerous breaks in the text.

—Michael Peters

Books: *The Thirteenth Woman*. New York: Living Hand, 1976; *Sketches for a Life of Wassily*. Barrytown, New York: Station Hill, 1981; *Story and Other Stories*. Great Barrington, MA: The Figures, 1983; *Break It Down*. New York: Farrar, Straus, and Giroux, 1986; *End of the Story*. New York: Farrar, Straus, and Giroux, 1995; *Almost No Memory*. New York: Farrar, Straus, and Giroux, 1997.

DAVIS, Stuart

(7 December 1894–24 June 1964).

Beginning as a realist, Davis created some of the earliest American pseudo-collages in the early 1920s, incorporating *trompe l'oeil* depictions of cigarette packs and lettering drawn from advertising art into his paintings (much as NICOLAS SLONIMSKY, say, incorporated jingles into his music compositions around that time). As one of the first Americans to understand European CUBISM, particularly FERNAND LÉGER and PABLO PICASSO, Davis created by the end of the 1920s a series of paintings of two mundane objects, the percolator and eggbeater, implicitly forecasting POP ART.

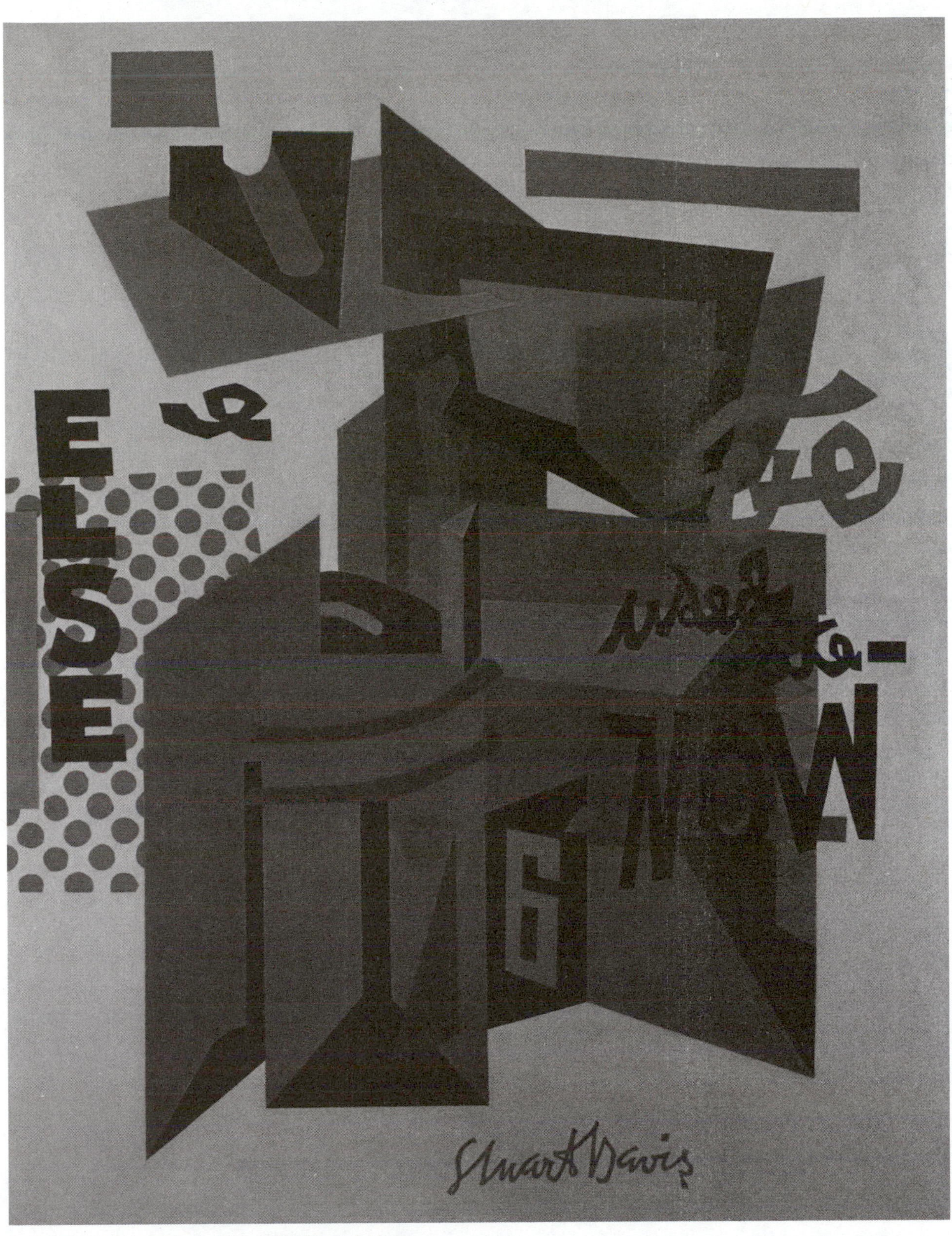

Stuart Davis, *Owh! In Sao Paolo*, 1951. CORBIS/Francis G. Mayer.

From the thirties to his death, Davis's work took an original, if limited, direction in emphasizing colorful shapes arrayed in flat, posterlike patterns that emulated the rhythms of JAZZ music. Perhaps the most interesting departure in his later works was the addition of words, arrayed without syntactic or semantic connections, across the canvas.

—with Richard Carlin

Paintings: *Egg Beater Series*, 1927–28.

Writings: *Stuart Davis*. New York: American Artists Group, 1945.

Books: *Stuart Davis Sketchbooks*. New York: Taplinger, 1987.

Exhibition Catalog: *Abstract Painting in America*. Intro. Stuart Davis. New York: Whitney Museum, 1935; Sweeney, James Johnson. *SD*. New York: MOMA, 1945; *SD*. Minneapolis, MN: Walker Art Center, 1957; *SD Memorial Exhibition*. Washington, DC: Smithsonian Institution, National Collection of Fine Arts, 1965; Lane, John R. *SD: Art & Art Theory*. Brooklyn, NY: Brooklyn Museum, 1978; *SD: Black and White*. New York: Salander-O'Reilly, 1985; *SD: Scapes, 1910–1923*. New York: Salander-O'Reilly, 1990; Sims, Lowery. *SD: American Painter*. New York: Metropolitan Museum, 1991; *SD: Landscapes*. New York: Salander-O'Reilly, 1998.

Interpretation: Baur, John I. H. *Revolution and Tradition in Modern American Painting*. Cambridge: Harvard University Press, 1954; Blesh, Rudi. *Stuart Davis*. New York: Grove, 1960; Goosen, E. C. *Stuart Davis*. New York: Braziller, 1959; Kelder, Diane, ed. *Stuart Davis*. New York: Praeger, 1971; Wilkin, Karen. *Stuart Davis*. New York: Abbeville, 1987.

DAWKINS, Daryl

(11 January 1957).

My publisher for this *Dictionary*, who previously edited books about dance, suggested that I include an entry on this African-American basketball player, whose great choreographic innovation was the Slam Dunk. Nearly seven feet tall and propulsively athetic, Dawkins was able to get his hand so far above the basket that he could propel the ball downwards with thunderous aplomb. It was a choreographic feat that others quickly imitated. So strong was Dawkins that his slam dunk would sometimes make the hoop come away from its glass moorings, shattering the backboard glass (and, needless to say, bringing the game to a halt until it could be replaced). The practice was initially banned by the NBA. The fact that slam dunks were crowd-pleasers kept basketball officials from raising the hoop a foot or two. In a dance sequel, the choreographer ELIZABETH STREB concludes her program with a dancer diving fist-first through a pane of glass. As when watching likely slam dunks, don't blink, or you might miss it. I suspect that someone has published a "highlight" videotape of choice slam dunks.

DE ANDREA, John

(24 November 1941).

De Andrea, among others, has created awesomely lifelike sculptures of people, especially nudes with nothing to hide. Such sculptures reflect as they transcend the illusions typical of the traditional wax museum. Hyperrealism is more successful in sculpture than in painting or photography, in part because three-dimensionality is unavailable to the latter artforms, but mostly because of new materials, as well as new intelligence, that have become available to sculptors.

De Andrea has an unusual ability to give his sculptures humanity. It was the British poet-critic Edward Lucie-Smith who pointed out, "They somehow give away both their class and their national origin through details of posture, hair style, and expression." The cleverest de Andrea in my experience involved three figures—two nude women and a clothed man facing them. You knew the women were "fake," so to speak, but you had to look and think twice to realize that the man with his back to you was a sculpture as well.

Exhibition Catalog: Goodyear, Frank. *John De Andrea: Sculpture*. New York: Carlo Lamagna Gallery, 1987.

Interpretation: Lucie-Smith, Edward. *Art Now*. Rev. ed. New York: Morrow, 1981.

DE KOONING, Willem

(24 April 1904–19 March 1997).

Born in Holland, de Kooning emigrated to America as a young man and worked as a W.P.A. muralist. His midlife innovation came from imaginatively developing and extending a major stylistic contribution of European CUBISM, breaking up the representational plane to portray an object or field as seen from two or more perspectives simultaneously. The initial paintings in his *Women* series, done in the early fifties, evoke in impulsive and yet well-drawn strokes (and colors identical to those in the environment portrayed) a single figure regarded from a multitude of perspectives, both vertical and horizontal, in several kinds of light and, therefore, implicitly at various moments in time. Not only are the differences between figure and setting, past and present, and background and foreground all thoroughly blurred, but nearly every major detail in this all-over and yet focused field suggests a different angle of vision or a different intensity of light. De Kooning never did as well again, even in roughly similar styles, though his admirers were forever hailing later works with the wish that he had.

Selected Works: *Working Man*, c. 1938; *Seated Figure (Classic Male)*, c. 1940; *Seated Woman*, c. 1940; *Pink Angels*, c. 1945; Black-and-white Abstractions, 1945–50; *Willem Woman*, 1948; *Excavation*, 1950; *Woman I*, 1950–52; *Woman as Landscape*, 1955; *Gotham News*, c. 1955; *Door to the River*, 1960; *Woman, Sag Harbour*, 1964; *Seated Woman on a Bench*, 1972; *Untitled Series*, 1975–79.

Writings: *The Collected Writings*. Ed. George Scrivani. New York: Hanuman, 1988.

Exhibition Catalogs: *De Kooning Retrospective*. Boston: Boston Museum School, 1953; Hess, Thomas B. *Willem de Kooning*. New York: MOMA, 1968; Kertess, Klaus and Robert Rosenblum. *Willem de Kooning: An Exhibition of Paintings*. New York: Salander-O'Reilly Gallery, 1990; Prather, Marla. *Willem de Kooning: Paintings*. With essays by David Sylvester and Richard Schiff. Washington, DC: National Gallery of Art, 1994; *Willem de Kooning: The Late Paintings, the 1980's*. San Francisco: MoMA, 1995.

Website: http://www.artincontext.org/artist/d/willem_de_kooning/

Interpretation: Gaugh, Harry. *De Kooning*. New York: Abbeville, 1983; Hess, Thomas B. *De Kooning: Recent Painting*. New York: Walker & Co., 1967; Janis, Harriet, and Rudi Blesh. *De Kooning*. New York: Grove, 1960; Rosenberg, Harold. *De Kooning*. New York: Abrams, 1974; Sylvester, David. *Willem de Kooning: Paintings*. New Haven: Yale University Press, 1994; Waldman, Diane. *Willem de Kooning*. New York: Abrams, 1988; Yard, Sally. *Willem de Kooning*. New York: Rizzolli, 1997.

DE MARIA, Walter

(1 October 1935).

A true eccentric, de Maria first made sculptures that posed genuine dangers to viewers, such as a bed of spikes pointed upwards, and pioneered CONCEPTUAL ART with *Mile Long Drawing* (1968), for which he drew two parallel lines, twelve feet apart, in the Mojave Desert. (Because the original is inaccessible, this is commonly seen and experienced through documentary photographs.) In 1968, de Maria filled an entire Munich gallery with earth a few feet deep, which was such a good idea that he was asked to do it again, first at another gallery in Cologne, and then in a former gallery in SoHo, where it has been on museum-like display for over twenty years as The New York Earth Room. Nearby in SoHo is another apparently permanent de Maria installation, *The Broken Kilometer* (1979), where the entire floor of an 11,000-square-foot space has highly polished brass rods arrayed in parallel rows.

Works: *Mile Long Drawing*, 1968; *The New York Earth Room*, 1977; *Lightning Field*, 1977; *The Broken Kilometer*, 1979.

Writings: "Meaningless Work" (1960). In Richard Kostelanetz, *Esthetics Contemporary*. 2nd Ed. Buffalo, New York: Prometheus, 1989.

Exhibition Catalogs: *Walter de Maria: Large Rod Series Rectangles 1984–86*. New York: Xavier Fourcade, 1986; Nittve, Lars. *Walter de Maria 5 7 9: The 5 7 9 Series*. New York: Gagosian, 1992; *Walter de Maria: The 2000 Sculpture*. Zurich, Switzerland: Kunsthaus, 1992.

d

DE STIJL

(1917–1931).

A Dutch periodical of art and esthetics edited by THEO VAN DOESBURG until his premature death, *De Stijl* was commonly considered the most influential avant-garde art magazine of its time, representing not just Dutch CONSTRUCTIVISM but a rationalist approach to art and society. Its title, meaning "the style," is pronounced (in English) as, roughly, "duh style." Among the member-contributors were PIET MONDRIAN , GEORGES VANTONGERLOO, EL LISSITZKY, GEORGE ANTHEIL, JEAN/HANS ARP, and lesser-known architects and industrial designers. "This periodical hopes to make a contribution to the development of a new awareness of beauty," van Doesburg wrote in the initial issue. "It wishes to make modern man receptive to what is new in the visual arts." This "new" they called the "new plasticism," which not only rejected representation (Mondrian having once specialized in flowers) but, instead, strictly limited painting to straight lines, 90-degree angles, and the three primary colors of red, yellow, and blue (along with the neutrals of black, white, and gray). Thinking their art socially redemptive, they wanted to convey its significance to a larger public. As H. L. C. Jaffe wrote in the principal history of the magazine, "The purification of the plastic means of expression should also serve to solve various actual problems of our present time." Because van Doesburg as a POLYARTIST was as much a writer as a painter, one of *De Stijl's* issues was devoted to literature that was avant-garde at the time; and because he became involved with DADA, a 1922 issue had a Dada supplement titled *Mecano*. (This could have been alphabetized under S.)

Primary Sources: Jaffe, H. L. C., ed. *De Stijl 1917–1931*. Cambridge: Harvard University Press, 1986. (This has a large bibliography of Dutch sources.); Mondrian, Piet. *The New Art—The New Life* (1986). Ed. & trans. Harry Holzman and Martin J. James. New York: Da Capo, 1993; Vantongerloo, Georges. *Paintings, Scuptures, Reflections*. New York: Wittenborn, 1948; Warnke, Carsten-Peter. *The Ideal as Art: De Stijl 1917–1931*. Köln: Taschen, 1991.

Exhibition Catalog: *De Stijl*. Amsterdam: Stedelijk Museum, 1951; *De Stijl*. New York: MOMA, 1953.

Interpretation: Banham, Reyner. *Theory and Design in the First Machine Age* (1960). New York: Praeger, 1967; Blotkamp, Carel. *De Stijl: The Formative Years 1917–1922*. Tr. Charlotte, I. and Arthur L. Loeb. Cambridge: MIT, 1986; Overy, Paul. *De Stijl*. New York: Thames & Hudson, 1991.

DEAN, Laura

(3 December 1945).

As a choreographer once closely associated with STEVE REICH, Dean created highly inventive dances that depended upon simple repeated moves. In *Jumping Dance* (1973), twelve performers, lined up in three rows of four, jump up and down, making their own noises, until everyone is exhausted, incidentally illustrating JOHN CAGE'S classic remark about doing something again and again until it is no longer boring but interesting. *Circle Dance* (1972) has ten performers shuffling their feet around four concentric circles in unison. However, since they move around four completely different circumferences, the performers go in and out of visible phase (the work thus resembling early Reich music). As in *Jumping Dance*, the music comes only from sounds made by the performers themselves.

Works: *Circle Dance*, 1972; *Square Dance*, 1972; *Stamping Dance*, 1972; *Jumping Dance*, 1973; *Changing Pattern Steady Pulse*, 1973; *Response Dance*, 1974; *Spinning Dance*, 1974; *Changing*, 1974; *Drumming*, 1975; *Song*, 1976; *Dance*, 1976; *Spiral*, 1977; *Music*, 1979; *Tympani*, 1980; *Night*, 1980.

Interpretation: McDonagh, Don. "Laura Dean. " In *The Complete Guide to Modern Dance*. Garden City, NY: Doubleday, 1976.

Video: *Tympani*. Minneapolis, MN: Twin Cities Public Television-UC Video, 1985.

DEFAMILIARIZATION

(c. 1920s).

One of the great modernist esthetic ideas, sometimes translated as "making strange" and other times as "estrangement," this was coined by the Russian formalist critic Viktor Shklovsky (1893–1984) to honor the process of disrupting conventional forms of literary presentation and thus habitual forms of literary experience—in his phrases, "to make objects unfamiliar, to make forms difficult, to increase the difficulty and length of the perception process." Defamiliarization comes from deviations in literary devices such as language, syntax, narrative, or point of view. (Writing in the 1920s, Shklovsky cites Leo Tolstoy's story "Kholsomer," which is told from a horse's perspective. Later literature has more extreme examples.) The principle of defamiliarization is applicable to the nonliterary arts as well. It is scarcely surprising that in this century's late teens, as he came to maturity, Shklovsky was personally close to the poets who made RUSSIAN FUTURISM.

Bibliography: Shklovsky, Viktor. *Theory of Prose* (*O teorii prozy*, 2d ed., 1929). Trans. Benjamin Sher. Elmwood Park, IL: Dalkey Archive, 1990; Shklovsky, Victor. "Art as Technique" (1947). In Lee T. Lemon and Marion J. Reese, trans. & eds. *Russian Formalist Criticism: Four Essays*. Lincoln: University of Nebraska Press, 1965.

DENCKER, Klaus Peter

(1941).

A German visual poet and cultural administrator, he has produced books composed entirely of newspaper headlines and clippings— . . . *grünes erlangen* (1979)—as well as a pioneering German anthology of VISUAL POETRY (*Text-Birder Visuelle Poesie International* [1972]) and a wonderfully thick, annotated collection of *Deutsche Unsinnspoesie* (1978), or nonsense poetry. For a while in the 1970s, Dencker promoted *Poesia vivisa*, a mostly Italian art that depended upon mixing language with photographs large enough to hang in art galleries, as distinct from the primarily linguistic, smaller-scale orientations of both VISUAL POETRY and CONCRETE POETRY.

Website: http://www.thing.net/~grist/l&d/dencker/dencker.htm (this site displays Denker's work, "Wortkœpfe").

Edited Books: *Text-Bilder; visuelle Poesie international*. Köln: Dumont, 1972; *Deutsche Unsinnspoesie*. Stuttgart, Germany: Reclam, 1978.

DEPERO, Fortunato

(1892–1960).

Born an Austrian citizen in northern Italy, he was a precocious toy designer as a child. He moved to Rome in 1913 and participated in Futurist exhibitions, becoming a leader of the movement's second phase. After collaboraing with Giacomo Balla (1871–1958) on *Ricostruzione Futurista dell'Universo* (The Futurist Reconstruction of the Universe, 1915), Depero produced kinetic sculpture and mechanical theater, along with stunning theatrical texts, some of which were collected in Michael and Victoria Nes Kirby's pioneering anthology, *Futurist Performance* (1971). Historians of the history of book art credit Depero with preceding George Maciunas in using bolts to bind a book.

Exhibition Catalog: *Fortunato Depero: Opere 1911–1930*. Torino: Martano/due, 1969.

Interpretation: Kirby, Michael and Victoria Nes, eds. *Futurist Performance*. New York: Dutton, 1971.

DEPEW, Wally

(5 January 1938).

An experimental poet-publisher from his professional beginnings, Depew published *Nine Essays on Concrete Poems* (1974), which are not conventional expositions but substantial visual-verbal self-reflective displays of qualities unique to CONCRETE POETRY, which he defines as I do here—dealing with the elements of language apart from syntax or semantics. In his own VISUAL POETRY, he tends to favor images in sequence, at times verging on visual fiction, using rubber-stamp letters in his recent books.

d

Books: *Once*. Paradise, CA: Dustbook, 1971; *Ladderbook piece*. Sacramento, CA: Poetry Newsletter, 1972; *Lobelia*. Sacramento, CA: Poetry Newsletter, 1973; *Series*. Sacramento, CA: Poetry Newsletter, 1974; *100 Poems*. Sacramento, CA: Poetry Newsletter, 1974; *ironwhoresbook*. Sacramento, CA: n.p. (P.O. Box 232, Patagonia, AZ 85624), n.d.

Visual Writings: *Nine Essays on Concrete Poetry*. Alamo, CA: Holmgangers Press, 1974.

Website: *www.dakota.com.net/~wdepew/*

DERRIDA, Jacques

(15 July 1930).

A Frenchman from North Africa, Derrida has become in some academic literary circles the most influential critical theorist since NORTHROP FRYE. His dense and often confusing books seem designed for the classroom, which means that they are most successfully read with a guide, in concert with other seekers. Where they are comprehensible, at least in my experience, their ideas are obvious; where they are incomprehensible, Derrida's theories of Deconstruction offer the cognoscenti rich opportunities for the kinds of one-upmanship endemic to such hierarchical societies as the military and most universities.

I quote one summary, from Philip M. W. Thody's contribution to the encyclopedia *Twentieth-Century Culture* (1983), not because I agree with it but because Thody, who once wrote a good book on Albert Camus, seems to know what he's talking about (and I can't confidently summarize it):

> Philosophers have gone wrong in trying to make sense of experience by looking for essential truth lying with the 'essence of things.' What they should do is look at language itself, but without seeing individual words as having a meaning because of the link which they are alleged to have with the object, concepts, or activities they designate. Instead they should follow out the full implications of Saussure's remark that language contains only difference and that meaning is created by the distinction between the sounds of e.g, "pin" and "pen." The task of the philosopher is to examine how language works both by the differences within it and by the chain of expectations which the writer or speaker sets up and which require the listener to defer the moment when she or he decides what a particualar sentence may nor may not mean.

Got it? If not, don't ask me to get it any clearer for you.

To my mind, Derrida's originality comes from his way of expressing his thoughts, which I discovered not from reading his works but from hearing him speak. In Jerusalem several years ago, I witnessed a question/answer performance before a mostly academic audience, most speaking, as he does, non-native English. Whenever Derrida took a question, you could see him fumble for the beginnings of an answer, but once he got on track, an elaborate digression followed, at once elegant and idiosyncratic, until he reached a pause. Having followed him so far, you wondered whether he would then turn to the left or to the right, each direction seeming equally valid, only to admire the next verbal flight that led to another roadstop, with similarly arbitrary choices before continuing or concluding. In response to the next question, Derrida improvised structurally similar rhetorical gymnastics.

What separates Derrida from traditional literary theorists is this commitment to improvisatory thinking, with all of its possibilities and limitations. Should you have a taste for highflown intellectual flights, consider MARSHALL McLUHAN, whose similarly improvised perceptions were sociologically more substantial. If you think improvisation is "no way to play music," you might judge that Derrida's example is no way to think.

Writings: *Of Grammatology* (1976). Trans. G. C. Spivak. Baltimore: Johns Hopkins University Press, 1998; *Writing and Difference*. Chicago: University of Chicago Press, 1980; *Dissemination*. Chicago: University of Chicago Press, 1983; *Margins of Philosophy*. Chicago: University of Chicago Press, 1984; *The Archeology of the Frivolous*. Lincoln: University of Nebraska Press, 1987; *Limited Inc*. Evanston: Northwestern University Press, 1988; *Acts of Literature*. New York: Routledge, 1991; *Of Spirit: Heidegger and the Question*. Chicago: University of Chicago Press, 1991; *Cinders*. Lincoln: University of Nebraska Press, 1991; *Given Time: I. Counterfeit Money*. Chicago: University of Chicago Press, 1994; *Aporias*. Stanford: Stanford University Press, 1994; *Points . . . Interviews 1974–1994*. Ed. Elisabeth Weber. Stanford: Stanford University Press, 1995; *The Gift of Death*. Chicago: University of Chicago Press, 1996; *Deconstruction in a Nutshell*. New York: Fordham University Press, 1997; *Politics of Friendship*. New York: Verso, 1997; *Monolingualism of the Other; or, the Prosthesis of Origin*. Stanford: Stanford University Press, 1998; *Resistances of Psychoanalysis*. Stanford: Stanford University, 1998; *Archive Fever: A Freudian Impression*. Chicago: University of Chicago Press, 1998.

Anthology: *The Derrida Reader*. Ed. Julian Wolfreys, Lincoln: University of Nebraska Press, 1998.

Website: http://www.mii.kurume-u.ac.jp/~leuers/Derrida.htm (Links and other information).

Interpretation: Hartmann, Geoffrey A. *Saving the Text: Literature, Derrida, Philosophy*. Baltimore: Johns Hopkins University Press, 1981; Sokal, Alan D., and Bricmont, Jean. *Fashionable Nonsense: Postmodern Intellectuals' Abuse of Science*. New York: St. Martin's Press, 1998.

Interpretation of Interpretation: Critchley, Simon & Mouffe, Chantal. eds. *Deconstruction and Pragmatism*. New York: Routledge, 1996; Sallis, John. ed. *Deconstruction and Philosophy: The Texts of Jacques Derrida*. Chicago: University of Chicago Press, 1989; Wigley, Mark. *The Architecture of Deconstruction*. Cambridge: MIT Press, 1995; Wood, David. ed. *Derrida: A Critical Reader*. New York: Blackwell, 1992.

DER STURM.

See **WALDEN, Herwarth.**

di SUVERO, Mark

(18 September 1933).

Born in Shanghai of Italian–Jewish parents, di Suvero moved with his family to California in 1941 and majored in philosophy at the University of California at Berkeley. Taking off from DAVID SMITH'S sense of sculpture as an outdoor art and FRANZ KLINE'S taste for thick lines and odd angles, di Suvero fabricated monumental sculptures initially of wood and then of scrap steel beams gathered from demolished buildings and junkyards. Asymmetrical and to the eye precariously balanced, these sculptures sometimes contain seats inviting the spectator to gain a more intimate experience of the work. Though CUBIST in syntax, they look like nothing found in life and could thus be considered CONSTRUCTIVIST as well. A distinguished older sculptor, Sidney Geist (1914), greeted di Suvero's first exhibition in 1960 with this generous encomium: "I myself have not been so moved by a show of sculpture since the Brancusi exhibition of 1933." In a classic of appreciative criticism, Geist continued: "History is glad to record the arrival of any new artist, the creation of a new beauty, or the presence of a singular work of art; but the real stuff of history is made of those moments at which one can say:

from now on *nothing will be the same."* Geist added, "Constructivism is Cubism with the object left out." After leaving America in protest against the Vietnam War, di Suvero returned to Long Island City, where he located his studio in an abandoned waterfront pier and later established on shorefront property an outdoor sculpture park.

Exhibition Catalog: Monte, James K. *Mark di Suvero*. New York: Whitney Museum, 1975; *Mark di Suvero: 25 Years of Sculpture and Drawings*. Mountainville, NY: Storm King Art Center, 1985; *Mark di Suvero: Retrospective 1959–1991*. Nice: Musée d'art moderne et d'art contemporain, 1991; *Mark di Suvero: Open Secret: Sculpture 1990–92*. New York: Gagosian-Rizzoli, 1993; *Mark di Suvero: Recent Work*. San Francisco: John Berrgruen Gallery 1994; *Mark di Suvero at Storm King Art Center*. New York: Harry A. Abrams, 1996.

Interpretation: Geist, Sidney, "A New Sculptor: Mark di Suvero" (1960). In *Mark di Suvero*. Stuttgart, Germany: Württemburgischer Künstverein, 1988; Kozloff, Max. "Mark di Suvero," *Artforum* (November 1972).

DIAGHILEV, Sergei Pavlovich

(19 March 1872–20 August 1929).

One of the greatest organizers of innovative artistic events, Diaghilev first became known as a leading figure in the Petersburg World of Art Group, as founder and editor of the journal *World of Art* (*Mir iskusstva*, 1899–1904), which introduced important new European art movements to the Russian public in an elegantly printed format, setting a high standard for subsequent Russian art and literary journals. Diaghilev ceaselessly promoted native Russian achievements, as well as innovative trends in the fields of art, music, opera, and ballet. His most significant accomplishment was the creation and management of the renowned Les Ballets Russes, which, beginning in 1909, produced some of the most brilliant spectacles in the history of ballet. To do this, he engaged the services of the most talented avant-garde artists, composers, choreographers, and dancers of Russia and France, including Leon Bakst (1866–1924), Aleksandr Benois (1870–1960), Natalia Goncharova (1881–1962), Mikhail Larionov (1881–1964), PABLO PICASSO, Henri Matisse (1869–1954), Georges Braque (1882–1963), IGOR STRAVINSKY, Sergei Prokofiev (1891–1953), Maurice Ravel (1875–1937), Claude Debussy (1862–1918), Mikhail Fokine (1880–1942), Vaslav Nijinsky (1890–1950), Anna Pavlova (1881–1931), and Tamara Karsavina (1885–1978). Perhaps his most artistically successful production was *Petrushka* (1912), with music by Stravinsky, stage design by Benois, choreography by Fokine, and Nijinsky dancing the title role. His most scandalous success occurred in May 1913, with the premier of Stravinsky's *The Rite of Spring*. Nijinsky's unusual choreography, evoking pagan rituals in pre-Christian Russia, plus the wild music, caused a riot during the performance. Diaghilev's role was to stimulate, in fact to demand, innovative work from his collaborators and to provide them with the resources to stage the results. His motto was "surprise me."

—Gerald Janecek

Biographies: Haskell, Arnold Lionel. *Diagileff: His Artistic and Private Life* (1935). New York: Da Capo, 1977; Kodicek, Ann. *Diagilev: Creator of the Ballets Russes*. London: Lund Humphries, 1996; Kochno, Boris. *Diaghilev and the Ballets Russes* (1970). Freeport, NY: Books for Libraries, 1980; Lifar, Serge. *Serge Diagilev, His Life, His Work, His Legend: An Intimate Biography* (1940). New York: Da Capo, 1977; Sokolova, Lydia. *Dancing for Diaghliev*. Ed. Richard Buckle. London: Murray, 1960; Buckle, Richard. *Diaghilev*. New York: Atheneum, 1979.

Interpretation: Bowlt, John E. *The Silver Age: Russian Art of the Early Twentieth Century and the "World of Art Group."* Newtonville, MA: Oriental Research Partners, 1979; Garafola, Lynn. *Diaghilev's Ballets Russes*. New York: Oxford University Press, 1989; Grigoriev, S. L. *The Diaghilev Ballet 1909–1929*. Trans. & ed. Vera Bowen. London: Constable, 1953; Percival, John. *The World of Diaghilev*. New York: Dutton, 1971; Pozharskaya, M. N., and Tatiana Volodina. *The Russian Seasons in Paris*. Trans. V. S. Friedman. New York: Abbeville, 1991; Spencer, Charles. *The World of Serge Diaghilev*. New York: Penguin, 1974; Benson, Carl. "The Ballets Russes: Two 'S's or Four?" in *Thoughts Contemporary*. Glen Ridge, NJ: Kit Kat, 1998.

DIGITAL

(1960s).

This term is a euphemism for any mechanism, commonly computer-assisted, that converts an input to numerical quantities, which are positive or negative impulses (commonly characterized as 0/1). The term is applicable to visual and video as well as audio machines. Digital-to-analog conversion refers to the process of taking material stored in a computer medium, such as on a tape or a floppy disc, and making it more accessible, whether on paper or on analog audiotape.

Analysis: Dodge, Charles, and Jerse, Thomas A., *Computer Music: Synthesis, Composition, and Performance*. 2d ed. New York: Schirmer, 1997.

DIGITAL ARCHIVES

There exist no digital archives that I know of for avant-garde art, and few digital archives for any kind of cultural material. At first, this seems unimportant: the avant-garde art of the twentieth century has been ignored or despised at its birth, then sometimes refound and cherished later. But with the advent of computer art (performance and poetry for the computer screen) the need for such archives is greater than ever, though not likely. The computer works of the 1980s are probably already disappearing or unintelligible. During the mid-1980s, a number of poets wrote kinetic computer poems in BASIC for the Apple IIe computer. Many of these computers still exist, abandoned in the basements of elementary schools, but the media needed to run these (5.25-inch computer disks) are rarer still, and it's unlikely that many of them are still intelligible. And transfer to videotape was difficult and unimpressive for such systems, so few (if any) people attempted this as a form of preservation. I abandoned the attempt to save my own computer poems a few generations of computers ago, and printed out the code as a means of preservation. Here are a few lines from the long poem "Havoc":

```
440 VTAG 8: HTAB 8; PRINT 'ENDEMIC"/450 VTAB 16:
HTAB 9: PRINT "ALGORITHM"/460 VTAB 13: HTAB 25:
PRINT "RHYTHM" /470 VTAB 21: HTAB 4: PRINT
"LAYER"/480 VTAG 2: HATB 17: PRINT "AFTER".
```

As you might imagine, reading lines of code doesn't have the same emotional effect on a person as seeing a wave of language surge over the screen.

The preservation of computer-aided art is a problem that will continue to grow, because art designed to take advantage of the possibilities of the computer will be sacrificed on the altar of computer evolution. What this may mean is that much of the avant-garde art of our age will be lost to the future and be remembered only through description.

—Geof Huth

Bibliography: *The Alchemist*, a periodical of computer poetry and fiction, published during the early '90s on 5.25 inch diskettes for Apple computers; Nichol, bp. *First Screening: Computer Poems by bp Nichol*. Toronto: Underwhich, 1984.

DISNEYLAND (1955)/DISNEY WORLD (c. 1971)

Besides his landmark animated feature *Fantasia*, Walt Disney must surely be counted among the few visionaries who actually created a parallel, fantasy world. While others have proposed creating self-contained environments, Disney's Disneyland and, later, Disney World, Euro-Disney, and Disneyland-Tokyo, were among the first alternate worlds created and operated successfully. Not only business models for later developments (the so-called "themeparks" that now dot the landscape promoting various commercial operations), Disney's parks have also become neat universes where visitors can enter not only the childlike world of Disney's characters but also experience, through subparks like Epcot Center, various world cultures (without the tedium or danger of world travel). Just as American culture has invaded the world, Disney has scooped up the world and Americanized it, making it palatable for the mass audience. Disney's success relies on total control of the environment, so that ideally visitors must stay in Disney-operated hotels, eat at Disney-operated concessions, and see only Disney-operated attractions. To do otherwise would be to explode the mythic power of Disney's creation (and also rob corporate Disney of its stranglehold on your pocketbook). While LAS VEGAS is an artificial city, it has many owners and a real population; Disneyland and Disney World are more perfect because the entire artificial reality is maintained consistently through one owner—and the only real population are tourists.

—Richard Carlin

Interpretation: Centre canadien d'architecture/Canadian Centre for Architecture. *Designing Disney's Theme Parks*. Paris/New York: Flammarion, 1997; Wade, Judy. *Disneyland and Beyond*. Berkeley, CA: Ulysses Press, 1994; Koenig, David. *Mouse Tales*. Irvine, CA: Bonaventure Press, 1994; Bryman, Alan. *Disney and his Worlds*. London & New York: Routledge, 1995.

Website: http://disney.go.com/Disneyland/

DODECAPHONIC MUSIC

(1924).

In historical perspective, dodecaphonic music is the product of a luxuriant development of chromatic melody and harmony. A conscious avoidance of all tonal centers led to the abolition of key signature and a decline of triadic harmony. The type of composition in which all tonal points of reference have been eliminated became known as ATONALITY. It was from this paludous atmosphere of inchoate atonality that the positive and important technical idiom of dodecaphonic composition was gradually evolved and eventually formulated by ARNOLD SCHOENBERG as the "method of composing with 12 tones related only to one another." Schoenberg's first explicit use of his method occurs in his Serenade, op. 24, written in 1924. Five fundamental ideas underlie Schoenberg's method: (1) Dodecaphonic monothematism in which the entire work is derived from a 12-tone row (*Tonreihe*), which comprises 12 different notes of the chromatic scale. (2) The tone-row is utilized in four conjugate forms: original, retrograde, inversion, and retrograde inversion. (3) Although the order of the notes in the tone-row is rigidly observed, the individual members of the series can be placed in any octave position, a peculiar feature of dodecaphonic music which results in the wide distribution of the thematic ingredients over the entire vocal or instrumental range of a single part or over sections of different parts. (4) Since each of the 4 forms of the basic 12-tone series can be transposed to any starting point of the chromatic scale, the total of all available forms is 48. (5) Melody, harmony, and counterpoint are functions of the tone-row, which may appear in all its avatars, horizontally as melody, vertically as harmony and diagonally as canonic counterpoint. It may also be distributed partly in melodic progressions, partly in harmonic or contrapuntal structures, creating dodecaphonic meloharmony or melocounterpoint. Because of the providential divisibility of the number 12, the 12-tone row can be arranged in 6 groups in 2-part counterpoint, 4 groups in 3-part counterpoint (or harmony), 3 groups in 4-part harmony, or 2 groups in 6-part harmony.

In a communication sent to NICOLAS SLONIMSKY in 1939, Ernst Krenek describes the relationship between atonality and the method of composing with 12 tones as follows: "Atonality is a state of the musical material brought about through a general historical development. The 12-tone technique is a method of writing music within the realm of atonality. The sense of key has been destroyed by atonality. The method of composing with 12 tones was worked out in order to replace the old organization of the material by certain new devices."

Schoenberg was not alone in his dodecaphonic illumination. Several musicians, mostly in Austria and Germany, evolved similar systems of organizing the resources of the chromatic scale in a logical and self-contained system of composition. JEF GOLYSCHEFF, Russian composer and painter who lived in Germany and eventually settled in Brazil, worked on the problem as early as 1914, and in 1924 published a collection which he called 12 Tondauer Musik, making use of 12 different tones in thematic structures. At about the same time, Nicolas Obouhov invented a system that he called "Absolute Harmony," which involved the use of all 12 chromatic tones without doubling; he played his piano pieces written in this system at a concert in Petrograd on 3 February 1916.

Passages containing 12 different notes in succession, apart from the simple chromatic scale, are found even in classical works. There is a highly chromaticized passage in Mozart's *G Minor Symphony* derived from three mutually exclusive diminished-seventh chords, aggregating to 12 different notes. The main subject in the section "Of Science" in the score of *Also sprach Zarathustra* by Richard Strauss contains the 12 different notes of the chromatic scale, but they remain uninverted, untergiversated and otherwise unmetamorphosed, and thus cannot be regarded as a sampler of dodecaphonic writing.

Liszt's *Faust Symphony* opens with a theme consisting of four successive augmented triads descending by semitones, comprising the 12 different tones, but it cannot be meaningfully described as an anticipation of the dodecaphonic method. CHARLES IVES uses a 12-tone series of different chromatic notes in his instrumental piece *Tone Road No. 3*, which he wrote in 1915. This intuitive invention is important not only as an illustration of his prophetic genius, but also as another indication that dodecaphonic ideas appeared in the minds of musicians working in different parts of the world, completely independently of each other.

Among scattered examples of 12-tone composition of the pre-dodecaphonic years is *L'adieu à la vie* for piano by Alfredo Casella, which ends on a chord of 12 different notes. An amusing example of dodecaphonic prevision is the *Hymn to Futurism* by Cesar Cui, written in 1917, when the last surviving member of the Russian Mighty Five was 82 years old. Intended as a spoof, the piece contains a passage of three mutually exclusive diminished-seventh chords in arpeggio adding up to 12 different notes, and another passage comprising two mutually exclusive augmented triads with a complementary scale of whole tones passing through the unoccupied six spaces, forming another series of 12 different notes. The fact that Cui had two dodecaphonic series in his short composition demonstrates that even in a musical satire the thematic use of 12 different notes was a logical outcome of the process of tonal decay, serving as a fertilizer for the germination of dodecaphonic organisms.

The method of composing with 12 tones related only to one another did not remain a rigid dogma. Its greatest protagonists, besides Schoenberg himself, were his disciples Alban Berg (1889–1935) and ANTON VON WEBERN. Somewhat frivolously, they have been described as the Vienna Trinity, with Schoenberg the Father, Berg the Son, and Webern the Holy Ghost. Both Berg and Webern introduced considerable innovations into the Schoenbergian practice. While Schoenberg studiously avoided triadic constructions, Alban Berg used the conjunct series of alternating minor and major triads capped by three whole tones as the principal subject of his last work, the *Violin Concerto op. 36* (1936). Schoenberg practically excluded symmetric intervallic constructions and sequences, but Alban Berg inserted, in his opera *Lulu*, a dodecaphonic episode built on two mutually exclusive whole-tone scales. Anton von Webern dissected the 12-tone series into autonomous sections of 6, 4, or 3 units in a group, and related them individually to one another by inversion, retrograde, and inverted retrograde. This fragmentation enabled him to make use of canonic imitation much more freely than would have been possible according to the strict Schoenbergian doctrine.

d

The commonly used term for dodecaphonic music in German is *Zwölftonmusik*. In American usage it was translated literally as 12-tone music, but English music theorists strenuously object to this terminology, pointing out that a tone is an acoustical phenomenon, that dodecaphony deals with the arrangement of written notes, and that it should be consequently called 12-note music. In Italy the method became known as *Dodecafonia* or *Musica dodecafonica*. Incidentally, the term Dodecafonia was first used by the Italian music scholar Domenico Alaleona in his article "L'armonia modernissima," published in *Rivista Musicale* in 1911, but it was applied there in the sense of total chromaticism as an extension of Wagnerian harmony.

The proliferation of dodecaphony in Italy was as potent as it was unexpected, considering the differences between Germanic and Latin cultures, the one introspective and speculative, the other humanistic and practical. Luigi Dallapiccola was one of the earliest adepts, but he liberalized Schoenberg's method and admitted tonal elements. In his opera *Il Prigioniero*, written in 1944, he made use of four mutually exclusive triads.

The greatest conquest of Schoenberg's method was the totally unexpected conversion of IGOR STRAVINSKY, whose entire esthetic code had seemed to stand in opposition to any predetermined scheme of composition; yet he adopted it when he was already in his seventies. Many other composers of world renown turned to dodecaphonic devices as a thematic expedient, without full utilization of the four basic forms of the tone-row. Bela Bartók made use of a 12-tone melody in his Second Violin Concerto op. 112 (1937–38), but he modified its structure by inner permutations within the second statement of the tone-row. Ernest Bloch, a composer for whom the constrictions of modern techniques had little attraction, made use of 12-tone subjects in his *Sinfonia Breve* and in his last string quartets. English composers who have adopted the technique of 12-tone composition with various degrees of consistency are Michael Tippett, Lennox Berkeley, Benjamin Frankel, Humphrey Searle, and Richard Rodney Bennett. William Walton makes use of a 12-tone subject in the fugal finale of his Second Symphony. Benjamin Britten joined the dodecaphonic community by way of tonality. In his Expressionist opera *The Turn of the Screw*, he adopts a motto of alternating perfect fifths and minor thirds (or their respective inversions), aggregating to a series of 12 different notes. The Spanish composer Roberto Gerhard, who settled in England, wrote in a fairly strict dodecaphonic idiom. In France the leader of the dodecaphonic school is René Leibowitz, who also wrote several books on the theory of 12-tone composition. Wladimir Vogel, a Russian-born composer of German parentage, making his home in Switzerland, has adopted Schoenberg's method in almost all of his works. The Swiss composer Frank Martin has extended the principles of dodecaphonic writing to include a number of tonal and modal ramifications.

In America, Schoenberg's method has found fertile ground, not only among his students but also among composers who initially had pursued different roads. ROGER SESSIONS, VIRGIL THOMSON, and David Diamond followed Schoenberg's method with varying degrees of fidelity. Aaron Copland used the dodecaphonic technique in some of his chamber music works; in the orchestral compositions entitled *Connotations*, commissioned for the opening concert of Lincoln Center, New York, in 1962, he applied the totality of dodecaphony to characterize the modern era of music. Walter Piston interpolated a transitional 12-tone passage in his ballet suite *The Incredible Flutist*. He resisted integral dodecaphony until his septuagenarian calendae, when in his Eighth Symphony he adopted Schoenberg's method in all its orthodoxy. Leonard Bernstein inserted a 12-tone series in the score of his *Age of Anxiety* to express inner agitation and anguished expectancy of the music. Samuel Barber made an excursion into the dodecaphonic field in a movement of his Piano Sonata. Gian Carlo Menotti turned dodecaphony into parody in his opera *The Last Savage* to illustrate the decadence of modern civilization into which the hero was unexpectedly catapulted from his primitivistic habitat.

—Nicolas Slonimsky

Bibliography: Schoenberg, Arnold. "Aesthetic Evaluation of Chords with Six or More Tones." In *Composers on Modern Musical Culture*, ed. Bryan Simms. New York: Schirmer Books, 1999; ——. "Composition with Twelve Tones." In *Style and Idea*, ed. Leonard Stein. Berkeley: University of California Press, 1984; Ernest Krenek, "Serialism." In *Dictionary of Contemporary Music*, ed. John Vinton. New York: Dutton, 1974.

DODGE, Charles

(5 June 1942).

One of the first trained composers to work with computers in the creation of digital information that was then transferred to audiotape, Dodge produced several pieces whose claims to originality depended less upon their structures and thus acoustic experiences than upon the computer-assisted means used to produce them. Exceptions to that generalization include *Earth's Magnetic Field* (1970), in which readings of the Earth's magnetic field were serendipitously translated into musical notes (a method structurally comparable to the sun-based sculptures of CHARLES ROSS); *The Days of Our Lives* (1974), which is a kind of operatic dialogue for male and female voices that are resynthesized with computer assistance; and *Any Resemblance* (1981), his masterpiece, in which a computer was used to take away the accompanying instruments from a tenor resembling Enrico Caruso. Dodge then composed fresh accompaniments, each insufficient, until the theme of this eight-minute acoustic comedy becomes the singer's search for an appropriate backing. He is credited with discovering speech SAMPLING and resynthesis in *Speech Songs* (1973) and *In Celebration* (1964). More recently, Dodge has been using the concepts of fractal geometry for fairly familiar music, creating works that are again further ahead technically than esthetically.

Selected Works: *Composition in 5 Parts*, for cello and piano, 1964; *Solos and Combinations*, for flute, clarinet, and oboe, 1964; *Folia*, for chamber orchestra, 1965; *Rota*, for orchestra, 1966; *Changes*, for computer synthesis, 1970; *Earths Magnetic Field*, 1970; *Speech Songs*, for computer-synthesized voice, 1972; *The Days of Our Lives*, for computer synthesized voice, 1974; *In Celebration*, for computer-synthesized voice, 1975; *Cascando*, for a radio play by Samuel Beckett, 1978; *He Met Her in the Park*, for radio play by Richard Kostelanetz, 1982; *The Waves*, for soprano and computer synthesis, 1984; *A Postcard from the Volcano*, for soprano and computer synthesis, 1986; *Song without Words*, for computer synthesis, 1986; *A Fractal for Wiley*, for computer synthesis, 1987; *Imaginary Narrative*, for computer synthesis, 1989; *The Village Child*, puppet theater, 1992.

Recordings: *Any Resemblance is Purely Coincidental*. Albany, CA: New Albion, 1992.

Writings: and Jerse, Thomas A. *Computer Music: Synthesis, Composition, and Performance*. 2d ed. New York: Schirmer, 1997.

DORIA, Charles

(18 April 1938).

A poet and translator, initially trained in classical languages, Doria turned his profound knowledge of contemporary avant-garde poetry toward finding precursors in ancient writing, compiling anthologies by himself and in collaboration with others, as well as writing critical articles about previously unexamined classical examples. In *The Game of Europe* (1983), his own book-length poem, each section expires as it extrapolates a different writing convention, beginning with that of the novel, passing through Greek chorus, medieval sequence, ballad, literary epistle, newspaper article, and shaped poems/text-sound, concluding with riddles, graffiti, and broken texts from the Tibetan and Egyptian Books of the Dead, all of which indicates that the range of its allusion includes forms as well as content. (Another translator from the classical languages, likewise reflecting avant-garde intelligence, is Geoffrey Cook [1946].) Paul Schmidt (1932–1999) had few peers as an excellent translator of innovative poetry by ARTHUR RIMBAUD, VLADIMIR KHLEBNIKOV, and many others.

Works: *The Tenth Muse: Classical Drama in Translation*. Athens: Ohio University Press, 1980; *Short*. Brooklyn: Assembling, 1982; *Short R*. Brooklyn: Assembling, 1983; *The Game of Europe*. Athens: Swallow-Ohio University Press, 1983; *Selected Poems, June 1988*. Barrytown, NY: Left Hand, 1989; *The Toy Palace*. Barrytown, NY: Left Hand, 1990; *Giordano Bruno: On the Composition of Images, Signs, and Ideas*. Trans. Charles Doria. Ed. and annotations by Dick Higgins. New York: Willis, Locker, & Owens, 1991; *Bagdad Bones*. New York: Posy (506 Ft. Washington Ave., 10033), 1993.

Anthologies: and Harris Lenowitz, eds. and trans. *Origins*. Garden City, New York: Doubleday Anchor, 1976.

DOVE, Arthur

(2 August 1880–November 1946).

Dove gets the credit for being the first American artist to paint a work of nonrepresentational abstraction. He is perhaps the first artist in the world to do so. His five small, numbered *Abstraction* paintings (1910–11) are roughly contemporaneous with the earliest efforts at pure abstraction by WASSILY KANDINSKY, and may well precede them. Dove's five paintings are compositions of oval, rectangular, and curving forms, rendered in earth tones and vibrant reds with short, hatching brush strokes. They vaguely resemble images of trees, hills, and buildings, but none of them can be fully resolved into a coherent landscape. Despite this moment of artistic prescience, most of the work that followed is remarkably unimpressive. Simplifications of natural scenery, such as mountains, streams, sunrises, and storms, they reduce landscape painting to crude arrangements of ovals, triangles, and rectangles that lack any formal ingenuity or visual resonance but are notable for appearing dull and inert. Dove is more successful when he attempts to render nonvisual sensations by visual means. In his *Fog Horns* (1929), the piercing blare of the horns appears to blast forward from the surface of the work.

—Mark Daniel Cohen

Selected Works: *Abstraction No. 1* through *5*, 1910–11; *Pagan Philosophy*, 1913; *Thunderstorm*, 1921; *Fog Horns*, 1929; *Moon*, 1935; *That Red One*, 1944.

Exhibition Catalogs: Johnson, Dorothy Rylander. *Arthur Dove: The Years of Collage*. College Park: University of Maryland Art Gallery, 1967; Potter, Margaret. *AD: An Exhibition*. New York: MoMA, 1968; Haskell, Barbara. *AD*. San Francisco: San Francisco Museum of Art, 1974; DePietro, Anne Cohen. *AD & Helen Torr: The Huntington Years*. Huntington, New York: Heckscher Museum, 1989; Balken, Debra Bricker. *Arthur G. Dove: Pastels, Charcoals, Watercolor: February 6-March 13, 1993*. New York: Terry Dintenfass, 1993; Balken, Debra, Agee, William C., and Turner, Elizabeth Hutton. *AD: A Retrospective*. Andover, MA: Addison Gallery of American Art & Cambridge, MA: MIT Press in association with the Phillips Collection, Washington, DC, 1997.

Catalog Raisonné: Morgan, Ann Lee. *Arthur Dove, Life and Work: with a Catalogue Raisonné*. Newark: University of Delaware Press, 1984.

Arthur Dove, *The Inn*, 1942. Oil on canvas. CORBIS/Francis G. Mayer.

Interpretation: Wright, Frederick Stallknecht. *Arthur G. Dove*. Berkeley: University of California, 1958; Cohn, Sherrye. *Arthur Dove: Nature As Symbol*. Ann Arbor, Michigan: UMI Research Press, 1985.

"DOWNTOWN"

(1970s).

This epithet, based on New York City geography, arose initially in talk about classical music to distinguish work produced below 14th Street from that more typical of "uptown," which refers pointedly to culture produced on the West Side between Lincoln Center in the south and Columbia University to the north. If uptown composers were affiliated with institutions such as universities, those downtown were customarily independent. Audiences at uptown concerts tended to be older and better dressed than those downtown. If uptown composers tended to write serial music for their university colleagues to play, those residing downtown tended to MODULAR or other kinds of alternative music for themselves and their similarly unaffiliated friends to play. The uptown composer Milton Babbitt (who curiously lived most of his Manhattan life downtown, south of 23rd Street), told me in 1997 that "midtown composers" were the New Yorkers who, regardless of where they actually lived, "get the token commissions from provincial orchestras." The remark was fresh enough at the time for me to tell it to others.

So applicable was this binary New York geographical distinction that it was extended to other cultural domains. Here the stylistic measure is difference, if not "deviance," in form and/or content, particularly literature. The sorts of writing anthologized in, say, *Unbearables* (1995), would never appear in uptown journals, even if their authors were famous. Similarly, it makes symbolic sense that the Fales Special Collections at New York University, once specializing in nineteenth-century British fiction, should now concentrate on downtown New York writing, much as its music library collects downtown scores and recordings, as New York University is the only major Manhattan academic institution located south of Tenth Street.

Refining this theme of geographical difference down to finer details, I once identified several strains *within* downtown Manhattan literature, distinguishing that produced in the West Village from East Village writing, which in turn differed from SoHo literature. Specifically, as the East Village literature extended developments in poetry, SoHo writing reflected advanced visual and musical arts. Its fairly broad strokes notwithstanding, downtown/uptown defines clear differences in New York City dance and even visual art. The point of the 1976 Berlin exhibition, *SoHo*, was introducing Europe to artistic styles that then could not prosper above 14th Street.

Geographical differences are probably applicable to arts in other cities as well, though their fault lines might be different (east vs. west, lakefront vs. interior, etc.).

Anthology: Kolm, Ron, et al., eds. *Unbearables*. Brooklyn, NY: Autonomedia, 1995.

Exhibition Catalogs: *New York Downtown Manhattan Soho*. Ed. René Block. Berlin: Akademie der Kunste, 1976; *A Secret Location on the Lower East Side*. Curated Steven Clay & Rodney Phillips. New York: New York Public Library, 1998.

Interpretation: Banes, Sally. *Greenwich Village 1963: Avant-Garde Performance and the Effervescent Body*. Durham: Duke University Press, 1993; Kostelanetz, Richard. "Downtown Writing and the Literature of SoHo." New York: Fales Lecture, 1997; McDarrah, Fred W., and Patrick J. *The Greenwich Village Guide*. Pennington, NJ: a cappella books, 1993.

DOYLE, Tom

(23 May 1928).

After practicing a style of floor-hugging, linoleum sculpture that seemed to wave across an exhibition space, Doyle turned to the creation of large wooden architectural structures that were concerned with carving out volumes of space. Assembled from members hewn out of logs of cherry and oak, his works brought the concept of the arch into modern art. Sinewy and highly organic in appearance due to Doyle's retention of the natural forms of the wood, the delicately poised timbers seem to be arranged by expressive impulse, suggesting the influence of ABSTRACT EXPRESSIONISM. Yet, they display a subtle and ingenious use of geometry, indicating concerns that match those of CONSTRUCTIVISM. Although the majority of his arches stand on three points and appear to be designed strictly out of triangles, looking at them from a variety of angles reveals an array of implied geometric forms: squares and rectangles that emerge from changing perspectives.

—Mark Daniel Cohen

Selected Works: *Over Owl's Creek*, 1966; *Stillwater*, 1979; *Ballymaloe*, 1985; *Togher*, 1991; *Samhin*, 1996.

Exhibition Catalogs: Hering, Karl Heinz. *Tom Doyle: 6. August bis 17. Oktober, 1965*. Dusseldorf: Der

Kunstverein, 1965; *Marcel Duchamp; Wassily Kandinsky; Kasimir Malewitsch; Josef Albers; Tom Doyle: Kunsthalle Bern, 23. Oktober-29. November 1964*. Bern, Switzerland: Kunsthalle, 1964; Squiers, Carol. *Sculpture Yesterday/Today: Mark di Suvero, Tom Doyle, Peter Forakis, Charles Ginnever*. New York: Sculpture Now, 1977; Ratcliff, Carter. *Tom Doyle: Spring 1999*. New York: Kouros, 1999.

DUBUFFET, Jean

(31 July 1901–12 May 1985).

The son of a wealthy wine merchant, Dubuffet had little serious artistic training and spent little of his early life painting before beginning a life in Paris as a rich dilettante. After World War II, he took up painting again, developing a technique in which he loaded the canvas with a heavy paste made of plaster, putty, asphalt, concrete, and glue, and in which he embedded pebbles, broken glass, and various kinds of rubbish. Onto this dense paste, he scrawled and scratched crude renderings of figures reminiscent of the drawings of children and, to some extent, the childlike drawings of Paul Klee. He also championed the artworks of the insane, the untutored, and children, which he viewed as directly and intimately expressive and unencumbered by the stultifying (in his view) traditions of art history. He collected and exhibited the art works of the mentally handicapped and gave them the title "Art Brut." His own work did not advance. Although he briefly turned to sculpture in the 1950s, he showed little ability for it, and he lacked the training and wherewithal to develop artistically in any way. Critics and art historians have disagreed sharply over the worth of his work. Some find it valueless. Others see Dubuffet as a pioneer of anti-art and of the movement away from the use of traditional materials. Certainly, it can be said that his work provides hope and an unfortunate impetus to many artists in the late twentieth century who possess insufficient talent to have flourished at any other time.

—Mark Daniel Cohen

Selected Works: *Childbirth*, 1944; *Knoll of Visions*, 1952; *The Spotted Cow*, 1954; *The Substance of Stars*, 1959; *Life Without Man*, 1960; *Fruits of the Earth*, 1960.

Biographies: Franzke, Andreas. *Dubuffet*. New York: Abrams, 1981.

Exhibition Catalogs: Dubuffet, Jean and Selz, Peter. *The Work of Jean Dubuffet, with texts by the artist*. New York: MOMA, 1962; Allen, Virginia. *JD: Drawings*. New York: Metropolitan Museum of Art, 1968; *JD: A Retrospective*. New York: Guggenheim Museum, 1973; Schjeldahl, Peter. *JD: Recent Paintings, October 31–29 November 1980*. New York: Pace, 1980; Kernan, Beatrice. *Dubuffet, Works on Paper*. New York: MOMA, Department of Drawings, 1986.

Interpretation: Taipé, Michel. *Mirobolus Macadam & Cie; Hautespates de J. Dubuffet*. Paris: R. Drouin, 1946; Ragon, Michel. *Dubuffet*. New York: Grove Press, 1959; Cordier, Daniel. *The Drawings of Jean Dubuffet*. New York: G. Braziller, 1960; Berne, Jacques. *Dubuffet*. Paris: L'Herne, 1973; Dubuffet, Jean, Glimcher, Mildred, and Marc. *Jean Dubuffet: Towards an Alternate Reality*. New York: Pace Publications: Abbeville Press, 1987; Danchin, Laurent. *Jean Dubuffet*. Lyon: La Manufacture, 1988.

DUCHAMP, Marcel

(28 July 1887–2 October 1968).

The grandson of a painter, this Duchamp had three siblings who were also visual artists; but unlike his relatives, he turned his ironic skepticism about art into an extraordinary career built on the smallest amount of work. Indeed, it was his unique and improbable talent to endow, or get others to endow, even his inactivity with esthetic weight. Ostensibly, he went to Paris at sixteen to study art. From 1905 to 1910 he contributed cartoons to French papers. Early paintings, from 1910 and 1911, depict members of his family. His next paintings reflect an interest in movement, presaging the themes of Italian Futurist work; the epitome is the multiframe *Nude Descending a Staircase No. 2* (1913), which became the single most notorious work at the Armory Show in New York City. Abandoning

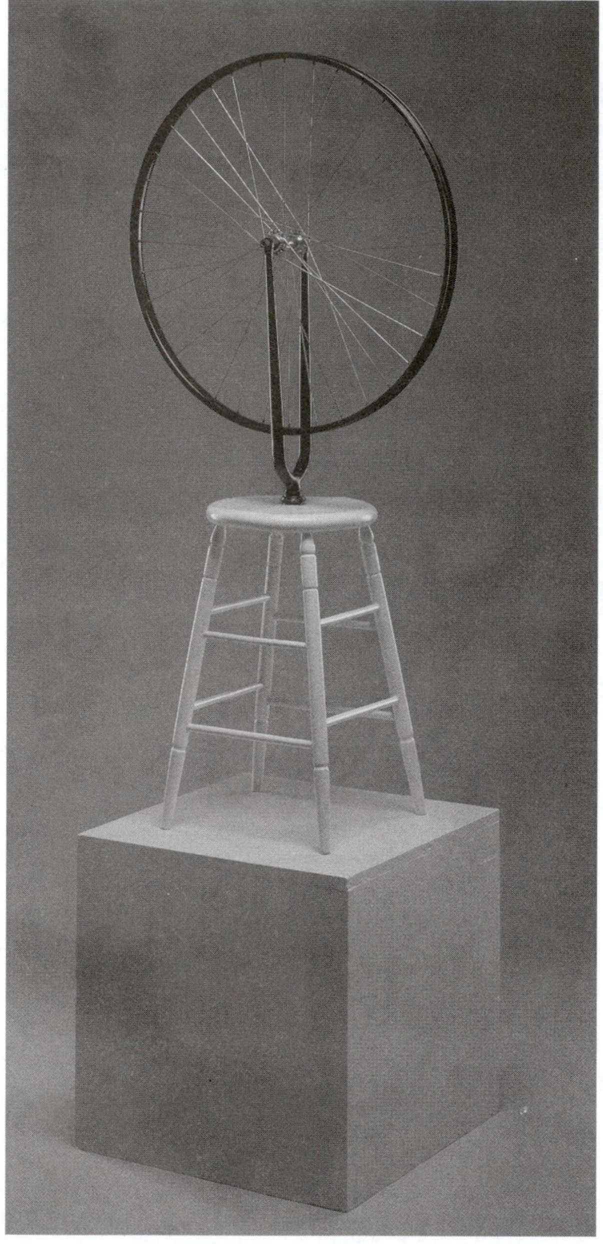

Marcel Duchamp, *Bicycle Wheel*. Reconstruction, 1964.
CORBIS/Philadelphia Museum of Art.

painting for three-dimensional art, Duchamp offered such everyday objects as a *Bicycle Wheel* (1913) and *Bottle Rack* (1914) as "readymades." Moving to New York in 1915, he spent several years working on *Large Glass: The Bride Stripped Bare by Her Bachelors, Even* (1915–23), which is often regarded as his single most monumental piece. Built from lead wire and tinfoil affixed to a sheet of glass, it is nearly nine feet high and six feet wide. Exhibited at the Brooklyn Museum in 1926, it was later found shattered and then restored in 1936 with repaired glass for permanent installation at the Philadelphia Museum of Art. (Facsimiles were made for Duchamp exhibitions in London in 1966 and in Venice in 1993.)

Meanwhile, Duchamp became the modern master of the provocative and resonant esthetic gesture. With courage based upon self-confidence, he submitted a urinal titled *Fountain* to the 1917 exhibition of the Society of Independent Artists, which he had cofounded and whose vice president he was. When the exhibition organizers refused to accept it, he resigned. (The implication, subsequently developed by others, was that esthetic value could be bestowed upon commonly available objects.) Similarly, to a DADA exhibition in Paris in 1920 Duchamp submitted a full-color reproduction of Leonardo's *Mona Lisa* to which he had added a beard and mustache; its official title was *L. H. O. O. Q. (Elle a chaud au cul)*, whose French is loosely translated as she has a hot arse. Whereas successful visual artists are encouraged to repeat themselves by their dealers and collectors, Duchamp alternatively established the avoidance of repetition as a laudatory professonal principle. By the mid-1920s, Duchamp had publicly abandoned painting in favor first of chess, his principal pastime, and then certain experiments in kineticism: *Rotary demisphere precision optics* (1925), film collaborations with MAN RAY, and *Rotoreliefs* (c. 1935), or discs with regular lines that create three-dimensional illusions when rotated like a phonograph record.

Returning to New York in 1942, Duchamp became a presence, even in his inactivity, especially at exhibitions including his early work. He worked on the contents of his *Boîte-en-Valise/Box in a Valise*, which he designed in the 1930s and began selling in the 1940s as a kind of autobiographical container with miniatures of his most important works, even adding *Paysage fauif* (1946, Wayward

Landscape) which appears to contain semen, probably his own, as a representation of frustrated love at age 59.

Yet so controversial was his art, and so generally unacceptable to the reigning authorities, that not until 1963, past his own seventy-fifth year, did Duchamp have an institutional retrospective, which was not in New York or Paris but in Pasadena, California. After he died, even Duchamp aficionados were surprised to find in his studio a tableau, *Ètant données*, on which he had secretly worked for many years. The viewer must peer through a crack in a door to see a diorama of a nude young woman (which must be seen firsthand at the Philadelphia Museum, because photographs of it are forbidden); this work culminates Duchamp's erotic obsessions, for which he was also famous. (As the poet Mina Loy remembered, "Marcel was slick as a prestidigitator; he could insinuate his hand under a woman's bodice and caress her with utter grace.")

Selected Works: *Nude Descending a Staircase No. 2*, 1913; *Bicycle Wheel*, 1913; *Erratum Musical*, 1913; *Three Standard Stoppages*, 1913–14; *Bottle Rack*, 1914; *In Advance of the Broken Arm*, 1915; *Large Glass: The Bride Stripped Bare by Her Bachelors, Even* (1915–1923); *L. H. O. O. Q. (Elle a chaud au cul)*, 1920; *Rotary Glass Plates (precision optics)*, 1920; *Rotary Demisphere (precision optics)*, 1925; *Rotoreliefs*, c. 1935; *Given: 1° The Waterfall; 2° The Illuminating Gas*, 1946–66.

Website: http://www.marcelduchamp.org/

Further Reading: Perhaps because Duchamp's works are so few in number and so initially inscrutable, they have generated an incomparable wealth of interpretations, offering different things to different commentators. In no other modern artist can sophisticated writers find such a variety, if not a wealth, of deep meanings. (By this measure, Duchamp resembles Leonardo da Vinci of all artists and James Joyce among his contemporaries.) With characteristic cunning, Duchamp accredited the Duchamp critical industry with a passing remark made in a lecture delivered in 1957 to the American Federation of the Arts in Houston, Texas: "The spectator brings the work in contact with the external world by deciphering and interpreting its inner qualifications and thus adds his contribution to the creative art." Because new discoveries are still being made, it is appropriate to provide admittedly incomplete guidance to the Duchamp literature:

The subtitle of *Salt Seller: The Writings of Marcel Duchamp* (1973; New York: Da Capo, 1989), edited by Michel Sanouillel and Elmer Peterson, suggests a completeness that is not entirely true. Besides, Duchamp the writer does not illuminate much about Duchamp the artist. *The Bride Stripped Bare by Her Bachelors, Even* (London: Percy Lund Humphries, 1960) is Richard Hamilton's "typographical version" of Duchamp's notes and sketches about his masterpiece. Ecke Bonk's *Marcel Duchamp: Box in a Valise* (New York: Rizzoli, 1989) itemizes the artist's boxed (and thus alternative) artistic autobiography.

Pierre Cabanne's *Dialogues with Marcel Duchamp* (1971; New York: Da Capo, 1988) transcribes conversations held in French just before Duchamp's death. It includes one of those stupendous bibliographies for which the Museum of Modern Art's librarian at the time, Bernard Karpel, was justly famous, itemizing published texts, interview transcripts, and secondary literature to 1970. Duchamp's remark valorizing the Duchamp critical industry appears in "The Creative Act" in Gregory Battcock's anthology *The New Art* (New York: Dutton, 1966).

Robert Lebel's *Marcel Duchamp* (New York: Grove, 1959) is a substantial introduction, including an early catalogue raisonné and a French-centered bibliography. A paperback edition (New York: Paragraphic, n.d. [1967]) omits the color plates but updates the documentation to 1967. Calvin Tomkins's *The World of Marcel Duchamp* (New York: Time-Life, 1966) is a well-illustrated introduction. Three decades later, Tomkins published *Duchamp: A Biography* (New York: Holt, 1997).

Arturo Schwarz's *The Complete Works of Marcel Duchamp* (New York: Abrams, 1969, 1970) includes a critical catalogue raisonné and an exhaustive descriptive bibliography. Incredible though it seems with an artist prominent so long and now long dead, a third, expanded edition of this book attributes 253 additional works to

Duchamp. New York: Delano Greenridge; London: Thames & Hudson, 1997.

The Mexican Nobelist Octavio Paz's *Marcel Duchamp or the Castle of Purity* (New York: Grossman, 1970) is an unpaginated chapbook written while its author was a diplomat in India. Paz also contributed one of the strongest essays to the catalog *Duchamp* edited by Anne d'Harnoncourt and Kynaston McShine for the Museum of Modern Art in 1973 (reprinted 1989), along with LUCY R. LIPPARD, DAVID ANTIN, Richard Hamilton, and Bernard Karpel, with a fuller bibliography.

Shigeko Kubota's *Marcel Duchamp and John Cage* (Tokyo: Takeyoshi Miyazawa, n.d) includes thirty-six photos of the two subjects playing chess on an amplified board, taken only a few months before Duchamp's death. It comes in a sleeve, accompanied by a small, plastic, long-playing recordlette.

New York Dada, edited by Rudolf E. Kuenzli (New York: Willis, Owens & Locker, 1986), contains Craig Adcock's "Marcel Duchamp's Approach to New York: 'Find an Inscription for the Woolworth Building as a ReadyMade.'" Adcock's book about Duchamp's use of geometry is *Marcel Duchamp's Notes from the Large Glass: An N-Dimensional Analysis* (Ann Arbor: UMI Research, 1983). Kuenzli collaborated with Francis M. Naumann in editing *Marcel Duchamp: Artist of the Century* (Cambridge: MIT Press, 1990), which contains an introduction to William A. Camfield's spectacularly elaborate essay on "Marcel Duchamp's *Fountain*" (aka the urinal), which, as he points out, survived only in a photograph that was ignored until the conceptual assumptions of the work became relevant to esthetic issues established in the 1960s. The book concludes with a yet fuller "Selective Bibliography." The full Camfield essay appeared as *Marcel Duchamp's Fountain* (Houston: The Menil Collection/Houston Fine Art Press, 1989). Naumann curated *Making Mischief: Dada Invades New York*, featuring Duchamp, in addition to editing with Beth Venn the Whitney Museum's catalog for that exhibition (1996). Jo-Anne Birnie Danzker's *Duchamp Readymades* (Vancouver Art Gallery, 1978) is an exhibition catalog.

Jennifer Gough-Cooper & Jacques Caumont's *Marcel Duchamp: Work and Life* (Cambridge: MIT Press, 1993) is a two-front publication, reading from one cover (Work) as a catalog of the exhibition held at Palazzo Grassi, Venice, and from the other (Life) as a day-by-day chronology of the artist's life with over 3,600 items arranged by astrological signs. Joseph Maschek's *Marcel Duchamp in Perspective* (Englewood Cliffs, NJ: Prentice-Hall, 1975) reprints criticism unavailable elsewhere, including an interview with John Cage about Duchamp. Theirry de Duve's anthology *The Definitively Unfinished Marcel Duchamp* (Cambridge: MIT Press, 1991) recycles many of the same scholars.

Other Duchamp Interpretation: Hulten, Pontus, ed. *Marcel Duchamp: Work & Life*. Cambridge: MIT Press, 1993; Joselit, Dave. *Infinite Regress: Marcel Duchamp 1910–1941*. Cambridge: MIT Press, 1998; Mink, Janis. *Marcel Duchamp 1887–1968: Art as Anti-Art*. Köln: Taschen, 1996; Nixon, Mignon, and Martha Buskirk, eds. *The Duchamp Effect*. Cambridge: MIT Press, 1996; Seigel, Jerrold. *The Private Worlds of Marcel Duchamp: Desire, Liberation, and the Self in Modern Culture*. Berkeley: University of California Press, 1995.

DUCKWORTH, William

(13 January 1943).

An unusual university composer, Duckworth produced one piece of such brilliance and originality that it has become a hard act for him to top. Especially in the NEELY BRUCE recording, which remains superior to other renditions, *The Time Curve Preludes* (1979) reflects MODULAR MUSIC, as well as the popular concern with generating audible overtones, without resembling any previous music conceived in those ways. Composed for a specially retuned piano, the *Preludes* are brief pieces, twenty-four in sum, based upon the Fibonacci series (in which each number is the sum of the two preceding it, in a continuous sequence), one hour in total length, rich with allusions to both contemporary and pre-Renaissance music. Very much in the great tradition of exhaustive modernist compositions for solo piano (including Dmitri Shostakovitch's [1906–1975] *Preludes and Fugues*, Paul Hindemith's [1895–1963] *Ludus Tonalis*, and JOHN CAGE'S *Sonatas and Interludes), The Time Curve Pre-*

ludes are also lushly beautiful. Duckworth has also published a collection of his extended interviews with his contemporaries.

Selected Compositions: *An Unseen Action*, for flute, prepared piano, and 4 percussion, 1966; *A Mass for These Forgotten Times*, for chorus, 1973; *The Time Curve Preludes*, 1977–78; *Southern Harmony*, for chorus, 1980–81; *Imaginary Dances* for piano, 1985; rev. 1988; *Gathering Together*, for 2 keyboards and 2 mallet percussion, 1992.

Internet Work: *Cathedral* (http://www.monroestreet.com/Cathedral/).

Selected Recordings: *The Time Curve Preludes*. New York: Lovely Music, 1990.

Books: *Talking Music: Conversations with John Cage, Philip Glass, Laurie Anderson, and Five Generations of American Experimental Composers*. New York: Schirmer, 1995; *20/20: 20 New Sounds of the 20th Century*. New York: Schirmer, 1999; ———, ed, *Sound and Light: La Monte Young, Marian Zazeela*. Lewisburg, PA: Bucknell University Press, 1996; ———, and R. Fleming, eds. *John Cage at Seventy-Five*. Lewisburg, PA: Bucknell University Press, 1989.

DUDEK, Louis

(6 February 1918).

"Context is criticism" is an insight that sheds light on the life and work of Louis Dudek. The Montreal-born poet and critic, who taught at McGill University from 1951 until his retirement in 1982, advanced the causes of modern, contemporary, and Canadian literature through teaching, writing, and publishing. In a Canadian context, Dudek is a proponent of new poets and poetries ("Is it the destiny of Montreal to show the country from time to time what poetry is?"). In a Western context, he stands as a literary modernist, a sometime correspondent of Ezra Pound, and a critic of the ideology *du four* and *de la patrie*. In the context of the avant-garde, his writings are intransigently intelligent, idiosyncratically free-flowing, and unfashionably humanistic. Book-length poetic meditations like *Atlantis* are characteristic; so are needling aphorisms that shed both light and friends: "Of all sad fates, the Avant-Garde's the worst: / They were going nowhere, and they got there first."

—John Robert Colombo

Poetry: *East of the City*. Toronto: Ryerson, 1946; *The Searching Image*. Toronto: Ryerson, 1946; *Twenty-Four Poems*. Toronto: Contact, 1956; *Collected Poetry*. Montreal: Delta Canada, 1971; *Selected Poems*. Ottawa: Golden Dog, 1975; *Epigrams*. Montreal: DC, 1975; *Cross-Section Poems 1940–1980*. Toronto: Coach House, 1980; *Continuation I*. Montreal: Véhicule, 1981; *Zembla's Rocks*. Montreal:Véhicule, 1987; *Infinite Worlds*. Ed. Robin Blaser. Montreal: Véhicule, 1989; *Continuation II*. Montreal: Véhicule, 1990; *Some Perfect Things*. Montreal: DC, 1991; *A Last Stand: Poems*. Montreal: Véhicule, 1995.

Prose: *Literature and the Press: A History of Printing, Printed Media, and Their Relation to Literature*. Toronto: Ryerson & Contact, 1960; *Selected Essays and Criticism*. Ottawa: Tecumseh, 1978; *In Defense of Art: Critical Essays and Reviews*. Ed. Aileen Collins. Kingston, Ont: Quarry, 1988; *Paradise: Essays on Myth, Art & Reality*. Montreal: Véhicule, 1992.

Anthologies: With Irving Layton. *Canadian Poems 1850–1952* (1952). Rev. ed. Toronto: Contact, 1953; and Michael Snarowski, eds. *The Making of Modern Poetry in Canada: Essential Articles on Contemporary Canadian Poetry in English*. Toronto: Ryerson, 1967.

Interpretation: Davey, Frank. *Louis Dudek and Raymond Souster*. Vancouver: Douglas & McIntyre, 1980; Goldie, Terry. *Louis Dudek and His Works*. Toronto: E.C.W., 1985; Stromberg-Stein, Susan. *Louis Dudek: A Biographical Introduction to his Poetry*. Ottawa: Golden Dog Press, 1983.

DUFRÊNE, François

(1930–12 December 1982).

Initially an associate of Lettrism, he developed in the l950s "cri-rhythmes," as he called them. Though these word-based wails initially reflect Antonin Artaud, their style acoustically resembles the 1960s Expressionist jazz of

ORNETTE COLEMAN and ALBERT AYLER. They were quite spectacular, whether performed live (say, at sound poetry festivals) or on a record. At times he overdubbed his voice, creating a level of declamatory intensity that, even after his premature death, remains unsurpassed. Dufrêne also published Lettristic CONCRETE POETRY and poster poems.

Exhibition Catalogs: *François Dufrêne*. Rouen: Centre d'Art Contemporain, 1981; *Pour FD*. Paris: Association Polyphonix-Centre Georges Pompidou 1983; *FD*. Sables d'Olonne, France: Musée de l'Abbaye Ste. Croix, 1988. (This includes a discography and filmography.)

Interpretation: Chopin, Henri. *Poésie sonore internationale*. Paris, France: Jean-Michel Place, 1979.

DUGUAY, Raoul

(1939).

Since the middle 1960s, no other French–Canadian poet has so completely reflected international avant-garde activities. As Caroline Bayard summarizes his "writing techniques":

> The first is the breaking down of sentences and words into atomized units. The second is his use of simultaneity—words or phonemes being projected at the same time, by different voices, from different places. The third is the search for a notation system, a score—words being placed on bars with annotations which indicate measure, tonality, and length. In effect, the poem becomes a musical score, the notes being either words or phonemes. The fourth is the need for a visual presentation, one which, however, has little to do with visual concrete principles. Most of his poems present a typography similar to that of old illuminated texts. Graphic designs form the background, words the foreground.

Bayard continues, "On the whole, Duguay's contribution to international concrete theory is his exploration in the areas of sound, phonetics, and phonology."

Writing: "On the Vibrant Body." *Open Letter* III/8 (Spring 1978).

Interpretation: Bayard, Caroline. *The New Poetics in Canada and Quebec*. Toronto: University of Toronto Press, 1989.

DUKE, Jas H.

(16 October 1939–16 June 1992; b. James Heriot D.).

Duke was an Australian poet I know mostly through extraordinary recordings. A note accompanying his declamation of "Nikola Tesla" says, "Since starting to write sound poetry in 1966, Jas Duke produced a large and varied body of work including the publication of two books and innumerable performances. His recitals often employed simple modifications to the acoustic of his voice, achieved, for example, by filling his mouth with paper." Another "modification" clearly audible is speech unique to Australia. From sketchy information, I gather that Duke went as a young man to England, where he edited *Archduke* (1968–74) and *Brighton Head and Freak Mag* (1969–70) and made experimental films with Jeff Keen before returning to his native Australia. Once back home, he became the principal advocate for literary and performance art that extended the historical avant-gardes, as well as becoming a devout anarchist.

Books: *Poems of War and Peace*. Melbourne, Australia: Collective Effort (GPO 2340v, 3001), 1987; et al. *Industrial Women*. Melbourne: Women's Collection, 1986; *Poems of Life and Death*. Ed. (T. T. O. Melbourne: Collective Effort, forthcoming.

Recordings: *Tribute* (unnumbered CD), in *Going Down Swinging* 13 (P.O. Box 64, Coburg, Victoria, Australia 30S8), 1993.

Website: http://www.thing.net/~grist/l&d/thalia/au-jd.htd

DUNCAN, Isadora

(27 May 1877–14 September 1927).

Isadora Duncan won notoriety for her flamboyant lifestyle, memorialized first in her autobiography and then in a pop movie, and genuine fame for her artistic evocation of a "natural" style of dance that contradicted the

Isadora Duncan's dance company, known as The Isadorables. Photo: Frances Benjamin Johnston, CORBIS.

ballet conventions of her time. Though Duncan had in fact received some ballet training and performed on vaudeville stages, she questioned the validity of established modes of dance movement, seeking her inspiration instead in her perceptions of nature (for example, the motions of the sea) and antiquity (Greek art and architecture). She believed all movement originates from the solar plexus and acknowledges the force of gravity (in this last respect, in particular, differing from ballet). Her dance vocabulary included loose, graceful, flowing gestures and childlike runs, skips, and leaps. An expressive dancer, who thought movement alone could articulate emotion, Duncan touched people through the deep passion of her performances. She cherished great music and chose to perform to masterpieces (at a time when some ballet dancers were frequently performing to mediocre scores). Duncan was associated with some of the great artists of her time, including the innovative stage designer EDWARD

GORDON CRAIG (by whom she bore a child) and the Russian poet Sergei Esenin (1895–1925, whom she married). Although born in Oakland, California, she spent most of her adult life in Europe, where she died in an unfortunate automobile accident.

—Katy Matheson

Compositions: Unlike other dancer/choreographers, Duncan customarily did not name her pieces. She is believed to have created over 200 pieces.

Books: *My Life* (1927). New York: Liveright, 1996; *The Art of Dance* (1928). Ed. Sheldon Cheney. New York: Theatre Arts, 1977; *Isadora Speaks: Writings and Speeches*. Ed. & intro. Franklin Rosemont. San Francisco: City Lights, 1981.

Biography: Daly, Ann. *Done into Dance: Isadora Duncan in America*. Bloomington: Indiana University Press,1995; Desti, Mary. *The Untold Story: The Life of Isadora Duncan 1921–27*. New York: Da Capo, 1981; Duncan, Irma. *Duncan Dancer: An Autobiography*. Middletown: Wesleyan University Press, 1965; Duncan, Irma, and Allan Ross Macdougall. *Isadora Duncan's Russian Days and her Last Years in France*. New York: Covici-Friede, 1929; Seroff, Victor. *The Real Isadora*. New York: Dial, 1971; Lowenthal, Lillian. *The Search for Isadora: Legend and Legacy of Isadora Duncan*. Pennington, NJ: Princeton Book, 1993; McVay, Gordon. *Isadora and Esenin*. Ann Arbor: Ardis, 1976; Duncan, Doree, ed. *Life into Art: Isadora Duncan and Her World*. New York: Norton, 1993.

Website: www.isadoraduncan.org

DUNCAN, Robert

(7 January 1919–3 February 1988).

Although his deservedly high reputation as a poet depends almost entirely on norm-clinging collections like his *Roots and Branches*, Duncan flirted with innovation throughout his career. Steinianly repetitive automatic writing, Surrealism, Dada, Cummingsesque visual-poetic techniques, and his friend Charles Olson's composition by field were part of his early repertoire, and in *Letters* (1953–56) he anticipated LANGUAGE-CENTERED POETRY with such passages as "He was one like him that in grown out cast over bearing under done far fetchd near by all most quite all ways never with out full filld part time close spaced semi-literate multi-phase of a face of him her." In the same collection he broke the phrase "old grey matter" infra-verbally into "old greym attar"—grimness plus fragrance. And we are reminded that it was Duncan who made the famous selection of ARAM SAROYAN's splendid pwoermd (i.e., one-word poem), "lighght," a decade later for the NEA grant that imbeciles in Congress are still using as an example of aesthetic insanity.

—Bob Grumman

Books: *Selected Poems*. Ed. Robert Bertholf. New York: New Directions, 1997.

Biography: Fass, Ekbert. *Young Robert Duncan: Portrait of the Poet as Homosexual in Society*. Santa Barbara, CA: Black Sparrow, 1983.

Bibliography: Bertholf, Robert J. *Robert Duncan: A Descriptive Bibliography*. Santa Rosa, CA: Black Sparrow, 1986.

DYLAN, Bob

(24 May 1941; b. Robert Allen Zimmerman).

Consider Dylan an avant-garde artist on several grounds. He broadened the subject matter of popular vocal music beyond young love and cars, incidentally extending the length of the typical pop song; he also broke down the structure of verse-chorus-bridge typical of other pop artists. His manner is everything other than that of an earlier teen idol. Dylan demonstrated that a singer-guitarist of only modest natural abilities could be a better interpreter of his own material than a more attractive and virtuosic "star."

Previous to the arrival of Dylan, most "songwriters" wrote material for pop singers to perform; Dylan was the first to show that a songwriter could be a performer, even if he had rather limited vocal qualities. Dylan also created several musical genres, including folk-rock (the melding of folk-protest lyrics with rock instrumentation and beat), and country-rock (the combining of country-style songs into the rock mold).

Dylan's greatest avant-garde act is his constant changing of personae; although not a new idea, it was certainly new to popular music. As soon as listeners and critics became comfortable with one "Dylan," he would unveil another. So he alienated his folk audience by "going electric" in 1965; he then surprised his rock-pop audience by taking up country music in the late '60s (and adopting a smoother form of his nasal voice); he then switched to being a confessional singer-songwriter in the '70s; a born-again Christian prophet in the late '70s; a rock-arena artist in the mid-'80s; back to acoustic-folk in the early '90s; and most recently a roots-rock revivalist. Dylan has also reworked his songs, changing the arrangements and sometimes rewriting lyrics, so that his "hits" are not always recognizable to his audience.

Dylan also experimented with free-form poetry and prose, inspired by sources as diverse as the Bible, JAMES JOYCE, and ALLEN GINSBERG. *Tarantula* (1966) collects his early literary experiments.

—Richard Carlin

Select Recordings: *The Freewheelin' Bob Dylan*. New York: Columbia, 1963; *Times they are A-Changin'*. New York: Columbia, 1964; *Blonde on Blonde*. New York: Columbia, 1966; *Blood on the Tracks*. New York: Columbia, 1975; *Biograph*. New York: Columbia Records, 1987; *The Bootleg Series Vols. 1–3 1961–1991*. New York: Sony, 1997.

Books: *Tarantula*. New York: Macmillan, 1971; *Writings and Drawings*. New York: Knopf, 1973; *Lyrics, 1962–1985*. New York: Knopf, 1986; *Drawn Blank*. New York: Random House, 1994.

Biographies: Shelton, Robert. *No Direction Home*, New York: Beech Tree, 1986; Heylin, Clinton. *Bob Dylan: Behind the Mask*, New York: Summit, 1991; Scaduto, Anthony. *Bob Dylan: An Intimate Biography*. New York: Grosset & Dunlap, 1971; Spitz, Bob. *Bob Dylan: A Biography*. New York: McGraw-Hill, 1989;

Sessionography: Heylin, Clinton. *Bob Dylan: Complete Recording Sessions*. New York: St. Martin's Press, 1995.

Interpretation: Bauldie, John. ed. *Wanted Man: In Search of Bob Dylan*. New York: Citadel, 1991; Benson, Carl, ed. *Bob Dylan Companion: Four Decades of Commentary*. New York: Schirmer, 1998; Cott, Jonathan. *Dylan*. New York: Doubleday, 1984; Marcus, Griel. *Invisible Republic: Bob Dylan and the Basement Tapes*. New York: Holt, 1996; McGregor, Craig. *Bob Dylan The Early Years: A Retrospective* (1972). New York: Da Capo, 1990; Miles, Barry, ed. *Bob Dylan in His Own Words*. New York: Quick Fox, 1978; Williams, Paul. *Watching the River Flow*. London: Ominbus, 1996.

Website: www.bobdylan.com

DYMSHITS-TOLSTOYA, Sof'ya (Isaakovna)

(23 April 1889–30 August 1963).

According to John Bowlt (1943), the pioneering scholar of Russian futurist art, Dymshits-Tolstoya made several painted glass reliefs exhibited in Tatlin's Moscow exhibition *The Store* in 1916. "It was within this enterprise [of reliefs] that many of the avant-garde came together, particularly those working in three dimensions: Bromirsky, Bruni, Dymshits-Tolstoya, Rodchenko, Tatlin, et al." The populous traveling exhibition, *The Great Utopia: The Russian and Soviet Avant-Garde, 1915–1932* (1992–93), included a small work of hers ("ca. 1920") from the period featuring abstract shapes painted on two pieces of thick glass, securely framed. Married in 1907 to the novelist Aleskei Tolstoy, she lived in Paris, where she worked closely with VLADIMIR TATLIN, but returned to Russia after the Revolution and became active in Soviet cultural activities. In 1919 she reportedly organized the Moscow fireworks display for the second anniversary of the October Revolution. In a familiar photograph of Tatlin working on his projected *Monument to the Third Communist International*, she is the woman on the far left. *The Great Utopia* also included *Compass* (1920), which Jane A. Sharp regards as "undoubtedly her best work on canvas [where] string is woven into an abstract surface, the curvilinear forms of which only barely suggest the implement [the compass] that is the work's subject." Dymshits-Tolstoya wrote a memoir that lies in manuscript in the Russian Museum in St. Petersburg. Later she retired from administrative work and produced Soviet-style graphics celebrating women in agriculture and heavy industry. Her name is so unfamiliar, even to those who should know, that in an unfortunate caption on the wall of a 1991 KAZIMIR MALEVICH exhibition at New York's Metropolitan Museum she was cited as "Symshits-Tolstoya." I initially knew about her as my grandmother's sister.

Exhibition Catalog: *The Great Utopia: The Russian and Soviet Avant-Garde, 1915–1932*. New York: Guggenheim Museum, 1992.

Interpretation: Bowlt, John. "The Construction of Spaces in *Von der Flache zum Raum/From Surface to Space*. Köln, Germany: Galerie Gmurzynska, 1974; Sharp, Jane A. "Dymshits-Tolstoya." In *The Dictionary of Women Artists*. Ed. Delia Gaze. London & Chicago: Fitzroy Dearborn, 1997; Goodman, Susan Tumarkin, ed. *Russian Jewish Artists*. Munich, Germany: Prestel, 1995.

E-ZINE

(1990s).

One of the hallmarks of the micropress in the 1990s has been its insistent movement away from the paper copy culture and into cyberspace. From the mid-1990s on, there has been a definite and inexorable migration of the avant-garde press from the difficulties and anonymity of the paper press to the moderate ease and the greater exposure of the INTERNET. This change has occurred, of course, concurrent with a similar change in American culture away from books and towards the liquid paper screen of the computer. At the beginning of this transition, the term "e-zine" was born, meaning a zine presented over the Internet. Sometimes these zines were distributed via e-mail, but most frequently they were loaded onto the World Wide Web for viewing by the entire world. Such e-zines still flourish, but the term has been appropriated by the Internet community at large, and the term now refers merely to any electronic periodical at all, most of which are commercial in nature.

—Geof Huth

Reference: Rucker, Rudy, et al. *Mondo 2000: A User's Guide to the New Edge*. New York: HarperPerennial, 1992.

EAMES, Charles and Ray

(17 June 1907–21 August 1978; 15 December 1912–21 August 1988, b. Berniece Kaiser).

In addition to being prominent industrial designers, very much for hire, the Eameses, husband and wife working with equal credit long before such acknowledgment became more frequent in art, made several innovative films for their clients. *Glimpses of USA* (1959) consisted of seven films, composed from still photos projected simultaneously on seven screens that were twenty by thirty feet in size. It was shown continuously for twelve-minute stretches at the Moscow World's Fair. *House of Science* (1962) was a six-screen film, fifteen and one-half minutes long, created for the Seattle World's Fair. *Think* (1964–65), made for the New York World's Fair, featured twenty-two screens of various shapes.

A Rough Sketch for a Proposed Film Dealing with the Powers of Ten and the Relative Size of Things in the Universe (1968) became the preliminary version of *Powers of Ten* (1977), both of which films deal concretely with questions of scale. (The later videotape produced by Charles Eames's grandson, Eames Demetrios, reverses the sequence of the films.) Though these two shorts were made for instructional purposes (with funding from IBM, no less), the concept of enlargements (and then contractions) by powers of ten (at a quick and regular speed) is so original and breathtaking that the results attain esthetic quality. After pulling back continuously from the hand of a sleeping man into the galaxies (10 to the 24th power), in each ten seconds moving ten times the distance traveled in the previous ten seconds, the camera returns at a yet faster pace, entering the man's skin, revealing finally the structure of the atom (10 to the minus-13th power), in sum traversing the universe and the microcosm, all in

Charles Eames. L: *Molded plywood chair*, 1946; R: *Molded fiberglass chair*, 1952. Courtesy Herman Miller Archives.

less than eight minutes. On the left side of the screen in the earlier film are three chronometers measuring distance and time. This sort of conceptual tripping makes even *2001*, say, seem as elementary as scientific exposition.

The French arts historian Frank Popper credits Charles Eames alone with constructing a *Do-Nothing Machine* (1955) powered by solar energy, while several histories of contemporary architecture acknowledge the residential house that the Eameses built for themselves in Santa Monica, California. Charles is also credited with the inventive design of chairs and the discovery of alternative materials, particularly moulded plywood, for their manufacture. A traveling exhibit of Eames's works opened at the Library of Congress in Summer 1999.

Select Works: *Glimpses of U.S.A*, 1959; *House of Science*, 1962; *Think*, 1964–65; *A Rough Sketch for a Proposed Film Dealing with the Powers of Ten and the Relative Size of Things in the Universe*, 1968; *Powers of Ten*, 1977.

Videotapes: *Films of Charles & Ray Eames Vol.1*. Pyramid Home Video, 1989; *Vol. 2 Black Top House*. Pyramid, 1989; *Vol. 3 World of Franklin & Jefferson*. Pyramid, 1998; *Vol. 4 Films of Charles & Ray Eames*. Pyramid, 1994.

Website: http://www.eamesoffice.com/

Interpretation: Albrecht, Donald. *The Work of Charles and Ray Eames: A Legacy of Invention*. New York: Abrams, 1997; Caplan, R. *Connections: The Work of Charles and Ray Eames*. Los Angeles: UCLA Arts Council, 1976; Kirkham, Pat. *Charles & Ray Eames: Designers of the 20th Century* (1995). Cambridge: MIT Press, 1998; Morrison, Philip, and Phylis Morrison, and the Office of Charles and Ray Eames. *Powers of Ten*. San Francisco: Scientific American Library–W. H. Freeman, 1982; Newhart, John, et al. *Eames Design: the Work of the Office of Charles and Ray Eames*. New York: Abrams, 1989; Schrader, Paul. "The Films of Charles Eames." *Film Quarterly* XXIII/3 (Spring 1970); Steele, James. *Eames House*. London: Phaidon, 1994.

EARTH ART

(1960s, aka "earthworks" and "land art").

Perhaps as a reaction to the visual tedium and the sleek, boxy technological polish of Minimalist sculpture, or perhaps in an effort to break out of the commercial system that treated works of art as commodities, a number of artists in the late 1960s began executing enormous projects that altered the land in areas remote from civilization. Earth Art works existed primarily *in situ* and involved large excavations, the transferral of earth and stone to new sites in artificial configurations, and the burial of objects. These works became publicly known through exhibiting of photographic records of the projects, which often did not long survive their completion. Earth Art made its first appearance in an exhibition in 1968 at the Dwan Gallery in New York City with Sol LeWitt's *Box in a Hole* (1968), in which a steel cube was, presumably, buried in the ground in the Netherlands, and Walter de Maria's *Mile Long Drawing* (1968), in which two parallel white lines were drawn in the desert in Nevada. Other artists involved in Earth Art were Robert Smithson, Robert Morris, Michael Heizer, Richard Long, and Richard Serra. Regardless of the initiating motivation, Earth Art certainly was an expression of the typical Romantic impulse to combine art and nature, and the congenitally American urge to return to the wilderness. However, Earth Art projects lacked any Huckleberry-Finn deliberate naiveté. They often were guided by complex, attenuated, and elusive intellectual programs, so elusive that this form of art did not continue for long after the early death of Smithson in 1973. By the end of the 1970s, Earth Art was going out of fashion, and later artists who followed the inspiration to fuse together art and nature, like David Nash, returned to the creation and exhibition of object-based art. If there is one work by which Earth Art is primarily remembered through its photographic records, it is Smithson's *Spiral Jetty* (1970), which was a piled-up runway of basalt rock and dirt that corkscrewed its way along the surface of the Great Salt Lake in Utah.

—Mark Daniel Cohen

Works: de Maria, Walter, *Mile Long Drawing*, 1969; Heizer, Michael. *Displaced/Replaced Mass*, 1969; Heizer, Michael. *Double Negative*, 1969; Heizer, Michael. *City: Complex One*, 1972–74; Heizer, Michael. *Effigy Tumuli*, 1983–85; Heizer, Michael. *City: Complex Two*, 1980–88; LeWitt, Sol, *Box in a Hole*, 1969; Long, Richard. *Turf Circle*, 1969; Long, Richard. *Three Circles of Stones*, 1972; Long, Richard. *192 Pieces of Wood*, 1975; Long, Richard. *Sandstone Circle*, 1977; Serra, Richard, *Shift*, 1970–72; Smithson, Robert. *Spiral Jetty*, 1970; Smithson, Robert. *Spiral Hill*, 1971; Smithson, Robert. *Amarillo Ramp*, 1973.

Interpretation: Sonfist, Alan (ed.). *Art in the Land: A Critical Anthology of Environmental Art*. New York: Dutton, 1983; Beardsley, John. *Earthworks and Beyond: Contemporary Art in the Landscape*. New York: Abbeville, 1984; Bourdon, David. *Designing the Earth: The Human Impulse to Shape Nature*. New York: Abrams, 1995; Oakes, Baile (ed.). *Sculpting with the Environment: A Natural Dialogue*. New York: Van Nostrand Reinhold, 1995; Tiberghien, Gilles A. *Land Art*. New York: Princeton Architectural, 1995; Weilacher, Udo. *Between Landscape Architecture and Land Art*. Basel & Boston: Birkhauser, 1996; Korp, Maureen. *Sacred Art of the Earth: Ancient and Contemporary Earthworks*. New York: Continuum, 1997; Kastner, Jeffrey. *Land and Environmental Art*. London: Phaidon, 1998.

EASTMAN, George

(12 July 1854–14 March 1932).

As the inventor of photographic film that could be put on a spool and rolled through a camera, he changed not only the production of visual art but the perceptual and cultural experience of everyone. Forming the Eastman Dry Plate and Film Company in 1884, Eastman patented film that depended upon a paper roll. In 1889, he replaced the paper roll with celluloid and, in 1924, improved his invention futher with cellulose acetate. Once a camera could roll film, professional photographers could take numerous shots in quick succession, while the avoidance of cumbersome procedures encouraged amateurs to take a lot more pictures, incidentally enriching his company. Eastman's invention enabled THOMAS EDISON to develop a camera for moving film. No dope, Eastman gave away more than $75 million to various scientific, educational, and cultural organizations, including the Rochester-based School of Music that still bears his name. The other great inventor in photography was Edwin H. Land (1909–91), who invented after World War II rolled film that could be developed, so to speak, within the camera, producing a positive print within a short time, thus enabling the photographer to decide within a short time if he or she wanted to make another shot.

Bibliography: Coe, Brian. *George Eastman and the Early Photographers*. London: Priory, 1973; Brayer, Elizabeth. *George Eastman: A Biography*. Baltimore: John Hopkins University Press, 1996.

Website: www.eastman.org

EASTMAN, Julius

(1940–1990).

A mercurial African–American musician, born in New York and educated in composition at the Curtis Institute in

Philadelphia, Eastman became prominent, first in Buffalo, then in New York, in the 1970s, working with both pop music structures and free improvisation in a classical context. Also a singer with both a strong bass voice and an aptitude for falsetto, he was a brilliant performer for MEREDITH MONK, among others. According to Kyle Gann, who was also in Buffalo around that time, Eastman "developed a composing technique he called 'organic music,' a cumulatively overlapping process in which each section of a work contains, simultaneously, all sections which preceded it." By the early 1980s, he was titling his pieces provocatively—*Evil Nigger, Crazy Nigger*, and *Gay Guerrilla*, all of which were scored for several pianos, building up, in Gann's recollection, "emotive power through the incessant repetition of rhythmic figures." By the middle of the decade, Eastman became notorious for making unreasonable demands of his colleagues, as well as for drug and alcohol abuse. When he was evicted from his apartment, much of his music was lost. For a while he was reportedly homeless.

Works: *She is Alive* for solo voice with amplification [n.d.]; *Trumpet* for seven trumpets [n.d.]; *If You're So Smart Why Ain't You Rich?* for 4 trumpets, 4 french horns, 2 double basses, trombone and tuba [n.d.]; *Nigger Faggot* for strings, percussion, and bell [n.d.]; *Humanity and Not Spiritual Beings* 1. Solo for voice 2. Pianos & instruments, 1981.

Interpretation: Gann, Kyle. *American Music in the Twentieth Century*. New York: Schirmer, 1997.

EDGERTON, HAROLD

(6 February 1903–4 January 1990).
See **STROBE LIGHT.**

EDISON, Thomas

(11 February 1847–18 October 1931).

If GEORGE EASTMAN belongs here, so does his near-contemporary, Edison, an inventor who contributed not only to such pure technologies as the telephone, electric light, and the wireless telegraph, but to such artistic machines as the phonograph and the motion-picture projector. If not for Edison, modern life would have been different; likewise, modern art. Edison's life resembles that of some avant-garde artists in that he was thought uneducable and taken out of school. Aged only twelve, he took odd jobs, becoming, while a teenager, a telegraph operator whose deafness enabled him to concentrate on the telegraph's clicks, much as some advanced artists learn to exploit personal incapacities to practical advantage (e.g., JOHN CAGE, GERTRUDE STEIN). Inventing the phonograph in 1877, he found it a dead end until he developed a wax-coated cylinder on which sounds could be encoded, and then a floating stylus for playing back the sounds, and

Thomas Alva Edison in his West Orange laboratory, c. 1920.
CORBIS/Bettmann.

finally an electroplated master recording from which copies could be pressed, completing the processes necessary for dissemination. Accumulating teams of engineers and researchers, Edison founded the first industrial laboratory, incidentally establishing a corporate model that, in later hands, created other inventions with esthetic applications.

Biography: Josephson, Matthew. *Edison: A Biography* (1959). New York: Wiley, 1992; Baldwin, Neil. *Edison: Inventing the Culture.* New York: Hyperion, 1995.

Website:
http://home.earthlink.net/~zummos/edison/index.htm

EGGELING, Viking

(21 October 1880–19 May 1925).

Born in Sweden, Eggeling moved to Paris before the end of the nineteenth century and then to Switzerland, where he became an early contributor to the DADA movement. In collaboration with HANS RICHTER, he worked initially with abstract picture strips, hoping to discover "rhythm in painting" through all the possible permutations of certain linear and spatial relationships. After making scroll paintings, the two artists put their scrolls onto animated films. Producing more than a thousand drawings by his own hand, Eggeling made the classic film *Diagonalsymphonien* (1924, *Diagonal Symphony*), in addition to two other films completed just before his premature death.

Films: *Horizontal-Vertical Orchestra* (c. 1919); *Diagonal Symphony*, 1924.

Videotapes: *Symphonie Diagonal* (1921). In *The Experimental Avant-Garde Series: Dada Doo Doo* . New York Film Annex.

Interpretation: O'Konor, Louise. *Viking Eggeling 1880–1925: Artist and Filmmaker, Life and Work*. Trans. Catherine G. Sundstrom and Anne Bibby. Stockholm, Sweden: Almqvist & Wiksell, 1971.

EINSTEIN, Carl

(26 April 1885–5 July 1940).

Trained in philosophical esthetics, Einstein published at the beginning of the century a pioneering book on African sculpture that influenced both CUBISM and DADA. His novel *Bebuquin* (1912), subtitled "The Dilettantes of Miracles," incorporated principles of pictorial cubism into prose narrative, broaching incoherence. "Too few people have the courage to talk complete nonsense," he wrote. "Nonsense which is frequently repeated becomes an integrating force in our thought; at a certain level of intelligence we are not at all interested in what is correct or rational any more." As *Bebuquin* became a milestone of advanced fiction, a limerick written about another German with the same surname is applicable to this writer as well: "Remarkable family Stein, there's Ep and there's Gert, and there's Ein. Ep's sculpture is junk, Gert's poetry is bunk, and nobody understands Ein." Carl Einstein fought on the Loyalist side in the Spanish Civil War (1936–39), after which he went to Paris. When it fell to the Nazis, he escaped to southern France; but, unable to emigrate to America because of his prior service against Franco, he committed suicide (as did his near contemporary and countryman in roughly the same place, WALTER BENJAMIN).

Writings: *Gesammelte Werke*. Ed. Ernst Nef. Wiesbaden: Limes Verlag, 1962; *Werke*. 4 vols. Berlin, Germany: Fannei & Walz; *Correspondence 1921–39* Ed. Lilliane Meffre. Marseilles, France: A. Dimanche, 1993.

Interpretation: Brockington, Joseph L. *Vier Pole Expressionistischer Prosa: Studies in Modern German Literature IV*. New York: Peter Lang, 1998; Donahue, Neil H. "Analysis and Construction: The Aesthetics of Carl Einstein." In *Forms of Disruption: Abstraction in Modern Germany Prose*. Ann Arbor: University of Michigan Press, 1993; Schulte-Sasse, Jochen. "Carl Einstein: or, The Postmodern Transformation of Modernism." In Andreas Huyssen & David Bathrick, eds. *Modernity and the Text: Revisions of German Modernism*. New York: Columbia University Press, 1989.

e

EISENSTEIN, Sergei Mikhailovich

(23 January 1898–11 February 1948).

His *Battleship Potemkin* (1925; aka, simply, *Potemkin)* was the first distinctly Soviet film to receive international acclaim. Exemplifying the power of montage, or the rapid cutting between scenes to portray conflict, this film showed how radically different the medium of film could be from the theatrical stage, or from the filming of staged activities. His reputation established, Eisenstein became enough of a cultural celebrity for Soviet officials to worry about and thus restrict his subsequent activities. While the original negative of *Battleship Potemkin* was mutilated, his next film, *October* (1927), had to be reedited after Leon Trotsky's demotion, reportedly under Joseph Stalin's personal scrutiny. Invited to work in Hollywood in 1930, Eisenstein made several film proposals that were not accepted. With the help of the American writer Upton Sinclair (1878–1968), he began a feature film about Mexico that was not finished until decades after Eisenstein's death, albeit in incomplete form. Returning to the Soviet Union, Eisenstein was allowed to work on only a few of several possible projects, and then production was often halted before the films were complete. Before his death at fifty, of a second heart attack, Eisenstein also wrote classic essays that have been read by everyone seriously interested in film.

Selected Films: *Battleship Potemkin*, 1925; *October*, 1927; *Alexander Nevsky*, 1938. (Out of copyright, these are available in several versions on videotape.)

Books: *Film Form/The Film Sense* (1949, 1942). Ed. and trans. Jay Leyda. New York: Meridian, 1957; *The Complete Films of Sergei Eisenstein*. Trans. John Hetherington. New York: Dutton, 1974; *Immoral Memories: An Autobiography*. Trans. Herbert Marshall. Boston: Houghton Mifflin, 1983.

Biography: Bergan, Ronald. *Sergei Eisenstein: A Life in Conflict*. New York: Overlook, 1999; Leyda, Jay, and Zina Voynow. *Eisenstein at Work*. New York: Pantheon/MOMA, 1982.

Website: http://www.carleton.edu/curricular/MEDA/classes/media110 (Links page).

Exhibition Catalog: Van Norman Baer, Nancy, et al. *Theatre in Revolution: Russian Avant-Gade Stage Design, 1913–1935*. San Francisco: Fine Arts Museum, 1991.

Interpretation: Burdwell, David. *The Cinema of Eisenstein*. Cambidge: Harvard University Press, 1994; Goodwin, James. *Eisenstein, Cinema, and History*. Urbana: University of Illinois Press, 1996; Mayer, David. *Eistenstein's Potemkin: A Shot-by-Shot Presentation*. New York: Grossman, 1972.

EISLER, Hanns

(6 July 1898–6 September 1962).

Generally ranked after Alban Berg and ANTON WEBERN among ARNOLD SCHOENBERG'S more distinguished early pupils, Eisler had a different sort of musical career. Reportedly influenced by his brother and sister, who were devout communists, he moved to Berlin in 1925, joined the Communist party the following year, and wrote songs for communist choirs and plays. By 1929, he was regularly collaborating with the communist playwright Bertolt Brecht. Leaving Germany in 1933, he moved first to Moscow, then to New York, where he taught at the New School from 1935 to 1942, and finally to Hollywood, where he became involved in composing for film, collaborating with Charlie Chaplin, even coauthoring with THEODOR ADORNO a short book about the subject. (Meanwhile, some of Schoenberg's Los Angeles pupils, such as Leonard Rosenman [1924], were beginning to incorporate serial music into film scores, popularizing Schoenberg, so to speak, without ever making Schoenberg more popular.) Here, in the heart of capitalist culture, Eisler also wrote the national anthem for East Germany—*Aufstanden aus Ruinen*. When their sister Ruth Fischer testified against them before the House Un-American Activities Committee, the Eisler brothers both emigrated to East Berlin, where Hanns resumed his collaboration with Bertolt Brecht, his music nontheless reflecting his serial training. Because major modern composers were scarce in East Germany (and his brother headed the radio station), Hanns Eisler became more prominent there than he could have been in the West. The tragedy was that, in both his politics and esthetics, he made wrong moves.

Selected Compositions: *Johannes Faustus*, opera, 1953; some 38 scores of incidental music to Bertolt Brecht plays.

Books: *The Rebel in Music: Selected Writings* (1976). Ed., with an intro. Manfred Grabs. [East] Berlin: Seven Seas, 1978; and T. W. Adorno. *Composing for Film*. New York: Oxford University Press, 1947.

Biography: Betz, Albrecht. *Hanns Eisler: A Political Musician* (1976). Trans. William Hopkins. New York: Cambridge University, 1982.

EL TEATRO CAMPESINO

(1965; Farmworkers' Theater, aka ETC).

Formed by Luis Valdez (1942), who had worked with the SAN FRANCISCO MIME TROUPE and retained the SFMT's love of signs and songs, ETC recruited untrained, instinctive performers, initially to publicize a grape strike in California and, by extension, to organize Mexican–American itinerant farm laborers into the United Farm Workers union. Addressing Chicano audiences during the working summers, ETC presented short plays, called "actos," in a mixture of Spanish and English, showing stereotypes of workers and bosses in the manner of *commedia dell'arte*. ETC staged such highly original theater that, thanks to prompt critical recognition, it toured American universities during the off-farm seasons. A skilled scenarist-director, Valdez subsequently produced the play *Zoot Suit* (1978), which transferred from Los Angeles to Broadway, in addition to feature-length films, such as *La Bamba* (1987), which was likewise about Chicano culture.

El Teatro Campesino, *Simply Maria*, 1992. L to R: Linda Lopez, Dena Martinez, Wilma Bonet. Photo: Brad Shirakawa, courtesy California Artists Management.

Books: Valdez, Luis. *Zoot Suit and Other Plays*. Arte Publico Pr., 1992; —— y El Teatro Campesino. *Actos*. San Juan Bautista, CA: Cucaracha, 1971.

Webpage: http://www.mercado.com/grupos/campesin/campesin.htm

Anthologies: Weisman, John. *Guerilla Theater: Scenarios for Revolution*. Garden City, NY: Doubleday, 1973.

Interpretation: Elam, Harry J. *Taking It to the Streets*. Ann Arbor: University of Michigan Press, 1997.

ELDRIDGE, Aethelred

(21 April 1930).

Working with both text and images, this eccentric American artist creates simplistic black-and-white images with near-biblical stylistic certitude. As a professor of art at Ohio University in Athens, Ohio since 1957, Aethelred has self-published thousands of his image/textual works with various technologies, including the hectograph, the mimeograph, and more recently, the photocopier. These self-described *invective pamphlets* are both cryptically pedantic, and at times autobiographical, all within his own

e

Aetheled Eldridge. *One of the Golgonoozas*. Courtesy the artist.

mythopoeia. Larger works include earlier paintings and an expansive mural-in-progress that adorns an archway of Seigfred Hall on the OU campus. The black and white mural has been repainted several times since it first appeared in 1966. Similar to the texts accompanying his images (e.g. "Were you there when your feet came out all fittingly abluted?"—*Golgonooza* #20), his class lectures are themselves works of art. Aethelred weaves playful, sometimes invective speech tapestries with outlandish word associations, electrically charged phonetics, and scrambled catchphrases that succeed or fail with his often-baffled listeners. He also founded the Church of William Blake on his property outside of Athens near Mt. Nebo, a spiritualist mecca since the 1830s. In the restored Koons Cabin, a building dating back to the 1850s, Aethelred regularly hosted "happening-like" gatherings and ceremonies for nearly three decades until the late 1980s.

—Michael Peters

Writings: *Golgonooza*. Millfield, OH (13951 Mill Creek, 45761), n.d.

Documentary: Kortlander, John, and John Douglas. *Aethelred*. Columbus, OH: John Kortlander (c/o Columbus College of Art and Design, 107 N. 9th Street, 43215-1758), 1997.

ELECTRO-ACOUSTIC MUSIC

See **MUSIQUE CONCRÈTE; HANSON, Sten.**

ELECTRONIC BOOKS

See **HYPERTEXT.**

ELECTRONIC MUSIC

(c. 1910).

Used accurately, Electronic Music describes not one new thing but many new things that are still appearing; for music, of all the arts, has been the most constant beneficiary of recent technological developments. These inventions offer not only new instruments but technically superior versions of older ones for both composers and performers, in addition to editing and structuring technologies far handier than their predecessors. Do not forget that modern technologies created new listening situations for music, beginning, of course, with the capacity to record musical sound to be played back at a later date (initially through a phonograph), and then with the capacity (initially provided by radio) to transmit in live time musical sound from one source to many outlets. Neither of those capabilities existed in the nineteenth century.

The same American who co-invented night lights for outdoor sports arenas, Thaddeus Cahill (1867–1934), also built at the beginning of this century the Telharmonium, a 200-ton machine that could synthesize musical sounds for distribution over telephone lines. The machine had to be big and loud, because Cahill did not know the principle of acoustic amplification. Nowadays, even a common home-audio system can radically transform an existing instrumental sound, not only making it louder but also accentuating its treble or bass, if not redefining its timbre and extending the duration of such redefined sound to unlimited lengths.

By the 1960s, microphone pickups were incorporated into a whole range of instruments—guitar, double bass, piano, saxophone, clarinet, flute—to give each more presence than it previously had. Whereas early electronic pop musicians performed with only single speakers, groups new to the 1960s used whole banks of huge speakers to escalate their sounds to unprecedentedly high volumes, thereby also creating such technical dysfunctions as distortion, hum, buzzing, and ear-piercing feedback. Among classical musicians, Philip Glass and Mauricio Kagel exploited the volume controls and mixing panel of a standard recording studio to radically modify the music made by live performers, so that what the audience heard—what became available on record—would be radically different from the sounds originally made.

Electronic Music also includes wholly new instruments, beginning with the Theremin in the early 1920s. In 1928, the French inventor Maurice Martenot (1898–1980) introduced the Ondes Martenot ("Martenot's Waves"), a keyboard that electronically produces one note at a time and can slide through its entire tonal range. In 1930 came Frederick Trautwein's (1888–1956) Trautonium, another electronic one-note generator that could be attached to a piano, requiring the performer to devote one hand to each instrument.

Unlike the Ondes Martenot and the Theremin, which were designed to produce radically different sounds, the Hammond organ was invented in the 1930s to imitate electronically the familiar sounds of a pipe organ, but musicians discovered the electronic organ had capabilities for sustained reverberation and tremolo that were impossible before. The original synthesizers were essentially electronic organs designed to generate a greater range of more precisely specified (and often quite innovative) musical sounds. Synthesizers became something else when they could incorporate sounds made outside of the instrument and process them into unprecendented acoustic experiences. This tradition became the source in the 1970s for Live Electronic Music and, later, for sampling.

Another line of Electronic Music depended upon the development of magnetic audiotape that could be neatly edited and recomposed; audiotapes also became the preferred storage medium for electronic compositions. Sounds previously recorded in the environment could be enhanced by being played at a faster speed or a slower speed, or by being passed through filters that removed certain frequencies or added echo or reverberation. Extended echoing dependent upon tape-delay was also possible. *Musique concrète* was based upon these techniques.

The next step was to work entirely with electronically generated sounds, beginning with those from elementary sound generators, such as sawtooth, triangular, and variable rectangular waves. One of the best early endeavors in this vein was Bulent Arel's *Music for a Sacred Service* (1961). The step after that involved mixing sounds that were originally live with artificial sources on a single fixed tape. Once stereophonic and then multitrack tape became available, sounds from separate sources, even recorded at separate times, could be mixed together. When played back, these acoustic compositions could be distributed to speakers that could surround the spectator with sound; materials in individual speakers could conduct pseudo-conversations with one another.

Because wholly Electronic Music did not depend upon instruments, it eschewed conventional scoring. Indeed, if a piece were created entirely "by ear," so to speak, there would be no score at all, initially creating a problem with the American copyright office, which would accept scores but not tapes as evidence of authorship. Partly to deal with this problem, tape composers developed all kinds of inventive timeline graphings in lieu of scores.

A quarter-century ago, the composer Virgil Thomson (1896–1989) suggested, in the course of an article on JOHN CAGE, that any sound emerging from loudspeakers (and thus electronic at some point in its history) was fundamentally debased. Although his opinion was dismissed and is perhaps forgotten, can I be alone in having the experience, usually in a church, of hearing music that initially sounds funny? I know why, I must remind myself—no amplification.

Since the arrival of Robert Moog's SYNTHESIZER in the late 1960s and then the PERSONAL COMPUTER in the 1970s brought other kinds of Electronic Music, they are discussed separately in this book.

Bibliography: Appleton, Jon, and Ronald Perera, eds. *The Development and Practice of Electronic Music*. Englewood Cliffs, NJ: Prentice-Hall, 1974; Boon, Michael. *Music through MIDI*. Redmond, WA: Microsoft, 1987; Darter, Tom. *The Art of Electronic Music*. Ed. Greg Armbruster. New York: Morrow, 1984; Chadabe, Joel. *Electric Sound: The Past and Promise of Electronic Music*. Upper Saddle River, NJ: Prentice-Hall, 1997; DeForia, Steve. *The MIDI Book*. Milwaukee, WI: Hal Leonard, 1988; Dunn, David. "A History of Electronic Music Pioneers (1992/1996)." In Richard Kostelanetz & Joseph Darby, eds., *Classic Essays on Twentieth-Century Music: A Continuing Symposium*. New York: Schirmer, 1996; Ernst, David. *The Evolution of Electronic Music*. New York: Schirmer, 1977; Holmes, Thomas B. *Electronic and Experimental Music*. New York: Scribner, 1985; Howe, Hubert S., Jr. *Electronic Music Synthesis*. New York: Norton, 1975; Keane, David. *Tape Music Composition*. Oxford, England: Oxford University Press, 1980; Manning, Peter. *Electronic and Computer Music*. Oxford, England: Clarendon, 1985; Mathews, Max. *The Technology of Computer Music*. Cambridge: MIT Press, 1969; Naumann, Joel, and James D. Wagoner. *Analog Electronic Music Techniques*. New York; Schirmer, 1985; Rhoads, Curtis, ed. *The Music Machine*. Cambridge: MIT Press, 1989; Schwartz, Elliott. *Electronic Music: A Listener's Guide*. New York: Praeger, 1973; Thomson, Virgil. "Cage and the Collage of Noises," *A Virgil Thomson Reader*. New York: Dutton, 1981; Welles, Thomas. *The Technique of Electronic Music*. New York: Schirmer, 1981.

ELIOT, Karen

(c. 1989).

No one knows exactly when Karen Eliot was born, but by 1989 she was a presence in the Neoist circle of cultural workers who were planning for the ART STRIKE, 1990–93. Karen Eliot was nothing more than a mouthpiece for the Neoists and others as they propounded their ideas about that strike, but she was a mouthpiece who could be anyone. Everyone, as a matter of fact, could take on her identity. Eliot was merely the female version of the Neoists' MONTY CANTSIN. Though less common a figure than her alter-ego Monty Cantsin, Eliot was a frequent voice in support of the Art Strike, so much so that those people who questioned the value of the Art Strike often attacked Karen herself—who could be anyone but was certainly also no one. The Strike/Strike, 1990–93 was one short-lived reaction to the Art Strike: "First there was the Art Strike, Then there was the Word Strike, Now, there is the Strike/Strike. Three Strikes And You're Out." The brainchild of the typogram-magicians Don Baker and Jeff Brice, the Strike/Strike was a "strike against all other psuedo[sic]-intellectual strikes involving creative activity between the years 1990–1993." One neat twist of this strike was how it approved of itself in the persona of Karen Eliot, having her say on their behalf, "The STRIKE/STRIKE is the most comprehensive statement on the condition of modern art that I have ever seen."

—Geof Huth

Bibliography: *Yawn: Sporadic Critique of Culture*. Iowa City, 1989–1992; Baker, Don and Jeff Brice. *Strike/Strike, 1990–1993*. Seattle: Strike/Strike Headquarters, 1990.

ELIOT, T. S.

(26 September 1888–4 January 1965; born Thomas Stearns E.).

Where and when was Eliot avant-garde? Not in his pseudo-juvenile *Old Possum's Book of Practical Cats* (1939), or in the solemn footnotes at the end of *The Waste Land* (1922). One could make a case for *Sweeney Agonistes* (1932) as a conceptual play, because it cannot be staged as is; but to my mind, Eliot's greatest departure was publication, even in his initial *Collected Poems* (1930), of several works that are explicitly introduced as "Unfinished." The heirs and editors of a dead poet might have made that qualifying term, but rarely has a living poet done it, especially in his or her early forties. The assumption is that even in an admittedly unfinished state a text such as "Coriolan" can be read on its own.

Advocates of poems composed from words "found" in the works of others, rather than wholly created from within, have cited Eliot's essay on Thomas Massinger for this rationale:

> Immature poets imitate; mature poets steal; bad poets deface what they take, and good poets make it into something better, or at least something different. The good poet welds his theft into a whole of feeling which is unique, utterly different from that from which it was torn; the bad poet throws it into something which has no cohesion.

However, by no measure was Eliot a pioneering FOUND POET.

Relevant Books: Eliot, T. S. *The Complete Poems and Plays*. New York: Harcourt, Brace, 1962; *Selected Prose of T. S. Eliot*. Ed. Frank Kermode. New York: Harcourt, Brace & Farrar, Straus, 1975; *Essays on Poetry and Poets*. London: Faber, 1985.

Biography: Ackroyd, Peter. *T. S. Eliot: A Life*. New York: Simon & Schuster, 1984; Gordon, Lyndall. *Eliot's Early Years* (1977). New York: Oxford University Press, 1989; *Eliot's New Life*. New York: Farrar, Straus, 1988.

Website: http://people.a2000.nl/avanarum/index.html (Online hypertext project; there are other sites)

Interpretation: Kenner, Hugh. *The Invisible Poet: T. S. Eliot*. New York: McDowell Obolensky, 1959; Martin, Mildred. *A Half-Century of Eliot Criticism*. London: Associated University, 1979; Menand, Louis. *Discovering Modernism: T. S. Eliot in His Context*. New York: Oxford University Press, 1987; Moody, A. David. *The Cambridge Companion to T. S. Eliot*. Cambridge: Cambridge University Press, 1994; Tate, Allen, ed. *T. S. Eliot: The Man and His Work*. London: Chatto & Windus, 1967.

ELUARD, Paul

(14 December 1896–18 November 1952; b. Eugène-Emile-Paul Grindel).

Generally regarded as the second most important Surrealist poet after André Breton, whom he first met around 1920, Eluard was also a political activist who joined the Communist Party and kept reminding his literary colleagues of his politics. Nonetheless, his best poems portray heterosexual passion. In a translation by the American poet Michael Benedikt (1935), "Ecstasy" opens:

> Before this feminine landscape I feel
> As if I were a child standing before a fireplace
> Full of delight with my eyes full of tears

And closes:

> Before this feminine landscape I feel
> As if I were some green branch in a fire.

In addition to publishing his own poems, many of which purportedly transcibed his dreams, Eluard collaborated with MAX ERNST on two pioneering visual-verbal books in 1932 and with Breton in writing *L'Immaculée conception* (1930), which attempts to portray a variety of mental disturbances.

> The hundred and fifty castles where we were going to make love were not enough for me a hundred thousand more will be built for me tomorrow I have chased out from the boabab forests of your eyes the peacocks and panthers and lyre-birds I will shut them in my strongholds and we shall go walking together in the forests of Asia of Europe of Africa and America which surround our castles in the admirable forests of your eyes which are accustomed to my splendour.

To some this is an authentic psychological representation; to others, it epitomizes studied affectation, either because of or despite the absence of internal punctuation.

Eluard's French reputation gained from more traditional poems collected into books published during World War II, as he, unlike Breton, chose to remain in Europe. He also collaborated with painters such as Max Ernst and PABLO PICASSO in producing not VISUAL POETRY but fields in which text and image complement each other. What should be made of the fact that his first wife Gaia went on to marry SALVADOR DALI and become the Svengali behind her new husband's progressively more dubious career?

Books: *Selected Writings*. Trans. Lloyd Alexander. New York: New Directions, 1948; *Oeuvres complètes*. 2 vols. Paris: N. R. F., 1968; with André Breton. "The Immaculate Conception," trans. Jon Graham. In *The Automatic Message*. London: Atlas (BCM Atlas (WC1N 3XX), 1997.

Anthologies: Benedikt, Michael, ed. & trans. *The Poetry of Surrealism*. Boston: Little, Brown, 1974.

Interpretation: Caws, Mary Anne. *The Poetry of Dada and Surrealism*. Princeton, NJ: Princeton University Press, 1970.

EMSHWILLER, Ed

(16 February 1925–22 July 1990).

Emshwiller began as an illustrator, particularly of science fiction, before producing his first film, *Dance Chromatic* (1959), combining live action with animated abstract painting. In addition to working as a cameraman on numerous television documentaries and independent films, he produced *Relativity* (1966), which he called a "film poem." While continuing to work with film, he pioneered video art, particularly in *Scape-mates* (1972), which uses an animation technology partly of his own design and ranks among the earliest artistic videotapes that can still be screened without embarrassment. Independent for most of his professional life, Emshwiller became in 1979 a dean at the California Institute of the Arts where he remained to his death. His wife, Carol E. (1921) has published several collections of scrupulously strange experimental short fiction.

Works: *Dance Chromatic*, 1959; *Relativity*, 1966; *Scape-mates*, 1972.

Videotapes: *Totem*. New York: Grove Press Film, 1964 (a dance by ALWIN NIKOLAIS, dir. by E. E.); *George Dumpson's Place*. New York: Filmmaker's Co-operative, 1965; *Scapemates*. New York: Electronic Arts Intermix, 1972; *Sunstone*. New York: Electronic Arts Intermix, 1979.

Related Writings: Emshwiller, Carol. *Joy in Our Cause*. New York: Harper & Row, 1974.

Interpretation: Russett, Robert, and Cecile Starr. *Experimental Animation*. New York: Van Nostrand, 1976.

ENO, Brian

(15 May 1948).

A prolific producer of recordings, though formally untrained in music, Eno adapts avant-garde ideas for more popular purposes; only occasionally do they survive as consequential innovative art. He collaborated on GAVIN BRYARS's recordings; Eno also recruited Bryars and CORNELIUS CARDEW, among others, to make "1, 2, 1-2-3-4" (for Eno's Obscure label), in which several musicians, each wearing headphones, hear music that they must try to reproduce in live performance. One Eno classic is *Portsmouth Sinfonia* (1974), for which musically subamateur art-school students were recruited to perform such classical warhorses as Rossini's *William Tell Overture* and Johann Strauss's *Blue Danube Waltz*. Though the joke may be simple, the result is complex humor. The idea was not to create chaos but to establish preconditions that could only result in chaotic and highly original comic semblances of familiar originals.

Recordings: *Here Come the Warm Jets*. (1973), eg. CD, 1989; *Taking Tiger Mountain (by Strategy)* (1974), eg. CD, 1989; *Another Green World* (1975), eg. CD, 1989; *Before and After Science* (1977), eg. CD, 1989; and David Byrne, David. *My Life in the Bush Ghosts*. Warner Brothers, 1981; *Thursday Afternoon* (1985), eg. CD, 1989; *Desert Island Selections*. eg. CD, 1989; et al. *Portsmouth Sinfonia*. New York: Columbia (KC 33049), 1974.

Writings: "Generating and Organizing Variety in the Arts" *Studio International* (Nov.–Dec. 1976).

Website: http://www.hyperreal.org/music/artists/brian_eno/

ENVIRONMENT

(forever).

This term describes an enclosed space that is artistically enhanced. The materials defining the space might be visual, sculptural, kinetic, or even acoustic, or may contain combinations of all these elements, but they give the space an esthetic character it would not otherwise have. To put it differently, thanks to what the artist does, the space itself becomes a surrounding work of art. Among the classic Environments are St. Peter's Church in Rome and the Dome of the Rock in Jerusalem. In more recent art, consider Stanley Landesman's multiply mirrored room, *Walk-In Infinity Chamber* (1968), in which spectators inside the Environment see themselves infinitely reflected; the kinetic galleries mounted by the artists' collective known only as USCO in the late 1960s; CLAES OLDENBURG'S *The Store* (1962), which was filled with ironic renditions of seedy objects; and JOHN CAGE'S *HPSCHD*, which filled a 15,000-seat basketball arena with sounds and images for several hours (but could have gone on forever). An Environment differs, on one hand, from a MIXED-MEANS theatrical piece that has a definite beginning and an end and, on the other, from an INSTALLATION, which describes art made for a particular site, theoretically to inhabit it forever or be destroyed when the exhibition is over.

Bibliography: Kostelanetz, Richard. "Artistic Environments." In *Metamorphosis in the Arts*. New York: Assembling, 1980; USCO." In *On Innovative Art(ist)s*. Jefferson, NC: McFarland, 1992.

ERDMAN, Jean

(1917).

As a member of MARTHA GRAHAM'S dance company in the early 1940s, Erdman collaborated with MERCE CUNNINGHAM, who also danced with Graham at the time. On her own, Erdman wrote, directed, and choreographed *The Coach with the Six Insides* (1962), which ranks among the most extraordinary theatrical productions in my lifetime. Initially an adaptation of JAMES JOYCE'S *FINNEGANS WAKE*, on which her husband, the writer/mythologist Joseph Campbell (1908–89), had incidentally coauthored the first critical book, *The Coach* faithfully portrays the technique of multiple reference that defines Joyce's classic, even if a woman, Anna Livia Plurabelle, played by Erdman herself, replaces H. C. Earwicker at the center of Joyce's five-person mythology. As the dance critic Don McDonagh remembers, "At one moment she is the keening Irishwoman bemoaning the sorrows of her life and her race's difficulties. At another moment she is Belinda the hen, who scratches and reveals a letter that no one can read, and she transforms herself into a dancing rain." The piece offered a flood of puns and striking turns of phrase that, in my experience even after several visits, were never entirely assimilated. It was magnificent; I'd see it again tomorrow.

Works: *Transformations of Medusa*, 1942; *Creature on a Journey*, 1943; *Daughters of the Lonesome Isle*, 1944;

Passage, 1946; *Ophelia*, 1946; *Hamadryad*, 1948; *The Perilous Chapel*, 1949; *Solstice*, 1950; *Changing Woman*, 1951; *Perriot, the Moon*, 1954; *Fearful Symmetry*, 1957; *The Coach with the Six Insides*, 1962.

Videotapes: *Dance & Myth* (3 tape set). New York: Mystic Fire, 1995.

Interpretation: McDonagh, Don. *The Complete Guide to Modern Dance*. Garden City, NY: Doubleday, 1976.

ERNST, Max

(2 April 1891–1 April 1976; b. Maximilian E.).
After six years studying philosophy, Ernst fought in World War I; soon after his demobilization, he became a leader of Cologne DADA, personally dubbed "Dadamax" by 1919. Quickly moving over to Parisian SURREALISM, Ernst is credited with having introduced the techniques of COLLAGE and PHOTOMONTAGE to Surrealist art. Surrealist collage differed from Dada in aiming not to juxtapose dissimilars but to weave from "found" pictures a coherent subconscious image. Ernst's best collages draw upon banal engravings, some of which he incorporated into book-art narratives that I rank among his strongest works: *La Femme 100 Têtes* (1929) and *Une semaine de bonté* (1934). The latter, subtitled *A Surrealist Novel in Collage*, is actually a suite of separate stories that depend upon pasting additions onto existing illustrations. Ernst developed *frottage*, which comes from tracing patterns found in an object (e.g., the grain of a floorboard, the texture of sackcloth) as a technique for freeing the subconscious by relieving the author of direct control, becoming the visual analog for ANDRÉ BRETON'S automatic writing. More handsome than most, Ernst went during World War II to New York, where he married successively PEGGY GUGGENHEIM, a major patron of the avant-garde, and Dorothea Tanning (1910), herself an important artist and writer, he remained in America until 1952. While in the United States, Ernst collaborated with Breton and MARCEL DUCHAMP on the periodical *VVV* (1942).

Max Ernst, image from *Une semaine de bonté*, 1934. Courtesy Libraire Kostelanetz/Wordship.

Works: *Crucifixion*. 1913; *Stratified Rock Gift of Nature Composed of Gnosis*, 1920; *Hat Makes the Man*, 1920; *Parole*, 1921; *Sacra conversazione*, 1921; *Elephant Celebs*, c. 1921; *Oedipus Rex*, 1921–22; *Oedipus Rex*, 1923; *La Belle Jardinère*, 1923; *Woman, Old Man, and Flower*, 1923–24; *Two Children Are Threatened by a Nightingale*, 1924; *Robing of the Bride*, 1939–41; *Europe after the Rain*, 1940–42; *Temptation of St. Anthony*, 1945; *Father Rhine* (Old Man River), 1954.

Sculpture: *Capricorn*, 1948.

Books: *Une Semaine de bonté* (A Week of Goodness, 1934). New York: Dover, 1976; *La Femme 100 Têtes* (1929). New York: Braziller, 1981; *Histoire naturelle* (1926). London: Arts Council of Great Britain, 1982;

Beyond Painting and Other Writings by the Artist and His Friends. New York: Wittenborn, Schultz, 1948.

Website:
http://www.mcs.csuhayward.edu/~malek/Ernst.html (includes many images).

Exhibition Catalogs: Lippard, Lucy R. *Max Ernst: Works on Paper*. New York: MoMA, 1967; *Max Ernst: A Retrospective*. New York: Guggenheim Museum, 1975; *Exposition Max Ernst: peintures, sculptures, collages, frottages*. Bruxelles: Galerie Isy Brachot, 1977; Rainwater, Robert, ed. *Max Ernst Beyond Surrealism: A Retrospective of the Artist's Books and Prints*. New York: New York Public Library, 1986; *Max Ernst: a Retrospective*. Ed. & intro., Werner Spies. London: Tate Gallery, 1991.

Interpretation: Camfield, William. *Max Ernst: Dada and the Dawn of Surrealism*. Intro. Werner Spies. Preface Walter Hopps. New York: te Neues 1993; Diehl, Gaston. *Max Ernst*. New York: Crown, 1973; Russell, John. *Max Ernst: Life and Work*. New York: Abrams, 1967; Tanning, Dorothea. *Birthday*. Santa Monica, CA: Lapis, 1986.

Anthologies: *Max Ernst, 1891–1976: Beyond Painting*. Köln: Taschen, 1994; *Ernst (Great Modern Masters)*. Ed. Jose Maria Faerna. New York: Abradale, 1997.

ESCHER, M. C.

(17 June 1898–27 March 1972, b. Maurits Cornelis E.). The art cognoscenti can be divided almost evenly into those who appreciate Escher and those who think his visual art is slick kitsch. What is interesting about this particular dichotomy is that, unlike other opinion-splitters, this test bears no ostensible relation to anything else. After establishing a style of repeated symmetrical configurations of animals, Escher made geometrical illusions, such as a stairway that appears to be constantly ascending or a water sluice that is constantly descending, using images based on reason to portray what is, as a whole, not credible, which is to say that he made a rational art to portray irrationality. As these images became more familiar in the late sixties, when they appeared on T-shirts, posters, and even coffee mugs, Escher's work was dismissed as decorative—a kind of contemporary Dutch equivalent of Irish illuminated manuscripts (e.g., *The Book of Kells* [c. 8th–9th century]). The simplest measure of Escher's originality is a visual intelligence that is easily identifiable as his.

Books: *Escher on Escher: Exploring the Infinite*. New York: Abrams, 1989; *M.C. Escher: His Life and Complete Graphic Works*, ed. J. L. Locher. New York: Abrams, 1992; MacGillivray, Caroline H. *Fantasy & Symmetry: The Periodic Drawings of M. C. Escher*. New York: Abrams, 1976; Schattschneider, Doris. *Visions of Symmetry: Notebooks, Periodic Drawings and Related Works of M. C. Escher*. New York: W.H. Freeman, 1990; *M.C. Escher: The Graphic Work*. Köln: Taschen, 1996; *M. C. Escher: Book of Boxes 100 Years 1898–1998*. Köln: Taschen, 1998.

Website: http://www.djmurphy.demon.co.uk/escher.htm (includes many images).

Exhibition Catalogs: *The Graphic Works of M. C. Escher*. The Hague: Gemeentemuseum, 1967; Smith, Brydon. *M. C. Escher: Landscapes to Mindscapes*. Ottawa: National Gallery, 1995.

Video: *The Life and Work of M. C. Escher*. Acorn Media, 1999.

EUROPERA

(1987).

John Cage's first opera produced with the assistance of Andrew Culver (1953), is an encompassing pastiche of sounds and costumes from the repertoire of traditional (i.e., European) operas that are no longer protected by copyright. The title, a shrewd verbal invention, incorporates not only "Europe" and "opera," but it also sounds like "your opera," which is to say everyone's opera. From the score library of New York's Metropolitan Opera, Cage pulled music pages to be photocopied at random. Though flutists, say, each received music previously composed for their instrument, each flutist was given different scores.

Thus, motifs from various operas could be heard from the same instruments simultaneously.

Noticing that operatic voices are customarily classified under nineteen categories (for sopranos alone, for instance, coloratura, lyric coloratura, lyric, lyric spinto, and dramatic), Cage requested nineteen singers, each of whom is allowed to select which public domain arias are appropriate for him or her; but only in the performance itself would each find out when, where, or if they could sing them. So several arias, each from a different opera, could be sung at once, to instrumental accompaniment(s) culled from yet other operas.

The costumes were likewise drawn from disparate sources, and these clothes were assigned to individual singers without reference to what they would sing or do onstage. From a wealth of opera pictures, Cage selected various images that were then enlarged and painted, only in black and white, for the flats. These flats are mechanically brought onstage from left, right, or above with an arbitrariness reminiscent of the changing backdrops in the Marx Brothers' A *Night at the Opera* (1935). Once a flat or prop is no longer needed, it is simply laid to rest beside the performing area, visibly contributing to the chaotic mise-en-scène. A computer program ensures that the lighting of the stage will be similarly haphazard.

For the libretti offered to the audience, Cage simply extracted sentences from traditional operatic plot summaries, replacing specific names with pronouns like "he" and "she." These sentences were scrambled to produce twelve different pseudo-summaries, each two paragraphs long (to coincide with the two acts), none of which has any intentional connection with what actually occurs on stage. Each program distributed at *Europera's* premiere contained only one of the twelve synopses, which meant that people sitting next to each another had different guides, further contributing to the elegant chaos.

What *Europera* is finally about, from its transcriptions of phrases and images to its libretti, is the culture of opera, at once a homage and a burlesque, offering a wealth of surprises with familiar material; its theme could be defined, simply, as the conventions of nineteenth-century European opera after a twentieth-century avant-garde American has processed it. *Europera* has two parts, subtitled *I* and *II*, the second being half the length of the former. As with *HPSCHD*, Cage made "chamber" versions— *Europera 3 & 4* (1990) and *Europera 5* (1991)— that, if only for their diminished scale, are less successful. Nicolas Slonimsky, historically knowledgeable, sees them representing "a unique theatrical genre."

Musical Score: *Europera I & II*. New York: C. F. Peters (373 Park Ave. S., 10016), 1987.

Interpretation: Kostelanetz, Richard. "*Europera*: Before and After (1988)." In *Thirty Years of Critical Engagements with John Cage*. New York: Archae, 1997; Slonimsky, Nicolas. "Europera." In *Lectionary of Music*. New York: McGraw-Hill, 1989.

EVRIENOV, Nikolai

(1879–1953).

Succeeding Vsevolod Meyerhold as the director of the Vera Komisarjevskaya's theater at the beginning of the century, Evrienov published in 1908 an article proclaiming that the purpose of theater was the "theatricalization of life," by which he meant all human experience. It became his mission to revive the tradition of spectacles, beginning with medieval miracle plays and sixteenth-century farces. To stage a thirteenth-century pastorale, Adam de la Halle's *Robin and Marion*, the theater was transformed nto a castle hall filled with knights, their ladies, servants, and minstrels, which is to say the typical audience of the play's period. The players arrive later, setting up their stage (within-a-stage), unpacking their props, etc. Evrienov's most spectacular production, by common consent, occurred after the Revolution. In 1920, he staged in Petrograd (aka St. Petersburg) *The Storming of the Winter Palace,* which was a major Soviet victory a few years before. In James Roose-Evans' summary:

> Eight thousand people took part in the show, an orchestra of 500 played revolutionary songs, while a real blast from the warship *Aurora*, anchored on the Neva River, added to the theatricality of the occasion.

I can't be alone in wishing I was there, because there has hardly been anything like it since. Evrienov emigrated to western Europe in 1925, only to find his work decline. His name is sometimes spelled in the West as Everinoff.

Books: *The Theatre of the Soul: A Monodrama in One Act*. London: Hendersons, 1915; *The Chief Thing*. Garden City, New York: Doubleday, Page & Co. for the Theater Guild, 1926; *The Theatre in Life*. Ed. & trans. Alexander I. Nazaroff. New York: B. Blom, 1970; *Life as Theatre: 5 Modern Plays*. Trans. & ed. Christopher Collins. Ann Arbor: Ardis, 1973.

Interpretation: Carnicke, Sharon Marie. *The Theatrical Instinct*. New York: Peter Lang, 1989; Golub, Spencer. *Everinov, The Theater of Paradox and Transformation*. Ann Arbor: UMI Research, 1984; Roose-Evans. James. *Experimental Theatre* (1970). New York: Avon, 1971.

EXPRESSIONISM

(c. 1895).

(This concept is so unsympathetic to me that I fear misrepresentation, but here goes.) The central assumption is that, through the making of a work, the artist transfers his or her emotions and feelings, customarily anguished, to the viewer/reader. Such art is judged "expressive" to the degree that feelings and emotions are projected by it; therefore, the success of such communication often depends upon the use of images or subjects familiar to the audience, the artist thus always skirting vulgarity. The social rationale was breaking down the inhibitions and repressions of bourgeois society. (The trouble is that different viewers get different messages, especially in different cultures and at different times. That difficulty perhaps accounts for why the concept of Expressionism is scarcely universal, being almost unknown in Eastern art.) Arising from Romanticism that tied expression to the notion of "genius," the term became popular around the turn of the century, beginning with Edward Munch's (1863–1944) famous woodcut depicting a face proclaiming terror. Indeed, the term "Expressionistic" became an honorific, implicitly excluding whatever arts lacked such quality. It characterized work produced by disparate individuals, rather than a self-conscious group (such as Dada or Surrealism). Responding to the examples of Munch and Van Gogh in painting, as well as Oskar Kokoschka (1886–1980) and Egon Schiele (1890–1918) after them, critics began to confine the epithet Expressionism to art (and sometimes thought) produced in Northern and/or Teutonic European countries, in contrast to French and/or Mediterranean traditions. This last notion legitimized German Expressionism of the 1920s and 1930s, in poetry as well as visual art, and perhaps American ABSTRACT EXPRESSIONISM afterwards. The German dancer MARY WIGMAN appropriated Expressionist esthetics for her dance works.

Anthologies: Kandinsky, Wassily, and Franz Marc, eds. *The "Blaue Reiter" Almanac* (1912). New York: Viking, 1974; Long, Rose-Carol Washton, ed. *German Expressionism* (1993). Berkeley: University of California Press, 1995; Meisel, Victor H., ed. *Voices of German Expressionism*. Englewood Cliffs, NJ: Prentice-Hall, 1970.

Exhibition Catalogs: *Expressionism: A German Institution*. New York: Guggenheim Museum, 1980

Interpretation: Cheney, Sheldon. *Expressionism in Art* (1934). New York: Liveright, 1958; Myers, Samuel Bernard. *The German Expressionists: A Generation in Revolt* (1957). New York: McGraw-Hill, 1963; Richard, Lionel. *Phaidon Encyclopedia of Expressionism*. London: Phaidon, 1978; Whitford, Frank. *Expressionism*. London & New York: Hamlyn, 1970; Willett, John. *Expressionism*. New York: McGraw-Hill, 1970; Zigrosser, Carl D. *The Expressionists*. New York: Braziller, 1957; Dieter-Dube,

Wolf. *The Expressionists*. London: Thames & Hudson, 1985; Gordon, Donald E. *Expressionism: Art & Idea*. New Haven: Yale University Press, 1991.

EXTER, Alexandra

(6 January 1882–17 March 1949).

Exter's earliest distinguished paintings, from the time of the Russian Revolution, display geometric shapes in a larger field, somewhat more reflective of ITALIAN FUTURISM than other Russian Abstract Art in that period. For these planes that appear to float around one another, she favored the primary colors of red, yellow, and blue. The Parisian art historian Andrei B. Nakov, who published the first contemporary monograph on Exter's work, speaks of a "centrifugal structure . . . based on a center of energy within the work. For this possibility is based not on the static weight of the mass but rather on its own dynamic potential whose principal role is to counteract the immobility of forms." For Yakov Protazanov's science fiction film *Aelita* (1924), based on an Aleksei Tolstoy story about Russians transported to Mars, Exter designed costumes that emphasized geometric asymmetry, black-and-white contrasts, and the use of shiny materials. Because *Aelita* was at the time the most popular Russian film in the West, Exter emigrated to Paris, where she worked mostly as a designer for stage, fashion, and architectural interiors. Her surname is sometimes spelled Ekster.

Works: *Colour Dynamism*, 1916–17; *Construction*, 1922–23.

Exhibition Catalogs: Nakov, Andrei B. *Alexandra Exter*. Paris: Galerie Jean Chauvelin, 1972; *Russian Constructivism: "Laboratory Period."* London: Annely Juda, 1975; *Russian Pioneers at the Origins of Non-Objective Art*. London: Annely Juda, 1976; *Alexandra Exter: Artist of the Theatre*. Four essays, with an illustrated checklist of scenic and costume designs. New York: New York Public Library, 1974; *Alexandra Exter: Marionettes Created 1926*. New York: Leonard Hutton Gallery, 1974; Van Norman Baer, Nancy, et al. *Theatre in Revolution: Russian Avant-Garde Stage Design, 1913–1935*. San Francisco: Fine Arts Museum, 1991; *The Great Utopia: The Russian and Soviet Avant-Garde, 1915–1932*. New York: Guggenheim Museum, 1992.

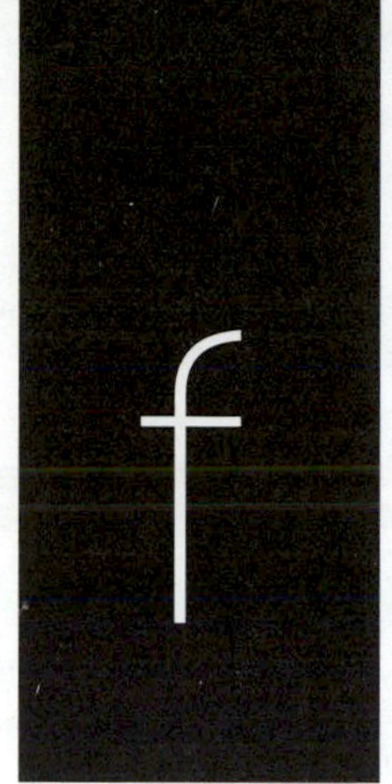

FAHLSTRÖM, Öyvind

(28 December 1928–8 November 1976).

A Swede born in Brazil, Fahlström moved to Sweden in 1939 and began his artistic career with theater and CONCRETE POETRY. About the latter he wrote a manifesto about a language art that "kneaded" language apart from conventional meanings. Next came long narrative paintings that implied theatrical events. By the end of the 1950s, his use of comic-strip imagery, so different from ROY LICHTENSTEIN'S subsequent exploitations, made Fahlström seem a progenitor of POP ART. In the early 1960s, Fahlström made "playable" pictures whose parts the spectator could move about with magnets. Once he moved to America in 1966, where ROBERT RAUSCHENBERG became his principal sponsor, Fahlström's paintings became journalistic cartoons. He died too soon to capitalize on his genuine innovations.

Works: *Ade-Ledic-Nander II*, 1955–57; *Sitting*, 1962; *The Planetarium*, 1963; *Dr. Schweitzer's Last Mission*, 1964–66.

Exhibition Catalogs: *Öyvind Fahlström*. New York: Sidney Janis Gallery, 1971; *Garden: A World Model, 1973*. Köln: Aurel Scheibler, 1991; Hulten, K. G. Pontus, and Bjorn Springfeldt. *Öyvind Fahlström*. Paris: Centre Georges Pompidou, 1980; *Öyvind Fahlström*. New York: Guggenheim Museum, 1982; *Öyvind Fahlstrom: Ivan Centre Julio Gonzàlez, 10 junio/23 agosto 1992*. Valencia: El Centre Generalitat Valenciana Conselleria de Cultura Educació i Ciéncia, 1992.

FANTASIA

(1940).

Aside from what you might think of Walt Disney (1901–65), a *schlockmeister* if ever there were one, consider his most ambitious film for its virtues: luscious animation, pioneering stereo sound, and the visualizing of classical music (the last element making it a precursor of MTV'S "rock videos"). Even though this last idea was "stolen" from OSKAR FISCHINGER, who had come to Hollywood only a few years before (and who worked on the project before resigning because his designs were compromised), Disney went far beyond previous schemes for filming classical music. Remember that *Fantasia* has sections, each produced by a different army of Hollywood technicians, and that some sections are better than others; the original soundtrack conducted by LEOPOLD STOKOWSKI is superior to that used for the 1982 release. There has been nothing quite like *Fantasia* before or since (as it makes rock videos seem inelegant and impatient). The only films to come close, in my considered opinion, are TEX AVERY'S *The Magical Maestro* (1951); Robert Clampett's *A Corny Concerto* (1943) produced under the banner of Bugs Bunny, typically having a sharper edge, by the competing Warner Bros. studio; Bruno Bozzetto's *Allegro Non Troppo* (1976), an Italian feature combining rather mundane live action with some clever animation (particularly to Maurice Ravel's *Bolero*); and several shorts collected under the generic title *Opera Imaginaire*. Rereleased every few years since its premiere, *Fantasia* has recently become available, fortunately with the original Stokowski soundtrack, on both videotape and videodisc.

Video: *Fantasia* (1940). Buena Vista Home Video, 1991.

Interpretation: Finch, Christopher. *The Art of Walt Disney*. New York: Abrams, 1973; Culhane, John. *Walt Disney's Fantasia*. New York: Abrams, 1983; Thomas, Frank, & Ollie Johnston. *Disney Animation: The Illusion of Life*. New York: Abbeville, 1983.

Biography: Thomas, Bob. *Walt Disney: An American Original*. New York: Simon & Schuster, 1978.

f

FANZINE or "ZINE"

(c. 1970s).

With the increased availability of copying machines ('70s and '80s), followed by the personal computer revolution (late '80s-'90s), new technologies enabled fanatics with a passion for a circumscribed underground topic to self-publish small magazines or "fanzines." Not to be completely confused with related aesthetics of the MICROPRESS, which have also been called "zines," fanzines in particular associate with a genre or subgenre of underground popular music. They are read and distributed by the select crowd that their fanzine of choice champions. The fanzine, unlike popular large-scale magazines, is usually a one-person operation located in areas outside major cities where the more established, larger presses and publications are based. Although fanzine prototypes existed as early as the 1920s, *Sniffin' Glue*, a London-based photocopied PUNK fanzine (c. 1977), displayed all the characteristics of today's music-related fanzines and is usually considered to be the first true contemporary fanzine. By the mid-90s, fanzines reached epic popularity. Some were self-published once and never heard from again, but in every case, new technologies enabled their publishers to disseminate variously subversive or not so subversive text and images with alarming speed through a music-related network. This would not have been possible through the existing empire of magazines and newspapers, and thus, fanzines continue the *samizdat* tradition. Whereas layout and graphics were more primitive in the early cut-and-paste days, the computer created a sudden increase in well-designed, attractive layouts. Some of these fanzine publishers are paying extra for a good-looking print job, selling ads to small "indie" or independent record labels, and sending their publications to distributors. For example, the music magazine *Alternative Press* (aka *AP*) out of Cleveland began as a small photocopied fanzine, and is now a well-circulated magazine with cigarette/alcohol ads and a large readership. *Sweet Portable You* (McLean, VA) prefers a low-fi disdain for fanciful computer layouts, usually consisting of one photocopied legal-sized sheet of paper, double-sided, with "indie" record reviews in the form of short fiction or poetry. *Monozine* (Baltimore, MD) publishes true, often disturbingly comic accounts of maladies—sicknesses or injuries—and also promotes underground popular music shows. *Chunklet* (Athens, GA) is a more comically informative barometer of underground popular culture. *Badaboom Gramophone* publishes intelligent, hipster-centric articles and comes with a compilation CD of varying underground musical forms.

—Michael Peters

Selected Bibliographies: *Badaboom Gramophone*: P.O. Box 204, Leonia, NJ 07605; *Chunklet*: Chunklet Magazine, P.O. Box 2814, Athens, GA 30612; *Monozine*: P.O. Box 598, Reisterstown, MD 21136; *Sweet Portable You*: #T2 1937 Kennedy Drive, McLean, VA 22102–1937.

FAULKNER, William

(25 September 1897–6 July 1962).

Faulkner seemed so stupid, in person and at times in print, while conservative critics were predisposed to overpraise his conventional virtues, that we tend to forget he wrote some of the greatest avant-garde fiction of the twentieth century. I'm thinking initially of *The Sound and the Fury* (1929) and *As I Lay Dying* (1930), both with multiple narrators, each so radically different in intelligence (and thus style) from the others, and then of *Absalom, Absalom!* (1936), with its inimitable prose, composed of words rushing over one another, initially with complementary adjectives, devoid of commas. From the book's opening sentence, Faulkner is discovering enriched language:

> From a little after two oclock until almost sundown of the long still hot weary dead September afternoon they sat in what Miss Coldfield still called the office because her father had called it that—a dim hot airless room with the blinds all closed and fastened for forty-three summers because when she was a girl someone had believed that light and moving air carried heat and that dark was always cooler, and which (as the sun shone fuller and fuller on that side of the house) become latticed with yellow slashes full of dust motes which Quentin thought of as being flecks of the dead old dried paint itself blown inward from the scaling blinds as wind might have blown them.

No one wrote English like this before, and no one has quite done so since (though several have tried). A style so strong makes any plot, in this case about a Southern dynasty in the nineteenth century, seem secondary. Some of this extraordinary prose style also appears in Faulkner's short story "The Bear" (1940).

Selected Books: *The Sound and the Fury*. New York: Random House, 1929; *As I Lay Dying*. New York: Random House, 1930; *Absalom, Absalom!* (1936) Corrected text. New York: Vintage, 1987; *Big Woods* (contains "The Bear"). Random House, 1955.

Anthologies: Cowley, Malcolm, ed. *The Portable Faulkner* (1946). Rev. ed. New York: Viking, 1967; —. *The Faulkner-Cowley File: Letters and Memories 1944–1962*. New York: Viking, 1966; *The Faulkner Reader*. New York: Random House, 1954; Kawin, Bruce. *Faulkner's MGM Screenplays*. Knoxville: University of Tennessee Press, 1982; Meriwether, James B., ed. *Essays, Speeches & Public Letters*. New York: Random House, 1965.

Biography: Blotner, Joseph Leo. *Faulkner: A Biography*. 2 vols. (1974). New York: Vintage, 1984; Coughlan, Robert. *The Private World of William Faulkner*. New York: Harper & Bros., 1954; Karl, Frederick. *William Faulkner: American Writer*. New York: Weidenfeld, 1989.

Correspondence: Blotner, Joseph, ed., *Selected Letters of William Faulkner* (1977). New York: Vintage, 1978.

Interviews: Meriwether, James B., and Michael Millgate, eds. *Lion in the Garden: Interviews with William Faulkner*. Lincoln: University of Nebraska Press, 1968.

Website: http://www.utep.edu/mortimer/faulkner/mainfaulkner.htm (online journal and links).

Interpretation: Brooks, Cleanth. *William Faulkner: Toward Yoknapatawpha and Beyond*. New Haven: Yale University Press, 1978; Hoffman, Frederick J., and Olga W. Vickery, eds. *William Faulkner: Three Decades of Criticism*, New York: Twayne, 1996; Kinney, Arthur F. ed. *Critical Essays on William Faulkner*. East Lansing: Michigan State University Press, 1960; Millgate, Michael. *The Achievement of William Faulkner* (1966). Lincoln: University of Nebraska Press, 1978; Sensibar, Judith. *The Origins of Faulkner's Art*. Austin: University of Texas Press, 1984; Wagner, Linda W., ed. *William Faulkner: Four Decades of Criticism*. East Lansing: Michigan State University Press, 1973; Weinstein, Phillip M. *The Cambridge Companion to William Faulkner*. Cambridge, England: Cambridge University Press, 1995.

FEDERMAN, Raymond

(15 May 1928).

Born in France, Federman came to the U.S. after World War II, a survivor of distinctly modern disasters. After completing one of the first academic monographs about Samuel Beckett, Federman published a bilingual collection of poems, some first written in French, others initially written in English, with all translations by himself, and then

Double or Nothing (1971), which is a highly inventive sequence of typewritten pages. The bilingual prose of *Take It or Leave It* (1976) portrays in both languages the narrator's coming to America. Here he is in Times Square:

> I was on Broadway now j'arrive au bon moment in my Buickspecial which was parked illegally of course on a side street elles me parurent d'autant mieux divines ces apparitions qu'elles no semblaient point du tour but not at all s'aperçevoir que j'existais moi là à côté tout baveux tired gâteau dumbfounded d'admiration tout érotico-mystique of fatigue hunger desire ready to burst out of my fly. . . .

Federman's subsequent fiction has been less innovative. The new typeset edition (1992) of *Double or Nothing* is decidedly inferior to the original, apparently reflecting the devices of a university professor who is trying to be acceptable in spite of his wayward imagination.

Federman: A Recyclopedia Narrative (1998) is a rich alphabetical compendium, written by many hands, that represents a distinct conceptual advance in the genre of literary criticism/biography.

Fiction & Poetry: *Double or Nothing: A Real Fictitious Discourse*. Chicago: Swallow, 1971. Rev. ed. Boulder, CO: Fiction Collective Two, 1991; *Take It or Leave It*. New York: Fiction Collective, 1976; *The Voice in the Closet/La Voix dans le Cabinet de Débarras*, bilingual, with Maurice Roche. Madison, WI: Coda, 1979; *The Twofold Vibration*. Bloomington: Indiana University Press, 1982; *Smiles on Washington Square*. New York: Thunder's Mouth, 1985; *To Whom It May Concern*. Boulder, CO: Fiction Collective 2, 1990.

Critical Works: *Journey to Chaos: Samuel Beckett's Early Fiction*. Berkeley: University of California Press, 1965; *Critifiction: Postmodern Essays*. Albany, New York: SUNY Press, 1993; Ed. *Surfiction: Fiction Now—and Tomorrow*. Chicago: Swallow, 1975.

Recordings: *Take It or Leave It*. Sound design by Erik Belgum. Red Wing, MN: Voys, 1998.

Interpretation: *Federman: A Recyclopedia Narrative*. Ed. Larry McCaffery, Thomas Hartl, and Doug Rice. San Diego: San Diego State University Press, 1998.

FELDMAN, Morton

(12 January 1926–3 September 1987).

Initially regarded as a composer working in the wake of JOHN CAGE, Feldman eventually forged a different sort of career, first as a tenured professor, mostly at SUNY-Buffalo, and eventually in his compositional style. His characteristic scores of the fifties and sixties are graphic notations (within fixed pagination) that merely approximate dimensions and relationships of pitches, registers, and attacks, all of which the individual performer is invited to interpret to his or her taste. Nonetheless, the sounds of Feldman's music tend to be soft and isolated, with a consistency that is audibly different from the chaos cultivated by Cage. This aural pointillism, indebted in part to Feldman's interest in contemporary painting, superficially sounds like ANTON WEBERN'S music, but the compositional choices owe more to personal intuition and thus a sense of *taste* (which is a key word in Feldman's vocabulary, unlike Cage's) than either SERIAL systems or strictly Cagean indeterminate vocabulary. Once he became a professor surrounded by aspiring musicians, Feldman composed several very long pieces, at once austere and self-indulgent, that are belatedly becoming available (e.g., *For Philip Guston* [1984], which runs 265:16 in its first recording, or over four hours).

Selected Works: *Intersection I* for orchestra, 1951; *II* for piano, 1951; *III* for piano, 1953; *IV* for cello, 1953; *Projection I* for cello, 1950; *II* for flute, trumpet, piano, violin, and cello, 1951; *III* for two pianos, 1951; *IV* for violin and piano, 1951; *V* for three flutes, trumpet, two pianos, and three cellos, 1951; *Durations I* for alto flute, piano, violin, and cello, 1960; *II* for cello and piano, 1960; *III* for tuba, piano, and violin, 1961; *IV* for violin, cello, and vibraphone, 1961; *V* for horn, celesta, piano, harp, vibraphone, violin, viola, and cello, 1963; *Intervals* for bass-baritone, trombone, cello, vibraphone, and percussion, 1961; *Vertical Thoughts I* for 2 pianos, 1963; *II* for violin and piano, 1963; *III* for soprano, flute, horn, trumpet, trombone, tuba, 2 percussion, piano, celesta, violin, cello, and double bass, 1963; *IV* for piano, 1963; *V* for soprano, tuba, celesta, percussion and violin, 1963; *Cello and Orchestra*, 1972; *String Quartet and Orchestra*, 1973; *Piano and Orchestra*, 1975; *Flute and Orchestra*, 1977–78; *Patterns in a Chromatic Field* for cello and piano. 1981; *3 Voices* for 3 sopranos or 3 solo voices and tape, 1982; *Violin and String Quartet*, 1985.

Recordings: *American Masters: The Music of Morton Feldman*. CRI, 1993; *Feldman Edition Vol. 1*. Mode, 1996; *Feldman Words and Music*. Montaigne, 1997; *For Philip Guston*. Therwil, Switzerland: Hat Hut, 1992; *Why Patterns?/Crippled Symmetry*. Therwil, Switzerland: Hat Hut, 1991.

Writings: Feldman, Morton. *Essays*. Kerpen, Germany: Beginner, 1985.

Interpretation: DeLio, Thomas. *The Music of Morton Feldman*. Westport, CT: Greenwood, 1996; ——. *Circumscribing the Open Universe*. Lanham, MD: The University Press of America, 1983.

FENOLLOSA, Ernest

(18 February 1853–21 September 1908).

An American writer and scholar, he arrived in Japan in 1879 to teach at the Imperial University in Tokyo, perhaps at the apex of the westernization that followed the Meiji Restoration. Becoming an admirer of Japanese art, he persuaded Japanese intellectuals not to neglect their own heritage, and so contributed to the development of the New Nihonga movement in Japanese painting in the 1890s. Returning to America in 1890, Fenollosa helped form the oriental art collection at the Museum of Fine Arts in Boston. After his death, his widow asked the young poet Ezra Pound to edit Fenollosa's papers. One result was an essay, "The Chinese Written Character as a Medium for Poetry," that had a great impact not only on Pound's poetic practice but on other poets to this day. Fenollosa contributed to the avant-garde less on his own initiative than through someone else's channel.

Books: *Epochs of Chinese & Japanese Art* (1912). New York: Dover, 1963; with Ezra Pound. *"Noh," or, Accomplishment: A Study of the Classical Stage of Japan* (1916). Westport, CT: Greenwood, 1977; *The Instigations of Ezra Pound*. New York: Boni & Liveright, 1920.

Biography: Brooks, Van Wyck. *Fenollosa and His Circle*. New York: Dutton, 1962; Chisholm, Lawrence. *Fenollosa, The Far East, and American Culture*. New Haven: Yale University Press, 1963.

Interpretation: Miyake, Akiko; Sanehidee Kodama, & Nicholas Teele. *A Guide to Ezra Pound and Ernest Fenollosa's Classic Noh Theater of Japan*. Orono: University of Maine Press, 1994.

FERRARI, Luc

(5 February 1929).

One of the most distinctive figures in the history of electronic music, this French composer developed musique concrète in a unique direction, taking it to what could be seen as its logical conclusion. He has also composed impressive instrumental music, and in general has remained unpredictable and uncommitted to any particular style, though his work certainly has unifying concerns, many of them not typically considered musical.

Born in Paris, he studied piano with Alfred Cortot (1877–1962) and composition with Arthur Honegger (1892–1955) at the École Normale de Musique (1948–50), then transferred to the Paris Conservatoire and Olivier Messiaen's music theory class (1953–54). Initially he wrote instrumental and vocal works influenced by Messiaen, Arnold Schoenberg, and Edgard Varèse, but in 1958 he turned to tape music, and joined Pierre Schaeffer's Groupe de Musique Concrète. During 1958–59, he helped Scha-

f

effer establish the Groupe de Recherches Musicales. At first he conceived of *concrète* music in instrumental terms, and followed what had become the standard approach to treating *concrète* material—transforming it until it became an abstract musical sound. But by the early sixties he had begun working with sounds that maintained their "natural" character, formulating his concept of "anecdotal music": music structured like a literary narrative, and made out of recognizable sounds from daily life. These ideas were first manifested in *Hétérozygote* (1963–64), which was built out of snippets of conversation, bits of interviews, natural sounds, and city noises, blended together but still clearly intelligible. In Konrad Boehmer's words, the piece "suggest[s] possible stories without developing them."

If some of Ferrari's electroacoustic works seem like literary narratives, others more closely resemble documentaries or psychological investigations. *Presque rien no. 1, le lever du jour au bord de la mer* (1967–70) is a sound portrait of a fishing village stirring into activity at the beginning of the day; it is so "realistic," so discreetly shaped, it could almost be heard as straight audio reportage. Nonetheless, the sounds *have* been artfully arranged and enhanced in the studio, to create a hybrid form that is simultaneously "music" and documentary. *Presque rien no. 2, ainsi continue la nuit dans ma tête multiple* (1977) adopts a multiple perspective, both objective and subjective. The piece, Ferrari comments, is a "description of a nightscape which the sound engineer tries to pick up with his microphone, but the night takes the 'sound hunter' by surprise and slips into his head. So then we have a double description: the inner landscape alters the outer nightscape. It composes it, juxtaposing its own reality to it (imagination of reality)—a psychoanalysis, you might say, of its own nightscape."

It would be a mistake, though, to think of Ferrari as a specialist in a certain kind of electroacoustic soundscape; in fact, his creative output has been so diverse it is hard to summarize. He has written works combining tape and live instrumentalists—such as *Programme commun* (1972), *Cellule 75* (1975), and *A la recherche du rythme perdu* (1978)—which explore repetition and the "conflict of rhythm's instinctive force with the mechanization of society." He has written scores that incorporate improvisation (for example, *Ce qu'a vu le Cers* [1977]), and also fully notated pieces, such as the powerful orchestral work *Histoire du plaisir et de la désolation* (1981). He has also made video documentaries, and during the 1960s produced a series of films about the rehearsal process of works by Varèse, KARLHEINZ STOCKHAUSEN, Olivier Messiaen, CECIL TAYLOR, and others.

—Tony Coulter

Discography: *Hétérozygote/J'ai été coupé*. Philips, n.d; *Presque Rien No. 1/Société II*. Hamburg: Deutsche Grammophon, n.d; *Und so weiter/Music Promenade*. Mainz: Wergo, n.d; *Interrupteur/Tautologos 3*. Paris: Pathé Marconi, n.d; *Presque Rien No. 2/Promenade symphonique à travers un paysage musical*. Paris: INA-GRM, 1980; *Cellule 75/Collection 85*. Adda, n.d; *Brise-Glace*. Adda, n.d; *Ce qu'a vu le Cers*. Adda, 1988; *Matin et Soir*. Adda, 1989; *Electronic Works*. Amsterdam: BvHaast, n.d; *Unheimlich Schön*. Fontaine, France: Metamkine, 1993; *Presque Rien*. Paris: INA-GRM, 1995; *Piano - Piano*. Auvidis, 1997; *L'escalier des aveugles*. Alfortville, France: La Muse en Circuit, n.d.; *Cellule 75/Place des Abbesses*. New York: Tzadik, 1998.

FERRER, Rafael

(c. 1933).

An innovation in site-specific sculpture, Ferrer's work was based upon creating preconditions for natural processes to occur. For a 1969 "Anti-Illusion" show at New York's Whitney Museum, he made *Hay Grease Steel*, which consisted of what remained after hay was tossed against a steel frame along a museum wall to which wet glue had just been applied. *Ice* (1969), an even less permanent piece, consisted of leaves piled on blocks of ice that slowly melted away. "The act of conceiving and placing the pieces takes precedence over the object quality of the works," wrote this show's cocurator James Monte. "The fact of [the unusual materials'] inclusion in the art work is much less interesting than the way in which they are used." Since the late 1970s, Ferrer has concentrated on easel paintings that mostly depict his native Puerto Rico.

Selected Works: *Leaf Pieces*, 1968; *Hay Grease Steel*, 1969; *Ice*, 1969; *50 Cakes of Ice*, 1970; *Deflected Fountain*, 1970; *For Reba Stewart*, 1971; *Whale-Skin-Boat-(Flying)*, 1973; *Deseo*, 1973; *Patagonia*, 1973.

Exhibition Catalogs: *Deseo: An Adventure, Rafael Ferrer*. Cincinnati, OH: Contemporary Arts Center, 1973; Prokopoff, Stephen. *Rafael Ferrer: Recent Work and an Installation*. Boston: Institute of Contemporary Art, 1978; *Rafael Ferrer Impassioned Rhythms*. Austin TX: Laguna Gloria Art Museum, 1982; *Drawing/Rafael Ferrer*. New York: Nancy Hoffman Gallery, 1995; Monte, James, and Marcia Tucker. *Anti-Illusion: Procedures/Materials*. New York: Whitney Museum, 1969.

FINCH, Peter

(6 March 1947).

Since the early 1970s, Finch has been the principal innovator in Welsh poetry, the most genuine successor to Dylan Thomas; but instead of florid, drunken Thomasian rhetoric, Finch has favored a variety of tight sober structures, including parodies of other poets, VISUAL POEMS, TONE/SOUND POEMS, and, say, verbal imitations of PHILIP GLASS's music. The strongest work in his *Selected Poems* (1987) is "Some Blats," which is a world of interrogations, printed as individual lines without punctuation, beginning "is England green," including "is a lawnmower an object of beauty," continuing with "is really chum chuzz" and "is gadsass," and concluding "is sssssssss," in an implicit parody of drunken writing (and you know who). Finch also edited *Second Aeon* (1967–74) which was the only Welsh magazine of its time to swim with the international avant-garde, not only for what it printed but for Finch's considered, small-print reviews of publications both straight and wayward. If not for him and the aforementioned Mr. Thomas, Wales wouldn't appear in this book at all; for that alone (and since no living Irish person is here), Finch deserves a Welsh knighthood.

Books: *Beyond the Silence*. Cardiff, Wales: Vertigo, 1970; *Selected Poems*. Mid Glamorgan, Wales: Poetry Wales, 1987; ——. ed. *Typewriter Poems*. Millerton, NY: Something Else, 1972; *Whitesung*. Birmingham: Aquila, 1972; *Antarktika*. London: Writers Forum, 1972; *Trowch Eich Radio 'mlaen*. London: Writers Forum, 1977; *Blues and Heartbreakers*. Newcastle: Galloping Dog, 1981; *Reds in the Bed*. Newcastle: Galloping Dog, 1987; *Selected Poems*. Bridgend: Poetry Wales Press, 1987; *Make*. Newcastle: Galloping Dog, 1990; *Useful*. Bridgend: Seren Books, 1997; *Dauber*. London: Writers Forum, 1997; *Antibodies*. Exeter: Stride, 1997.

Website: http://dialspace.dial.pipex.com/peter.finch

FINLAY, Ian Hamilton

(28 October 1925).

I wish I liked Finlay's work more, because he is among the few contemporaries to be honored in the histories of both contemporary poetry and contemporary visual art. He began as a conventional Scottish poet whose first book, *The Dancers Inherit the Party* (1960), contained traditional rhymed sentiments about people in the Scottish outlands. Within a few years, he had become the principal Scottish participant in international CONCRETE POETRY, often writing poems that were just collections of nouns. An example is "Little Calendar":

april light light light light
may light trees light trees

june trees light trees light
july trees trees trees trees
august trees light trees light
september lights trees lights trees

His next development was VISUAL POEMS that transcended the limitations of the printed page, some of them created in collaboration with professional visual artists. Many of these pieces began as additions to his home garden in Lanarkshire, a remote area he rarely leaves because he regards it (and thus the works collected there) as a refuge from the cruel modern world. Many of his poems have military images reminiscent of World War II. As Finlay's work assumed more political themes in the 1980s (and he came into conflict with cultural officials over one thing or another), his pieces have often been included in thematic exhibitions that were installed outdoors.

Writings: *Rapel*. Edinburgh: Wild Hawthorn Press,1963; *The Blue and The Brown Poems*. New York: Atlantic Richfield-Jargon, 1968; *Poems To Hear and See*. New York: Macmillan, 1971; *A Sailor's Calendar*, New York: Something Else Press, 1971; *Honey by the Water*. Los Angeles: Black Sparrow, 1973; *Heroic Emblems*. Calais, VT: Z Press, 1977; *The Anaximander Fragment*, Wild Hawthorn Press, 1981; *I Sing for the Muses and Myself*. Green River, VT: Longhouse, 1991; *The Dancers Inherit the Party and the Glasgow Beasts*. Polygon, 1997.

Visual Art: *Works in Europe, 1972–1995*. Ed. Zdenek Felix and Pia Simig. Ostfildern, Germany: Cantz, 1995; *Prints 1963–1997 Druckgrafick*. Ed. Rosemarie E. Pahlke and Pia Simig. Ostfildern Germany: Cantz, 1998.

Exhibition Catalog: Abrioux, Yves. *Homage to Ian Hamilton Finlay: An Exhibition of Works*. London: Victoria Miro, 1987.

Interpretation: Abrioux, Yves. *Ian Hamilton Finlay: A Visual Primer* (1985). Cambridge: MIT Press, 1992; Finlay, Alex. ed. *Wood Notes Wild: Essays on the Poetry and Art of Ian Hamilton Finlay*. Edinburgh: Polygon, 1997; Morgan, Edwin. *Ian Hamilton Finlay and the Wild Hawthorn Press 1958–91*. Edinburgh: Graeme Murray, 1991.

FINLEY, Karen

(1956).

Finley is such a limited and thus repetitious writer that it is easy to wonder about the reasons for her 1990s celebrity. Her subject and theme are anger, particularly in exposing what she thinks men do to women; and, though her critique is often right, she is not immune from exaggerations unfortunately devoid of irony. Her principal talent as a writer is heavy, very heavy satire. Her celebrity seems the result of a complimentary publicity campaign involving the implicit collaboration between two publicly opposed cultural groups. When the conservative columnists Evans and Novak, among others, vociferously objected to the NATIONAL ENDOWMENT FOR THE ARTS funding of her work, they gave Finley the best free publicity, making her more important than she really was. On another side, the folks at the NEA, by trying to deny subsequent panel-awarded grants to Finley and comparable performers, contributed to the publicity push. (It was not for nothing that commercial publishers fifty years ago would try to have their new books banned in Boston; the publicity would guarantee increased sales everywhere else, so easily were the Boston censors manipulated, exploited, and duped.) All this notoriety prompted cultural liberals to respond by inflating Finley's importance initially with publicity, especially in *The Village Voice*, and then by sponsoring her presentations (more than recompensing her for lost NEA funds), even though her art invariably disappoints those not predisposed to Finley's particular ideology. The question raised is whether tax money should pay public officials, such as Jesse Helms and the NEA chiefs, who successfully promote mediocre anti-erotica while pretending to do otherwise. The second tragedy was that the others also denied NEA grants did not receive such success, in part because their work was too profoundly deviant to be publicized.

Predisposed to exploitation, she once fronted "1-900-ALLKAREN," which offered around the clock "a new message daily" for "$1.75 first minute, $1.25 thereafter," which represents, I suppose, a kind of alternative publishing.

Books: *Shock Treatment*. San Francisco: City Lights, 1990; *Enough Is Enough: Weekly Meditations for Living Dysfunctionally*. New York: Poseidon, 1993; *Living It Up: Humorous Adventures in Hyperdomesticity*. New York: Doubleday, 1996.

Interpretation: Bolton, Richard, ed. *Culture Wars*. New York: New Press, 1992; Carr, C. "Unspeakable Practices, Unnatural Arts: The Taboo Art of Karen Finley," *Village Voice* (June 24, 1986). In *On Edge: Performance at the End of the Twentieth Century*. Middletown: Wesleyan University Press, 1993; Zeigler, Joseph Wesley. *Arts in Crisis: The National Endowment for the Arts vs. America*. Pennington, NJ: A Cappella books, 1994.

FINNEGANS WAKE

(1939).

One reason why JAMES JOYCE's final book remains a monumental masterpiece is that its particular inventions have

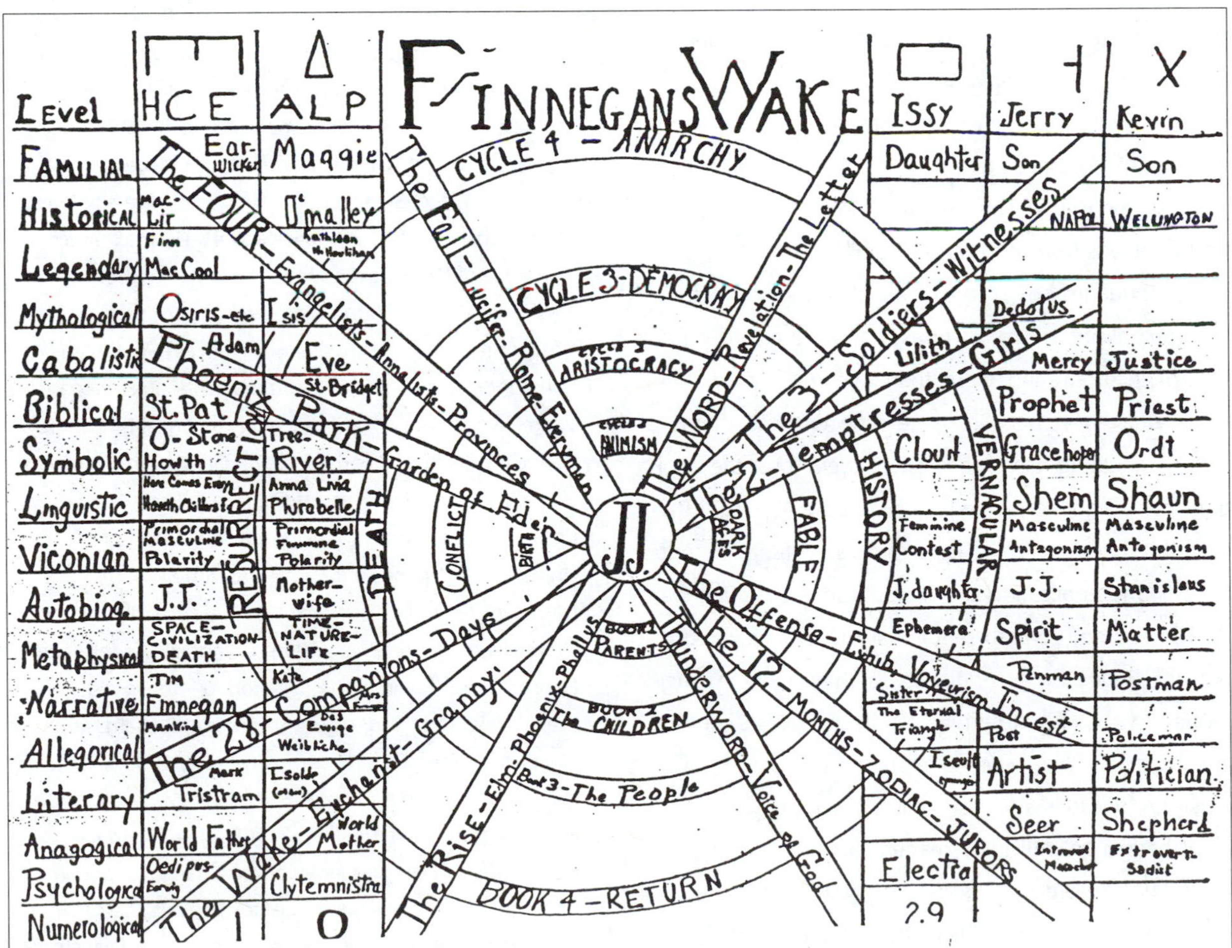

László Moholy-Nagy. Chart of *Finnegans Wake*. Courtesy Librarie Kostelanetz/Wordship.

never been exceeded. Unlike journalism, which tries to render complex experience in the simplest possible form, the *Wake* tells a simple story in an exceedingly complex form. Its subject is familial conflict—among two brothers, a sister, and their two parents. Exploiting the techniques of literary Symbolism, Joyce portrays numerous conflicts taking the same familial forms. The metaphors for the two brothers include competing writers, such as Pope and Swift, or competing countries, such as Britain and America, among other antagonistic pairs of roughly equal age and/or authority. This interpretation of human experience hardly ranks as "original" or "profound," but thanks to the techniques of multiple reference, incorporating innumerable examples into every part of the text, the theme is extended into a broad range of experience. No other literary work rivals the *Wake* in allusive density; in no other piece of writing known to me are so many dimensions simultaneously articulated.

Congruent with his method, Joyce coins linguistic portmanteaus that echo various familiar words; the use of many languages serves to increase the range of reference and multiplicity. He favors puns that serve a similar function of incorporating more than one meaning within a single unit—a verbal technique reflecting the theme of history repeating itself many times over. Thus, the book's principal theme is entwined in its method. As SAMUEL BECKETT put it, back in 1929, "Here form is content, content is form." One implication of this method is that *Finnegans Wake* need not be read sequentially to be understood. A principal index of its originality is that no other major modern work, except perhaps GERTRUDE STEIN'S *Geography and Plays*, is still as widely unread and persistently misunderstood, decades after its initial publication.

Whether an individual reader "accepts" or "rejects" Joyce's final masterpiece is also, in my observation, a fairly reliable symbolic test of his or her sympathy toward subsequent avant-garde writing. (Another similarly useful test can be carried out with the more experimental writings of Gertrude Stein.) The addition of an apostrophe to the book's title is not just a spelling mistake, happen though it often does; it is a red flag reflecting literary illiteracy.

Bibliography: Joyce, James. *Finnegans Wake*. New York: Viking, 1939. 3d ed. London: Faber, 1964.; *A Shorter Finnegans Wake*. Ed. Anthony Burgess. New York: Viking, 1968; *Scribbledehobble: The Ur-Workbook for Finnegans Wake*. Ed. Thomas E. Connolly. Evanston: Northwestern University Press, 1961.

Interpretation: Atherton, James S. *The Books at the Wake: A Study of Literary Allusions in James Joyce's Finnegans Wake* (1959). Carbondale: S. Illinois University Press, 1974; Bauerle, Ruth, and Hodgart, Matthew J.C. *Joyce's Grand Operoar: Opera in Finnegans Wake*. Urbana: University of Illinois Press, 1996; Beckett, Samuel. "Dante . . . Bruno . Vico . . Joyce." It. *Our Exagmination Round His Factification for Incamination of Work in Progress* (1929). New York: New Directions, 1962; Begnal, Michael H. *Dreamscheme: Narrative and Voice in Finnegans Wake*. Syracuse, NY: Syracuse University Press, 1988; Benstock, Bernard. *Joyce-again's Wake*. Seattle: University of Washington Press, 1965; Bishop, John. *Joyce's Book of the Dark*. Madison: University of Wisconsin Press, 1986; Bolderoff, Frances. *Hermes to His Son Thoth: Joyce's Use of Giordano Bruno in Finnegans Wake*. Woodward, PA: Classic Non-Fiction Library, 1968; Bonheim, Helmut, *A Lexicon of the German in Finnegans Wake*. Berkeley: University of California Press, 1967; Brivac, Sheldon. *Joyce's Waking Women*. Madison: University of Wisconsin Press, 1995; Burrell, Harry. *Narrative Design in Finnegans Wake*. Gainesville: University of Florida Press, 1996; Campbell, Joseph, and Henry Morton Robinson. *A Skeleton Key to Finnegans Wake*. New York: Viking, 1944; Ellmann, Richard. *James Joyce*. New York: Oxford University Press, 1959; Glasheen, Adaline. *A Second Census of Finnegans Wake*. Evanston: Northwestern University Press, 1963; ——. *Third Census of Finnegans Wake: An Index of the Characters and Their Roles*. Berkeley: University of California Press, 1977; Hart, Clive. *Structure and Motif in Finnegans Wake*. Evanston: Northwestern University Press, 1962; ——. *A Concordance to "Finnegans Wake"*. Minneapolis:

University of Minnesota Press, 1963; Hayman, David. *A First Draft Version of Finnegans Wake*. Austin: University of Texas Press, 1962; Hodgart, Matthew J. C., and Mabel P. Worthington. *Song in the Works of James Joyce*. New York: Columbia University Press, 1959; Hofheinz, Thomas. *Joyce and the Invention of Irish History: Finnegans Wake in Context*. Cambridge, England & New York: Cambridge University Press, 1995; Lernout, Geert. *Finnegans Wake: Fifty Years*. Amsterdam & Atlanta, GA: Rodopi, 1989; Margot, Norris. *The Decentered Universe of Finnegans Wake*. Baltimore: Johns Hopkins University Press, 1976; McCarthy, Patrick. *The Riddles of Finnegans Wake*. Madison, NJ: Fairleigh Dickinson University Press, 1980; ——, ed. *Critical Essays on Joyce's Finnegans Wake*. New York: G. K. Hall, 1992; McHugh, Roland. *The Sigla of Finnegans Wake*. Austin: University of Texas Press, 1972; *Annotations to Finnegans Wake*. Baltimore: Johns Hopkins University Press, 1980; *Finnegans Wake Experience*. Berkeley: University of California Press, 1982; McLuhan, Eric. *The Role of Thunder in Finnegans Wake*. Toronto: University of Toronto Press, 1997; Mink, Louis O. *A "Finnegans Wake" Gazeteer*. Bloomington: Indiana University Press, 1979; O Hehir, Brendan. *A Gaelic Lexicon for "Finnegans Wake."* Berkeley: University of California Press, 1967; ——, and John M. Dillon. *A Classical Lexicon for Finnegans Wake*. Berkeley: University of California Press, 1977; Patell, Cyrus R. K. *The Use of History in Finnegans Wake*. Cambridge: Harvard University Press, 1985; Sailer, Susan Shaw. *On the Void to Be: Incoherence and Trope in Finnegans Wake*. Ann Arbor: University of Michigan Press, 1993; Tindall, William York. *A Reader's Guide To "Finnegans Wake." New York: Farrar, Straus, 1969.*

FISCHINGER, Oskar

(22 June 1900–31 January 1967).

Initially a painter precociously interested in abstract interpretations of music and poetry, Fischinger produced his first animated shorts in 1920 with a wax-cutting machine of his own design. In 1926, he presented a series of shorts called "absolute film studies," individually named *Study 1*, *Study* 2, and so on, in the tradition of ABSTRACT EXPRESSION. With the arrival of sound, such kinetic abstractions could accompany music. In 1933, Fischinger began working in color with a special process he helped to develop, and in 1935 he won an international prize for his *Komposition in Blau/Composition in Blue*. After emigrating to Hollywood, he made *Allegretto* (1936) to accompany JAZZ and later worked with Walt Disney on the J. S. Bach segment of *FANTASIA* (1940). However, because his original designs were dismissed as too abstract and modified against his wishes, Fischinger acquired a deserved reputation as an animator with more artistic integrity than Disney. His *Motion Painting No. 1*, which accompanies Bach's *Brandenburg Concerto No. 3*, won the Grand Prix at the Brussels Exhibition of 1949.

Works: "Absolute film studies" (aka Study 1, Study 2, etc.), 1926; *Komposition in Blau/Composition in Blue*, 1935; *Allegretto*, 1936; *Radio Dynamics*, 1942; *Motion Painting No. 1*, 1949.

Video Anthology: *The Films of OF, Vol. 1*. Los Angeles: Jack Rutberg Fine Arts, 1998.

Exhibition Catalog: Nordland, Gerald. *Fischinger: A Retrospective of Paintings and Films*. Denver, CO: Gallery 609, 1980.

Interpretation: Starr, Cecile. "Oskar Fischinger" In Robert Russett and Cecile Starr. *Experimental Animation*. New York: Van Nostrand, 1976; Stauffacher, Frank, ed. *Art in Cinema: A Symposium on the Avant Garde Film* (1947). New York: Arno, 1968.

FLAIR

(1950–51, 1952).

By the measure of design alone, this was by far the most innovative magazine of its times. Founded by Fleur Cowles (c. 1922), a sometime painter who was at the time married to an heir to the Cowles family that published *Look*, among other slick magazines, *Flair* was initially a monthly that sold on newsstands for fifty cents (until killed after a year), and then a single annual that was copyrighted 1952. I know first the latter, which is essentially a clothbound book, 10" wide by 14" high, with a rectangular hole in its elegantly patterned cover. In the pages of the book are many sections, as in a conventional periodical; however, each is designed quite differently from all the others, sometimes on paper perceptibly different in texture and/or size from the sections around it. Just as some sections of *Flair* include pages that fold out or upwards, others have partial cutaways whose loose edges must be lifted to reveal imagery underneath. Bound into the book are small booklets, each with a single subject. No one would dispute the magazine's one-word title, which seems, in retrospect, an understatement.

As the table of contents is only minimally informative, the *Flair Annual 1953*, as it is called, must be read from beginning to end. Different in appearance, the short sections are likewise culturally different from one another; so that, for instance, a two-page spread about translations of the German poet Rainer Maria Rilke precedes a single page announcing new recordings of the music of EDGARD VARÈSE, which is followed in turn by the score of a nineteenth century musical exercise for children. Elsewhere in the *Flair Annual 1953* is a reproduction of three pages of "The Great Paris Polyglot," which is a sixteenth-century Bible with Genesis in parallel columns of Hebrew, Chaldean, and Greek, with separate Latin translations of all three. Tightly bound into the book's gutter is a twelve-page booklet, 6" high and 9" wide, of Katharine Anne Porter's prose text, *The Flower of Flowers*. Saul Steinberg drawings of New York City precede turn-of-the-century New York City photographs by Percy C. Byron, who was apparently still alive at the time.

In her introduction to a retrospective published decades later, *The Best of Flair* (1996), Cowles wrote of wanting to realize in her magazine "a sense of surprise instead of the rigid magazine make up." In that sense of establishing identity through wild variety, *Flair* resembles (and presages) an ASSEMBLING more than a standard magazine. Appearing more than four decades after its death, this large book, 34 cm. high and 25 1/2 cm wide (or 13 1/4" by 10") is a spectacular self-retrospective, in the respectable tradition of a magazine remembering its strongest front, effectively epitomizing *Flair*'s alternative editing strategy and reproducing design departures that still look fresh. Perhaps because of its origins in commercial publishing, *Flair* is rarely mentioned in the histories of significant American magazines. Indicatively, when *The Best of Flair* appeared, it was scarcely noticed and quickly remaindered (for $100 instead of $250), its legendary reputation among print designers notwithstanding.

Publications: Cowles, Fleur, ed. *Flair Annual 1953*. New York: Cowles, 1952; ——. *The Best of Flair*. New York: HarperCollins, 1996.

FLAVIN, Dan

(1 April 1933–29 November 1996).

Perhaps the epitome of the avant-garde MINIMAL artist, Flavin at his best used the simple means of fluorescent lamps (manufactured not by himself but by others) to produce complex effects. He typically runs his lamps, sometimes various in color, along walls or locates them in corners of darkened spaces to induce a meditative atmosphere. His early works range in complexity from simple rows of vertical tubes to quite intricate arrangements of crossing tubes of green, pink, orange, and blue on the ceiling of a long corridor in his untitled piece (dedicated to Elizabeth and Richard Koshalek) shown at the Castelli Gallery in New York in 1971. Not only are the tubes in this piece set at right angles to one another and in four layers, but two of the colors are placed with their diffuser pans facing out, so that they are seen only as reflected light. One theme is visual qualities peculiar to pure fluorescent light (in contrast to the more familiar incandescent lamp).

Because Flavin used light to transform radically (and brilliantly) an architectural space, he has received many commissions. Though his preference for rectangular formats inevitably suggests the medium of painting (and the color shadings of MORRIS LOUIS and Jules Olitski [1922], among others), the final experience of his exquisite art broaches qualities closer to those produced by such sacred objects as stained glass and religious icons.

Works: *Icon I*. 1961; *Daylight and Cool White* (to Sol LeWitt), 1964; *Red and Green Alternatives*, 1964; *Fluorescent Light*, 1964; *Alternating Pink and Gold*, 1967–68; *An Artificial Barrier of Green Fluorescent Light* (to Trudie and Enno Develing), 1968–69; *Untitled*, (to S.M.) 1969; *Three Sets of Tangented Arcs in Daylight and Cool White* (to Jenny and Ira Licht), 1969; *Untitled* (monument to Vladimir Tatlin), 1969; *Untitled* (monument to Vladimir Tatlin), 1970; *Untitled*, (for Tracy Harris), 1992; *Untitled* (for Buck), 1993; *Untitled* (for Greta Garbo), 1993.

Exhibition Catalogs: Smith, Brydon. *Dan Flavin, Fluorescent Light, etc.* Ottawa: National Gallery of Canada, 1969; *Monuments for V. Tatlin from Dan Flavin 1964–1982*. Los Angeles: Museum of Contemporary Art, 1989; *Dan Flavin: Untitled (for Lucie Rae master potter) 1990: Themes and Variations*. London: Waddington, 1990; *Dan Flavin tall cornered fluorescent light*. New York: Pace Wildenstein, 1993.

Interpretation: Muller, Gregory. *The New Avant-Garde: Issues for Art of the Seventies*. New York: Praeger, 1972.

FLEISCHER, Dave and Max

(14 July 1894–June 1979; 17 July 1889–11 September 1972). These two brothers were principal innovators in cinematic animation, developing films with human rather than animal characters and, in Betty Boop, creating the epitome of the sophisticated urban woman (who even today makes human sex symbols look reserved). In contrast to Walt Disney's crew, who were largely farm boys working in the bright light of Hollywood, the Fleischers were immigrants' children, the elder born in Vienna, with a studio was located in New York City. It was the brothers' good fortune that the censors who restricted live action films were slow to discover what was happening in cartoons. Eventually forced to clean up Betty Boop's highly erotic act, the Fleischers developed several technical innovations, such as creating the illusion of depth by filming their protagonists on clear cells against a background diorama. What most impresses me, as a sometime dance critic, is the choreography of the Fleischers' people, whose continuous movements are at once evocative and delicate. My own feeling is that the Fleischers' post-censorship films, such as *Gulliver's Travels* (1939), while longer and more ambitious, are less original and less consequential. Additionally, the Fleischer studio also initiated the characters of Popeye the Sailor, whose superhuman strength depends upon spinach, and Grampie, who lives in a world of RUBE GOLDBERG inventions. Perhaps because I come from the culture of reading, I've always found conventional Hollywood films terribly slow, if not soporifically languid, in ways that cartoons by the Fleischers or TEX AVERY and his associates are not. The tragedy is, that while books about Disney continue to appear, appreciations of the Fleischers are comparatively scarce.

Interpretation: Cabarga, Leslie. *The Fleischer Story* (1976). Rev. ed. New York: Da Capo, 1988.

Documentary: Maltin, Leonard. *Cartoon Madness: The Fantastic Max Fleischer Cartoons* (1993).

Website: http://pw1.netcom.com/~dself/boopfan.html (Betty Boop page with many links).

Anthology: Fleischer, Max. *Betty Boop's Sunday Best: The Complete Color Comics 1934–36*. Ed. Bill Blackbeard. Kitchen Sink, 1995.

FLUXUS

A multi-art group, both formed and decimated by GEORGE MACIUNAS, roughly on the hierarchical model of SURREALISM, though in the irreverent spirit of DADA. Fluxus included at various times DICK HIGGINS, Robert Watts (1923–88), Ken Friedman (1949), Jean Dupuy (1926), Wolf Vostell (1932–98), Ay-O (1931), and ALISON KNOWLES, among others. The myth of Fluxus has always had more success in Europe, which is more predisposed to understand the concept of an artists' group than America, even though most of its participants were Americans. Many of the best works displayed under the Fluxus banner are ingeniously comic, prompting some critics to classify it as "neo-Dada," though some of the participants were scarcely so.

f

Website: http://www.fluxus.org/

Exhibition Catalogs: Sohm, Hans, and Harald Szeeman. *Happening und Fluxus: Materialen*. Köln: Koelnischer Kunstverein, 1970; *1962 Wiesbaden FLUXUS 1982*. Berlin: DAAD-Harlekin Art, 1983; *Fluxus, etc.: The Gilbert & Lila Silverman Collection*. Cranbrook, MI: Cranbook Academy of Art, 1981; *Fluxus, etc./Addenda II: The Gilbert & Lila Silverman Collection*. Ed. Jon Hendricks. Pasadena, CA: Baxter Art Gallery/California Institute of Technology, 1993; *In the Spirit of Fluxus*. Minneapolis, MN: Walker Arts Center, 1993; *Ubi Fluxus ibi motus 1990–1962*. Ed. Achille Bonito Oliva. Milano: Mazzotta, 1990.

Anthologies: *Fluxus, etc./Addenda II: The Gilbert & Lila Silverman Collection*. Ed. Jon Hendricks. New York: Ink &, 1983; Friedman, Ken, ed. *The Fluxus Reader*. London: Academy, 1998.

Interpretation: Hendricks, Jon, & Kellein, Thomas. *Fluxus*. London: Thames & Hudson, 1995; Higgins, Dick. *Horizons: The Poetics and Theory of the Intermedia*. Carbondale: S. Illinois University Press, 1983; Pijnappel, Johan. *Fluxus: Today & Yesterday*. London: Academy, 1993; Smith, Owen F. *Fluxus: The History of an Attitude*. San Diego: San Diego State University Press, 1998; Williams, Emmett, and Ann Noël, eds. *Mr. Fluxus: A Collective Portrait of George Maciunas 1931–1978*. London: Thames & Hudson, 1997.

Documentary: Movin, Lars. *The Misfits: 30 Years of Fluxus*. Copenhagen, Denmark: Cinnamon Film & The National Danish Film Board, 1993.

FONTANA, Lucio

(19 February 1899–7 September 1968). Born in Argentina of Italian parents, Fontana moved to Milan in 1905. He began as an abstract sculptor, prolific through the 1930s; but with World War II, he relocated to Buenos Aires, where he published his *Manifesto Blanco* (1946), which advocated a new art that would exploit such recent technologies as neon light and TELEVISION. Once he returned to Italy, Fontana issued additional manifestos advocating *Spazialismo*. In 1947, he pioneered ENVIRONMENTAL ART with a room painted entirely black; two years later came his *Ambiente Spuziale*, with ultraviolet light that deliberately disoriented the viewer's perception. In the early 1950s, he made monochromatic canvases to which by the late 1950s he added a clean slit that became his trademark, purportedly suggesting not the desecration of art but space behind the canvas. In the 1960s, he made massive sculptures that were slashed open like his canvases. Though one may disagree about the final value of his work, it is clear that Fontana anticipated many ideas that others developed later.

Works: *Manifesto Blanco*, 1946; *Spatial Environment*, 1949; *Spatial Concept*, 1952; *Nature*, 1959–60.

Exhibition Catalogs: *Lucio Fontana 1899–1968: A Retrospective*. New York: Guggenheim Museum, 1977; *Lucio Fontana*. Eds. Enrico Crispotli and Rosella Siligato. Milano: Electra, 1998.

FORD, Charles Henri

(10 February 1909).

Born in Mississippi, in a year he had successfully kept unknown into his late 80s, Ford edited the first issues of the literary periodical *Blues* in Columbus, Mississippi, in

Charles Henri Ford. From *Silver Flower Coo*. Courtesy the author.

1929–30 before moving to Paris in the early thirties, in time to be noticed favorably in Gertrude Stein's *The Autobiography of Alice B. Toklas* (1933). He subsequently collaborated with the film-critic-to-be Parker Tyler (1904–74) on *Young and Evil* (1933, in Paris), a pioneering fictional exploration of homosexuality, more courageous in its choice of subject than in its esthetic moves. Once back in America, Ford edited from 1940 to 1947 *View*, a journal of American SURREALISM. Ford's most innovative literary art is to be found in his VISUAL POEMS, largely made from newspaper clippings, appearing first in the self-published and extremely colorful *Spare Parts* (1966), then in *Silver Flower Coo* (1968, printed in black and white). He has also exhibited his photographs, his paintings, and his film *Johnny Minotaur* (1971).

Books: *Sleep in the Nest of Flames*. New York: New Directions, 1949; *Spare Parts*. New York: New View, 1966; *Silver Flower Coo*. New York: Kulchur, 1968; *Flag of Ecstasy: Selected Poems*. Ed. Edward B. Germain. Los Angeles: Black Sparrow, 1972; *Out of the Labyrinth: Selected Poems*. San Francisco: City Lights, 1990.

Anthologies: Ed. *View: 1940–47*. New York: Thunder's Mouth, 1991; ——. and Parker Tyler. *The Young and Evil* (1933). New York: Richard Kasak, 1996.

Films: *Johnny Minotaur*, 1971.

FORD, HENRY

(30 July 1863–7 April 1947).

Despite his late-life anti-Semitism, Ford was a true visionary for the introduction of mass production and the assembly line. The crowning achievement of this vision was the Model T, created in 27 million copies, all nearly identical, all originally available in "any color you want—as long as it's black." Ford's standardization of a single model pressaged such radical ideas as the COPY CULTURE of the '60s and ANDY WARHOL's mass production of celebrity images. His next radical concept was the "$5.00 day"; Ford realized that if his workers were paid a good wage, they'd be able to afford to spend more money on consumer products—such as cars. Thus, by paying his employees more, he was actually lining his own pockets! Further, the idea of an industrial city—the River Rouge plant—to be a self-contained production center making everything from raw steel through the finished product was another radical concept. Ford's need for near total control of the work process—and his dogged insistence that style was not as important as function—nearly led to the downfall of the Ford empire. Thus, new ideas can quickly become old; Ford sadly lacked the ability to see beyond his original innovations.

—Richard Carlin

Interpretation: Batchelor, Ray. *Henry Ford, Mass Production, Modernism, and Design*. Manchester,

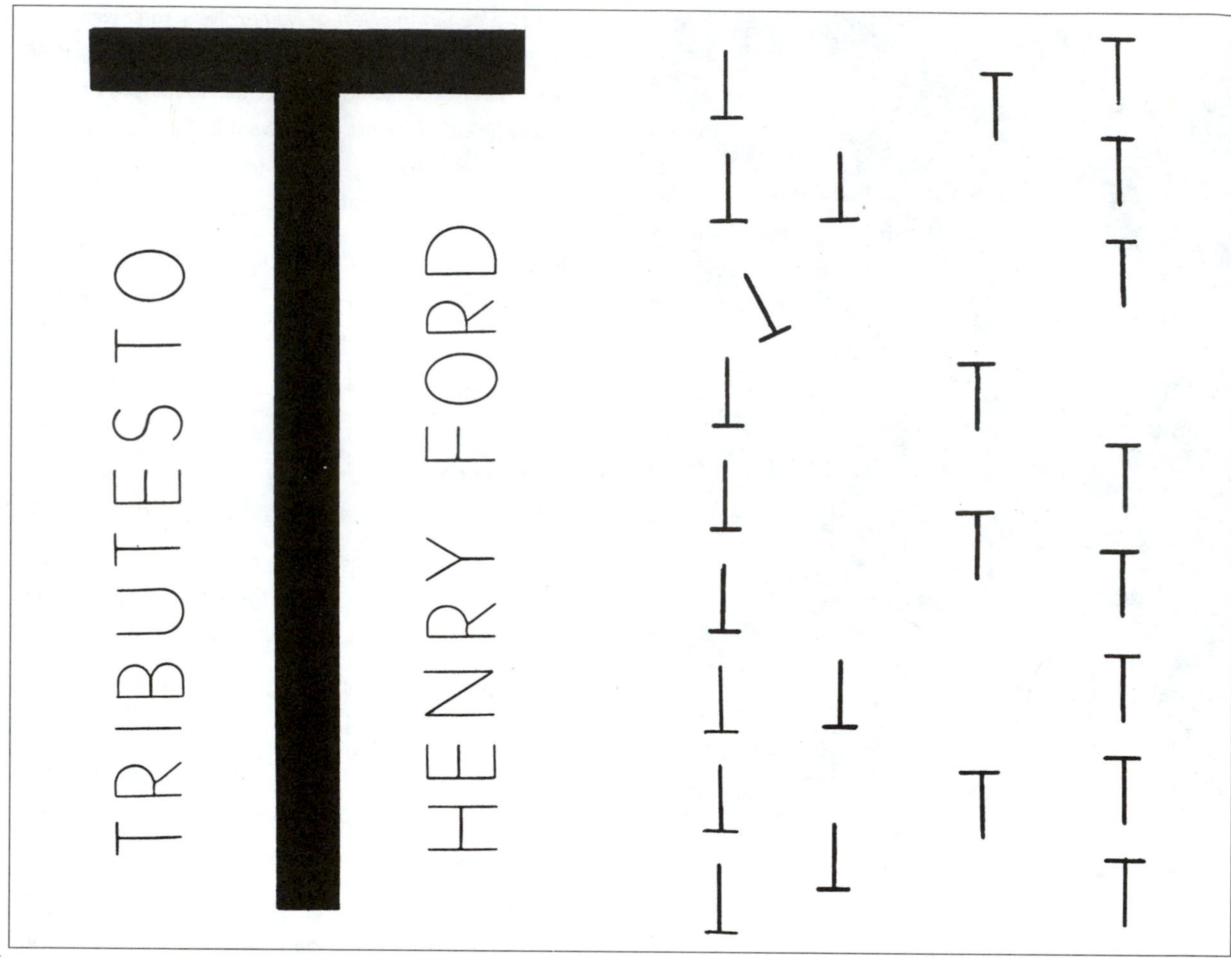

Richard Kostelanetz. From "Tributes to Henry Ford." Courtesy the author.

England: Manchester University Press, 1994; Middleton, Haydn. *Henry Ford*. New York: Oxford University Press, 1997; Kostelanetz, Richard. "Homage to Henry Ford" (1967) in *Visual Language* New York: Assembling Press, 1970.

Website: www.ford.com (Ford Motor Co. site)

FOREGROUNDING

(1920s).

Along with DEFAMILIARIZATION, this is a key concept in the radical esthetics of RUSSIAN FORMALISM, identifying the emphasizing or making visible of a literary element customarily secondary. Examples include works that are primarily about qualities unique to language, such as the tongue-twister, "Peter Piper picked a peck of pickled peppers," which is not about agriculture but the plosive sound of the letter P. Acknowledging its relevance to all the arts, an unidentified slave behind *The Oxford Companion to Twentieth-Century Literature in English* writes:

> Rhyme foregrounds the possibilities of echoes in language, of clashes and consonances between sound and meaning; jokes foreground the role of play in interpretation; a plot full of coincidences reveals and foregrounds the controlling hand of the author. What

is foregrounded—either by the writer or by the reader—is usually what was previously thought to be absent, or only a background element, or a technical support system. A film, for example, might foreground the placing of the camera; a painting may foreground the painter's own presence in his or her work [of, in a better example, color alone in monochromic canvases].

What makes foregrounding avant-garde is the generally unprecedented emphasis upon elements indigenous to an artistic medium.

Interpretation: Stringer, Jenny, ed. *The Oxford Companion to Twentieth Century Literature*. New York: Oxford University Press, 1996.

FOREMAN, Richard

(10 June 1937).

Because I have known Foreman since high school (and he was a few years ahead of me in college as well), I have followed his work sympathetically from its very beginnings and so feel obliged to say something special here. However, every time I begin to write anything, I find myself so impressed by his own statements that, remembering my vow never to do anything professionally that anyone else can do better, I reprint one of them here:

> In 1968, I began to write for the theater that I wanted to see, which was radically different from any style of theater that I had seen. In brief, I imagined a theater which broke down all elements into a kind of atomic structure—and showed those elements of story, action, sound, light, composition, gesture, in terms of the smallest building-block units, the basic cells of the perceived experience of both living and art-making. The scripts themselves read like notations of my own process of imagining a theater piece. They are the evidence of a kind of effort in which the mind's leaps and inventions may be rendered as part of a process not unique to the artist in question (myself) but typical of the building-up which goes on through all modes of coming-into-being (human and nonhuman). I want to refocus the attention of the spectator on the internals, gaps, relations, and rhythms which saturate the objects (acts and physical props) which are the "givens" of any particular play.

Perhaps because his work is not easily understood by others, Foreman customarily directs his texts, as well as designing both the stage and the sound. He also also made films and published unusual fiction.

Works: *Angelface*, New York: 1968; *Elephant-Steps*, New York: 1970; *Total Recall: Sophia = (Wisdom) Part 2*, New York: 1970; *Rhoda in Potatoland (Her Fall-starts)*, New York: 1975.

Books: *Plays and Manifestos*. Ed. Kate Davey. New York: New York University Press, 1976; *Reverberation Machines: The Later Plays and Essays*. Barrytown, NY: Station Hill, 1985; *Love & Science: Selected Music-Theater Texts*. New York: Theatre Communications Group, 1991; *Unbalancing Acts* (1992). New York: Theatre Communications Group, 1995; *My Head Was a Sledgehammer*. Woodstock, NY: Overlook, 1995; *No-Body: A Novel in Parts*. Woodstock, NY: Overlook, 1997.

Interpretation: Davy, Kate. *Richard Foreman and the Ontological-Hysteric Theatre*. Ann Arbor: UMI Research, 1981.

FORMALISTS, RUSSIAN

(1914–28).

In the years around World War I, several Russian linguists and literary critics attempted to define rigorously the devices and conventions that distinguish literary language from common talk. The name of their group was OPOYAZ, which was an acronym for the Society for the Study of Poetic Language. According to their pioneering principal historian Victor Ehrlich, they represented "the first critical movement in Russia which attacked in systematic fashion the problems of rhythm and meter, of style and composition." The major figures were Roman Jakobson (1896–1982) and Viktor Shklovsky (1893–1984). Whereas

Jakobson's specialty was the elaborate close analysis of innovative poetry, beginning with VELIMIR KHLEBNIKOV'S, Skhlovsky concentrated on prose, particularly contributing the useful concept of DEFAMILIARIZATION, which is also translated as "making strange," which he identified as a quality distinguishing literary language from practical. Another insightful epithet is FOREGROUNDING.

The historian Ehrlich wrote: "The Formalist movement had ever since its inception made common cause with the artistic avant-garde. In their early writing, Shklovsky and Jakobson sought to elevate the Futurist experiments into general laws of poetics." In their disregard of biography and history, the Russian Formalists resembled the New Critics, who became prominent in America in the 1930s.

Because of their emphasis on form over content, the Russian Formalists fell to the wrath of the Stalinist demand for a literature of socialist realism. While Shklovsky stayed behind in Leningrad (aka St. Petersberg), producing semi-autobiographical texts that incidentally illustrated his theories, Jacobson emigrated first to Prague, where he joined the literary scholar René Wellek (1903–1995), among others, in the Prague Linguistic Circle, which survived until World War II, where both men emigrated to America. Wellek became at Yale the principal English-language historian of literary criticism, while Jakobson, eventually at Harvard, became the dean of American Slavic Professors, applying some of his Russian formalist experience to many linguistic and literary problems. Meanwhile, Wellek joined an American New Critic, Austin Warren (1899–1986), in writing *Theory of Literature* (1949, subsequently revised), for many years a popular textbook that advocated the autonomy of the literary work and critical analysis based on "intrinsic" or "specifically literary" qualities. My recollection is that the professors teaching it to me four decades ago said nothing about the book's conceptual origins in Russian Formalism and Russian Futurism, which I had to discover on my own.

Books: Shklovsky, Viktor. *Mayakovsky and His Circle*. Trans. Lily Feiler. New York: Grossman, 1972; *Theory of Prose* (2d ed., 1929). Trans. Benjamin Sher. Elmwood Park, IL: Dalkey Archive, 1990; *Third Factory* (1926). Trans. & ed. Richard Sheldon. Ann Arbor, MI: Ardis, 1977; Jakobson, Roman. *Selected Writings*, 8 vols. The Hague: Mouton, 1962–88; ——. *Six Lectures on Sound and Meaning*. Trans. John Mepham. Cambridge: MIT Press, 1978; —— & Morris Halle. *Fundamentals of Language*. The Hague: Mouton, 1956; —— & Linda R. Waugh. *The Sound Shape of Language*. Bloomington: Indiana University Press, 1979; "The Newest Russian Poetry" (Velimir Klebnikov, 1919), trans. E. J. Brown, in his anthology, *Major Soviet Writers: Essays in Criticism*. New York: Oxford University Press, 1973; Wellek, René. *A History of Modern Criticism 1750–1950*. 4 vols. New Haven: Yale University Press, 1955–66; Wellek, René, and Austin Warren. *A Theory of Literature*. New York: Harcourt, Brace, 1949.

Anthologies: Lemon, Lee T., and Marion J. Reese, trans. *Russian Formalist Criticism: Four Essays*. Lincoln: University of Nebraska Press, 1965; Bann, Stephen, and John E. Bowlt, eds. *Russian Formalism*. New York & Edinburgh: Barnes & Noble & Scottish Academic, 1973.

Memoirs: Jakobson, Roman. *My Futurist Years*. Trans. Stephen Rudy. Ed. Bengt Jangfeldt. New York: Marsilio, 1996; ——, and Krystyna Pomorska. *Dialogues*. Cambridge: MIT Press, 1983; Shklovsky, Viktor. *Third Factory*. Ed. & trans. Richard Sheldon. Ann Arbor, MI: Ardis, 1977. (This contains, as an appendix, Fyldor Grits's extended essay on "The Work of Viktor Shklovsky.")

Interpretation: Ehrlich, Victor. *Russian Formalism* (1955). 3d ed., revised. New Haven: Yale University Press, 1981; Holenstein, Elmar. *Roman Jakobson's Approach to Language*. Bloomington: Indiana University Press, 1976; Jackson, Robert Louis, & Stephen Rudy. *Russian Formalism: A Retrospective Glance*. New Haven: Yale Center for International and Area Studies, 1985; Wellek, René. *The Literary Theory and Aesthetics of the Prague School*. Ann Arbor: University of Michigan Press, 1969; Winner, Thomas G. "Roman Jakobson and Avant-Garde

Art." In *Roman Jakobson: Echoes of His Scholarship*. Ed. D. Armstrong and G. H. Van Schooneveld. Lisse, the Netherlands: Peter de Ridder, 1977.

FORTI, Simone

(25 March 1935).

Italian-born, American-raised, this dancer/choreographer studied with ANNA HALPRIN and collaborated with her husbands ROBERT MORRIS and ROBERT WHITMAN in their MIXED-MEANS performances. Some of her dances reflect MINIMALISM in their simple organizational structures and their use of everyday movements to accomplish particular tasks (thereby meriting the term "task dances"). In *Slant-Board* (1961), for instance, dancers maneuver on a slanted board by holding onto ropes to prevent total slippage. *Huddle* (1961) involves dancers huddling in a mass to form a base for members to emerge from and climb over. While continuing to work with improvisational forms, Forti became increasingly interested in childlike and animal movements as a basic vocabulary for her works.

—Katy Matheson

Selected Dances: *See-Saw*, 1960; *Rollers*, 1960; *Slant-Board*, 1961; *Huddle*, 1961; *Face Tunes*, 1967; *Planet*, 1976; *Jackdaw Songs*, 1982.

Writings: *Handbook in Motion*. Halifax, NS, and New York: Nova Scotia College of Art & Design and New York University Press, 1974.

FOUND ART

(c. 1910s).

One of the principal innovations of avant-garde visual arts in the century's teens was the introduction of real objects into an artistic context. In America, while CHARLES IVES incorporated hymn tunes into classical music, MARCEL DUCHAMP insisted through his "readymades" that a *Bicycle Wheel* (1913), a *Bottle Rack* (1914), and even a urinal he called *Fountain* (1917) be regarded as art. Back in Europe, painters introduced ticket stubs and newspaper clippings into collages that were exhibited as paintings. Not until the 1960s did visual artists become so concerned with estheticizing mundane objects that GEORGE MACIUNAS for one coined the term "Concretism," which he defined as "the opposite of abstraction." He continued:

> The realistic painting is not realistic; it's illusionistic. You can have illusionistic music; you can have abstract music, you can have concrete music. In music, let's say if you have an orchestra play, that's abstract music, because the sounds are all done artificially by musical instruments. But if that orchestra is trying to imitate a storm, say, like Debussy or Ravel do it, that's illusionistic; it's still not realistic. But if you're going to use noises like the clapping of the audience or farting or whatever, now that's concrete. Or street car sounds, or a whole bunch of dishes falling from the shelf. That's concrete—nothing illusionist or abstract about it.

By the 1980s, found sculptural objects became an over-publicized movement that, at least to those who knew history, seemed terribly derivative. On the other hand, appropriation of another composer's music, which was a minor development in modern music, became more feasible in the 1990s with computer-assisted SAMPLING.

Bibliography: Rosenblum, Robert. *Cubism and Twentieth-Century Art* (1961). New York: Abrams, 1977; Maciunas, George. "Transcript of a Videotaped Interview by Larry Miller, March 24, 1978." In *FLUXUS, etc./Addenda I*, ed. Jon Hendricks. New York: Ink, 1983.

FOUND POETRY

The found poet discovers poetry in language not her or his own. The simplest strategy is to break apart prose into lines, with appropriately sensitive line-breaks. William Butler Yeats took Walter Pater's prose evocation of the *Mona Lisa* and, retyping it into free verse, made it the initial poem in his *The Oxford Book of Modern Verse* (1936).

f

Some of the COMTE DE LAUTRÉAMONT's *Les Chants de Maldoror* (posthumously published in 1890) were, scholars discovered, direct quotations from an 1853 encyclopedia of natural history. With this likewise posthumous discovery in mind, consider this rationale for poetic plagiarism found elsewhere in Lautréamont's writings: "It stays close to the words of an author; it uses his expressions, erasing a false idea and replacing it with a correct one."

The *Times Literary Supplement* in 1965 published a serial debate over the Scottish poet HUGH MACDIARMID's authoring of a poem that begins with a verse arrangement of words from another poet's short story. In introducing MacDiarmid's *Selected Poems* (1993), the critic and translator Eliot Weinberger finds that much of MacDiarmid's *Cornish Heroic Songs for Valda Trevlyn* (1937–38) is drawn from "long passages from obscure travel and science books, reviews in the *Times Literary Supplement*, Herman Melville's letters, the writings of Martin Buber, Thomas Mann's *Tonio Kroger*." JOHN ASHBERY acknowledged that his major early long poem "Europe" contains phrases lifted randomly from a 1917 children's book by William LeQueux, *Beryl of the Biplane*.

The Canadian practitioner JOHN ROBERT COLOMBO identifies the first book wholly composed of found poetry as John S. Barnes's *A Stone, A Leaf, A Door* (1945), which consists entirely of the novelist Thomas Wolfe's prose, broken apart to look like poetry. BERN PORTER composed his "founds" from words in advertising, appropriating typography as well as language, while JOHN CAGE has drawn on Henry David Thoreau and JAMES JOYCE, among others, for his shrewdly chosen source texts. RICHARD KOSTELANETZ has scrambled the opening pages of literary classics in his prose-looking *Aftertexts* (1987) and the opening pages of his own essays in *Recyclings* (1973, 1984), which he considers to be implicitly a kind of "literary autobiography." Though recent developments in the visual arts have given to "appropriation" a new authority that has, curiously, scarcely extended into literary appreciation, writers continue to remember T. S. Eliot's advice: "Immature poets imitate; mature poets steal; bad poets deface what they take and good poets make it into something better, or at least something different."

Bibliography: Ashbery, John. "Europe." In *A Tennis Court Oath*. Middletown: Wesleyan University Press, 1962; Colombo, John Robert. "Found Poetry." In *The Avant-Garde Tradition in Literature*, ed. Richard Kostelanetz. Buffalo, NY: Prometheus, 1982; Kostelanetz, Richard. *Recyclings*, Vol. I. New York: Assembling, 1973; complete. New York: Assembling, 1984; *Aftertexts/Prose Pieces*. San Diego: Atticus (POB 927428, 92192), 1987; MacDiarmid, Hugh. *Selected Poems*. Intro. Eliot Weinberger. Manchester, England: Carcanet, 1993.

THE FOUR HORSEMEN

(1970–1989).

They were four Canadians of independent literary reputation who came together to jam, much as freelance jazz musicians do: BP NICHOL; Paul Dutton (1943), who has worked solo in various experimental modes; Rafael Barreto-Rivera (1944), born in Puerto Rico, who has likewise published both texts and tapes; and Steve McCaffery (1948), a London-born writer who deserves a separate entry here, if I could figure out how to summarize his difficult, perhaps excessively obscure work (and so refer curious readers to Marjorie Perloff's 1991 book, *Radical Artifice)*. The Horsemen's initial TEXT-SOUND works were collected on a record called *CaNADAda* (1972), in which the strongest piece is a fugue ("Allegro 108") that opens, "Ben den hen ken len men pen ken fen men yet," with one voice chanting alone on a single note. Then a second voice enters, at first chanting nonsynchronously, but then in unison with the initial voice, as a third voice enters, chanting along on a single note. "Allegro 108 " develops a steady, emphatic rhythm typical of voices clearly accustomed to working with one another, all devoid of instrumental accompaniment. Other Horsemen collaborations incorporate sentences and fully written texts. After Nichol's sudden death, the Horsemen fulfilled prior commitments as a trio and then disbanded. Another Canadian sound poetry group with a similar multi-man makeup called itself Owen Sound.

Works: *CaNADAda*. Toronto: Griffin House, 1972; *Horse d'Oeuvres*. Toronto: General Publishing, 1975; *The Prose Tattoo: Selected Performance Scores*. Kenosha, WI: Membrane (P.O. Box 4190, 53141), 1983.

FRANCIS, LINDA

(8 January 1943).

In the Agnes Martin tradition of subtle abstract drawing, Linda Francis has worked on various surfaces (mostly paper, including fiberglass) with various chalks and charcoal for diverse visual effects. Initially using grids, she turned to circular imagery, particularly spirals derived from photographs of the stars, often intersected with curving lines. Another theme of her work is different sizes that require different physical movements. As she told an interviewer:

> When I draw the small notes with a paintbrush, the relationship I have with the page is that of writing. The movements are at the scale of the brush (the quantity of ink it can hold) as well as that of my hand, or even that of my fingers holding it, for the whole hand need not move. The wrist is the center of my arcs. For the middle-size drawings, on the contrary, the movement I have to make requires the whole arm. The scale is different, and the pastel, chalk, or charcoal require more energy. . . . Finally, when I use the large format, my whole body must move, and the way the chalk is used becomes an extension of the body.

Needless to say perhaps, Francis's drawings reflect these unusual sensitivities about physicality and scale.

Works: *Shadow*, 1996; *Equatorial Precession*, 1996; *Spiral*, 1996.

Exhibition Catalog: Bois, Yves-Alain. *Linda Francis*. Wayne, NJ: Ben Shahn Gallery, William Patterson College, 1996.

FRANK, Peter

(3 July 1950).

The JAMES GIBBONS HUNEKER of his generation, Frank is a polymathic critic, better at enthusiasm than discrimination, who has written about all the arts. More skilled at reviews than books, he should have become an interdepartmental newspaper critic; but, since this has not occurred, there is reason to believe that newspaper executives today are not as culturally sophisticated as they were in Huneker's times. Thus, at various times, Frank has written for innumerable art and music magazines. In the late 1980s, this native New Yorker moved to California, editing a new journal there. His books include an intelligently annotated bibliography of the Something Else Press and a less intelligent survey of visual arts in the 1980s.

Writings: *The Travelogues*. Los Angeles: Sun & Moon, 1982; *Something Else Press*. New Paltz, NY: McPherson & Co., 1983; ——. and Michael McKenzie. *New, Used & Improved*. New York: Abbeville, 1987; *Theater of the Object*. New York: Alternative Museum, 1988.

FREE JAZZ

(c. 1960).

This type of JAZZ was supposed to be free of any preconceived notions of melody, harmony, or rhythm. The crucial example was the 1960 ORNETTE COLEMAN LP, *Free* Jazz, in which a pair of four-man ensembles were invited to play simultaneously, supposedly with no preconceived score. Actually, group passages were preplanned, while the rhythm section never drops out completely. Because all eight musicians never improvise at once, usually a solo voice emerges from the crowd only to be reabsorbed into the ensemble.

Recordings: Coleman, Ornette. *Free Jazz*. New York: Atlantic SD-1364/-2 (IT/CD), 1960.

Interpretation: Budds, Michael J. *Jazz in the 60's: The Expansion of Musical Resources and Techniques*. Iowa City: University of Iowa Press, 1978; Jost, Ekkehard. *Free Jazz*. New York: Da Capo, 1994.

FREYTAG-LORINGHOVEN, Elsa van

(1874–1927).

Born in eastern Germany, the daughter of a contractor, she married a baron whose hyphenated family name she appropriated. Arriving in the New York art world before the beginning of World War I, she became known as the "Baroness," producing new art and writing in her second language, English—the most hysterical, EXPRESSIONIST poetry to appear in avant-garde magazines at that time. A typical title is "Mineself-Minesoul-and-Mine-Cast-Iron Lover," which includes such lines as this: "Heia! ja-hoho! hisses mine starry-eyed soul in her own language." (She also wrote German poems that remain untranslated.) Freytag-Loringhoven collaborated with the American artist Morton Schamberg (1881–1918) in his classic sculpture *God* (1916), made out of a plumbing trap and miter, perhaps, as some suggest, selecting the object herself, while Schamberg only took the legendary photograph. Though she had not participated in any European DADA, Freytag-Loringhoven became a center of its New York incarnation, curiously realizing a celebrity here that was unavailable to her back home.

Though scarcely young when she came to America, the Baroness's displays of her nude self became legendary among her contemporaries (and incidentally make subsequent artist-exhibitionists seem esthetically slight). In his *Life Among the Surrealists* (1962), Matthew Josephson remembers: "She decorated her own person in a mechanistic style of her own device, shaving her head and painting it purple; wearing an inverted scuttle for a hat, a vegetable grater as a brooch, long ice-cream spoons for earrings, and metal teaballs attached to her pendulant breasts. Thus adorned and clad in an old fur coat, or simply a Mexican blanket, and very little underneath, Freytag-Loringhoven would saunter forth to serve as one of the truly curious sights of the 'Village' forty years ago." In *An American Artist's Story* (1939), George Biddle recalls:

> Having asked me in her high-pitched German stridency, whether I required a model, I told her I should like to see her in the nude. With a royal gesture she swept apart the folds of a scarlet raincoat. She stood before me quite naked—or nearly so. Over the nipples of her breasts were two tin tomato cans, fastened with a green string around her back. Between the tomato cans hung a very small bird cage and within it a crestfallen canary. One arm was covered from wrist to shoulder with celluloid curtain rings, pilfered from a furniture display in Wanamaker's. She removed her hat, trimmed with gilded carrots, beets, and other vegetables. Her hair was close-cropped and dyed vermillion.

Decades later, someone not too swift coined the term "Body Art" for self-decoration of this sort.

Autobiography: Hjartarson, Paul I., and Douglas O. Spettigue, eds. *Baroness Elsa*. Ottawa: Oberon, 1992.

Interpretation: Biddle, George. *An American Artist's Story*. Boston: Little, Brown, 1939; Josephson, Matthew. *Life Among the Surrealists*. New York: Holt, 1962; Reiss, Robert. "'My Baroness Elsa van Freytag-Loringhoven." In *New York Dada*, ed. Rudolf E. Kuenzli. New York: Willis, Locker, & Owens, 1986.

FRYE, Northrop

(14 July 1912–23 January 1991, Herman W. F.).

A loyal Canadian, Frye spent his entire professional life in the country where he was born and mostly educated, even though he became for a time the most influential literary theorist in the English-speaking world. Perhaps because his first major book dealt with WILLIAM BLAKE, Frye had a broad conception of literary possibility; and with an extraordinary memory for literary detail, as well as a capacity to view the largest cultural terrain from the greatest critical distance, he could make generalizations appropriate to many examples. He belongs in this book less for his major theories, which remain influential, than for passing insights into avant-garde writing that remain freshly persuasive: "Literature seems to be intermediate between music and painting: its words form rhythms which approach a musical sequence of sounds at one of its boundaries, and form patterns which approach the hieroglyphic or pictorial image at the other. The attempt to get as near to these boundaries as possible forms the main body of what is called experimental writing." One virtue of these sentences is accurately placing VISUAL POETRY and TEXT-SOUND in the largest artistic context.

Writings: *Fearful Symmetry: A Study of William Blake*. Princeton: Princeton University Press, 1947; *Anatomy of Criticism*. Princeton: Princeton University Press, 1957; *Fables of Identity*, New York: Harcourt Brace, 1963; *The Well-Tempered Critic*. Bloomington: Indiana University Press, 1963; *The Stubborn Structure; Essays on Criticism & Society*. Ithaca: Cornell University Press, 1970; *The Eternal Act of Creation: Essays 1979–1990*. Bloomington: Indiana University Press, 1993.

Biography: Ayre, John. *Northrop Frye: A Critical Biography*. Toronto: General Publishing, 1988.

Website: http://www.orc.ca/~delite/fri.htm (Links site)

Interpretation: Hamilton, A. C. *Northrop Frye: Anatomy of His Criticism*. Toronto: University of Toronto Press, 1990; Kostelanetz, Richard. *Three Canadian Geniuses*. Toronto: Colombo & Co., 2000.

Bibliography: Denham, Robert D. *Northrop Frye: An Enumerative Bibliography*. Metuchen, NJ: Scarecrow, 1974.

FULLER, Buckminster

(12 July 1895–1 July 1983).

The architectural historian Wayne Andrews identified, in *Architecture, Ambition, and Americans* (1955), two indigenous architectural traditions, producing buildings as fundamentally different as their rationales. One, typified in American thought by William James (1842–1910), holds that a beautiful building will enhance the lives of all who dwell within and around it, as elegant architecture supposedly doth elegant people make. The second tradition, from Thorstein Veblen (1857–1929), holds that, because a building's usefulness as a human habitat is primary, technical efficiency and human considerations create architectural quality and perhaps a certain kind of beauty.

The most original and profound Veblenian was Fuller, who based his architecture upon the "dymaxion" principle (the maximalization of dynamic performance), which he related to industrial ephemeralization: the achievement of increasingly more production from increasingly fewer materials; the practical advantages of mass production; and the universal applicability of architectural solutions. Because Fuller came to architecture from an education in engineering and experience in the construction-materials business, his designs lack discernible stylistic antecedents.

Fuller's Dymaxion House (1927) is a circular multiroom area fifty feet in diameter, suspended by cable from a central unit, forty feet high, that can be set into the ground anywhere on earth. The living space is partitioned into several rooms, while the volume between its floor and the ground can be curtained and filled to the owner's taste—its most likely use being an indoor parking place. Above the living space is an open-air landing partially shaded from the sun by a suspended roof. A later version, built closer to the ground, was the Wichita House, a circular aluminum shell-plus-utility-core that Fuller tried to mass produce after World War II. The dymaxion principle also informed the Kleenex House, a fifteen-foot surrogate tent designed for the U.S. Marine Corps. Fuller claimed it would be "one-third the weight of a tent, cost one-fifteenth as much, use less than ten dollars' worth of materials, and be packed into a small box," in sum exemplifying his three principles.

f

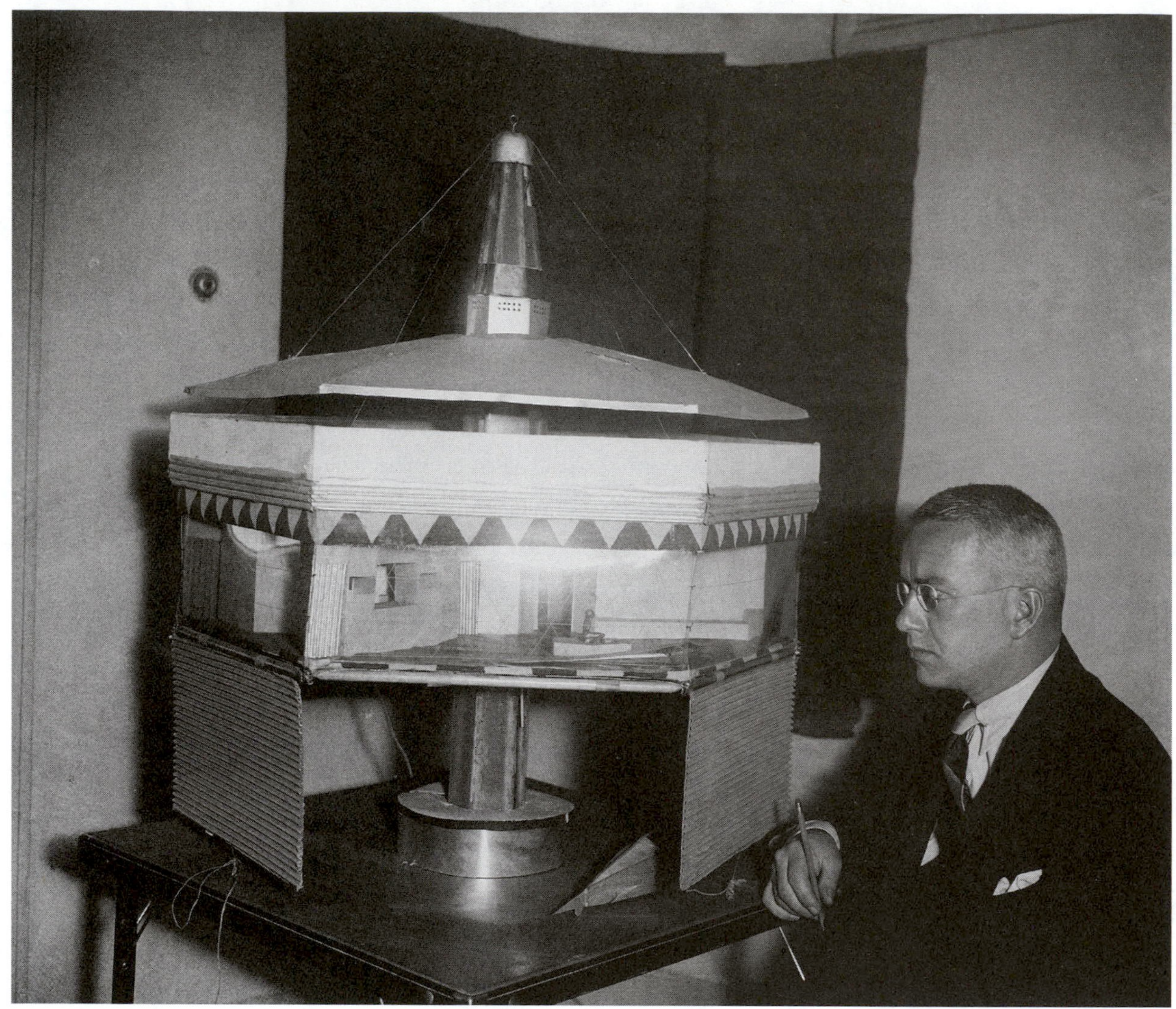

Buckminster Fuller with his Dymaxion House, 1929. CORBIS/Bettmann.

With his bias for doing more with less, Fuller suggested that distances commonly bridged by cables or girders should instead be spanned by a network of three-dimensional triangles (actually, tetrahedrons) often built up into larger networks; for Fuller's innovative truth, strangely not recognized by earlier builders, was that the triangular tetrahedron more effectively distributes weight and tension than the rectangular shapes traditionally favored. The most effective overarching form for these tetrahedrons was the geodesic dome, which could span spaces of theoretically unlimited diameters with an unprecedentedly lightweight structure, demonstrating the dymaxion principle of high performance per pound. The first full realization of this last innovation was the 93-foot rotunda for a Ford plant in Detroit (1953); the most successful is the nearly complete sphere, over 200 feet in diameter, that Fuller built for Expo '67 in Montreal. This has a grandeur that, in my experience, was implicitly Jamesian, particularly since several interior levels made its tetrahedrons visible from various angles and the lucite skin changed color in response to the outside climate. Because other structures were as large as 384 feet in diameter, enclosing two-and-a-half acres, Fuller proposed constructing domes miles in diameter over whole cities or neighborhoods. One proposal for a dome over midtown Manhattan would have weighed 80,000 tons and cost 200 million dollars.

Don't forget Fuller's writings, which are in their coinages and complex sentences as stylistically original as his thinking: "Living upon the threshold between yesterday and tomorrow, which threshold we reflexively assumed in some long ago yesterday to constitute an eternal now, we are aware of the daily-occurring, vast multiplication of experience-generated information by which we potentially may improve our understanding of our yesterday's experiences and therefrom derive our most farsighted preparedness for successive tomorrows." It is not surprising that Petr Kotik , who had previously composed an extended choral piece to a difficult Gertrude Stein text, *Many Many Women* (1978/80), did likewise with selected passages from Fuller's two-volume *Synergetics* (1976, 1979).

Architecture: *Dymaxion House*, c. 1927; *Geodesic Dome*, c. 1950.

Writings: *Nine Chains to the Moon* (1938). Carbondale: S. Illinois University Press, 1963; *Operating Manual for Spaceship Earth*. New York: E.P. Dutton, 1963; *No More Secondhand God*. Garden City, NY: Doubleday, 1963; *Ideas and Integrities*. Englewood Cliffs, NJ: Prentice-Hall, 1963; *Education Automation*. Garden City, NY: Doubleday, 1963; *Synergetics I*. New York: Macmillan, 1976; *Synergetics II*. New York: Macmillan, 1979; *Critical Path* New York: St. Martin's Press, 1981; *Synergetics Dictionary: The Mind of Buckminster Fuller*. Compiled & ed. E. J. Applewhite. New York: Garland, 1986.

Anthology: Meller, James, ed. *The Buckminster Fuller Reader*. London, England: Cape, 1970.

Documentary: Snyder, Robert. *The World of Buckminster Fuller* (1971). New York: Mystic Fire Video, 1995.

Website: http://www.lsi.usp.br/usp/rod/bucky/buckminster_fuller.html

Exhibition Catalog: *Three Structures by Buckminster Fuller in the Garden of the Museum of Modern Art*. New York: MOMA, 1960.

Interpretation: Baldwin, J. *Bucky's Works: Buckminster Fuller's Ideas for Today*. New York: John Wiley, 1997; Kenner, Hugh. *Bucky*. New York: Morrow, 1973; Marks, Robert W. *The Dymaxion World of Buckminster Fuller*. Carbondale: Southern Illinois University Press, 1960; Pawley, Martin. *Buckminster Fuller*. New York: Taplinger, 1990; Rosen, Sidney. *Wizard of the Dome—R. Buckminster Fuller, Designer of the Future*. Boston: Little, Brown, 1969.

Musical Setting: Kotik, Petr, and the S.E.M. Ensemble. An excerpt from *Explorations in the Geometry of Thinking*. Berlin, Germany: EarRational (ECD 7553), 1989.

FULLER, Loïe

(22 January 1862–2 January 1928; b. Louie F.).

An American dancer and theater artist, Fuller achieved great fame in Europe, especially in France, where she made her debut at the Folies-Bergère in 1892 and where, at the 1900 Paris World Fair, a special theater was built to house her performances. Fuller was renowned for spectacular stage effects that she accomplished through the use of colored lights, transparent cloth (such as silk), and mechanical devices (such as the use of wooden sticks to extend the lines of her arms). For her popular *Fire Dance*, she reportedly required fourteen electricians who, responding to her taps and gestures as she danced on glass, would change the light emanating from below, creating the illusion of smoke and flame. She put her performers on pedestals with glass tops so that, when illuminated from underneath, they "would appear to be mysteriously suspended in air," to quote a contemporane-

Loie Fuller. Poster for the *Folies Bergère* by Jules Cheret, 1893. CORBIS/Historical Picture Archive./© 2000 Artists Rights Society (ARS), New York/ADGAP, Paris.

ous reviewer. Her recent biographers Richard and Maria Ewing Current credit Fuller with "another invention [:] an arrangement of mirrors set at an angle to one another, with a row of incandescent bulbs along each of the joined edges, so as to reflect a 'bewildering maze of dancers, skirts, and colors.'" Fuller was so popular that Parisian couturiers sold dresses based on her costumes. Although she apparently had little dance training, improvised movement became an important element in her performances. Portraying herself as tall and lovely, the master illusionist was actually short and stumpy, her features, plain. She billed herself as "Le Loïe Fuller," adding an umlaut to an unfamiliar place, because, according to the Currents, "without those two dots above the 'ï' [her name] would be "Lwah" in French and the word 'the goose,' or 'law.'" Notwithstanding all her years and fame abroad, she retained her American citizenship. Because many leading artistic figures found Fuller's work enchanting—among them Anatole France, Auguste Rodin, and STEPHANE MALLARMÉ—and more than seventy artists in ten countries potrayed her in lithographs, pastels, and sculptures, her performances were remembered long after she ceased presenting them.The Italian arts historian Giovanni Lista has reportedly written the fullest reconstructions of her performances.

—With Katy Matheson

Works: *Serpentine Dance*, c. 1890; *Violet*, c. 1892; *La Danse du Feu*, c. 1895; *L'Homme au Sable*, c.1924; *L'Ombres Gigantesques (La Danse de la Sorciere)*, c.1924; *La Grande Voile (La Mer)*, c. 1925.

Autobiography: *Fifteen Years of A Dancer's Life*. London: Herbert Jenkins, 1913.

Exhibition Catalog: Harris, Margaret Haile. *Loïe Fuller: Magician of Light*. Richmond, VA: The Virginia Museum, 1989.

Biography: Current, Richard Nelson, and Maria Ewing Current. *Loïe Fuller: Goddess of Light*. Boston: Northweastern University Press, 1997; Lista, Giovanni. *Loïe Fuller: Danseuse de la Belle Epoque*. Paris: Stock, 1994.

FURNITURE MUSIC

See **AMBIENT MUSIC**

FURNIVAL, John

(29 May 1933).

Trained as a visual artist and for many years a professor at the Bath Academy in western England, Furnival in the early sixties developed a highly original and indubitably personal style of building up layers of words, usually chosen with taste and literacy, into architecturally representational structures, done not on small sheets of paper but on pieces of wood (doors, actually), six feet high and a few feet wide. In the words that make the shape of *La Tour Eiffel* (1964) are, for instance, the puns "eye full" and "Evefall." The word "lift" turns into "ascenseur" where the elevator is, and among other representational markings is "échafaudage" (or "scaffolding") on the other leg. If only for its scale and scope of reference, *Tours de Babel Changées en Ponts* (1964) is Furnival's great work, if not the masterpiece of its kind. In six panels, each originally a wooden door onto which Furnival drew and stamped words in ink, all together twelve feet in length and six and one-half feet high (and usually displayed in a semicircular form), this work tells of the evolution of language. A key image is a succession of word bridges (with here and there the names of the great nineteenth-century bridge builders) connecting the otherwise isolated towers. The panels can be read from left to right as well as from right to left, and from top to bottom and back again. As they contain more secrets than anyone can count, Furnival's visually arranged words must be read as closely and completely as those of any modern poet.

Work: *La Tour Eiffel*, 1964; *Tour de Babel Changées en Ponts*, 1964.

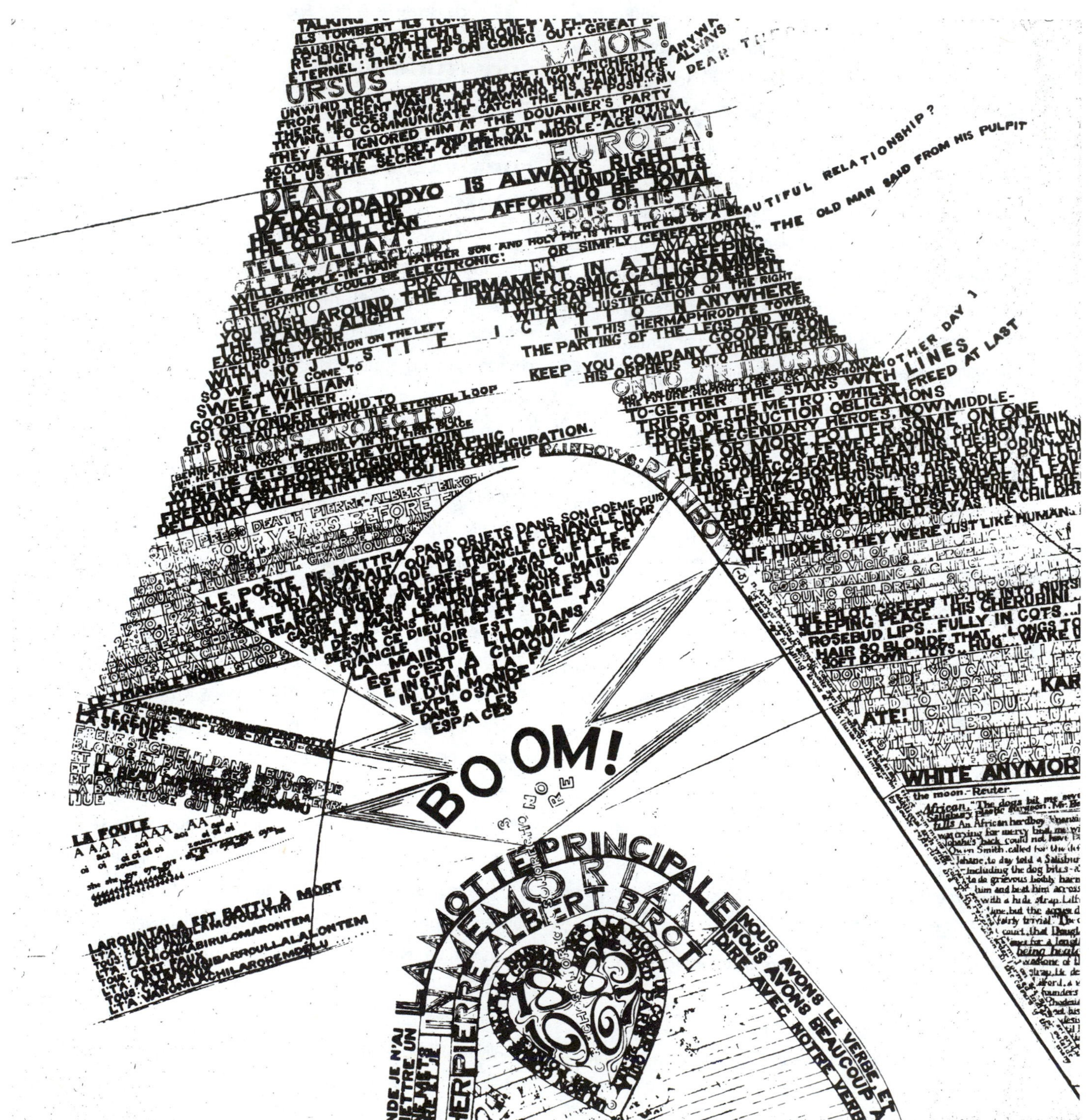

John Furnival. *Eyeful Tower*. Screen in the collection of the Arts Council of Great Britain. Courtesy the artist.

Exhibition Catalogs: *Ceolfrith 14*. Sunderland, England: Coelfrith, 1971; *Astrid & John Furnival*. Roswell, NM: Roswell Museum & Art Center, 1984.

Anthologies featuring his work: Bory, Jean-François. *Once Again*. New York: New Directions, 1968; Kostelanetz, Richard, ed. *Imaged Words or Worded Images*. New York: Outerbridge & Dienstfrey, 1970; Solt, Mary Ellen, ed. *Concrete Poetry: A World View*. Bloomington: Indiana University Press, 1970; Williams, Emmett, ed. *An Anthology of Concrete Poetry*. New York: Something Else Press, 1967.

FUTURISM (ITALIAN)

(1909).

Italian Futurism began with the poet F. T. MARINETTI publishing in, of all places, the Parisian newspaper *Le Figaro* on 20 February 1909 a manifesto that, in bombastically provocative language, proclaimed the birth of a new literary and social movement purportedly of the young. In what remains a masterpiece of manifesto writing (apart from its impact), Marinetti exalted movement and change, in addition to appealing to Italian pride. "Courage, audacity, and revolt will be essential elements of our poetry" is his second tenet. "A racing car" is portrayed as "more beautiful than the *Victory of Samothrace*." What began in literature was seen to have more currency in visual art, with the *Manifesto of the Futurist Painters* signed the following year by the painters Giacomo Balla (1871–1958), Umberto Boccioni (1882–1916), Carlo D. Carrà (1881–1966), Gino Severini (1883–1966), and LUIGI RUSSOLO.

While his associates continued to publish manifestos with titles like *Futurist Photodynamism* (1911), *Technical Manifesto of Futurist Sculpture* (1912), *Chromophony—The Colors of Sounds* (1913), *The Painting of Sounds, Noises and Smells* (1913), and *Futurist Manifesto of Men's Clothing* (1913), Marinetti's subsequent declarations focused upon literature: *Destruction of Syntax—Imagination without Strings—Words in Freedom* (1913), *The Variety Theatre* (1913), *The Futurist Synthetic Theater* (1915), and *The Futurist Cinema* (1916, with others). Apart from what one might think of individual Futurist artists and works, it is hard to dispute the opinion that no other group published so many brilliant manifestos, filled as they are with lines that remain no less radical today than seventy-five years ago.

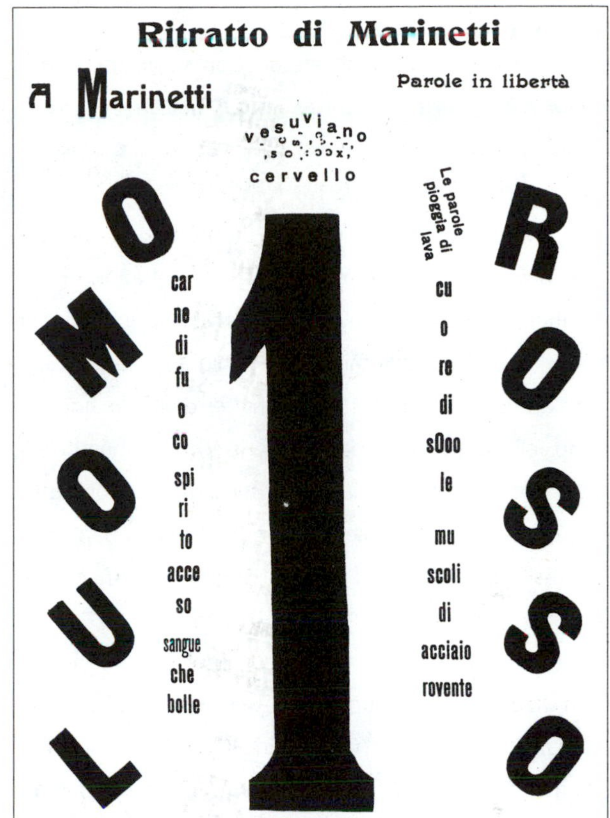

Marietta Angelini, *Ritratto di Marinetti*, 1916. Courtesy Libraire Kostelanetz/Wordship.

It was in painting, more than any other art, that Futurist ideas generated major work. Needing devices for portraying movement within two-dimensional frames, the painters turned to CUBISM for overlapping planes that, since Cubism was new at the time, contributed to Futurism's avant-garde image. However, Futurism distinguished itself from Cubism by a visual agitation that was perceived to represent heightened expression. Among the masterpieces of Futurist painting are Boccioni's *The Forces of a Street* (1911), Severini's *Nord-Sud* (1912), Carra's *Interventional Demonstration* (1914), and Boccioni's sculpture *Unique Forms in Space* (1913).

Energized by one another, these Futurist painters developed so rapidly that, by 1915, they had individual identities, united only by memories of the initial manifestos. It is commonly said that the highest phase of Italian Futurism ended in 1916 with the death of Boccioni (who fell from a horse during World War I). Nonetheless, thanks to frequent translations of those manifestos, Futurist ideas had a discernible influence, especially upon artists in Russia, but also upon those in England, Germany, and America.

In the small Italian city of Bassano del Grappa, the Galleria Dieda in 1997 mounted an exhibition titled *Da Pagina a Spazio* of creditable visual and visual-verbal works by women involved with Italian Futurism, among them Marietta Angelini (1868–1942), Emma Marpillero (1896–??), Irma Valeria (1897–1988), Rosa Rosà (1884–1978), Benedetta (1897–1977), Alzira Braga (1900–1930), and Regina (1894–1974), all of whose names were previously unknown, at least to me. Such feminist exhibitions implicitly remind us that in every modernist movement were women, often wives or lovers, whose work was unjustifiably neglected during macho times, who remain to be discovered, albeit decades later.

Books: Apollonio, Umbro, ed. *Futurist Manifestos*. Trans. Robert Brain, et al. New York: Viking, 1973; Kirby, Michael. *Futurist Performance*. New York: Dutton, 1971.

Website: www.unknown.nu/futurism (Features many of the Futurist manifestos in their full text.)

Exhibition Catalogs: Taylor, Joshua C. *Futurism*. New York: MoMA, 1961; *Futurismo 1909–1919*. Newcastle upon Tyne, England: Northern Arts, 1972; *Words-in-Freedom: Drawings by the Italian Futurists*. New York: T. J. Arts, 1985; *Da Pagina a Spazio*. Prefaced by Mirella Bentivoglio. Bassano del Grappa (Vicenza), Italy: Galleria Dieda (Via Roma 98), 1997.

Interpretation: Banham, Reyner. *Theory and Design in the First Machine Age* (1960). New York: Praeger, 1967; Bentivoglio, Mirella, and Franco Zoccoli. *The Women Artists of Italian Futurism*. New York: Midmarch Art, 1997; Blum, Cynthia Sartini. *The Other Modernism: F.T. Marinetti's Futurist Fiction of Power*. Berkeley: University of California Press, 1996; Clough, Rosa Trillo. *Looking Back at Futurism*. New York: Cocce, 1942; De Villers, Jean-Pierre A. *Le Premier Manifeste du Futurisme*. Ottawa: University de Ottawa, 1986; Martin, Marianne W. *Futurist Art and Theory, 1909–1915*. Oxford: Clarendon, 1968; Poggi, Christine. *Cubism, Futurism, and the Invention of Collage*. New Haven: Yale University Press, 1993.

FUTURISM (RUSSIAN)

(1909–1917).

The premier avant-garde movement in Russian literature, Futurism was in part a reaction to Symbolism, which nonetheless shared the latter's interest in the sound texture of the word and in the work's suggestive power beyond its denotative meaning. Russian Futurism is customarily divided into two wings. Ego-Futurism, centered in St. Petersburg, focused upon romantic hyperbolization of the poet-ego. Its chief figures were Igor Severyanin (1887–1941, who gave the movement its name in 1911), Konstantin Olimpov (1889–1940), and Ivan Ignatyev (1892–1914). The last was particularly important as a publisher of a series of Futurist miscellanies. While the Ego-Futurists' imagery could be extravagant, they were verbally less experimental than the second group, the CUBO-FUTURISTS, centered in Moscow. This group numbered among its members three of the most important and innovative poets of the twentieth century: VELIMIR KHLEBNIKOV, ALEKSEI KRUCHONYKH, and VLADIMIR MAYAKOVSKY. Vasilisk Gnedov (1890–1978), nominally associated with the Ego-Futurists, demonstrated some of the same verbal inventiveness as the Cubo-Futurists.

While both groups had been active since 1909 and were to some extent familiar with the activities of the Italian FUTURISTS, they developed independently of the Italian movement and did not share its militaristic aspirations. What finally caught the attention of the Russian public was "A Slap in the Face of Public Taste" (1912), signed by Kruchonykh, Khlebnikov, and Mayakovsky, along with David Burliuk (1882–1967), if only for this oft-quoted line: "Throw Pushkin, Dostoevsky, Tolstoy, etc. etc., overboard from the Ship of Modernity." Other statements in the manifesto argued for the poet's right to create "arbitrary and derivative words (word-novelty)" and for the "self-sufficient word." This soon led to the rise of ZAUM (translational language), the most radical development in twentieth-century poetry. Kruchonykh's "dyr but shchyl" (1913) and his opera *Victory Over the Sun* (1913) epitomize early Zaum. The Cubo-Futurists were also innovative in introducing visual effects into Russian literature, ranging from primitive manuscript books to floridly typographed works.

The year 1913 was the high point of Russian Futurism, the most important events and publications all occurring in that year, which ended with a well-publicized tour of the provinces. By 1917, a new center had formed in the Georgian capital of Tiflis with ILIA ZDANEVICH (AKA ILIAZD), Kruchonykh, and Igor Terentyev (1892–1937) as the core of a group called 41°. This group produced particularly radical examples of Zaum and innovative visual effects in their texts.

In 1921, Kruchonykh joined forces once again in Moscow with Mayakovsky, around whom the group Left Front of the Arts (LEF) formed; they published a journal of the same name. They propagandized for the role of Futurism as the truly revolutionary art most appropriate for the new socialist society. However, neither the Bolshevik government nor proletarian writers and critics were sympathetic. By the later 1920s, the movement had disappeared, its members succumbing to the demand to produce less radical and politically more acceptable writing.

Futurism is credited with having a strong impact on the development of RUSSIAN FORMALISM, CONSTRUCTIVISM, and OBERIU, an acronym for a group of writers formed in the late 1920s. Futurism's achievements are still being discovered by a new generation of Russian avant-gardists who were ignorant of the movement until recent liberalization under glasnost.

—Gerald Janecek

f

Anthology: Bowlt, John, ed. *Russian Art of the Avant-Garde: Theory and Criticism, 1902–1934* (1976). 2d ed. London: Thames & Hudson, 1988.

Intrepretation: Compton, Susan. *The World Backwards: Futurist Books 1912–16*. London: The British Library, 1978; Janecek, Gerald. *The Look of Russian Literature*. Princeton: Princeton University Press, 1984; *Zaum: The Transrational Poetry of the Russian Futurists*. San Diego: San Diego State University Press, 1996; Lawton, Anna. *Russian Futurism through Its Manifestoes 1912–1928*. Ithaca: Cornell University, 1988; Livshits, Benedikt. *The One and a Half-Eyed Archer*. Newtonville, MA: Oriental Research Partners (P.O. Box 158, Newtonville, MA 02160), 1977; Markov, Vladimir. *Russian Futurism: A History*. Berkeley: University of California Press, 1968.

FUTURIST MUSIC

FUTURISM is a modern movement in the arts that emerged in Italy early in the twentieth century, under the aegis of the Italian poet F. T. MARINETTI. Its musical credo was formulated by Balilla Pratella in his Manifesto of Futurist Musicians issued in Milan on 11 October 1910 and supplemented by a Technical Manifesto of Futurist Music of 11 March 1911. On 11 March 1913 LUIGI RUSSOLO published his own Futurist Manifesto. In these declarations the Italian Futurists proclaimed their complete disassociation from classical, romantic, and IMPRESSIONIST music and announced their aim to build an entirely new music inspired by the reality of life in the new century, with the machine as the source of inspiration. And since modern machines were most conspicuous by the noise they made, Pratella and Russolo created a new art of noises, ARTE DEI RUMORI. Russolo designed special noise instruments and subdivided them into six categories. His instruments were rudimentary and crude, with amplification obtained by megaphones, but there is no denying that the Futurists provided a prophetic vision of the electronic future of fifty years later. It is interesting to note that most Futurist musicians and poets were also painters. Their pictures, notably those of Luigi Russolo, emphasized color rather than machinelike abstractions, and generally approximated the manner of ABSTRACT EXPRESSIONISM. In the music by Pratella and others we find a profusion of modern devices of their Futurist day, with a foremost place given to the WHOLE-TONE SCALE. The Futurists gave monody preference over polyphony, and steady rhythm over asymmetry. The future of the Futurists appears passé, but they opened the gates to the experimenters of the actual chronological future, which none of them lived to witness.

—Nicolas Slonimsky

Bibliography: Russolo, Luigi. "The Art of Noise." In *Futurist Performance*, ed. Michael Kirby. New York: Dutton, 1971.

Recordings: *Futura. Poesia Sonora*. Milan: Cramps Records, 1978; *Dada for Now*. Liverpool, England: Ark, 1985; *Musica futurista*. Milan: Cramps Records/Fonitcetra, 1986; *Futurism & Dada Reviewed*. Brussels: Sub Rosa, 1988.

GABO, Naum

(5 August 1890–23 August 1978; b. Naum Neemia Pevsner). Born in Russia, Gabo studied medicine and engineering in Germany before returning to his homeland in 1920. Back in Russia, he joined his older brother Antoine Pevsner (1886–1962) in drafting a *Realistic Manifesto* (1920) that established the principles of what became European CONSTRUCTIVISM, in contrast to the Constructivism that VLADIMIR TATLIN, among others, advocated in Russia. While in Russia, Gabo made *Virtual Kinetic Volume* (1920, also known as *Kinetic Sculpture*), a vibrating strip of steel that is customarily identified as the first artwork to incorporate a motor. Objecting to the Soviet government's regimentation of artistic activities, Gabo moved west, first to Berlin, then to

Naum Gabo, *Construction*, 1938. CORBIS/Burstein Collection.

Paris and to England, until he came to the United States in 1946, becoming an American citizen in 1952. Once in America, Gabo specialized in monuments, which often remained proposals, and monumental sculptures for new buildings.

Works: *Column*, 1920–21; *Kinetic Construction*, 1919–20; *Kinetic Sculpture*, 1920; *Translucent Variation on Spheric Theme*, 1937 (New York: Guggenheim); *Spiral Theme*, 1941 (London: Tate); *Construction in Space* I, 1942–43. (London: Tate).

Writings: *Of Divers Arts* (1962). Princeton: Princeton University Press, 1971.

Exhibition Catalogs: Olson, Ruth, and Abraham Chanin. *Naum Gabo—Antoine Pevsner*. New York: Museum of Modern Art, 1948; *Naum Gabo: The Constructive Process*. London: Tate, 1976.

Biography: Pevsner, Alexei. *A Biographical Sketch of My Brothers Naum Gabo and Antoine Pevsner*. Amsterdam: Augustin & Schooman, 1964.

Interpretation: Ford, Andrew. *An Appreciation of Naum Gabo*. Biddenden, Kent, England: Florin, 1985; Read, Herbert. *Gabo*. Cambridge: Harvard University Press, 1957.

Catalog Raisonné: Nash, Steven A., ed. *Naum Gabo: Sixty Years of Constructivism*. Munich, Germany: Prestel, 1985.

GABURO, Kenneth

(5 July 1926–26 January 1993).

Gaburo was a problematic artist who was rarely written about, in part because he did many good things only fairly well. As a composer, he produced a number of pieces for both instruments and electronic media, of which the most ambitious, *Lingua I–IV* (1965–70), deals with language used in a variety of once original ways. As a performer, Gaburo founded and directed the New Music Chorale Ensemble. As a publisher, Gaburo established Lingua Press (once in San Diego, later in Iowa City), which issued scores by composers, mostly university-based, whose work reflected avant-garde activities without contributing to them. He also edited in *Allos* (1980) a spacious antholgy of writing eccentrically combining poetry and music. The British critic Nicholas Zurbrugg attributes to Gaburo a classic aphorism on the prerequisites for avant-garde creation that I've not seen anywhere else: "I frankly don't know what an audience is, and so I can't possibly imagine writing for one."

Works: *Antiphony I (Voices)* for three string groups and tape, (1958); *II (Variations on a Poem of Cavafy)* for soprano, chorus, and tape (1961); *III (Pearl-White Moments)* for chamber chorus and tape (1963); *IV (Poised)*, for piccolo, trombone, double bass, and tape (1967); *V*, for piano and tape (1968–89); *VI (Cogito)* for string quartet, slides, and 2- and 4-channel tape (1971); *VII (—And)*, for 4 video systems and 4-channel tape (1974–89); *VIII (Revolution)*, for percussionist and tape (1983–84); *X (Winded)*, for organ and tape (1985–89).

Recordings: *Music for Voices, Instruments & Electronic Sounds*. New York: Nonesuch H-71199, (c.1969); *Lingua II: Maledetto* (1967–68). New York: CRI (SD 316), 1974.

Anthology: Ed. *Allos: "Other" Language*. La Jolla, CA: Lingua, 1980.

Interpretation: Zurbrugg, Nicholas. "Multimedia Art in the Age of Mechanical Reproduction: Gaburo and Ashley." In *The Parameters of Postmodernism*. Carbondale: S. Illinois, 1993.

GALÀS, Diamanda

(29 August 1955).

Drawing upon experience of both JAZZ and opera, as well as her ease with languages other than English, Galàs has created a highly aggressive singing style that can exploit not only her wide vocal range but new technologies to create "songs" of unprecedented hysteria. The result is high-tech emotive singing in the tradition of Screamin' Jay

Hawkins and Johnny Ray on the one hand and Maria Callas on the other. Anger is the principal emotion of Galàs's performances, such as *Plague Mass* (1990), in memory of her brother, Philip-Dimitri Galàs (1954–86), a playwright who died of AIDS. Typical Diamanda Galàs titles hum with barbed wire: *Litanies of Satan* (1982) and *Wild Women with Steak Knives* (1981–83). Inspiring controversy, her performances have been banned, which is neither frequent nor easy in our time, especially in Italy.

Works: *Medea tarantula* for voice, 1977; *Song from the Blood of Those Murdered* for voice and tape, 1981; *Litanies of Satan*, 1982; *Wild Women with Steak Knives*, 1981–83.

Recordings: *Plague Mass* (1990). New York: Mute 9610432,1991; *The Singer*. New York: Mute A.D.A., 1992; *Masque of the Red Death Trilogy*. New York: Mute A.D.A, 1993; *Malediction and Prayer*. New York: Asphodel (P.O. Box 51, Chelsea Station, 10113), 1998.

Website: www.diamandagalas.com

GANCE, Abel

(25 October 1889–10 November 1981).

Initially an actor, Gance made unsuccessful short silent films before returning to the stage. Resuming his film career during World War I, he experimented with close-ups and tracking shots, which were at the time thought to be confusing techniques. By 1917, according to the film lexicographer Ephraim Katz (1932–92), "He was considered important enough as a director for his picture to appear ahead of the stars in a film's title sequence. This was to become a personal trademark of all Gance's silent films." He made the first major film about the horrors of the Great War, *J'accuse/I Accuse* (1919) with footage he shot with real soldiers in real battles, for successful release just after Armistice Day. His technique of quickly cutting from scene to scene, from horror to horror, influenced filmmakers coming of age at that time. After the commercial failure of *La Roue* (1923), which began as thirty-two reels (over five hours) before being abridged to twelve, he made his most stupendous film, *Napoleon* (1927), which remains a monumental masterpiece. Initially an epic on the scale of D. W. Griffith's *Intolerance* (1918), it is also technically innovative. The concluding sections of the film were shot by three synchronized cameras to be shown simultaneously on three screens, in a technique resembling Cinerama, which came thirty years later. When these additional images appear, toward the end of the film, they produce a gasp of awe, even now. Other parts were shot in two-camera 3-D and in color, but not used. Unfortunately, the film failed commercially. According to Katz, the three-screen format was seen in only eight European cities. The version shown at the time in America was so drastically butchered it was incomprehensible. Several years later, Gance recorded stereophonic sound effects that he wanted to add to the master print. Beginning in the 1930s, he made melodramas on familiar historical subjects (e.g., Lucrezia Borga, Beethoven, Cyrano and D'Artagnan). Only in the 1970s, thanks to the culturally responsible Hollywood director Francis Ford Coppola (1939), was the original three-screen version of *Napoleon* made available to American audiences. Though Gance lived long enough to see his innovations exploited elsewhere, he was never again encouraged to make innovative film.

Films: *J'accuse/I Accuse*, 1919; *La Roue*, 1923; *Napoleon*, 1927. Universal City, CA: MCA Home Video 80086, 1986.

Webpage: http://www.hrsk.edu.fi/ccf_hki/fr-fenetres/presentation/visite/salle-6.htm (in French).

GANGEMI, Kenneth

(23 November 1937).

An early Minimalist writer, Gangemi published a "novel" called *Olt* (1969) that was only sixty pages long. It was written not as a sequence of paragraphs but as a collection of highly resonant sentences, all about a man with minimal emotional affect. His next book, *Lydia* (1970), has even more severe fictions, some of them merely listings of elements in a narrative; some poems consist of only a single word. He has also published prose poems, a novel in the form of an unrealized film script *(The Interceptor Pilot*, 1980), and a memoir of traveling in Mexico *(Volcanoes from Puebla*, 1979). His books are typically published abroad before they appear in his native America.

Writings: *Olt*. New York: Orion Press, 1969; *Lydia*. Santa Barbara, CA: Black Sparrow, 1970; *Corroboree: A Book of Nonsense*. New York: Assembling Press, 1977; *The Volcanoes from Puebla*. London: Boyars, 1979; *The Interceptor Pilot*. London: Boyars, 1980.

Interpretation: Caramello, Charles. "On the Guideless Guidebooks of Postmodernism: Reading *The Volcanoes from Puebla* in Context," *Sun & Moon*, 9 & 10 (1980).

g

GARDNER, Martin

(21 October 1914).

A truly independent writer for most of his life, noted mostly for his books about science and pseudoscience, Gardner is also a primary scholar of truly eccentric literature, beginning with elaborately annotated and introduced editions of Lewis Carroll: *The Annotated Alice* (1960) and *The Annotated Snark* (1962), the latter dealing with a less intelligible text. Some of Gardner's appreciations of OULIPO, among other avant-garde writers mentioned here, appeared in his regular column in *The Scientific American*, illustrating the principle that literacy about advanced science might be good preparation for understanding advanced literature, and vice versa. His *The New Ambidextrous Universe* (1964) influenced, among others, VLADIMIR NABOKOV, who mentions the book on page 542 of his novel *Ada* (1969). In 1992, when JOHN ROBERT COLOMBO edited an anthology of stories less than fifty words long, he sent copies to several like-minded enthusiasts, asking in part for suggestions for a future edition. The most nominations came from Martin Gardner. Don't be surprised to find that no other book about contemporary art or literature mentions his name.

Works: *Fads and Fallacies in the Name of Science* (1952). New York: Dover, 1957; *The Annotated Alice*. New York: Potter, 1960; *The Annotated Snark* (1962). Harmondsworth, England: Penguin, 1967; *Mathmatical Carnival*. New York: Knopf, 1975.

GARRARD, Mimi

(16 March 1936).

Early in Garrard's choreographic career, this former ALWIN NIKOLAIS dancer produced a brilliantly original work, *Flux* (1968). To a score by Bülent Arel (1918–90), one of the more accomplished tape composers of the 1960s, and a foreground film made in collaboration with her husband James Seawright, several Garrard dancers move themselves and some tall panels as the quickly cut color film, composed entirely of kinetic geometric patterns (verticals, horizontals, dots, rainbows, etc.), continually rearticulates the hues of their leotards and the visual activity on the stage. The result is a theatrical field whose overwhelming intensity is typical of SERIAL MUSIC. The elements are quite precisely integrated and yet nonsynchronous, for one theme is the qualitative differences between live and filmed movement.

Works: *Flux*, 1968.

Interpretation: Kostelanetz, Richard. *On Innovative Performance(s)*. Jefferson, NC: McFarland, 1994.

GAUDÍ, Antoni

(25 June 1852–10 June 1926).

By the measure of image alone, Gaudí was the most original architect of early modern times. Influenced by Catalonian philosophers who glorified earlier Spanish arts and crafts, Gaudí developed a taste for undulating lines, ornamental details, ornate additions, colorful materials, and

Antoni Gaudi, Casa Batllo in Barcelona, c. 1984–87. CORBIS/O. Alamany & E. Vicens.

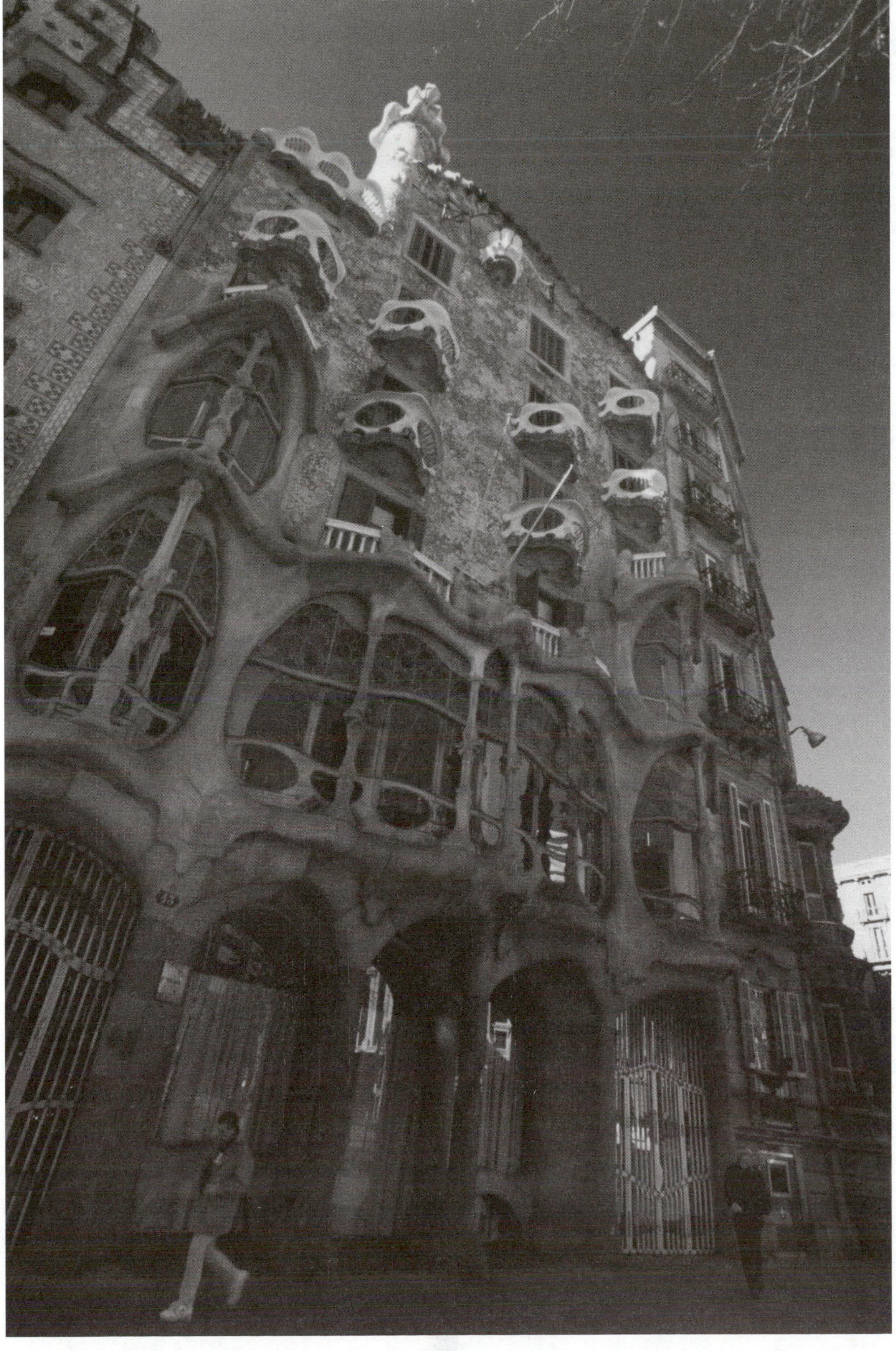

paint—all in sharp contrast to the esthetic that informed the streamlined INTERNATIONAL STYLE. For instance, Gaudí's Church of the Sagrada Familia (1883–1926, Sacred Family) has three open doorways leading to four towers intertwined at their bases, their diagonal spires rising to a height over 100 meters. At the top of each tower is an ornate echo of a flower. One Gaudí assumption, made particularly clear in his later years, was that, whereas the straight line belonged to man, the curved line was God's. Because Gaudí's style is so eccentric, it had scarce acceptance and little influence. Curiously, the later structure most resembling Gaudí is the Los Angeles *Watts Towers* of SIMON RODIA, an Italian-American handyman who may or may not have known of Gaudí's work.

Works: *Palau Güell House*, 1886–91; *Casa Mila*, Barcelona: 1906–1910; *Casa Calvet*, 1898–1904; *Casa Batlló*, 1904–1906; *Templo Expiatorio de la Segrada Familia*, 1883–1926.

Exhibition Catalogs: *The Design and Space of Gaudí*. Japan: Cultural Project Dept., Asahi Shimbun, 1990; Hurtado, Victor. *Antoni Gaudí*. Madrid: Fundación Caja de Pensiones, 1985.

Bibliography: Collins, George R. *Antonio Gaudí*. New York: Braziller, 1960.

GAUDIER-BRZESKA, Henri

(4 October 1891–5 June 1915).

A French sculptor who added his Polish wife's name to his own (as she added his to hers), Gaudier-Brzeska went to London in 1911, befriending influential British writers and artists who supported and exhibited his work. Beginning with abstracted modeling that reflected Auguste Rodin (1840–1917), he rapidly assimilated VORTICISM, contributing both essays and illustrations to Wyndham Lewis's *BLAST*. Enlisting in the French Army in 1914, Gaudier-Brzeska was killed in battle in the following year. His late sculptures are commonly credited as influencing subsequent abstraction, particularly in England. EZRA POUND memorialized him in a classic essay.

Sculptures: *Mermaid,* 1912–13; *The Wrestler*, 1913; *The Dancer*, 1913; *Young Man with Lifted Arms*, 1913; *Mother and Child*, 1913; *Sleeping Fawn*, 1913; *Dog*, 1914; *Sitzende,* 1914.

Exhibition Catalog: *Henri Gaudier-Brzeska Sculpture & Drawings*. New York: Gruenebaum, 1977.

Interpretation: Cole, Roger. *Gaudier-Brzeska: Artist and Myth*. Bristol: Sansom, 1995; Pound, Ezra. *Gaudier-Brzeska: A Memoir* (1916). New York: New Directions, 1970; Silber, Evelyn. *Gaudier-Brezeska: Life and Art. London: Thames & Hudson, 1996.*

GENDER

Along with the general acceptance of homosexuality and bisexuality (among other behaviors previously regarded as "deviant"), the avant-garde has long stretched the notion of gender. Famous female avant-garde artists have adopted male attire (GERTRUDE STEIN, for one), while others, both male and female, have created their own unisexual image (ANDY WARHOL). This has degenerated in pop culture into "gender-bender" fashions—from the "moptop" long-haired male rock stars of the 1960s to the shaved-head look of the popular female Irish singer Sinead O'Connor (1967). The visual assault of gender-bending is meant to make the viewer question his or her own sexual preconceptions while expanding social acceptance for alternative ways of interhuman relating. In the best sense, these artists transform themselves into living artistic statements, to shock, to amuse, or to befuddle the general public. In the worst sense, as in the case of commercial celebrities like Madonna (1958; b. M. Ciccone), outré sex is used as the ultimate tool to sell a bill of goods.

—Richard Carlin

In contrast to my loyal publisher, usually a smart guy, I think gender one of many current categories that really

Henri Gaudier-Brzeska. *Seated Woman*, c. 1910. CORBIS/Burstein Collection.

don't belong in this book, because its terms relate to journalism, which by definition lasts only a day, rather than to books, which are meant to last for years. My own opinion is that understandings based on gender have become the great heresy of an emerging generation, just as intelligence based on psychotropic drugs was the great heresy of my contemporaries and alcoholic unintelligence sabotaged the best minds of a previous generation, all of which provide the illusion of insight only to those who indulge.

Bibliography: Too many references are applicable to make invidious distinctions.

g

GERZ, Jochen

(4 April 1940).

Though Gerz has been a friend of mine for nearly a quarter-century, I barely understand his work and career, perhaps because we live in different cities, mostly because we have pursued drastically different directions from similar beginnings. Born in Berlin and raised in Dusseldorf, Gerz began as a VISUAL POET whose first exhibition (1968) was held in conjunction with JEAN-FRANÇOIS BORY; and, like Bory, Gerz made some striking book-art. From here he moved into one-person performances, presented nearly entirely in Europe, which depend upon a striking narrative. A recurring motif involves burying something in the earth, so that only a memory of the piece survives. Gerz has made photographs and videotapes, both distinguished more for their conceptual/documentary resonance than for their mediumistic artistry.

Works: *Caution: Art Corrupts*, Piazza della Signoria, Firenze, 1968; *The Book of Gestures*, 1969; *Piece for 1, 2, 3, 4*, 1971; *Speaking of Her*, 1972–93; *To Cry Until Exhaustion*, 1972; *Photo/Text 65*, 1976; *Le Grand Amour #1* (fiction), 1980; *The Sleeping Dog #1*, 1984; *The Poisoned Tongue*, 1985; *The U.S. Doubt*, 1989; *I Had a Dream #7*, 1992; *The Opposite*, 1994.

Books: *Footing*. Paris: Agentzia, 1968; *Replay*. Paris: Agentzia, 1969; *Resurrection*. Brescia, Italy: Amodulo, 1970; *Annonceteil*. Neuwied, Germany: Luchterhand, 1971; *Die Beschreibung des Papiers*. Darmstadt, Germany: Luchterhand, 1973; *Die Zeit der Beschreibung*. Lichtenberg, Germany: Klaus Ramm, 1974; *Blue or Real Life*. Lille, France: A. Buyse, 1990.

Exhibition Catalogs: *Jochen Gerz: Foto/Texte, The French Wall & Stücke*. Karlsruhe, Germany: Badischer Kunstverein, 1975; *Jochen Gerz: Griechische Stacke*. Ludwigshafen, Germany: Heidelberger Kunstverein, 1984; Gerz, Jochen, et al. *2146 Steine Mahnmal Gegan Rassismus Saarbrücken*. Verlag Gerd Hatje, 1993; *Jochen Gerz People Speak*. Vancouver, BC: Vancouver Art Gallery, 1994.

GIANAKOS, Cristos

(4 January 1934).

Influenced on one hand by the broad lines of the American painter FRANZ KLINE and, on another side, by the scuptures of VLADIMIR TATLIN, Gianakos has produced unadorned ramps that cut across spaces both indoors and out with a sure elegance. They typically reveal their scaffolding, whose crosshatched braces have visual charm. The *Maroussi Ramp* (1995), over one hundred feet long and made from painted steel, is perhaps the most spectacular, permanently crossing a ravine in the Emfietzoglou Art Center in Athens. Another interesting, original move in his work involves imposing geometric shapes on photographs or drawings of classic Greek architecture and sculpture. As an American of Greek descent, Gianakos has done more major work in his parents' native country than in his own. His brother Steve G. (1938) is also an artist, working mostly in two dimensions in entirely different ways.

Installations: *White Powder Piece*, Spring & Greene Sts., New York, 1970; *White Powder Piece*, Central Park, New York, 1972; *Ramp #2*, Kenne, NY, 1977; *Ramp #3*, Plattsburgh, NY, 1977; *Ramp #7*, Ward's Island, NY, 1978;

Sitesights, Brooklyn, NY, 1980; *Sculpture Now*, Malmo, Sweden, 1985; *Eclipse*, New York, 1982; *Diver*, New York, 1983; *Gemeni*, Sweden, 1985; *Styx*, New York, Long Island University, 1987; *Deja Vu V*, Crete, 1988; *Wanas Ramp*, Sweden, 1990; *Morpheus II*, New York, 1994; *Maroussi Ramp*, Athens, 1995.

Exhibition Catalog: *Cristos Gianakos*. Roslyn, NY: Nassau County Museum of Fine Art, 1979; *Cristos Gianakos: Rampworks*. Amherst, MA: University Gallery/ University of Mass. at Amherst, 1989; *Gridlock: Cristos Gianakos*. Thessaloniki, Greece, 1997.

GIBSON, Jon

(11 March 1940).

As an experienced improviser before becoming a lifelong flutist in the PHILIP GLASS Ensemble, he also performed at various times with LA MONTE YOUNG, TERRY RILEY, and STEVE REICH—the entire pantheon of pioneering MINIMAL and MODULAR composers. His own music typically mixes repeated elements with free improvisation, at times with environmental sounds, in extended linear strucutures, often in performances for his wife, the choreographer Nancy Topf (1942–98). Two of Gibson's strongest earlier pieces, *Cycles* (1973) and *Untitled* (1974), appeared on a single disc, recently reissued as *Two Solo Pieces*. He has also produced extraordinary book-art books of his abstract systemic drawings.

Other Works: *Melody IV*, Part 1 for nine players, 1975; *Call* for alto flute, 1978; *Extensions II* for saxophone and tape, 1981, 1992; *Rainforest*, 1982.

Recordings: *Two Solo Pieces* plus *Melody IV Part I* (1975), *Melody III* (1975), and *Song 1* (1972). San Germano, Italy: Robi Droli (Strada Roncaglia 16, I-15040), 1997; *In Good Company*. New York; Point Music (434 873-2), 1992; *Visitation I* (1973), *Visitations II* (1973), *Thirties (30s)* (1970). New York: New Tone, 1996.

Books: *Melody III Book II*. New York: Printed Matter (77 Wooster St., 10012), 1977.

GILBERT and GEORGE

(G. Proesch, 17 September 1943; and G. Passmore, 8 January 1942).

Meeting as sculpture students at the St. Martin's School of Art in 1967, these two men, known only by their first names, have lived and worked together ever since. Their innovation was to exhibit themselves as "living sculptures," cleanly dressed in identical grey suits, their faces and hands usually painted silver, one bespectacled and the other not. In vaudeville-like, scheduled performances that had announced beginnings, they would typically sing "Underneath the Arches," a British music-hall tune, again and again. Or they would pose on a museum's stairway for several hours straight, earning newspaper articles with titles like "Living Sculptures" or "They Keep Stiff for Hours." They issued statements: "Being living Sculpture is our life blood." In the early 1970s, Gilbert and George were ubiquitous, illustrating how rapidly and internationally a truly original idea can find acceptance in visual-arts venues. In 1970 alone, they had over a dozen solo exhibitions in venues as various as museums in Düsseldorf, Krefeld, Oxford, Copenhagen, Stuttgart, Turin, and Oslo, and private galleries in Milan, London, Berlin, Cologne, and Amsterdam. Not unlike celebrities in other areas, they exploited their fame to produce book-art, videotapes, drawings, and, especially large photographs arrayed in photogrids, most of which portrayed them in various posed circumstances, some of which portray naked young males. *Hellish* (1980), among the strongest (appearing on the cover of a 1980 exhibition catalog) has one man in profile, colored yellow, sticking his tongue out toward the other, in contrary profile, his face evenly red, with his mouth open only inches away, as though he would soon receive his colleague's tongue. The work measures 240 cm by 300 cm (or roughly 8 feet by 11 feet), in 24 separate panels. Gilbert and George's "book as a sculpture," *Dark Shadow* (1974), portrays in pho-

Gilbert and George at the Sonnabend Gallery, New York, 25 September 1971. Copyright © Fred W. McDarrah.

tographs and texts a decadent world that seems to lie behind their self-consciously neat appearance. Catalogues about Gilbert and George resemble hagiography in glorifying what would normally seem trivial. (As photographers, they were curiously far less successful than ROBERT MAPPLETHORPE at making nude bodies appear sculptural in a two-dimensional medium.)

Works: *Postal Sculptures*, 1969–75; *Magazine Sculptures*, 1969–73.

Living Sculpture Presentations: *Underneath the Arches*. London: St. Martin's School of Art (as "Our New Sculpture"), 1967; London: Cable Street, 1969; Düsseldorf, Germany: Kunsthalle, 1970; Hannover, Germany, Kunstverein, 1970; Torino, Italy: Museum of Modern Art, 1970; New York: Sonnabend Gallery, 1970; Aachen, Germany: Gegenverkehr, 1970; Oslo: Sonja Henie Niels Onstad Foundation, 1970; Stuttgart: Württembergischer Kunstverein, 1970; *Posing on Stairs*. Amsterdam, Holland: Stedelijk Museum, 1969; *The Red Sculpture*. Tokyo: Art Agency, 1975; New York: Sonnabend, 1976; London: Robert Self Gallery, 1977; Brussels: MTL Gallery; Ghent, Belgium: Museum van Hedenaagse Kunst, 1977; Amsterdam: Stedelijk Museum, 1977, etc.

Publications: *A Day in the Life of George & Gilbert*. London: Gilbert & George, 1971; *Side by Side*. Köln: König Bros., 1971; *Dark Shadow*. London: Nigel Greenwood, 1976; *Lost Day* 1972. 2d ed. Köln: Oktagon, 1996; *Oh, The Grand Old Duke of York* (1972). 2d ed. Köln: Oktagon, 1996.

Exhibition Catalogs: *Gilbert and George: The Complete Pictures 1971–1985*. Bordeaux, France: Musée d'art contemporain, 1986; *Gilbert & George, 1968–1980*. Eindhoven, Holland: Municipal Van Abbemuseum, 1980.

GILLESPIE, Abraham Lincoln

(11 June 1895–10 September 1950).

Commonly regarded as the most eccentric of the literary Americans gathered in Paris in the 1920s, Gillespie produced prose so unique it must be read to be believed; excerpts are not sufficient. He made VISUAL POETRY; he worked with neologisms in a piece/poem characteristically titled "A Purplexicon of Dissynthegrations (Tdevelop abut Earfluxsatisvie-thru-Heypersieving)," which typically tells almost everything that need be known about Gillespie in an introductory entry. It is indicative that no book of his writings appeared until thirty years after his death.

Interpretation: Milazzo, Richard, ed. *The Syntactic Revolution: Abraham Lincoln Gillespie*. New York: Out of London, 1980.

GILLETTE, Frank

(26 July 1941).

A pioneering video artist, Gillette collaborated with Ira Schneider (1938) in producing *Wipe Cycle* (1969), one of the first video installations to create the illusion of art responding to the spectator. Hidden in a bank of nine television screens (arrayed three by three) is a camera that constantly photographs in live time the area in front of the work (including, in a matter of course, the work's spectators). This image is instantly broadcast through the middle monitor. The same image is rebroadcast eight seconds later on two screens (varying between the horizontal and vertical axis) and then, after a sixteen-second delay, over the other monitors on the perpendicular axis. In the four corner monitors are two different sets of identical images from previously taped materials. To make the system more complex (and the perceptual experience more ambiguous and involving), the delayed live images switch their axes at periodic intervals, as do the corner images, and the monitors are all wiped blank one at a time in a regular cycle. The spectator feels caught in an intelligent, watchful, oblivious system whose incessant and variable observations remain compelling and mysterious even after their operation is explained. I saw *Wipe Cycle* in New York in 1969, and again twenty years later in Berlin, recreated as part of a traveling exhibition of "video sculpture" using color monitors, and it was no less compelling. After producing other acclaimed videotapes, Gillette later became the first noted video artist to give his professional renunciation of video (in his case for painting, no less) a DUCHAMPIAN significance.

Works: With Ira Schneider, *Wipe Cycle*. New York: 1969.

Writings: *TV as a Creative Medium*. New York: Howard Wise Gallery, 1969; "Masque in Real Time." In Ira Schneider & Beryl Korot, eds. *Video Art: An Anthology*. New York: Harcourt, Brace, 1976.

Exhibition Catalogs: *Frank Gillette: Video, Process and Meta-Process*. Ed. Judson Rosebush. Syracuse, NY: Everson Museum of Art, 1973; *Aransas: Axis of Observation*. Houston, TX: Point of View, 1978; *Frank Gillette*. Washington, DC: Corcoran Gallery of Art, 1980.

Website: www.limulus.org

GINS, Madeline

(7 November 1941).

It is hard to explain how Gins's first novel *Word Rain* found a commercial publisher in 1969, because its theme is the epistemological opacity of language itself. The first sign of the book's unusual concerns is its subtitle: "(or a Discursive Introduction to the Philosophical Investigations to G,R,E,T,A, G,A,R,B,O, It Says)"; a second is the incorporation of several signs of new fiction: special languages, expressive design, extrinsically imposed form—most of these devices reiterating, in one way or another, the book's theme. What distinguishes the book are numerous inventive displays of printed material: lists of unrelated words with dots between them, entire pages filled mostly with dashes, where words might otherwise be, pseudological proofs, passages in which the more mundane expressions are crossed out, an appendix of "some of the words (temporary definitions) not included," even a photographed hand holding both sides of a printed page, and a concluding page of dense print-over-print that reads at its bottom: "This page contains every word in the book." I've found Gins's later books comparably obscure, though perhaps less ambitious, even when her subject is presidential politics; but because no one else risks writing about her work, let alone reading it critically, there is no one other than yourself, dear reader, with whom you can compare my impression. It may or may not be important that she has been married for over three decades to the painter (Shusaku) ARAKAWA, with whom Gins has collaborated on an extremely opaque, large format visual/verbal book that has gone through three highly different editions, *The Mechanism of Meaning*.

The body is composed 98% of water.
This page contains every word in the book.

Madeline Gins. Last page of *Word Rain*. Courtesy the author.

Books: *Word Rain*. New York: Grossman, 1969; *What the President Will Say and Do!!!* Barrytown, NY: Station Hill (Station Hill Rd., 12507), 1984; *Helen Keller or Arakawa*. Santa Fe, NM: Burning Books (P.O.Box 2638, 87504), 1994; ——, and Arakawa. *The Mechanism of Meaning*. 3d ed. New York: Abbeville, 1989; ——, and Arakawa.

Architecture: *Sites of Reversible Destiny (Architectural Experiments after Auschwitz-Hiroshima)*. London: Academy, 1994.

Interpretation: Lakoff, George & Taylor, Mark. *Reversible Destiny: Arakawa/Gins*. New York: Abrams, 1997.

GINSBERG, Allen

(3 June 1926–5 April 1997).

The avant-garde Ginsberg is the author not of post-Whitmanian lines that survive in the head of every literate American but of certain sound poems that he published without musical notation. (Remember that he has also published, as well as sung, many conventionally configured songs.) One of them, "Fie My Fum," appears in his *Collected Poems* (1984), while most do not. An example is "Put Down Yr Cigarette Rag," whose verses conclude with variations on the refrain "dont smoke dont smoke dont smoke dont smoke": "Nine billion bucks for dope/ approved by Time & Life/ America's lost hope/ The President smokes his wife/ Dont Smoke dont smoke dont smoke dont smoke dont smoke nope/ nope nope nope." Especially when I heard Ginsberg perform this, I wished there were more poems like it.

Selected Writings: *Howl and Other Poems* (1956). San Francisco: City Lights, 1991; *Wichita Vortex Sutra*. San Francisco: Coyote, 1966; *First Blues*. New York: Full Court, 1975; *Collected Poems 1947–1980*. New York: Harper, 1984; *Allen Verbatim: Lectures on Poetry, Politics, Consciousness*. Ed. Gordon Ball. New York: McGraw-Hill, 1974.

Recordings: *Holy Soul Jelly Songs and Poems* (4 cassettes). Los Angeles: Rhino, 1994.

Biographies: Miles, Barry. *Allen Ginsberg*. New York: Simon & Schuster, 1989; Morgan, Bill, and Bob Rosenthal, eds. *Best Minds: A Tribute to Allen Ginsberg*. New York: Lospecchio, 1986.

Interpretation: Tytell, John. *Naked Angels* (1976). New York: Grove, 1991; Hyde, Lewis, ed. *On the Poetry of Allen Ginsberg*. Ann Arbor: University of Michigan Press, 1984.

Website: http://www.naropa.edu/ginsberg.html (Sponsored by Naropa Institute)

Bibliography: Kraus, Michelle P. *Allen Ginsberg: An Annotated Bibliography 1969–1977*. Metuchen, NJ: Scarecrow, 1980; Morgan, Bill. *The Works of Allen Ginsberg, 1941–1994: A Descriptive Bibliography*. Westport, CT: Greenwood, 1995.

GIORNO, John

(4 December 1936).

Giorno's principal poetic innovation extended FOUND POETRY by chopping apart a prose sentence so that its words are repeated in different linear arrangements, with different line breaks, and often duplicated in adjacent columns. As a strong performer of his own texts, Giorno turned to electronic technology for a single capability—echoing—so that variations other than those he was saying could be electronically reproduced as faint replicas of his initial voice, thereby increasing the potential for *after-sound* analogous to the afterimage of the visual arts. His contributions to later records in his own *Dial-A-Poem* anthologies have yet more complicated kinds of echoing. Because Giorno's poems generally have a distinct subject, as well as syntax, semantics, and narrative, they represent not TEXT-SOUND but inventively amplified poetry that no doubt contrasts with the general decadence of the principal current forms of literary recital. Every time I see the much-touted KAREN FINLEY, I'm reminded of how much her performance resembles in both style and content those of Giorno.

Works: *Poems by John Giorno*. New York: Mother Press, 1967; *Cancer in My Left Ball*. W. Glover, VT: Something Else Press, 1973; *You Got to Burn to Shine: New and Selected Writings*. New York: Serpents Tail, 1994.

Recordings: *John Giorno and William S. Burroughs*. New York: Giorno Poetry Systems (222 Bowery, 10012), 1975.

GLASS, Philip

(31 January 1937).

Traditionally trained, not only at Juilliard but with the legendary teacher Nadia Boulanger in Paris, Glass began as a conventional composer before creating music of distinction: a sequence of pieces that included *Strung Out* (1967), *Music in Similar Motion* (1969), *Music in Contrary Motion* (1969), and *Music in Fifths* (1969). Essentially monophonic, these compositions have lines of individual notes, with neither harmonies nor counterpoint; they are tonal without offering melodies, accessible without being seductive. What made this music seem radical in the 1960s was its avoidance of all the principal issues that preoccupied nearly all contemporary composers at that time—issues such as chance and control, serialism and atonality, improvisation and spontaneity. It is scarcely surprising that before his music was performed in concert halls it was heard in art galleries and in art museums. Though this music was frequently characterized as MINIMAL, the epithet "MODULAR" is more appropriate in that severely circumscribed bits of musical material are repeated in various ways. One minor innovation is that even in live concerts Glass's music would always be heard through amplifiers, the man at the electronic mixing board (Kurt Munkasci) becoming one of the acknowledged "musicians."

Within *Music with Changing Parts* (1970), Glass moved progressively from monophony, in its opening moments, to a greater polyphonic complexity and then, toward its end, into the kinds of modulations that would inform his next major work, *Music in Twelve Parts* (1974), an exhaustive four-hour piece that epitomizes Glass's compositional ideas at that time and remains, in my opinion, the zenith of his avant-garde art. Glass subsequently moved into operatic collaborations, beginning with *Einstein on the Beach* (1976, with ROBERT WILSON) and then *Satyagraha* (1980, based upon Mahatma Gandhi's early years), among other operas. The requirements of music theater, as he prefers to call it, made his music more accessible and more popular, as it did for AARON COPLAND before him. Glass's composing in the 1980s became more lyrical and more charming, which is to say devoid of those earlier characteristics that might make it problematic to his new, larger audience.

Selected Works: *Strung Out*, 1967; *Music in Similar Motion*, 1969; *Music in Contrary Motion*, 1969; *Music in*

Fifths, 1969; *Music with Changing Parts*, 1970; *Music in Twelve Parts*, 1974; *Another Look at Harmony, Parts One & Two*, 1975; *Einstein on the Beach*, 1976; *Satyagraha*, 1980; *A Madrigal Opera*, 1980; *Koyaanisqatsi*, a film score, 1982; *The Photographer*, 1982; *Akhnaton*, an opera 1984; *A Descent into the Maelstrom*, a theater piece, 1986; *The Making of the Representative for Planet 8*, an opera, 1986; *Powaqqatsi*, film score, 1987; *1000 Airplanes on the Roof*, an opera, 1988; *Hydrogen Jukebox*, an opera, 1990; *The Voyage*, an opera, 1992; *Low Symphony*, 1992; *Orphée*, an opera, 1993; Symphony # 2, 1994; *La Belle et la Bëte*, an opera, 1994.

g

Recordings: *Music with Changing Parts*. Glass Ensemble. New York: Atlantic/Nonesuch, 1994; *Two Pages, Contrary Motion, Music in Fifths*. New York: WEA Atlantic, 1994; *Music in Twelve Parts*. Glass Ensemble. New York: Atlantic/Nonesuch, 1996.

Books: *Music by Philip Glass*. Ed. Robert T. Jones. New York: Harper & Row, 1987.

Website: http://www.schirmer.com/composers/glass_bio.html

Interpretation: Kostelanetz, Richard, ed. *Writing on Glass*. New York: Schirmer, 1997.

GLAUGNEA

(c. 1971).

An artificial language that is both hermetic and all-encompassing, Glaugnea is an invention of the poet Michael Helsem (1958). The language grew out of Helsem's teenage experimentation with language invention. Starting with the concept that everything had one true name (the concept that drove some of the earliest inventors of artificial languages), Helsem eventually transformed his language into one where every word in any language, any character in any script, any sound in any tongue was part of Glaugnea. This bizarre fact might make it appear that Glaugnea is not a language at all, but merely a concept. However, the tongue comes complete with pronunciations, grammatical rules, with, in short, the structure that makes language a possible means of communication. Glaugnea has a complete set of pronouns—and all persons and genders of those pronouns exist in singular, plural, and (the rare) dual forms. Glaugnea has an intricate set of "answer-words" (yes, no, maybe, and combinations of these), a detailed set of suffixes denoting negation (including "no longer," and "opposite of" as well as "not"), and an almost runic alphabet, the members of which look suspiciously like Christograms. An interesting feature of the tongue is that Helsem designed it with the dictionary in mind, for his precise and often poetic definitions are part of the gestalt of the language. Take these examples from his *Giyorbicon* (which roughly translates as "A Dictionary of Hitherto-Unarticulated Nuance"): **oolongphaeic**: dusky as the taste of oolong tea; **peguc**: the joy of precision; **hooth**: a chance happening which becomes meaningful in retrospect.

—Geof Huth

Bibliography: [Helsem, Michael.] *Giyorbicon: Volquardsen Svinmol; Chabd, Haply Yallifer*. np: self-published, 1990; Helsem, Michael. *Glaugnea: On the Choice Not to Utter Sense*. Published as taboo jadoo # 4 (Winter 1991/Summer 1992).

GOBER, Robert

(12 September 1954).

The installations of Gober are the most consistently recognizable examples of the theme of abjection: the conception and rendition of the human body as the site of poisons and morbid excretions, making the body emblematic of death and marking the physical person as repulsive to society and an outcast. Gober evokes the theme by creating stiff and partial figures that he punctures with holes and frequently metal sink drains and then lays on the floor in hallucinatory environments. In an untitled 1991 installation at the Jeu de Paume in Paris, he embedded a male figure into the wall so that it was visible only from the waist down. The wall was painted with a lush forest scene, and candles were placed into holes in the trousers. Gober's damaged figures—open to the poisons of the environment and sometimes, as in the Jeu de Paume exhibition, portrayed in a self-memorializing state—are clearly images of a deeply emotional response to the AIDS crisis. Even so, from the point of view of formal innovation and expressive articulation of the human form, his figures add nothing to the artistic language of human gesture. Gober does not render the figure; he cites it as a point of reference.

—Mark Daniel Cohen

Works: *Installation*: Paula Cooper Gallery, New York City, 1989; *Installation*: Jeu de Paume, Paris, 1991; *Forest*, 1991; *Installation*: Dia Center for the Arts, New York City, 1992; *Installation*: Larry Aldrich Foundation Award Exhibition, The Aldrich Museum of Contemporary Art, Ridgefield, Connecticut, 1995–97.

Exhibition Catalogs: Indiana, Gary, and Wool, Christopher. *A Project*. New York: 303 Gallery, 1988; Marta, Karen. *Robert Gober: Dia Center for the Arts, September 24, 1992–June 20, 1993*. New York: Dia Center for the Arts, 1993; Schimmel, Paul, and Foster, Hal. *Robert Gober*. Los Angeles: Museum of Contemporary Art & Zurich: Scalo, 1997; Philbrick, Harry. *Robert Gober: The 1996 Larry Aldrich Foundation Award Exhibition: January 18–May 24, 1998.* Ridgefield, CT: Aldrich Museum of Contemporary Art, 1998; Flood, Richard, Garrels, Gary; and Temkin, Ann. *Robert Gober, Sculpture and Drawing*. Minneapolis: Walker Art Center, 1999.

GODARD, Jean-Luc

(3 December 1930).

While working toward a Certificate in Ethnology at the Sorbonne, Jean-Luc Godard regularly attended meetings and screenings at the Ciné-Club du Quartier Latin. By all accounts, the young Godard was obsessed by movies, developing a taste for American films that struggled against the Hollywood system (the cigar-munching Samuel Fuller appears in Godard's *Pierrot le Fou* [1965] as himself and defines "movies"). Godard also developed an immediate dislike and, more importantly, *distrust* of overt commercial cinema, particularly of French origins. By 1950, he met the people who would develop a cinematic revolution: André Bazin (1918–58), François Truffaut (1932–84), Claude Chabrol (1930), Eric Rohmer (1920), and Jacques Rivette (1928). Watching films and discussing them, they became critics. By 1952, Godard was writing for *Cahiers du Cinéma*. Thus began what later became known as the French New Wave.

Godard's contribution to the New Wave was always the most experimental, most confrontational, and most political of those of the directors in the movement. His New Wave films attacked the very grammar of traditional cinema. His first film was a shock to the system of movies: *À Bout de Souffle* (*Breathless*) (1960) is a "gangster" film that reshapes the language of the commercial film through technical experimentation—jump cuts, a shaky camera, a wild pace—at the same time that it questions the form.

All of Godard's films of the '60s work in this manner because a Godard film is always an *essay* on film; Godard stated in an interview for *Cahiers* that appeared at the end of 1962:

> As a critic, I thought of myself as a filmmaker. Today I still think of myself as a critic, and in a sense I am, more than ever before. Instead of writing criticism, I make a film, but the critical dimension is subsumed. I think of myself as an essayist, producing essays in novel form: only instead of writing, I film them. Were the cinema to disappear, I would accept the inevitable and turn to television; were television to disappear, I would revert to pencil and paper.

Between the years 1960–67, Godard produced a staggering fifteen films, including some of the classics of the New

Wave: *Vivre sa Vie* (1962), *Les Carabiniers* (1963), *Une Femme Mariée* (1964), and *Alphaville* (1965). Always essays on the medium, his films were also political critiques, exemplified by the examination of the war in *Le Petit Soldat* (1960), which was banned by the French government until 1963, and *La Chinoise* (1967). *Weekend* (1967) ended the first phase of Godard's career at the same time that it depicted the end of Western civilization. Denouncing cinema as "bourgeois," Godard made the art "disappear" as he turned to a new form: "revolutionary films for revolutionary people."

From 1968–73 Godard made films as a part of the Marxist filmmaking collective known as the Dziga-Vertov group. If Bertolt Brecht had been an influence on Godard's "alienation" of traditional cinema, then it was Brecht's political example that pushed Godard into making films such as *One Plus One* (*Sympathy for the Devil*) (1968) and *See You at Mao* (1969). The former work featured factory noise so excruciating that it is difficult to listen to. In defense of his soundtrack, Godard remarked: "The workers have to listen to that noise all day, every day, for weeks, months and years, and a bourgeois audience can't stand to listen to it for more than a few seconds." *One Plus One* (*Sympathy for the Devil*) was famous for featuring the Rolling Stones working on an record album; it was also an infamous film for the fight Godard waged with the film's producer over the final cut. Godard's cut had the Stones working on a set of songs without any conclusion to their efforts— the revolution is not complete. But Godard's producer wanted a complete version of "Sympathy for the Devil" in the film and he tacked it on at the end. When Godard's producer introduced the "producer's version" of the film in front of a packed audience in London, Godard reportedly leaped onto the stage and punched him in the face. Godard then called for the audience to demand their money back and donate it to the Eldridge Cleaver Fund.

The early '70s marked Godard's break with the Marxist group, although he still kept his confrontational politics. He began experiments with mixing film and video in works entitled *Numeró deux* (1975), which he said was a "remake" of *Breathless*, and *Comment ça va?* (1975). This mixture of film and video led to his first feature film in almost eight years: *Sauve qui peut* (1980). The main character of this return to film is a Godard alter ego who teaches a class on cinema; he writes on the board: "CAIN ET ABEL, CINÉMA ET VIDEO." This kind of critical awareness of the evolution of film Godard brought to the films that follow, most notably the controversial retelling of the immaculate conception in *Je vous salue, Marie* (*Hail Mary*) (1984), and the story of a God in a man's body that is *Hélas pour moi* (1993).

Godard's latest project is a video work begun in 1989 called *Histoire(s) du cinéma.* A history of film, Godard's ongoing video, whose latest segments were completed in 1997, combines images from painting, film, and sculpture to form a collage of ideas and impressions. It is an unfinished essay on watching film by someone who destroyed movies before breathing avant-garde life back into them.

—John Rocco

Films: *À bout de souffle (Breathless)*, 1960; *Le Petit soldat* (*The Little Soldier*), 1960; *Une Femme est une femme* (*A Woman Is a Woman*), 1961; *Vivre sa vie* (*My Life to Live*), 1962; *Les Carabiniers* (*The Riflemen*), 1963; *Le Mépris* (*Contempt*), 1963; *Bande à part* (*Band of Outsiders*), 1964; *Une Femme mariée* (*A Married Woman*), 1964; *Alphaville*, 1965; *Pierrot le fou*, 1965; *Masculin/Féminin*, 1966; *Made in the U.S.A.* 1966; *2 ou 3 Choses que je sais d'elle (2 or 3 Things I Know About Her)*, 1966; *La Chinoise*, 1967; *Weekend*, 1967; *Ciné-Tracts*, 16mm. 1968; *One Plus One (Sympathy for the Devil)*, 1968; with Dziga-Vertov Group, *Un Film comme les autres (A Film Like the Others)*, 16mm. 1968; with Dziga-Vertov Group, *See You at Mao (British Sounds)*, 16mm, 1969; with Dziga-Vertov Group, *Pravda*, 16mm, 1969;

with Dziga-Vertov Group, *Vladimir et Rosa*, 16mm, 1971; *Tout va bien*, 1972; *Letter to Jane: Investigation of a Still*, 16mm, 1972; *Numéro deux*, 35mm, video, 1975; *Sauve qui peut (Every Man for Himself)*, 1980; *Passion*, 1982; *Prénom: Carmen*, 1983; *Je vous salue, Marie (Hail Mary)*, 1985; *Détective*, 1985; *King Lear*, 1987; *On s'est tous défilé*, Video, 1988; *Le Rapport Darty*, Video, 1989; *Nouvelle vague*, 1990; *Allemagne année 90 neuf zéro (Germany Year 90 Nine Zero)*, 1991; *Hélas pour moi (Oh Woe Is Me)*, 1993; *JLG/JLG*, 1994; *2 X 50 ans de cinéma français (2 X 50 Years of French Cinema)*, Video, 1995; *For Ever Mozart*, 1997; *Histoire(s) du cinema*, Video, 1989–97.

Interviews & Writings: *Godard on Godard*. Ed. Tom Milne. New York: Da Capo, 1972; Sterritt, David, ed. *Jean-Luc Godard: Interviews*. Jackson: University of Mississippi Press, 1998.

Criticism: Brown, Royal S., ed. *Focus on Godard*. Englewood Cliffs, NJ: Prentice-Hall, 1972; Cameron, Ian, ed. *The Films of Jean-Luc Godard*. New York: Praeger, 1969; Hiller, Jim, ed. *Cahiers du Cinéma: The 1960s: New Wave, New Cinema, Reevaluating Hollywood*. Cambridge: Harvard University Press, 1986; Lellis, George. *Bertolt Brecht, Cahiers du Cinéma, and Contemporary Film Theory*. Ann Arbor: UMI Research, 1982; MacBean, James Roy. "Godard and the Dziga Vertov Group: Film and Dialectics." *Film Quarterly* 26, 1 (Fall 1972); White, Armond. "Double Helix: Jean-Luc Godard." *Film Comment* 32, 2 (March/April 1996).

Website: http://contempt.net/godard-new.html

GOFF, BRUCE

(8 June 1900–4 August 1982).

Influenced by FRANK LLOYD WRIGHT, Goff built numerous houses in the Middle and far West that blend structure into the environment. His masterpiece, the Bavinger House (1950) in Norman, Oklahoma, has a ninety-six-foot wall that follows a logarithmic spiral into the living space and ultimately around a steel pole, from which the entire roof, interior stairway, and living areas are suspended. Plants inside the structure duplicate those outside, so that the environment seemingly flows into the home, or vice versa. "They wanted a large open space, and liked the idea of living on different levels," Goff told an interviewer. "They wanted many interior plants, and preferred natural rather than synthetic materials." In *Bizarre Architecture* (1979), the critic Charles Jencks locates Goff in a "Pantheon," particularly praising the Joe Price House (1956) in Bartlesville, Oklahoma, where windows are hidden behind a facade of "triangular and hexagonal shapes [that] explode into copper roofs, a sun-screen of white stars, green-blue crystal and strange yellow spikes."

Works: *Bavinger House*, Oklahoma: 1950–55; *Bartman House*, Kentucky: 1941–42; *Ledbetter House*, Oklahoma: 1947–48; *Joe Price House*, 1956 (interior additions, 1976); *Gryder House*, Mississippi, 1959–60; *Duncan House*, Illinois, 1965–67.

Interpretation: Birkerts, Gunnar. *Process and Expression in Architectural Form*. Norman: University of Oklahoma Press, 1994; Jencks, Charles. *Bizarre Architecture*. New York: Rizzoli, 1979; Saliga, Pauline. *The Architecture of Bruce Goff 1904–1982*. Chicago: Art Institute of Chicago, 1997.

Interviews: Welch, Phillip. ed. *Goff on Goff: Conversations and Lectures*. Norman: University of Oklahoma Press, 1996; Heyer, Paul. "Bruce Goff." In *Architects on Architecture*. New York: Walker, 1966.

GOFFMAN, Erving

(11 June 1923–19 November 1982).

In his first major book, *The Presentation of the Self in Everyday Life* (1959), this remarkable sociologist suggested that social life is a kind of theater and thus that human beings are always performing for audiences, playing different roles, or projecting different selves, in various situations. Doing his field work in exotic situations, including a hotel in the Shetland Islands and a gamblng casino, Goffman generated a wealth of original and largely persuasive sociological perceptions. Some of his ideas were relevant to art, particularly to performance art, particularly to Allan Kaprow, who wrote the following appreciation:

> In this book and subsequent ones, he describes greetings, relations between office workers and bosses, front-of-the-store and back-of-the store behavior, civilities and discourtesies in private and public, the maintenance of small social units on streets and in crowded gatherings, and so forth as if each situation had a prescribed scenario. Human beings participate in these scenarios, spontaneously or after elaborate preparations, like actors without stage or audience, watching and cuing one another.

If all life were theater, then mundane activities could be considered theatrical. "Intentionally performing everyday life is bound to create curious kinds of awareness." This last thought became the foundation of Kaprow's own explorations after 1970.

Books: Goffman, Erving. *The Presentation of the Self in Everyday Life*. Garden City, NY: Doubleday, 1959; Kaprow, Allan. *The Blurring of Art and Life*. Ed. Jeff Kelley. Berkeley: University of California Press, 1993.

Anthology: *The Goffman Reader*. Eds. Charles Lement and Ann Branaman. Cambridge, MA: Blackwell, 1997.

GOLDBERG, Rube

(4 July 1883–7 December 1970; b. Reuben Lucius G.). Do not dismiss Goldberg as a mere cartoonist, because his pictures tell within single frames complicated stories, filled with unobvious moves sometimes defying reality, mostly about the ironic relation between effort and result. By no measure are they "cartoons" whose point can be understood instantly, which is to say that, for all their resemblance to popular art, they approach more serious work by requiring time merely to go back and forth between the verbal and the visual. It is not for nothing that his influence can be observed in the kinetic sculpture of GEORGE RHOADS and the poetic art of DAVID MORICE, among others.

Works: *Rube Goldberg vs. the Machine Age*. New York: Hastings House, 1968; *Rube Goldberg: Inventions and Comics*. New York: Truman Gallery, 1977; *The Best of Rube Goldberg*. Compiled by Charles Keller. Englewood Cliffs, NJ; Prentice–Hall, 1979; *Rube Goldberg: A Retrospective*. New York: Putnam, 1983.

Website: http://www.rube-goldberg.com/

WEIGHT OF CIGARETTE BUTT LOWERS ASH-STAND AND CAUSES POINT (A) TO RISE AND PUNCTURE BALLOON (B)-POLICEMAN (C), HEARING REPORT LIKE GUN, OPENS WINDOW (D), WHICH PULLS STRING (E) AND TURNS ON GAS STOVE (F) AND STARTS ONIONS AND GARLIC COOKING - PARROT (G) IS SOON GASSED AND FALLS TO PLATFORM (H), CAUSING TIN CAN (I) TO FLY UP IN AIR PAST GOAT(J) AND OUT OF HIS REACH- THIS CAUSES GOAT KEEN DISAPPOINTMENT AND HE CRIES BITTERLY- TEARS (K) FALL ON CIGARETTE BUTT AND EXTINGUISH IT COMPLETELY.
A
B
C
D
E
F
G
H
I
J
K

Rube Goldberg. Untitled drawing. Courtesy Libraire Kostelanetz/Wordship.

GOLDSWORTHY, Andy

(1956).

Like DAVID NASH, Goldsworthy has helped to reorient recent British sculpture to natural materials and forms. What distinguishes Goldsworthy's works in the late 1980s and 1990s is his expansion of the range of craft and his mixing of natural materials and natural forms that do not belong together. Working with elements of nature such as twigs, stones, leaves, even snow, Goldsworthy makes intimate observations of natural processes, which he then duplicates as he fashions objects that his chosen materials never generated on their own, such as a bee's nest woven together from leaves. Goldsworthy works in the wild rather than the studio, creating his works while wandering about, in a manner similar to that of RICHARD LONG. However, he has a heavier touch than Long, and a tendency to impose artificial appearances on the terrain, covering stones with autumn leaves of garish colors, or cutting concentric circles into slabs of frozen snow. Such practices seem an imposition on—rather than a response to—the land, and a direct contradiction of the initial impulses of EARTH ART. In the end, Goldsworthy can be credited with expanding the range of techniques available to sculptors and with giving new emphasis to working by hand.

—Mark Daniel Cohen

Works: *Sycamore Leaves Stitched Together with Stalks Hung from a Tree*, 1986; *Clearly Broken Pebbles Scratched White*, 1987; *Slate Hole*, 1988; *Beech Leaves*, 1992; *Oak Tree Snowball*, 1994.

Exhibition Catalogs: Friedman, Terry. *Hand To Earth: Andy Goldsworthy Sculpture, 1976–1990*. Leeds, England: Henry Moore Centre for the Study of Sculpture, 1990; *Sand Leaves: September 16–November 4, 1991*. Chicago: The Arts Club, 1991; *Mid-Winter Muster: Sculptures at Mount Victor Station: Andy Goldsworthy, 23rd May–4th July, 1993*. Harwood, England: Harwood Academic Publishers, 1993; *Black Stones, Red Pools*. London & New York: Pro Arte Foundation, in association with Michael Hue-Williams Fine Art and Galerie Lelong, 1995; *Alaska Works*. Anchorage: Anchorage Museum of History and Art, Alaska Design Forum, 1996.

GOLYSCHEFF, Jef

(20 September 1897–25 September 1970; b. Jefim G.).

A scarcely remembered POLYARTIST, Golyscheff was a Russian who happened to be in Berlin at the beginnings of DADA and understood its implications for music. An early Berlin Dada exhibition included a performance of his *Anti-Symphony* (1919), subtitled "Musical Circular Guillotine," which included movements emblazoned "Provocational Injections," "Chaotic Oral Cavity, or Submarine Aircraft," and "Clapping in Hyper F-sharp Major." For another Dada concert later that year, Golyscheff offered *Keuchmaneuver* (Cough Maneuver). Five years before, while still a teenager, he composed a string trio containing "Zwölftondauer-Komplexen," as he called them—passages in which the twelve tones of the chromatic scale have different durations; this work is considered protoSERIAL. Golyscheff also worked as a chemist and, in 1956, moved to Brazil, where he devoted himself exclusively to paintings. It is appalling how many histories of Dada neglect music in general and Golyscheff's work in particular.

Works: *Anti-Symphony*, 1919; *Keuchmaneuver*, 1919.

Interpretation: Slonimsky, Nicolas. *Music Since 1900*. 5th ed. New York: Schirmer Books, 1993.

GOMEZ DE LA SERNA, Ramón

(3 July 1888–12 January 1963).

A Spanish writer whose specialty was a fictional aphorism (as distinct from a philosophical one) that he called *gregueria*, Gomez de la Serna was probably the most original author of his generation in Spain (whose contemporaries included José Ortega y Gasset and Miguel de Unamuno). Though he published essays, short stories, plays, novels, biographies, memoirs, and even chronicles of the gatherings at his favorite literary café in Madrid, Gomez de la Serna is best remembered for his thousands of *gregueria*, which he claimed to have invented around 1910: "The little girl wants to dance because she wants to fly"; "Moon and sand are mad for each other"; "Tigers of somnambulists and they cross rivers of sleep over bridges of leaps"; "We should take more time to forget; thus we would have a longer life." (No one would ever confuse these with philosophical aphorisms.) Miguel Gonzalez-Gerth writes, "He opposed esthetic hierarchies, advocating instead that the artist should have complete freedom and start with everything at zero level." Though Gomez thought of *gregueria* as a combination of "metaphor + humor," Spanish-English dictionaries translate his key word as "irritating noise, gibberish, or hubbub," which is less nonsense than a kind of inspired ridiculousness.

Works: *Some Greguerias*. Trans. Helen Granville-Barkes. New York: W. E. Rudge's Sons, 1944; *Greguerias, selección 1910–1960*. Madrid: Espasa-Calpe, 1972; *Aphorisms*. Trans. Miguel Gonzalez-Gerth. Pittsburgh, PA: Latin American Literary Review, 1989; *Greguerias: The Wit and Wisdom of Ramon Gomez de la Serna*. Ed. & trans. Philip Ward. Cambridge, NY: Oleander, 1982; *Paris/Ramon Gomez de la Serna*. Ed. Nigel Dennis. Valencia: Pre-Textos, 1986.

GOMRINGER, Eugen

(20 January 1925).

A Swiss-German born in Bolivia, Gomringer pioneered the idea of CONCRETE POETRY, publishing early examples and writing the most visible early manifesto. His key idea was the "constellation," or words in standard typography connected by qualities apart from syntax, freely distributed within the space of the printed page. Given his polyglot background, Gomringer was able to write his poems in Spanish, French, English, and German. For instance, down a single page are widely spaced three words: "berg land see," or "mountain," "land" (i.e., territory, ground), "sea," preceding by several years comparable MINIMAL poems by CLARK COOLIDGE, among others. The English poems reprinted in Gomringer's 1969 retrospective include "butterfly," nine lines divided into three stanzas, which would be striking in any American poetry magazine even today:

mist
mountain
butterfly

mountain
butterfly
missed

butterfly
meets
mountain.

Perhaps because the initial American anthologies of Concrete Poetry were not as good as they should have been, Gomringer failed to have as much influence here as he deserved.

Books: *Die Konstellationen=Les Constellations=The Constellations*. Frauenfeld, Switzerland: E. Gomringer, 1962; *Book of Hours and Constellations*. New York: Something Else, 1968; *Worte Sind Schatten: Die Konstellationen, 1951–68*. Hamburg, Germany: Rowohlt, 1969; *konstellationen ideogramme stundenbuch*. Stuttgart, Germany: Reclam, 1977; *das stundenbuch/the book of hours/le libre d'heures/el libro de las horas/timbak*. Stamberg, Germany: Josef Keller Verlag, 1980; Ed. *Koncrete Poesie*. Stuttgart, Germany: Reclam, 1972.

GONZÁLEZ, Julio

(21 September 1876–27 March 1942).

Born into a family of Barcelona metal artisans, González learned techniques that, after a decade of painting, he put to esthetic use in sculpture, beginning with masks. He first forged sculpture in iron in 1927, and, the following year, though already in his early fifties, he decided to devote himself exclusively to sculpture whose innovations depend upon the use of welding. González was a close friend of his countryman PABLO PICASSO, to whom he introduced the possibility of metal sculpture, and González's works initially reflected the influence of CUBISM. Later assimilating the radical example of ALEXANDER CALDER, the Spaniard made open works defined less by solidity than by an assembling of rods and ribbons of metal. All subsequent welded sculpture, including DAVID SMITH'S, implicitly acknowledges González's influence.

Works: *Polished Iron Head*, 1930; *Harlequin*, 1930; *Woman Combing Her Hair*, 1934 (Stockholm: Modern Museum); *Maternity*, 1934 (London: Tate); *Standing Figure*, 1935; *Cactus Man I*, 1939; *Cactus Man II*, 1939.

Exhibition Catalogs: Ritchie, Andrew Carnduff. *Sculpture of Julio González*. New York: MoMA, 1956; *JG*. London: Tate, 1970; Rowell, Margit. *JG: A Retrospective*. New York: Guggenheim, 1983; *JG: Sculptures & Drawings* London: The South Bank Centre–Whitechapel, 1990.

GOREY, Edward

(22 February 1925).

Gorey is the master of visual fiction, which is to say images, generally composed of pictures mixed with words, whose sequences suggest narrative. Superficially similar to comic books in their use of panels, Gorey's stories are

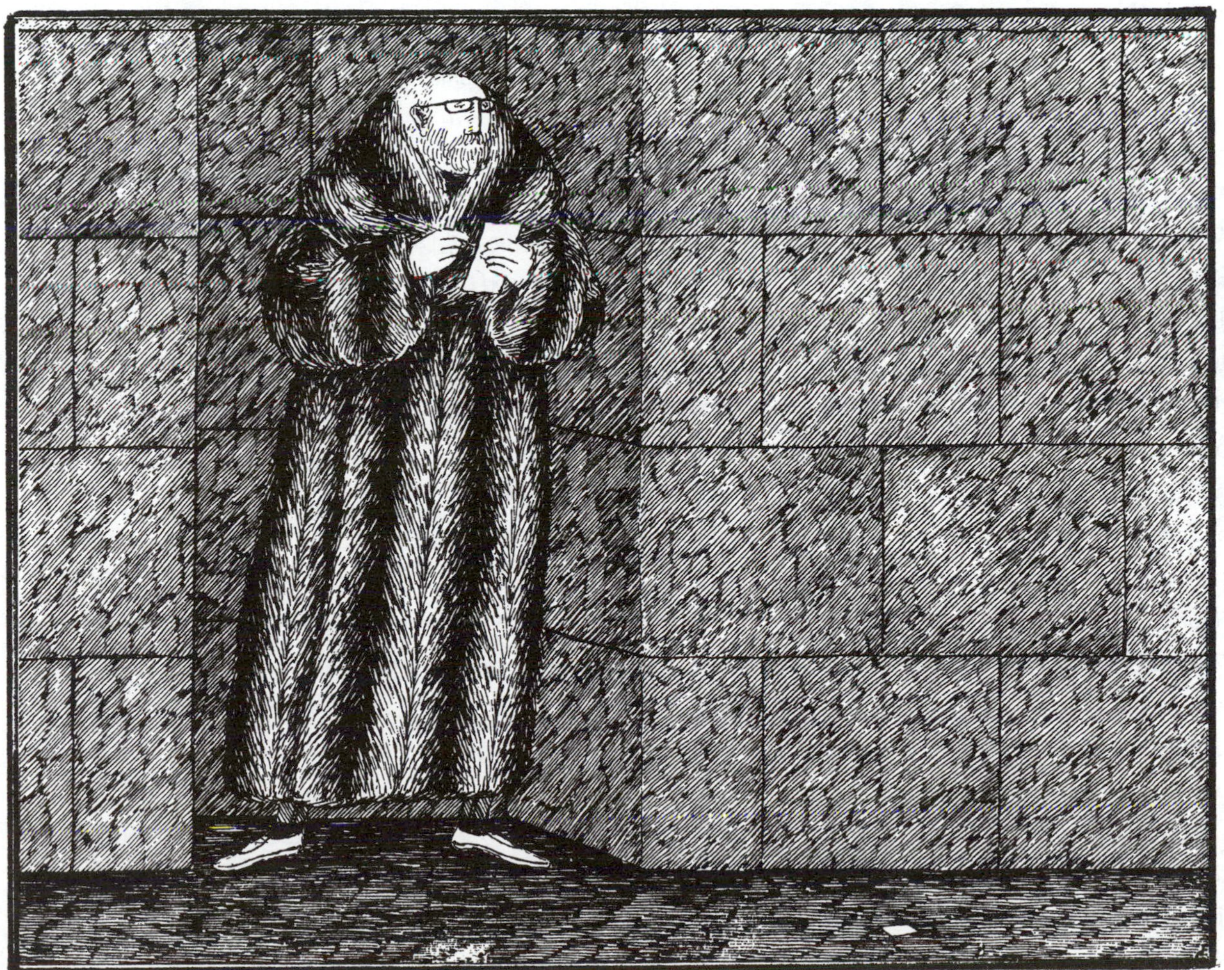

Edward Gorey. *Self-Portrait*. Courtesy Andreas Brown, Gotham Bookmart.

more profound in theme and more serious in subject, with an adult use of language and more detailed pictures. In an extreme Gorey work, like "The West Wing," the images appear without words; for "The Wuggly Ump," he added color. Gorey has also produced literary ballets or scenarios for dance. His works are superficially similar as well to FRANS MASEREEL'S, but he is a far superior craftsman with a superior narrative imagination. Though Gorey's works are well known, thanks to their publication in prominent magazines, they are not acknowledged in histories or encyclopedias of American fiction.

g

Books: *Amphigorey: Fifteen Books* (1973). New York: Perigee, 1980; *Amphigorey Too* [twenty books] (1975). New York: Perigee, 1977; *Amphigorey Also* (1983). New York: Harcourt Brace, 1993.

Biography: Ross, Clifford, and Karen Wilkin. *The World of Edward Gorey*. New York: Abrams, 1996.

Website: http://www.goreyography.com/west/west.htm

GORMLEY, Antony

(1950).

The British artist Gormley and ROBERT GOBER have been the two principal young sculptors to focus on figurative work through the 1980s and 1990s, a period in which sculptors have largely moved away from representation of the human form and experimented with found materials arranged in large installations. Whereas Gober builds tableaux that frequently, but not always, include the figure, Gormley works almost exclusively with the human form. By casting in lead, he creates life-sized figures that are usually stiffly upright, almost mummified, and softly defined. The grey, characterless images wear a grid work of highly visible horizontal and vertical white seams where the parts have been assembled, and Gormley distributes them in odd positions around the exhibition space. They lie flat on their backs, float horizontally with feet against the wall, hang with their heads embedded in the ceiling. On occasion, they roll up in a ball, lie spreadeagled with arms and legs thrown out, or sit on their haunches. And sometimes Gormley turns to other images: airplanes, fish, enormous spheres. But these works stand apart from his principal thrust. Gormley has observed that he is interested in "materializing perhaps for the first time, the space within the body. . . . To realize embodiment, without really worrying too much about mimesis, about representation in a traditional way." His purpose is to instigate a sense of the body's inner cavity as the focus of a meditative state. The evident seams on his figures give them the appearance of being hollow, vessels containing something within. Their lack of animation makes them seem less like living beings and more like shells of life, and their frequent hovering suggests an otherworldliness.

—Mark Daniel Cohen

Works: *Home*, 1984; *Edge*, 1985; *Still Running*, 1986; *Learning to Think*, 1991; *Learning to See*, 1993.

Exhibition Catalogs: Cooke, Lynne. *Antony Gormley*. New York: Salvatore Ala, 1984; *AG, Five Works*. London: Serpentine Gallery, 1987; Independent Art Space. *AG: Body and Light and Other Drawings, 1990–1996*. London: J. Jopling, 1996.

Interpretation: Hutchinson, John, and Gombrich, E. H. *Antony Gormley*. London: Phaidon Press, 1995.

GORMAN, LeRoy

(7 August 1949).

The editor of a newsletter of the organization *Haiku Canada*, and contributor to a wide variety of conventional haiku publications, Gorman shares the quietly haiku-centric background of many of the best avant-garde poets active today. "fencepo st air to s now," "ctric ning ash," and "sp air g" are three randomly chosen specimens of his work in fissional infraverbal poetry. In another of his infraverbal haiku he breaks "c," "r" and "o" upward out of the word, "carrion," and adds to them a high-flying, visually potent "w." He's been quietly ingenious with mathematics in his poetry, as well—as in "the day," which works wonders on the theme of night as an "un" and the sun as a form of "up" in the two simultaneous equations, "un + s = up," and "up - s = un."

— Bob Grumman

Writings: *Beautiful Chance*. London, Ont.: South Western Ontario Poetry (396 Berkshire Drive, N6J 3S1), 1984; *where sky meets sky*. Toronto: Nietzsche's Brolly (745 Markham Street, M6G 2M4), 1987; *glass bell*. Pointe Claire, Que.: King's Road (148 King's Road, H9R 4H4), 1991; *Heavyn*. Port Charlotte, FL: The Runaway Spoon Press (Box 3621, 33949), 1992.

GOULD, Glenn

(25 September 1932–4 October 1982).

While Gould's piano performances represented a departure from standard classical interpretation, especially in his recordings of J. S. Bach, they gained immediate acceptability not available to his creative works, which were audiotape compositions of speech and sound done mostly for the Canadian Broadcasting Corporation. The first three portray isolation in Canada: *The Idea of North* (1967) focuses on individuals who live near the Arctic Circle; *The Latecomers* (1969) depicts Newfoundland; and *Quiet in the Land* (1973) portrays religious fundamentalists. A second trilogy deals with the musicians Arnold Schoenberg, Leopold Stokowski, and Richard Strauss (1864–1949), again incorporating interviews into an audio montage that gives the illusion of a live symposium with ingeniously appropriate musical backgrounds. While discs of his piano playing continue to appear, Gould's avant-garde compositions remain less available, nearly two decades after his death. Gould also collaborated with the French musician Bruno Mon-

Glenn Gould playing the piano, c. 1960. CORBIS/Bettmann.

saingeon in producing what remains, in my judgment, the most exquisite and unaffected film/video ever of a musical performance, *The Goldberg Variations* (1981).

Compositions: *The Idea of North*, 1967; *The Latecomers*, 1969; *Quiet in the Land*, 1973.

Writings: *The Glenn Gould Reader*. Ed. Tim Page. New York: Summit, 1985.

Biography: Friedrich, Otto. *Glenn Gould: A Life and Variations*. New York: Random House, 1989; Ostwald, Peter. *Glenn Gould: The Ecstacy and the Tragedy*. New York: Norton, 1997.

Website: http://www.gould.nlc-bnc.ca/egould.htm

Interpretation: Kazdin, Andrew. *Glenn Gould at Work: Creative Lying*. New York: Dutton, 1989; Kostelanetz, Richard. "Glenn Gould." In *On Innovative Music(ian)s*. New York: Limelight, 1989; McGreevy, John, ed. *Glenn Gould: By Himself and His Friends*. Garden City, NY: Doubleday, 1983; Payzant, Geoffrey. *Glenn Gould: Music and Mind*. Toronto: Van Nostrand Reinhold, 1978; Girard, François and Don McKellar. *Thirty-Two Short Films about Glenn Gould: The Screenplay*. Toronto: Coach House, 1995.

GRAHAM, Dan

(31 March 1942; b. Daniel Henry G.).

Though I have known Graham most of my adult life and followed his activities as often as I could, my sense of his achievement remains incomplete. As a critical writer, Graham published some of the most insightful essays about sixties avant-garde sculpture; as the director in the mid-sixties of a New York gallery bearing his name in part (John Daniels), he also exhibited advanced work. As a creator of original language structures, he published highly unprecedented conceptual poems that were anthologized in my *Possibilities of Poetry* (1970) (and others that I have critically discussed). The art historian Thomas Crow, in his book on the 1960s, credits Graham with exhibiting his art in a magazine's pages "as conveniently as an art gallery," which is a curious distinction. His best performances are remembered long after their premieres. According to RoseLee Goldberg:

> Dan Graham explored Bertolt Brecht's principles of alienation, connecting performer and viewer by designing situations that had discomfort built into the work. In *Performance, Audience, Mirror* (1977), the audience, seated on chairs in front of a large mirror, were forced to become witness to their own movements and to read each other's self-conscious body language. To increase their unease, Graham walked back and forth in front of them, scrutinizing their actions and commenting into a microphone on what he saw.

Graham was early into video, with pieces in which he taped himself taking a picture of himself. *Video–Architecture–Television* (1979) documents his individual moves without becoming as generally edifying as his best writing about others. One difference between the world of visual art and that of literature is that the former is far more receptive to genuine eccentrics such as Graham.

Works: *Selected Works 1965–1972*. New York: Privately published, 1972; *Textes*. Brussels: Galerie 17 et Daled, 1974.

Books: *Video–Architecture–Television*. Halifax, Canada and New York: Nova Scotia College of Art and Design & New York University Press, 1979; *Rock Is My Religion*. Ed. Brian Wallis. Cambridge: MIT Press, 1983; with Marie-Paul Macdonald. *Wild in the Streets/The Sixties*. Ghent, Belgium: Imschoot, 1993.

Exhibition Catalogs: *Dan Graham: Pavilions*. Ed. Jean-Hubert Martin. Bern: Kunsthalle, 1983; *DG Public/Private* Phildelphia, PA: Goldie Paley, 1993.

Interpretation: Antin, David. "Dan Graham," *Studio International* (July 1970); Charre, Alain. *Dan Graham*. Paris: Editions Dis Voir, 1995; Goldberg, RoseLee. *Performance: Live Art since 1960*. New York: Abrams, 1998.

Documentary: *Video/Architecture/Performance*. Dir. Michael Shamberg. Vienna: EA-Generali Foundation, 1995.

GRAHAM, John

(9 January 1881–1961; b. Ivan Dombrowsky).

Active among New York artists from the time of his arrival in the United States in 1920, Graham became influential not just because he was older but because of his direct experience of avant-garde developments in both his native Russia and elsewhere in Europe. According to the anonymous author of the *Oxford Dictionary of Twentieth-Century Art*, "He discussed the automatism of the Surrealists before this was generally understood in America, and he anticipated the doctrines of minimalism. In his *System and Dialectics of Art* (Paris, 1937), he elaborated his doctrines of the occult, his mysticism, and his aesthetics of contemporary art. He is chiefly remembered today for the great influence he had on the evolution of modernism in the U.S.A." Graham's paintings were mostly CUBIST in style.

Writings: *System and Dialectics of Art* (1937). Ed. Marcia Allentuck. Baltimore: Johns Hopkins University Press, 1971.

Exhibition Catalog: *John Graham: Artist and Avatar*. Washington, DC: Phillips College, 1987.

GRAHAM, Martha

(11 May 1894–1 April 1991).

Initially noted for her dynamic performing presence, this American modern-dance pioneer also developed a unique technique for movement. Trained with the Denishawn company, she broke from its style, which was indebted to ballet and François Delsarte (1811–71), to explore deep motions of the torso, especially "contraction and release." A barefoot modern to the end (despite an occasional sandal), she nonetheless increasingly encouraged performing virtuosity in her dancers.

In her long, sustained career as a choreographer, Graham created over 200 works, including such early ABSTRACT and EXPRESSIONIST pieces as *Lamentation* (1930), in which, enshrouded in fabric and poised on a bench, she enacted grief distilled through her movements and gestures. She explored American forms and themes in *Primitive Mysteries* (1931), inspired by Native American ritual, and in *Letter to the World* (1950), which was based on Emily Dickinson's poetry and life. Graham developed narrative dances exploring Jungian theory and Greek mythology in works such as *Cave of the Heart* (1946) and the evening-length *Clytemnestra* (1958). She explored alternative narrative devices such as flashback in *Seraphic Dialogue* (1955). Although the predominant feeling of her work was dark and serious, notable exceptions include the joyous *Diversion of Angels* (1948) and her last work, the surprising *Maple Leaf Rag* (1990) to music by Scott Joplin, which poked fun at her own stylistic conventions. She also collaborated with many notable artists, including ISAMU NOGUCHI in set design. Due to her significance, longevity, and relative accessibility, more has been written about her than anyone else in American modern dance.

—Katy Matheson

Selected Works: *Lamentation*, 1930; *Primitive Mysteries*, 1931; *Cave of the Heart*, 1946; *Diversion of Angels*, 1948; *Letter to the World*, 1950; *Seraphic Dialogue*, 1955; *Clytemnestra*, 1958; *Maple Leaf Rag*, 1990.

Writings: *Blood Memos*. New York: Doubleday, 1991; *The Notebooks of Martha Graham*. Ed. Nancy Wilson Ross. New York: Harcourt Brace, 1973.

Biographies: McDonagh, Don. *Martha Graham: A Biography*. New York: Praeger, 1973; De Mille, Agnes. *Martha*. New York: Random House, 1991.

Interpretation: Armitage, Merle, ed. *Martha Graham* (1937). New York: Da Capo, 1978; Horosko, Marian. *Martha Graham: The Evolution of Her Dance Theory and Training, 1926–1991*. Pennington, NJ: A Cappella, 1991.

g

GRAND UNION

(1970–1976).

This collaborative improvisational dance group grew out of the JUDSON DANCE THEATER of the early 1960s and YVONNE RAINER'S *Continuous Project Altered Daily* (1970). Though membership varied, with nine people participating at various times, the core group included Rainer, TRISHA BROWN, David Gordon (1936), Douglas Dunn (1942), STEVE PAXTON, and Barbara Lloyd (1938; b. B. Dilley), most of whom would sustain independent choreographic careers. Always unpredictable, a typical Grand Union performance would have a casual tone. The performers were usually dressed in street or rehearsal clothes (although they might play with costumes or props). They talked, chatting with one another, reciting, giving one another visible cues. As performances were not planned in advance, the playful, process-oriented evening was supposedly as fun for the participants as for the audience.

—Katy Matheson

Bibiliography: Banes, Sally. "The Grand Union." In *Terpsichore in Sneakers (1980)*. Middletown: Wesleyan University Press, 1987; Ramsey, Margaret Hupp. *The Grand Union*. New York: Peter Lang, 1991.

GRAPHIC NOTATION

(1920s).

Ever since 1000 A.D., when Guido d'Arezzo drew a line to mark the arbitrary height of pitch, musical notation has been geometric in its symbolism. The horizontal coordinate of the music staff still represents the temporal succession of melodic notes, and the vertical axis indicates the simultaneous use of two or more notes in a chord. Duration values have, through the centuries of evolution, been indicated by the color and shape of notes and stems to which they were attached. The composers of the avant-garde eager to reestablish the mathematical correlation between the coordinates of the musical axes have written scores in which the duration was indicated by proportional distance between the notes. Undoubtedly such geometrical precision contributes to the audio-visual clarity of notation, but it is impractical in actual usage. A passage in whole-notes or half-notes followed by a section in rapid rhythms would be more difficult to read than the imprecise notation inherited from the past. In orchestral scores, there is an increasing tendency to cut off the inactive instrumental parts in the middle of the page rather than to strew such vacuums with a rash of rests. A graphic system of tablature notation was launched in Holland under the name Klavarskribo, an Esperanto word meaning keyboard writing. It has been adopted in many schools in Holland.

New sounds demanded new notational symbols. HENRY COWELL, who invented tone-clusters, notated them by drawing thick vertical lines attached to a stem. Similar notation was used for similar effects by the Russian composer Vladimir Rebikov. In his book *New Musical Resources*, Cowell tackled the problem of non-binary rhythmic division and outlined a plausible system that would satisfy this need by using square, triangular, and rhomboid shapes of notes. Alois Haba of Czechoslovakia, a pioneer in microtonal music, devised special notation for quarter-tones, third-tones, and sixth-tones.

As long as the elements of pitch, duration, intervallic extension, and polyphonic simultaneity remain in force, the musical staff can accommodate these elements more or less adequately. Then noises were introduced by the Italian Futurists into their works. In his compositions, the Futurist LUIGI RUSSOLO drew a network of curves, thick lines, and zigzags to represent each particular noise. But still the measure and the proportional lengths of duration retained their validity. The situation changed dramatically with the introduction of ALEATORY processes and the notion of indeterminacy of musical elements. The visual appearance of aleatory scores assumes the aspect of ideograms. JOHN CAGE, in particular, remodeled the old musical notation so

Martha Graham, *Salem Shore*. CORBIS/Hulton-Deutsch Collection.

as to give improvisatory latitude to the performer. The score of his *Variations I* suggests the track of cosmic rays in a cloud chamber. His *Cartridge Music* looks like an exploding supernova, and his *Fontana Mix* is a projection of irregular curves upon a strip of graph paper. The Polish avant-garde composer KRZYSZTOF PENDERECKI uses various graphic symbols to designate such effects as the highest possible sound on a given instrument, free improvisation within a certain limited range of chromatic notes, or icositetraphonic tone-clusters.

g

In music for mixed media, notation ceases to function per se, giving way to pictorial representation of the actions or psychological factors involved. Indeed, the modern Greek composer Jani Christo introduces the Greek letter psi to indicate the psychology of the musical action, with geometric ideograms and masks symbolizing changing mental states ranging from complete passivity to panic. The score of *Passion According to Marquis de Sade* by Sylvano Bussotti looks like a surrealistic painting with musical notes strewn across its path. The British avant-garde composer CORNELIUS CARDEW draws black and white circles, triangles, and rectangles to indicate musical action. IANNIS XENAKIS prefers to use numbers and letters, indicating the specific tape recordings to be used in his musical structures. Some composers abandon the problem of notation entirely, recording their inspirations on tape.

The attractiveness of a visual pattern is a decisive factor. The American avant-garde composer EARLE BROWN draws linear abstractions of singular geometric excellence. KARLHEINZ STOCKHAUSEN often supplements his analytical charts by elucidatory (or tantalizingly obscurative) annotations. The chess grandmaster Tarrasch said of a problematical chess move: "If it is ugly, it is bad." *Mutatis mutandis*, the same criterion applies to a composer's musical graph.

—Nicolas Slonimsky

Bibliography: Cage, John, ed. *Notations*. New York: Something Else, 1969; Johnson, Roger, ed. *Scores: An Anthology of New Music*. New York: Schirmer, 1981; Cowell, Henry. *New Musical Resources*, (1930). New York: Something Else, 1969.

GRAYSON, Richard

(4 June 1951).

In the late 1970s, Grayson was the most prolific and interesting young fiction writer in America, working with several good ideas and publishing in a variety of magazines, much as JOYCE CAROL OATES did at the beginning of her career. Though some of Grayson's fictions were more experimental than others, two qualities distinguishing his work were weighty sentences and the appearance of names similar to those of real people, including himself. Intentionally confusing fiction with reality, he acted out the fiction of running for president, issuing press releases that were picked up by newspapers, even though he was underage. I use the past tense in talking about Grayson here, not because he has passed, but because he published less and less through the 1980s until he took a law degree. Essays and perhaps books will no doubt be written accounting for the premature disappearance of such a prodigal talent from contemporary literature.

Books: *With Hitler in New York and Other Stories*. New York: Taplinger, 1979; *Lincoln's Doctor's Dog and Other Stories*. Havre de Grace, MD: Thunder Bass, 1982; *I Brake for Delmore Schwartz*. Somerville, MA: Zepher, 1983; *Narcissism and Me*. n.p.: Male & Mule, 1990; *I Survivied Caracas Traffic: Stories from the Me Decades*. Greensboro, NC: Avison, 1996.

GREENBERG, Clement

(16 January 1909–7 May 1994).

By common consent, Greenberg was the great American art critic of the middle twentieth century, the one whose essays on the ABSTRACT EXPRESSIONIST painting of the postwar decade seem as smart today as they did then (as does his 1939 classic on "Avant-Garde and Kitsch"). Whereas his colleague and competitor HAROLD ROSENBERG emphasized the act of freely applying paint to canvas and surrogate revolution for failed Marxism, Greenberg focused on "all-over" imagery extending evenly to the edges of the painting. Though he presented himself as a rational, dispassionate observer, some of his particular judgments seem, especially in retrospect, highly subjective. In subsequent decades, he advocated painterly painting, not necessarily abstract, especially against those who preferred painting that incorporated performance, philosophy, or something else. Though Greenberg stopped publishing in the mid-1970s, he remained influential, not only as an occasional lecturer but as the touchstone that his successors are continually citing, either inflating or rejecting.

Writings: "Avant-Garde and Kitsch," *Partisan Review* VI/5 (1939); *Art and Culture*. Boston: Beacon, 1961; *The Collected Essays and Criticism*. 4 vols. Ed. J. O'Brien. Chicago: University of Chicago Press, 1986–93.

Biography: Rubenfield, Florence. *Clement Greenberg: A Life*. New York: Scribner's, 1998.

Interpretation of Interpretation: Kuspit, Donald B. *Clement Greenberg: Art Critic*. Madison: University of Wisconsin Press, 1979; Orlon, Fred, and Griselda Pollock. *Avant-Gardes and Partisans Reviewed*. Manchester: Manchester University Press, 1996.

GREENFIELD, Amy

(8 July 1940).

Elementary actions like spinning, falling, and rising to one's feet are laden with meaning in Greenfield's cinema. Greenfield believes such physical movements can evoke primal experiences recalled by individuals and cultural memories held by generations. Her *Element* (1973) is a glistening meditation on a solitary female figure struggling through a sea of total mud, but also a metaphor for perseverance and survival. Coming to film from modern dance, Greenfield understands the latent meanings of simple gestures. Though her cinema draws energy from dance, it does not resemble theater. In *Element*, mud spatters onto the camera lens, reminding us of its presence. In *Dervish* (1974), a real-time spinning ritual-dance that was videotaped with two cameras, images of the whirling figure dissolve into each other, building a picture that is unique to video. Greenfield consistently tailors the subjects of her films, videotapes, or HOLOGRAMS to the special characteristics of each medium. In her 1979 *Videotape for a Woman and a Man*, a couple whirls at the end of the work, freezing into immobility and then rushing back to life in shared moments that are electronic and ecstatic. Greenfield's short film *Tides* (1980) and her feature-length *Antigone* (1989) continue the concerns of her earlier works: ordeal; human movement registered and magnified by an active camera; and a fluid treatment of narrative that retroactively upsets our sense of space and time. Quite remarkably, in a 1968 essay for *Filmmakers' Newsletter*, Greenfield outlined an artistic agenda very similar to what she would actually do, from *Encounter* (1969), which echoes STAN BRAKHAGE, to all of her other films.

—Robert Haller

Works: *Antigone (1989)*. New York: Mystic Fire Video, 1990; *Videotape for a Woman and a Man* (1979). New York: Filmmakers' Cooperative (175 Lexington Ave. 10016), 1990.

GRIFFITH, D. W.

(22 January 1875–23 July 1948; b. David Llewelyn Wark G.).

Initially the most prolific director of early silent films, Griffith belongs here less for his general achievement than for a single film, *Intolerance* (1916), which in crucial respects utterly transcended everything made before it. Among the film's innovations was its structure of telling four separate but interwoven stories ("The Modern Story," "The Judean Story," "The French Story," and "The Babylonian Story") that were linked by the common theme announced in its title and explained in an opening statement. The technical departure of interweaving four stories (more than a decade before WILLIAM FAULKNER'S structurally similar *The Sound and the Fury*, 1929) gives the film a fugal form, a grand scope, and a historical resonance previously unknown and subsequently rare.

As Seymour Stern pointed out, Griffith worked without a script, even editing from memory, meaning there was nothing for his bosses to approve prior to his making the film. The spectacle is a reflection, in Stern's luminous phrases, of "a creative titan's hand, moving puppet-forces, but moving them in a resplendent esthetic of coordinated masses, counterpointed rhythms, orchestrated tempos, parallel movements, structured multiple movement-forces, configurations both static and dynamic, visual confluences of timeless space, imagistic symphonies of people, objects, and light: the filmic architecture of history and tragedy beyond emotion and beyond criticism." The surviving print has subtitles, contrary to Griffith's original intention of making a purely visual film with the integrity of a

D. W. Griffith. Scene from *Intolerance*. Courtesy Kino International Corporation.

Beethoven string quartet. Griffith also varied the size and shape of the screen, forecasting images of alternative projection, including circular screens and the ratios of CINEMASCOPE. Perhaps because of the commercial failure of *Intolerance*, he subsequently made only more modest films. Much of his energies were then devoted to finding better ways for serious directors to fund their films, first by cofounding the collaborative United Artists Corporation (with Charlie Chaplin, Mary Pickford, and Douglas Fairbanks), later by legally incorporating himself, all without sufficient success to permit him to control his subsequent filmmaking. He died alone and forgotten in a Hollywood hotel room.

Selected Works: *The Birth of the Nation*, 1915; *Intolerance*, 1916.

Biographies: Henderson, R. M. *D. W. Griffith: The Years at Biograph* (1970). New York: Noonday, 1971; *D. W. Griffith: His Life and Work*. New York: Farrar, Strauss, 1972; Schickel, Richard. *D. W. Griffith: An American Life* (1984). New York: Limelight, 1996; Williams, Martin. *Griffith: First Artist of the Movies*. New York: Oxford University Press, 1980.

Video Anthology: *Corner in Wheat & Selected Biograph Shorts Vol.1*. Kino Video, 1993.

Exhibition Catalog: Barry, Iris. *D. W. Griffith: American Film Master* (1940). New York: MoMA, 1965.

Web Site: http://www.uno.edu/~drcom/Griffith/ (links and film clips).

Interpretation: Stern, Seymour. "D.W. Griffith's *Intolerance*" (1974). In *The Essential Cinema*, ed. P. Adams Sitney. New York: Anthology Film Archives and New York University Press, 1975.

GRÖGEROVÁ, Bohumila

(7 August 1921), and **Josef HIRSAL** (24 July 1920).

They edited the anthology *experimentální poezie* (1967), which (even though it was published in Czechoslovakia) ranks among the best anthologies of CONCRETE POETRY. It included the strongest works not only from their contemporaries, such as EUGEN GOMRINGER, JEAN-FRANÇOIS BORY, and JOHN FURNIVAL, but from earlier writers, including MICHEL SEUPHOR, RAOUL HAUSMANN, and PIERRE-ALBERT BIROT, only some of which they translated into Czech. Their book even has a good visual poem by Vaclav Havel (1938), who a quarter-century later was elected leader of their country. Grögerovà has also produced poetic objects and drawings, in addition to experimental prose, radio plays, and cycles of diaries in the form of literary montages. Hirsal has published several books of poetry. Not unlike other prominent writers in minority languages, they have both translated from the major Western tongues.

Anthology: and Josef Hirsal, eds. *experimentální poezie*. Prague, Czechoslovakia: Odeon, 1967.

GROSS, Milt

(4 March 1895–28 November 1953).

Gross was a cartoonist, famous in his time, with sufficient literary ambition to write a book-length narrative that had, as its title page boasted, "not a word in it—no music, too." In a series of finely drawn pictures various in size (and thus structurally different from a standard cartoon strip), *He Done Her Wrong* (reprinted as *Hearts of Gold*) tells of a frontier trapper going into the woods to earn enough money to marry his girlfriend who, while he is gone, succumbs to a city slicker who cons the woman into believing the trapper has died. (JOHN BARTH once quoted the Latin poet Horace saying that if an experimental writer wants to use an unfamiliar form, he or she would be wise to choose a familiar plot, which is what Gross did.) As representational images devoid of words, this Gross novel is very much the precursor of, among other books, several marvelous, strictly visual narratives of Martin Vaughn James (1943), whose books *Elephant* (1970) and *The Projector* (1971) were published in Canada in the early seventies; more recently, Vaughn-James's special fictions

FOREWORD: THEY LAUGHED WHEN I SAT DOWN TO DRAW A NOVEL, BUT THEY DIDN'T LAUGH WHEN I FIN — — OOPS! THAT DIDN'T SOUND SO GOOD. WELL ANYWAY, ONCE UPON A TIME — —

ROOMS

Milt Gross, Image from *He Done Her Wrong*, 1930. Courtesy Libraire Kostelanetz/Wordship.

(which need not be translated) have appeared in the French literary periodical *Minuit*.

Works: *Nize Baby*. New York: Doran, 1926; *Hiawatta, Witt No Odder Poems*. New York: Doran, 1926; *Dunt Esk!!* New York: Doran, 1927; *He Done Her Wrong: The Great American Novel*. Garden City, NY: Doubleday Doran, 1930 (reprinted as *Hearts of Gold*. New York: Abbeville, 1983).

Website: www.bpib.com/gross.htm

GROTOWSKI, Jerzy

(11 August 1933–14 January 1999).

From modest professional beginnings directing a theatrical company in the small Polish city of Opole and then another in Wroclav (formerly Breslau), Grotowski quickly became known for radical stagings. He put the audience for Calderon de la Barca's *The Constant Prince* on a four-sided shelf behind a high wooden fence, so that spectators had to stand and peer like voyeurs over the barrier. His production of Stanislaw Wyspianski's (1869–1907) *Akropolis* (1904) has the performers build structures through the audience. For his 1969 New York production of several plays, Grotowski limited attendance to 100 people and the performance to an hour. He also cut and transposed texts, resetting their action. He was so influential that, when he returned to America the following year, he gave lectures titled "Misconceptions in the United States about the Grotowski Method." He wrote provocatively: "The actors can play among the spectators, directly contacting the audience and giving it a passive role in the drama." The theme of Grotowski's book *Towards a Poor Theater* (1970) was that theater could exist without lights, music, or scenery. All it needed was one performer and one spectator. Grotowski also developed an innovative program for training actors for extraordinary, almost superhuman (e.g. trancelike) performances and inhuman sounds. Much of the influence of the pedagogy depended at the time upon the extraordinary actor Richard Cieslak. Sometime in the seventies, Grotowski became, no joke, a Southern California academic, before resettling in Pontedera, Italy, where he died. He was also one of the few individuals featured in this book to get a MacArthur "genius" grant, perhaps because avant-garde stars are more acceptable to American funders if they are foreign-born.

Writings: *Towards a Poor Theatre*. New York: Simon & Schuster, 1970.

Bibliography: Richards Thomas, with Jerzy Grotowski. *At Work with Grotowski on Physical Actions*. New York: Routledge, 1995; Schechner, Richard and Wolford, Lisa, eds. *The Grotowski Source Book*. New York: Routledge,

1997; Burzynski, Tadeusz and Osinski, Zbigniew. *Grotowski's Laboratory.* Warsaw: Interpress, 1979; Wohlford, Lisa. *Grotowski's Objective Drama Research.* Jackson, MI: University Press of Mississippi, 1996.

GRUMMAN, Bob

(2 February 1941).

With his regular contributions to the periodical *Small-Press Review* and his book *Of Manywhere-at-Once* (1990), Grumman has become a major critic of avant-garde American poetry. His strengths are, first, relating new developments to the high modernist tradition and, then, elaborate, penetrating close readings of texts that would strike most readers as initially impenetrable. For instance, looking at George Swede's "graveyarduskilldeer," Grumman notices, "Here three words are spelled together not only to produce the richly resonant 'double-haiku,' graveyard/dusk/killdeer//graveyard/us/killdeer, but strikingly to suggest the enclosure (like letters by a word) of two or more people (a couple—or, perhaps *all* of us) by an evening—or some greater darkening." Very keen on distinctions, Grumman coins useful discriminatory categories where previous commentators saw only chaos: "infraverbal" and "alphaconceptual" are two examples. He has also published many books of poetry, some of them featuring poems that mix words and numbers, which, with typical readiness to classify, he calls "alphanumeric." Not only does his micropress Runaway Spoon rank among the most active publishers of the best experimental writing but his press's catalog demonstrates how witty the conventions of a book list can be.

Diana
32 ft./sec.^{2} MOON
ACCB
June

Bob Grumman. "Mathemaku for Ron Johnson." Courtesy the author.

Works: *Poems* (1966). Port Charlotte, FL: Runaway Spoon (P.O. Box 3621, 33946–3621), 1990; *An April Poem*. Port Charlotte, FL: Runaway Spoon, 1989; *Spring Poem No. 3,719,242*. Port Charlotte, FL: Runaway Spoon, 1990; *Mathemaku 1–5*. Charleston, IL: Tel-Let, 1992; *Of Poem*. Schenectady, NY: dbqp (875 Central Parkway, 12309), 1995; *Of Manywhere-at-Once* (1990). Port Charlotte, FL: Runaway Spoon, 1998.

GUERRILLA ART ACTION GROUP

(1969–80; aka GAAG).

In the late 1960s they were classic political artists, led by Jon Hendricks (1939), later a curator of private collections, and Jean Toche (1932), a Belgian then living in America. Their specialty was a provocative event in an artistic space, accompanied by press releases, manifestoes, and a photographer. On 15 October 1969, Touche and Hendricks lay down in the doorway of the Metropolitan Museum for an hour, protesting the Museum's refusal to take a stand against the Vietnam war. The following month, 18 November 1969, they surprised spectators at the Museum of Modern Art by ripping at one another's clothes and taking out concealed bags of animal blood that they then poured over one another in the museum lobby. On 18 October 1971 came this manifesto:

> An artist is like a plumber. It is a question of trade and tools. The plumber fixes the toilet of the rich, the artist beautifies it. But a plumber can also be subversive and clog up the drain. What will the artist do now?

On 6 December 1980, GAAG sponsored at a SoHo art space *Blow the Lid off the FBI: Public Service-Information Action*, inviting participants:

Come and Apply for Your Own FBI File. Approved forms, notary public, free lawyers on hand to help you fill in the form. We provide the stamps.

This artful political protest was PERFORMANCE ART in an art context. GAAG's retrospective book documents dozens of provocations that, decades later, still seem radical and imaginative. I assume that in the ways of art-out-of-art the GUERRILLA GIRLS chose a moniker that honors this predecessor.

g

Books: GAAG. *The Guerilla Art Action Group 1969–1976: A Selection*. Photographs by Jan van Ray. New York: Printed Matter (77 Wooster St., 10012), 1978.

GUERRILLA GIRLS

(1985).

The speciality of this scrupulously anonymous collective is the provocative poster, customarily realized with considerable irony and wit. Such posters appear wherever they can be placed, beginning with the walls of New York's SoHo but including other venues, such as pages of magazines. The posters customarily have a large-type headline over a series of short assertions. My favorite is headlined "Relax Senator Helms, the Art World *Is* Your Kind of Place" (1989). Among the assertions, each preceded by a bullet, in ironic reference to advertising styles, are: "Museums are separate but equal. No female black painter or sculptor has been in a Whitney Biennial since 1973. Instead, they can show at the Studio Museum in Harlem or the Women's Museum in Washington"; "The majority of exposed penises in major museums belong to the Baby Jesus." These statements are not only true, but stylishly presented; and when you're appealing to people receptive to art, that last quality helps.

Books: *Confessions of The Guerrilla Girls*. New York: Harper Perennial, 1995; *The Guerrilla Girls' Bedside Companion to the History of Western Art*. New York: Penguin, 1998.

Website: http://www.proactivist.com/links_peo/Guerrilla_Girls/

GUERILLA THEATER

See **THE SAN FRANCISCO MIME TROUPE**.

GUGGENHEIM, Peggy

(26 August 1898–23 December 1979; b. Marguerite G.).

In spite of her personal extravagances and absurdities, she ranks among the great patrons of avant-garde painting. In addition to purchasing works by emerging artists, she also gave them stipends and even for a while sponsored a gallery that showed their work. The historical measure of her success as a patron was that many of those early receiving her beneficence later earned greater recognition. Indeed, good wagering is finally the truest measure for patronage, whether by private individuals, public institutions like universities, or state cultural agencies, most of whom have a record of unsuccessful judgment at the service of good intentions. In Alvin Toffler's classic warning, "Patrons who were stupid enough or uncultivated enough to support the mediocrities of their period fade into richly deserved obscurity. Only those who guessed right are remembered. The history of patronage is thus biased and selective." As a family, the De Menils, mostly of Houston, TX, rank among the best. Few recent individuals have equaled David Bermant (1919), a shopping-center developer who has single-handedly supported technological art at a time when galleries displaying it were few. One theme of the museum established in Peggy Guggenheim's villa in Venice is that she was among those who "guessed right." Her cousin, Solomon R. Guggenheim (1861–1949), likewise a good guesser, established the Guggenheim Museum in New York.

Autobiography: *Out of This Century* (1946). New York: Universe, 1979; *Confessions of an Art Addict*. New York: Macmillan, 1960.

Exhibition Catalog: *The David Bermant Collection: Color, Light, Motion*. Hartford, CT: Wadsworth Athenæum, 1984.

Interpretation: Toffler, Alvin. *The Culture Consumers*. New York: St. Martin's Press, 1964.

GUGGENHEIM FOUNDATION

(c. 1925).

It was an extraordinary move, really, for an independent entity to give modest sums to artists (and scholars) to do whatever they wished for a year or two, and in this respect the Foundation established by the Guggenheim family, in memory of a son died young, set a good example. Based on private money, rather than state money (or royal money), this foundation was accountable only to itself. This differed from private patronage, such as PEGGY GUGGENHEIM's (from the same family), wherein rich people support someone they know, whose work or company pleases them personally, for several years at least. Rather than rely on their own tastes or a single trusted advisor, as most private patrons do, the Guggenheim Foundation established selection committees that would review applications in which supplicants describe the projects each wishes to pursue.

Over the years, the Guggenheim Foundation has supported avant-garde artists, including many mentioned in this book. Of course, it missed opportunities, as when ARNOLD SCHOENBERG applied in the mid-1940s to complete the third act of his opera *Moses und Aron*; and it wasted profligately, as in awarding four fellowships in the 1930s to a middling composer named Dante Fiorello (1906), who vanished physically in the early 1950s.

Whereas Guggenheim grants at the beginning funded those who were young and barely known, it was thought in the 1960s and 1970s that the Guggenheim Foundation, less secure in its decision making, would fund only people whose work had been recognized elsewhere, the Foundation in effect putting its rubber stamp on someone, probably in mid-career, already approved (in implicit exchange for their subsequently acknowledging the Guggenheim in their biographies). Like all arts funders, the Fund should get credit for what it actually does, not what it says it wants to do. The best that can be said is that the Guggenheim Foundation has made things happen that would not otherwise have happened; since many of those things were good, the beneficiaries ultimately included a public larger than the initial artist.

Of the later independent foundations, few have equalled the Pollock-Krasner, established by JACKSON POLLOCK's widow in the 1980s (with money earned from art, not commerce), in supporting a large number of needy artists (mostly painters and sculptors). Too many other funding programs, by contrast, support remarkably few people, often of indistinct quality, with too much fanfare (aka "publicity"), so that a skeptic inevitably wonders why its beneficiaries, rather than others more deserving, whose work is already superior, were chosen.

Bibliography: The annual reports of the Guggenheim Foundation (90 Park Avenue, New York, NY 10016). (It's curious that a history of funding American avant-garde arts has not yet been written.)

Website: http://www.gf.org/

GUTAI

(1954–1972).

A group of Japanese artists, trained in various disciplines including law and literature, founded in Osaka by Jiro Yoshihara (1905–72), they produced collective paintings and MIXED-MEANS theater pieces, some of them quite spectacular. The first Gutai exhibition in Tokyo, October 1955, included Saburo Murakami's *Paper Tearing* and Kazuo Shiraga's *Challenging Mud*, both of which were influential. Yoshihara founded a journal that lasted a decade (1955–65) and issued *The Gutai Manifesto* in 1956.

Among the participants were Atsuko Tanaka (1931), Sadamasa Motonaga (1922), Kazuo Shiraga (1924), and Minuro Yoshida (1935). The theatricist MICHAEL KIRBY describes them as expanding "the means used in the action of painting. One artist tied a paintbrush to a toy tank and exhibited the marks it left on the canvas; others painted with their feet, with boxing gloves made of rags and dipped in paint, or by throwing bottles filled with paint at a canvas with rocks under it." Kirby continues:

> In 1957 the Gutai presented more formal theater works for an audience. A large plastic bag filled with red smoke was pushed through a hole at the back of the stage and inflated. Smoke puffed out through holes in the side. Another presentation employed a large box with three transparent plastic walls and one opaque white wall. Performers inside the box dropped balls of paper into buckets of paint and threw them against the white wall, coloring the surface. Then colored water was thrown against the plastic walls that separated the spectators from the performers.

The critic Udo Kultermann writes,

> The Gutai artists built huge figures after designs by Atsuko Tanaka and lighted them from the inside with strings of colored lamps. The lamps flashed rhythmically, suggesting such disparate effects as outdoor advertising and blood circulation. A moving strip covered with footprints snaked across the forest floor and up a tree. There were also spatial constructions that could be entered, traffic signs, jellyfish-shaped mounds of mud, plastic, and rope, stuffed sacks hanging from trees tied with ribbons.

Allan Kaprow included photographs of Gutai performances in his *Assemblage, Environments & Happenings* (1966). As far as I can tell, this major avant-garde group mostly disbanded by the middle 1960s, the individual members pursuing separate, less consequential careers. Yoshihara's death in 1972 ended it.

Interpretation: Falk, Ray. "Japanese Innovators." *New York Times* (8 December 1957); Goldberg, RoseLee. *Performance: Live Art Since 1960*. New York: Abrams, 1998; Kirby, Michael. *Happenings*. New York: Dutton, 1965; Kaprow, Allen. *Assemblage, Environments, and Happenings*. New York: Abrams, 1966; Kultermann, Udo. *Art and Life*. New York: Praeger, 1971.

GYSIN, Brion

(19 January 1916–13 July 1986).

An Anglo-Canadian who became an American citizen by virtue of service in the U.S. Army, where he studied Japanese, Gysin went to France on a Fulbright in 1946 and, instead of coming back, moved to Tangier. A lesser POLYARTIST, he painted as well as wrote. He collaborated with WILLIAM BURROUGHS on experiments in cutting apart and recomposing texts. He also produced a great permutational poem, "I Am That I Am," in which those five words are subjected to all 120 of their combinations, which he then read aloud for the BBC in 1959. Fortunately reproduced on the initial *Dial-A-Poem* record (1972), this performance remains among the indisputable classics of SOUND POETRY. The Parisian critic Marc Dachy (1952) remembers Gysin as the most generous elder supporter of the young French avant-garde.

Writings: *To Master A Long Goodnight*. New York: Creative Age Press, 1946; *The Process*. London, England: Cape, 1970; *Brion Gysin Let the Mice In*. W. Glover, VT: Something Else, 1973; *The Last Museum*. Boston, MA: Faber, 1986; with William Burroughs. *The Exterminator*. San Francisco: Auerhahn, 1960; *The Third Mind*. New York: Viking, 1978.

HAACKE, Hans

(12 August 1936).

Born in Germany, Haacke came to America as an art-school teacher. His principal esthetic achievement has been getting galleries to display artworks that emphasize highly pointed social exposé and commentary. Descending from CONCEPTUAL ART, Haacke began in the early 1970s exhibiting maps with highlighted neighborhoods along with photographs of buildings held by Manhattan slumlords he viewed as particularly unctuous. (This prompted the cancellation of an announced exhibition of his work at the Guggenheim Museum and the firing of its curator, the critic Edward Fry [1935–1992], in a scandal that decades later is not forgotten.) Subsequent work often uses the slogans from art-supporting corporations for ironic ends, such as a single horizontal aluminum plaque on which are polished letters with Alcoa's president's declaration, "Business could hold art exhibitions to tell its own story." Naming names, Haacke is skilled at satirical retitling, such as calling PBS the "Petroleum Broadcasting Service." His recurring theme is exposing the connections between corporate bullies and art institutions. Though Haacke's admirers claim he is making "unacceptable art," his work is exhibited and discussed respectfully while he remains professionally employed, perhaps because exposé exhibitions—in contrast, say, to publication especially in newspapers—epitomize the safe enterprise of preaching to the converted.

Installations: *Isolation of News Broadcasting Systems*, 1969; *Visitor's Profiles* (A Series), 1972; *The Goodwill Umbrella*, 1976; *Helmsboro County*, 1990; *A Breed Apart*. Oxford: 1978.

Books: *Framing and Being Framed: 7 Works 1970–73*. Halifax, N. S., and New York: Nova Scotia College of Art & Design and New York University Press, 1975.

Exhibition Catalogs: *Hans Haacke: Four Works*. New York: John Weber, 1979; Wallis, Brian, ed. *HH: Unfinished Business*. With contributions by Rosalyn Deutsche, Frederic Jameson, Leo Steinberg, et al. Cambridge, MA-New York: MIT-New Museum, 1986; *Business as Usual*. New York: John Weber, 1988; *Helmsboro County*. New York: John Weber, 1990.

Interpretation: Burnham, Jack. "Hans Haacke's Cancelled Show at the Guggenheim" (1971). In *Looking Critically: 21 Years of Artforum*. Ann Arbor, MI: UMI Research, 1984.

HALPRIN, Anna

(13 July 1920, b. Anna Shuman).

After studying with Margaret H'Doubler (1889–1982), a pioneer dance educator at the University of Wisconsin, Halprin emphasized nondance "natural" movements, improvisation, and process in both workshops and performances beginning in the late 1950s. Though she lived and worked in San Francisco, Halprin's work was first recognized in European festivals in the early 1960s. Her *Parades and Changes* (1965), a complex and ever-varying piece, caused a scandal in the mid-1960s for its total nudity. Halprin became more interested in the therapeutic aspects of dance—in how it feels to the participant—than how it looks to an audience. In 1980, she began a community workshop called *Search for Living Myths* with her husband, LAWRENCE. She became committed to creating modern-day rituals—in exploring collective power, archetypal forms that emerge from groups, and the possibility for concrete results from the process of creation and performance. One such ritual—a performance of *Planetary Dance* (19 April 1987)—involved seventy-five groups in thirty-five countries.

h

—Katy Matheson

Selected Works: *Parades and Changes*, 1965; *Ceremony of Us*, 1969; *New Time Shuffle*, 1970; *Male and Female Rituals*, 1978; *Search for Living Myths*, 1980.

Writings: *Moving Towards Life: 5 Decades of Transformational Dance*. Middletown: Wesleyan University Press, 1995.

Interpretation: Kostelanetz, Richard. "Anna Halprin." In *The Theater of Mixed Means* (1968). New York: Archae, 1980; Schechner, Richard. "Interview with Anna Halprin." *The Drama Review* 122 (Summer 1989).

HALPRIN, Lawrence

(1 July 1916).

The husband since 1940 of ANNA HALPRIN, he studied conventional architecture before taking his advanced degree in landscape design. Commonly credited with helping develop "the California garden concept," Halprin subsequently expanded his range to, to quote his succinct summary of his career, "group housing, suburban villages, shopping centers. Gradually these issues have aggregated into larger ones—how people, in regions, can live together in towns and villages without raping the land and destroying the very environment they live in. This led to concerns about transportation, both freeways for cars and mass transportation (BART), with particular concern for how these mammoth constructions could do more than just function as carriers, but go further and become forms of sculpture (as well as sociology) in the landscape." Halprin's ideas reflect, as they continually quote, such artists as BUCKMINSTER FULLER and JOHN CAGE, among others featured in this *Dictionary.*

Books: *Cities* (1963). Cambridge: MIT Press, 1972; *Freeways*. New York: Reinhold, 1966; *RSVP Cycles: Creative Processes in the Human Environment*. New York: Braziller, 1970; *Notebooks of Lawrence Halprin 1959–1971*. Cambridge: MIT Press, 1972.

Exhibition Catalog: *Changing Places*. San Francisco Museum of Modern Art, 1986.

HANSEN, Jefferson

(8 February 1965).

Representative (with Mark Wallace, Elizabeth Burns, and others) of the first generation of "post-langpo" poet/critics who evolved from their SUNY, Buffalo, firsthand experience with language-centered poetry into openness to other forms of the art. Thus, in *Red Streams of George through Pages*, Hansen uses a minor visual-poetry technique to run a wandering stream of primary text down his book's pages between isolated patches of secondary texts. The primary text is fairly straightforwardly about a suicidal character named George; the secondary texts—well, here's one: "mine derived of/ from to (them)/ dance steps/ pull singular into whirl/ seemly shipwreck/ of lost/ mining." Meaningless? Almost—until (for me, at least) "mine" shifted from standard noun to first person possessive pronoun, and "mining" started having something to do with George as that pronoun acting as a verb. Ergo: visually treated narrative poetry splotched with language-centered poetry. Hansen also deserves mention for his coeditorship of *Poetic Briefs* (1992–98), one of the few critical zines of the time that covered practically the entire range of innovative poetry extant.

—Bob Grumman

Lawrence Halprin and Associates, Sea Ranch, San Francisco. CORBIS/G.E. Kidder Smith.

Books: *Red Streams of George through Pages*. Port Charlotte, FL: Runaway Spoon (P.O. Box 3621, 33949–3621), 1992; *The Dramatic Monologues of Joe Blow only Artsy*. Norman, OK: Texture Press (3760 Cedar Ridge Drive, 73072), 1994.

HANSON, Sten

(1936).

Born in northern Sweden, Hanson was initially an experimental poet before turning to audiotape composition, in which he is largely self-taught. His earliest electroacoustic works were short collages of text and sound, usually with a political theme. ("Electroacoustic" music differs from purely ELECTRONIC MUSIC in using prerecorded sounds that are processed and mixed.) Subsequently, Hanson realized AUDIO ART that could be comic for much the same reason that animation is, because it portrays humans performing in superhuman ways. Formerly recognized as a promising poet, he became a composer, even writing for live instrumentalists. A natural publicist, calling himself a "sonophosopher," Hanson has organized TEXT-SOUND festivals, served as chairman of the Swedish Composers Society, and traveled around the world representing Swedish culture.

Recordings: *Text-Sound Compositions*. Stockholm: Fylkingen, 1978; *The John Carter Song Book* (1979–1985). Stockholm: Phono Suecia (PS CD 30), 1987; *The Pioneers*. Stockholm: Phono Suecia, 1992; et al. *Constellations: Electroacoustic Music from Sweden*. Stockholm: Phono Suecia, 1997.

HAPPENING

(1958).

Coined by ALLAN KAPROW, a gifted wordsmith as well as an innovative artist, for his particular kind of nonverbal, MIXED-MEANS theatrical piece, this term came, in the late sixties, to characterize any and every chaotic event, particularly if it wasn't immediately definable. Especially because the epithet had been vulgarized elsewhere, it became, within the community of visual performance, exclusively the property of Kaprow, who defined it thus:

> An assemblage of events performed or perceived in more than one time and place. Its material environments may be constructed, taken over directly from what is available, or altered slightly, just as its activities may be invented or commonplace. A Happening, unlike a stage play, may occur at a supermarket, driving along a highway, under a pile of rags, and in a friend's kitchen, either at once or sequentially. If sequential, time may extend to more than a year. The Happening is performed according to a plan without rehearsal, audience, or repetition.

Like all good definitions, this excludes more than it encompasses, beginning with some examples that one might think belong.

Bibliography: Becker, Jürgen, and Wolf Vostell. *Happenings, Fluxus, Pop Art, Nouveau Réalisme*. Reinbeck bei Hamburg: Rowohlt, 1968; Kaprow, Allan. *Assemblage, Environments & Happenings*. New York: Abrams, 1966; Kirby, Michael. *Happenings: An Illustrated Anthology*. New York: Dutton, 1965; Kostelanetz, Richard. *The Theatre of Mixed Means* (1968). New York: Archae Editions, 1980; Lebel, Jean-Jacques. *Le Happening*. Paris: Denoël, 1966; Vostel, Wolf. *Happening & Lieben*. Neuwied: Luchterhand, 1970.

Exhibition Catalog: Sohm, Hans, & Harald Szeemann. *Happening und Fluxus: Materialen*. Köln: Kölnischer Kunstverein, 1970.

HARD-EDGE ABSTRACTION

See **COLORFIELD PAINTING**.

HAUBENSTOCK-RAMATI, Roman

(27 February 1919–3 March 1994).

The avatar of graphic notation for musical peformance, he was music director at the state radio station in native Kraków from 1947 to 1950. Emigrating to Israel, he directed the State Music Library in Tel-Aviv from 1950 to 1956. In 1957, he settled for keeps in Vienna, working for the music publisher Universal Edition before becoming a professor of composition at the Vienna Academy of Music, as another internationally renowned avant-garde Jewish artist who found professional life better outside Israel. His mature catalog acknowledged few pieces composed prior to his settling in Vienna. In 1959, Haubenstock-Ramati organized, in Donaueschingen typically, the first large exhibition of musical scores in GRAPHIC NOTATION. For his own scores, he developed, according to Slonimsky, "an imaginative type of modern particella in which the right-hand page gives the outline of musical action for the conductor while the left-hand page is devoted to instrumental and vocal details. This type of notation combined the most advanced type of visual guidance with an aide-memoire of traditional theater arrangements. Several of his works bear the subtitle 'Mobile' to indicate the flexibility of their architectonics." Haubenstock-Ramati spoke of wanting to realize the multidirectionality and multidimensionality of an ALEXANDER CALDER mobile. In *Mirrors/Miroirs I* (1984) for sixteen pianos, each pianist has sixty pages which can be reordered, while the motifs on each page can be read in sixteen possible ways. In *Pour Piano* (1973), which was recorded, the score, according to Art Lange in the accompanying notes, "is a collage of overlapping and intersecting geometric shapes, lines, and shades, totally without introduction or instruction. To perform this, the pianist must rely on one's past experiences with the composer's music for insight ('memory' and 'intention'), or discover their own situational response and develop a formal entity ('improvisation')." Though performances of Haubenstock-Ramati's work can vary widely, given the permissions implicit in graphic notation, the common critical quip about his scores is that they are better seen than heard.

Works: *Ricercari* for string trio, 1950; *Blessings* for voice and 9 players, 1952; *Papageno's Pocket-Size Concerto* for glockenspiel and orchestra, 1955; *Chants et Prismes* for orchestra, 1957; *Séquences* for violin and orchestra, in 4 groups, 1957–58; *Interpolation* "mobile" for flute, 1958; *Liasons* "mobile" for vibraphone and marimbaphone, 1958; *Petite musique de nuit* "mobile" for orchestra, 1958; *Credentials* or *"Think, Think Lucky"* for speech-voice and 8 players, after Beckett, 1960; *Decisions*, 10 pieces of musical graphics for variable instrumentation, 1960–68; *Divertimento* text collage for actors, dancer, and/or mime, and 2 percussionists, 1968; *Alone* for trombone and mime, 1969; *Shapes (in Memory of Stravinsky) I* for organ and tape, and *II* for organ, piano, harpsichord, and celesta, both, 1973; *Mirrors/Miroirs I*, "mobile" for 16 pianos, 1984; *Sotto voce* for chamber orchestra, 1986.

Recordings: *Pour Piano*, with Carol Morgan. Therwil, Switzerland: Hat Hut (1961–62), 1997; *Interpolation* (1957), mobile for 1, 2, and 3 flutes. Eberhard Blum, flute, alto flute, and bass flute. Therwil, Switzerland: Hat Hut, 1995.

Bibliography: Slonimsky, Nicolas, et al. *Baker's Biographical Dictionary of Twentieth-Century Musicians*. New York: Schirmer, 1997.

HAUSMANN, Raoul

(12 July 1886–1 February 1971).

Born in Vienna, Hausmann spent his teen years in Berlin, where as a young man he met JOHANNES BAADER, who joined him and RICHARD HUELSENBECK in founding the DADA Club in 1918. Before long Hausmann became, in Marc Dachy's summary, "painter, craftsman, photographer, creator of photomontages, visual concrete poet, sound poet, theoretician, prose writer, technician, journalist, historian, magazine editor, dancer, and performer," which is to say a POLYARTIST. In 1919, Hausmann started the periodical *Der Dada* and organized the first Dada exhibition in Berlin. Politically radical, he allied with Baader in placing fictitious articles in Berlin daily newspapers and in proposing a Dada Republic in the Berlin suburb of Nikolassee, announcing political activities through eye-catching posters. Hausmann invented the Optophone, which was a photoelectric machine for translating kaleidoscopic forms into sound, and also created the Dada "phonetic poem" before KURT SCHWITTERS took the idea to a higher level, the former's performance in 1921 of his "FMSBW" reportedly influencing the latter. "The sound poem," according to Hausmann, "is an art consisting of respiratory and auditive combinations. In order to express these elements typographically, I use letters of different sizes to give them the character of musical notation," preceding ERNEST ROBSON, among others. Hausmann probably invented PHOTOMONTAGE before MOHOLY-NAGY and JOHN HEARTFIELD. His polyartistic career is best defined by an epithet more popular in Europe than America: "multiple researches."

Works: *OFFHEAHBDC*, 1918; *L' Inconnu*, 1919; *Optophone*, 1919; *The Art Critic*, 1920; *Abstract Image-Idea*, 1921; *ABCD*, 1923.

Exhibition Catalogs: *Raoul Hausmann: Collages*. Rochechouart, France: Musée départmental d'art contemporain de Rochechouart, 1988; *Raoul Hausmann: fotoarbeiten: photographic works*. München: Goethe-Institute, 1993.

Anthology: Bory, Jean-François. *Raoul Hausmann*. Paris: L'Herne, 1972.

Interpretation: Benson, Timothy O. *Raoul Hausmann and Berlin Dada*. Ann Arbor, MI: UMI Research, 1987; Dachy, Marc. *The Dada Movement*. New York: Rizzoli, 1990.

HAYS, Sorrel

(6 August 1941; b. Doris H.).

Initially a contemporary pianist, renowned for her interpretations of HENRY COWELL, among others, Hays turned in the late 1970s to multimedia performance and audiotape composition. The epitome of her multimedia work is

M.O.M.'n P.O.P. (1984, which means "Music Only Music, and Piano Only Piano"); this is a fantasized reflection (with film, taped sounds and narration, three pianos, and mimes) on the comic difficulty of reconciling nineteenth-century virtuosic pianism with twentieth-century cultural ideals. By contrast, the audiotape *Southern Voices* (1981) is an extraordinarily rich interweaving of speech rhythms and melodies indigenous to the American South (included in Hays's album *Voicings*). In the early 1980s, Hays confused historians by changing her first name to that of "an edible stubborn wild plant" (with which she identifies). She has since composed a piece about the sounds of feminist affirmation, *A Celebration of No* (1983), and an opera, *The Glass Woman* (1992).

Compositions: *Hands and Lights* for piano and lights, 1971; *In-de-pen-dance* for chanter and nylon string, 1979; *Celebration of No* for tape, film and optional violin or soprano or piano trio, 1983; *M.O.M.'n P.O.P.* for three pianos, tape, film, slides, and mime, 1984; *Love in Space*, radio opera/music theater, 1986; *Hei-Ber-Ny-Pa-To-Sy-Bei-Mos* for soprano, flute, and percussion, 1989; *The Glass Woman*, opera, 1989–95; *Dream in Her Mind*, opera (for Westdeutscher Rundfunk), 1994–95.

Recordings: *Voicings*. New York: Folkways (FTS 37476), 1983; *Dreaming the World*, with *Structure 123*, *U Mah Ah Sur*, *Circling Around*, *Water Bug*, *Song for the Dying*, *For the Children*, *Take a Back Country Road* (1988), *Tunings* (1981). New York: New World, 1996.

As Performer: *The Piano Music of Henry Cowell*. New York: Finnadar (SR 9016), 1983.

HEARTFIELD, John

(19 June 1891–26 April 1968; b. Helmut Herzfeld).

The son of a socialist poet, he anglicized his names as a protest against forced military service in World War I. A founding member of Berlin DADA, Heartfield differed from his politically dissenting colleagues by actually joining the Communist party. An early adventurer in PHOTOMONTAGE, he specialized in cutups that ridiculed Fascist politicians. These were published as cartoons, posters, book covers, and illustrations—wherever he could, in his aspiration to be a popular political artist. Heartfield's most famous image is *Adolf, Der Übermensch: Schluckt Gold und redet Blech* (1932), depicting Hitler swallowing large coins and spewing junk. Once Hitler took power, Heartfield fled to Prague and then to London (while his brother, Wieland Herzfelde, a prominent publisher, escaped to New York). After settling in East Germany in 1950, Heartfield received all the benefits and privileges a communist state could offer.

Works: "I've got millions behind me" *Arbeiter-Illustrierte-Zeitung* 1932; "Adolph the Superman Swallows Gold and Sports Junk" *Arbeiter-Illustrierte-Zeitung* 1932; *Photomontages of the Nazi Period*. Ed. Peter Selz. New York: Universe, 1977.

Anthologies: Siepmann, Eckhard. *Montage: John Heartfield*. Berlin, Germany: Elefanten, 1977; *John Heartfield*. Peter Pachnicke and Klaus Honnef, eds. New York: Abrams, 1992.

Exhibition Catalogs: *John Heartfield Photomontage*. London: Arts Council of Great Britain, 1969; Evans, David. *JH A12/VI 1930–38*. New York: Kent Gallery, 1992.

Interpretation: Kahn, Douglas. *John Heartfield: Art and Mass Media*. New York: Tanam, 1985; Evans, David and Gohl, Sylvia. *Photomontage: A Political Weapon*. London: G. Fraser, 1986; Willet, John. *Heartfield vs. Hitler*. Paris: Hazan, 1997.

HECKERT, Matt

(18 March 1957).

One of the advantages offered by amplification is making music loud, not only to spread its sound but also, by LA MONTE YOUNG, among others, to reveal overtones that would not be available at lower volumes. The principal innovation of Matt Heckert's self-constructed unamplified instruments is an unprecedented loudness. In his Mechanical Sound Orchestra are "Oscillating Rings" that generate rhythmic whirring sounds whose pitch varies with speed, "Resonators" made from disemboweled water heaters whose membranes thunder when tickled at their most resonant frequencies, and the "Boxer," an inverted wok that bounces around a steel table. Scarcely a technophobe, Heckert "conducts" his instruments through a computer that sends commands to the electric motors that power his band. This obviously epitomizes what LUIGI RUSSOLO had in mind for *The Art of Noise*, but did not know how to do. Heckert must be seen to be heard; no recording can capture the physically overwhelming presence of his "natural" sound.

Interpretation: Dery, Mark. "The Art of Crash, Hum, and Hiss." *New York Times* (15 March 1992).

Recording: *Mechanical Sound Orchestra*. Los Angeles: Cata Sonic (P. O. Box 2727, 90078), 1995.

HEIDSIECK, Bernard

(30 November 1928).

A pioneering sound poet, whose spoken work has a propulsive sound instantly identifiable as his, Heidsieck has since the early 1950s pursued a singular path, devoted to French language and French history, usually with identifiable subjects, producing many tapes and records as well as books that include seven-inch records and even films. He coined the epithets "poésie sonore" in 1955 and "poésie action" in 1962, the first an approximation of SOUND POETRY, the second of performance poetry. He began to work with audiotape recorders as early as 1959. Heidsieck is one of the few writers mentioned in this book who has won a major prize from his own government (in his case, the Grand Prix National de la Poésie [1991]); the explanation was that the literary judges, initially divided over more conservative candidates, picked Heidsieck to take revenge on one another. Fortuitous accidents like that appear to be the only way that prize-givers ever reward vanguard writers.

Recordings: *Partition V*. Paris, France: Soleil Noir, 1973.

Books: *Foules*. Ed. Guy Schraenen. Antwerp: Van de Velde, 1974.

Interpretation: Bobillot, Jean-Pierre. *Bernard Heidsieck: Poésie Action*. Paris: Jean-Michel Place, 1996.

HEISSENBüTTEL, Helmut

(21 June 1921–19 September 1996).

Initially a student of architecture, art history, and "Germanistik," he was regarded as one of the foremost exponents of post-World War II German avant-garde poetry. An influence upon the new poets of the 1960s (Peter Handke [1942] and FRANZ MON), he approached poetry, as well as his prose, from, in his words, a linguistically "an-anarchic" point of view. His poems are calculated, experimental, and carefully crafted, occasionally including lines in English or French; he called them "texts," and thus his collections, literally, "textbooks." His writings often deal with trivia, with thoughts anyone could have in the course of a day, in a language as ungrammatical as everyday language can be; once spelled out, such thoughts become generalized and yet are alienating.

Heissenbüttel has been a renowned essayist, who worked from 1959 to 1981 as the director of "Radio-Essays" at the Stuttgart radio station. His novels, usually called "projects," are mostly parodies of historical events. In *Wenn Adolf Hitler den Krieg nicht gewonnen hätte* (If Adolf Hitler Had Not Won the War), Hitler and Stalin have triumphed, and Europe has become a socialist computer society whose totalitarian government lets superfluous people die for the sake of economic advantage. Triangular relationships among Friedrich Nietzsche, Paul Rée, and Lou von Salomé become the center of *1882. Eine historische Novelle* (1882, an Historical Novella). *Das Ende der Alter-*

native, Fast eine einfache Geschichte (The End of the Alternative, Almost a Simple Story) tells about a beautiful, tall woman, the "alternative," who commits suicide by drowning herself in the ocean after several attempts to kill her have failed.

—Michal Ulrike Dorda

Works: *Kombinationen: Gedichte, 1951–1954*. Esslingen, Germany: Bechtle, 1954; *Topographen: Gedichte, 1954–1955*. Esslingen, Germany: Bechtle, 1955; *Über Literatur: Aufsätze*. Olten, Germany: Walter, 1966; *Das Textbuch*. Neuwied & Berlin: Luchterhand, 1970; *Gelegenheitsgedichte und Klappentexte*. Darmstadt: Luchterhand, 1973; *Texts*. Trans. and ed. Michael Hamburger. London, England: Marion Boyars, 1977; *Textbucher 1–6*. Stuttgart: Klett-Cotta, 1980.

Interpretation: Waldrop, Rosmarie. *Against Language*. The Hague: Mouton, 1971.

h

HEIZER, Michael

(4 November 1944).

Along with ROBERT SMITHSON and RICHARD LONG, the American artist Heizer has been one of the principal proponents and practitioners of Earth Art. He shares with Smithson a taste for executing projects on a grand scale. What distinguishes his work from that of Smithson is the paradigm from which it proceeds. Smithson's projects accompanied a complex intellectual program built on sophisticated aesthetic and scientific ideas. Heizer's alterations of the landscape are designed to reinvigorate the traditional sensibility of the sublime, invoking the breathless and expansive sense of awe instigated by the monumentality of mountain vistas. The shortcoming of his method is that, as with most works of Earth Art, his projects are generally seen through photographs in gallery exhibitions, and there they have the dryness of documentary records. In Heizer's *Displaced/Replaced Mass* (1969), three boulders were dynamited nine thousand feet up in the Sierra Mountains, and the pieces were carted down to a desert plain and loaded into prepared holes. For the typical viewer, the project is just an idea, and the photographs convey an experience others have had. His *Double Negative* (1969), in which two deep trenches were cut into a desert cliff, might well induce a sense of natural wonder in the face of its towering walls, but only if one were actually there. Unlike many Earth Artists, Heizer continued to execute his large-scale projects into the 1980's, most notably in *Effigy Tumuli* (1983–85) and *City: Complex Two* (1980–88). Since that time, he has focused on object-based sculptures presented in gallery spaces. They have been, for the most part, works in stone and in steel, large and simple forms such as large, smooth boulders and enormous biomorphic shapes perforated with holes.

—Mark Daniel Cohen

Works: *Compression Line*, 1968; *Displaced/Replaced Mass*, 1969; *Double Negative*, 1969; *City: Complex One*, 1972–74; *Effigy Tumuli*, 1983–85; *City: Complex Two*, 1980–88; *Chaotic Geometric Sculpture*, 1987; *Perforated Object*, 1990–91; *Stele I*, 1996.

Exhibition Catalogs: Brown, Julia, and Heizer, Barbara. *Michael Heizer, Sculpture in Reverse*. Los Angeles: Museum of Contemporary Art, 1984; *Dragged Mass Geometric*. New York: Whitney Museum of American Art, 1985; Whitney, David. *Michael Heizer*. London: Waddington, 1990; Celant, Germano. *Michael Heizer*. Milano: Fondazione Prada, 1996.

Interpretation: McGill, Douglas C. *Michael Heizer: Effigy Tumuli: The Reemergence of Ancient Mound Building*. New York: Abrams, 1990.

HELMES, Scott

(27 October 1945).

An architect by training and by trade, Helmes has made strong visual poems since the 1970s, beginning with simple word-images and progressing through more complex word-based works realized in a variety of ways—some of them, for instance, suggesting motion by rubber-stamping the same letters across a page, often making the familiar strange. "Some work concentrates on letter shape and connections to other letter poems," he writes. "Others are based upon the patterns of letters, words on pages, rather than lines and paragraphs." Helmes speaks of his most recent poems as "tautological texts deconstructed from repetitive patterns in order to jar memories and force the reader into evaluating how they see and construct their language frameworks." Though his poems appear widely in exhibitions and periodicals, he has yet to collect them into a big book.

Works: *Visual Poems/Scott Helmes*.Vandergrift, PA: Zelot, 1986; *Autistext: Poetry Before I Learned To Read*. St. Paul, MN: privately published (862 Tuscarora, 55102), 1987; *Poems: 1972–1997*. St. Paul, MN: Stamp Pad, 1997.

Exhibition Catalog: *Scott Helmes: Visual Rubber Stamp Poems*. San Francisco: Stampart Gallery (466 Eighth St., 94103), 1993.

HELMS, Hans G.

(1932).

Around 1969, I met this German writer who, in the course of discussing something else, claimed to have written a polylingual novel. Skeptical, I replied, "not bilingual, like Anthony Burgess's *A Clockwork Orange* [1961]." His response was in an awesome number of languages. This book, *Fa:m' Ahniesgwow* (1959), comes in a box with a ten-inch record on which the author reads selected pages. Some pages are predominantly German, others predominantly English. My own sense is that, like JAMES JOYCE before him, Helms made linguistic decisions based on sound and rhythm. The disc reveals that Helms hears white space as silence. The book concludes with extensive notes (in German only, alas) by Gottfried Michael Koenig (1928), himself a noted German composer, who sees the title, for instance, combining English, Danish, Swedish, South American Spanish, and North American slang. Around the same time, Helms produced *Golem*, a speech performance that he characterizes as "polemics for nine solo vocalists." More recently, Helms has written Marxist social criticism.

Books: *Fa:m' Ahniesgwow*. Köln: DuMont, 1959.

HENDRIX, Jimi

(27 November 1942–18 September 1970).

I have this audio bootleg of a Jimi Hendrix performance in the Manhattan club The Scene from 1968. Hendrix's guitar is stunningly inventive as he pushes sounds from it that one would think came from at least *two* different guitars and maybe a synthesizer as well. Hendrix gave many notable performances during his short career: the "break-out" at Monterey when he set his guitar on fire (remembered in the classic D. A. Pennybaker films, *Monterey Pop* [1967] and *Jimi Plays Monterey* [1967]); the ethereal space music of his 1968 Isle of Wight performance (recalled in Murray Lerner's films, *Jimi Hendrix at the Isle of Wight* [1990] and *Message to Love* [1996]); the recreation of the American War of Independence—complete with bombs bursting, horses screaming, and even bullets tearing through flag fabric—during his rendition of "The Star-Spangled Banner" at Woodstock (remembered in a 1970 film of the same title); and the transformation of his sound during the four shows at the Fillmore East, with the backing of the bassist Billy Cox and the drummer Buddy Miles, in 1970. The performance on my bootleg is notable as a microcosm of the effect of Hendrix on a rock audience.

As the greatest innovator on the electric guitar since Charlie Christian (1917–41), Hendrix redefined how the instrument could be used at the same time that he shattered expectations of *live* sound. On my bootleg, Hendrix drives one member of his audience into a Dionysian ecstasy that mimics the larger effect Hendrix had on rock culture. The audience member was no stranger to Dionysian excess; his name was Jim Morrison and Hendrix drove him mad with sound.

Morrison is drunk or stoned or both and Hendrix provokes him, lashes out at him, holds him up, and then knocks him down with his guitar. Morrison evidently climbed onto the stage; and for intruding on his act, Hendrix plays *him* as he plays his guitar. As the lead singer of the Doors, Morrison was not new to the stage or intoxication (by stimulants or sound), but Hendrix's guitar was new and it pushed him in his own subsequent performance from singing to grunting, from shouting to screaming. And this was the effect Hendrix had on rock as a whole: he interrupted its commercialization and provoked from it a new sound, a new way of using the main tool of rock.

Completely self-taught on his instrument, Hendrix never learned how to read musical notation. More amazingly, innately left-handed, he played upside-down the standard guitar made for right-handed people (making him handicapped, or at least physically challenged, much as two other major guitarists were—Django Reinhardt, who was missing fingers, and LES PAUL whose injured right arm was fixed in a perpendicular joint). One of Hendrix's first jobs as a Seattle teenager was in a backing band for a touring Little Richard, and he played the club circuit in Greenwich Village in his early twenties. Only in England, in the middle sixties, was he first recognized as the avant-garde representative of what rock could become. He came back to the United States in 1967 with two Englishmen named Mitch Mitchell on drums and Noel Redding on bass, calling themselves the Jimi Hendrix Experience. From the moment that his album *Are You Experienced?* (1967) appeared, he reigned as the preeminent rock guitarist in the world. His ferocious left-handed playing was abetted by his interest in guitar technology, beginning with the power of distortion and feedback, and the Marshall amplifier stack he made famous. *Extending* the power of the guitar, Hendrix in his solos created "sheets of sound" reflecting John Coltrane. BRIAN ENO regards Hendrix's approach to the guitar as nothing short of revolutionary: "He really understood that there was a relationship between the room acoustics and the amplifier he was using, the whole situation." The handful of albums recorded in his very short lifetime mixed blues, jazz, and rock that propelled rock and popular music as a whole to its fusion at least three years before Miles Davis released the seminal fusion of rock and jazz on *Bitches Brew* (1970).

Several months before his untimely death at 27, Hendrix had this to say in an interview about the possibilities of his music: "I want a big band. I don't mean three harps and fourteen violins. I mean a big band full of competent musicians that I can conduct and write for. And with the music we will paint pictures of Earth and space, so that the listener can be taken somewhere." He didn't live to experiment further, but his influence runs throughout the electric music that he helped create and shape. In 1981, Miles Davis introduced his new band at the Kool Jazz Festival. Mike Stern on guitar remembers Davis coming over to his amp and turning it way up, saying: "Play some Hendrix! Turn it up or turn it off!" The guitar of Hendrix is still provocative, still explosive, still maddening.

—John Rocco

Recordings: *Are You Experienced?* New York: Reprise RS 6261, 1967; *Axis: Bold As Love*. New York: Reprise RS 6281, 1968; *Electric Ladyland*. New York: Reprise 2RS 6307, 1968; *Smash Hits*. New York: Reprise RS 2276, 1969; *Jimi Plays Monterey*. New York: Reprise 25358–1, 1986; with Buddy Miles and Billy Cox. *Band of Gypsies*. New York: Capitol STAO-472, 1970; *Hendrix: Live at the Fillmore East*. New York: MCA MCAD2-11931, 1999.

Biography: Hopkins, Jerry. *Hit & Run: The Jimi Hendrix Story*. New York: Perigee, 1983; McDermott, John, and Eddie Kramer. *Hendrix: Setting the Record Straight*. New York: Warner, 1992; Mitchell, Mitch, and John Platt. *The Hendrix Experience*. London: Pyramid, 1990; Redding, Noel, and Carol Appleby. *Are You Experienced?* London: Fourth Estate, 1990; Shapiro, Harry and Caesar Glebbeek.

Jimi Hendrix: Electric Gypsy. New York: St. Martin's Griffin, 1995.

Documentaries: Pennebaker, D. A. *Jimi Plays Monterey*, 1967; ——. *Monterey Pop*, 1967; Michael Wadleigh, *Woodstock*, 1970; Palafian, Peter. *Jimi Plays Berkeley*, 1971; *Jimi Hendrix*, Warner Home Video, 1973; Douglas, Alan. *Johnny B. Goode*, 1985; Lerner, Murray. *Jimi Hendrix at the Isle of Wight*, 1990; ——. *Message To Love*, 1996.

Website: http://www.jimi-hendrix.com/ (Official site; there are many "unofficial" ones as well.)

Interpretation: Henderson, David. *Jimi Hendrix: Voodoo Child in the Aquarian Age*. New York: Doubleday, 1978; Murray, Charles S. *Crosstown Traffic: Jimi Hendrix and Post-War Pop*. London: Faber and Faber, 1989; Potash, Chris, ed. *The Jimi Hendrix Companion*. New York: Schirmer Books, 1996.

HENNINGS, Emmy

(1885–1948; b. Emma Maria Cordsen).

Long regarded as the eccentric and proto-promiscuous wife of the Dada poet HUGO BALL, who followed him into Catholicism and kept his memory alive, Hennings has in recent years been portrayed as a more substantial figure, who was probably the star of the first Dada venue, the CABARET VOLTAIRE in Zurich in 1915. Though her own writings were closer to Expressionism than the emerging Dada alternative, she was reportedly skilled at reciting, singing, and dancing, and was as well a popular organizer. She was one of seven voices in the premiere of the classic simultaneous poem by TRISTAN TZARA. As Hubert van den Berg put it, "[Hennings] was the central figure in that cabaret, and it became a cabaret *as a result* of her participation," which is another way of identifying her as responsible for the performance element in Dada. Hennings arranged for a tour of "Moderne Literarische Cabaret-Abende" [modern literary cabaret evenings] elsewhere in Switzerland in 1916. As a sometime nightclub hostess, morphine consumer, and streetwalker who was once imprisoned "for robbing a nocturnal guest," Hennings brought to Dada her experience with the Zurich demimonde. To quote van den Berg again, "She was also responsible for the mixture of 'high' and 'low' culture—without a doubt to be considered an important element in the cabaret's character of protest."

Writings: *Das flüchtige Spiel, Wege und Umwege einer Frau*. Frankfurt am Main: Suhrkamp, 1988; *Ruf und Echo: Mein Leben mit Hugh Ball* (1953). Frankfurt am Main: Suhrkamp, 1990.

Interpretation: Rugh, Thomas F. "Emmy Hennings and Zurich Dada," *Dada/Surrealism* 10/ll (1982); Van den Berg, Hubert. "The Star of the Cabaret Voltaire." In Brigitte Pichon and Karl Riha, eds. *Dada Zurich: A Clown's Game from Nothing*. New York: G. K. Hall, 1977.

HENRY, Pierre

(9 December 1927).

Pierre Henry has specialized in MUSIQUE CONCRÈTE for the past fifty years, producing many of its classics; today he is still creating works remarkable for their liveliness and originality. Born in Paris, he grew up in the countryside, then studied composition with Nadia Boulanger and OLIVIER MESSIAEN at the Paris Conservatoire (1938–48), where he also trained as a pianist and percussionist. From the beginning his interests turned toward rhythm and "noise"—placing him in the tradition of LUIGI RUSSOLO and EDGARD VARÈSE. Henry experimented not only with percussion instruments, but also with preparing the piano, which he began doing in the late 1940s, initially without any knowledge of JOHN CAGE. Henry's approach to preparing the piano was quite different from Cage's, as his preparations were more extreme and deliberately crude, and incorporated larger objects; the result was not the delicate, controlled gamelan-like effects of Cage's prepared piano, but sounds that were clattering, chaotic, and noisy. This distinctive element has recurred in Henry's compositional universe ever since; it was centrally featured, for example, in his homage to Russolo, *Futuristie* (1975).

In 1949 Henry met Pierre Schaeffer (1910–95), a radio engineer who the year before had produced the earliest examples of musique concrète—short studies created out of manipulated recordings of environmental or instrumental sounds. Schaeffer invited Henry—who in the end proved a far more fertile composer—to join him at his studio, and together they produced the first masterpiece of musique concrète (and of ELECTRONIC MUSIC in general): *Symphonie pour un homme seul* (1949–50). This title, which translates as Symphony for a Man Alone, is not intended to suggest the isolation of man in modern times, but refers, rather, to the fact that a single person could "perform" all the parts of this new kind of symphony. In fact, the piece, like most of Henry's later work, is remarkably free of existential angst, and free as well of pretensions of high-minded scientific seriousness. It is lively, sensual, and humorous. Predictably, music with these qualities was dismissed as lightweight during the 1950s, and to this day the various and rich tradition that grew out of these early musique concrète experiments (for example, the works of LUC FERRARI, François Bayle, Bernard Parmegiani, and MICHEL CHION) is slighted or ignored in most English-language histories of electronic music.

From its relatively modest beginnings in the late 1940s, Henry's musique concrète—or, as the genre is now usually referred to, electroacoustic music—grew in complexity and power. In Henry's large body of work there is great variety, but also a certain recurring atmosphere of ritual and incantation. It is no accident that several of his pieces are secular masses, i.e., the *Messe de Liverpool* (1967–70) and the *Messe pour le temps présent* (1967). There is also an underlying physicality, expressed in strong rhythms and reflecting the origin of much of Henry's electroacoustic music in recordings of his own instrumental performances. This has led him to create scores for many ballets (notably for choreographer Maurice Béjart) and theatrical events, the latter sometimes conceived in their entirety by himself. He has also shown great open-mindedness in his collaborations with rock and pop musicians, which are sometimes successful (*Messe pour le temps présent*, or *Paradise Lost* [1982]), and sometimes not (*Cérémonie* [1969]). Finally, it is interesting to note that he has occasionally incorporated sound poetry into his pieces, as in *Messe de Liverpool* (with poet Jacques Spacagna) and *Fragments pour Artaud* (from 1970, with poet François Dufrêne).

—Tony Coulter

Selected Discography: *La Noire à soixante/La Noire à soixante + Granulométrie*. Philips; *Le Voyage*. Philips/Limelight, n.d; *Orphée-Ballet*. Philips; *Musique pour la reine verte*. Philips; *Mise en musique du Corticalart*. Philips; *Musiques pour une fête*. Philips; *Messe de Liverpool*. Philips, 1970 [with one section deleted from the CD reissue]; *Machine-danse*. Philips; *Symphonie pour un homme seul* (with Pierre Schaeffer)/*Concerto des ambiguités*. Philips, 1972; *Corticalart 3*. Philips; *Prismes*. Philips; *Le Microphone bien tempéré*. Paris: INA-GRM, n.d.; *Dieu*. Philips, 1978; *Futuristie*. Philips, 1980; *La Dixième Symphonie*. Philips; *Paradise Lost* (with Urban Sax). Philips, 1982; *Variations pour une Porte et un Soupir/Voile d'Orphée*. Arles: Harmonia Mundi, 1987; *Messe de Liverpool/Pierres réfléchies*. Charenton, France: Mantra, n.d.; *Mouvement-Rythme-Étude*. Charenton, France: Mantra, n.d.; *Des Années 50*. Charenton, France: Mantra, 1991; *Le livre des morts égyptien*. Charenton, France: Mantra, n.d.; *Apocalypse de Jean*. Paris: Mantra, 1994; *L'homme à la caméra*. Paris: Mantra, 1994; *La Ville. Die Stadt*. Mainz: Wergo, 1994; *Noire à soixante/Variations pour une porte et un soupir* (ballet version)/*Gymkhana*. Paris: Mantra, 1995; *Fragments pour Artaud/Prismes*. Paris: Mantra, 1996; *Intérieur/Extérieur*. Philips, 1997; *Messe pour le temps présent*. Philips, 1997.

Interpretation: Chion, Michel. *Pierre Henry*. Paris, Fayard/Sacem, 1979.

HEPWORTH, Barbara

(10 January 1903–20 May 1975).

Along with Henry Moore, Hepworth was one of the two premier British sculptors of the middle of the twentieth century. Their works were very similar: smooth, simple, biomorphic shapes that both artists frequently pierced through. Hepworth often ran parallel lines of strings through the center hole, giving her sculpture a further similarity to the works of Naum Gabo. The closeness to Moore is the most evident, but what Moore was to the figure, Hepworth was to landscape. Moore almost always abstracted the human form, leaving it sufficiently evident that his subject matter is unmistakable. Hepworth dealt in pure abstraction, developed out of her experience in nature. She extracted the properties of topography: open shapes, enveloping curves, cavernous concavities, the stretching arms of a coastline. Re-creating these properties as pure form, Hepworth aestheticized the landscape mode, which was an accomplishment utterly different from Moore's.

—Mark Daniel Cohen

Works: *Pierced Form*, 1931; *Two Forms*, 1937; *Two Figures*, 1943; *Wave*, 1943–44; *Pelagos*, 1946; *Hollow Form (Penwith)*, 1955.; *Single Form (Memorial)*, 1961–62; *Single Form*, 1964; *Spring*, 1966.

Autobiography: Hepworth, Barbara. *Barbara Hepworth: A Pictorial Autobiography*. New York: Praeger, 1970.

Exhibition Catalogs: *Barbara Hepworth: Carvings and Drawings, 1937–1954*. New York: Martha Jackson Gallery, 1955; Read, Herbert. *BH*. New York: Marlborough-Gerson, 1966; Wilkinson, Alan G. *BH: The Art Gallery of Ontario Collection*. Toronto: Art Gallery of Ontario, 1991; Curtis, Penelope and Wilkinson, Alan G. *BH: A Retrospective*. London: Tate Gallery, 1994; Wilkinson, Alan G. *BH: Sculptures from the Estate*. New York: PaceWildenstein, 1996; *BH: Carvings and Bronzes*. New York: Marlborough, 1979; Thistlewood, David. *BH Reconsidered*. Liverpool: Liverpool University and Tate Gallery Liverpool, 1996.

Interpretation: Browse, Lillian, ed. *Barbara Hepworth*. London: Faber, 1946; Hammacher, Abraham Marie. *Barbara Hepworth*. New York: Thames and Hudson, 1998; Hodin, J. P. *Barbara Hepworth*. New York: David McKay, 1962; Read, Herbert. *Barbara Hepworth: Carvings and Drawings*. London: Lund, Humphries, 1952.

HERRIMAN, George

(22 August 1880–25 April 1944).

Herriman's *Krazy Kat* comic strip is the zenith of the form. Krazy Kat (sometimes male, but more frequently female) loved Ignatz Mouse, and the scatterbrained Krazy always believed that a brick thrown at her head by Ignatz was a sign of his love. The newspaper-reading public did not eat this up. All of the adventures of Krazy Kat took place in the mythical Kokonino Kounty, a desert decorated with weird geological and botanical forms. Herriman's genius, however, accounted for more than the strangeness of the physical landscape he developed or the emotional landscape of his characters. His experiments with the form of the comic strip were what made his work remarkable. Panels were inserted into panels, overlaid upon panels that served as establishing shots, or laid askew of the defining grid. Colors were used not logically but brashly. The fiction of the comic strip was laid bare by visual puns that broke through the wall of the newspaper and made clear the other reality that the characters lived within. Herriman explored, as fully as anyone has, the esthetic possibilities of the comic strip through design, language, color, and characterization. The sense that no one has ever surpassed his work indicates how confining the modern strip format is—remember that Herriman had a whole newspaper page to work with, and occasionally only one panel filled that space—and how conservative the comic-strip syndicates have become.

—Geof Huth

Anthologies: O'Connell, Karen, and Patrick McDonald. *The Comic Art of George Herriman* (1986). New York: Abrams, 1999; *George Herriman's Krazy & Ignatz*.

Forestville, CA: Eclipse, 1988; Blackbeard, Bill, and Martin Williams, eds. *The Smithsonian Collection of Newspaper Comics*. Washington, DC: Smithsonian Institution, 1977.

Web Site: www.krazy.com/krazy.htm (reproduces the strip and has information on Herriman).

HERTZBERG, Hendrik

See **O'Rourke, P. J.**

HESSE, Eva

(11 January 1936–29 May 1970).

Born in Hamburg, Hesse fled in 1957 to New York with her educated and cultured family. In her brief career as a sculptor, cut short by terminal brain cancer, Hesse discovered the feasibility of using several materials previously unknown to three-dimensional visual art. After dark gouaches of 1960–61, whose motifs presage later sculptures, she made reliefs and sculptures in greys and blacks. The classic Hesse work, *Expanded Expansion* (1969), has vertical fiberglass poles, several feet high, with treated cheesecloth suspended horizontally across them; her rubberizing and resin treatment gives cloth a density and tension previously unavailable to it. Given the essential softness of her materials, the sculpture would necessarily assume a different look each time this work was exhibited. Though *Expanded Expansion* is already several feet across, there is a suggestion, which the artist acknowledged, that it could have been extended to surrounding, thus ENVIRONMENTAL, length. Reportedly destroyed, the work may never be exhibited again, its mythic status notwithstanding. Hesse also used latex. In part because she was, along with LEE BONTECOU (1930), among the first American women

Dick Higgins, *How I Move*. Performed at the Avant-Garde Festival, Floyd Bennett Field, New York, 27 September 1975. Copyright © Fred W. McDarrah.

sculptors to be generally acclaimed, Hesse also became, posthumously alas, a feminist heroine.

Works: *Expanded Expansion*. New York: Guggenheim, 1969; *Right After*, 1969.

Exhibition Catalogs: Shearer, Linda. *Eva Hesse: A Memorial Exhibition*. New York: Guggenheim Museum, 1972; *EH: Sculpture*. London: Whitechapel, 1979; Barrette, Bill. *EH: Sculpture: Catalogue Raisonné*. New York: Timken, 1989; *EH: A Retrospective*. New Haven: Yale University Art Gallery, 1992; *EH: Drawing in Space—Paintings and Reliefs*. Ulm, Germany: Ulm Museum, 1994.

Interpretation: Lippard, Lucy R. *Eva Hesse*. New York: New York University Press, 1976; Spector, Naomi. "Eva Hesse." In *Jewish Woman in America: An Historical Encyclopedia*. New York: Carlson, 1997.

Eva Hesse, *Tori*, 1969. Fibreglass on wire mesh. CORBIS/Philadelphia Museum.

HIGGINS, Dick

(15 March 1938–25 October 1998).

A truly precocious artist and writer, Higgins was producing original adult art while still a teenager, some of which was collected in *Selected Early Works 1955–64* (1982). Higgins wrote mature arts criticism and founded a major avant-garde publishing house, Something Else Press, while still in his mid-twenties. Though his work had little academic or commercial success (and typically earned more recognition in Germany and Italy than in his native country), it should not be forgotten. Before he died prematurely, Higgins had realized one of the great artistic lives in America—the rich experience of which biographies are made.

Though his abundant output may be conventionally divided into such categories as writing, theater, music, film, criticism, and book publishing, it is best to regard Higgins not as a specialized practitioner of one or another of these arts, but as a true POLYARTIST—a master of several nonadjacent arts, subservient to none. In over thirty years, he has produced a wealth of work, both large and small, permanent and ephemeral, resonant and trivial—uneven, to be sure; but no two people familiar with his activities agree on which are best (other than book publishing, his Something Else Press being revered almost universally as the most substantial avant-garde publisher ever in America).

All of his diversity notwithstanding, Higgins reveals five fundamental ways of dealing with the materials of each art he explores. These procedures are COLLAGE, representation, permutation, ALEATORY, and EXPRESSIONISM. In nearly all his works, one or two of these procedures are dominant. Briefly, collage is the juxtaposition of dissimilars; representation is the accurate portrayal of extrinsic reality; permutation is the systematic manipulation of limited materials; aleatory depends upon chance; and Expressionism reflects personality or personal experience.

Among Higgins's many works are *7.7.73* (1973), a series of 899 unique prints of various visual images, both abstract and representational, with forms repeated from one print to the next. *Amigo* (1972) is a book-length poetic memoir of Higgins's love for a young man. "Danger Music #17 (May 1962)" reads in its entirety: "Scream! Scream! Scream! Scream! Scream! Scream!" *Postface* (1962) is a percipient and prophetic critical essay about advanced arts in the early 1960s. *Saint Joan at Beaurevoir* (1959) is a complicated, long scenario that includes such incongruities as Dr. Johnson and Saint Joan appearing on the same stage. *Men & Women & Bells* (1959) is a short film that incorporates footage made by both his father and his grandfather. *Foew&ombwhnw* (1969)—pronounced F,O,E,W, for short—is a book with four vertical columns across every two-page horizontal spread. One column continuously reprints critical essays, a second column poetry, a third theatrical scenarios (including *Saint Joan at Beaurevoir)*, a fourth drawings. Though the experience of reading *Foew* is that of collage, the book as a whole is an appropriate representation of a multifaceted

Higgins's Five Methods

	COLLAGE	REPRESENTATION	PERMUTATION	ALEATORY	EXPRESSIONISM
Visual Arts	7.7.73 (1973) Intermedia (1976)	Some Poetry	7.7.73 (1973)	Graphis (1957 to present)	A Thousand Symphonies (1967)
Writing	Foew&ombwhnw (1969)	Postface (1962)	Modular Poems (1975)	A Book About Love & War & Death (1965, 1969, 1972)	Amigo (1972)
Theater	St. Joan at Beaurevoir (1959)	Act (1969)	The Freedom Riders (1962)	Stacked Deck (1958)	Death and the Nickel Cigar (1973)
Music	In Memoriam (1961)		To Everything its Season (1958) Glasslass (a text-soundpiece, 1970)	Graphic Sources	"Danger Music No. 17" (May 1962)
Film	Men & Women & Bells (1969)	Flaming City (1962)	Hank and Mary without Apologies (1969)	Men & Women & Bells (1969)	Flaming City
Publishing	Emmett William's *An Anthology of Concrete Poetry* (1967)	Henry Cowell's *New Musical Resources* (1930, 1962)	Gertrude Stein's *The Making of Americans* (1926, 1965)	John Cage's *Notations* (1968) Merce Cunningham's *Changes* (1969)	Geoff Hendricks's *Ring Piece (1973)*

man. Higgins also published a historical study of *Pattern Poetry* (1987) which is, by common consent, the definitive book on its multicultural subject. He died in action, so to speak, soon after performing to exhaustion his "Danger Music #17," whose text reads in is entirety: "Scream! Scream! Scream! Scream! Scream! Scream!"

Works: *Jefferson's Birthday/Postface*. New York: Something Else, 1964.; *Foew&ombwhnw*. New York: Something Else, 1969; *Amigo*. Barton, VT: Unpublished Editions, 1972; *Modular Poems*. W. Glover, VT: Unpublished Editions, 1975; *Legends & Fishnets*. Barton, VT, and NY: Unpublished Editions, 1976; *George Herbert's Pattern Poems: In Their Tradition*. W. Glover, VT: Unpublished Editions, 1977; *The Epickall Quest of the Brothers Dichtung and Other Outrages*. W. Glover, VT: Unpublished Editions, 1977; *A Dialectic of Centuries*. New York: Printed Editions, 1978; *Selected Early Works 1955–64*. Berlin, Germany: Galerie Arts Viva, 1982; *Horizons: The Poetics and Theory of the Intermedia*. Carbondale: S. Illinois University Press, 1983; *Poems Plain & Fancy*. Barrytown, NY: Station Hill, 1986; *Pattern Poetry: Guide to an Unknown Literature*. New York: SUNY Press, 1987; *The Journey*. Barrytown, NY: Left Hand, 1991.

Visual Art: *7.7.73*, 1973; *Properties of the Four Winds*, 1990; *On the Creation of the Universe by Means of Sound*, 1990; *St. Anthony and the Fishes*, 1991; *Fish Music: Homage to Paul Klee*, 1991; *A Danish Earthquake Shakes Europe*, 1992.

Films: *The Flaming City*, 1961–62; *Mysteries*, 1969; *Men & Women & Bells*, 1970.

Compositions: *Graphis*, a series of pieces for varying groups, 1958; *Danger Music*, a series of pieces for varying groups, 1961–64; *The 1000 Symphonies*, a series for orchestra, 1968; *Piano Album 1962–1984*, 1980; *Trinity* for piano and percussion, 1981.

Web Site: http://www.fluxus.org/higgins/

Exhibition Catalogs: *Dick Higgins*. Ed. Ina Blom, with essays by Daniel Charles, S. S. Bauerbier, Jacques Donguy and Piotr Rypson. Oslo: Henie Onstad Art Center, 1995; *DH*. Milano: Archivio di Nuova Scrittura, 1995.

Interpretation: Frank, Peter, ed. *Something Else Press: An Annotated Bibliography*. New Paltz, NY: McPherson & Co, 1983; Woods, Gerald, et al. *Art Without Boundaries*. New York: Praeger, 1972.

HIJIKATA, Tatsumi

(9 March 1928–21 January 1986).

The leading figure and principal founder of the Japanese dance-theater form BUTOH, Hijikata determined that established dance forms did not satisfy the concerns of his generation or survivors of the shock and horror of Hiroshima. He evolved Butoh from a wide variety of influences, including his own extensive readings and studies of European avant-garde writers, artists, and performers. His presentation of *Kinjiki* (Forbidden Colors, 1959), based on a novel by Yukio Mishima (1925–1970), at the time one of Japan's most famous authors, is considered to be the founding event in the development of Butoh. In it, a dancer appears to have sexual relations with a chicken and is subjected to sexual advances from another man. Both subject matter and tone shocked the Japanese establishment. In 1960, Hijikata applied the term "ankoku buyo" ("darkness dance") to the evolving form; in 1963 he renamed it "Butoh" (based on a nearly obsolete term for dance that connotes something more basic than "buyo"). His *Rebellion of the Flesh* (1968) was another milestone that was also shocking because he killed a chicken as part of the performance. He collaborated with KAZUO OHNO, who was his student (though more than twenty years his senior), and taught and worked with almost all the younger performers who are now continuing the Butoh movement.

—Katy Matheson

Works: *Kinjiki* (Forbidden Colors), 1959; *650 Dance Experience no Kai*, 1960; *Rebellion of the Flesh*, 1968; *Shiki No Tameno 27 Ban* (27 Nights for Four Seasons), 1972.

Bibliography: Viala, Jean, and Nourit Masson-Sekine. *Butoh: Shades of Darkness*. Tokyo, Japan: Shufonotomu, 1988; *Butoh: Dance of the Dark Soul*. New York: Aperture, 1987; *The Drama Review* T110 (Summer 1986).

Documentary: Blackwood, Michael. *Butoh: Body on the Edge of Crisis*. New York: Michael Blackwood Productions, 1990.

HIRSAL Josef

See **GRÖGEROVÁ, Bohumila**

h

HILL, Crag

(25 August 1957).

As much at home in LANGUAGE-CENTERED as VISUAL POETRY, Hill suggests what can sometimes be achieved by combining the best discoveries of those two sometimes rancorously opposed schools. His *Dict*, a reworking of a dictionary by leaving out portions of it to get definitions like "distance/ between escapes" for "effusion," "used as a/ knife" for "on," or "an essential// is divisible/ machine/ falling// paper/ assigned/ stresses// bread/ implication// applies/ cleavage// rest/ the fragments" for "part," proved the worth of his language-centered poetry, while his full-color *Trans-Forms*, in which he visually reshaped words or phrases a highly-connotative step at a time into new words (deriving "experience" in nine steps, for instance, from "knowledge"), did the same for his visual poetry. Meanwhile, he was coediting the still active *Score* (which his wife Laurie Schneider, he, and Bill DiMichele cofounded 1983), a periodical second only to *Kaldron* (1976–present) in this country for its coverage of visual poetry.

—Bob Grumman

Books: *I Chings and Prototypes*. Madison, WI: Xexoxial (now at Rt. 1, Box 131, LaFarge, WI 54639), 1983; *Dict*. Madison, WI: Xexoxial, 1989; *Trans-Forms*. Oakland: Score (now located at 1015 NW Clifford Street, Pullman, WA 99163), 1989; *Yes, James, Yes Joyce & Other Poems*. Arroyo Grande, CA: Loose Gravel (262 Phelan Ranch Way, 93420), 1994; *Another Switch*. San Francisco: Norton Coker (Box 640543, 94164), 1994; ——. and John Byrum, eds. *CORE: A Symposium on Contemporary Visual Poetry*. Mentor, OH and Mill Valley, CA: Generalorscore, 1993.

HIVNOR, Robert

(19 May 1916).

Hivnor's play *Too Many Thumbs* (1948) tells of an exceptionally bright chimpanzee with a large body and a comparatively small head. In the course of the play, this figure moves up the evolutionary ladder to become, first, an intermediate stage between man and beast, and then a normal man, and ultimately a godlike creature with an immense head and a shriveled body. The university professors who keep him also attempt to cast him as the avatar of a new religion, but unending evolution defeats their designs. The play's ironically linear structure is original (preceding by a few years EUGÈNE IONESCO'S use of a similar form in *The New Tenant* [1957]). By pursuing the bias implicit in evolutionary development to its inevitable reversal, the play pointedly questions mankind's claim to a higher stage of existence.

Plays: *Too Many Thumbs*. Minneapolis: University of Minnesota Press, 1949; *The Ticklish Acrobat*, 1954. In *Playbook: Five Plays for a New Theatre*. New York: New Directions, 1954; *The Assault on Charles Sumner*, 1964. In *Plays for a New Theatre: Playbook 2*. New York: New Dirctions, 1966; "Love Reconciled to War," 1968. In *Breakout! In Search of New Theatrical Environments*. Ed. James Schevill. Chicago: Swallow, 1973.

HOFFMAN, Abbie

(30 November 1936–12 April 1989; b. Abbot H.).

His politics aside, Abbie Hoffman was a brilliant radical performer whose best shows were always recognized for their theatrical qualities. It was a brilliant move to go to the observation balcony of the New York Stock Exchange and toss handfuls of dollar bills onto the floor below. Likewise sensational was his decision, when he didn't want to be filmed for evening television news, to write the word "Fuck" in lipstick on his forehead. He could also be a brilliant writer (or talker, whose words were sometimes committed to print), as in this memoir of being Jewish in a traditional Christian prep school in the 1950s:

> My favorite hymn was 'Onward Christian Soldiers.' You know the part that goes, 'With the Cross of Jesus, going as to war.' Jewish kids weren't supposed to say the name of Christ out loud, so we all had to sing 'with the cross of Hum Hum, going as to war.' I did a two-year stretch at Worcester Academy, and by the second year Hum Hum was giving Jesus a run for his money.

Allan Kaprow appreciates Hoffman, attuned to avant-garde art, for working the intermedium between radical agitation and stand-up comedy. "It makes no difference whether what Hoffman did is called activism, criticism, pranksterism, self-advertisement, or art. The term *intermedia* implies fluidity and simultaneity of roles." So entertaining was Hoffman as a performer that, in comparison, nearly all his radical colleagues seem like schoolteachers.

Realizing that writing could be a form of radical action, he published several books other than memoir. My own opinion is that *Steal This Book* (1971) ranks among the most profoundly incendiary texts ever published in this country.

Books: *Revolution for the Hell of It*. New York: Dial, 1968; *The Conspiracy*, NY: Dell, 1969; *Woodstock Nation*. New York: Vintage Books, 1969; *Steal This Book* (1971). New York: Four Walls Eight Windows, 1995; *Soon to be a Major Motion Picture*. New York: Putnam's, 1980; *Square Dancing in the Ice Age: Underground Writings*. New York: Putnam's, 1982; *Steal This Urine Test*. New York: Penguin Books, 1987; The *Best of Abbie Hoffman*. New York: Four Walls Eight Windows, 1989; ——. and Anita Hoffman. *To America with Love*. New York: Stonehill, 1976; ——, Jerry Rubin, and Ed Sanders. *Vote!*. New York: Warner, 1972.

Selections: *The Best of Abbie Hoffman*. New York: Four Walls Eight Windows, 1989.

Biography: Hoffman, Jack, and Daniel Simon. *Run Run Run: The Lives of Abbie Hoffman*. New York: Tarcher/Putnam, 1994; Raskin, Jonah. *For the Hell of It: The Life and Times of Abbie Hoffman*. Berkeley: University of California Press, 1996; Sloman, Larry. *Steal This Dream: Abbie Hoffman and the Countercultural Revolution in America*. New York: Doubleday, 1998.

Web Site: www.abbiehoffman.com

HOLOGRAPHY

A technology new to the 1960s, drawing upon scientific discoveries of the late 1940s, holography superficially resembles photography in representing an image on two-dimensional photoemulsion (film), but it differs in capturing an image in different situations (and thus, at least implicitly, at different times) and then in situating that image in illusory space. That is to say that the principal feature of holography is creating the illusion that things are located where they are not. (A variant, called a multiplex or stereogram, is created by shooting an image with motion-picture film that is then compressed anamorphically into vertical slivers that, once illuminated from below, create the illusion of an image suspended in space.)

Exploiting a laser split-beam process to register information on a photographic plate, holography is also a far more recalcitrant medium than either photography before it, or video, which arrived around the same time. The fundamental measure of its recalcitrance is this statistic. Whereas there are millions of photographers and millions of video users, nearly all of them amateur, there are only a few dozen holographers, nearly all of them professionals.

Incidentally, what they make is a *hologram*, which is not the same as a "holograph." That word, at least in English, refers to a document wholly written, usually by hand, by the person who is its author. Among the most distinguished hologram artists are Margaret Benyon (1940), Rudie Berkhout (1946), Arthur David Fonari (1949), Dieter Jung (1940), Sam Moree (1946), Dan Schweitzer (1946), Fred Unterseher (1945), and Doris Vila (1950).

Books: Iovine, John. *Homemade Holograms: The Complete Guide to Inexpensive, Do-It-Yourself Holography*. Blue Ridge Summit, PA: TAB, 1990; Smith, Howard. *Principles of Holography*. New York: Interscience 1969; Unterseher, Fred, et al *The Holography Handbook*. Berkeley, CA: Ross Books, 1982.

Exhibition Catalog: *Holography (re)defined*. New York: Museum of Holography, 1984.

h

HOLZER, Jenny

(29 July 1950).

Holzer is included only because some readers might expect to find information and insight into her work here; by no measure known is it avant-garde. Her use of language is prosaic, bordering on dull; there is no invention in either syntax or diction. Holzer's departures, scarcely significant, are to make her words large (without the afterimage resonance of, say, ROBERT INDIANA), and then to use signage technologies that are scarcely unfamiliar. Holzer's language style descends from slogans; her sentences are designed to impress not for any linguistic excellence but as counter-adages for the cognoscenti whose prejudices, for another measure of kitschiness, are assuaged rather than challenged. Invariably as dumb and unoriginal as possible, her art cons an audience predisposed to the obvious, becoming thereby the litmus test for identifying the unsophisticated, which is the inadvertent but beneficial "political" function of her work. If you see a Jenny Holzer in a gallery, in a museum, in a private collection, or illustrated in a magazine, you know a dummy is lurking somewhere. Do not dismiss the social value of such art, for every profession needs an idiot-identifier if it is to remain a profession.

Books: *Truisms and Essays*. Halifax: Nova Scotia College of Art & Design, 1983; and Peter Nadin. *Eating Through Living*. New York: Tanam, 1981.

Exhibition Catalogs: Holzer, Jenny. *Signs*. Des Moines, IA: Des Moines Art Center, 1986; Waldman, Diane. *JH*. New York: Guggenheim Museum, 1989.

Web Site: http://adaweb.walkerart.org/context/artists/holzer/holzer.html (selected images of Holzer's works).

Interpretation: Auping, Michael, *Jenny Holzer*. New York: Universe, 1992.

HOME PAGE

(c. 1990).

The INTERNET has given virtually everyone the possibility of self-advertisement (or aggrandizement) through the creation of a "home page." The idea is that, within the vast world of the World Wide Web, your "home" is where you "live"—and where others can come and "visit" you. The home page has been used for various purposes; individuals may post their own likes and dislikes ("Bob's Home Page"), pictures, fantasies, and usually links to "favorite sites." Corporations use home pages as entry points to their goods and services. The idea is to offer enough new and changing information to encourage people to make regular "visits" and thereby keep them within your own "domain." Poets and writers, of course, use home pages both to mount their works and to advertise their more conventional wares—such as publications—for sale. Academics also have created home pages as spots to disseminate their research, and thereby win the kudos of colleagues. An anthology of home pages would make for fascinating viewing/reading. I am unaware of any archive that saves homepages for future study.

—Richard Carlin

Web Searchers: Common Web searchers such as YAHOO are the best portal to the world of home pages.

HOME THEATER

(1990s).

This new epithet describes the possibility for the homeowner to purchase enough audio and video equipment to simulate the experience of a moviehouse. This requires not a monitor, like traditional television, but a screen that receives a projected video image (either from in front or from behind), in addition to several loudspeakers of varying capabilities distributed over the seating area. Designed principally for watching home movies, such a system also enhances the sound of compact discs, to the degree that six speakers are better than two. Fans of science-fiction movies or movies with many stereophonic effects (such as airplanes swooping across the sound field) are particularly enamored of the sound quality available through having a subwoofer and more speakers spread around the room. My own experience of a large video screen (six feet at the diagonal, taking three projections from an old Kloss perpendicularly in front of it) is that it works best for sports events and old movies. It is less successful at reproducing television produced in a studio or films produced since the mass dissemination of television, which favor closeups designed eventually to be seen on small screens. As film theaters housed within a "cineplex" become smaller and smaller, the home theater maven will go to the moviehouse not for superior reproduction but only to see new films not yet available on tape—or perhaps to make new friends.

Bibliography: Ferstler, Howard. *The Home Theater Companion*. New York: Schirmer, 1997; Harley, Robert, and Holman, Tomlinson. *Home Theater for Everyone: A Practical Guide to Today's Home Entertainment Systems*. Albuquerque, NM: A Capella, 1997; Wolenik, Robert. *Build Your Own Home Theater*. Boston: Newnes, 1997.

HÖRSPIEL

See **RADIO ART**.

HOUÉDARD, Dom Sylvester

(16 February 1924–15 January 1992).

Born in the Channel Islands, Dom Sylvester became in 1949 a Benedictine monk, thereafter residing in Prinknash Abbey in Gloucester, England. A leading English-language theorist of CONCRETE POETRY in the 1960s, he published and exhibited elaborate, typewriter-composed visual poems that his colleague EDWIN MORGAN called typestracts, speaking of them as "ikons for contemplation, topological tantric forms linked to language or 'poetry' only by the lingering literary hookup anything typewritten still tends to retain." Because Dom Sylvester's poetry has been scattered through numerous chapbooks, among them *Kinkon* (1965) and *Tantric Poems Perhaps* (1966), while his religious humility deflected his innate idiosyncrasy, what is needed now is a thicker book representing his unique achievement.

Houédard published a good deal of criticism, as eccentric in its typography as his learning, for instance succinctly defining his personal poetic tradition as:

> benedictine baroque as contrasted with the Jesuit—& poetmonks in the west [who] have always cultivated what [Cardinal] newman calls "the alliance of Benedict & Virgil," eg: s-abbo s-adelhard agobard b-alcuin s-adlhelm (the concretist) s-angilbert s-bede s-betharius (caedmon) s-dunstan (another concretist) flaws fridoard gerbert (sylvester II) heiric hepidamn-the-newsallust herimann v-hildebert hincmar b-hrabanus-maurus (concrete).

Houédard also collaborated in editing the *Jerusalem Bible* (1961).

Works: *Frog-Pond-Plop*. Openings Press, 1965; *(Poems)*. Ed. Charles Verey. Sunderland, England: Ceolfrith, 1972; *Begin Again: A Book of Reflections & Reversals*. Brampton, Cambria: LYC Museum & Gallery, 1975.

Interpretation: Woods, Gerald, et al. *Art Without Boundaries*. New York: Praeger, 1972.

HPSCHD

(1969).

One of JOHN CAGE'S most abundant pieces, created in collaboration with the pioneering computer composer Lejaren Hiller (1924–94), *HPSCHD* was premiered at Assembly Hall at the University of Illinois's Urbana campus, 16 May 1969, for five hours. The venue's name is appropriate, because Cage assembled an immense amount of visual and acoustic materials. On the outside walls were an endless number of slides projected by fifty-two projectors. In the middle of the circular sports arena were suspended several parallel sheets of Visquine, each 100 by 40 feet, and from both sides were projected numerous films and slides whose collaged imagery passed through several sheets. Running around a circular ceiling rim was a continuous 340-foot screen on which appeared a variety of smaller images, both representational and abstract. Beams of light spun around the upper reaches, both rearticulating the concrete supports and hitting mirrored balls that reflected dots of light in all directions. Lights shining directly down upon the asphalt floor also changed color from time to time. Complementing the abundance of images was a sea of sounds that had no distinct relation to one another—an atonal and astructural chaos so continuously in flux that one could hear nothing more specific than a few seconds of repetition. Most of this came from fifty-two tape recorders, each playing a computer-generated tape composed to a different scale, divided at every integer between five and fifty-six tones to an octave. Fading in and out through the mix were snatches of harpsichord music that sounded more like Mozart than anything else. These sounds came from seven harpsichordists on platforms raised above the floor in the center of Assembly Hall. Around these islands were flowing several thousand people. *HPSCHD* was an incomparably abundant visual/aural uninflected ENVIRONMENT, really the most extravagant of its kind ever presented. A few years later, Cage mounted a "chamber version," with far fewer resources, at New York's Brooklyn Academy of Music. Literally abridged, this *HPSCHD* did not have a comparable impact.

Score: *HPSCHD*. New York: C. F. Peters, 1969.

Interpretation: Kostelanetz, Richard. "Environmental Abundance." In *John Cage* (1970), ed. Richard Kostelanetz. 2d ed. New York: Da Capo, 1991.

HUELSENBECK, Richard

(23 April 1892–20 April 1974).

Incidentally residing in Zurich in 1916, this young German doctor participated in the beginnings of DADA, which he continued to support in Berlin in 1918. Huelsenbeck wrote the first history of Dada in 1920–21 and edited the *Dada Almanach* (1920), an anthology so well selected it was reissued in the original German by SOMETHING ELSE PRESS in 1966. After years as a ship's doctor cruising the world, Huelsenbeck landed in 1936 in New York, where he became a psychiatrist (taking the name Charles R. Hulbeck) and, after World War II, the only first-rank participant in Dada based in New York. His 1916 poem "End of the World" resembles GUILLAUME APOLLINAIRE'S "Zone" in its disconnected lines, universal scope, and lack of punctuation. Huelsenbeck's *Memoirs of a Dada Drummer* (1969) is very candid, not only about his colleagues but about his success as a New York shrink who, as he boasts, sent his children to the best schools. Given the scant rewards for avant-garde art in New York, it is always gratifying to learn that its creators can find other vehicles of patronage.

Works: *Dada Almanach*. Berlin: 1920, New York: 1966; *Memoirs of a Dada Drummer* (1969). Berkeley: University of California Press, 1991.

HUNEKER, James Gibbons

(31 January 1857–9 February 1921).

Educated in music in Paris, initially a music critic for Philadelphia and New York newspapers, Huneker became a distinguished commentator on all of the arts, the polyartistic critic who popularized European avant-gardes on these alien shores from the 1880s until his premature death. Huneker wrote books about music, literature, and drama, in addition to short fictions and a novel. His two-volume autobiography, *Steeplejack* (1920), is about enthusiastic living with all the arts. He became an immediate model for the next generation of polyartistic critics, such as GILBERT SELDES. There are few like Huneker today.

Books: *Mezzotints in Modern Music*. New York: Scribner's, 1899; *Melomaniacs* (1902). Westport, CT: Greenwood, 1969; *Overtones: A Book of Temperaments* (1904). Freeport, NY: Books for Libraries, 1970; *Iconoclasts: A Book of Dramatists*. New York: Scribner's, 1909; *Ivory Apes and Peacocks* (1915). New York: Sagamore, 1957; *Essays by James Huneker*. Ed. by H. L. Mencken. New York: Scribners, 1929; *Americans in the Arts: Critiques by James G. Huneker 1890–1920*. Ed. Arnold T. Schwab. New York: AMS Press, 1985.

Autobiography: *Steeplejack*. New York: Scribners, 1920.

Biography: Schwab, Arnold T. *James Gibbons Huneker: Critic of the Seven Arts*. Stanford, CA: Stanford University, 1963; Kammen, Michael. *The Lively Arts: Gilbert Seldes and the Transformation of Cultural Criticism in the United States*. New York: Oxford University, 1996.

HUTH, Geof

(25 May 1960).

As a poet and sometime small publisher in and around Schenectady, New York, Huth has produced an abundance of work based upon linguistic invention by himself and others, as well as radically unusual formats, including SEMI-OBJECTS as he calls them. Rather than quote examples, why don't I mention that his periodicals are called *Alabama Dogshoe Moustache, A Voice Without Sides*, and, most indicatively, *The Subtle Journal of Raw Coinage*. His imprint, "dbqp," which is a pseudoacronym for "goodbooqpres" (and also is identical if inverted), specializes in "language, visual, and conceptual poetry, comics, prose, and other artistic investigations into language and meaning." For its 101st publication, Huth produced an anecdotal history that came in a plastic box slightly less than four-inches square.

Huth the poet focuses, as he puts it, "on the smallest units of language—words or letters," sometimes discovering "how little a bit of a word can have some extractable meaning," extending the range of classic CONCRETE POETRY. This poem from *Perisyle* (1989) recalls ancestors who came to live in Swansea, Massachusetts:

swansea
seaswan
swamsea
seeswan
swansee
seeswam
swarmss
sswarms
warmsss
ssswarm
swarsms
seawarm
warmsea
sowarms
warmsss
seaworn
wormsea
swarmss
seaworm
sswarms
seawarm
warnsee
swansea
beswans

swanbee
beeswam
swamsee
beswarm
swarmbe
beswand
swarmbs

His multi-media *The Dreams of the Fishwife* (1990) appeared in three formats: as a long multi-part visual poem; as an aural poem (as the text is a score for the spoken word); and as a combined visual/aural poem published in the CD-ROM issue of *The Little Magazine* by the Department of English at SUNY-Albany.

Huth was also a regular reviewer for *Factsheet Five* (1982–91), the Michael Gunderloy (1959) periodical that, in its lifetime, provided the most complete review of alternative products in print and electronic media.

Works: *Wreadings*. Port Charlotte FL: Runaway Spoon, 1987; *Perisyle*. Seattle, WA: EmPO (1002 East Denny Way, # 202, 98122), 1989; *Ghostlight*. Port Charlotte, FL: Runaway Spoon, 1990; *An Introduction to the History and Data Base of dbqp*. Schenectady, NY: dbqp, 1990; *The Dream of the Fishwife. Madison*, WI: Xexoxial, 1990; *Interior Definitions*. Vancouver, BC: Fingerprinting Inkoperated (Box 74567, Kitsilano PO, V6K 4P4), 1992; *Analphabet*. Lakewood, OH: Burning, 1993.

HYDE, Scott

(10 October 1926).

A professional photographer who incidentally had studied with John Cage, Hyde reacted to the cult of the "autograph club," as he called it, by exploring offset/lithographic printing as a photographic medium. He gave publishers black-and-white negatives, sometimes complementary and other times contrary, to be printed with different colors over one another. "I regard the picture printed in this way as a kind of 'original' print, since no 'reproductive' steps are involved. If I am satisfied with the way the picture looks, I do not permit that picture to be published [i.e., printed] again." Needless to say, perhaps, Hyde's pictures look like no one else's. "Synthetic color, variations on themes, montages created directly on the press, and a simple but effective form of stereographic imagery" are among "the technical and structural issues" that the seminal critic A. D. Coleman (1943) finds in Hyde's work, citing especially his influence on "many younger photographers and artists who have come to see the photographic print as an intermediary step en route to an offset print or book." Hyde has also made brilliant meta-photomontages, which he calls "mosaics," differing from traditional photo-pastiche by piecing together bits from many photographs of a single subject, thereby transforming its appearance. Around 1970 I remember seeing elaborate redesigns of New York's Washington Square Arch that were not publicly exhibited or published, at first because they were thought to be too original, later because the British painter David Hockney (1937) produced photo works that are similar, albeit less distinguished.

Books: *The Real Great Society Album*. Jersey City, NJ: Bayonne Press, 1971; *Scott Hyde, Offset Lithographs 1965–1989*. New York: Bound & Unbound, 1989.

Interpretation: Coleman, A. D. "Scott Hyde." In *Contemporary Photographers*, ed. Colin Naylor, et al. Chicago: St. James's Press, 1988.

HYDROPATHES

(1878).

In a late 1990s traveling exhibition called "Counter Culture: Parisian Cabarets and the Avant-Garde, 1875–1905," the organizers claim that The Hydropathes, organized around 1878 by the young poet Emile Goudeau, became the first group of artists and writers to transform "casual get-togethers into significant sites of group entertain-

Scott Hyde. *Washington Square Arch*, ca. 62/67. Courtesy the artist.

ment, collaboration, and self-promotion." They met every Wednesday and Saturday in a particular café. "For a year-and-a-half the group published a bi-monthly journal, *L'Hydropathe*, and its meeting would formalize the role of the café as a non-institutional showplace for members of the Parisian literary and art world." In this respect, the Hydropathes became a model for subsequent tightly organized and self-conscious Parisian groups of various sizes, ambitions, and consequence, though the model has had less impact elsewhere in Europe and none in America, where artists belonging to clubs that meet regularly, excluding as they induct, are generally dismissed as loathsome snobs.

Exhibition Catalog: *The Spirit of Montmartre*. Ed. by Phillip Dennis Cate & Mary Shaw. New Brunswick, NJ: Jane Voorhees Zimmerli Art Museum-Rutgers University Press, 1996.

HYKES, David

(2 March 1953).

In concerts with his Harmonic Choir, Hykes produces sustained open chords that, like earlier LA MONTE YOUNG music with a similar structure, generate overtones; and by favoring performance spaces where overtones can last several seconds, such as the Cathedral of St. John the Divine in New York, the Harmonic Choir can fill a theater with sounds other than those currently produced. This is MINIMAL music that gains from doing more with much less. It reflects Hykes's travels to Mongolia in the early 1980s. Though the initial impact is stunning, whether live or on record, Hykes's music does not become richer within itself, at least in my experience. Anyone initially familiar with the recordings is invariably surprised that so few performers—five in one concert I saw—can generate so many sounds.

Compositions: *Hearing Solar Winds*, 1977–83; *Current Circulation*, 1983–84; *Harmonic Meetings*, 1986.

Recordings: —— and the Harmonic Choir. *Harmonic Meetings*. Wilton, CT: Celestial Halmonies, n.d. (c. 1985); —— and The Harmonic Choir. *Earth to the Unknown Prayer*. New York: BMG/Catalyst, 1996.

HYPERTEXT

Coined by researcher Theodor Holm Nelson (1938), this term defines writing done in the nonlinear or consequential verbal structures made possible by the computer, for a true computer exposition—whether an essay or a story—offers multiple paths of alternate routes in linking segments. In his radical redefinition, Nelson chracterizes literature as "a system of interconnecting documents."

"With its network of alternate routes (as opposed to print's fixed unidirectional page-turning)," writes the novelist Robert Coover (1934) (a fan but not a practitioner), "hypertext presents a radically divergent technology, interactive and polyvocal, favoring a plurality of discourses over definitive utterance and freeing the reader from domination by the author." Though multipath fiction appeared before in *Hopscotch* (1963) by JULIO CORTÀZAR and Charles Platt's "Norman vs. America," which was reprinted in my anthology *Breakthrough Fictioneers* (1973), as well as in a new kind of juvenile adventure story available through the 1980s, it becomes more feasible with computers. (Hypertext also enables scholars to find linkages through tracing key words, not just through single books, but through whole bodies of scholarship, better illustrating Nelson's redefinition.)

In his introductory survey, Coover credits Michael Joyce's *Afternoon* (1987) as the "granddaddy of full-length hypertext fictions" (though the year before, PAUL ZELEVANSKY published on disc *Swallows*, which is a mostly visual fiction of immeasurable length). Hypertext literature frequently appears in literary periodicals that are published on computer discs, such as *Postmodern Culture* (1990) in Raleigh, North Carolina (Box 8105, 27695), and Richard Freeman's *PBW* (1990) in Yellow Springs, Ohio (130 W. Limestone, 45387). The Art Com Electronic Network (ACEN) that is connected to the WELL (Whole Earth Lectronic Link) makes works by JIM ROSENBERG, FRED TRUCK, and JOHN CAGE, among others, available gratis through the home modem.

Website: www.eastgate.com (Extensive catalog of publications plus many examples of hypertext in fiction and poetry.)

Fiction and Poetry: Joyce, Michael. *Twilight: A Symphony*. Watertown, MA: Eastgate, 1990; ——. *Afternoon: A Story*. Watertown, MA: Eastgate, 1990; Malloy, Judy, and Cathy Marshall. *Forward Anywhere*. Watertown, MA: Eastgate, 1996; Strickland, Stephanie. *True North*. Watertown, MA: Eastgate, 1999.

Interpretation: Bolter, Jay David. *Writing Space: The Computer, Hypertext, and the History of Writing*. Hillsdale, NJ: Lawrence Erlbaum Assoc., 1991; Joyce, Michael. *Of Two Minds: Hypertext Pedagogy and Poetics*. Ann Arbor: University of Michigan Press, 1995; Landow, George P. *Hypertext 2.0: The Convergence of Contemporary Critical Theory and Technology* (1992). 2d ed. Baltimore: Johns Hopkins University Press, 1997; ——, ed. *Hyper/Text/Theory*. Baltimore: Johns Hopkins University Press, 1994; Murray, Janet H. *Hamlet on the Holodeck:*

The Future of Narrative in Cyberspace. New York: Free Press, 1997; Nelson, Ted H. *Literary Machines* (1984). Sausalito, CA: Mindful (% Eastgate, 134 Main St., Watertown, MA 02172), 1992; Snyder, Llana. *Hypertext: The Electronic Labyrinth*. New York: N.Y.U. Press, 1997; Tuman, Myron D., ed. *Literary Online*. Pittsburgh: University of Pittsburgh Press, 1992; Baron, Naomi S. "Thinking, Learning, and the Written Word." In *Visible Language*, XXX/1 (1997); Coover, Robert. "The End of Books." *The New York Times Book Review*, 20 June 1992.

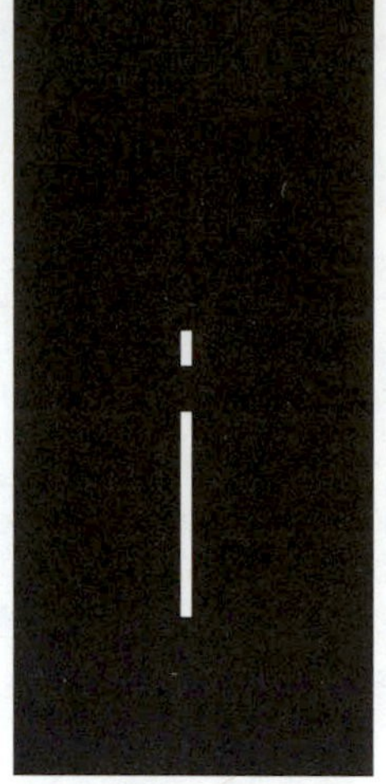

ILIAZD

(21 April 1894–25 December 1975;
b. Ilia Mikhailovich Zdanevich).

One of the most radical of Russian CUBO-FUTURISTS, Iliazd grew up in Tiflis on the Caucasus, the son of a professor of French, and by 1911, while still a teenager, became an active proponent of ITALIAN FUTURISM. While studying law in St. Petersburg, he became especially close to the painters Mikhail Larionov (1881–1964), Natalia Goncharova (1881–1962), and Mikhail Le-Dantiu (1891–1917) and wrote the first monograph on Larionov and Goncharova in 1913 under the pseudonym Eli Eganburi. He developed the theory of "Everythingism," an early manifestation of postmodernism, which declared "all forms of art past and present, here and elsewhere, are contemporary for us"—thus an artist was free to use them as desired. Beginning in 1913, he composed a series of five one-act "dras" called "Dunkeeness" that use ZAUM (transrational language) as an important ingredient. The action of these plays is satirical-absurdist, in the style of ALEKSEI KRUCHONYKH'S *Victory Over the Sun* (1913) and ALFRED JARRY'S *Ubu Roi* (1896). They feature a donkey as a character, either explicitly or metphorically. Themes range from political power to the role of free artistic creativity. In contrast to other Russian poets who used Zaum, Iliazd adopted phonetic spelling to facilitate correct pronunciation of his invented words. He arranged them in quasi-musical ensembles, such as duets, trios, and choruses of increasing complexity, concluding the fifth dra, *Le-Dantiu as a Beacon* (Paris, 1923), with an ensemble of eleven separate simultaneous voice lines. Collectively, Iliazd's dras constitute the largest work of Zaum yet composed. For *Le-Dantiu* alone, he coined over 1,600 new words. As Iliazd was also an expert typographer, these works, *Le-Dantiu* in particular, are also noteworthy for their visual elaborateness.

Instead of pursuing a law career in St. Petersburg, Iliazd in 1917 returned to Tiflis where, with Kruchonykh and Igor Terentyev (1892–1937), he formed the group 41° and created the Fantastic Little Inn cabaret, which became a focal point for Futurist- and Dada-style evenings and lectures. The first four dras were performed in Tiflis and Iliazd's typographical creativity was applied to publishing his own works and those of his colleagues, the most spectacular being his 1919 anthology dedicated to the local actress Sofia Melnikova.

In 1921, Iliazd moved to Paris and for several years led the Russian avant-garde there, giving lectures publicizing the achievements of the RUSSIAN FUTURISTS and allying with the Paris Dadaists. He organized the famous "Coeur ‡ barbe," a ball at which the split between DADA and SURREALISM erupted. Thereafter he led a quieter life, writing several innovative novels, only one of which was published during his lifetime, and cycles of poems that were formally conservative, if unusual in content and style. He devoted the later part of his life to the creation of elegantly designed limited editions of rare literary works with original illustrations by artists such as Pablo Picasso, Max Ernst, and Joan Mirò (1893–1983).

—Gerald Janecek

Works: *Yanko Krul' Albanskai* (Yanko, King of Albania), 1918; *Ostraf Paskhi* (Easter Eyeland), 1919; *zgA YAkaby* (As if Zga), 1920.

Exhibition Catalogs: Chapon, François. *La recontre Iliazd-Picasso homage à Iliazd*. Paris: Musée d'Art Moderne de la ville de Paris 1976; *Iliazd*. Paris, France: Centre Pompidou, 1978; Isselbacher, Audrey. *Iliazd and the Illustrated Book*. New York: MOMA, 1987.

Interpretation: Gayraud, Regis. Il'ja Zdanevich (1894–1975): L'Homme et l'oeuvre. *Rev. Étud. slaves* (1991); Janecek, Gerald. *The Look of Russian Literature*. Princeton: Princeton University Press, 1984; ——. *ZAUM: The Transrational Poetry of Russian Futurism*. San Diego: San Diego State University Press, 1996; Markov, Vladimir. *Russian Futurism: A History*. Berkeley: University of California Press, 1968.

IMAX

(1970).

This is a registered pseudo-acronym, written entirely in capitals, even if it means "Maximum Image," of a new projection technology that the Canadian Graeme Ferguson (7 October 1929) developed in the wake of the brilliantly successful multiscreen films shown at Expo '67 in Montreal. Using special cameras (and thus special projectors as well), a 70-millimeter film runs sideways through the camera, so that the equivalent space of three frames is shot at once. Producing a negative image nine times the size of the standard 35-millimeter frame, such footage offers far finer detail on large screens than the prior expanded projection techniques of Cinerama and CinemaScope. In specially installed theaters around the world, such films are customarily screened with six-channel sound. The paradox is that, in this age of ever smaller public motion picture theaters, certain developments exploit the possibilities of bigger screens. OMNIMAX is a derivative technology for smaller spaces, with a wide, deeply dished, concave, almost spherical screen. The IMAX company has also developed three-dimensional film projection more popular than the cumbersome system briefly popular in the 1950s, and IMAX HD, which doubles the speed at which its film passes through the camera.

Articles About: Elmer-Dewitt, Philip. "Grab Your Goggles, 3-D Is Back!" *Time*, 16 April 1990.

Web Site: http://www.theatres.sre.sony.com/imax/imax.html

IMPRESSIONISM

(1874).

The innovations introduced by Impressionist techniques are as significant in the negation of old formulas as in the affirmation of the novelties. They may be summarized in the following categories:

MELODY:

(1) Extreme brevity of substantive thematic statements. (2) Cultivation of monothematism and the elimination of all auxiliary notes, ornaments, melodic excrescences, and rhythmic protuberances. (3) Introduction of simulacra of old Grecian and ecclesiastical modes calculated to evoke the spirit of serene antiquity in stately motion of rhythmic units. (4) Thematic employment of pentatonic scales to conjure up imitative sonorities and tintinnisonant Orientalistic effects. (5) Coloristic use of the scale of whole tones for exotic ambience. (6) Rapid iteration of single notes to simulate the rhythms of primitive drums.

HARMONY:

(1) Extension of tertian chord formations into chords of the eleventh, or raised eleventh, and chords of the thirteenth. (2) Modulatory schemes in root progressions of intervals derived from the equal division of the octave into

2, 3, 4, 6, and 12 parts in preference to the traditional modulations following the order of the cycle of fourths and fifths. (3) Motion by block harmonies without transitions. (4) Preferential use of plagal cadences, either in triadic harmonies or extended chordal formations. (5) Quartal harmonies used as harmonic entities which move in parallel formations. (6) Modal harmonization in root positions of perfect triads within a given mode, with the intervallic relationships between the melody notes and the bass following the formula 8, 3, 5, 8, etc. when harmonizing an ascending scale or mode, and the reverse numerical progression 8, 5, 3, 8, etc. when harmonizing a descending scale or mode, excluding the incidence of the diminished fifth between the melody and the bass; the reverse numerical progression, 8, 5, 3, 8, 5, etc. for an ascending scale results in a common harmonization in tonic, dominant, and subdominant triads in root position; the same common harmonization results when the formula 8, 3, 5, 8, 3, etc. is applied to the harmonization of a descending scale; this reciprocal relationship between a modal and a tonal harmonization is indeed magical in its precise numerical formula. (7) Intertonal harmonization in major triads, in which no more than two successive chords belong to any given tonality, with the melody moving in contrary motion to the bass; since only root positions of major triads are used, the intervals between the melody and the bass can be only a major third, a perfect fifth, and an octave. In harmonizing an ascending scale, whether diatonic, chromatic, or partly chromatic, the formula is limited to the numerical intervallic progression 3, 5, 8, 3, 5, etc., and the reverse in harmonizing a descending scale, i.e., 8, 5, 3, 8, 5, 3, etc. Cadential formulas of pre-Baroque music are often intertonal in their exclusive application of major triads in root positions. A remarkable instance of the literal application of the formula of intertonal harmonization is found in the scene of Gregory's prophetic vision in Mussorgsky's opera *Boris Godunov*, in which the ascending melodic progression, itself intertonal in its peculiar modality, B, C-sharp, E, F-sharp, G, is harmonized successively in the major triads in root positions, E major, C-sharp major, A major, F-sharp major, E-flat major. Another instance of intertonal harmonization occurs in the second act of Puccini's opera *Tosca*, in which the motto of the chief of police, a descending whole-tone scale in the bass, is harmonized in ascending major triads in root positions, in contrary motion; the intervallic relationship between the melody and the bass follows the formula 8, 3, 5, 8, 3, 5, 8,. (8) Parallel progressions of inversions of triads, particularly second inversions of major triads, with the root progression ascending or descending in minor thirds, so that the basses outline a diminished seventh chord. (9) Parallel progressions of major ninth chords, also with a bass moving by minor thirds. (10) Parallel progressions of inverted dominant-seventh chords, particularly 6/5/3 chords. (11) Free use of unattached and unresolved dissonant chords, particularly suspensions of major sevenths over diminished-seventh chords. (12) Cadential formulas with the added major sixth over major triads in close harmony.

COUNTERPOINT:

(1) A virtual abandonment of Baroque procedures; abolition of tonal sequences and of strict canonic imitation. (2) Reduction of fugal processes to adumbrative thematic echoes, memos, and mementos. (3) Cultivation of parallel motion of voices, particularly consecutive fourths and organum-like perfect fifths.

FORM:

(1) Desuetude of sectional symphonies of the classical or romantic type, and their replacement by coloristic tone poems of a rhapsodic genre. (2) Virtual disappearance of thematic development, its function being taken over by dynamic elements. (3) Cessation in the practice of traditional variations, discontinuance of auxiliary embellish-

ments, melodic and harmonic figurations whether above, below, or around the thematic notes and the concomitant cultivation of instrumental variations in which the alteration of tone color becomes the means of variegation. A theme may be subjected to augmentation or diminution, and in some cases to topological dislocations of the intervallic parameters. Thus, the tonal theme of Debussy's *La Mer* is extended in the climax into a series of whole tones. (4) Homeological imitation of melorhythmic formulas of old dance forms, often with pandiatonic amplification of the harmony. (5) A general tendency towards miniaturization of nominally classical forms, such as sonata or prelude.

—Nicholas Slonimsky

History: Simms, Bryan R. *20th Century Music*. 2d ed. New York: Schirmer Books, 1996.

IMPROVISATION

See **JAZZ**.

INAUDIBLE MUSIC

(1918).

Since electronic instruments are capable of generating any frequency, it is possible to reproduce sounds below and above the audible range. The first work for infrasonic and ultrasonic wavelengths was the inaudible symphony entitled *Symphonie Humaine* by the French composer Michel Magne, conducted by him in Paris on 26 May 1955. Its movements were entitled Epileptic Dance, Thanatological Berceuse, and Interior View of an Assassin. The inaudible version was unheard first, followed by a hearing of an audible transcription. The mystical Russian composer Nicolas Obouhov devised in 1918 an inaudible instrument which he named Ether, theoretically capable of producing infrasonic and ultrasonic sounds ranging from five octaves below the lowest audible tone to five octaves above the highest audible tone. But Obouhov's instrument was never constructed. Avant-garde composers working in mixed media often compose visual music, which can be seen but not heard. A poetic example is the act of releasing a jar full of butterflies "composed" by La Monte Young. Imagination plays a crucial part in the appreciation of inaudible music. An interviewer on a broadcast of the British Broadcasting Corporation was sent a defective copy of *John and Yoko's Wedding Album* (John Lennon was a member of a Liverpudlian vocal quartet, since fallen into innocuous desuetude, known as The Beatles) in which two sides were blank except for an engineer's line-up tone. The broadcaster gave it a warmly favorable review, noting that the pitches differed only by microtones, and that "this oscillation produces an almost subliminal uneven beat which maintains interest on a more basic level," and further observing that the listener could improvise an Indian raga, plainsong, or Gaelic mouth music against the drone. John and his Japanese bride Yoko sent him a congratulatory telegram, announcing their intention to release the blank sides for their next album. "Heard melodies are sweet, but those unheard are sweeter."

—Nicolas Slonimsky

Bibliography: Young, La Monte, ed. *An Anthology* (1963). 2d ed. Munich: Heiner Friedrich, 1970.

INCOMPREHENSIBLE CRITICAL PROSE

(forever).

Always with us, alas, incomprehensible writing about culture and the arts became more frequent, if not more acceptable, in the wake of intellectual invasions from France, beginning in the 1970s, continuing into the 1980s and perhaps into the 1990s. Examples are so plentiful nowadays, not only in books but pretentious magazines, that I fear singling out examples, because readers might think I chose one or another example out of revenge or personal distaste.

The theme of incomprehensible critical prose is pride in privilege, no matter what its writer is trying or pretending to say (including the exposure of privilege in others); its implicit purpose is demonstrating that its author can brazenly write (or talk) as you and I can't, for fear we might be criticized, demoted, or dismissed. Incomprehensible authors customarily benefit from belonging to one or another social class, to which compensatory intellectual privileges are extended—whether female, black, or third-world-born (or, ideally, at least two of the three, if not all three)—the recital of which can be turned into a shield against obvious criticism.

Rest assured, dear reader, that the following excerpts come from people I don't know and, in truth, would rather not know, thinking, as I do, that incomprehensible prose is a sympton of more serious intellectual and moral defects.

> If, for a while, the ruse of desire is calculable for the uses of discipline soon the repetition of guilt, justification, pseudo-scientific theories, superstition, spurious authorities, and classifications can be seen as the desperate efforts to 'normalize' formally the disturbance of a discourse of splitting that violates the rational, enlightened claims of its enunciatory modality.

(In this context, a book titled *Locations of Culture* [1994], Homi Bhabha's final phrase packs a particularly mighty fluff punch.)

Consider this about the German-American Dada baroness Elsa van Freytag-Loringhoven, who reportedly made a plaster cast of a penis (since lost), and the French American Marcel Duchamp:

> It was imperative that the New Woman, per Picabia, be contained within the anxiety-reducing mechanomorphic forms of the facetious machine image, not parading freely through the streets wielding a penis clearly disattached from its conventional role as guarantor of male privilege. The baroness' performative (rather than biological) penis, along with Marcel's erotically invested *garçonne*-esque eros/rose-as-commodity, were the ultimate weapons against the bourgeois norms that Dada in general is thought of as radically antagonizing.

I also suspect that anyone who reads widely has his or her favorite bête-noirs.

Incidentally, the best antedote for such contagiously bad medicine is reading or rereading George Orwell's fifteen-page "Politics and the English Language" (1946), whose clearly expressed insights into peculiar language are more prophetically true than he could have foreseen.

Bibliography: Bhabha, Homi. *Locations of Culture*. New York: Routledge, 1994; Jones, Amelia. "Eros, That's Life, or the Baroness' Penis." In Francis M. Naumann, with Beth Venn. *Making Mischief: Dada Invades New York*. New York: Whitney Museum, 1996; Orwell, George. "Politics and the English Language" (1946). Reprinted widely, thankfully.

INDETERMINACY

(c. 1954).

Incidentally the title of John Cage's first solo record (1957), this term refers to music composed with the assistance of chance operations—such as throwing dice in order to make decisions, observing the imperfections in paper to discover notes on staves, or using random tables—and to the use of musical instructions likely to produce radically unpredictable results. In the latter case, the composer may provide only generalized directions; or collections of notes that may be played in any order, at any speed, in any combination, etc.; or allow for a surprise that, if observed, will necessarily redirect the performance. Indeterminate performance differs from improvisation in providing ground rules that will prevent its performers from seeking familiar solutions. Indeterminacy differs from aleatory music, which was an alternative popularized by Pierre Boulez in the 1960s, with compromises typical of him, purportedly to represent a saner avant-garde. In my experience, indeterminacy, aka "chance," functioned as a divisory issue in talking, say, about John Cage's music until the late 1970s, when everyone both opposed and predisposed realized that it wasn't as important as it once seemed.

Bibliography: Childs, Barney. "Indeterminacy." In *Dictionary of Contemporary Music*, ed. John Vinton. New York: Dutton, 1974; Kostelanetz, Richard. *Conversing with Cage*. New York: Limelight, 1989.

Discography: Cage, John and David Tudor. *Indeterminancy* (1958). Washington, DC: Smithsonian/Folkways, 1994.

INDIANA, Robert

(13 September 1928; b. R. Clarke).

Initially classified among the Pop Artists, Indiana is actually a word painter, which is to say that the innovation of his very best paintings comes from making them mostly, if not exclusively, of language. Using bold letters and sometimes numbers, rendered in the clean-edge tradition of American commercial sign painting, Indiana exposes very short Americanisms to art, or vice versa, establishing himself as a master of color, shape, and craftsmanship (though repetitiously favoring Roman letters and numerals within circles, as well as circles within circles), well before Jenny Holzer, among others. Indiana's single most famous work, *Love* (1966), depends upon tilting the letter O, which in this heavy Roman style evokes the sexuality embodied in its shape, and then upon the fact that all four letters are literally touching each of their adjacent letters. One version is a painting, since reproduced on a postage stamp, with the red, blue, and green so even in value that the foreground does not protrude from the background. Four of these LOVE shapes, each five by five feet, were grouped into a magisterial *LoveWall* (1966), ten feet by ten feet of rearrangeable panels, each deployed perpendicularly to its companions, all of which can be rotated so that different common letters meet at the center of the field. My favorite numerical Indiana is *Cardinal Numbers*, an extended vertical progression from zero to nine that was

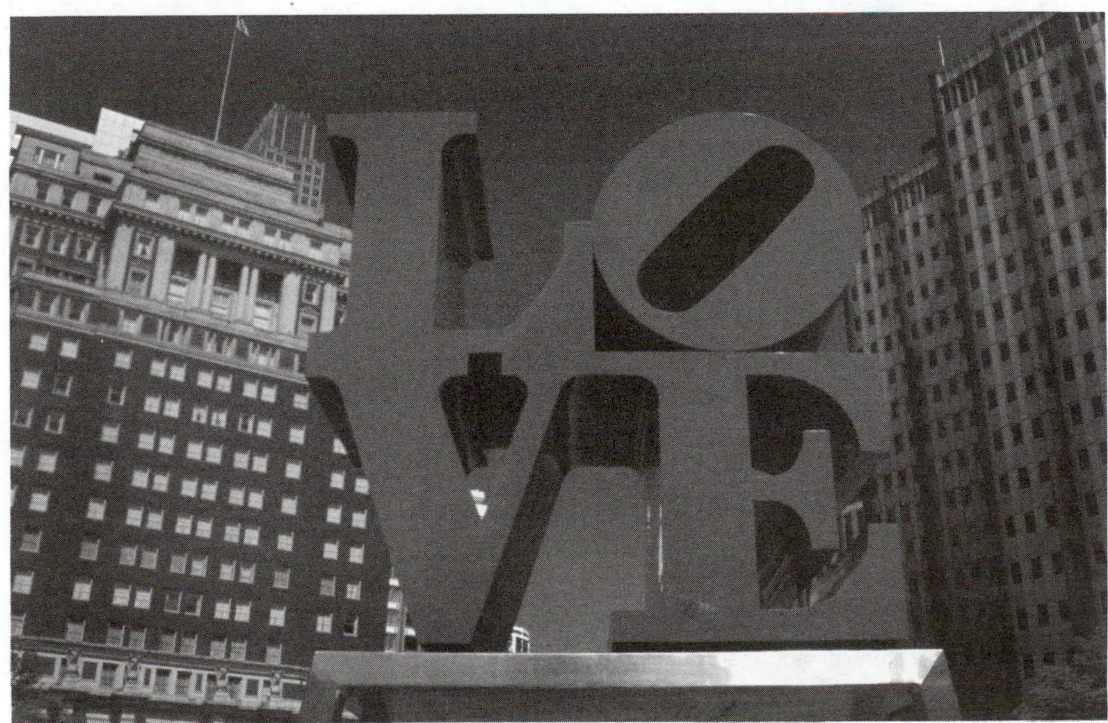

Robert Indiana. *Love.* Sculpture. CORBIS/Lee Snider.

displayed at Expo '67. I think Indiana's design for the basketball court at the Milwaukee Mecca (1977) is the best floor done by an American artist in recent memory.

Visual Art: *The American Dream, 1960–61; Mother and Father*, 1963–67; *The Brooklyn Bridge*, 1964; *Love*, 1966; *Cardinal Numbers*, 1966; *LoveWall*, 1966; *Love Cross*, 1968.

Exhibition Catalogs: *Robert Indiana*. Intro. Jan van der Marck. Minneapolis, MN: Dayton's, 1966; *RI*. Introduction John W. McCoubrey. Philadelphia, PA: Institute of Contemporary Art, 1968; *RI * Graphics*. Intro. Richard-Raymond Alasko. Notre Dame, IN: Dept. of Art, Saint Mary's College, 1969; *Indiana's Indians: 20 Year Retrospective*. Rockland, ME: William A. Farnsworth Library and Art Museum, 1982; *RI: Retrospective 1958–1998*. Nice, France: Musée d'art moderne et d'art contemporain, 1998.

Interpretation: Weinhardt, Carl J., Jr. *Robert Indiana*. New York: Abrams, 1990.

Catalog Raisonné: Sheehan, Susan. *Robert Indiana Prints: A Catalog Raisonné 1951–1991*. New York: Susan Sheehan, 1991.

INFRAVERBAL POETRY

(1990).

Another taxonomical poetic term of mine, this one has to do with poetry in which what is done inside words becomes significant. I divide the class into the following four subclasses: (1) fissional poetry (e.g., RICHARD KOSTELANETZ's "TheRapist"); fusional poetry (e.g., GEOF HUTH's "shadowl"); microherent poetry (e.g., MICHAEL BASINSKI's "cedkwmeyme"); and alphaconceptual poetry (e.g., ARAM SAROYAN's "lighght," which exploits the concept of silent letters). The intentional misspelling of words for poetic effect probably began with LEWIS CARROLL's portmanteau words in the latter part of the nineteenth century, though he was probably aiming more for comedy than poetry (e.g., "slithy toves" to suggest slimy/slippery/lithe toads/cloves/coves/groves). The first genuine genius of the art was JAMES JOYCE, particularly in *FINNEGANS WAKE* (1939) where he used such coinages as "cropse," "trwth," "pftjschute," and "sylble." Some twenty years later Aram Saroyan took the simple-seeming but crucial step of making poems, one to a page, of single infraverbally enhanced words, like his famous "lighght" and "blod." Since then, many have followed his example, among them Kostelanetz (an inventor of such bilingual pwoermds as the "Spanglish" "dmionneeryo," in which the fusion of "money" and "dinero" glistens with appropriate connotations), KARL KEMPTON, Huth, and JONATHAN BRANNEN—Huth, among several, expanding to longer lyrics in which infraverbalisms are embedded naturally, as simply one kind of the many devices available for use, as it was for Joyce, albeit in prose rather than lyric poetry.

—Bob Grumman

Reference: Grumman, Bob. "MNMLST POETRY: Unacclaimed But Flourishing." At *Light & Dust*. The Internet, 1997 (http://www.thing.net/~grist/l&d/lighthom.htm).

INSTALLATION

(c. 1980).

The term "installation" identifies art made for a particular space, which need not be a gallery. Such art theoretically exploits certain qualities of that space that it will inhabit forever, or that will be destroyed when the exhibition is terminated. The category arose in the 1980s as an open and yet debased term for what had previously been called "site-specific art," as exemplified by the sculptors Nancy Holt (1938) and Mary Miss (1944), among others. Examples include WALTER DE MARIA's Earth Room (1968), which, in its third incarnation (or installation), has been permanently on display in New York City since the late 1970s. Both installations and site-specific art differ from an ENVIRONMENT, which is an artistically enhanced, circumscribed space.

Bibliography: *Land Marks*. Annandale, New York: Bard College Center, 1984.

INTERMEDIA

(1966).

This term was coined by DICK HIGGINS to define new genres of art that combined the aspects of two heretofore separate types of art. (Only later did Higgins become aware of Samuel Taylor Coleridge's earlier uses of the epithet.) Intermedia is different from "multimedia," which implies something much less dramatic—the inclusion of various art media, such as different kinds of material, within one work. One frequently cited example of intermedia is VISUAL POETRY, which results from the combination of the literary and visual arts. Although there is a long (and mostly unknown) tradition of visual literature, the modern fusion of the two arts becomes a distinct intermedium, something not conventional literature and not exclusively visual art. During the twentieth century, experimentation with intermedia became more common as artists searched for radically alternative modes of expression.

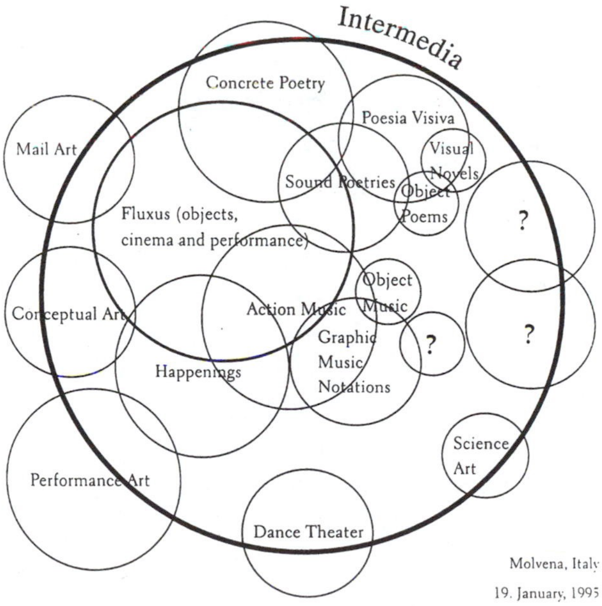

Other genres of intermedia are artistic machines (combining scupture with technology), sound poetry (combining music and literature), and artistically enclosed spaces (combining architecture with music,. sculpture, or painting). It is possible, however, that sometime in the future such intermedia will be considered perfectly usual forms of art and that other intermedia will appear on the continuum of art forms. My own considered opinion (RK) is that, just as collage was the great fertile interart esthetic invention of the early twentieth century, so will intermedia in its various forms come to represent retrospectively the end of the century. My own sense of the larger history of the past forty years is that the radical developments in art came either from purifying the materials of a traditional form (whether printing or music) or from mixing forms. As colorfield painters represented purification, so Robert Rauschenberg explored miscegenation; as Milton Babbitt and Elliott Carter purified, so John Cage pushed his initially musical ideas into other arts.

—With Geof Huth

Dick Higgins. *Intermedia Chart*. Molvena, Italy, 19 January 1993. Courtesy the author.

Interpretation: Higgins, Dick. *Horizons: The Poets and Theory of the Intermedia*. Carbondale: Southern Illinois University Press, 1983; ——. *Modernism since Postmodernism: Essays on Intermedia*. San Diego: San Diego State University Press, 1997; Kostelanetz, Richard. *Metamorphosis in the Arts*. New York: Assembling, 1980.

INTERNATIONAL STYLE

(c. 1920).

Born in Germany, mostly at the BAUHAUS, this kind of architecture was popularized in America, first with the publication of Henry-Russell Hitchcock's and Philip Johnson's book *The International Style* (1932), and then with exhibitions at the MOMA, which became its principal publicist. To quote the cultural historian Russell Lynes, "If few people liked the International Style when it first appeared in America, it was the MOMA that did more than any other institution to bring about its acceptance." With the immigration to the U.S. of Walter Gropius (1883–1969) and MIES VAN DER ROHE, both masters of the mode, the International Style became the dominant architectural fashion, particularly in office buildings, in the 1950s.

Also known as the Functional Style and the Machine Style, International Style stood for six general principles: the marriage of art and the latest technology; geometric CONSTRUCTIVIST forms whose "streamlining" symbolized the spirit of the machine more than intrinsic technological quality; the building as a volume rather than a mass (thus the penchant for glass walls that visually denied a building's massive weight); a rejection of axial symmetry typical of classic cathedrals, in favor of noncentered, asymmetrical regularity, as epitomized by, say, rows of glass walls; the practice of making opposite sides, if not all four sides, resemble one another so that, formally at least, the building has no obvious "front" or "back"; and, finally, a scrupulous absence of surface ornament.

For these reasons, buildings cast in the International Style suggest no-nonsense efficiency and economy, if not a physical environment consonant with both modern technology and bureaucratic ideals, all tempered by geometric grandeur and numerous subtle visual effects produced, for instance, by colors in the glass or intersecting lines and planes.

What was initially called "POSTMODERN" in architecture represented various conscious reactions against the purported sterility of this International Style.

Interpretation: Giedion, Siegfried. *Space, Time and Architecture*. Cambridge: Harvard University Press, 1941; Hitchcock, Henry-Russell, and Philip Johnson. *The International Style* (1932). New York: Norton, 1966; Lynes, Russell. *The Lively Audience*. New York: Harper & Row, 1985; Riley, Terence. *The International Style: Exhibition 15 and the MOMA*. New York: Rizzoli, 1992.

INTERNET

(1969).

The amazing truth is that the Internet began its existence as ARPAnet, a computer network developed for the U.S. Department of Defense's Advanced Research Projects Agency (ARPA) as a prototype of a computer network that couldn't be bombed out of existence. The original idea was that the network would be so large and robust that it could function even after some of its important nodes were destroyed. But the Internet could not stay true to its intended nature. By the late 1980s and then dramatically so in the early 1990s, the Internet became a network for the outsider on the fringe of society. At that time, the prevalent "netiquette" was that the Internet was for ideas and fun, not for financial gain. But that brief pioneering fling with the fringe was quickly overwhelmed by the peddlers, and now our concept of the Internet is primarily that of a giant multi-territorial mall with a quirky little automated encyclopedia thrown into the mix. Regardless, the Internet remains a multifarious presence, providing for both commerce and art. For some types of art, including kinetic poetry, it provides an easy and cheap method of distribution. By the late 1990s, there was a real and perceptible move of North American MICROPRESS away from print media and onto the Internet. We have yet to see what long-term effects this will have on the art that is produced.

—Geof Huth

Bibliography: Cotton, Bob, and Richard Oliver. *The Cyberspace Lexicon: An Illustrated Dictionary of Terms from Multimedia to Virtual Reality*. London: Phaidon Press, 1994; Kelly-Bootle, Stan. *The Computer Contradictionary*. 2d ed. Cambridge: MIT Press, 1995.

INTERNET ART

(1980s).

Artists interested in concepts were the first to use the Internet to create art, because computer technology supported text, a medium they had used extensively before. Art on the Internet has developed in three broad phases. From 1977 to 1984, conceptual artists explored the possibilities of text, asynchronous time and its effects on message-sending, and various properties of place as they related to the network. From 1985 to approximately 1991, after artists had mastered the technology—use of the network itself—its mapping capabilities and its global, borderless properties were explored in terms of performance on-line, in extended narratives and database techniques, and in the use of text to set up special environments and spaces. Finally, with the advent of the Web, artists interested in images, animation, and video joined in to explore all the foregoing, using art's full orchestral possibilities. Additionally, two other general features of art on the Internet emerged: project-based art and network-based art. Project-based art has a duration determined by the length of time the project takes. Network-based art has an open-ended duration and is terminated only when the network structure is eliminated or destroyed. The ebb and flow of interaction, and the growth and contraction of its reach thus become metaphors for the organic process and a major focal point. (See *Art Com Electronic Network*, below.) Most art on the Internet has been project-based, as it has been generally difficult for artists to have sufficient control of the technology to set up very long-term works.

Following is a listing of artists who have done significant work on the Internet, arranged chronologically by date of their earliest works. Where appropriate, URLs (Universal Resource Locators, a type of computer addressing that allows users to find information on-line anywhere in the world) are included. This may cause problems over time, because servers fold, artists move, and so move their Web pages to other servers, and so on. Still, since the works cited are sometimes only visible on the Web, latest addresses are included for the sake of being as useful as possible.

Carl Loeffler was one of the very earliest organizers of telecommunications events. Always a collaborator, he worked with Willoughby Sharp, Liza Bear, and Sharon Grace to realize *Send/Receive* in 1977. In 1985, he founded the *Art Com Electronic Network* with Fred Truck. In 1991, working at Carnegie Mellon University, he successfully realized a form of networked virtual reality. Loeffler's main contribution to art on the Internet has been his organizing energy and his knack for accessing resources to provide an environment for others to do their work in.

Roy Ascott always seemed to be a step ahead of everyone in anticipating directions art would take on the net. Correctly intuiting the performance potential inherent in the Internet, he launched *La Plissure du Texte: A Planetary Fairytale* in 1983. In this work, nodes (practically speaking, anyone participating in the project became a node in the Net) represented various fairytale characters, and through interaction, developed a story. Ascott's 1989 work, *Aspects of Gaia: Digital Pathways across the Whole Earth* featured an Upper Level, on which viewers could receive, change, and send incoming messages on horizontal screens. On the Lower Level, lying on an electronic carriage, the viewer passed through a long tunnel carrying overhead LED messages relayed from the worldwide network. *Aspects of Gaia* echoed other works of the period which were making use of the network's ability to penetrate the Iron Curtain and reach heretofore unreachable countries. In fact, as this work was presented at Ars Elekctronika in Austria in 1989, the Iron Curtain was crashing down.

Fred Truck (1946) has put his art on the Internet since 1982, when he assembled information about performance art and artists, created a large database called *The Electric Bank,* and made the information available gratis on-line. As cofounder and programmer of the *Art Com Electronic Network* (1985) he continued and expanded these efforts, which culminated in the *E-Mall* (1990), an on-line shopping mall he programmed in collaboration with Carl Loeffler and Anna Couey. This shopping environment, created entirely with text, could be navigated aisle by aisle; purchases were tracked, and checkouts were made. While this was a commercial enterprise, it was also viewed as art and performance because much attention was paid to creating an environment with its layout and design, so the performer, the shopper, would be comfortable in this new territory. In 1998, Truck launched *The Badge of Quality* Web pages, which tell the story through interaction, animation, sound, and text of the fictional Badge of Quality Corporation and its spokesperson, Mr. Milk Bottle.

—Fred Truck

Web Site: http://www.fredtruck.com/frontend.html

Art Com Electronic Network (ACEN). The *Art Com Electronic Network* was cofounded in 1985 by Carl Loeffler and Fred Truck. They were soon joined by Anna Couey. Unlike all other artists' network projects of limited duration, *ACEN* was conceived of as open-ended in duration because the network obtained space on the WELL (Whole Earth 'Lectronic Link), Stuart Brand's computer conferencing service which was an extension of his *Whole Earth Catalog* activities. *ACEN* was officially opened to the public on April 15, 1986 and quickly became involved in electronically publishing *Métier*, a Canada-based art publication, and distributing art projects such as Judy Malloy's *Bad Information Base* and John Cage's *The First Meeting Of The Satie Society*. In 1986, *ACEN* also participated in *The Planetary Network*, Roy Ascott's Internet project for the Venice Biennale.

Judy Malloy's work uses fundamental programming techniques, such as randomization and database structuring in conjunction with carefully orchestrated texts to create a state-of-mind image that can be read sequentially as well as by keyword-searching. Malloy is one of the very few artists who has managed to issue the same work in both CD-ROM and network formats, because the network is a physical extension of her basic ideas. Although Malloy's writing on the net can be conventionally described as hypertext, she has combined database and narrative and coined the term "narrabase" to define her work. *The Roar of Destiny Emanated from the Refrigerator* is Malloy's most technically and visually sophisticated work for the Web to date, while carrying on her hallmark tradition of intense, compact writing.

Web Site: http://www.well.com/user/jmalloy/control.html

Anna Couey, in addition to her work with the *ACEN*, has realized telecommunications art on her own. Beginning in 1992 with *Cultures in Cyberspace* (an open-participation virtual panel organized to address the impact of cyberspace on distinct cultural groups and vice versa, run across five different networking systems), she quickly showed an interest in the political, and how the Internet can reach across geographic and cultural boundaries. Additional projects include *Virtual Culture* (1990), *Virtual Country* (1990), and *Imagining the Information Age* (1993).

Fred Forest is best known for his 1995 Internet work called *Parcelle/Réseau*. *Parcelle/Réseau* was auctioned at Druout, a gallery, by Maître Binoche, an auctioneer. The art work was present only on the Internet. What was actually sold was an address on the Internet, which gave only the buyer access to the work. The buyer of the address could then use it and the work contained there at his or her discretion for private or public good. Prints of the work found at the address could also be made and distributed by the owner, who thereby would become a publisher. Fred Forest has pioneered a number of works similar to this one, such as *Video-Portrait of a Collector in Real Time* (1974), *The Artistic Square Meter* (1978), and *The Lost Work of Art* (1990), all of which involved auction sales. Forest established the notion of the buyer becoming publisher through the Internet.

Web Site: http://www.monaco.mc/exhib/territories/0gb.html

Eduardo Kac is a longtime worker in a variety of network technologies, such as fax, slow-scan TV, and videotex, an early form of text transmission using cable TV technology rather than computers. Kac's project-based work with the Internet is notable for its use of telepresence. Through the net he gives the user visual and sonic input from a remote site. In *Rara Avis* (1996), users experience an aviary from the point of view of a telerobotic macaw. In *Ornitorrinco, the Webot* (1996), users inhabited the perceptions of the webot, which shared a nest with two turkeys. A webot is, in this case, a point-of-view computer construct governing what users see on their monitors.

Web Site: http://www.ekac.org

Bibliography: *Connectivity: Art And Interactive Telecommunications*, ed. Roy Ascott and Carl Eugene Loeffler. *Leonardo,* Vol. 24, No. 2, 1991; Gidney, Eric. *The artists's* [sic] *use of telecommunications*. Paddington [NSW] Australia: City Art Institute, 1984; *Im Netz Der Systeme: Für Eine Interaktive Kunst: Ars Electronica. Linz*, ed. Gerhard Johann Lischka and Peter Weibel. *Kunstforum*, no. 103, September/October, 1989. Cologne: Kunstforum International; Kac, Eduardo. *Holopoetry: Essays, Manifestoes, Critical and Theoretical Writings*. Lexington: New Media Editions, 1995; *"New media poetry": Poetic Innovation and New Technologies*. *Visible language*, v. 30, no. 2. Providence: Rhode Island School of Design, 1996; Grundmann, Heidi, ed. *Art Telecommunication*. Vancouver, BC: The Western Front, 1984.

IONESCO, Eugène

(26 November 1912–28 March 1994).

Born in Rumania of a French mother, Ionesco grew up in both his parents' countries before moving permanently to France in 1938. Most famous for his plays, he has also written fiction and criticism. Ionesco's play *The Chairs* (1952) is the epitome of the THEATRE OF THE ABSURD. Ionesco also has a keen ear for authoritarian lingo that, for all its fashionable propriety, does not make sense. This example comes from *The Lesson* (1951):

> That which distinguishes them, I repeat, is their striking resemblance which makes it so hard to distinguish them from each other—I'm speaking of the neo-Spanish languages which one is able to distinguish from one another, however, only thanks to their distinctive characteristics, absolutely indisputable proofs of their extraordinary resemblance, which renders indisputable their common origin, and which, at the same time, differentiates them profoundly—through the continuation of the distinctive traits which I've just cited.

And, of course, the student responds: "Oooh! Ye-e-e-e-s-s-s. Professor!" The tragedy of his career was that nothing Ionesco had written after the early 1950s, in any genre, equalled those few short plays for satirical edge and weighty originality.

Drama: *Four Plays* [including *The Chairs: A Tragic Farce; The Bald Soprano, Anti-Play; The Lesson, A Comic Drama; Jack, or The Submission, A Naturalistic Comedy*]. Trans. Donald M. Allen. New York: Grove, 1958; *Three Plays: Amédée, A Comedy; The New Tenant; Victims of Duty: A Pseudo-Drama*. New York: Grove, 1958; *The Killer and Other Plays*. New York: Grove, 1960; *A Stroll in the Art & Frenzy for Two, or More: Two Plays*. New York: Grove, 1965; *Hunger and Thirst and Other Plays*. New York: Grove, 1969; *Killing Game* (1970). Trans. Helen Gary Bishop. New York: Grove, 1974.

Fiction: *The Colonel's Photograph and Other Stories*. London: Faber, 1967; *The Hermit*. New York: Seaver, 1980.

Essays: *Notes and Counter Notes; Writings on the Theatre*. Trans. Donald Watson. New York: Grove, 1964; *Present Past, Past Present: A Personal Memoir* (1972). Trans. Helen R. Lane. New York: Da Capo, 1997.

Biography: Hayman, Ronald. *Eugène Ionesco*. London: Heinemann, 1972.

Interpretation: Lamont, Rosette C., & Melvin Friedman. *Two Faces of Ionesco*. Troy, NY: Whitston, 1978; Lamont, Rosette C. ed. *Ionesco: A Collection of Critical Essays*. Englewood Cliffs, NJ: Prentice–Hall, 1973.

IRCAM

See **BOULEZ, Pierre**.

IRELAND, Patrick

See **O'DOHERTY, Brian**.

IRWIN, Robert

(12 September 1928).

The classic Robert Irwin work, *No Title* (1967), is a white circular plate, five feet in diameter, mounted from behind to stand several feet away from the background wall. When illuminated by four spotlights distributed to the corners of a rectangle in front of the disc, an illusion is formed on the background wall of four overlapping discs, creating a three-dimensional tension between the original and its shadows, as well as faint concentric bands of color on the real disc's face. The supporting wall, the surrounding space, and the quality of the light all become as important as the disc. Because he regarded perception as the principal subject of art, he favored circumstances with little substance. "Inquiry" is a favorite work for his own activity. In 1992 at New York's Pace Gallery, Irwin made an untitled installation where one initially sees a black rectangle behind several layers of rectangular gauze. As the illumination in the spaces between the gauze changes color, so does the black. Because the spectator is allowed to go between the layers, he or she can look back on the piece in different ways. In discussing Irwin, as well as his colleague JAMES TURRELL, simple descriptions scarcely convey the remarkable experience of light transformations, apart from any object. For obvious reasons, photographs of Irwin's art are rarely sufficient.

Visual Art: *No Title*, 1967; *No Title* (Ace Gal. L.A.), 1972; *No Title* (Pace Gal., New York), 1973; *No Title*, (Mizuno Gal. L.A.), 1973; *Column*, 1973; *No Title* (Wright State University, Dayton, OH), 1974.

Writings: *Being and Circumstances: Notes Toward a Conditional Art*. Larkspur Landing, CA: Lapis, 1985.

Installations: *Eye Level Wall Division*, Pace Gal., 1973; *Three-Plane Triangulation*, University California-Berkeley Art Museum, 1979; *Floating Hallway*, San Francisco Museum of Modern Art, 1985; *Nine Spaces Nine Trees*, Seattle, 1983; *Pure Space*, Los Angeles Museum of Contemporary Art, 1990; *Sentinel Plaza*, Pasadena, 1990.

Biography: Wechsler, Lawrence. *Seeing and Forgetting the Name of the Thing Once Seen: A Life of the Contemporary Artist Robert Irwin*. Berkeley: University of California, 1982.

Exhibition Catalog: Compton, Michael. *Larry Bell, Robery Irwin, Doug Wheeler*. London: Tate, 1970; Feinberg, Jean E. *Perceiving the Garden: Robery Irwin at Wave Hill*. Bronx, NY: Wave Hill, 1987; Ferguson, Russell, ed. *Robert Irwin*. Los Angeles: The Museum of Contemporary Art, 1993; *Robert Irwin*. Madrid: Museo Nacional Centro de Arte Reina Sofia, 1995.

IVES, Charles

(20 October 1874–19 May 1954).

It is perhaps typically American that an avant-garde composer so neglected in his own time should be so widely acclaimed by later generations. Though Ives's works were so rarely played during his lifetime that he never heard some of his major pieces, nearly all of his music is currently available on disc; and though he taught no pupils and founded no school, Ives is generally considered the progenitor of nearly everything distinctly American in American music. He was not an intentional avant-gardist, conscientiously aiming for innovation, but a modest spare-time composer (who spent most of his days as an insurance salesman and then as a long-term convalescent).

A well-trained musician, who worked as a church organist upon graduating from college, Ives was essentially a great inventor with several major musical patents to his name. While still in his teens, he developed his own system of polytonality—the technique of writing for two or more keys simultaneously. In a piece composed when he was twenty (*Song for Harvest Season*), he assigned four different keys to four instruments. Ives was the first modern composer who consistently didn't resolve his dissonances. Many contemporary composers have followed Ives's *The Unanswered Question* (1908) in strategically distributing musicians over a physical space, so that the acoustic source of the music affects not only theatricality but the sounds actually heard. For the *Concord Sonata*, composed between 1909 and 1915 (and arguably his masterpiece), Ives invented the tone cluster, where the pianist uses either his forearm or a block of wood to sound simultaneously whole groups, if not octaves, of notes.

He originated the esthetics of POP ART, for Ives, like CLAES OLDENBURG and ROBERT INDIANA after him, drew quotations from mundane culture—hymn tunes, patriotic ditties, etc.—and stitched them into his modernist artistic fabric. Though other composers had incorporated "found" sounds prior to Ives, he was probably the first to allow a quotation to stand out dissonantly from the context, as well as the first, like the Pop Artists after him, to distort a popular quotation into a comic semblance of the original. Just as Claes Oldenburg's famous *Giant Hamburger* (1962)—seven feet in diameter, made of canvas, and stuffed with kapok—creates a comic tension with our memory of the original model, so Ives, decades before, evoked a similar effect in his *Variations on a National Hymn* ["America"] (1891, composed when he was seventeen!). In juxtaposing popular tunes like "Columbia, the Gem of the Ocean" in the same musical field with allusions to Beethoven's *Fifth Symphony*, Ives employed another Pop strategy to create a distinctly American style suggesting that both classical music and popular, both formal and informal cultures, are equally immediate and perhaps equally relevant.

Other Ivesian musical innovations include polyrhythms—where various sections of the orchestra play in wholly different meters, often under the batons of separate conductors, all to create multiple cross-rhythms of great intricacy. In his rhythmic freedom, as well as his unashamed atonality, Ives clearly fathered the chaotic language of modern music, a tradition that runs through HENRY COWELL and early EDGARD VARÈSE to JOHN CAGE. Indeed, Ives anticipated Cage by inventing INDETERMINANCY—where the scripts offered the musicians are so indefinite at crucial points that they could not possibly play exactly the same sounds in successive performances. In *The Unanswered Question*, Ives further discouraged musical unanimity by placing three separate groups of musicians in such a way that one could not necessarily see the others.

As one of the first modern composers to develop a distinctly eccentric music notation, Ives anticipated contemporary composers' practices of using graphs, charts, and abstract patterns—manuscripts that resemble everything but traditional musical scores—to make their works available to others. He also wrote notes that he knew could not be played, such as a 1/ 1,024 note in the *Concord Sonata*, followed by the words "Play as fast as you can." Indeed, Ives's scripts were so unusually written, as well as misplaced and scrambled in big notebooks, that editors have labored valiantly to reconstruct definitive versions of his major pieces, some of which had their debuts long after his death. The independent scholar Maynard Solomon (1930), among others, has questioned the dates commonly attributed to some Ives compositions.

There is a remarkable conceptual similarity between Ives and GERTRUDE STEIN, who, born in America in the same year, was as radically original in her art as Ives was in his. While we can now identify what each of them did quite precisely, given our awareness of the avant-garde traditions to which they significantly contributed, it is not so clear to us now what either of them thought they were doing—what exactly was on their minds when they made their most radical moves—so different was their art from even innovative work that was done before or around them.

Musical Compositions: *The Unanswered Question*, 1906; *Sonata No. 2, "Concord,"* for piano, 1910–15; Symphony No. 2, 1900–01; *"Holidays" Symphony*, 1912; *Three Places in New England* (aka Orchestral Set No. 1), 1908–14; Symphony No. 4, 1909–16. (Since most of Ives's works were premiered long after they were written, dates are necessarily unverifiable. A 26-page small-print list of other Ives compositions appears in *The New Grove Twentieth-Century American Masters*. New York: Norton, 1977.)

Books: *114 Songs*. New York: Privately published, 1922; *Essays Before a Sonata & Other Writings*. Selected and ed. Howard Boatwright. New York: Norton, 1962; *Charles E. Ives Memos*. Ed. John Kirkpatrick. New York: Norton, 1972.

Recordings: *Concord Sonata*, John Kirkpatrick (Columbia o.p.); Gilbert Kalish (Elektra/Nonesuch); *Songs,* Greg Smith Singers, Ithaca College Choir, American Symphony Orchestra, cond. Leopold Stokowski (Sony); Dora Ohrenstein, Phillip Bush, 4 vols (Albany); *Charles Ives: Piano Pieces.* Herbert Henck & Deborah Richards. Wergo; *Sonatas for Violin & Piano, 1–4,* Gregory Fulkerson & Robert Shannon, Bridge; *Symphony No. 2.* New York Philharmonic, cond. Leonard Bernstein (Sony Classical); *Symphony No. 4.* American Symphony Orchestra, cond. Leopold Stokowski (Sony); Three Quarter-Tone Pieces for Two Pianos (1921), *American Festival of Microtonal Music* (Newport Classics); *Unanswered Question*, *Central Park in the Dark*, *Three Places in New England*, Symphony No. 2, St. Louis Symphony, cond. Leonard Slatkin (RCA).

Biography: Block, Geoffrey. *Charles Ives: A Bio-Bibliography*. Westport, CT: Greenwood, 1988; Perlis, Vivian. *Charles Ives Remembered: An Oral History*. New Haven: Yale University Press, 1974; Rossiter, Frank R. *Charles Ives and His America*. New York: Liveright, 1975; Swofford, Jan. *Charles Ives: A Life with Music*. New York: Norton, 1996.

Interpretation: Block, Geoffrey, and J. Peter Burkholder, eds. *Charles Ives and the Classical Tradition*. New Haven: Yale University Press, 1996; Burkholdler, J. Peter. *Charles Ives: The Ideas Behind the Music*. New Haven: Yale University Press, 1985; ——. *All Made of Tunes: Charles Ives and the Uses of Musical Borrowing*. New Haven: Yale University Press, 1995; ——. ed. *Charles Ives and his World*. Princeton: Princeton University Press, 1996; Nicholls, David. *American Experimental Music, 1890–1940*. Cambridge, England & New York: Cambridge University Press, 1990; Reed, Joseph W. *Three American Originals: John Ford, William Faulkner, and Charles Ives*. Middletown: Wesleyan University Press, 1984; Starr, Lawrence. *A Union of Diversities: Style in the Music of Charles Ives*. New York: Schirmer, 1992.

Bibliography: De Lerma, Doninique-René. *Charles Ives, 1874–1954: A Bibliography of His Music*. Kent: Kent State University Press, 1970; Kirkpatrick, John. *A Temporary Mimeographed Catalogue of the Music Manuscripts and Related Materials of Charles Edward Ives*. New Haven: Library of the Yale School of Music, 1960.

JAKOBSON, Roman

See **FORMALISM (RUSSIAN)**.

JANCO, Marcel

(24 May 1895–21 April 1984).

Born in Bucharest, Janco happened to be studying architecture and painting in Zurich in 1915, at the beginnings of the DADA movement, joining HUGO BALL, RICHARD HUELSENBECK, and his fellow Rumanian, TRISTAN TZARA. A few years before he had co-founded a literary journal, *Simbolul* (The Symbol) with the latter, its title reflecting an esthetic trend popular in European literature at the time. While a DADA active in Zurich, Janco made paintings and reliefs that are still regarded as his strongest visual art, as well as neo-African masks and woodcut illustrations to a Tzara poem. He is remembered primarily for his 1916 painting of the CABARET VOLTAIRE, the initial Dada venue. Going to Paris in 1919, Janco soon broke with Tzara over politics and returned to Rumania, where he founded *Contimporanul* (1922–40) and worked as an architect. Meanwhile, nearly all of Janco's Dada work disappeared, including the Voltaire painting mentioned above, which was last exhibited in his native Bucharest, to be remembered only in photographs or, less fortunately, exhibition catalogs and lists. (Only one early Dada work is known to survive, *Bal à Zurich*.) By 1941 Janco was safely in Palestine, where he remained until his death, in a country so inhospitable to avant-garde art (in contrast to avant-garde science, say) that its more pioneering creative personalities necessarily make their careers abroad, much as comparable Americans did in the nineteenth century.

Selected Works: *Relief au Miroir*, 1916; *Blanc Sur Blanc*, 1917; *Bal à Zurich*, 1917 (Jerusalem: Israel Museum); *Architecture*, 1917; *La secrure*, 1918; *Coup De Dé, Zürich*, 1919; *Collage pour Jean Arp*, 1920; *Fugue Majeure*, 1950; *Fugue Formation*, 1950; *Tour et Muraille*, 1960; *Nouveau Trophée*, 1960; *Oasis-Couleur*, 1970.

Architecture: Janco, Marcel, and his brother. *Wexler House*, Bucharest 1931.

Interview: Naumann, Francis M. "Janco/Dada, An Interview with Marcel Janco," *Arts Magazine*, 57/3 (November 1982).

Exhibition Catalogs: *Dada, documents et telmoignages, 1916–1958.* Tel Aviv: Musée TelAviv, 1958; *Marcel Janco*. Paris: Denise René Gallery, 1963.

Bibliography: Dachy, Marc. *The Dada Movement*. New York: Rizzoli, 1990; Yoffe, A. B. *Marcel Janco*. Tel Aviv: Masadah, 1982; Seiwert, Harry. *Marcel Janco*. Frankfurt am Main & New York: P. Lang, 1993; "Marcel Janco." In *Dada Zurich: A Clown's Game from Nothing*. New York: G. K. Hall, 1997.

JANECEK, Gerald

(15 August 1945).

One of the few full-time academics to write successfully on avant-garde subjects, he authored *The Look of Russian Lit-*

erature (1984), which documents the development of visual devices mostly in FUTURIST writing of 1900–30. In contrast to previous commentators, such as Vladimir Markov (of *Russian Futurism: A History*, 1968), who tended to favor the poetry of VELIMIR KHLEBNIKOV, Janecek concentrates upon the most radical figure, ALEKSEI KRUCHONYKH, finding more sense than anyone else previously unearthed in his innovations and extravagances. What makes Janecek's avant-garde criticism special is his willingness to understand the most extreme: not only the most advanced individual in a group but his or her furthest departures. His principal sequel deals thoroughly with ZAUM, or "transrational language," which Markov before him called "the most extreme of all Futurist achievements."

Bibliography: *The Look of Russian Literature*. Princeton: Princeton University Press, 1984; *Zaum: The Transrational Poetry of Russian Futurism*. San Diego: San Diego State University Press, 1996. (Portions from this can be found at www.thing.net/~grist/l&d/kruch/lkrucht1.htm.); ——, trans. *Kotik Letaev*, by Andrei Bely. Ann Arbor, MI: Ardis, 1971.

JARGON

In critical writing, the function of jargon is not to illuminate but to suggest that its author is "verbally correct." So, should you come across a piece of criticism filled with imposing terms (such as "ambiguity," "tension," and "metonymy" in days gone by; "dialectical," "signifier," "disruption," "confrontation," "contradiction," "deconstruction," "difference" [sic], "logocentrism," "asymptotic," "indexical," "decentering," and the like nowadays), to all appearances used in unfathomable ways, do not worry and, most of all, don't be intimidated (unless you're a student or an untenured professor, whose function in the academic hierarchy is to be predisposed to intimidation). You're not supposed to understand anything, but merely to be impressed by the author's modish choice of lingo, much as, in other contexts, you might be awed by his or her choice of dress, shoes, car, or something else superficial.

It was the American sociologist Thorstein Veblen (1857–1929) who pointed out a century ago that inefficient expression is meant to reflect "the industrial exemption of the speaker. The advantage of the accredited locutions lies in their reputability; they are reputable because they are cumbrous and out of date, and therefore argue waste of time and exemption from the use and the need of direct and forcible speech." That is to say, you must be economically comfortable to talk that way and, by doing so, are explicitly announcing that you are. The reason why Leftish jargon amuses working people is that they know instantly, as a measure of their lower economic class, what its real purpose is.

Bibliography: Veblen, Thorstein. *The Theory of the Leisure Class* (1899). New York: New American Library, 1953.

JARRY, Alfred

(8 September 1873–1 November 1907).

An eccentric's eccentric, who lived modestly and needed collegial support to make his works known, Jarry wrote plays and fiction so different from the late Victorian conventions that they are commonly regarded as having anticipated SURREALISM, DADA, the THEATRE OF THE ABSURD, JAMES JOYCE, and much else, which is to say that Jarry was a slugger in spite of himself. His play *Ubu Roi* (King Ubu, 1896) opens with the word *Merdre*, which is customarily translated as "Shittr," proclaiming from the start its ridicule of bourgeois false propriety. The freewheeling movement from line to line, and scene to scene, makes it different from any plays written before. Yet more innovative, to my mind, are Jarry's novels, such as *Gestes et Opinions du Dr Faustroll, Pataphysicien* (1911), and *Le Surmâle (The Supermale*, 1902), in which ridiculousness is raised to a higher level. The former begins as a satire on Lawrence

Sterne's *Tristram Shandy* (1759–67), if that is possible, but it ends in the modern world with pseudo-mathematics in an extraordinary chapter "Concerning the Surface of God," which concludes: "GOD IS THE TANGENTIAL POINT BETWEEN ZERO AND INFINITY."

Though Jarry was a limited writer, the image of the man and his work had a great influence upon his avant-garde betters; in this respect, he resembles his near-contemporary compatriot, RAYMOND ROUSSEL, and his successor, ANTONIN ARTAUD. (Another useful divide within avant-garde consciousness is separating those who treasure Jarry from those who worship Artaud—those valuing invention over madness.) After initiating a *COLLÈGE DE 'PATAPHYSIQUE*, Jarry died young of tubercular meningitis aggravated by alcoholism, which was in its time no more avant-garde, alas, than drug abuse is today.

Works: *Ubu Roi*, 1896; *Ubu Enchaîné*, 1900; *Gestes et Opinions du Docteur Faustroll, Pataphysicien*, 1911; *The Supermale* (*Le Surmâle*, 1902). Trans. Barbara Wright. New York: New Directions, 1977.

Anthology: Shattuck, Roger, and Simon Watson Taylor, eds. *Selected Works of Alfred Jarry*. New York: Grove, 1965; *Ceasar Antichrist: The Collected Works of Alfred Jarry*. Trans. by Antony Melville. London: Atlas, 1992.

Interpretation: Beaumont, Keith. *A Critical and Biographical Study*. New York: St. Martin's Press, 1984; Shattuck, Roger. *The Banquet Years*. New York: Harper, 1958.

Website:
http://www.ukans.edu/~sma/almanac/almanac.htm

JAZZ

(c. 1885).

Arising from obscure origins in the American South, this indigenous music first became prominent in New Orleans at the beginning of the twentieth century. While reflecting African and African-American concepts of alternative rhythm and group participation, early jazz initially followed black gospel music in observing European harmonies. Nonetheless, other musical strategies seem peculiar to jazz in its many forms: melodic improvisation within a predetermined harmonic range; continuous harmonies either within a solo instrument or a backup band; and certain kinds of instrumentation and thus timbre and intonation. Even when adopted by musicians other than African-Americans, such as BIX BEIDERBECKE, a master improvising cornetist from Iowa, or Jewish Klezmer musicians, the result is called jazzy—or, in the Klezmer example, "Jewish jazz." Though many prominent jazz musicians had compositional careers, jazz has remained essentially a performer's music.

Avant-garde jazz is the fringe that was initially unacceptable because of formal deviations, beginning historically with LOUIS ARMSTRONG's transcending the piano-based ragtime predominant between 1900 and 1920 by featuring the trumpet as a solo instrument. This departure created the foundation for the "big bands" of the 1930s that featured brass instruments customarily played in harmonic unison. The principal alternative to this style came in the 1940s with the dissonance cultivated by CHARLIE PARKER in smaller bands. Behind him came in the next decades ORNETTE COLEMAN and ALBERT AYLER, among others, who eschewed any metronomic beat while often playing as rapidly as possible.

The development of jazz is [to my editor, Richard Carlin] a paradigm for American avant-garde growth. Instead of moving linearly from folk blues to Dixieland jazz through big band jazz to BEBOP and FREE JAZZ to jazz/rock fusion to new acoustic jazz (in emulation of a European model of avant-garde development), jazz both moves forward and looks backwards. Although the heyday of New Orleans jazz was the 1920s, New Orleans jazz continues to be played today, both by musicians raised in this style and by others who emulate it. In this sense, each new style does not replace the old ways, but rather complements them. [RK would be remiss if he didn't acknowledge his disagreement with this formulation.]

From the beginning of the 1920s, classically trained composers could hardly resist the influence of jazz, as many of them incorporated one or another jazz device (or, sometimes, a live jazz musician) into their own works. Though such fusions are sometimes hailed for representing a "third stream" between classical music and jazz, that epithet has never had much acceptance with either the jazz public or that devoted to modernist classical music. The real influence of jazz on classical avant-garde music lies in the acceptance of kinds of rhythms, beginning with syncopation, indigenous to North America. (Even today, recordings of some American classical music made in Europe reveal that the otherwise conscientious musicians are missing rhythmic deviations more prevalent in America than in Europe.)

One recent myth that must be disspelled is that jazz is an African-American monopoly. Elsewhere in this book is an entry on Bix Biederbecke, whose improvisations represented jazz at its best. Nicolas Slonimsky, from the perspective of classical music, thinks that whites in the 1920s "developed a modern type of jazz dsigned for concert performance. Among them were Benny Goodman, Woody Herman, Guy Lombardo, and Paul Whiteman. The most important contribution to concert jazz was made by George Gershwin, whose *Rhapsody in Blue* became a modern classic." Few jazz keyboardists have been as brilliant as George Shearing (1919), who was born blind in the Battersea section of London. The first great jazz guitarist was a Belgian gypsy named Django Reinhardt (1910–53).

A subsidiary effect of jazz's success was new kinds of dancing, not only between couples in social situations but on a stage, beginning with percussive tap dancing that complements jazz to the same degree that classical music complements ballet. Within this general rubric of jazz dance are a wide variety of alternatives with unique names, such as Black Bottom, Shimmy, Charleston, Cakewalk, Strut Step, Hucklebuck, Mashed Potato, about which an encyclopedia could no doubt be written. Marshall and Jean Stearns' *Jazz Dance* (1968) includes graphic notations documenting how various parts of the body should be positioned for each dance, in addition to a list of films and kinescopes dating back to the end of the nineteenth century.

One interesting measure of jazz's cultural success is that, since 1950, most purportedly comprehensive histories of American music acknowledge jazz.

—with Richard Carlin

Bibliography: Berendt, Joachim. *The Jazz Book: From Ragtime to Fusion and Beyond*. 5th ed. Brooklyn, NY: Lawrence Hill, 1992; Gridley, Mark C. *Jazz Styles: History and Analysis*. 3d ed. Englewood Cliffs, NJ: Prentice-Hall, 1987; Hitchcock, H. Wiley. *Music in the United States* (1969). 3d ed. Englewood Cliffs, NJ: Prentice-Hall, 1988; Schuller, Gunther. *Early Jazz: Its Roots and Musical Development* (1968). New York: Oxford University Press, 1986; Stearns, Marshall & Jean. *Jazz Dance* (1968). New York: Da Capo, 1994; Such, David G. *Avant-Garde Jazz Musicians*. Iowa City: University of Iowa Press, 1997; Williams, Martin T., ed. *The Art of Jazz*. New York: Oxford University Press, 1960.

JOHNS, Jasper

(15 May 1930).

Though he was initially paired with his friend ROBERT RAUSCHENBERG, who is five years his senior, Johns is a different sort of artist, concerned less with exploring unfamiliar materials than with creating objects that pose esthetic questions. In looking at his early and prototypical *Target with Four Faces* (1955), one cannot help but ask: Is this a replica of a target? A collection of concentric circles? Or something else? What relationship do those four sculpted bottoms of heads (noses and mouths, to be precise) have to the two-dimensional picture? Why is the target-image represented so realistically and yet the heads so surrealisti-

Jaspar Johns preparing for his exhibit at the Whitney Museum, 14 October 1977. Copyright © Fred W. McDarrah.

cally? Is there some symbolism here, or do all meanings exist within the picture? "I thought he was doing three things," JOHN CAGE once wrote, "five things he was doing escaped my notice." By painting a realistic image without a background, Johns followed JACKSON POLLOCK in abolishing the discrepancy between image and field that is the core of traditional representational art, again raising the question of whether the target image was a mechanical copy of the original target, or a nonrepresentational design (and what in this context would be the difference anyway?). Later Johns works develop this love of images and objects unfamiliar to painting, as well as displaying his taste for ambiguity, puzzle, and enigma. Given such a high level of exploratory richness, it is not surprising that the first major critic of his work should have been Leo Steinberg (1921), an art history professor whose forte has been the exhaustive examination of meanings available in a single picture. Johns's work is generating a secondary literature approaching in size that devoted to MARCEL DUCHAMP, so that even catalogs accompanying his exhibitions physically resemble thick books.

Select Paintings: *Target with Four Faces*, 1955; *Green Target*, 1955; *Three Flags*, 1958; *False Start*, 1959; *According to What?* 1964; *Flag*, 1965; *Scent*, 1973–74; *Between the Clock and the Bed*, 1981; *Perilous Night*, 1982; *Racing Thoughts*, 1983; *The Seasons*, 1985–86.

Select Sculptures: *The Critic Smiles*, 1959; *Painted Bronze*, 1960.

Exhibition Catalogs: Solomon, Alan R. *Jasper Johns*. New York: Jewish Museum, 1964; Goldman, Judith. *JJ: 17*

Monotypes. West Islip, NY: ULAE, 1982; Castleman, Riva. *JJ: A Print Retrospective*. New York: MOMA, 1986; *Foirades/Fizzles: Echo and Allusion in the Art of Jasper Johns*. Los Angeles: Wright Art Gallery: University of California, 1987; Rosenthal, Mark. *JJ: Work Since 1974*. Philadelphia: Philadelphia Museum of Art, 1988; Rosenthal, Nan, and Ruth E. Fine. *The Drawings of JJ*. Washington, DC: National Gallery of Art, 1990; *JJ: Printed Symbols*. Ed. Phil Freshman. Minneapolis, MN: Walker Art Center, 1990; Bernstein, Roberta. *JJ: The Seasons*. New York: Brooke Alexander, 1991; *JJ /35 Years/Leo Castelli*. Ed. Susan Brundage. New York: Leo Castelli Gallery, 1993.

Interpretation: Bernstein, Roberta. *Jasper Johns' Paintings and Sculptures 1954–194: The Changing Focus of the Eye*. Ann Arbor, MI: UMI Research, 1985; *Jasper Johns*. New York: Rizzoli, 1992; Crichton, Michael. *Jasper Johns* (1977). Revised & expanded ed. New York: Abrams, 1994; Johnson, Jill. *Jasper Johns: Privileged Information*. New York: Thames & Hudson, 1996; Kozloff, Max. *Jasper Johns*. New York: Abrams, 1967; Orton, Fred. *Figuring Jasper Johns*. Cambridge: Harvard University Press, 1994; Shapiro, David. *Jasper Johns: Drawings 1954–1984*. New York: Abrams, 1984; Steinberg, Leo. "Jasper Johns: The First Seven Years of His Art" (1962). In *Other Criteria*. New York: Oxford University Press, 1972.

Catalog Raisonné: *The Prints of Jasper Johns, 1960–93: A Catalog Raisonné*. Text by Richard Field. West Islip, NY: Universal Limited Art Editions, 1994.

JOHNSON, B. S.

(5 February 1933–13 November 1973; b. Bryan Stanley J.). The most experimental British novelist of his generation, Johnson began with *Traveling People* (1963), in which narrative gives way to impressionistic stream-of-consciousness, and *Albert Angelo* (1964), which, telling of an impecunious architect working as a substitute teacher, includes a section where spoken thoughts on the right side of the page become a counterpoint to the monologue on the left-hand side. Pages 149–53 of the latter book contain a hole that is purportedly caused by the knife that killed Christopher Marlowe (how British!). "Why do the vast majority (it must be over 95 per cent at a reasonable guess) of novelists writing now still tell stories," Johnson asked in *Books and Bookmen* (1970), "still write as though *Ulysses* (let alone *The Unnameable)* had never happened?" Johnson's greatest departure was *The Unfortunates* (1967), which came in a box whose opening and closing chapters were fixed, while the remaining twenty-five were loose, to be read and reread in any order.

Johnson also published poems and stories, in addition to making a film that won several prizes, *You're Human Like the Rest of Them* (1968). Of the ten books he published before his suicide, only one, his first collection of poems, was republished in America in his lifetime.

Novels: *Traveling People*. London: Constable, 1963; *Albert Angelo*. London: Constable, 1964; *Trawl*. London: Secker & Warburg, 1966; *The Unfortunates*. London: Secker & Warburg, 1969; *House Mother Normal: A Geriatric Comedy* (1971). New York: New Directions, 1986; *Christie Malry's Own Double Entry* (1973). New York: New Directions, 1985.

Short Stories: *Statement Against Corpses*, with Zulfikar Ghose. London: Constable, 1964.

Prose: *Aren't You Rather Young To Be Writing Your Memoirs?* London: Hutchinson, 1973.

Poems: *Poems*. New York: Chilmark, 1964; *Poems Two*. London: Trigram, 1972.

Film Script in Verse: *You're Human Like the Rest of Them* (1967). In *New English Dramatists 14*. Harmondsworth: Penguin, 1970.

JOHNSON, Bengt Emil

(12 December 1936).

His *Hyllningarna* (Greetings, 1963) is said to be the first book of CONCRETE POETRY in Sweden, containing a "Homage to John Cage" (1962) that, as miscellaneous words typed to the edge of the page, reflects an accurate understanding of Cagean esthetics rare at the time. While Johnson's later poetry has moved closer to traditional lyricism that draws upon his respect for nature in rural Sweden, his music, initially composed of words for audiotape, has assumed a more radical edge. More recently, he has composed texts and music for live instrumentalists, especially his wife, the singer Kersten Stahl.

Works: *Hyllningarna* 1963; *Im Time Vittringar Escaping*. Stockholm, Sweden: Caprice, 1979.

JOHNSON, Carla Rae

(9 March 1947).

An extremely witty sculptor, working in a tradition mixing prodigious construction with social satire, she specializes in large installations filled with various objects on a theme. What looked like shelves of uniformly designed books in *Grey Matters: The Last Library* (1990) turned out to contain facsimiles made of styrofoam, the lightness of the material reflecting ironically on the weight, both intellectual and physical, customarily associated with the original. *The Last Chance Salon: Games for the Millennium* (1997), an even more elaborate installation, has a pool table, a roulette wheel, and other objects associated with a casino, all illuminated by green-shaded lamps and yet somewhat askew, as an elaborate satire on competition in modern society. As Johnson has written, "Verbal play, humor, social comment, and attention to detail are some characteristics which remain constant throughout my ongoing production of sculpture. In the past ten years, my work has begun to focus on issues of social consciousness." Ever audacious, Johnson once opened the season at a women's art gallery by posing at the front door dressed like a street tart, successfully shocking (or mocking) patrons both male and female.

Installations: *Grey Matters: The Last Library*, 1990; *Spirit and Substance: Sculptural Lecterns and the Spoken Word*, 1994; *The Last Chance Salon*, 1997.

JOHNSON, Sarah East

(18 September 1967).

A short and broadly built woman initially trained in dance, Sarah East Johnson has spoken of her early wish to "perform with MERCE CUNNINGHAM, ELIZABETH STREB, and Circus Oz." Instead, she made performance pieces that reflect not only her remarkably powerful female body but her diverse performance mentors: Cunningham for nonrepresentational movement, Streb for athleticism, and the circus for her use of trapeze swings and other props. Her dancers frequently perform like acrobats while hanging onto cross bars, suspended ropes, or one another, but the

Sarah East Johnson performing "Double Trapeze" from *Volcano Love*, at the Kitchen; Adrienne Truscott is shown below her. January 1999. Copyright © Tom Brazil.

pacing of Johnson's work especially reflects her origins in modern dance. Some of her innovations come from slowing down circus-like movements, better to display their choreographic beauty; and in this respect, in particular, she differs from Streb, who favors speed. "Dance is my world," she once told a reporter. "I just use a different vocabulary than most choreographers." My single favorite Johnson move, "Hoop Diving," involves two thick-sided hoops, stacked one atop the other, so that her dancers approaching them perpendicularly can decide to dive through either the lower or upper one, in either case the prop forcing them to move their bodies in choreographically remarkable ways. Another masterpiece is the majesterial duet *Adagaio*. The dance involves Johnson supporting a slighter woman dancer on her shoulders, thighs, hands, and back, much as male dancers traditionally supported women, but here more acrobatically. Because all her performers are women, one Johnson theme is the potentialities of female athleticism. Though her programs have different titles, they frequently incorporate routines used before.

Works: *Topographies*, 1994; *Dirty Wings*, 1995; *Girls and Volcanos*, 1997; *Groundwork*, 1998; *Volcano Love*, 1999; *Lava Love Cabaret*, 1999.

JOHNSON, Scott

(1952).

For *John Somebody* (1983), he collected spoken sounds whose ostinatos resembled those of rock and roll. Analyzing these samples for inadvertent qualities of pitch and rhythm, he used audiotape editing to evoke, as he wrote, "musical regularities that my ear imposed on these spontaneous sounds. The fragments were then looped and layered in synchronization on a multitrack tape machine, and the resultant whole was carved into by mixing processes." His unique achievement there is a speech-based pre-RAP electro-acoustic dance music that preceded rap music.

Recordings: *John Somebody* (1983). New York: Icon-Nonesuch, 1986; *Rock Paper Scissors: Scott Johnson Ensemble*. New York: Pgd/Point Music, 1996.

JOHNSON, Tom

(18 November 1939).

Notwithstanding having earned not one but two degrees from Yale University, Johnson has been an innovative composer working with a variety of severe constraints, or, in his words, "logical progressions and highly predictable structures." *The Four Note Opera* (1972) is what it says it is (like other Johnson work), using only the pitches D, E, A, and B, with the singers incidentally announcing details about the mechanics of the producion. *Music for 88* (1988) is actually nine pieces for all the keys of the standard piano. For *The Chord Catalogue* (1987) Johnson spends two hours playing all 8,178 chords available within a single octave; the experience depends upon the audience's appreciation of his CONCEPTUAL feat. Another vein of Johnson's work requires an instrumentalist to follow instructions that appear suddenly on a screen, purportedly as new to him or her as to the audience. I remember a skilled pianist, performing before a sophisticated audience, being subjected to the repeated instruction that he play a "yet more spectacular cadenza" than the one before. *Falling* (1975) requires a string bass soloist to declaim a prepared text as he or she plays. Like much of Johnson's other performance pieces, this can be profoundly comic in unfamiliar ways.

From 1971 to 1982, Johnson was, as the music reviewer for the *Village Voice*, New York's most sympathetic and knowledgeable regular critic of new music, and the best of these notices have been collected in a book, *The Voice of New Music*, published not in his native country but in Holland. Since 1983 Johnson has lived mostly as an American in Paris. His successor as the *Voice*'s new-music critic has been Kyle Gann (1955), who incorporated his notices into the richest book yet on contemporary composers, *American Composers in the Twentieth Century* (1997).

Works: *An Hour for Piano*, 1971; *The Four-Note Opera*, 1972; *Falling: A Very Difficult Piece for String Bass (and Narrator)*, 1975; *Rational Melodies*, 1982; *The Chord Catalogue*, 1987; *Music for 88*, 1988.

Book: *The Voice of New Music*. Eindhoven, Holland: Apollohuis (Tongelrestraat 81, NL-5613 DB), 1989.

Recordings: *Falling*, with Robert Black, string bass (CRI); *Rational Melodies*. Eberhard Blum, flute (Hat Hut).

Interpretation: Gann, Kyle. *American Music in the Twentieth Century*. New York: Schirmer, 1997.

JOLAS, Eugene

(26 October 1894–26 May 1952).

Born in New Jersey, Jolas grew up in Lorraine, France (near Germany), before returning to the United States in 1911. Back in Paris in the 1920s, he worked for newspapers and then edited *transition* (1927–38), which was the most distinguished avant-garde magazine of its time. It published not only episodes from James Joyce's *Finnegans Wake* among other literature that was avant-garde at the time, but illustrations of advanced paintings and even, in a departure rarely imitated, scores by comparably vanguard composers.

The most distinctive Jolas poems draw upon his multilingual background, some like "Mountain Words" broaching self-invented language:

mira ool dara frim
oasta grala drima
os tristomeen.

Others combine German, French, and English, such as this opening of "Weltangst en Chevauchant une Frontiere," a polylingual prose poem:

The earth is troubled es geistert dans les cavernes her disalogues der draklings lopent through the the griefhours it is so icy in the eyes in the world of and streets are tired with waitng for kinderlieder et hymns
singmourn the legends le matin is droguegrey die hirne hungern nach paradis the lonely hunting horns are tenebrating in the miserere of rooks dans la chronique de forces dans le deesert évanoui

all reflecting the sensibility of a man who said he dreamt in three languages.

Books of Jolas's poetry have long been out of print, and the only anthologists to reprint him recently are Jerome Rothenberg and myself. *Man from Babel* (1998) draws from autobiographical manuscripts drafted a half century before. His daughter, Betsy J. (1926), is a distinguished American composer who, though she went to college in America, has resided mostly in France.

Works: *Cinema: Poems*. NY: Adelphia, 1926; *The Language of Night*. The Hague: Servire, 1932; *I Have Seen Monsters and Angels*. Paris: Transition, 1938; ——, ed. *transition workshop*. New York: Vanguard, 1949.

Autobiography: *Man from Babel*. Ed. & intro. Andreas Kramer and Rainer Rumold. New Haven: Yale University Press, 1998.

JOPLIN, Scott

(24 November 1868–1 April 1917).

An itinerant Midwestern pianist, Joplin is generally credited with composing the first popular piano piece to sell a million copies of sheet music, "Maple Leaf Rag" (1899). Although the term "ragtime" was meant to be semiderogatory, Joplin's piano pieces were as classically rigorous as Chopin's études, with four parts, composed AA-BB-AA-CC (trio)-DD. Joplin's music also incorporated dissonant harmonies, intuitively expanding the musical idioms of popular composition; his "Stop Time Rag" was the first sheet music to include markings for foot-tapping.

One misfortune of Joplin's life is that, not unlike George Gershwin (1898–1937), after him, Joplin thought himself worthy of more ambitious music, composing a ballet based on ragtime, and then a full-scale opera, *Treemonisha* (1911), which everyone wishes were better than it is. He died just short of fifty, a full half-century before his music was revived, first in brilliant records in the early 1970s by the conductor-pianist-musicologist-arranger Joshua Rifkin (1944), then in the popular film *The Sting* (1974).

—with Richard Carlin

j

Selected Compositions: *Maple Leaf Rag*, 1899; *The Ragtime Dance*, 1902; *Sycamore*, A Concert Rag, 1904; *Treemonisha*, 1911.

Recordings: Rifkin, Joshua. *Piano Rags of Scott Joplin*, Vols. I–III. New York: Nonesuch, 1970–74; *King of the Ragtime Writers* [piano roll transcription]. Port Chester, NY: Biograph, c. 1988.

Bibliography: Berlin, Edward A. *King of Ragtime*. New York: Oxford University Press, 1996; Curtis, Susan. *Dancing to a Black Man's Tune: The Life of Scott Joplin*. Columbia, MO: University of Missouri Press, 1994.

Discography: Jasen, David A. *Recorded Ragtime, 1897–1958*. Hamden, CT: Archon /Shoestring, 1973.

Website: http://www.scottjoplin.org/

Interpretation: Blesh, Rudi, and Harriet Janis. *They All Played Ragtime* (1950). 4th ed. New York: Oak Publications, 1971; Gammond, Peter. *Scott Joplin and the Ragtime Era.* New York: St. Martin's Press, 1976. [This concludes with an elaborate bibliography.]; Schafer, William J., and Johannes Riedel. *The Art of Ragtime: Form and Meaning of an Original Black American Art.* Baton Rouge: Louisiana State University Press, 1973; Williams, Martin, ed. *The Art of Jazz.* New York & London: Oxford University Press, 1972.

JOSHUA LIGHT SHOW

(1967–1972).

Of all the late 1960s light shows, as they were called at the time, the Joshua Light Show, in residence at New York's Fillmore East, a former movie palace seating 2,500 or so spectators, was the strongest. The esthetic innovation was to expand the concept of the Lumia, or the THOMAS WILFRED light box, to fill, in live time, a large translucent screen hung behind performing rock musicians. These lights were projected from several sources *behind* the screen, which at the Fillmore measured thirty feet by twenty and was always filled with bright and moving imagery. In the middle, usually within a circular frame (reflecting the glass bowl necessary to make it), nonrepresentational, brilliantly colored shapes pulsated in beat to the music, changing their forms unpredictably (thanks to the fact that the colors were composed of oil, water, alcohol, glycerine, and other materials that do not mix). Around that frame was a less blatant, fairly constant pattern whose composition and color mysteriously changed through variations repeated in a regular rhythm (these coming from slides fading over one another). Across the entire screen flashed rather diaphanous white shapes that irregularly fell in and out of patterns (these coming from an individual situated apart from the others, using a collection of mirrors to reflect white light onto the screen). From time to time representational images also appeared on the screen—sometimes words, at other times people; sometimes still, at other times moving. For instance, when musicians were tuning their instruments on stage, on the screen appeared a gag image of, say, Arturo Toscanini hushing his orchestra. (Those pictures came from slides and sometimes films.) For good reason, the Joshua Light Show received a billing line directly under the musicians, for what it achieved in fact contributed enormously to the theatrical experience, which wouldn't have been the same without it.

Interpretation: Kostelanetz, Richard. "Joshua Light Show" (1968). In *Fillmore East: Recollections of Rock Theater*. New York: Schirmer, 1995.

JOYCE, James

(2 February 1882–13 January 1941).

My job in a book like this is to distinguish the avant-garde Joyce from the more traditional writer. *FINNEGANS WAKE* obviously belongs and, if only to measure its excellence, deserves a separate entry. For Joyce's stories, *Dubliners* (1914), the innovation was the concept of the epiphany, which is the revelatory moment, customarily appearing near the end, that would give meaning to the entire fiction. "The epiphany is, in Christian terms, the 'showing forth' of Jesus Christ's divinity to the Magi," writes Martin Seymour-Smith. "They are 'sudden revelation[s] of the whatness of a thing,' 'sudden spiritual manifestation[s]—in the vulgarity of speech or gesture or in a memorable phase of the mind itself." Thus the departure of a Joycean story is the form not of an arc, where events proceed to a climax before retreating to a denouement, but of continuous events that establish a flat form until the flashing epiphany.

One innovation of *Ulysses* (1922) is the elegant interior monologue, also called stream-of-consciousness. Retelling in many ways the story of an oafish Jew, who has as much resemblance to the classic Ulysses as a bulldog to a greyhound, this thick book incorporates a wealth of parodies, epiphanies, allusions, extended sentences, and contrary philosophies within a fairly conventional story.

What also distinguishes Joyce's career is the escalation of his art, as each new book proved ever more extraordinary than its predecessor. The culmination was *Finnegans Wake* (1939). One's mind boggles at the notion of what Joyce might have produced had he lived twenty years longer. Indeed, this sense of esthetic awe, if not incredulity, is intrinsic in our appreciation of Joyce's continuing high reputation.

Works: *Dubliners*. London: Grant Richards, 1914; *Portrait of the Artist as a Young Man*. New York: Huebsch, 1916; *Ulysses* (1922). Paris: Shakespeare & Co., 1922 and New York: Random House, 1934; *Finnegans Wake*. New York: Viking, 1939; *Collected Poems*. New York: Viking, 1957; *Stephen Hero*. Ed. John J. Slocum and Herbert Cahoon. New York: New Directions, 1963.

Scholarly Texts: *"Dubliners": Text, Criticism, and Notes*. Ed. Robert Scholes & A. Walton Litz. New York: Viking, 1969; *"A Portrait of the Artist as a Young Man": Text, Criticism, and Notes*. Ed. Chester G. Anderson. New York: Viking, 1968; *Ulysses*. Ed. Hans Walter Gabler with Wolfhard Steppe and Claus Melchior. New York: Vintage, 1986.

Anthologies: Ellmann, Richard. *Letters of James Joyce*. Vols. II & III. New York: Viking, 1966; *Selected Letters of James Joyce*. Ed. Richard Ellmann. New York: Viking, 1975; Gilbert, Stuart, ed. *The Letters of James Joyce*. New York: Viking, 1957; Levin, Harry, ed. *The Essential James Joyce*. London: Jonathan Cape, 1948; Mason, Ellsworth, and Richard Ellmann, eds. *The Critical Writings of James Joyce*. New York: Viking, 1959.

Biography: Costello, Peter. *James Joyce: The Years of Growth, 1882–1915*. New York: Pantheon, 1992; Ellmann, Richard. *James Joyce* (1959). Rev. ed. New York: Oxford University Press, 1982; ——. *Four Dubliners*. New York: George Braziller, 1988; Epstein, Edmund L. "James Augustine Aloysius Joyce." In *A Companion to Joyce Studies*. Ed. Zack Bowen and James F. Carens. Westport, CT: Greenwood Press, 1984; Hutchins, Patricia. *James Joyce's World*. London: Methuen, 1957; Maglaner, Marvin, and Richard M. Kain. *Joyce: The Man, the Work, the Reputation*. London: Calder, 1957; Mercanton, Jacques. "The Hours of James Joyce" in *Portraits of the Artist in Exile: Recollections of James Joyce by Europeans*. Trans. Lloyd C. Parks. Ed. Willard Potts. New York: Harcourt Brace, 1979.

Website: www.jough.com/joyce

Interpretation: Beckett, Samuel, et al. *Our Exagmination Round His Factification For Incamination of Work in Process*. New York: New Directions, 1972; Beja, Morris. "One Good Look at Themselves: Epiphanies in *Dubliners*" in *Work in Progress: Joyce Centenary Essays*. Eds. Richard F. Peterson, Alan M. Cohn, and Edmund L. Epstein. Carbondale: S. Illinois University Press, 1983; Cheng, Vincent. *Joyce, Race, and Empire*. Cambridge & New York: Cambridge University Press, 1995; Cixous, Hélène. "At Circe's, or the Self-Opener." Trans. Carol Bove. *Boundary 2*, 3 (1979): 387–97; ——. "Joyce: The (R)use of Writing" in *Post-Structuralist Joyce: Essays From the French*. Trans.

Judith Still. Ed. Derek Attridge and Daniel Ferrer. Cambridge & New York: Cambridge University Press, 1984; Dettmar, Kevin J. H. *The Illicit Joyce of Postmodernism: Reading Against the Grain.* Madison: University of Wisconsin Press, 1996; Ellmann, Richard. *The Consciousness of James Joyce*. New York: Oxford University Press, 1972; Epstein, Edmund L. *The Ordeal of Stephen Dedalus*. Carbondale: S. Illinois University Press, 1971; Fairhall, James. *James Joyce and the Question of History*. Cambridge & New York: Cambridge University Press, 1993; Gillespie, Michael Patrick. *Reading the Book of Himself: Narrative Strategies in the Works of James Joyce*. Columbus: Ohio State University Press, 1989; Givens, Seon, ed. *James Joyce; Two Decades of Criticism*. New York: Vanguard, 1963; Kenner, Hugh. *Dublin's Joyce* (1956). Boston: Beacon, 1962; —— *Joyce's Voices*. Berkeley: University of California Press, 1978; —— *Ulysses*. Rev. ed. Baltimore, MD: The Johns Hopkins University Press, 1987; —— "Notes Toward an Anatomy of 'Modernism'" in *A Starchamber Quiry: A James Joyce Centennial Volume 1882–1982*. Ed. E. L. Epstein. London: Methuen, 1982; Kershner, R. B. *Joyce, Bakhtin, and Popular Literature: Chronicles of Disorder*. Chapel Hill: University of North Carolina, 1989; Levin, Harry. *James Joyce: A Critical Introduction*. New York: New Directions, 1941; MacCabe, Colin. *James Joyce and the Revolution of the Word*. New York: Harper and Row, 1979; Manganiello, Dominic. *Joyce's Politics*. London & Boston: Routledge & Kegan Paul, 1980; Miller, J. Hillis. "From Narrative Theory to Joyce; From Joyce to Narrative Theory." In *The Seventh of Joyce*. Ed. Bernard Benstock. Bloomington: Indiana University Press, 1982; Pound, Ezra. In *Pound/Joyce*. Ed. Forrest Read. New York: New Directions, 1967; Riquelme, John Paul. *Teller and Tale in Joyce's Fiction: Oscillating Perspectives*. Baltimore & London: The Johns Hopkins University Press, 1983; Scholes, Robert. "Stephen Dedalus, Poet or Aesthete?" In *In Search of James Joyce*. Urbana and Chicago: University of Illinois Press, 1992; Vanderham, Paul. *James Joyce and Censorship*. New York: New York University Press, 1997; Walzl, Florence L. *"Dubliners"* in *A Companion to Joyce Studies*. Ed. Zack Bowen and James F. Carens. Westport, CT: Greenwood, 1984.

Bibliography: Staley, Thomas. *An Annotated Critical Bibliography of James Joyce*. New York: St. Martin's Press, 1989.

JUDD, Donald

(3 June 1928–12 February 1994).

A pioneer of MINIMALIST sculpture, Judd established his canonical reputation with the display of simple forms, devoid of any base, that were distributed in evenly measured ways, such as protruding three-dimensional rectangles up the side of a wall. Viewed from various angles, such definite forms suggest a variety of interrelated shapes, for Judd's point was to make one thing that could look like many things. With success, he used more expensive metals fabricated to his specifications, often with seductive monochromatic coloring, and produced many variations, only slightly different from one another, on a few ideas. As a writer, Judd contributed regular reviews to the art magazines of the early sixties, urging the move away from emotional EXPRESSIONISM toward intellectual structuring, and away from an earlier sense of art, particularly sculpture, as interrelated parts toward an idea of a single "holistic" image. Quite radical and influential in the sixties, Judd's art has neither changed nor significantly developed in his later years.

Selected Sculpture: *Light Cadmium*, red oil on wood with violet plexiglass, 1963; *Light Cadmium,* red oil on wood with metal lathe, 1963; *Light Cadmium,* red oil and black oil on wood with galvanized iron, 1963; *Untitled*, cold-rolled steel with green enamel, 1968; *Untitled,* anodized aluminum and brushed aluminum, 1970; *Untitled,* brass and painted aluminum, 1975; *Untitled,* anodized fast blue aluminum with clear plexiglass top and bottom, 1989.

Writings: *Complete Writings, 1959–1975*. Halifax, NS, & New York: Nova Scotia College of Art and Design/New York University Press, 1975.

Exhibition Catalogs: Agee, William C. *Don Judd*. New York: Whitney Museum, 1968; *DJ*. Eindhoven,

Donald Judd, *Untitled*, 1968. Stainless steel and amber plexiglass. CORBIS/State of New York. © Donald Judd Estate/Licensed by VAGA, New York, NY.

Netherlands: Stedelijk VanAbbe Museum, 1970; *DJ*. Pasadena, CA: Pasadena Art Museum, 1971; Haskell, Barbara. *DJ*. New York: Whitney Museum, 1988; Agee, William. *DJ: Sculpture/Catalogue*. New York: Pace Wildenstein, 1994.

Catalogues Raisonnés: Smith, Brydon. *Donald Judd: Catalogue Raisonné of Paintings, Objects, and Wood Blocks, 1960–1974*. Essay by Roberta Smith. Ottawa, Ont.: National Gallery, 1975; Josephus Jitta, Mariette & Schellman, Jörg, ds. *Prints and Works in Editions*. Cologne & New York: Edition Schellman & Munich: Schirmer/Mosel, 1993.

j

JUDSON DANCE THEATER

(1962–1964).

Out of the composition classes taught in the early 1960s by Robert Ellis Dunn (1928–96) at the MERCE CUNNINGHAM Studio came young dancers wanting to create their own pieces. The Judson Memorial Church—a Greenwich Village landmark, which had already gained cultural fame, rare for a church at that time, by making its space available for a Poet's Theater—was receptive to aspiring choreographers. The result was, in Sally Banes's succinct summary, "the first avant-garde movement in dance theater since the modern dance of the 1930s and 1940s. The choreographers of the Judson Dance Theater radically questioned dance aesthetics, both in their dances and in their weekly discussions. They rejected the codification of both ballet and modern dance. They questioned the traditional dance concert format and explored the nature of dance performance. They also discovered a cooperative method for producing dance concerts." The result was a rich succession of choreographic experiments, some more successful than others. In addition to involving dancers who subsequently had distinguished choreographic careers, such as YVONNE RAINER, TRISHA BROWN, LUCINDA CHILDS, and STEVE PAXTON, the Judson Dance Theater hosted performances authored by such predominantly visual artists as ROBERT RAUSCHENBERG and ROBERT MORRIS.

Bibliography: Banes, Sally. *Democracy's Body: Judson Dance Theater 1962–1964* (1983). Durham: Duke University Press, 1993; McDonagh, Don. *The Rise & Fall & Rise of Modern Dance* (1970). Rev. ed. Pennington, NJ: A Cappella, 1990.

KAC, Eduardo

(3 July 1962).

A Brazilian experimental poet since his teens, Kac was among the first writers to realize that HOLOGRAPHY, a visual technology new to our times, could be a medium for language. In the 1980s, he created holograms in which, among other clever constructions, words from two languages meld into one another, the same letters are reorganized to create different words, a cylinder reveals a series of words, seen only in parts, that reads differently clockwise from counterclockwise ("Quando?" ["When?" 1987]). For art such as this Kac coined the epithet "holopoetry," whose significance he has explained in several manifestos: "The perception of a holopoem takes place neither linearly nor simultaneously, but rather through fragments seen at random by the observer, depending upon his or her [physical] position relative to the poem." Originally from Rio de Janeiro, Kac moved to Chicago in 1989, taking an advanced degree at its Art Institute and subsequently teaching there. He has worked with various new media, in addition to editing a special issue on "New Media Poetry: Poetic Innovation and New Technologies" for the seminal magazine *Visible Language* (1997). I think of him as a post-2000 artist.

Works: *Holopoetry: Essays, Manifestoes, Critical and Theoretical Writings*. Lexington, KY: New Media Editions (now c/o Prof. Kac, Art Institute of Chicago), 1995; and Orrneo Botelho. *Holofractal*. Rio de Janeiro, Brazil: Galeria de Fotografia da Funarte, 1988; ed. "New Media Poetry: Poetic Innovation and New Technologies." *Visible Language*, XXX/2 (1997), with contributons from John Cayley on Literary Cybertext, Philippe Bootz on Poetic Machinations, and JIM ROSENBERG on "The Interactive Diagram Sentence; Hypertext as a Medium of Thought."

Interpretation: Dobrila, Peter Tomaz and Kostic, Aleksandra, eds. *Eduardo Kac: Teleporting An Unknown State*. Maribor, Slovenia: KIBLA, 1998.

Website: www.ekac.org

KAGEL, Mauricio

(24 December 1931).

A theatrical composer far better known in Europe than in the Americas, Kagel, born in Buenos Aires, has lived in Cologne since 1957 and become one of the most prominent German composers. Possessed of a fecund imagination, he has created instrumental music as well as ELECTRONIC MUSIC, produced films as well as new scores to classic silent films, and authored books and produced gallery exhibitions. One of his specialties is music in which his own performance is key, such as a "Requiem," wherein he is a conductor who collapses on stage while the musicians play on. Another specialty is to draw upon classical texts, as often of literature as music. Thus, *Aus Deutschland* (1977–1980) is a "Lieder-Oper" about nineteenth-century Germany; *Sankt-Bach-Passion* (1983–85) portrays the life of J. S. Bach as resembling that of Jesus

Christ; *Ensemble* (1967–70), an opera without words (or orchestra) is described as "a satirical look at the previous history of opera"; and *Ludwig van* (1970) is "a Kagelian montage of Beethoven motifs." A principal esthetic idea is metacollage in which disparate materials are all drawn from a single source.

Compositions: *Ensemble*, 1967–1970; *Ludwig van*, 1970; *Aus Deutschland* Lieder-Oper 1977–1980; *Sankt-Bach-Passion* for mezzo-soprano, tenor, baritone speaker, chorus, speaking chorus, boy's chorus, and orchestra, 1981–85.

Recordings: *Nah und Fern/Near and Far*, radio piece for bells and trumpets with background (Montaigne, 1995); *String Quartets 1–3* (Montaigne, 1994); *Sankt-Bach-Passion* (Montaigne, 1996); Die Stücke der Windrose; Osten, Süden, Nordosten, Nordwesten, Sñdosten; Phantasiestück (Montaigne); *Zwei Akke; rrrr . . . 5 Jasssücke; Blue's Blue* (Montaigne).

Books: Schnebel, Dieter, ed. *Mauricio Kagel: Musik Theater Film*. Köln, Germany: DuMont, 1970; Küppelholz, Werner. *Maricio Kagel: 1970–1980*. Köln, Germany: DuMont, 1981; *Kagel: . . . ./1991*. Köln, Germany: DuMont, 1991.

Interpretation: Kostelanetz, Richard. "Mauricio Kagel (1988)." In *On Innovative Art(ist)s.* New York: Limelight, 1989.

KANDINSKY, Wassily

(4 December 1866–13 December 1944; b. Vasi'yevich K.). Born in Moscow, Kandinsky studied law and social science at the local University, where he later taught law. Impressed by the first Russian exhibition of French Impressionists in 1895, he traveled in 1897 to Munich to study painting. Older than the other students, Kandinsky quickly progressed professionally, organizing exhibitions throughout Europe. By 1909, he became a founding member of *Neue Künstlervereinigung* (NKV), which initially represented the style of the Fauves against the German version of Art Nouveau called *Jugendstil*. By the following year, the NKV exhibition included a broader range of advanced European painting. By 1912, Kandinsky belonged to a dissident group that published the *Blaue Reiter Almanach*, which he coedited; in the same year, he authored *Über das Geistige in der Kunst (Concerning the Spiritual in Art)*, which still ranks among the major essays in the development of nonrepresentational painting for insisting upon the primacy of expressive and compositional elements in art. During World War I, Kandinsky returned to Russia, where he worked in arts administration, until he was invited in 1921 to teach at the BAUHAUS, remaining there until it was closed by the Nazis. He then moved to Paris, where he lived until his death.

Kandinsky's own mature paintings emphasized bright color, an intentionally flat field, and irregular abstract forms whose unfettered exuberance seems reminiscent of the art of his sometime colleague at the Bauhaus, Paul Klee (1879–1940). Perhaps because of the softness of their abstraction, both Klee and Kandinsky are now less influential than they used to be.

Selected Works: *Compositions I–X*, 1910–1939; *Several Circles*, 1926; *Yellow-Red-Blue*, 1925; *Thirty*, 1937; *Accompanied Contrast*, 1937; *Reciprocal Award*, 1942.

Books: *Concerning the Spiritual in Art* (1912, 1914, 1947, 1964). New York: Dover, 1977; *Kandinsky: Complete Writings on Art* . Lindsay, K.C., Vergo, P., eds., Boston: G. K. Hall, 1982; ——. and Franz, Marc, eds. *The Blaue Reiter Almanac* (1912). Ed. & intro. Klaus Lankheit. New York: Viking, 1974.

Autobiography: *Reminiscences*. In Robert L. Herbert, ed. *Modern Artists on Art*. Englewood Cliffs, NJ: Prentice-Hall, 1964.

Intrepretation: Grohman, Will. *Wassily Kandinsky: Life and Work*. Trans. Norbert Guterman. New York: Abrams, 1958; Weiss, Peg. *Kandinsky in Munich: The Formative Jugendstil Years*. Princeton: Princeton University Press, 1979; Barnett, Vivian Endicott. *Kandinsky Watercolors*. 2

vols. Ithaca, NY: Cornell University Press, 1992–94; Bill, Max, et al. *Wassily Kandinsky*. Paris: Maeght, 1951; Levin, Gail. *Theme and Improvisation: Kandinsky & the American Avant-Garde 1912–1950*. Boston: Bullfinch, 1992; Long, Rose-Carol Washton. *Kandinsky: The Development of an Abstract Style*. New York: Oxford University, 1980; Overy, Paul. *Kandinsky: The Language of the Eye*. New York: Praeger, 1969.

Exhibition Catalogs: *Wassily Kandinsky, 1866–1944: A Retrospective Exhibition*. New York: Guggenheim Museum, 1962; *WK*. Edinburgh: Scottish National Gallery of Modern Art, 1975; *Kandinsky in Munich, 1896–1914*. New York: Guggenheim Museum, 1982; Dabrowski, Magdalena. *Kandinsky Compositions*. New York: Abrams, 1995.

Web Sites: http://metalab.unc.edu/cjackson/kandinsky/

KAPROW, Allan

(23 August 1927).

To the claim that American universities are inhospitable to avant-garde art and artists, Kaprow will always be cited as a principal counter-example, as well he should be, having taught at universities (albeit four of the more sophisticated—Rutgers, SUNY-Stony Brook, Cal Arts, UCSD) for forty years while inventing the HAPPENING as a form of alternative performance. Beginning around 1956 with ASSEMBLAGES incorporating materials found in public places, he progressed to ENVIRONMENTS, or artistically defined enclosures, and MIXED-MEANS performance pieces he called Happenings. The last typically involved people following instructions to unexpected results, initially in gallery spaces, later in public places. By the late 1960s, Kaprow's elegantly written and masterfully designed book, *Assembling, Environments & Happenings*, had appeared; and his term "Happening" was being used indiscriminately by the media to define anything chaotic. Relocating in California (which can be hazardous to the artistic output of New Yorkers), Kaprow turned to more intimate situations he called successively "Work Pieces" and "Activities," which are reportedly more psychological than spectacular in effect. Few artists are as effective in talking about their own work and esthetic purposes. Kaprow combines adventurous thinking with a broad vision, in well-turned sentences stylistically indebted to his graduate school mentor, the art historian Meyer Schapiro (1904–96).

Writings: *Assemblage, Environments & Happenings*. New York: Abrams, 1966; *Some Recent Happenings*. New York: Something Else, 1966; *Essays on the Blurring of Art and Life*. Ed. Jeff Kelley. Berkeley: University of California Press, 1993.

Exhibition Catalogs: *Allen Kaprow: Collagen, Environments, Videos, Broschüren, Geschichten, Happening-and Activity-Dokumente 1956–1986*. Dortmond, Germany: Museum am Ostwall, 1986; Marter, Joan, ed. *Off Limits: Rutgers Uniersity and the Avant-Garde, 1957–1963*. Newark, NJ: The Newark Museum & Rutgers University Press, 1999.

Web Site: http://www.fluxus.org/FLUXLIST/kaprow.htm

KASPER, Michael

(7 January 1947).

While working as a reference librarian at Amherst College, Kasper has produced a series of tart chapbook-length visual/verbal fictions, mostly self-published, that his fellow book-artists commonly rank among the best. The third "expanded" edition of his *All Cotton Briefs* (1992), his biggest collection yet, contains his strongest work. A brief interview with Kasper, along with an illustration, appears in GEORGE MYERS JR.'s *Alphabets Sublime* (1986).

Works: *Odds 'n' Ends from the Lost 'n' Found*, 1980; *20 Trial Briefs*, 1981; *Billy! Turn Down That TV*, 1983; *Verbo-Visuals*, 1985; *Plans for the Night*, 1987; *All Cotton Briefs* (1981, 1985). Florence, MA: Benzene-Left Lane (106 High St., 01060), 1992.

KAWARA, On

(2 January 1933).

An austere CONCEPTUAL ARTIST, Kawara has spent his professional life doing (or redoing) only a few works: painting in sans-serif letters the words for the day's date (in the language of wherever he is currently staying), sending local picture postcards on whose backsides he stamps "I got up at [at whatever time]," recording separate sheets with the names of the individuals he met that day, and posting telegrams that read "I am still alive/On Kawara." (Editions Rene Block in Berlin once published a book of that quoted title, consisting wholly of reproductions of telegrams.)

I have in the course of my life saved works from many artists, some by purchase and others as gifts, but you can imagine my surprise when the first works from my collection to tour in an international show were unsolicited picture postcards that Kawara had sent me for several weeks, several years before.

Works: *Bathroom*, 1953–54; *Date Paintings* (series), 1965–; *I Got Up . . .*, 1968–; *I Am Still Alive*, 1970; *One Million Years* (past), 10 vols. 1970–71; *One Million Years* (future), 1980.

Exhibition Catalogs: *On Kawara: Continuity/Discontinuity 1963–79*. Stockholm: Moderna Musset, 1980; *Again and Against*. Nagoya, Japan: Inst. of Contemporary Art, 1989; *OK: Whole and Parts, 1964–1995*. Eds. Xavier Douroux and Franck Gautherot. Paris: Les presses du réel, 1996.

Buster Keaton. Still from *Steamboat Bill Jr.*, 1928. Courtesy Kino video.

KEATON, Buster

(4 October 1895–1 February 1966; b. Joseph Francis K.).

Among the most innovative of all silent film directors, Keaton created a character with so little external affect that much of his comedy depends upon his deadpan reaction to the catastrophes occurring around him. Nicknamed "Stoneface," the Keaton persona remained unchanged whether he was in the midst of a hurricane (as at the end of his classic *Steamboat Bill, Jr.* [1928]) or fleeing from Union troops in the Civil War *(The General* [1927]). Keaton's comic conceptions often bordered on DADA, as in the famous short *(One Week* [1920]) in which a newly married couple struggle to build their dream house. A villain has so scrambled the directions that the house comes out resembling a wild CUBIST construction. (Because the main entry is on the second floor, one continuing gag in the film is Keaton's pratfalls when he exits the house.)

Keaton was among the first to experiment with the nature of reality and illusion in film. His 1922 short *The Play House* features some of the earliest trick photography, in which Keaton, through multiple exposures, portrays an entire orchestra, performing troupe, and audience. The protagonist of *Sherlock, Jr.* (1924), his first feature-length film, is a film projectionist who, in his dreams, leaps into the film that he is showing, becoming unwittingly involved with the action on screen. As his own director, Keaton was also a masterful film editor, often working with striking juxtapositions. In *Cops* (1922), he created a classic chase sequence in which gangs of police appear and disappear (almost magically) as they pursue the unwitting hero through a busy city landscape. Much of the comedy depends upon the cuts between scenes where the lone Keaton is shown running down a street and then, moments later, a sea of policemen run through the same space.

With the advent of sound (and thus more expensive productions), Keaton unfortunately lost creative control of his films, appearing in a series of lame MGM features, often paired with the hopelessly overbearing Jimmy Durante. Late in his life, when his silent masterpieces were rediscovered, Keaton starred again in some wonderful short films, including a dialogue-less film portraying him traveling across Canada on a small handcar *(The Railroader* [1965]) and the SAMUEL BECKETT-scripted short, entitled simply *Film* (1965) that was incomplete at the time of Keaton's death.

—Richard Carlin

Selected films (Starring & Directed by): *Neighbors*, 1920; *One Week*, 1920; *The Haunted House*, 1921; *Hark Luck*, 1921; *The Play House*, 1922; *Cops*, 1922; *Sherlock, Jr.*, 1924; *The Navigator*, 1924; *Seven Chances*, 1925; *Go West*, 1926; *The General*, 1926; *Steamboat Bill, Jr.,* 1928.

Film Appearances: *Film* (dir. Alan Schneider), 1965; *The Railrodder* (dir. Gerald Patterson), 1965; *Buster Keaton Rides Again* (dir. John Spotton), 1965; *The Great Stone Face* (dir.-ed., Vernon P. Becker), 1968; *Buster (*aka *The Golden Age of Buster Keaton)* (prod. Raymond Rohauer), 1975. (The last two are compilation films with choice historic Keaton footage.)

Autobiography: with Charles Samuels. *My Wonderful World of Slapstick* (1960). New York: Da Capo, 1982.

Biography: Blesh, Rudi. *Keaton*. New York: Macmillan, 1966; Dardis, Tom. *Keaton: The Man Who Wouldn't Lie Down* (1979). New York: Limelight, 1988; Meade, Marion. *Buster Keaton: Cut to the Chase*. New York: HarperCollins, 1995.

Web Site: http://www.netbistro.com/buster/buster.htm (check yahoo—there are more).

Interpretation: Kline, Jim. *The Complete Films of Buster Keaton*. New York: Citadel Press, 1993; Oldham, Gabriela. *Keaton's Silent Shorts: Beyond the Laughter*. Carbondale: Southern Illinois University Press, 1996.

KEITH, Bill

(20 January 1929).

Initially a painter, long a photographer as well as a poet, Keith has recently produced VISUAL POETRY discernibly different from what others are doing and have done. (Can the same be said for the latest practitioners of free verse?) Drawing upon African and African-American traditions, he has "written" a highly original alphabet and "Harlequinode," which I would gladly anthologize if I still edited poetry anthologies. *Pictographs* is an appropriate title for

Bill Keith. From *Pictographs*, 1996. Courtesy the author.

Keith's collection of images, pictures, and words. Keith has also organized exhibitions of visual poetry.

Books: *Sphinx*. Lafarge, WI: Xerolage (Rt. 1, Box 131, 54639), 1992; *Wisdom*. Port Charlotte, FL: Runaway Spoon, 1993; *Pictographs: Poems*. Barrytown, NY: Left Hand, 1996.

KELLY, Ellsworth

(31 May 1923).

A veteran of U.S. Army camouflage units, who studied in France under the GI Bill, Kelly began in the early 1950s to make paintings divided into rectangular panels that were identical in size but different in color. Because these colors were usually bright and unmodulated, they produced a shimmer along the straight edge where they touched each other. Such work customarily requires the painter to apply the paint thickly and evenly and the viewer to find an optimal viewing distance. Because Kelly uses two or more colors, this is customarily called COLOR-FIELD or hard-edge painting. (Were there only one color, the epithet "monochromic" would be more appropriate.)

Selected Works: *Black Form*, 1967; *Green Black*, 1970–72; *Black Curve I (White Curve I)*, 1973; *Two Yellows*, 1973–75; *Fontenay*, 1973–76; *Moissac*, 1973–76; *Jacmel*, 1978–80; *Concorde I (State)*, 1981–82; *Cupecoy* 1983–84.

Exhibition Catalogs: Goosen, E. C. *Ellsworth Kelly*. New York: MoMA, 1973; Sims, Patterson. *EK, Sculpture*. New York: Whitney Museum, 1982; *EK: At Right Angles 1964–1966*. Los Angeles, San Francisco & New York:

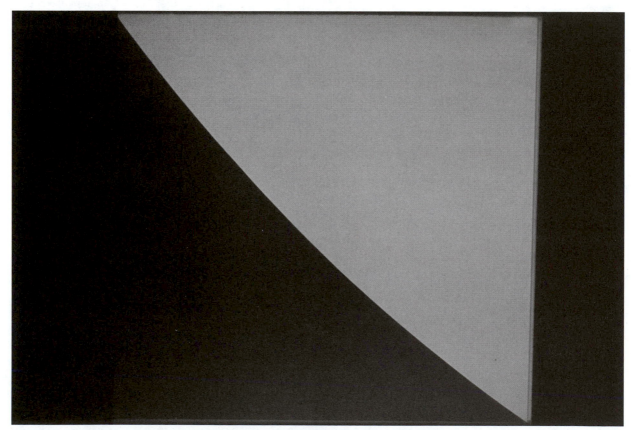

Ellsworth Kelly. *White Curve V*, 1973. Oil on canvas. CORBIS/Seattle Art Museum.

Margo Leavin, John Berggruen, and Paula Cooper, 1991; Bois, Yve-Alain, Jack Cowart, and Alfred Paquement. *EK: The Years in France, 1948–1954*. Washington, DC: Natonal Gallery of Art, 1992; *EK: A Retrospective*. Ed. Diane Waldman. New York: Guggenheim, 1996.

Interpretation: Parola, Rene. *Optical Art: Theory and Practice*. New York: Reinhold, 1969.

Catalog Raisonné: Axson, Richard H. *The Prints of Ellsworth Kelly: A Catalogue Raisonné, 1949–1985*. New York: Hudson Hills-Am. Federation of the Arts, 1987.

KEMPTON, Karl

(1 July 1943).

Since the early seventies, Kempton has edited *Kaldron*, North America's foremost and longest-lasting visual poetry publication (in print from 1976–1990, but currently still going at the LIGHT & DUST Website), and has composed some of this century's best poetry. His art ranges from all-text short lyrics to highly sophisticated visio-verbo-musico-mathematical hybrids. Though particularly strong in infraverbal poetry (as in a four-liner that ends "a we/ awe" to capture near-perfectly the way "a we," or group of people, transcendently fuses—audibly as well as visually—to form something higher), he is best-known for his "typoglifs." These (visually chanted) repeated-letter typewriter poems are the basis of the ongoing series of Runes Kempton has been working on since the late seventies. On the surface they seem simple, though Kempton often gives them dimensionality and motion through op-art techniques he was among the first visual poets to exploit. Examined in depth, however, they are seen to be widely referential reworkings of patterns found in knotted seaweed and elsewhere in Nature, and in American Indian, Celtic, and numerous other cultures all the way back to rock art. In short, they intricately as well as uniquely celebrate the final awe that, for Kempton, underlies all things.

—Bob Grumman

Selected Books: *Lost Alfabet Found*. Reno, NV: West Coast Poetry Review (1335 Dartmouth Drive, 89509), 1979; *Black Strokes White Spaces*. Madison, WI: Xerox Sutra Press, 1984; *KO*, with Loris Essary. Pullman, WA: Score, 1984; *Alignment*. Calexico, CA: Atticus Press (720 Heber Avenue, 92231), 1985; *Charged Particles*. Port Charlotte, FL: Runaway Spoon (P.O. Box 3621, 33949–3621), 1991; *Rune: a Survey*. Kenosha, WI: Light and Dust Books (7112 27th Avenue, 53143), 1992; *Water from the Mountains of Light*. Orcutt, CA: White Crow (4773 Harmony Lane, 93455), 1995.

Website: http://www.thing.net/~grist/l&d/lighthom.htm

KENNER, Hugh

(7 January 1923; b. William Hugh K.).

From his beginnings an audacious, independent, and prolific literary critic-scholar, Kenner has produced two kinds of books—eccentric and often oblique studies of the accepted literary modernists and less oblique books about such avant-garde figures as EZRA POUND (back in 1951, when his subject was still imprisoned and academically unacceptable), WYNDHAM LEWIS, and BUCKMINSTER FULLER. This means that Kenner exhibits courage not only in his choice of subjects but in his interpretations. Among the more iconoclastic of the latter is his demolition of Sigmund Freud, a modern icon if ever there were one, in "Tales of the Vienna Woods," collected in Kenner's *Gnomon* (1958). It is indicative that this sometime student of MARSHALL MCLUHAN, likewise born Canadian and likewise Catholic, should write sensitively in *The Mechanic Muse* (1987) about the computer as a successor to the typewriter, and that he should be among the first of his cultural generation to become familiar enough with computers to produce programs that are widely used. Though common opinion regards *The Pound Era* (1972) as Kenner's best book, my own sense is that his essays and books on more avant-garde subjects represent his greater achievement.

Writings: *The Poetry of Ezra Pound*. New York: New Directions, 1951; *Wyndham Lewis*. New York: New Directions, 1954; *Dublin's Joyce*. London: Chatto & Windus, 1955; *Gnomon: Essays on Contemporary Literature*. New York: McDowell, Obolensky, 1958; *The Invisible Poet: T. S. Eliot*. New York: McDowell, Obolensky, 1959; *Samuel Beckett*. New York: Grove, 1961; *The Stoic Comedians: Flaubert, Joyce, and Beckett*. Boston: Beacon, 1962; *The Counterfeiters: An Historical Comedy*. Bloomington: Indiana University Press, 1968; *The Pound Era*. Berkeley: University of California Press, 1971; *Bucky: A Guided Tour of Buckminster Fuller*. New York: Morrow, 1973; *A Homemade World: The American Modernist Writers*. New York: Knopf, 1975; *Geodesic Math and How to Use It*. Berkeley: University of California Press, 1976; *The Mechanic Muse*. New York: Oxford University Press, 1987; *Dublin's Joyce* (1956). New York: Columbia University Press, 1987; *A Sinking Island: The Modern English Writers*. New York: Knopf, 1988; *A Colder Eye: The Modern Irish Writers* (1983). Baltimore: Johns Hopkins University Press, 1989; *Chuck Jones: A Flurry of Drawings*. Berkeley: University of California Press, 1994; *Historical Fictions: Essays*. Athens: University of Georgia Press, 1995; *Mazes: Essays*. Athens: University of Georgia Press, 1995; *A Reader's Guide to Samuel Beckett* (1973). Syracuse, New York: Syracuse University Press, 1996; *The Elsewhere Community*. Concord, Ont.: Anansi, 1998.

Criticism: Borklund, Elmer. *Contemporary Literary Critics*. New York: St. Martin's Press, 1977.

KERN, Richard

(20 December 1954).

The nurse who takes care of Jimmy Stewart in Alfred Hitchcock's *Rear Window* has a line that cuts to the heart of the film viewing experience: "We've become a race of Peeping Toms." Hitchcock's movie about a voyeur who stares out the window at his neighbors has been taken as an allegory of spectatorship itself. The desire to look runs throughout Hitchcock's work and is literalized in *Psycho*, when Norman peeps through a hole in the wall at Marion Crane undressing for the shower. We look with Mr. Bates and we take the bait and become implicated in his voyeurism. In the same year as *Psycho*—1960—MICHAEL POWELL released his infamous *Peeping Tom*, a film about a filmmaker who literally kills with his camera as he records the action. This fascination with the dark side of looking—with the dynamics and aesthetics of voyeurism—is Richard Kern's theme and it runs through his films and photography. In many ways, Kern's work is a culmination of self-referential approaches to depicting the artist's relationship to his "subject." And his subject is a kind of seeing.

The allusion to mainstream films is important for a discussion of Kern's early work because in many ways his movies are responses to popular film and commercial culture as a whole. Kern has made this relationship clear: "I take what interests me in the movies and put it in a shorter format so I don't get bored. What interests the American public are sex and violence and the seamy side of life." In his effort not to be bored, Kern moved to the Lower East Side and began a series of Super-8 films that eventually became associated with the Cinema of Transgression. His first Super-8, *Goodbye 42nd Street* (1983), is indicative of his approach to moviemaking: the camera moves down the fabled street of vice and takes in store signs and marquees of porno and exploitation movies. Spliced into this movement down the street are scenes of strippers in booths, a man putting a cigarette out on his face (Kern himself—the Auteur as Ashtray), various killings (a woman turns LUIS BUÑUEL on his head by stabbing her male lover in the eye) and suicides.

Kern's early career was spent making his films—movies like *Zombie Hunger* (1984) which depicted a group of people shooting up and then vomiting—and screening them, accompanied by outrageous performance pieces that created a Grand Guignol for the Lower East Side. In the tradition of ANDY WARHOL and John Waters (1946), Kern employs actors from his immediate social world who reappear throughout his films. Some of these denizens of the Kern Super-8 universe include Lydia Lunch, Clint Ruin (aka Jim Thirlwell), David Wojnarowicz, Lung Lee, Karen Finley and a filmmaker who is credited as the founder and first promoter of the Cinema of Transgression, Nick Zedd. What this evolving cast depicted in Kern films such as *The Right Side of My Brain* (1984), *The Manhattan Love Suicides* (1984), *You Killed Me First* (1985), and the glorious dark ride of *Submit to Me* (1985) was nothing short of an assault upon the conventions of filmmaking and spectatorship. *Submit to Me* consists of a series of scenes depicting bondage, violence, sex, and suicide, many of which were suggested to Kern by the actors themselves.

As the underground reflection of Ronald Reagan's America, Kern's films embraced the subculture of the Lower East Side and the avant-garde impulse of those on the fringe of the established art world. However, a split occurred in Kern's career around 1987 when he decided to quit the Lower East Side to remove himself from its drug culture. This split is depicted in *The Evil Cameraman* ('87–'90), an allegory of Kern's evolution as a visual artist. The first part of the film is made up of two segments depicting Kern "arranging a model" in provocative S&M scenarios; the imagery and music is dark and the threat of violence is palpable. Then the title "2 Years Later" appears and we are given two very different segments of a different Kern—back from his hiatus—who works with two "models" who do not play into his "control" as photographer. The film ends with a rejected Kern looking into the camera. This new relationship to the women in his films—playful, puzzling, rejecting the anticipatory action of "pornography"—colors Kern's later films: *X = Y* (1990), *Nazi* (1991), *Catholic* (1991), *Horoscope* (1991), and *The Bitches* (1992). During this period Kern also shifted his attention to a different visual form.

Although he has continued work on his own films and on music videos, Kern has lately concentrated on photography. His pictures have moved from the gore and "splatter" effects of his early films to a concentration on the women he photographs. The pictures themselves are more fluid than his films: they easily cross over into the world of pornography (he has contributed work to magazines such as *Hustler* and *Barely Legal*). But what distinguishes Kern's pictures from prosaic porno is that his work is remarkably beautiful and, more important, it continues his play with the force of voyeurism. Each of Kern's photographs is a mini-movie, a story the viewer steps into and "sees." This "seeing" of a Kern photo is fascinating because after the viewer takes in the picture s/he must take in the effect of such looking. In his preface to *New York Girls*, Kern describes the feeling he has about taking pictures: "For me, nothing compares to the experience of building an environment with light then adding a living person as an unknown to make a temporal image." The "unknown" here is the Kern model, but it is also the Kern viewer: we are the unknown looker encountering an image and trying to decipher its "story." Kern's pictures tell us we are voyeurs and we are then forced to look at our own looking. Each of Kern's photographs tell a different story—his entire artistic output could be called "The Story of His Eye"—but all of them tell us something he once admitted in an interview: "The best part of anything is watching."

—John Rocco

Documentation: *New York Girls*. Köln: Taschen, 1997; *XXGirls*. Tokyo: Fiction, Inc., 1996.

Interpretation: Paparoni, Demetrio. *Richard Kern*. Milan: Charta, 1998; Sargent, Jack. *Deathtripping: The Cinema of Transgression*. London and San Francisco: Creation Books, 1995.

Website: www.richardkern.com

KERN, W. Bliem

(24 November 1943).

A sometime student of Norman Henry Pritchard II, Kern adapted the idea of the rapidly repeating phrase in his sound poetry to his own purposes, reiterating, for example, "belief in the illusion of" until it sounds like something else. His printed texts range from "straight" poetry to visual texts of words and letters to poems that mix familiar words with unfamiliar, some of which come from an entirely fictitious language that Kern calls "Ooloo." Whereas most sound poetry is static, Kern's pieces often suggest a narrative direction, as in "Dream to Live," a long poem that tells in words, phrases, and phonemes of the end of a love affair. His principal collection (1973) appeared as a box with both a book and an audiotape, one element no less important than the other. Rarely publishing any more, Kern works as an astrologer and an ordained interfaith minister.

Book & Recording: *Meditationsmeditationsmeditations-meditations: Selected Poems 1964–73*. New York: New Rivers, 1973.

KEROUAC, Jack

(12 March 1922–21 October 1969).

The avant-garde Kerouac is not the chronicler of hitchhiking through America in *On the Road* (1957) or the embarrassing drunk of his later years, but the author of certain abstract prose in which words are strung together not to describe a subject but for qualities indigenous to language. *Visions of Cody* (1972, though written many years before) and, especially, "Old Angel Midnight" are thought to be examples of "automatic writing," Kerouac purportedly transcribing words at the forefront of his consciousness. Whether that last claim is true, the result is extraordinary prose, as in the following from the latter title:

> Stump—all on a stump the stump—accord yourself with a sweet declining woman one night—I mean by declining that she lays back & declines to say no—accuerdo ud. con una merveillosa—accorde tue, Ti Pousse, avec une belle fe'Tune folle pi vas, t'councer—if ya don't understand s t t and tish, that language, it's because the langue just bubbles & in the babbling void I Lowsy Me I's tihed.

Like other Kerouac writing, this is about the possibilities of memory and language, but differs from most other Kerouac in being about the limitless *intensities* of each. Kerouac's major experimental poems are "Sea," which initially appeared as an appendix to *Big Sur* (1962), and *Mexico City Blues (242 Choruses)* (1959), which displayed linguistic leaps similar to those quoted from "Old Angel Midnight."

Selected Works: *Mexico City Blues (242 Choruses)*, (1959). New York: Grove, 1990; *Big Sur* (1962). New York: Penguin, 1992; *Visions of Cody*, (1972). New York: Penguin, 1992; "Old Angel Midnight [Part II]" and "Sea." In *Text-Sound Texts* (1980), ed. Richard Kostelanetz. New York: Archae, 1984; *Old Angel Midnight*. San Francisco: Grey Fox, 1993.

Biography: Charters, Ann. *Kerouac*. New York: Warner, 1974; Clark, Tom. *Jack Kerouac*. New York: Harcourt, Brace, 1984; Gifford, Barry, and Lawrence Lee. *Jack's Book*. New York: St. Martin's Press, 1978; McNally, Dennis. *Desolate Angel: A Biography of Jack Kerouac*. New York: Random House, 1979; Nicosia, Gerald. *Memory Babe: A Critical Biography of Jack Kerouac*. New York: Grove, 1983.

Web Site: http://porter.appstate.edu/~kh14586/links/beats/kerouac/ (Links)

Interpretation: Beaulieu, Victor-Levy. *Jack Kerouac: A Chicken Essay*. Toronto, Ont.: Coach House, 1979; Hipkiss, Robert A. *Jack Kerouac: Prophet of the New Romanticism*. Lawrence, KS: Regents Press, 1976; Tytell, John. *Naked Angels: Kerouac, Ginsberg, Burroughs* (1976). New York: Grove 1991; Weinreich, Regina. *The Spontaneous Prose of Jack Kerouac*. Carbondale: S. Illinois University Press, 1987.

Bibliography: Charters, Ann. *A Bibliography of Works by Jack Kerouac* (1967). Rev. ed. New York: Phoenix Bookshop, 1975.

KHARMS, Daniil

(17 December 1905–2 February 1942). Born into the family of a left-wing writer in St. Petersburg, the Russian poet Daniil Ivanovich Kharms (Yuvachov) in 1925 met Aleksandr Vvedensky(*), who, though only a year older, Kharms identified as his teacher. While Vvedensky departed from the esthetics of Zaum (*) in the mid-1920s, Kharms used Zaum elements in his own poetry: modifying words by vowel/consonant substitution and creating a strong effect of DEFAMILIARIZATION within a traditional rhymed poem. He also used invented words as imaginary archaisms from strange dialects/Oriental languages ("Trr ear of my hairs," "Daughter of daughter of daughters of daughter of Peh . . ."). The poet's early interest in children's poetry (and poetry for children) influenced his more serious writing. The "narrator" of Kharms's poems is often a "primitive," a child, or a retarded person.

In 1926 Kharms, Vvedensky and several other young poets formed a group called OBERIU. Kharms's outstanding achievement during OBERIU years (1926–1931) was the play "Elizaveta Bam," first staged in 1928. After his first arrest in 1930 and the demise of OBERIU, Kharms's writing became more daring, venturing far out of his favorite trochee meters into irregular and even free verse.

Having written most of his best poetry by 1935, he then concentrated on writing short fiction, creating what many consider to be his defining work—a series of very short stories called "Accidents." In the summer of 1941 Kharms was arrested again and died, according to KGB archives, six month later in Gulag mental asylum, faking madness to escape execution.

The relative accessibility of Kharms's prose, compared to the difficulties of translating his (and, for that matter, other OBERIU) poetry into English, led to his recognition in the West as a master of very short fiction. This, unfortunately, came at the expense of any appreciation of his brilliant poetics.

—Igor Satanovsky

Selected Works: Gibian, George, ed. and trans. *Russia's Lost Literature of the Absurd, A Literary Discovery: Selected Works of Daniil Kharms and Alexander Vvedensky*. Ithaca; London: Cornell University Press, 1971; Meylakh, B., and V. I. Erl', eds. *Poety Gruppy "OBERIU."* St. Petersburg: Sovetskiy Pisatel', 1994 (in Russian).

KHLEBNIKOV, Velimir

(28 October 1885–28 June 1922; b. Viktor Vladimirovich K.).

The brilliant pathfinder of RUSSIAN FUTURISM and one of the greatest Russian poets of the twentieth century, Khlebnikov was a quiet, reclusive man who led a nomadic existence, in contrast to the brash behavior of the other CUBO-FUTURISTS. They nonetheless recognized him as the genius of the movement, one whose ceaseless innovation and great poetic achievement served as a creative stimulus in the areas of both practice and theory.

His earliest poems (1906–08) already show the marks of originality and innovation that made Khlebnikov a leader of Futurism when the movement began to form in 1910. One of his most famous early poems is "Incantation on Laughter," a series of neologisms based on the root *smekh* ("laughter") and published in 1910. Khlebnikov's major poetic quest was to uncover the true creative roots of language that existed in primitive times, when presumably there was a close iconic link between linguistic signs and their meaning. Many of Khlebnikov's theoretical works are devoted to uncovering these links in the Slavic language, and many of his poems are partly illustrations of his theories.

Khlebnikov was a Slavophile in his attitude toward language, and he avoided borrowings from European languages (especially from French and German, which are heard frequently in spoken and literate Russian). The goal of many of his coinages was to demonstrate the capacity of Slavic to generate all the words necessary for present and future needs, not only to replace foreign borrowings in current use but also to name new phenomena. While the term "ZAUM" was used by him and others to describe these linguistic inventions, Khlebnikov, in contrast to ALEKSEI KRUCHONYKH, intended his coinages to be clearly understood and not to be indeterminate in meaning, at least in the long run. Often he provided keys to their interpretation either explicitly by giving definitions or implicitly by providing analogies to known words within the same context.

Khlebnikov's innovations were not limited to word-creation, but covered a full linguistic range, from attempting to define the universal meanings of individual sounds and letters to new ways of creating metaphors, to rhythmic and syntactic experiments, and to new syntheses of all of these elements in larger forms called "supersages," one of the most noted of which is *Zangezi* (1922). Khlebnikov was also a significant writer of prose fiction and theater texts. His "The Radio of the Future" (1921) is filled with suggestions that still seem radical today.

He preferred to depict the primitive state of man in close contact with nature, a state analogous to primitive man's close contact with the roots of language. Slavic mythology is a notable element. Khlebnikov was not as enamored of modern technology and urban life as other Futurists. However, in addition to his principal concern of creating a perfect language for the future, he penned a number of Utopian descriptions of futuristic life. As he was a trained mathematician, his favorite project was attempting to discover the mathematical laws governing human destiny, according to which the pattern of historical events could be understood and future events predicted.

Because of his nomadic existence and personal eccentricity, publications of Khlebnikov's works during his lifetime were often to some degree faulty, filled with typographical errors, misreadings, and variant or fragmentary versions, the author's final wishes being to varying degrees uncertain. These problems continued in posthumous editions until very recently, when more rigorously edited volumes have begun to appear. Khlebnikov was fortunate, however, to have had champions throughout the Soviet period when his work appeared with some regularity, though not abundantly. As the difficulty of his poetry still challenges even the most sophisticated reader, he has never been and is unlikely ever to become broadly popular; he will remain a "poet's poet" whose work continues to inspire new generations of Russian writers.

—Gerald Janecek

Writings: *The King of Time: Selected Writings of the Russian Futurian*. Trans. Paul Schmidt. Cambridge: Harvard University Press, 1985; *Collected Works: Letters and Theoretical Writings*. Trans. Paul Schmidt. Ed. Charlotte Douglas. Cambridge: Harvard University Press, 1988; *Collected Works: Prose, Plays, and Supersagas*. Trans. Paul Schmidt. Ed. Ronald Vroon. Cambridge: Harvard University Press, 1990; *Collected Works: Selected Poems*. Cambridge: Harvard University Press, 1998; *Tvoreniia*. Ed. M. Poliakov. Moscow, Russia: Sovetskii Pisatel', 1989.

Interpretation: Cooke, Raymond. *Velimir Khlebnikov: A Critical Study*. New York: Cambridge University Press, 1987; Janecek, Gerald. *The Look of Russian Literature*. Princeton: Princeton University Press, 1984; ——. *Zaum: The Transrational Poetry of Russian Futurism*. San Diego: San Diego State University Press, 1996; Markov, Vladimir. *The Longer Poems of Velimir Khlebnikov*. Berkeley: University of California Press, 1962; Petrivskii, Dmitrii. *A Story about Velimir Khlebnikov*. St. Bruno, Que.: Baoum, 1994; Vroon, Ronald. *Velimir Khlebnikov's KRYSA*. Stanford: Stanford University Slavic Studies, 1989.

KIENHOLZ, Edward

(23 October 1927–10 June 1994).

An American original, Kienholz made tableaux, usually with decrepit detritus, of people living at the margins of society—in a homely bar, in a state hospital, etc. He typically placed life-sized maimed figures in such real settings as a double bunk bed in *State Hospital* (1966), a chopped-apart 1930s automobile in *Back Seat Dodge '38* (1964), and a bar counter in the mammoth *Beanery* (1965), where almost all the figures have clocks for heads. Because he incorporated various sub-art materials into three-dimensional constructions, Kienholz was initially classified as a master of ASSEMBLAGE; but what he really did was design static theatrical sets, sometimes as INSTALLATIONS meant for a particular location. The suggestion is that spectators could enter them, even if they are blocked off, perhaps because Kienholz's "human" figures are customarily less lifelike than their surroundings. In *State Hospital* (1966), installed at the national museum in Stockholm, viewers peer through a small barred window into a room containing a double-decker bed with two naked, emaciated men facing the window. Their hands are tied to the bed. In place of their faces are fishbowls. For its original installation, Kienholz infused a hospital smell into the scene. Often living in Berlin since the middle 1970s, Kienholz once mounted an installation of old radios that, when activated, played raucous Wagnerian music reminiscent of a discredited era. In 1981, he decided that the name of his wife, Nancy Reddin K. (1943), should retroactively accompany his own on all works produced after 1972.

Selected Constructions/Installations: *Triptych*, 1956; *Roxy's*, 1961; *History as Planter*, 1961; *Back Seat Dodge '38*, 1964; *The Wait*, 1964–65; *Beanery*, 1965; *State Hospital*, 1966; *Still Live*, 1974; *The Ladder*, 1976; *Portrait of a Mother with Past Affixed Also*, 1980–1981.

Writings: *Documentation Book: Five Car Stud and Sawdy*. Los Angeles: Gemini G.E.L., 1972.

Web Site:
http://www.sas.upenn.edu/~vbell/kienholz.html

Exhibition Catalogs: Tuchman, Maurice. *Edward Kienholz*. Los Angeles: Country Museum of Art, 1966; *Art in Los Angeles: Seventeen Artists in the Sixties*. Los Angeles: Country Museum of Art, 1981; *EK: Work from the 1960s*. Washington, DC: Washington Gallery of Modern Art, 1968; *Hulten*, K. G. Pontus. *11 + 11 Tableaux*. Stockholm: Moderna Museet, 1970; *EK*. Zürich: Kunsthaus, 1975; Scott, David. *Tableaux 1961–1979*. Dublin: Douglas Hyde Gallery, Trinity College, 1981; Hopkins, Henry T., ed. *Edward and Nancy Kienholz—Human Scale*. San Francisco: MoMA, 1984; Edward and Nancy Kienholz: *Werk aus den 90er Jahren*. Düsseldorf: Kunsthalle, 1989; Harten, Jürgen and Schmidt, Hans-Werner. *Edward & Nancy Kienholz:1980's*. Düsseldorf: Kunsthalle Düsseldorf, 1989; *Keinholz: A Retrospective*. New York: Whitney Museum, 1996.

Interpretation: Pincus, Robert L. *On a Scale That Competes with the World: The Art of Edward and Nancy Reddin Kienholz*. Berkeley: University of California Press, 1990.

KIESLER, Frederick

(22 September 1890–27 December 1965).

An Austrian who came to the United States in 1926, Kiesler was a visionary architect whose proposals were mostly unrealized. His few projects that were built were commonly judged to be "ahead of their time": peripatetic scenery and a theater in the round in 1924; a long, cylindrical space for Peggy Guggenheim's "Art of This Century" gallery in 1942; and an egg-shaped white grotto made of fabric over curved stretchers for the last major SURREALIST exhibition. His art seemed to hypothesize an INTERMEDIUM incorporating architecture and theater along with painting and sculpture. One great architectural proposal was endlessness, or infinite continuity, first conceived for a theater in 1923 and then exhibited as the *Endless House* at New York's Museum of Modern Art in 1960: a series of concrete shells with no structural members. Others remember *Galaxies* (1952), also at MOMA, which Irving Sandler describes as "environmental 'clusters' of painting and sculpture." Kiesler coined the term "Corealism" to acknowledge continuity of time and space, as well as the idea that artwork depends upon its environmental context. From 1933 to 1957 he worked as Scenic Director at the Juilliard School of Music.

Architecture: Plan for the Endless Theatre, 1923–25; Plan for Place de la Concorde, 1925; *Nucleus House*, 1926–28; *Utility Towers*, c. 1930; *The Universal*, a theater for Woodstock, NY, 1931; *Paris Endless*, 1947; *Tooth House*, 1948; *Endless House*, 1950–60; *The Shrine of the Book*, Jerusalem, 1959–65; *The Universal Theater*, 1960–61; *Endless House for Mary Sisler*, West Palm Beach, FL, 1961; *Grotto for Meditation*, New Harmony, IN, 1963.

Exhibition Design: *Art of this Century*, New York, 1942; *Salle de Superstition*, Galerie Maight, Paris, 1947.

Sculpture: *Galaxy*, 1948–51; *The Last Judgment*, 1955–63; *Birth of a Lake*, 1960; *Landscape: The Savior Has Risen*, 1964.

Books: *Inside the Endless House: Art, People, and Architecture.* New York: Simon & Schuster, 1966.

Exhibition Catalogs: *Frederick Kiesler (1890–1965): Visionary Architecture, Drawings and Models, Galaxies and Paintings, Sculpture*. New York: Andre Emmerich, 1979; Pincus-Witten, Robert. *FK: Galaxies (1890–1965)*. New York: Alfred Kren and Jason McCoy, 1986; Bogner, Dieter, et al. *FK: Architekt, Maler, Bildhauer, 1890–1965*. Vienna, Austria: Museum Moderner Kunst, 1988; *FK: Environmental Sculpture*. New York: Guggenheim Museum, 1964; Phillips, Lisa. *FK*. New York: Whitney Museum, 1989.

Interpretation: Bottero, Mario. *Frederick Kiesler: arte, architettura, ambiente*. Milano: Electra, 1995; Held, Roger L. *Endless Innovations: Frederick Kiesler's Theory and Scenic Design*. Ann Arbor: University of Michigan [doctoral thesis], 1977.

KINETIC ART

(c. 1920).

Several artists between 1910–1920—among them, NAUM GABO, Alexander Archipenko (1887–1964), MARCEL DUCHAMP, and Giocomo Balla (1871–1958)—came up with the idea of making art move, utilizing motors to propel their initially sculptural works. In a famous 1920 manifesto, Gabo joined his brother Antoine Pevsner in suggesting, "In place of static rhythm in the plastic arts, we announce the existence of a new element, kinetic rhythm, which is to be the basis of a new perception of real time." In his book *The Origins and Development of Kinetic Art* (1969), the French critic Frank Popper distinguishes among several genres of kinetic art. One depends upon some kind of machinery (e.g., the artists already cited, POL BURY and MOHOLY-NAGY). A second, called mobiles, realizes movement without motors (e.g., ALEXANDER CALDER and GEORGE RICKEY). A third depends upon moving light (e.g., THOMAS WILFRED and CLYDE LYNDS). A fourth, such as that made by JULIO LE PARC and YAACOV AGAM, depends upon spectators shifting themselves for the illusion of movement to occur in the work of art. Certain holograms also depend upon spectator movement. A fifth is a kind of Optical Art that, if stared at fixedly, will generate the illusion of movement; the exemplars here are BRIDGET RILEY and VICTOR VASARELY. To Popper's list I would add a genre of machines that respond to outside influences (such as works by James Seawright [1936] and ROBERT RAUSCHENBERG) and a second of kinetic sculptures that function autonomously. One contemporary master in the last category is GEORGE RHOADS, who uses a motor to lift a small ball to the top of a multi-route contraption that then depends upon pretechnological forces of gravity to make the artwork move. The sculptures of WEN-YING TSAI transcend Popper's categories by incorporating both motors and changing light. Some contemporary kinetic art has been produced by collectives, such as USCO. Some examples are permanently installed (such as the George Rhoads *42nd Street Ballroom* in Manhattan's Port Authority Bus Terminal); others, such as JEAN TINQUELY'S *Hommage à New York* (1960), were meant to survive only for an evening. Some recent kinetic art exploits computers, at times to make the activity more various than was possible in the mechanical age, or to make it respond to viewers' presence.

Some Examples of Kinetic Art: Agam, Yaacov. *Nouveau soffège*, 1966; Bury, Pol . . . *Boules en mouvements* (Balls in Motion), 1963; Calder, Alexander. Innumerable mobiles (a generic term), 1930s–1970s; LeParc, Julio. *Light Continuum*, 1962; Lye, Len. *Steel Fountain*, 1959; Moholy-Nagy, L. *Lichtrequisit* (Light-Space Modulator), 1923–30; Okamoto, Rikuro. *Moving Rock # 11*, 1979; Rhoads, George. *42nd Street Ballroom* (at the Port Authority Bus Terminal, New York), 1985; ——. *The Magic Clock*, 1980; Reiback, Earl. *Lumia*, 1967; Riley, Bridget. *Current*, 1964; Schöffer, Nicolas. *Microtemps*, 1965; Seawright, James. *Scanner*, 1996; Spellins, Art. *New Frontier*, 1984; Tsai, Wen-Ying. Dancing rods (another generic term for a group of works), 1968; ——. *Harmonic Field*, 1975: ——. *Computer Light Array*, 1975; ——. *Upwards-Falling Fountain*, 1979; Victoria, Ted. *Tom and Lucy Left Their Mark Here*, 1984.

Exhibition Catalogs: Hulten, K. G. Pontus. *The Machine as Seen at the End of the Mechanical Age*. New York: MoMA, 1968; *The David Bermant Collection: Color, Light, Motion*. Hartford, CT: Wadsworth Atheneum, 1984; *Cybernetic Sculptures: The World of Tsai Wen-Ying*. Beijing, China: Center Art and Science Foundation, 1997; *Electrus by Babis Vekris*. Athens, Greence: Gazi Art Center, 1997.

Interpretation: Brett, Guy. *Kinetic Art: The Language of Movement*. London & New York: Studio Vista, 1968; Malina, Frank, ed. *Kinetic Art: Theory and Practice*. New York: Dover, 1974; Popper, Frank. *The Origins and Development of Kinetic Art*. Greenwich, CT: New York Graphic Society, 1969; *Art of the Electronic Age*. New York: Abrams, 1993; Rickey, George. *Constructivism: Origins and Evolution*. New York: Braziller, 1968; "The Morphology of Movement: A Study of Kinetic Art." In Gygory Kepes, ed. *The Nature and Art of Motion*. New York, G. Braziller, 1965; Selz, Peter. *Directions in Kinetic Sculpture*. Berkeley: University of California Press, 1966; Tovey, John. *The Technique of Kinetic Art*. New York, Van Nostrand Reinhold, 1971.

KING, Kenneth

(Unknown, at his request).

A profoundly original mind from the beginnings of his professional career, King has worked inventively in both

Kenneth King in *Dancing Wor(l)ds*, 1990. Copyright © Johan Elbers, courtesy Kenneth King.

dance and writing. For *Camouflage* (1966), he jumped in place for several minutes, and the most spectacular passages of *Blow-Out* (1966) had him dressed in dark glasses, his hands in gloves attached by elastic strings to the side walls, his feet firmly planted, his body contorting within the severely constraining frame. In *M-o-o-n-b-r-a-i-n with SuperLecture* (1966), King emerges in the costume of an old man, which he proceeds to remove piece by piece, later putting a few items back on. Midway through this work begins an audiotape of prose written and spoken by King in a style that imitates and parodies both JAMES JOYCE and MARSHALL MCLUHAN, and laments the impossibility of choreography in the electronic age. At one point King takes a single familiar dance step, only to return to plodding around the stage, concluding his danceless dance about the difficulties, if not the death, of modern dancing. That last theme informed *Printout* (1967) in which King, dressed in black from head to toe, supervised the playing of a tape on which he reads a prose essay whose Joycean words are simultaneously projected on a screen. While the *SuperLecture* was reprinted in my anthology *The Young American Writers* (1968), the text of *Printout* appears in my selection of *Future's Fictions* (1971).

As an innovative dancer, King developed an extremely light flutter step; he has also performed solos entirely to his own live spoken accompaniment. Perhaps because he initially publishes in contexts far from literary magazines and even conventional theater, his brilliant writings are scarcely noticed. When I was directing a SMALL PRESS, we applied regularly for grants to publish a book of his prose, without success.

Selected Choreographies: *Camouflage*, 1966; *Blow-Out*, 1966.

Writings: "SuperLecture"(1967). In *The Young American Writers* (1968). New York: Archae, 1984; "Space Dance and the Galactic Matrix." In Richard Kostelanetz, ed. *Merce Cunningham: Dancing in Space and Time* (1992). New York: Da Capo, 1998; *Dancing W-o-r-d-s*. New York: Privately published (201 East 28th St., 5-L, New York, NY 10016), 1990; *Five Appreciations/Concretics X*. New York: Privately published, 1992; "Autobiopathy," in *Footnotes*. Ed. Elena Alexander. Amsterdam: G+B Arts, 1998.

KING, Philip

(1 May 1934).

In the early 1960s, King was the leading representative of the New Generation sculptors, a group of young British artists who turned against the emotional expressiveness and the emphasis on craft, on figuration, and on truth to materials that had characterized sculpture during the previous ten years. In reaction, King developed a style of work that focused on simple unitary forms such as cones and boxes, bold colors, stability rather than implied movement, and the use of fiberglass in lieu of traditional materials. His most influential work was *Rosebud* (1962), a simple, wide, pink conic section, looking very much like a teepee, with a vertical slit running down the front that revealed a bright green surface behind it. The slit was curved and came to a point halfway down its length, so as to vaguely resemble the pointed edge of a rose leaf. In their geometric simplicity and stasis, such works clearly precede the Minimalist sculptures of CARL ANDRE and DONALD JUDD created later in the 1960s. But with the passage of time, the loud colors and King's preference for the look of manufacture, instead of a sculpture of modeling and carving, make his art seem to be more the antecedent of another development of the later 1960s: POP ART.

—Mark Daniel Cohen

Works: *Rosebud*, 1962; *Genghis Khan*, 1963; *Slit*, 1966; *Slant*, 1966; *Angle Poise*, 1973.

Exhibition Catalogs: Robertson, Bryan. *Philip King: Sculpture 1960–68, September–October 1968*. London: Whitechapel Gallery, 1968.

KIRBY, Michael

(13 January 1931–24 February 1997).

Kirby's early critical writings include an introduction to *Happenings* (1965), and essays, such as his classic "The Aesthetics of the Avant-Garde," which became *The Art of Time* (1969). As a sculptor, Kirby took six sets of photographs from four sides of six subjects and then printed them on cubes that, if turned in complementary ways, would show different sides of six different subjects. As a theater artist, he made MIXED-MEANS pieces that depended upon the appearance of a double for himself (his identical twin brother, E. T. Kirby [1931–1985], who also published books about alternative theater), and scripted plays whose principal subject is their structure, which is "played out," as he puts it, in ways unusually rigorous for live theater. These were so original, in both writing and staging, that it is scarcely surprising that even the latest *Contemporary Dramatists* (1993) lacks an entry on Michael Kirby's work.

Books: *Happenings*. New York: Dutton, 1965; *The Art of Time*. New York: Dutton, 1969; *A Formalist Theatre*. Philadelphia: University of Pennsylvania Press, 1990; and Kirby, Victoria Nes. *Futurist Performance* (1971). New York: Performing Arts Journal, 1987; Kirby, E. T., ed. *Total Theatre*. New York: Dutton, 1969.

KIRSTEIN, Lincoln

(4 May 1907–5 January 1996).

A writer and effective arts activist, Kirstein made many contributions that benefit American culture, beginning with the founding and editing of the literary magazine *Hound and Horn* (1927–1934). In 1928, while an undergraduate at Harvard, he also cofounded a Society of Contemporary Art that leased a two-room suite above the Harvard Co-op Bookstore and mounted the first American exhibitions of CONSTANTIN BRANCUSI, BUCKMINSTER FULLER, and ALEXANDER CALDER, among others. Also the founder of the School of American Ballet, Kirstein helped bring George Balanchine (1903–83) to America and supported his reign as choreographer for the New York City Ballet. Kirstein was also one of the first American dance critics (as distinct from newspaper reviewer), a writer on the visual arts, and a poet.

Books: *Ballet: Bias and Belief*. Brooklyn, NY: Dance Horizons, 1982; *Three Pamphlets Collected* [*Blast at Ballet*, 1937; *Ballet Alphabet*, 1939; *What Ballet Is About*, 1959]. Brooklyn: Dance Horizons, 1967; *Nijinsky Dancing*. New York: Knopf, 1975; *By With To & From: A Lincoln Kirstein Reader*. Ed. Nicholas Jenkins. New York: Farrar, Straus, 1991; *Mosaic: Memoirs*. New York: Farrar, Straus, 1994; Hamovitch, Mitzi Berger, ed. *The Hound and Horn Letters*. Athens: University of Georgia Press, 1982.

Interpretation: Weber, Nicolas Fox. *Patron Saints: Five Rebels Who Opened America to a New Art, 1928–1943*. New York: Knopf, 1992.

KLEIN, Yves

(28 April 1928–6 June 1962).

A sometime jazz musician who also wrote a book about judo (at which he earned a black belt), this French artist purportedly made in 1946 monochromic canvases, painted edge to edge in a single color. Though he claimed to have exhibited them privately as early as 1950, they were not publicly shown until 1956. Succès de scandale prompted him to devote his activities to "International Klein Blue," as he called it, a distinctive hue which was applied not only to canvases but sculpted figures and even nude models, who then imprinted it onto canvases. Though his blue was lush, Klein claimed to favor metaphysical resonances. In 1958, he enhanced his reputation with a PRE-CONCEPTUAL ART "exhibition" in an empty gallery painted white. He also claimed (but typically could not document) that in 1957 he mounted in Milan an exhibition entirely of identical, blue, monochrome canvases with different prices, purportedly reflecting different qualities in surface texture. Klein is commonly identified as among the first artists to exploit publicity to make himself, as well as the photograph of himself (especially flying through the air), more important than any of his works.

Selected Paintings: *Propositions monochromes*, 1956; *Sponge Reliefs*, 1958; *Anthropometries of the Blue Period*, 1960; *Anthropométrie sans titre*, 1961; *Planetary Relief RP23*, 1961; *Moon No.1*, 1961.

Sculpture: *Blue Rain*, 1957; *Sponge Sculpture*, 1957.

Writings: *Selected Writings*. Ed. Jacques Caumont and Jennifer Gough-Cooper. London: Tale Gallery, 1974.

Exhibition Catalogs: *Yves Klein*. New York: Jewish Museum, 1967; *Yves Klein*. Berne, Switzerland: Kunsthalle, 1971; *1928–1962: A Retrospective*. Houston, TX: Institute for the Arts, Rice University, 1982; *Yves Klein/Sidra Stich*. London: Hayward Gal., 1994; *Yves Klein*. Oslo, Norway: Museet for Samtidskunst, 1997.

Interpretation: Restany, Pierre. *Yves Klein*. New York: Abrams, 1982.

KLINE, Franz

(23 May 1910–13 May 1962).

Initially a painter of urban silhouettes as shadowless forms, Kline in the 1950s developed an extremely original style of abstraction with broad brushstrokes assuming the quality of ideograms. It is said that he projected an image of one of his drawings onto a wall, and in the contrast between large black and white fields saw his mature painting. Precisely because so many of Kline's paintings are black, the untainted white areas attain the status of independent images. In their avoidance of colors typical of Nature, these canvases could be regarded as an epitome of a New York City sensibility. As a native New Yorker, I once suggested that only two colors are worthy of art—black and white; all other colors are appropriate for illustrations.

Selected Works: *Untitled*, 1947; *Untitled*, 1950; *Cardinal*, 1950; *Wotan*, 1950–51; *Black and White*, 1951; *Untitled*, 1952; *Untitled*, 1955; *Untitled* 1957; *Mycenae*, 1958; *Requiem*, 1958; *Mars, Black and White*, 1959; *Black Sigma*, 1960; *Flanders*, 1961.

Exhibition Catalogs: de Kooning, Elaine. *Franz Kline Memorial Exhibition*. Washington, DC: Washington Gallery of Modern Art, 1962; O'Hara, Frank. *Franz Kline*. London: Whitechapel, 1964; Gordon, John. *Franz Kline: 1910–1962*. New York: Whitney Museum, 1968; Gaugh, Harry F. *The Vital Gesture: Franz Kline*. Cincinnati: Cincinnati Art Museum, 1985; Anfam, David. *Franz Kline, Black & White, 1950–1961*. Houston, TX: Menil Col., 1994.

Interpretation: Dawson, Fielding. *An Emotional Memoir of Franz Kline*. New York; Pantheon, 1967.

KLINKOWITZ, Jerome

(24 December 1943).

In addition to many conventionally written expositions mostly about contemporary American fictioners, Klinkowitz has produced one extraordinary book that is so different that neither he nor anyone else has done anything like it since. The chapters of *The Life of Fiction* (1973) introduce a new form for literary criticism, mixing fragments of textual quotation from both primary and secondary sources, transcribed interviews, personal letters, biography both formal and informal, and Klinkowitz's own comments, all presented at a speed roughly comparable to film montage, in an attempt to provide a "more complete picture" than that available by drawing from only one of those materials. The book's square pages are imaginatively designed by his colleague at the University of Northern Iowa, Roy H. Behrens, who often mixes type more than six inches wide with double columns half as wide, adding oblique illustrations. The book's problem is less its method, which is avant-garde, than Klinkowitz's choice of subjects, including, as it does, several writers who are not—among them Russell Banks, Jonathan Baumbach, Ishmael Reed, and Kurt Vonnegut, Jr. More than a quarter-century later, Klinkowitz hasn't progressed, most recently writing memoirs of of his scant relations with the same writers he discussed critically decades ago (Kurt Vonneget yet again, Jerzy Kosinski, Donald Barthelme, Gilbert Sorrentino, et al.).

Books: *The Life of Fiction*. Urbana, IL: University of Illinois Press, 1973; *Keeping Literary Company: Working with Writers since the Sixties*. Albany, NY: SUNY, 1998.

KLUCIS, Gustav

(4 January 1895–c.1944).

A Latvian who arrived in Moscow in 1918 as a part of a Latvian regiment assigned to guard the Kremlin, Klucis became active in art, producing, in collaboration with his wife Kulagina, a lithograph called *Dynamic City* (1919), in which, over the background of a filled-in circle, planes appear to extend forward and backward. He produced PHOTOMONTAGES for VLADIMIR MAYAKOVSKY'S *V. I. Lenin* (1925); he co-designed ALEKSEI KRUCHONYKH'S book *Chetrye foneticheskikh romana* (Four Phonetic Novels, 1924). Klucis produced model "Radio Announcers" designed to serve, within one structure, as both a newspaper stand and a platform for public speakers (which would still look innovative if displayed today). In 1928 he became a founding member of the group October, which had a major show in 1930. Though always a loyal Communist, Klucis was arrested in 1938 as a Latvian and sentenced to a labor camp in Siberia, where he died several years later.

Works: *Dynamic City*, 1919; Construction, 1921; Design for a Screen, 1922; Design for a Stand, 1922; *Project for a Construction for the Fifth Anniversary of the October Revolution*, 1922; *Study for Poster of Lenin and Socialist Reconstruction*, 1927; *Spartakiada (Divers)*, 1928; Posters and studies for posters of various Soviet efforts, 1930–32.

Exhibition Catalogs: Nakov, Andrei. *Russian Pioneers at the Origins of Non-Objective Art*. London: Annely Juda, 1976; *Art into Life: Russian Constructivism 1914–1932*. New York: Rizzoli, 1990; Gassner, Hubertus and Nachtigäller, Roland. *Gustav Klucis: Retrospektive* Stuttgart: G. Hatje, 1991; *The Great Utopia: The Russian & Soviet Avant-Garde, 1915–1932*. New York: Guggenheim Museum, 1992.

KNOWLES, Alison

(29 April 1933).

One of the founders of FLUXUS, Knowles has been mainly concerned with re-creating and conceptualizing the act of reading. In her *Big Book* (1966), she gestalts the book as a gigantic stage construct, through, around, and into which the performers crawl, slide, slip, hop, and bend, thus realizing as activity the many stages, psychic and emotional, that we as readers undergo when encountering a book. In her later *Finger Book* (1986), the book is imaged as a small tactile ASSEMBLAGE, composed of representative elements from all over the planet—shells, mirrors, tablets, coins, etc.—all uniting to form a book object that is covered with a crystallized Braille text. Knowles has also produced radio plays for Westdeutscher Rundfunk.

—Charles Doria

Book-Art: *Big Book*, 1966; *The Identical Lunch*, 1966–1981.

Recordings: *Frijoles Canon*. Santa Fe, NM: What Next? (P.O. Box 2638, 87504), 1992.

Books: *By Alison Knowles* (Great Bear pamphlet No.1), New York: Something Else Press, 1965; *Spoken Texts*. Barrytown, NY: Left Hand (Station Hill, 12507), 1992; *Event Scores*. Barrytown, NY: Left Hand, 1992; *Bread and Water*. Barrytown, NY: Left Hand, 1995.

Book-Art: As compiler, *A Bean Concordance vol. 1*. Barrytown, NY: Printed Editions, 1983; *Gem Duck*. Berkeley: Unpublished Editions, 1977; *More*. New York: Unpublished Editions, 1976.

KOCH, Kenneth

(27 February 1925).

Not unlike that of his Harvard College buddy JOHN ASHBERY, Koch's early poetry was more experimental than what he later produced. His classic avant-garde text is *When the Sun Tries to Go On*, which was written in 1953, first published in a one-shot magazine, *The Hasty Papers* (1960), and later reprinted as a book. Many pages long, it offers interminable unintelligibility in a regularly irregular meter, evenly measured lines, and consistent diction. The critic Jonathan Cott (1942) wrote long ago that it "defies explication or even persistent reading." Koch has also written plays, some considerably more experimental (and substantial) than others. At their best, such as *Pericles* (1960) and *Bertha* (1959), they include inspired parodies and nonsensical writing. In *George Washington Crossing the Delaware* (1962, which originated as a response to a Larry Rivers painting of the same title), Koch swiftly ridicules the myths of American history, the language of politicians, war films, military strategies, patriotism, and much else, the theme of his burlesques being that accepted familiar versions are no more credible than his comic rewritings. Also a Professor of English at Columbia University, Koch has written popular treatises on the teaching of poetry. Though Stephen Koch (1941) is likewise a writer and a Columbia professor who also pronounces his surname "Coke" (in contrast to former New York City mayor "Kotch"), they are not related.

Books of Poetry: *Ko; or, A Season on Earth*. New York: Grove, 1960; *Thank You and Other Poems*. New York: Grove, 1962; *When the Sun Tries to Go On* (1953, 1960). Los Angeles: Black Sparrow, 1969; *Sleeping with Women*. Los Angeles: Black Sparrow, 1969; *The Art of Love*. New York: Random House, 1975; *The Duplications*. New York: Random House, 1977; *Days and Nights*. New York: Random House, 1982; *Seasons on Earth*. New York: Viking, 1987; *Selected Poems 1950–1982*. New York: Random House, 1985; *On the Great Atlantic Rainway: Selected Poems 1950–88*. New York: Knopf, 1994.

Plays: *Bertha and Other Plays*. New York: Grove Press, 1966; *A Change of Hearts: Plays, Films, and Other Dramatic Works*. New York: Random House, 1973; *One Thousand Avant-Garde Plays*. New York: Knopf, 1988.

Fiction: *The Red Robins*. New York: Random House, 1975; *Hotel Lambosa*. Minneapolis: Coffee House, 1993.

Pegagogy: *Wishes, Lies, Dreams: Teaching Children To Write Poetry*. New York: Random House, 1970; *Rose, Where Did You Get That Red? Teaching Great Poetry to Children*. New York: Random House, 1973; *I Never Told Anybody: Teaching Poetry Writing in a Nursing Home*. New York: Random House, 1977.

Interpretation: Lehman, David. *The Last Avant-Garde*. New York: Doubleday, 1998.

KOLÁŘ, JIŘI

(24 September 1914).

If one's name is one's fate, then it was inevitable that this Czech, whose family name is pronounced like "ko-large," should produce the most original COLLAGE of the past two decades. Initially a poet, who had published books as early as 1941, Kolář was progressing toward LETTRISM and CONCRETE POETRY when, during the post-World War II Soviet occupation of his country, he incorporated other materials into his works. "Screws and razor blades, nuts and bolts took the place of words, thereby creating a poetry of things," recalls Thomas Messer, himself a Czech who for many years headed the Guggenheim Museum in New York. "By controlled crumpling of reproduced images borrowed mostly from art history he created the *crumplage*; by introducing into the collage composition movable parts that could be lifted, the *ventilage*; and through the fragmentation and reconstitution of written and printed texts (which often used occult and arcane alphabets) he created his plastic style through the Greek-lettered *chiasmage*." In *rollage*, thin strips from one image are interspersed with thin strips taken from another image so that, especially if both images are familiar, one comments on the other. Eventually a fully conscious visual artist, Kolář has extended his compositional principles into reliefs and even three-dimensional objects. Some Kolář work is funny; all of it is indubitably clever and identifiable as his. Perhaps because Kolář is self-taught in visual art, he works exclusively with texts and images that have already been printed. In 1975, the Guggenheim Museum mounted a retrospective so filled with surprises that I rank it, over two decades later, among the strongest one-artist exhibitions I have ever seen.

Visual Art: *Always Beautiful*, 1960; *The Ballroom*, 1961; *Times Past*, 1963; *Japan's Sun*, 1964; *Meditating Girl*, 1964; *Bloody Money*, 1965; *Compote Tray with Pear*, 1965; *Apple*, 1965; *The Parable of the Blind (after Bruegel)*, n.d.; *Daydreaming Boy*, n.d.; *St. Francis Preaching to the Bird (after Giotto)*, n.d.; *Duchamp's Vest*, n.d.; *Sign for the Bricklayer's Mess*, 1968; *Restless Salome*, 1969; *Salon of Remembrances*, 1970; *Planets-Universe*, 1973; *Hommage à Matisse*, 1981.

Books: *Birth Certificate*. Prague, 1941; *Limb and Other Poems*. Prague, 1945; *Odes and Variations*. Prague, 1946; *The Chance Witness*. Prague, 1964; *Hinauf und Hinter*. Hanover, Germany, 1969; *Das Sprechende Bild*. Frankfurt: Suhrkamp, 1971.

Exhibition Catalogs: *Jiří Kolář*. New York: Guggenheim Museum, 1975; Kotik, Charlotta. *Jiří Kolář*. Buffalo, New York: Albright Knox, 1978; *Homage á Jiří Kolář: Tagebuch 1968*. Nürnberg, Germany: Die Kunsthalle, 1984; *Jiří Kolář: objetos y collages* Madrid: Museo Nacional Centro de Arte Reina Sofia, 1996.

KOMAR & MELAMID

(11 September 1945 & 14 July 1943, b. Vitaly K., and Alexander M.)

Emerging from the Soviet Union in the mid-1970s, their art made a strong impact, in absentia, in the West, initially among Russian emigrés, who were particularly enthusiastic, later for a larger art public. Their forte were parodies of Soviet heroic imagery and Social Realist representation, beginning with a classic oil painting (1973) of themselves in overlapping profile, replicating a prominent prior image of Lenin cheek to cheek with Stalin. Later images include a "Passport from TransState" (1977), with a parody inscription about privileges granted by the fictitious document. "Don't Babble" (1974) has a severe face with a perpendicular finger over his closed lips, but since the image is off-center, it looks less like a threat than a mistake. *Double Self-Portrait as Young Pioneers* (1982–83) had their adult faces in short pants blowing a bugle at a chest-up statue of Joseph Stalin. *The Origin of Socialist Realism* (1982–83) portrays a draped naked woman fondling Stalin's impassive face. And so on.

Though Komar and Melamid were allowed (i.e., encouraged) to leave the Soviet Union initially for Israel and later for the United States, they continued to make Sots Art, as the critic Margarita Tupitsyn called it, through the 1980s. However, once the fearsome Soviet Union collapsed into a bumbling state, their satire lost its edge. One of the risks of basing art, even good art, upon an unstable social circumstance is that it might change. (Imagine what would happen to feminist art if everyone learned that sexism had ended.) For a while, Komar and Melamid made works in several media about Bayonne, New Jersey, an industrial suburb of New York. More recently, they've been working with George Washington and his resemblances with Marcel Duchamp and Vladimir Lenin, initiating an opera titled *Naked Revolution* (1997) about the historic trio. Though both men have wives, their partnership has remained intact, along with their preference for Russian, through two emigrations.

Books: *Komar & Melemid's Scientific Guide to Art*. Ed. JoAnn Wypijewski. Berkeley: University of California Press, 1999.

Interpretation: Nathanson, Melvyn B., ed. *Komar/Melamid: Two Soviet Dissident Artists*. Intro. Jack Burnham. Carbondale: S. Illinois University Press, 1979; Tupitsyn, Margarita. *Margins of Soviet Art*. Milan, Italy: Giancarlo Politi, 1989.

KONSTRIKTOR, Boris

(30 October 1950; b. B. Mikhailovich Axelrod)

As with the other TRANSFUTURISTS, Konstriktor operates in a variety of media, but places somewhat more weight on

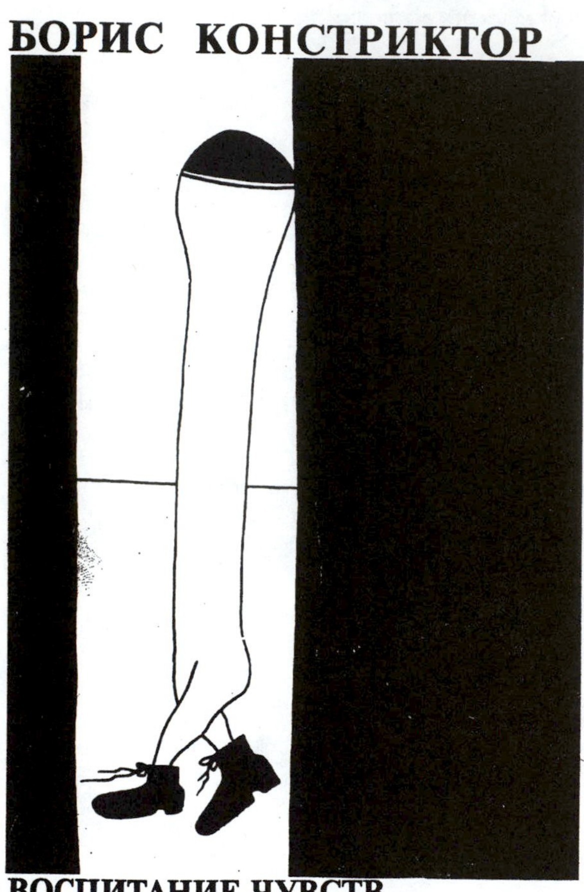

Boris Konstriktor. From *Education of Feelings*, 1994. Courtesy the author.

drawing and painting. He often begins with chance patterns from black washes that he then peoples with human figures in these surreal-abstract spacial settings. He has a special gift for grotesquerie and black humor in which his native St. Petersburg plays a notable role. In many instances, the influence of the Petersburg absurdist movement OBERIU is evident. His earliest poetry, written in the mid to late seventies under the pen name of Boris Vantalov, is not formally innovative, but revives OBERIU absurdism with an additional dose of black humor and sexual imagery that remain his hallmarks. In the early 1990s he began a collaboration with the virtuoso St. Petersburg violinist Boris Kipnis resulting in a series of sound tapes in which Konstriktor recites poetry in a funerial voice while Kipnis improvises on the violin as an accompaniment. Another favorite recent genre of Konstriktor's is the transformation of preprinted items such as picture postcards by overdrawing and overpainting, so as to bring out the ironies of the the original. Konstriktor spent the first half of 1993 at the Schloss Solitude Academy, Stuttgart, Germany on a residency fellowship, resulting in the book *Musikhochschule. 15 Grafiken* (1993), which combines his drawings with a letter from Edmonton, Canada, by Kipnis. He has also written prose and essays on Russian theater.

—Gerald Janecek

Books: *Vospitanie chuvstv. Saga*. Moscow: Izd. E. Pakhomovoi, 1994; *Stikhotvoreniia*. St. Petersburg: Prisma-15, 1993.

KOSTELANETZ, Richard

(14 May 1940).

"The taken name of a collective composed of twelve industrious elves," Kostelanetz has produced countless books of poetry, fiction, experimental prose, criticism, cultural history, and book-art, in addition to audiotapes, videotapes, HOLOGRAMS, and films. By his own admission less a POLYARTIST than a *writer* influenced by the ideal of polyartistry, he thinks of all his creative work, in every medium, as "essentially writing." *Wordsand* was the title of a traveling retrospective exhibition of his art (1978–81); "Wordship" is the name of the urban castle (loft) in which he lives. His poetry, in particular, is a record of formal inventions, beginning with VISUAL POEMS, subsequently including permutational poems, recompositions of familiar words, FOUND POEMS, video poems, poetic holograms, and other alternatives not yet classifiable. Even his set of documentary films about the great Jewish Cemetery of Berlin (with soundtracks in six different languages, made in collaboration with Martin Koerber [1956], 1984–88) is in part about the visual poetry of gravestones. One distinction of Kostelanetz's video art is

J. Nebraska Gifford. *Mind of the Master*, 1991. Collection Richard Kostelanetz.

that his tapes are produced mostly without any cameras, using instead electronic sources such as computers and synthesizer. Since some of them are visual accompaniments to his electroacoustic audio compositions, he classifies them, distinctively, as audiovideotapes.

Kostelanetz's fiction favors such departures as several narratives interwoven into a single continuous text, stories in which each sentence contains one word more or one word less than its predecessor, single-sentence stories, three-word, two-word, and one-word stories, permutational prose, and sequences of ABSTRACT drawings, among other departures. Appearing in scores of literary magazines, his fictions have barely become available in books. They also exemplify his taste for comedy. Some of Kostelanetz's productions are more successful than others, but detractors as well as admirers disagree about which is which.

Not unlike his heroes MOHOLY-NAGY, JOHN CAGE, and AD REINHARDT, Kostelanetz writes frequently, and accessibly, about his esthetic ambitions. Numerous anthologies, many of and about new art/literature, bear his name. One recurring concern is alternative historiography, both in forms and in content (e.g., several autobiographies, this *Dictionary*). Kostelanetz is no less radical in his professional politics than in his art, his single most famous critical book being an elaborate examination of literary politics in america, *The End of Intelligent Writing* (1974). A libertarian anarchist in both word and deed, he even founded an annual of "otherwise unpublishable" graphic work, *Assembling*, whose implicit purpose was the abolition of editorial power. Kostelanetz's devotion to the idea and subject of the avant-garde, as well as to critical standards, has survived changing fashions. His uncle Andre K. (1901–80) was a pioneering conductor/arranger of classical music for recording media, beginning with radio in the early 1930s, when other musicians of similar background scorned the new channel. Following the example of the dedicatee, NICOLAS SLONIMSKY, in his *Baker's* compendiums, Kostelanetz contributed this entry on himself.

Creative Writing: *Wordworks: Poems Selected & New*. Rochester, NY: BOA, 1994; *Solos, Duets, Trios, & Choruses*. Kenosha, WI: Membrane (P.O. Box 4190, 53141), 1983; *Minimal Fictions*. Paradise, CA: Asylum Arts, 1994; *Autobiographies*. New York: Future, 1981; *3-Element Stories*. New York: Archae, 1998; *Vocal Shorts: Collected Performance Texts*. Tarpon Springs, FL: Dramatika, 1998.

Criticism: *The End of Intelligent Writing: Literary Politics in America* (1974). New York: Archae, n.d; *The Old Poetries and the New*. Ann Arbor: University of Michigan Press, 1981; *The New Poetries and Some Olds*. Carbondale: S. Illinois University Press, 1991; *An ABC of Contemporary Reading*. San Diego: San Diego State University Press, 1995; "Andre Kostelanetz." In *On Innovative Music(ian)s*. New York: Limelight, 1989.

Audio Art: *Die Evengelien/The Gospels*, 1982 (Westdeuscher Rundfunk); *The Eight Nights of* Hanukah, 1983 (CBC); *New York City*, 1984 (Westdeutscher Rundfunk); *America's Game*, 1986; *Kaddish*, 1991 (Westdeutscher Rundfunk).

Photography: *Reincarnations*. New York: Future, 1981.

Holography: *On Holography*, 1978; *Antithesis*, 1985; *Hidden Meanings*, 1989.

Recordings: *Invocations*. New York: Folkways, 1983; *The Gospels Abridged*. Santa Monica, CA: Peter & Eileen Norton Foundation, 1990.

Films: *Constructivist Fictions*, with Peter Longauer, 1976–77; *Openings & Closings*, with Bart Weiss, 1976–78; *Ein Verlorenes Berlin* (1983); *Ett Forlorat Berlin* (1984); *A Berlin Lost* (1985); *Berlin Perdu* (1986); *El Berlin Perdido* (1987); *Berlin Sche-Einena Jother* (1988), all with Martin Koerber; *Epiphanies*, 1981–1993.

Videotapes: *Three Prose Pieces*, 1975; *Kinetic Writings*, 1989; *Stringtwo*, 1990.

Audiovideotapes: *Invocations*, 1987; *Onomatopoeia*, 1990.

Exhibition Catalogs: *Wordsand*. Burnaby, Canada: The Gallery at Simon Fraser University, 1978; *Language & Structure in North America*. Toronto: Kensington Arts, 1975.

Interpretation: "Richard Kostelanetz." In *A Reader's Guide to Twentieth-Century Writers*. Ed. Peter Parker. New York: Oxford University Press, 1996; *Richard Kostelanetz's Monumental Birthday Book* (forthcoming); *Ecce Kosti*, New York: Archae, 1996.

KOSUGI, Takehisa

(24 March 1938).

Born in Tokyo, Kosugi came to America in 1962 to do MIXED-MEANS theatrical pieces, often in collaboration with FLUXUS artists. In 1969, he founded the Taj Mahal Travelers to perform group improvisations in various venues, and toured with them during 1971–72. He also belonged to the group Transition, founded in Brussels in the early seventies by Jacques Bekaert (11 May 1940) with Marc Dachy (1952), Ryo Koike, and Michael Herr. In 1977, he joined DAVID TUDOR among the musicians producing "live electronic music" in concerts with the MERCE CUNNINGHAM Dance Company. Kosugi's sound installations have been exhibited around the world.

Works: *Anima I*, event for a long string, 1961; *Organic music*, mixed media performance, 1962; *Ear-Drum-Event*, event for a window and a door, 1962; *g Music g*, mixed-media music, 1966; *Heterodyne*, live electronic instrumental music, 1972; *Interspersion (for 54 Sounds)*, sound installation,1980; *Cycles for 7 sounds*, multi-space performance,1981; *Spacings*, audiovisual version, 1985; + - , a multipurpose event, 1987; *Loops*, 1988.

Recordings: *Violin Improvisations*. New York: Lovely Music, 1990.

Exhibition Catalogs: *Four Devices: Takehisa Kosugi*. Tokyo, Japan: P3 Art and Environment, 1991; *Takehisa Kosugi: Interspersions*. Berlin: DAAD Berliner Künstler Programm, 1992.

KOSUTH, Joseph

(31 January 1945).

Kosuth's principal achievement is such a unique art career it is hard to imagine anyone forecasting it. Whereas other artists had exhibited bits of language and sometimes even sentences, Kosuth in his early twenties showed whole paragraphs, not only in art magazines but, audaciously, on gallery walls. His prose reflected a dense, implicitly pretentious intellectual style derived from late writings of the philosopher Ludwig Wittgenstein (1889–1951), coupled with polemical disdain for nearly everyone else. Kosuth insisted, successfully, that these thoughts about art constitute his entire oeuvre. As the general response at the time was negative, there were doubts whether Kosuth would be visible as an artist a decade later. So the second miracle of Kosuth's career is that he didn't renounce an earlier self and nonetheless survived professionally for three decades.

Books: *Art After Philosophy and After: Collected Writings, 1966–1990*. Ed. Gabriele Guercio. Cambridge: MIT Press, 1991; *Within the Context: Modernism and Critical Practice*. Ghent, Belgium: Coupure, 1977; *Joseph Kosuth: Interviews*. Preface by Charles LeVine. Stuttgart: Edition Patricia Schwarz, 1989.

Exhibition Catalogs: Ramsden, Mel. *Joseph Kosuth: Art Investigations and "Problematics" since 1965*. Lucerne, Switzerland: Kunstmuseum, 1973; Freedberg, David. *The Play of the Unmentionable: An Installation by Joseph Kosuth at the Brooklyn Museum*. New York: Brooklyn Museum/New Press, 1992; *(Eine Grammatische Bemerkung)/(A Grammatical Remark)*. Stuttgart: Württembergischer Kunstverein-Edition Canz, 1993.

Interpretation: Damsch-Wiehager, Renate, ed. *Joseph Kosuth: No Thing, No Self, No Form, No Principle (Was Certain)*. Stuttgart, Germany: Edition Cantz, 1993.

KOTIK, Petr

(27 January 1942).

Born in Prague, Kotik came to America in 1969, where his composing flourished. The principal signature of his best work is a quasi-polyphonic structure of overlapping solos, sometimes proceeding in parallel perfect intervals (i.e., fourths, fifths, and octaves). One departure was adapting his compositional style to the setting not of poetry but of prose, and then not classic prose, like the Bible, say, but high modernist prose. By this departure Kotik produced a sound wholly different from that established for the contemporary singing of words. Perhaps his most distinctive signature comes from the use of parallel fourths and fifths for harmony. The texts he chooses are not simple, easily understood stories, but more difficult writing, sometimes prompting him to write to epic lengths. His masterpiece is *Many Many Women* (1976–78), to a GERTRUDE STEIN text of the same title, which in Kotik's hands becomes polyphonic and antiphonal. His second major work in this genre is *Explorations in the Geometry of Thinking* (1978–80), to passages from BUCKMINSTER FULLER's two-volume *Synergetics* (1976, 1979). Kotik's instrumental music, performed mostly under the elastic umbrella of the S.E.M. Ensemble (its initials meaning, he says, nothing), confronts the post-Cagean problem of writing nonclimactic, uninflected music that nonetheless moves forward.

Recordings: *Many Many Women*. New York: Labor LAB-6/10 (c/o S.E.M., 25 Columbia Place, Brooklyn, NY 11201), 1981; *Petr Kotik/S.E.M. Ensemble: Wilsie Bridge* (1986–87), *Solos and Incidental Harmonies* (1983–85), *Explorations in the Geometry of Thinking* (1978–1980). Berlin, Germany: Ear-Rational Records (Kolonierstr. 25a, D-1000Berlin 65), 1989; *Integrated Solos III* (1986–88) on *Virtuosity with Purpose*. Berlin, Germany: Ear-Rational (c/o S.E.M., 25 Columbia Place, Brooklyn, NY 11201), 1992.

KOVACS, Ernie

See **TELEVISION**.

KRASSNER, Paul

(9 April 1932).

Back in the 1960s, Krassner was probably the most audacious comic writer around. Not unlike other way-out literary comedians (e.g., Karl Kraus, H. L. Mencken), he had his own magazine, *The Realist* (1958), which at times seemed an adult, prose version of *MAD Magazine*, where in fact he had once worked. Krassner's literary specialty has been the fictional anecdote, particularly about politicians, done with details that bestow credibility. This description of Lyndon Johnson was introduced in a passage about Jackie Kennedy that was purportedly removed from William Manchester's best-selling *Death of the President* (1967):

> That man was crouching over the corpse, no longer chuckling but breathing hard and moving his body rhythmically. At first I thought he must be performing some mysterious symbolic rite he'd learned from Mexicans or Indians as a boy. And then I realized—there is only one way to say this—he was literally fucking my husband in the throat. In the bullet wound in front of his throat. He reached a climax and dismounted. I froze. The next thing I remember, he was being sworn in as the new President.

Widely considered objectionable at the time, especially by those initially accepting the "story" as credible, it has become a model for political humor. For instance, when Jay Leno says, as he did, on his national late-night television program that Queen Elizabeth's children celebrated her seventieth birthday "by sleeping with commoners, as they usually do," he was implicitly acknowledging stylistic liberties established by Krassner, no one else.

Books: *How a Satirical Editor Became a Yippie Conspirator.* New York: Putnam's, 1971; *Tales of Tongue Fu*. Berkeley, CA: And/Or (P.O. Box 2246, 94702), 1981; *Best of the Realist*. Philadelphia: Running Press, 1984; *Confessions of a Raving Unconfined Nut: Misadventures in the Counter-Culture*. New York: Simon & Schuster, 1993; *The Winner of the Slow Bicycle Race: The Definitive Satirical Writings*. New York: Seven Stories, 1996.

Recordings: *We Have Ways of Making You Laugh*. Mercury, 1996.

KŘENEK, Ernst

(23 August 1900–23 December 1991).

A precocious musician in Vienna, he became prominent while still in his mid-twenties with the production in Leipzig of his opera *Jonny spielt auf* (1927) which portrays, in mostly atonal music, a black jazz musician pronouned "Yonny," who became so famous he concludes the opera sitting atop a gigantic globe. Soon afterwards, the work was reproduced around the world and translated into over a dozen languages; it was even staged in New York at the Metropolitan Opera with the protagonist as a black-faced white, sooner than racially integrate that august venue at that time. In the 1930s, Křenek adopted SERIAL music, even producing in the new musical language an historical opera *Karl V* (1933) that was, needless to say, less popular than his first foray. Though not Jewish, he found his music banned by the Nazis and so came to America, where he became a professor in backwoods universities, finally ending in Palm Springs, which is a long way, culturally as well as geographically, from Vienna.

Operas: *Zwingburg*, 1924; *Der Sprung über den Schatten*, 1924; *Orpheus und Euyrike*, 1926; *Jonny spielt auf*, 1927; *Der Diktator, Das geheime Königreich, Schwergewicht*, 1928; *Leben des Orest*, 1930; *Karl V*, 1938; *Der goldene Bock*, 1964; *Sardakai*, 1970.

Recordings: *Jonny spielt auf* (1927), with Vienna State Opera cond. H. Hollreiser (Vanguard Classics); *Lamenatio Jeremiae Prophetae*, for mixed chorus a cappella, Op. 93 (1941). RIAS Chamber Choir cond. Marcus Creed (Harmonia Mundi France); *Concerto No. 3 for Piano & Orchestra* (1946). New York Philharmonic cond. Dmitri Mitropoulos (AS Disc).

Books: *Exploring Music*. New York: October House, 1966; *Horizons Circled: Reflections on My Music*. Berkeley: University of California Press, 1974.

Bibliography: Stewart, John L. *Ernst Křenek: The Man and his Music*. Berkeley: University of California Press, 1991.

Autobiography: A voluminous manuscript, reportedly completed in 1950, was deposited at the Library of Congress, not to be opened until fifteen years after his death—wait until 2005.

KRIWET, Ferdinand

(1942).

A precocious VISUAL POET, Kriwet made typewriter poems in 1960 and a few years later "Rundscheibe," which are brilliantly composed lines of overlapping words put into roughly concentric circles. His book about his own early work, *Leserattenfaenge* (1964), includes impressively detailed analyses of those complex early word-image texts. He also produced "poem-paintings" entirely of words drawn in dramatically different letters, usually to fracture familiar and recognizable words ("Beat Us"); constructed columns imprinted with words and letters in various typefaces; made films animated with words; and created audiotape collages that are still rebroadcast over German radio. *Textroom* (1969) extends his way with words into an entire room, whose walls, ceiling, and floor are filled with rows of metal plates, each embossed with two eleven-letter combinatory words.

Books: *Durch die Runse auf den Redder*. Berlin: Fietkau, 1965; *Apollo America*. Frankfurt, Germany: Suhrkamp, 1969; *Kriwet 69*. Köln: Köloischer Künstverein, 1969; *Decomposition of the Literary Unit*. San Francisco, CA: Nova Broadcast, 1971; *Campaign: Wahlkamph in der USA*. With a recording. Düsseldorf: Droste, 1974.

Interpretation: Woods, Gerald, et al. *Art Without Boundaries*. New York: Praeger, 1972.

KRONOS QUARTET

See **ARDITTI QUARTET**.

KRUCHONYKH, Aleksei Eliseevich

(9 [21] February 1886–17 June 1968).

The wild man of RUSSIAN FUTURISM, notorious for his ZAUM poetry, Kruchonykh began his career as an art teacher but became associated with the Hylaea branch of the Russian Futurists and, in 1912, began publishing a series of lithographed primitivist booklets with his own and other Futurists' poetry, with illustrations by Mikhail Larionov (1881–1964), Natalia Goncharova (1881–1962), KAZIMIR MALEVICH, and others. Kruchonykh's most famous poem, "Dyr bul shchyl," is the first Russian poem written explicitly in an "indefinite" personal language.

Although the idea of writing poetry in "unknown words" was suggested to him by David Burliuk (1882–1967), it was Kruchonykh who developed this form of poetry in all its ramifications. His most elaborate creation was the opera *Victory Over the Sun*, performed in St. Petersburg in December 1913, with music by MIKHAIL MATIUSHIN and sets and costumes by Kazimir Malevich. A scandalous success, the performances were sold out. Kruchonykh continued to experiment in various ways to create indeterminacy in language on all levels from the phonetic to the narrative, until the early 1920s. Throughout this period, he was often the critical whipping boy of Russian Futurism; his works were treated as examples of the most ridiculous extremes of the movement. While VLADIMIR MAYAKOVSKY and VELIMIR KHLEBNIKOV were sometimes granted reluctant respect, Kruchonykh was always treated as beneath serious consideration. His anti-esthetic imagery, crude eroticism, and deliberately clumsy language contributed to an impression of a lack of talent and culture. His most famous poem, when acknowledged, was (and still is) almost always misquoted.

During World War I, Kruchonykh was drafted to work on the southern railroad, which brought him into contact with ILIAZD and Igor Terentev (1892–1937) in Tiflis, and he formed with them the avant-garde group 41°. At this time his works consisted of a long series of handmade ("autographic") booklets duplicated by carbon copy or hectograph; others were elegantly typographed by ILIAZD. In the former, his ZAUM poetry reached a Minimalist level in sparse compositions of individual letters and lines and even blank pages. For Kruchonykh, the visual appearance of poetry was always important, as was its sound texture.

In 1921, Kruchonykh moved permanently to Moscow, where he attempted to enter literary life by arguing for the usefulness of his literary experiments for the new socialist culture and producing a series of valuable theoretical texts. However, his poetry was already less adventurous. Because of his reputation and a certain residual thickness of texture, his efforts to create works that would appeal to the common reader or theatergoer were unsuccessful. Though shunned by Soviet publishers after 1930, Kruchonykh continued to write significant poetry afterward; he survived into the 1960s by collecting and trading in avant-garde and mainstream poetic materials.

Kruchonykh remained the most consistent publicist for Futurist views. His works are still largely unknown to the Russian reader, in part because the sole edition of his work has appeared in Germany (1973); only in the past decade have his works begun to receive serious scholarly attention, initially in the West but now in Russia as well.

—Gerald Janecek

Works: *Igra v Adu* (A Game in Hell). Moscow,1912; *Mirskontsa* (The World Backwards). Moscow, 1912; *Utinoye gnezdyshko . . . durnykh slov* (A Ducks Nest . . . of Bad Words). St. Petersburg, 1913; *Te Li Le*. St. Petersburg, 1914; *Zaumnaya Kniga* (Transrational Book). Moscow, 1915; *Voyna* (War). Petrograd, 1915, Petrograd, 1916; *Izbrannoe*. Ed. Vladimir Markov. Munich, Germany: Funk, 1973; *La Victoire sur le soleil* (Victory Over the Sun, opera) Lausanne: L'Age d'homme, 1976. (Text in Russian, rept. 1913, original & French translation.)

Bibliography: Janecek, Gerald. *The Look of Russian Literature*. Princeton: Princeton University Press, 1984; ——. *Zaum: The Transrational Poetry of Russian Futurism*. San Diego: San Diego State University Press, 1996; Markov, Vladimir. *Russian Futurism: A History*. Berkeley: University of California Press, 1968.

Website: http://www.thing.net/~grist/l&d/kruch/lkrucht1.htm

KRUGER, Barbara

(26 January 1945).

Kruger has made a large-scale visual art of advertising imagery, customarily enlarged to monstrous proportions, coupled with commercial slogans in billboard type. The pretence is saying something significant about consumer culture; yet art-world viewers have no difficulty deciphering Kruger's accessible, if not familiar, messages. (And it is highly unlikely that such paintings ever affected anyone who was not already converted.) Kruger's works are thus best viewed as advertisements for themselves—or perhaps herself.

Books: *Remote Control: Power, Cultures, and the World of Appearances*. Cambridge: MIT Press, 1993.

Website: http://www.geocities.com/SoHo/Cafe/9747/kruger.html

Exhibition Catalogs: *We Won't Play Nature to Your Culture*. London: Inst. of Contemporary Arts, 1983; *Jenny Holzer, Barbara Kruger*. Jerusalem: The Israel Museum, 1986; Harper, Jenny, and Lita Barrie. *Barbara Kruger: The Temporary-Contemporary*. Wellington: New Zealand National Gallery of Art, 1988.

Interpretation: Linker, Kate. *Love for Sale: The Words and Pictures of Barbara Kruger*. New York: Abrams, 1990; Mann, Paul. *The Theory-Death of the Avant-Garde*. Bloomington: Indiana University Press, 1991.

KUBRICK, Stanley

See **2001**.

KUENSTLER, Frank

(17 April 1928–11 August 1996).

In 1964, from the imprint of Film Culture, a New York publisher noted for its film magazine of the same title, appeared *Lens*, a book so extraordinary that it was completely unnoticed at the time. It opens with a single-page "Emblem," a sort of preface that establishes in six sections that anything might happen in the following pages, including the destruction of both sense and syntax. The last section of "Emblem" reads: "aura.Dictionary. aura.Crossword Puzzle. aura.Skeleton. aura.Poem./Once upon a time." What follows are eighty long paragraphs so devoid of connection, from line to line, from word to word, that you realize only a human being could have made them; even the most aleatory computer program would have put together, even inadvertently, two words that made sense. The book concludes with the tag "New York, N. Y., 1952–64," suggesting that *Lens* took a full dozen years to write; I can believe it, because anyone who thinks such writing easy to do should try it sometime (and send me the results). Kuenstler's later publications include *13 1/2 Poems* (1984), which is a progression of increasingly experimental poems (though none as radical as *Lens*). Toward the end of his life he sold antiquarian books on the street in New York, usually on Broadway north of 86th Street.

Works: *Lens*. New York: Film Culture, 1964; *Fugitives, Rounds*. New York: Eventorium, 1966; *Paradise News*. New York: Eventorium, 1966; *13 1/2 Poems*. New York: SZ, 1984; *In Which*. New York: Cairn Editions (P.O. Box 573, Old Chelsea Station, 10011), 1994; *The Seafarer, B.Q.E, and Other Poems*. New York: Cairn, 1996.

KURYOKHIN, Sergey

(10 June 1954–9 July 1996).

A classically trained piano player extraordinaire, the Russian musician Sergey Kuryokhin embraced early on a global musical culture, striving for extreme eclecticism. Being instrumental in jump-starting St. Petersburg rock-n-roll and new jazz in the late seventies, Kuryokhin in the eighties formed his own eclectic band, Pop-Mechanics. Including both human and animal musicians, Pop-Mechanics pursued large-scale improvised neo-Dada performances, mixing classical music, rock-n-roll, jazz, and the Soviet propaganda music with the most "inappropriate" absurd theatrics. As the Cold War receded, Kuryokhin began to tour extensively in Europe, Japan, and the United States. His last recording, *Friends Afar*, made with Keshavan Maslak, is a testament of his subversive genius. An early death cut short Kuryokhin's brilliant career at the height of his creative powers.

—Igor Satanovsky

Recordings: *Introduction to Pop-Mechanics*. UK: Leo Rec; *Popular Science*. USA: Rykodisc; ——. and Maslak, Keshavan. *Friends Afar*. Sound Wave Records, Japan.

KUZMINSKY, Konstantin Konstantinovich

(16 April 1940).

A multilingual Russian poet, essayist, art collector/historian, visual/performance artist, and all around "enfant terrible" of contemporary Russian letters, Kuzminsky became one of the central figures in the St.Petersburg literary/artistic underground scene in the sixties and early seventies. His impressive organizing skills helped to integrate what could have been several groups of independently minded writers/poets/artists into a movement that rediscovered and extended the legacy of Russian Avant-garde/Russian Modernism. He was one of "five young poets from Leningrad" featured in a 1972 book by Suzanne Massie; another was his contemporary (only six weeks younger), Joseph Brodsky (1940–96), whose work is more self-consciously traditional.

As a poet, Kuzminsky came to maturity in the early seventies, with the long poem "Babylon Tower," wherein he drew on his different influences, from eighteenth-century Russian poetry to Russian Futurism and beyond. This poem put forward not one, but several literary styles that can be identified as Russian Imagism (not to be confused with Russian Imaginism), Russian Beat, and Russian jazz poetry, serving, in effect, as a

Konstantin Konstantinovich Kuzminsky, Cover of *Babylon Tower* (Limited Edition, PODVAL publishing, 1992). © K. K. Kuzminsky & V. Mishin-Bukovsky, 1968.

blueprint for later developments in his writing. "Babylon Tower" also showed Kuzminsky's first forays into multilingual poetry. What started as his early interest in various Russian dialects, evolved into "writing in tongues," transcending European languages to include exotic African and Polynesian dialects. Kuzminsky's outstanding short work "Leopold Havelka" mixes twenty-four languages into a coherent page-long poem, demonstrating his taste for the outrageous, as well as his mastery of sound textures: "Welcome, You, lotry und shabery, Bielorussians mit Ukrainische geshriben das Kunstler und painter sans l'oeil. Yomkippurisch Blit monster Sie Branchen Teobaldus Grossier mit Poline zum Aliosha geschlossen - Potz und tausend Potz - meine herren und Damen, genuk . . . ."

Pushed out of his country by the K.G.B. in 1974, Kuzminsky settled in the United States. In the following fifteen years he edited and introduced (with G. Kovalev) *The Blue Lagoon*, a definitive nine-volume anthology of the underground Russian poetry from World War II to the seventies. Inclusion of juicy details, conflicting accounts, anecdotes of bohemian lifestyles, and tales of literary intrigue that would be shunned by most academians put his selections in the larger social/historic context, set a high standard yet to be matched by any academic scholar, and made *The Blue Lagoon* the most memorable Russian anthology of the century.

—Igor Satanovsky

Bibliography: Massie, Suzanne. *The Living Mirror: Five Young Poets from Leningrad*. Garden City, NY: Doubleday, 1972; Kuzminsky, K., and G. Kovalev, eds. *The Blue Lagoon: An Anthology of Modern Russian Poetry*. Newtonville, MA: Oriental Research Partners (P.O. Box 158, 02160). 1980–1986 (in Russian).

LA BARBARA, Joan

(8 June 1947; b. J. Linda Lotz).

Initially a vocalist adept at "extended" vocal techniques, including "circular breathing" while producing sound, La Barbara became a composer, mostly of pieces for herself, sometimes as continuous sound installations. She also has written articles and reviews of avant-garde music. Her second husband is the composer MORTON SUBOTNICK, whose art is roughly as moderately innovative as his wife's. It is one of the mysteries of artists' marriages that two people who have pursued independent careers, once together in midlife, come to resemble each other.

Compositions: *Hear What I Feel* for voice, 1974; *Vocal Extensions* for voice and live electronics, 1975; *Thunder* for voice, six timpani and electronics, 1975; *Space Testing* for acoustic voice, 1976; *Chords and Gongs* for voice, cimbalom, and gongs, 1976; *Cathing* for voice and tape, 1977; *Twelve for Five in Eight* for 5 voices, 1979; *Erin*, radio work, 1980; *Time(d) Trials and Unscheduled Events* for voice on tape, 1984; *Loose Tongues* for 8 solo voices and tape, 1985; *Prologue* to *The Book of Knowing . . . (and) of Overthrowing*, aria for voice and tape with visual environment and costumes, 1987–88; *"to hear the wind roar"* for voice, percussion, and tape, 1991; *The Misfortune of the Immortals*, interactive media opera, 1994–95.

Recordings: *Shaman Song*. New York: New World Records, 1998. *Sound Paintings*. New York: Lovely Music, 1999.

Interview: Zimmermann, Walter. "Joan La Barbara." In *Desert Plants*. Köln: Beginner, 1981.

LA GRAN SCENA OPERA CO.

(1981).

The idea of men playing female operatic roles is not new, but never before has it been so elaborate and sustained. The effect is initially that of parody and thus of camp, which comes from being so awful it is good. (By the late twentieth century, all nineteenth-century opera seems campy, while many noticed that Maria Callas, for one, often seemed to be a man playing a woman, or perhaps a woman playing a man playing a woman.) However, the Gran Scena performance transcends those effects, being lovingly done, with strong falsetto voices that take pride in their ethereal resonance. The company's founder and mastermind, Ira Siff (1946), by profession a vocal coach, is the best example of esthetic and vocal virtuosity.

The typical Gran Scena program consists of excerpts from classic operas, usually just scenes, sometimes whole acts. The sections are framed by "Miss Sylvia Bills," who has the verbal jokes. Precisely because it must be seen that men are playing women, their productions succeed on videotape but not on audio discs. The work of two all-male ballet companies, *The Trockadero Gloxinia Ballet* (1972) and its descendent and rival, the sumptuously named *Les Ballets Trockadero de Monte Carlo* (1974), is esthetically similar.

Bibliography: *La Gran Scena Opera Co.* New York: Video Artists' International, 1986.

LA MAMA EXPERIMENTAL THEATRE CLUB (E.T.C.)

(1961).

Founded by Ellen Stewart (1919), a born impresario, and the playwright Paul Foster (1931), it became the exemplar of off-off-Broadway, producing plays that, not only for reasons of avant-garde difference, were not acceptable to producers on Broadway and an increasingly commercialized off-Broadway. Though most of its productions belong to the tradition of staged drama, La Mama became a receptive venue for many touring productions of more performance-oriented theater. As Ellen Stewart once wrote, "The plays that we're doing are the plays I want to do. I don't interfere in how they get to be that way."

Bibliography: Stewart, Ellen. "La Mama Experimental Theatre Club." In *Eight Plays from Off-Off-Broadway*, eds. Nick Orzel and Michael Smith. Indianapolis: Bobbs Merrill, 1966.

Web Site: http://www.nytheatre-wire.com/LMhome.htm

Documentary: *La Mama: Ellen Stewart.* New York: NET American Playhouse, 1987.

LAFFOLEY, Paul

(c.1936).

Trained in classics and architecture before turning to painting, Laffoley makes work so eccentric it is innovative by virtue of its waywardness. He is essentially a visionary painter, in the great American tradition, whose paintings represent both verbally and visually unseen forces, mostly cosmological. Some of Laffoley's paintings have a density of words and symbols that reflect charts as they transcend charting. *The Levogyre* (1976), which he describes as "nested shells connected by gimbals," is, he says, "an attempt to model a photon creating light, and in turn an atom of consciousness. The structure of the Levogyre derives from the structure of the Universe proposed by Eudoxus (the astronomer pupil of Plato). Eudoxus stated that the Universe is a series of nested crystalline spheres which contained the stars as fixed, the planets which moved, down to the central nonrotating Earth. Each sphere is connected to the next by gimballike axes which are randomly distributed." Other thoughtful and thought-filled paintings portray *The Orgone Motor* (1981), *The Astrakakiteraboat* (1983), *De Rerum Natura* (1985), *The Aetheiapolis* (1987), and *Thanaton III* (1989). Some of Laffoley's activities are conducted under the name of The Boston Visionary Cell, Inc. His illustrated book about his own work—more precisely, his own imagination—ranks among the richest artist's self-expositions.

Paul Laffoley, *Get Thee Behind Me, Satan*, 1974. Courtesy Paul Laffoley of The Boston Visionary Cell, Inc. [1974]/The Kent Gallery.

Paintings: *The Levogyre*, 1976; *The Orgone Motor*, 1981; *The Astrakakiteraboat*, 1983; *De Rerum Natura*, 1985; *The Aetheiapolis*, 1987. *Thanaton III*, 1989.

Writings: *The Phenomenology of Revelation*. Ed. Jeanne Marie Wasilik. New York: Kent, 1989.

LANGUAGE-CENTERED POETRY

(aka "Language" poetry, c. 1975).

Whether this constitutes a genuine artistic category or simply an opportunistic banner is a good question. Excessive mutual backslapping, very much in imitation of earlier "New York Poets," raises suspicions, especially in America, because the work of those paraded under this newer rubric is quite various (while the work of others working in esthetically similar veins, but not included, is often superior). The interior mental states of Hannah Weiner's (1929–96) poetry, for instance, scarcely resemble the dry experimentalism of Bruce Andrews (1948), whose poetry has little in common with the fragmented, elliptical narratives of Michael Palmer (1943) or Barrett Watten's (1948) extracting phrases from ulterior texts. (If any artists' group lacks esthetic principle, it is really functioning as an exclusive club more worthy of acknowledgment in a history of false snobbery. Willfully excluding individuals who might by esthetic right belong smacks too much of elitism for common comfort. And people behaving like an army inevitably raises questions about what others think of military mentalities.) In the earlier edition of this *Dictionary*, I questioned whether this entry would ever be reprinted—whether the term would survive; the doubt is raised again.

Anthologies: Andrews, Bruce, and Charles Bernstein, eds. *The L-A-N-G-U-A-G-E Book*. Carbondale, IL: Southern Illinois, 1984; Messerli, Douglas, ed. *"Language" Poetries: An Anthology*. New York: New Directions, 1987; *From the Other Side of the Century*. Los Angeles: Sun & Moon, 1994; Silliman, Ron, ed. *In the American Tree*. Orono, ME: National Poetry Foundation, 1986.

Criticism: Andrews, Bruce. *Paradise & Method: Poetics & Praxis*. Evanston, IL: Northwestern University Press, 1996; Watten, Barrett. *Total Syntax*. Carbondale: S. Illinois University Press, 1985.

Interpretation: McGann, Jerome. *Black Riders: The Visible Language of Modernism*. Princeton: Princeton University Press, 1993.

Hartley, George. *Textual Politics and the Language Poets*. Bloomington: Indiana University Press, 1989.

Perelman, Bob. *The Marginalization of Poetry*. Princeton: Princeton University Press, 1996.

LANSKY, Paul

(14 June 1944).

Lansky's strongest work uses the computer to create a pseudospeech reminiscent of the best acoustic poetry of CHARLES AMIRKHANIAN while also exemplifying the principle that, with a sophisticated computer, the composer can realize speech-music that is beyond the capabilities of live human beings and even earlier electronic techniques. Lansky's *Idle Chatter* (1985) creates the illusion of thousands of people speaking, each at roughly equal volume. The notes accompanying its CD release speak of an eloquent attempt to say nothing without taking a breath for 565.9 seconds, 9.43 minutes, 31,690,400 samples, or 63,380,800 bytes—take your pick. Knowing a good idea when he invents one, Lansky has produced *Justmoreidlechatter* (1987) and *Notjustmoreidlechatter* (1988), as well as *Small Talk* (1988). Formerly a French hornist, currently a professor of music at Princeton University, he has composed in other ways with speech and with instruments.

Works: *Idle Chatter*, 1985; *Justmoreidlechatter*, 1987; *Notjustmoreidlechatter*, 1988; *Small Talk*, 1988.

Recordings: *Six Fantasies on a Poem by Thomas Campion (1978–79)* & *Still Time*. New York: CRI, 1994; *Idle Chatter,* on *New Computer Music*. Mainz, Germany: Wergo, 1987; *Small Talk & August*, *Guy's Harp & Not So Heavy Metal*. Albany, CA: New Albion, 1991; *Homebrew*. New York: Bridge, 1992; *More than Idle Chatter*. New York: Bridge, 1994; *Conversation Pieces*. New York: Bridge, 1998.

LARDNER, Ring

(6 March 1885–25 September 1933).

Lardner is remembered mostly as a lightweight writer whose baseball stories were recently collected into a book,

Ring Around the Bases (1992). However, it was the critic Martin Esslin (1916), in *The Theatre of the Absurd* (1961), who discovered a more experimental writer in his very short plays. "Some of their funniest lines occur in the stage directions, so that the little plays become more effective when read than when seen," Esslin writes. "How, for example, is a stage direction like the following, in *Clemo Uti (The Water Lilies)*, to be acted? '(Mama enters from an exclusive waffle parlor. She exits as if she had had waffles.)"' Another play is credited as "translated from the Squinch," while a third compresses five acts into a few minutes. Precisely in broaching the unperformable, these resemble GERTRUDE STEIN's plays, written about the same time. Until a publisher collects these theatrical texts into a single book, they remain hard to find.

Works: "The Tridget of Greva"; "Abend di Anni Nouveau." In *Theatre Experiment*, ed. Michael Benedikt. Garden City, New York: Doubleday Anchor, 1967; *Ring Around the Bases: The Complete Baseball Stories of Ring Lardner*. Ed. with an intro. by Matthew J. Bruccoli. New York: Scribner's, 1992.

Biography: Elder, Donald. *Ring Lardner: A Biography*. Garden City, NY: Doubleday, 1956.

LAS VEGAS

(c. 1947).

Las Vegas represents a continuing collective attempt to create a city as a unique work of art. As a 1940s frontier town in the middle of an otherwise empty desert but near the construction site that became the Hoover Dam, Las Vegas initially benefited from the absence of laws forbidding gambling. When enterpreneurs decided to build hotels initially for southern Californians on a holiday, it began to assume its current identity. After a dormant period, consruction increased rapidly in the 1990s. As the hotels were built to have unique identities, rather than restrictive uniformity, Las Vegas itself became a work of avant-garde art. The kind of shameless eccentricity of Hollywood architecture, so aptly satirized in Nathaniel West's *The Day of the Locust* (1939), is in Las Vegas extended to a higher level, if not to infinity. Simply to walk down its main tourist street, Las Vegas Boulevard, customarily called the Strip, is to experience not only impressive kinetic signage (itself a public art form insufficiently appreciated) but, on one stretch, a building styled after medieval England next to an Egyptian pyramid adjacent to another hotel meant to recreate neighborhoods within New York City. Elsewhere on the Strip, next to a hotel that has a pseudo-volcano fronting the street that "erupts" every twenty minutes is another hotel that mounts a fight between two eighteenth-century pirate ships every ninety minutes. Even on foot, one is continually moving through different worlds (or their surrogates). Another hotel on the Strip, new in 1998, houses an art gallery with classic sculptures and paintings. It was not for nothing that Robert Venturi (1925), an academically trained architect, boosted his reputation by publishing back in 1972 an influential essay titled *Learning from Las Vegas*.

In the hotels are, in addition to casinos devoid of clocks, spectacularly spacious theatrical venues that sponsor live entertainments ranging in quality from semipro magicians to the world-class performance troupe, Cirque du Soleil. The surprise is that the gambling moguls have become modern-day Medicis who support the traditional art of live performance in the age of mass media. As a continuous show in itself, the Las Vegas Strip is always changing, as hotels only a few decades old are razed to make space for new ones with yet more extravagant images (northern Italy, Venice, etc.). Because no one could have imagined this by himself, Las Vegas represents a collective effort that has the character of folk art and yet differs from traditional folk art in its corporate sponsorship. Obviously, profits from gambling, which is rigged to fleece, finance this mammoth eccentricity; but don't forget that it is possible to experience Las Vegas as an everchanging INSTALLATION without ever losing a penny to vice.

Bibliography: *Planet Vegas*. Ed. Rick Browne and James Marshall. San Francisco: Collins, 1995. Land, Barbara & Myrick. *A Short History of Las Vegas*. Reno: University of Nevada Press, 1999; Venturi, Robert. *Learning from Las Vegas* (1972). 2d Ed. Cambridge, MA: MIT Press, 1977.

Web Site: http://www.las-vegas-guide.com/

LAUTRÉAMONT, Comte de

(4 April 1846–24 November 1870; b. Isidore Ducasse).

Born in Uruguay of French parents, Lautréamont came to Paris to prepare for the polytechnical high school. Failing in this mission, and plagued by poverty, he began a prose poem, *Les Chants de Maldoror* (posthumously published in 1890), which, while reflecting classical literature, became a precursor of SURREALISM. As his protagonist, Maldoror, suffers gruesome misfortunes, Lautrémont's language becomes extremely hallucinatory: "Who could have realized that whenever he embraced a young child with rosy cheeks he longed to slice off those cheeks with a razor, and he would have done it many times had he not been restrained by the thought of Justice with her long funereal procession of punishments."

Books: *Maldoror*. Trans. Guy Wernham. New York: New Directions, 1946; *Maldoror & the complete works of the Comte de Lautréamont*. Trans. Alexis Lykiard. Cambridge, MA: Exact Change, 1994.

LAX, Robert

(30 November 1915).

A Columbia College chum of both AD REINHARDT and THOMAS MERTON, Lax has sought linguistic purity comparable to the visual purity of the former and the spiritual purity of the latter. It is fair to say that Lax writes the poetry that Merton should have written, were he a true Trappist artist. Lax's poetry is extremely reductive, sometimes with only a few words arrayed in various ways. In his great long poem *Black and White* (1966), the total vocabulary consists of only three different words and an ampersand. Because Lax resides on a Greek island and does not actively submit his poems to publishers, it is not surprising that they have appeared sparingly, first in chapbooks from Emil Antonucci's Journeyman Press in Brooklyn and then in perfectbound bilingual books from Pendo Verlag in Zurich, Switzerland. In the mid-1990s, two American commercial publishers recently issued collections, the Grove larger than the Overlook, that were scarcely noticed.

Books: *Circus of the Sun/Circus/Cirque Circo*. Trans. into German by Alfred Kuoni; French by Catherine Mauger; Spanish by Ernesto Cardenal. Zürich: Pendo, 1974; *Selections*. Hove, England: X-Press, 1978; *Episodes/Episoden*. Ed. Robert J. Buttmann. Zürich: Pendo, 1983; *Fables/Fabeln*. Zürich: Pendo, 1983; *21 Pages/21 Seiten*. Zürich: Pendo, 1984; *Journal A/Tagebuch A*. Zürich: Pendo, 1986; *33 Poems*. New York: New Directions, 1987; *Journal B/Tagebuch B*. Zürich: Pendo, 1988; *The Light/The Shade*. Zürich: Pendo, 1989; *Journal C/Tagebuch C*. Zürich: Pendo, 1990; *Psalm & Homage to Wittgenstein*. Zürich: Pendo, 1991; *Mogador's Book/Für Mogador*. Ed. Paul J. Speath. Zürich: Pendo, 1992; *Journal D/Tagebuch D*. Zürich: Pendo, 1993; *Notes/Notizen*. Zürich: Pendo (% Paul Spaeth, Friedsam Library, St. Bonaventure University, NY 14778), 1995; *Love Had a Compass*. Ed. James J. Uebbing. New York: Grove, 1996; *A Thing That Is: New Poems*. Woodstock, NY: Overlook, 1997.

LE CORBUSIER

(6 October 1887–27 August 1965; b. Charles-Édouard Jeanneret).

A prime mover behind the INTERNATIONAL STYLE, Le Corbusier made one construction so different from prevailing ideas, as well as so original, that it expands any

Le Corbusier. "Notre-Dame-du-Haut Chapel," CORBIS/Patrick Ward.

earlier sense of his architecture: the Chapel of Notre-Dame-du-Haut in Ronchamp, France. Built between 1950 and 1955, it has a tower reminiscent of a grain silo, along with a sweeping roof that resembles a floppy hat, covering curved walls with rectangular apertures of various sizes and shapes, in sum reflecting le Corbusier's taste for articulated light and reinforced concrete, as well as qualities sparse and ascetic. Because one wall is set several feet inside the edge of the roof, it is possible to be under the roof and yet open to the elements. About the interior of this chapel, Russell Walden has written: "He used the east wall as a cyclorama against which the public and more private altars were set, incorporating a swiveling virgin in the reredos wall." The forms of this building remind us that Le Corbusier began as a CUBIST painter who initially signed his works "Jeanneret" and that he continued to produce twodimensional visual art throughout his career. Marc Treib's *Space Articulation in Seconds* (1997) remembers Corbusier's remarkable structure for EDGARD VARÈSE's *Poème électronique* the Philips Pavilion at the 1958 Brussels World's Fair. This pioneering environment of continuously kinetic sound and images, color and voice, in an eight-minute cycle, reportedly attracted nearly two million spectators, most of them no doubt passing through it as part of a larger show.

Architecture: Catrohan House, 1921; Le Pavillon de L' Esprit Nouveau, 1925, rebuilt in Bologna, 1977; Villas at Garches, 1927; and Poissy, 1929–31; United Nations Headquarters, with others. New York, 1947; Unité d'Habitation, Marseille, France, 1947–52; Chapel of Notre-Dame-du-Haut, Ronchamp, 1950–55; Phillips Pavilion at the Brussels Exhibition, 1958; Museum of Modern Art, Tokyo, 1957; Dominican Friary of La Tourette, 1957–60; Carpenter Centre for the Visual Arts, Harvard University, Cambridge, MA, 1961–64.

Christo, *Running Fence* (1976). Photo Morton Beebe. © 1976 CORBIS/ Morton Beebe, S.F.

Wassily Kandinsky, *Composition*. © 2000 Artists Rights Society (ARS), New York/ ADGAP, Paris.

B

J

Carla Rae Johnson, "POVERTY: Field of Dreams Deferred" from *The Last Chance Salon: Games for the Millennium* (1997).

F

Dan Flavin, *Untitled (for you Leo, in long respect and affection) 2* (1977). Photo © 1991 Dorothy Zeidman, courtesy Leo Castelli Gallery.

Elliott Barowitz, *The Art Critic* (1996–97). Courtesy the artist.

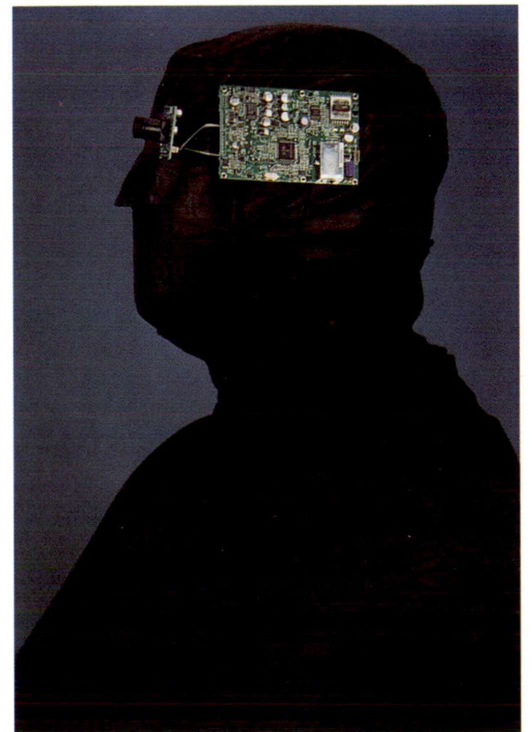

Eduardo Kac, *Telepresence Garment* (1995–96). Photo: Anna Yu.

Edward Kienholz, *Backseat Dodge* (1938). Courtesy the Pace Gallery.

W

Andy Warhol, *Campbell's Soup* (1966). © 2000 Andy Warhol Foundation for the Visual Arts/ARS, New York.

Piet Mondrian, *Composition No. II* (1922). © 2000 Artists Rights Society (ARS), New York/Beeldrecht, Amsterdam.

Kazimir Malevich, *Sportsmen* (1928). CORBIS/The State Russian Museum, St. Petersburg.

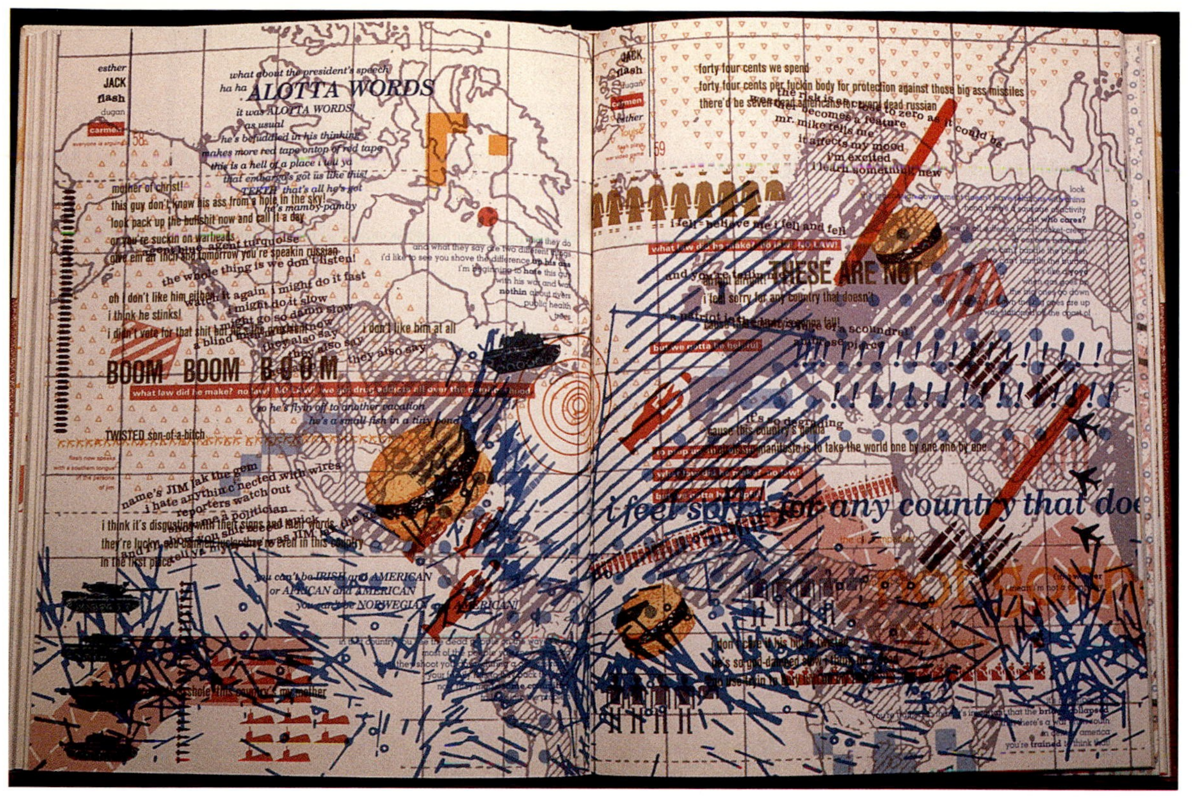

L

Warren Lehrer from *French Fries* (1985). Courtesy the artist.

L

Morris Louis, *Alpha Gamma* (1960–61). CORBIS/Burstein collection.

K

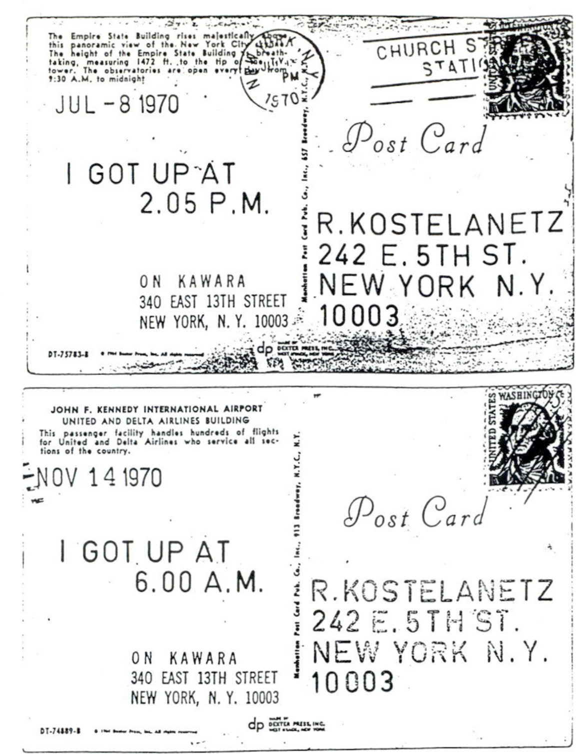

On Kawara. *I Am Alive.*
Collection R. Kostelanetz.

George Rhoads, *Ball City* (1985). 27′ X 10′ X 10′,
Triple Five Corp., West Edmonton Mall, Edmonton, Alberta.
Courtesy Bob McGuire/Rockstream Studios.

Alwin Nikolais. *The Crystal and the Sphere,* April 1990, Kennedy Center performance. Photo © Nan Melville, courtesy Nikolais and Murray Louis Dance.

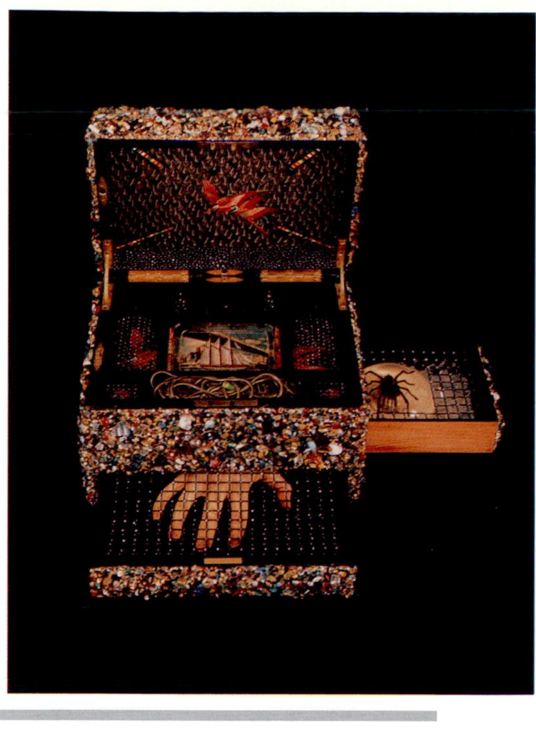

Lucas Samaras, *Box 124,* 1988.
Photo: Bill Jacobson, courtesy the Pace Gallery.

Aleksandr Rodchenko, *Red and Yellow* (c.1918).
CORBIS/State Russian Museum St. Petersburg.

Carolee Schneemann, *Meat Joy (*1964). Premiere performance.
Photo © 1993 Al Giese.

SITE. *Ghost Parking Lot*, 1978. Hamden, CT. National Shopping Centers, Inc. Materials: Cars, concrete, asphalt. Courtesy SITE Projects.

S

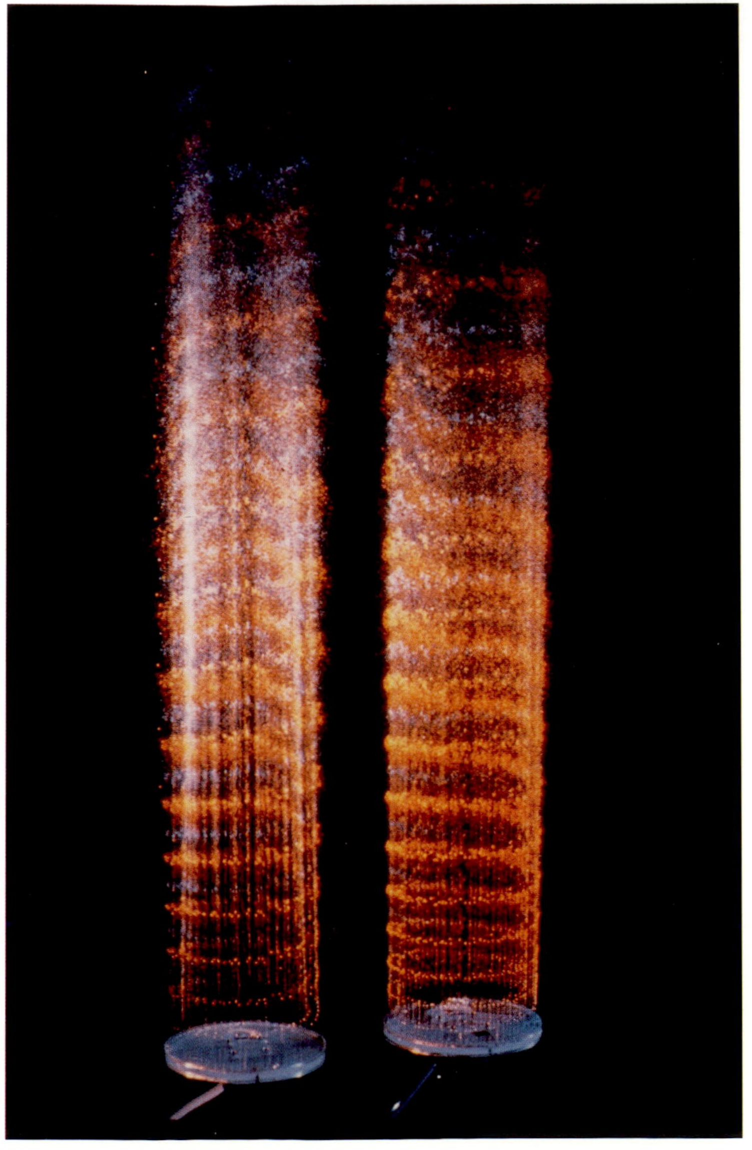

Wen-Ying Tsai, *Upwards-Falling Fountain* (1979). Courtesy the artist.

Town Planning: Ville Contemporaine, 1922; Plan Voisin, 1925; Ville Radieuse, 1935; Plan for Algiers, 1930; Chandigarh, India, 1951–56.

Designs not executed: League of Nations, Geneva, 1927.

Books: *Towards a New Architecture* (1927; English trans. 1931. Tr. Frederick Etchells. London: Architectural Press, 1946). New York: Dover, 1986; *Precisions: On the Present State of Architecture and City Planning* (1930). Cambridge: MIT Press, 1991; *New World of Space*. New York: Reynal and Hitchcock, 1948; *The Chapel at Ronchamp*. London: Architectural Press, 1957; *Creation Is a Patient Search*. New York: Praeger, 1960; *Last Works*. Ed. Willy Boesiger. New York: Praeger, 1970; *Sketchbooks* Vols. 1–4. Cambridge, MA: Architectural History Foundation: 1981–82.

Interpretation: Baker, Geoffrey. *Le Corbusier: An Analysis of Form*. New York: John Wiley & Sons, 1996; Banham, Reyner. *Theory and Design in the First Machine Age* (1960). 2d ed. New York: Praeger, 1967; Bentone, Tim. *The Villas of Le Corbusier*, 1920–1930. New Haven: Yale University Press; Cohen, Jean-Louis. *Le Corbusier and the Mystique of the U.S.S.R.* Princeton: Princeton University Press, 1992; Curtis, William J. R. *Le Corbusier: Ideas and Forms*. Oxford: Phaidon Press, 1986; Jencks, Charles. *Le Corbusier and the Tragic Vision of Architecture*. Cambridge: Harvard University Press, 1974; Padaki, Stamo. *Le Corbusier: Architect, Painter, Writer*. New York: Macmillan, 1948; Trieb, Marc. *Space Articulation in Seconds: The Philips Pavilion Le Corbusier Edgard Varèse*. Princeton: Princeton University Press, 1996; Walden, Russell. "Le Corbusier." In *Contemporary Masterworks*, ed. Colin Naylor. London: St. James's Press, 1991; ——, ed. *The Open Hand: Essays on Le Corbusier*. Cambridge, MA: MIT, 1982.

LE PARC, Julio

(23 September 1928).

An Argentine who held off going to Paris until 1958, Le Parc joined several groups working with optical abstraction and kineticism, including Groupe de Recherche d'art Visuel, commonly known as GRAV. His art developed static surface patterns that generated radically different appearances if viewed from different angles, which is to say that it offers not one principal "look" but several, all of them equally legitimate. Le Parc also made reliefs of different materials that rotated at various speeds. He used other materials to vary the reflection of light and made objects with adjustable parts that respond to spectators' manipulations. Because I have not seen any of these latter pieces at first hand, I quote Edward Lucie-Smith's testimony in *Late Modern* (1969):

> Le Parc creates devices which belong partly to the laboratory, partly to the funfair. They are experiments with mechanisms and also experiments upon the psychology of the spectator. Mirrors, distorting spectacles, balls which run through complicated labyrinths—he has made use of all these things.

At the intersection of the amusement park and the laboratory is probably a good place for advanced art to be.

Works: *Light-Continuum*, 1962; *Continuel-lumière*, 1962; *Continuel-luz cilindro*, 1962–66; *Círculos fraccionados*, 1965; *Continuidad Luminosa con Formas en Contorsión*, 1966; *Continuel-mobil plateado*, 1967; *Modulación 413*, 1980; *Modulación 496*, 1981; *Modulación 535*, 1982; *Modulación 668*, 1984; *Modulación 718*, 1985; *Modulación 996*, 1987.

Exhibition Catalogs: *Le Parc Couleur 1959*. Paris: Denise Rene, 1959; *Julio Le Parc: Experiencias 1959–1977*. Madrid: Patronato Nacional de Museos, 1978; *GRAV: Groupe de recherche d'art visuel 1960–68*. Milan: Electra Editrifice, 1975; *Julio Le Parc, experiencias, retrospectiva*. Santiago de Chile: Centro de Extensión y Escuela de arte de la Pontificia Universidad Católica de Chile, 1989.

Bibliography: Lucie-Smith, Edward. *Late Modern*. New York: Praeger, 1969.

LEAR, Edward

(12 May 1812–29 January 1888).

When you consider how wary contemporary editors are of any writing faintly unclear, it is amazing that this Vic-

torian writer had such encouraging publishers, prompting him to produce several editions of *A Book of Nonsense* (1845), *A Book of Nonsense and More Nonsense* (1862), *Nonsense Songs, Stories, Botany and Alphabets* (1871), *More Nonsense, Pictures, Rhymes, Botany, Etc.* (1872), and *Laughing Lyrics, a Fresh Book of Nonsense Poems* (1877), which, all would agree, is a ridiculous bibliography for an adult writer. The mark of Lear's verse is a limerick that turns back on itself, the last line echoing, if not repeating, the first: "There was an Old Person of Rhodes,/Who strongly objected to toads;/He paid several cousins/To catch them by dozens,/ That futile Old Person of Rhodes." (This gains from its "POLITICALLY CORRECT" gender usage, a century in advance.) Lear was also a travel writer and a landscape painter.

Works: *A Book of Nonsense*, (1845). London: Everyman's Library, 1992; *A Book of Nonsense and More Nonsense*. 1862; Jackson, Holbrook, ed. *The Complete Nonsense of Edward Lear* (1947). New York: Dover, 1951.

Biography: Kamen, Gloria. *Edward Lear: King of Nonsense*. New York: Atheneum, 1998.

Web Site: http://www2.pair.com/mgraz/Lear/index.html

Interpretation: Chesterton, G. K. "A Defense of Nonsense." *The Defendant*, 1901.

LEFTWICH, Jim

(1956).

Of the many poets who have worked in poems by JOHN M. BENNETT—with or after him—Leftwich may be the only one who's produced anything the non-Bennettic feel of which holds its own with the Bennettic, which suggests the magnitude of his poetic presence. A speck of infraverbal evidence for this that glistens with spins off of rain, spring, and nakedness is the following passage from his variation on Bennett's "END AGO": "raw in du itc spr mple"—with "ked" (which is what, with "raw," suggests nakedness) directly beneath "spr." Leftwich travels a wide range of

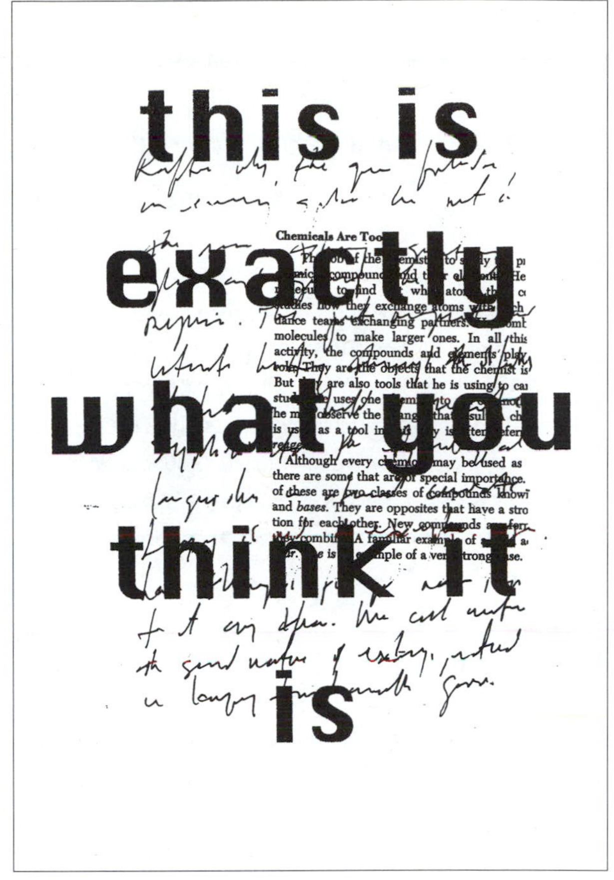

Jim Leftwich. Page from Jim Leftwich's *Sample Example*. Courtesy Luna Bisonte Productions.

other linguistically norm-breaking and visual routes to equally resonant precincts in his other poems.

—Bob Grumman

Books: *Dirt*. Columbus, OH: Luna Bisonte (137 Leland Avenue, 43214), 1995; *Khawatir*. Port Charlotte, FL: Runaway Spoon (P.O. Box 3621, 33949–3621), 1995; *Bodies Knot*. Charlottesville, VA: Juxta (977 Seminole Trail, #331, 22901), 1996.

LÉGER, Fernand

(4 February 1881–17 August 1955).

An early CUBIST painter, Léger belongs to avant-garde history first for portraying both machinery and warfare in modern ways. He was also a renowned stage designer

whose work is remembered mostly through insufficient photographs, and then a filmmaker whose *Ballet mécanique* (1924), exploring rhythm and motion, survives as classic avant-garde cinema. During World War II, Léger, very much an ebullient personality, lived in America, collaborating with HANS RICHTER on part of the latter's *Dreams That Money Can Buy* (1944–46), at various times teaching at American universities, along with such distinguished French refugees as the art historian Henri Focillon, the essayist André Maurois, and the composer Darius Milhaud.

Works: *Contraste de Formes*, 1914; *Le Moteur*, 1918; *La Ville*, 1919; *Les Maisons*, 1922; *Élément mécanique*, 1924; *Peinture Murale*, 1926; *Composition*, 1927; *Composition en bleu*, 1927; *Composition jaune*, 1928; *Composition Murale*, 1929; *Nature Morte*, 1930; *Le Triangle Rouge*, 1930.

Books: *Functions of Painting*. New York: Viking, 1973.

Exhibition Catalogs: *Fernand Léger: Five Themes and Variations*. New York: Guggenheim Museum, 1962; *Fernand Léger*. Paris: Centre Georges Pompidou, 1997.

Bibliography: Saphire, Lawrence. *Fernand Léger: The Complete Graphic Work*. New York: Blue Moon, 1978; *Fernand Léger 1911–1924: The Rhythm of Modern Life*. ed. Dorothy Kosinski, München: Prestel, 1994.

Catalogue Raisonée: Bauquier, Georges. *Fernand Léger: A Catalogue Raisoneé*. 5 vols. Paris: A. Maeght, 1990.

Interpretation: De Francia, Peter. *Fernand Léger*. New Haven: Yale University Press, 1983; Green, Christopher. *Léger and the Avant-Garde*. New Haven: Yale University, 1976; Kuh, Katharine. *Fernand Léger*. Urbana: University of Illinois Press, 1953; Lawder, Standish D. *The Cubist Cinema*. New York: New York University Press, 1975.

LEHRER, Warren

(22 July 1955).

One of the most imaginative bookartists of our time, Lehrer has produced several largeformat, elegantly printed, self-published volumes filled with a wealth of images and words. The latter sometimes come from himself, at other times from collaborators such as the poet Dennis Bernstein (1950). Technically scripts, they address major cultural issues, typically in a style more intimidating than communicative. One of the thoughtful technical depatures of *French Fries* (1984), perhaps Lehrer's most sumptuous work, is that a summary of its obscure pages appears continuously in the upper outside corners. *The Portrait Series: A Suite of Four Books About Men* (1995) is Lehrer's most ambitious work, a quadrology of portraits, apparently fictions, with language and pictures both written and designed by the author (in a striking size of 10.5" high and 4" wide). His four narrators are Brother Blue, a black street poet; Claude Debs, a well-heeled adventurer; Nicky D., a retired dock-worker; and Charlie, a musician victimized by mental-health institutions. *The Portrait Series* is unique, like all art reflecting truly avant-garde ambition. (Whereas Flannery O'Connor once reportedly said that she'd put aside anything looking peculiar on a page, my own predisposition is a desire to read everything that comes in alternative packaging.) Lehrer also works in audio, co-composing with Harvey Goldman the song cycle *The Search for It & Other Pronouns* (1991), a full-length compact disc that has the most intelligently and imaginatively designed (not to mention legible) accompanying CD booklet to come my way, reminding us that the secondary elements of any artifact deserve as much attention as the primary ones. Lehrer's wife, Judith Sloan (1958), is a provocative PERFORMANCE ARTIST.

Books: *willow weep, don't*. Mattapoisett, MA: Lehrer/Baker, 1979; *Versations*. Purchase, NY: Ear/Say (Main P.O. Box 299, 10577), 1980; Lehrer, Warren. *I mean you know*. Rochester, NY: Visual Studies Workshop, 1983; Lehrer, Warren, and Dennis Bernstein. *French Fries*. Purchase, NY: Ear/Say, 1984; *GRRRHHHH: A Study of Social Attitudes*. With chants and scores by Dennis Bernstein. Purchase, NY: Ear/Say, 1988; *The Portrait Series:*

A Suite of Four Books About Men. 4 vols. Seattle, WA: Bay Press (115 W. Denny Way, 98119–4205), 1995.

Recordings: *The Search for IT and Other Pronouns*, with Harvey Goldman. Westport, MA: LaLa Music, 1991.

LENNON, John

(9 October 1940–8 December 1980).

At the height of the success of the Beatles (1962–69), for which he initially played rhythm guitar, Lennon published two self illustrated books of free form prose, *In His Own Write* (1965) and A *Spaniard in the Works* (1966), that reflect the influences of EDWARD LEAR, LEWIS CARROLL, and JAMES JOYCE, but these did not sell enough copies to persuade publishers to hound the celebrated singer for more. Lennon reportedly initiated the Beatles' experiments with feedback (in "I Feel Fine"), backwards tape (in "Rain" and "Tomorrow Never Knows"), and AUDIO ART ("Strawberry Fields Forever" and "A Day in the Life"). Later, working in collaboration with his second wife, YOKO ONO, Lennon created less successful self-consciously experimental music beginning with the tape montage "Revolution No. 9" featured on *The Beatles* (1969; commonly known as "The White Album") and the Lennon/Ono albums *Two Virgins* (1968) and *Life with the Lions* (1969).

—with Richard Carlin

Books: *In His Own Write* and *A Spaniard in the Works* (1966). New York: New American Library, 1967.

Recordings: *Anthology*. Boxed set. Capitol, 1998.

Biography: Coleman, Ray. *Lennon: The Definitive Biography*. New York: Harper Perennial, 1992; Goldman, Albert. *The Lives of John Lennon*. New York: Bantam, 1988; Wiener, Jon. *Come Together: John Lennon in His Time*. New York: Random House, 1984.

Web Site:
http://members.tripod.com/~crayola123/ring.html (Links); www.instantkarma.com (online fan magazine).

Interpretation: Kozinn, Allan. *The Beatles*. London: Phaidon, 1995; Thomson, Elizabeth, ed. *The Lennon Companion* New York: Schirmer, 1990.

LETTRISM

(mid-1940s).

Founded in Paris by Isidore Isou (1925; b. Jean-Isidore Goldstein), himself a young refugee recently arrived from Rumania, Lettrism is perhaps the epitome of a circumscribed European literary group, with its untitled head, its insiders, its hangerson, and its excommunications. Lettrist work seems based on calligraphy, initially for books but also for visual art, and thus in the age of print seems quite innovative (though it might not have fared as well in preprint times). One recurring device is letters that resemble verses, even though they are devoid of words. Jean-Louis Brau (1930), Gil J. Wolman (1929), Maurice Lemaître (1926), Roberto Altmann (1942), Roland Sabatier (1942), and Jean-Paul Curtay (1951) were among the other prominent writer/artists based in France who were associated with the group at various times. Not unlike other selfconscious agglomerations, Lettrism has been particularly skilled at the production of manifestos, which can be read with varying degrees of sense. By discounting semantic and syntactical coherence for language art, Lettrist works can be seen as precursors of CONCRETE POETRY. Among the alumni are Guy Ernest Debord (1931–94), who, under the name Guy Debord, is commonly credited with initiating the Situationatist International (c. 1958–72), which can be seen as representing artists' most profound, courageous, and, it follows, most successful involvement in radical politics. While Situationist writings have been translated into English, Lettrist texts barely have—to our loss.

Books: Curtay, Jean-Paul. *La Poésie Lettriste*. Paris: Seghers, 1974; Isou, Isadore. *Introduction à l'esthetique imaginaire*. Paris: Centre de Créativité, 1977.

John Lennon and Yoko Ono during their famous "Bed-In for Peace" in Amsterdam, 25 March 1969. CORBIS/Bettmann.

Exhibition Catalogs: Foster, Stephen C. *Lettrisme: Into the Present*. Iowa City, IA: University of Iowa Museum of Art, 1983; Sussman, Elizabeth, et al., *On the Passage of a Few People Through a Rather Brief Moment in Time: The Situationist International 1957–1972*. Cambridge, MA: MIT, 1989.

Anthology: Knabb, Ken, ed. and trans. *The Situationist International*. Berkeley, CA: Bureau of Public Secrets (POB 1044, 94701), 1981.

Website: www.thing.net/~grist/l&d/lettrist/lettrist.htm (features work from Roland Sabatier, Isidore Isou, and Alain Satié).

LEVENDOSKY, Charles

(4 July 1936).

His *perimeters* (1970) ranks among the very best long poems of recent times, achieving what Walt Whitman suggested, what MICHEL BUTOR attempted (in *Mobile)*, and what ALLEN GINSBERG projected (in "These States")—a comprehensive panoramic portrait of the forty-eight continental states. Its success stems not only from Levendosky's attention to suggestive details, but also from its distinctive visual and verbal rhythms, the excellence of particular passages, and the sustained coherence of the encompassing whole. At that time, I heard that he was planning a comparably long poem about Middle America. A collection, *Hands & Other Poems* (1986), appeared instead. Levendosky subsequently became a prominent editorial writer and columnist in Wyoming.

Books: *perimeters*. Middletown: Wesleyan University Press, 1970; *Aspects of the Vertical*. Norman, OK: Point Riders, 1978; *Hands & Other Poems*. Norman, OK: Point Riders Press (P.O. Box 2731, 73070), 1986; *Circle of Light*. Gendo, WY: High Plains, 1995.

LEVY, d.a.

(29 October 1942–24 November 1968).

In a life so short he seems to have been the American ARTHUR RIMBAUD, d.a.levy, in his preferred orthography, published all sorts of poetry, including VISUAL POEMS, obliterated texts, COLLAGES, and BLAKEAN mixtures of pictures with calligraphy, in addition to more conventional lyrics and visionary prose. Some of his Blakean texts are particularly marvelous; along with KENNETH PATCHEN levy ranks among the few who have worked that vein without seeming too derivative of the master. Levy made poems from advertising print, or "FOUND ART", similar to BERN PORTER's, just as his cover for the thirteenth issue of *The Buddhist Oracle* resembles AD REINHARDT's comics. Living in relative isolation in Cleveland, levy was not included in any of the late 1960s anthologies of visual poetry, even though, on its intrinsic merits, his work deserved being there. Harassed by the police, arrested for publishing poetry purportedly obscene, levy took his own life. A recent collection of his poetry, lovingly edited, thankfully features his more experimental work.

Works: *Red Lady*. Cleveland: Para-shakti, 1969; *Barking Rabbit*. Cleveland: Falling Down, 1976; *Collected Poems*. Ephraim, WI: Druid (Jon Reilly, 5421), 1976; *Zen Concrete & Etc*. Ed. Ingrid Swanberg. Madison, WI: Ghost Pony Press (2518 Gregory St., 53711), 1991.

Website: www.thing.net/~grist/l&d/dalevy.htm

LEVY, Julien

(22 January 1906–February 1981).

An approximate Harvard classmate of LINCOLN KIRSTEIN, Everett Austin, Jr., and Alfred Barr, all of whom became elevated impresarios of advanced American culture, Levy had the foresight to open in the early 1930s an art gallery near the Museum of Modern Art, founded only a few years before, complementing its program on advancing American taste. In addition to early exhibitions of SURREALISM (1932), ALEXANDER CALDER, and MAN RAY, he sponsored the first American shows of JOSEPH CORNELL and SALVADOR DALI, in addition to the photographers Walter Evans, George Platt Lynes, and Henri Carter-Bresson. Early in 1932, Levy began exhibiting avant-garde films, including

Fernand Léger's *Ballet mécanique*, accompanied by George Anthiel's piano roll, and Man Ray's *L'Étoile de Mer*. This program became a foundation for the permanent film department at the Museum of Modern Art. Levy also published the first American book on Surrealism (1936).

Books: *Surrealism* (1936). New York: Da Capo, 1995; *Memoirs of an Art Gallery*. New York: G. P. Putnam's Sons, 1977; Barr, Alfred H. *Defining Modern Art: Selected Writings*. Ed. Irving Sandler & Amy Newman. New York: Abrams, 1986.

Exhibition Catalog: *A. Everett Austin, Jr.: A Director's Taste and Achievement*. Hartford, CT: Wadsworth Atheneum, 1957.

Interpretation: Schaffner, Ingrid, and Lisa Jacobs. *Julien Levy: Portrait of an Art Gallery*. Cambridge: MIT Press, 1998; Jones, Caroline. *Modern Art at Harvard*. New York: Abbeville, 1985; Lynes, Russell. *Good Old Modern: An Intimate Portrait of the Museum of Modern Art*. New York: Atheneum, 1973; Marquis, Alice Goldfarb. *Alfred Barr: Missionary for the Modern.* Chicago: Contemporary,1989; Weber, Nicolas Fox. *Patron Saints: Five Rebels Who Opened America to a New Art, 1928–1943*. New York: Knopf, 1992.

LEWIS, Wyndham

(18 November 1882–7 March 1957; b. Percy W. L.).

Born off the Canadian coast on his British father's yacht, Lewis studied at the Slade School of Art in London before becoming an Abstract painter and the founder of Vorticism, a British sort of Italian Futurism favoring geometrical recompositions and aggressive colors. In 1914, Lewis founded and edited two issues of *Blast*, one of the great avant-garde magazines, not only for its content but for its typography (which still looks avant-garde, more than eighty years later). He later edited more modest magazines to which he was likewise also a prominent contributor, *The Tyro* (1921–22) and *The Enemy* (1927).

Initially the author of plays and short stories, collected in various volumes, Lewis eventually wrote novels, beginning with *Tarr* (1918), which some think had an influence on James Joyce and continuing with a tetralogy, *The Human Age*, which Martin Seymour-Smith for one ranks as "the greatest single imaginative prose work in English of this century." (It includes *The Childermass* [1928; rev. ed.1956], *Malign Fiesta, Monstre Gai* [1955], and the incomplete *Trial of Man.) One-Way Song* (1933) is a stylistically unique anti-progressive political poem whose 2,000-plus lines were fortunately reprinted in *Collected Poems and Plays* (1979). Lewis also wrote criticism and scintillating polemics, and painted highly evocative portraits of his contemporaries, including T. S. Eliot and Ezra Pound.

Lewis spent World War II underrecognized in Canada and his postwar years in London as an art critic for the weekly *Listener*. Not unlike other avant-garde writers of his generation, he is continually being rediscovered with new editions, as well as new selections, of his works. He is not to be confused with D. B. Wyndham Lewis (1894–1969), who wrote polite biographies.

Fiction: *Mrs. Dukes' Million* (1908–10). Toronto: Coach House, 1977; *Tarr*. New York: Knopf, 1918; *The Childermass*. New York: Covici Friede, 1928; *The Wild Body*. New York: Harcourt, Brace, 1928; expanded as *The Complete Wild Body*. Ed. Bernard Lafourcade. Santa Barbara, CA: Black Sparrow, 1982; *The Apes of God* (1930). Santa Barbara, CA: Black Sparrow, 1981; *Revenge for Love* (1937). Chicago: Regnery, 1952; *Self-Condemned* (1954). Afterword by Rowland Smith. Santa Barbara, CA: Black Sparrow, 1983.

Nonfiction: *The Art of Being Ruled* (1926). Ed. Reed Way Dasenbrock. Santa Barbara, CA: Black Sparrow, 1989; *The Lion and the Fox*. New York: Harpers, 1927; *Time and Western Man*. New York: Harcourt, Brace, 1927; *Paleface, The Philosophy of the Melting-Pot*. London: Chatto & Windus, 1929; *The Diabolical Principle and the Dithyrambic Spectator*. London: Chatto & Windus, 1931; *Men without Art* (1934). Ed. with notes by Seamus Cooney. Santa Rosa, CA: Black Sparrow, 1987; *The Hitler*

Cult. London: Dent, 1939; *America, I Presume*. New York: Howell, Soskin & Co., 1940; *The Writer and the Absolute*. London: Metheun, 1952; *America and Cosmic Man*. New York: Doubleday, 1948; *Rotting Hill*. Chicago: Regnery, 1955; *The Demon of Progress in the Arts*. Chicago: Regnery, 1955.

Autobiography: *Blasting and Bombardiering*. London: Eyre & Spottiswoode, 1937; *America, I Presume*. New York; Howell, Soskin & Co., 1940; *Rude Assignment: An Intellectual Autobiography* (1950). Ed. Toby Foshay Santa. Santa Barbara, CA: Black Sparrow, 1984.

Other Books: *Collected Poems and Plays*. Ed. Alan Munton. New York: Persea, 1979.

Anthology: *Wyndham Lewis the Artist: From Blast to Burlington House*. London: Laidlaw & Laidlaw, 1939; *A Soldier of Humor and Selected Writings*. Ed. Raymond Rosenthal. New York: New American Library, 1966; *Wyndham Lewis: An Anthology of His Prose*. ed. E. W. F. Tomlin. London: Methuen, 1969; Michel, Walter. *Wyndham Lewis: Paintings and Drawings*. Berkeley: University of California Press, n.d. (c. 1971); *Enemy Salvos: Selected Literary Criticism*. London: Vision, 1975; *Essential Wyndham Lewis: An Introduction to His Work*. Ed. Julian Symons. London: Deutsch, 1989; *Creatures of Habit and Creatures of Change: Essays on Art, Literature and Society 1914–1956*. Ed. Paul Edwards. Santa Rosa, CA: Black Sparrow, 1989.

Magazines Edited: *Blast*. 2 vols, (1915). Santa Barbara, CA: Black Sparrow, 1981.

Biography: Meyers, Jeffrey. *The Enemy*. London: Routledge & Kegan Paul, 1980.

Web Site: http://tori.ic.h.kyoto-u.ac.jp/pub/Lewis/Lewis.html

Interpretation: Porteus, Hugh Gordon. *Wyndham Lewis*. London: Desmond Harmsworth, 1932; Gawsworth, John. *Apes, Japes, and Hitlerism*. London: Unicorn, 1932; Hadley-Read, Charles. *The Art of Wyndham Lewis*. London: Faber, 1951; Kenner, Hugh. *Wyndham Lewis*. New York: New Directions, 1954; Meyers, Jeffrey, ed. *Wyndham Lewis: A Revaluation New Essays*. Montreal: McGill-Queens University, 1980; Sherry, Vincent. *Ezra Pound, Wyndham Lewis, and Radical Modernism*. New York: Oxford University Press, 1993; Wagner, Geoffrey. *Wyndham Lewis: A Portrait of the Artist as the Enemy*. New Haven: Yale University Press, 1957; Dasenbrock, Reed Way. *The Literary Vorticism of Ezra Pound & Wyndham Lewis: Towards the Condition of Painting*. Baltimore: Johns Hopkins University Press, 1985.

Bibliography: Morrow, Bradford, & La Fourcade, Bernard. *Bibliography of the Writings of Wyndham Lewis*. Santa Barbara, CA: Black Sparrow, 1978.

Le WITT, Sol

(9 September 1928).

An ABSTRACT artist from his beginnings, a geometricist interested in systems, and a prolific producer with a generous collection of assistants, Le Witt is best known for his sculptures, his wall drawings, and his writings on CONCEPTUAL ART. The theme of the first, especially in sum, is variations on the cube, which over the years have been arrayed, stacked, and left partially incomplete, among other unprecedented moves. Le Witt's wall drawings, which are customarily executed in his absence, affix a geometric scheme—say, different sets of curved lines a few inches apart—to a space from which it will be removed at an exhibition's end. His is a rigorously nonreferential art that is concerned with purity of both concept and execution, precisely by suggesting nothing that is not obviously perceptible. Le Witt's much-reprinted "Paragraphs on Conceptual Art" rationalizes work where "all of the planning and decisions are made beforehand and the execution is a perfunctory affair. The idea becomes a machine that makes the art. This kind of art is not theoretical or illustrative of theories; it is intuitive; it is involved with all types of mental processes and it is purposeless."

Sol Lewitt installing his exhibit at the Jewish Museum, 26 April 1966. Copyright © Fred W. McDarrah.

Two developments within Le Witt's wall art are the addition of colors other than black and white and verbal titles that are more poetic than descriptive (if not informative). It is said that over his entire career he has never missed opening a show on time. My own alternative opinion holds that, good as his other work has been, Le Witt's masterpieces are bookart books that he has been producing since the early 1970s. The first masterpiece is *Arcs, Circles & Grids* (1972), which has 195 progressively denser combinations of the linear geometric images announced in its title. Though Le Witt may have had something else in mind, I see this book as an elegantly simple narrative about increasing linear density. *Autobiography* (1980) has a large number of square black-and-white photographs, each two and five-eighths inches square, of every object in Le Witt's living and working space, none of them featured over any others; and although no photograph of the author or any of his works appears, the book does indeed portray not only a life but the roots of his particular imaginative sensibility. Among Le Witt's many books and booklets are *Incomplete Open Cubes* (1974), *The Location of Lines* (1974), *Lines & Color* (1975), *Squares with Sides and Corners Torn Off* (n.d.), *Red, Blue and Yellow Lines from Sides, Corners and the Center of the Page to Points on a Grid* (1975), *Photogrids* (1977), and *Sunrise and Sunset at Praiano* (1980), all of which accurately reflect their titles. Throughout the 1970s, Le Witt cleverly made it his custom to do fresh book-art in lieu of catalogs for his exhibitions.

Books & Booklets: *49 Three-Part Variations Using Three Different Kinds of Cubes, 1967–68*. Zürich: Bruno Bischofberger, 1969; *Four Basic Kinds of Lines & Colour*. London: Lisson, 1971; *Arcs, Circles & Grids*. Bern, Switzerland: Kunsthalle & Paul Biancini, 1972; *Incomplete Open Cubes*. New York: John Weber, 1974; *The Location of Lines*. London: Lisson, 1974; *Arcs and Lines*. Lausanne & Paris: Massons & Yvon Lambert, 1974; *The Location of Eight Points*. Washington, DC: Max Protech, 1974; *Red, Blue and Yellow Lines from Sides, Corners and the Center of the Page to Points on a Grid*. Jerusalem: Israel Museum, 1975; *Lines & Color*. Zürich & Basel: Annemarie Verna & Rolf Breisig, 1975; *Five Cubes and Twenty-Five Squares*. Bari, Italy: Bonomo, 1977; *Geometric Figures & Color*. New York: Harry N. Abrams, 1979; *Open Geometric Structures*. London: Nicholas Fiona Logsdail/Lisson, 1979; *Autobiography*. New York & Boston, MA: Multiples, Inc., and Lois and Michael K. Torf, 1980; *Variations of I am Still Alive On Kawara*. Florence, Italy: Firenze & Lugo, 1988; *Cube*. New York: John Weber, 1990.

Exhibition Catalogs: *Sol Le Witt*. The Hague: Gemeentemuseum, 1970; Legg, Alicia, ed. *Sol Le Witt*. New York: MoMA, 1978; Hanson, Bernard. *The Graphics of Sol Le Witt*. New Britain, CT: The New Britain Museum of Art, 1979; *Sol Le Witt Wall Drawings*. Amsterdam: Stedelijk & Hartford, CT: Wadsworth Atheneum, 1984; Singer, Susana, ed. ——. *Sol Le Witt: Wall Drawings 1984–1988*. Bern: Kunsthalle, 1989; *Sol Le Witt Books, 1966–1990*. Köln: W. König, 1990; *Sol Le Witt: Drawings 1958–1992*. The Hague, Netherlands: Haags Gemeentemuseum, 1992; *Sol Le Witt: Structures, 1962–1993*. Oxford, England; Museum of Modern Art, 1993; Reynolds, Jock and Miller-Keller, Andrea. *Twenty-Five Years of Wall Drawings 1968–1993*. Andover, MA: Addison Gallery, 1994; *Prints 1970–1986*. London: Tate Gallery, 1997.

LICHTENSTEIN, Roy

(28 October 1923–29 September 1997).

Lichtenstein's name is most familiar from his Pop Art canvases of the early sixties, often consisting of blowups of single frames from comic strips, bubblegum wrappers, and advertising art images. His use of exaggerated dot screens (imitating newspaper printing), bold colors, and even comic-strip bubbles to portray his characters' "thoughts" all contribute to an essentially ironic vision of his subject matter. Later Lichtenstein paintings parody twentieth-century masters, including Picasso, Mondrian, and Abstract Expressionist painters in deadpan canvases that reproduce their typical themes and techniques.

—Richard Carlin

Selected Works: *Spray*, 1962; *Tension*, 1964; *Foot and Hand*, 1962; *Sandwich and Soda*, 1964; *Mirrors*, 1970–72.

Exhibition Catalogs: Beeren, Wim. *Roy Lichtenstein*. Amsterdam: Stedelijk Museum, 1967; Coplans. John. *Roy Lichtenstein*. Pasadena: Pasadena Art Museum, 1967; Waldman, Diane. *Roy Lichtenstein* New York: Guggenheim, 1969; Pincus-Witten, Robert. *Roy Lichtenstein: A Drawing Retrospective*. New York: Goodman, 1984; *Roy Lichtenstein Pop Masterpieces 1961–64*. New York: Blum Helman, 1987; Marter, Joan, ed. *Off Limits: Rutgers University and the Avant-Garde, 1957–1963*. Newark, NJ: The Newark Museum & Rutgers University Press, 1999.

Interpretation: Waldman, Diane. *Roy Lichtenstein: Drawings and Prints*. New York: Chelsea House, 1973; Alloway, Lawrence. *Roy Lichtenstein*. New York: Abbeville, 1983; *The Art of Roy Lichtenstein: Mural with Blue Brushstroke*. Photos & interview Bob Adelman; intro. Calvin Tompkins. New York: Arcade, 1994.

Catalogue Raisonné: Corlett, Mary Lee. *The Prints of Roy Lichtenstein: A Catalogue Raisonné 1948–1993*. New York: Hudson Hills, 1994.

LIGETI, György

(28 May 1923)

Born in Transylvania, educated at the Budapest Music Academy, Ligeti left Hungary in 1956, reportedly walking to Cologne; within fifteen years, he was a professor at the Hamburg music school. His most successful pieces incorporate clusters of closely related sounds, aggregations literally, resembling acoustic bands more than traditional separate notes, articulated with a strong sense of instrumental texture, he says to produce "acoustic motionlessness." The most familiar is the "Kyrie" from *Requiem*, which incidentally appeared in the soundtrack to the Stanley Kubrick film *2001*. Among Ligeti's more eccentric pieces is *Poème symphonique*, its title alluding to Edgard Varèse, except that Ligeti's is for 100 metronomes, all running at different speeds. His son, Lukas L. (1965), is a remarkably different, but similarly innovative, composer/percussionist living in both Vienna and New York.

Works: Cello Sonata 1948–53; *Musica ricercata*, 1951–53; *Romanian Concerto* for small orchestra, 1952; *Pápainé* for chorus, 1953; *Glissandi*, 1957; *Artikulation*, 1958; *Apparitions*, 1958–59; *Fragment* for chamber orchestra, 1961; *Trois bagatelles*, 1961; *Volumina*, 1961–62; *Poème symphonique* for 100 metronomes, 1962; *Requiem* for soprano, mezzo-soprano, 2 choruses, and orchestra, 1963–65; *Ramifications* for string orchestra or 12 solo strings, 1968–69; 10 Pieces for Wind Quintet, 1968; *Continuum*, 1968; *San Francisco Polyphony*, 1973–74; *13 Études*, 1985–93; *Nonsense Madrigals* for 6 men's voices 1988–1993; *Macabre Collage*, 1991;

Recordings: *Requiem, Lontano for Full Orchestra, Continuum for Harpsichord*. New York: Helidor-Polydor, 1970; *Aventures (1962), Nouvelles Aventures (1962–65) & Requiem (1965)*, Darmstadt Int'l Chamber Ensemble. Mainz, Germany: Wergo; *Concerto for 13 Chamber Instruments* (1970). Ensemble Modern. Sony Classical; *Concerto for Piano & Orchestra* (1985–88). Ensemble Intercontemporain, cond. Pierre Boulez. DGG; *Kammerkonzert for 13 Musicians*. Nouvelle Ensemble Moderne. Ummus; *Quartets #1 & # 2*. Arditti Q. Mainz, Germany: Wergo; *Ten Pieces for Wind Quintet* (1968) & *Six Bagatelles for Wind Quintet* (1953). Berlin Philharmonic Wind Quintet. Sweden: Bis.

LIGHT & DUST

(1995).

Essentially an eclectic, multicultural, multilingual, international, growing, revisable anthology of poetry, Karl Young's *Light & Dust* (l&d) Website has been in operation since 1995, two years after Young began electronic publishing as a member of Spunk Anarchist Collective—and with John Fowler on Fowler's *Grist On-Line* magazine. For the previous 29 years, Young had been active in print publication, putting out work by people like Karl Kempton, Barbara Einzig, bp Nichol, and Jackson Mac Low. Amazingly, *l&d* averages 1000 hits a day, its craft-extending material drawing at least half of them. A quieter source of encouragement is its increasing use in classrooms and galleries as an adjunct to lectures and other demonstrations.

One of its specialties is republishing books, particularly ones that, for various reasons, have never before been printed, such as dissident Clemente Padin's *Art and People*, censored in his native Uruguay—present at *l&d* not in Spanish but in Harry Polkinhorn's English translation. Young's site also has areas devoted to individual artists, at times expanding on symposiums Young published through *Margins* and other magazines in the '70s. One of the most important is a d.a.levy memorial site, co-curated by Ingrid Swanberg, that extends and amplifies levy's *Zen Concrete & Etc.* (notably through the use of color). *l&d* includes, as well, a survey co-curated by Young, along with Alain Satie, and David W. Seaman of the French verbo-visual school, Lettrism (acting, in fact, as its far-from-Paris Official Site), a survey of Australian verbo-visual work co-curated by Young and thalia, and a survey of Web-specific poetry. A useful collection of criticism, essays, manifestos, and other forms of commentary, mainly by poets, is there, too. Although some subsites, such as Michael McClure's home page, almost automatically attract a wide audience, *l&d* generally emphasizes writers and genres (especially verbo-visual art) that have been abused, ignored, or otherwise marginalized. It is easily the most valuable source of important avant-garde and other poetry, and writing about poetry, on the Internet.

—Bob Grumman

Website: http://www.thing.net/~grist/l&d/lighthom.htm

LIGHT ART

(c. 1900).

It seems odd, in retrospect, that visual artists were slow to realize the esthetic possibilities of electric light—that light had been around for many years before artists recognized that it could become the principal material of their work. The principal innovator of light art is commonly considered to be Thomas Wilfred, whose specialty was projections from behind a translucent screen; among subsequent projection-light artists were the Joshua Light Show, Gyorgy Kepes (1905), and Earl Reiback (1943), who purchased Wilfred's studio after the latter's death.

Subsequent light artists have used fluorescent lamps, such as Dan Flavin; neon lamps, such as Chryssa and Stephen Antonakis; or small bulbs so transparent that their flickering filaments are visible, such as Otto Piene (1930); lamps of various colors, programmed to change constantly, such as Boyd Mefferd (1941); or lasers, as in Rockne Krebs's (1938) *Aleph [squared]* (1969), where intense, narrow beams, either red or green, projected over one's head, bounce off mirrored walls in a dark room. Some light art depends upon reflecting or refracting materials, such as Moholy Nagy's *Light-Space Modulator* (1930), which is a kinetic sculpture designed to redirect projected light in various ways, and Clyde Lynds's use of fiber optics to make light turn corners. Though individual light artists have had major exhibitions over the past decades, I'm not aware of any recent comprehensive overview, either in books or a museum.

Exhibition Catalogs: *Light, Motion, Space*. Minneapolis, MN: Walker Art Center, 1967; Doty, Robert. *Light: Object and Image*. New York: Whitney Museum, 1968.

Interpretation: Kostelanetz, Richard. "Artistic Machines." In *Metamorphosis in the Arts*. Brooklyn, NY: Assembling, 1980; Malina, Frank, ed. *Kinetic Art: Theory and Practice*. New York: Dover, 1974; Sharp, Willoughby. "Luminism and Kineticism." In Gregory Battcock, ed. *Minimal Art* (1968). Berkeley: University of California Press, 1995.

LINDSAY, Vachel

(10 November 1879–5 December 1931; b. Nicholas V. L.).
More than any American before him, more than any of his contemporaries (except perhaps Gertrude Stein, five years his senior), Lindsay discovered what we now call text-sound in poetic onomatopoeia. You can hear it on reading the following text aloud to yourself (aside from the unfortunate racist implications): "Walk with care, walk with care, /Or Mumbo Jumbo, god of the Congo, /And all of the other gods of the Congo, /Mumbo-Jumbo will hoodoo you. /Beware, beware, walk with care, /Boomlay, boomlay, boomlay, boom. [repeated two additional times] /Boomlay, boomlay, boomlay, BOOM." For a fuller experience of Lindsay's acoustic poetry, listen to the recording that he made shortly before his suicide.

Educated mostly in fine art, Lindsay also published in 1915 the first intelligent book on the esthetics of film, as distinct from stage and photography, declaring prophetically that, "The motion picture art is a great high art, not a process of commercial manufacture," and then percipiently noting that, "The keywords of the stage are *passion* and *character*; of the photoplay, *splendor* and *speed*."

Recordings: Lindsay, Vachel. *Reads the Congo and Other Poems* (1931). New York: Caedmon, n.d.

Books: *The Congo and Other Poems* (1914). New York: Dover, 1992; *The Golden Book of Springfield*. New York: Macmillan, 1920; *Collected Poems*. New York: Macmillan, 1925; *Selected Poems*. Ed. Hazelton Spencer. New York: Macmillan, 1931; *The Art of the Moving Picture* (1915). New York: Liveright, 1970; *Poetry of Vachel Lindsay*. Ed. Dennis Camp. 2 vols. Granite Falls, MN: Spoon River Poetry (PO Box 6, 56241), 1984; *The Progress and the Poetry of the Movies: A Second Book of Film Criticism*. Ed. Myron Lounsbury. Lanham, MD: Scarecrow Press, 1995.

Biography: Masters, Edgar Lee. *Vachel Lindsay: A Poet in America* (1935). New York: Biblo & Tannen, 1969; Ruggles, Eleanor. *The West-Going Heart: A Life of Vachel Lindsay*. New York: Norton, 1959.

Interpretation: Harris, Mark. *City of Discontent* (1952). Urbana: University of Illinois Press, 1992; Wolfe, Glenn Joseph. *Vachel Lindsay: The Poet as Film Theorist*. New York: Arno, 1973.

LIPPARD, Lucy R.

(14 April 1937).
Lippard was for many years the first major independent female art critic in America (as distinct from newspaper-

based female art reviewer), and her early books, beginning with *Changing* (1968) and continuing perhaps through *Overlay* (1983), rank among the best at understanding new art. Her brilliant monograph on *Ad Reinhardt* (published in 1981, but written a decade before) makes all subsequent writing on this avant-garde American seem amateur. I use the past tense, even though Lippard is still alive, because around 1975 she "got religion," as we would say, which in her case was a leftist feminism that generated articles and books that, in my considered opinion, won't survive the times. *Mixed Blessings* (1989), perhaps the most absurd, advocates artists of privileged birth, in this case females "of color," who are introduced with their appropriate racial/ethnic/tribal tags (much like individuals in the old *Social Registers* were), as though these tags should compensate, in Lippard's mind as well as the reader's, for any persuasive appreciation of their individual art. It is unfortunate that some of these recent books have sold more copies than Lippard's better ones (and probably won her more ancillary jobs as well), because in America that sort of success can make a writer think nothing has been lost.

Works: *Pop Art*, with others (1966). New York: Thames & Hudson, 1985; *Changing: Essays in Art Criticism*. New York: Dutton, 1968; *Eva Hesse* (1976). New York: Da Capo, 1992; *Ad Reinhardt*. New York: Abrams, 1981; *Overlay: Contemporary Art and the Art of Prehistory*. New York: Pantheon, 1983; *The Pink Glass: Selected Feminist Essays on Art*. New York: New Press, 1995; *On the Beaten Path*. New York: New Press, 1999.

LISSITZKY, El

(23 November 1890–30 December 1941; b. Eliezer Markowich L.).

Born in Smolensk, Russia, Lissitzky studied engineering in Germany before returning to Russia during World War I. After collaborating with Marc Chagall (1887–1985) on the illustration of Jewish books and with Kazimir Malevich in establishing Russian Constructivism, Lissitzky moved to Berlin, where he published *The Story of Two Squares* (1922), which, as its title says, is a pioneering abstract visual fiction, as well as a modest masterpiece of modern typography. Lissitzky then finished a series of Constructivist paintings that he called *Proun*. In 1928, for a museum in Hanover, he designed an "abstract gallery," a proto-Environment that Alexander Dorner described in *The Way Beyond "Art"* (1958):

> The walls of that room were sheathed with narrow tin strips set at right angles to the wall plane. Since these strips were painted black on one side, grey on the other, and white on the edge, the wall changed its character with every move of the spectator. The sequence of tones varied in different parts of the room. This construction thus established a supraspatial milieu of the frameless compositions [i.e., suspended paintings].

Dorner continues, "This room contained many more sensory images than could have been accommodated by a rigid room." By current categories, this was a proto Environment. Lissitzky also made innovative photomontages and wrote about architectural possibilities *(An Architecture for World Revolution*, 1930) before returning in the 1930s to Russia, where he confined himself mainly to typography and industrial design (e.g., the Soviet Pavilion at the New York World's Fair in 1939) until his premature death.

Lissitzky also designed *Die Kunstismen/Les ismes de l'art/The Isms of Art* (1925), a cunningly illustrated anthology of illustrations exemplifying cubism, neoplasticism, futurism, constructivism, dada, suprematism, expressionisms, simultaneity, etc., as represented by Mondrian, Moholy-Nagy, Man Ray, Malevitch, Kandinsky, Tatlin, Richter, Picasso, Van Doesburg, Vantongerloo, et al. (In retrospect, we can judge that the selection of individuals reflected sure taste.) Published in Switzerland, this is the first modern art book known to me (conceding there

El Lissitzky. *Construction—Proun 2*, 1920. Oil, colored tin, papers, etc. CORBIS/Philadephia Museum.

might have been predecessors) to have parallel texts in French, English, and German (none of which was Lissitzky's mother tongue). Not solely an antique, this book was reprinted intact recently, likewise in Switzerland. So were the two issues, likewise initially in several languages, now with elaborate annotations in English, of the spectacularly prophetic magazine *Gegenstand* (1922) that Lissitzky co-edited with the Russian writer Ilya Ehrenburg (1891–1967).

Visual Art: *Beat the Whites with the Red Wedge*, 1919–20; *Proun 2C*, 1920; *Proun*, 1922; *Proun 12E*, 1923; *Proun*, 1924–25.

Books: *Russia: An Architecture for World Revolution* (1930). Trans. Eric Dluhosh. Cambridge: MIT Press, 1970; ——, and Hans Arp. (1925). *Die Kunstismen/Les ismes de l'art/The Isms of Art.* Baden, Switzerland: Lars Muller (CH-5401), 1990; ——, and Ilya Ehrenberg. *Veŝĉ Objet Gegenstand.* Ed. Roland Nachtigäller and Hubertus Gassner; annotations by Rita Frommenwiler. Baden, Switzerland: Lars Muller (CH-5401), 1990.

Exhibition Catalogs: Nakov, Andréi B. *Russian Pioneers at the Origins of Non-Objective Art.* London: Annely Juda, 1976; *El Lissitsky, 1890–1941.* Cambridge: Harvard University Art Museum, 1987; *El Lissitsky Retrospektive.* Frankfurt am Main & Berlin: Propyläen, 1988; *The Great Utopia: The Russian & Soviet Avant-Garde, 1915–1932.* N.Y: Guggenheim Museum, 1992.

Interpretation: Lissitzky-Küppers, Sophie. *El Lissitzky: Life, Letters, Texts* (1967). Intro. Herbert Read. London: Thames & Hudson, 1980; Lubbers, Frank. *El Lissitsky: 1890–1941 Architect, Painter, Photographer, Typographer.*

New York: Thames & Hudson, 1991; Mansbach, Steven. *Visions of Totality: Laszlo Moholy-Nagy, Theo van Doesburg, and El Lissitzky*. Ann Arbor, MI: UMI Research, 1978; Margolin, Victor. *The Struggle for Utopia: Rodchenko Lissitzky Moholy-Nagy, 1917–1946*. Chicago: University of Chicago Press, 1997.

LIVING THEATRE

(1947).

Founded by Judith Malina (1926) and Julian Beck (1925–1985), longtime wife and husband, the Living Theatre has forever epitomized whatever might be radical in American theater. At their beginnings, at a time when naturalistic theater predominated, their specialty was poet's plays (e.g., GERTRUDE STEIN, KENNETH REXROTH, W. B. Yeats, Paul Goodman, et al.); that perhaps accounts for why they spell "theater" to this day in the British way. By the 1960s, they had assimilated *The Theatre and Its Double* by ANTONIN ARTAUD, creating in their productions of Jack Gelber's *The Connection* (1961) and especially Kenneth Brown's *The Brig* (1963) theater that moved audiences, in Artaud's words, "with the force of the plague." In 1963, after their home theater was seized by the Internal Revenue Service for nonpayment of withholding taxes, they moved to Europe where, in Eric Mottram's words, "they developed the idea of a theater company as creative political critics and emotional gurus." They returned to the United States in 1968 with *Paradise Now*, which was a series of scripted provocations that succeeded in involving theatrical audiences like nothing before or since.

Though Beck died in 1985, with Hanon Reznikov becoming both Malina's husband and principal partner, the company persists at various temporary locations, including Manhattan's Times Square, where, in the 1990s, they performed street theater after every prison execution in America. Though new productions invariably disappoint those who remember previous masterpieces, the Living Theatre has, after fifty years, survived longer than any other theater company of its avant-garde and politically radical kind, incidentally outliving nearly all of its imitators; for this alone, the Living Theatre deserves national honors.

Theatrical Texts: The Living Theatre. *Paradise Now*. New York: Random House, 1971.

Autobiography: Beck, Julian. *The Life of the Theater*. San Francisco: City Lights, 1972; Malina, Judith. *The Enormous Despair*. New York: Random House, 1972; *The Diaries of Judith Malina*. New York: Grove, 1984.

Living Theater. *Paradise Now*, presented at the Brooklyn Academy of Music, 14 October 1968. Photograph © Fred W. McDarrah.

Interpretation: Biner, Pierre. *The Living Theatre*. New York: Horizon, 1972; Tytell, John. *The Living Theatre: Art, Exile, and Outrage*. New York: Grove, 1995.

Documentary: Silvestro, Carlo, ed. *The Living Book of the Living Theatre*. Greenwich, CT: New York Graphic Society, 1971.

Videos: *The Brig: A Film* (1964). Dir. Jonas and Adolfus Mekas. New York: Mystic Fire, 1986; *Paradise Now: A Videofilm* (1970). Dir. Sheldon Rochlin. New York: Mystic Fire, 1986; *The Connection* (1961). Written by Jack Gelber, Dir. Shirley Clarke. New York: Mystic Fire, 1987.

LONG, Richard

(2 June 1945).

The projects of British Earth Artist Richard Long are distinguished from those of ROBERT SMITHSON and MICHAEL HEIZER by the lightness of Long's touch. Whereas Smithson and Heizer have engaged in large-scale excavation works, Long generally marks the environment tentatively, arranging sticks or rocks in geometrical patterns during his walks, gently carving out small circles and short lines in the terrain, and reporting his doings through gallery installations of documentary photographs. He is, like Heizer, cut out of the Romantic mold. But, unlike Heizer, Long is more in the English model: something of a saunterer who respectfully explores nature, *à la* William Wordsworth. What is more significant is that Long has devised a way of returning Earth Art to the gallery. Bringing back elements such as stones and wood from his journeys, he orders them into geometric patterns on the gallery floor, often into long rectangles that look too much like the well-tooled, highly industrial floor works of CARL ANDRE to retain the tie to nature that characterizes Earth Art. However, Long frequently arranges the natural, rough-hewn shapes of his stones into circular patterns that bear a distinct resemblance to megalithic circles. Despite their relatively small scale, the association endows them with a quality of the mythic, an effect completely foreign to the Minimalist aesthetic that Andre represents.

—Mark Daniel Cohen

Works: *A Line Made by Walking*, 1967; *Turf Circle*, 1969; *Three Circles of Stones*, 1972; *192 Pieces of Wood*, 1975; *Sandstone Circle*, 1977; *A Hundred Sticks Placed on a Beaver Lodge*, 1985.

Exhibition Catalogs: Compton, Michael. *Some Notes on the Work of Richard Long*. London: British Council, 1976; *The North Woods*. London: Whitechapel Art Gallery, 1977; Jeppson, Gabriella. *Richard Long*. Cambridge, MA: Fogg Art Museum, 1980; *Surf Roar*. La Jolla, CA: La Jolla Museum of Contemporary Art, 1989; Brades, Susan Ferleger. *Richard Long: Walking In Circles*. London: South Banke Centre, 1991; Brettell, Richard R., and Friis-Hansen, Dana. *Richard Long: Circles, Cycles, Mud, Stones*. Houston: Contemporary Arts Museum, 1996.

Criticism: Fuchs, Rudolf Herman. *Richard Long*. New York: Guggenheim Museum & London: Thames and Hudson, 1986.

LOUIS, Morris

(28 November 1912–7 September 1962; b. M. L. Bernstein).

Louis's innovation was self-referential paintings that emphasized not the forms of gestural abstraction but the textures of variously applied paints, the relationships of colors within the field, and, in some cases, the possible subtle shadings of a single hue. Adapting JACKSON POLLOCK's alternative way of applying paint to his own ends, Louis in the mid-1950s poured thinned-out acrylic paint directly on unprimed cottonduck canvas. For a series called *Veils* (1954, again in 1957–60), the thinned paints were poured onto canvas in overlapping patterns that are patently beautiful. The curator-critic John Elderfield finds that, "With Louis . . . fully autonomous abstract painting came into its own for really the first time, and did so in paintings of a quality that matches the level of their innovation." One appropriate epithet was COLORFIELD PAINTING, whose later advocates included Kenneth Noland (1924) and Jules Olitski (1922).

Works: *Veils*, 1954; *Veils II*, 1958–59; *Unfurleds*, 1959–61; *Stripes*, 1961–62.

Exhibition Catalogs: Greenberg, Clement. *Three New American Painters: Louis, Noland, Olitski*. Regina, Canada: McKenzie Art Gallery, 1963; Alloway, Lawrence. *Morris Louis: 1912–1962*. New York: Guggenheim Museum, 1963; Solomon, Alan. *Morris Louis*. London: Whitechapel, 1965; Rosenblum, Robert. *Morris Louis*. Amsterdam: Stedelijk Museum, 1965; Fried, Michael. *Morris Louis: 1912–1962*. Boston: Boston Museum of Fine Arts, 1967; *Morris Louis*. London: Tate Gallery, 1974; Elderfield, John. *Morris Louis*. New York: MoMA, 1986.

Interpretation: Fried, Michael. *Morris Louis*. New York: Abrams, 1969.

Catalogue Raisonné: Upright, Diane. *Morris Louis: The Complete Paintings*. New York: Abrams, 1985.

LOUIS, Murray

(4 November 1926).

For many years the principal male dancer in the ALWIN NIKOLAIS company, Louis became the only prominent modern dancer influenced by Charlie Chaplin, which is to say that his choreography tends to stylized movements and parody, making as much fun of its ostensible subjects as of numerous styles of dance. In his classic *Junk Dances* (1964), the set is a mockery of POP ART; one sequence parodies the courtship mannerisms evident in 1930s movies; another sequence, as brilliantly performed by Phyllis Lamhut, satirizes the standard theatrical rendition of the busy secretary; another episode mocks Nikolais's propheavy choreography. The piece closes with Louis himself draped in Christmas tinsel and a network of lights that actually illuminate as the COLLAGE tape plays the opera star Galli-Curci hitting her final high note. I have seen *Junk Dances* perhaps a dozen times, never with decreasing pleasure.

Dances: *Junk Dances*,1964; *Chimera*,1966; *Hoopla*, 1971; *Porcelain Dialogues*, 1974; *Schubert*, 1977; *Déjá Vu*, 1977; *Afternoon*, 1980; *Four Brubeck Pieces*, 1984.

Books: *Inside Dance*. New York: St. Martin's Press, 1981; *On Dance*. Pennington, NJ: A Cappella, 1992.

LUCIER, Alvin

(14 May 1931).

Interested in the musical resonances of ambient sounds, particularly in live electronic performance, Lucier composed *I Am Sitting in a Room* (1970), which begins with him reading a 100-word prose statement that is recorded on tape. This recorded version is then played in the same place in which the original statement was made and rerecorded on new tape one generation away from the initial live statement. This procedure of broadcasting and re-recording is continued through several generations, as distortion progressively obliterates the text with the increasingly amplified sounds not of the composer's voice but of the acoustic space.

I remember his *Chambers* (1968), in which four musicians played conch shells through the auditorium, down the stairs, and out into New York's 57th Street, where Lucier himself stood on the double white line in the middle of the street. As cars whizzed by in both directions, a taxicab honked a horn that was louder and perhaps more musical than the sounds Lucier was producing. Then out of a building came a uniformed doorman—a "found player," so to speak—to tell Lucier to move on. Lucier has also worked creatively with devices to amplify alpha brain waves in live musical performance, as an example of live ELECTRONIC MUSIC, with sound vibrations to generate visual imagery, with instrumentalists accompanying electronically generated sound, and with sustained sounds in continually rearticulated microtonal relations. A reporter interviewing Lucier writes that he typically speaks of "making" works rather than composing them

Works: *Action Music* for piano, 1962; *Music for Solo Performer* for amplified brain waves and percussion, 1965; *"I am sitting in a room"* for voice and electromagnetic tape, 1970; *Outlines of persons and things* for microphones, loudspeakers, and electronic sounds, 1975; *Bird and Person Dyning* for a performer with microphones, amplifiers, loudspeakers, and sound-producing objects, 1975; *Music on a Long Thin Wire* for audio oscillators, and electric monochord, 1977; *Solar Sounder I*, electronic music system powered and controlled by sunlight, 1979; *Seesaw* sound installation, 1983; *Music* for pure waves, bass drums, and acoustic pendulums, 1980; *Spinner* sound installation, 1984; *Sound on Paper* sound installation, 1985; *Kettles* for 5 timpani and 2 pure wave oscillators, 1987; *Amplifier and Reflector I* for open umbrella, ticking clock, and glass over dish, 1991.

Writings: *Chambers*. With Douglas Simon. Middletown: Wesleyan University Press, 1980; *Reflections: Interviews, Scores, Writings.* Köln: Musik Texte, 1995.

Recordings: *Clocker* for Amplified Clock, Galvanic Skin Response Sensor & Digital Delay System (1978–88). New York: Lovely Music; *Crossings* for Small Orchestra with Slow-Sweep Pur Wave Oscillator (1982–84). New York: Lovely; *I Am Sitting in a Room* (1969). New York: Lovely Music/Vital Records, 1981; *Music on a Long Thin Wire*. New York: Lovely; 1999.

Web Site: http://www.wesleyan.edu/course/faculty/lucieralvina.htm

Interpretation: Kozinn, Allan. "Music Reconceived as Acoustical Sculpture." In *New York Times* (13 April 1997).

LUDLAM, Charles

(12 April 1943–28 May 1987).

Ludlam gladly accepted the epithet "Theatre of the Ridiculous," which represented an extension at once appropriate

Charles Ludlam, photographed on 23 March 1972. Copyright © Fred W. McDarrah.

and ironic of the THEATRE OF THE ABSURD; for, if the latter used absurd means to portray worldly absurdity, Ludlam took the satirical impulse a step further, using ridiculous means to portray worldly ridiculousness. "We have passed beyond the Absurd," wrote his colleague and sometime collaborator Ronald Travel (1941), "Our position is absolutely preposterous." Ludlam's manifesto typically emphasizes "axioms to a theater for ridicule," including "the things one takes seriously are one's weaknesses." Even though most of his plays drew upon classical models, they were filled with bad taste, sexual confusion, phallic worship, and operatic extravagance. Success encouraged him to inflate these aberrations. Of the plays familiar to me, the most inspired is *Der Ring Gott Farblonjet* (1977), subtitled "A Masterwork," which it truly is. Initially a takeoff on Richard Wagner's *Ring* cycle of operas, it deflates their pomposity first with a Yiddish euphemism for getting hopelessly lost (*Farblonjet*, which is pronounced "farBLAWNjit"). The characters all have atrociously Teutonic names (the Valkyries being "Brunnhilda," "Helmvige," "Schwertheita," "Valtrauta," etc.); and, as is typical in Ludlam plays, female roles are often assumed by men. Ludlam makes language work in ways ironically reminiscent of *Finnegans Wake*, opening his *Ring* with: "Weia! Water! Waga! Waves of wasser! Waves of wasser! Wagalawei! Wallalla weiala weia!" True to his means, Ludlam also wrote ridiculous stage directions: "(The weaves giftoff to scrimmist sheerest parting until all is clear, clearing on a mountain's height. Lustering Blistering tamples pinnacles of casteln hinterground.)" He died prematurely of complications from AIDS, which is not avant-garde—just a deadly disease.

Writings: *The Complete Plays*. New York: Harper & Row, 1989; *Ridiculous Theater: Scourge of Human Folly*. New York: TCG, 1992.

Interpretation: Roemer, Rick. *Charles Ludlam and the Ridiculous Theatre Company*. Jefferson, NC: McFarland, 1998.

LUENING, Otto

(15 June 1900–2 September 1996).

Born in Milwaukee, the son of a German-American musician, Luening was educated in the United States, Germany, and Switzerland. One among many American avant-garde composers in the 1930s and 1940s, better known as a flutist and for his administrative skills, Luening established a unique reputation in the 1950s as a pioneer of Electronic Music. On 28 October 1952, he played the flute in *Fantasy in Space* to a prerecorded (i.e., precomposed) audiotape accompaniment; two other premieres on that program, *Low Speed* and *Invention in 12 Tones*, were audiotapes wholly of electronically manipulated instrumental sounds. Luening later collaborated with his Columbia University, colleague, Vladimir Ussachevsky (1911–1990) in producing tapes that would function as soloists in orchestral concerts, their *Rhapsodic Variations* (1954) preceding by months an Edgard Varèse piece that worked similarly. Compared to what followed, Luening remains a traditional electronic composer. (Ussachevsky, curiously, spent his last years in Utah, composing music reflective of Russian Romanticism.) Luening was also a successful arts politician, not only in establishing an early electronic music studio at Columbia University, but in advising foundations to support the more avant-garde younger composers.

Works: *Fantasy in Space*, flute on tape, 1952; *Low Speed*, flute on tape, 1952; *Invention in 12 Tone*, flute on tape, 1952; *Rhapsodic Variations*, with Vladimir Ussashevsky, tape and orchestra, 1954; *Of Identity* ballet for organ on tape 1954; *A Poem in Cycles and Bells* with Vladimir Ussachevsky, for tape and orchestra, 1954; *Carlsbad Caverns* (electronic television theme for *Wide, Wide World*),1955; *Concerted Piece* for tape and orchestra, 1960; *Electronic Fanfare* for recorder, sound synthesizer, and percsussion on tape, 1962–65.

Recordings: *Music of Luening: Orchestral Works, 1917–1992*. Manhattan Chamber Orchestra cond. Richard Auldon Clark (Newport Classics); *Sonatas for Piano*. New York: Composers Recordings, 1996; *Incantation for Electronic Tape* (1953, with Vladimir Ussachevsky). On *Electronic Music: The Pioneers* (New York: CRI).

Autobiography: *The Odyssey of an American Composer*. New York: Scribner's, 1980.

Biography: Hartsock, Ralph. *Otto Luening: A Bio-Bibliography*. Westport, CT: Greenwood, 1991.

LYE, Len

(5 July 1901–15 May 1980).

Born in New Zealand, Lye lived in the South Sea Islands in the 1920s, assimilating Polynesian art, before moving to

London. Working with John Grierson's documentary film unit at the General Post Office, he invented around 1934 a technique for painting directly on film, producing the short *Color Box* (1935). In later films, Lye developed this technique, which consequently influenced the Canadian Norman McLaren (1914–87), among others. Rarely profiting from filmmaking, Lye abandoned that art for equally innovative, if esthetically different, work in kinetic sculpture.

Films: *Tusalava*, 1928; *Color Box*, 1935; *Rainbow Dance*, 1936; *Color Cry*, 1952.

Sculptures: *Fountain*, 1963; *Universe*, 1963; *Flip and Two Twisters*, 1967.

Writings: *Figures of Motion: Selected Writings* eds. Wystan Curnow and Roger Horrocks. Auckland, New Zealand: Auckland University, 1984.

Exhibition Catalog: *Len Lye: A Personal Mythology: Paintings, Steel-Motion Compositions, Films*. Ed. Ron Brownson. Auckland, New Zealand: Auckland City Art Gal., 1980.

Interpretation: Russett, Robert, and Cecile Starr. *Experimental Animation*. New York: Van Nostrand, 1976.

LYNDS, Clyde

(22 June 1936).

After training in classical painting, Lynds seized upon a new technology called "fiber optics" to open up new esthetic territory. Fiber optics uses translucent cable as thin as a strand of hair to transmit light or data. More important for Lynds's purposes is its capacity to carry light around corners, which is to say that light entering at one end or tip of this thin cable will emerge at the other tip, no matter how the cable is twisted and turned. What Lynds does is to distribute these ends to strategic points in a concrete surface, so that they become visible only when illuminated from within. The hidden element responsible for the continuous variations in surface light—for the appearance of endlessly changing "painting"—is color wheels, which are plastic discs whose sections are treated with various colored gels, including black. Situated between the strong light source and the interior ends of the fiber optic strands, the gels determine not only whether light is propelled to the exterior ends (black, of course, preventing this), but also what color the light will be. By introducing two discs, each rotating at different speeds, Lynds further varies the communication, literally, of light to the fiber optic terminals. The visible result is slowly metamorphosing combinations of dots of light, in continuously varying patterns, with minimal repetition, so that the principal afterimage for Lynds's kinetic paintings becomes not one or another stilled pose but flow itself.

Works: *Stele CIII*, 1992; *Stele CIV*, 1992; *Lustral Basin*, 1992; *Stele XCIV*, 1992; *Alabama Moon, for Betty*, 1989; *American Sunrise*, 1990; *Stele XLVI Icon*, 1988; *Stele XIV*, 1985; *Stele XXIC*, 1986; *Tympanum—Detail*, 1985; *Stele XLIII, Quetzalcoatl—Detail*, 1987; *Maiden Japan*, 1984; *Radium Night*, 1981.

Exhibition Catalog: *The David Bermant Collection: Color, Light, Motion*. Hartford, CT: Wadsworth Athenæum, 1984; *Lynds, Stelae*. Washington, DC: Wallace Wentworth, 1987; *Clyde Lynds Buddha's Seat*. Trenton: N.J. State Museum, 1993.

MAC LOW, Jackson

(12 September 1922).

As a poet, composer, and dramatist, Mac Low has used INDETERMINANCY in the creation of his works. In his own words, "My work, especially that of 1954–80, is closely related to that of such composers as JOHN CAGE, MORTON FELDMAN, EARLE BROWN, CHRISTIAN WOLFF, and LA MONTE YOUNG." He describes his writing from 1954 as "incorporat[ing] methods, processes, and devices from modern music, including the use of chance operations in composition and/or performance, silences ranging in duration from breath pauses to several minutes, and various degrees of improvisation by performers. Many of the works are 'simultaneities'—works performed by several speakers and/or producers of musical sounds and noises at once." Some of these texts are based on grids whose words (both horizontally and vertically arrayed) are spoken in an order determined by chance operations. Avowedly eclectic, Mac Low also writes fairly conventional free verse and even EXPRESSIONISTIC lyrics.

Mac Low stated in *Talisman* 8 (Spring 1992), "Open to all poetries, I'm shipwrecked amid terms such as 'avant-garde' and 'experimental'—words largely abandoned by many who share my universe of discourse. On the superficial—that is, the most serious—level, I hate the military provenance of 'avant-garde.' And to this noxious connotation the authoritarian split off from democratic Marxism added the concept of the 'vanguard party.'" As a veteran anarchist who uses those epithets generously (as in this book) and has written whole books about opening the professional field, I find it odd that anyone purportedly advocating openness would want to push some positions (and thus people) off the map. It's unfortunate to see Mac Low take this abnegating position, because he has for some fifty years been producing genuinely experimental, avant-garde poetry and theater.

—with Richard Carlin

Books: Mac Low, Jackson. *22 Light Poems*. LA: Black Sparrow Press, 1968; *Stanzas for Iris Lezak*. Barton, VT: Something Else Press, 1971; *21 Matched Asymmetries*. London; Aloes, 1978; *Asymmetries 1–260: The First Section of a Series of 501 Performance Poems*. New York: Printed Editions 1980; *Bloomsday*. Barrytown, NY: Station Hill, 1984; *Representative Works 1938–1985*. New York: Roof, 1986; *Words nd Ends from Ez*. Bolinas, CA: Avenue B., 1989.

MacDIARMID, Hugh

(11 August 1892–3 September 1978;
b. Christopher Murray Grieve).

A monumentally truculent literary character, he was expelled from the Scottish Nationalist Party in the 1930s for his Communism and soon afterwards bounced from the Communist Party for his Scottish Nationalism. His earliest major work, *A Drunk Man Looks at the Thistle* (1926), is frequently credited with awakening nationalistic consciousness in Scottish writers. Taking his own advice, MacDiarmid produced poems in self-taught Scots that are barely comprehensible to English-speaking readers—a literary lingo that seems more indebted to his *Irish* contemporary JAMES JOYCE than to his Scottish predecessor Robert Burns. Epitomizing DEFAMILIARIZATION to some and gibberish to others, the results include this stanza from "Overinzievar":

The pigs shoot up their gruntles here,
The hens staund hullerie,
And a' the hinds glower roond about
Wi' unco dullery.
Wi sook-the-bluids and switchables
The grund's fair crottled up,'
And owre't the forkit lichtnin' flees
Like a cleisher o' a whup.

(Does it help to know that gruntles=snots; hullerie=with ruffled feathers; hinds are farmhands; sook-the-bluids=little red beetles; switchables=earwigs; crottled=crumbled; owre't=over it; cleisher=lash; and, to less surprise, whup=whip, and wi=with and perhaps we.)

As his *First Hymn to Lenin* (1931) had a broader influence, the ever-truculent MacDiarmid also wrote "Epitaph on British Leftish Poetry, 1930–40," which mocks the effete political writings of his more prominent British contemporaries:

Auden, MacNeice, Day Lewis, I have read them all
Hoping against hope to hear the authentic call.

When he also got caught appropriating someone else's esoteric prose for his own verse, MacDiarmid replied more arrogantly than contritely, his reputation for higher-than-thou integrity undermined. One always felt that Christopher Murray Grieve, much like the man behind "Louis-Ferdinand Céline," used a PSEUDONYM for a more audacious (more political and less responsible) part of himself.

Poetry: *A Drunk Man Looks at the Thistle* (1926). Ed. John C. Weston. Amherst: University of Massachusetts Press, 1971; *First Hymn to Lenin and Other Poems*. London: Unicorn, 1931; *Stony Limits and Other Poems* (1932). London: Gollancz, 1934; *Selected Poems*. London: Macmillan, 1934; *Collected Poems*. New York: Macmillan, 1962; *Selected Poems*. Ed. David Craid and John Monson. Hammondsworth: Penguin, 1970; *Complete Poems 1920–1976*. Ed. Michael Grieve & W. R. Aitken. London: Martin Brian & O'Keeffe, 1978.

Prose: *The Islands of Scotland*. London: Batsford, 1939; *Burns Today and Tomorrow*. Edinburgh: Castle Wynd, 1959; *The Company I've Kept*. London: Hutchinson, 1966; *The Uncanny Scot*. Ed. Kenneth Buthlay. London: McGibbon & Kee, 1968; *Selected Essays*. Ed. Duncan Glen. London: Cape, 1969; *The Thistle Rises: An Anthology of Poetry and Prose*. Ed. Alan Bold. London: Hamish Hamilton, 1984.

Biography: Bold, Alan. *MacDiarmid: The Terrible Crystal*. London: Routledge, 1983; Wright, Gordon. *MacDiarmid: An Illustrated Biography*. Edinburgh: Gordon Wright, 1977.

Interpretation: Duval, K. D., and Sydney Goodsir Smith. *Hugh MacDiarmid: A Festschrift*. Edinburgh: K. D. Duval, 1962; Buthlay, Kenneth. *Hugh MacDiarmid (C.M. Grieve)*. Edinburgh: Oliver & Boyd, 1964; Glen, Duncan. *Hugh MacDiarmid and the Scottish Renaissance*. Edinburgh: Chambers, 1964.

MACIUNAS, George

(8 November 1931–9 May 1978).

A legendary character to all who knew him, Maciunas, a Lithuanian-born American who seemed forever an immigrant, was at once the founder and sometime generalissimo of FLUXUS and the developer/renovator of artists' cooperatives in SOHO. His own art consisted of ingenious architectural proposals, small boxes accumulating debris similar in some way (such as excrement), and audacious graphic designs. His artistic masterpiece is the *Expanded Arts Diagram* (1966), which is a complex graphic history portraying the relationships of the new arts to the old arts (aka INTERMEDIA). Using lists turned at various angles and flow-chutes, Maciunas identified the roles of DADA, Vaudeville, MARCEL DUCHAMP, church processions ("Baroque Multi-Media Spectacle"), circuses, fairs, and the BAUHAUS as precursors to such activities as "acoustic theater," "kinesthetic theater," "expanded cinema," "events—neo-haiku theater," "verbal theater," "HAPPENINGS", etc.—all positioned in the sans-serif type that always marked his graphic work. To quote Ken Friedman on Maciunas, "He saw the artists fulfilling in their work a long evolution of ideas, fluid rather than rigid, part of a millennia-long human dialogue. The chart reveals a designer with an eye for broad historical scope and a visual humor." I own a larger, later chart, some six feet by two, that Friedman says is an incomplete draft "published in Sweden after Maciunas's death," even though my recollection is that Maciunas gave it to me a few years before.

Works: Maciunas, George. *Expanded Arts Diagram*, 1966.

Biography: Williams, Emmett. *Mr Fluxus: A Collective Portrait of George Maciunas 1931–1978*. New York: Thames & Hudson, 1998.

Web Site: http://www.fluxus.org/FLUXLIST/georgem.htm (links).

Interpretation: Friedman, Ken, "George Maciunas." In *Contemporary Masterpieces*, ed. Colin Naylor. London, England: St. James, 1991.

Portrait of Loren MacIver by Carl van Vechten. CORBIS.

MACIVER, Loren

(2 February 1909).

Largely self-educated as a painter, with only one year of formal training at the age of ten, MacIver developed an individual style that defies categorization within mainstream artistic currents. By the 1940s, she had become one of the best-known women artists in the United States. Her subject was the atmospheric effect of light. She portrayed commonplace objects of urban life, and on occasion cityscapes, with a luminosity that seems to emanate from them and blend together, suffusing the entire canvas with a glistening illumination. Votive candles, oil slicks, jars, bottles, bouquets of flowers, buildings, and skylines were rendered as softly defined, out of focus, and aglow with colors of gem-like intensity. Sticking to her subject, MacIver gave a poetic sense of wonder to otherwise ordinary imagery. In fact, she associated with avant-garde poets as much as with visual artists, and the poet Elizabeth Bishop (a friend of MacIver) described her work as a "divine myopia." What distinguishes MacIver's style is its combination of realism and abstraction. In her best work, she organizes her wavering visions in strict geometric patterns, as if a planar structure inherent in the light were replacing the details of observation.

—Mark Daniel Cohen

Works: *Decalomania*, 1934; *Strunsky House*, 1935; *Hopscotch*, 1940; *The City*, 1941; *Red Votive Lights*, 1943; *New York*, 1952; *Manhattan*, 1959; *Byzantium*, 1965; *Skylight Moon*, 1968; *Green Votive Lights*, 1981.

Exhibition Catalogs: *MacIver, Paintings: October 1949*. New York: Pierre Matisse Gallery, 1949; *Loren MacIver, Paintings, Pastels, Drawings: March 22–April 16, 1966*. New York: Pierre Matisse, 1966; Frash, Robert M. *Loren MacIver: Five Decades: Newport Harbor Art Museum, Newport Beach, California, April 14–June 12, 1983*. Newport Beach, CA: Newport Harbor Art Museum, 1983; Marshall, Richard D. *Loren MacIver: October 7–November 6, 1993*. New York: Terry Dintenfass Gallery, 1993; Balken, Debra Bricker. *Loren MacIver: A Retrospective*. New York: Tibor de Nagy Gallery, 1998.

Criticism: Garbrecht, Sandra. *Loren MacIver: The Painter and the Passing Stain of Circumstance*. Washington, DC: Georgetown University Press, 1987.

MAD MAGAZINE

(1952).

On second thought, it is scarcely surprising that one of the most influential radical magazines in America should have begun as a sort of comic book for sophisticated teenagers. And it has remained a sort of comic book, internal improvements notwithstanding. Whenever nosy parents tried to censor it, *MAD*'s reputation gained. *MAD Magazine* has pioneered all kinds of satire and irreverant humor, all without the benefit of advertisers (which made it different from most other large-circulation magazines and purportedly immune from corporate meddling), and even without advertising itself. In addition to a periodical that appeared eight times a year, the *MAD* men produced small-format paperback books where, as in the periodical, every detail became a platform for humor. Even in a purportedly straight book by a *MAD* writer, such as Dick DeBartelo's memoir, there are classic passages such as this, explaining how the anarchic medium should now be owned by Time Warner:

> [The publisher] sold EC Publications, MAD's parent company, to Premiere Industries. They sold it to Kenney Corporation, which was originally in the rent-a-car and the rent-a-hearse business. Then Kinney merged with Warner, and became part of Amalgamated By-Products. They merged with World Wide Rust, a division of International House of Flannel. MAD was spun off into the cooking division until three years later, when it was discovered that MAD was not edible. . . . Then one morning we all woke up to find we were owned by Time Warner.

I thought of writing more here about its typical art, beginning with the reincarnations of its anti-logo "Alfred E. Neuman/What—Me Worry?" Then I figured that most people reading this *Dictionary* already know whatever I might say, as *MAD* is remembered first in nearly everyone's memories and then in several well-selling anthologies, on uncharacteristically fine book paper, of choice materials from its newsprint pages.

Self-Anthologies: *Mad About the Fifties*. New York: Little, Brown, 1997; *Mad About the Sixties*. New York: Quality Paperback Book Club, 1996; *Mad About the Seventies*. New York: Little, Brown, 1996; *The Half-Wit and Wisdom of Alfred E. Neuman*. New York: Warner, 1997.

History: Reidelbach, Maria. *Completely MAD*. Boston: Little, Brown, 1991.

Memoir: DeBartolo, Dick. *Good Days and Mad*. New York: Thunder's Mouth, 1994; Gaines, William. *The Mad World of William Gaines*. Secaucus, NJ: L. Stuart, 1972.

Web Site: http://www.dccomics.com/mad/

MAGRITTE, René

(21 November 1898–15 August 1967; b. René-François-Ghislain M.).

Magritte aligned himself with the Parisian SURREALISTS in the late 1920s, and subsequently became, along with SALVADOR DALI, one of the two Surrealist painters beloved by the general public. Again, like Dali, Magritte used strictly

Rene Magritte. *Hegel's Holiday*, 1958. CORBIS/Archivo Iconografica, S.A. © 2000 C. Hersvocivi, Brussels/Artists Rights Society (ARS), New York.

realistic imagery (which probably accounts for the shared popularity); but unlike Dali, he did not paint particularly well, and he never distorted his images with a nightmare logic. Magritte presented normal objects and figures in absurd situations: enormous boulders floating like clouds, a railroad train emerging from the back wall of a fireplace (presumably an escalation of imagined smoke with the smoke of burning wood), landscape paintings in ornate frames depicted as standing before "real" landscapes that continue the image within the frame, an image of a smoking pipe above the words: "This is not a pipe" (which has sent hordes of postmodern thinkers who study linguistic theory into intellectual genuflection). Magritte does not display a visual sensibility; his imagination is literary and theoretical. He is stylistically an illustrator conveying irrational anecdotes and posing logical conundrums. And he did more than any other artist, and much more than Dali, to tone down Surrealism's excesses and make it palatable: to make Surrealism seem intriguing, and nothing more than strange, and in no sense psychologically dangerous or disorienting.

—Mark Daniel Cohen

Works: *This Is Not A Pipe*, 1928–29; *The Unexpected Answer*, 1933; *The Dominion of Light*, 1954; *Where Euclid Walked*, 1955; *The Castle in the Pyrenees*, 1959; *The Listening-Room*, 1959; *The Son of Man*, 1964.

Exhibition Catalogs: *Magritte: 27 September–24 October 1961*. London: Grosvenor Gallery, 1961; Soby, James Thrall. *René Magritte*. New York: The MoMA; Distributed by Doubleday, 1965; Colinet, Paul. *The 8 Sculptures of Magritte*. London: Hanover Gallery, 1968; Sylvester, David. *Magritte*. New York: Praeger, 1969; *Magritte*. London: Marlborough Fine Art, 1976; Whitfield, Sarah. *Magritte*. London: South Bank Centre, 1992.

Catalogues Raisonnés: Kaplan, Gilbert E. and Timothy Baum. *The Graphic Work of René Magritte*. New York: Il Editions, 1982; Sylvester, David (ed.) and Whitfield, Sarah. *René Magritte, Catalogue Raisonné*. Houston, Texas: Menil Foundation, & London: Philip Wilson, 1992–1994.

Web Page: http://ruesch.addict.de/~lynx/magritte/ (gallery of images).

Interpretation: Gablik, Suzi. *Magritte*. Greenwich, CT: New York Graphic Society, 1970; Larkin, David, ed. *Magritte*. Intro. Eddie Wolfram. New York: Ballantine, 1972; Hammacher, Abraham Marie. *René Magritte*. New York: Abrams, 1974; Noll, Bernard. *Magritte*. New York: Crown, 1977; Michals, Duane. *A Visit with Magritte*. Providence, RI: Matrix, 1981; Sylvester, David. *Magritte: The Silence of the World*. New York: Abrams, 1992; Spitz, Ellen Handler. *Museums of the Mind: Magritte's Labyrinth and Other Essays in the Arts*. New Haven: Yale University Press, 1994.

MAIL ART

Out of the reasonable assumption that the commercial gallery system is limited, many artists emerging in the 1970s and 1980s around the world decided it would be more feasible to exhibit their work not through galleries and ancillary museums but through the postal system, especially if they lived in areas where galleries and other artists were scarce. For the production of imagery, they drew often upon XEROGRAPHY and the earlier graphic technology of rubber stamps. They would also announce exhibitions in venues previously devoid of art, such as city halls in remote parts of the world, ideally accepting everything submitted and issuing a catalog with names, usually accompanied by addresses and selected reproductions. While such work had little impact upon commercial galleries (and the "art magazines" dependent upon galleries' ads), one result was a thriving alternative culture, calling itself "The Eternal Network," as intensely interested in itself as serious artists have always been.

Bibliography: Crane, Mike. *Correspondence Art*. San Francisco: Contemporary Arts, 1984; Welch, Chuck. *Eternal Network*. Calgary, Canada: University of Calgary, 1996.

MALEVICH, Kazimir

(26 February 1878–15 May 1935).

Malevich came to Moscow in his late twenties, initially working as an Impressionist painter. Befriending political radicals in the pre-World War I decade, Malevich produced paintings depicting rural peasants in a deliberately primitive style. Working with flat planes of unmodulated color, Malevich called his art CUBO-FUTURISM. Changing his style again, he made COLLAGES and juxtapositions of realistically rendered details in the manner of PABLO PICASSO and Georges Braque (1882–1963). In 1913, he designed stage sets and costumes for MIKHAIL MATIUSHIN's and ALEKSEI KRUCHONYKH's opera *Victory Over the Sun*, by common consent a monument of FUTURIST theater. By 1915–1916, Malevich reached his most radical style of non-objective painting which he called Suprematism, best regarded as a radical development within CONSTRUCTIVISM. A 1915 oil painting titled *Red Square (Painterly Realism: Peasant Woman in Two Dimensions)*, 53 cm square, has a large, unmodulated red square set against a white background, the title alone implying representational intentions. (Indicatively, a reproduction of this crucial work became not only the cover but the opening illustration of *The Great Utopia* [1992], the richest recent exhibition of Russian avant-garde art from 1915 to 1932.) Not unlike his near contemporary PIET MONDRIAN, Malevich, in writing about his art, made claims that are hard to verify: for example, "Suprematism is pure feeling." In their fields of unmodulated color, these works resemble monochromic paintings that became more familiar after 1960.

In the 1920s, Malevich extended Suprematist principles to sculpture. A supporter of the Soviet Revolution, he became head of the Viebsk art school. Everyone acknowledged his exceptional organizational skills, as well as his capacity to forge professional alliances. Shrewdly sensing trouble, he traveled in 1927 to Germany, leaving some of his more radical paintings there, to remain undiscovered until the 1970s. Back in Leningrad, he returned to figurative painting, concluding his career with portraits of friends and family. Given all the rapid changes (through, in Valentine Marcade's sweeping summary, "Impressionism, NeoPrimitivism, Fauvism, Futurism, Cubism, Alogism, Suprematism, the *arkhitekton* constructions and then, in the 1930s, back to figurative art"), the critical question posed by all the changes in Malevich's career was whether he was mercurial or opportunistic.

Works: *Four Squares*, 1915; *Suprematist Painting*, 1915; *Suprematist Painting: Eight Red Rectangles*, 1915; *Red Square (Painterly Realism: Peasant Woman in Two Dimensions)*, 1915; *Dynamic Suprematism (Supremus No. 57)*, 1916; *White Square on White Finish*, 1918.

Writings: *The Non-Objective World*. Chicago: Theobald, 1959; *Essays on Art*. 4 vols. Ed. Troels Anderson: Copenhagen: Borgen, 1978.

Exhibition Catalogs: *Kazimir Malevich, 1875–1935*. London: Whitechapel, 1959; Karshan, Donald H. ed. *Kasimir Malevich: The Graphic Work, 1913–1930: Print Catalogue Raisonné*. Jerusalem: Israel Museum, 1975; Nakov, Andre B. *Russian Pioneers at the Origins of Non-Objective Art*. London: Annely Juda, 1976; *Malevich*. London: Tate Gallery, 1976; *Kazimir Malevich*. Amsterdam: Stedelijk Museum, 1989; *Kazimir Malevich, 1878–1935*. Los Angeles: Armand Hammer Museum of Art & Cultural Center, 1990; *The Great Utopia: The Russian and Soviet Avant-Garde, 1915–1932*. New York: Guggenheim Museum, 1992.

Interpretation: Crone, Rainer. *Kazimir Malevich: The Climax of Disclosure*. Chicago: University of Chicago Press, 1991; Douglas, Charlotte. *Swans of Other Worlds: Kazimir Malevich and the Origins of Abstraction in Russia*. Ann Arbor, MI: UMI Research, 1976; *Kazimir Malevich*. New York: Harry Abrams, 1994; Marcade, Valentine. "The Peasant Theme in the Work of Kazimir Severinovich Malevich." In *Kasimir Malewitsch*. Köln, Germany: Galerie Gmurzynska, 1978; Milner, John. *Kazimir Malevich and the Art of Geometry*. New Haven: Yale University Press,

1996; Zhadova, Lariss A. *Malevich: Suprematism and Revolution in Russian Art, 1910–30*. London: Thames & Hudson, 1982.

MALLARMÉ, Stéphane

(18 March 1842–9 September 1898).

Mallarmé's avant-garde masterpiece is the long poem *Un Coup de Dés* (1897). The radical idea for this work was making the page a field receptive to various typographies and verbal relationships both syntactical and spatial, and in this respect, Mallarmé foreshadowed GUILLAUME APOLLINAIRE and CHARLES OLSON, among many other poets, who developed a similar idea. "The word image-complex," Charles Mauron wrote, "is the fundamental quality of poetry, and melody is ancillary to that." Because the theme of *Un Coup* seems to be that everything perishes unless it is remembered in print, the form complements the content. Mallarmé's short poems are so precious and obscure that they are still treasured by those who regard preciosity and obscurity as the essence of poetic art. (Not I.) As Mauron puts it, "This cumulative effect of the auras of words is the essential quality of the poetic act." The fact that the standard French edition of Mallarmé's complete works contains less than 100 poems abets this image of preciousness. A teacher of English by trade, he is frequently credited with revolutionizing French narrative and with an Olympian detachment utterly contrary to the EXPRESSIONISTS who followed him. The Anthony Hartley translations are prose footnotes to the French, while Roger Fry's follow the structure of verse. Jean-Paul Sartre (1905–1980), frequently obsessed with writers profoundly unlike himself, produced an inspired monograph on Mallarmé that was translated only recently.

Works: *Poems*. Trans. Roger Fry, with commentaries by Charles Mauron. New York: New Directions, 1951; *Selected Prose Poems, Essays, & Letters*. Trans. Bradford Cook. Baltimore: Johns Hopkins University Press, 1956; *Selected Poems*. Trans. C. F. MacIntyre. Berkeley: University of California Press, 1957; *Mallarmé*. Ed., intro., prose trans. Anthony Hartley. Hammondsworth, England: Penguin, 1965; *Selected Poetry and Prose*. Ed. Mary Ann Caws. New York: New Directions, 1982; *Collected Poems*. Trans. Henry Weinfield. Berkeley: University of California Press, 1996.

Biography: Milan, Gordon. *A Throw of the Dice: The Life of Stéphane Mallarmé*. New York: Farrar, Straus & Giroux, 1994.

Interpretation: Block, Haskell. *Mallarmé and the Symbolist Drama*. Detroit: Wayne State University Press, 1963; Cohn, Robert Greer. *Toward the Poems of Mallarmé*. Berkeley: University of California Press, 1965; Fowlie, Wallace. *Mallarmé*. Chicago: University of Chicago Press, 1951; Sartre, Jean-Paul. *Mallarmé or the Poet of Nothingness* (1980). Trans. Ernest Strum. University Park: Penn State University Press, 1988.

MAN RAY

(27 August 1890–18 November 1976; b. Emmanuel Rudnitsky).

A minor POLYARTIST, Man Ray was considerably more skilled at some of his arts than others. Largely self-taught, he made COLLAGES and CUBIST paintings before World War I. In 1915, he published out of a New Jersey artists' colony a PROTODADA magazine, *The Ridgefield Gazook*, and after meeting MARCEL DUCHAMP later that year, Ray became a principal participant in New York Dada. Moving to Paris in 1921, he joined organized SURREALISM and moved from photography into film, producing in *Emak Bakia* (1927), his closest claim to a classic. "Man Ray was adamant that there be no script for *Emak Bakia*, no discernible narrative progression," his biographer Neil Baldwin writes, "in keeping with his belief that there generally was no progress in art. Nevertheless, there *are* motifs in the film, repetitions of patterns of light as Man Ray paints with light, exploring more deeply dazzling contrasts engineered

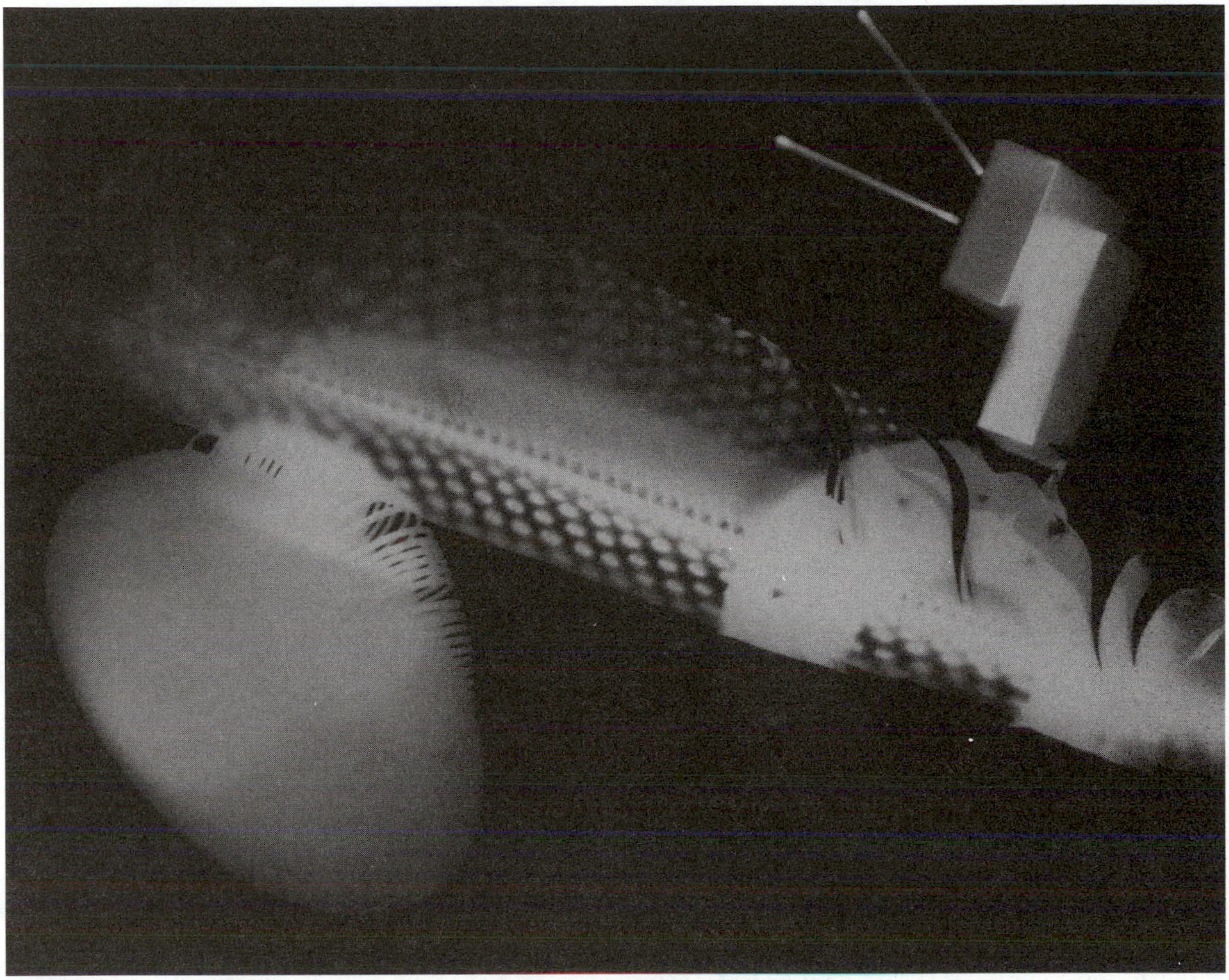

Man Ray, *#3 With Feather*. CORBIS/Burstein Collection. © 2000 Man Ray Trust/Artists Rights Society, NY/ADAGP, Paris.

to stir the viewer's emotions . . . dark objects upon light backgrounds, light faces against dark backdrops, dark words against light paper." Man Ray challenged Moholy-Nagy's claim to have invented the photogram, in which a photograph is made by placing objects directly on photographic paper and then exposing it to light; he called these works "rayographs." He also worked, with considerable commercial success, as a fashion photographer. Indeed, Man Ray may have been the first painter-photographer whose photographs were superior—more original, more thoughtful—than his paintings, implicitly establishing in the 1920s and 1930s an esthetic legitimacy for the newer medium. *Self-Portrait* (1963) is Man Ray's immodest, incomplete autobiography. His nom-de-art is Man Ray, not Ray, Man—even though a recent catalog about New York Dada mistakenly alphabetizes him under R.

Paintings: *Observatory Time—The Lover*, 1932–34; *La Fortune*, 1938; *The Poet (King David)*, 1938; *La Femme et son Poison*, 1938; *Imaginary Portrait of D.A. F. de Sade*, 1938; *The Wall*, 1938; *Le Beau temps*, 1939.

Photograph Portfolios: Man Ray. *Photographs*. Milan, Italy: Electa Editrice, 1982; *Man Ray: Photography and its*

Double. Eds. Emmanuelle de L'Ecotais and Alain Sayag. Corte Madera, CA: Gingko, 1998.

Films: *Le Retour à la Raison*, 1923; *Emak Bakia*, 1927; *L'Etoile de Mer*, 1928; *Les Mystères du Château de Dé/The Mystery of the Chateau of the Dice*, 1929; ——, with others. *Dreams That Money Can Buy*, 1944–46.

Autobiography: *Self Portrait* (1963). New York: McGraw-Hill, 1979.

Anthologies: Baum, Timothy. *Man Ray's Portraits: 1921–39*. Albuquerque: University of New Mexico Press, 1990; *Man Ray Photographs* (1982). London: Thames & Hudson, 1997.

Biography: Baldwin, Neil. *Man Ray: American Artist*. New York: Clarkson Potter, 1988.

Website: www.manraytrust.com

Exhibition Catalogs: *Man Ray*. Los Angeles: County Museum of Art, 1966; *Man Ray*. New York: Cultural Center, 1975; Foresta, Merry A. *Perpetual Motif: The Art of Man Ray*. Washington, DC: National Museum of American Art, 1988; Nauman, Francis M. *Man Ray: The New York Years, 1913 to 1921*. New York: Zabriskie Gallery, 1988; *Man Ray in America*. Milwaukee, WI: Haggerty Museum of Art, Marquette University, 1989; *Man Ray: Paris, L.A.* Santa Monica, CA: Smart Art, 1996; Perlein, Gilbert. *Man Ray: a rétrospective 1912–1976*. Nice: Musée d'art moderne et d'art contemporain, 1997.

Interpretation: Penrose, Ronald. *Man Ray*. Boston: New York Graphic Society, 1975; Schwartz, Arturo. *Man Ray: The Rigour of the Imagination*. London: Thames & Hudson, 1977; Stauffacher, Frank, ed. *Art in Cinema: A Symposium on the Avant Garde Film* (1947). New York: Arno, 1968.

MANN, Chris

(9 March 1949).

One of the few Australian poets to have acquired an international avant-garde reputation, Mann has also produced highly inventive prose; unusual books, such as *On Having Words* (1978), which is actually a single sheet of paper approximately sixty inches by forty-two inches, printed on both sides, folded to fit between a pseudo-book cover; and *Quadraphonic Cocktail* (1987), multitrack radio programs that were broadcast over different Australian channels simultaneously; among other audacious inventions. He is *not* the South African poet of the same name who appears in the 1996 edition of the otherwise encyclopedic *Contemporary Poets* (St. James's Press).

Works: Mann, Chris. *On Having Words*. Melbourne, Australia: Outback, 1978; *Words and Classes*. Melbourne, Australia: Outback, 1978; *doin 2s*. Melbourne, Australia: phon'm, 1982; *Word for word*. New York: Christine, 1983; *Subjective beats metaphor*. Melbourne, Australia: NMA 1985; *LA DE DA*. Melbourne, Australia: collective effort, 1985; *The Rationales*. Melbourne, Australia: NMA/postneo, 1986; *of course*. Melbourne, Australia: collective effort, 1988; *Birth of Peace*. Melbourne Australia: NMA 1990; *Chris Mann and Grammar*. N.p.: Lingua, 1990; *Working Hypothesis*. Barrytown NY: Barrytown Ltd.,1998.

Recordings: *On second thoughts*. Black Rock, CT: OO Discs, 1994; *Chris Mann and the Impediments*. Black Rock, CT: OO Discs.

Criticism: Chopin, Henri. "Concerning Chris Mann." In *Electronic Arts in Australia*. Ed. Nicholas Zurbrugg. Murdoch, WA: Continuum, 1994.

MANZONI, Piero

(13 July 1933–6 February 1963).

A sometime student of Lucio Fontana, Manzoni extended his mentor's taste for radical challenges within the art-world context, signing his name on the lower backside of a nude model (1961), purportedly to guarantee the natural beauty of the woman's skin (which was unlikely), producing balloons inflated with "artist's breath" and tins containing "artist's shit [in truth, his own]," exhibiting "achromes," as he called them, made of polystyrene soaked in cobalt chloride, and making "tubes containing kilometers of lines designed to mock the idea of space." According to Giulio Carlo Argan, Manzoni was "the first to see that Duchamp was one of the most important protagonists of the century, the first artist for whom there was no work of art that wasn't also an idea about the essence and historical condition of art." If you think Argan is attributing too much philosophical weight to Manzoni's second-generation protoconceptual gestures, you might begin to understand why remarkably few Anglo-American critics, to different degrees predisposed to the ethics of verification, have written about Manzoni's work. Jes Petersen's *Piero Manzoni: Life and Work* (1969) epitomizes conceptual criticism as a blank book of transparent pages.

Works: *Achrome*, 1959; *Line 1000 m. Long*, 1961; *Socle of the World*, 1961.

Exhibition Catalogs: *Piero Manzoni: Catalogo Generale*. Milan: A. Mondadari arte, 1975; *Piero Manzoni*. Paris: Galerio Karsten Greve, 1992; Celant, Germano, ed. *Piero Manzoni*. Lonon: Serpentine Gallery, 1991.

Interpretation: Argan, Ginlio Carlo. "Reconstruction: Art in Postwar Italy." In *Breakthroughs*. New York: Rizzoli, 1991; Petersen, Jes. *Piero Manzoni: Life and Work*. Berlin: Verlag Peterson, 1969.

Catalogue Raisonné: Battino, Freddy and Luca Palazzoli. *Piero Manzoni: Catalogue Raisonné*. Milano: V. Scheiwiller, 1991.

MAPPLETHORPE, Robert

(4 November 1946–9 March 1989).

A minor studio photographer whose trick was lighting and shooting in ways that rendered his subjects sculptural, Mapplethorpe was made famous by dumb and/or devious reactionaries vociferously deploring him. Not much more can be said about him as an artist. Whereas an earlier generation of photographers kept some distance from the subcultures they portrayed (think of Walker Evans or Paul Strand in the 1930s), Mapplethorpe, like Nan Goldin after him, made no secret of his physical and emotional involvements, such admissions supportedly lending credibility to his photographs. (Is the surest diagnostician the doctor or the person who has had all the diseases?) Mapplethorpe's subject range was limited but disparate—nude males and females, flowers, himself. Since most of his early advocates were gay, the acceptance of Mapplethorpe by arts institutions and then the larger public was seen, along with the needling of the noisy yahoos, to reflect a sociopolitical agenda. Meteorically successful, Mapplethorpe died young of AIDS-related diseases, leaving behind a lot of expensive prints and books, as well as a foundation that supposedly benefits from them. From such short artists' lives are pop biographies made.

Photograph Collections: *Lady, Lisa Lyon*. Text by Bruce Chatwin; foreword by Sam Wagstaff. New York: Viking, 1983; *Flowers*. Foreword by Patti Smith. Boston: Bulfinch, 1990; *Mapplethorpe*. Essay by Arthur C. Danto. New York: Random House, 1992.

Biography: Morrisroe, Patricia. *Mapplethorpe: A Biography* (1995). New York: Da Capo, 1997.

Exhibition Catalogs: Amaya, Mario. *Robert Mapplethorpe: Photographs*. Norfolk, VA: Chrysler Museum, 1978; Barents, Els. *Robert Mapplethorpe*. Amsterdam: Stedelijk Museum, 1988; Celant, Germano. *Robert Mapplethorpe*. Venice: Centro di Documentazione de Pallazzo Fortuny, 1983; Marshall, Richard, et al., *Robert Mapplethorpe*. New York: Whitney Museum, 1988; Morgan, Stuart, and Alan Hollinghurst. *Robert Mapplethorpe, 1970–1983*. London: Institute of Contemporary Arts, 1983.

Web Site: http://www.ocaiw.com/mapple.htm (images).

Interpretation: Danto, Arthur C. *Playing with the Edge: The Photographic Achievement of Robert Mapplethorpe*. Berkeley: University of California Press, 1996.

MARINETTI, Filippo Tommaso

(22 December 1876–2 December 1944).

The founder of ITALIAN FUTURISM, Marinetti wanted to be known as a poet and playwright; he is remembered mostly as a reportedly personable publicist who authored some of the strongest sentences advocating alternative art: "Literature having up to now glorified thoughtful immobility, ecstasy, and slumber, we wish to exalt the aggressive moment, the feverish insomnia, running, the perilous leap, the cuff, and the blow." The principal effect of Marinetti's rhetoric was making a few good artists famous—Giacomo Balla (1871–1958), FORTUNATO DEPERO, etc.—at least for a while. His reputation suffered from his early support of Benito Mussolini and Fascism, while some of his remarks are embarrassing decades later, beginning with the declaration to "fight moralism, feminism [sic], every opportunistic or utilitarian cowardice."

Works: Marinetti, F. T. *Selected Writings*. Ed. R. W. Flint. New York: Farrar, Straus, 1972; *La Cucina Futurista/Futurist Cookbook* (1932). Ed. Lesley Chamberlain. San Francisco: Bedford Arts, 1989.

Interpretation: Blum, Cinzia Sartini. *The Other Modernism*. Berkeley: University of California Press, 1996.

MARISOL

(22 May 1930; b. Marisol Escobar).

Although a member of the artistic generation that included ROBERT RAUSCHENBERG and JASPER JOHNS, Marisol was less concerned with exploiting the materials of contemporary culture or posing subtle esthetic questions than with adopting the methods and materials of folk art, reflecting in part her Venezuelan birth. Her wooden sculptures have been influenced by pre-Columbian pottery, Mexican picture boxes, and Egyptian and Mayan mythology. The tall, hieratic figures have their features frequently painted on, rather than carved in, and are generally arranged in tableaux. Marisol's intent is satiric, and she aims her biting sarcasm or gentle mockery at politicians, celebrities, and even fellow artists. Marisol's work is notable for being highly individual and instantly recognizable, though it has had little, if any, influence on other sculptors. Marisol is one of a small handful of artists, including ROBERT ARNESON and LOUISE BOURGEOIS, whose distinction is their distinctiveness—their works look like those of no other.

Portrait of Marisol Escobar. CORBIS/Oscar White.

—Mark Daniel Cohen

Works: *The Kennedys*, 1960; *The Family*, 1962; *Andy (Warhol)*, 1962–63; *LBJ*, 1967; *Willem de Kooning*, 1980; *Self-Portrait Looking at the Last Supper*, 1986.

Exhibition Catalogs: *Marisol*. Chicago: Arts Club, 1965; *Figures of State, Sculptures by Marisol: an Exhibition in London and New York*. London: Hanover Gallery; New

York: Sidney Janis Gallery, 1967; Loring, John. *Marisol: Prints, 1961–1973*. New York: New York Cultural Center in association with Fairleigh Dickinson University, 1973; *New Sculpture by Marisol*. New York: Sidney Janis Gallery, 1973; *Marisol*. New York: Sidney Janis, 1989; Grove, Nancy. *Magical Mixtures: Marisol Portrait Sculpture*. Washington, DC: Published by the Smithsonian Institution Press for the National Portrait Gallery, 1991; *Marisol: September 20–October 21, 1995*. New York: Marlborough Gallery, 1995; Ratcliff, Carter. *Marisol, Recent Sculptures: March 4–28, 1998, Marlborough*. New York: Marlborough, 1998.

MARSHALL, Ingram

(10 May 1942).

Not unlike ELLIOTT CARTER before him, Marshall passed through undistinguished beginnings to bloom in his forties, mostly with pieces that mix taped accompaniments with live instrumentalists in harmonious ways different from and more elegant than earlier (and other) tape-live mixes. One reason is Marshall's use of unfamiliar sounds, such as the slamming of a huge steel door at Alcatraz prison, a funeral procession in Yugoslavia, and exotic church bells. *Hidden Voices* (1989) draws upon tapes made in Mordovian Russia, Rumania, and Hungary; *Three Penitential Visions* (1986), upon a colleague's saxophone playing in a large church at Eberbach in Germany's Rheingau province.

Works: *Transmogrification* for tape 1966; *Cortez*, text-sound, 1973; *Vibrosuperball* for 4 amplified percussion, 1975; *Non confundar* for string sextet, alto flute, clarinet, and electronics, 1977; *Addendum: In aeternam* for clarinet, flute, and string sextet, 1979; *Spiritus* for 6 strings, 4 flutes, harpsichord, and vibraphone 1981; *Fog Tropes* for brass sextet and tape, 1982; *Voces resonae*, string quartet, 1984.

Recordings: *Fog Tropes* for brass sextet, fog horns, and tape (1982). Albany, CA: New Albion, 1989; *Alcatraz* (1982–84). Albany, CA: New Albion, 1991; *Evensongs*. Albany, CA: New Albion, 1997; *Three Penitential Visions* (1986) & *Hidden Voices* (1989). New York: Nonesuch, 1990.

Extended Interview: Strickland, Edward. "Ingram Marshall." In *American Composers*. Bloomington: Indiana University Press, 1991.

MARTIN, Agnes

(22 March 1912).

Born in Saskatchewan, she emigrated to the United States in 1932 to attend college in Washington State and New York. In the early 1960s, a few years after relocating from New York to New Mexico, Martin began producing paintings of grids composed of horizontal bricks, so to speak, that run from edge to edge, both vertically and horizontally. Perhaps sensing that she had reached an ultimate image, much as her near-contemporary AD REINHARDT had, she stopped painting for several years before returning to grids that were even more subtle in making thin, straight parallel lines that shimmer, and thus evoke a spiritual experience outside of themselves. Not unlike Reinhardt again, Martin is also an assertive writer: "Art work is a representation of our devotion to life. Everyone is devoted to life with an intensity far beyond our comprehension. The slightest hint of devotion to life in art work is received by all with gratitude." Especially in group exhibitions, in my experience, her work shines through the strength of subtlety.

Works: *Drift of Summer*, 1957; *Untitled*, 1960; *White Flower*, 1960; *Journey*, 1963; *Morning*, 1965; *Grass*, 1967; *On a Clear Day*, 1971; *Untitled #7*, 1974; *Untitled #12*, 1977; *Desert Flower*, 1985; *Lemon Tree*, 1985; *Untitled #9*, 1989.

Writings: *Schwarz, Dieter, ed.* Writings—Schriften/Agnes Martin. *Winterhur, Germany: Kunstmuseum Winterthur, 1992.*

Exhibition Catalogs: *Agnes Martin: Paintings and Drawings = Peintures et dessins, 1974–1990.* Amsterdam: Stedelijk Museum, 1991; Haskell, Barbara. *Agnes Martin.* New York: Whitney Museum of American Art, 1992.

Interview: Gruen, John. "Agnes Martin." In *The Artist Observed.* Pennington, NJ: A Cappella, 1991.

MARTIN, Stephen-Paul

(19 September 1949).

The Flood, a satirical verbo-visual epic poem weaving surrealistic commentary on Ronald Reagan with a warped take on Noah, ought to have made Martin's reputation long ago. In it, he maximizes the possibilities of typewriter poetry by (to give just one of countless instances), forming columns out of dashes and parentheses four lines high and placing a description of Ronald Reagan in crisis in lower-case letters at the top of the columns and Noah in crisis in uppercase letters at the bottom; then suddenly, after nine "stanzas," jolting the narrative by halving the columns' height for one stanza; then at once halving it again for one stanza, and following that with a series of indented, shortened stanzas. The payoff from such devices in the establishment of tone and rhythm, visual connotativeness, and degrees of innerness and outerness, is revelatory. Martin has also flourished as a surrealistic satirist in short story collections like *Fear and Philosophy* and *Not Quite Fiction*, and as a leading avant-garde critic in *Open Form and the Feminine Imagination*.

—Bob Grumman

Works: *Open Form and the Feminine Imagination*. Washington, DC: Maisonneuve, 1988; *Corona 2500*. Oakland: Score, 1989; *The Gothic Twilight*. Mission Hills, CA: Asylum (Box 8234, 91346), 1992; *The Flood*. Port Charlotte, FL: The Runaway Spoon (P.O. Box 3621, 33949–3621), 1992; *Fear and Philosophy*. St. Paul, MN: Detour (1506 Grand Avenue, #3, 55105), 1994; *Not Quite Fiction*. San Francisco: Vatic Hum, 1997.

MASEREEL, Frans

(30 July 1889–3 January 1972).

Born in Flemish Belgium, Masereel began as an illustrator of books written by others, but because his drawings were strong enough to stand apart from any texts, he made them in masterful sequences that suggested narratives, such as *Mein Stundenbuch* (subtitled variously "a novel without words" or "a novel told in 165 pictures"); thus he became the precursor of such later visual fictioneers as the Americans LYND WARD, MILT GROSS, EDWARD COREY, Giacomo Patri (1898), and the sometime Canadian MARTIN VAUGHN-JAMES. Masereel was a leftist and a pacifist.

Books: *Passionate Journey [Mein Studenbuch]* (1920). Intro. Thomas Mann. San Francisco: City Lights, 1988; *The City (Die Stadt) 100 Woodcuts* (1925). New York: Dover, 1972; Patri, Giacomo. *White Collar* (1940). Millbrae, CA: Celestial Arts, 1975.

Exhibition Catalog: *Retrospective Frans Masereel.* Antwerp: Koninklijke Academie voor Schone Kunsten, 1958.

MASLAK, Keshavan

(26 February 1947; a.k.a. Kenny Millions).

Born Keshavan Maslak in a family of Ukrainian immigrants in Detroit, Michigan, this "talented but slightly enigmatic" (in the *Penguin Guide to Jazz*) musician was influenced by Eastern European folk music, Motown, free jazz, and Chicago blues. A virtuoso saxophone/clarinet player, Maslak is also known as the inventor of Hum-Ha horn (a trombone-trumpet-saxophone hybrid). His idiosyncratic musical style combines elements of classical music, free and new jazz, extreme R&B honking, and hard-boiled blues, all spiced up by his great sense of the absurd. He has been called everything from "R&B terrorist" to "eclectic-dada avant-gardist." His recent recordings, *Friends Afar* (1996), a collaboration with Russian avant-gardist SERGEY KURYOKHIN, and *Without/With Kuryokhin* (1998), with Japanese noise/turntable artist Otomo Yoshihide, show Maslak widening his range.

—Igor Satanovsky

Bibliography: Davis, Francis. *In The Moment: Jazz in the 1980's* (1986). New York: Da Capo, 1996.

Recordings: And Sergey Kuryokhin. *Friends Afar*. Sound Wave Records, 1996.

Web Page: http://www.sushiblues.com/kenny.html

MATHEMATICAL POETRY

(1969).

There has been little if any scholarship done on the origins of true mathematical poetry—which is poetry that does mathematics rather than merely discusses mathematics (or uses mathematical algorithms to choose its content, as in the OULIPO movement)—but it may be that LOUIS ZUKOFSKY'S *A* (1969) contains the first specimen of the form, an integral symbol out of calculus with the word, "music" at its top, and "speech" at its bottom, to provide the reader with a working mathematical description of Zukofsky's concept of poetry. In the following decade SCOTT HELMES experimented surrealistically with words as fractions, the square root of words, and the like, notably in his "Non-additive Postulations." An anthology of mathematical poems, *Against Infinity*, appeared (and disappeared) in 1979, though it contained as many or more poems about mathematics as poems that *did* mathematics, including an arresting visual poem, "Eye of History," by Robert Stodola, in which 3.14152, etc., in the shape of a circle surrounds 3.0000, etc., in the shape of a figure that is part circle and part straight line to illustrate the history of pi. His book also had a pair of numerical rectangles by RICHARD KOSTELANETZ (a pioneer of *numerical* poetry as opposed to mathematical poetry) that arithmetically mirror each other in a droll manner. Since *Against Infinity* other poets have worked with math, notably LEROY GORMAN (who once defined "the birth of tragedy" as the quantity "!" plus "?" squared; KARL KEMPTON, who has done fascinating things with the square root of minus one; JAKE BERRY, in his *Equations*, which HARRY POLKINHORN called, "(t)he mixing of registers which purists have always feared (Berry) has pushed to an extreme," and BOB GRUMMAN, with a series of poems he calls "mathemaku" under way that predominantly investigate the results of the long division of such quantities as the actual color blue by such quantities as the dictionary definition of "blue."

—Bob Grumman

Non-additive postulations

random order + perposterous outcry = negative time

negative time^2 = relationships +3

$$\text{relationships} = \frac{\text{rudders}}{\text{udders}} + \sqrt{\frac{\text{alphswakes}}{\text{oscillations}}}$$

$\phi + \pi =$ blueberryohio to the tenth power

$$\text{Ohio} = \sum_{0}^{\infty} \frac{+\text{antioch}}{\text{trying} \sqrt{\text{power} + \phi}}$$

equality + three equality +5 = race^2

without (recognition) + negative se x = tomorrow

$$\text{Jefferson} + \frac{\text{airplane}}{6+3\text{pee}} = \frac{\text{pee} + \infty}{\text{green ddt}}$$

$$\frac{\text{negative}}{\text{sex}} + \text{i.u.d.} = \sqrt{\frac{\text{time}}{\text{communicate}}} + 1^2 + c$$

$$\frac{\text{time}}{\text{telepathy}} = 2' + c = \frac{\text{noosphere}}{\text{RBF}} =$$

terminate

Scott Helmes. "Non-additive postulations." Courtesy the author.

Books: Robson, Ernest, and Jet Wimp, eds. *Against Infinity*. St. Peter's, PA: Primary Press (Box 83, 19470), 1979; Grumman, Bob. *Mathemaku 13–19*. Charleston, IL: tel-let, 1996; Kostelanetz, Richard. *Numbers: Poems & Stories*. New York: Assembling, 1976; ——. *Exhaustive Parallel Intervals*. New York: Future, 1979; Weiss, Irving. *Number Poems*. Port Charlotte, FL: Runaway Spoon (P.O. Box 3621, 33949–3621), 1997.

MATHEWS, Harry

(14 February 1930).

Educated in music at Harvard and then at the École Normale de Musique in Paris, Mathews has, not unlike other experimental American writers before and since, lived most of his adult life abroad. At the service of prosaic plots, Mathews uses highly original and playful language, as would be expected of the only active American member of OULIPO who is based in Paris; and, like other experimental writers, he works in more than one genre. Linguistic possibilities appear to be his principal theme, and he is predisposed to extremes. Commercially published novels include *The Conversions* (1962), *Tlooth* (1966), *The Sinking of the Odradek Stadium* (1975, once bound into a single paperback volume along with its two predecessors), and *Cigarettes* (1987). From smaller presses have come *Selected Declarations of Independence* (1977) and *20 Lines a Day* (1988). Mathews co-compiled *Oulipo Compendium* (1998), which stands as a model of rich and witty documentation.

Writings: *The Sinking of the Odradek Stadium and Other Novels*. New York: Harper & Row, 1975; *Selected Declarations of Independence*. Calais, VT: Z Press, 1977; *Country Cooking and Other Stories*. Providence, RI: Burning Deck, 1980; *Cigarettes* (1987) . Normal, IL: Dalkey Archive, 1998; *Armenian Papers: Poems, 1954–1984*. Princeton: Princeton University Press, 1987; *20 Lines a Day*. Normal, IL: Dalkey Archive, 1988; *Out of Bounds*. Providence, RI: Burning Deck, 1989; *Immeasurable Distances: The Collected Essays*. Venice, CA: Lapis, 1991; *A Mid-Season Sky: Poems 1954–1991*. Manchester, England: Carcenet, 1992; *The Journalist* (1994). Normal, IL: Dalkey Archive, 1997.

Documentation: and Allastair Brotchie, compilers. *Oulipo Compendium*. London: Atlas, 1998.

Web Site: http://jhunix.hcf.jhu.edu/~deschene/phosphor.html

MATHIEU, Georges

(27 January 1921).

Among the originators of post-World War II Parisian Expressive ABSTRACTION, Mathieu worked rapidly, purportedly without sketches or other plans, often on large canvases whose imagery sometimes reflected calligraphy. "The only true creation," he once wrote, "is one which invents its means on the spot, calling everything into question." Even though Mathieu organized as early as 1950 an exhibition joining Parisian and New York EXPRESSIONISTS, his work remains less familiar than, say, JACKSON POLLOCK's or FRANZ KLINE's, so that the comparative neglect of his art can serve as a measure of recent American dominance in this area. Mathieu preceded HAROLD ROSENBERG in formulating the image of painting as the result of physical action. Educated in law and philosophy, Mathieu has also published books about contemporary art.

Works: *Hommage à Pierre de Montaigu*, 1960; *Guermantes*, 1964; *Gradlon*, 1964; *La Ferté*, 1965; *Fermail*, 1965; *Farcheville*, 1965; *Maintenon*, 1965; *Ammon*, 1967; *Extractum*, 1967; *Babylone*, 1970; *Corydon*, 1971; *Phoebus*, 1971; *Borée*, 1971; *Frenilly*, 1971; *Ennus*, 1971; *Necténabo*, 1971; *Enigme*, 1982.

Exhibition Catalogs: *Mathieu*. Paris: Museé des BeauxArts de la Ville de Paris, 1963; *Georges Mathieu*. Zurich: Gimple & Hanover, 1968; *Georges Mathieu: The Art of Lyrical Abstraction*. New York: Wally Findlay, 1985.

Book: Quignon-Fleuret, Dominique. *Mathieu*. Paris: Flammarion, 1973.

MATIUSHIN, Mikhail

(1861–14 October 1934).

Matiushin was the fourth collaborator, along with ALEKSEI KRUCHONYKH, KAZIMIR MALEVICH, and VELIMIR KHLEBNIKOV in the pathbreaking opera *Victory Over the Sun* (1913). Though Matiushin was at the time a violinist in the Court Orchestra, where he had worked for the previous twenty years, his music For *Victory* includes dissonances and sounds evocative of cannon shots and airplanes. Turning to writing and publishing, Matiushin in 1914 established a press, The Crane, printing vanguard texts by VELIMIR KHLEBNIKOV and Kazimir Malevich, among others, in addition to his own translations of French theoretical writings. Because less is known about him, at least in English, I quote from Andrei B. Nakov's history of Russian avant-garde art 1915–21:

> Taking off from certain presuppositions of the famous 'fourth dimension,' he situated man at the center of a new cosmic image. While taking into account the interaction of the visible and the audible, in his plastic system a very special place was reserved for psychocensorial sensation. The superseding of the synthesist theories of the symbolists led him to the conception of synthetic images, the formulation of which was carried out with the intermediary of abstract-geometrical images.

Some of these findings appeared in Matiushin's 1932 book whose title translates as "The Rules and Variability in Color Combinations," which he thought would be applicable to various applied arts.

Works: *Movement in Space*, 1917–18; *Painterly Musical Construction*, 1918; *Crystal Moscow*, 1919–20.

Interpretation: Nakov, Andrei B. *Avant-garde Russe*. New York: Universal, 1986.

MATTA, Roberto

(11 November 1911).

In Paris in 1936, after working for two years at the architectural studio of LE CORBUSIER, Matta turned to painting and associated himself with the SURREALISTS. He quickly became one of the principal practitioners of automatism, painting spontaneously and in an improvisational manner, without the intercession of conscious control, directed by deep impulses so as to render visual metaphors for the reality of inner experience. He called his early paintings "inscapes" and "psychological morphologies." Unlike the collages, dream landscapes, and nightmare narratives of the other Surrealists, Matta's paintings were vistas of seemingly infinite and luminescent space, filled only with small biomorphic shapes, free-floating angular surfaces, and disembodied outlines of rectangles and ovals, drawn in bright colors but signifying nothing. Despite the vast emptiness he portrayed, Matta seemed to load his expanses with vigorous movement, as if the void itself were suffering cataclysm. His spaces are at once both psychological and cosmic, depicting both the profundity of the spirit and of the universe. In 1946, Matta changed his style and began painting large canvases with images of creatures half-biological and half-machine, engaged in inexplicable activities, indeed often engaged in violent struggles. But it is his early paintings, his "inscapes," that are his most effective, and among the most successful works by any artist in practicing the Surrealist intent of bringing unconscious experience into consciousness.

—Mark Daniel Cohen

Works: *Inscape*, 1939; *Le Prisonniere de Lumière*, 1943; *Le Vertige d'Eros*, 1944; *Splitting the Edge*, 1946; *Eros Océan*, 1960; *Instinct Caliban*, 1961; *Explosant Fixe*, 1974.

Exhibition Catalogs: *Matta*. New York: Pierre Matisse Gallery, 1947; Breton, André. *Préliminaires sur Matta*. Paris: René Drouin, 1947; *Matta*. London: Institute of Contemporary Arts, 1951; *The Sculpture of Matta*. Chicago: Allan Frumkin, 1962; Calas, Nicolas. *Matta: A Totemic World: Paintings, Drawings, Sculpture, January 11–February 15, 1975*. New York: Andrew Crispo Gallery, 1974; *Matta, The Early Years: a selection of paintings and drawings from the years 1937–1947: November 10–December 19, 1981, Maxwell Davidson Gallery*. New York: Maxwell Davidson Gallery, 1981; Miller, Nancy. *Matta, The First Decade*. Waltham, MA: Rose Art Museum at Brandeis University, 1982; *Matta*. Fort Lauderdale: Museum of Art, 1983; *Matta: The Logic of Hallucination*. London: Arts Council of Great Britain, 1984; *Matta: "Paradise Now": March 25–April 26, 1997*. New York: Jeffrey H. Loria & Maxwell Davidson Gallery, 1997; Uribe, August O. *Matta, Paintings & Drawings: February 20–March 22, 1997*. New York: Andre Emmerich, 1997.

Catalogue Raisonné: Sabatier, Roland. *Matta: Catalogue Raisonné de l'Oeuvre Gravé, 1943–1974*. Stockholm: Sonet, 1975.

Interpretation: Ferrari, Germana. *Matta*. London: Sistan, 1987.

MATTA-CLARK, Gordon

(22 June 1943–27 August 1978).

Matta-Clark's projects involved the excision of large holes from buildings in urban centers, revealing the layering of floors above and below and the vistas of surrounding buildings, along with brief moments of sky framed by the crowded and encroaching cityscape. Although at first glance it would seem otherwise, Matta-Clark's exercise of cutting sections out of existing structures has more to do with the transformations of the natural terrain by EARTH ARTISTS such as ROBERT SMITHSON, for whom he once worked, than with the reconfigurations of institutional spaces of MICHAEL ASHER. Matta-Clark has simply moved the reconfiguration procedure from the natural to the artificial environment. But where Earth Art's exposure of previously unseen geological layers may be viewed as revelatory—as capable of instigating new sensations—Matta-Clark's projects were exercises in social criticism. His deletions from human-made structures conveyed suggestions of the social hierarchies and the economic stratification that are represented by the tiers of floors that recede in seemingly endless repeating patterns.

—Mark Daniel Cohen

Works: *Splitting*, 1974; *Days End*, 1975; *Conical Intersect*, 1975; *Office Baroque*, 1977; *Circus*, 1978.

Exhibition Catalogs: *Circus: The Caribbean Orange*. Chicago: Museum of Contemporary Art, 1978; Jacob, Mary Jane, and Pincus-Witten, Robert. *Gordon Matta-Clark: A Retrospective*. Chicago: Museum of Contemporary Art, 1985; Jacobs, Mary Jane. *Gordon Matta Clark: Splitting*. New York: Holly Solomon Gallery, 1990; Deegan-Day, Joseph. *Museo Matta 3/2/3+1*. Los Angeles: Reeves Press, 1995; Noever, Peter. *Anarchitecture: Works by Gordon Matta-Clark: 17 November 1997–18 January 1998, Schindler House L.A.* Los Angeles: MAK Center for Art and Architecture, 1997.

MAYO

See **MURAYAMA, Tomoyoshi**.

MAXIMAL ART

(c. 1970).

This was my coinage, which I'd be the first to admit has scarcely taken, for works that, in contrast to MINIMAL ART, contain more of the stuff of art than previous art. A principal literary example of maximal art is JAMES JOYCE's *FINNEGANS WAKE*, which, though it relates a simple story, has a wealth of words and, by extension, a wealth of references. Another is MILTON BABBITT's multiple SERIALIZATION, where each note contributes to several musical developments. (I remember telling Babbitt that another composer claimed his work presented several hundred "musical events" within a few minutes; as true to his esthetic as ever, Babbitt thought that number was not particularly high.) Influenced by James Joyce, the playwright CHARLES LUDLAM used "Maximal" to measure his own ambitions. The term "Maximal art" is also applicable to my favorite JOHN CAGE pieces: *Williams Mix*, which likewise offers several hundred acoustic events in only a few minutes; *EUROPERA*, which draws upon dozens of classic operas; and *HPSCHD*, which comes from a large number of independent sound sources. Maximality in visual art might be harder to measure. It is certainly implied in the multiple references of JASPER JOHNS; it is explicit in the several Plexiglas levels of John Cage's *Not Wanting To Say Anything About Marcel* (1969) and in the kinetic sculptures of GEORGE RHOADS. I find Maximality in AD REINHARDT's cartoons about the art world (in sharp contrast to his Minimal paintings) and in MERCE CUNNINGHAM's choreography, though others may disagree.

Exhibition Catalog: Hess, Thomas B. *The Art Comics and Satires of Ad Reinhardt*. Düsseldorf, Germany: Kunsthalle, 1975.

MAYAKOVSKY, Vladimir

(19 July 1893–14 April 1930).

Born in Russian Georgia, Mayakovsky studied art before turning to poetry, which made him famous, initially among the FUTURIST painters and poets before the Revolution, then as one of the first avant-gardists to support the Revolution actively, and later as a favored beneficiary of the new Soviet state. He visited New York in the mid-1920s and wrote a memorable poem about it. Mayakovsky collaborated with major avant-garde artists in poster designs and, in his own poetry, broached enough visual devices to warrant an extended analysis by GERALD JANECEK in his classic book *The Look of Russian Literature*. Among Mayakovsky's minor inventions was the "stepladder poem," since popularized by Lawrence Ferlinghetti (1919), among others, in which narrow lines run diagonally down a wider page. Though his poetry was never as deviant as that of VELIMIR KHLEBNIKOV and, especially, ALEKSEI KRUCHONYKH, the other principals in Futurist poetry, it was popular (for reasons that remain mysterious to the reader of English translations). Precisely because he was a statefavored poet, much as Dmitri Shostakovich (1906–75) became a state-favored composer, every new work of Mayakovsky's was subjected to excessive critical scrutiny, as often by ignorant commissars as by knowledgeable critics. Perhaps because his last two plays, *The Bedbug* (1929) and *The Bath House* (1930) were negatively received, Mayakovsky committed suicide in 1930. (Shostakovich chain-smoked and struck Westerners as insufferably nervous.) The poet's name, long spelled in America as I have it, is now sometimes spelled Maiakovskii.

Works: *The Bedbug and Selected Poetry*. Ed. Patricia Blake. New York: Meridian, 1960; *Wi the Haill Voice*. Trans. into Scots by Edmund Morgan. S. Hinksey, Oxford, England: Carcanet, 1972; *Listen: Early Poems 1913–1918*. San Francisco: City Lights, 1991; *Plays*. Evanston, IL: Northwestern University, 1995.

Anthology of Poetry & Interpretation: *Vladimir Mayakovsky: Innovator*. Moscow: Progress, 1976.

Biography: Brown, Edward J. *Mayakovsky: A Poet in the Revolution*. Princeton: Princeton University Press, 1973.

Interpretation: Brown, E. J. "Mayakovsky's Futurist Period." In *Russian Modernism: Culture and the Avant-Garde, 1900–1930*. Ed. George Gibian and H. W. Tjalsma. Ithaca: Cornell University Press, 1976; Janecek, Gerald. *The Look of Russian Literature*. Princeton: Princeton University Press, 1984; Jangfeldt, Bengt. *Majakovskij and Futurism, 1917–1921*. Stockholm: Almqvist and Wiksell, 1976; Kalb, Jonathan. "Mayakovsky's Tragic Comedy," *Free Admissions*. New York: Limelight, 1993; Markov, Vladimir. *Russian Futurism: A History*. Berkeley: University of California Press, 1968; Stapanian, Juliette R. *Mayakovsky's Cubo-Futurist Vision*. Houston: Rice University Press, 1986; Terras, Victor. *Vladimir Mayakovsky*. New York: Twayne, 1983.

MAYER, Peter

(1935).

Born in Berlin, Mayer was taken at a very young age to England, where he became the principal scholar of avant-garde poetries, both visual and aural. His taxonomies and bibliographies, the latter sometimes produced in collaboration with others, are particularly brilliant and incomparable. He has also made three-dimensional poems and film poems. Among his publications are *'Yin Yang' Cube* (1968), *Gamma de gamma* (1970), and *Earmouth* (1972). Along with DOM SYLVESTER HOUÉDARD and BOB COBBING, Mayer co-edited the periodical *Kroklok* (1971). He was the sole editor of *Alphabetical and Letter Poems* (1978), a truly pioneering anthology. He is not related to someone with the same name, born around the same time, who once headed the corporation owning Penguin Viking, nor to Peter R. Meyer, a younger language artist who works at Swedish radio.

Books: ——and Bob Cobbing, eds. *Concerning Concrete Poetry*. London, England: Writers Forum, 1978 (continually updated); —— ed. *Alphabetical and Letter Poems: A Chrestomathy*. London, England: Menard, 1978.

McBRIDE, Henry

(25 July 1867–31 March 1962).

Not until he was forty-three did Henry McBride begin the career that made him important, becoming the first major American reviewer of visual art at the New York *Sun*, a newspaper where JAMES GIBBONS HUNEKER, wrote mostly about music. Through the medium of a short notice, there and elsewhere, McBride had the critical foresight to welcome not only THE ARMORY SHOW but ALFRED STIEGLITZ, GEORGIA O'KEEFFE, GERTRUDE STEIN, FERNAND LÉGER, HENRI MATISSE, and Florine Stettheimer (1871–1948), among his generation; and JACKSON POLLOCK and MARK ROTHKO in the next. He contributed regularly to *The Dial*, the most distinguished revived cultural journal in the 1920s, and, after leaving the *Sun* in 1950, in his own early eighties, wrote monthly for *Art News* until 1955. For forty years McBride provided good guidance, though the limitations of journalistic media kept his insights few. *The Flow of Art* (1975) is a model retrospective, including not only many of McBride's short notices but reproductions of "Some of Henry McBride's Favorites."

Books: *The Flow of Art: Essays and Criticism of Henry McBride* (1975). Selected, with an intro. by Daniel Catton Rich. New Haven: Yale University Press, 1997; *Three American romantic painters*. New York: Arno Press, 1969; *Florine Stettheimer*. New York: MoMA, 1946.

McCAFFERY, Steve

See **FOUR HORSEMEN, THE.**

McCAY, Winsor

(26 September 1869–26 July 1934).

McCay was one of the comics's most skillful craftsmen, producing Sunday strips so visually dazzling that they would be inconceivable in today's newspapers. They were filled with colorful details and experiments with visual distortion, all of which were simply the dreams of Little Nemo. McCay's strip (variously called "Little Nemo in Slumberland" or "In the Land of Wonderful Dreams," depending upon whom he was working for at the time) had serious weaknesses, induding bland storylines, boring writing, and predictable conclusions (as each strip ended with Nemo awaking from his dream in a little square at the bottom corner of the page). Despite these shortcomings, McCay expanded the visual repertoire of the comic strip as no one else had (since his talents as a craftsman far outshone those of his contemporary GEORGE HERRIMAN). One of the first people to experiment with film animation in the first decade of this century, McCay did not have the advantage of background cels, so he had to redraw completely the scene for each frame of his black-and-white cartoon *Gertie, the Trained Dinosaur* (1909). Though lacking much of a story, the cartoon has a stunning visual reality, even as the entire background (and Gertie herself) shimmers with each slight misstep of his pen.

—Geof Huth

Works: *Dreams of the Rarebit Fiend* (1905). New York: Dover, 1973.

Anthologies: *Little Nemo*. Franklin Square, NY: Nostalgia, 1972; *Daydreams & Nightmares: The Fantastic Visions of Winsor McCay*. Ed. Richard Marshall. Westlake Village, CA: Fantagraphics, 1988; Blackbeard, Bill, and Martin Williams, eds. *The Smithsonian Collection of Newspaper Comics*. Washington, DC: Smithsonian Institution, 1977.

Biography: Canemaker, John. *Winsor McCay*. New York: Abbeville, 1987.

McFERRIN, Bobby

(11 March 1950).

Initially a virtuoso vocalist, McFerrin is the first human singer to resemble the electronic SAMPLER, a technology new to the 1980s that "stores sounds," as they say, remembering them, to be instantly evoked at a later time.

What is most remarkable is the sheer number and variety of sounds in McFerrin's acoustic inventory. With the assistance of audio overdubbing, he can vocally accompany himself, in addition to producing with his voice alone the sounds of percussion and other instruments. I've seen a videotape in which McFerrin pulls classic pop albums off the shelf and evokes sounds characteristic of each, and heard a live performance in which he renders, both accurately and ironically, all the sounds at the end of *The Wizard of Oz*. You would think that no sound was beyond McFerrin's instant vocal recall until you realize that he must have spent a good deal of time learning how to make his mouth reproduce each of them. In the mid-1990s, he found a new career as an orchestral conductor of the classical repertory.

Recordings: *Spontaneous Inventions* (Blue Note, 1987); *The Voice* (WEA/Elektra 1988); *Simple Pleasures*. New York: EMIMusician, 1988; *Bobby McFerrin*. New York: Electra/Asylum, 1982; *Circlesongs*. New York: Sony, 1997; ——, and Yo-Yo Ma. *Hush*. New York: Sony, 1992.

Web Site: www.bobbymcferrin.com

Interpretation: Kostelanetz, Richard. "Bobby McFerrin." In *More on Innovative Music(ian)s*. Berkeley, CA: Fallen Leaf, 2000.

McLUHAN, Marshall

(21 July 1911–31 December 1980).

Beginning with *The Mechanical Bride* (1951), McLuhan examined mass-cultural artifacts and then mass culture itself with a critical sensibility honed on the close rhetorical analysis of English literature. This approach generated a wealth of original insights, such as the perception that the representational discontinuity distinguishing modernist painting and literature resembled the newspaper's front page, with its discontinuous field of unrelated articles, oversized headlines, and occasional captioned pictures. One theme of *Understanding Media* (1964) holds that this discontinuity reflects the impact of electronic information technology and that, differences in quality notwithstanding, "the great work of a period has much in common with the poorest work." All this insight into mass culture did not prevent McLuhan from proposing a necessary and persuasive measure for distinguishing esthetic quality from kitsch: "How heavy a demand does it make on the intelligence? How inclusive a consciousness does it focus?" The great paradox of McLuhan personally was that he had remarkably little firsthand experience of the new media that he seemed to understand so brilliantly. Hugh Kenner wondered somewhere if his former teacher ever sat through an entire movie. He rarely watched television. If one definition of a "genius" is someone with great insight into things he knows little about, McLuhan epitomizes that sort of higher mentality. His medium was books, which he read adventurously and which he wrote brilliantly. Not unlike other literary adventurers, he cofounded a literary magazine, *Explorations* (1953–59), and then edited an anthology drawn from its pages, *Explorations in Communication* (1960). In the 1960s, he also collaborated with the book designer Quentin Fiore (1920) in producing imaginatively designed books that looked fresh when they were reprinted intact in the 1990s by the computer-waving magazine *Wired*, which incidentally lists McLuhan on its masthead as "patron saint." Since one book McLuhan knew thoroughly was James Joyce's *Finnegans Wake*, he wrote insightfully about its general structure and operation. *The Essential McLuhan* (1995) is a rich recent selection of his thoughts, both heavy and light, on various subjects.

Writings: *The Mechanical Bride*. New York: Vanguard Press, 1951; *The Gutenberg Galaxy: The Making of Typographic Man*. Toronto: University of Toronto Press, 1962; *Understanding Media*. New York: McGraw-Hill, 1964; *The Interior Landscape*. Ed. Eugene McNamara. New York: McGraw-Hill, 1969; *Counterblast*. New York:

Harcourt, Brace, 1969; *Culture Is Our Business*. New York: McGraw-Hill, 1970; ——, ed. *Explorations in Communication*. Boston: Beacon, 1960; ed. *Verbi-Voco-Visual Explorations*. New York: Something Else Press, 1967; ——and Quentin Fiore. *The Medium Is the Massage* (1967). San Francisco: HardWired, 1997; *War and Peace in the Global Village* (1968). San Francisco: Hard/Wired, 1997; ——, with Harley Parker. *Through the Vanishing Point: Space in Poetry and Painting*. New York: Harper & Row, 1968; ——, with Wilfred Watson. *From Cliché to Archetype*. New York: Viking, 1970; ——, with Eric McLuhan. *Laws of the Media: The New Science*. Toronto: University of Toronto Press, 1988; ——, with Bruce R. Powers. *The Global Village*. New York: Oxford University Press, 1989.

Anthologies: *Letters of Marshall McLuhan*. Selected & ed. Matie Molinaro, Corinne McLuhan, & William Toye. Toronto: Oxford University Press, 1987; *Essential McLuhan*. Eds. Eric McLuhan & Frank Zingrone. New York: HarperCollins, 1995.

Biography: Gordon, W. Terrence. *Marshall McLuhan: Escape into Understanding, A Biography*. New York: Basic Books, 1997.

Web Site: http://www.beaulieuhome.com/McLuhan/default.htm

Interpretation: Grosswiler, Paul. *Method Is the Message: Rethinking McLuhan through Critical Theory*. Montreal: Black Rose, 1998; Marchand, Phillip, & Neil Postman. *Marshall McLuhan: The Medium and the Messenger*. Cambridge: MIT Press, 1998; Miller, Jonathan. *Marshall McLuhan*. New York: Viking, 1971; Neil, S. D. *Clarifying McLuhan*. Westport, CT: Greenwood, 1993; Powe, B. W. *Outage: A Journey into Electric City*. Toronto: Random House, 1995; Rosenthal, Raymond, ed. *McLuhan Pro and Con*. New York: Pelican, 1969; Stearn, Gerald Emanuel, ed. *McLuhan: Hot & Cool*. New York: Dial, 1967; Theall, Donald F. *Understanding McLuhan: The Medium Is the Rear View Mirror*. Montreal: McGill-Queen's University Press, 1971.

Documentary: *The Video McLuhan*. Written & narr. Tom Wolfe. Toronto: McLuhan Prods., 1996.

McPHEE, Colin

(15 March 1900–7 January 1964).

A Canadian composer who lived mostly in the United States and spent several years in Bali, McPhee, more than anyone else, introduced the intelligence of Indonesian music to Western composers, initially with his own music, but also with such publications as the memoir *A House in Bali* (1946) and *Music in Bali* (1966), which appeared after his death. In this respect, his implicit influence upon subsequent avant-garde music is immeasurable. Thanks to the reputation of his books, McPhee's own compositions, particularly *Tabuh-Tabuhan* (1936), are remembered. The concise biography by Carol Oja (1953) is a model of its scholarly kind.

Compositions: *Pastorale and Rondino* for 2 flutes, clarinet, trumpet, and piano, 1925; *Sarabande*, 1927; *Tabuh-Tabuhan*, for 2 pianos, orch. and exotic percussion, 1936; *4 Iroquois Dances*, 1944; *Invention*, 1926; *Kinesis*, 1930; *Balinese Ceremonial Music* for 2 pianos, 1934–38; *Transitions*, 1954; Concerto for Wind Orchestra, 1959.

Recordings: *Symphony No. 2, Concerto, Nocturne*. New York: BMG/Music Masters 1996; *Tabuh-Tabuhan: Music of Colin McPhee*. Toronto: CBC Records, 1998.

Books: *A House in Bali*. New York: John Day, 1946; *Music in Bali*. New Haven: Yale University Press, 1966.

Interpretation: Oja, Carol. *Colin McPhee*. Washington, DC: Smithsonian, 1990.

MEDICINE SHOW THEATRE ENSEMBLE

(1970).

Founded by Barbara Vann (1938) and James Barbosa (1932), previously founding members of the OPEN THEATRE, it remains among the strongest off-off-Broadway theater companies, staging the best modernist work—including texts by GERTRUDE STEIN, Paul Goodman (1911–1972), WILLIAM CARLOS WILLIAMS, E.E. CUMMINGS's *him* (1927)—and indicatively resisting "postmodern" fashions. Their name comes from a uniquely American form of entertainment, popular around the turn of the century, that was particularly successful at involving its audience. In the tradition of the Open Theatre, the Medicine Show performances favor physical presence, and the juxtaposition of styles and forms, along with rapid shifts of focus.

MERTON, Thomas

(31 January 1915–10 December 1968).

A Frenchman who became an American, a Protestant who became a Roman Catholic and then a Trappist monk, Merton was also an extremely various and prolific writer whose work falls into many categories. There is a classic young man's autobiography, *The Seven Storey Mountain* (1948); there are pacifist polemics; there are sympathetic explanations of the monastic life and Catholic faith. After his death, Merton's principal American literary publisher issued not only a thick book of *Literary Essays* (1981) but a yet thicker book of poems (1977).

Merton's avant-garde masterpiece is a novel written in 1941, inspired by his friendship with two Columbia College classmates, ROBERT LAX and Edward Rice, not to mention the publication of *FINNEGANS WAKE* two years before. Likewise released after his death as *My Argument with the Gestapo* (1969), this novel has the subtitle *A Macaronic Journal*, that adjective referring to the occasional mixing of languages in the text (from p. 228):

> Rouse. Weck. Sturz. Bekom. Gross lettercatchers is the orders of the day. Guess you no comprenny, you jigsfrench. Youse of the lapin races, aside, hide in your lascivious newspapers. Faz dolor di honta rossu figuro. Ėcartez vous, cheaps. Hoc es fe Trowel-spiel, or the Roarspiegel. Begins in the first with Latin declensions, fur monstrar la natura clásica de la fiesta. Continua mit whole speeches from imitation marble paradigms, eventually concatenating intself upwards into a durchbruch of the meistens evotive hocking and choking: it y a des scènes dance la rue, e d'autres encore dans la maison.

More examples of this other Merton style appear in his extraordinary letters to Lax, collected as *A Catch of Anti-Letters* (1978), a classic of its genre (literary correspondence), which is implicitly about the stylistic influence of 1930s experimental literature, particularly JAMES JOYCE and GERTRUDE STEIN, upon writers who were young at the time of its publication. Here is Merton acknowledging the early passing of another college buddy, the painter AD REINHARDT:

> Just heard today by clipping from Schwester Therese about Reinhardt. Reinhardt he daid. Reinhardt done in. He die. Last Wednesday he die with the sorrows in the studio. Just said he died in a black picture he said. The sorrows here said that he has gone into the black picture for he is dead.

I would recommend, as an aside, that anyone in the vicinity of Lexington, Kentucky, pay a visit to the Trappist monastery, Gethsemane, in which Merton spent most of his life. The place and its setting are magnificent and sacred.

Works: *The Seven Storey Mountain*. New York: Harcourt, Brace, 1948; *Confessions of a Guilty Bystander*. Garden City, NY: Doubleday, 1966; *My Argument with the Gestapo*. New York: New Directions, 1969; *Collected Poems*. New York: New Directions, 1977; *Selected Poems* (1959). Enlarged ed. New York: New Directions, 1967; *The Literary Essays*. Ed. Brother Patrick Hart. New York: New Directions, 1981; —— and Robert Lax. *A Catch of Anti-Letters*. Kansas City, KS: Sheed, Andrews, & McMeel, 1978.

Anthologies: *A Thomas Merton Reader*. Ed. Thomas P. McDonnel. New York: Harcourt, 1962; *Thomas Merton Spiritual Master: The Essential Writings*. Paulist Press, 1992.

Biography: Mott, Michael. *The Seven Mountains of Thomas Merton*. Boston: Houghton Mifflin, 1984.

MERZ

See **SCHWITTERS, Kurt**.

MESSIAEN, Olivier

(10 December 1908–27 April 1992).

While Messiaen is among the most widely recorded, and highly regarded, of twentieth-century composers, he is still frequently mischaracterized, particularly in the United States. Certain elements of his style—the use of repetition, the incorporation of birdsong—have been deemed banal or perverse by those who lack a proper understanding of his basic orientation. Most fundamentally, Messiaen was unconcerned with forward-moving harmonic development, with theme and variation—the traditional strategies of western classical music. What he sought to achieve in his music was a kind of mystical timelessness; his pieces are contemplations—of the divine, of nature, of human love—rather than narratives. Many of his most distinctive characteristics—the use of modes, of so-called *non-retrogradable rhythms* (symmetrical units that are the same played forwards and backwards), of massive blocks of sound, of rythmic cycles, of repetition, of birdsong—are used precisely to *prevent* a sense of forward movement. At the same time, Messiaen is not the soothing new age mystic certain record labels have tried to market—his music is far too complex for that; and while some of it is tender, it can also be frenetic and abrasive.

Messiaen's output was large, and is divisible into certain distinct phases, though each phase builds on the previous one, rather than negating it. His most avant-garde works, and the greatest as well, date from the mid-1940s to the late-1960s. While retaining signature elements of his early mode-based, somewhat post-Debussyean style, Messiaen added rhythms and melodies derived from birdsong, adapted elements from various Asian traditions, and experimented with abstract methods of construction (as in the *Mode de valeurs et d'intensités* from 1950, which systematized volume, duration, and attack into the equivalent of scales, and thus greatly influenced the development of 1950s total serialism by KARLHEINZ STOCKHAUSEN and PIERRE BOULEZ). Messiaen's use of birdsong was far from bucolic and picturesque, in the manner of nineteenth century program music. Indeed, in its purest form, as in *Réveil des oiseaux* (1953) and *Oiseaux exotiques* (1955–56), it was not embellishment, but an organizing principle, and led to music of surpassing originality—and to the evocation of an otherworldly suprareality, a hidden face of nature.

Messiaen's last phase, beginning around 1970, was one of reconciliation, in which all the most characteristic elements of earlier periods were blended together. Unfortunately, the pieces of these years often seem nothing more than pastiches of his earlier work, and there is a marked decline in quality, despite the production of some of his most large-scale works, such as the opera *Saint François d'Assise* (1975–82).

Finally, in this, of neccessity, too brief summing-up, I should mention Messiaen's large output of works for solo organ, for which he was the twentieth century's most significant composer, and his great influence as a teacher: among many students one could list Stockhausen, IANNIS XENAKIS, PIERRE HENRY, LUC FERRARI, and Boulez.

—Tony Coulter

Selected Works: Opera: *St. Francois d'Assise* (1983). Orchestra: Fugue in D minor (1928); *Le Banquet eucharistique* (1928); *Simple chant d'une âme* (1930); *Les Offrandes oubliées* (1930); *Le Tombeau resplendissant* (1931); *Hymne au Saint Sacrement* (1932); *L'Ascension* (1933); *3 Talas* for piano and orchestra (1948); *Turangalîla-Symphonie* (1946–48); *Réveil des oiseaux* for piano and orchestra (1953); *Oiseaux exotiques* for piano, 2 wind instruments, xylophone, glockenspiel, and percussion (1956); *Chronochromie* (1960); 7 Hai-kai for piano, 13 wind instruments, xylophone, marimba, 4 percussion instruments, and 8 violins (1962); *Couleurs de la cité céleste* for large orchestra, with imitations of 2 New Zealand birds and 1 from Brazil (1964); *Et expecto resurrectionem mortuorum* for 18 woodwinds, 16 brass instruments, and 3 percussion instruments (1964); *Des canyons aux étoiles* (1970–74). Chamber Music: Thème et variations for violin and piano (1932); *Quatuor pour la fin du temps* for violin, clarinet, cello, and piano (1941); *Le Merle noir* for flute and piano (1951); *Le Tombeau de Jean-Pierre Guézec* for horn (1971). Also various vocal works, and works for piano and organ.

Pedagogy: 20 leçons de solféges modernes (Paris, 1933); 20 leçons d'harmonie (Paris, 1939); *Technique de mon langage musical* (2 vols., Paris, 1944; Eng. tr. as *The Technique of My Musical Language*, 2 vols., 1957); individual articles on musical ornithology and other subjects.

Discography: *Harawi, Chant d'amour et de mort*. Djursholm, Sweden: BIS, 1978; *Turangalîla-Symphonie*. Forlane, 1983; *Cinq Rechants*. Erato, n.d.; *Quatre Études de rythme* [on *Piano Etudes by Bartók, Busoni, Messiaen, Stravinsky*]. New York: Nonesuch, 1976; *Messe de la Pentecôte*. Paris: EMI/Pathé Marconi/Ducretet-Thomson, n.d.; *Livre d'Orgue*. Paris: EMI/Pathé Marconi/Ducretet-Thomson, 1972; *Le Merle noir* [on Music for Flute and Piano]. New York: Time Records, n.d.; *Réveil des oiseaux/Oiseaux exotiques*. Prague: Supraphon, 1967; *Catalogue d'oiseaux*. Erato, n.d.; *Chronochromie*. Angel, 1965; *Sept Haïkaî*. Century City, CA: Everest, n.d.; *Couleurs de la Cité Céleste/Et Exspecto resurrectionem mortuorum*. Erato/CBS, n.d.; *Méditations sur le mystère de la Sainte-Trinité*. Erato, 1973.

Selected Writings: *Technique de mon langage musical*. Paris: Leduc, 1944; English translation, Leduc, 1957; Conférence de Bruxelles. Paris: Leduc, 1958; Conférence de Notre-Dame. Paris: Leduc, 1978.

Web Site: http://www.composers.net/general/links/Messiaen_Links.html (links).

Interpretation: Goléa, Antoine. *Rencontres avec Olivier Messiaen*. Paris: Julliard, 1960; Griffiths, Paul. *Olivier Messiaen and the Music of Time*. Ithaca, NY: Cornell University Press, 1985; Halbreich, Harry. *Olivier Messiaen*. Paris: Fayard/SACEM, 1980; Johnson, Robert Sherlaw. *Messiaen*. (1975). Berkeley: University of California Press, 1989; Mari, Pierrette. *Olivier Messiaen*. Paris: Seghers, 1965; Nichols, Roger. *Olivier Messiaen* (1974). 2d ed. London: Oxford University Press, 1986; Périer, Alain. *Messiaen*. Paris: Seuil, 1979; Reverdy, Michele. *L'Oeuvre pour orchestre d'Olivier Messiaen*. Paris: Leduc, 1988; Rostand, Claude. *Olivier Messiaen*. Entretiens avec Olivier Messiaen. Paris: Samuel, Claude. Paris: Pierre Belfond, 1967; English translation. London, 1976; Waumisley, Stuart. *The Organ Music of Olivier Messiaen*. Paris: Leduc, 1968.

METRIC MODULATION

(1910s).

In a general sense of the word, metric modulation is a change of time signature. In special modern usage, proleptically applied by CHARLES IVES and systematically cultivated by ELLIOTT CARTER, metric modulation is a technique in which a rhythmic pattern is superposed on another, heterometrically, and then supersedes it and becomes the basic meter. Usually, such time signatures are mutually prime, e.g., 4/4 and 3/8, and so have no common divisors. Thus the change of the basic meter decisively alters the numerical content of the beat, but the minimal denominator (1/8 when 4/4 changes to 3/8; 1/16 when, e.g., 5/8 changes to 7/16, etc.) remains constant in duration.

—Nicolas Slonimsky

Compositions: Carter, Elliott. *String Quartets* No.1, 1950–51; No. 2, 1959; No. 3, 1971; No. 4, 1985–86; No. 5, 1995.

MEV—MUSICA ELETTRONICA VIVA

(1966, "Live Electronic Music").

Formed in Rome by expatriate American composers ALVIN CURRAN, ALLAN BRYANT, Jon Phetteplace (1940), and Frederic Rzewski (1938), this group pioneered the use of electronic instruments, beginning with keyboards and amplifying processors, later including early SYNTHESIZERS in live concerts. Descending from JOHN CAGE, they were predisposed to perform in public spaces, allowing outside noises to infiltrate their concert space, and to incorporate into their collective improvisations music both highbrow and lowbrow, formal and informal musics, as well as both formal and informal sounds. At various times, other musicians were included, such as the American RICHARD TEITELBAUM and the Hungarian Ivan Vandor (1932), MEV describing itself as "a performing group, a way station, and a school where older and younger learn from one another and play together on the same stage." MEV resembled AMM, which was formed by CORNELIUS CARDEW with British musicians in London, also in the late 1960s.

Recordings: MEV and AMM. *Live Electronic Music Improvised*. New York: Mainstream (MS 5002), 1970.

MEYERHOLD, Vsevolod

(28 January 1874–2 February 1939; b. Karl-Theodor-Kasimir M.).

The more innovative of the two great early Soviet directors (the other being Constantin Stanislavsky [1863–1938]), Meyerhold was a sophisticated eclectic who drew upon sources both traditional and alternative. (In this balance, he resembled his contemporary Max Reinhardt, who worked out of pre-Hitler Germany.) Learning from the circus and other forms of vaudeville, Meyerhold came to see mime as superior to speech, and he tried alternative seating arrangements. In The House of Interludes, a theater designed for his experiments, the hall was arranged like a restaurant bar with the audience seated at tables while the action occurred around them.

James Roose-Evans describes a 1911 production of Molière's *Don Juan*, where Meyerhold "removed the front curtains and the footlights and built a semicircular proscenium. The stage was lit by a huge candelabra and chandeliers, and all the lights in the auditorium were on so that it resembled a vast ballroom." After the Soviet Revolution, which he supported, even heading the state theater organization until 1921, Meyerhold developed a theory of biomechanics, which he incorporated into theatrical training, that made aspiring actors part athletes, part acrobats, part robots. The result was not only that every theatrical movement could be planned in advance, down to tiny details, but that human feelings would be eliminated.

Roose-Evans also recalls a 1926 production of Gogol's popular *The Government Inspector* that was set not in a small town, as in the original, but in Moscow:

> There was a semi-circular-shaped set, like the inside of a drum, in which were fifteen doors. The main action took place on a sloping platform which emerged out of the darkness for each scene. In the scene where the officials arrive to bribe Kheslakov secretly, Meyerhold achieved one of his most startling effects. Suddenly, all the doors in the circular wall opened and in each appeared an official offering money. At the end, as the General was carried off in a strait-jacket on a stretcher, a white curtain was lowered, announcing in gold letters the arrival of the real Inspector General. When it was raised, instead of the live actors there were painted dummies arranged like a tableau of the final scene.

All of this sounds quite marvelous, even today.

Not unlike other theater directors, Meyerhold had many assistants who subsequently established their own distinguished careers, including SERGEI EISENSTEIN. However, once Joseph Stalin assumed control of Soviet culture, socialist realism became the norm and then the rule in Moscow theater. By 1932, the principal Soviet newspaper, *Pravda*, began an endless attack on all experiment in art as representing capitalist decadence. By 1938, Meyerhold's theater was closed, its director left unemployed. Invited in June 1939 to the All-Union Convention of Theater Directors to make a public display of submission, he gave instead an impassioned speech defending theatrical experiment and denouncing government-imposed uniformity. A few days later, Meyerhold was arrested and deported to an Arctic concentration camp which, scarcely young at the time, he did not leave. Shortly after his arrest, his wife, a noted actress, was found dead with her throat cut, her face disfigured, and her body punctured with knife wounds. The lesson of their deaths was not lost on those concerned with theater, both within the Soviet Union and outside it.

Books: Braun, Edward. *The Theatre of Meyerhold: Revolution on the Modern Stage* (1974). New York: Dramabook Specialists, 1979; Carter, Huntley. *The New Spirit of the Russian Theater 1917–1928* (1929). New York: Arno, 1970; Hoover, Majorie L. *Meyerhold: The Art of Conscious Theater*. Amherst: University of Massachusetts Press, 1974; Houghton, Norris. *Moscow Rehearsals: The Golden Age of the Soviet Theatre* (1936). New York: Grove, 1962; Leyda, Jay. *Kino: A History of the Russian and Soviet Film*. (1960). New York: Collier, 1973; Roose-Evans, James. *Experimental Theatre* (1970). New York: Avon, 1971; Schmidt, Paul. ed. *Meyerhold at Work*. Austin: University of Texas Press, 1980; Slonim, Marc. *Russian Theater from the Empire to the Soviets*. Cleveland: World, 1961.

Anthology: Braun, Edward, ed. *Meyerhold on Theatre*. Hill & Wang, New York, 1969.

Exhibition Catalog: *Art in Revolution: Soviet Art and Design Since 1917*. London: Arts Council, 1971.

MICHALS, Duane

(18 February 1932).

Michals has produced sequences of photographic images not to document stages in an event but to evoke a story. Two qualities that make these stories appropriate for photography, rather than film or print, are that the distance between images approximates the time it takes the reader to turn the page, and that the mystery of the plot depends upon actions that must have happened between the images. As MARTIN VAUGHN-JAMES said of his own visual fiction, "Between one frame and the next something has happened—an unknowable event." In Michals's book of wordless photographic *Sequences* (1970) is a set of six pictures entitled "The Lost Shoe." The first image shows a deserted urban street with the fuzzy backside of a man walking away from the camera and up the street. In the second frame he drops on the pavement a blurred object that in the third frame is seen to be a lady's shoe; and this frame, as well as the next two, suggests that he departs up the street in a great hurry. In the sixth frame, the man is nowhere to be seen, while the shoe is mysteriously burning. The realism of all the photographs starkly contrasts with the mysteriousness of the plot, while the large changes between the frames reveal the absolute immobility of the camera. For this last reason, the authorial perspective is as Chekhovian as both the work's title and its passive acceptance of something inexplicably forbidding.

Realizing the marvelous title of "A Man Going to Heaven," Michals in five images portrays from behind a nude man climbing a stark staircase that by the concluding frame feels his absence. In later sequences, Michals began writing on the surface of the photographs words that either added or detracted. Another classic single Michals photograph has the nude standing bodies of a man and a woman, approximately similar in height and girth, melting into each other, the photographer exploiting the medium's device for double exposure. One of the more suggestive sentences in Marco Livingston's prefaces to a recent Michals anthology distingushes him from "most photographers, who direct attention to things as they supposedly are. Michals is far more stimulated by what could be. Consequently, he depends not so much on his eyes as on his imagination." To me, this is another way of saying that for Michals, telling stories through image sequences takes precedence over photography's traditional mission of representing reality.

Works: *Sequences*. New York: Doubleday, 1970; *The Journey of the Spirit After Death*. New York: Winter

House, 1971; *Things are Queer*. Köln: A. & J. Wilde, 1972; *Duane Michals: The Photographic Illusions*. Text Ronald Bailey. New York: Crowell, 1975; *Real Dreams*. Danbury, NH: Addison House, 1976; *Sleep and Dream*. New York: Lustrum, 1984; *Album: The Portraits of Duane Michals 1958–88*. Pasadena, CA: Twelve Trees, 1989; *Eros & Thanatos*. Santa Fe: Twin Palms, 1993.

Anthologies: *Upside Down, Inside Out, and Backwards*. New York: Fotofolio 1993; *The Essential Duane Michals*. Ed. Marco Livingston. Boston: Little, Brown-Bullfinch, 1997.

Exhibition Catalog: *Duane Michals: Photographs, Sequences, Texts, 1958–1984*. Oxford, England: Museum of Modern Art, 1984.

Interpretation: Kozloff, Max. *Duane Michals: Now Becoming Then*. Altadena, CA: Twin Palms, 1990.

Web Site: http://www.artincontext.com/listings/pages/artist/i/fb8l20li/menu.htm

MICHAUX, Henri

(24 May 1899–18 October 1984).

Allegorical is perhaps the best stab at describing the Belgium-born Frenchman Henri Michaux. Although living through the heyday of modernism and the crossover into postmodernism, Michaux resisted the invitation of renowned movements, such as Surrealism, and bequeathed a legacy of cryptic images and prose poems that defy simple explanation. Michaux fancied himself a novice and aimed to avoid professionalism (in 1965 he refused the French Grand Prize for Letters). Michaux shares with Antonin Artaud the concerns of the psyche and the refusal to be incorporated; but whereas Artaud is maniacal and combative, Michaux is subtle in his choice of battles. He employs a lyrically vivid imagination in such enterprises as malady-inspired beasts or fictive cultures that rival Borges' dictionary of magical beings. In "Fantastic Animals" he writes, "A trembling weasel with skull split open lets a small, toothed, metallic wheel be seen in a brain that is running with blood. . . . For the sick man, no species are extinct." Some of Michaux's allegorical prose poems sound gracefully poetic, while others read like quick, perverted fables. He describes the events of his imagination with contrapuntal perversity: when it's a physical sickness, it ís described in a psychological way; and when it's related to the mind, it is described as physical symptom. Michaux was also known for paintings and prints that were abstractly based upon the shape of texts—both Arabic-influenced and hieroglyphic-like—forming a unique pictorial vocabulary that on occasion was assisted by the use of a hairdryer. In forays and experiments with drugs, most notably mescaline, Michaux wrote about their effects, and, on occasion, created under their influence. A reserved man of excess, well-traveled, an abstract expressionist, and beat before the beats, Michaux was prototypical and definitively protean.

—Michael Peters

Bibliography: *Selected Writings*. Trans. Richard Ellmann. New York: New Directions, 1968.

MICROPRESS

(c. 1965).

The micropress revolution came of age in the 1980s, although such publishing had begun earlier. Smaller than the literary-cultural small press, the micropress depends on cheaper methods of reproduction and distribution: xerography (and the postal system) and the World Wide Web being the common methods in the 1990s. From the 1960s until the 1980s, other forms of reproduction were common, including mimeography, spirit-duplicating, and even handwriting. These cheap varieties of printing permitted the almost instantaneous reproduction of text and image. Since the 1980s, literally thousands of publications have been produced, both chapbooks and periodicals (customarily called "zines"), in print runs rarely exceeding 100, across the United States and the rest of the world.

True, much of the output from these publishers is (as with art everywhere) ill-formed, but in the United States, some of these micropresses have become the major avenue for the publication of advanced writing, now that all the major publishers and nearly all the established small presses have no contact with the literary avant-garde. With the advent of the Internet as a cultural behemoth in the mid-1990s, Web-based e-zines and other forms of "samiznet" distribution have become the main avenues for broadcasting micropress output. This development is both hopeful (in that it provides greater access to this material than did the former print-based distribution) and disturbing (in that there is no likelihood of the development of any system for preserving the often computer-reliant output of these presses).

—Geof Huth

Books: Gunderloy, Mike, and Cari Goldberg Janice. *The World of Zines*. New York: Penguin, 1992; Rowe, Chip, ed. *The Book of Zines*. New York: Henry Holt, 1997.

MICROTONALITY

(c. 1920).

In the first half of the twentieth century, composers around the world separately began to explore intervals smaller than the halftone, which is traditionally the smallest interval in Western music, including quarter tones (or more precisely, half of a halftone) and even slighter fractions. Though musicologists were aware of such microtones, especially in Asian music, it is only in the twentieth century that self-conscious composers have systematically investigated the possibilities of using them in their works. Among the pioneers were the Czech Alois Haba (1893–1973), the Mexican Julian Carrillo (1875–1965), the American Harry Partch, and Ivan Wyschnegradsky (1893–1980), a Russian long resident in Paris. Charles Ives wrote a choral in strings for quarter tones in 1914. All these composers except Ives either made their own instruments or had instruments specially constructed to play microtones. Carrillo had a "harpzither" built that reportedly had ninety-seven tones within an octave.

I saw in 1997 a stunning concert organized by the Swiss pianists Thomas Bächeli and Gertrud Schneider that make me think that two normal pianos, tuned a quarter tone apart, constituted a distinct keyboard instrument. Among older living composers, Easley Blackwood (1933) is perhaps the most prominent microtonalist. Though microtonal music is infrequently performed, in part because it sounds strange to Western ears (and is not conveniently available to instruments with fixed pitches), it remains one of those secondary innovative ideas that have had more influence than is commonly acknowledged.

The New York bassoonist Johnny Reinhard (1956), who has been sponsoring his American Festivals of Microtonal Music since 1981, honors all these composers, the unevenness of their works notwithstanding. His most consequential concert was an evening-length reconstruction in 1996 of Charles Ives's *Universe Symphony*, which was for decades thought to be incomplete. As eccentric and overwhelming as the best Ives, this begins with perhaps twenty-five minutes of languid percussion and concludes with stately sonorities. It should be performed around the country, if only because I'd like to hear and see it again, while the recording of the premiere cannot be sold (because of legal restrictions).

Interpretation: Kostelanetz, Richard. "Microtonal Concerts." In *More On Innovative Music(ian)s*. Berkeley, CA: Fallen Leaf, 2000; Read, Gardner. *Twentieth-Century Microtonal Notations*. Westport, CT: Greenwood, 1990.

MIES VAN DER ROHE, Ludwig

(27 March 1886–17 August 1969).

The son of an Aachen stonemason, he moved to Berlin as a teenager, apprenticing himself to an established architect and then working as an assistant before establishing his

Mies van der Rohe, Seagram Building, New York. CORBIS/Bettman.

own office in 1913, incidentally adding his mother's name to his father's for presence. Emigrating from Hitler's Germany, Mies had the foresight to settle in Chicago, which had traditionally been more supportive of advanced architecture than other cities, and to teach at its technological institute, rather than, say, at a liberal arts university. Unlike LE CORBUSIER, Mies van der Rohe did not deviate from the glass-walled, strictly geometric INTERNATIONAL STYLE in any consequential way. *Contemporary Masterworks* (1991) includes a case for the Farnsworth House (1945–1950), designed early in Mies's stay in America, as an example of his break, even though it displays unadorned geometries and glass walls. The book's contributor makes a claim for "the placement of furniture": "Functional and aesthetic requirements were carefully balanced. With sophistication and subtlety, beds, chairs, and tables served as counterpoints to the fixed elements, animating the total composition and enhancing the total spatial experience." This sounds like the International Style to me, and persuades me that, even in America, Mies's buildings have epitomized it. Of those I've seen first-hand, the strongest is the Neue Nationalgalerie in Berlin. (The Seagram Building in New York, by contrast, suffers from the imitators surrounding it.) Among this architect's subsidiary interests was furniture design, including distinctive chairs. Though he didn't write as much as LE CORBUSIER and FRANK LLOYD WRIGHT, the other modernist masters with whom he is customarily grouped (as in Peter Blake's classic introduction, *The Master Builders* [1960]), Mies also coined one of modernism's most popular aphorisms, "Less is more," which is only sometimes true.

Architecture: Kroller house project, The Hague, Holland, 1912; Glass office building project, Berlin, 1919; Glass skyscraper project, 1920–21; Monumunt to Karl Liebknecht and Rosa Luxemburg, Berlin, 1926; Tugendhat House, Brno, Czech Republic, 1928–30; Barcelona Pavilion, 1929; Barcelona Chair, 1929; Perlstein Hall, Illinois Institute of Technology, Chicago, 1945–46; Farnsworth House, Plano, IL, 1945–50; 860 Lake Short Drive Apartments, Chicago, 1948–51; Crown Hall (College of Architecture), Illinois Institute of Technology, Chicago, 1950–56; with Philip C. Johnson. Seagram Building, New York, 1958; Administration building for Bacardi Company, Santiago, Cuba, 1958; Pavilion and Colonade Apartments, Newark, NJ, 1958–60; Chicago Federal Center, IL, 1959–63; Lafayette Park [a housing complex], Detroit, 1960; Toronto-Dominion Centre, 1963–69; Neue Nationalgalerie, Berlin, 1968.

Exhibition Catalog: *Mies Reconsidered: His Career, Legacy, and Disciples*. Chicago: Art Institute, 1986; *Mies van der Rohe: Stuttgart, Barcelona, and Brno: Furniture & Architecture*. New York: Abbeville, 1999.

Biography: Schulze, Franz. *Mies van der Rohe: A Critical Biography*. Chicago: University of Chicago Press, 1985; Hochman, Elaine S. *Architects of Fortune: Mies van der Rohe and the Third Reich*. New York: Weidenfeld & Nicolson, 1989.

Interpretation: Arsenault, Andrea Kalish. "Ludwig Mies van der Rohe. " In *Contemporary Masterworks*, ed. Colin Naylor. London, England: St. James's Press, 1991; Blake, Peter. "Mies van der Rohe and the Mastery of Structure." In *The Master Builders* (1960). New York: Norton, 1976; Blaser, Werner. *Mies van der Rohe: The Art of Structure*. New York: Whitney Library of Design, 1994; Mertins, Detlef, ed. *The Presence of Mies*. New York: Princeton Architectural, 1994; Schulze, Frank, ed. *Mies van der Rohe: Critical Essays*. New York: MoMA, 1989; Spaeth, David. *Mies van der Rohe*. New York: Rizzolli, 1985.

Bibliography: Spaeth, David A. *Ludwig Mies van der Rohe: An Annotated Bibliography*. New York: Garland, 1979.

Web Site: http://studwww.rug.ac.be/~jvervoor/architects/mies/index.html

MILLER, Henry

(26 December 1891–7 June 1980).

Perhaps because he didn't start writing seriously until he passed forty, Miller made the principal theme of his books his liberation from an earlier life. This liberation involved a rejection not only of the workaday world, but of its proper language. For three decades, his books were regarded as pornography; their importation into the United States was forbidden by law (and Customs officials would confiscate them from tourists). Once they were published here, in the early 1960s, abolishing state censorship with their presence, they came to seem quite tame. Since few wrote about sexual intercourse as often as Miller, it was assumed that this was his principal subject; but now that most of us have read other writers on heterosexual experience, we see that Miller's copulating is less realistic than mythic. It thus becomes another element in his central story, told through numerous books, which is self-liberation. Since his works are finally understood easily, the critical literature about them is slight. Perhaps because I did my B.A. honors thesis on Miller, using books that were contraband, a version of which was reprinted decades later in the Ronald Gottesman anthology noted below, I think I've outgrown him.

Books: *Tropic of Cancer* (1934). New York: Grove, 1961; *Black Spring* (1936). New York: Grove,1963; *Tropic of Capricorn* (1939). New York: Grove, 1962; *The World of Sex* (1940). New York: Grove, 1965; *The Air-Conditioned Nightmare*. New York: New Dircctions, 1945; *The Books in My Life*. Norfolk, CT: New Directions, 1952; *My Life and Times*. Chicago: Playboy, 1972.

Anthologies: *Henry Miller on Writing*. Ed. Thomas H. Moore. New York: New Directions, 1964; *The Paintings of Henry Miller*. Ed. Noel Young. San Francisco: Chronicle, 1982.

Biography: Martin, Jay. *Always Merry and Bright: The Life of Henry Miller*. Santa Barbara, CA: Capra, 1978; Dearborn, Mary. *The Happiest Man Alive*. New York: Simon & Schuster, 1991.

Bibliography: *Henry Miller: A Bibliography of Primary Sources*. Compiled & ed. Lawrence J. Shifreen and Roger Jackson. Ann Arbor, MI: Roger Jackson (339 Bookside Drive, 48105) & Glen Arm, MD: Lawrence J. Shifreen (12008 Deer Bit Lane, 21057), 1993.

Interpretation: Gottesman, Ronald, ed. *Critical Essays on Henry Miller*. New York: G. K. Hall, 1992.

Web Site: http://www.geocities.com/SoHo/Cafe/1538/henry.htm

MINIMAL MUSIC

See **MODULAR MUSIC; YOUNG, La Monte.**

MINIMALISM

(c. 1965).

The idea of doing more with less was so persuasive that, once Minimalism was articulated in the late 1960s (first by whom remains a question of dispute), it conquered not only the arts but arts writing. The term particularly refers to work with a usually low degree of differentiation, which is to say a monochromic (or nearly monochromic) canvas or a piece of music composed with only a few notes, ideally to suggest, at times by critical inference, meanings that would otherwise be unavailable. (Processes of intellectual inference could function to locate a work's ultimate meanings outside of itself, say in the contexts of art history.)

Once the idea of Minimalism won adherents, many earlier artists could be identified as proto Minimalists—among others, KAZIMIR MALEVICH in painting, or TONY SMITH in sculpture. Back in his *System and Dialectics of Art* (1937), the Russian-born American painter JOHN GRAHAM mentioned the "reducing of painting to the minimum ingredients for the sake of discovering the ultimate, logical destination of painting in the process of abstracting." At first the term also referred to work that revealed a meager amount of artist's work, such as MARCEL DUCHAMP'S exhibition of a urinal, but most art reflecting that kind of strategy has since assumed other names. I have used it to characterize poems, such as certain texts by YVOR WINTERS and ROBERT LAX, among others, with drastically few words. Used sometimes to refer to fiction that by most measures is scarcely Minimal, containing as it does full pages of conventional sentences, the term fell (much like "HAPPENINGS" just before it) into the mouths of opportunistic publicists who, for their success, necessarily depended upon ignorance of what the term really meant and honored.

Exhibition Catalogs: *Minimal Art*. The Hague: Gemeentemuseum, 1968; *La Couleur Seule*. Lyon, France: Musée d'art contemporain, 1987.

Interpretation: Battcock, Gregory, ed. *Minimal Art: A Critical Anthology* (1968). Berkeley: University of California Press, 1995; Baker, Kenneth. *Minimalism*. New York: Abbeville, 1988; Strickland, Edward. *Minimalism*. Bloomington: Indiana University Press, 1993.

MIXED-MEANS THEATER

(c. 1960).

This was my epithet, in a book of that title, for performances that de-emphasize speech in the course of using a variety of means, including human bodies, lights, film, objects, and stagecraft. Even though the term did not become common parlance, I find it useful for encompassing pure HAPPENINGS, which were only certain kinds of participational pieces performed by ALLAN KAPROW, along with the film-based staged performances of ROBERT WHITMAN and the kinetic environments of, say, USCO or LA MONTE YOUNG. To distinguish among various genres, my book proposed this typology.

TYPES OF MIXED-MEANS THEATER

GENRE	SPACE	TIME	ACTIONS
Pure Happenings	Open	Variable	Variable
Staged Happenings	Closed	Variable	Variable
Staged performance	Closed	Fixed	Fixed
Kinetic environments	Closed	Variable	Fixed

"Closed" space was my euphemism for a theater, which could also be any kind of enclosed performance space; "variable" time could range from a few seconds to infinity, depending upon the performance. The assumption of a "Happening" was that generalized instructions could generate unforeseen results. The chapters of my book are extended interviews with practitioners who seemed major at the time: ROBERT RAUSCHENBERG, ANN HALPRIN, CLAES OLDENBURG, JOHN CAGE, Ken Dewey (1934–1972), and the artists mentioned before. Not unlike the classic old fogey, I think this mixed-means theater superior to that performer-centered PERFORMANCE ART that became more prominent in the 1980s; and, as a contrarian resistant to fads, I think I'm right.

Interpretation: Kostelanetz, Richard. *The Theatre of Mixed-Means* (1968). New York: Archae Editions, 1980.

MNATSAKANOVA, Elizaveta Arkadievna

(31 May 1922; German pen name Elisabeth Netzkowa).

Mnatsakanova has produced a large body of Russian poetry that successfully uses musical procedures as a major compositional factor. She was born in Baku and received a musical education at the Moscow Conservatory (graduating in 1950); she earned a living in Moscow writing articles and books on classical music. In the late 1940s she began to write original poetry in combination with abstract colored drawings. She never attempted to get any of her poetry published in the Soviet Union and in 1975 emigrated to Vienna, where she now lives.

Mnatsakanova's first published poem, "Autumn in the Lazaret of Innocent Sisters. Requiem in Seven Parts" (written in Moscow 1971, published in Paris in 1977) is modeled on the traditional requiem mass and employs repetition, motivic development, polyphony, paronomasia, and unusual layouts to create an edifice of significant complexity akin, in her view, to a musical score. A second major work, *Das Buch Sabeth*, a love poem written in May 1972, synthesizes verbal, visual, and musical features in an even more complex and extended way. The book consists of six parts, composed of up to twenty-five individual numbered poems, each with an unique elaboration of its basic thematic material, mostly in a nonlinear form, ranging from unbroken stream of consciousness to word fragments scattered across the page. Part Five recreates the form of a passacaglia with a column of repeating and evolving italicized words on the right creating the effect of an organ pedal line, while the center of the page provides variations on fragments of everyday themes. A third book, *Metamorphosen* (Vienna, 1988) was written in emigration and can be compared to Bach's *Goldberg Variations*. Its subject is music itself and life's transigence. Mnatsakanova's first collection to come out in Russia, *Vita Breve* (Perm, 1994), served as the basis of a theater piece created by a Perm theatrical group and performed in Moscow in May 1998, on the occasion of her first return to Moscow since her emigration.

—Gerald Janecek

Writings: "Osen' v lazarete nepovinnykh sester. Rekviem v semi chastiakh." *Apollon-77*. Paris: n.p., 1977; *Shagi i vzdokhi. Chetyre knigi stikhov*. Vienna: *Wiener Slawistischer Almanach*, Sonderband 6, 1982; *Beim tode zugast/U smerti v gostiakh*. Vienna: n.p., 1986; *Das Buch Sabeth. Kniga v piati chastiakh*. Vienna: n.p., 1988; *Metamorphosen. 20 Vernderungen einer vierzeiligen Strophe und Finale*. Vienna: n.p., 1988; *Vita Breve*. Perm: Izd. Permskogo universiteta, 1994.

Interpretation: Janecek, Gerald. "Paronomastic and Musical Techniques in Mnacakanova's 'Requiem,'" *Slavic & East European Journal*. 31/2 (1987); "Elizaveta Mnatsakanova," *Russian Women Writers*, ed. Christine Tomei. New York: Garland, 1999, Vol. 2.

MODERN MUSIC

(1924–1946).

One of the great art magazines, it was founded by Minna Lederman (1896–1995), a true servant of art, to enable composers of all persuasions, including avant-garde ones, to write at length and with consideration about one another and issues relevant to all. The fact that the musical profession had such an outlet, while visual artists or choreographers didn't, perhaps accounts for why composers, at least in America, have always been better writers than other artists. Had *Modern Music* not existed, the intellectual and even the professional world of American composers would have been different. That is a fundamental measure of why it is remembered (or why an entry on it belongs here). To read through its issues, as I have done, is to be continually awed by the range and seriousness of the writing in its pages. Most other arts magazines seem, by contrast, too limited, too partisan, too academic, too parochial, too small, and/or too compromised by hidden agendas or commercial considerations. When a colleague and I edited an anthology of *Classic Essays on Twentieth-Century Music* (1996), two of the selections originally appeared in *Modern Music*, while we seriously considered including several more originally published there.

Though Lederman wrote a memoir, no selection from its pages has ever appeared.

Histories: Lederman, Minna. *The Life and Death of a Small Magazine (Modern Music, 1924–1946)*. Brooklyn, NY: Institute for Studies in American Music, 1983; Reis, Claire R. *Composers, Conductors, and Critics*. New York: Oxford University Press, 1955; Salzman, Eric. "*Modern Music* in Retrospect," *Perspectives of New Music*, II/1 (Spring–Summer 1964).

MODERNISM

What this book is about: art reflecting modern times, which includes the development of new technologies, the spread of alternative ideas, the influence of new arts upon one another, the transcendence of transient content and transience-based media (aka journalism), unprecedented appreciation of innovation, among other processes that continue, indicating that modernism has not ended, any more than "modern times" have ended. Any theory that advocates the end of modernism in art, usually for the purpose of justifying retrograde and probably inferior work, should not be called "POSTMODERNIST" but "antimodernist." The most authentic history of modernism today will be the one that ignores "postmodernism" for the opportunism that it is. Accept no substitutes.

One reason for writing this *Dictionary* has been to defend modernism and modernist standards not only from traditionalists, who have scarcely disappeared, but from their de facto allies, the Philistines disguised as sophisticates. To define my position, consider this from the critic Paul Mann: "Studies that focus on the similarity or partnership between modernism and the avant-garde tend to emphasize aesthetic issues, whereas studies that argue for the distinction between them tend to emphasize ideology." With this caveat in mind, consider how many prominent "critics" proclaiming the death of the avant-garde vulgarize their polemic with one or another ideological bias.

Bibliography: Bradbury, Malcolm, and James McFarlane, eds. *Modernism*. New York: Penguin, 1976; Kolocotroni, Vassiliki, Jane Goldman, and Olga Taxidou, eds. *Modernism: an Anthology of Sources and Documents*. Edinburgh: Edinburgh University Press, 1998; Mann, Paul. *The Theory-Death of the Avant-Garde*. Bloomington: Indiana University Press, 1991.

MODULAR MUSIC

(late 1960s).

In the middle seventies, most of this work was first called MINIMAL music, in acknowledgment of self-imposed severe limitations on the use of musical materials (and perhaps to capitalize upon the growing reputation of Minimal visual art); but since all of its practitioners (other than LA MONTE YOUNG) produced work far more various in surface texture than monochromic paintings or simple geometrical shapes, another epithet would be more appropriate. I prefer "modular" in that composers/performers such as PHILIP GLASS, STEVE REICH, TERRY RILEY, MEREDITH MONK, JON GIBSON, John Adams (1947), and the Canadian composer Lubomyr Melnyck (1948), among others, tend to use circumscribed musical materials, such as a limited number of phrases (e.g., Terry Riley's *In C*), as modules that are repeated either in different ways or in different combinations with other instruments.

Recordings: Adams, John. *Shaker Loops* for 7 strings. San Francisco Symphony Orchestra, cond. Edo De Waart (Phillips); Melnyck, Lubomyr. *KMH: Piano Music in the Continuous Mode*. Toronto, Canada: Music Gallery 18, 1978.

Interpretation: Dreier, Ruth. "Minimal Music." In *The New Grove Dictionary of American Music*, eds. H. Wiley Hitchcock and Stanley Sadie. New York: Macmillan, 1986; Schwarz, K. Robert. *Minimalists*. London: Phaidon, 1996.

MOHOLY-NAGY, Laszlo

(20 July 1895–24 November 1946).

Born in Hungary, Moholy, as he was commonly called, produced masterful paintings as well as writing first-rate books. While residing in Berlin during the 1920s, he produced innovative and influential book designs, photographs that are sometimes exhibited and reprinted, films that are still screened, sculptures that are in MOMA and other major museums—all while developing a revolutionary program of artistic education. Moholy worked across the constraints of professional training and the disciplinary conventions still associated with artists' standard careers. He created art he was not expected to and produced work in domains where he had neither specialized schooling nor apprenticeship.

The key ideas of Moholy's sensibility had their origins in the BAUHAUS/CONSTRUCTIVIST synthesis. Nearly everything he did favored rectangular and circular forms. As the designer of the first great series of modern art books, the Bauhaus editions, he repudiated both "gray inarticulate machine typesetting" on the one hand and highly ornamental beaux-arts affectations in typography on the other. His alternative was the now familiar hyperrectangular "modern" style, in which illustrations and occasional epigraphs mix with paragraphs sometimes prefaced by boldface subheadings in two-page spreads of rectangular blocks of uniform, justified, sans-serif type that are always much narrower than the width of the page. Visually the design of a typical Moholy page could be characterized as rectangles within rectangles, with no disruptive ornaments. One virtue of his style is placing illustrations in close proximity to commentary about them. The epitome is Moholy's overlooked masterpiece, *Vision in Motion* (1946), a book he designed and wrote in American English while living in Chicago.

In his paintings are rectangles, straight lines, and the regular curves of circles, parabolas, and spirals, sometimes overlapping. Even in his artistic inventions—such as the *Space Modulator,* made by putting a sheet of Plexiglas a few inches above a background canvas so that shapes painted on or cut out of the Plexiglas make shadows on the canvas—Moholy favored his idiosyncratic iconography. It can be found as well in his photography: not only in the representational pictures he took in various cities but in his photograms and PHOTOMONTAGES. Even for commissioned assignments, such as the photographs for *John Betjeman's Oxford* (1938), Moholy put a geometric image in the center of every picture. These Moholyan forms also appear in his stage designs; in his poster art for all sorts of commercial products, including conveniently geometric automobile tires; and in his 1946 extraordinarily brilliant charting of multiple referents in James Joyce's *FINNEGANS WAKE*, which had been published only a few years before.

This last artifact appeared in *Vision in Motion*, the book which I take to be Moholy's single greatest creation, representing better than anything else the sum of his imagination and intelligence. Not only is it the single most insightful survey I know of avant-garde modernism in the arts (including literature, in a chapter often ignored), *Vision in Motion* is also an "artist's book" of the very highest order, demonstrating that few practitioners of any art ever wrote as well or as truly about their own esthetic aspirations. Appearing posthumously, it concludes an artist's life as only a book can do.

Visual Art: *Light Display Machine*, 1930; *Space Modulator* (The Ovals), 1943–45; *Space Modulator—Red Over Black*, 1946; *Dual Form with Chromium Rods*, 1946.

Books: *Painting, Photography, Film* (1925). Cambridge: MIT Press, 1969; *The New Vision: From Material to Architecture* (1929). 3d ed. (including "Abstract of an Artist"). New York: George Wittenborn, 1946; *Moholy-Nagy: 60 Fotos*. Ed. Franz Roh. Berlin: Klinkhardt & Bierman, 1930; *The Street Market of London*. London: John Miles, 1936; *Eton Portrait*. London: John Miles, 1937; *An Oxford University Chest*. London: John Miles, 1939; *Vision in Motion*. Chicago, IL: Paul Theobald, 1947; ——, with Ludwig Kassak. *Buch Neuer Künstler* (1922). Baden, Switzerland: Lars Muller (CH-5401), 1991; ——, with Oskar Schlemmer & Farkas Molnar. *The Theater of the Bauhaus* (1925). Middletown, CT: Wesleyan University Press, 1961.

Lazlo Moholy-Nagy. *Composition #19*, 1921. CORBIS/Burstein Collection. © 2000 Artists Rights Society (ARS), New York/VG Bild-Kunst, Bonn.

Selected Films: *Marseilles Vieux Port* (The Old Port of Marseilles), 1929; *Grossstadt Zigeuner* (Big City Gypsies), 1932; *Life of the Lobster*, 1935.

Anthologies: Haus, Andreas. *Moholy-Nagy: Photographs and Photograms* (1978). New York: Pantheon, 1980; Kostelanetz, Richard, ed. *Moholy-Nagy* (1970). 2d ed. New York: Da Capo, 1991.

Biography: Moholy-Nagy, Sibyl. *Experimental in Totality* (1950). Cambridge: MIT Press, 1969.

Exhibition Catalogs: *Laszlo Moholy-Nagy*. Chicago: Museum of Contemporary Art, 1969; *Photographs of Moholy-Nagy*. Claremont, CA: Galleries of Claremont College, 1975; *Moholy-Nagy Fotoplastiks: The Bauhaus Years*. Ed. Julie Saul. Bronx, NY: Bronx Museum of the Arts, 1983; Hight, Eleanor M. *Moholy-Nagy: Photography and Film in Weimar Germany*. Wellesley, MA: Wellesley College Museum, 1985; *Moholy-Nagy: A New Vision for Chicago*. Ed. Terry Suhre. Springfield, IL: Illinois State Museum,1990; *In Focus. Laszlo Moholy-Nagy*. Malibu, CA: J. Paul Getty Museum, 1995.

Interpretation: Caton, Joseph. *The Utopian Vision of Moholy-Nagy*. Ann Arbor, MI: UMI Research, 1985; Coke, Van Doren. *Avant-Garde Photography in Germany 1919–1939*. New York: Pantheon, 1982; Kaplan, Louis. *Laszlo Moholy-Nagy: Biographical Writings*. Durham: Duke University Press, 1995; Kostelanetz, Richard. "Two Ways of Polyartistry," "To End in a Book," "The Truest Polyartist," *On Innovative Art(ist)s*. Jefferson, NC: McFarland, 1992; Mansbach, Steven. *Visions of Totality: Lazslo Moholy-Nagy, Theo van Doesburg, and El Lissitzky*. Ann Arbor, MI: UMI Research, 1978; Margolin, Victor. *The Struggle for Utopia: Rodchenko Lissitzky Moholy-Nagy, 1917–1946*. Chicago: University of Chicago Press, 1997; Passuth, Krisztina. *Moholy-Nagy*. New York: Thames & Hudson, 1985; Traub, Charles, ed. *The New Vision: Forty Years of Photography at the Institute of Design*. New York: Aperture, 1982.

MOHR, Manfred

(8 June 1938).

A pioneering computer artist, Mohr owned his own PDP11 computer well before most writers had their word processors. Trained in fine art, married to a mathematician, he began as a concrete (rather than mystical) CONSTRUCTIVIST committed to rational structures in black-and-white art. His BOOK-ART BOOK, *Artificiata I* (1968), contains a succession of geometric shapes on a continuous field of horizontal lines, broaching narrative in the transitions from page to page.

Soon afterwards, Mohr began to use the computer not to execute drawings (which has become its predominant use) but to find possible shapes through inventing algorithms, or logical sets of rules, to generate results that he could then realize initially on a computer-assisted plotter. "Generative art" was an appropriate term he used for such work. One of his principal subjects has been the hypercube, a geometric figure incorporating many dimensions, which he typically subjects to exhaustive alternatives.

A principal paradox of Mohr's work is that it can be rationally understood, with generally verifiable perceptions more typical of scientific processes, even though at first glance it may appear inscrutable. He is an extremely intelligent artist in the sense that he knows how best to realize his purposes, and his works represent what he says they should. In Mohr's work, the critic Richard Gassen finds a search "for the 'integrated artwork,' as he calls it, a structure from which all works can be derived, a 'hyperstructure' that one day will encompass all his works." *Manfred Mohr* (1994) is a rich monograph with texts and pictures recapitulating a quarter-century of highly intelligent art. Though Mohr has lived in New York for over two decades, his work is customarily exhibited entirely in Europe, where it wins him prizes.

Texts: *Artifacta I*. Paris: Agentsia, 1968; "Programmed Esthetics." In *Esthetics Contemporary*, ed. Richard Kostelanetz. 2d ed. Buffalo, NY: Prometheus, 1989; *Manfred Mohr*. Zürich: Waser-Verlag, 1994.

Exhibition Catalogs: Gassen, Richard, et al. *Fractured Symmetry: Algorithmic Works 1967–1987*. Ludwigshafen,

P-480/010000 ink on paper 1991 80x80 cm

Manfred Mohr. *P-480/010000*, 1991. Ink on paper. Courtesy the artist.

Germany: Wilhelm-Haack-Museum, 1988; *Manfred Mohr: Arbeiten 1960–1988*. Pforzheim, Germany: Reuchlinhaus, 1988; *Manfred Mohr: Algorithmische Arbeiten/Algorithmic Works*. Texts by Eugen Gomringer and Lauren Sedofsky. Bottrop, Germany: Josef Albers Museum, 1998.

MON, Franz

(1926; b. F. Lofferholz).

One of the most persistent and consistent German avant-garde writers, Mon has produced collections and selections of his poems, in addition to radio plays, that for one measure of their excellence are frequently rebroadcast. He also collaborated with two colleagues in editing *Movens* (1960), one of those rare landmark anthologies that announced accurately several more experimental directions to come. Mon's typographic texts have been exhibited around the world.

Books: *Artikulationen*. Pfullingen: Günter Neske, 1959; *Lesebuch*. Rev. ed. Neuwied & Berlin: Luchterhand, 1972; *Horen ohne aufzuhoren*. Linz: H. Backer, 1982; *Es liegt noch naher*. Spenge: K. Ramm, 1984; *Works 1994*. Berlin: Janus, 1994; ——, et al., eds. *Movens*. Wiesbaden, Germany: Lines, 1960.

Recording: *Lautpoesie*. Obermichelbach: G. Scholz, 1987.

MONDRIAN, Piet

(7 March 1872–1 February 1944; b. P. Mondriaan). Though the best geometric paintings resemble one another more than anything else, any sense of a single family is an illusion. Whereas one line reflects a rational CONSTRUCTIVISM that includes MOHOLY-NAGY, SOL LE WITT, FRANÇOIS MORELLET, and MANFRED MOHR, another strain, epitomized by traditional Islamic art and among the moderns Mondrian, regards geometries as a key to ultimate truths.

It should first be said that Mondrian came to his mature, familiar style after many years of doing something else. His first known paintings are landscapes; he painted flowers; he passed through CUBISM to a style that abstracted lines and rectangles from naturalistic scenes. Joining those artists, mostly Dutch, gathered around *DE STIJL* in 1917, he developed a compositional style, limited to horizontals and verticals, that he called Neo-Plasticism. Making precision an ideal, he eliminated from these paintings all signs of brushstrokes and individual technique. A purist in temperament, Mondrian objected to VAN DOESBURG's use of diagonals, and over that issue, incredible though it seems, broke with *De Stijl*. His last years were spent in America, where his painting changed with the introduction of colored lines instead of black ones and blocks of contrasting colors that were thought to reflect his enthusiasm for American jazz. To some, these New York paintings marked new possibilities; to earlier Mondrian admirers, they represented a step back.

Should you think Mondrian's geometries reflect a dogged rationalist, consider his writings, which include his "opposition to art which is purely abstract. In removing completely from the work all objects, 'the world is not separated from the spirit,' but is on the contrary, *put into a balanced opposition* with the spirit, since the one and the other are purified. This creates a perfect unity between the two opposites." He continues, "Precisely by its existence non-figurative art shows that 'art' *continues always on its true road*. It shows that 'art' is *not the expression of the appearance of reality such as we see it, nor of the life which we live*, but that *it is the expression of true reality and true life . . . indefinable but realizable in plastics*." Surprised, aren't you? Incidentally, Mondrian's collected writings include an extraordinary appreciation of "Italian Futurists' *Bruiteurs*" (1921), as he called them, which is perhaps the only major essay on modernist music written by someone known primarily for visual art.

Selected Paintings: *Lozenge with Gray Lines*, 1918; *Composition: Bright Color Planes with Gray Lines*, 1919; *Composition in Diamond Shape*, 1918–1919; *Diamond Painting in Red, Yellow, and Blue*,1921–1925.

Books: *The New Art—The New Life* (1986). Ed. and trans. Harry Holtzman and Martin S. James. New York: Da Capo, 1993; "Plastic Art and Pure Plastic Art." In *Circle*, eds. J. L. Martin, et al. London, England: Faber, 1937.

Exhibition Catalogs: Sweeney, James Johnson. *Piet Mondrian*. New York: MOMA, 1948; *Piet Mondrian, 1872–1944*. London: Whitechapel, 1955; *Piet Mondrian, 1872–1944*. Toronto: Art Gallery of Ontario, 1966; *Piet Mondrian, 1872–1944 Centennial Exhibition*. New York: Guggenheim Museum, 1971; Bois, Yve-Alain, et al. *Piet Mondrian, 1872–1944*. Boston: Little, Brown, 1995.

Web Site: http://www.usinternet.com/users/glenedwards/mondrian.html

Interpretation: Faerna, Jose Maria, ed. *Mondrian*. New York: Cameo/Abrams, 1997; Gay, Peter. *Art and Act*. New York: Harper & Row, 1976; Seuphor, Michel. *Piet Mondrian: Life and Work*. New York: Abrams, 1957.

Catalogue Raisonné: Joosten, Joop M. *Piet Mondrian: Catalogue Raisonné*. New York: Abrams, 1998.

MONK, Meredith

(20 November 1942).

A major MIXED-MEANS performance artist, Monk has, since her breakthrough *16 Millimetre Earrings* (1966), created a rich series of performance pieces incorporating choreography, music, language, and film customarily produced mostly, if not entirely, by herself. She has explored alternative theatrical spaces, performing the three parts of *Juice* (1969) weeks apart in a museum, a university, a theater, and a downtown loft. Much of Monk's work is autobiographical to differing degrees; much, epitomized by *Education of the Girlchild* (1974), has content congruent with feminism. Working separately in various arts, Monk is most successful as a composer, especially when she sings her own compositions in her eerily unique voice. She has also produced discrete films and, with less success, an opera, *Atlas* (1991).

Selected Performances: *16 Millimetre Earrings*, 1966; *Juice*, 1969; *Education of the Girlchild*, 1974; *Atlas*, 1991.

Recordings: *Key*. Los Angeles, CA: Increase 2008, 1971; *Dolmen Music*. Munich, Germany: ECM,1981.

Extended Interview: Strickland, Edward. "Meredith Monk." In *American Composers*. Bloomington: Indiana University Press, 1991.

Videos: *Meredith Monk: Composer, Singer, Dancer, Filmmaker, Choreographer, Performance Artist*. South Burlington, VT: Mystic Fire, 1989; *Meredith Monk's Paris*. Prod. & dir. by Mark Lowry and Kathryn Esher. St. Paul, MN: KTCA TV, 1982.

Web Site: http://www.shaganarts.com/html/monk.html

Interpretation: Jowitt, Deborah. *Meredith Monk*. New York: PAJ, 1997.

MONK, Thelonious Sphere

(10 October 1917–17 February 1982).

Emerging on the margins of Bebop as an inventive pianist who also behaved eccentrically, wearing scullcaps and dark glasses, occasionally arising from the piano to do a tap dance, Monk could smoke a cigarette while improvising, his hand going to the ashtray and coming back to the keyboard to continue an earlier complex rhythm at exactly the right micro-moment. To the classical musicologist Nicolas Slonimsky, who was likewise a pianist, Monk "experimented with discordant harmonies [angular rhythms and asymmetrical bar sequences], searching for new combinations of sounds. Paradoxically, he elevated his ostentatious ineptitude to a weirdly cogent modern idom, so that even deep-thinking jazz critics could not decide whether he was simply inept or prophetically innovative." Most experienced jazz listeners can instantly identify Monk's music after only a few bars. Verbally true to his music, Monk also had a taste for idiosyncratic titles such as *Epistrophy, Misterioso*, and *Rhythm-a-ning*. Leslie Gourse's biography lists 91 compositions, including the legendary "'Round Midnight," which Monk registered with BMI, as well as a "Sessionography," which documents sixty occasions with identification of his musical colleagues and the pieces played.

Recordings: *Misterioso*. New York: Columbia, c. 1958; *The Complete Blue Note Recordings*. Emd/Blue Note, 1982; *The Complete Riverside Recordings*, with 13 tracks on 15 cds & notes by Orrin Keepnews, 1986.

Biography: Gourse, Leslie. *Straight, No Chaser: The Life and Genius of Theolonious Monk*. New York: Schirmer, 1997.

Documentaries: *Straight, No Chaser*. Produced by Charlotte Zwerin & Bruce Ricker. Warner Brothers, n.d.; *Thelonious Monk, American Composer*. Toby Byron/Multiprises, 1991; *Jazz on a Summer's Day* (1959). Raven Films, 1987; *Monk in Oslo*, 1966.

Web Site: http://www.achilles.net/~howardm/tsmonk.html

Interpretation: Schuller, Gunther. *The Swing Era*. New York: Oxford University Press, 1989; Williams, Martin, ed. *The Art of Jazz: Essays on the Nature and Development of Jazz*. New York: Oxford University Press, 1959.

MONTMARTRE

(c. 1875).

This Parisian neighborhood was probably the first example in history of professional artists settling in previously underinhabited real estate, in this case a quiet, somewhat hilly district quite far from the center of the city, giving the enclave an avant-garde identity. Artists, writers, and performers who felt that the Left Bank of the Seine was becoming too bourgeois or expensive seized on this opportunity, defining themselves as alternative, not only artistically but geographically, the fact of the latter perhaps lending credence to more tenuous claims for the former.

Whole groups of artists established themselves in Montmartre by the 1880s, while organizations such as the Chat Noir (black cat) were founded for the publication of an illustrated magazine and the presentation for performances. It was here in 1882 that the artist Paul Bilaud exhibited "the first documented monochrome painting, a black rectangle with the facetious title *Negroes Fighting in the Cellar at Night*," implicitly presaging not only painterly minimalism but DADA. (Indicatively, that title would still cause controversy today, though for a different reason.) In a Montmartre apartment in that same year Jules Lévy organized an *Art incohérent* (Incoherent Art) exhibition that included, in addition to the Bilaud monochrome, "a painting of a garlic sausage, the sculpture made of cheese, a landscape painted by a dancer on a ballet slipper, and a drawing done by an artist with his foot," to quote a recent account. In Montmartre, not on the Left Bank, was the first performance on 9 December 1896 of Alfred Jarry's monumentally challenging play *Ubu Roi*, with sets and costumes by Pierre Bonard and Henri de Toulouse-Lautrec.

By the twentieth century, nonartists arrived to join the real-estate pioneers in Montmartre, typically driving up the rents and making the neighborhood less distinctively avant-garde. In these respects, the evolution of Montmartre became a model for Greenwich Village in the 1920s, Fire Island in the 1940s, and SoHo in the 1970s, to cite comparable New York City enclaves—not to mention less prominent frontier neighborhoods settled by artists with similar ambitions around the western world.

Books: Émile-Bayard, Jean. *Montmartre Past and Present*. New York: Brentano, n.d.; Parry, Albert. *Garrets and Pretenders: A History of Bohemia*. New York: Dover,1960.

Exhibition Catalog: *The Spirit of Montmartre*. New Brunswick, NJ: Jane Voorhees Zimmerli Art Museum–Rutgers University, 1996.

MOOG, Robert

(23 May 1934).

Moog invented the first generally available Electronic Music SYNTHESIZER. Whereas the previous comprehensive music-making machines were unique behemoths that filled whole rooms, Moog combined his experience as a builder of THEREMINS (a touch-sensitive continuous sound generator) in the '50s with the transistor technology new to the '60s. As a synthesizer in the purest sense of the word, Moog's machine worked by combining discrete parts into an aural whole, producing sounds that represented, literally, syntheses of different specifications of elements. By no means a composing (i.e., decision-making) machine, in that it makes no musical choices, a synthesizer merely executes musical designs that, like the traditional score, customarily precede the composer's contact with the instrument. The initial Moogs of the late 1960s were monophonic, which is to say capable of producing only one note at a time; later Moogs were polyphonic. Among the most expert Moogists was WENDY CARLOS. By the 1980s, there were so many synthesizers, most of them technically more advanced, that Moogs became antiques, while Moog himself became an advisor to some of the successor manufacturers.

Website:
http://www.trax.ro/synths/machines/moog/index.html

Interpretation: Darter, Tom, compiler. *The Art of Electronic Music*. New York: Morrow, 1984; Kostelanetz, Richard. "Robert Moog (1970)." In *On Innovative Music(ian)s*. New York: Limelight, 1989.

MOORE, Henry

(30 July 1898–31 August 1986).

Moore dominated British sculpture in the middle of the twentieth century, and in so doing, he created the first British sculpture of distinction since the Middle Ages. Despite the evident influences of JEAN ARP and CONSTANTIN BRANCUSI in his smoothed and simplified forms, Moore followed his own path. He combined nearly abstract but clearly recognizable renderings of human figures with what he called "universal shapes": forms that can be considered essential in that they are those, in Moore's own words, "to which everyone is subconsciously conditioned and to which they can respond." His figures were matched to his formal concerns, in that they were limited to a few archetypal motifs: reclining figures, mother and child, and the family. It can be objected that Moore hedges his bet on the universal recognizability of form by incorporating the human figure, something generally not done by BARBARA HEPWORTH, a near-contemporary whose sculpture is otherwise remarkably similar to Moore's. Nevertheless, Moore went further than any other artist of his time in fusing together pure form and precise, identifiable feeling.

—Mark Daniel Cohen

Works: *Reclining Woman*, 1927; *Reclining Figure*, 1936; *Stringed Figure*, 1937; *Family Group*, 1948–49; *Time-Life Screen*, 1952–53; *Upright Internal/External Form*, 1952–53; *Warrior with Shield*, 1953–54; *UNESCO Reclining Figure*, 1957–58; *The Arch*, 1963–64; *Atom Piece*, 1964–65; *Large Animal Form*, 1969–70.

Writings: James, Philip, etc. *Henry Moore on Sculpture*. New York: Viking, 1966.

Biography: Read, Herbert. *Henry Moore: A Study of his Life and Work*. New York: Praeger, 1966; Hall, Donald. *Henry Moore: The Life and Work of a Great Sculptor*. New York: Harper & Row, 1966; Read, John. *Henry Moore: Portrait of an Artist*. London: G. Whizzard, 1979; Berthoud, Roger. *The Life of Henry Moore*. New York: Dutton, 1987.

Exhibition Catalogs: Epstein, Jacob. *Catalogue of an Exhibition of Sculpture and Drawings by Henry Moore*. London: E. Brown & Phillips, 1931; *Sculpture and Drawings by Henry Moore*. London: Tate Gallery, 1951; Russell, John. *Henry Moore Stone and Wood Carvings*. London: Marlborough Fine Arts; New York: M. Knoedler, 1961; Sylvester, David. *Henry Moore*. London: Arts Council of Great Britain, 1968; M. Knoedler & Co. *Henry Moore: Carvings 1961–1970, Bronzes 1961–1970*. New York: M. Knoedler & Co. Inc., 1970; Serpentine Gallery. *Henry Moore at the Serpentine: 80th Birthday Exhibition of Recent Carvings and Bronzes*. London: Arts Council of Great Britain, 1978; *Henry Moore, Drawings, 1969–79*. New York: Wildenstein, 1979.

Catalogues Raisonnés: Sylvester, David. *Henry Moore, Sculpture and Drawings: Volume 1: 1921–1948*. London: Lund, Humphries: A. Zwemmer, 1957; Moore, Henry. *Henry Moore, Sculpture and Drawings: Volume 2: 1949–1954*. London: Lund, Humphries: A. Zwemmer, 1965.

Henry Moore. Reclining Figure. Bronze. CORBIS/Burstein Collection.

Interpretation: Read, Herbert. *Henry Moore, Sculptor*. London: A. Zwemmer, 1934; *Henry Moore, Sculpture and Drawings*. New York: C. Valentin, 1949; Neumann, Erich. *The Archetypal World of Henry Moore*. New York: Pantheon Books, 1959; Russell, John. *Henry Moore*. New York: Putnam, 1968; Argan, Giulio Carlo. *Henry Moore*. New York: Abrams, 1973; Clark, Kenneth. *Henry Moore Drawings*. New York: Harper & Row, 1974; Finn, David. *Henry Moore: Sculpture and Environment*. New York: Abrams, 1976; Spender, Stephen. *Henry Moore Sculptures in Landscape*. New York: Clarkson N. Potter, 1979; Wilkinson, Alan G. *The Drawings of Henry Moore*. New York: Garland, 1984.

MOORMAN, Charlotte

(18 November 1933–8 November 1991).

After beginning her New York career as an orchestra pit cellist, Moorman became in the early 1960s involved with avant-garde performance, working principally with the video artist Nam June Paik, who typically made for her a brassière with video monitors in place of cups. Her most extraordinary creation was the New York Avant-Garde Festival, which she organized almost annually from 1963 to 1982. Once a year, Moorman would invite artists to do whatever they wanted within space available for certain hours. As no admission was charged, one assumption was that spectators would go wherever they wanted, for as long as they wished. As she refused to recognize stars (in the John Cagean anarchist tradition), everyone received equal billing, even, in one year, for Sun Ra, who appeared with his Arkestra in a flatbed truck that inched down Central Park West. One festival was held in Shea Stadium, another on a boat docked in the East River, a third on a platform of Grand Central Station, otherwise empty on Sundays. One never regretted attending or participating. A tenacious woman beneath her Southern-belle veneer, Moorman was particularly adept at getting New York City politicians and administrators to accede to her designs.

Interpretation: Gruen, John. *The New Bohemia* (1966). Pennington, NJ: A Cappella books, 1991.

MORELLET, François

(30 April 1926).

Though for most of his adult life the manager of a family factory, Morellet has been a prolific and consistent artist specializing in rationally derived, superficially simple, and yet awesomely clever geometric works that generate complex structures. Implicitly rejecting MONDRIAN's reliance upon intuition, Morellet has worked with systems, which are customarily announced in the titles of his pieces (e.g., "6 Canvases with a 5m Perimeter and a Horizontal Diagonal," 1973), and it follows that Morellet denies Mondrian's obsession with hidden meanings. Indeed, he speaks of families of systems: juxtaposition; superimposition; random; interference; fragmentation; and destabilization. As a painter and book-artist, Morellet has worked almost exclusively in black and white.

Morellet has also made light objects and kinetic sculptures. Edward Lucie-Smith (1933) describes *"sphéretrames* (sphere-webs)—a sphere made up of rods laid at right angles to one another to form a cellular structure which, through its multiple perspectives, has strange effects on light. A related work is a lattice of fluorescent tubes, which seems to dissolve the wall behind it." In significant respects, Morellet's art predates similar developments in the work of FRANK STELLA, DONALD JUDD, and SOL LE WITT among others. Morellet has written about wanting to "reduce my arbitrary decisions to a minimum. To put limits on my 'artist's' sensibility, I among others have made use of simple and obvious systems, of pure chance, and of spectator participation."

Visual Art: *Peinture*, 1952; *Rectangles*, 1953; *2 trames de lignes perpendiculares*, 1952; *2 trames de tirets 0°, 14°*, 1956; *4 double trames 0°, 22.5°, 45°, 67.5°*, 1958.

Sculpture: *Sphere-trames*, 1962; *Interférence avec mouvements ondulatoires*, 1965.

Exhibition Catalogs: *François Morellet*. Berlin, Germany: Nationalgalerie, 1977; Kotik, Charlotta, et al. *François Morellet: Systems*. Buffalo, NY, & Brooklyn, NY: Albright-Knox and Brooklyn Museum, 1984.

Interpretation: Hill, Anthony, ed. *DATA: Directions in Art, Theory and Aesthetics*. London: Faber, 1968; Parola, Rene. *Optical Art: Theory and Practice*. New York: Reinhold, 1969.

MORGAN, Edwin

(27 April 1920).

A Glasgow academic, Morgan has produced, along with scholarship, several deviant poems that rank among the best of the era. "Opening the Cage" is a sonnet based upon fourteen variations of the fourteen words in JOHN CAGE's "I have nothing to say and I am saying it and that is poetry." "The Chaffinch Map of Scotland" uses a few typically Scottish words to represent the shape of his native land. "Pomander" uses words that sound like the title word to make that fruit's shape, the visual prosody (such as the repeated *p*'s) complementing the aural. (This updating of the George Herbert shape poem is superior to the American poet John Hollander's [1929] forays in the same direction in *Types of Shape* [1969, 1991], which suffer, curiously, from prosaic language.) "Seven Headlines" finds English words embedded in the French phrase "il faut etre absolument moderne." "Space Poem 1" mixes English words with Russian, the latter apparently chosen for their sounds. One virtue of Morgan's experimental poems is that each invention is unique to one poem; none of his alternative devices are repeated. In *Wi the Haill Voice* (1972), he translated the Russian poet VLADIMIR MAYAKOVSKY, not into English but Scots.

Count Morgan among the few poets among the dozens acknowledged in this book also to merit an entry in Ian Hamilton's smugly conservative *Oxford Companion to Twentieth-Century Poetry* (1994), where the entries on avant-garde subjects such as sound poetry, "concrete poetry," and even "language poetry" are consistently ignorant and insufficient.

Poetry: *Second Life: Selected Poems*. Edinburgh, Scotland: Edinburgh University Press, 1967; *Wi the Haill Voice*. S. Hinksey, Oxford, England: Carcanet, 1972; *Poems of 30 Years*. Manchester: Carcanet, 1982; *Selected Poems.* Manchester, England: Carcanet, 1985; *Collected Poems*. Manchester: Carcenet, 1990; *Nothing Not Giving Messages: Reflections on His Work and Life*. Ed. Hamish Whyte. Edinburgh: Polygon, 1990; *Sweeping Out the Dark*. Manchester: Carcenet, 1994.

Prose: *Hugh MacDiarmid*. London: Longman, 1976; *Crossing the Border: Essays in Scottish Literature*. Manchester: Carcanet, 1990.

Interpretation: Crawford, Robert, and Hamish Whyte, eds. *About Edwin Morgan*. Edinburgh: Edinburgh University Press, 1990.

Bibliography: Whyte, Hamish. *Edwin Morgan: A Selected Bibliography 1950–1980*. Glasgow: Mitchell Library, 1980.

MORGENSTERN, Christian

(6 May 1871–31 March 1914).

Though he might have intended otherwise, Morgenstern is best remembered for his nonsense poems and a certain wordless poem composed entirely of typographical marks (dashes and parentheses tilted 90 degrees and thus arrayed horizontally, like inverted umbrellas) and customarily translated as "Fish's Nightsong." Martin Seymour-Smith credits Morgenstern with anticipating "most of the modern tendencies that came after his early death from tuberculosis, [among them] the realization that bourgeois 'values' are mechanisms for self-evasion, experiments with words as things-in-themselves as well as (arbitrary?) symbols of things they denote." The American translation mentioned below curiously omits the classic Morgenstern sound/nonsense poem "Des grosse Lalula," which begins: "Kroklowafzl? Semememl!/ Selokrontro—prafriplo:/ Bifzl, bafzl: hulalemi:/ quastl bastl ho . . . / Lalu lalu lalu lalu la!"—perhaps because no translation is necessary.

Books: *Galgenleider*, 1905; *Palmström*, 1910; *Gallows Songs*. Trans. W. D. Snodgrass and Lore Segal. Ann Arbor: University of Michigan Press, 1967; *Selected Poems of Christian Morgenstern*. Trans. Alfred Feiner. Walton-on-Thames, England: Outposts, 1973.

Interpretation: Hofacker, Erich P. *Christian Morgenstern*. Boston: Twayne, 1978.

MORICE, Dave

(10 September 1947).

One of Morice's original ideas was a poetry marathon in which he would write as many poems as possible within an extended period of time, usually in a public place. Morice claims to have written "a thousand poems in twelve hours, a mile-long poem, and a poem across the Delaware River." His questionable feats belong in the *Guinness Book of World Records*, among other competitors to this *Dictionary*. Remembering two principles—that a special mentality can produce special work and that if you write a lot you increase the likelihood that something might be good—I would wager that somewhere in this mountain of produce is some remarkable poetry.

A second Morice move was to cast the words of poems, both classic and contemporary (ALLEN GINSBERG, W. C. WILLIAMS, JOHN CAGE), into comic strips of various styles, at once introducing the poems and, largely through images, making his own ironic commentary on the texts. Under the heading "abuse the muse," these poetry comics first appeared as a photocopied periodical and then in an oversize book that, since it came from a hypercommercial publisher, quickly disappeared from public view.

A third Moricean idea was the creation of a female pseudonym, Joyce Holland (1969–78), whose specialty was MINIMAL poems, in contrast to Morice's garrulous predisposition. The classic, in collaboration with the late Darrell Gray (1945–80), is "Days of the Week": "mungday.

twosday. weedsday. thirty. fryday. sat her day. someday." An actress claiming to be Ms. Holland often appeared, usually with Morice in tow, at art festivals and at conferences. Holland was also the editor-in-name of *Matchbook* (1973–74), in which one-word poems by many authors were stapled into a matchbook cover. He is one of the few writers mentioned in this book to have an M.F.A. from the mass-production lines of the Writer's Workshop at the University of Iowa.

Works: Holland, Joyce. *The Final E: Selected Poems 1969–73*. Iowa City, IA: X Press, 1978; Morice, Dave. *Poetry Comics*. New York: Simon & Schuster, 1982; *A Visit from St. Alphabet*. Pennington, NJ: A Cappella, 1993; *More Poetry Comics*. Pennington, NJ: A Cappella, 1994; *Alphabet Avenue*. Chicago: Chicago Review, 1997.

MORRIS, Robert

(9 February 1931).

A radical sculptor and sculptural theorist, working with a variety of alternative ideas, Morris produced in the late 1960s a series of works, accompanied by several essays, that challenge previous ideas in several ways. In his criticism Morris favored sculptors working outside of the studio, with materials offered by Nature, such as earth; the use of previously neglected materials, such as felt, whose shapes necessarily depend upon gravity; and the creation of easily comprehended structures, which he called "unitary" forms, in contrast to the CUBIST complexity of, say, DAVID SMITH. The result is work that presented a single image, rather than interrelated parts. "Such are the simpler forms that create strong gestalt sensations," Morris wrote at the time. "Their parts are bound together in such a way that they offer the maximum resistance to perceptual separation. In terms of solids, or forms applicable to sculpture, these gestalts are the simpler polyhedrons." Unlike DONALD JUDD, who has similar biases, Morris eschewed modular formats. He also collaborated in MIXED-MEANS performance.

Writings: *Continuous Project Altered Daily: The Writings of Robert Morris*. Cambridge: MIT Press, 1993.

Sculptures: *Box with the Sound of Its Own Making*, 1961; *Untitled "Mirrored Cubes"* c. 1960s; *Card File*, 1963; *Metered Bulb*, 1963; *Corner Piece*, 1964; *Observatory*, 1971; *Hearing*, 1972.

Exhibition Catalogs: Michelson, Annette. *Robert Morris*. Washington, DC: Corcoran Gallery, 1969; Tucker, Marcia. *Robert Morris*. New York: Whitney Museum, 1970; Compton, Michael, & David Sylvester. *Robert Morris*. London: Tate Gallery, 1971; *Robert Morris: Selected Works 1970–1980*. Houston: Contemporary Arts Museum, 1981; *Robert Morris: The Felt Works*. New York: Grey Art Gallery & Study Center NYU, 1989; Sultan, Terrie. *Robert Morris: Inability to Endure or Deny the World*. Washington, DC: Corcoran, 1990.

Interpretation: Berger, Maurice. *Labyrinths: Robert Morris, Minimalism, and the 1960s*. New York: Harper & Row, 1989.

MOSCOW SUBWAY STATIONS

(1931–).

This was reportedly Joseph Stalin's pet art project and perhaps the only surviving compensation for all the prominent artists and writers his regime killed in mid-career. Not only are the stations esthetically more magnificent than those in other cities, but they were individually designed in a variety of styles with chandeliers, statuary, and reliefs. The trackside pillars in some stations incorporate columnar designs, while those in other stations have flat, rectangular shapes. Some stations also have street-level entrances that are likewise magnificent. Because Moscow subways ran more frequently than those elsewhere, in 1981, when I was last there, I could get out at any stop, admire the station's interior design, and expect another train to come along within a few minutes. The Moscow Subway stations represents collective art, much like LAS VEGAS, but whereas the latter was constructed by independent entrepreneurs in competition with one another, the Moscow Subway stations reflect a plan officially initiated by the Soviet Central Committee. During my 1981 visit to Moscow, I purchased a paperback with color illustrations that was produced for the 1980 Olympics (in which the USA did not participate) that effectively represents the whole work. No other city known to me has even tried to build subway stations of comparable individuality and esthetic quality, preferring instead a grim uniformity.

Books: *Moscow Metro: A Pictorial Guide*. Text by Valentine Berezin. Photos by Alexander Terziev. Moscow: Planeta, 1980.

MOSOLOV, Alexander

(11 August 1900–12 July 1973).

His contribution to the avant-garde tradition was the use of shaking sheet metal to suggest the sound of a working factory in his composition *Zavod* (Iron Foundry, 1927). Like the composer NICOLAS SLONIMSKY, Mosolov wrote songs to the texts of newspaper advertisements. Slonimsky the lexicographer reports that such explicitly proletarian music "elicited a sharp rebuke from the official arbiters of Soviet music. On 4 February 1936, Mosolov was expelled from the Union of Soviet Composers for staging drunken brawls and behaving rudely to waiters in restaurants. He was sent to Turkestan to collect folk songs as a move toward his rehabilitation." (If not for the historic Soviet Union, we could regard the U.S.A. as incomparably inhospitable to the avant-garde.) Mosolov does not rate an entry in John Vinton's *Dictionary of Contemporary Music* (1974), perhaps because, unlike many of the lesser composers included there, Mosolov was not connected to an American university that purchases books.

Works: *Zavod*, 1927; *Geroy* (The Hero), 1927; Piano Trio 1927; 2 Piano Concertos, 1927, 1932; Dance Suite for piano trio, 1928; *Plotina* (The Dam), 1929; *Maskarad* (Masquerade), 1940; *M. I. Kalinin*, 1940; *The Signal*, 1941; *Ukraine* for soloist, chorus, and orchestra, 1942; *Moscow*, 1948.

Recordings: *Piano Music: Selections*. France: Le Chant du Monde, 1991; *String Quartet: On Themes of 1812*. Triton, 1996; *Four Newspaper Advertisements, Op. 21; Three Children's Sketches, Op. 18*. Moscow, Russia: Melodiya,1990.

MOSS, David

(21 January 1949).

A large man, trained in percussion, Moss has been concerned with alternatives in the placement of his drums and thus with different physical strategies in using available soundmakers. Meanwhile, Moss developed a unique kind of propulsive scat singing, reflecting a variety of declamatory styles but commonly identifiable as uniquely his. Usually in conjunction with amplifiers that he controls while he sings (sometimes playing percussion as well), he succeeds at what many other composers have tried to do far less effectively—making music that suggests the end of the world. Not unlike others active on the current "performance scene," Moss tours widely and collaborates generously, reportedly having given over a thousand discrete concerts. In the 1990s, he lived as an American in Berlin.

Works: *Light No.18*, 1983; *Full House* (duets), 1983; *King Lear*, Incidental Music 1983; *N.Y. Objects and Noise Nos. 1 & 2*, 1984; *Vox Box*, 1984; *Mossmen*, 1984; *Operadio*, 1986; *Slow Talking*, 1987; *Operadio #2*, 1987; *That Tempest*, 1989; *After That Tempest*, 1989; *Stolen Voice*, 1990.

Recordings: *Full House*. Moers, West Germany: Moers Music, 1984; *Dense Band*. Moers, West Germany: Moers Music, 1985; *Texture Time*. Zurich: Intekt, 1994; *Time Stories*. Zurich: Intekt, 1998; "Language Linkage" (1988). In *The Aerial* #1. Santa Fe, NM: Nonsequitur Foundation (P.O. Box 15118, 87506), 1990; ——, et al. *The Day We Forgot*. Würzburg, Germany: No Man's Land, 1991.

MOSTEL, Rafael

(11 August 1948).

Mostel's innovation comes from using ancient Eastern artifacts, namely Tibetan singing bowls, to play distinctly contemporary music. Actually made to receive sounds rather than make them, the small bowls respond to wooden mallets run around their rims. Realizing that the different acoustics of various venues can affect the humming sound of these bowls, Mostel has performed in New York's Central Park, which has little echo amid an abundance of natural sounds, and in the humongous Cathedral of St. John the Divine, which has a rich, extended echo. In these performances, Mostel adds such Eastern instruments as wooden and clay flutes, thigh-bone trumpets, a ram's horn, and various kinds of non-Western percussion.

Compositions: *Passage Time*, 1971; *In the Theatre of the Absurd*, 1971; *Eclipse*, 1972; *Dances for Anton Chekhov*, 1979; Sonata for Two Cassette Machines, Found Material, and Noisemakers, 1983; *A Passage to Light* for Tibetan singing bowls, 1984; *Prologues/Secrets/Hymn of the Sun* for Tibetan singing bowls and ram's horn, 1985; *Ceremonial for the Equinox*, for 40 musicians, 1986; *Ascent to the Lullwater* for voice, rasp, bow, double clay flute, and Tibetan singing bowls, 1988; *Wyrd: In Memoriam Morton Feldman* for Aztec clay flutes, Tibetan singing bowls 1990; *Travels of Babar, an Adventure in Scales and the Circle of Fifths*, for slides, narrator, 8 musicians, 1994.

Recordings: Mostel, Rafael. *Nightsongs*, with title composition (1989) & *Jacob's Ladder* (1989). New York: Digital Fossils (P.O. Box 1066, Cooper Station, 10276), 1992; *Blood on the Moon*, with *The River* (1987) & *Swiftly, How Swiftly . . .* (1987). New York: Digital Fossils, 1992; *Music for the October Moon*, with title composition and *Prologues/Secrets/Hymn of the Sun* (1985). New York: Digital Fossils, 1994; *Travels of Babar/An Adventure in Scales* (in Japanese). Japan: Toshiba/EMI, 1994; *Ceremonial for the Equinox*. New York: Digital Fossils, 1995.

Exhibition Catalog: *Metal Earth Wood Styrofoam= Music*. New York: Vincent Astor Gallery, New York Public Library for the Performing Arts at Lincoln Center, 1996.

MOTHER MALLARD'S PORTABLE MASTERPIECE COMPANY

(1969–78; 1999–).

Founded by the musician David Bordon (1938), they were among the first to play MOOG synthesizers live, performing mostly MODULAR MUSIC, successfully demonstrating that an instrument thought to belong exclusively to the recording studio (thanks to WENDY CARLOS) could also be used on a concert stage. In their first New York City concert, three musicians played several Moogs, incorporating a variety of rifts that overlapped one another, each musician beginning his or her bit before the other was finished. Not unlike other early compositions for the Moog, their music relied heavily upon the "sequencer," as it was called, which could easily generate the repetition characteristic of MODULAR MUSIC. The group survived in spite of unjustified neglect, caused in part by residing in Ithaca, rather than New York City, and by changing personnel. MMPMC set a precedent not only for other live synthesists but for later groups like *The Hub*, which is composed of Chris Brown, John Bishoff, Mark Trayle, Tim Perkins, Scott Gresham-Lancaster, and Phill Stone sitting before cathode-ray tubes, not only generating computer music in live time but also silently sending one another word-messages that appear on their screens, supposedly altering their collaborative performance. David Borden revived Mother Mallard along with his sons early in 1999.

Recordings: *Mother Mallard's Portable Masterpiece Co.* Ithaca, NY: Earquack EQ0001 (1191 East Shore Drive, 14850), 1973; *Mother Mallard's Portable Masterpiece Co. 1970–1973*. Silver Spring, MD: Cuneiform (P.O. Box 8427, 20907–8427), 1999; Borden, David. *Places, Times & People*. Silver Spring, MD: Cuneiform, 1994.

MOTOWN

(1959–1975).

Label founder Berry Gordy Jr. (1929) recognized early on a new market for recordings: teenagers. He also realized that black music—if packaged in a palatable way—would appeal to a middle-class, white audience. Modeling his recording company on Detroit's other leading industry—the modern automobile assembly line where he had briefly worked—Gordy hired a "stable" of songwriters and musicians to create product in a specific mold. He then hired elocution and etiquette teachers to teach his artists how to perform. Using as raw material the many vocal groups already performing in local schools, Gordy was able to create his own stars. Nicknamed "Hitsville, USA," Motown resembled a small town where Gordy was absolute monarch, or a family where Gordy-the-father ruled in an absolute, unquestioned manner. It was only when a few Motown artists—such as Marvin Gaye and Stevie Wonder—rebelled against his absolute authority and demanded artistic freedom that the Motown empire began to crumble. Further, Gordy was unable to keep up with changing tastes in popular music. Although Motown still exists as a label today, it is owned by others and no longer defines a "sound."

—Richard Carlin

Sources: Gordy, Berry. *To Be Loved: The Music, the Magic, the Memories of Motown: An Autobiography*. New York: Warner Books, 1994; Morse, David. *Motown & the Arrival of Black Music*. London: Studio Vista, 1971; Waller, Don. *The Motown story*. New York: Scribner's, 1985; Allyn, Douglas. *Motown Underground*. New York: St. Martin's Press, 1993.

MTV

(1982).

Its technical innovation, to stretch that noun, is presenting music-based video art in which no scene is more than a few seconds long, purportedly because its viewers have the attention span of prepubescent children. Although the songs behind the video might have a few *minutes* of unbroken sound, the picture hops from image to image, from singer(s) to accompanying scene, with a rapidity more typical of commercials (making it hard for the MTV viewer to distinguish between the official commercials and the programming). The epitome of this MTV style in my experience is *Decade: MTV's Review of the 1980s* (1989), billed as "a sight and sound explosion"—a two-hour "documentary" that must be seen to be believed, as history is compressed, or chopped apart, into scenes as short as those in commercials. Nothing, not even interviews with distinguished informants, is given sufficient time (or space) to be more important than anything else. Those of us accustomed to structured exposition, even expositions as short as those in this book, question the efficacy of this lightning-fast style in conveying understanding. It is unfortunate that the MTV intelligence has infiltrated not only soap operas, or daytime television serials, where both scenes and speeches are shorter than before, but VIDEO ART, where any extended, continuous shot has come to represent, merely by contrast, a measure of mature intelligence.

Source: Available from your local cable television company.

Web Site: www.mtv.com

MULTICULTURAL

(c. 1990).

A modish academic term for a group of people who look superficially various but think pretty much alike about major issues of politics and art. A current synonym is "diversity," though both words had different meanings in the past and will probably have yet other meanings in the future. The fallacy here is that people are not what they are but what they were at birth, a while ago—a fallacy that is for some too reminiscent of fascism, which believed, to be precise, that Jewish soldiers, say, were catgorically different (and thus death-destined) only because they were different at birth from other soldiers. George Orwell once quipped about something else: "One has to belong to the intelligentsia to believe things like that; no ordinary man could be such a fool." Beware of anyone using either of these words affirmatively in the course of selling you something; you'll be stuck with something you don't need.

Bibliography: Examples are too many for selection.

MULTITRACKING

(c. 1960).

This is one of the great technical innovations in the development of recorded music, comparable to the development of the typewriter in the production of writing. The original recording technologies—first, the wax cylinder, then discs, then wire, and finally audiotape—were monophonic in the sense that they could record only one line of sound. Two-track tape recorders arrived in the 1950s, to record simultaneously live sound through two separate microphones, each of which purportedly had a different perspective (comparable to that of two eyes). It later became possible to record or modify each track separately without affecting the other.

In the 1960s came four-track tape, with the possibility of four-line recording, which was what THE BEATLES used to create their *Sgt. Pepper's Lonely Hearts Club Band* album, and thus the opportunity to produce in the late 1960s "quadraphonic" records for those listeners with four loudspeakers.

In the 1970s came tape with sixteen, twenty-four, thirty-two, and even sixty-four tracks, each of which could be recorded independently of the others, so that sound producers were offered the possibility of adding sounds well after the original tapings were made. Sounds from each of these tracks could then be modified in the "mixing down" process to the stereophonic (two-track) tape required for standard distribution. Needless to say, perhaps, each of these technological developments generated alternative musical possibilities.

With the advent in the late 1980s of DIGITAL consoles, such as the Lexicon Opus, a simulation of multitracking could appear on a computer screen; so that instead of going through the cumbersome process of rerecording a sound on, say, track two to have it begin a few seconds earlier, the audio engineer/computer operator needed only to punch a few instructions into his machine, greatly accelerating the re-editing process.

Resource: Holmes, Thomas B. *Electronic and Experimental Music*. New York: Scribner's, 1985.

MUNRO, Thomas

(15 February 1897–14 April 1974).

An encyclopedic art historian, Munro championed as early as 1928 "Scientific Method in Esthetics," which he defined as "broadly experimental and empirical, but not limited to quantitative measurement; utilizing the insights of art criticism and philosophy as hypotheses, but deriving objective data from two main sources—the analysis and history of form in the arts, and psychological studies of the production, appreciation, and teaching of the arts." However, to establish the preconditions for such an esthetics, Munro, very much a positivist, wrote a prodigiously exhaustive, valuable, needlessly forgotten study of the categories of artistic endeavor, *The Arts and Their Interrelations* (1949), and then historiographical theory in *Evolution and Art* (1963). His interest in establishing "scientific" esthetics parallels that of the Harvard mathematician GEORGE BIRKHOFF. Munro's daughter Eleanor (1928), likewise an art historian, produced in 1985 a stylish memoir of her father's culture, including these memorable sentences: "The goal of Modernist art and art education has been an evangelistic one, right for an optimistic age in which cultural opportunities offered at the bottom of the economic scale seemed to promise profit for the whole nation." She continued, "He wouldn't be alone, in coming decades, to feel bewilderment, then painful disappointment, as he saw the tissue of modernist confidence come apart in alternate phases of social conformity, then disorientation, in the course of which emerged new art and behavioral styles that were uncongenial to him."

Writings: *Scientific Method in Aesthetics*. New York: Norton, 1928; *The Future of Aesthetics*. Cleveland: Cleveland Museum of Art, 1942; *The Arts and Their Interrelations* (1949). Rev. ed. Cleveland: Case Western Reserve University, 1967; *Form and Style in the Arts*. Cleveland: Case Western Reserve University, 1970; *Toward Science and Aesthetics*. New York: Liberal Arts, 1956.

Biography: Munro, Eleanor. *Memoir of a Modernist's Daughter*. New York: Viking, 1988.

MURAYAMA, Tomoyoshi

(18 January 1901–22 March 1977).

Murayama introduced DADA to Japan. After spending several months of 1922 in Berlin, he returned with an esthetic platform he called "Conscious Construction," even though it resembled Dada more than CONSTRUCTIVISM. Once home, he quickly mounted several exhibitions, mostly of small works, because, as Tsutomu Mizusawa writes, "He could not wait for larger pieces to arrive by sea freight. He called the show "Exhibition of Small Conscious Constructivist Works by Tomoyoshi Murayama Dedicated to the Overbearing Beauty of Niddy Impekoven." The last two words supposedly identified a teenage dancer in Berlin. Mizusawa continues, "Looking at the catalog made of art paper, which was unusual for the time, we see four photographs. The three photographs of the works are a valuable record since most of them were destroyed during the war, but the photograph of the artist himself is even more interesting. We see Murayama here as a dancer. He appears with long hair cut in the *Buben-kopf* style (a kind of Dutch-boy), which was to become the trademark of the Mavo group, bare feet, and wearing a dark-colored tunic, posing self-consciously for the camera." Mizusawa concludes, "There was probably no other artist who had made his debut in the Japanese art world quite this way before."

Murayama's ideas spawned a group called Mavo, which, according to Mizusawa, "broke down the boundaries of the art system, and carried out activities on the stage of Tokyo quite different in character from anything done by the established art societies." One associate made a "sound constructor" of oil cans, logs, and wire, while Murayama designed modernist stage sets, especially for productions in translation of German avant-garde plays. After publishing several issues of a monthly magazine, Mavo fell apart. By the late 1920s, Murayama had assimilated Marxism and moved into making political theater that was esthetically less significant.

Works: Construction Tokyo. National Museum of Modern Art, 1925; "Japanese Dada and Constructivism: Aspects of the Early 1920s"; and Toshiharu Omuka, "To Make All of Myself Boil Over." In Andrei B. Nakov, Marc Dachy, et al. *Dada Constructivism*. Tokyo, Japan: Seibu Museum of Art, 1988.

MUSIQUE CONCRÈTE

(c. 1947).

This epithet arose after World War II, in the wake of the development of magnetic audiotape. Sound had previously been recorded on wax cylinder, shellac disc, or magnetic wire, none of which offered the opportunity for neat editing. Tape, by contrast, could be cut with a razor blade, much like film, its loose ends spliced together with a minimum of audible signs. *Musique concrète* differs from subsequent ELECTRONIC MUSIC in drawing only upon the sounds of the world, rather than artificial sound generators. These natural sounds could then be played at faster or slower speeds, modifying not only pitch and rhythm but timbre, while parts separately recorded could be spliced together. Once stereo and then MULTITRACK tape were developed, the composer could mix and play back separately produced sounds simultaneously. One practical advantage was that the tape composer did not need to know how to read music.

As the epithet suggests, the prime movers of musique concrète were based in Paris, often working at European radio stations: Pierre Henry and Pierre Schaeffer (1910). One masterpiece in this mode is John Cage's *Williams Mix* (1953), which consists of six tapes, each made from the tiniest feasible fragments, that are designed to emerge from six transducers/speakers simultaneously (but not synchronously) as a kind of prerecorded chorus. One familiar example of musique concrète is John Lennon's "Revolution No. 9" (1968), which is as close to contemporary avant-garde music as any Beatle ever came; it purportedly has a different sound if played backwards (a feat possible only with reel-to-reel audiotape). A later term for audiotape produced mostly from live sources is "electroacoustic," as distinct from Electronic Music.

Discography: Henry, Pierre. *Des Années 50*. Charenton, France: Mantra, 1991; —— *Le Microphone bien tempéré*. Paris: INA-GRM, n.d.; —— *Orphée-Ballet*. Philips, n.d.; —— *Variations pour une Porte et une Soupir/ Voile d'Orphée*. Harmonia Mundi, 1987; —— *Le Voyage*. Philips, n.d.; U.S. release: Limelight, n.d.; Schaeffer, Pierre. *L'Oeuvre musicale*. Albany, NY: Electronic Music Foundation, 1999; Xenakis, Iannis. *Electronic Music*. Albany, NY: Electronic Music Foundation, 1997; *Images Fantastiques*. Limelight, n.d.; *Musique Concrète*. Paris: Disques BAM, n.d.; *Musique Concrète*. Philips, n.d.; *Musique Concrête* [sic]. Candide, n.d.; *Musique Expérimentale*. Paris: Disques BAM, n.d.; *Musique Expérimentale 2*. Paris: Disques BAM, n.d.; Cage, John. *Williams Mix*. In *The 25-Year Retrospective Concert of the Music of John Cage* (1958). Mainz, Germany: Wergo, 1994; *Electronic Music/Musique Concrète* [with twelve composers]. N.p.: Mercury SR29123, n.d.

MUYBRIDGE, Eadweard

(9 April 1830–8 May 1904; b. Edward James Muggeridge). Born in England, Muybridge came to America in 1852 and settled in San Francisco in 1855. As a pioneering photographer, Muybridge took early pictures of Yosemite Valley

Eadweard Muybridge. Action Series: Pole Vaulter, 1881. CORBIS.

and, in 1867, became Director of Photographic Surveys for the U.S. Government. Influenced by American landscape painting, he became interested in representing photographically unusual atmospheric effects. Beginning in 1878, Muybridge used several still cameras to portray movement, initially of a galloping horse, later of nude men and women. This led to his development of a "zoopraxiscope," as he called it, in which motion could be reproduced through a sequence of photographs mounted on the inside of a rotating cylinder. Thanks to his photographic ingenuity, Muybridge proved for the first time that a galloping horse had at certain points all four feet off the ground. The books collecting his motion studies, at once accurate and evocative, remain in print.

Anthology: *Muybridge's Complete Human and Animal Locomotion* (1887). New York: Dover, n.d. (c. 1975); *Eadweard Muybridge in Guatemala 1875: The Photographer as Social Recorder*. Text E. Bradford Burns. Berkeley: University of California Press, 1986.

Exhibition Catalog: *Motion and Document, Sequence and Time: Eadweard Muybridge and Contemporary American Photography*. Andover, MA: Addison Gallery of American Art, 1991.

Biography: Haas, Robert Bartlett. *Muybridge: Man in Motion*. Berkeley: University of California Press, 1976; Hendricks, Gordon. *Eadweard Muybridge: Father of the Motion Picture*. New York: Grossman, 1975.

Web Site: http://www.masters-of-photography.com/M/muybridge/muybridge.html

MYERS, George, Jr.

(10 July 1953).

Myers began as a SMALL-PRESS publisher who worked nights at a local newspaper in Harrisburg, Pennsylvania. On the side Myers wrote the essays that became *An Introduction to Modern Times* (1982), which was then, and still remains, a good and true guide to emerging esthetic alternatives. He also produced the abstract VISUAL POEMS that became *The News* (1985) and *SubText* (1987). *Alphabets Sublime* (1986) is a book of interviews with BERN PORTER, PAUL ZELEVANSKY, JOHN M. BENNETT, KENNETH GANGEMI, and CAROLEE SCHNEEMANN, among others. In 1984 Myers became a book editor and occasional columnist at the Columbus (Ohio) *Post-Dispatch* and subsequently the winner of a state award for "criticism," but neither his poetry nor his criticism of the avant-garde has been the same since. He introduced an on-line literary magazine titled *George, Jr.,* in the mid-1990s, which prompted a name-infringement lawsuit from a slick magazine of the same first name. The only other American newspaperperson known to be doing advanced writing and publishing is Jerry Madson in Bemidji, Minnesota. Perhaps there are others.

Books: *An Introduction to Modern Times*. N.p. (Grosse Point Farms, MI): Lunchroom (P.O. Box 36027, 48236), 1982; *Nairobi*. Havre de Grace, MD: Thunderbaas, 1978; *The News*. Dublin, OH: Cumberland (P.O.Box 2962, Columbus, OH 43216), 1985; *Natural History*. Baltimore, MD (3938 Colchester Rd. #364, 21299-5010): Paycock, 1985; *Alphabets Sublime*. Baltimore, MD: Paycock, 1986.

NABOKOV, Vladimir

(23 April 1899–2 July 1977).

An aristocratic Russian emigré of profoundly conservative, anti-Soviet prejudices, Nabokov nonetheless wrote one truly avant-garde novel, a book so original and subtle that it is easily misunderstood, even by his academic biographers. Produced in the wake of the success of *Lolita* (1958) and Nabokov's early retirement from university teaching, *Pale Fire* (1962) consists of a long poem, attributed to an American poet named John Shade, followed by an elaborate commentary by Kinbote, an African-born scholar teaching in America. Though some commentators, including at least one Nabokov biographer, have praised the poem as masterful, it strikes me as a subtle parody of Robert Frost in particular and of American poetics in general.

Kinbote's commentary, on the other hand, is the work of a megalomaniac, whose typical extravagance is to see himself and his experience as a deposed African prince writ large in lines that don't ostensibly refer to him at all. This mad misreading becomes a sustained joke that only gets bigger with each Kinbote abuse of Shade's text, all abetted by the reader's suspicion that if Kinbote were a sufficiently titled academic, his juniors would no doubt kowtow to his delusions. My own hunch is that, in the course of writing his elaborate commentary to Pushkin's *Eugene Onegin*, Nabokov, as a profound ironist, decided to write a fiction about a madman (an aristocratic exile whose background superficially resembles his own) writing a skewed commentary. The result of that clever creative move is classic.

Buried in Nabokov's huge oeuvre are probably other comparably innovative texts that I haven't found, perhaps they were originally written in another language and remain untranslated (say, a fiction in the form of a chess problem or an entomological discovery, to mention two other Nabokov hobbies), because the paradox of Nabokov's career is that he was a fairly conservative fictioner who, perhaps incidentally, wrote a subversive masterpiece.

Once he began to be a celebrity, Nabokov accepted invitations to be interviewed, or at least write out responses to questions; and one reason why *Strong Opinions* (1973) is better than most collections of conversations, incidentally setting a good example, is that his published texts were not just written but rewritten.

Selected Writings: *Pale Fire*. New York: Putnam, 1962; *Strong Opinions*. New York: McGraw-Hill, 1973; Ed. with a commentary, Alexsander Pushkin. *Eugene Onegin: A Novel in Verse*. Princeton: Princeton University Press, 1964.

Autobiography: *Speak, Memory* (1951). Rev. ed. New York: G.P. Putnam's Sons, 1966.

Anthology: *The Portable Nabokov*. Ed. Page Stegner. New York: Viking, 1968.

Biography: Boyd, Brian. *Vladimir Nabokov: The Russian Years*. Princeton: Princeton University Press, 1990; ——.

Vladimir Nabokov: The American Year. Princeton: Princeton University Press, 1992; Field, Andrew. *Nabokov: His Life in Art*. Boston: Little Brown, 1967; ——. *Nabokov: His Life in Part*. New York: Viking, 1977.

Web Site: http://www.libraries.psu.edu/iasweb/nabokov/zembla.htm

Interpretation: Wood, Michael. *The Magicians Doubts Nabokov and the Risks of Fiction*. Princeton, NJ: Princeton University, 1998.

Bibliography: Field, Andrew. *Nabokov: A Bibliography*. New York: McGraw-Hill, 1973.

NAGY, Paul

See **PAPP, Tibor**.

NAKIAN, Reuben

(10 August 1897–4 December 1986).

Of all the sculptors influenced by Abstract Expressionist painting, Nakian was the freest and most expressive in his use of form. Avoiding all suggestions of the slick industrial look, he developed in his bronze sculptures a personal style that appeared at the same time both rocky and ageless, and spontaneously conceived. Works such as *Olympia* (1962) seem to have been constructed quickly, out of sudden gestures that were never retouched. Large slabs of bronze lean against each other and make what, at first glance, seems to be nothing more than a simple triangular arrangement of individual sections. Nevertheless, the form coheres before the viewer's eyes into the suggestion of a human figure, holding itself in a heroic pose. Even Nakian's more overtly figurative works, such as *The Goddess of the Golden Thighs* (1964–65), look at first as if they were modeled rapidly in a mound of clay and then abandoned, with all the thumbprints and the excess material still evident on the surface of the form. Nevertheless, there is an intricacy and a mythological power to the gesture of the goddess, who sits with legs spread wide as the embodiment of fecundity itself. In their immediacy and impulsive energy, the masses out of which his works are assembled have distinct similarities to the brushwork of Franz Kline and Willem de Kooning.

—Mark Daniel Cohen

Works: *Head of Marcel Duchamp*, 1943; *Europa and the Bull*, 1949–50; *Leda and the Swan*, 1960; *Olympia*, 1962; *Voyage to Crete*, 1960–62; *Goddess with the Golden Thighs*, 1964–65.

Exhibition Catalogs: Hess, Thomas B. *Nakian: January 8 through February 18, 1963: The Washington Gallery of Modern Art*. Washington, DC: Washington Gallery of Modern Art, 1963; O'Hara, Frank. *Nakian*. New York: MoMA, 1966; Nordland, Gerald. *Reuben Nakian: Recent Works, October 7–November 3, 1982*. New York: Marlborough Gallery, 1982; *Reuben Nakian: Sculpture and Drawings*. Milwaukee: Milwaukee Art Museum, 1985; Metzger, Robert P. *Reuben Nakian: Centennial Retrospective, 1897–1986*. Reading, PA: Reading Public Museum, 1998.

NANCARROW, Conlon

(27 October 1912–10 August 1997).

Born in Arkansas, initially a trumpeter in jazz orchestras, Nancarrow studied modernist composition with Nicolas Slonimsky and Roger Sessions. Having fought with the Abraham Lincoln Brigade on the Loyalist side in Spain, he emigrated to Mexico City, where he lived until his death, becoming a Mexican citizen. After producing undistinguished music for conventional instruments, Nancarrow began in the late 1940s to compose directly on player-piano rolls, perforating the special paper to mark notes and rhythms, incidentally rescuing an instrument commonly scorned. Thanks to such painstaking procedure, Nancarrow produced a kind of proto-electronic composition in the sense that he was using machines to make piano sounds whose rapid articulations and multiple voicings were beyond human capabilities and could as well be

n

permanently fixed. In his notes to Nancarrow CDs issued in Germany, JAMES TENNEY writes: "The two most distinctive characteristics of Nancarrow's work as a whole are his *rhythmic procedures* and his exploration of manifold types of *polyphonic texture* and thereby, *polyphonic perception*. The most prominent of Nancarrow's explicit compositional concerns has always been rhythm. But an exploration of polyphonic texture, which follows almost of necessity from the fullest development of rhythm, may one day be seen as the area of his greatest achievement." Though Nancarrow began just before his death to receive greater recognition in the country of his birth, including a MacArthur Fellowship, his music is heard more often in Europe than America.

Works: *Studies for Player Piano*. New York: Columbia, 1970; *Studies for Player Piano*. Vols. I–V. Mainz, Germany: Wergo, 1988–1991.

Interpretation: Carlsen, Phillip. *The Player Piano Music of Conlon Nancarrow*. Brooklyn, NY: Institute for Studies in American Music, 1988; Gann, Kyle. *The Music of Conlon Nancarrow*. New York: Cambridge University Press, 1995.

NASH, David

(14 November 1945).

Along with ANDY GOLDSWORTHY, Nash is one of the two principal sculptors to take the urge to return to Nature that typifies EARTH ART and practice it in object-based works, thereby also returning to sculpture crafted after the emphasis on manufacture that characterized MINIMALISM. Nash's early wood sculptures from the 1970s and 1980s combine cultural and natural forms: window frames that emerge like strange growths from the ends of tree limbs, chairs and tables that bristle with branches and twigs, which extend from them like tentacles. These works blur the clarity of the nature/culture distinction, suggesting the artificiality of the division. Nash's later works of the 1990s take on religious overtones. He chars tall tree trunks, burns crosses onto their surfaces, and cuts deep vertical crevices into them, creating Christian symbols that seem distinctly Celtic for being rendered in elements from Nature. (Nash currently lives in Wales.) The crevices become nearly black and mysterious recesses, and are remarkably effective in a time when many people confuse the urban with the urbane and believe themselves to be too sophisticated for an authentic religious emotion.

—Mark Daniel Cohen

Works: *Roped Arch*, 1972; *Branch Frame*, 1977; *Ash Stick Chair*, 1979; *Flying Frame*, 1980; *Red Shrine*, 1989; *Threshold Column*, 1990; *Charred Cross Egg*, 1994.

Exhibition Catalogs: Juda Rowan Gallery. *Tree to Vessel: David Nash Sculpture*. London: Juda Rowan Gallery, 1986; Lynton, Norbert. *David Nash, Sculpture 1971–90*. London: Serpentine Gallery, 1990; *At the Edge of the Forest: David Nash: Sculpture and Projects 1989–1993: 22 April–19 June 1993*. London: Annely Juda Fine Art, 1993; *David Nash: Recent Sculpture: 17 October–21 December 1996*. London: Annely Juda Fine Art, 1996; *David Nash: The Language of Wood*. London: Annely Juda Fine Art, 1998.

Interpretation: Andrews, Julian. *The Sculpture of David Nash*. London: Henry Moore Foundation/Lund Humphries, 1996.

NASH, Ogden

(19 August 1902–19 May 1971).

Surprise. Nash's prosaic subjects and corny sentiments notwithstanding, he was an inventive poet, beginning with campy couplets uniquely identifiable as his: "I think it very nice for ladies to be lithe and lis-some,/ But not so much so that you cut yourself if you happen to embrace and kissome." Writing out of the traditions of conventional verse, Nash played not only with formal fulfillment and violation but with symmetry and asymmetry, as in couplets such as: "I know another man who is an expert on everything from witchcraft and demonology to the Elizabethan drama,/ And he has spent a week-end with the Dalai Lama." This, like all good wit (as well as much avant-garde art), depends upon unexpected shifts.

As an alternative poet, Nash avoided what his contemporaries were doing—there are no myths, no symbolism, no enjambment, no obscurity, no deep mysteries or anything else that academic critics influential at the time would have thought particularly important. Nonetheless, the best Nash epitomizes Robert Frost's definition of poetry as that which cannot be translated. Just as limericks are unique to English, so is the best Nash, who made qualities indigenous to our language a favorite subject: "English is a language than which none is sublimer/ But it presents certain difficulties for the rhymer/ There are no rhymes for orange or silver/ Unless liberties you pilfer."

So strong is Nash's poetry that few remember that he also wrote stories, a kind of avant-garde skeletal fiction that depended not upon linguistic play but narrative ellipses (and incidentally makes subsequent so-called MINIMAL fictions seem verbose). This is the opening of "The Strange Case of Mr. Donnybrook's Boredoms":

> Once upon a time there was a man named Mr. Donnybrook.
>
> * * *
>
> He was married to a woman named Mrs. Donnybrook.
>
> * * *
>
> Mr. and Mrs. Donnybrook dearly loved to be bored.
>
> * * *
>
> Sometimes they were bored at the ballet, other times at the cinema.

From this introduction follows a wild story about fantasies incurred during insomnia.

Needless to say perhaps, this more deviant Nash has been less acceptable to anthologists and diehard Nashians (otherwise unfamiliar with everyone else mentioned in this book) than the pap-master.

Anthology: *The Pocket Book*. New York: Pocket, 1962; *I Wouldn't Have Missed It* (1975). Ed. Linell Smith and Isabel Eberstadt. London: Deutsch, 1983; *Selected Poetry of Ogden Nash: 650 Rhymes, Verses, Lyrics and Poems.* New York: Black Dog & Leventhal, 1995.

THE NATIONAL ENDOWMENT FOR THE ARTS

(1965; aka NEA).

Founded as a minor contribution to Lyndon Johnson's Great Society, as a means of underwriting the development of all the arts in America, the NEA has been uneven in its support of the American avant-garde, mostly because of different levels of sophistication in its various departments. On this issue, Media Arts and Visual Arts, say, have better records than Literature and Music, both of which in over thirty years have rarely supported the writers and composers mentioned in this book, almost taking pride in their dogged Yahooism. Thus, the problem becomes that nobody at the higher NEA levels seems to care about persistent retrograde deviance in particular departments, which is another way of measuring an absence of cultural leadership that would be unacceptable, say, at even the CANADA COUNCIL across the border. Secondly, in contrast to more sophisticated European governmental cultural agencies, which often support avant-garde Americans (particularly in Germany), the NEA rarely supports comparable Europeans, to the detriment of our cultural reputation abroad. (You get the impression of administrators working overtime to look Bush league.)

The NEA's companion, the National Endowment for the Humanities (aka NEH), has an even sorrier record when presented with opportunities to support criticism/scholarship about avant-garde art and literature. I've written elsewhere that the NEH's outlook and politics—its devotion to hierarchy and a circumscribed collection of approved authorities, its enthusiasm for embarrassing America—are essentially Stalinist. The fact that Senator Jesse Helms,

Patrick Buchanan, and their ilk have missed this last ripoff of the American taxpayer tells everyone all that need be known about *their* unfortunate ignorance and innocence. (My suspicion, which I've put into print before, is that these "conservatives"' attacks on the NEA look like a classic example of a KGB diversionary tactic.) The surest way to find out what the NEA and the NEH have actually done, rather than what people say they have done, is to get their *Annual Reports*, which are public documents.

Bibliography: Kostelanetz, Richard. *The Grants-Fix*. New York: Archae Editions (P.O. Box 444, Prince St., 10013), 1987; NEA and NEH *Annual Reports*. Washington, DC (1100 Pennsylvania Ave., N.W., 20506), 1967 to the present; Jarvik, Lawrence, et al. *The National Endowments: A Critical Symposium*. Los Angeles: Second Thoughts (Center for Popular Culture, P. O. Box 67398, 90067), 1995; Zeigler, Joseph Wesley. *Arts in Crisis: The National Endowment for the Arts vs. America*. Pennington, NJ: A Cappella, 1994.

Web Site: http//arts.endow.gov/

NAUMAN, Bruce

(6 December 1941).

Since his entry into installation art in the early 1970s, Nauman's works have been the most aggressive critiques by an artist of the standard expectations people have for art. His arrangements of constructed corridors leading nowhere, videos of visual static and of shrieking clowns, and casts of oddly combined and seemingly mutated body parts, have been devised to frustrate typical expectations of clearly defined art objects that offer some form of information and enlightenment. However, as "critiques," Nauman's installations are themselves uninformative and unenlightening, for they merely turn artistic definitions on their head without offering any specific ideas or criticisms. Furthermore, if art can be considered to be, at minimum, a manner of communication between the artist and the viewer and an enhancement of the felt human connection between them, Nauman's shrill, simplistic, adversarial style can be considered the ultimate example of "anti-art," and even, in its abuse of the audience, anti-human.

—Mark Daniel Cohen

Selected Works: *A Cast of the Space Under my Chair*, 1965–68; *Tony Sinking into the Floor, Face Up and Face Down*, 1973; *Sex and Death*, 1985; *Double Poke in the Eye*, 1985; *Clown Torture*, 1987; *Untitled (Three Small Animals)*, 1989; *Untitled (Hand Circle)*, 1996; *Partial Truth*, 1997.

Exhibition Catalogs: Whitney, David. *Bruce Nauman*. New York: Leo Castelli Gallery, 1968; Nicholas Wilder Gallery. *Flayed Earth/Flayed Self (Skin/Sink)*. Los Angeles: Nicholas Wilder Gallery, 1973; Livingston, Jane and Marcia Tucker. *Bruce Nauman: Work from 1965 to 1972*. Los Angeles: County Museum of Art, 1973; Brundage, Susan. *Bruce Nauman, 25 years*. New York: Rizzoli, 1994; Storr, Robert. *Bruce Nauman: March 1–May 23, 1995*. New York: MoMA, 1995; *Elliott's Stones*. Chicago: Museum of Contemporary Art, 1995; Snyder, Jill and Schaffner, Ingrid. *Bruce Nauman, 1985–1996: Drawings, Prints, and Related Works: The 1995 Larry Aldrich Foundation Award Exhibition*. Ridgefield, CT: Aldrich Museum of Contemporary Art, 1997.

Catalogues Raisonnés: Yau, John. *Bruce Nauman, Prints 1970–89: A Catalogue Raisonné*, New York: Castelli Graphics, Lorence-Monk Gallery; Chicago: Donald Young Gallery, 1989; Benezra, Neal David, Joan Simon, and Robert Storr. *Bruce Nauman: Exhibition Catalogue and Catalogue Raisonné*. Minneapolis: Walker Art Center, 1994.

NEVELSON, Louise

(23 September 1899–17 April 1988).

Nevelson's innovation was a sculptural image—more precisely, a rectangular relief, best viewed perpendicularly from the front. These reliefs are divided into smaller rectangular compartments containing miscellaneous scraps of wood, ranging from newel posts to pegs, sometimes including chair legs and other discarded wooden pieces and then painted entirely in a single color, usually black, sometimes white or gold. Though Nevelson did not change her compositional style after 1955, it did become more complex in internal relationships, culminating perhaps in the grandiose *Homage to the World* (1966). In the late sixties, Nevelson favored Plexiglas for open rectangles within a larger frame or smaller assemblages of geometric wooden parts within a Plexiglas case. Nevelson also reworked this characteristic style for outdoor sculptures in aluminum and steel.

Sculptures: *Sky Cathedral*, 1958; *Moon Garden Plus One*, 1958; *Dawn's Wedding Chapel*, 1959; *Homage to the World*, 1966.

Books: *Dawns and Dusks*. Ed. Diana MacKown. New York: Scribner's, 1976.

Web Site:
http://www.plgrm.com/history/women/N/Louise_Nevelson.HTM

Exhibition Catalog: *Louise Nevelson*. New York: Whitney Museum, 1967; *Louise Nevelson: Prints & Drawings*. Brooklyn, NY: Brooklyn Museum, 1967; *Louise Nevelson: Cascades, Perpendiculars, Silence, Music*. New York: Pace Gallery, 1983; *Louise Nevelson*. Rockland, ME: William A. Farnsworth Library & Art Museum, 1979; *Louise Nevelson: Atmospheres & Environments*. New York: Clarkson N. Potter, 1980; *Louise Nevelson*. Curated by Germano Celant. Milano: Charta, 1994.

Biography: Lisle, Laurie. *Louise Nevelson: A Passionate Life*. New York: Summit,1990.

Interpretation: Glimcher, Arnold. *Louise Nevelson*. New York: Dutton, 1976.

NEW DIRECTIONS

(1936).

Commonly thought to be a book publisher predisposed to avant-garde writing, New Directions was actually something else. Founded by James Laughlin IV (1914–97), heir to a steel fortune, while he was still a Harvard undergraduate, it loyally served certain major avant-garde figures at least a generation older than he: EZRA POUND, WILLIAM CARLOS WILLIAMS, JORGE LUIS BORGES, and KENNETH REXROTH, at minimum until other book publishers rescued them. Toward avant-garde figures of his own generation, Laughlin was less faithful, publishing at times KENNETH PATCHEN and CHARLES HENRI FORD, until their work was dropped, needlessly disappearing, to everyone's misfortune. In his voluminous perfect-bound semiannual publication, likewise called *New Directions* (1936–91), Laughlin could sometimes be more adventurous.

Remarkably few avant-garde writers of the next generations appeared under New Directions' imprint. Acknowledging limitations and peculiarities, Pound often referred to the imprint as "Nude Erections." In the "Publisher's Foreword" to *A New Directions Reader* (1964), a self-retrospecive in mid-career, Laughlin speaks of "no editorial pattern beyond the publisher's inclinations," which is another way of accounting for the essentially personal base of his selections. "The name New Directions," he continued, "is as often as not misleading in its implication of the experimental, the avant-garde, and the 'offbeat.'" Considering this accurate self-appraisal, Laughlin could just as well have avoided the avant-garde moniker and instead followed the example of Alfred A. Knopf, for instance—naming his publishing house after himself.

Books: Carruth, Hayden, and J. Laughlin, eds. *A New Directions Reader*. New York: New Directions, 1964; Peabody, Richard, comp. *Mavericks: Nine Independent Publishers*. Washington, DC: Paycock,1983.

Correspondence: *Kenneth Rexroth & James Laughlin: Selected Letters*. Ed. Lee Bartlett. New York: Norton, 1991; *Ezra Pound & James Laughlin: Selected Letters*. Ed. David M. Gordon. New York: Norton, 1994.

NEW YORK SCHOOL, SCHOOL OF PARIS, BLACK MOUNTAIN POETS, etc.

Any purportedly categorical classifications based upon geography, sex, race, or academic background do not belong in art criticism, as they rarely say anything significant about the style of an individual artist's work. Such epithets customarily function as sales slogans, capitalizing upon pre-established favorable auras of key words (e.g., New York, Paris, feminism, etc.) in the marketing both of works and of opinions (and even of "critical" books), mostly to establish significance for art or artists about which and whom nothing more substantial can be said.

Beware of any artist who opens his or her biography with sexual, racial, geographic, or academic tags designed to substitute for genuine credentials, artistic styles, or achievements. Whereas some consumers of art lap up these sorts of deceptions, others avoid them like a plague. *Caveat emptor*.

Sources: Too many examples, many of them book-length, to cite.

NEWMAN, Barnett

(29 January 1905–4 July 1970).

Though a painting contemporary of WILLEM DE KOONING and JACKSON POLLOCK, Newman created a different sort of work, proceeding from different assumptions, which was thus not acknowledged until the 1960s. Typical paintings consist of a predominantly monochromatic canvas interrupted by only a few contrasting marks that often take the form of vertical stripes. *The Wild* (1950), for instance, was a canvas nearly eight feet high but only one and five-eighths inches wide. Because Newman's first one-person exhibitions in 1950 and 1951 aroused hostile responses, he did not show again in New York until 1959, when he was in his mid-fifties.

Only with a 1966 exhibition at the Guggenheim Museum, featuring his *Stations of the Cross*, was his genius fully acknowledged. In the fourteen paintings comprising that last work, each six and one-half feet by five feet, the traditional Biblical narrative is "told" through vertical stripes of various widths and shapes, against a background field of raw canvas, so that the absence of familiar iconography becomes a commentary on the classic myth, as well as an echo of the simple cosmological forms of primitive art.

His most notable sculpture, *Broken Obelisk* (1963–67), is similarly vertical, with a ground-based pyramid on whose pointed top is balanced a rectangular volume whose bottom comes to a point. (This looks technically impossible and no doubt required sophisticated engineering.) In retrospect, Newman can be regarded as a primary precursor of COLOR-FIELD PAINTING, monochromic painting, the conundrum art of JASPER JOHNS, and much else. He was also a strong writer and talker whose prose was posthumously collected into a book.

Selected Paintings & Sculptures: *Onement*, 1948; *The Wild*, 1950; *Cathedra*, 1951; *Broken Obelisk*, 1963–67; *Stations of the Cross*, 1966.

Books: *Selected Writings and Interviews*. Ed. John P. O'Neill. New York: Knopf, 1990.

Exhibition Catalogs: Greenberg, Clement. *Barnett Newman: First Retrospective Exhibition*. Bennington, VT: Bennington College, 1958; Alloway, Lawrence. *Stations of the Cross*. New York: Guggenheim Museum, 1966; Hess, Thomas B. *Barnett Newman*. New York: Walker & Col, 1969; ——., *Barnett Newman*. New York: MoMA, 1980; *Barnett Newman*. London: Tate Gallery, 1972; Rosenberg, Harold. *Barnett Newman*. New York: Abrams, 1978; *Barnett Newman: The Complete Drawings*. MD: Baltimore Museum of Art, 1979; Strick, Jeremy. *The Sublime is Now: The Early Work of Barnett Newman*. New York: Pace Wildenstein, 1994.

Web Site: http://www.artincontext.org/artist/n/barnett_newman/

NICHOL, bp

(30 September 1944–25 September 1988; b. Barrie Phillip N.).

Perhaps the most prolific notable Canadian poet of his generation, Nichol worked in several veins, only some of which were avant-garde. *Konfessions of an Elizabethan Fan Dancer* (1967) contains typewriter poems. Later visual writing incorporates press-on type. *Still Water* (1970) is a box of poems. Of the last, his fellow Canadian Michael Andre (1946) writes, "Many are funny, like this rap at high coo: '2 leaves touch/bad poems are written.' Others are one-liners using onomatopoetic permutations: 'beyond a bee yawned abbey on debby Honda beyond."'

Though Nichol's poetry won a Canadian Governor General's Literary Award in 1970, by international avant-garde standards he ranked among neither the best nor the worst. Even in his strivings for profundity, he tended toward the superficial. Nichol also participated in the FOUR HORSEMEN, the most prominent SOUND-POETRY quartet of its time, and in the collective compositions of the Toronto Research Group. Among his less experimental masterworks is *The Martyrology* (1972, 1976, 1977, 1982), five volumes about imaginary saints. In his success—with one bibliography listing over seventy titles, nearly all of them published in his native country—Nichol demonstrated that no English-speaking country can match Canada in supporting experimental poetry.

Works: *Konfessions of an Elizabethan Fan Dancer*. London: Writers Forum, 1967; *bp*. Toronto: Coach House, 1967; *Dada Lama: A Sound Sequence in Six Parts*. London: Cavan McCarthy, 1968; *Andy and For Jesus Lunatic: Two Novels*. Toronto: Coach House, 1969; *Still Water*. Vancouver: Talonbooks, 1970; *ABC: The Aleph Best Book*. Ottawa: Oberon, 1971; *The Martyrology*. Toronto: Coach House, 1972; *Zygal: A Book of Mysterses and Translations*. Toronto: Coach House, 1984; *The Martyrology*. 5 vols. Toronto: Coach House, 1972, 1976, 1977, 1982.

Interpretation: Scobie, Stephen. *bp Nichol: What History Teaches* (1984). Vancouver, Canada: Talonbooks, 1993.

Web Site: www.thing.net/~grist/l&d/bpnichol/bp.html. Curated by Karl Young, who writes that it includes poetry and essays, scores by the FOUR HORSEMEN Performance Group, and a continuation of Nichol's participatory TTA 29 project. "Some of these are web-specific, exploring a medium Nichol would have loved to play with had he lived long enough to work with it."

NIDITCH, B.Z.

(8 January 1943, b. Ben Zion N.).

Niditch is one of those frequent contributors to American literary magazines whose work is invariably more advanced and distinctive than the common run; and rather than confining himself to coterie publications (as would writers with little confidence in their work's presence in any larger world), Niditch publishes widely, working out of classic avant-garde traditions. Given that his favorite subject is the recurring disasters of European history, typical titles of his very best poems, some of them adopting numerative forms, are "Thoughts Before Dachau," "1944," "Vienna's Last Waltz," and "1944: Mid Europa." Niditch has also written plays that have mostly been produced in and around Boston. He writes me, "I am active in the Boston Avant-Garde Society—BAGS."

Works: *Unholy Empire*. Browns Mills, NJ: Ptolemy (Box 98, 08015), 1982; *Exile*. Novato, CA: Heritage Trails (94 Santa Maria Drive, 94947), 1986; *On the Eve*. Hyde, Cheshire, England: New Hope Int'l (20 Werneth Ave, Gee Cross, SK 14 5NL). 1989; *Milton*. Miami, FL: Earthwise, 1992; *Lost and Found Tribes*. Arcadia, FL: JVC (509 N.12th Ave., 34266–8966), 1993; *The Lot of the Poet*. Arcadia, FL: JVC, 1994.

Related Web Site: www.teleport.com/~jaheriot/authors.htm.

n

NIKONOVA, Rea

(25 June 1942; b. Anna Alexandrovna Tarshis).

Nikonova is arguably the premier Russian avant-gardist of today, having created an enormous and varied body of innovative work, some of which clearly relates to the FUTURIST tradition, but much of which is entirely new. She received a musical education in Sverdlovsk, was one of the main organizers of the Uktus School there, and of the manuscript journal *Nomer*. She began to write seriously in 1959 and to paint in 1962, producing numerous pictures and drawings per day. With her husband SERGE SEGAY, she founded the group TRANSFUTURISTS and the journal *Transponans*. Mikonova has authored some of the earliest Russian examples of MINIMALIST and CONCEPTUALIST POETRY (mid-1960s). She has been particularly interested in exploring the possibilities of what she calls "vacuum poetry," where text or words are expected but absent. These can range from printed texts with absent components to performance pieces. Among her other inventions are vector poems (where arrows indicate movement), gesture poems (performed only with hand motions), architectural poems (treatments of pre-existing or new poems in which equivalent letters are lined up vertically in a grid with added vectors and coloration to create a unique visual artifact), and "Pliugms" (series of variations on several set phrases that employ all possible manipulations from shuffling of letters to the substitution of geometric figures for words). The last also exist in audiotaped versions.

Nikonova has written theater pieces, as well as prose and criticism. Among her largest projects to date have been a work called "Mutology," which describes several hundred kinds of pieces in which silence is the main ingredient, and the *System of Interrelated Styles with Illustrations and Commentaries for Them* in ten volumes, which is a compendium of virtually any imaginable literary technique, with examples provided mostly from her own works. Nikonova began an international mail-art journal, *Double* (1991—five issues to date) designed in the "rea-structure" used for some of the latter issues of *Transponans*, and in recent years she has contributed to numerous Western and Russian journals. Her first book to appear in Russia, however, came out only in 1997 in connection with her performance at the Sidur Museum in Moscow. Since 1998 she has lived in Germany.

—Gerald Janecek

OUTLINE OF STORIES

No. thoughts	MEN			No. thoughts	WOMEN		
	Nikolai	Aleksei	Fyodor		Anna	Maria	Larisa
1	Let's have a smoke	Let's	Me, too	1	He a-dores me	Me, too	Me, too
2	One more each	Friends	Enough	2	I love him so	I do, too	I do, too
3	Let's get a drink ?	Where?	Enough for me	3	I'm tired of him	Why	I am, too

Rea Nikonova. *Outline of Stories*. Translations by Gerard Janacek. Courtesy the author.

Writings: *Protsess nad shotlandtsem*. Trento: Edizioni Serge Sigej in Italia, 1989; *Architectural treatment of Daniel Plunkett's letter to Serge Segay*. Yeisk: Serge Segay, 1994; *Gesture Poem. terraz mowie* 10, n.d.; "Nemotologiia," sbornik *Move/Mova*, ed. Iurko Malinochka. Dnepropetrovskk: Artikl, 1996; *epigraf k Pustote. Vakuumnaia poeziia*. Moscow: Vadim Sidur Museum, 1997.

NIKOLAIS, Alwin

(25 November 1910–8 May 1993).

Though initially trained in dance, Nikolais worked as an accompanist for silent films and with marionettes before developing a dance theater in which the movements of individuals are subordinated to larger theatrical patterns established by scenery, costumes, and lights. His major works use all kinds of props, most of which function as dramatic extensions of the dancers' limbs, and brightly colored costumes that puff out from the natural lines of the body, to generate what he called a "direct kinetic state-ment." Technologically more advanced than other choreographers, Nikolais composed his own electronic scores (he was historically the first customer for a Moog synthesizer), and developed original theatrical illuminations, including portable lights carried by performers. Perhaps because his choreography as such was not as innovative as his spectacular stage images, a typical Nikolais piece tends to be experienced as a series of episodes that establish breathtaking new scenes for less engaging movements.

Selected Dances: *Kaleidoscope*, 1953, redone in 1956; *Forest of Three*, 1953; *Masks, Props and Mobiles*, 1953; *Prism*, 1956; *Allegory*, 1959; *Totem*, 1960; *Imago*, 1963; *Vaudeville of the Elements*, 1963; *The Mechanical Organ*, 1980; *Persons and Structures*, 1984; *Contact*, 1985.

Recordings: *Electronic Dance Music*. New York: Composers Recordings, 1993.

Writings: "Growth of a Theme" In *The Dance Has Many Faces*, 3d ed.; ed. Walter Sorrell. Pennington, NJ: A Cappella, 1992.

Interpretation: Siegel, Marcia B., ed. "Nik: A Documentary Study of Alwin Nikolais." *Dance Perspectives* 48 (Winter 1971).

NOGUCHI, Isamu

(17 November 1904– 30 December 1988).

Born in Los Angeles, the son of an American writer named Leonie Gilmore (1873–1933) and a Japanese poet who abandoned her before their son was born, Noguchi grew up in Japan and studied (as "Sam Gilmour") at an Indiana high school. After taking courses in art in both New York and Paris, where he befriended Constantin Brancusi, and then studied further in both China and Japan. It is often said that his art synthesized Eastern and Western influences more profoundly than anyone else's. His early stone and metal sculptures favored a post-Brancusi reduction of forms to simple, smooth surfaces that assumed organic qualities. Beginning in the 1940s, he sometimes placed electric lamps inside his works. Noguchi experimented with various base supports. In a fully productive long career, he also designed gardens, furniture, and lamps. His decors for ballets by George Balanchine (1904–83) and Martha Graham are remembered as among the best in that genre. Perhaps because Noguchi was moderately famous for so long, little was written about his later exhibitions. In Long Island City, just over the East River from Manhattan, he made his studio-home into a museum that survived his death.

Works: *Sphere Section*, 1927; *The Queen*, 1931; *Kouros*, 1945; *Nightland*, 1947; *The Family*, 1956–57; *Red Cubes*, 1968.

Books: *A Sculptor's World*. New York: Harper & Row, 1968; *Space of Akari and Stone*. San Francisco: Chronicle Books, 1986; *Essays and Conversations*. Ed. Diane Apostolos-Cappadona and Bruce Altshuler. New York: Abrams, 1994.

Exhibition Catalogs: Friedman, Martin. *Noguchi's Imaginary Landscapes*. Minneapolis, MN: Walker Art Center, 1978; Gordon, John. *Isamu Noguchi*. New York:

Isamu Noguchi, *Fishface*, 1945. Black slate, six elements, 30 X 14 1/2 X 8 3/4". Reproduced with permission of the Isamu Noguchi Foundation, Inc.

Whitney Museum, 1968; *The Isamu Noguchi Garden Museum*. New York: Abrams, 1987.

Web Site: www.noguchi.org

Interpretation: Altshuler, Bruce. *Isamu Noguchi*. New York: Abbeville, 1994; Ashton, Dore. *Noguchi: East and West*. Berkeley: University of California Press, 1992; Hunter, Sam. *Isamu Nogachi*. New York: Abbeville, 1978.

Documentation: Grove, Nancy, and Diane Botnick. *The Sculpture of Isamu Noguchi 1924–1979*. New York: Garland, 1980.

"NONSENSE"

(forever).

Actually there is no such thing, for any human creation that can be defined in one way, rather than another way, has by that fact of definition a certain amount of esthetic sense. Indeed, some of the most inspired avant-garde writing, from Edward Lear through *Finnegans Wake* to the present, has struck many who should have known better, if only as a measure of esthetic intelligence, as "nonsense." That means that the use of that word as derogatory criticism indicates that the writer/speaker is none too smart about contemporary art. The anthology of criticism noted below contains essays on Edward Lear, Lewis Carroll, the Marx Brothers, Flann O'Brien, and Stefen Themerson, as well as a useful bibliography.

Interpretation: Stewart, Susan. *Nonsense: Aspects of Intertextuality in Folklore and Literature* (1980). Baltmore: Johns Hopkins University, 1989; Tigges, Wim, ed. *Explorations in the Field of Nonsense*. Amsterdam, Holland: Rodopi, 1987.

NOUVEAU ROMAN

(c. 1958; "New French Novel").

European critics and cultural audiences are more predisposed than Americans to identify groups, whether they be composed of artists who consciously band together (e.g., Surrealists, Fluxus) or of artists whose works are perceived to be similar, perhaps because they arrived at roughly the same time (e.g., "Generation of '98"). The epithet "New French Novel" identifies several French fiction writers who first became prominent in the late 1950s, differences among them notwithstanding. Nathalie Sarraute (1900) portrays the subtleties of consciousness, very much in the tradition of Henry James. Claude Simon's (1913) specialty was capturing the mind's awareness of the dynamic relationship between memory and present experience, much as William Faulkner attempted to do. Michel Butor turned out to be the most innovative, exploring various formal alternatives for narrative. Alain Robbe-Grillet initially seemed the most original, his narrator assimilating a scene very much as a movie camera does, catching lots of details, regardless of their relevance; in contrast to Simon and Sarraute, both psychological novelists, Robbe-Grillet believes that surfaces reveal as much human truth as we are likely to know. His style is both original and haunting, although limited; *La Jalousie* (1957; *Jealousy*, 1959), as the most accessible of his novels, is the best introduction to his peculiar sensibility. After publishing *Pour un nouveau roman* (1963), which is filled with healthy, quotable, audacious prejudices, he became more active in filmmaking.

Interpretation: Mauriac, Claude. *The New Literature*. Trans. Samuel I. Stone. New York: Braziller, 1959; Mercier, Vivian. *Reader's Guide to the New Novel*. New York: Farrar, Straus, 1971; Sturrock, John. *The French New Novel*. New York: Oxford University Press, 1969.

NYMAN, Michael

(23 March 1944).

Given his current reputation as one of the best composers for feature-length films (including several directed by Peter Greenaway and Jane Campion's *The Piano* [1994]), do not forget that Nyman once composed austere innovative music, in addition to writing *Experimental Music: Cage and*

Beyond (1974), which is still a good survey of compositional INDETERMINACY and early MODULAR music. Perhaps the epitome of the former is a piece whose title has only numerals, *1–100* (1976). For "multiple pianos," this work is designed, in Nyman's words, to "demonstrate a curious confluence of free and fixed musical systems." Each pianist is instructed to read the same scored sequence of 100 sustained chords, moving ahead to the next chord only when the previous one decays; and as the chords move down the scale, their overall pitch gets increasingly lower. "The free(ish) process is designed to create *unwritten* harmonic (and rhythmic) divergences by overlapping and juxtaposition brought about by the fact that each individual reading of the chordal text is independent of those of the other players." *1–100* is a stunning piece, paradoxically brilliant in its austerity, perhaps gaining from the recollection of the far slicker music that Nyman has composed since.

Recordings: *1–100*. On *Piano Circus* (Argo 433522–2 ZH); *The Piano Concerto*. Kathryn Stott, soprano; Royal Liverpool Orchestra, cond. the composer; *MGV (Musique à Grand Vitesse),* Michael Nyman Band & Orchestra. London: Argo/Decca, 1994; *Quartets for Strings Nos. 1–3*, Balanescu Quartet (Argo 433093–2); *The Music of Michael Nyman* (with selections from his film scores); *The Essential Michael Nyman Band* (Argo 436820–2 ZH); *Noises, Sounds & Sweet Airs*. Ensemble Instrumental de Basse-Normandie. London: Argo/Decca (D 102265), 1995.

Books: *Experimental Music: Cage and Beyond*. New York: Schirmer, 1974.

Web Site: http://www.december.org/nyman.htm

n

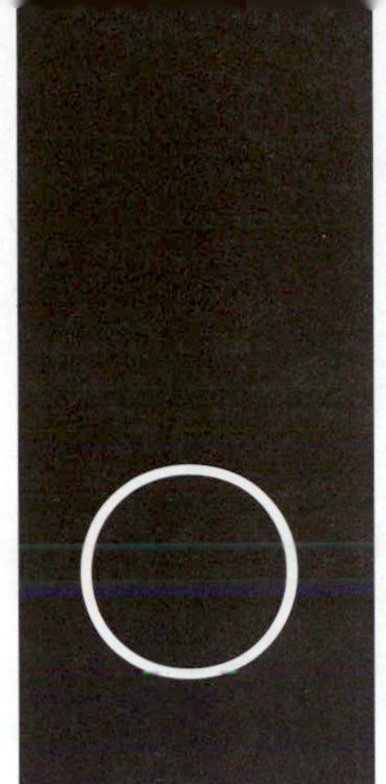

OATES, Joyce Carol

(16 June 1938).

Buried in Oates's bottomless bibliography are several genuinely experimental stories, most of them ironic take-offs on conventional forms, such as the contributors' notes in the back of a literary magazine. Quite wonderful, such fictions suggested a direction for Oates's work far more avant-garde and fundamentally more distinguished than those she has since pursued. As far as I can tell, these stories haven't been collected in any of her books, perhaps because they represent the kind of departures that an upwardly mobile, self-consciously "acceptable" novelist would find it opportune to discard.

Very Selected Writings: *Where Are You Going, Where Have You Been? Selected Early Stories.* Princeton, NJ: Ontario Review, 1993; "Notes on Contributors" (1971), in *Seduction & Other Stories.* Los Angeles: Black Sparrow, 1975.

Bibliography: Lercangé, Francine. *Joyce Carol Oates: An Annotated Bibliography*. New York: Garland, 1986.

Web Sites: http://storm.usfca.edu/~southerr/jco.html; http://www.ontarioreviewpress.com/ (Ontario Review Press site.)

A poster from an OBERIU theatricalized evening, *Three Left Hours*, presented on 24 January 1928. It involved poetry reading, staging of D. Kharms's play ***Elizaveta Bam,*** movie shorts presentation, and a jazz band playing in intermissions. From V.I.Erl' (St.Petersburg, Russia) private collection. ©V.I.Erl', 1994.

OBERIU

(late 1920s).

An acronym for "Union of the Real Art," this turned out to be the last important development of the Russian avant-garde in the first half of the twentieth century. A group of poets who came together in St. Petersburg in the late twenties, this consisted of Aleksandr Vvedensky, Daniil Kharms, Nikolai Zabolotsky, Igor Bakhterev and sometime collaborators Konstantin Vaginov and Nikolai Oleynikov.

While sharing ideals and goals of the most radical Futurists like KASIMIR MALEVICH and ALEXEI KRUCHONYKH, the OBERIU poets found their own direction exploring concepts of nonsense and the absurd. Their influences, besides Futurism, included "outsider" genres like Russian nonsense folklore, children's poems, poems of the mad, and even bad amateur poetry. Unlike ZAUM, OBERIU writing stayed mostly within the limits of Russian traditional vocabulary and meter, and yet was infinitely inventive in juxtaposing different semantic layers of language. Filled with dark humor of the most subversive kind, their works were particularly unacceptable to Stalin's regime.

Because few of OBERIU members' major works appeared in print in the late twenties, their greater immediate impact was in performance and theater. OBERIU plays like Vvedensky and Kharms's "All in Clocks My Mother Walks" (1926) or Kharms's "Elizaveta Bam" (1928) defined THEATER OF THE ABSURD well before this term was invented.

Though most of the OBERIU poets were arrested and prosecuted by 1931, individual members continued to create innovative works well into the late 1930s, before perishing in the Soviet Gulags. Their works were rediscovered by the younger generation of Russian poets in the sixties, in large part thanks to the only surviving OBERIU member, Igor Bakhterev (b. 1907).

—Igor Satanovsky

Selected Works: Meylakh, B., and V. I. Erl', eds. *Poety Gruppy "OBERIU."* St. Petersburg: Sovetskiy Pisatel', 1994 (in Russian); Gibian, George, ed. and trans. *Russia's Lost Literature of the Absurd, A Literary Discovery: Selected Works of Daniil Kharms and Alexander Vvedensky*. Ithaca & London: Cornell University Press, 1971.

O'BRIEN, Flann

(5 October 1911–1 April 1966; b. Brian O'Nolan; aka Myles na Copaleen, Brian O Nuallain).

As a civil servant who wrote a newspaper column under the name Myles na Copaleen, Brian O'Nolan needed yet another pseudonym for his fiction, and so chose Flann O'Brien. His clever masterpiece is *At Swim-Two-Birds* (1939), a novel about an author whose characters turn against him by writing a novel about him. Because the initial narrator is a student writing a book, *At Swim-Two-Birds* has three beginnings and three endings. The extremely witty writing includes this interrogation of a cow: "State your name. . . . /That is a thing I have never attained, replied the cow. Her voice was low and guttural and of a quality not normally associated with the female mammalia." This novel initially failed in the marketplace, but became a genuine underground classic that is reissued from time to time. Its sequel, written around the same time, was posthumously published as *The Third Policeman* (1967). About another novel, *The Dalkey Archive* (1964), HUGH KENNER writes: "Neither James Joyce nor he ever surpassed the nested ingenuity of its contrivances, the insidious taut language to make everything at all seem plausible, or the unforced beauty of such episodes as our man's dialogue with his soul, when, not knowing he's already dead, he supposes he's about to be hanged." O'Brien also published another novel entirely in Gaelic. Some would nominate him to be the final wing of the Irish trinity of JAMES JOYCE and SAMUEL BECKETT. It is said that Myles na sCopaleen's newspaper column had a stylistic distinction similar to, though greater than, Art Buchwald's.

Works: At *Swim-Two-Birds* (1939). Normal, IL: Dalkey Archive, 1998; *The Third Policeman*. London: MacGibbon & Kee, 1967; *The Dalkey Archive*. London: MacGibbon & Kee, 1964.

Anthologies: Jones, Stephen, ed. A *Flann O'Brien Reader*. New York: Viking, 1973; O'Brien, Flann. *The Best of Myles: A Selection from "Cruiskeen Lawn."* Ed. Kevin O'Nolan. London: Grafton, 1987.

Biography: Cronin, Anthony. *No Laughing Matter: The Life & Times of Flann O'Brien*, New York: Fromm Int'l., 1998.

Interpretation: Clissmann, Anne. *Flann O'Brien: A Critical Introduction to his Writings*. Dublin, Ireland: Gill & Macmillan, 1975; Shea, Thomas. *Flann O'Brien's Exorbitant Novels*. Lewisburg, PA: Bucknell University Presss, 1992.

OCKERSE, Tom

(20 April 1940).

Born Dutch, Ockerse came to America in the late 1950s and was initially active among those producing VISUAL POETRY at Indiana University in the middle 1960s. Trained in visual art, he differed from other early visual poets in using colors, at the same time respecting the literary convention of eight and one-half inch by eleven inch sheets of paper. One distinguishing mark of his first major collection, the self-published T. O. P. (or Tom Ockerse Project; 1970), is design solutions so various that the book as a whole lacks stylistic character. However, in his works that are most frequently reproduced elsewhere, there is a distinct signature reflecting verbal-visual elegance and CONSTRUCTIVIST simplicity.

Around this time, Ockerse also produced *The A–Z Book* (1970), an awesomely inventive alphabet, a foot square, in which he used die-cutting to produce a sequence of pages in which the portion cut away from a foreground page belongs to the letter behind it.

Works: *The A–Z Book*. New York: Colorcraft-Brussel, 1970; *T. O. P.* Bloomington, IN: Self-published (now 37 Woodbury, Providence, RI 02906), 1970; *Documentracings: Printed Matter*. Providence, RI: Tom Ockerse, 1973; *POST ART*. Providence, RI: Tom Ockerse, 1978; *Son of Fury: A Documentracing*. Providence, RI: Tom Ockerse, 1973; *Time: A Documentracing*. Providence, RI: Tom Ockerse, 1973; *TV Documentracing*. Providence, RI: Tom Ockerse, 1973.

O'DOHERTY, Brian C.

(1934).

Born in Ireland, educated in England, O'Doherty began as an art critic and has worked primarily as an administrator, most recently for the NATIONAL ENDOWMENT FOR THE ARTS as the director of the esthetically most progressive department, apparently with political skill, because little, if any, of the negative attention aimed at the NEA mentioned him. As an artist customarily exhibiting under the name Patrick Ireland, he has realized a highly original, rigorously relational CONSTRUCTIVISM, at times in drawings on paper, at other times with installations of taut strings stretched to the edges of a space, interacting in geometric ways. As elaborate investigations of the new circumstances of art galleries and museums, the essays he collected as *Inside the White Cube* are true avant-garde criticism.

Writings: *Object and Idea*. New York: Simon & Schuster, 1967; *Museums in Crisis*. New York: Braziller, 1972; *The Voice and the Myth*. New York: Random House, 1972; *Inside the White Cube*. San Francisco: Lapis, 1986.

Exhibition Catalog: *Patrick Ireland: labyrinths, language, pyramids, and related acts*. Curated by Russell Panczenko. Madison: Elvehjem Museum of Art, University of Wisconsin Press, 1993.

O'HARA, Frank

(27 June 1926–25 July 1966).

A man not just of letters but of the visual arts, who curated exhibitions in addition to publishing poems and writing plays, Frank O'Hara is often portrayed as the American semblance of Guillaume Apollinaire, who likewise died too young. However, this claim doesn't hold. As a poet, O'Hara was associated with the "New York School," whose masters were JOHN ASHBERY and KENNETH KOCH, both of whom were stronger poets. As a writer on visual art, O'Hara mastered the sort of obscure enthusiasm that acceptably fills exhibition fliers but doesn't survive well in books. Artists predisposed to flatter his power as a curator at the Museum of Modern Art could praise his poetry, most of which was reportedly written in spare moments and published in first draft. (His celebrity set a bad example for younger writers predisposed to be off-handed.) However,

O'Hara wrote, as far as I can tell, only one major poem, "In Memory of My Feelings." The title of an early collection, it became the token poem that was inevitably cited whenever anyone was asked to confirm O'Hara's legitimacy as a poet. For all of O'Hara's personal charm, he didn't write essays as strong or influential as the best of Apollinaire and didn't produce poems as innovative as, say, Apollinaire's "Zone." His few plays now seem embedded in the 1950s. The first biography of O'Hara repeats the Apollinaire myth without confirming it, suggesting, instead of an innovative force, the image of a hanger-on.

Selected Books: *The Collected Poems of Frank O'Hara*. Ed. Donald Allen. New York: Knopf, 1971; *The Selected Poems of Frank O'Hara*. Ed. Donald Allen. New York: Knopf, 1974; *Art Chronicles 1954–66*. New York: Braziller, 1975; *Amorous Nightmares of Delay: Selected Plays*. Baltimore: Johns Hopkins University Press, 1997; *What's With Modern Art*. New York: Blue Press, 1999.

Interpretation: Lehman, David. *The Last Avant-Garde*. New York: Doubleday, 1998; Perloff, Marjorie. *Frank O'Hara: Poet Among Painters* (1977). Chicago: University of Chicago Press, 1998.

Biography: Gooch, Brad. *City Poet: The Life and Times of Frank O'Hara*. New York: Knopf, 1993.

OHNO, Kazuo

(27 October 1906).

Considered to be the soul and cofounder of BUTOH, Ohno began dance studies with Baku Ishii (1886–1962) in 1933 and later studied with Takaya Eguchi (1900–1977), who had been a pupil of the German EXPRESSIONIST dancer MARY WIGMAN. In 1977, Ohno created and performed *Admiring La Argentina*, in which, dressed in a flowing gown, he impersonated and honored the Spanish dancer Antonia Merce (1888–1936), whose performances had inspired Ohno early in his career. Ohno's son, Yoshita, is also a Butoh performer.

—Katy Matheson

Works: Ohno, Kazuo. *Admiring La Argentina*, 1977.

Documentary Film: Sempel, Peter. *Just Visiting This Planet*. Hamburg, Germany: Peter Sempel, 1991.

O'KEEFFE, Georgia

(15 November 1887–6 March 1986).

Apparently learning from photography about the esthetic advantages of enlargement, O'Keeffe discovered formal qualities and radiant colors in the extremely close observations of biomorphic objects, such as flowers, plants, and pelvic bones. O'Keeffe often painted similar objects many times over, in series. Moving to rural New Mexico in the late 1940s, she again echoed photography by using the contrary strategy of painting broad expanses in a compressed scale. These paintings in turn echo her remarkably stark and lyrical 1920s horizontal views of New York. The thin paint of her early watercolors presages the innovations of MORRIS LOUIS, among others. O'Keeffe lived long enough to become a feminist exemplar whose celebrity could support a commercial publisher releasing a strong collection of images accompanied by her writings.

Selected Paintings: *59th Street Studio*, 1919; *Inside Red*, 1919; *Petunia*, 1924; *City Night*, 1926; *Black Cross, New Mexico*, 1929.

Books: *Georgia O'Keeffe*. New York: Studio-Viking, 1976.

Anthology: Lane, James W. *The Work of Georgia O'Keeffe: A Portfolio of Twelve Paintings*. New York: Knight, 1937; Callaway, Nicolas. *One Hundred Flowers*. New York: Knopf, 1990; Benke, Britta. *Georgia O'Keeffe 1887–1986: Flowers in the Desert*. Köln: Taschen, 1995.

Exhibition Catalog: *Alfred Stieglitz Presents Fifty-One Recent Pictures: Oils, Watercolors, Pastels, and Drawings by Georgia O'Keeffe, American*. New York: Anderson, 1924; *Georgia O'Keeffe: Exhibition of Oils and Pastels*. New York: American Place, 1939. (This includes the autobiographical "About Myself."); Arrowsmith, Alexandra, and Thomas West, eds. *Two Lives: Georgia O'Keeffe and Alfred Stieglitz*. New York: HarperCollins/Callaway, 1992; Goodrich, Lloyd, and Doris Bry. *O'Keeffe*. New York: Whitney Museum, 1970; Rich, Daniel Catton. *Georgia O'Keeffe*. Chicago: The Art Institute, 1943; *Georgia O'Keeffe: Forty Years of Her Art*. Worcester, MA: Worcester Art Museum, 1960; Wilder, Mitchell, ed. *Georgia O'Keeffe*. Ft. Worth, TX: Amon Carter Museum, 1966; *Georgia O'Keeffe: Works on Paper*. Santa Fe, NM: Museum of University of New Mexico, 1985.

Biography: Lisle, Laurie. *Portrait of an Artist: Biography of Georgia O'Keeffe* (1980). New York: Washington Square Press, 1997; Pollitzer, Anna. *A Woman on Paper: Georgia O'Keeffe*. New York: Simon & Schuster, 1988; Peters, Sarah Whitaker, *Becoming O'Keeffe: The Early Years*. New York: Abbeville, 1991; Eldredge, Charles E. *Georgia O'Keeffe: American and Modern*. New Haven: Yale University Press, 1993; Udall, Sharyn. *O'Keeffe in Texas*. New York: Abrams, 1992; Dijksra, Bram. *O'Keeffe and the Eros of Place*. Princeton: Princeton University Press, 1998; Robinson, Roxana. *Georgia O'Keeffe: A Life* (1989). Hanover, NH: University Press of New England, 1999.

Web Site: http://www.okeeffemuseum.org/

Interpretation: Buckley, Chris. *Blossoms and Bones: On the Life and Work of Georgia O'Keeffe*. Nashville, TN: Vanderbilt University Press, 1989; Lynes, Barbara Buhler. *O'Keeffe, Stieglitz, and the Critics, 1916–1929*. Chicago: University of Chicago Press, 1989.

OLDENBURG, Claes

(28 January 1929).

Born in Sweden, raised in Chicago as the son of a Swedish diplomat, educated in English literature at Yale, Oldenburg mounted a 1959 exhibition of sculpture made from urban junk and soon afterward created his first truly memorable works: semblances of such common objects as ice-cream cones, hamburgers both with and without an accompanying pickle, cigarette ends, pastries, clothespins, toasters,

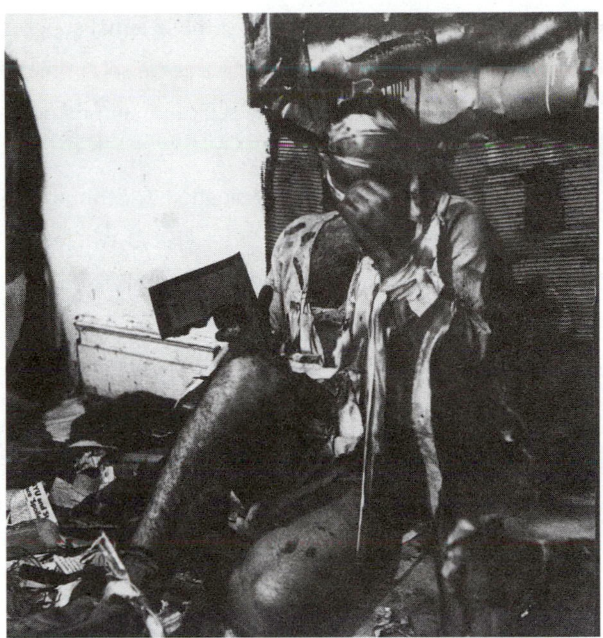

Claes Oldenburg in *Ray Gun*. Judson Memorial Church, 1 March 1960. Photograph © Fred W. McDarrah.

telephones, plumbing pipes, and so forth. Compared to their models, his fabrications are usually exaggerated in size, distorted in detail, and/or dog-eared in texture. By such transformations, these pedestal-less sculptures usually gained, or accentuated, several other, less obvious resonances, most of them archetypal or sexual in theme, in the latter respect echoing Francis Picabia. Epitomizing Pop Art, Oldenburg's *Ice Cream Cone* (1962) is indubitably phallic; *Soft Wall Switches* (1964) looks like a pair of nipples; the soft *Giant Hamburger* (1963), several feet across, is distinctly vaginal; and so forth. "Appearances are not what counts," he once wrote, "it is the forms that count."

After 1962, Oldenburg's strategy of ironic displacement took another elaborate form in his "soft" sculpture, in which semblances of originally hard objects are fabricated in slick-surfaced, nonrigid materials different from the traditional sculptural staples. These representations of a toilet, a bathtub, a typewriter, and a drum set are so flabby that they behave contrary to the original object's nature and thus customarily need some external support for effective display. They also create a perversely ironic, if not ghostly, relation between the sculpture and its original model.

Thanks to an adventurous imagination, Oldenburg has worked in various media. *The Store* (1962) was a real Lower East Side store-front filled with artistically fabricated but faintly representational (storelike) objects. Because regular hours were kept, people could browse through the place and even purchase objects, so that *The Store* was indeed an authentic store, but it was also an artistically defined space, an ENVIRONMENT, wholly in Oldenburg's early sixties style of colorful but ironic renditions of seedy objects. As an ingenious writer, Oldenburg authored *Store Days* (1967), a large-format, glossy book that contains a disconnected collection of prose and pictures as miscellaneous in form as the stuff of his store: historical data, replicas of important printed materials (such as a business card), sketches, price lists for the objects, photographs, scripts for his staged performances, various recipes, esthetic statements, parodies, declarations, and even an occasional aphorism (which may not be entirely serious). The result is an original open-ended potpourri of bookish materials that, unlike a conventional artist's manifesto, "explains" Oldenburg's Environmental art less by declarative statements than by implied resemblances. He has also published books of his theatrical scripts, some of which were staged as MIXED-MEANS performance.

Selected Sculptures: *Ice Cream Cone*, 1962; *The Store*, 1962; *Giant Hamburger*, 1963; *Soft Wall Switches*, 1964; *Profile Airflow*, 1969; *Giant Trowel*, 1976.

Books: *Store Days*. New York: Something Else Press, 1967; *Proposals for Monuments and Buildings*. Chicago: Big Table, 1969; *Raw Notes*. Halifax, NS: Nova Scotia College of Art & Design, 1973; *Photo Log/Press Log May 1974–August 1976*. 2 vols. Stuttgart & London: Hansjörg Mayer, 1976.

Exhibition Catalogs: Rose, Barbara. *Claes Oldenburg*. New York: MoMA, 1969; Celant, Germano, and Mark Rosenthal, et al. *Claes Oldenberg: An Anthology*. New York: Guggenheim Museum, 1995.

Interpretation: Johnson, Ellen. *Claes Oldenburg*. Baltimore: Penguin, 1971; Kostelanetz, Richard. "Claes Oldenburg." In *The Theatre of Mixed Means* (1968). New York: Archae, 1980.

Web Page: http://www.fi.muni.cz/~toms/PopArt/Biographies/oldenburg.html.ISO-8859–1

Documentation: Baro, Gene. *Claes Oldenberg: Drawings and Prints*. London & New York: Chelsea House-Paul Bianchini, 1969; Axsom, Richard H., and David Platzker. *Printed Stuff: A Catalogue Raisonné 1958–1996*. New York: Hudson Hills, 1997; Saroff, Raymond. *Claes Oldenburg's Store Days Happenings 1962* [video]. Kingston, NY: McPherson, 1995; Platzker, David. *Claes Oldenburg: Multiples in Retrospect 1964–1990 with the Soap at Baton Rouge*. Essay by Thomas Lawson. Cincinnati, OH: Carl Solway, 1991; Van Bruggen, Coosje. *Large-Scale Projects*. New York: Monacelli, 1994.

OLIVEROS, Pauline

(30 May 1932).

Long an academic, Oliveros threw up, as the British would say, a full professorship at the University of California to become an itinerant musician, working with a wealth of superficially divergent ideas, including feminist consciousness, improvisation, meditative experience, and possibilities for playing the accordion (which is her instrument of virtuosity). She writes that "All of my work emphasizes attentional strategies, musicianship, and improvisational skills." Oliveros's most stunning recordings were produced in reverberant caves with the Deep Listening Band (mostly the trombonist Stuart Dempster). Through the Oliveros Foundation (156 Hunter Street, Kingston, NY 12401), she has also organized the independent distribution of avant-garde music.

Compositions: *Sound Patterns*, for Chorus, 1961; *Double Basses at 20 Paces*, theatre piece for 2 basses, their seconds, and a referee with slide and tape, 1968; *Meditations on the Points of the Compass*, for chorus, 1970; *Sonic Meditations*, for voices and instruments, 1971; *Music for Stacked Deck*, for four players, 1979; *The Wanderer*, for accordian ensemble and percussion, 1982; *Gathering Together*, for piano, and 8 hands, 1983; *Portraits*, for solo or any ensemble, 1987.

Books and CD: *The Roots of the Moment*. Jersey City, NJ: Drogue (111 1st Street, 07302), 1998.

Recordings: *Crone Music*. New York: Lovely Music, 1990; *In Memoriam Mr. Whitney*, for accordion, voice, and vocal ensemble. New York: Mode, 1994; *Deep Listening*, with Stuart Dempster and Paniotis. Albany, CA: New Albion, 1989; *Alien Bog, Beautiful Soop*, Pogus 1998.

Website: www.artswire.org/newmusicnet/index.html

Interpretation: Gunden, Heidi van. *The Music of Pauline Oliveros*. Metuchen, NJ: Scarecrow, 1983.

OLSON, Charles

(27 December 1910–10 January 1970).

Olson was an American poet whose lifework was his *Maximus* poems, the title reflecting his goal of creating a MAXIMAL literary art. Like EZRA POUND in his *Cantos* or LOUIS ZUKOFSKY in his *A*, Olson attempted to incorporate his entire life experience and a fair amount of literary history into the framework of a single, ever-expanding megapoem. Not unlike those other poets, Olson was doomed to failure, creating an open-ended work that could never be satisfactorily completed. He differed from other writers of his generation in viewing the page as a field, upon which he could spread his words. This notion, as well as his experimental typography, influenced later poets. He also wrote criticism distinguished for luminous sentences.

—with Richard Carlin

Books: *The Maximus Poems*. Berkeley: University of California Press, 1986; *The Post Office: A Memoir of His Father*. San Francisco: Grey Fox, 1966; *The Human Universe and Other Essays*. New York: Grove, 1967; *The Fiery Hunt and Other Plays*. Bolinas, CA: Four Seasons, 1977; *Muthlogies*. 2 Vols. Bolinas, CA: Four Seasons, 1978, 1979; *Collected Prose*. Ed. Donald Allen. Berkeley: University of California Press, 1997; *Collected Poems of Charles Olson: Excluding the Maximus Poems*. Ed. George Butterick. Berkeley: University of California Press, 1997; *Call Me Ishmael* (1939). Baltimore: Johns Hopkins University Press, 1997.

Recordings: *Reads from the Maximus Poems*. New York: Folkways 9738, c. 1958.

Biography: Clark, Tom. *Charles Olson: The Allegory of a Poet's Life*. New York: Norton, 1991; Maud, Ralph. *Charles Olson's Reading: A Biography*. Carbondale: S. Illinois University Press, 1996.

Interpretation: Butterick, George F. *Guide to the Maximus Poems*. Berkeley: University of California Press, 1981; Maud, Ralph. *What Does Not Change: The Significance of Charles Olson's "The Kingfishers."* Madison, NJ: Fairleigh Dickinson University Press, 1998; Paul, Sherman. *Olson's Push: Origin, Black Mountain, and Recent American Poetry*. Baton Rouge: Louisiana State University Press, 1978; Sitney, P. Adams. "Out via Nothing: Olson's Genealogy of the Proper Poem," *Modernist Montage*. New York: Columbia University Press, 1990.

ONO, Yoko

(18 February 1933).

Born in Japan, she came of age in upper-middle-class America; and though she has returned to Japan for visits and speaks English with a Japanese accent, she has been an American CONCEPTUAL artist who gained international celebrity from her 1969 marriage to the pop singer-songwriter JOHN LENNON. Ono's strongest avant-garde works are the performance texts collected in her book *Grapefruit* (1964). For "Beat Piece" (1965), the entire instruction is

Yoko Ono performing *Cut Piece* at the Avant-Garde Festival, Central Park, 9 September 1966. Photograph © Fred W. McDarrah.

"Listen to a heartbeat." Her "Cut Piece" requires the performer, usually herself, to come on the stage and sit down, "placing a pair of scissors in front of her and asking the audience to come up on the stage, one by one, and cut a portion of her clothing (anywhere they like) and take it." (One charm of this piece is that the spectator courts as much embarrassment as the performer-author.) Ono's films customarily have the same audacious image repeated to excess (e.g., human butts). She also collaborated with Lennon on musical works in which her highly expressionist singing, part chanting and part screaming, continues to excessive duration (and for that reason influenced PUNK musicians in the mid–1970s). It is unfortunate that, for too many, Ono will never be more than a famous pop singer's widow.

Books: *Grapefruit* (1964). New York: Simon & Schuster, 1970; *Instruction Painting*. New York: Weatherhill, 1995.

Recordings: *Yoko Ono & The Plastic Ono Band* (1970). Ryko, 1997; *Fly* (1971). Ryko, 1997; *Onobox*. Lee's Wharf, MA: Rykodisc, 1992.

Interview: In Melody Sumner, et al., eds. *The Guests Go into Supper*. San Francisco: Burning Books, 1986.

Exhibition Catalog: Haskell, Barbara, and John G. Hanhardt. *Yoko Ono: Objects, Films*. New York: Whitney Museum, 1989.

Web Sites: http://www.cam.org/~rjoly/yoko/onoweb.html; www.instantkarma.com (online fan magazine for John Lennon and Yoko Ono).

THE OPEN THEATRE

(1963–1973).

Founded by Joseph Chaikin (1935), a charismatic antileader who had previously worked with the LIVING THEATRE, the Open Theatre began with plays, such as Jean-Claude van Itallie's *America Hurrah* (1966), before focusing upon predominantly physical performances that were collectively developed. (As Robert Pasolli explained, "The writer is defined not by the fact that he has written a script on which the work is based . . . but on the fact that he *will* write a script related to the work which the troupe is improvising.") The most memorable production was *Terminal* (1969), which opens with a verbal fugue that repeats the word "dead" over and over until it becomes percussive sound; its subject (strange for a company so young) is attitudes about death. A horrifying portrayal of embalming is repeated, as visual fugues complement verbal fugues. The principal props are rolling platforms of various heights and large pieces of plywood, both props serving as beds, embalming tables, and graves. The play is divided into sections, each with its own title, which are announced by the performers: "The Calling Up of the Dead"; "The Last Biological Rites"; and "The Dying Imagine Their Judgment." *Terminal* ends in just over an hour with all the performers crawling along the floor, their voices becoming progressively more incoherent. The group's final production, *Nightwalk* (1973), investigated sleep. Some of its members formed a new group called the Talking Band.

Writings: Chaiken, Joseph. *The Presence of the Actor*. New York: Theater Communications Group, 1991.

Interpretation: Pasolli, Robert. *A Book on the Open Theatre*. Indianapolis, IN: Bobbs Merrill, 1970; Shank, Theodore. *American Alternative Theatre*. New York: Grove, 1982.

OPTICAL ART (aka Op Art)

See **KINETIC ART**; **RILEY, Bridget**; **VASARELY, Victor**.

O'ROURKE, P.J.

(14 November 1947; b. Patrick Jake O'R.).

What is *he* doing here, I can hear you say. Well, in 1975 he published (perhaps self-published under an otherwise unfamiliar imprint) a loose-leaf collection of TYPEWRITER POEMS printed on legal-size (eight and one-half inch by fourteen inch) pages, and dedicated to the actress Shelly Plimpton. They are carefully wrought, witty, and at times delicate, especially in the opening dedication piece, which is as good as any typewriter poem done anywhere. O'Rourke subsequently worked as a columnist for *The National Lampoon* and *Rolling Stone*, among other mass magazines, contributing witty, anti-liberal, political criticism that, while esthetically less distinguished and certainly less avant-garde, has been more remunerative, America being America. In this respect, his career resembles that of Hendrik Hertzberg (1940), who coauthored *One Million* (1970), an imaginatively designed BOOK-ART essay on size and number, before he became a speechwriter for Jimmy Carter and an editor at, successively, *The New Republic* and *The New Yorker*. (And, wonders of wonders, *One Million* was reprinted two decades later to even less acclaim the second time around, the author's greater presence notwithstanding, to no surprise.)

Works: *Our Friend the Vowel*. Aspers, PA: Stone House, 1975; Hertzberg, Hendrik. *One Million* (1970). New York: Times, 1993.

Web Site: http://www.pjorourke.com/index2.html

OROZCO, José Clemente

(23 November 1883–7 September 1949).

A one-armed painter who identified passionately with the Mexican Revolution of 1910, Orozco developed a highly stylized representational art that rendered Mexican people at once simply and heroically, especially rural working people, *campesinos*, who were the Revolution's heroes. A principal Mexican influence on him and the other muralists was the engraver Jose Guadalupe Posada (1852–1913), whose last great subject was the Mexican Revolution.

Though Orozco made paintings, his most effective surface was the extended mural. Most of these survive not in art museums but in public buildings throughout Mexico. Among the most successful, dating from the late 1930s, are those in the former chapel of the Hospicio Cabañas in Guadalajara, the capital of the Jalisco state. The Mexican art historian Justino Fernandez wrote in 1961 that the Orozco murals at Dartmouth College from the early 1930s are "the most important contemporary mural paintings in the United States," incidentally marking "a beginning of a new and splendid period in Orozco's work." Since he refused to join the Communist party, which had captured his muralist colleague DIEGO RIVERA, Orozco was in his own lifetime often dismissed as a "bourgeois skeptic." About the Mexican Revolution he reportedly wrote, "To me the Revolution was the gayest and most diverting of carnivals."

Orozco's work had far more presence and influence in the States in the 1930s than now, especially upon those coming of age at the time, such as JACKSON POLLOCK. In Orozco's style of representing people and the world I find an esthetic precusor for the "magic realism" commonly associated with a later generation of Latin American writers, beginning with Gabriel García Márquez (1928), a Colombian who, incidentally, lives mostly not in his native country but in Mexico.

Works: *Omniscience*, 1925; *The Trench*, 1926; *Friar and the Indian*, 1926; *The Strike*, 1926; *Prometheus*, 1930; *Catharsis*, 1934; *Creative Man*, 1936; *People and its False Leaders*, 1936; *Hidalgo and National Independence*, 1937–38; *Allegory of Mexico*, 1940; *Dive Bomber*, 1940; *National Allegory*, 1947–48.

Autobiography: Orozco, Jose Clemente. *An Autobiography*. Trans. John Palmer Leeper. Austin: University of Texas Press, 1962; Orozco, José Clemente. *The Artist in New York*. Austin: University of Texas Press, 1974.

Interpretation: Charlot, Jean. *The Mexican Mural Renaissance 1920–1925*. New Haven: Yale University Press, 1967; Fernandez, Justino. *A Guide to Mexican Art* (1961). Trans. Joshua C. Taylor. Chicago: University of Chicago Press, 1969; Hulburt, Laurence. *The Mexican Muralist Movement in the United States*. Albuquerque: University of New Mexico Press, 1989; Reed, Alma. *The Mexican Muralists*. New York: Crown, 1960; Rochfort, Desmond. *Mexican Muralists: Orozco, Rivera, Siqueiros*. New York: Universe, 1994; Rodriguez, Antonio. *A History of Mexican Mural Painting*. New York: Putnam, 1969.

Documentation: Hopkins, Jon H. *Orozco: A Catalog of His Graphic Work*. Flagstaff: N. Arizona, 1967.

OTTINGER, Ulrike

(1942).

Initially a visual artist who became a filmmaker without formal training (which is far less available in Germany than, say, in the U.S.), Ottinger has become the writer, producer, director, and cinematographer of most of her films, which are sometimes renowned for remarkable lighting and color. One recurring theme in her work is rebellion against alienated forms of living and working. One of her early feature-length films, *Madame X—Eine absolute Herrscherin* (1977, 141 minutes), portrays the lesbian matriarchy of a pirate queen named Madame X, who rules in the China Sea. Thanks in part to the quality of support available in Germany, Ottinger has been able to work at extended lengths. *The Image of Dorian Gray in the Yellow Press* (1984), runs 150 minutes; *Johanna D'Arc of Mongolia* (1989), 165 minutes; and *Exile Shanghai* (1997), about Jewish immigration to the Chinese mainland during World War II, a whopping 275 minutes. Ottinger seems at times the female semblance of another German director, only a few years her elder, who is likewise predisposed to Wagnerian durations: Hans Jürgen Syberberg (1936). Thanks again to support of adventurous excellence typical of Germany, all of Ottinger's distinctly noncommercial films are available with English subtitles. Were she forced to leave Germany, as an earlier generation of major directors were, it is doubtful that she would ever find employment in America.

Other films: *Laokoon und Söhne/Laocoon and Sons*, 1972–73; *Die Betönung der blauen Matrosen/The Bewichment of Drunken Sailors*, 1975; *Bildnis einer Trinkerin—aller jamais retour/Portrait of a Female Alcoholic—Ticket of No Return*, 1979; *Freak Orlando: Kleines Welttheater in fünf Episoden/Freak Orlando: Small Theatre of the World in Five Episodes*, 1981; *China—Die Kunst—Her Alltag/China—The Arts—Everyday Life*, 1985.

Interpretation: Kuhn, Annette, with Susanna Radstone, eds. *The Women's Companion to International Film*. London: Virago, 1990.

OULIPO

Founded on 24 November 1960 by RAYMOND QUENEAU and François Le Lionnais (1901–84), this Parisian-based group began with the intention of basing experimental writing on mathematics. Its name is an acronym for Ouvroir de Littérature Potentielle (Workshop for Potential Literature). Once others came aboard, the group's theme became the use, at times the invention, of highly restrictive literary structures. According to HARRY MATHEWS, its principal American participant, "The difference between constrictive and ordinary forms (such as rhyme and meter) is essentially one of degree." Jean Lescure (1912) took texts written by someone else and by rigorous methods substituted, say, each noun with the seventh noun to appear after it in a common dictionary. Others wrote "recurrent literature," as they called it, which was defined as "any text that contains, explicitly or implicitly, generative rules that invite the reader (or the teller, or the singer) to pursue the production of the text to infinity (or until the exhaustion of interest or attention)." One associate, by trade a professor of mathematics, wrote a sober analysis of "Mathematics in the Method of Raymond Queneau."

No other literary group, in any language known to me, has produced quite so many extreme innovations; and perhaps because Oulipo does not distinguish among members living and dead, its influence continues to grow. Among the contributors to its first major self-anthology, *Oulipo, la littérature potentielle* (1973), were Queneau, GEORGES PEREC, Jean Queval (1913–90), Marcel Bénabou (1939), Jacques Roubaud (1932), and Noel Arnaud (1919), all of whom are, by any measure, consequential experimental authors. MARCEL DUCHAMP joined Oulipo in 1962, while Oskar Pastior (1927), a German-speaking Rumanian long resident in Berlin, joined as recently as 1995. In the American translation of much of this initial anthology is a new name: Italo Calvino (1923–85), whose celebrity made his association untypical and finally marginal. The *Oulipo Compendium* (1998) is a witty and masterful guide both to the entire movement and its constituents. I wanted to spell it OuLiPo, acknowledging the component words, but Mathews himself insisted that I do otherwise.

Translations into English: Bénabou, Marcel. *Why I Have Not Written Any of My Books*. Trans. David Kornacker. Lincoln: University of Nebraska Press, 1997; *Jacob, Ménahem, and Mimoun: A Family Epic*. Trans. Steven Rendall. Lincoln: University of Nebraska Press, 1998; Caradec, François. *Le Pétomane*. London: Souvenir, 1967; Fournel, Paul. *Little Girls Breathe the Same Air As We Do*. Trans. Lee Sahnestock. New York: Braziller, 1979; Pastior, Oskar. *Poempoems*. London: Atlas Press (BCM, England WC1N 3XX), 1990; Perec, Georges. *A Void* (*La Disparition*). Trans. Gilbert Adair. New York: HarperCollins, 1994; Roubaud, Jacques. *Our Beautiful Heroine*. Trans. David Kornacker. Woodstock, New York: Overlook, 1987; *The Great Fire of London* (1989). Trans. Dominic Di Bernardi. Normal, IL: Dalkey Archive, 1991; *The Plurality of Worlds of Lewis*. Trans. Rosmarie Waldrop. Normal, IL: Dalkey Archive, 1995.

Anthologies: Oulipo. *La littérature potentielle*. Paris, France: Gallimard, 1973; Matte, Warren F., Jr., ed. *Oulipo: A Primer of Potential Literature* (1986). Normal, IL: Dalkey Archive, 1998; *Oulipo Compendium*. Compiled Harry Mathews and Alastair Brotchie. London: Atlas, (BCM, England WC1N 3XX), 1998; *Oulipo Laboratory. Texts from Bibliothèque Oulipiènne*. Trans. Harry Mathews and Ian White. London: Atlas, 1995.

Web Site: http://jhunix.hcf.jhu.edu/~deschene/phosphor.html

Interpretation: Mathews, Harry. "Vanishing Point [G. Perec and the Oulipo]." In *The Avant-Garde Tradition in Literature*, ed. Richard Kostelanetz. Buffalo, New York: Prometheus, 1982.

OUTSIDER ART

(c. 1995).

This term has become popular among "insiders"—museum curators, academics, critics, and other middle-class folks—to describe art created by people traditionally "outside" the accepted museum categories: inmates; drug users; folk artists; handicapped people, etc. It all smacks of a certain smug complacency, an "aren't they quaint" anthropology that used to infect academic thought when it came to studying tribes people of the lower Congo. Exhibits of outsider art, in an attempt to be all-inclusive, often end up looking like a rummage sale gone wrong, with everything from primitive watercolors to hand-stitched socks showing scenes from the Bible. And, since it has become popular, many groups are clamoring to get inside the "outside" status: women; gays; African-Americans; and other ethnics all say "we're outsiders, too," in an effort to garner funding, recognition, and academic cachet for their works (which might otherwise be judged against some other standards, such as quality or innovation). Like other academic fads—think of POLITICAL CORRECTNESS, such a hot-button issue a few short years ago—this, too, will pass with yesterday's news.

—Richard Carlin, emulating Richard Kostelanetz

Sources: Recent museum and gallery exhibits in trendy spots across the country.

PADIN, Clemente

(8 October 1939).

Long a political activist of note in Uruguay, his homeland, Padin was jailed for two years and three months in the eighties for crimes as an artist and exhibitor of other artists against "the morale and reputation of the Army." A Pound-like generator of, and publicist for, avant garde work, worldwide, for over a quarter of a century now, he may be personally in touch with more major artists than anyone else, ever! In the best of his own always craft-extending work in performance art, fax art, sound poetry, mail art, book-art, installation art, and visual and video poetry, a lyric simplicity generally presides—as in one infraverbal visual poem in which he's depicted a window boarded up with planks forming an "N" and placed it between the "I" and "D" of the word "WIDOW" to capture nearly all one could about widowhood. Henry Polkinhorn's translation of Padin's *Poetry and People: Latin American Poetry in Our Time* is available at www.concentric.net/~lndp/padin/lcptitle.htm.

—Bob Grumman

Bibliography: Padin, Clemente. *Action Works.* Montevideo, Uruguay: Ovum, 1988.

PAIK, Nam June

(20 July 1932).

Born in Korea, educated in music in Japan and then Germany, where his work earned support from both JOHN CAGE and KARLHEINZ STOCKHAUSEN, Paik came to America in 1964 as a celebrated young international artist. His initial forte was ELECTRONIC MUSIC, thanks to three years of work at a Cologne studio. On the side, he did other things that assumed more importance in his career. After several outrageous performance pieces in Europe, many of them in FLUXUS festivals, some of them involving genuine danger (e.g., leaving a stage on which a motorcycle engine was left running, thus filling a small space with increasing amounts of carbon monoxide), Paik, in 1963, installed the first exhibition of his video work in a gallery in Wuppertal, Germany—thirteen used television sets whose imagery he altered by manipulating the signal through the use of magnets, among other techniques. Paik was among the first to realize a lesson since lost—that training in high-tech music might be a better preparation for video art than education in film and visual art, and thus that video programs belong in music schools rather than art schools. (REYNOLD WEIDENAAR is another major VIDEO ARTIST who began in Electronic Music, initially depending upon a competence required there—the ability to decipher complicated technical manuals.)

Though Paik continued producing audacious live PERFORMANCE ART, his video activities had greater impact. Late in 1965, he showed a videotape made with a portable video camera he had purchased earlier that day, and soon afterward held an exhibition that depended upon a videotape recorder. He was among the first artists-in-residence

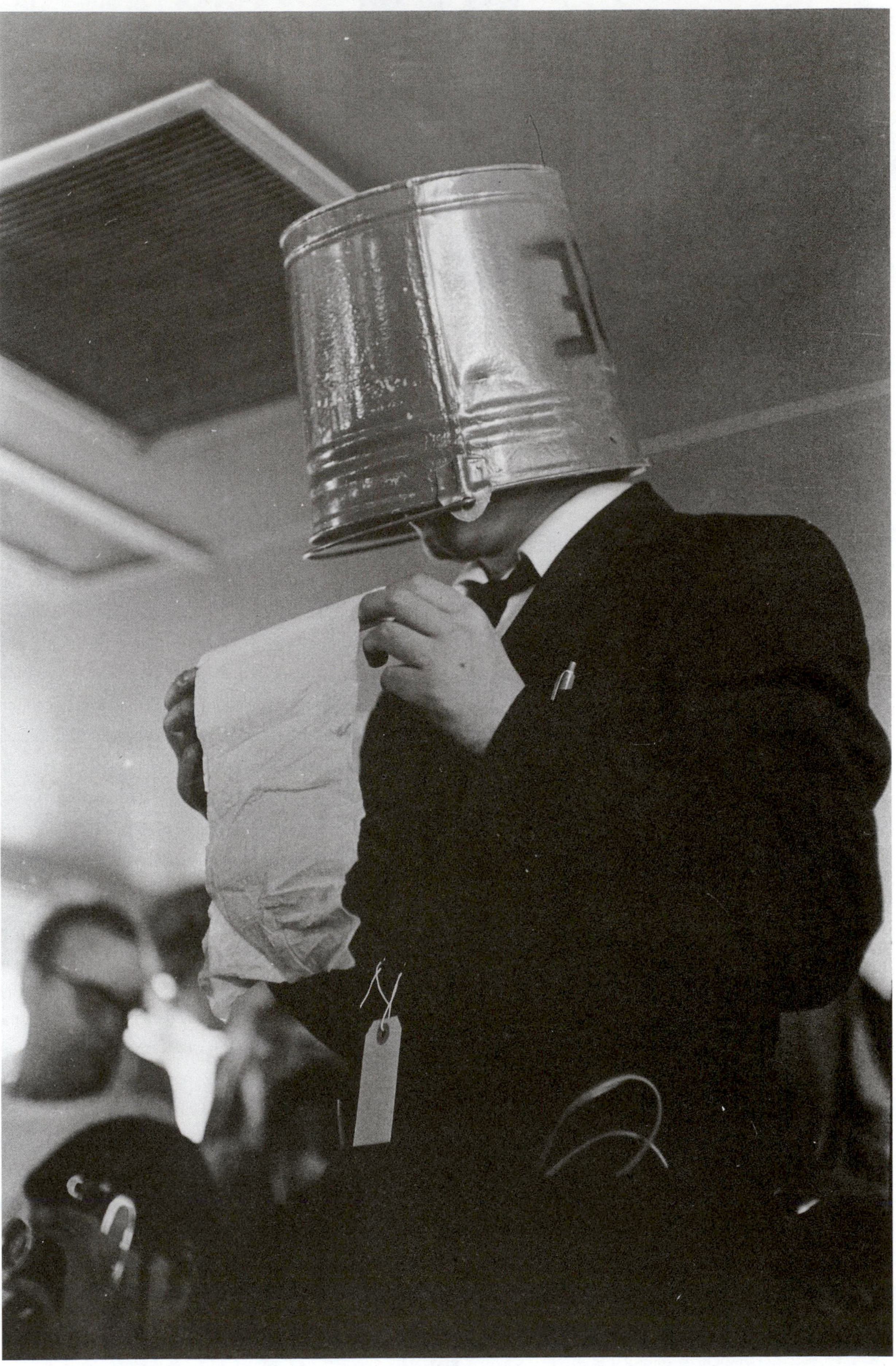

at the Boston Public Television station WGBH, where Paik also developed a video SYNTHESIZER that, extending his original video-art principle, could radically transform an image fed into it. Another oft-repeated move involved incorporating television monitors into unexpected places, such as on a bra worn by the cellist CHARLOTTE MOORMAN, amid live plants, or in a robot. Into the 1970s, if any museum exhibition included some video art, the token representative was usually Paik.

Precisely because the most sophisticated American television stations and private foundations have concentrated so much of their resources on Paik's video career, there has been reason for both jealousy and disappointment. From the beginning, his art had remarkably few strategies, most of them used repeatedly: performances that are audacious and yet fundamentally silly; tapes that depend upon juxtapositions of initially unrelated images, which is to say COLLAGE, which has become old-fashioned in other arts; installations depending upon accumulations of monitors that show either the same image or related images; unexpected placements of monitors (such as in a bra). Nonetheless, Paik was the first video artist to be given a full-scale retrospective at the Whitney Museum of American Art.

His American base notwithstanding, Paik's work has been recognized around the world. In 1979, he was awarded a professorship at the Staatliche Kunstakademie in Düsseldorf; in 1987, he was elected to the Akademie der Künste in Berlin; in 1988, he was commissioned to erect a tower with 1,003 monitors for the Olympic Games in his native Seoul. Because of an incapacitating stroke in 1996, Paik has recently been living mostly in Miami.

Paik's wife Shigeko Kubota (1937 in Japan), has likewise produced distinguished video, particularly with agglomerations of monitors varying in imagery ("multichannel") and other objects in a genre called "video sculpture." In addition, from 1974 to 1983, she curated the video program at New York's most important venue for screening alternative film, the Anthology Film Archives.

Compositions: *Hommage à John Cage*, 1960; *One for violin solo*, 1962; *Read Music—Do It Yourself*, 1962; *Piano for All Senses*, 1963; *Prelude for Audience*, 1964; *Sonata No. 1 for Adults Only*, 1965; *Opéra Sextronique*, 1967; *Variations on a Theme by Saint-Saens*, 1968.

Selected Videos: *Electronic Opera No 1* (New York: Public Broadcasting Laboratory), 1969; *Electronic Opera No. 2* (Boston: WGBH), 1970; *Global Groove*, 1973; *Tribute to John Cage* (Boston: WGBH), 1973; *Merce by Merce by Paik*, 1975; *Video-Buddha* 1976; *Moon is the Oldest T.V.*, 1976; *Video Thinker*, 1976; *Video Jungle*, 1977; *Lake Placid '80*, 1980; *Tri-Color Video*, 1982; *Good Morning, Mr. Orwell*, 1984; *Beuys-Voice*, 1987; *V-Matrix with Beuys Voice am Seibu*, 1988; *Literature is Not Book*, 1988.

Writings: *Aphorismen, Briefe, Texte*. Ed. Edith Decker: Köln: DuMont, 1992.

Exhibition Catalogs: *Nam June Paik: Electronic Art*. Essay John Cage. New York: Bonino, 1965; *Nam June Paik: Electronic Art II*. Essay Allan Kaprow. New York: Bonino, 1968; *Paik-Abe Video Synthesizer with Charlotte Moorman: Electronic Art III*. Essays John Cage and Russell Connor. New York: Bonino, 1971; *Nam Jun Paik: Videa 'n' Videology, 1959–73*. Ed. Judson Rosebush. Syracuse, NY: Everson Museum of Art, 1974; *Peter Campus*. Essays James Harithas and David A. Ross. Syracuse, NY: Everson Museum, 1974; Hanhardt, John G., et al. *Nam June Paik*. New York: Whitney Museum and W. W. Norton, 1982; *Family of Robot*. Cincinnati: Carl Solway, 1986; Nam June Paik: *eine DATA base*. Ed. Klaus Bussmann and Florian Metzner. Ostfilden, Germany: Cantz, 1993. (This reprints in their original languages essays by David Bourdon, Grace Glueck, Otto Hahn, Wolf Herzogenrath, Achille Bonito Oliva, David Ross, Irving Sandler, and Calvin Tomkins, among others.); *Shigeko Kubota: Video Sculptures*. Essen, Germany: Folkwang, 1982; *Shigeko Kubota: Video Sculpture*. Ed.

Nam June Paik in a performance at the Fifth Annual New York Avant-Garde Festival on the John F. Kennedy Ferry Boat, 29 September 1967. Photograph © Fred W. McDarrah.

Mary Jane Jacob. Astoria, NY: American Museum of the Moving Image, 1991; Stooss, Toni, and Thomas Kellein, eds. *Nam June Paik: Video Time/Video Space* (1991). New York: Abrams, 1993.

Web Site: http://www.artincontext.com/listings/pages/artist/f/0wy9rkpf/menu.htm

Interpretation: Decker, Edith. *Paik Video* (1988). Barrytown, NY: Barrytown Ltd., 1998; Fargier, Jean-Paul. *Nam June Paik*. Paris: Art Press, 1989.

Documentary: *Nam June Paik Video Works 1963–1988*. London: South Bank Board, 1988.

p

PALESTINE, Charlemagne

(c. 1945).

A POLYARTIST of sorts, Palestine was particularly distinguished at energetically performing elegant MODULAR MUSIC on the carillon and on a Boisendorfer grand piano. In *Strumming Music* (1970–75), he pounded away frenetically, realizing rapidly transforming clouds of overtones. Kyle Gann remembers "three- to four-hour performances on church organs in a series called the *Spectral Continuum Drones*; he was searching, he said, for 'the Golden Sonority.'" Typically dressed flamboyantly, surrounding himself with stuffed animals and drinking cognac, Palestine could also give embarrassing performances that could lose an audience, not just for a single evening, but forever. He has recently been working more on visual art.

Compositions: *Strumming Music*, 1970–75; *Two Fifths*, 1973.

Interview: Zimmerman, Walter. "Charlemagne Palestine." In *Desert Plants*. Cologne, Germany: Beginner, 1981.

PAOLOZZI, Eduardo

(7 March 1924).

The most inventive member of the first generation of British sculptors sufficiently young to avoid the dominating influence of HENRY MOORE, the Edinburgh-born Paolozzi introduced the metaphor of the machine into his art form. Unlike John Chamberlain and RICHARD STANKIEWICZ, who arranged and welded together the debris of the industrial environment, Paolozzi in the 1950s began embossing his bronze sculptures with intricate patterns cast from cog wheels and small machine parts. His large works, covered with the hieroglyphics of the machine age, loom like monumental totemic spirits, idols representing the logic of technology that holds the modern world in its grip like the wisdom of the gods, and which Paolozzi said he found "as fascinating as the fetishes of a Congo witch doctor." He continued his machine-inspired works into the mid-1960s, at which time he turned to producing simpler biomorphic sculptures, strongly reminiscent of JEAN ARP, as well as collages, painted ceramics, and even films. In the 1950s, Paolozzi had been touted as the leading sculptor of his generation by such people as the art historian HERBERT READ. However, none of the work from after his "machine sculpture" period has had much impact. Although he is still alive, his name is now largely relegated to art history books.

—Mark Daniel Cohen

Works: *Head*, 1957; *Japanese War God*, 1958; *Hermaphroditic Idol, no. 1*, 1962; *The City of the Circle and the Square*, 1963; *Medea*, 1964; *As Is When: Wittgenstein the Soldier*, 1964–65; *Etsso*, 1967.

Films: *The History of Nothing*, with Denis Postle, 1960–62; *Kakafon Kakkoon*, with Peter Leake's animation, 1965.

Exhibition Catalogs: *Paolozzi, Sculpture: 11 November–31 December, 1958*. London: Hanover Gallery, 1958; *Paolozzi, New Works: 5 September–28 September 1963*. London: The Waddington Galleries, 1963; *Eduardo Paolozzi Recent Sculpture: September 15–October 18, 1964*. London: Robert Fraser Gallery, 1964; Museum of Modern Art. *Eduardo Paolozzi*. New York: MoMA, 1964; *Eduardo Paolozzi, Sculpture and Graphics, 14 June–21*

July, 1967. London: Hanover Gallery, 1967; *Eduardo Paolozzi*. London: Hanover Gallery, 1968; Spencer, Robin. *Eduardo Paolozzi, Recurring Themes*. New York: Rizzoli, 1984; *Eduardo Paolozzi: Recurring Themes*. Lyon, France: Octobre Desarts, 1985.

Catalogue Raisonné: Miles, Rosemary. *The Complete Prints of Eduardo Paolossi: Prints, Drawings, Collages, 1944–77*. London: Victoria & Albert Museum, 1977.

Interpretation: Alloway, Lawrence and John Munday. *The Metallization of a Dream*. London: Lion and Unicorn Press, 1963; Finch, Christopher. *Image as Language: Aspects of British Art, 1950–1968*. Baltimore: Penguin, 1969; Middleton, Michael. *Eduardo Paolozzi*. London: Methuen, 1963; Kirkpatrick, Diane. *Eduardo Paolozzi*. Greenwich, CT: New York Graphic Society, 1970; Boyarsky, Alvin and Peter Cook. *Underground Design*. London: Architectural Association, 1986.

Documentary: Lauder, Al. *The Paolozzi Story*, 1980.

PAPP, Tibor (1936), and Paul NAGY (1935)

These two Hungarians, long residents of Paris, rank, as far as I can tell, among the most interesting VISUAL POETS currently working in France. Beginning their collaboration as part of a group called L'Atelier, which was also the title of their magazine, they have produced a series of highly inventive books and poster-books (drawing in part upon their common experience as working typographers) in addition to the richest edition known to me of STÉPHANE MALLARMÉ's avant-garde classic *Un coup de dés*, which includes commentaries both visual and verbal. They have also published in Hungarian not only a French-sponsored magazine but books of their own poems that Hungarians tell me are quite marvelous, both visually and verbally. Papp has also written a pioneering book on computer literature (whose title translates as "With or Without Muse?") that is currently available only in Hungarian, alas.

Works: Papp, Tibor. *Vendègszövegek 2, 3*. Paris, France: Magyar Mühely, 1984; *Mùzsával Vagy Mùzsa Nélkül?* Budapest, Hungary: Balassi Kiado, 1992; ——, et al. *Un coup de dés*. Paris, France: Change errant/d'atelier, 1980; Nagy, Paul. *Sadisfactions*. Paris, France: D'Atelier-New York: Future, 1977; *Journal in Time, 1970–1984*. Paris, France: Magyar Mühely, 1984.

PANDIATONICISM

(1937).

The term pandiatonicism was coined by NICOLAS SLONIMSKY and was initially used in the first edition of his book *Music since 1900*, published in 1937. It is a technique in which all seven degrees of the diatonic scale are used freely in democratic equality. The functional importance of the primary triads, however, remains undiminished in pandiatonic harmony. Pandiatonicism possesses both tonal and modal aspects, with a distinct preference for major keys. The earliest pandiatonic extension was the added major sixth over the tonic major triad. A cadential chord of the tonic major seventh is also of frequent occurrence. Independently from the development of pandiatonicism in serious music, American jazz players adopted it as a practical device. Concluding chords in piano improvisations in JAZZ are usually pandiatonic, containing the tonic, dominant, mediant, submediant and supersonic, with the triad in open harmony in the bass, topped by a series of perfect fourths. In C major, such chords would be, from the bass up, C, G, E, A, D, G. It is significant that all the components of this pandiatonic complex are members of the natural harmonic series, with C as the fundamental generator, G is the third partial, E the fifth partial, D the ninth, B the fifteenth, and A the twenty-seventh. The perfect fourth is excluded both theoretically and practically, for it is not a member of the harmonic series—an interesting concordance of actual practice and acoustical considerations. With the dominant in the bass, a complete succession of fourths, one of them an augmented fourth, can be built: G, C, F, B, E, A, D, G, produc-

ing a satisfying pandiatonic complex. When the subdominant is in the bass, the most euphonious result is obtained by a major triad in open harmony, F, C, A, in the low register, and E, B, D, G in the upper register. Polytriadic combinations are natural resources of Pandiatonicism, with the dominant combined with the tonic, e.g., C, G, E, D, G, B, making allowance for a common tone; dominant over the subdominant, as in the complex, F, C, A, D, G, B, etc. True polytonality cannot be used in Pandiatonicism, since all the notes are in the same mode. Pedal points are particularly congenial to the spirit of Pandiatonicism, always following the natural spacing of the component notes, using large intervals in the bass register and smaller intervals in the treble. The esthetic function of Pandiatonicism is to enhance the resources of triadic harmony; that is the reason why the superposition of triads, including those in minor keys, are always productive of a resonant diatonic bitonality. Although Pandiatonicism has evolved from tertian foundations; it lends itself to quartal and quintal constructions with satisfactory results. Pandiatonicism is a logical medium for the techniques of neo-classicism. Many sonorous usages of pandiatonicism can be found in the works of Debussy, Ravel, IGOR STRAVINSKY, Casella, Malipiero, Vaughan Williams, AARON COPLAND and Roy Harris. The key of C major is particularly favored in piano music, thanks to the "white" quality of the keyboard. Indeed, pandiatonic piano music developed empirically from free improvisation on the white keys. Small children promenading their little fingers over the piano keyboard at the head level produce pandiatonic melodies and pandiatonic harmonies of excellent quality and quite at random.

—Nicolas Slonimsky

Interpretation: Slonimsky, Nicolas. *Music Since 1900* (1937). 5th ed. New York: Schirmer, 1994.

PARKER, Charlie

(29 August 1920–12 March 1955; b. Charles Christopher P.; aka Yardbird, Bird).

Essentially self-taught on the alto saxophone, Parker became the premier jazzman of his generation, beginning his professional life at fifteen, coming to New York in 1939, and recording when he was twenty-one, in an initially precocious career. As one of the progenitors of the new style of the 1940s called BEBOP, he excelled, in Nicolas Slonimsky's summary, at "virtuosic speed, intense tone, complex harmonies, and florid melodies having irregular rhythmic patterns and asymmetric phrase lengths."

Rejecting the big bands characteristic of the preceding generation of jazzmen, Parker and his closest colleagues favored smaller "combos," as they are called, in a kind of chamber art that was precious to some and pathbreaking to others. Parker turned JAZZ into a modernist art of a quality distinctly different from its slicker predecessor; and knowing where he had gone, he once asked EDGARD VARÈSE for lessons in composing. It is hard to imagine ORNETTE COLEMAN's subsequent departures without Parker's foundation. He had recurring trouble with everyday life and died young, essentially of self-abuse. One of the more interesting appreciations of him appears in a scholarly history of modern music by William Austin (1920).

Recordings: *Bird: The Complete Charlie Parker on Verve*, 1988; *The Genius of Charlie Parker*, Savoy, 1992; *The Complete Charlie Parker*, Dial Jazz Classics, 1996; *Yardbird Suite: The Ultimate Charlie Parker*, WEA/Atlantic/Rhino 1997; *The Masters*, Cleopatra, 1999; *The Complete Savoy Live Performances*, Savoy, 1998.

Web Site: www.charlieparker.com

Bibliography: Austin, William W. *Music in the Twentieth Century*. New York: Norton, 1966; Giddins, Gary. *Celebrating Bird*. New York: Morrow, 1986; Reisner, Robert G. ed. *Bird: The Legend of Charlie Parker*. New York: Da Capo, 1988; Woideck, Carl. *Charlie Parker: His Music and Life*. Ann Arbor: University of Michigan Press, 1998; —— ed. *The Charlie Parker Companion*. New York: Simon & Schuster, 1998.

PÄRT, Arvo

(11 September 1935).

Initially a tonal composer and then one of the few SERIAL composers in his native Estonia, Pärt developed in the mid-1970s his "tintinnabuli style," derived from tintinnabulation, or the sound of ringing bells. These pieces are tonal, with gradual scalar shifts and resounding rhythms in the tradition of plainsong and Russian liturgical music; they also incorporate repetition and extended structures that are totally absent from serial music. Like ringing bells, they are filled with overtones and undertones. Pärt's best works are profoundly sacred: *Cantus in Memory of Benjamin Britten* (1976), where the repeated sound of bells comes to epitomize his tintinnabuli style; and *Stabat Mater* (1985), which echoes his earlier *Passio* (1982), which is probably his strongest single work. Fully entitled *Passio Domini nostri Jesu Christi secundum Joannem*, the latter opens with a choral chord reminiscent of Bach. With gorgeous writing for voices alone, especially in the highest and lowest registers, this seventy-minute oratorio fully intends to stand beside Bach's work. Because *Passio* has a single movement that runs without pause, the CD has no sections; perversely or not, it can be heard only from the beginning. Pärt is among the few composers featured in this book to benefit from the ideal arrangement of loyal support from a single recording company.

Works: *Nekrolog*, 1960; *Maailma samm* (The Worlds Stride), oratorio for chorus and orchestra, 1961; *Perpetuum Mobile*, 1963; *Collage über B-A-C-H*, for strings, oboe, harpsichord, and piano, 1964; *Pro et contra*, cello concerto, 1966; *Credo*, for chorus, piano, and orchestra, 1968; Symphony No. 3, 1971; *Laul armastatule* (Song for the Beloved), for 2 solo voices, chorus, and orchestra, 1973; *Für Alina*, 1976; *Cantus in Memory of Benjamin Britten*, for strings and bells, 1976; *Tabula Rasa*, double concerto for 2 violins or violin and viola, strings, and prepared piano, 1977; *Missa Syllabica*, for voices and instruments, 1977–91; *Arbos*, for 7 flutes and 3 triangles ad libitum, 1977; *Pari intervallo*, for 4 flutes, 1980; *Summa*, for string quartet, 1980–91; *Stabat Mater* for soprano, alto, tenor, violin, viola, and cello, 1985; *7 Magnificat-Antiphonen*, for chorus 1988; *The Introductory Prayers*, for strings, 1992.

Recordings: *Tabula Rasa, Frates, Cantus in Memory of Benjamin Britten*. München: ECM, 1984; *Arbos*. The Hilliard Ensemble, Gidon Kramer, Vladimir Mendelssohn, Thomas Demenga, Brass Ensemble Staatsorchester Stuttgart, cond. Dennis Russell Davies. München: ECM, 1987; *Passio Domini Nostri, Jesu Christi Secundum, Joannem*. The Hilliard Ensemble, cond. Paul Hillier. Münich, Germany: ECM, 1988; *Symphonies 1, 2, & 3, Cello Concerto*. Bamberg Symphony Orchestra cond. Neeme Jarvi. Djursholm, Sweden: Bis, 1989; *Miserere, Festina Lente, Sarah Was Ninety Years Old*. The Hilliard Ensemble cond. Paul Hillier; Orchester der Beethovenhalle, Bonn, cond. Dennis Russell Davies. München: ECM, 1991; *Trivium, Mein Weg hat Gipfel und Wellentäler, Annum per annum, Pari intervallo*. Christopher Bowers-Broadbest, organ. München: ECM, 1992; *Te Deum, Silouans Song, Magnificat, Berliner Messe*. Estonian Philharmonic Chamber Choir, Tallin Chamber Orchestra cond. Tönu Kaljuste. München: ECM, 1993; *Collage, Festina Lente, Credo, Frates, Summa, Symphony # 2*. Philharmonia, cond. Neeme Jarvi. Essex, England: Chandos, 1993; *De Profundis*. Theatre of Voices, Paul Hillier. München: ECM, 1996; *Litany, Psalm, Trisagion*. Estonian Philharmonic Chamber Choir; Lithuanian Chamber Orchestra. München: ECM, 1996; *Kanon Pokajanen*. Estonian Philharmonic Chamber Choir cond. Tönu Kaljuste. München: ECM, 1998.

Interpretation: Hillier, Paul. *Arvo Pärt*. New York: Oxford University Press, 1997; Kostelanetz, Richard. "Arvo Pärt." *More On Innovaive Music(ian)s*. Berkeley, CA: Fallen Leaf, 2000.

PARTCH, Harry

(24 June 1901–3 September 1974).

An eccentric western American, Partch was a self-taught musician who repudiated his earliest compositions and then, in the 1930s, developed a forty-three tone scale. Patiently building his own instruments, mostly percussive,

Harry Partch performing on stage, 8 September 1968, seen through his Crychord. Photograph © Fred W. McDarrah.

most of them striking in appearance, on which to play his microtones, Partch christened his inventions with such appropriately outlandish names as zymoxyl, chromalodeon, kithara, and cloud-chamber bowls. Based on an ancient Greek instrument of the same name, the kithara, for instance, is a tall harp with seventy-two strings grouped in twelve vertical rows of six apiece. The cloud-chamber bowls come from 12-gallon Pyrex glass bottles that have been sawed down; they are played with a mallet. Partch's MICROTONAL scales produced interesting relationships, and his instruments fresh timbres; yet the forms of Partch's music seem archaic, and his rhythms are too regular, while his arrangements are perhaps too reminiscent of the Indonesian gamelan. In short, radical innovations in tonality did not induce comparable revolutions in other musical dimensions. The texts that Partch customarily wrote for his spoken compositions likewise seem old-fashioned today. The words in *U.S. Highball* (1943), for instance, reflect to excess 1930s writing by John Dos Passos, among others.

Not unlike other indigent musicians during the 1930s, Partch lived as a hobo for several years; and since he is remembered, while others are forgotten, his life becomes the epitome of the heroic American composer who survived in spite of institutional neglect. Partch's forceful expository writings have perhaps had more influence than his music; that befits an aphorist who can write: "Originality cannot be a goal. It is simply inevitable." Kyle Gann in his *American Music in the Twentieth Century* provides an accessible introduction to Partchian scales, incidentally testfiying that Partch's mammoth book, *Genesis of a New Music* (1949), "its delightful vernacular tone notwithstanding, remains the best, most insightful one-volume history of tuning available."

Partch's instruments now belong to Dean Drummond (1949), a composer/performer whose Newband ensemble plays them, in addition to commissioning other composers to write for them.

Compositions: *17 Lyrics by Li Po*, for voice and adapted viola, 1930–33; *2 Psalms*, for voice and adapted viola, 1931; *The Potion Scene from Romeo and Juliet*, for voice and adapted viola, 1931; *The Wayward Barstow: 8 Hitchhiker Inscriptions from a Highway Railing at Barstow, California*, for voice and adapted guitar, 1941; *U.S. Highball: A Musical Account of a Transcontinental Hobo Trip*, for voices guitar, kithara, chromelodeon, 1943; *San Francisco: A Setting of the Cries of 2 Newsboys on a Foggy Night in the 20's*, for 2 baritones, adapted viola, kithara, and chromelodeon, 1943; *2 Settings from Joyce's* Finnegans Wake, for soprano, kithara, 2 flutes, 1944;

Yankee Doodle Fantasy, for soprano, tin flutes, tin oboes, flex-a-tones, and chromelodeon, 1944; *Plectra and Percussion Dances*, for voices and original instruments, 1949–52; *Oedipus* dance music for 10 solo voices and original instruments, after Sophocles, 1951; *Two Settings from Lewis Carroll*, for voice and original instruments, 1954; *The Bewitched*, dance satire for soprano and ensemble of traditional and original instruments, 1955; *Revelation in the Courthouse Park*, for 16 solo voices, 4 speakers, dancers, and large instrumental ensemble, 1960; *Rotate the Body in All Its Planes*, film score, 1961; *Water! Water!* farsical intermission, 1961; *And on the Seventh Day Petals Fell in Petaluma*, for large ensemble of original instruments, 1963–66.

Recordings: *Harry Partch Collection*. 4 Vols. New York: Composers Recordings, 1997; *Historic Speech-Music Recordings from the Harry Partch Archives*. St. Paul, MN: Innova-Bayside, 1995; *17 Lyrics of Li Po*. With Stephen Kalm and Theodore Mook. New York: Tzadik, 1995.

Writings: Partch, Harry. *Genesis of a New Music* (1949). 2d ed., revised and augmented. New York: Da Capo, 1974; *Bitter Music*. Ed. by Thomas McGeary. Urbana: University of Illinois Press, 1991.

Biography: Gilmore, Bob, *Harry Partch: A Biography*. New Haven: Yale University Press, 1998.

Website: http://www.corporeal.com/cm_main.html

Interpretation: Gann, Kyle. *American Music in the Twentieth Century*. New York: Schirmer, 1997.

PATAPHYSICS

(c. 1900; 1949–75).

In May 1960, *Evergreen Review*—in some respects the most influential American avant-garde magazine of its time—published an issue headlined "What Is 'Pataphysics'?" Co-edited and introduced by Roger Shattuck (1923), it included contributions from ALFRED JARRY (purportedly Pataphysics's founder); RAYMOND QUENEAU; and EUGÈNE IONESCO, among other less familiar but comparably wayward writers, all of them identified as "Satraps" of the Collège de Pataphysique. In his introduction, Shattuck defines "Pataphysics" as "the science of imaginary solutions. 'Pataphysics' is the science of the realm beyond metaphysics; or, 'Pataphysics' lies as far beyond metaphysics as metaphysics lies beyond physics—in one direction or another." From this assertion follow these corollaries, which Shattuck states without reservation: "Life is, of course, absurd, and it is ludicrous to take it seriously. Only the comic is serious." As an extension of DADA, officially inaugurated at the end of 1948, Pataphysics suggested the kind of ludicrous paradox-loving intelligence informing absurd literature. Pataphysics did not die so much as move underground, way underground, until it recently surfaced in Australia, in a magazine of that title, indicating that Australia is perhaps becoming the Western world's cultural frontier, much as America was through most of the twentieth century.

Bibliography: Shattuck, Roger, and Simon Watson Taylor, eds. "What Is 'Pataphysics'?" *Evergreen Review* IV/13 (May–June 1960); *Pataphysics*. (G.P.O. 171 8P, Melbourne, Victoria, Australia 3001).

PATCHEN, Kenneth

(13 December 1911–8 January 1972).

Patchen was an inspired EXPRESSIONIST writer with attractive sympathies, as well as a more original VISUAL POET who, in the tradition of WILLIAM BLAKE, combined pictures with his own handwritten words in works that are as much idiosyncratic as innovative. There are reasons to regard his greatest achievement as two books of extended prose, *The Journal of Albion Moonlight* (1941), *Memoirs of a Shy Pornographer* (1945), and *Sleepers Awake* (1946), which, though they have always been in print, are, shame of shame, rarely mentioned in histories of American literature. (Indeed, any purportedly comprehensive survey of American literature that omits Patchen's name should be

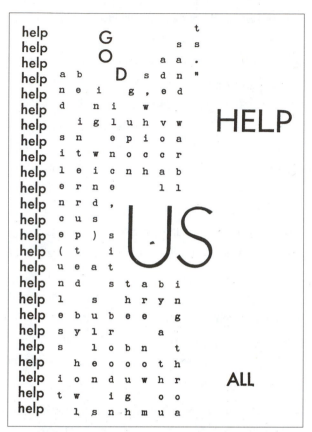

Kenneth Patchen. From *Sleeper's Awake*. Courtesy New Directions Publishing Corp.

discarded unread; the latest offender to come my way is Richard Ruland and Malcolm Bradbury's *From Puritanism to Post-modernism* [1991].) Patchen was also among the first poets to read publicly, along with jazz accompaniments, making several recordings combining poetry and jazz, and thus inspiring other poets to perform in nightclubs to musicians' accompaniment.

Works: *The Journal of Albion Moonlight* (1946). New York: New Directions, 1961; *Memoirs of a Shy Pornographer: An Amusement*. New York: New Directions, 1945; *Sleepers Awake*. New York: New Directions, 1946; *Selected Poems*. New York: New Directions, 1946; *Doubleheader: Poemscapes, A Letter to God; Hurrah for Anything*. New York: New Directions, 1958; *Because It Is*. New York: New Directions, 1960; *The Collected Poems*. New York: New Directions, 1967; *Patchen's Lost Plays*. Selected, with an intro. by Richard G. Morgan. Santa Barbara, CA: Capra, 1977; *A Collection of Essays*. Ed. Richard G. Morgan. New York: AMS, 1978.

Recordings: *Reads with Jazz*. New York: Folkways 9718, 1960.

Visual Art: *Hallulujah Anyway*. New York: New Directions, 1966; *But Even So: Picture Poems*. New York: New Directions, 1968; *The Argument of Innocence: A Selection from the Arts of Kenneth Patchen*. Ed. Peter Veres. San Francisco: Scrimshaw, 1976.

Web Site: http://ourworld.compuserve.com/homepages/Patchen; Patchen's visual poetry may be viewed at www.thing.net/~grist/l&d/patchen.htm

Interpretation: Smith, Larry. *Kenneth Patchen*. Boston: Twayne, 1978.

PATTERN POETRY

(c. 325 B.C.).

This term is most appropriate in defining poems, usually conventional in syntax, whose typography represents a shape that may be figurative or abstract. The term thus defines lines of poems whose ends suggest, say, the shape of a horse; the epithet defines as well the classic geometric shape poems of the seventeenth-century British poet George Herbert (1593–1633). It differs from VISUAL POETRY, which is generally nonsyntactical, and POESIA VIVISA, which customarily incorporates photographs along with words. Thanks to DICK HIGGINS's prodigious research, we know that the tradition goes back to classical times in the West, that it appears in all Western literatures from time to time, and that similar works were produced in China, India, and the Middle East—all of which is to say that it has been a recurring alternative stream in the history of literary writing.

Interpretation: Higgins, Dick. *Pattern Poetry*. Albany, NY: SUNY Press, 1987.

PATTERSON, Clayton

(9 October 1948).

With his videotape *Tompkins Square Park Police Riot* (1988), Patterson revealed how video as a documentary medium can differ from film. On a hot summer Saturday night, after five weeks of 90° days, the City of New York decided to close Tompkins Square Park in the East Village at one o'clock in the morning. The implicit purpose was to evacuate the squatters who had been sleeping in the park, after parks elsewhere in the city were closed to them. Well before the 1:00 A.M. curfew, protesters opposed to the park's closing began to gather on Avenue A, and plenty of police came as well, as did Patterson, a Canadian who lived nearby, carrying the battery-powered lightweight video camera he makes an extension of his body. When walking among people, he carries his camera on his hip, which means that the camera (and thus the spectator) participates in the events to the same degree that Patterson participates (for example, when others ran from the rampaging police, his camera ran as well). Since Patterson's camera has no light and makes slight noise, people are generally not aware that they are being intimately recorded. Patterson has learned from experience how to refocus distance without actually looking through the lens, capturing as well the peculiar light of New York at night. Patterson's tape, more than anything else I've seen, shows how video is far more effective than film at realizing the informal "cinema vérité" ideal of a quarter-century ago.

Videography: Patterson, Clayton. *Tompkins Square Park Police Riot* (1988). New York: Privately published (P.O. Box 103, Prince St. Station, 10012–0002), 1991.

PAXTON, Steve

(21 January 1939).

Though a member of the MERCE CUNNINGHAM Dance Company from 1961 to 1964, Paxton also participated in the JUDSON DANCE THEATER and, later, in the GRAND UNION improvisational ensemble. A skilled performer, improviser, and polemicist, Paxton developed a form of dance that by 1972 he called "contact improvisation." Drawing on a movement vocabulary that evolved from martial arts, social dances, sports, and child's play, Paxton's contact improvisation has a relaxed, easy-going quality. Although some training in this form is necessary for safety (when, say, one dancer's body becomes the "floor" or support for another's in a free-flowing exchange), participation has been open to people of all backgrounds. Because it has become both a theatrical and a social dance form, there is now an international network of contact improvisers.

—Katy Matheson

Selected Works: *Proxy*, 1961; *Flat*, 1964; *Jag Ville gorna telefonera*, 1964; *Physical Things*, 1966; *Satisfyin' Lover*, 1967.

Bibliography: Novack, Cynthia. *Sharing the Dance: Contact Improvisation and American Culture*. Madison: University of Wisconsin Press, 1990; Banes, Sally. "Steve Paxton: Physical Things." In *Terpsichore in Sneakers* (1980). 2d ed. Middletown: Wesleyan University Press, 1987.

PENDERECKI, Krzysztof

(23 November 1933).

An idiosyncratic Polish composer, Penderecki has appropriated a variety of avant-garde ideas in ways that may or may not be original. His *String Quartet* (1960) had old instruments resonating in new ways, while his genuinely moving *Threnody for the Victims of Hiroshima* (1960) displays fifty-two strings realizing smoothly modulated frequency bands, mostly at their highest possible pitches, superficially resembling GYORGY LIGETI's stunning *Atmospheres* (1961) and *Lux Aeterna* (1966). As Penderecki gained recognition, his music became slickly pretentious, if not simplistic and derivative; his *Passion and Death of Our Lord According to St. Luke* (1965) is highly congenial to listeners who don't much like modern music (much as Carl

Orff's [1895–1982] *Carmina Burana* was, a few decades before). NICOLAS SLONIMSKY credits Penderecki with inventing "an optical notation, with symbolic ideograms indicating the desired sound; thus a black isosceles triangle denotes the highest possible pitch; an inverted isosceles triangle, the lowest possible pitch; a black rectangle represents a sonic complex of white noise within a given interval;" etc. It is unfortunate that such innovative intentions do not always produce comparably innovative results.

p

Selected Compositions: *Tren pamieci ofiarom Hiroszimy* (Threnody for the Victims of Hiroshima) for 52 strings, 1959–60; *3 Miniatures* for violin and piano, 1959; *Wymiary czasu i ciszy* (Dimensions of Time and Silence) for chorus strings and percussion, 1959–60; *2 String Quartets No. 1*, 1960, *No. 2*, 1968; *Fonogrammi*, for 3 flutes, strings, and percussion, 1961; *Polymorphia*, for 48 strings, 1961; *Fluorescences*, 1961–62; *Stabat Mater*, for 3 choruses, 1962; *Kanon* for strings and 2 tapes 1962, *3 Pieces in Olden Style* for strings, 1963; *Dies Ire (Oratorio Dedicated to the Memory of Those Murdered at Auschwitz)*, for soprano, tenor, bass, orchestra, and chorus, 1967; *De natura sonoris No. 1*, 1966, *No.2*, 1971; Symphony No. 2, "Christmas Symphony," 1979–80; *Polish Requiem*, for SATB soloists, orchestra, and chorus, 1984; Trio for Strings, 1990–91; 2 violin concertos: No. 1 (1976–77), No. 2 (1992–95); *Benedictus* for chorus, 1993.

Recordings: *Passion and Death of Our Lord According to St. Luke/ Threnody for the Victims of Hiroshima*. Krakow Philharmonia, cond. Henryk Czyz. N.p.: Philips PHS2–901, n.d.; *Dies Irae* (Auschwitz Oratorio)—(1967), *Polymorphia*, for 48 String Instruments (1961), *De Natura Sonoris*, for Orchestra (1966). Chorus and Orchestra of the Cracow Philharmonia, cond. Henryk Czyz. Phillips; Choral Music, with National Philharmonic Choir of Warsaw cond. Henryk Wojnowski. Mainz, Germany: Wergo, 1995; Choral Music [different selection], at Penderecki Sixtieth Birthday Gala Concert (1993). New York: Sony Classical; Concerto for Viola and Orchestra (1983). Kim Kashkashian and Stuttgart Chamber Orchestra cond. Dennis Russell Davies. Munich: ECM; Chamber Music, with Silesian String Quartet. Mainz, Germany: Wergo; Music of Penderecki, with *Threnody for the Victims of Hiroshima*; *Fonogrammi*; *De Natura Sonoris 1 & 2*; *Capriccio for Violin & Orch*.; *Canticum Canticorum Salomonis*; *The Awakening of Jacob*. Polish Radio National Symphony Orchestra. London: EMI Classics.

Biography: Schwinger, Wolfram. *Krzysztof Penderecki: His Life and Work*. Trans. William Mann. London & New York: Schott, 1989.

PEREC, Georges

(7 March 1936–3 March 1982).

Perhaps the most ambitious experimental French writer of his generation, Perec began as an author of crossword puzzles, which perhaps accounts for why few writers, ever, could match his dexterity with innovative linguistic structures. A major member of OULIPO, he wrote many books, including *La Disparition* (1969), a novel totally devoid of the most popular letter in both English and French—the *E*—only to discover that the stunt had been done years before, with less literary distinction, by the American Ernest Vincent Wright in *Gadsby*, 1939. "By the end of *La Disparition,"* writes HARRY MATHEWS, "e has become whatever is unspoken or cannot be spoken—the unconscious, the reality outside the written work that determines it and that it can neither escape nor master. *E* becomes whatever animates the writing of fiction; it is the fiction of fiction."

Works: *La Disparition*. Paris: Editions Denoël, 1969; *Les Choses: A Story of the Sixties*. Trans. Helen Lane. New York: Grove, 1967; *Life: A User's Manuel*. Trans. David Bellos. Boston: Godine, 1987; *W or the Memory of Childhood*. Trans. David Bellos. Boston: Godine, 1988; *Things: A Story of the Sixties* & *A Man Asleep*. Trans. David Bellos. Boston: Godine, 1990; *"53 Days."* Trans. David Bellos. London: Harvill, 1992; *A Void (La Disparition) (1969)*. Trans. Gilbert Adair. New York: HarperCollins, 1994; *Three*. Trans. Ian Monk. Intro. David Bellos. London: Harvill, 1996.

Biography: Bellos, David. *George Perec: A Life in Words*. Boston: David R. Godine, 1994.

Interpretation: Schwartz, Paul. *George Perec: Traces of His Passage*. Birmingham, AL: Summa, 1988.

PEREIRA, I. Rice

(5 August 1902–1 January 1971; b. Irene R. P.).

Pereira's work was perhaps too avant-garde to be incorporated into the recent feminist revival. After beginning with paintings of machines, Pereira then favored abstract shapes on transparent materials that were customarily hung without a frame. In the 1940s, she used layers of glass to explore resonating light sources, which she regarded as extending painting. A geometric mystic in the tradition of MONDRIAN, Pereira thought her trapezoidal shapes subsumed spiritual presences. During the 1950s, her textures became thicker, featuring floating rectilinear forms. This work was so different from what others were doing that it remains memorable. Pereira also wrote books whose titles tell all: *Light and the New Reality* (1951), *The Transformation of "Nothing" and the Paradox of Space* (1955), *The Nature of Space* (1956), *The Lapis* (1957), and *The Crystal of the Rose* (1959). Karen A. Bearor's monograph (1993) investigates not only her art but its continuing unjustified neglect, even among those predisposed toward women's art.

I Rice Pereira. *Rectangles*, 1940. Courtesy The C. Leonard Pfeiffer Collection of American Art. University of Arizona.

Works: *Transversion*, 1946; *White Rectangle* No. 1, 1938; *Ascending Scale*, 1937; *The Diagonal*, 1938; *Pendulum*, 1937; *Pillar of Fire*, 1955.

Books: *Crystal of the Rose*. New York: I. Rice Periera & Nordness Gallery, 1959; *The Transcendental Formal Logic of the Infinite*. New York: I. Rice Pereira, 1966; *The Finite versus the Infinite*. New York: I. Rice Periera, 1969; *The Lapis* (1957). Washington, DC: Corcoran, 1970; *The Nature of Space, Metaphysical an Aesthetic Inquiry* (1956). New York: I. Rice Periera, 1968.

Exhibition Catalog: *Loren MacIver—Rice Pereira*. New York: Whitney Museum, 1953; *Space, Light, and the Infinite*. New York: Nordness Gallery, 1961; Baur, John I. H. *I. Rice Pereira*. New York: Whitney Museum of American Art, 1976.

Interpretation: Bearor, Karen A. *I. Rice Pereira: Her Paintings and Philosophy*. Austin: University of Texas Press, 1993.

PERELMAN, S.J.

(1 February 1904–17 October 1979; b. Sidney Joseph P.).

Not unlike other highly original American writers who appeared largely in slick media (e.g., OGDEN NASH and

ROBERT BENCHLEY), Perelman had an avant-garde streak that is insufficiently appreciated, perhaps because examples are buried in his collected writings, rather than segregated into separate books. This element of his style depended upon destroying clichés with inspired non sequiturs:

> Six months of revelry and an overzealous make-up man have left their stamp on the Fool when we again see him; the poor chap is shipping water fast. He reels around the mansion squirting seltzer at the help and boxing with double-exposure phantoms, and Theda, whose interest in her admirers wanes at the drop of a security, is already stalking a new meatball. Apprised of the situation, Kate goes to her husband bearing an olive branch, but their reunion is thwarted by his mistress, who unexpectedly checks in and kisses him back into submission.

By any measure, few other writers have incorporated so many imaginative leaps into so few sentences.

Selected Books: *The Most of*. New York: Fireside, 1980; Wilk, Max. *And Did You Once See Sidney Plain? A Random Memoir of S. J. Perelman*. New York: Norton, 1986.

Web Site: http://rpu.com/tribute_to_perelman.htm

PERFORMANCE ART

(c. 1975–).

This is a 1980s epithet for a presentational genre that had previously been called HAPPENINGS or MIXED-MEANS THEATER, which is to say a live performance, drawing upon dance, music, drama, and sometimes motion pictures. Performance art shares two elements. The various parts function disharmoniously, in the tradition of COLLAGE, which is based upon the principle of assembling elements not normally found together; aliveness, because a recorded piece, whether on video or audiotape, lacks spontaneity. Performance art may also involve members of the audience, voluntarily or involuntarily. Allan Kaprow developed his coinage Happenings to describe a one-time event, generally held outdoors, in which people come together to execute instructions they have not seen before. The art depended upon discovery and surprise. In JOHN CAGE'S untitled 45-minute piece staged at Black Mountain College in 1952, one person read a text, another performed choreography, and a third produced sounds, all with minimal rehearsal.

While performance art extends this tradition of alternative theater, the term came to identify more modest theatrical events, often involving one performer who was customarily her or his own director. Much depended upon the paradoxical treatment of language. If the performer was trained in theater, words, if used at all, play a secondary role to the articulation of image and movement. If, however, the performer was trained in dance, language might predominate over movement. Performance Art differs esthetically from the masterpieces of 1960s mixed-means theater in reflecting later the influence of MINIMALISM and CONCEPTUAL ART.

Anthologies: Dupuy, Jean, ed. *Collective Consciousness: Art Performances in the Seventies*. New York: Performing Arts Journal, 1980; Gray, John. *Action Art*. Wesport, CT: Greenwood Press, 1993; McAdams, Dona. *Caught in the Act*. New York: Aperture, 1996; Loeffler, Carl, ed. *Performance Anthology*. San Francisco: Contemporary Arts, 1980; Roth, Moira, ed. *The Amazing Decades: Women and Performance Art in America 1970–1980*. Los Angeles: Astro Artz, 1983.

Exhibition Catalog: *Outside of the Frame: Performance and the Object, A Survey History of Performance Art in the USA Since 1950*. Cleveland, OH: Cleveland Center for Contemporary Art, 1994.

Interpretation: Kultermann, Udo. *Art and Life*. New York: Praeger, 1971; Popper, Frank. *Art, Action and Participation*. New York: New York University Press, 1975; Goldberg, Roselee. *Performance Art* (1979). Rev. and enlarged ed. New York: Abrams, 1988; ——. *Performance: Live Art Since 1960*. New York: Abrams,

1998; Battcock, Gregory, and Robert Nickas, eds. *The Art of Performance: A Critical Anthology*. New York: Dutton, 1984; Kostelanetz, Richard. *On Innovative Performance(s): Three Decades of Recollections of Alternative Theater*. Jefferson, NC: McFarland, 1994.

PERFORMANCE GROUP

(1967–1980).

Organized by Richard Schechner (1934), a drama professor at New York University, this began as the resident company for a downtown New York alternative space called the Performance Garage (because it previously housed large trucks) that was renovated with wooden platforms and rafters that allowed everyone to sit where he or she wished. The group's best production, *Dionysus in '69* (1968), followed the academic tradition of adapting classic texts, in this case Euripides's *The Bacchae*, rather than creating theater wholecloth. It begins with company members performing various exercises in the middle of a carpeted floor. After an exchange of words between one performer and the woman tending the door, the actors begin to "perform," moving in and out of Euripides's lines and characters. Now and then they shift into contemporary speech and use their real names. They move at times among the audience, occasionally challenging individual spectators. Early in the play, a Dionysian dance is performed, which members of the audience are invited to join, and also a stunning birth ritual, in which Dionysus's body, clad in a minimum of clothing (sometimes none), is passed through five pairs of female legs and over a carpet of similarly semi-clothed male bodies. In a concluding Dionysian frenzy, the audience is again invited into a melee of stroking figures. The title refers to a line in the election-year play—a vote for the lead male actor would "bring Dionysus in '69." Out of the Performance Group came the Wooster Group (1976), cofounded by Elizabeth Le Compte (1944) and Spalding Gray (1941), who later became a distinguished monologist. Initially utilizing many of the same performers, the Wooster Group took over the Performance Garage.

The Performance Group in *Dionysius in '69*: "Birth Ritual." Photograph © Fred W. McDarrah.

Books: Schechner, Richard, ed. *Dionysus in '69*. New York: Farrar, Straus, 1970; Savran, David. *Breaking the Rules: The Wooster Group* (1986), New York: Theatre Communications Group, 1988.

PESSOA, Fernando

(13 June 1888–30 November 1935).

The most distinguished modern user of multiple literary pseudonyms—"heteronyms" was his name for them—

this Portuguese poet descended from Marranos, or Jews who were forcibly converted to Christianity after the Spanish Inquisition. After his father died and his mother remarried, Pessoa grew up in Durban, South Africa, where his stepfather was the Portuguese consul. Isolated and improverished back in his native country, he reportedly filled his life with imaginary figures, who became literary characters and then creators. Femando Pessoa coined, in addition to his own name, Alberto Caeiro, Ricardo Reis, and Álvaro de Campos, each for a different sort of poetry. (A linguistic ventriloquist, he also wrote poems in seventeenth-century English.) As Pessoa explained, "I put into Caeiro all my power of dramatic depersonalization, into Ricardo Reis all my intellectual discipline, dressed in the music that is proper to him, into Álvaro de Campos, all the emotion that I do not allow myself in my living." These are less pseudonyms than literary creations, each apparently producing for Pessoa what could not be written under his own name.

Selected Books: *Selected Poems*. Trans. Edwin Honig. Chicago: Swallow, 1971; *Always Astonished*. Trans. Edwin Honig. San Francisco: City Lights, 1988; *Book of Disquietude*. Riberdaleron-Hudson, NY: Sheep Meadow Press, 1996; *Poems of*. San Francisco: City Lights, 1998; *Selected Poems*. Trans. Richard Zenith. New York: Grove, 1998; *Works and Texts*. New York: Thames & Hudson, 1992; Pessoa's complete works are available in Portuguese in several volumes (1942–69).

Interpretation: Tabucchi, Antonio. *Fernando Pessoa*. Trans. Simon Pleasance. Paris: Hazan, 1997.

PHILLIPS, Michael Joseph

(2 March 1937).

Though a Ph.D., Phillips writes monumentally simple poems that, if only for their audacious simplicity, are instantly recognizable as his. His intentionally limited vocabulary and his penchant for exact repetition represent radical repudiations of two traditional values of English poetry; for whereas even Gertrude Stein claimed that nothing she wrote was ever repeated precisely, Phillips often repeats exactly. The most successful of his poems in this mode is "On Claudia Cardinale," in which the phrase "I have never seen so much so well put-together" is repeated in a staggered visual form that generates an erotic complement. In contrast to Aram Saroyan, who gave up poetic Minimalism for commercial prose, Phillips continues mining his idosyncratic vein.

Works: *9 Concrete Poems*. Bloomington, IN: Privately published, 1967; *7 Poems for Audrey Hepburn*. Bloomington, IN: Flowers Publ., 1968; *Kinetics & Concretes*. Bloomington, IN: Michael Joseph Phillips Editions (238 N. Smith Rd. #25 47408–3188), 1971; *Selected Love Poems*. Indianapolis, IN: Hackett, 1980; *Imaginary Women*. Huron, OH: Cambric (208 Ohio St. 44839–1514), 1986; *Selected Concrete Poems*. Bloomington, IN: Michael Joseph Phillips, 1987; *Dreamgirls*. Huron, OH: Cambric, 1989.

PHILLIPS, Tom

(24 May 1937).

Educated in English literature, trained as a composer, Phillips became a visual artist, not only as a gallery painter but as the author of one of the great book-art books of our time, *A Humument* (1980). What Phillips did was take a Victorian novel, W. H. Mallock's *A Human Document*, and paint or draw over most of its pages so that only certain words from the original text were visible, in effect composing his own visual-verbal poems with another man's text. (Phillips's title comes from *removing* the middle letters from Mallock's original.) Over the missing words Phillips put an endless wealth of designs, made in a wide variety of ways. The results appeared in several forms, beginning with publication of sample pages in literary magazines in the late 1960s, then as suites from a graphics publisher, later in a book of black-and-white reproductions (*Trailer*, 1971), and finally as a full-color book (1981) that seven years later, and then eleven years later reappeared in revised forms. Phillips has meanwhile recorded a musical version of pages from A *Humument* and made another visual-verbal creation with Blakean echoes, an illustrated edition of his own translation of Dante's *Inferno*, in addition to curating and introducing a traveling exhibit of African art.

Books: *A Humument*. London, England, & New York: Thames & Hudson, 1980; First rev. ed. London: Thames & Hudson, 1987. 3d ed. London: Thames & Hudson, 1998; *Works. Texts to 1974*. Stuttgart, Germany: Hansjörg Mayer, 1975; *Dante's Inferno*. London: Talfourd, 1983.

Exhibition Catalog: *Tom Phillips*. London: Marlborough Fine Art, 1973; *Human Documents*. Philadelphia: University of Pennsylvania Press, 1993; *Bookworks by Tom Phillips*. New York: Center for the Book Arts, 1983.

Paintings: *Fragment from a Humument*, 1970; *From the Stanzas of the Graves*, 1972.

Recordings: *A Humument*. Stuttgart, Germany: Hansjörg Mayer, 1975.

PHOTOMONTAGE

(late 1910s).

Literally, a photomontage is made by using splicing techniques to assemble photographic images. Technically, photomontage should really be called photocollage, as collage means glueing in French and montage implies sequence, as in film. (True photomontage would thus exhibit two images from *different* times, as in superimpositions.) For me at least, the epitome of photomontage is Paul Citroen's (1896–1983) *Metropolis*, which is the name not for one image but several that he composed around 1923. Taking bits of distinctly metropolitan images, particularly buildings whose height exceeded their width, he filled a vertical rectangle, from top to bottom, from side to side, making a persuasive image of an all-encompassing urban world (that has no relation to primary nature). Though the image itself is frequently reprinted, there is no book in English about Citroen.

To other critics, the great photomontagist is John Heartfield, a German who took an English name for publishing photomontages that resembled political cartoons, really, by customarily mixing the faces of politicians, particularly Adolf Hitler, with critical imagery, such as coins replacing Hitler's spinal structure, and captions that became part of the picture as the image was rephotographed, so to speak. As Richard Huelsenbeck writes of Heartfield's photomontage: "It has an everyday character, it wants to teach and instruct, its rearrangement of parts indicates ideological and practical principles."

Books: *Paul Citroen en het Bauhaus*. Utrecht & Antwerp: Bruna, 1974; Heartfield, John. *Photomontages of the Nazi Period*. New York: Universe, 1977; Ades, Dawn. *Photomontage*. London: Thames & Hudson, 1986.

Exhibition Catalog: *Montage and Modern Life 1919–1942*. Boston: Institute of Contemporary Art, 1992.

PICABIA, Francis

(22 January 1879–30 November 1953).

Born in Paris of a Cuban father and a French mother, Picabia grew up a French artist, beginning as an Impressionist, becoming a Cubist, and by 1912 following Robert Delaunay's (1885–1941) Orphism. Traveling to New York in 1913, he collaborated with his compatriot Marcel Duchamp, who was by 1915 also in New York, in establishing American Dada. Having contributed to Alfred Stieglitz's periodical *291* in 1916, Picabia published in 1917 the first number of his Dada review *391* in Barcelona, participating in Dada both there and in New York, creating "mechanothropomorphic" fantasies, such as *La Parade Amoureuse* (1917). Returning to Paris in the 1920s, Picabia denounced Dada and joined the Surrealists, collaborating with Erik Satie on the ballet *Relâche* (1924) and with René Clair (1898–1981) on the film *Entr'acte* (1925). Departing to

Provence in 1925, Picabia produced lyrical COLLAGES made from cellophane, which he called Transparencies, before returning to Paris two decades later.

Selected Works: *Sunlight on the Banks of the Loing*, 1905; *Red Tree*, 1912; *Star Dancer and her School of Dancing*, 1913; *Edtaonisl*, 1913; *Udnie (Young American Girl)*, 1913 (Paris: Pompidou); *Je revois en souvenir ma chère udnie*, 1914; *Very Rare Painting on the Earth*, 1915; *Amorous Parade*, 1917; *Machine Turn Quickly*, 1916–18; *Child Carbuettor* c. 1919; *Wet Paint*, 1917–19; *Straw Hat* c. 1921; *Cacodylic Eye*, 1921; *Toothpicks* c. 1924; *Feathers*, 1924–25; *First Meeting*, 1925–1926; *The Kiss* c. 1924–27; *Ganga* c. 1929; *Spring*, 1935; *Composition*, 1939; *The Mexican*, 1937–38; *Women with Bulldog*, 1940–42; *I Ask Myself*, 1949; *Cynicism and Indecency*, 1949.

Writings: *Who Knows? Poems and Aphorisms*. Trans. Remy Hall. New York: Hanumen, 1986; *Yes No*. New York: Hanumen, 1990.

Performances: Costume and stage design, with Erik Satie and Ballets Suédois. *Relâche*, 1924.

Films: With René Clair and Erik Satie. *Entr'acte* 1925; *Ganga*, 1929.

Interpretation: Hunt, R. *Picabia*. London: ICA, 1964; Borràs, Maria Luïsa. *Picabia*. New York: Thames & Hudson, 1985; Camfield, William. *Francis Picabia: Art, Life and Times*. Princeton: Princeton University Press, 1979.

Exhibition Catalogs: Camfield, William. *Francis Picabia*. New York: Guggenheim Museum, 1970; Nauman, Francis. *Making Mischief: Dada Invades New York*. New York: Whitney Museum, 1996; Schwarz, Arturo. *New York Dada: Duchamp, Man Ray, Picabia*. Münich: Städtische Galerie im Lenbachhaus, 1973; *Francis Picabia: exposició antològica*. Barcelona: Fundació Caixa de Pensions, 1985; *Picabia 1879–1953*. Edinburg: Scottish National Gallery of Modern Art; Frankfurt am Main: Galerie Neuendorf, 1988; Wilson, Sarah. *Accommodations of Desire: Transparencies 1924–32*. New York: Kent Gallery, 1989; *Late Works 1933–53*. Zdenek Felix, ed. Ostfildern-Ruit: Hatje, 1998.

PICASSO, Pablo

(25 October 1881–8 April 1973).

Picasso began his career as an exceptionally talented realistic Spanish painter. His first genuine breakthrough came after he settled in France. He is generally credited with initiating CUBISM in the first decade of this century. Over the years, until World War II, he passed through a succession of artistic styles, mirroring the rapidly changing art world with its many "isms" (Analytic Cubism, Synthetic Cubism, Neo-Classicism, SURREALISM, and so forth). Some of Picasso's many innovative contributions to world art include the assimilation of African art into Western painting, incorporating several vantage points into a single portrait, and introducing into his still lifes such found objects as newspaper headlines, wallpaper fragments, and ticket stubs. His constant changing is considered avant-garde, because it reflected a restlessness and dissatisfaction with the status quo, even when that status quo reflected his own creations.

Historians also identify Picasso as initiating Cubist sculpture, and his subsequent three-dimensional art took a variety of forms. A whimsical sculpture of a gorilla whose face was sculpted around one of his children's toy cars predicted later POP ART. His many Cubist constructions of guitars brought the intersecting planes of Cubist painting into three dimensions; they also utilized scrap metal, wire, and scrap wood, among other materials not often found in fine-art sculpture at the time.

Picasso also worked for a brief period as a stage designer for SERGEI DIAGHILEV's Ballets Russes, contributing Cubist back-drops and costumes to innovative productions, most notably *Parade* (1917). As an aspiring POLYARTIST, Picasso spent two years mostly writing poetry and plays that, though experimental, are now forgotten.

—with Richard Carlin

Pablo Picasso. *Violin and Guitar*, 1913. CORBIS/Alexander Burkatowski. © 2000 Estate of Pablo Picasso/Artists Rights Society (ARS), New York.

Selected Visual Art: *Three Women*, 1907; *Man with Violin*, 1910–12; *Women with Guitar*, 1911–12; *Violin and Sheet of Music*, 1912; *Geometric Composition: The Guitar*, 1913; *Harlequin*, 1915; *Man Leaning on a Table*, 1916; *Three Musicians*, 1921; *The Dance*, 1925; *Figure*, 1928; *Women in the Garden*, 1929–30; *Women Throwing a Stone*, 1931.

Writings: Ashton, Dore, ed. *Picasso on Art*. New York: Grove, 1972.

Exhibition Catalogs: Barr, Alfred. *Picasso: Fifty Years of His Art*. New York: MoMA, 1946; Rubin, William S., ed. *Picasso: A Retrospective*. New York: MoMA, 1980; ——, ed. *Picasso in the Collection of the Museum of Modern Art*. New York: MoMA, 1972; *Picasso and Portraiture*. New York: MoMA, 1996.

Anthology: Warnke, Carsten-Peter, and Ingo F. Walther. *Pablo Picasso 1881–1973*. 2 vols. Köln: Taschen, 1998.

Biography: Huffington, Arianna Stassinopoulos. *Picasso: Creator and Destroyer*. New York: Simon & Schuster, 1988; O'Brian, Patrick. *Pablo Ruiz Picasso: A Biography*. New York: Putnam, 1976; Richardson, John. *A Life of Picasso*. 2 vols. New York: Random House, 1991; Russell, Frank. *Picasso's Guernica*. Montclair, NJ: Allanheld & Schram, 1980; Spies, Werner. *Picasso Sculpture*. Trans. Jo Maxwell Brownjohn. London: Thames & Hudson, 1972.

Web Site: http://www.clubinternet.com/picasso/

Interpretation: Baldessari, Anne. *Picasso and Photography: The Dark Mirror*. Houston: Museum of Fine Arts, 1997; Cooper, Douglas. *Picasso Theatre*. New York: Abrams, 1968; Frank K. Elgar, and Robert Maillard. *Pablo Picasso* (1955). New York: Tudor, 1972; FitzGerald, Michael. *Making Modernism: Picasso and the Creation of the Market for Twentieth-Century Art*. New York: Farrar, Straus, 1995; Gedo, Mary Mathews. *Picasso: Art as Autobiography*. Chicago: University of Chicago Press, 1981; Krauss, Rosalind E. "In the Name of Picasso," *The Originality of the Avant-Garde and Other Modernist Myths*. Cambridge: MIT Press, 1996; ——. *The Picasso Papers*. New York: Farrar, Straus, 1998; Leighton, Patricia. *Re-Ordering the Universe*. Princeton: Princeton University Press, 1989; Leymarie, Jean. *Picasso: The Artist of the Century*. New York: Viking, 1972; McCully, Marilyn, ed. *A Picasso Anthology: Documents, Criticism, Reminiscences*. London: Thames & Hudson, 1981; Penrose, Ronald. *Picasso* (1971). London: Phaidon, 1991; ——. *The Sculpture of Picasso*. New York: MoMA, 1967; Schiff, Gert, ed. *Picasso: In Perspective*. Englewood Cliffs, NJ: Prentice-Hall, 1976.

PIETRI, Pedro

(21 March 1943).

To the pioneering anthology of *The Puerto Rican Poets/Los Poetas Puertorriqueños* (1972) Pietri contributed "The Broken English Dream," which consists entirely of punctuation marks (that are different in Spanish *en face*, of course). The "last edition" of *Invisible Poetry* (n.d.) is twenty-eight blank pages; in my copy Pietri inscribed on the opening page, "Read this and pass on the message to others . . . and others." He once sent me *I Never Promised You a Cheeseburger*, which is a box with unbound but numbered pages, all cut into the shape of an ellipse, each with discrete writing in various styles. Pietri's stand-up poetry readings rank among the more inspired, incorporating theatrics that, while they have little to do with poetry, reflect his unfettered imagination. Pietri has also written plays that, while eccentric in parts, are comparatively more conventional.

Works: *Puerto Rican Obituary*. New York: Monthly Review, 1973; *The Masses are Asses*. Maplewood, NJ: Waterfront, 1984; *Illusions of a Revolving Door: Plays Teatro*. Rio Piedras, PR: University of Puerto Rico Press, 1992.

Recordings: *Loose Joints*. New York: Folkways Records 1979.

PISCATOR, Erwin

(17 December 1893–20 March 1966).

An actor and director in pre-Nazi Berlin, Piscator is credited with introducing PHOTOMONTAGE, slides, and film into his stagecraft. Becoming Bertolt Brecht's collaborator in Epic Theater, he published an influential book, *Das politische Theater* (1929) in which "political" was a euphemism for Communist. Among epic characteristics his widow Maria Ley-Piscator identified "a theatre for vast audiences, a theatre of action, whose objective is to bring out the stirring questions of our time and to bring about a total re-education of both men of the theatre and the audience." Emigrating to America in 1938, after stops in Russia and Paris, Piscator became an influential teacher, counting among his prominent pupils the founders of the LIVING THEATRE. He returned to (West) Germany in 1951, struggling for a decade until he became artistic director of the Berlin Volksbühne in 1962. Among those younger directors acknowledging Piscator's influence are Judith Malina (1926) of THE LIVING THEATRE in New York and Peter Stein (1937) in (West) Berlin.

Books: *The Political Theatre* (1929). Trans. Hugh Rorrison. London: Eyre Methuen, 1980.

Exhibition Catalog: *Erwin Piscator: 1893–1966*. Berlin: Akademie der Künste, 1977. [In English.]

Interpretation: Innes, C. D. *Erwin Piscator's Political Theatre: The Development of Modern German Drama*. Cambridge, England: Cambridge University Press, 1972; Ley-Piscator, Maria. *The Piscator Experiment* (1967). Carbondale: Southern Illinois University Press, 1970; Probst, Gerhard F. *Erwin Piscator and the American Theater*. New York: Peter Lang, 1992; Willet, John. *The Theatre of Erwin Piscator* (1978). New York: Holmes & Meier, 1979.

PISTOLETTO, Michelangelo

(23 June 1933).

Through much of the 1960s and 1970s, the Italian artist Pistoletto mounted a series of installations, works of "sculpture," and other personal artistic inventions that, taken together, provide a case study of faint thinking and a shift of the burden of ingenuity from the artist to the interpreting audience. His early efforts involved the use of vertical mirrored surfaces with life-sized figure drawings attached, behind which viewers saw themselves reflected, thereby making some vague point about the relationship between art and life. Pistoletto moved on to work with piles of rags. In *Golden Venus of Rags* (1967–71), a statue of the goddess painted gold stands before a heap of multicolored rags. In *Orchestra of Rags* (1968), clothing is piled around a boiling kettle beneath a sheet of glass. The viewer is left to guess the symbolic meaning of the rags. With no clue given, perhaps they mean nothing at all. Pistoletto was a leading figure in ARTE POVERA. The lack of clear thinking in his works gives a new meaning to the name of the group, and the only mystery in his art is why he never used smoke in his mirrored projects.

—Mark Daniel Cohen

Works: *Person Seen from the Back*, 1962; *Vietnam*, 1962–65; *A Reflected World*, 1966; *Golden Venus of Rags*, 1967–71; *Orchestra of Rags*, 1968; *Wall of Rags*, 1968; *Welcome to New York*, 1979.

Exhibition Catalogs: *Pistoletto*. Paris: Ileana Sonnabend, 1964; Walker Art Center. *Michelangelo Pistoletto: A Reflected World*. Minneapolis: Walker Art Center, 1966; *Pistoletto*. New York: Sidney Janis Gallery, 1974; Hickey, Dave. *Michelangelo Pistoletto*. Houston, TX: Institute for the Arts, 1983; Celant, Germano, and Alanna Heiss. *Pistoletto: Division and Multiplication of the Mirror*. Long Island City, NY: Institute for Contemporary Art, P.S. 1 Museum; Milano: Fabbri Editori, 1988.

Interpretation: Celant, Germano. *Pistoletto*. New York: Rizzoli, 1989.

PLAGIARISM

(timeless).

T. S. Eliot's statement in 1920 is an early indication that someone considered the issue: "Immature poets imitate; mature poets steal." Think of MARCEL DUCHAMP'S "L.H.O.O.Q." from 1919: The Mona Lisa with a moustache and goatee painted on it and a flourish that is Duchamp's signature in the lower right corner. Found art, but particularly FOUND POETRY, continues the thought: the appropriation and manipulation of bits of text, usually not a single word of your own making, and ending up with a new work. JOHN GIORNO's found poetry provides us with a good example: he takes text, usually from journalistic sources, and through a system of repetition and visual placement of the text, devises poems of incredible power and humanity. But beginning at least by the 1980s and possibly earlier, Western avant-garde artists working in the reprographic arts (xerographics and tape-recording) began to promote the idea that plagiarism (occasionally called "plagiartism") was a valid form of artistic expression. Despite the rhetoric promulgated by the MONTY CANTSINS, KAREN ELIOTS, mail artists, and others, the goal of this artistic urge was never pure plagiarism, which requires an attempt to fool the audience. With esthetic plagiartism, the audience understands the source of the work, either implicitly or explicitly, and the plagiarism is merely the manipulation of the stolen sources. Even the SAMPLING of RAP music reflects this urge towards plagiarism. Part of the impetus for this type of work was a reaction to the hyper-anonymity of the modern, postindustrial world where, rather than being lost in a mass of humanity billions strong, we discovered ourselves singled out: our actions, purchases, and connections recorded and tracked by networks of computers, both governmental and corporate. In such a world, a retreat to group pseudonymity (in the form of Monty Cantsin) and a reliance on plagiarism as an esthetic helps to tie people together into a single structure (we, the people of the world, now, then, and forever).

—Geof Huth

Resources: *The Plagiarist Codex: An Old Maya Information Hieroglyph*. Madison, WI: Xexoxial Editions, 1988.

PLURALISM

One assumption behind the individual selections in this book, not to mention its title, holds that there is not one and only one avant-garde in any art, but several; and, because monopoly is impossible in an open, plural society, where culture develops mostly apart from state influence, these avant-gardes move in different, if comparably original, directions. For instance, the field of painting has in the past thirty years witnessed POP ART, OP ART, shaped canvases, monochromic fields, nonhierarchical pastiche, conundrum art (associated with JASPER JOHNS), CONCEPTUAL ART as well as ASSEMBLAGE, space-encasing ENVIRONMENTS, and works that resemble paintings but are not, such as the light pieces of JAMES TURRELL. Whereas only the followers of ARNOLD SCHOENBERG on one side and JOHN CAGE on the other were identified with avant-garde music three decades ago, now we can speak of ALEATORY, MODULAR, MICROTONAL, and MULTI-TRACK and SAMPLING tape developments as each generating new art.

Indeed, it seems that a period of pluralism in all the arts has succeeded an era of dichotomies. Although avant-garde is a useful general measure for distinguishing the new from the old, and thus one work can be more avant-garde than another (even if created by the same artist), beware of anyone who says that one or another decidedly innovative direction is necessarily "more" avant-garde than others. Likewise, beware of anyone or any group declaring itself the sole avant-garde, especially if s/he excludes or ignores people doing work that is roughly similar or closely related. Be even more wary if such monopolists try to sell you anything, intellectual as well as physical. Suspect this to be a road map directing all traffic to a dead end.

One fundamental difference in the current avant-gardes is that some would isolate the processes, capabilities, and materials of the established medium—say, the application of paint to a plane of canvas—while the other would mix painting with concerns and procedures from the other arts, such as working in three dimensions or using light. Similarly, the new music descending from Schoenberg would isolate phenomena particular to music—pitch, amplitude, timbre, dynamics, and duration—and then subject each of these musical dimensions to an articulate ordering, creating pieces of exceptionally rich musical interactivity. The other new music, traditionally credited to John Cage, would combine sound with theatrical materials in original ways, creating an experience not just for the ear but for the other senses too. In dance, one avant-garde would explore the possibilities of movement alone—Yvonne Rainer and Molissa Fenley (1954), for two—while the other favors theatrical conceptions, mixing in unusual ways such means as music, props, lights, setting, and costumes: Alwin Nikolais, Anna Halprin, or Meredith Monk. Paradoxically, Merce Cunningham, who was in his beginnings avant-garde in the first sense, switched his emphasis in the early sixties to become an innovating figure in mixed-means dance, only to return after 1967 to pieces predominantly about movement.

The avant-garde is thus not a single step built upon an old house but a diversity of radical and discontinuous alternatives to previously established paradigms. The result is not worldwide stylistic uniformity but numerous pockets of exponents of one or another innovative style. It has been the bias of art historians to portray one style as succeeding another (thus fresh artists gain reputations by climbing over their predecessors' backs), whereas the contemporary truth holds that several new styles can develop and thrive simultaneously and that there is not "progress" in art but an expansion of possibilities.

Bibliography: Kostelanetz, Richard. *Metamorphosis in the Arts* (1970). New York: Assembling, 1980; Kubler, George. *The Shape of Time*. New Haven: Yale University Press, 1962; Kuhn, Thomas S. *The Structure of Scientific Revolutions*. Chicago: University of Chicago Press, 1962; Munro, Thomas. *The Arts and Their Interrelations*. Cleveland, OH: Case Western Reserve University Press, 1969; Peckham, Morse. *Man's Rage for Chaos*. Philadelphia, PA: Chilton, 1965.

POLITICAL CORRECTNESS

(aka "PC," c. 1985).

Beginning as a reaction against the ethnocentricism and male-dominated language of the West, PC has spawned a noisy debate about what should be taught in American colleges. Initially this was an argument over linguistic propriety, especially on isolated college campuses; so that it is not "PC" to call a young woman a "babe," for example. Later in the 1980s arose a cultural argument, with self-conscious old fogeys, such as the late University of Chicago professor Allan Bloom, dismissing current popular culture as trash, while compusive list-makers, such as University of Virginia professor E. D. Hirsch, Jr., itemized "What Every American Needs to Know, " to cite the subtitle of his best-selling book. On the other side are "radical," "feminist," and "third-world" critics insisting that anyone who reads Charles Dickens must be hopelessly Western-culture-centric retrograde. The PC controversy has inspired collegiate humor, such as numerous "PC dictionaries" that attack cultural awareness by mocking it, in addition to a popular daily television symposium proudly calling itself Politically Incorrect. Sadly, PC issues have become a sledgehammer for both sides, with conservative academics bashing more liberal ones, and vice versa. A valid question is whether either group has emerged with greater intelligence or sensitivity from the process.

—with Richard Carlin

Bibliography: Beard, Henry, and Christopher Cerf. *The Official Politically Correct Dictionary and Handbook*. New York: Villard Books, 1993; Bloom, Allan. *The Closing of the American Mind*. New York: Simon & Schuster, 1988; Hirsch, E. D., Jr., et al. *The Dictionary of Cultural Literacy*. Boston: Houghton Mifflin, 1988.

POLKINHORN, Harry

(3 March 1945).

Among the strongest of the new VISUAL POETS to emerge in the 1980s, Polkinhorn also writes traditional verse, having produced a highly original antiwar epic, *Anaesthesia* (1985), which is composed of phrases, rather than poetic "lines," and is marked by unobvious turns. *Bridges of Skin Money* (1986) collects his early visual poetry. *Mount Soledad* (1997) is a textually rich recollection of a disappointing love affair with passages like this:

> march of history to a grand finale with trap doors and retreating women at work in beehives and industrial parks conscious abdication and abduction I've observed as if from up close or a distance indistinguishable war lords, another generation sets out on a juggernaut to deceive and lie as if time and circumstance the dripping lard of abuse that only a general famine could interrupt her full-blown consumption of steel plastic energy foodstuffs paper and water because they told her to take now on credit if necessary which some even admire.

Polkinhorn has also exhibited paintings, drawings, and photographs. Formerly a professor at the Imperial Valley campus of San Diego State University (and currently the director of its press), he translated an invaluable anthology of statements by Spanish and Portuguese-language experimental poets, *Corrosive Signs* (1990). His critical essays on avant-garde literature rank among the best. Unable to find a publisher for his collected criticism of literature and art, *Seeing Power*, Polkinhorn distributed the text in 1997 on the Internet.

Books: *Anaesthesia*. Clarence Center, New York: Textile Bridge, 1985; *Bridges of Skin Money*. Madison, WI: Xeroxial Editions, 1986; *Mount Soledad*. Barrytown, NY: Left Hand (USA 12507), 1996; *Corrosive Signs*. Ed. by Cesar Espinosa. Washington, DC: Maisonneuve (P.O. Box 2980, 20013), 1990; Alfredo Velasco, and Mal Lambert. *El Libro de Caló/Pachuco Slang Dictionary*. San Diego, CA: Atticus (P.O. Box 92728, 92192), 1983; —— et al., eds. *Open Signs: Language and Society on the U.S.-Mexico Border*. San Diego: San Diego State University Press, 1993; ——. ed. and trans. *Bodies Beyond Borders*. Calexico, CA: Binational, 1994.

Web Site: www.thing.net/~grist/l&d/hpsp-00.htm. (full text of *Seeing Power*).

POLLOCK, Jackson

(28 January 1912–11 August 1956).

Following his oldest brother's ambition for a painting career, Jackson Pollock went to New York as a young man, studying with the prominent Americanist painter Thomas Hart Benton (1889–1975), among others, who taught him realisms that Pollock quickly outgrew. Lacking conventional facility, Pollock was not a good student. Befriending the Russian-American painter JOHN GRAHAM, Pollock learned not only about modern European painting but primitive art that purportedly reflected unconscious dimensions of human experience.

Whereas DE KOONING radically extended CUBISM, Pollock initially developed another major innovation of early twentieth-century European art—EXPRESSIONISM. Pollock's departure depended upon innovative methods of applying paint to canvas. He laid it on the floor and then, in a series of rapid movements with sticks and stiffened brushes, literally poured and splattered paint all over the surface. He worked on his canvases from all sides, dripping paint at various angles, mixing enamels with oil pigments squeezed directly from its tubes, varying the rhythms of his movements. Some of the brilliance of *Blue Poles: Number 11, 1952* (1952), perhaps Pollock's last great painting, comes from adding aluminum paint. Though Pollock rejected many of the canvases produced by these impulsive and purposeful actions, certain pictures realized an overwhelming density of visual activity. One radical innovation is that such Expressionist intensity is visible *all over* the nonhierarchical, nonfocused canvas, thereby not only realizing the principle that any part epitomizes the whole but creating the sense that the imagery could have extended itself well beyond the painting's actual edges, if not forever. Wishing to overwhelm, Pollock reportedly "explored with the architect Peter Blake the idea of an 'ideal museum' in which his paintings would act as freestanding walls within an open architectural space."

Pollock's best paintings, like de Kooning's, suggest different levels of illusionistic space, but Pollock's decisively differed from de Kooning's by finally eschewing any reference to figures outside of painting. Such a complete meshing of image and field, content and canvas, even stasis and movement, creates a completely integrated, autonomous, and self-referential work that differs radically from the fragmented, allusive, and structured field of post-Cubist painting. Since he had undergone Jungian psychoanalysis, it was said that the only experience represented in Pollock's art was his mind at the time(s) of actually painting.

Whereas some of these expressionist canvases were big—often nine feet by eighteen, recalling Pollock's earlier interest in murals, others were small. He eschewed using the same size twice. Among the masterpieces in the latter vein is a favorite of mine, *Full Fathom Five* (1947), 50 7/8" by 30 1/8", whose dark, closely articulated surface includes not only paint thickly applied, but buttons, nails, tacks, coins, cigarettes, matches, etc. Whereas early Pollock paintings had poetic titles, some of which came from solicitous friends, by 1948 he followed the precedent established by Moholy-Nagy, among others, of simply numbering his works within each year, sometimes adding poetic prefixes or suffixes as subtitles.

Once Pollock's innovations earned sudden international acclaim in the early 1950s (along with the inevitable negative notices from dissenters), the self-destructive painter stopped producing, regrettably succumbing to the alcoholism that had earlier contributed to his unraveling. John Cage, among other sometime friends, spoke of how they would avoid contact with him in social situations. As few paintings were produced in the last four years of his life, Pollock's premature death in an auto accident seems, in retrospect, almost a narrative convenience.

A 1998 traveling retrospective, initiated at the Museum of Modern Art, belongs among the greatest exhibitions, including not only a wealth of works from Pollock's entire career but also demonstrating how certain familiar images, often reproduced, look not only so different, but so much more impressive, on walls, in their original sizes. Another virtue of this exhibition was including the classic Hans Namuth and Paul Falkenberg film about Pollock at work, some of it shot from a glass below, which ranks among the classic documentaries of artistic process (so superior to the more familiar form of an earnest head jabbering about his or her work).

Pollock's work was so well understood soon after its first appearance that commentary on it has hardly developed or changed in the decades since; and in this respect, Pollock criticism differs from that gathering around other avant-garde artists.

Selected Works: *Full Fathom Five*, 1947; *Alchemy,* 1947; *Summertime Number 9A*, 1948; *Cut Out Figure*, 1948; *White Cockatoo: Number 24A*, 1948; *The Wooden Horse*, 1948; *Number 1A*, 1948; *Number 13A,* 1948; *Arabesque*, 1948; *Out of the Web*: *Number 7*, 1949; *Autumn Rhythm #30*, 1950; *One: Number 31*, 1950; *Autumn Rhythm: Number 30, 1950*, 1950; *Number 32*, 1950; *Convergence: Number 10*, 1952; *Blue Poles: Number 11, 1952*, 1952.

Biography: Friedman, B. H. *Jackson Pollock: Energy Made Visible*. New York: McGraw-Hill, 1972; Naifeh, Seven, and Gregory White Smith. *Jackson Pollock: An American Saga*. New York: Harper, 1991.

Exhibition Catalogs: Sweeney, J. J. *Jackson Pollock*. New York: Art of this Century, 1943; Ossorio, Alfonso.

Jackson Pollock. New York: Betty Parsons Gallery, 1951; Greenberg, Clement. *Retrospective Exhibition of Jackson Pollock*. Bennington, VT: Bennington College, 1952; O'Connor, Francis V. *Jackson Pollock*. New York: MoMA, 1967; Rose, Bernice. *Jackson Pollock: Works on Paper*. New York: MoMA, 1969; Varnadoe, Kirk, with Pepe Carmel. *Jackson Pollock*. New York: MoMA, 1998.

Catalogue Raisonné: O'Connor, Francis V., and Eugene Victor Thaw. *Jackson Pollock: A Catalogue Raisonné of Paintings, Drawings, and Other Works*. 4 vols. New Haven: Yale University Press, 1978.

Web Pages: http://metalab.unc.edu/wm/paint/auth/pollock/; www.pkf.com (Pollock/Krassner foundation home page.)

Interpretation: Robertson, Bran. *Jackson Pollock*. New York: Abrams, 1960; Greenberg, Clement. *Art and Culture*. Boston: Beacon, 1961; O'Hara, Frank. *Jackson Pollock*. New York: Braziller, 1959; Landau, Ellen G. *Jackson Pollock*. New York: Harry N. Abrams, 1989.

POLYARTIST

(1969).

This is my honorific, coined back in 1969 and occasionally used by others, for the individual who excels at more than one nonadjacent art or, more precisely, is a master of several unrelated arts. The principal qualifier in my definition is "nonadjacent." In my understanding (sometimes missed by others using the term), painting and sculpture are adjacent, as are both film and photography, and both poetry and fiction (as many individuals excel at each pair). However, poetry and music are not adjacent. Nor are painting and fiction.

Thus, John Cage was a polyartist for excelling at music and poetry. So, in different ways were Wyndham Lewis, Moholy-Nagy, Theo van Doesburg, Kurt Schwitters, Jean (Hans) Arp, Jean Cocteau, and William Blake. Among contemporaries other than Cage I would rank Yvonne Rainer, Dick Higgins, and Kenneth King.

I distinguish the polyartist from the individual who excels at one art but not in another, such as Pablo Picasso, who quit painting for eighteen months in order to write modest poetry and plays, from the artist who incorporates several media into a single performance, in the tradition of the Wagnerian *Gesamtkunstwerk* (literally, "total artwork"); and from the dilettante who, as I understand that epithet, excels at nothing. "No one capable of genuine polyartistry," I once wrote, "should want to be merely an 'artist' anymore." One critical advantage of the term is forbidding the interpretation of work in one art with the terms of another (such as "poet's paintings").

Consider too that the great movements of classic modernism—Dada, Surrealism, Futurism, the Bauhaus—were all essentially polyartistic enterprises. True polyartistic criticism attempts to identify the esthetic ideas that are reflected in a polyartist's various works.

Interpretation: Kostelanetz, Richard. "Two Ways of Polyartistry." In *On Innovative Art(ist)s*. Jefferson, NC: McFarland, 1992.

POP ART

(c. 1960).

It was quite stunning at the beginning—the first post-World War II representational reaction to Abstract Art that was not primarily conservative (or antimodernist) in spirit. As the creation of painters conscious of art history, who had assimilated and revealed the influence of Abstraction, these paintings and sculptures of popular icons are primarily about "Art" (in contrast to commercial art, which is thoroughly worldly). One Pop style, exemplified by James Rosenquist (1933), uses both the scale and flat color, as well as the sentimentally realistic style and visible panel-separating lines, of billboard art to create large, glossy paintings that, like his classic ten-foot by eighty-eight-foot *F-111* (1965), are full of incongruous images. As the critic Harold Rosenberg once cracked, "This was advertising art advertising itself as art that hates advertising." Another Pop artist, ROY LICHTENSTEIN, painted enlarged comic-strip images, which are so refined in their realism that they even reproduce the dots characteristic of comic-book coloring. This theme of ironic displacement—the incongruous relation between the identifiable image and its model—informs not only Lichtenstein's highly comic paintings but also the Pop sculpture of CLAES OLDENBURG and certain paintings of ANDY WARHOL. To Barbara Rose (1937), at that time as sharp a critic as any, "These artists are linked only through subject matter, not through stylistic similarities."

Exhibition Catalogs: *The Popular Image Exhibition*. Washington, DC: Washington Gallery of Modern Art, 1963; *Mixed Media and Pop Art*. Buffalo, NY: Albright Knox, 1963; *American Pop Art*. Amsterdam: Stedelijk Museum, 1964; Alloway, Lawrence. *American Pop Art*. New York: Whitney Museum & Collier, 1974; Haskell, Barbara. *Blam! The Explosion of Pop, Minimalism, and Performance: 1958–1964*. New York: Whitney Museum, 1984; Umland, Anne, et al. *Pop Art: Selections from MoMA*. New York: MoMA, 1998.

Interpretation: Alloway, Lawrence, et al. *Modern Dreams: The Rise and Fall and Rise of Pop*. Cambridge: MIT Press, 1988; Finch, Christopher. *Pop Art*. New York: Dutton, 1968; Lippard, Lucy R., et al. *Pop Art*. New York: Praeger, 1966; Livingstone, Marco *Pop Art: A Continuing History*. London: Thames & Hudson, 1990; Madoff, Steven Henry, ed. *Pop Art: A Critical History*. Berkeley: University of California, 1998; Pierre, José. *Pop Art: An Illustrated Dictionary.* London: Eyre Methuen, 1976; Russell, John, and Suzi Gablik. *Pop Art Redefined.* New York: Praeger, 1969; Rose, Barbara. *Autocritique*. New York: Weidenfeld & Nicholson, 1988.

Web Site: http://www.fi.muni.cz/~toms/PopArt/index.html

PORTER, Bern

(14 February 1911).

Think of Porter as a twentieth-century Walt Whitman, a sometime printer and courageous publisher, a longtime servant of both U.S. letters and his own very American muse. He began as a physicist, only to become disillusioned with science during World War II. By its end, he published the first critical anthology on HENRY MILLER. *The Waste Maker* (1972) represents Porter's assiduous discovery of America writ large in the smallest "found" details, which he exposes in the guise of VISUAL POETRY that is formally similar to that of his contemporary CHARLES HENRI FORD. Collecting native waste into artlessly designed pages, Porter reflects not only his love and bitterness, but exposes cultural insights and perspectives. *The Waste Maker* ranks with MICHEL BUTOR'S *Mobile* (1963) as an encompassing pastiche of modern America. A yet bigger book, *Found Poems* (1972), measuring (in its original hardback edition) eight-and-a-half by eleven inches, with several hundred pages, collects all sorts of witty and incisive word-based poetic images. Though recognitions of Porter's greatness surface now and then, customarily in independent literary journals based in New England, his name does not appear in *Contemporary Poets* or, shamefully, in the standard histories of American literature.

Books: *I've Left* (1963). 2d ed. Millerton, NY: Something Else, 1971; *What Henry Miller Said and Why It Is Important*. Pasadena, CA: Marathon, 1964; *The Manhattan Telephone Book*. Somerville, MA: Abyss, 1972; *Found Poems*. Millerton, NY: Something Else, 1972; *The Book of Do's*. Hulls Cove, ME: Dog Ear/Tilbury House (132 Water St., 04345), 1982; *Here Comes Everybody's Don't Book*. Gardiner, ME: Dog Ear/Tilbury House, 1984; *Neverends*. Pt. Charlotte, FL: Runaway Spoon, 1988; *Numbers*. Pt. Charlotte, FL: Runaway Spoon, 1991.

Anthology: *Sounds That Arouse Me: Selected Writings*. Ed., with intro. by Mark Melnicove. Gardner, ME: Tilbury House, 1993.

Biography: Schevill, James. *Where To Go, What To Do, When You Are Bern Porter: A Personal Biography*. Gardner, ME: Tillbury House, 1992.

p

PORTER, Donald

(16 April 1939).

Educated in classics at the University of the South and in English literature at King's College, Cambridge, Porter wrote in the early seventies several highly original and complicated stories. The most visible, *As If a Footnote* (1974), is a fiction in which elaborate footnotes, beginning with numbers, continuing as letters (and then numbers doubled), become a comic counterpoint to the principal text. Porter remains one of the few to do what JOHN BARTH could not—elaborate on the advanced, highly literary position established in the latter's *Lost in the Funhouse* (1968). Finding familiar resistances to experimental fiction, Porter subsequently wrote several pop paperbacks and less innovative fictions, which is unfortunate, because *As If a Footnote* remains a classic, by any standards.

Books: *As If a Footnote*. New York: Assembling (P.O. Box 444, 10012–0008), 1974; *Jubilee Jim and the Wiz of Wall Street*. New York: Patton, 1990.

POSTMODERN

(c. 1949).

This term is included here not because it belongs but because too many people think it might belong. It is commonly used to characterize work that is not avant-garde at all but still purportedly contemporary, usually because of its journalistic subject matter (the assumption being that MODERNISM has died, to be replaced by something else). My personal opinion holds that anything characterized as postmodern, whether by its author or its advocates, is beneath critical consideration, no matter how immediately popular or acceptable it might be. The assumption of this book is that the revolutions implicit in modernism continue, and thus that current avant-garde art simply extends modernism, which is dead only to dodos. Charles Jencks proposes the term "late modern" as separate from early modern and postmodern, and while I accept Jencks's term as a useful antidote, I wish it were not necessary.

Just as this second edition was going to press, I looked into Mark C. Taylor's *Hiding* (1997), which is marvelously designed, with typography running both vertically and horizontally on the same pages, printing in various colors, paper differing in quality from section to section, faded photos of tattooed people, various colors, etc. After noticing on a copyright page that its author and/or his publisher wished the book to be classified under "Postmodernism," my crap-detector, as Ernest Hemingway called it, turned itself on. Thinking to test my resistance to that red flag against the text itself, I found on page 95 the following:

> European modernism invents itself by inventing primitivism. The modern is what the primitive is not, and the primitive is what the modern is not. Far from preceding the modern temporally and historically, primitivism and modernism are mutually constitutive and, therefore, emerge together.

Aside from approaching double-talk in the folding back of the concluding sentence, this is simply wrong historically. Modernism arose in response to prior developments in art and culture. Only later did some (and only some) modernists, such as MARSHALL MCLUHAN, come to identify certain primitivistic elements. Beware of anything billed as "postmodernist."

Bibliography: Jencks, Charles. *What Is Postmodernism?* New York: St. Martin's Press, 1986; Taylor, Mark C. *Hiding*. Chicago: University of Chicago Press, 1997.

POTAMKIN, Harry Alan

(1900–19 July 1933).

One of the first film critics in America, Potamkin had only a brief life in the field. From 1927 to his sudden death (from a botched operation), a period that witnessed the end of silent film and the birth of sound movies, Potamkin wrote extended, literate, thoughtful essays on American cinema, more frequently on French and Soviet films, on Chaplin, on the earliest American avant-garde filmmakers, and on the creative use of the movie-camera. A posthumous collection of Potamkin's texts is *The Compound Cinema* (1977), edited by Lewis Jacobs (1906) (who would in turn fulfill Potamkin's unfulfilled objective of writing the first important history of American film). Potamkin stressed the internal analysis of films, not their social or historical context—a position that set him apart from his peers, Marxist and otherwise. And he had a vision of cinema evolving: "Years hence, a Joyce will not think of attempting his compounds with words. He will go into cinema which unifies the verbal and aural with the visual and ultimately the spatial. . . ." It was appropriate that the most sophisticated British film journal of the period, *Closeup* (1927–33) chose Potamkin in 1929 to be its correspondent. Potamkin's nephew MILTON BABBITT is a distinguished American composer.

—Robert Haller

Anthology: *The Compound Cinema*. Ed. Lewis Jacobs. New York: Teachers College, 1977.

History: Jacobs, Lewis. *The Rise of the American Film* (1939). Rev. ed. New York: Teachers College, 1968.

POUND, Ezra

(30 October 1885–1 November 1973).

Pound's innovation was poetic COLLAGE, in which an abundance and variety of both experiential and linguistic materials are pulled together into a poetically integral mosaic—so that, even where striking images are evoked, the effect of their structural principle is unfamiliar, perhaps pointed juxtapositions. The achievement of the final edition of *The Cantos* (1970), which were begun over fifty years before, is a wealth of reference and language, both historic and contemporary, incorporated into a single sustained pastiche. The paradox of the poem's long history is that the collage form that seemed so innovative when the poem was begun had become familiar, if not old-fashioned, by the time it was complete. Back in 1970, I was compelled to moan, "More bad poetry in America today is indebted to Pound than anyone else." Pound's translations of Chinese and classic Latin and Greek poetry were innovative in that he did not attempt literally to translate these works. Though he often "translated" poems from languages he could not read, his nonliteral versions were often thought better at capturing the essence of the originals than more "accurate" translations. Pound was also a strong literary publicist who identified early in their careers the best writers of his generation, such as T. S. ELIOT and JAMES JOYCE, and even visual artists such as HENRI GAUDIER-BRZESKA. Pound's classic literary essay, *ABC of Reading*

Ezra Pound, photograph: Boris de Rachewiltz. Courtesy of New Directions Publishing Corp.

(1935), is no less provocative today. HUGH KENNER, who wrote the first influential introduction to Pound in 1951, produced in *The Pound Era* a rich interpretation of Pound's centrality to literary modernism.

Selected Books: *Gaudier-Brzeska: A Memoir* (1916). New York: New Directions, 1970; *Pavannes and Divisions*. New York: Knopf, 1918; *Instigations of Ezra Pound*. New York: Boni & Liveright, 1920; *Anthiel and the Treatise on Harmony*. Paris: Three Mountains, 1924; *Personae: The Collected Poems of Ezra Pound*. New York: Boni & Liveright, 1926; *Imaginary Letters*. Paris: Black Sun, 1930; *ABC of Economics*. London: Faber, 1933; *ABC of Reading* (1934). New York: New Directions, 1960; *Make It New*. London: Faber, 1934; *Jefferson and/or Mussolini* (1935). New York: Liveright, 1970; *Guide to Kulchur*. London: Faber, 1938; *The Pisan Cantos*. New York: New Directions, 1948; *Money Pamphlets*. London: Peter Russell, 1960; *Translations*. New York: New Directions, 1963; *A Lune Spento and Other Early Poems*. New York: New Directions, 1965; *Drafts & Fragments of Cantos CX-CXVIII*. New York: New Directions, 1969; *The Cantos*. New York: New Directions, 1970; *Plays Modelled on the Noh* (1916). New York: New Directions, 1987.

Compilations: *Literary Essays*. Ed, with an intro. by T. S. Eliot. London: Faber, 1954; *Impact: Essays on Ignorance and the Decline of American Civilization*. Ed. Noel Stock. Chicago: Regnery, 1960; *Selected Prose 1909–1965*. Ed. William Cookson. London: Faber, 1973; *Ezra Pound and Music: The Complete Criticism*. Ed. R. Murray Schafer. New York: New Directions, 1977; *"Ezra Pound Speaking": Radio Speeches of World War* II. Ed. Leonard Doob. Westport, CT: Greenwood, 1978; *Ezra Pound and the Visual Arts*. Ed. Harriet Zinnes. New York: New Directions, 1980; *The Collected Early Poems of Ezra Pound*. Ed. Michael John King. New York: New Directions, 1982; *Machine Art and Other Writings*. Ed. Maria Luisa Ardizzone. Durham: Duke University Press, 1996.

Correspondence: *The Letters of Ezra Pound*. Ed. D. D. Paige. New York: Harcourt, Brace, 1950; *Pound/Joyce: Letters and Essays*. Ed. Forrest Read. New York: New Directions, 1967; *Pound/Ford, the Story of a Literary Friendship: The Correspondence Between Ezra Pound and Ford Madox Ford and Their Writings About Each Other*. Ed. Brita Lindberg-Seyersted. New York: New Directions, 1982; *Ezra Pound and Dorothy Shakespear: Their Letters, 1909–1914*. Ed. Omar Pound and A. Walton Litz. New York: New Directions, 1984; *Pound/Lewis: The Letters of Ezra Pound and Wyndham Lewis*. Ed. Timothy Materer. New York: New Directions, 1985; *Pound/Zukofsky: Selected Letters of Ezra Pound and Louis Zukofsky*. Ed. Barry Ahearn. New York: New Directions, 1987; *Pound/The Little Review: The Letters of Ezra Pound to Margaret Anderson*. Ed. Thomas L. Scott, et al. New York: New Directions, 1988; *Ezra Pound & James Laughlin: Selected Letters*. Ed. David M. Gordon. New York: Norton, 1994.

Biography: Carpenter, Humphrey. *A Serious Character: The Life of Ezra Pound*. Boston: Houghton Mifflin, 1988; Doolittle, Hilda. *End to Torment: A Memoir of Ezra Pound*. New York: New Directions, 1985; Stock, Noel. *The Life of Ezra Pound*. New York: Routledge, 1970; Tytell, John. *Ezra Pound: The Solitary Volcano*. New York: Doubleday Anchor, 1987; Wilhelm, J. J. *Ezra Pound in London and Paris: 1908–1925*. University Park: Pennsylvania State University Press, 1990.

Web Page: http://www.english.udel.edu/mkraus/pound.html (links).

Interpretation: Bush, Ronald. *The Genesis of Ezra Pound's "Cantos."* Princeton: Princeton University Press, 1976; Kenner, Hugh. *The Poetry of Ezra Pound*. New York: New Directions, 1951; ——. *The Pound Era*. Berkeley: University of California Press, 1972; Fraser, G. S. *Ezra Pound*. New York: Grove, 1961; Kostelanetz, Richard. "Impounding Pound's Milestone" (1970). In *The Old Poetries and the New*. Ann Arbor, MI: University of Michigan, 1981; Nadel, Ira Bruce. ed. *The Cambridge Companion to Ezra Pound*. New York: Cambridge University Press, 1999; Terrell, Carroll F. *A Companion to the Cantos of Ezra Pound*. 2 vols. Berkeley: University of California, 1993.

Bibliography: Gallup, Donald. *A Bibliography of Ezra Pound*. London: Rupert Hart-Davis, 1963; ——. *On*

Contemporary Bibliography with Particular Reference to Ezra Pound. Austin: University of Texas Humanities Research Center, 1970.

POWELL, Michael

(30 September 1905–19 February 1990) and **Emeric Pressburger** (5 December 1902–5 February 1988).

Powell, born in England, began as a slick director, reportedly producing twenty-three films between 1931 and 1936. Pressburger, born in Hungary, had worked as a scriptwriter in Germany, Austria, and France before arriving in England in 1936. The London producer Alexander Korda (1893–1956) brought them together, initially for *The Spy in Black* (1939), a thriller about espionage that had success in America as *U-Boat 29*. Calling their production company The Archers, Powell and Pressburger collaborated for seventeen years, sharing credits for writing, directing, and producing.

Their masterpiece is *The Tales of Hoffman* (1951), a lushly beautiful feature that has been described as either the most eccentric and successful film adaptation of an opera or as the classiest musical film ever made. (It makes most Hollywood musicals look tawdry.) Even in excerpts, which are often seen on American cable television on the "Classical Arts Showcase" (where I discovered it), the film is continuously bizarre and impressive.

Working on his own, Powell directed *Peeping Tom* (1960), which portrays a psychopathic killer who records on film the dying moments of his female victims. Reviled at the time and thus terminating Powell's career prematurely, this film is frequently revived, often with apologies from critics who remember dismissing it before. Nowadays it is praised, in Ephraim Katz's phrases, as "a complex film-within-film essay on voyeurism and the psychology of motion-picture viewing."

The influence of Powell and Pressburger survives in the musical films of Peter Greenway (1942), an Englishman who also produces paintings, novels, illustrated books, and gallery exhibitions, in addition to staged operas—*Rosa: A Horse Drama* (1994) with music by the Dutchman Louis Andriessen (1939) and *100 Objects To Represent the World—a Prop Opera* (1997) with Jean-Baptiste Barrière's music. Powell's second wife, Thelma Schoonmaker (1945), is a major American film editor renowned particularly for her work with Martin Scorsese.

Other Films: *The Life and Death of Colonel Blimp*, 1943; *Black Narcissus*, 1947; *The Red Shoes*, 1948; *The Small Back Room*, 1949; *Gone to Earth, The Elusive Pimpernel*, 1950; *Ill Met by Moonlight*, 1957.

Videotapes: *Tales of Hoffman* (1951), Home Vision Cinema, 1993; *Black Narcissus* (1947), Hallmark Home Entertainment, 1996; *Peeping Tom* (1960), Home Vision Cinema, 1996; *Gone to Earth, The Elusive Pimpernel* (1950), Home Vision Cinema, 1998.

Writings: and Emeric Pressburger. *The Life and Death of Colonel Blimp*. London: Faber & Faber, 1994.

Autobiography: Powell, Michael. *A Life in the Movies*. New York: Knopf, 1987.

Biography: Macdonald, Kevin. *Emeric Pressburger: The Life and Death of a Screenwriter*. London: Faber, 1994.

Web Site: http://members.aol.com/DavAbs/DavAbs/index.html

Interpretation: Christie, Ian. *Arrows of Desire: The Films of Michael Powell and Emeric Pressburger* (1985). London: Faber, 1994; Salwolke, Scott. *The Films of Michael Powell and the Archers*. Lanham, MD: Scarecrow, 1997.

PRAECISIO

(timeless, formless, motionless, beingless).

You won't find this term in any dictionary. *The Oxford English Dictionary* specifically excludes Renaissance rhetorical terms, and praecisio (pronounced "pray-KEY-see-oh") is one of these. Praecisio is the figure of speech one step beyond aporia, the figure of speech wherein, instead of speaking, one makes one's point by holding one's tongue: It is the silence that is the message and the method. This silence, or the suggestion of silence, is often a strong message, one that avant-gardists have used for years. Examples of avant-garde praecisio include the pataphysical "Passage de la Mer Rouge par les H–breux" (a "drawing") from 1965, JOHN BYRUM's "Batesville, Indiana" (a visual poem consisting of four empty rectangles), various nonperformances of G. X. Jupitter-Larsen and The Haters, poems that consist of nothing but titles, and the international Art Strike (1990–93). Even Jean Arp's famous line ("a knifeless blade which is missing its handle") is a deft little conceptual praecisio, surprising us with its absence.

—Geof Huth

Resources: Quinn, Arthur. *Figures of Speech: Sixty Ways to Turn a Phrase*. Davis, CA: Hermagoras, 1993.

PREPARED PIANO

(c. 1938).

JOHN CAGE coined this term to describe his internal modifications to the standard piano in order to change the sounds it produces. Typically, he inserted pieces of metal, paperclips, erasers, rubber bands, wooden spoons, and other objects between the strings. He played both the keys and the strings, sometimes depressing the keyboard in order to free the strings from the dampers. These modifications transformed the piano from primarily a melodic instrument into a percussive one. Among the other American composers to use variations on this contemporary instrument are Lou Harrison (1917—who merits an entry in this book, did he not personally tell me that his work wasn't avant-garde), August M. Wegner (1941), Stephen Scott (1944), Samuel Pellman (1953), Alan Stout (1932), and Richard Bunger (1942), who recorded an album wholly of compositions for prepared piano before his departure from the music profession.

Recordings: Bunger, Richard. *Prepared Piano: The First Four Decades*. Tinton Falls, NJ: Musical Heritage, 1983; Cage, John. *Sonatas & Interludes for Prepared Piano* (1947–49). Many other recordings.

Interpretation: Bunger, Richard. *The Well-Prepared Piano*. Sebastopol, CA: Litoral Arts, 1981.

PRITCHARD, Norman Henry II

(22 October 1939–8 February 1996).

A New Yorker of West Indian descent, Pritchard published in 1970 and 1971 two books of innovative poetry. The first, *The Matrix Poems: 1960–70* (1970), includes VISUAL POEMS along with MINIMAL poems and TEXT-SOUND TEXTS. His style in the last vein depends upon repeating the same phrase until something other than the original phrase results. In the only conveniently recorded example, "Gyre's Galax," the phrase " above beneath" is rapidly repeated, with varying pauses between each line. (The reader repeating these two words rapidly aloud to himself or herself will get a faint sense of the effect.) Pritchard stopped publishing in the early 1970s, and before his early death from cancer was residing in rural eastern Pennsylvania.

Recordings: "Gyre's Galax. " On *New Jazz Poets*, ed. Walter Lowenfels. New York: Folkways/Broadside 9751, 1967.

Books: *The Matrix Poems 1960–70*. Garden City, NY: Doubleday, 1970; *Eecchhooeess* New York: N.Y.U. Press, 1971.

PROJECTION TELEVISION

(c. 1967).

It was at a Janis Joplin concert in the late 1960s that I first saw a face projected live onto a large television screen, and this has since become a common sight at rock concerts. In the mid-1970s, a projection TV with a distant screen was common particularly in educational institutions, on airplanes, and in bars featuring sporting events. A three-lens, three-color system situated several feet away from a screen projected the image.

The next development came in the early 1990s, when Sharp offered a projection system that differs from the earlier versions in several respects. Whereas the heavy old two-piece systems had to be kept permanently in place, SharpVision (at thirty-one pounds) could be moved about easily; whereas the old system required the installation of a fixed screen especially designed for it, SharpVision could be projected onto any flat surface, such as a clean wall. Thanks to liquid crystal display (LCD) panels (similar technologically to those in digital watches), the picture emerges from a single source.

All of these two-piece projection systems differ from the single-piece rear-projection boxes with screens measuring from forty inches, diagonally, to seventy; because they weigh upwards of 200 pounds, rear-projection systems are nearly always mounted on the floor. What they gain in scale for the viewer they lose in detail. In my own experience of a large separate screen, which I placed directly above a normal monitor, I found my eye preferring the smaller monitor for most television programs, but the screen for movies, especially if made before 1960, and for sports, where television directors have less control over the scale of the images on the screen. Once projection systems outnumber monitors, as I expect they will, you can assume that television directors will shoot live images to a scale more familiar to motion pictures. I wrote in the first edition of this *Dictionary* that a good book on this subject has yet to be written; it still hasn't appeared, to my knowledge.

PROLETARIAN MUSIC

(1917).

The ideological upheaval that accompanied the Soviet Revolution of 1917 posed an immediate problem of creating arts that would be consonant with the aims and ideals of socialist society. Since the political structure of the Soviet government was that of the dictatorship of the proletariat, it was imperative to postulate a special type of literature, drama, art, and music that would be proletarian in substance and therefore accessible to the popular masses. Some Soviet theoreticians proposed to wipe off the slate of the arts the entire cultural structure that preceded the Revolution and to create a tabula rasa on which to build a new proletarian edifice. Among suggestions seriously offered by some musicians in the early days of the Soviet Revolution was confiscation of all musical instruments in order to abolish the tempered scale and to construct new instruments based on acoustically pure intervals. A more appropriate suggestion was made to compose music which included sounds familiar to a proletarian worker. A symphony of the factory was actually staged in an experimental demonstration, with singers and players placed on rooftops. Shostakovich included a factory whistle in the score of his *May First Symphony*. Alexander Mossolov wrote a ballet called *Iron Foundry*, in which a large sheet of steel was shaken to imitate the sound of the forge. Unsuccessful attempts were made to proletarianize the librettos of old operas. In one production, Puccini's opera *Tosca* was advanced from Napoleonic times to those of the Paris Commune. Tosca kills not the chief of the Roman police but the anti-Communard general Gallifet, disregarding the fact that the actual general Gallifet died in bed long after the fall of the Commune. Meyerbeer's opera *The Huguenots* was renamed *The Decembrists* and the action transferred to December 1825 to celebrate the rebellion of a group of progressive-minded aristocrats against the accession to the throne of the Czar Nicholas I.

The notorious Russian Association of Proletarian Musicians (RAPM) was founded in 1924 to pass judgment on the fitness and unfitness of all music for proletarian consumption. It stipulated an arbitrary code of desirable musical attributes, among them unrelenting optimism, militant socialism, proletarian class-consciousness, representational programmaticism, and the preferential use of major keys.

Beethoven was commended by the RAPM for his rebellious spirit; among Russian composers, Mussorgsky was singled out as a creator of realistic art. A difficult problem was posed by Tchaikovsky. His profound pessimism and fatalism, his reactionary political views, and particularly his homosexuality seemed an insurmountable barrier for the RAPM theoreticians to overcome. But Tchaikovsky was a favorite composer, not only of the popular masses, but also of the entire Presidium of the Soviet of People's Commissars. However, even from the purely musical standpoint, Tchaikovsky was theoretically unacceptable. His preference for minor keys and for melancholy moods in his operas and symphonies are the very antinomy of all that the new society of Soviet Russia stood for. In their attempt to rationalize the popularity of the *Pathétique Symphony,* the RAPM reached the acme of casuistry. In this work, so the argument went, Tchaikovsky delivered a magnificent funeral oration on the tomb of the bourgeoisie, and the superb artistic quality of this lamentation could not fail to please proletarian listeners. But soon the dialectical self-contradictions became evident even to the most obdurate members of the RAPM, and factional strife pulled their ideology apart. There were also signs of repugnance against the vicious attacks led by the RAPM against the surviving composers of pre-revolutionary times, greatly esteemed Conservatory professors, and any others who dared to oppose the new untenable ideology. The entire controversy was suddenly resolved when the Soviet government summarily disbanded the RAPM. As one composer expressed the nearly unanimous satisfaction at this action, "We could once again dare to write music in 3/4 time," alluding to the RAPM's ridiculous insistence that proletarian music ought to be written in march time.

The valid residue of proletarian music found its way to Germany and to America, assuming special national idioms. Simplicity of form, utilization of popular dance rhythms and, in theatrical music, a selection of subjects from Revolutionary history or class warfare, were the main characteristics of music for the proletariat. In America, proletarian opera flourished briefly in the 1930s with MARC BLITZSTEIN as its chief proponent. In Germany, KURT WEILL, working in close collaboration with the dramatist Bertolt Brecht (1898–1956), created a type of music drama that, in its social consciousness, had a strong affinity with proletarian music. In Russia itself, after the disbandment of the RAPM, viable ideas of proletarian music were absorbed in the doctrine of Socialist Realism.

—Nicolas Slonimsky

Related Reading: Gordon, Eric A. *Mark the Music: The Life and Work of Marc Blitzstein*: New York: St. Martin's Press, 1989.

PROUST, Marcel

(10 July 1871–18 November 1922).

In his multivolume fiction, *A la Recherche du temps perdu (Remembrance of Things Past*, 1913–27), this French author transcended earlier conventions of novel-writing. Drawing upon Henri Bergson's theories of time—chiefly the difference between historical or chronological time and interior or psychological time—Proust weaves a story that is as much about the processes of memory (voluntary, involuntary, rational, and especially sensate) as it is about its main characters (Charles Swann and the wealthy Guermantes family). The novel amplifies late nineteenth-century realism with rich and abundant detail, for example using many pages to describe lying in bed or taking a piece of cake with a cup of tea. At the same time, "real" objects and events assume "symbolic" and mythic import in Proust's poetic evocation.

Although dealing with issues of morality and decadence in its depiction of French culture at the turn of the century, Proust's work consciously displays the power of art to fix permanently what in life, time, and memory are always in flux. Originally published in sixteen French volumes, Proust's masterpiece was available in English first in C. K. Scott Moncrieff's translation (1927–32) and now in Terence Kilmartin's revision of Scott Moncrieff's text. Proust's influence on subsequent writers such as WILLIAM FAULKNER and JACK KEROUAC is immeasurable.

—Katy Matheson

Writings: *Swann's Way*. Trans. C. K. Scott-Moncrieff. 2 vols. New York: Henry Holt & Co., 1922; *Within a Budding Grove*. Trans. C. K. Scott-Moncrieff. 2 vols. New York: Boni, 1924; *Guermantes Way*. Trans. C. K. Scott-Moncrieff. New York: Seltzer, 1925; *Cities of the Plain*. Trans. C. K. Scott-Moncrieff. 2 vols. New York: Boni, 1927; *Sweet Cheat Gone.* Trans. C. K. Scott-Moncrieff. New York: Boni, 1930; *The Past Recaptured.* Trans. Fredrick Blossom. New York: Boni, 1932; *Time Regained.* Trans. Stephen Hudson. London: Chatto & Windus, 1932; *Remembrance of Things Past.* Trans. C. K. Scott Moncrieff and Terence Kilmartin. New York: Random House, 1981; *On Art and Literature 1896–1919* (1954, 1957). Trans. and ed. Sylvia Townsend Warner. New York: Carroll & Graf, 1984; *On Reading Ruskin.* Trans. and ed. Jean Autret, et al. New Haven, CT: Yale University Press, 1987.

Biography: Painter, George D. *Marcel Proust* (1959, 1965). New York: Random House, 1990; Heyman, Ronald. *Marcel Proust.* New York: HarperCollins, 1990.

Web Page: http://www.library.uiuc.edu/kolbp/

Interpretation: Brée, Germaine. *Marcel Proust and Deliverance of Time* (1960). 2d ed. Westport, CT: Greenwood, 1982; Bucknall, Barbara, ed. *Critical Essays on Marcel Proust.* Boston: G. K. Hall, 1987; Fowlie, Wallace. *A Reading of Proust.* Garden City, NY: Anchor, 1964; Frank, Joseph. *The Widening Gyre.* New Brunswick, NJ: Rutgers University Press, 1963; Kilmartin, Terence. *A Guide to Proust.* London, England: Chatto & Windus, 1983.

PSEUDONYMS

(forever).

Though human beings have forever been taking other names for professional purposes, the most familiar literary precedents being nineteenth-century women who assumed male names to make their writing publicly acceptable (e.g., George Eliot, George Sand), only in modern times, as far as I can tell, have pseudonyms functioned to identify alternative artistic identities. If the name Vernon Duke identified the light music of Vladimir Dukelsky (1903–69), so the names Patrick Ireland and FLANN O'BRIEN grace works by civil servants BRIAN O'DOHERTY and Brian O'Nolan, respectively, in each case signing work that probably could not have been done as well under their own names. At their most effective, pseudonyms enable their authors to do something considerably different from their normal activity, P. D.Q. BACH becoming not only a container for Peter Schickele's comedy but creating a more interesting composer, HUGH MACDAIRMID becoming a more aggressive Scottish presence than Christopher Murray Grieve's. (Pseudonyms have also functioned to hide the identities of writers who were politically blacklisted, as during the McCarthyite 1950s in Hollywood, when an Academy Award was offered to someone who, in a DADAISH mockery, could not show up to receive it.)

Marc Dachy reminds us that Arthur Cravan (1887–1918), a true free spirit, wrote the entire issue of a proto-Dada magazine, *Maintenant* (1915), by himself: "W. Cooper for articles on Oscar Wilde, Eduard Archinard (almost a phonetic anagram of *anarchie)* for a poem in classical alexandrines, Marie Lowitska for aphorisms, Robert Miradique for literary criticism. The boxer-poet signed his own name to his apocryphal encounters with André Gide and to his detailed, mordant comments upon the artists exhibiting at the Salon des Independants." The Portuguese poet FERNANDO PESSOA likewise used several pseudonyms for various compartments of his multiple creative personality.

Related Readings: Atkinson, Frank. *Dictionary of Literary Pseudonyms.* London: Bingley, 1982; Cushing, William. *Initials and Pseudonyms: A Dictionary of Literary*

Disguises (1885). Waltham, MA: Mark Press, 1963; Dachy, Marc. *The Dada Movement*. New York: Rizzoli, 1990; Room, Adrian. *Naming Names: Stories of Pseudonyms and Name Changes with a Who's Who*. Jefferson, NC: McFarland, 1981; Schickele, Prof. [sic] Peter. *The Definitive Biography of P.D.Q. Bach*. New York: Random House, 1976; Scroggins, Daniel C. *20,000 Spanish American Pseudonyms*. Lanham, MD: Scarecrow, 1997.

PSYCHEDELIC ART

(1960s).

This epithet arose in the 1960s, in the wake of increasing recreational use of lysergic acid, commonly called LSD, along with related "psychedelics" that produced colorful hallucinations in the user's mind and had an obvious attraction to those predisposed to otherworldly experience. Psychedelic art purported to represent such heightened mental states, customarily on canvas, sometimes with lights. One critical claim made for this work was that it represented deeper unconscious states than could be reached without such stimulants. Most psychedelic art in retrospect looks either like a highly stylized Expressionism or colorful updated religous art that didn't survive into the 1970s. For all the work's innovative strength when it first appeared, the principal contemporaneous book about the style features names that are now forgotten, some of them perhaps lost to drug excesses which had a deleterious effect upon those coming of age in the 1960s comparable to that caused by alcohol for earlier generations.

Interpretation: Masters, Robert E. L., and Jean Houston. *Psychedelic Art*. Ed. Marshall Lee. New York: Grove Press-Balance House, 1968.

PUNK ROCK

(c. 1975).

Punk developed in England as a reaction of those musicians born in the 1950s and 1960s to the increasingly slick, commercial popular music associated with the first generation of rock stars born in the 1940s. (It is awesome to recall that the Rolling Stones, so raucously offensive in 1965, especially to older people, could be perceived a decade later as slick.) One assumption of punk was that anybody could play or write music—indeed, that musical talent might even be a liability. Punk clubs made little distinction between performer and audience. While the performers often held their audiences in contempt, the audience responded by ignoring the performance on stage, all in reaction to the mutual seductiveness of earlier popular music. British punk also had a political dimension as a reaction to increasingly conservative British politics. When punk came to lower Manhattan in the mid-1970s, it had more impact on fashion than music, as new kinds of hairstyles, clothing, makeup, and demeanor seemed stronger than any musical message. Griel Marcus (1945), among the more literate of the American rock critics, once wrote a fat, pretentious, but ultimately unpersuasive book that regarded punk as the legitimate heir of avant-garde radicalism.

—with Richard Carlin

Bibliography: Marcus, Griel. *Lipstick Traces*. Cambridge: Harvard University Press, 1988; Heylin, Clinton. *From the Velvets to the Voidoids*. New York: Penguin, 1993; McNeil, Legs, ed. *Please Kill Me: The Uncensored Oral History of Punk*. New York: Penguin, 1997.

PYNCHON, Thomas

(8 May 1937).

I would love to write an entry that portrays Pynchon's spectacular development from precociously sophisticated short stories about scientific concepts, such as "Entropy" (1960), through the absurdist vision of history portrayed in his first novel *V.* (1963), which I featured in a 1965 essay on "The American Absurd Novel," to *Gravity's Rainbow* (1973), which parades many signs of an avant-garde masterpiece. The problem is that, though purportedly "a good reader," I have never been able to finish that last 600-plus-

Punk Rock. The Sex Pistols, 1976. CORBIS/Hulton-Deutsch Collection.

page book (having taken it on airplanes, to the beach, even to Europe!) and would not, on my own authority, begin to introduce it. I am told its subject is conspiracies, which is certainly unfashionable intellectually. I hear that *Vineland* (1990) represents a falling away from its predecessor, much as Pynchon's second novel, *The Crying of Lot 49* (1966), is a much slighter book than *V*. Given my problems, it is scarcely surprising that even in mid-career Pynchon has become one of those rare writers who has inspired a critical literature whose total wordage greatly exceeds the number of words in his own books. This is an inadvertant achievement not to be dismissed.

Works: "Entropy" (1960). In *Slow Learner*. Boston: Little, Brown, 1984; *V*. Philadelphia, PA: Lippincott, 1963; *The Crying of Lot 49*. Philadelphia, PA: Lippincott, 1966; *Gravity's Rainbow*. New York: Viking, 1973; *Vineland*. Boston: Little, Brown, 1990; *Mason & Dixon*. New York: Holt, 1997.

Web Site: http://www.hyperarts.com/pynchon/

Interpretation: Clerc, Charles. *Approaches to Gravity's Rainbow*. Columbus: Ohio State University Press, 1983; Cooper, Peter L. *Thomas Pynchon and the Contemporary World*. Berkeley: University of California Press, 1983; Cowart, David. *Thomas Pynchon: The Art of Allusion*. Carbondale: Southern Illinois University Press,1980; Dugdale, John. *Thomas Pynchon: Allusive Parables of Power*. London: Macmillan, 1990; Eddins, Dwight. *The Gnostic Pynchon*. Bloomington: Indiana University Press, 1990; Fowler, Douglas. *A Reader's Guide to Gravity's*

Rainbow. Ann Arbor, MI: Ardis, 1980; Grant, J. Kerry. *A Companion to the Crying of Lot 49*. Athens, GA: University of Georgia Press, 1994; Hite, Molly. *Ideas of Order in the Novels of Thomas Pynchon*. Columbus: Ohio State University Press, 1983; Levine, George, and David Leverenz, eds. *Mindful Pleasures: Essays on Thomas Pynchon*. Boston: Little, Brown, 1976; Mackey, Douglas. *The Rainbow Quest of Thomas Pynchon*. San Bernadino, CA: Borgo, 1980; McHoul, Alec and Wills, David. *Writing Pynchon: Strategies in Fictional Analysis*. London: Macmillan, 1990; Mendelson, Edward, ed. *Pynchon: A Collection of Critical Essays*. Englewood Cliffs, NJ: Prentice–Hall, 1978; O'Donnell, Patrick, ed. *New Essays on the Crying of Lot 49*. Cambridge, England, & New York: Cambridge University Press, 1991; Pearce, Richard. ed. *Critical Essays on Thomas Pynchon*. Boston: G. K. Hall, 1981; Plater, William M. *The Grim Phoenix: Reconstructing Thomas Pynchon*. Bloomington: Indiana University Press, 1978; Schaub, Thomas. *Pynchon: The Voice of Ambiguity*. Urbana: University of Illinois Press, 1981; Seed, David. *The Fictional Labyrinths of Thomas Pynchon*. London: Macmillan, 1988; Siegal, Mark Richard. *Pynchon: Creative Paranoia in Gravity's Rainbow*. Port Washington NY: Kennikat, 1978; Slade, Joseph V. *Thomas Pynchon*. New York: Warner, 1974; Stark, John O. *Pynchon's Fictions: Thomas Pynchon and the Literature of Information*. Athens: Ohio University Press, 1980; Tanner, Tony. *Thomas Pynchon*. London: Methuen, 1982; Weissenburger, Steven. *A Gravity's Rainbow Companion*. Athens: University of Georgia Press, 1988.

Bibliography: Mead, Clifford. *Thomas Pynchon: A Bibliography of Primary and Secondary Materials*. Normal, IL: Dalkey Archive, 1989.

QUANT, Mary

(11 February 1934).

Credit her with inventing the miniskirt and the companion minidress, which, by bringing hemlines above the knee, gave women more genuine freedom of lateral movement than previous fashions. The miniskirt depended, like so much else new in art, upon a technological development, in this case low-cost tights (aka panty hose) as a replacement for cumbersome thigh-high stockings that required a garter belt. The miniskirt represented a revolution comparable to the development in the early 1920s of the Maiden Form, which was the first uplifting brassiere, radically reshaping the female form in public. (That accounts for why bra-burning became a liberating theatrical event for certain radical women.) As legs clad in panty hose became more visible, designers gave them patterns and colors bolder than those previously associated with stockings. Miniskirts also forced the elimination of girdles and looked better with low-heeled, "sensible" shoes. Sociologically, miniskirts permitted *young* women to become the trendsetters in fashion. Though some of Mary Quant's sketches from 1958–61 reportedly included short-length dresses, she did not manufacture for a mass market until 1962. Negative reaction was vociferous, if shortlived; by the end of 1966, Quant herself wore a miniskirt to receive her OBE from the Queen. Though fashion publicists are forever predicting repudiation of the mini styles, they have survived.

Autobiography: *Quant by Quant. New York:* Putnam's, 1966.

QUENEAU, Raymond

(21 February 1903–25 October 1976).

Very much a smart writer's smart writer, Queneau was brilliant beyond measure, working in a variety of mostly original ways. After SURREALIST beginnings, he became involved with PATAPHYSICS, an avant-garde parody-philosophy calling itself the "science of imaginary solutions." In 1960, Queneau cofounded *Ouvroir de Littérature Potentielle*, commonly known as OULIPO, along with the mathematician François Le Lionnais. In addition to working as a publisher, as a translator into French (of books such as *The Palm Wine Drinkard* by AMOS TUTUOLA), and as the principal editor of the Pléiade encyclopedia, Queneau published comic pop novels, such as *Zazie dans le metro* (1959; *Zazie*, 1960), along with such experimental works as *Exercises de style* (1947; *Exercises in Style*, 1958), a tour de force, or farce, in which the same scene is described in ninety-nine different ways.

His avant-garde masterpiece, so audaciously extraordinary it will never be transcended or remotely repeated, is *Cent mille milliards de poèmes* (100,000 billion poems, 1961), in which he writes ten sonnets whose lines (in place) are interchangeable, because they are die-cut into strips bound to the book's spine, creating combinatorial sonnet possibilities numbering ten to the fourteenth power. The result is the creation of preconditions for the reader to discover a multitude of relationships not intended.

Works in English: *Le Chiendent* (1933). Trans. Barbara Wright as *The Bark-Tree*. New York: New Directions, 1971; *Un rude hiver* (1939). Trans. Betty Askwith as *A Hard Winter*. London: John Lehmann, 1948; *Pierrot mon ami* (1942). Trans. J. Maclaren-Ross as *Pierrot*. London: John Lehmann, 1950; *Loin de Rueil* (1944). Trans. by H. J. Kaplan as *The Skin of Dreams*. Norfolk, CT: New Dirctions, 1948; *Zazie dans le Metro* (1959). Trans. Barbara Wright as *Zazie*. New York: Harpers, 1960; *Exercises in Style* (1947; rev. ed. 1964). Trans. Barbara Wright. New York: New Directions, 1958; *Les Fleurs bleues* (1965). Trans. Barbara Wright as *Blue Flowers*. New York: Atheneum, 1967; *The Flight of Icarus*. Trans. Barbara Wright. New York: New Directions, 1973; *The Sunday of Life*. Trans. Barbara Wright. New York: New Directions, 1977; *We Always Treat Women Too Well*. Trans. Barbara Wright. New York: New Directions, 1981; *Cent mille milliards de poèmes* (1961). Trans. John Crombie as *One Hundred Million Poems*. Paris: Kickshaws, 1983; *Pounding the Pavements, Beating the Bushes, and other Pataphysical Poems*. Trans. Teo Savory. Greensboro, NC: Unicorn, 1985; *Odile*. Trans. Carol Sanders. Normal, IL: Dalkey Archive, 1988; *The Last Days*. Trans. Barbara Wright. London & Normal, IL: Atlas & Dalkey Archive, 1990; *Saint Glinglin*. Trans. James Sallis. Normal, IL: Dalkey Archive, 1993; *Children of Clay*. Trans. Madeleine Velguth. Los Angeles: Sun & Moon, 1998.

Interpretation: Cobb, Richard. *Raymond Queneau*. Oxford, England: Clarendon, 1976; Esslin, Martin. "Raymond Queneau. " In *The Novelist as Philosopher*, ed. John Cruickshank. New York: Oxford, 1962; Guicharnaud, Jacques. *Raymond Queneau*. New York: Columbia University Press, 1965; Hale, Jane Alison. *The Lyric Encyclopedia of Raymond Queneau*. Ann Arbor: University of Michigan Press, 1989; Mercier, Vivian. *A Reader's Guide to the New Novel from Queneau to Pinget*. New York: Farrar, Straus, 1971; Shorley, Christopher. *Queneau's Fiction: An Introductory Study*. Cambridge, England, & New York: Cambridge University Press, 1985.

RADIO ART

(1920s).

Radio art exploits capabilities unique to audio broadcasting. Mark E. Cory tells of Richard Hughes's 1924 radio play set in a mine after a cave-in had extinguished all light. As Cory writes, "Listeners and characters work out the consequences of being trapped in darkness in a bond no other dramatic medium could forge as well. NBC would later exploit the principle in its *Lights Out* series of ghost stories." ORSON WELLES's celebrated *War of the Worlds* broadcast depended upon the convention, used even in 1938, of interrupting a program with on-the-scene news bulletins. More recently, the Australian CHRIS MANN simultaneously broadcast his *Quadraphonic Cocktail* over two mono AM stations and one stereo FM station, depending upon the fact that even in Australia listeners are likely to have three radios in fairly close proximity to one another.

Within broadcasting institutions in the past three decades, radio art matured mostly in Germany, usually in departments called *Hörspiel*, or "hear-play." The principal development is away from reproducing the illusion of live theater or poetic monologues, with their literary base, toward audio experience based in sound. In *Der Monolog der Terry Jo* (Saarländischen Rundfunks, 1968), by Ludwig Harig and Max Bense, the voice of an unconscious accident victim is rendered by an electroacoustic vocoder, which is able to create approximations of human speech until recognizable words appear. One theme is the kind of message communicated by incomprehensible speech. Other radio works, such as my own *Invocations* (Sender Freies Berlin, 1981), bring into the same acoustic space sounds that would normally be heard separately—in my piece, prayers spoken by ministers of various (even antagonistic) faiths. The principal sponsor of this *Akustische Kunst* ("acoustic art") has been Klaus Schöning (1936), who has also edited books of scripts and criticism. More recently, German stations have broadcast radio art designed to be heard through earphones, *Kunstkopf* (literally, "art-head") stereo, surrounding the listener with stereophonic effects. Though such special audio experience might be made available in the United States on discs or cassettes, in Germany at least it is more likely to be heard over the acoustic airwaves.

Histories and Related Readings: Cory, Mark E. *The Emergence of an Acoustic Art Form*. Lincoln, NE: University of Nebraska Studies, 1974; ——. "New Radio Drama as Acoustic Art." In *Esthetics Contemporary*, ed. Richard Kostelanetz. Buffalo, New York: Prometheus, 1989; Kostelanetz, Richard. *Radio Writings*. Union, NJ: Further States of the Art (741 Park Ave, # 3, Hoboken, NJ 07030), 1995; Schöning, Klaus, ed. *Neues Horspiel*. Frankfurt, Germany: Suhrkamp, 1969; Strauss, Neil, ed. *Radiotext(e)*. New York: Semiotext(e), 1993.

RAINER, Yvonne

(24 November 1934).

Originally a dancer, she choreographed pieces that incorporated movements previously unknown to dance, such as running, climbing, tumbling, and other elementary athletic activities. In one sequence of *The Mind Is a Muscle* (1966), perhaps Rainer's greatest single dance, a professional juggler commands the left side of the stage, while the company of six mill uninterestedly on the right side of the stage. In another part, behind a movie screen filled with the image of someone's legs, the dancers execute mundane movements and at one point dribble a basketball. Another section, known as "Trio A," includes Rainer's choreographic innovation of circular swinging of both arms and a concomitant shifting of the body's weight in an intrinsically endless phrase. In the 1970s, Rainer became a filmmaker whose reels, never too experimental to begin with, have turned increasingly slick.

Selected Dances: *Room Service*, 1964; *Trio A*, 1966; *The Mind is a Muscle*, 1966; *Continuous Project—Altered Daily*, 1970; *Grand Union Dreams*, 1971; *Inner Appearances*, 1972.

Films: *Volleyball*, short, 1968; *Hand Movie*, short, 1968; *Rhode Island Red*, short, 1968; *Trio Film*, short, 1969; *Line*, short, 1969; *Lives of Performers: A melodrama* (1972). New York: First Run/Icarus Films, 1988; *Film about Women who . . .* (1974). New York: First Run/Icarus, 1988; *Kristina Talking Pictures*. New York: Zeitgeist, 1976; *Journeys from Berlin/1971*. New York: Zeitgeist, 1980; *The Man Who Envied Women*. New York: First Run/Icarus, 1985; *Privilege*. New York: Zeitgeist, 1990; *Murder and Murder*. New York: Zeitgeist, 1996.

Books: *Work 1961/73*. Halifax, Canada, & New York: Nova Scotia College of Art and Design & New York University, 1974; *The Films of Yvonne Rainer*. With contributions by others. Bloomington: Indiana University, 1989.

Bibliography: McDonagh, Don. "Why Does It Have to Be That Way?" In *The Rise and Fall and Rise of Modern Dance*. Rev. ed. Pennington, NJ: A Cappella, 1990.

Web Site: http://www.zeitgeistfilm.com/current/murder/rainerbio.html (covers Rainer's film career).

Interpretation: Green, Shelly. *Radical Juxtaposition: The Films of Yvonne Rainer*. Metuchen, NJ: Scarecrow, 1994.

RANDALL, J. K.

(16 June 1929).

After taking his M.F.A. at Princeton, Randall became a pioneering computer composer, whose *Mudgett: Monologues of a Mass Murderer* (1965) ranked among the best work produced for "converted digital tape" at the time. However, by the 1980s he gave up this sort of composing in favor of eccentric improvisations that are self-published on cassettes that he and his esthetic compatriot Benjamin Boretz (1934) distribute to an interested few. Even more eccentric are his highly visual essays "Compose Yourself: A Manual for the Young," which have been published from time to time in the university-based periodical *Perspectives of New Music* and will someday appear as the book they are meant to be.

Compositions: *Slow Movement*, for piano 1959; *Improvisation on a Poem by E.E. Cummings*, for soprano, clarinet, saxophone, trumpet, guitar, piano, or soprano, and piano, 1960; *Pitch-derived Rhythm: 7 Demonstrations* for flute, clarinet, piano, and 2 cellos, 1961–64; *Quartets in Pairs*, for computer, 1964; *Mudgett: Monologues by a Mass Murderer*, for taped violin and computer, 1965; *Lyric Variations*, for taped violin and computer, 1968; *Quartersines*, for computer, 1969; *Music for Eakins* film score for computer, 1972; *. . . such words as it were vain to close . . .* for piano, 1974–76; *Troubador Songs* for voice and percussion, 1977; *Meditation on Rossignol*, for piano, 1978; *Soundscroll 2*, for piano, 1978; *Greek Nickel I* and *II* for piano, 1979.

Recordings: Randall, J. K. *Mudgett: Monologues by a Mass Murderer*, 1965; *Quartersines*, for computer, 1969; *Lyric Variations*, for taped violin and computer, 1968; ——, Benjamin Boretz, et al. Numerous cassettes and CDs. Red Hook, New York: Open Space (R.D. 2, Box 45e, 12571), 1983–ongoing.

RAP

(c. 1975).

Rap music originally wed two distinct traditions: the African-American tradition of "toasting" or reciting long, semi-boastful poetry, often critical of a rival while celebrating the prowess (sexual and otherwise) of the toaster; and the modern technology of recordings, particularly turntables and sound systems, as operated by a DJ. Rap scholar Steven Stancell traces the artform to the late '40s in Jamaica, when street DJs, traveling in sound trucks equipped with record players and speakers, would play music for passersby, while reciting nonsense rhymes or making announcements between the records. Mobile DJs began showing up in Brooklyn, NY, in the early 1970s, attracting large crowds of people who would dance and party to their music. One of the most innovative of these early DJs was Jamaican-born Kool DJ Herc, who had one of the most powerful sound trucks around. He is also credited with being among the first to play just the instrumental "breaks" from a song, repeating it over and over. He did this by using two turntables, playing the section of the record first on one, then switching to the other, and then returning to the first. This style became known as "break-beat deejaying." Herc attracted a crowd of acrobatic dancers, who specialized in combining unusual gymnastic-like moves with rhythmic movement, whom he called his "b-boys" because they danced to the "breaks" in the record. This style later became known as break-dancing. Herc was also among the first to employ a second person, Coke La Rock, who served as an announcer/MC for his events. Coke would speak in between numbers while Herc prepared the next records, praising Herc while criticizing others who did not live up to Herc's prowess as a record spinner. Another prominent early DJ was DJ Hollywood, who performed in Manhattan discos in the mid-'70s. He is credited with expanding the MC patter into rhymed stories, a kind of proto-rap. He also used the nonsense syllables "hip, hop" to fill out his recitations, and this in turn became another early term for the musical form.

The first major figure to introduce break-beat deejaying was Afrika Bambaataa (aka Afrika Bambaataa Aasim, born c. 1955, Bronx, NY). A former leader of a street gang known as the Black Spades, Bambaataa was recognized as "Master of Records," because he drew on recordings from around the world, introducing reggae, soca, and other world-beat styles into the rap soundscape. He was renowned for his elaborate parties, attracting dancers, rappers, graffiti artists, and other street denizens. In 1982, he was hired to work at Manhattan's trendy Mudd Club, exposing him for the first time to a nearly all-white crowd. His success there led to engagements at many other midtown clubs and dance halls. Bambaataa's greatest success came with his 1982 hit "Planet Rock," a rap record he coproduced with Arthur Baker, based on the European electronic rock group Kraftwerk's "Trans-Europe Express."

That same year, he took his collective of artists, now known as the Zulu Nation, on a European tour. He was also involved with the anti-Apartheid movement of the '80s, performing on the "Sun City" record and organizing a huge concert at London's Wembley Stadium to celebrate the freeing of Nelson Mandela.

Grandmaster Flash (b. Joseph Sadler, c. January 1957, Bronx, NY) is credited with perfecting several important deejaying techniques, including "cutting (repeating a beat or musical phrase by moving the record back and forth); backspinning (repeating a beat or phrase on a record, by alternately spinning both records backward to the desired beat or phrase; thus, repeating it); and punch-phrasing (playing certain parts of a record on one turntable in quick volume surges, while the same record plays on the other turntable)," in Stancell's words. Flash had his own dancers, the Furious Five, along with various MCs, including Melle Mel. Their early hits included 1981's "Adventures of Grandmaster Flash on the Wheels of Steel" and "The Message," which featured the ominous refrain "Don't push me, 'cause I'm close to the edge." Another DJ, Grand Wizard Theodore, is credited with creating "scratching," the percussive spinning and backspinning of a turntable, which turns it into a true rhythm instrument. Often Theodore would play a break on one turntable, while "scratching" the same record on a second turntable.

Neighborhood gatherings of DJs soon developed into contests, in which the DJ with the flashiest ensemble, greatest technique, or loudest sound system would vanquish his opposition. Rappers would trade insults or comment on each other's songs in their own rhymes—thus making rap a truly collaborative art. This responsive interplay spread to rap records. UFTO made one of the first anti-female rap records called "Roxanne, Roxanne," which expressed the male rapper's frustration with his girlfriend, the fictional Roxanne. In answer to this record, a real woman (taking the name of Roxanne) recorded "Roxanne's Revenge," responding venomously to the original record. This "dissing" war spread over several records, and several women came forward claiming to be the "real Roxanne" with their own answers to the original insult.

Rap entered popular music in the late '70s through a series of successful records. The Sugarhill Gang's 1977 "Rapper's Delight" is generally cited as the first successful rap single, and its party-time atmosphere influenced other groups like the Fat Boys. The second major breakthrough for popular rap came in the mid-'80s, beginning with Run-DMC's successful collaboration with the white rock group Aerosmith on "Walk this Way."

Meanwhile, a new, more potent version of rap was developing in the slums of Los Angeles, called "Gangsta Rap." This rap focussed on social commentary, urging armed resistance to the often racist forces in the community, particularly the police. Ice-T's 1992 release "Cop Killer" was the most controversial of these releases, giving conservative groups—both black and white—ammunition in their fight to suppress the musical style. Increasingly, the popular image of the rapper as an ex-gangster became an albatross around the neck of the music. Several stars tried to live up to this image, even those who were not necessarily gang members in their youth. The most prominent casualties of this confusion of pop persona with real life were Tupac Shakur and Biggie Smalls (the Norotious B.I.G.), both of whom were gunned down by rivals.

By the mid-'90s, however, mainstream rappers dominated MTV airplay, and rap elements were heard in many top-forty releases. The political edge of the earlier rappers was mostly gone from this music, as was the street-level creativity. Rap as an innovation was replaced by rap as a business—just another profit center for the major recording companies.

—Richard Carlin with Steven Stancell

Resources: Stancell, Steven. *The Rap Whoz Who*. New York: Schirmer Books, 1996.

Recorded Anthologies: *Best of Sugar Hill Records*. Los Angeles: Rhino Records 75472, 1995.

RAUSCH, Mechthild

(5 January 1940).

A German critic and freelance media producer, Rausch is one of the few who have a sure sense of the difference between genuinely avant-garde work and its pretenders, for instance distinguishing in an elaborate essay between the highly avant-garde VIENNA POETS and the more derivative writers associated with the Austrian city of Graz, epitomized by Peter Handke (1942). Not unlike other independent German writers, Rausch has produced films and radio features as well as essays, most notably about the art critic–novelist CARL EINSTEIN and PAUL SCHEERBART, in addition to authoring several volumes of and about the latter. Rausch's criticism remains as untranslated as the writing of her principal enthusiasms, so backward is the English-speaking world.

Selected Works: Scheerbart, Paul. *70 Trillionen Weltgrüsse*. Ed. Mechthild Rausch. Berlin, Germany: Argon-Verlag, 1991.

RAUSCHENBERG, Robert

(25 October 1925).

His innovations were based upon two principles: that literally everything could be incorporated into painterly art, and that one part of a picture need not dominate, or even relate to, the others. In the first respect, he painted his own bed, transforming a sub-esthetic object into something that was purchased and displayed by the Museum of Modern Art (*Bed*, 1955); he put a whole stuffed Angora goat into a painted field (*Monogram*, 1959); added a live radio to another (*Broadcast*, 1959); and even added a clock to yet another (*Third Time Painting*, 1961). For a while, Rauschenberg seemed the most inventive visual artist since PABLO PICASSO.

Rauschenberg's earlier *White Painting* (1951) has reflective surfaces designed to incorporate lights and images from the surrounding environment (in contrast to AD REINHARDT, say, whose monotonal canvases were intentionally nonreflective). About this early work, Allan Kaprow wrote a decade later:

> They were taken as a joke by most of the committed artists of the New York school. Yet they are the pivotal works of the artist, for in the context of Abstract Expressionist noise and gesture, they suddenly brought us face to face with the humbling devastating silence.

For painted ASSEMBLAGES that had three dimensions and yet were not quite sculpture, Rauschenberg coined the term "combine." In the late sixties, he worked with technology and theatrical pieces.

Otherwise, the typical Rauschenberg painting (or graphic) is a disparate collection of images, some of them painted, others applied in other ways (such as silkscreen or glue), in which no image is more important than any other, though they may comment upon one another. Rauschenberg's initial adventurousness notwithstanding, he never developed much beyond his early innovations, perhaps because by the 1970s he had forsaken New York, which seemed an inspiration for his art, for residence on an isolated island off the west coast of Florida.

By the 1980s, he had become the Leonard Bernstein (1918–90) of visual art, a sort of elder statesman whose public activities were exemplary and publicized, even though his art ceased being interesting or influential.

Selected Visual Art: *Female Figure (Blue Print)*, c. 1949; *Automobile Tire Print*, 1951; *White Paintings*, 1951; *Black Paintings*, 1951–52; *Red Paintings*, 1953; *Erased de Kooning Drawing*, 1953; *Charlene*, 1954; *Bed*, 1955; *Odalisque*, 1955; *Monogram*, 1959; *Broadcast*, 1959; *Pilgrim* 1960; *Third Time Painting*, 1961; *Black Market*, 1961.

Exhibition Catalogs: Solomon, Alan R. *Robert Rauschenberg*. New York: Jewish Museum, 1963; Forge, Andrew. *Robert Rauschenberg*. Amsterdam: Stedelijk Museum, 1968; *Robert Rauschenberg: Paintings, Drawings, and Combines, 1949–1964*. London: Whitechapel, 1964; Swanson, Dean. *Robert Rauschenberg*. Minneapolis, MN: Walker Art Center, 1965; *Rauschenberg Currents*. Minneapolis, MN: Dayton's, 1970; *Rauschenberg*. Washington: Smithsonian Institution, 1977; *Robert Rauschenberg*. London: Tate Gallery, 1981; *Photographs*. New York: Random House, 1981; Feinstein, Roni. *Robert Rauschenberg: The Silkscreen Paintings, 1962–64*. New York: Whitney Museum, 1990; *Rauschenberg 96: New Works*. Singapore: Wetterling Teo Gallery, 1996; Hopps, Walter, and Susan Davidson. *Robert Rauschenberg*. New York: Guggenheim Museum, 1997; Craft, Catherine. *Robert Rauschenberg Haywire: Major Technological Works of the 1960s*. Ostfildern-Ruit, Germany: Hatje, 1997.

Web Page: http://www.artchive.com/artchive/ftptoc/rauschenberg_ext.html

Interpretation: Forge, Andrew. *Robert Rauschenberg*. New York: Abrams, 1970; Klotz, Mary Lynn. *Robert Rauschenberg*. New York: Abrams, 1990; Tomkins, Calvin. *Off the Wall: Robert Rauschenberg and the Art World of Our Time*. Garden City, New York: Doubleday, 1980.

READ, Herbert

(4 December 1893–12 June 1968).

From provincial origins, Read went not to Oxford-Cambridge but to Leeds University before serving in World War I, where he earned medals. Moving to London in the 1920s, he cofounded the short-lived magazine *Arts and Letters* and worked at the Victoria and Albert Museum and later in commercial publishing. In his off hours, he produced not only an endless stream of essays and reviews but numerous books about literature and the visual arts, including applied arts—no false snob he. As the most visible advocate of modern abstract visual art in England, he was particularly skilled at catalogue introductions. As a sometime publisher, he had an enviable talent for giving his books seductive titles that no doubt contributed to their being reprinted widely. Often portrayed during his lifetime as advocating the most avant-garde work, he seems in retrospect too self-consciously accommodating to retrograde fashions. Typically, he championed the sculptor Henry Moore over more radical artists. Indicatively, T. S. Eliot accepted Read while reportedly keeping the books of William Carlos Williams unpublished in England during their common lifetimes.

A true man of letters, Read also published books of poetry, autobiography, and a single novel. Politically, he declared himself an anarchist, a kind of agricultural utopian, and was perhaps the most prominent British anarchist until at sixty he accepted a knighthood, becoming "Sir Herbert" and reportedly sending the movement into disarray. (This always happens when the figurehead is publicly co-opted.) By current standards, he seems less interesting and less radical than, say, his near-contemporary Wyndham Lewis, accounting for why he is for some a youthful enthusiasm that is outgrown.

Arts Criticism: *English Stained Glass*. London & New York: G. P. Putnam's Sons, 1926; *Art Now: An Introduction to the Theory of Modern Painting and Sculpture* (1933). London: Faber & Faber, 1960; *Art and Society* (1937). Rev. ed. New York: Schocken, 1966; *Contemporary British Art* (1951). Harmondsworth, England: Penguin, 1964; *The Philosophy of Modern Art: Collected Essays* (1952). New York: Horizon, 1952; *Art and Industry* (1953). Bloomington: Indiana University Press, 1961; *Icon and Idea* (1955). New York: Schocken, 1965; *The Art of Sculpture* New York: Pantheon, 1956; *A Concise History of Modern Painting*. New York: Praeger, 1959; *The Form of Things Unknown* (1960). New York: Meridian, 1963; *A Concise History of Modern Sculpture*. New York: Praeger, 1964; *Henry Moore* (1965). New York: Praeger, 1966; *The Origins of Form and Art*. New York: Horizon, 1965; *Art and Alienation: The Role of the Artist in Society*. New York: Horizon, 1967; *Arp*. New York: Praeger, 1969.

Literary Criticism: *Wordsworth* (1930). Rev. ed. London: Faber & Faber, 1958; *Form in modern poetry* (1932). London: Vision, 1948; *English Prose Style* (1932). Boston: Beacon, 1955; *Collected Essays in Literary Criticism*. London: Faber & Faber, 1938; *A Coat of Many Colors: Occasional Essays* (1945). Rev. ed. New York: Horizon, 1956.

Poetry: *Collected Poems* (1946). Rev. ed. New York: Horizon, 1966; *The Tenth Muse: Essays in Criticism*. New York: Horizon, 1958; *Truth is More Sacred*. New York: Horizon, 1961.

Fiction: *The Green Child: A Romance*. 1935. New York: New Directions, 1948.

Memoir: *Annals of Innocence and Experience* (1940). Rev. ed. London: Faber & Faber, 1946; *The Contrary Experience: Autobiographies*. New York: Horizon, 1963.

Political Essays: *Poetry and Anarchism*. London: Faber & Faber, 1938; *Education Through Art* (1943). London: Faber & Faber, 1958; *Anarchy and Order: Essays in Politics*. London: Faber & Faber, 1945; *The Politics of the Unpolitical* (1953). Rev. as *To Hell with Culture*. New York: Schocken, 1964.

Anthology: *Selected Writings: Poetry and Criticism*. New York: Horizon, 1964.

Biography: Woodcock, George. *Herbert Read: The Stream & the Source*. London: Faber & Faber, 1972.

Interpretation: Treece, Henry, ed. *Herber Read: An Introduction to His Work by Various Hands*. London: Faber & Faber, 1944; Skelton, Robin, ed. *Herber Read: A Memorial Symposium*. New York: Barnes & Noble, 1970; Thistlewood, david. *Herbert Read: Formlessness and Form, An Introduction to His Aesthetics*. London & Boston, Routledge & Kegan Paul, 1984.

REDOLFI, Michele

(1951).

An eccentric, second-generation electroacoustic composer, the Frenchman Michel Redolfi has specialized in bringing performances of tape music to places other than the concert hall. Despite his fondness for state-of-the-art digital equipment (some of which he has developed himself), Redolfi has never been a sterile technology fetishist; his sound world is always rich and sensual, his outlook romantic. He is also not a conceptual artist—irrespective of the novel circumstances of much of his music's performance, his pieces stand on their own as highly musical and sophisticated creations.

Born in Marseilles, Redolfi in 1969 cofounded the Groupe de Musique Expérimentale de Marseille (GMEM), one of the first independent electronic music studios in France. From 1973 to 1984 he lived in the United States, where he worked at several of the major centers for computer music; the Dartmouth electronic composer Jon Appleton (1939) commented in 1983 that Redolfi was "the only composer to reconcile the French and American styles of electronic music." During the 1970s Redolfi began trying to develop novel ways of experiencing electronic music, reflecting his utopian desire to create total sensory environments—and also, presumedly, his dissatisfaction with the experience of staring at loudspeakers on an empty concert stage. In 1976 he introduced the *homo-parleur* (body speaker)—a live-electronics device worn like a jacket—and in 1984 he presented a series of concerts of music for sleeping (*L'écume de la nuit*). What he has most thoroughly explored, however, is the idea of creating music underwater—to be listened to by an audience floating in pools or in the ocean. He has staged "underwater concerts" around the world, and has even written an underwater opera, *Crysallis* (1992); other pieces in the series include *Pacific Tubular Waves* (1979), *Immersion* (1980), *Sonic Waters* (1981), and *Nausicaä* (1991).

Redolfi has also composed pieces inspired by various dramatic and remote natural settings; these use location recordings gathered by him as source material, though the digital transformation of this material is so complete that the result is more metaphysical portraiture than sound reportage. These pieces include *Desert Tracks* (1987–88) (made out of recordings gathered in Death Valley, the Mojave, and Palm Canyon) and *Carnets Brésiliens* (1990–93) (built from material recorded in the Brazilian rainforest).

In recent years Redolfi has produced a series of pieces for soloists and tape—for example, *Portrait de Jean-Paul Celea avec contrebasse* (1991), in which the tape part is conceived of as a portrait of the performer, and has also designed permanent sound installations in art and science museums around the world. Since 1986 he has been the director of the CIRM (Centre International de Recherche Musicale) in Nice.

—Tony Coulter

Discography: *Hardscore* (with André Jaume). Paris: CBH Records/Côte d'Azur, n.d.; *Immersion/Pacific Tubular Waves*. Paris: INA-GRM, 1980; *Sonic Waters*. Therwil, Switzerland: Hat Hut Records, 1983; *Desert Tracks*. Paris: INA-GRM, 1988; *Sonic Waters II*. Therwil, Switzerland: Hat Hut Records, 1990; *Nausicaä*. Nice: CIRM, 1991; *Jungle*. Paris: Albin Michel/Paris-Musées/CIRM, 1991 [book and CD]; *Crysallis*. Mirage Musical, 1996; *Appel d'Air*. Paris: INA-GRM, 1993; *Songes drolatiques* (on GMEB compilation *Le sixte livre dit électroacoustique de François Rabelais*). Bourges, France: GMEB, 1995.

REICH, Steve

(3 October 1936).

Not unlike his Juilliard classmate and sometime colleague PHILIP GLASS, Reich began as a daunting avant-garde composer whose work has become more accessible and popular over the years. What *Music in Twelve Parts* (1974) is for Glass, *Drumming* (1971) is for Reich, which is to say the apex of his radical style—a composition that benefits from being longer and thus more ambitious than his previous works. Reich's original radical idea was a strain of MODULAR MUSIC, in which bits of material would be repeated, customarily in slightly different forms, until through repetition alone they generated a pulsing sound. The clearest example was *It's Gonna Rain* (1965), where that three-word phrase becomes a chorus of itself, as Reich working in an early electronic music studio realized an incantatory intensity unequaled in audio language art. Another, similarly composed work, *Come Out* (1966) depends upon more violent language, as initially spoken by a black teenager who had suffered a police beating. Whereas Glass is a melodist, the best Reich, as in *Drumming*, marks him as a rhythmicist. Of the later Reich, I like *Tehillim* (1981) for its imaginative setting of a Hebrew text. His most ambitious later work, *The Cave* (1993), based on the Biblical story of Abraham, Sarah, and their sons, includes multiscreen video made by his wife Beryl Korot (1945) in a kind of multimedia oratorio.

In 1997 Reich's latest record label, Nonesuch, produced a box of 10 CDs, with an accompanying book running 136 pages, that ranks Reich among the major living composers and Nonesuch high among those companies supporting the best contemporary composers.

Selected Compositions: *Pitch Charts*, for any instruments, 1963; *Plastic Haircut*, film score for tape, 1963; Music for 3 or more pianos or piano and tape, 1964; *It's Gonna Rain*, for tape, 1965; *Come Out*, for tape, 1966; *Slow Motion Sound*, for tape, 1967; *Piano Phase*, for two pianos and two marimbas, 1967; *Drumming*, for 2 women's voices, piccolo, 4 pairs of tuned bongo drums, 3 marimbas, and 3 glockenspiels, 1971; *Clapping Music*, for 2 performers, 1972; *Six Pianos*, 1973; *Music for Pieces of Wood*, for 5 pairs of tuned claves, 1973; *Music for Mallet Instruments, Voices and Organ*, for three women's voices, 3 marimbas, 3 glockenspiels, vibraphone, and electric organ, 1973; *Eight Lines* for chamber orch., 1979; *My Name Is*, for tape, 1980; *Tehillim (Psalms)*, for 3 sopranos, alto, and chamber orchestra, 1981; *The Desert Music*, 1984; *New York Counterpoint*, 1985; *Sextet*, 1985; *The Four Sections*, 1997; *Different Trains*, for string quartet and tape, 1988; *Three Movements*, for orchestra, 1986; *The Cave*, 1993; *City Life*, for 17 performers with concrète urban sounds from 2 sampling keyboards, 1994;

Hindenberg, 1998, from *Three Tales*, a "documentary video opera" (in progress).

Recordings: *Works 1965–1995*. New York: Nonesuch, 1997. (These 10 cds contain, in roughly chronological sequence, *It's Gonna Rain*; *Come Out*; *Piano Phase*; *Four Organs*; *Drumming*; *Clapping Music*; *Six Marimbas*; *Music for Mallet Instruments, Voices, and Organ*; *Music for 18 Musicians*; *Eight Lines (Octet)*; *Tehillim*; *The Desert Music*; *Sextet*; *New York Counterpoint*; *Three Movements*; *The Four Sections*; *Electric Counterpoint*; *Different Trains*; *The Cave* (excerpts); *Nagoya Marimbas*; *City Life*; *Proverb*, performed mostly by his own group.); *Reich Remixed*. New York: Nonesuch (7559–79552), 1999.

Books: Reich, Steve. *Writings about Music*. Halifax, NS, & New York: College of Art and Design & New York University Press, 1974.

Extended Interview: Strickland, Edward. "Steve Reich." In *American Composers*. Bloomington: Indiana University Press, 1991.

Documentary Film: *Steve Reich: A New Musical Language*, produced by Mary Jane Walsh and directed by Margaret Williams (NET: Great Performances).

Web Page: http://www.slis.keio.ac.jp/~ohba/srhome.html (in English and Japanese).

REINHARDT, Ad

(24 December 1913–30 August 1967; b. Adolf R.).

A college chum of both Robert Lax and Thomas Merton, Reinhardt was, from his professional beginnings, a scrupulous Abstractionist, perhaps the only major American Abstract artist of his generation never to have exhibited representational paintings. His most distinctive early paintings had geometric shapes on a multicolored field, while works of the late forties favored less definite abstract shapes. By 1953, he offered canvases painted entirely in different shades of the same color—all red, all blue, all black, in one case, all white—usually divided into geometric shapes whose slight differences in hue became more visible with the spectator's increased attention. Reinhardt's *Black Paintings* of the early sixties, each five feet square, contain not a sole black color evenly painted from edge to edge, but many rectilinear forms, each painted a slightly different hue of black. Viewing Reinhardt's work from the perspective of subsequent art history (which generally clarifies earlier innovations), the critic Lucy R. Lippard judges that his "innovations consist largely of the establishment of a valid function for nonrelational, monotonal concepts, progressive elimination of texture, color contrast, value contrast and eventually of color itself, which was replaced by a uniquely nonillusionistic painted light."

In addition to being a masterfully sophisticated cartoonist, critically portraying ideas and life in the New York art world, Reinhardt was also a witty and aphoristic writer, declaring, for instance, "An avant-garde in art advances art-as-art or it isn't an avant-garde"—an adage that would have been an epigraph to this book, did it not seem more appropriate here.

Works: *Abstact Painting*, 1940; *Number 18*, 1949; *Red Painting*, 1952; *Black Painting*, 1952; *Abstract Painting, Blue*, 1953; *Abstract Painting, Red*, 1953; *Abstract Painting*, 1956; *Abstract Painting, Black*, c. 1954–56; *Painting 1956*, 1956; *Abstract Painting, 1954–59*, 1954–59; *Black Painting*, 1962; *Abstract Painting 1964*, 1964.

Books & Booklets: *Art-as-Art: Selected Writings* (1975). Ed. Barbara Rose. Berkeley: University of California Press, 1991; *Art Comics and Satires*. New York: Truman Gallery, 1976.

Exhibition Catalogs: *Ad Reinhardt: 25 Years of Abstract Painting*. New York: Betty Parson Gallery, 1960; Lippard, Lucy R. *Ad Reinhardt*. New York: Jewish Museum, 1966; *Ad Reinhardt: Black Paintings 1951–67*. New York: Marlborough, 1970; *Ad Reinhardt: A Selection from 1937–1952*. New York: Marlborough, 1974; *Seventeen Works*. Washington, DC: Corcoran, 1984; Rowell, Margit.

Ad Reinhart in his studio with his Black on Black Paintings, 3 April 1961. Photograph © Fred W. McDarrah.

Ad Reinhardt and Color. New York: Guggenheim Museum, 1980; Inboden, Gudrun, and Thomas Kellein. *Ad Reinhardt*. Stuttgart, Germany: Staatsgalerie, 1985; *Ad Reinhardt*. New York: MoMA, 1991.

Interpretation: Hess, Thomas B. *The Art Comics and Satires of Ad Reinhardt*. Düsseldorf & Rome: Kunsthalle & Marlborough, 1975; Lippard, Lucy R. *Ad Reinhardt*. New York: Abrams, 1981.

REINIGER, Lotte

(2 June 1899–19 June 1981).

Among the pioneering film animators, she designed distinctive intertitles for another director's film in 1916, while she was still a student in her native Berlin, and made her first film in 1919. In 1923 Reiniger began directing one of the earliest feature-length animated films, *The Adventures of Prince Achmed* (1926), which is based upon the familiar *Arabian Nights*. Her signature technique involved paper cutouts that were illuminated from behind to create moving silhouettes on screen. For this style of animation Reiniger drew disparately upon Chinese shadow puppets and the Expressionist theater lighting of the theatrical director Max Reinhardt, with whom she briefly studied. Even though *Prince Achmed* had international success, it includes several abstract sequences that depend upon experimental techniques involving sliced wax and sand on glass likewise illuminated from behind. The music biographer Eric Walter White, who compiled the music for *Harleken/Harlequin* (1931), published in 1931 a charming booklet, *Walking Shadows*, that, describing Reiniger's animation technique, incidentally established her reputation in England.

In the mid-1930s, Reiniger emigrated to London where she stayed after World War II, producing many short films, mostly for British children's television. Her husband Carl Koch produced and photographed her films from 1921 until his death in 1963. Reiniger's reputation for adult filmmaking had to be revived in post-post-War Germany, just before her death. In part because no one afterwards used Reiniger's silhouette technique as well (silhouetting is neglected by younger artists), those 1920s films invariably look fresh on first viewing today.

Films: *Das Ornament des verliebten Herzens/ The Ornament of the Loving Heart*, 1919; *Aschenputtel/Cinderella*, 1922; *Die Abenteuer des Prinzen Achmed/The Adventures of Prince Achmed*, 1926; *Doktor Dolittle und seine Tiere/The Adventures of Dr. Dolittle*, 1928; *Harleken*, 1931; *Carmen*, 1933; *Das Gestohlene Herz/The Stolen Heart*, 1934; *Papageno*, 1935; *Das Kleine Schornsteinfeger/The Little Chimney Sweep*, 1935.

Books: *Shadow Theatres and Shadow Films*. New York: Watson-Guptill, 1970.

Documentaries: *The Art of Lotte Reiniger*. London: Primrose, 1971.

Interpretation: White, Eric Walter. *Walking Shadows*. London: Leonard and Virginia Wolff, 1931; Russett, Robert, and Cecile Starr. *Experimental Animation* (1976). New York: Da Capo, 1988.

REXROTH, Kenneth

(22 December 1905–6 June 1982).

I'd like to think Rexroth belongs here, because anyone who is radical in both his literary and social politics serves as an avant-garde model. However, Rexroth's poems at their best were fairly conventional and accessible, usually in appreciation of nature, with scarcely any interest in the possibilities of poetry. I have scoured them, hoping to find avant-garde aberrations comparable to those existing in, say, Cummings and Ogden Nash, but have uncovered one and only one, "Fundamental Disagreement with Two Contemporaries," which is indicatively dedicated "for Tristan Tzara & Andre Breton" and opens with fragmented language ("gonaV/ ; /ing evIT / dras pRoG") before returning into the underpunctuated declarative phrases more typical of Rexroth's poetry.

Poetry: *In What Hour*. New York: Macmillan, 1940; *The Art of Worldly Wisdom*. Prairie City, IL: Decker, 1949; *The Signature of all Things; Poems, Songs, Elegies, Translations, and Epigrams*. New York: New Directions, 1950; *The Dragon and the Unicorn*. New York: New Directions, 1952; *Natural Numbers: New & Selected Poems*. New York: New Directions, 1963; *The Collected Shorter Poems*. New York: New Directions, n.d. (c. 1966); *The Heart's Garden, The Garden's Heart*. Cambridge, MA: Pym-Randall, 1967; *The Collected Longer Poems*. New York: New Directions, 1968; *The Morning Star*. New York: New Directions, 1979; *The Selected Poems of Kenneth Rexroth*. Ed. Bradford Morrow. New York: New Directions, 1984.

Plays: *Beyond the Mountains* [with *Phaedra*, *Iphigenia*, *Haemaios*, *Berenike*]. New York: New Directions, 1951.

Prose: *Bird in the Bush*. New York: New Directions, 1959; *Assays*. New York: New Directions, 1961; *Classics Revisited* (1969). New York: New Directions, 1986; *The Alternative Society: Essays from the Other World*. New York: Herder & Herder, 1970; *With Eye and Ear*. New York: Herder & Herder, 1970; *American Poetry in the Twentieth Century*. New York: Herder & Herder, 1971; *The Elastic Retort: Essays in Literature and Ideas*. New York: Seabury, 1973; *Communalism: From Its Origins to the Twentieth Century*. New York: Seabury, 1974; *World Outside the Window: The Selected Essays of Kenneth Rexroth*. New York: New Directions, 1987.

Anthologies: Mottram, Eric, ed. *The Rexroth Reader*. London: Jonathan Cape, 1972.

Autobiography: Rexroth, Kenneth. *An Autobiographical Novel* (1964). Revised and expanded ed. New York: New Directions, 1991.

Correspondence: *Kenneth Rexroth & James Laughlin: Selected Letters*. Ed. Lee Bartlett. New York: Norton, 1991.

Biography: Hamalian, Linda. *A Life of Kenneth Rexroth*. New York: Norton, 1992.

Web Page: http://www.charm.net/~brooklyn/People/KennethRexroth.html

Interpretation: Gardner, Geoffrey, ed. *For Rexroth: The Ark 14*. New York: The Ark, 1980.

RHOADS, George

(1926).

As a painter incidentally skilled at fixing watches, Rhoads began in the 1970s to create kinetic sculptures that use a minimum of technology by mostly depending upon gravity for their effects. Rhoads typically uses a motor to bring a single kind of ball (billiard balls, golf balls, etc.) to the top of a structure. The balls flow randomly down one of several available paths, customarily hitting a succession of noisemakers and moving parts until they reach a bottom level, from which they are, by machine, carried back to the top. These audiokinetic sculptures, as Rhodes calls them, are customarily placed in shopping centers (two in West Edmonton, Canada; one in Plattsburg, New York, etc.), public institutions (Boston's Science Museum), bus stations (New York's Port Authority), and airport terminals (Logan C in Boston)—which is to say places where people congregate. It is not unusual to see individuals fixated for minutes at a stretch, intent on discovering a sculpture's many possible movements.

No other public art succeeds as well with the general public, perhaps explaining why, in contrast to unpopular public art, Rhoads's machines are rarely, if ever, defaced. My own favorite is an untitled piece installed at the Allendale Shopping Center in Pittsfield, Mass., where golf balls are propelled into the air. As they fall into different channels, they activate various switches that open different organ pipes, producing a wealth of sounds. I consider Rhoads's machines to be a kind of mechanical theater in the tradition of OSKAR SCHLEMMER and thus note that, because the only technology they require is a simple motor, they would have been technically feasible long ago.

Interpretation: Kostelanetz, Richard. "George Rhoads." In *On Innovative Performance(s)*. Jefferson, NC: McFarland, 1994.

RIBEMONT-DESSAIGNES, Georges

(19 June 1884–9 July 1974).

Initially a painter, Ribemont-Dessaignes focused primarily on writing without ever abandoning visual art. Active in DADA, he wrote innovative plays, an early book about MAN RAY, and several novels. From 1929 to 1931 he edited the magazine *Bifur* which, in its short life, made a remarkable synthesis in publishing TRISTAN TZARA, JAMES JOYCE, RAMÓN GÓMEZ DE LA SERNA, and WILLIAM CARLOS WILLIAMS, along with statements by BUSTER KEATON and the Russian Formalist Victor Shklovsky (1893–1983). Ribemont-Dessaignes's history of Dada, initially written in 1931 for a Parisian magazine, became a 1958 book.

Works: *The Oceanic Spirit*, 1918; *Great Musician*, 1920.

Interpretation: Dachy, Marc. *The Dada Movement*. New York: Rizzoli, 1990.

RICHIER, Germaine

(16 September 1904–31 July 1959).

A precursor of the group of sculptors who emerged after World War II and whose works critic HERBERT READ referred to as the "geometry of fear," Richier may be the most unnerving sculptor in the modern era. The scabrous, diseased, eaten-away metal forms of this French sculptor bear a resemblance to the works of Alberto Giacometti (1901–66), and her concern with anxiety matches his. But where Giacometti was interested in the human figure distorted by anxiety, Richier developed a sculptural style that was aimed at creating metaphoric images of anxiety itself. She portrays sinister and decomposing creatures that observe no natural distinctions. The images break down the boundaries between the animal, vegetable, and mineral realms. As images of a frightening mental chaos, Richier's creatures are symbols for unknown depths of the imagination, for unconscious qualities of sensation and emotion. In this pursuit, she shows a relationship to SURREALISM, but where Surrealism most often sought to evoke unconscious states of mind through the anomalous arrangements of familiar objects, Richier fused elements from nature into unnatural combinations. Perhaps a response to the carnage of the war, perhaps a register of the discontent of the technological world, Richier's sculptures are piercing renditions of the imagination of terror.

—Mark Daniel Cohen

Works: *The Spider*, 1946; *The Storm*, 1948; *The Hurricane*, 1949; *Ogre*, 1951; *The Bat*, 1952; *Tauromachy*, 1953; *Thistle (Sun)*, 1956–59; *Horse*, 1957–58.

Exhibition Catalogs: *The Sculpture of Germaine Richier: First American Exhibition*. Chicago: Allan Frumkin, 1954; *The Sculptures of Germaine Richier*. New York: Martha Jackson, 1957; *Sculpture by Germaine Richier*. Minneapolis: Walker Art Center, 1958; *Sculpture by Germaine Richier*. Boston: Division of Art, Boston University, 1959.

Criticism: Cassou, Jean. *Germaine Richier*. New York: Universe Books, 1961.

RICHTER, Hans

(6 April 1888–1 February 1976).

A POLYARTIST of sorts, Richter is now remembered for his pioneering films and his books, beginning with his 1921 abstract film *Rhythmus 21*, which focuses upon a single formal element, the rectangle. In Germany, he worked with VIKING EGGELING and with SERGEI EISENSTEIN. In *Vormittagsspuk/Ghosts before Breakfast* (1927–28), bowler hats fly through the landscape in articulate formations, Richter replicating in human action footage the animator's trick of creating on film comic effects that could not be done on stage. Once settled in America, where he became director of the Institute of Film Techniques at New York's City College (1942–52), Richter organized *Dreams That Money Can Buy* (1946), a feature-length color film that drew upon scenarios by ALEXANDER CALDER, MARCEL DUCHAMP, MAX ERNST, and MAN RAY, among others. Another longer film, *8 x 8* (1957), made after his return to Switzerland, involved JEAN COCTEAU, among others. Richter compiled a two-part self-retrospective, *Forty Years of Experiment* (1951, 1961), in addition to writing histories featuring his own involvements in the arts. In the concluding two decades of his life, much of them spent back in Europe, he worked principally as a painter. He authored an early book-length history of DADA that, partly for a lack of competition, got widely translated and reprinted.

Visual Art: *Kurfürstendamm*, 1911; *Cello*, 1914. *Self-Portrait*, 1917; *Orchestration of Color*, oil on canvas, 1923; *Victory in the East (Stalingrad)*, oil on canvas roll, 1943–44; *Liberation of Paris*, oil and collage on canvas, 1944–45; *From Major to Minor*, mosaic, 1964; *Labyrinth #2*, wood and brass, 1965; *Pro and Contra*, painted wood, 1968.

Films: *Rhythmus 21*, 1921; *Rhythmus 23*, 1923; *Rhythmus 25*, 1925; *Filmstudie*, 1926; *Inflation*, 1927–28; *Vormittagsspuk/Ghosts before Breakfast*, 1927–28; *Rennsymphonie/Race Symphony*, 1928–29; *Alles Dreht Sich, Alles Bewegt Sich!/Everything Turns, Everthing Revolves*, 1929; *Philips-Radio/Industrial Symphonie*, 1931; *Dreams That Money Can Buy*, 1944–47; *Alexander Calder: From the Circus to the Moon* (c. 1947; released 1962); *Dadascope I*, 1956–61; *Dadascope II*, 1967; —— with others. *8 X 8*, 1955–58.

Books: *Dada, Kunst und Antikunst*. Köln: DuMont, 1964. 3d rev. and expanded ed., 1973. First ed. trans. as *Dada: Art and Anti-Art*. New York: McGraw-Hill, n.d. (c. 1965); *Hans Richter*. Ed. Cleve Gray. New York: Holt, Rinehart, and Winston, 1971.

Exhibition Catalogs: *Hans Richter. Ein Leben für Bild und Film*. Berlin, Akademie der Künst, 1958; *Hans Richter. Art: 1905–1966*. New York: Finch College Museum of Art, 1968.

Interpretation: Foster, Stephen C., ed. *Hans Richter: Activism, Modernism, and the Avant-Garde*. Cambridge: MIT Press, 1998; Stauffacher, Frank, ed. *Art in Cinema: A Symposium on the Avant Garde Film* (1947). New York: Arno, 1968.

RICKEY, George

(6 June 1907–).

Alexander Calder's innovation (of a nonmechanical, kinetic, three-dimensional art) was so different from traditional sculpture that his sort of work, apparently requiring competences different from those learned in art school, had remarkably few successors. The most important, as well as original, successor has been George Rickey, a Scotsman who has spent most of his life in the United States (and learned mechanics in the U.S. Army Air Corps). His delicately poised pieces move, like Calder's, in response to the gentlest shifts of air (even drafts within museums). Whereas Calder usually suspends his floating and spatially intersecting parts from a central point (itself usually suspended from the ceiling), providing a pivotal axis, Rickey either suspends his metal pieces individually from several axes or pitches them up from an axial point close to the ground, as in his classic *Two Lines* (1964), where intersecting blades, like scissors, run thirty-five feet high into the open air. Though Rickey's *oeuvre* may not be as rich as Calder's, it suggests that the medium of nonmechanical kinetic art is scarcely exhausted. Rickey also published one of the strongest critical histories of Constructivism.

Sculptures: *Flag-Waving Machine with Quarterings*, 1954; *Tree*, 1956. *Twenty-four Lines*, 1963; *Two Lines Temporal I*, 1964; *Space Churn—Steel*, 1968; *Two Open Rectangles, Excentric, Honolulu*, 1976; *Forty Triangles in Three Movements*, 1982; *Eight Triangles, Two Squares, Hommage à Albers*, 1984.

Exhibition Catalogs: *George Rickey: Retrospective Exhibition 1971–1972*. Los Angeles: UCLA Art Council, 1971; *George Rickey*. Berlin: Nationalgalerie, 1973; *George Rickey in Berlin 1967–1992*. Berlin: Berlinische Galerie, 1992; *George Rickey, Recent Sculpture*. New York: Maxwell Davidson, 1997.

Books: *Constructivism: Origins and Evolution* (1967). New York: Braziller, 1995.

RIEFENSTAHL, Leni

(22 August 1902; b. Helene Bertha Amalie R.).

Riefenstahl was the Eadweard Muybridge of film, which is to say that she mastered, as no one before her had, the art of capturing human motion. Her masterpiece is *Olympia* (1938), a four-hour documentary ostensibly about the 1936 Berlin Olympics, but stylistically a glorification of human athletic performance at its highest. Generously supported by the Nazi government, Riefenstahl used forty-five cameras, some of which were sunk in holes in the ground, others of which were in balloons, and then spent over a year editing over two hundred hours of footage. (Ironically, the African-American sprinter Jesse Owens always credited a female follower of Hitler with making him famous through her portrayal of his victories.) If only for directorial decisions about shooting individual events, nearly every major sports film since seems in some way or another indebted to Riefenstahl. (To her credit, she eschewed the post-victory, talking-head interviews that plague American television's coverage of sports. Since her soundtrack wasn't synchronized with the action, Riefenstahl could redo her work in different languages without changing her brilliant footage.) The book of still phor

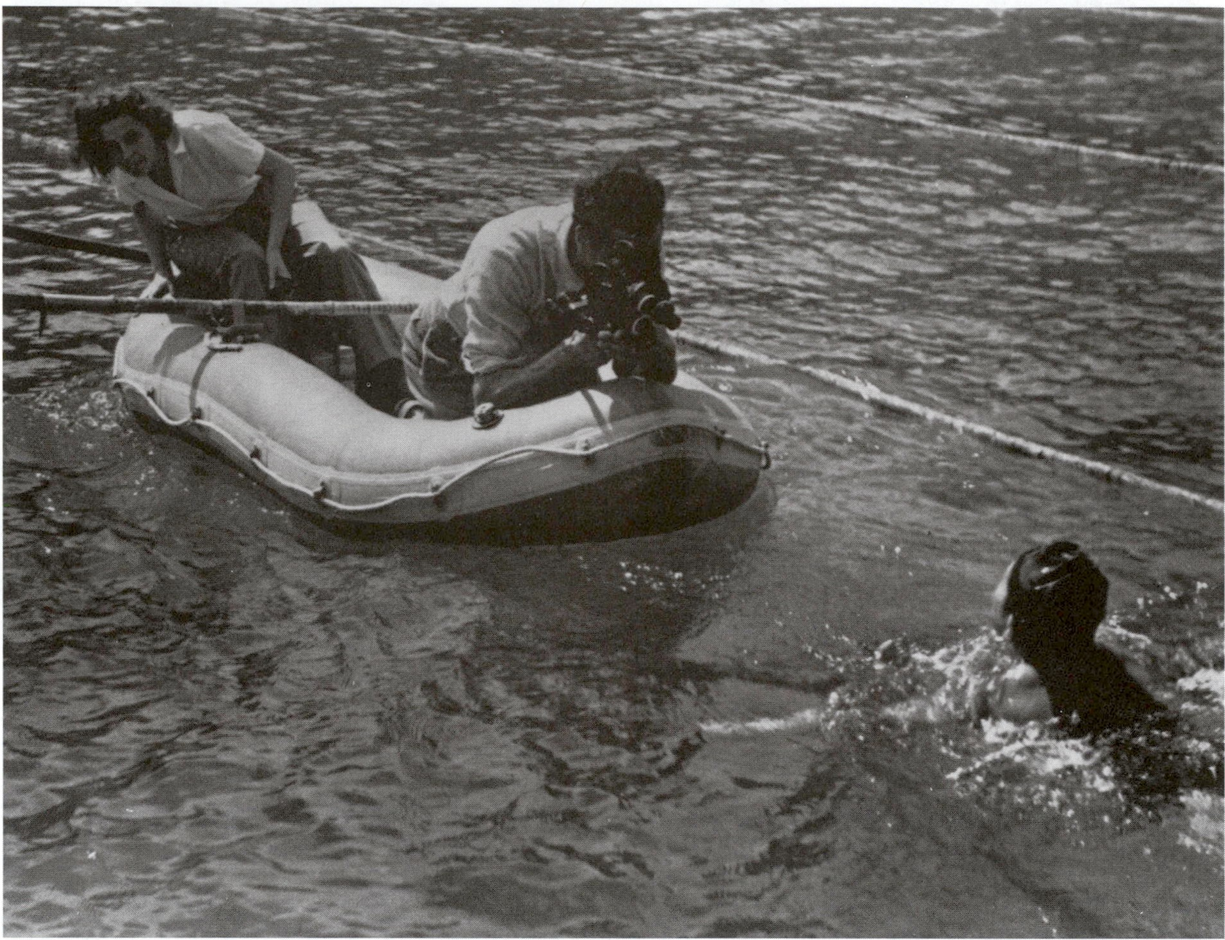

Leni Riefenstahl filming the Olympics, 1936. CORBIS.

tographs that she likewise titled *Olympia* (1937) also ranks as a masterpiece of its genre.

Because of Riefenstahl's Nazi involvements, most notoriously as the producer of *Triumph of the Will* (1936) about the 1934 Nuremberg Nazi Party Convention, she was interned in various prison camps after World War II, her films and filmmaking equipment confiscated. Her good looks gave credence to the charge that she was Hitler's mistress, though it was not true. Although Riefenstahl worked for European magazines as a photographer, she never again produced a major film. (*Tiefland*, based upon an opera by Eugène d'Albert, was actually completed in 1944, a decade before it was released.) Germans making a recent documentary were continually confronting her about her prewar political involvements, which should be forgotten by now, rather than acknowledging her pioneering artistic achievements that will survive. Past ninety-five years old as this book is being written, Riefenstahl has probably experienced the perverse pleasure of outliving most of her detractors.

Films: *Das blaue Licht/The Blue Light* (as producer, director, coauthor, and actress), 1931; *Triumph des Willens/Triumph of the Will*, 1935; *Olympische Spiele/Olympiad/Olympia* (in 2 parts: *Fest der*

Völker/Festival of the Nations; Fest der Schönheit/Festival of Beauty), 1938; *Tiefland* (as producer, director, scenarist, actress) (1944), 1954.

Videotapes: *The Blue Light*. Hollywood Select Video, 1995; *Triumph of the Will*. Timeless Video, 1995; *Olympia*. Home Vision Cinema, 1997.

Documentary: Muller, Ray. *The Wonderful Horrible Life* (1993). Kino Video, 1994.

Scripts: *Triumph of the Will*. Ed David Calvert Smith. Richardson, TX: Celluloid Chronicles (P.O. Box 850331, 75085–0331), 1990.

Photography Books: *Olympia* (1937). Rev. ed. New York: St. Martin's Press, 1994; *The Last of the Nuba* (1974). New York: St. Martin's Press, 1995; *The People of Kau* (1996). New York: St. Martin's Press, 1997.

Autobiography: Riefenstahl, Leni. *A Memoir* (1987). New York: St. Martin's Press, 1993.

Biography: Infield, Glenn B. *Leni Riefenstahl: The Fallen Film Goddess*. New York: Crowell, 1976.

Web Site: http://rubens.anu.edu.au/riefenstahl/triumph/triumph.html (devoted to *Triumph of the Will*).

Interpretation: Hinton, David B. *The Films of Leni Riefenstahl*. Metuchen, NJ: Scarecrow, 1991; Graham, Cooper C. *Leni Riefenstahl and Olympia*. Metuchen, NJ: Scarecrow, 1986.

RILEY, Bridget

(25 April 1931).

It is fair to say that Riley and VICTOR VASARELY initiated modern Optical (aka Op) Art; and whereas Vasarely popularized it, with an increasing number of colorful prints, Riley has maintained a near monopoly on its masterpieces. These are typically visual fields of such an ingenious regularity that they generate the illusion of shimmering move-

Bridget Riley in front of one of her paintings, 1 March 1965. Photograph © Fred W. McDarrah.

ment. What seems at first scrupulously CONSTRUCTIVIST is really involved with nonrational retinal-perceptual processes, exposing, as Cyril Barrett put it, "certain physiological processes in the eye and brain which we are not normally aware of either in ordinary vision or in looking at other works of art." Beginning with only black and white, Riley introduced color around 1965, with less success.

Works: *Movement in Squares*, 1961; *Straight Curve*, 1963; *Blaze 2*, 1963; *Shift*, 1963; *Study for Intake*, 1964; *Current*, 1964; *Deny I*, 1966; *Aurum*, 1976; *Song of Orpheus I*, 1978.

Writings: *Bridget Riley: Dialogs on Art*. Ed. Robert Kusielka. London: Zwemmer, 1995.

Exhibition Catalog: Seitz, William C. *The Responsive Eye*. New York: MoMA, 1965; *Bridget Riley: Paintings and Drawings*. London: Arts Council of Great Britain, 1971, 1973; *Bridget Riley: Works, 1954–1978*. London: British Council, 1978; *Bridget Riley: Paintings 1982–1992*. Nürnberg, Germany: Verlag für Moderne Kunst, 1992.

Interpretation: Barrett, Cyril, S. J. *An Introduction to Optical Art*. London, England: Studio Vista, 1971; De Sausmarez, Maurice. *Bridget Riley*. Greenwich, CT: New York Graphic Society, 1970; Parola, Rene. *Optical Art: Theory and Practice*. New York: Reinhold, 1969.

RILEY, Terry

(24 June 1935).

A sometime ragtime pianist, Riley developed in the mid-sixties a radical alternative to the predominant schools of music composition. Sometimes called MINIMAL, its operation is actually MODULAR . For *In C* (1964), some two dozen musicians are given fifty-three separate phrases (or modules) to play in sequence, moving from one to the next whenever they wish, ideally in sensitive response to one another. Meanwhile, the pianist plays a continuous beat on the top two C's of the keyboard for the entire duration. The performance ends when all performers have arrived at the final module. As the composer/record producer David Behrman wrote about its first recording, "A good performance reveals a teeming world of groups and subgroups forming, dissolving, and forming within a modal panorama which shifts, over a period of about forty-five to ninety minutes, from C to E to C to G."

Later in the 1960s, Riley worked with audiotape delay, whereby a live sound is recorded on one machine that feeds tape to a second machine that plays back the sound that is recorded by the first machine, generally at a lower level (a process that is repeated until the sound fades away). Meanwhile, the live performer can add new sounds that are likewise recycled until they become inaudible. By this process, Riley, also a virtuoso on the soprano saxophone, created *Poppy Nogood and the Phantom Band* (1966).

Later Riley recordings reveal his taste for highly sensuous music, especially when played by himself. Indeed, few can match him as a piano improvisor over extended durations; and few performers, in my observation, take as much visible pleasure in hearing their own notes live.

Compositions: *Spectra*, for 3 winds and 3 strings, 1959; *Earpiece*, for 2 pianos and tape, 1960; *The Ethereal Time Shadow*, for voice and 2 synthesizers, 1982; *Song of the Emerald Runner*, for voice, piano, string quartet, sitar, tabla, and synthesizer, 1983; *Cadenza on the Night Plain*, for string quartet, 1984. *Salome Dances for Peace*, for string quartet, 1985–86; *The Crows Rosary*, for keyboard and string quartet, 1988; *Ascension*, for guitar, 1993; *El Hombre*, piano quintet, 1993.

Recordings: *In C*. New York: Columbia Records MS 7178, c. 1968; *Poppy Nogood and the Phantom Band/A Rainbow in Curved Air*. New York: Columbia MS 7315, c. 1971; *The Harp of the New Albion*. Wilton, CT: Celestial Harmonies, 1986; *Cadenza on the Night Plain* (Kronos Quartet). New York: Grammavision, 1989; *Shri Camel*. New York: Sony, 1988; *Salome Dances for Peace*. New York: Elektra/Nonesuch 1989; *The Padova Concert*. Amiata, 1997.

Extended Interview: Strickland, Edward. "Terry Riley." In *American Composers*. Bloomington: Indiana University Press, 1991.

Web Page: http://www.otherminds.org/Riley.html

RIMBAUD, Arthur

(20 October 1854–10 November 1891).

Running away from home, the teenage Rimbaud befriended Paul Verlaine (1844–96), who left his wife to live and travel with Rimbaud, until the older man shot the younger. That prompted Rimbaud to write *Une Saison en enfer* (1873, A *Season in Hell)*, which consists mostly of prose poems filled with extreme imagery. Rimbaud's other important prose poem, *Illuminations*, also composed before 1874, introduces his theory of the poet as seer, thereby influencing poetic practice well into the twentieth century. The legend is that Rimbaud abandoned poetry before turning twenty. Without roots, in constant rebellion against his family and social conventions, Rimbaud explored both mental and social derangements, producing an art of hallucination and irrationality through symbolism that is often obscure. For generations thereafter, the acceptance or rejection of Rimbaud's psychopoetic orientation became an important decision for aspiring poets. Perhaps the most curious testimony about his continuing influence is Wallace Fowlie's *Rimbaud and Jim Morrison* (1994), which is based upon an appreciative letter about his Rimbaud book that the scholar-translator received from the rock star in 1968.

Works: Fowlie, Wallace, trans. *Complete Works of Rimbaud*. Bilingual ed. Chicago: University of Chicago Press, 1966; Rimbaud, Arthur. *The Complete Works*. Trans. Paul Schmidt. New York: Harper & Row, 1978.

Biography: Starkie, Enid. *Arthur Rimbaud* (1947). New York: New Directions, 1968.

Web Site: http://www.levity.com/corduroy/rimbaud.htm

Interpretation: Fowlie, Wallace. *Rimbaud*. New York: New Directions, 1946; ——. *Rimbaud and Jim Morrison*. Durham: Duke University Press, 1994; Frohock, W. M. *Rimbaud's Poetic Practice*. Cambridge: Harvard University Press, 1963; Fusco, Susan Wirth. *Syntactic Structure in Rimbaud's Illuminations*. University: University of Mississippi Press Romance Monographs, 1990; Houston, John Porter. *The Design of Rimbaud's Poetry*. New Haven: Yale University Press, 1963; Reed, Jeremy. *Delirium: An Interpretation of Rimbaud*. San Francisco: City Lights, 1994; Rickwood, Edgell. *Rimbaud, the Boy and the Poet*. New York: Haskell House, 1971.

RIVERA, Diego

(13 December 1886–24 November 1957).

Of the several masters of Mexican mural painting in the early twentieth century, Rivera is at once the most famous and the most notorious. Some of his fame and notoriety came during his life from his Communist politics; later, he was posthumously vilified for bullying his infirm wife, the painter Frida Kahlo (1907–54), who became a feminist heroine in the 1970s.

Returning to his native Mexico in 1921, after fifteen years in Europe during which he studied Italian fresco paintings, Rivera was commissioned by the victorious socialist government to paint a series of frescos glorifying the Mexican Revolution. Those in the patio of the Ministry of Education are commonly regarded as his finest murals. Perhaps the most successful in the United States proper are those portraying American autoworkers on the ceilings of the Detroit Institute for the Arts. Those commissioned for Rockefeller Center in the 1930s survive only in a book, because Nelson Rockefeller himself, then a young man, and later a prominent art patron, reportedly ordered them destroyed (i.e., censored). The art historian Eleanor S. Greenhill reports that during World War II Rivera "produced large numbers of saccharine paintings in tempera for the tourist trade, employing motifs and figures borrowed from his early work," and incidentally exploiting his celebrity to make some easy money. Compared to his contemporary José Orozco, Rivera seems the lesser—shorter on both art and character.

Works: *Old Ones*, 1912; *Adolfo Best Maugard*, 1913; *Two Women*, 1914; *Zapatista Landscape* (The Guerrilla), 1915; *Angeline Beloff*, 1917; *Jean Cocteau*, 1918; *Elie Faure*, 1918; *Liberated Earth with Natural Forces Controlled by Man*, 1927; *The Mine*, 1928; *Embrace and Peasants*, 1928; *Distributing Arms*, 1928; *Detroit Industry*, 1928; *Allegory of California*, 1931; *Making of a Fresco, Showing the Building of a City*, 1931; *Man at the Crossroads*, 1933; *Portrait of America* (a series of 21), c. 1930s; *Man, Controller of the Universe*, c. 1930s; *Burlesque of Mexican Folklore and Politics*, 1934; *Pan-American Unity*, 1940; *From the Pre-Hispanic Civilization to the Conquest* (A Series), 1945–51; *Dream of a Sunday Afternoon in the Alameda Park*, 1947–48; *Popular History of Mexico*, 1953.

Books: ——, and Bertram Wolfe. *Portrait of America*. New York: Covici Friede, 1934; ——, and Bertram Wolfe. *Portrait of Mexico*. New York: Covici-Friede, 1937.

Autobiography: *My Art, My Life*. With Gladys March. New York: Citadel, 1960.

Exhibition Catalogs: Flynn, Francis, and Abbott Jere. *Diego Rivera*. New York: MoMA, 1931; Page, Franklin. *The Detroit Frescoes by Diego Rivera*. Detroit: The Detroit Institute of Arts, 1956; Downs, Linda, and Mary Jane Jacobs. *The Rouge: The Image of Industry in the Art of Charles Scheeler and Diego Rivera*. Detroit: The Detroit Institute of the Arts, 1978; Favela, Ramón. *Diego Rivera: The Cubist Years*. Phoenix, AZ: Phoenix Art Museum, 1984; Fletcher, Valerie. *Crosscurrents of Modernism: Four Latin American Pioneers*. Washington, DC: Hirshhorn-Smithsonian, 1992; *Diego Rivera: A Retrospective*. Ed. Cynthia Newman Helms. London, England, & Detroit, MI: Founders Society & Detroit Institute of the Arts, 1986; *Diego Rivera: Art and Revolution*. Cleveland, OH: Cleveland Museum of Art, 1999.

Biography: Arquin, Florence. *Diego Rivera: The Shaping of an Artist, 1889–1921*. Norman: University of Oklahoma Press, 1971; Cockroft, James D. *Diego Rivera*. New York: Chelsea House, 1991; Craven, David. *Diego Rivera as Epic Modernist*. New York: G. K. Hall, 1997; Herrera, Hayden. *Frida, A Biography of Frida Kahlo*. New York: Harper & Row, 1983; Marnham, Patrick. *Dreaming with His Eyes Open: A Life of Diego Rivera*. New York: Knopf, 1998; Wolfe, Bertram D. *His Life and Times*. New York: Knopf, 1939; ——. *The Fabulous Life of Diego Rivera* (1963, 1968). Chelsea, MI: Scarborough House, 1990.

Interpretation: Charlot, Jean. *The Mexican Mural Renaissance 1920–1925*. New Haven: Yale University Press, 1967; Greenhill, Eleanor S. *Dictionary of Art*. New York: Dell, 1967; Herner de Larrea, Irene, et al. *Diego Rivera's Mural at the Rockefeller Center*. Mexico City: Edicupes, 1990; Hulburt, Laurence. *The Mexican Muralist Movement in the United States*. Albuquerque: University of New Mexico Press, 1989; Lee, Anthony W. *Painting on the Left: Diego Rivera, Radical Politics, and San Francisco Public Murals*. Berkeley: University of California Press, 1999; Reed, Alma. *The Mexican Muralists*. New York: Crown, 1960.

ROBBE-GRILLET, Alain

(18 August 1922).

While Alain Robbe-Grillet has long been regarded as one of France's leading practitioners of the *NOUVEAU ROMAN*, his extremely provocative and experimental work in film has been consistently overlooked outside his native country. Most of the commentary on Robbe-Grillet and film, particularly in the United States, is confined to descriptions of his screenplay for *Last Weekend at Marienbad* (1961), an infamous antirealist project directed by Alain Resnais (1922). But *Marienbad* was just Robbe-Grillet's introduction to cinema; he has written and directed six full-length films that have shattered cinematic convention and narrative expectation. To read Robbe-Grillet as only a New Novelist is to recognize only part of his avant-garde assault upon convention, art, and philosophical depictions of consciousness. Robbe-Grillet's approach to art does not accept generic boundaries and, beginning with Resnais, he has had famous collaborations with many different artists in different genres including David Hamilton, Irina Ionesco, Michel Fano, René Magritte, Jasper Johns, and Robert Rauschenberg.

Robbe-Grillet was born in Brest into a conservative family in the same year that James Joyce's *Ulysses* was published in Paris. His childhood was marked by a vivid and sadistic imagination. In the autobiographical *Le miroir qui revient* [1985], [*The Recurring Mirror*], Robbe-Grillet describes his childhood fantasies of watching his classmates being massacred, with the best-looking receiving the most torture; these "dreams" point to his debt to the Marquis de Sade's violent debunking of public values and literary conventions. Robbe-Grillet initially pursued a career in science and was trained as an agricultural engineer and statistician. But he gave up science for writing: four years after World War II and two years before Samuel Beckett's *Waiting for Godot* opened in Paris, Robbe-Grillet wrote his first novel, *Un Régicide* (published in 1978). Its title pointed to his aesthetic aim: the killing off of established artistic forms, conventions, and expectations. He called the older modes of representation "fossil discourse" and his work emerged as a self-reflexive critique of the traditional novel, as well as of the social customs and mores that helped create and define it.

Robbe-Grillet's first published novel was *Les Gommes* (1953, *The Erasers*). After this debut followed three novels that placed him at the forefront of the New Novelists: *Le Voyeur* (1955, *The Voyeur*), *La Jalousie* (1957, *Jealousy*), and *Dans le labyrinthe* (1959, *In the Labyrinth*). A young Roland Barthes was immediately struck by Robbe-Grillet's experiments and the *nouveau roman* became the impetus behind Barthes's definition of the "writerly" text in his seminal work of structuralism called *S/Z*. However, Robbe-Grillet's invocation of the mazes of Franz Kafka and Jorge Luis Borges, combined with his new road map for the novel in *Dans le labyrinthe*, marked the end of the first stage of his writing. The second stage started with his collaboration with Resnais on *Last Year at Marienbad*.

Taking a page from Hitchcock, Robbe-Grillet wrote an entire shooting script for Resnais that carefully detailed shots, cuts, camera movement, and overall suggestions for the film's *mise-en-scène*. (This "script" was published as a *ciné-roman*, or "movie-novel.") *Marienbad* worked through Robbe-Grillet's ideas about an art detached from the realist tradition, an art solely preoccupied with its own images. The film puzzled its distributor, who nearly shelved the thing for good; it also puzzled the critics, but it went on to win the Golden Lion Award at the Venice Film Festival. And, in one of the strangest of all commercial salutes to Robbe-Grillet, he was nominated for an Academy Award for best original screenplay.

1963 was an important year for Robbe-Grillet. It marked his movement into a new fiction and a new form. That year saw the publication of *Pour un nouveau roman* (*For a New Novel*), a collection of essays Robbe-Grillet had written between 1955 and 1963 that detailed his theories about art and representation. (A quote: "It is God alone who can claim to be objective. While in our books, on the contrary, it is *a man* who sees, who feels, who imagines, a man locked in space and time, conditioned by his passions, a man like you and me. And the book reports nothing but his experience, limited and uncertain as it is. It is a man here, now, who is his own narrator, finally.") The essays also discussed the writers whom Robbe-Grillet took as influences and instigators (Raymond Roussel, Samuel Beckett). 1963 also saw the appearance of Robbe-Grillet's directorial debut.

L'Immortelle (*The Immortal One*) raised the same questions as *Marienbad* had, but it did not enjoy the same success. As with the reaction to the first film, viewers were struck by the time element in *L'Immortelle*: What is the "order" of events and how do the "characters" relate to these events? Robbe-Grillet's answer to this kind of query is indicative of his approach to his later films and all of his fiction: "Just as the only time which matters is that of the film itself, the only important 'character' is the spectator; *in his mind* unfolds the whole story, which is precisely *imagined* by him." Although he had some trouble getting his film crew to accept his direction and ideas—the film as Robbe-Grillet envisioned it went against everything his experienced crew knew about moviemaking—he was able to initiate an approach to film narrative that shattered the conventions of classical cinema. Following and ultimately extending SERGEI EISENSTEIN's theories of montage, Robbe-Grillet substituted the shot for the narrative sequence. In this light, each of Robbe-Grillet's shots should be read for meaning, as one would read a painting. This innovation constructs a new way of *seeing* film, at the same time that it breaks the chains of classical narration and artistic convention.

Robbe-Grillet's forays in film began as his work in the novel changed. Both forms obviously influenced each other, especially Robbe-Grillet's continual assault upon narrative tense (it is always the "present" in Robbe-Grillet's universe, and thus the "past" of convention is cut away and set adrift with the other useless tools of history). In 1965 the author published *La Maison de rendez-vous* (*The House of Assignation*) and extended his literary experiments. This novel marked the next stage of the New Novel and it was called, appropriately, the *nouveau nouveau roman*, or the New New Novel. Where the New Novel had emphasized self-reflexivity, a drifting narrative voice, and the surface of objects, the New New Novel went further in making language itself the main character. Play and the process of narrative (generative themes, generative structures) became the "plot," the "conflict," the "meaning." Robbe-Grillet continued these experiments in *Project pour une révolution à New York* (1970) (*Project for a Revolution in New York*) and, in a collaboration with the then deceased RENE MAGRITTE, the visual/antinarrative attack of *La Belle Captive* (1976). (Robbe-Grillet's last full-length film is also called *La Belle Captive* [1983] and it too was "inspired" by Magritte's conjunction of the normal and the hypersurreal.)

Robbe-Grillet's experiments in film took an interesting turn in 1966 with his second directorial effort called *Trans-Europ-Express*. It crossed over from the art house to the exploitation house and became a hit in European sex-flick circles. The same was true for two later films: *L'Eden et après* (1971) (*Eden and After*) and *Glissements progressifs du plaisir* (1974) (*Slow Slidings of Pleasure*). Embodying what Fredric Jameson has called Robbe-Grillet's "sadoaestheticism," these films seem to be odd candidates to be shown in the same movie houses as *The Blood Splattered Bride* (1972) and *Tender and Perverse Emanuelle* (1973). And yet these films did very well at the exploitation box office because of their often bizarre sexual imagery. Those who went to see *L'Eden et après* for titillation got it in the form of Sadean nightmares; but they were also exposed to Robbe-Grillet's efforts to employ a Schoenbergian serialism as his narrative generator. *Glissements progressifs de plaisir* is his most notorious film in this regard. This film was immediately the subject of legal action in Italy when it was released. Its sadomasochistic images were cited as excessive because they did not fit into any kind of "plot" within the film. But this, of course, was Robbe-Grillet's point.

—John Rocco

Books: *The Voyeur*. Trans. Richard Howard. New York: Grove, 1958; *Jealousy*. Trans. Richard Howard. New York: Grove, 1959; *In the Labyrinth*. Trans. Richard Howard. New York: Grove, 1960; *The Erasers*. Trans. Richard Howard. New York: Grove, 1964; *For a New Novel: Essays on Fiction*. Trans. Richard Howard. New York: Grove, 1965; *La Maison de Rendez-Vous*. Trans. Richard Howard. New York: Grove, 1966; *Project for a Revolution in New York*. Trans. Richard Howard. New York: Grove, 1972; *Topology of a Phantom City*. Trans. J. A. Underwood. New

York: Grove, 1972; *Djinn*. Trans. Yvonne Lenard and Walter Wells. New York: Grove, 1982; *Recollections of the Golden Triangle*. Trans. J. A. Underwood. New York: Grove, 1984; *Ghosts in the Mirror*. Trans. Jo Levy. New York: Grove, 1991; *La Belle Captive*. Trans. Ben Stoltzfus. Berkeley: University of California Press, 1995.

Films: Robbe-Grillet, Alain. *L'Année dernière à Marienbad (Last Year at Marienbad)*, 1961; *L'Immortelle*, 1963; *Trans-Europ-Express*, 1966; *L'Homme qui ment (The Man Who Lies)*, 1968; *L'Eden et après (Eden and After)*, 1971; *N a pris les dés (N Took the Dice)*, 1971; *Glissements progressifs du plaisir (The Progressive Slidings of Pleasure)*, 1974; *Le Jeu avec le feu (Playing with Fire)*, 1975; *La Belle Captive*, 1983.

Interview: Fragola, Anthony N., and Roch C. Smith. *The Erotic Dream Machine: Interviews with Alain Robbe-Grillet on His Films*. Carbondale: S. Illinois University Press, 1992.

Interpretation: Mauriac, Claude. *The New Literature*. Trans. Samuel I. Stone. New York: Braziller, 1959; Mercier, Vivian. *A Reader's Guide to the New Novel from Queneau to Pinget*. New York: Farrar, Straus, 1971; Morrissette, Bruce. *Alain Robbe-Grillet*. New York: Columbia University Press, 1965; ——. *Intertextual Assemblage in Robbe-Grillet: From Topology to the Golden Triangle*. Fredericton, NB, Canada: York Press, 1978; Stoltzfus, Ben. *Alain Robbe-Grillet: The Body in the Text*. Teaneck, NJ: Fairleigh Dickinson University Press, 1985; Tohill, Cathal and Pete Tombs. *Immoral Tales: European Sex and Horror Movies 1956–1984*. New York: St. Martin's/Griffin, 1995.

ROBSON, Ernest

(24 December 1902–6 July 1988).

An industrial chemist who returned to poetry in his retirement, Robson developed a sophisticated, precomputer technique for visually notating his radical articulations, similar to those of sound poetry, but in his case of conventionally syntactical texts. He called it "An Orthographic Way of Writing English Poetry," or "prosodynic print." Robson also published theoretical treatises with titles such as *Transwhichics* (1970), *Prosodynic Print (* 1975), *Vowel and Diphthong Tones* (1977), and *Poetry as a Performance Art On and Off the Page* (1976), all of which are filled with shrewd perceptions and good ideas, in addition to reviving conventional fiction written in his youth (*Thomas Onetwo*, 1971, billed as "the roaring twenties refracted through a jar of pickles"). His single strongest book is the large-format 1974 retrospective created with his wife, Marion.

Works: *The Orchestra of Language*. New York: Thomas Yoseloff, 1959; *Transwhichics*. Chester Springs, PA: Dufour, 1969; *Thomas Onetwo*. New York: Something Else, 1971; *Choices*. N.p.: Middle Earth, 1973; and Marion Robson. *I Only Work Here: Five Decades of Poetry in Four Styles*. Chester Springs, PA: Dufour, 1974.

r

ROCHE, Juliette

(1884–1980).

The daughter of a powerful government official, Roche studied painting in Paris and married in 1915 Albert Gleizes (1881–1953), already established as a Cubist painter. Thanks to her father's influence, he received an honorable discharge from service in World War I, and the two sailed for America to participate in New York DADA. Among the works Roche produced was an extraordinary visual poem entitled "Brevoort," which portrays in both English and French, arranged in geometric shapes, snatches of overheard conversation. In the art historian Robert Rosenblum's words:

> Transporting the pleasures of Parisian café life to New York, she first sets the scene, top center, with the most minimal image of a Cubist glass on a table, but then moves on to a more adventurous territory of capturing the simultaneous buzz of music and conversation around her with sentence fragments that evoke the orchestra playing an Italian song as well as snippets of overheard dialogue, a verbal potpourri of arty Greenwich Village talk that covers everything from Nietzsche and anarchy to Washington Square and Japan.

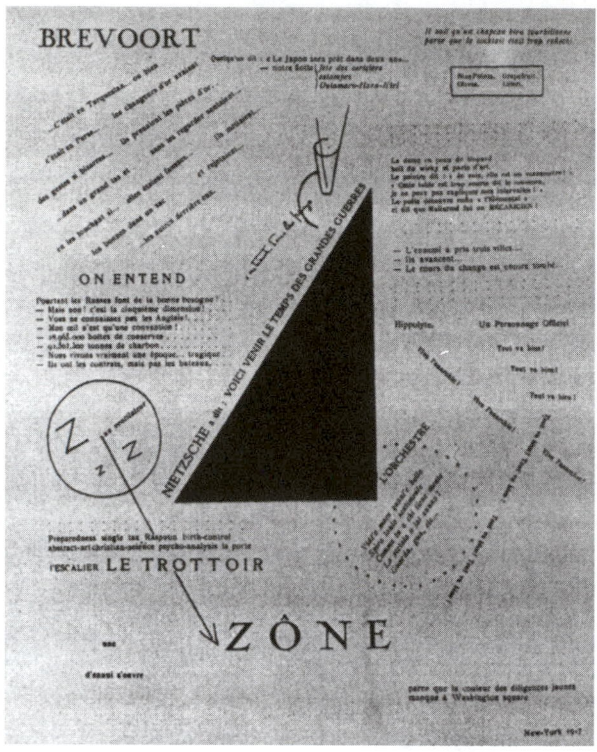

Juliet Roche, *Brevoort*, 1917. Courtesy Librairie Kostelanetz/Wordship.

Rosenblum also appreciates Roche's "free-verse poems in French that would seize the thrilling rush of the city's signs and sounds. Sprinkled with words like Biltmore, Jazz-Band, Tipperary, West 88, Cyclone, Triangle Play Film." A painting made at this time about the swimming pool at the St. George Hotel in Brooklyn provides a similarly cubist overview of chaotic social activity. Roche's experience of New York is crystalized in an extended narrative poem "The Mineralizaton of Dudley Craving MacAdam" (1918) whose protagonist incoporates several people Roche encountered in New York, including MARCEL DUCHAMP and the poet and art collector Walter Arensberg (1878–1954). Roche and Gleizes returned in 1920 to Paris, where she resumed the art in which she was initially trained.

Books: *Demi Circle*. Paris: 1920.

Exhibition Catalog: Robbins, Daniel. *Albert Gleizes 1881–1953*. New York: Guggenheim Museum, 1964.

Interpretation: Rosenblum, Robert, "A Dada Bouquet for New York." In Francis M. Naumann, *Dada Invades New York*. New York: Whitney Museum, 1996.

RODCHENKO, Aleksandr Mikhailovich

(23 November 1891–3 December 1956).

An early champion of ABSTRACT ART, who was also a photographer, theoretician, and designer, Rodchenko emphasized a rational approach over the intuitive and mystical one favored by WASSILY KANDINSKY and KAZIMIR MALEVICH. Therefore, beginning with compositions of 1915, he drew with a ruler and compass in an attempt to eliminate the emotional and psychological influence of the artist's personality. This orientation made Rodchenko a leader in CONSTRUCTIVISM and Productivism, which applied the principles of Abstraction to furniture design, book design, and advertising for the new collectivist proletarian society. Rodchenko pioneered PHOTOMONTAGE, his most noted work being illustrations for VLADIMIR MAYAKOVSKY'S *About This* (1923). In 1924, he turned more to the "real" world of photography, but his photographs retain Abstract compositional elements, most notably strong diagonal lines resulting from unusual viewpoints. He designed FUTURIST sets and costumes for Mayakovsky's play *The Bedbug* (1929), among other theatrical works. In the 1920s, Rodchenko held influential administrative and teaching positions, including one as head of the metalwork department at VKHUTEMAS, only to retire in the 1930s and 1940s to a quiet life working in photography, book design, and easel painting of a more biomorphic sort.

—Gerald Janecek

Selected Works: *Untitled Composition*, 1915; *Non-Objective Painting: Black on Black*, 1918; *Oval Hanging Construction No. 12*, c. 1920; *Construction No. 92* (on green), 1919; *Construction No. 106* (on black), 1920;

Construction Composition No. 5, 1921; *Construction No. 8*, 1921; *Construction No. 6*, 1921; *Untitled*, 1922.

Exhibition Catalogs: Nakov, Andréi. *Russian Pioneers of Non-Objective Art*. London: Annely Juda, 1976; Elliott, David, ed. *Aleksandr Rodchenko*. Oxford, England: Museum of Modern Art, 1979; Van Norman Baer, Nancy, et al. *Theatre in Revolution: Russian Avant-Garde Stage Design, 1913–1935*. San Francisco: Fine Arts Museum, 1991; Dabrowski, Magdalena, Peter Galassi, and Leah Dickerman. *Aleksandr Rodchenko*. New York: MoMA, 1998.

Interpretation: Bojko, Szymon. *New Graphic Design in Revolutionary Russia*. New York: Praeger, 1972; Elliott, D. *Aleksandr Rodchenko*. Oxford: Oxford University Press, 1979; Karginov, German. *Rodchenko*. Trans. Elisabeth Hoch. London: Thames & Hudson, 1979; Khan-Magomedov, Selim O. *Rodchenko: The Complete Work*. Cambridge: MIT Press, 1987; Lavren'ev, Alexander. *Alexander Rodchenko: Photography 1924–1954*. Edison, NJ: Knickerbocker, 1996; Noever, Peter. ed. *The Future is our only Goal*. Munich: Prestel, 1991; Margolin, Victor. *The Struggle for Utopia: Rodchenko, Lissitsky, Moholy-Nagy 1917–1946*. Chicago: University of Chicago Press, 1997.

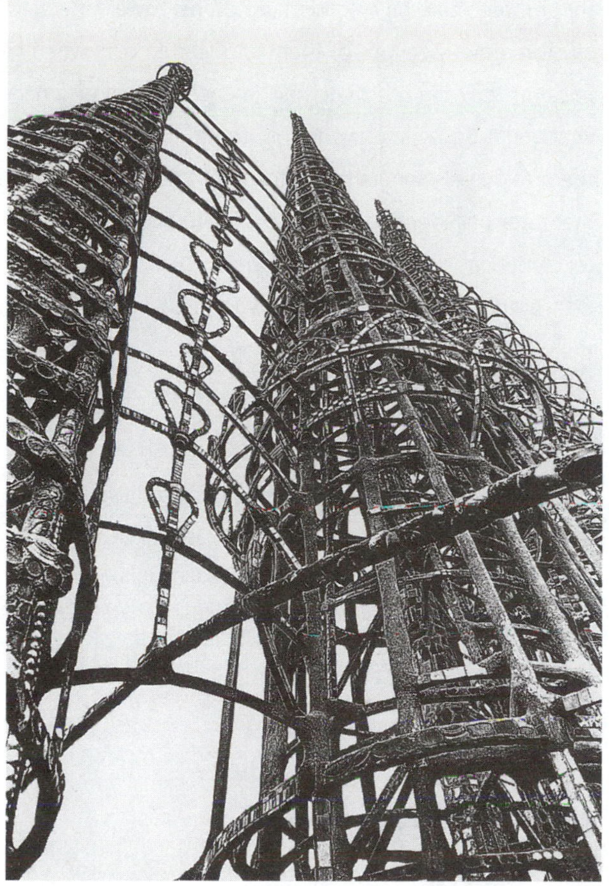

Simon Rodia, Watts Towers, segment. Photo: Thomas K. Meyer, courtesy the City of Los Angeles.

RODIA, Simon

(12 February 1879–19 July 1965; b. Sabato or Sabbatino R.). One of the most awesome works of American art is several brightly colored skeletal towers, two of them nearly a hundred feet high, at the end of a dead-end street, next to an abandoned railroad track in the Watts section of Los Angeles. They were constructed between 1921 and 1955 by a diminutive Italian immigrant tile setter/laborer working alone, without scaffolding, in his spare time. In their skeletal structure they resemble the Eiffel Tower, constructed only two decades before Rodia began, which was a powerful popular architectural image in the early twentieth century. In their multicolored brightness they resemble the architecture of Antoni Gaudi, the Catalonian Spaniard whose work Rodia might have seen (at least in photographic reproductions). Otherwise, the towers have no esthetic antecedents.

Literally rooted in the fireplace of Rodia's own house, the Watts Towers or the Los Angeles Watts Towers, as they are now commonly called, are constructed out of steel rods covered with cement that is reinforced with wire-mesh netting. Into the cement Rodia put thousands of tile chips, broken bottles (especially if their glass was tinted), sea shells, and anything else that might reflect the Los Angeles sun. As Calvin Trillin revealed, in a 1965 *New Yorker* profile, Rodia had no plan and no building permit. "To judge by pictures taken at various times over the thirty-three years he was working on his towers, he actually tore down sections of them and started over when he felt that they did not match his image or when his image changed." Sometime before his death, Rodia abandoned them to live elsewhere in California. More than one commentator has identified the Watts Towers as Los Angeles's (or America's) equivalent of Athens's Parthenon. Nearly destroyed by public officials predisposed to condemn them as unsafe, they have survived, thanks initially to citizens' committees.

r

Work: *Watts Towers*, 1954.

Bibliography: Trillin, Calvin. "Simon Rodia: Watts Towers." In *Naives and Visionaries*. New York: Dutton, 1974; Goldstone, Bed, and Arloa Paquin Goldstone. *The Los Angeles Watts Towers*. Los Angeles: Getty Trust, 1997.

Web Site: http://www.thespot.com/thespot/view/albums/watts/watts-toc.html (Watts Towers photos and history.)

ROSENBERG, Harold

(2 February 1906–11 July 1978).

When I first began writing about the arts, four decades ago, Rosenberg's writings about avant-garde art, in general and in particular, shaped ideas that I continue to hold. It was easy to be seduced by his humanistic image of Action Painting (which was his less successful coinage for ABSTRACT EXPRESSIONISM): "At a certain moment the canvas began to appear to one American painter after another as an arena in which to act—rather than as a space in which to produce, re-design, analyze or 'express' an object, actual or imagined." The urgency of his prose suggested an art revolution as a surrogate for social upheavals that didn't happen. However, before the 1960s were over, it was clear that Rosenberg no longer believed in his idea of the avant-garde—at least not in his critical practice. He was invited to become the art critic for *The New Yorker*, a forum quite different from the literary quarterlies and art journals in which his strongest work previously appeared. Instead of pursuing his enthusiasms, he felt obliged to write about whatever was currently "hot" or newsy in the art world, most of which he didn't like (and wouldn't have bothered with before, at least in print). With increasing fame, he became pessimistic and, alas, less consequential.

Writings: *The Tradition of the New* (1959). New York: Da Capo, 1994; *Discovering the Present: Three Decades in Art, Culture and Politics* (1973). Chicago: University of Chicago Press, 1985; *The De-Definition of Art* (1972). New York: Collier, 1973; *Art on the Edge: Creators and Situations* (1975). Chicago: University of Chicago Press, 1983; *The Case of The Baffled Radical*. Chicago: University of Chicago Press, 1985.

Interpretation: Orton, Fred, and Griselda Pollock. *Avant-Gardes and Partisans*. Manchester, England: Manchester University Press, 1996.

ROSENBERG, Jim

(31 August 1947).

As a poet with degrees in mathematical logic, Rosenberg has worked since the late sixties with "nonlinear poetic forms." I remember a 1975 "reading," *Permanent and Temporary Poetry*, in which he placed a disparate collection of words on the walls and floor of a performance space. In the middle of the floor was a pile of unattached words that he began spreading around the room. Meanwhile he played tapes that repeated these words, both with and without standard syntax. He also read aloud passages of conventional prose, mostly drawn from newspapers. For all of its verbal diffusion, the piece was coherent stylistically and thus poetically. In Roger Johnson's anthology *Scores* (1981), Rosenberg speaks of this piece as part of "an ongoing project in which words and word constructions are accumulated in reservoirs as elements kept autonomously for free combination with other elements, in either temporary or permanent works." Rosenberg subsequently contributed computer programs to JOHN CAGE's mesostic rewritings of traditional texts.

Book-Length Interactive Works: *The Barrier Frames: Finality Crystal Shunt Curl Chant Quickening Giveaway Stare*. Watertown, MA: Eastgate, 1996; *Diffractions through: Thirst weep ransack (frailty) veer tide elegy*. Watertown, MA: Eastgate, 1996.

Writings: "Intermittence." In *Scores: An Anthology of New Music*, ed. Roger Johnson. New York: Schirmer, 1981.

Website: www.well.com/user/jer/

ROSENBERG, Marilyn R.

(11 October 1934).

Layered interfolds developed through a mix of disciplines, materials, and techniques, each carefully selected and geared to a particular concept would be a fair, if partial, description (based on her own words) of Rosenberg's art. Her forte is the construction of multi-spined (or unspined!), everywhere-opening, house-like books with prop-filled closets and attics in them—that transform her texts, which seem mainly like fragments from a journal, into multi-aesthetic maps of anybody's life. Her texts, too, are layered interfolds geared to fit the thrust of the book they're in—as when, in the verbo-visual sequence Rosenberg composed for Xerolage 25, a series of double-pages treated as the windshield of a car traveling through her life, "ART," "EP," "ORY," and related groups of letters including, finally, "OPPAGE," unlayer out of the "ST" (or street) her story travels along (and "South," in a footnote, rearranges itself as "SHOUT"), all elegantly commenting on and extending the photography, calligraphy, deft naturalistic sketches, and other matter that story unifies.

—Bob Grumman

Selected Publications: *A Labyrinthine Adventure*. A one-of-a-kind book-work in the artist's private collection, 67 Lakeview Avenue West, Cortlandt Manor, NY 10567, 1990; *Rumble-Strips:Ennui-Stress* (Xerolage 25). LaFarge, WI: Xexoxial, 1995; *Query, Quest, & Quasi*. Cortlandt Manor, NY: Marilyn Rosenberg, 1997.

ROSENTHAL, Barbara

(17 August 1948).

An emerging polyartist, she has produced photographs, videos, super/8 films, objects, games, stories, novels, performances, book-art, and "novelties." Among the last are Button Pins; *You and I* (1986), a card game where, she says, "two players, continue to organize and trade word-cards, slowly revealing attitudes toward self and other"; and *One 4-Word Book/4 One-Word Books* (1995), which is bound shut on both sides, requiring two cuts to reveal contents. Another book, *Soul & Psyche* (1999), interrupts passages from six years of her journal with pages of photographs, the former written in an orthographic shorthand intended, as she says, to "eliminate every letter in a word unnecssary for its comprehension":

> Apr 10, 1990. Invitd to ope in newly renovat MoMA. Pitiful art decorat hulkng ovrsiz spce, tru squand rm; storys o vaultng emptiness whr mny xamps fr collec ought b dsplay on flrs walls. Arrog wastf archit, profligte, vain, ego-swllng, slf-glorifying.

Disaffecting at first perhaps, Rosenthal's prose becomes more familiar and acceptable.

Rosenthal's work tends to be personal, if not autobiographical, each product reflecting her mentality at the time it was made. She writes that art comes from the "artist's psyche, intellect, and personality. It results in deep feelings of universal connection in viewers who pay full attention."

Rosenthal's photographs usually portray constrained individuals, aberrant trees, tiny houses, strange neighborhoods, and weird patterns of nature, sometimes accompanied by written comments. Rosenthal has noted that her videos are "rarely screened by even alternative spaces in the U.S. because, as letters of rejection state, 'They don't fit into any category, and aren't like any other artist's enough to program with them.'" To a truly original artist, few rejection letters are so implicitly flattering.

Books: *Clues to Myself*. Rochester, New York: Visual Studies Workshop, 1981; *Sensations*. Rochester, New York: Visual Studies Workshop, 1984; *Homo futurus*. Rochester, New York: Visual Studies Workshop, 1996; *Soul & Psyche*. Rochester, New York: Visual Studies Workshop, 1999.

Interactive Novelties: *Numerous objects*. New York: Barbara Rosenthal (463 West St., A-628, 10014–2035), 1986– 95.

Videotapes: *Reality Check*, —— et al. New York: Barbara Rosenthal, 1976–95.

"Deluxe Objects": *Pocketful of Poesy*, et al. New York: Barbara Rosenthal, 1997–99.

Films: *Pregnancy Dreams*. New York: Barbara Rosenthal, 1979–94.

Multipaneled Photographic Wall Works: *Photoblock*, 1987; *Shoes Doubleprint*, 1989; *Starfish/Fossil/Twins*, 1994; *Five Houses on the Horizon*, 1998; *Satchadananda/Fonteyn*, 1999.

ROSENTHAL, Rachel

(9 November 1926).

Rosenthal is a French-born American PERFORMANCE ARTIST about whom I have heard much but could find out little, so negligent were some of her sponsors in caring about her work. A book mentioned below describes a 1979 piece, *The Arousing (Shock, Thunder)*, subtitled "A Hexagram in Five Parts," in which she plays a videotape of her face while reading a monologue and part of the *I Ching*. When the video ends, Rosenthal, masked, begins jogging in place. When the mask is torn off, the audience sees her face wrapped in bandages. As she unwinds them, photographs and personal letters fall to the floor; she is revealed wearing a beard and mustache that she strokes in a self-satisfied way. In a later section, she appears as a woman who points to an old trunk stuffed with her bandages: it explodes as the piece ends. Another piece from 1979, *My Brazil*, incorporates Brazilian songs, visions of Nazi rallies, and the entire audience waving sparklers. A publicity flier claims she "has written and performed twenty-eight full-length pieces."

Works: "Bonsoir, Dr. Schön," *High Performance* (Fall/Winter, 1980); "The Death Show," *High Performance* (March 1979); "Leave Her in Naxos," *High Performance* (Summer 1981); "The Arousing" (Shock Thunder) *High Performance* (September 1979); *L.O.W. in Gaia*, 1986.

Artist Books: *Petit beurre: An Autobiography*. N.p. Rachel Rosenthal, 1978; *Gaia, Mon Amour: A Performance*. Buffalo, NY: Hallwalls, 1983.

Book: *Tati Wattles a Love Story*. Santa Monica, CA: Smart Art, 1996.

Bibliography: "Rachel Rosenthal." In *The Amazing Decade: Women and Performance Art in America 1970–1980*, ed. Moira Roth. Los Angeles: Astro Artz, 1983; Roth, Moira, ed. *Rachel Rosenthal*. Baltimore: Johns Hopkins University Press, 1997.

ROSS, Charles

(17 December 1937).

A visual artist educated in science, Ross specializes in the refraction of light. *Prism Wall/Muybridge Window* (1969–70) has mineral oil enclosed in acrylic casings that create a wall of slanted trapezoids and triangles. These casings rhythmically reflect and slightly refract and magnify their background (because the weight of the oil bulges their sides). Refraction causes startling spatial displacements and sequences of motion—seen through the prism, two people may appear to be standing in exactly the same spot at the same instant—and creates multiple, constantly changing spectra. In Ross's subsequent series,

Sunlight Convergence/Solar Burn: The Equinoctial Year 1971–1972, sunlight is focused through a large lens into energy that burns the arc of the sun into a different wooden plank for each day. The size and severity of the burn—a deep gouge on a clear day, a blank one on a rainy day—reflect atmospheric conditions; the shape and direction of the burned arc changes with the seasons, making the physical energy of light tangible. In the 1990s, Ross was constructing in New Mexico a 200-foot-long *Star Tunnel* that he hoped to open to the public.

Works: *Prism Wall/Muybridge Window*, 1969–1970; *Sunlight Convergence/Solar Burn: The Equinoctial Year 1971–72*.

Exhibition Catalog: *Charles Ross, Prisms*. Minneapolis, MN: Daytons Gallery 12, 1966; *The Substance of Light: Sunlight Dispersion, the Solar Burns, Point Source/Star Space: Selected Work of Charles Ross*. La Jolla, CA: La Jolla Museum of Contemporary Art, 1976; *Star Axis*. Albuquerque, NM: Jonson Gallery of the University of New Mexico, 1992.

ROSZAK, Theodore

(1 May 1907–2 September 1981).

Roszak was one of the sculptors referred to by Herbert Read as a practitioner of the "geometry of fear." The spiky, often bone-like metal sculptures to which he devoted himself after 1946 have much in common with the work of Germaine Richier. However, where Richier drew her influence from Surrealism and employed natural forms combined in irrational congregations, Roszak drew from Abstract Expressionism and developed a style that evoked archetypal dimensions of the unconscious mind, while remaining purely abstract. His disconcerting, fear-ridden images are never more than mere suggestions of natural forms, such as tree roots, insect anatomy, and skeletal structures. His sculptures do not function like mythic symbols, evoking buried emotions. They seem instead to be mad creations directly extracted from the unconscious mind.

—Mark Daniel Cohen

Works: *Spectre of Kitty Hawk*, 1945–47; *Scavenger*, 1946–47; *Invocation*, I, 1947; *The Whale of Nantuckett*, 1952–53; *Prometheus*, 1955–56; *Thistle in the Dream*, 1955–56; *Sea Sentinel*, 1956; *Iron Gullet*, 1959.

Exhibition Catalogs: Arnason, H. Harvard. *Theodore Roszak*. Minneapolis: Walker Art Center, 1956; *Constructions, 1932–1945*. New York: Zabriskie, 1978; Wooden, Howard E. *Theodore Roszak: The Early Works, 1929–1943: an exhibition of sculptures, paintings and drawings: October 5 through November 30, 1986*. Wichita, KS: Wichita Art Museum, 1986.

ROT, Dieter

(21 April 1930–6 June 1998; b. Karl-Dietrich Roth, perhaps). The most original and fecund Swiss artist of his generation, Rot began as a graphic designer, and so it is scarcely surprising that he has published over a hundred books, many of which rank as extraordinary book-art. He has also exhibited organic materials that change color, not to mention odor, over the course of an exhibition. Allan Kaprow remembers this 1969 piece:

> Twenty-odd old suitcases filled with a variety of international cheese specialties. The suitcases—all different—were placed close together in the middle of the floor, as you might find them at a Greyhound bus terminal. In a few days the cheeses began to ripen, some started oozing out of the suitcases, all of them grew marvelous molds (which you could examine by opening the lids), and maggots were crawling by the thousands. Naturally, the smell was incredible.

Rot once collected two years of personal trash into transparent plastic bags that were stacked into two pyramids in Zurich's Helmhaus. In addition to giving concerts with instruments he was not trained to play (and frequently

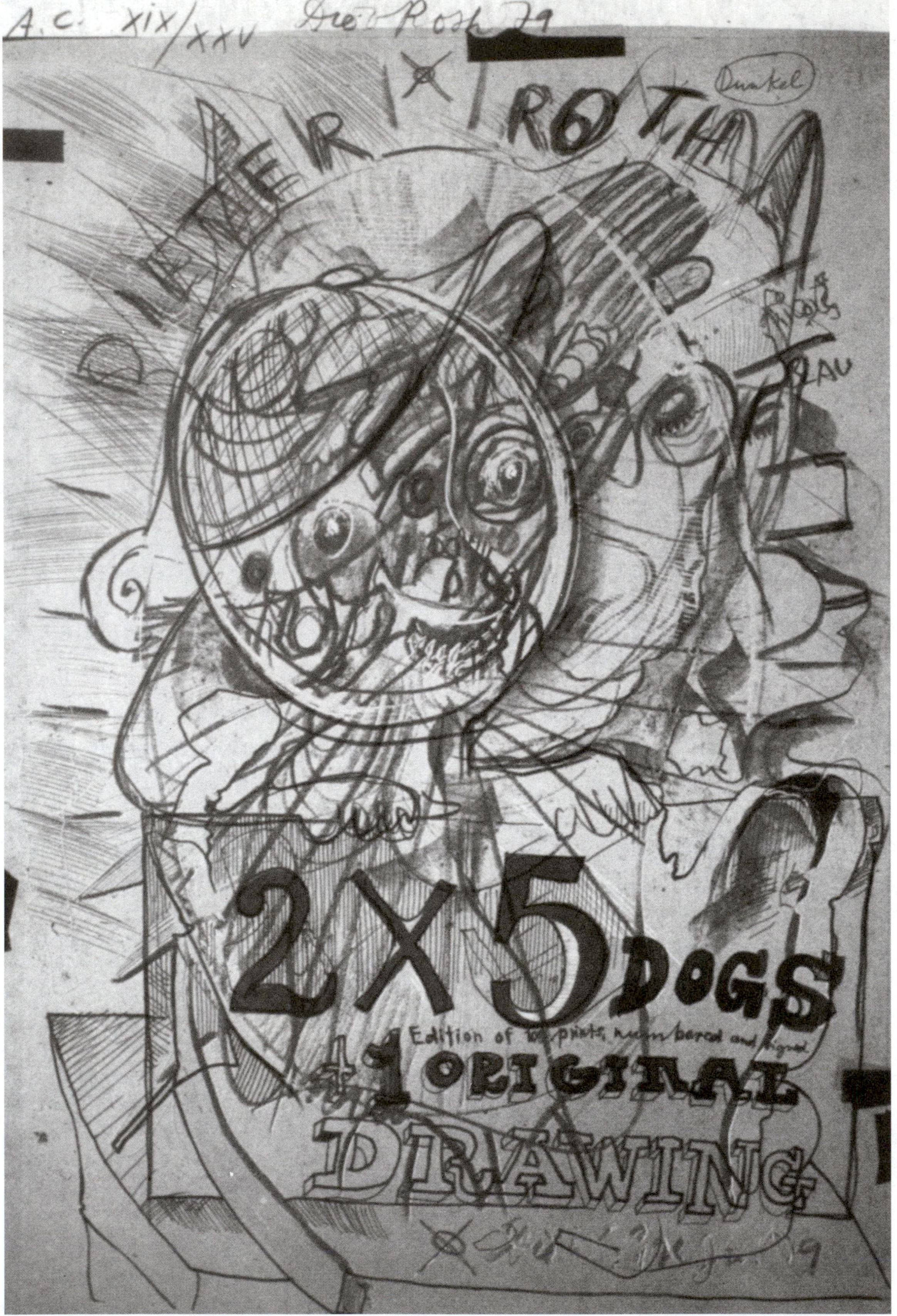

Dieter Rot. *2 Times 5 DOGS*, 1978/79. Offest print, artist's proof 19/25. Albertina Graphic Collection, Goldie Paley Gallery, Moore College of Art and Design.

concocting new versions of his name), Rot has published highly innovative prose in more than one language.

Books: *Die Blau Flut*. Stuttgart, Germany: Hansjörg Mayer, 1967; *246 Little Clouds*. New York: Something Else, 1968; *Books and Graphics (Part 1): from 1947 to 1971*. Stuttgart: Hansjörg Mayer, 1971; *120 Picadilly Postcards*. Stuttgart: Hansjörg Mayer, 1977; *Gesammelte Werke*. Vols. 1–20, 36, 38–40. Stuttgart: Hansjörg Mayer, 1969–86; *Munduculum*. Köln, Germany: Dumont Schauberg, 1967.

Exhibition Catalogs: Hamilton, Richard, and Dieter Roth. *Interfaces*. Bielefeld, Germany: Kunsthalle, 1979; *Dieter Roth, Zeichnungen*. Hamburg: Kunsthalle, 1987; *Dieter Roth*. New York: David Nolan, 1989; *Dieter Rot Druckgrafik und Bucher 1949–1979*. Wien: Graphische Sammlung Albertina, 1998.

ROTHENBERG, Jerome

(11 December 1931).

Initially a moderately radical and prolific poet, Rothenberg necessarily became an editor, first of the literary periodicals *Poems from the Floating World* (1960–64) and *some/thing* (1965–68), then of book-length collections that were designed to create new taste with mostly unfamiliar materials, rather than, like most anthologies, to clean up on established reputations. The purpose of *Technicians of the Sacred* (1968), subtitled *A Range of Poetries from Africa, America, Asia, and Oceania*, was opening the field in the wake of the oppressive influence of T. S. Eliot and his epigones in the decades after World War II. In this context, Rothenberg's sense of multicultural alternatives looked avant-garde. Extending his position into criticism and theory, he also coedited with his wife Diane, *Symposium of the Whole: A Range of Discourse Toward an Ethnopoetics* (1983).

His next major anthology, *Revolution of the Word: A New Gathering of American Avant-Garde Poetry 1914–1945* (1974), revived more alternatives to Eliot, in this case from among native radical predecessors, including many of the writers also acknowledged in this dictionary—Harry Crosby, Bob Brown, Eugene Jolas, Kenneth Patchen, Abraham Lincoln Gillespie, Louis Zukofsky, Kenneth Rexroth, Gertrude Stein—most of whom have become more acceptable in the two decades since *Revolution* appeared. The theme of *The Big Jewish Book* (1978) was the discovery of a mystical tradition different from the Yiddish and post-Yiddish prose commonly identified as Jewish (and Jewish-American) literature at the time. One measure of Rothenberg's anthological intelligence was that most of his books are cunningly organized, the ordering of the selections contributing to his theme. (By contrast, consider that an anthology whose selections appear in chronological or alphabetical order is ipso facto underedited.) He also provides extensive notes, in a prose that is, alas, too often more eccentric than clear.

By the 1990s, Rothenberg was no longer an outsider but an established professor at state universities, first in Binghamton, NY, and then in San Diego. In addition to continuing to publish his own texts, he coedited a two-volume *Poems for the Millennium* (1995, 1998) which, its avant-garde–sounding title notwithstanding, focused more on the multicultural themes of *Technicians of the Sacred*, representing a step back to some and an accommodation to current fashion to others. These latest books seem designed less to change taste, like Rothenberg's best anthologies, than to exploit sentiments established in part by his earliest anthologies.

Anthologies: *New Young German Poets*. Ed. and trans. San Francisco: City Lights, 1959; *Ritual: A Book of Primitive Rites and Events*. New York: Something Else, 1966; *Technicians of the Sacred: A Range of Poetries from Africa, America, Asia and Oceania*. Garden City, NY: Doubleday, 1972; *Shaking the Pumpkin: Traditional Poetry* of the Indian North America (1972). New York: Alfred van der Marck, 1986; —— with George Quasha. *America, a Prophecy: A New Reading of American Poetry from Pre-Columbian Times to the Present*. New York: Random House, 1973; —— with Harris Lenowitz and Charles Doria. *A Big Jewish Book: Poems and Other Visions of the Jews from Tribal Times to the Present*. Garden City, NY: Doubleday, 1978; —— with Pierre Joris. *Poems for the Millennium*. 2 vols. Berkeley: University of California Press, 1995, 1998.

Poetry: *Poems 1964–1967*. Los Angeles: Black Sparrow, 1968; *Poems for the Game of Silence 1960–90*. New York: Dial, 1971; *Poland/1931*. New York: New Directions, 1974; *A Seneca Journal*. New York: New Directions, 1978; *Vienna Blood and Other Poems*. New York: New Directions, 1980; *That Dada Strain*. New York: New Directions, 1983; *New Selected Poems 1970–1985*. New York: New Directions, 1986; *Khubin and Other Poems*. New York: New Directions, 1989; *The Gematria*. Los Angeles: Sun & Moon, 1990; *The Lorca Variations*. New York: New Directions, 1993.

Interpretation: Paul, Sherman. *In Search of the Primitive: Rereading David Antin, Jerome Rothenberg, and Gary Snyder*. Baton Rouge: Louisiana State University, 1986.

Bibliography: Polkinhorn, Harry. *Jerome Rothenberg: A Descriptive Bibliography*. Jefferson, NC: McFarland, 1988.

ROTHKO, Mark

(25 September 1903–25 February 1970).

Born in Russia, raised in Portland, Oregon, Rothko came to New York in 1925 and was for decades one among many serious painters struggling in New York. Finally, in the 1950s, he realized his original, mature style of large hand-shaped rectangles, usually stacked one above the other, together filling nearly the entire field of a canvas. The rectangles have only slightly different hues, while the background color differs only a little more from that of the rectangles. Each area has not a uniform color but ever-changing tones, whose gradations become more apparent if the work's visibly hand-painted strokes are looked at fixedly. Rothko painted around the edges of a canvas, leaving paintings unframed. He required that his paintings be displayed lower, closer to the ground, than is customary. What Rothko wanted to realize was unprecedented sublimity. His paintings became the foundation for subsequent artists' exploration of surface tensions, color relationships, and ways of negating suggestions of "depth." To my mind, the most visible sign of Rothko's influence has been the proliferation of nearly monochromic paintings in the past three decades.

Selected Works: *Untitled*, 1949; *Ochre and Red on Black*, 1954. *Red, Brown, and Black*, 1958; *Black on Maroon*, 1959.

Exhibition Catalogs: *Mark Rothko*. Houston: Contemporary Arts Museum, 1957; *Mark Rothko*. London: Whitechapel, 1961; Selz, Peter. *Mark Rothko*. New York: MoMA, 1961; *Mark Rothko*. Berlin: Nationalgalerie,1971; Waldman, Diane. *Mark Rothko*. New York: Guggenheim Museum, 1978; *Le Coleur seule*. Lyon, France: Musée d'art Contemporain, 1988; Weiss, Jefffrey, et al. *Mark Rothko*. Washington, DC, and New Haven, CT: Corcoran Gallery & Yale University, 1998.

Biography: Breslin, James E. B. *Mark Rothko: A Biography*. Chicago: University of Chicago Press, 1993; Seldes, Lee. *The Legacy of Mark Rothko*. New York: Holt, Rinehart and Winston, 1978.

Web Site: http://www.nga.gov/feature/rothko/rothkosplash.html

Interpretation: Ashton, Dore. *About Rothko* (1983) New York: Da Capo, 1996; Glimcher, Mark, ed. *The Art of Mark Rothko: Into an Unknown World*. New York: Clarkson N. Potter, 1991.

Documentation: Anfam, M. R. David. *Mark Rothko: The Works on Canvas: Catalogue Raisonné*. New Haven: Yale University Press, 1998.

ROUSSEL, Raymond

(20 January 1877–14 January 1933).

One of the great eccentrics of early modern French literature, Roussel was born rich and, shall we say, touched. A maniac in the true sense of the word, he wrote at nineteen a novel entirely in alexandrines (nearly 6,000 of them); he later used parentheses with an abandon that others find inspiring. An admirer of Jules Verne above all others, Roussel wrote about largely imaginary travels in Africa, first in prose and then (decades later) in verse, publishing both books under the same title, *Impressions d'Afrique* (1910, 1932; only the first has been translated, as *Impressions of Africa*, 1967). For the self-publication of the verse novel, he used only the right-hand pages, alternating his text with crude illustrations commissioned from a nobody selected by a private detective agency. Roussel's plays are disjunctive, their titles coming from concluding lines that, as Rayner Heppenstall points out, "are equally unrelated to all that has gone before." Because of his wealth, Roussel did not need to be popular, which he wasn't anyway. The posthumously published *Comment j'ai écrit certains de mes livres* (*How I Wrote Some of My Books*, 1935) accounts for the liberties of extreme imagination, even in recalling one's professional life and purposes. Perhaps because of his influence on ALAIN ROBBE-GRILLET, EUGÈNE IONESCO, and JOHN ASHBERY, among others, Roussel is continually revived.

Works: Roussel, Raymond. *Among the Blacks*. Trans. Ron Padgett. Bolinas, CA: Avenue B, 1988; *How I Wrote Some of My Books & Other Writings*. Trans. Harry Mathews and John Ashbery. Boston: Exact Change, 1995; *Impressions of Africa* (1910). Trans. Lindy Frood and Rayner Heppenstall. Berkeley: University of California Press, 1967; *Locus Solus*. Trans. Rupert Copeland Cunningham. Berkeley: University of California Press, 1970.

Interpretation: Foucault, Michel. *Death and Labyrinth: The World of Raymond Roussel*. Trans. Charles Ruas. Garden City, NY: Doubleday, 1986; Heppenstall, Rayner. *Raymond Roussel: A Critical Study*. Berkeley: University of California Press, 1967.

RUDHYAR, Dane

(25 March 1895–13 September 1985; b. Daniel Chennevière).

A Frenchman largely self-taught in music, he came to America in 1916 and soon afterwards changed his surname to Rudhyar, drawing upon a Sanskrit root conveying at once a sense of dynamic action and the color red. After premiering his *Poèms ironiques* and *Vision végétale* at the Metropolitan Opera in New York in 1917, he moved first to Canada and then to California, where he spent the 1920s as an active emerging composer of numerous pieces for orchestra, chamber groups, and the piano, which was his own instrument. By 1930, however, Rudhyar stopped making music, devoting most of his time instead to the field of astrology, where he became prominent, especially through popular books. In 1938 Rudhyar began a series of paintings whose titles reflected theosophic themes. Not until 1965, his eightieth year, did Rudhyar return to music composition, radically revising some of his earlier works and writing several new ones. While his compositions reflected Chinese, Japanese, and South Asian (Indian) influences, he favored Western instruments and notation. Inattention to his musical career notwithstanding, Rudhyar's better compositions have survived.

Compositions: *Vision végétale*, 1914; *Soul Fire*, 1920; *Three Poems*, for violin and piano, 1920; *To the Real (Syntony no. 1)*, 1920; *The Surge of Fire (Syntony no. 2)*, 1921; *The Warrior*, 1921–1976; *Tetragrams*, 1920–1967; *Pentagrams*, 1924–26; *The Human Way (Syntony no. 4)*, 1927; *Granites*, 1929; *Cosmic Cycle*, 1981.

Recordings: *Advent for String Quartet* (1976) and *Crisis & Overcoming for String Quartet* (1978), Kronos. New York: CRI, 1979; *Piano Music: Paeans* (1927), *Stars* (1926), *Granites* (1929), William Masselos. New York: CRI, n.d.

Books: *Claude Debussy et son oeuvre*. Paris: A. Durand et fils, 1913; *Art as Release of Power*. Carmel, CA: Hamsa, 1929; *The Astrology of Personality*. New York: Lucis, 1936; *The Astrological Houses*. Garden City, NY: Doubleday, 1977; *Culture, Crisis and Creativity*. Wheaton, IL: Theosophical, 1977; *The Astrology of Transformation*. Wheaton, IL: Theosophical, 1980; *The Magic of Tone and the Art of Music*. Boulder, CO: Shambala, 1982.

Web Site: http://www.matrix.com.au/life.html (About Rudhyar's life as an astrologer, not a composer.)

r

RUGGLES, Carl

(11 March 1876–24 October 1971; b. Charles Sprague R.). Perhaps the most painstaking of the modern composers, Ruggles produced relatively few works that were constantly revised and rearranged, so that the complete Ruggles could easily fit onto 2 compact discs (in contrast to his contemporary Charles Ives, who produced bundles of music and rarely revised). He worked for thirteen years on an opera designed for his singer-wife, titled it "The Sunken Bell," but never completed it. One reason why he finished so little was the lack of local support. Though his *Sun-Treader* was performed in Paris and Berlin in 1932 (in performances conducted by Nicolas Slonimsky), not until 1966, in Ruggles's ninetieth year, was it premiered in his native country.

Ruggles's music is at once dissonant, expansive, weighty, and elegant. Speaking more technically, the younger composer Lou Harrison (1917) wrote that Ruggles's music:

> is characterized by an absolute lack of negative spacing in the voices, which is to say that no voice is ever given over to repetitious arpeggiation or figuration of any kind. Each voice is a real melody, bound into a community of singing lines, living a life of its own with regard to phrasing and breathing, careful not to get ahead or behind in its rhythmic co-operation with the others, and sustaining a responsible independence in the whole polyphonic life.

In those classically brilliant phrases incidentally lies a definition of an American esthetic. Also a visual artist, Ruggles exhibited his paintings from time to time.

Compositions: *Men*, for Orchestra, 1920–21; *Angels*, for 6 Muted Trumpets, 1920–21, perf. as *Men and Angels*, 1922; *Angels*, rev. for 4 trumpets and 3 trombones, 1938; *Men and Mountains*, for Chamber Orchestra, 1924; rev. for large orchestra, 1936; rev. 1941; *Portals*, for 13 strings, 1925; rev. for string orchestra, 1929; rev. 1941 and 1952–53; *Sun-Treader*, for large orchestra, 1926–31; *Evocations: Four Chants for Piano*, 1937–43, rev. 1954; arr. for orchestra, 1944–47; *Organum*, for large orchestra, 1944–47; also arr. for 2 pianos, 1946–47.

Recordings: *The Complete Works of Carl Ruggles*. Cond. Michael Tilson Thomas. New York: CBS Masterworks, 1980.

Biography: Greene, Jonathan D. *Carl Ruggles: A Bio-Bibliography*. Westport, CT: Greenwood, 1995.

Web Site: http://www.diac.com/~herlin/ruggles.html

Interpretation: Harrison, Lou. *About Carl Ruggles*. Yonkers, NY: Oscar Baradinsky, 1946; Ziffrin, Marilyn J. *Carl Ruggles: Composer, Painter, and Storyteller*. Urbana, University of Illinois Press, 1994.

RUSCHA, Edward

(16 December 1937).

Though Ruscha's meticulous paintings of words, usually in a modestly expressive shape, echo Robert Indiana's without transcending them, his true innovations have been book-art books, mostly self-published. The single most successful contains standard black-and-white aerial photographs of Los Angeles parking lots, most of them empty; the only words beyond the title page identify each lot's location. Though one theme might be the peculiar beauty of such magnificent nonartistic edifices, *Thirty-Four Parking Lots* (1967) is a reiterated, scathing critique of Los Angeles urban design and its bondage to the automobile. Ruscha's formally most remarkable volume, likewise self-published, is a strip of heavy paper that folds into the shape of a book, becoming a ladderbook, which can be "read" in either direction. Along the entire length of each edge run amateurish photographs of buildings on both sides of *The Sunset Strip* (1966), arranged bottom to bottom, separated only by a white space down the middle of the paper.

Books: *26 Gasoline Stations*. Alhambra, CA: Cunningham, 1963; *Various Small Fires and Milk* (1964). Los Angeles: Edward Ruscha, 1970; *Some Los Angeles Apartments*. Los Angeles: Edward Ruscha, 1965; *Every Building on Sunset Strip*. Los Angeles: Edward Ruscha, 1966; *Thirty-Four Parking Lots*. Los Angeles: Edward Ruscha, 1967; *Nine Swimming Pools and a Broken Glass*. Los Angeles: Edward Ruscha, 1968; *Stains*. Hollywood, CA: Heavy Industry, 1969; *Crackers*. Hollywood, CA: Heavy Industry, 1969; *A Few Palm Trees*. Hollywood, CA: Heavy Industry, 1971; *Records*. Hollywood, CA: Heavy Industry, 1971; *Hard Light*, with Lawrence Weiner. Hollywood, CA: Heavy Industry, 1978; *Guacamole Airlines and Other Drawings*. New York: Abrams, 1980.

Exhibition Catalogs: *Edward Ruscha*. Paris: Musée National d'Art Moderne, 1989; Hickey, Dave, and Peter Plagens. *The Works of Ed Ruscha: Essays*. New York & San Francisco: Hudson Hills & San Francisco Museum of Art, 1982; *Edward Ruscha*. Lyon: Octobre Desarts, 1985; *Los Angeles Apartments, 1965*. Ed. Richard Marshall. New York: Whitney, 1990; Bois, Yves-Alain. *Edward Ruscha, Romance with Liquids: Paintings 1966–1969*. New York: Gagosian, 1993; *Edward Ruscha Editions 1962–1999*. 2 vols. Minneapolis: Walker Arts Center, 1999.

RUSSIAN FORMALISTS

See **FORMALISTS, RUSSIAN**.

RUSSOLO, Luigi

(30 April 1885–4 February 1947).

The notoriety of Russolo's book *L'arte dei rumori (The Art of Noise*, 1913) obscures the fact that he was mostly a painter (and one of five cosigners of "Futurist Painting: Technical Manifesto," 1910). His *Treno in velocità* (*Speeding Train*, 1911) is said to be the first FUTURIST painting to use a speeding machine as both its subject and theme. His major canvases of the next few years explored motion in both machines and people—crowds, thunderbolts, automobiles, political protesters, etc. In his famous manifesto on noise, he used capital letters to "take greater pleasure in ideally combining the noises of trains, explosions of motors, trains, and shouting crowds than in listening again, for example, to the 'Eroica' or the 'Pastorale.'" Russolo's appreciation of noises made by nonpitched machines, many of them new to his time, incidentally forecast the music of GEORGE ANTHIEL, EDGARD VARÈSE, and JOHN CAGE, among others. Russolo also invented several *intonarumori*, or noisemaking instruments, even writing music for them.

Paintings: *Street Light—Study of Light*, 1909; *Nietzche*, c. 1909; *Sleeping City*, 1909–10; *Woman Sewing*, 1909–10; *The Revolt*, 1911; *Treno in velocita* (*Speeding Train)*, 1911; *Plastic Synthesis of a Woman's Movement*, 1913.

Musical Invention: *Rumorarmonio* (noise-harmonium), c. 1920.

Texts: *The Art of Noise* (1913). Trans. Robert Filliou. New York: Something Else, 1967.

RUTMAN, Robert

(15 May 1931).

An American sculptor, composer, and performer now living in Berlin, Rutman began, around 1969, to develop several sound sculpture instruments, which consist of large sheets of curved metal, attached to stands, and acting as resonators for strings or rods. These include the *steel cello*, *bow chime*, and *buzz chime*. In the liner notes to his 1979 LP, *Bitter Suites*, Rutman describes two of these instruments (on which variations were later made): the steel cello

> consists of an eight foot sheet of stainless steel suspended vertically. . . . A wire is attached to the top and bottom right corners of the metal, [and is] pulled taut

> to form a generous curve. . . . [The wire is bowed] with a bass or cello bow, while [being] frett[ed] with the other hand. [The] sounds which can be produced [range] from low bass to the highest falsetto, [and are] rich in texture." The bow chime is "a six-foot sheet of stainless steel formed into a horizontal curve, with an iron bar attached to the top corners of the metal sheet. Five metal rods are attached to the iron bar at intervals along its length. The length of the rods is adjustable, which allows for tuning. . . . When bowed toward the center of the rods, the instrument produces deep resonant drones with . . . [distinctly audible] overtones. [When] bowed close to . . . the bar, high-pitched notes are produced, resulting in ringing, chiming sounds."

r

To showcase his newly developed sound sculptures, Rutman formed the U.S. Steel Cello Ensemble (now simply the Steel Cello Ensemble). Rutman's pieces—typically performed by quartets, trios, or duos—are occasionally active and clangorous, but are more usually meditative, emphasizing drones, overtones, and slowly evolving textures. This latter style makes Rutman seem spiritually aligned with other composers of drone-based music in the United States. Rutman, however, has yet to tap into the increasingly large audience for PAULINE OLIVEROS, LAMONTE YOUNG, TONY CONRAD, or some of the other experimental minimalists.

—Tony Coulter

Discography: *Sounds of Nothing*. Cambridge, MA: Art Supermarket, 1976; *Bitter Suites*. Cambridge, MA: Rutdog Records, 1979; *Music to Sleep By*. Tresor, n.d. [1990s]; *1939*. Chester, NY: Pogus, 1998 [4 of 5 CD tracks originally released by Pogus in 1989]; *Zuuhh!! Muttie Mum!!*. Bremen, Germany: Die Stadt, 1998.

RUTTMANN, Walter

(28 December 1887–15 July 1941).

Originally an architect and painter, Ruttmann turned to film after serving in the German army in World War I, initially producing in the early 1920s handpainted kinetic geometric films, which he gave such abstract titles as *Lightplay Opus One* (1921). His reputation is based upon an innovative 1927 documentary that captures a day in the life of a metropolis in less than one hour—*Berlin: Symphonie einer Große stadt (Symphony of a Big City)*. In addition to proceeding to a silent rhythmic beat, this film portrays scene after scene uniquely identifiable, even decades later, as Berlin; precisely by being always about its announced subject, Ruttmann's film remains a model for subsequent urban portraits throughout the world. Early in the 1920s, Ruttmann realized that the film soundtrack could be edited for its audio possibilities alone and so, a generation before the availability of editable audiotape, made an audio composition of sounds unique to *Week End* (in German as well as English) (1928), which remains a classic of avant-garde radio/electroacoustic art (still scarcely known, alas). Ruttmann advised LENI RIEFENSTAHL on the editing of *Olympia*, and in 1940 filmed the German invasion of France. The following year he was killed while making a newsreel at the warfront.

Films: *Opus 1, Die Sieger*, 1922; *Opus II, Das verlorene Paradies, Kantorowitz, Gesolei*, 1923; *Opus III*, 1924; *Opus IV*, 1925; *Berlin—Die Symphonie einer Großestadt*, 1927; *Deutscher Rundfunk*, 1928; *Melodie der Welt*, 1929; *Acciaio/Arbeit macht Frei/Steel*, 1933; *Hamburg: Welstrase See*, 1938; *Die deutsche Waffenschmiede*, 1940.

Audio Art: *Die tönnende Welle* [a sound film without images], 1921; *Week End*, 1928.

Exhibition Catalog: Goergen, Jeanpaul. *Walter Ruttmann: eine Dokumentation*. Berlin: Freunde der deutschen kinemathek, 1989.

Interpretation: Russett, Robert, and Cecile Starr. *Experimental Animation*. New York: Van Nostrand, 1976.

RUUTSALO, Eino

(19 September 1921).

A Finnish POLYARTIST who attended New York's Parsons School of Design in the early 1950s, Ruutsalo has made KINETIC ART considerably different from the common run, in part because he often uses language as his principal material. In his *oeuvre* are over forty short films (many of them made without a camera by painting directly on celluloid), numerous sculptures, paintings, and prints. Ruutsalo sometimes takes the same title through various media. A standard international history of film animation identifies him as "the most influential Finnish animator." Ruutsalo speaks creditably of wanting "to move freely among the different areas of art, depending upon which mode of expression is required at the time. My aim is to avoid becoming confined to a particular mode of art." By most measures, he ranks among the most under-known older polyartists of the Western world.

Exhibition Catalog: *Eino Ruutsalo: Kinetic Poems, Pictures and Paintings*. Helsinki, Finland: Aquarian, 1990.

RYMAN, Robert

(30 May 1930).

While art of one color no doubt remains a good avant-garde idea, it is hard to discern who in the second generation of monochromists is better and/or more original than the rest. There are general discriminations to be made between pure monochromists and those who would dilute their fields with alternative colors, and between those who use colors with varying degrees of seductive appeal, such as Marcia Hafif's (1929) *pink*, and those who work only with the noncolors of black and white. Ryman has favored the second side in both of these dichotomies, preferring a white painting adulterated with various degrees of grey shadings, often created in series of approximately similar appearance, generally in a square format. He experimented with different kinds of white paint and with a variety of surfaces, including plywood, fiberglass, and linen. While such works are individually impressive, a gathering of them makes clear, at least to me, that the better Ryman paintings are those with the faintest or most subtle shadings, especially if the monochromic fields are framed with edges painted a different color. However, at a 1992 exhibition, Ryman's second solo show at the Guggenheim Museum, the room in which they were displayed had at its ends tall, clean white curtains whose presence made the paintings look messy, if not uncharacteristically *schmutzik*.

Paintings: *Untitled*, 1965; *Untitled I*, 1965; *Nayco*, 1966; *Twin*, 1966; *Adelphi*, 1967; *Surface Veil*, 1970; *Surface Veil II*,1971; *Untitled Drawing*,1976; *Credential*, 1985; *Journal*, 1988.

Exhibition Catalogs: Waldman, Diane. *Robert Ryman*. New York: Guggenheim Museum, 1972; *Robert Ryman*. New York: Dia Art Foundation, 1988; *Robert Ryman: New Paintings*. New York: Pace Gallery, 1990; Storr, Robert. *Robert Ryman*. London: Tate, 1993.

r

SACHER, Paul

(28 April 1906–26 May 1999).

In his twenties, Sacher founded a chamber orchestra and a choir in his native city of Basel, Switzerland; in the fifties, he directed the local music academy. In between he toured as a conductor and incidentally married the widow of the founder of a large Swiss pharmaceutical firm. Thanks to her largess, Sacher commissioned over two hundred works from living composers. Later he began to collect original scores, typically purchasing for over five million dollars the entire IGOR STRAVINSKY archive soon after the composer's death. This collection is housed in the Paul Sacher Foundation building in Basel. There's no one else remotely like him as a modern-music philanthropist. Perhaps because such figures are personally modest and/or their efforts are taken for granted, extended appreciations of their contributions are scarce.

SAFDIE, Moshe

(14 July 1938).

The architectural star of the 1967 Montreal World's Fair was Safdie's *Habitat* '67 (1967), which was composed of prefabricated modular apartments stacked twelve high in various, apparently chaotic overlappings. As steel-reinforced modules whose exterior dimensions are seventeen and one-half feet by thirty-eight and one-half feet, with prefabricated bathrooms and kitchens, the apartments were nearly completely constructed before being lifted into place by cranes. Precisely because the modules were not placed directly atop one another, but literally strewn over land, most of the apartments have at least three exterior views. *Habitat* '67 was so clever that I have never ceased to wonder why it has not been replicated a thousand times; but perhaps, like his mentor BUCKMINSTER FULLER, Safdie made architecture too practical, too Veblenian, to succeed.

Buildings: Habitat '67, Montreal, Quebec, 1964–67; Manchat Housing Master Plan, Jerusalem, 1969–95; Science Center and Children's Museum, Wichita, Kansas (in progress), 1994–; Mamilla Center Jerusalem (in progress) 1972–; Hosh District Restoration Jerusalem, 1976–78; Hebrew Union College Jerusalem (final stages), 1976–99; Old Port of Montreal (partially built), 1977–90; Ottawa City Hall, Ontario 1988–94; Neve Ofer Community Center, Tel Aviv-Jaffa, Israel, 1989–95; West Jerusalem Master Plan, Israel (in progress), 1996–; Ardmore Habitat, Singapore, 1980–85; Cambridge Center, Massachusetts, 1980–88; Rowe's Wharf, Boston, Mass., 1981–82; Quebec Museum of Civilization, 1981–87; National Gallery of Canada, Ottawa, Canada, 1983–88; Montreal Museum of Fine Arts, Canada, 1985–91.

Projects (Conceptual Architecture): *A Three-Dimensional Modular Building System*, 1958–61; *City for Palestinian Refugees*, 1962; *Molson Center*, 1966; *Habitat New York*, 1967–68; *Habitat New York II*, 1967–68; *Lité de Illes*, 1968; *Habitat Puerto Rico*, 1968–71; *Habitat Israel*, 1969–70; *Pomipidou Center*, 1971; *Battery Park City*, 1972; *Western Wall Precinct*, Jerusalem, 1972.

Moshe Safdie. *Habitat 67*. CORBIS/Bettmann.

Books: *Beyond Habitat*. Ed. John Kettle. Cambridge: MIT Press, 1970; *For Everyone a Garden*. Ed. Judith Wolin. Cambridge: MIT Press, 1974; *Form and Purpose*. Ed. John Kettle. Boston: Houghton Mifflin, 1982.

Anthology: *Moshe Safdie: Buildings and Projects 1967–1992*. Irene Zantofska Murray, ed. Montreal & Buffalo, NY: McGill Queens University, 1996.

SALA, Oskar

(18 July 1910).

German composer/performer Oskar Sala is a fascinating figure not on account of his compositions—which are rather minor—but because of his nearly 70-year advocacy of a unique electronic instrument, the trautonium. Sala was a student of Paul Hindemith's in Berlin, and when, in 1930, Hindemith commissioned engineers connected to the experimental radio station of the Berlin Academy of Music to develop a new kind of electronic instrument, one utilizing strings, Sala quickly became involved. Initially, he was merely the assistant to Friedrich Trautwein (1888–1956)—the inventor of the prototype—but Trautwein quickly ceded further responsibility to Sala. The first version of the trautonium—which alters pitch in reaction to the movement of the player's finger along a wire—was monophonic and rather primitive, but Sala took the instrument through successive stages of complexity, making it polyphonic, adding effects, and renaming it along the way: first came the Telefunken-Trautonium, then the RadioTrautonium, then the Mixturtrautonium.

During the 1930s, Hindemith and Harald Genzmer (1909) composed several works featuring the trautonium, but after that it was left to Sala alone to create a repertoire for it. He has had his own studio since 1958, and has produced hundreds of pieces, including more than 300 for films. Typically, these compositions—as heard on a variety of commercial recordings—exhibit a peculiar kind of charm. Rather old-fashioned compositionally, they are nonetheless full of odd effects, and have a kind of likable excitement to them. Now in his late eighties, Sala is as passionate as ever about the instrument with which he has become almost exclusively identified.

—Tony Coulter

Selected Discography: A) as composer: *Electronics*. New York: Westminster, 1960s. [also includes work by Remi Gassmann]; *Electronic Virtuosity for Selected Sound* (1969). Reissued on CD as *Resonanzen*. Kiev: Originalton West, 1994; *Elektronische Impressionen*. Hamburg: Telefunken, 1979; *Electronique et Stéréophonie*. Paris: Erato; *Electronic Kaleidoscope*. Mainz: Wergo Schallplatten; *My Fascinating Instrument*. Eslohe, Germany: Erdenklang, 1990; *Subharmonic Mixtures*. Berlin: Erdenklang/Fax, 1997; B) as performer: Genzmer, Harald. *Trautoniumkonzerte*. Mainz: Wergo Schallplatten.

S

SALZMAN, Eric

(8 September 1933).

One of the clearest and most accurate writers of liner notes and reviews of avant-garde music, including a thrice-revised introductory book on the subject, Salzman is also a composer devoted to his own idea of an innovative "music theater," as he calls it, to distinguish his genre from opera, incidentally echoing the preferred coinage of the German director Felsenstein (1901–75). Salzman has collaborated with choreographers, as well as formed a performance company called Quog; he has codirected an annual music-theater festival. The stylistic pastiche of his *The Nude Paper Sermon* (1969) successfully eschews obvious juxtapositions (the primary fault of simplistic COLLAGES) to mix a huge variety of both historical styles and musical articulations, as well as a spoken narration (which provides, or parodies, a basso continuo) and electronic sounds, all around the unifying theme of "the end of the Renaissance—the end of an era and the beginning of another." Although sometimes performed live, *The Nude Paper Sermon* was originally written for stereophonic tape to exploit opportunities peculiar to recording, which, if you think about it, might finally be a far more feasible medium for musical theater than live performance.

Compositions: *Cummings Set*, for voice and piano, 1958; *Partita*, for Violin, 1958; *Queens Collage*, Academic Festival Overture for tape, 1966; *Larynx Music*, for actor, Renaissance consort, chorus, and electronics, 1967; *The Peloponnesian War,* mime-dance theater piece, 1967–68; *Feedback*, multimedia participatory environmental work for live performers, visuals, and tape, 1968; *Strophe/Antistrophe*, for keyboard and tape, 1969; *The Nude Paper Sermon*, verses for soprano, guitar, and 4-track tape, 1969; *Accord*, music theater piece for accordian, 1975; *Civilization and its Discontents*, music theater comedy, 1977; *The Passion of Simple Simon*, 1979; *Toward a New American Opera*, mixed-media piece, 1985; *Body Language*, for singers, dancers, violin, piano, and accordion, 1995–96.

Writings: *Twentieth-Century Music: An Introduction* (1967, 1974). 3d ed. Englewood Cliffs, NJ: Prentice-Hall, 1988; ——, and Michael Sahl. *Making Chances: A Practical Guide to Vernacular Harmony*. New York: McGraw-Hill, 1977.

SAMARAS, Lucas

(14 September 1936).

Born in Greece, Samaras came to America in 1948 and studied art and art history at Rutgers and then Columbia. Participating in early MIXED-MEANS THEATER, he recognized the artistic possibilities of his own body, which he later photographed promiscuously, mostly with a Polaroid camera, sometimes altering the image through pressure during developing or by the addition of ink. Narcissistic beyond belief, Samaras used extended exposures to make images of himself nude hugging his nude self and even making love to himself. Many of these photographs were collected in *Samaras Album* (1971), which ranks among the finest ARTIST'S BOOKS. As a sculptor, he began with boxed tableaux reminiscent of JOSEPH CORNELL, and then made geometric structures such as chairs or a cubed frame, commonly called "Untitled," with protruding knives, pins, and tacks, which become erotic imagery also evocative of terror.

In 1964, Samaras exhibited a replica of the small room in which he spent his teenage years (which he had just recently vacated, as his parents returned to Greece). Two years later he created a completely mirrored room that reflects everything inside it, including mirror-surface furniture, to infinity in all directions.

Even if one dislikes SURREALISM or EXPRESSIONISM as much as the author of this book, it is hard not to be impressed with Samaras's art. It was strong enough to overcome the anti-Expressionistic sentiments that were pervasive in the 1960s. Samaras's 1972 retrospective at the Whitney Museum ranks among the strongest ever from an artist less than forty years old.

Visual Art: *Box No. 3*, 1962–63; *Book No. 4 (Dante's Inferno)*, 1962; *Room*, 1964; *Reconstruction #30*, 1977; *Grand Couple I*, 1981; *Wire Hanger Chair (open shoe)*, 1986; *Box #118*, 1987.

Books: *Samaras Album*. New York: Whitney Museum, 1971; Ed. by C. Glenn Lucas. *Samaras: Sketches, Drawings, Doodles and Plans*. New York: Abrams,1987.

Films: *Self*, writtten, dir. and prod. Lucas Samaras, 1969.

Exhibition Catalogs: Alloway, Lawrence. *Samaras, Selected Works 1960–66*. New York: Pace Gallery, 1966; *Chair Transformation*. New York: Pace, 1970; *Lucas Samaras*. New York: Whitney Museum of American Art, 1972; *Photo-Transformations*. New York: Pace, 1974; *Lucas Samaras, chairs & drawings*. New York: Pace, 1987; *Crude Delights*. New York: Pace, 1980; *Self, 1961–1991*. Japan: Yomiuri Shimbun, 1991; *Lucas Samaras: Cubes, Pragmata, Trapezoids: October 22–November 26, 1994*. New York: Pace Wildenstein, 1994.

Web Site: http://www.pacewildenstein.com/samaras/

Interpretation: Levin, Kim. *Lucas Samaras*. New York: Abrams, 1975; Kuspit, Donald, et.al. *Lucas Samaras: Objects and Subjects 1969–86*. New York: Abbeville, 1988.

SAMPLING

(c. 1982).

The technique of taking short melodic or rhythmic fragments of limited durations and incorporating these "samples" into a new composition. This was made possible by the invention of electronic equipment that can record or "sample" external sounds, store them digitally, and then, in the course of recalling them, enable a composer to re-create and/or change their pitch, duration, or other musical qualities. (That is why BOBBY MCFERRIN is characterized as the "human sampler.") Its compositional significance is that sound sequences replace individual notes as the basic unit.

Commonly used by RAP artists, who prompt controversy by drawing upon copyrighted recordings, sampling has raised difficult questions about the value of cultural property on the one hand and the freedom of the artist on the other. For example, if a rap artist extracts the basic riff from a James Brown recording, should he or she be forced to pay a royalty to Brown (or at least acknowledge the source of the riff)? What's the difference between an artist filching a Chuck Berry riff on the guitar in a new composition and sampling the actual riff from a Chuck Berry recording? Didn't MARCEL DUCHAMP "sample" Da Vinci's *Mona Lisa*, not to mention a J. L. Mott Iron Works urinal? Such questions of authenticity versus artistic license recur in the history of avant-garde creation.

—with Richard Carlin

THE SAN FRANCISCO MIME TROUPE

(1962; aka SFMT).

Formed by R. G. Davis, who directed the company until 1970, SFMT has specialized in political plays, sometimes

S

called Guerrilla Theater because these plays were often performed outdoors on portable stages, supposedly attracting people who would not normally attend an enclosed performance space. SFMT performed pantomime in the raucous American tradition of Buster Keaton and Charlie Chaplin (1889–1977), rather than the more precious mime of, say, Marcel Marceau (1923). One mark of the SFMT performance style was the clever use of both large signs and songs. *Telephone* (1969) demonstrates how to cheat the telephone company by forging a credit-card number. After Davis's departure, SFMT became a commune, supporting its activities largely by asking spectators for money, in the great tradition of street theater. Their longest and most complex work, a critical memorial to the American Bicentennial, *False Promises/Nos Engañaron* (1976, the Spanish meaning "we've been had"), takes place in 1898–99, portray racism at the time of the Spanish-American War and incorporates, as its title suggests, both Spanish and English throughout. A book collecting several texts from 1970–76 gives individual credits that did not appear in the company's programs.

Bibliography: Davis, R. G. *The San Francisco Mime Troupe: The First Ten Years*. Palo Alto, CA: Ramparts, 1975; The San Francisco Mime Troupe. *By Popular Demand: Plays and Other Works by*. San Francisco: Privately published, 1980.

Web Site: http://www.sfmt.org/

SANDERS, Ed

(17 August 1939).

Initially a poet, he became both a novelist and then the lead voice in the counterculture band known as The Fugs

Ed Sanders at his Peace Eye Bookstore, 14 January 1966. Photograph © Fred W. McDarrah.

(c. 1965–70; 1984–89), whose typical songs had titles such as "Kill for Peace" and "Slum Goddess of the Lower East Side." Sanders also edited and published the broadside periodical, *Fuck You: A Magazine of the Arts*, while operating the Peace Eye Book Store on New York's Lower East Side. As a poet, he favors energized, outrageous language that sometimes works better in his prose, such as in *Shards of God* (1971): "He prayed over the sexual lubricant in the alabaster jar and swirled his cock directly into it, signaling to one of the air corps volunteers to grab her ankles as he oiled himself up like a hustler chalking a pool cue." The author of a commercially published investigative report on the notorious Charles Manson, *The Family* (1971), Sanders has also made cultural exposé a recurring purpose of his poetry and even his librettos.

Writings: *Poem from Jail*. San Francisco, City Lights, 1963; *The Toe-Queen*. New York: Fuck You Press, 1964; *Peace Eye*. Buffalo, NY: Frontier, 1965; *The Complete Sex Poems*. New York: Fug Press, 1965; *Shards of God*. New York: Grove, 1971; *The Family: The Story of Charles Manson's Dune Buggy Attack Battalion*. New York: Dutton, 1971; *20,000 AD*. Plainfield, VT: North Atlantic, 1976; *Investigative* Poetry. San Francisco: City Lights, 1976; *Thirsting for Peace in a Raging Century: Selected Poems 1961–1985*. Minneapolis, MN: Coffee House, 1987; *Tales of Beatnik Glory*. New York: Citadel Underground, 1990; *1968: A History in Verse*. Santa Rosa, CA: Black Sparrow, 1997.

Recordings: The Fugs *First Album*. Fantasy 1994.

Web Site: http://www.furious.com/perfect/fugs.html (Info on Fugs and interview with Sanders.)

SAPORTA, Marc

(20 March 1923).

In 1963, a hyperslick American publisher released an English translation of *Composition No. 1*, "a novel" apparently published the year before in Paris. It came as a box of loose pages that the reader is invited to shuffle "like a deck of cards," because "the pages of this book may be read in any order." More than once I've laid them out on the floor, picking up pages as one might colored sticks, reading scenes in the life of a Frenchman during World War II. Its pseudo-musical title acknowledges a debt to certain musical ideas new in the late 1950s. This combinatory book is so original it is not mentioned in Vivian Mercier's 1971 *Reader's Guide to the New [French] Novel*. Because *Composition No. 1* must have failed in the bookstores, no American commercial publisher has done anything similar since. Other shuffle books in my library, all but one self-published, are Peter H. Beaman's *Deck of Cards* (1989), Henry James Korn's (1945) *The Pontoon Manifesto* (1970), Elton Anglada's untitled box (1973), PEDRO PIETRI'S *I Never Promised You a Cheeseburger* (n.d.), Richard Hefter and Martin Stephen Moskof's juvenile *A Shuffle Book (* 1970), Arnold Skemer's *Momus* (1997), and my own long poem, *Rain Rains Rain* (1975). My suspicion is that as long as publishers ignore this form, its esthetic potential is scarcely exhausted.

Books: *Le Furet*. Paris: Editions du Seuil, 1959; *La Quête*. Paris: Seuil, 1961; *La Distribution*. Paris: Gallimard, 1961; *Les Invités*. Paris: Seuil, 1964.

Other Shuffle Books: Beaman, Peter H. *Deck of Cards*. Pittsburgh, PA: Peter H. Beaman (1500 Oliver Bldg., 15222), 1989; Hefter, Richard, and Martin Stephen Moskof. *A Shuffle Book*. New York: Golden, 1970; Kostelanetz, Richard. *Rain Rains Rain*. New York: Assembling, 1975; Saporta, Marc. *Composition No. 1*. Trans. Richard Howard. New York: Simon & Schuster, 1963; Skemer, Arnold. *Momus*. Bayside, NY: Phrygian (58-09 25th St., 11364), 1997.

SAROYAN, Aram

(25 September 1943).

Before he became a pop memoirist, Saroyan was briefly a visual poet whose specialty was running words together to create something else that must be seen, because it could not be read aloud: "lighght," "eyeye," for two instances,

Design for Erik Satie's Ballet *Relâche* by Francis Picabia. © 2000 Artists Rights Society (ARS), New York/ADGAP, Paris.

the ideographic effect of the latter additionally benefiting from the suggestion of eyeglasses. A pioneering Conceptual poet, Saroyan also "published" in the mid-1960s a book that was simply a box of blank paper.

Writings: *Aram Saroyan* (1967). New York: Random House, 1968; *Works*. New York: Lines, 1967; *Words and Photographs*. Chicago: Big Table, 1970; *Cloth: An Electric Novel*. Chicago: Big Table, 1971; *Pages*. New York: Random House, 1969; *The Street: An Autobiographical Novel*. Lenox, MA: Bookstore, 1974; *Genesis Angels: The Saga of Lew Welch and the Beat Generation*. New York: Morrow, 1979; *Last Rites: The Death of William Saroyan*. New York: Morrow, 1982; *Day and Night: Bolinas Poems*. Santa Rosa, CA: Black Sparrow, 1999.

SATIE, Erik

(17 May 1866–1 July 1925).

A slow starter, whose early adult years were devoted more to radical religion and politics than music (and his music mostly to tickling the ivories in Paris cabarets), Satie returned to music school in 1905 for three years of intensive study. Not until 1915 did his more serious music begin to receive recognition, and his reputation has grown enormously since his death. The last decade of Satie's life was consumed with such commissions as *Parade* (1917) for Serge Diaghilev's Ballets Russes; *Socrate* (1919), which is a symphonic drama for four sopranos and a small orchestra; and music for the René Clair (1898–1981) film of the ballet *Relâche* (1924), whose original form was a comic masterpiece that Satie produced in collaboration with Francis Picabia and Jean Borlin of the Swedish Ballet.

Satie's most popular compositions are short pieces for piano collectively known as *Gymnopèdies* (1888). Others have programmatic titles (e.g., in the shape of a pear). His music frequently depends upon unresolved chords; some works encourage unconventional distributions of musicians in a performance space. John Cage uncovered certain radical experiments ignored by most Satie scholars, such as *Vexations* (1892–93), which is a page of piano music meant to be repeated 840 times (typically performed in 1963 by five pianists working round the clock), and furniture music that, because it does not require conscious listening, presages not only Muzak but Brian Eno's ambient music. Satie was also a master of ironic aphorisms: "Although our information is incorrect, we do not vouch for it"; "I want to compose a piece for dogs, and I already have my decor. The curtain rises on a bone."

Compositions: *Trois Mélodies de 1886*, for voice and piano, 1886; *Trois Gymnopédies*. 1888; *Trois Gnossiennes*,

1890; *Trois Préludes* from *Le Fils des étoiles*, 1891; *Vexations*, 1892–1893; *2 Pièces froides*, 1897; *Valse, Je te veux*, c. 1900; *Jack in the Box*, 1900; *Le Poisson rêveur*, 1901; *Passacaille*, 1906; *En habit de cheval*, for piano, 4-hands, 1911; *3 Descriptions automatiques*, 1913; *Trois Valses du precieux degoûté*, 1914; *Cinq Grimaces*, 1914; *Choses vues à droite et à gauche (sans lunettes)*, for violin and piano, 1914; *Sonatine bureaucratique*, 1917; *Socrate*, for 4 sopranos and chamber orchestra, 1918; *Trois petites pièces montées*, 1919; *Premier Menuet*, 1920; *La belle exentrique*, 1920.

Recordings: *Satie: Piano Music*. Yuji Takahashi. Japan: Denon, 1985; *The Music of Satie*. E. Bonazzi; Frank Glazer, piano, Luxembourg Radio Symphony Orchestra, Die Reihe Ensemble. New York: Vox; *Orchestra Music*. London: Hyperion, 1989; *Gnossiennes*. Reinbert de Leow. Phillips, 1995; *Piano Music*. Aldo Ciccolini. London: EMI Classics.

Writings: Satie, Erik. *A Mammal's Notebook: Collected Writings*. Ed. Ornella Volta. London: Atlas, 1996; *Satie Seen through His Letters*. Ed. Ornella Volta. Trans. Michael Bullock. Intro. John Cage. New York: Marion Boyars, 1989; *The Writings of Eric Satie*. Trans. and ed. Nigel Wilkins. London: Eulenburg, 1980.

Bibliography: Gillmor, Alan M. *Eric Satie*. Boston: Twayne, 1988; Harding, James. *Erik Satie*. New York: Praeger, 1975; Myers, Rollo. *Erik Satie* (1948). New York: Dover, 1968; Perloff, Nancy. *Art and the Everyday: Popular Entertainment and the Circle of Erik Satie*. Oxford, England: Clarendon, 1991; Shattuck, Roger. *The Banquet Years* (1958). Garden City, NY: Doubleday Anchor, 1961; Templier, Pierre-Daniel. *Erik Satie*. Trans. Elena L. and David S. French. Cambridge: MIT Press, 1969; Whiting, Stephen M. *Satie the Bohemian: From Cabaret to Concert Hall*. Oxford: Oxford University Press, 1999.

Web Site: http://shift.merriweb.com.au/satie/

SCELSI, Giacinto

(8 January 1905–9 August 1988, b. Conte Giaconto Scelsi di Valva).

Trained in twelve-tone technique in pre-World War II Vienna, Scelsi also studied Eastern musical philosophy, in which scales and rhythms are regarded not as independent structures but as reflections of psychology. From Buddhism he took the concept that every point is the center of the universe and thus he explored fractional tones around a center sound. His compositions are at once eclectic and eccentric, typically sliding up, down, and around a single tone for attenuated durations. In addition to essays on music, he wrote poetry in French; one of his best-known and most ambitious works, *La Naissance du verbe* (The Birth of the Verb, 1950), is a setting of one of his poems. After his death, another Italian composer claimed to have "ghosted" some Scelsi compositions from twelve-tone sketches.

Compositions: *Rotative*, for 3 pianos, winds, and percussion, 1930; *Rapsodia romàntica*, 1931; *Sinfonietta*, 1932; *Preludio e fuga*, 1938; *Ballata*, for cello and organ, 1945; *La Nascita del verbo*, for chorus and orchestra, 1948; *Pwyll*, for flute, 1954; *Action Music*, 1955; *Yamaon*, for bass and 5 instruments, 1954–58; *Tre pezzi*, for trombone, 1957; *Trilogy*, for cello, 1957–65; *Elegia per Ty*, for viola and double bass, 1958; *Hurqualia*, 1960; *Wo-Ma*, for bass, 1960; *Aiôn*, 1961; *Chukrum*, for strings, 1963; *Hymnos*, for organs and 2 Orchestras, 1963; *Xnoybis*, for violin, 1964; *Ohoi*, for 16 strings, 1966; *Natura renovatur*, for 11 strings, 1967; *Voyages*, for cello, 1974; *Litanie*, for 2 women's voices or woman's voice and tape, 1975.

Recordings: *Suite No. 10 & No. 9*. Marianne Schroeder, piano. Therwil, Switzerland: Hat Hut, 1988; *Sonata No. 8, Bot-Ba*, for piano (1952), *Sonata No. 2* (1939), *Un Adieu for Piano* (c. 1978), etc. Marianne Schroeder, piano. Therwil, Switzerland: Hat Hut, 1992; *The Music of Scelsi*: *Maknongan for Low-Registered Instrument* (1976), *Tre pezzi*, for trombone (1956); *Wo-Ma*, for bass (1960), *C'est bien la nuit*, for double bass (1972); *Le reveil profond*, for double bass (1977); *Et Maintenant c'est à vous à jouer*, for cello and double bass (1974); *Okangon*, for harp, double bass, and tantam (1968); *Mantram*, for double bass (1987), etc. Therwil, Switzerland: Hat Hut, 1993.

SCHAFER, R. Murray

(18 July 1933).

A Canadian composer who shared a prominent Toronto teacher with his near-contemporary GLENN GOULD, Schafer was initially known for tape-recording "soundscapes" in various places around the world. This research informed a brilliant book about varieties of acoustic experience, *The Tuning of the World* (1977), which has the additional virtue of quoting past novels and plays to reveal what people heard at earlier times. As a true musician of letters, Schafer has produced other expository books, including *Creative Music Education* (1976), and several chapbooks of genuinely experimental poetry and prose, some of it very good, in addition to editing and elaborately annotating *Ezra Pound and Music: The Complete Criticism* (1977). As a composer, Schafer is best known for operas, such as *Patria II* (1966–74) and *Patria I* (1966–72), for which he wrote the libretto and produced picture-filled scores that, because of superlative visual qualities, can be read apart from any musical experience. Perhaps because his work is so various, considered critical writing about it is remarkably scarce.

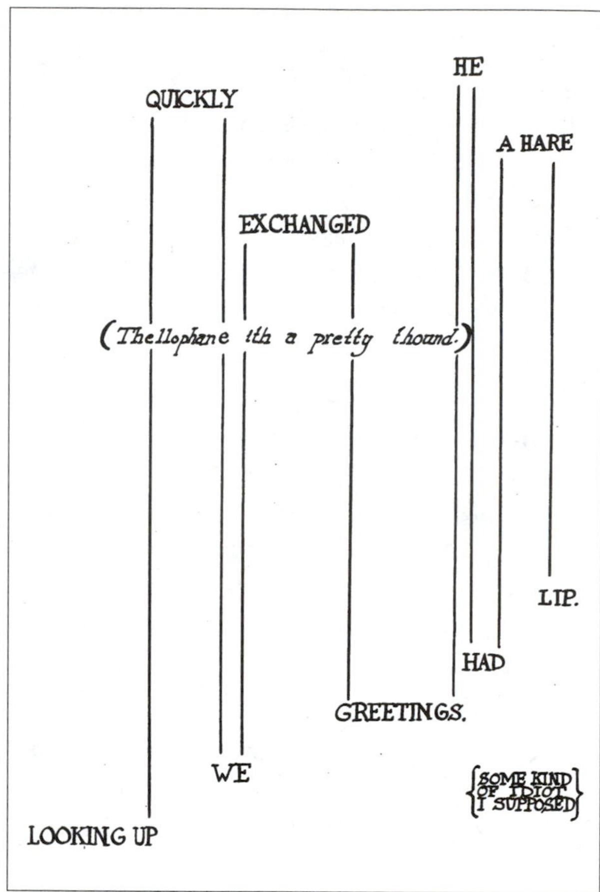

R. Murray Schafer. Page from *Ariadne*. Used by Permission of Arcana Editions.

Scores: *Protest and Incarceration*, for mezzo-soprano and orchestra, 1960; *Canzoni for Prisoners*, 1962; *Loving* or *Toi*, opera for four voices, two speaking roles, dancers, orchestra, tape, 1965; *Threnody*, for chorus, orchestra, and tape, 1966; *Kaleidescope*, for tape, 1967; *Minimusic*, for any combination of instruments and voices, 1967; *Epitaph for Moonlight*, SATB choir, optional bells, 1968; String Quartet No. 1. Vienna: Universal, 1970; *No Longer than Ten Minutes*, 1970; *North/White*, for orchestra and snowmobile, 1973; *Train*, for youth orchestra, 1976; *Jonah*, theater piece, 1979; *Apocalypsis*, musical/theater pageant, 1980; *Harbour Symphony*, for fog horns, 1983; *Ko wo kiku* (Listen to the Incense), 1985; *Le Cri de Merlin*, for guitar and tape, 1987; *The Death of Buddha*, for chorus, gongs, and bell tree, 1989.

Operas: *Patria I: The Characteristic Man* (1974). Toronto, Canada: Berandol Music (11 St. Joseph St., Toronto, Ont. M4Y 1J8), n.d.; *Patria II: Requiems for the Party Girl*. Toronto, Canada: Berandol Music, n.d.

Writings: Schafer, R. Murray. *E.T.A. Hoffman and Music*. Toronto: University of Toronto Press, 1975; *Creative Music Education*. New York: Schirmer, 1976; —— as editor: *Ezra Pound and Music: The Complete Criticism*. New York: New Directions, 1977; *Smoke: A Novel* (1976). Toronto: Ganglia, 1978; *The Tuning of the World* (1977). Philadelphia: University of Pennsylvania Press, 1980; *The Thinking Ear: Complete Writings on Music Education*. Toronto: Arcana (Indian River, Canada KOL 2BO), 1986; *Voices of Tyranny Temples of Silence*. Indian River, Ont.: Arcana, 1993.

Recordings: Concerto for flute and orchestra (1984), Concerto for harp and orchestra, *The Darkly Splendid Earth (The Lonely Traveler)*, for violin & orchestra. Toronto: CBC; *The Garden of the Heart*. Toronto: CBC, 1997.

Anthologies: *R. Murray Schafer: A Collection*. Toronto: Open Letter (Fourth Series, 4 & 5, Fall 1979).

Web Site: http://openingday.com/schafer.htm

SCHÄUFFELEN, Konrad Balder

(1929).

One of the more inventive European writers, he wrote classic German CONCRETE POEMS:

mon a de mo iselle
mon e te mo igner
mon i tor mo rast
mon o ton mo dell
mon u mento mo ri

before excelling at unusual containers for words. *Erdglobus* (1978) is a clay globe about sixteen inches in diameter onto which words have been stamped. *Schäuffelens lotterie romane* (1964, 1975) is a wooden box, six by four and one-quarter by two inches high, in which are tightly squeezed 365 pieces of light blue paper, each about six by two inches, tightly rolled, their ends up, which can be extracted with tweezers from the box in any order. On each sheet of paper are unpunctuated words. The principal problem of this *"entwicklungsroman"* (or novel-in-progess), as Schäuffelen calls it, is that the configuration of rolled up, light blue papers in the box is so elegant that one is reluctant to remove them from the box. Trained in medicine, Schäuffelen works as a psychiatrist in Munich.

Works: *Der stumme Traduktor*, 1968; *The Beast with Two Backs*, 1973; *Band 1–3*, 1974; *La Boucle*, 1974–76; *Big Murray*, 1976; *Präsenz-Flipper*, 1976; *Pestbuch*, 1979; *Gegen Stände Sätze*. Erlangen & München, Germany: Klaus G. Renner, 1979.

Exhibition Catalog: *Konrad Balder Schäuffelen: Sprache ist für wahrein koerper*. München: Städt Galerie im Lenbachhaus, 1976.

SCHECHNER, Richard

See **PERFORMANCE GROUP**.

SCHEERBART, Paul

(8 January 1863–15 October 1915).

A prolific German writer, active in Berlin, Scheerbart published stories, novels, poems, and plays. He also illustrated some of his own works with stylized, imaginary scenes, theorized about perpetual motion, and envisioned a new architecture. His artistic philosophy, explained in *Das Paradies, die Heimat der Kunst* (Paradise, the Home of Art, 1893), was based on fantasy, imagination, and a search for newness. Scheerbart's writings employ a wit and humor that sometimes becomes grotesque and nonsensical. He often wrote about the cosmos—his "Asteroid Novel," *Lesabéndio* (1913), presaging German science fiction. Other works were meant as social satire—*Revolutionäre Theater-Bibliothek* (1904) is a collection of twenty-two "revolutionary" theater pieces. In his plays Scheerbart advocated extreme reduction and simplification of stage setting, plot, and dialogue. Some works eschew language altogether, favoring pantomime, as in *Kometentanz* (Dance of the Comets, 1903), for which Scheerbart also created an accompanying score that would now be considered "noise music." He favored experiment in poetry, creating, in addition to other works, three SOUND POEMS; one, for example, begins, "Kikakoku! / Ekoralaps!" Scheerbart attempted to create a perpetual motion machine. His plan and sketches for this project

S

comprise the book *Das Perpetuum Mobile* (1910). Subtitled "The Story of an Invention," this book could be considered an early example of CONCEPTUAL ART. Though unschooled in architecture, Scheerbart worked closely with the architect Bruno Taut (1880–1938) on the highly influential Glass Pavilion displayed at the German Werkbund exhibition in Cologne in 1914. His manifesto *Glasarchitektur* (1914)—an important, prophetic work, if only for its influence on the INTERNATIONAL STYLE—remains the only book of his to be translated into English.

—H. R. Brittain

Writings: *Das Paradies, die Heimat der Kunst,* 1893; *Lesabéndio*, 1913; *Revolutionäre Theater-Bibliothek,*, 1904; *Kometentanz*, 1903; *Das Perpetuum Mobile,* 1910; *Glass Architecture* (1914). Ed. and intro. Dennis Sharp. New York: Praeger, 1972.

SCHILLINGER, Joseph

(31 August 1895–23 March 1943).

After studies at the St. Petersburg Conservatory, Schillinger taught in post-Revolutionary Russia before emigrating to the United States in 1928. Beginning with classes at New York's New School for Social Research, he established a reputation for teaching music composition based upon strict mathematical principles. George Gershwin (1898–1937) was one of his personal students; among those influenced by Schillinger are EARLE BROWN, the ragtime pianist/composer Eubie Blake (1883–1983), and the blues singer B. B. King (1926). As a composer, Schillinger is credited with the *First Airphonic Suite* (1929) for THEREMIN and orchestra.

Writings: Dowling, Lyle, and Arnold Shaw, eds. *The Schillinger System of Musical Composition* (1946). 2 vols. New York: Da Capo, 1978; Schillinger, Joseph. *Encyclopedia of Rhythm*, 1966; *The Mathematical Basis of the Arts* (1948). New York: Da Capo, 1976.

Compositions: Schillinger, Joseph. *March of the Orient*, for Orchestra, 1926; *First Airphonic Suite*, for theremin and orchestra, 1929; *North-Russian Symphony*, 1930; *The People and the Prophet*, ballet, 1931.

Biography: Schillinger, Frances. *Joseph Schillinger: A Memoir* (1949). New York: Da Capo, 1976.

Webpage: http://www.peabody.jhu.edu/current/js/js.htm

SCHLEMMER, Oskar

(4 September 1888–13 April 1943).

After undistinguished beginnings as a painter, Schlemmer made reliefs of concave and convex shapes and in 1921 exhibited abstract free-standing sculpture. On the faculty of the BAUHAUS from 1920 to 1929, he initially taught stonecarving and then theatrical design. Beginning with the *Triadischen Ballett* (Triadic Ballet, 1922), he made padded costumes that resembled figurines more than traditional ballet garb, giving props and lighting as much presence as performers (presaging ALWIN NIKOLAIS, among others). The result was a CONSTRUCTIVIST theater more attuned to Bauhaus ideals (and contrary to EXPRESSIONISM). "Theater is the concentrated orchestration," he wrote, "of sound, light (color), space, form, and motion. The Theatre of Totality with its multifarious complexities of light, space, plane, form, motion, sound, man—and with all the possibilities for varying and combining these elements—must be an organism." Any traditional "dramatic" script was thus a "literary encumbrance" lacking "the creative forms peculiar only to the stage." Schlemmer's 1926 plans for a "total theater," which would incorporate a deep stage and a center stage, in addition to a conventional proscenium and a fourth stage suspended above the others, still look radical today.

Sculpture: *JG Relief in Bronze*, 1919; *Relief H Bronze*, 1919; *Constructed Sculpture R*, 1919; *Ornamental Sculpture*, 1919; *Profile in Yellow*, 1922; *The Abstract* (from *The Triadic Ballet*), 1922; *Gold Sphere* (from *The Triadic Ballet*), 1922; *Grotesque II*, 1923.

Theatre: *Triadisches Ballet* (Triadic Ballet), 1922.

Set Design: *Solove* (by Igor Stravinsky), 1930; *Die Glückliche Hand* (by Arnold Schoenberg), 1930.

Writings: *Man: Teaching Notes from the Bauhaus*. Ed. Heimo Kuchling. Trans. Janet Seligman. Cambridge: MIT Press, 1971; ——, et al. *The Theater of the Bauhaus*. Ed. and intro. Walter Gropius, trans. Arthur S. Wensinger (1961). Baltimore: Johns Hopkins University Press, 1996.

Exhibition Catalogs: *Paintings, Watercolors, Drawings, Sculpture and Prints by Oskar Schlemmer*. Los Angeles: Felix Landau Gallery, 1970; Lidtke, Vernon L., et. al. *Oskar Schlemmer*. Baltimore: Museum of Art, 1986; *Oskar Schlemmer: Aquarelle*. Stuttgart: Cantz, 1988.

SCHMIDT, Arno

(18 January 1910–3 June 1979).

A prolific, innovative writer, Schmidt produced twenty-five novels or compilations of short stories that all deal with the author's life, feelings, and opinions, in addition to numerous radio features, essays on literature, and translations of a wide range of European and American authors. Often called the German JAMES JOYCE, Schmidt produced typescripts (camera-ready copies of elaborate texts that he typed himself): *Zettels Traum* (Bottom's Dream, 1970), which particularly reflects Joyce's *FINNEGANS WAKE; Schule der Atheisten* (School for Atheists, 1972); and *Abend mit Goldrand (Evening Edged in Gold*, 1975, 1979), all of which have at least two simultaneously continuous dialogues, adjacent to one another on a page, in a form reminiscent more of film scripts, drama, or even painting than a novel. Interspersed throughout these typographical feasts are quotations mostly from nineteenth-century literature, which was the German writing Schmidt felt closest to, probably because he found it filled with sexual overtones.

Like Joyce, Schmidt incorporated several languages (German, English, French, Latin) and German dialects (Silesian, Franconian, Alsatian, Low German, etc.) and then developed his "eytm"-theory (the art of misspelling), so that visual representation changed the meaning of certain words. To give an English example, to write "son" but mean "sin," Schmidt would have them appear as:

i
s-n
o

While his early work was quite EXPRESSIONISTIC, Schmidt's language became increasingly visual, his spelling phonetic, and his metaphors bolder.

A misanthrope and a cultural pessimist who (like his characters) could survive only amidst books and archives, Schmidt became a recluse at an early age, serving as a cartographer in the German occupation of Norway. He never overcame his proletarian upbringing, his sister's marriage to a Jewish merchant, his aborted study of mathematics and astronomy, the decade he lost at menial jobs and at war, the loss of his library and his early writings as a World-War II refugee from Silesia (now Poland), and his sense of having become a writer "too late."

Though most of Schmidt's work has been translated into English by John E. Woods, thanks to a generous grant from Jan Philip Reemtsma, an enlightened German philathropist, who owns the rights to Schmidt's work, many of these translations remain unpublished.

—Michal Ulrike Dorda

Writings: Schmidt, Arno. *Zettels Traum*, 1970; *Schule der Atheisten*, 1972; *The Egghead Republic: A Short Novel from the Horse Latitudes*. Trans. Michael Horovitz. Boston: Marion Boyars, 1979; *Evening Edged in Gold*. Trans. John E. Woods. New York: HBJ, 1980; *Scenes from the Life of a Faun: A Short Novel*. Trans. John E. Woods. New York: Marion Boyars, 1983; *Collected Novellas*. Trans. John E. Woods. Normal, IL: Dalkey Archive, 1994; *Nobodaddy's Children*. Trans. John E. Woods. Normal, IL: Dalkey Archive, 1995; *The Collected Stories of Arno Schmidt*. Trans. John E. Woods. Normal, IL: Dalkey Archive, 1996;

Two Novels: The Stony Heart, B/Moondocks. Normal, IL: Dalkey Archive, 1997.

Interpretation: Minden, Michael. *Arno Schmidt*. Cambridge, England, & New York: Cambridge University Press, 1995; Weninger, Robert. *Framing a Novelist: Arno Schmidt Criticism 1970–94*. Columbia, SC: Camden House, 1995; Ott, F.P., ed. "Arno Schmidt Number." *The Review of Contemporary Fiction* V111/1 (Spring 1988).

SCHNEEMANN, Carolee

(12 October 1939).

An exponent of messy EXPRESSIONISM in several media, Schneemann introduced its esthetic to MIXED-MEANS THEATER in her *Meat Joy* (1964), which was commonly ranked among the best of its kind and was thus frequently reproduced, not only on stage but as a script. After the stage lights go out, colored spotlights flash through the darkness, revealing the performers slowly undressing one another, down to feathered bikinis. The couples engage one another slowly, their bodies clustering on the floor, their legs sticking out. The performers are given flashlights that they suddenly shine on one another. Apart from this group, a woman dressed as a serving maid tosses dead fish and chickens and other food onto the scene, which assumes the image of chaos until the lights are turned on. Schneemann has written: "*Meat Joy* has the character of an erotic rite: excessive, indulgent, a celebration of flesh as material: raw fish, chickens, sausages, wet paint, transparent plastic, ropes, brushes, paper scrap. Its propulsion is towards the ecstatic." Perhaps because nothing she has done since has commanded as much respect, Schneemann titled a book-length retrospective of her work *More than Meat Joy* (1979).

Theater: *Meat Joy*, 1964; *Up to and Including Her Limits*, c. 1970s; *Homerunmuse*, 1977.

Writings: Schneemann, Carolee. *More than Meat Joy: Complete Performance Works and Selected Writings* (1979). New Paltz, NY: Documentext, 1997; "Parts of a Body House" in *Fantastic Architecture*, ed. Dick Higgins and Wolf Vostell. New York: Something Else, 1969.

Exhibition Catalogs: *Carolee Schneeman: I. Early Work. 1960/1970*. New York: Max Hutchinson Gallery & New Paltz, NY: Documentext, 1982; *Carolee Schneeman Up to and Including her Limits*. New York: New Museum, 1996.

Bibliography: McDonagh, Don. *The Rise and Fall and Rise Modern Dance* (1970). Rev. ed. Pennington, NJ: A Cappella, 1990; Roth, Moira. ed. "Carolee Schneeman" in *The Amazing Decade: Women and Performance Art in America 1970–80*. Los Angeles: Astro Artz, 1983.

SCHNEIDER, Ira

See **GILLETTE, Frank**, **VIDEO ART**.

SCHOENBERG, Arnold

(13 September 1874–13 July 1951).

An essentially self-taught composer, he produced in his native Vienna his first major work, the popular *Verklärte Nacht* (Transfigured Night) (1899) for string sextet, which is more commonly performed in an arrangement for string orchestra. Moving to Berlin in 1901, he worked at orchestrating operettas and directing a cabaret orchestra. Returning home in 1903 to teach, he befriended not only Gustav Mahler (1860–1911), the prominent Viennese composer and conductor who supported Schoenberg's activities, but two younger men who became his most prominent protégés, Alban Berg (1885–1935) and ANTON WEBERN. Because Schoenberg's harmonies in particular were so extreme, riots erupted at the premieres of his first two string quartets in 1905 and 1908. One result was to instill in Schoenberg a fear of public performances; he preferred instead that audiences at his concerts be restricted. Around this time, he began painting with a certain seriousness, in an Expressionist style that, differences in media notwithstanding, roughly resembled his music at the time.

In 1911, Schoenberg published his book *Harmonielehr* (Theory of Harmony), which he dedicated to Mahler's memory. He moved again to Berlin, where he composed *Pierrot Lunaire* (1912), which remains among his most influential works, composed in an idiom customarily called ATONAL because the music eschewed dependence upon tonics and dominants. Returning to Vienna during World War I, Schoenberg developed by 1923 his SERIAL method of composition, which is regarded as his extraordinary invention. (It is discussed in detail elsewhere in this book.) Invited to return to Berlin in 1925, where he was offered a professorship at the Academy of the Arts, the sometime self-taught avant-garde composer finally achieved bourgeois prestige and financial security

However, once the Nazis assumed power, Schoenberg, a Jew who had converted to Christianity, resumed his initial faith and departed for America, eventually settling in Los Angeles, where he taught at local universities. Though his arch-competitor IGOR STRAVINSKY had likewise emigrated to Los Angeles, the two men met only once, in passing. Becoming a naturalized American citizen in 1941, the composer incidentally Americanized the spelling of his surname from Schönberg to Schoenberg.

His serial innovation notwithstanding, most of Schoenberg's compositions reflect the Expressionistic esthetics of his youth, sometimes in his choice of literary texts, often in the ways these texts are sung. Those less enthusiastic about serialism like to point out that most of his compositions do not observe serial requirements and that his final compositions were less observant than those from the 1920s and 1930s.

Schoenberg was at times a strong writer, initially in German, later in English, his best writing reflecting the influence of Karl Krauss, an Austrian semblance of H. L. Mencken. Schoenberg wrote, in addition to his continuous textbook, essays uneven in quality. The most masterful, such as "Composition in Twelve Tones" (1941), deal with his esthetics and compositional processes. Schoenberg's example perhaps accounts for why composers are generally more predisposed than other kinds of artists (painters certainly, poets perhaps) to want to write well about their art. Like Richard Wagner before him, Schoenberg also wrote not only the libretto but highly detailed stage directions for his monumental opera *Moses und Aron* (begun in the early 1930s, but not premiered until 1957, after his death) and frequently revived since.

Selected Compositions: *Verklärte Nachte*, sextet for strings, Op. 4 (1899); arr. for string orchestra, 1917; rev. 1943; *Erwartung*, monodrama, op. 17, 1909; *Pierrot Lunaire*, for Sprechstimme with piano, flute, clarinet, and cello, op. 21, 1912; *Gurre-Lieder*, for soli, mixed chorus, and orchestra, 1900–09 (composed), 1910–11 (revised), 1913 (premiered); *Kol Nidre* for speaker, chorus, and orchestra, op. 39, 1938; *Das Buch der hängenden Gärten*, a cycle of 15 poems from Stefan George, 1908–09; *Moses und Aron*, biblical drama, to his own libretto, 1930–32 (for 2 acts); 1951 (for 3rd act begun but not completed); 1954 for radio premiere; 1957 for theatrical premiere.

Recordings: *Pierrot Lunaire*. Cond. Reinbert de Leeuw. Austria: Koch Schwann Musica Mundi, 1991; *Moses und Aron*. Cond. Pierre Boulez. Hamburg: Deutsche Grammophon, 1996; *Gurrelieder*. Cond. Giuseppe Sinopoli. Hamburg: Teldec, 1996; *Transfigured Night*. Cond. Esa-Pekka Salonen. New York: Sony Classical, 1997.

Books: *Harmonielehre/Theory of Harmony* (1911); *Models for Beginners in Composition*. New York: G. Schirmer, 1942; *Structural Functions of Harmony*. New York: W. W. Norton, 1954; *Letters* (1956, 1964). Ed. Erwin Stein. Berkeley: University of California Press, 1987; *Fundamentals of Musical Composition*. Ed. Leonard Stein. London: Faber, 1967; *1950.* 2d enlarged ed. by Leonard Stein (1975). Berkeley: University of California Press, 1984; *The Musical Idea and the Logic, Technique, and Art of Its Presentation*. Ed and trans. Patricia Carpenter and Severine Neff. New York: Columbia University Press, 1995.

Biography: Wellesz, Egon. *Arnold Schoenberg* (1925). Trans. W. H. Kerridge. Westport, CT: Greenwood, 1970; Stuckenschmidt, H. H. *Arnold Schoenberg* (1959). Trans. Edith Temple Roberts and Humphrey Searle. Westport, CT: Greenwood, 1979.

Web Site: http://www.primenet.com/~randols/schoenberg/schoenlinks.html (Many links.)

Interpretation: Bailey, Walter B., ed. *The Arnold Schoenberg Companion*. Westport, CT: Greenwood, 1998; Brand, Juliane, and Christopher Haily. *Constructive Dissonance: Arnold Schoenberg and the Transformations of 20th Century Culture*. Berkeley: University of California Press, 1997; Frisch, Walter. *The Early Works of Arnold Schoenberg 1893–1908*. Berkeley: University of California Press, 1993; Milstein, Silvina. *Arnold Schoenberg: Notes, Sets, Forms*, Cambridge, England, & New York: Cambridge University Press, 1992; Ringer, Alexander. *Arnold Schoenberg: The Composer as Jew*. New York: Oxford University, 1993; Rosen, Charles. *Arnold Schoenberg*. Chicago: University of Chicago Press, 1996; Shoaf, R. Wayne. *The Schoenberg Discography*. 2d rev. ed. Berkeley: Fallen Leaf, 1994.

Catalog: Rufer, Joseph. *The Works of Arnold Schoenberg: A Catalogue of His Compositions, Writings, and Painting*. London: Faber & Faber, 1962.

SCHÖFFER, Nicolas

(6 September 1912–8 January 1992).

Though Schöffer is commonly regarded as among the most distinguished European KINETIC sculptors, his work is hardly seen in the United States and, worse, rarely written about in English. Schöffer belonged to a group of Parisian artists, gathered around the Denise René Gallery in the late 1950s, who appropriated industrial methods as a prerequisite to eliminating the purported conflict between science and art. Alastair Mackintosh speaks of Schöffer's pieces having "two parts: a solid sculptural core and its reflection cast upon a suitable surface. The sculptural half usually moves and is made of many small pieces of reflective steel, put together in a CONSTRUCTIVIST manner. The whole edifice turns, and within his principal movement there is often other movement, creating a positive waterfall of light. Aimed at this are spotlights, often of different colors, which cast a huge shadow onto a screen." Mackintosh continues, "Frequently these pieces are equipped with CYBERNETIC systems that react to environmental influences. The largest outdoor pieces are often huge weathervanes reacting to wind speed, atmospheric pressure, sunlight, and so on." Born in Hungary, Schöffer lived in France after the mid–1930s. Nonetheless, the Hungarian government named a museum after him in his hometown of Kalocsa. He is also the prolific author of books that remain untranslated, some of which propose leisure cities constructed on pylons raised above the earth in large enclosed spaces similar to those envisioned by BUCKRNINSTER FULLER.

Works: *Spatiodynamic Reliefs* (1–6) 1950–51; *Polychrome spatiodynamic Sculptures* (1–15) 1949–53; *Cysp* (0–2), 1956; *Lux* (1–13) 1957–60; *Luminoscope I*, 1959; *Tower of Liège*, 1961; *Chronos* (1–6) 1960–61; *Anamorphosis* (1–2) 1961.

Architecture: *House with invisible inside walls*. Salon des Travaux Publics, 1956; *Plan for a Leisure City*, 1958.

Films: *Spatiodynamisme*, 1957; *Manola*, 1958.

Books: *La Ville Cybernétique*. Paris: Tchou, 1969.

Exhibition Catalogs: *Nicolas Schöffer: Space Light Time*. Text by Jacques Ménétrier and Guy Habasque. Neuchâtel, Switzerland: Griffon, 1963; *Two Kinetic Sculptors, Nicolas Schöffer and Jean Tinguely*. New York: Jewish Museum, 1965; *Schöffer*. Düsseldorf: Hans Mayer, 1968; *Nicolas Schöffer*. New York: Denise René, 1972.

Interpretation: Mackintosh, Alastair. "Nicolas Schöffer." In *Contemporary Artists*, ed. Colin Naylor. 3d ed. Chicago: St. James Press, 1989.

SCHOOL OF PARIS

See **NEW YORK SCHOOL**.

SCHONING, Klaus

See **RADIO ART**.

SCHWARTZ, Francis

(10 March 1940).

A Texan long resident in Puerto Rico, Schwartz has initiated and sponsored many avant-garde activities there, beginning in the late 1960s with his involvement with the Grupo Fluxus (which operated independently, if barely aware, of the principal FLUXUS activities), continuing with PERFORMANCE ART that incorporates odors as well as sounds, and speech compositions that typically exploit his polylinguistic competence. Extending the Wagnerian idea of the *Gesamtkunstwerk* ("total artwork"), Schwartz added audience participation (customarily conducted from the stage, with the performers functioning around him like cheerleaders). His mammoth *Cosmos* (1980), based on the University of Puerto Rico campus, incorporated several musical performance groups with gymnasts and aquatic ballerinas, in addition to telephone contact with collaborating artists around the world. His *Mon oeuf* (1979) was a construction seven feet high, three and one-half feet wide, and four inches deep that, he writes, "was at once a sculpture, a mini-theater, and an instrument that had electronic music, aromas, video, temperature manipulation, and tactile stimuli."

Compositions: Schwartz, Francis. *Auschwitz*, for tape, lights, odors, and movement (San Juan, 15 May 1968); *Geo-flux* electronic ballet, 1974; *Que reine la Paz*, for 4 guitars, 1987; *4 + 3 = Paris VIII*, didactic music for voice, violin, guitar, alto saxophone, trumpet, trombone, and percussion, 1978; *Musique pour Juvisi*, for tape, videotape, and synthesizer, 1979; *Ergo Sum*, for flute and tape, 1979; *Mon oeuf*, for tape, videotape, odors, sculpture, and audience, 1979; *Cosmos*, 1980; *Grimaces*, for voice, flute, alto saxophone, double bass, percussion, tape, and audience, 1985; *Dulce Libertad*, for soprano, violin, cello, and piano, 1988.

Books: *El Mundo de la Musica*. Rio Piedras: University of Puerto Rico Press, Department of Education Commonwealth of Puerto Rico, 1982; ——, and Donald Thompson, *Writings: Concert Life in Puerto Rico, 1957–1992: Views and Reviews*. Rio Piedras: University of Puerto Rico Press, 1999.

Recordings: *Caligula*. San Juan, PR: Institute of Puerto Rican Culture ICP-C 17, 1987.

SCHWARTZ, Tony

(19 August 1923).

A veteran American audio artist, Schwartz in the 1950s pioneered the use of the recently developed portable tape recorder to capture, literally on the street, sounds that previously could not be brought into a radio studio (and thus common acoustic experience). *Sound of My City* (1956), his audiotape portrait of New York people, won the Prix Italia for RADIO ART. Realizing that American radio after 1952 would be a less receptive medium for extended audio art than recordings, Schwartz produced several records, mostly about the sounds of his own neighborhood on New York's midtown West Side, that represent a unique achievement. He has also produced thousands of audio-based commercials for radio and television. Schwartz also wrote two provocative books on the media, extending MARSHALL MCLUHAN'S general ideas in specific ways.

Recordings: *1, 2, 3, and a Zing, Zing, Zing*. New York: Folkways, 1953; *Sound of My City*. New York: Folkways, 1956; *New York 19*. New York: Folkways, 1955; *Music in the Streets*. New York: Folkways, 1958; *Sounds of My City*. New York: Folkways, 1959; *You're Stepping on My Shadow*. New York: Folkways, 1962; *Tony Schwartz Records the Sounds of Children*. New York: Folkways, 1970; *Songs for Children from New York City*. New York: Folkways, 1978.

Writings: Schwartz, Tony. *Media: The Second God*. New York: Random House, 1981; *The Responsive Chord*. Garden City, NY: Doubleday, 1973.

Web Site: http://www.tony.schwartz.net

SCHWITTERS, Kurt

(20 June 1887–8 January 1948).

Born and raised in Hannover, a modest North Germany city roughly halfway between Berlin and Cologne, Schwitters was denied membership in the Berlin DADA Club and so took the word "Merz," which he made the title of his Hannover magazine (1923–27). (Marc Dachy characterizes it as "a verbal and semantic clone of Dada.") Schwitters's initial masterpieces were brilliantly colored COLLAGES composed of printed ephemera, such as ticket stubs, used toward abstract ends (that is, an appreciation of the composition as a composition, rather than, say, a political commentary). What most impressed me about his visual art, in an exhibition at MoMA in the mid–1980s, was the small size of most of his works, few of them being larger than a foot square.

Schwitters also built within his home the *Merzbau*, which was a CONSTRUCTIVIST ASSEMBLAGE of discarded junk

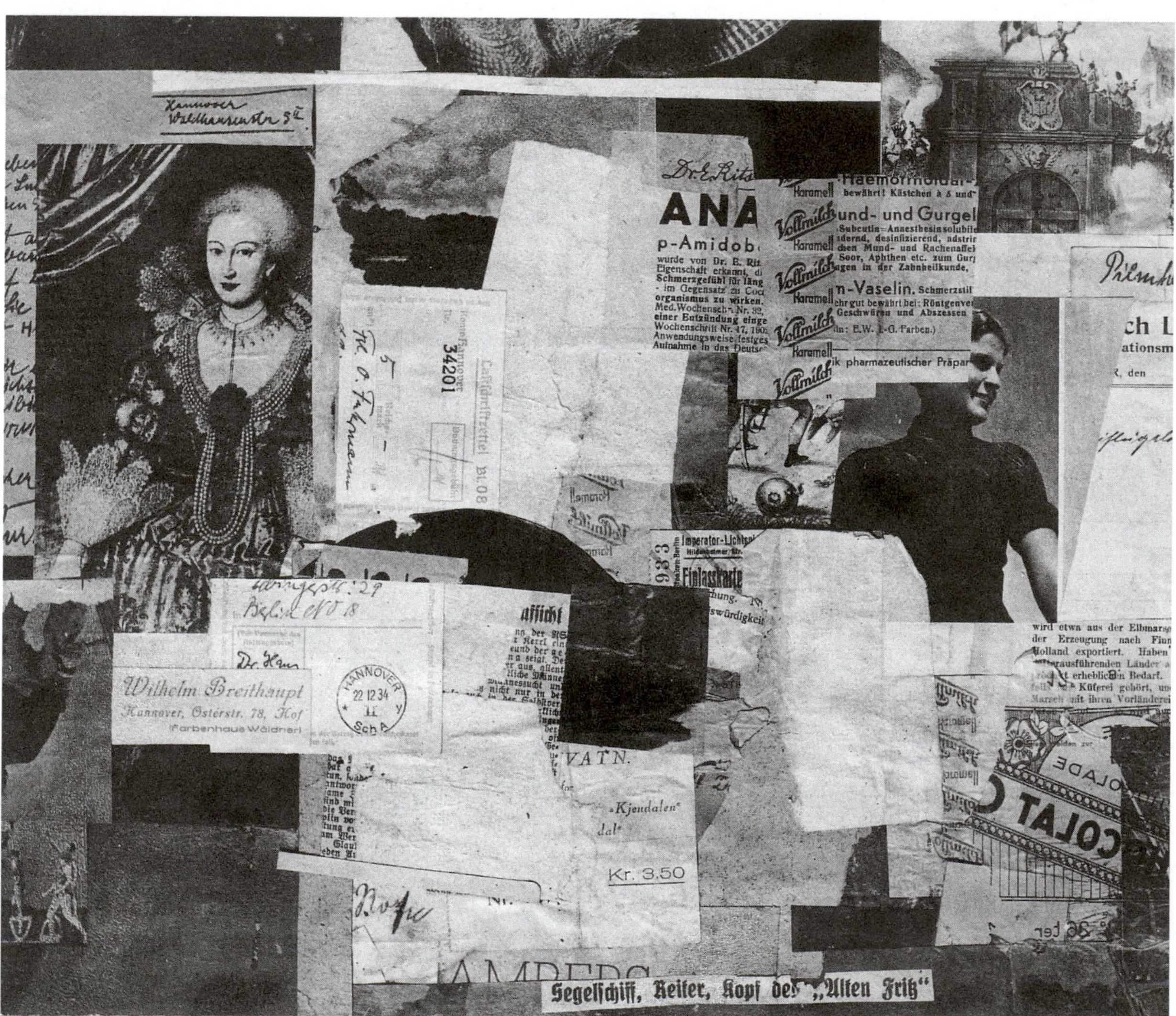

Kurt Schwitters, Paper collage, c. 1934. © 2000 Artists Rights Society (ARS), New York/VG Bild-Kunst, Bonn.

that eventually pierced the ceiling. Once the Nazis took hold, even the avowedly apolitical Schwitters fled to Norway, where he began a second *Merzbau* that was destroyed by fire after he left it, and then to England, where he began a third in a countryside barn, with funds from New York's Museum of Modern Art; it was incomplete at his death. Schwitters's first major poem, *Anna Blume* (1919), is a Dada classic in which the conventions of love poetry are rendered nonsensical. His literary masterpiece is *Ursonate* (1922–32), in which the musical form is filled with nonsemantic vocables for thirty-five minutes. Schwitters's previously uncollected writings, which appeared in Germany in five rich volumes—over 1,700 pages in total length (1973–81)—established him as a POLYARTIST.

Works: *Construction for Noble Ladies,*, 1919; *Merzbau*, 1923–36 (unfinished) destroyed, 1943; *Merz 42 (Like an Old Master)*, 1942.

Writings: *Die Blume Anna/Die Neue Anna Blume: Eine Gedichtsammlung aus den Jahren 1918–1922*. Berlin, Germany: Verlag der Sturn, n.d.; *Das Literarische Werk*. 5 Vols. Köln: DuMont, 1973–81; *Three Painter Poets: Arp, Schwitters, Klee*. Trans. Harriett Watts. Harmondsworth: Penguin, 1974; *Poems Performance Pieces Proses Plays Poetics: Kurt Schwitters*. Ed. and trans. Jerome Rothenberg and Pierre Joris. Philadelphia: Temple University Press, 1993; *Pin*. Ed. Jasia Reichardt. London: Gabberbochus, 1962.

Exhibition Catalogs: *Kurt Schwitters*. Intro Naum Gabo. New York: Pinacotheca Gal, 1948; *Kurt Schwitters*. Intro. Tristan Tzara. New York: Sidney Janis, 1952; *Kurt Schwitters*. Intro. Werner Schmalenbach. Hannover, Germany: Kestner-Gesellschaft, 1956; *Kurt Schwitters*. Pasadena, CA: Pasadena Art Museum, 1962; *Kurt Schwitters*. Köln: Wallraf-Richartz-Museum, 1963; *Kurt Schwitters*. Los Angeles: UCLA Art Gallery, 1965; *Kurt Schwitters*. Düsseldorf: Städtische Kunsthalle, 1971; *Kurt Schwitters in Exile: The Late Work 1937–1948*. Essay by Nicholas Wadley. London: Marlborough, 1981; *Kurt Schwitters*. Text Richard Humphreys. London: Tate Gallery, 1985.

Interpretation: Dietrich, Dorothea. *The Collage of Kurt Schwitters*. Cambridge, England, & New York: Cambridge University Press, 1993; Elderfield, John. *Kurt Schwitters*. New York: Thames & Hudson, 1985; Schmalenbach, Werner. *Kurt Schwitters*. New York: Abrams, n.d. (c. 1967); Steinitz, Käte T. *Kurt Schwitters: A Portrait from Life* (1963). Berkeley: University of California Press, 1968; Themerson, Stefan. *Kurt Schwitters in England*. London: Gabberbochus, 1958.

SCRIABIN, Alexander

(6 January 1872–27 April 1915).

Beginning as a composer-pianist in the tradition of Frederic Chopin and Franz Liszt, Scriabin established his reputation with piano music, including ten solo sonatas (1892–1913), before pursuing, roughly after 1902, more radical ways. *La poème de l'extase* (Poem of Ecstasy, 1907) incorporates original, complex harmonies on behalf of mystical notions derived from theosophy. NICOLAS SLONIMSKY summarizes Scriabin's avant-garde achievements in this way:

> Scriabin was a genuine innovator in harmony. . . . He gradually evolved in his own melodic and harmonic style, marked by extreme chromaticism; in his piano piece, *Désir*, Op. 57 (1908), the threshold of polytonality and atonality is reached; the key signature is dispensed with in his subsequent works; chromatic alternations and compound appoggiaturas [grace notes] create a harmonic web of such complexity that all distinction between consonance and dissonance vanishes. Building chords by fourths rather than by thirds, Scriabin constructed his 'mystic chord' of 6 notes (C, F-sharp, B-flat, E, A, and D), which is the harmonic foundation of *Promethée* (1911).

Also titled *Poéme du feu*, the latter included a score for a color keyboard designed to project changing colors programmed to individual notes (C major as red, F-sharp major as bright blue, etc.), because, to quote Slonimsky again, "at that time he was deeply immersed in the speculation about parallelism of all the arts in their visual and auditory aspects." Because few composers subsequently adopted either his ideas for enhancing music with color or his mystic chord, Scriabin's originality is currently regarded as a cul-de-sac. Just before his early death from blood poisoning, Scriabin was working on a "Mysterium" to be performed in the Himalayas. The American author and translator Faubion Bowers (1917) has produced several indispensable volumes about Scriabin.

S

Compositions: *Rêverie*, op. 24, 1898; *Le Poème divin*, 1902–04; *Le Poème de l'extase*, op. 54, 1905–08; *Poème du feu or Promethée*, op. 60, 1908–10; Piano Concerto, op. 20, 1896; *Romance*, for horn and piano, 1890; *Canon*, 1883; *Nocturne* in A-flat major, 1884; *Valse* in F minor, op. 1, 1885; *Sonate-Fantaisie*, 1886; *Valse* in G-sharp minor, 1886; *Valse* in D-flat major, 1886; 11 sonatas in E-flat major, 1887–89, op. 6 (1892), op. 19, *Sonata-Fantasy* (1892–97), op. 23 (1897–98), op. 30 (1903), op. 53 (1907), op. 62 (1911), op. 64 *Messe blanche* (1911), op. 66 (1913), op. 68, *Messe noire* (1913), and op. 70 (1913); *Fantasy*, for two pianos, 1889?; *2 Nocturnes*, op. 5, 1890; *Douze études*, op. 8, 1894; *Deux poèmes*, op. 32 1903; 4 *Préludes*, op. 31, 1903; *Poème satanique* op. 36, 1903; *Huit études* op. 42, 1903; *Feuillet d'album*, op. 58, 1910; *Trois études*, op. 65, 1912; *Deux Danses*, op. 73, 1914.

Recordings: Piano Music. Vladimir Horowitz, piano. New York: RCA Red Seal; Piano Music. Rec. by the composer, Samuel Feinberg, Alexander Goldenweiser, Neinrich Neuhaus, and Vladimir Sofronitsky. Paris: Chant de Monde; *Le Poème de l'extase* (Symphony No. 4, Op. 54) & Symphony No. 5. Philadelphia Orchestra cond. Leopold Stokowski. New York: Pearl; Symphony Nos. 1, 2, 3, 4, & 5. Philadelphia Orchestra, cond. Ricardo Muti. London: Angel; *The Complete Piano Sonatas*. 2 discs. Marc-Andre Hamelin, piano. London: Hyperion, 1996.

Biography: Bowers, Faubion. *Scriabin: A Biography of the Russian Composer*. 2 vols. Palo Alto, CA: Kodansha, 1969; Macdonald, Hugh. *Skryabin*. London/New York: Oxford University Press, 1978.

Web Page: http://gramercy.ios.com/~restemey/Scriabin/Scriabin.html

Interpretation: Baker, James M. *The Music of Alexander Scriabin*. New Haven: Yale University Press, 1986.

SEAWRIGHT, James

See **CYBERNETIC ART**.

SECOND VIENNESE SCHOOL

(c. 1910).

This epithet, formerly more popular, identified the composers gathered around ARNOLD SCHOENBERG, beginning with Alban Berg (1885–1935) and ANTON WEBERN, but also including former pupils who became prominent—among them, Roberto Gerhard (1896–1970, Spanish), René Leibowitz (1913–72, Polish-French), and Nikos Skalkottas (1904–49, Greek), even though the last studied with Schoenberg not in Vienna but in Berlin. Because these twentieth-century composers were customarily regarded as pioneers, it wasn't obvious that the *first* Viennese school was meant to identify F. J. Haydn, W. A. Mozart, L.von Beethoven, and Franz Schubert, who were, needless to say, a less cohesive bunch, since they lived in Vienna at different times and didn't even meet one another. The SVS description was finally pretentious, as geographical terms usually are in art, in this case capitalizing on the musical reputation of Vienna; because "The Schoenberg School" would have been a more appropriate, if less effective, banner.

Bibliography: Leibowitz, René. *Schoenberg and His School* (1949). New York: Da Capo, 1975; Neighbour, Oliver, Paul Griffiths, and George Perle. *The New Grove Second Viennese School*. New York: Norton, 1998; Rognoni, Luigi. *The Second Vienna School*. London: John Calder, 1977; Simms, Bryan R. ed. *Schoenberg, Berg,*

Webern: A Companion to the Second Viennese School. Westport, CT: Greenwood, 1999.

SEEGER, Charles

(4 December 1886–7 February 1979).

Born in Mexico City of American parents, educated at Harvard and then in Europe, Seeger returned to the United States to give the first courses in musicology in this country at the University of California at Berkeley in 1916, and later gave the first classes in ethnomusicology in 1932. A free spirit, Seeger worked at various times for the Resettlement Administration, the Federal Music Project of the Works Progress Adminsitation, and as chief of the music divison at the Pan-American Union. Very much a Communist, he contributed to the *Daily Worker* and edited two issues of *The Music Vanguard* (1934), which failed to compete with the venerable *MODERN MUSIC*. NICHOLAS SLONIMSKY credits Seeger as "a scholar whose uniquely universalist vision for the unification of the field of musicology as a whole continues to challenge the various, sometimes contentious contributing factions: musicology, ethnomusicology, and comparative musicology." In the mid-1990s, my coeditor Joseph Darby and I found Seeger's 1930 essay "On Dissonant Counterpoint" strong enough to reprint in *Classic Essays on Twentieth-Century Music* (1996). Also a composer who lost many of his early scores in a fire, Seeger is now best remembered for his arrangements of American folk songs for piano and voice. By his first wife he fathered the folksinger Pete Seeger (1919) and by his second wife, the composer RUTH CRAWFORD, he fathered the folksingers Peggy Seeger (1935) and Michael Seeger (1933). The aberration of Communism notwithstanding, he had the sort of career of which biographies are made.

Books: *Harmonic Structure and Elementary Compositon*, with Edward G. Stricklen. Berkeley, CA: Privately printed, 1916; *Studies in Musicology, 1935–75*. Berkeley: University of California Press, 1977.

Major Essays: "Carl Ruggles" and "Ruth Crawford." In *American Composers on American Music*, ed. Henry Cowell. Stanford: Stanford University Press, 1933.

Recordings: *The Music of Charles Seeger, 1886–1979*, with Ron Erickson, et al. Berkeley, CA: 1750 Arch, 1984.

Biography: Pescatello, Ann M. *Charles Seeger: A Life in American Music*. Pittsburgh: University of Pittsburgh Press, 1992.

Interpretation: Slonimsky, Nicolas. *Baker's Biographical Dictionary of Musicians*. 8th ed. New York: Schirmer, 1992.

SEGAL, George

(26 November 1924).

During the 1960s, Segal produced a style of figurative sculpture which he presented surrounded by elements drawn from the popular culture. He created his figures by casting: he wrapped live models in bandages soaked in plaster of Paris, cut the cast to release the model, reassembled it, and painted it white. He placed his figures among actual paraphernalia and furniture typical of the consumer society. Situated in environments such as soda fountains, gas stations, and bedrooms, which were filled with real counters, coffee machines, napkin holders, soda dispensers, gas pumps, chairs, and beds, his figures undramatically enact the mundane activities of daily living. Because of the roughness of the unfinished bandage-casts and their whiteness, the figures seem ghostly and lifeless among the real, colorful articles of their situations. They have an air of desolation. The effect is similar to the paintings of Edward Hopper, in which life feels empty and melancholic in the midst of a tawdry affluence. Once Segal found his formula, he stuck to it. He has continued to work for more than three decades, and his art has never changed. Since each of his environments essentially resembles the next, his works taken together amount to minor variations played on a single theme. The first you see is evocative, the rest redundant.

—Mark Daniel Cohen

S

George Segal. Setting up an exhibit at the Sidney Janis Gallery, 3 January 1964. Photograph © Fred W. McDarrah.

Works: *Legend of Lot*, 1958; *Woman Shaving Her Leg*, 1963; *Cinema*, 1963; *The Gas Station*, 1963–64; *The Moviehouse*, 1966–67; *The Execution*, 1967;B—. *Girl on Red Wicker Couch*, 1973; *Hot Dog Stand*, 1978; *The Expulsion*, 1986–87.

Exhibition Catalogs: *New Sculpture by George Segal*. New York: Sidney Janis Gallery, 1965; *George Segal, 12 Human Situations*. Chicago: Museum of Contemporary Art, 1968; *New Sculpture by George Segal*. New York: Sidney Janis, 1968; *George Segal: New Sculpture*. New York: Sidney Janis, 1980; *New Sculpture by George Segal*. New York: Sidney Janis, 1973; *New Sculpture by George Segal*. New York: Sidney Janis, 1974; *George Segal*. New York: Sidney Janis, 1978; *George Segal*. New York: Sidney Janis, 1980; *George Segal*. New York: Sidney Janis, 1986; Riva Yares Gallery. *George Segal: Selected Works*. Scottsdale, Arizona: Riva Yares Gallery, 1988; Sidney Janis Gallery. *George Segal*. New York: Sidney Janis, 1991; Janis, Carroll. *George Segal*. New York: Sidney Janis, 1994; *George Segal, Darkness and Light: New Photo-Sculpture*. New York: Sidney Janis, 1995; *George Segal: Sculpture and Works on Paper*. New York: Sidney Janis Gallery, 1997.

Criticism: Seitz, William Chapin. *Segal*. New York: Abrams, 1972; Van der Marck, Jan. *George Segal*. New York: Abrams, 1975; Tuchman, Phyllis. *George Segal*. New York: Abbeville, 1983.

SEGAY, Serge

(19 March 1947; b. Sergei Vsevolodovich Sigov)

Of the current Russian avant-gardists, Segay is perhaps closest to the roots of Russian Futurism. His higher education was in the area of theater at the Leningrad State Institute of Theater, Music, Art and Cinema (1979–85). He studied the original sources of the Russian avant-garde, sought out and became personally acquainted with surviving figures such as Vasilisk Gnedov, Igor Bakhterev, and Nikolai Khardzhiev, has gathered collections of their works, and has written scholarly studies of their contributions and those of other Futurists, with a special focus on theater. Consequently, his own poetry and book-works tend to resemble Futurist productions more so than the works of other Transfuturists. His careful explorations of Russian sources have nevertheless provided a solid base for his own further experiments and those of his wife, Rea Nikonova, who is more inclined to invent directly rather than checking for possible precedents. Segay is a master of Zaum, a brilliant performer of his own sound poetry, a vigorous user of mixed media in

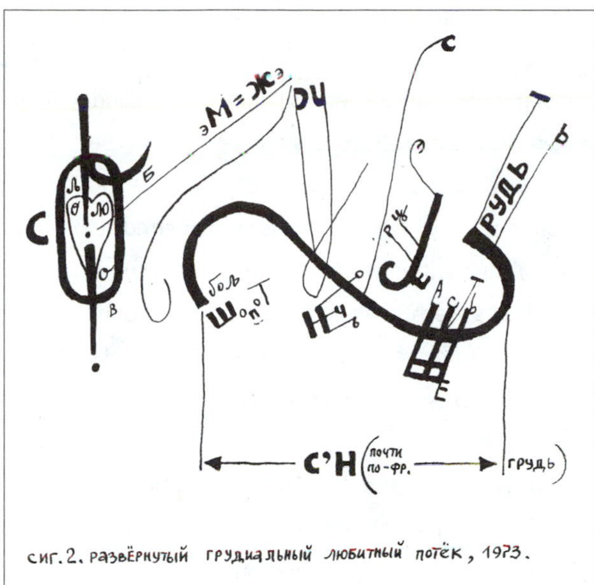

Serge Segay. From *Ekhona 1969/1982*. Courtesy the author.

book-works and visual poetry, and the inventor of rebus-like writing systems for poetry, ballet, and a variety of sign languages. His book-works are particularly inventive in form and medium, e.g. his anthology of Zaum uses a variety of materials (sandpaper, metal foil, etc.), and each section or word of text is hidden under a flap that the reader must lift in order to see the text. In the late 1980s and 1990s he became a pioneer MAIL-ARTIST from his provincial homebase in Yeisk, organized a series of avant-garde exhibits at the local city museum, and has collaborated with such Western figures as JOHN M. BENNETT, Johann W. Glaw, Jon Held, Carlo Belloli, H. R. Fricker, and Pierre and Elsa Garnier. In 1998 he and Nikonova emigrated to Germany.

—Gerald Janecek

Writings: Segay, Serge (Sergei Sigei). *Meil-Art. K vystavke v Eiskom muzee, iiul'-avgust*, 1989. Yeisk, 1989; *Poèmes pour Ballerines du Grand théâtre de l'U.R.S.S.* Orillia, Ont.: ASFi Editions, 1990; *Mezhdunarodnaia vystavka vizual'noi poezii*. Yeisk, 1990; *sound impressions*. Lafarge, WI: Xexoxial Editions, n.d.

SELDES, Gilbert

(3 January 1893–29 September 1970).

A unique intellectual figure as an arts critic who was also managing editor of the highly literary *The Dial*, a nonacademic until his sixties, a prolific writer who contributed to both literary journals and daily newspapers, Seldes established his reputation precociously with *The 7 Lively Arts* (1924), a book that argued that popular arts should and could be taken as seriously as high arts. Following his own advice, Seldes wrote pioneering appreciations of RING LARDNER, Charlie Chaplin, popular music, etc., generally extending the polyartistic precedent established by JAMES GIBBONS HUNEKER thirty years before. Consider this 1937 appreciation of early Walt Disney cartoons (which were much better than the stuff produced after 1941):

> No one else [in film animation] has created such interesting characters, no one else has taken the word "animation" to mean giving life, no one else has found so agreeable a color scheme, and no one else has so successfully integrated pictures and music. As these are four of the five fundamental things in animated cartoons, it is not hard to see why Disney remains so far ahead in the field, especially as in the fifth item, which is sheer, downright, unanalyzable fun, he is even farther ahead of them than in the others.

Courageous criticism sixty years ago, this remains sensitive and valuable today. One quality distinguishing Seldes from other prominent critics (and even the more literary book publishers) was that he was predisposed to American culture at a time when most cultural critics succeeded by publicizing the latest developments in Europe. (Given the recent academic success of various strains of Frogthink and Frogspeak, that Eurocentric bias is perhaps no less true today.)

If Seldes's near-contemporary Edmund Wilson was predominantly a *literary* critic, Seldes was an arts critic who looked at various media, seeing each in its own terms. At a time when nearly every critic is a specialist, whether in weeklies or dailies, it is hard for us to believe now that Seldes for years wrote about his enthusiasms in a regular column for a Hearst daily. In 1956, he published an ingenious reworking of his most celebrated early book. Needlessly taken for granted, in part because of his continuous prominence for four decades, Seldes had remarkably few imitators. Why polyartistic critics are so few nowadays, or rarely recognized, is perhaps another index of decline in the culture of American criticism. Seldes's brother George S. (1890–1996), ranked for decades among the great independent American muckrakers.

S

Books: *The 7 Lively Arts* (1924). 2d ed. New York: Sagamore, 1957; *The Stammering Century*. New York: 1928; *An Hour with the Movies and the Talkies*. Philadelphia & London: J.P. Lippincott, 1929; *The Years of the Locust*. Boston: Little, Brown, and Company, 1932; *Mainland*. N.Y.: C. Scribner's Sons, 1936; *The Movies Come from America* (1937). N.Y.: Arno Press, 1937; *The Great Audience*. Westport, CT: Greenwood, 1970.

Autobiography: Seldes, George. *Witness to a Century* (1987). New York: Ballantine, 1988.

Biography: Kammen, Michael. *The Lively Arts: Gilbert Seldes and the Transformation of Cultural Criticism in the United States*. New York: Oxford University Press, 1996.

SEMIOBJECT

(1960s).

Semiobjects are pieces of art made out of objects and signification. The poem-sculptures of some 1960s concrete poets are an example of this form, in which objects from the real world become encrusted with words, helping to bridge the distance between the physical world and the mind's world of meaning. The effectiveness of such realia is just that—that they force viewers to see themselves not just in a world of objects but in a semiotic universe, where the bits of the world surrounding them are not just objects but meanings.

Luigi-Bob Drake's *Male Art* (1989) is a self-published object consisting of a cassette tape case held closed with two rectangular yellow labels (one reading "MALE" and the other reading "ART"). Inside resides a blue plastic condom case (with the letters I, L, A, and M) and a single-edged razor blade. G. Huth's *the sentences* (1987, 1991) is an incomplete, seven-part, semiobjective work, each separate piece of which consists of pwoermds (one-word poems) handwritten on (and thereby defining) various natural objects. Each individual collection is "bound" differently (in petri dishes, in a suede pouch, in a plastic case, and, for *the leevs*, in a book) to extend the essence of the semiobject.

Miekal And's *Babbaly* (1990) is a publication so concrete, so much an object, that it becomes more than a text, more than the presentation of a text—a greater whole. *Babbaly* first appears to be a huge full-sized blueprint encrusted with weirdly formatted Zaumist neologisms. Glued to the back and folded within the blueprint is an envelope that holds a booklet and an audiotape. The booklet is two booklets, of a piece but folded into one another. The larger subbooklet reprints, in lavender, the neologistic matrix of the wording that covers the blueprint, and reprints this over the text of various poems, which, though foreign in syntax, are in English. The smaller subbooklet presents an almost bare text of "quantical fatherization." And the audiotape is an aural presentation of this grand "empoemation", with intentional audio distortion, wherein words (both semi- and nonsensible) are repeated in—strangely enough—the hypernormal Midwestern accent of And himself. The work, in this case, is more than the text alone (however presented) and more than the objects it inhabits. Together they form, as a semiobjective whole, a commentary on the possibilities not only of text and sound, but also of publishing.

—Geof Huth

Bibliography: And, Miekal. *Babbaly*. Cleveland Heights, OH: Burning, 1990; Drake, Luigi-Bob. *Male Art*. Cleveland Heights, OH: Burning, 1990; Huth, G. *the woords*.

Horseheads, NY: dbqp, 1987; Huth, G. *the stanes*. Horseheads, NY: dbqp, 1987; Huth, G. *the leevs*. Rotterdam, NY: dbqp, 1991; Huth, G. *the shlls*. Rotterdam, NY: dbqp, 1991; Solt, Mary Ellen, ed. *Concrete Poetry: A World View*. Bloomington: Indiana University Press, 1970.

SERIAL MUSIC

(c. 1910s).

It was an extraordinary invention, really, even if serial music is now widely criticized as esthetically convoluted. As a radically different way of cohering musical notes, this was, literally, a new musical language that had to discover its own rules for organizing musical sounds (its own "grammar," so to speak), its own patterns of procedures (syntax), and its own kinds of structures (sentences). In brief, ARNOLD SCHOENBERG postulated that the composer, working within the open range of twelve tones to an octave, could structure any number of tones (up to twelve), without repeating a tone, into a certain order of intervals that are called, variously, the "row," "series," or "set." The German epithet is *Zwölftonmusik*. Another name more common in the 1940s than now is Dodecaphony, which is sort-of Greek for twelve-toneness.

Once the composer chooses a row, it becomes his or her basic pattern for the piece. This sequence of intervals can be used in one of four ways: (1) in its original form; (2) in a reversed or retrograde order; (3) in an inverse order (so that if the second note in the original was three steps up, now it is three steps down, etc.); (4) in an inverted, reversed order. This row, we should remember, is less a series of specific musical notes than a pattern of intervallic relations. Suggesting that traditional musical notation is insufficient, the composer MILTON BABBITT, perhaps the foremost contemporary theorist of serial procedure, proposes instead that a row be represented in the following terms:

0,0; 1,1; 2,7; 3,5; 4,6; 5,4; 6,10; 7,8; 8,9; 9,11; 10,2; 11,3

with the first number of each pair marking the individual note's position in the entire set. Therefore, as the left-hand numbers in each pair escalate from 0 to 11, the second number in each pair refers to that particular note's intervallic relation to the first or base note of the row. (Because distances must be different, no number in the second part of each pair is duplicated.)

If we transpose this row up two intervals, we would then mark it as follows:

0,2; 1,3; 2,9; 3,7; 4,8; 5,6; 6,0; 7,10; 8,11; 9,1; 10,4; 11,5

This kind of notation illustrates the nature of the row, as well as how the elements relate to one another, more clearly than musical notes do; but these numbers, don't forget, are like notes on a staff, which is to say instructions for producing musical sounds.

Whereas note number 6 in the original numerical notation had the interval designation of 10, now it becomes 0, for what adds up to 12 becomes 0 (as 11 + 2 in note number 9 becomes 1). Once the row's pattern is imposed upon musical notes, the numbers refer not just to specific notes but to what Babbitt calls "pitch classes." That is, if note number 6 in this row produces C-sharp, then serial composers can designate any of the C-sharps available to their instruments. Second, just as the notes of a row can be strung out in a line, so they can be bunched into a single chord. The row used in this illustration comes from Arnold Schoenberg's opera *Moses und Aron* (1930–32). The fact that Schoenberg could successfully transform this basic material into various structures for a restricted evening-length opera demonstrates, quite conclusively, that the serial language is not as constricting as all the rules superficially suggest—tonal music, one remembers, has its rules too. Instead, just as twelve-tone procedure discourages the kind of repetition endemic in tonal music, so it creates its own kind of syntactical and grammatical possibilities.

The history of the twelve-tone language has been rather checkered and its development uneven. Soon after Schoenberg invented it, it attracted adherents throughout Europe; by the late 1920s, Schoenberg was invited to succeed Ferrucio Busoni (1886–1924) as professor of composition at the Berlin Academy of Art. However, once the Nazis assumed power, Schoenberg, born a Jew but raised a Christian, resigned his post, emigrating first to England and then to America, where he eventually taught at UCLA.

Once Fascist cultural authorities classified twelve-tone music as "degenerate," other musicians devoted to the new technique either left German territories or went culturally underground: the Spanish-born Roberto Gerhard (1896–1970) moved to England; Nikos Skalkottas (1904–49) returned to his native Greece; while ANTON WEBERN, deprived of his conducting jobs, nonetheless remained in Austria, where he eventually became a copyeditor and proofreader for the same firm that earlier published his music.

After Schoenberg arrived in America, several important composers who were previously counted among its opponents adopted the serial language: IGOR STRAVINSKY and ERNST KRENEK, among the immigrants; and among the American-born, ROGER SESSIONS, Arthur Berger (1912), and even AARON COPLAND toward the end of his compositional career. Meanwhile, in post-World War II Europe, temporary converts to serialism included such prominent young composers as KARLHEINZ STOCKHAUSEN and PIERRE BOULEZ, who differed from the Americans in declaring particular allegiance to Webern as purportedly the most consistent and rigorous serial composer (and thus more advanced than Schoenberg).

Bibliography: Babbitt, Milton. Numerous uncollected essays, but particularly *"Moses and Aron:* An Introduction to the Music." In *Perspectives on Schoenberg and Stravinsky*, eds. Benjamin Boretz and Edward Cone. New York: Norton, 1972; Basart, Ann Phillips. *Serial Music.* Westport, CT: Greenwood, 1976; Perle, George. *Serial Composition and Atonality (1963)*. 6th ed. Berkeley: University of California Press, 1991; *Twelve-Tone Tonality*. Berkeley: University of California Press, 1978; Smith-Brindle, Reginald. *Serial Composition*. New York: Oxford University Press, 1966; Wuorinen, Charles. *Simple Composition*. New York: Longman, 1979.

SERNER, Walter

(15 January 1889–1942).

A poet, art critic, and the author of erotic detective stories that have been recently revived in Germany, Serner published the magazine *Sirius* (1915–16). He joined Zurich DADA, to which he was already predisposed, and copublished *Zeltweg* (1919) in collaboration with TRISTAN TZARA. Described by HANS RICHTER as "the incarnation of revolt . . . the cynic of the movement, the declared anarchist," Serner could effectively climax an evening of short Dada performances. Manuel E. Grossman speaks of Serner making an entrance before an audience of a thousand carrying a headless dummy: "Placing the dummy down, he went back behind the curtain and returned bearing a bunch of artificial flowers which he motioned for the dummy to smell. Laying the flowers at the dummy's feet, he then proceeded to sit in a chair in the middle of the stage with his back to the audience and to recite from his nihilistic tract 'Final Dissolution.'" Richter remembers, "The tension in the hall became unbearable. At first it was so quiet that you could have heard a pin drop. Then the catcalls began, scornful at first, then furious. 'Rat, bastard, you've got nerve!' until the noise almost entirely drowned Serner's voice." Another account has him screaming "Viva Dada" during the premiere of Igor Stravinsky's *Le chant du rossignol*.

Most historians say Serner disappeared without a trace around 1928 (his Dada example thereby preceding the American composer Dante Fiorello [1905–?], who vanished around 1952, even though he had received an unsurpassed four Guggenheim fellowships *two* decades before). Both Marc Dachy and the catalog of a 1989 Berlin exhibition assert that, in August 1942, Serner "was shipped with other deportees from Prague to Theresienstadt." Dachy also reprints from the magazine 391 "Carpet [Notebook] du Docteur Serner," which has Serner's opinionated thumbnail sketches of his colleagues (e.g., "Tristan TZARA, très intelligent, pas assez DADA").

Anthology: *Dr. Walter Serner*. Berlin, Germany: Literaturhaus, 1989.

Interpretation: Dachy, Marc. *The Dada Movement*. New York: Rizzoli, 1990; Grossman, Manuel L. *Dada*. New York: Bobbs-Merrill, 1971.

SERRA, Richard

(2 November 1939).

Serra's innovation was to make three-dimensional visual art—sculpture—that emphazised presence over appearance and thus weight over even any illusion of lightness. He began by hanging a row of loops of rubber from nails in a wall (that even in their stillness resembled some of LEN LYE's motorized sculptures exhibited around the same time) and by pouring molten lead into the corners of an exhibition space before pulling away a lead island whose jagged edge corresponded to the part remaining against the wall—in both cases revealing process. Later, Serra took large sheets of lead and propped them precariously against each other or against a wall, at times injuring

S

Richard Serra, *Tilted Arc*, 1981. Installed Federal Plaza, New York; destroyed by the US government, 15 March 1989. Photograph © Fred W. McDarrah.

people when they were moved. As an example of art with an aggressive presence, the curving wall of his mammoth *Tilted Arc* (1981) bisected a public plaza in lower Manhattan. As the steel began to rust, assuming a color associated with decay, it became an affront to the people working there (and, incidentally, a blackboard for graffiti). People employed in the vicinity of the sculpture agitated for its removal and, after controversial hearings, in 1989 succeeded, illustrating the possibility of a distinguished artist making public sculpture that the public, alas, finds unacceptable.

Sculptures: *Verb List*, 1967; *Splash Piece*, 1968; *Casting*, 1969; *Tilted Arc*, 1981.

Exhibition Catalog: *Richard Serrra*. Pasadena, CA: Pasadena Art Museum, 1970; Krauss, Rosalind E. *Richard Serra Sculpture*. New York: MOMA, 1986; *Torqued Ellipses*. New York: Dia Center for the Arts, 1997; *Richard Serra Sculpture 1985–1998*. Los Angeles: Museum of Contemporary Art, 1998; *Richard Serra: Drawings 1969–1990 Catalogue raisonné*. Ed. Hans Jannsen. Berne, Switzerland: Benteli, 1990.

Web Site: http://home.sprynet.com/~mindweb/richard.htm (Photos of works.)

Interpretation: Guse, Ernst-Gerhard, ed. *Richard Serra*. New York: Rizzoli, 1987; Jordan, Sherrill, ed. *Public Art, Public Controversy*. New York: Americans for the Arts, 1988; Weyergraf-Serra, Clara, and Martha Buskirk, eds. *The Destruction of Tilted Arc Documents*. Cambridge: MIT Press, 1991.

SERRANO, Andres

(15 August 1950).

Serrano gained fame thanks to a cabal of conservative critics—including Senator Jesse Helms—who attacked his photograph "Piss Christ" when it was exhibited at a museum that received federal funding from the NATIONAL ENDOWMENT FOR THE ARTS. The photograph showed a store-bought Jesus-on-a-crucifix that was placed in a glass container filled with urine (some claimed the artist's own—as if this made a difference), and then photographed. The murky, rich amber color of this Jesus-under-hued-water, while certainly blasphemous, was also luminous and in a way mysterious—the way any good image of a savior should be. Besides his religiously objectionable images, Serrano has also photographed bodies in the morgue and other usually taboo subjects. Ironically, Serrano's images—often overlaid with human blood, urine, or other bodily fluids—are actually quite beautiful, featuring breathtaking colors. No reproduction of the photos does justice to them—you must see them, in their large-scale glory (these are not little 8x10s; they stretch over several feet), to really take them in. The shocking subject matter draws the crowds, but it is the craftsmanship of the images—and the fact that the surface beauty Serrano discovers in the most "ugly" or taboo elements—is what really makes his work interesting—at least to me.

—Richard Carlin

Exhibit Catalog: *Andres Serrano*. Ljubljana: Moderna galerija Ljubljana, 1994; *Andres Serrano, Works 1983–1993*. Philadelphia: Institute of Contemporary Art, University of Pennsylvania, 1994.

Photo Book: *Body and Soul*. New York: Takarajima Books, 1995.

Web Site: http://www.photology.com/serrano/ (Selected photographs)

SESSIONS, Roger

(28 December 1896–16 March 1985).

A brainy American composer who entered Harvard at fourteen, he later studied with Horatio Parker (who also taught CHARLES IVES) at Yale before beginning a teaching career at Smith College (1917–21) and the Cleveland Institute of Music (1921–25). Moving to Europe for several years, Sessions composed works reflecting the influence of IGOR STRAVINSKY and Ernst Bloch (1880–1959), a Swiss composer whom Sessions had assisted in Cleveland. Mostly in absentia, he collaborated in 1928–31 with Aaron Copland, likewise Brooklyn-born, in sponsoring in New York what came to be known as the Copland-Sessions concerts, which were very influential at the time. (Curiously, the two men were born on the same Brooklyn thoroughfare only four years apart—Sessions at 417 Washington Avenue and Copland at 630).

Frightened by Hitler's rise, which he saw firsthand, he returned home in 1933, teaching successively at Boston University, Princeton, the University of California at Berkeley, and then Princeton again. Retiring from there in 1965, Sessions then taught for nearly two decades more at Juilliard. He was among the first major American composers to realize that he could do his own work while teaching not at a "conservatory" but at a liberal arts university. (Among his contemporaries, Virgil Thomson, George Gershwin, Elliott Carter, and Aaron Copland all avoided teaching positions, while Howard Hanson and William Schuman ran music conservatories.)

A subsidiary benefit of teaching composition at an Ivy League university with a serious music program was teaching many bright and ambitious students who would later have their own careers. Retiring from Princeton in 1965, he later taught at Juilliard, whose graduate programs have always produced professionals. More than a decade after his death, Sessions is frequently cited in younger composers' biographies, where teachers are customarily acknowledged (as in dance, but not in painting). Among those featured in this book Sessions is acknowledged by CONLON NANCARROW, MILTON BABBITT, JAMES K. RANDALL, and ERIC SALZMAN. In Kyle Gann's incomparably populous survey of contemporary American composers, *American Music in the Twentieth Century* (1997), for instance, Sessions is mentioned for teaching David del Tredici (1937), Frederic Rzewski (1938), John Harbison (1938), Ellen Taafe Zwilich (1939), Daniel Lentz (1941), and Tod Machover (1953), most of whom produced music distinctly different from Sessions's own. Because few, if any, American arts professors, in any art, had so many distinguished students, Sessions became the model for younger composer/professors, though, if only because other universities are imitating Princeton's example in the 1950s and 1960s, it is doubtful that any contemporaries will have have as many pupils who subsequently became prominent.

Perhaps because so much of Sessions's time was spent teaching, the catalog of his works emphasizes substantial works, with remarkably few minor and occasional pieces. One theme of his music and musical career was increasing density, as Sessions progressed from works reflecting the influence of Igor Stravinsky in the 1920s to 12-tone compositions in the 1950s. His three piano sonatas (1930, 1946, 1965) exemplify this development, as the third is characterized justly as the "*Hammerklavier* of the twentieth century—half as long, with twice as many notes." Perhaps because he was fortunate enough to receive commissions to the end of his life, Sessions was especially productive in his seventies, when in John Harbison's phrase, "contrasts [in his music became] more sudden, transitions more swift, sections less balanced, and motivic connections less literal."

Compositions: *Lancelot and Elaine*, 1910; Piano Trio, 1916; 3 Violin Sonatas, 1916; Symphony in D major, 1917; *Nocturne*, 1921–23; *3 Chorale Preludes*, 1924–26; 9 Symphonies, 1926–27, 1944–46, 1957, 1958, 1964, 1966, 1967, 1968, 1975–78; *Pastorale*, for flute, 1927; *On the Beach at Fontana*, for soprano and piano, 1930; *3 Dirges*, 1933; Violin Concerto, 1930–35; *From My Diary*, 1937–39; *Chorale*, 1938; *Turn, O Libertad*, for chorus and piano, 4-hands or two pianos, 1944; *The Trial of Lucullus*, opera to a text by Bertolt Brecht, 1947; *Montezuma*, to a text by G. A. Borgese, 1941–63; *When Lilacs Last in the Dooryard Bloom'd*, to a Walt Whitman text, 1964–70; *Idyll for Theocritus*, for soprano and orchestra, 1953–54; *Mass*, for Unison Chorus, 1955; *Divertimiento*, 1959–60;

String Quintet, 1957–58; Concerto for Violin, Cello, and Orchestra, 1970–71; *Canons (to the Memory of Igor Stravinsky)*, for string quartet, 1971; *3 Choruses on Biblical Texts*, for chorus and orchestra, 1971–72; *5 Pieces*, 1975; *Concerto for Orchestra*, 1979–81.

Recordings: *Complete Piano Music*. Barry David Salwen, piano. New York: Koch, 1992; *Pianos Sonatas Nos. 1–3, from My Diary*. Robert Helps, piano. New York: CRI, 1998; Symphonies No. 6, 7, 9. Cond. Dennis Russell Davies. London: Argo, 1995; Quartet No. 1 in E (1938) & Quartet for Strings (1958), Six Pieces for Cello (1966). Perf. Group for Contemporary Music. New York: Koch; *Symphonies Nos. 1, 2, & 3*. Japan Philharmonic, cond. A. Watanbe. New York: CRI, 1993; *Symphonies Nos. 4 & 5*. Cond. Christian Badea. New York: New World; *When Lilacs Last in the Dooryard Bloom'd*. Boston Symphony Orchestra, cond. S. Ozawa. New York: New World, 1992.

Books: *The Musical Experience* (1950). New York: Atheneum, 1962; *Questions About Music*. Cambridge: Harvard University Press, 1970; *Roger Sessions on Music: The Collected Essays*. Ed. Edward T. Cone. Princeton: Princeton University Press, 1979; *Conversations with Roger Sessions*. Ed. Andrea Olmstead. Boston: Northeastern University Press, 1987; *Correspondence of Roger Sessions*. Ed. Andrea Olmstead. Boston: Northeastern University Press, 1992.

Web Site: http://www.netaxs.com/people/presser/sessions.html

Interpretation: Gann, Kyle. *American Music in the 20th Century*. New York: Schirmer, 1997; Harbison, John. "Roger Sessions." In *The New Grove Twentieth-Century American Masters*. New York: Norton, 1986; Olmstead, Andrea. *Roger Sessions and His Music*. Ann Arbor, MI: UMI Research, 1985; Slonimsky, Nicolas. "Roger Sessions." In Henry Cowell, ed. *American Composers on American Music: A Symposium* (1933). New York: Ungar, 1962.

SEUPHOR, Michel

(10 March 1901; b. Fernand-Louis Berckelaers).

Born in Antwerp of Flemish parents, Seuphor published in Belgium from 1921 to 1925 the journal *Het Overzicht*, which featured both art and writing. Moving to Paris, he took a French name that scrambles the letters in Orpheus and founded a group, that included PIET MONDRIAN, and published a magazine, *Cercle et carré*. In April 1930, he coorganized with JOAQUIN TORRES-GARCIA the first international exhibition of modernist ABSTRACT ART. Seuphor wrote *L'Art abstrait—ses origines, ses premiers maitres* (1949), which became a standard guide to Abstract Art in the French-speaking world, as well as *Dictionnaire de la Peinture Abstraite* (1957), which contains his "History of Abstract Painting." It is not surprising that in 1956 he wrote a major monograph on Mondrian, who influenced Seuphor's paintings and graphic art, which have been exhibited widely in Europe. Having also published experimental poetry, Seuphor could also be a brilliant aphorist, especially about esthetic issues: "As for myself, I confess to a preference for clear-cut situations," he once wrote, "for radical, and even extreme positions."

Writings: *Abstract Painting: Fifty Years of Accomplishment from Kandinsky to Jackson Pollock* (1949). New York: Abrams, 1964; *Piet Mondrian*. New York: Abrams, 1956; *Dictionary of Abstract Painting*. Trans. Lionel Izod, et al. New York: Paris Book Center, 1957; *The Sculpture of this Century*, Trans. Haakov Chevalier. New York: Braziller, 1960.

Exhibition Catalogs: *Poésie-Plastique*. Lodz, Poland: Muzeum Sztuki, 1967; *Cercle & Carré: Thought for the 1930s*. New York: Rachel Adler Gallery, 1990.

SHAPIRO, Joel

(27 September 1941).

Shapiro's early sculptures, created during the 1970s, stand in contrast to Minimalist works and their emphasis on self-reference: the presentation of a physical object whose presence is unmitigated by associations to other objects. Shapiro modeled small, rudimentary geometric forms that vaguely resembled houses, chairs, coffins, and bridges, demonstrating that any object, no matter how simple,

S

bears a resemblance to some familiar shape. Their miniature size (most were under a foot tall) made them seem objects of thought, almost Platonic ideals, the essential forms upon which the elements of the world are patterned. In the late 1970s, Shapiro's work changed to the style for which he is best known. He began arranging wood beams into assemblies that resemble the human figure in a wide variety of gestures and movements: running, sitting, dancing, crouching in despair, and stretching with exuberance. Initially as small as his earlier forms, these works seemed more like schematics of motion and gesture than like renderings of the human form; Shapiro soon started casting them in bronze and, in the 1990s, enlarged them to a scale larger than life. The use of simple rectangular beams echoed Minimalism, only here the association was not with familiar objects, but with the body. Although these sculptures seem at first like little more than stick figures, on a large scale they convey a sense of action, having been granted the precision of mathematics, as if one were seeing the Platonic ideals of human attitude and poise.

—Mark Daniel Cohen

Works: Note: All mature works of Joel Shapiro are untitled.

Exhibition Catalogs: Krauss, Rosalind E. *Joel Shapiro*. Chicago: Museum of Contemporary Art, 1976; Smith, Roberta. *Joel Shapiro, Sculpture and Drawing*. London: Trustees of the Whitechapel Art Gallery, 1980; Jordy, William H. *Joel Shapiro*. Providence, RI: Bell Gallery, List Art Center, Brown University, 1980; Smith, Roberta. *Joel Shapiro, Sculpture and Drawing*. London: Whitechapel Art Gallery, 1980; Ormond, Mark. *Joel Shapiro: Sculpture and Drawings 1981–85*. Sarasota, FL: Ringling Museum of Art, 1986; Leveton, Debora, and Donald B. Kuspit, *Joel Shapiro: Tracing the Figure*. Des Moines, IA: Des Moines Art Center, 1990; Reynolds, Jock. *Joel Shapiro: Sculpture in Clay, Plaster, Wood, Iron, and Bronze, 1971–1997*. Andover, MA: Addison Gallery of American Art, 1998; Kertess, Klaus. *Joel Shapiro: New Wood and Bronze Sculpture*. New York: PaceWildenstein, 1998.

Interpretations: Teicher, Hendel, and Brenson, Michael. *Joel Shapiro: Sculpture and Drawings*. New York: Abrams, 1998.

SHERMAN, Cindy

(19 January 1954).

In Sherman's distinctive self-portraits, she is dressed and made up to portray hundreds of different women and occasionally men, but never herself. Sherman says her art deals with female stereotypes, and they are portraits not of how she sees herself but of how she sees men seeing women. Born in Glen Ridge, New Jersey, she studied at the State University of New York at Buffalo (BA, 1976). As a teenager she began to wear makeup to look more glamorous and found that she could turn herself into a different person by changing her appearance. In college she started making photo narratives starring herself. Sherman moved to New York in 1977, when she was awarded a National Endowment for the Arts grant. Early recognition came in the late 1970s with a series of black-and-white photographs called "Untitled Film Stills," showing Sherman as a B-movie actress in various poses. She continued pursuing her art and earned her living at the Artists Space gallery. When the Metro Pictures Gallery opened in 1980, Sherman had one of the first shows, of her early color photos. It was the beginning of her success, and today Sherman is one of the highest-earning female artists. Over the years her repertoire of images has included movie stars, centerfold nudes, fairytale characters, victims of disasters, and historical figures. Some of Sherman's portraits have produced comic or grotesque effects with plastic body parts, dolls, and her own made-up body. Her work has been exhibited worldwide in numerous group and one-person shows, at such venues as the Los Angeles Museum of Contemporary Art, the Museum of Modern Art in New York, and the Pompidou Center in Paris. Among the collections holding her work are those of the Metropolitan and Brooklyn museums in New York and the

Tate Gallery in London. A selection of her photographs, Cindy Sherman Retrospective (1997), was published in conjunction with a major traveling exhibit.

—Gloria S. and Fred W. McDarrah

Collections of Photographs: *Cindy Sherman, 1975–1995*. New York: Rizzoli, 1993; *Fitcher's Bird*. New York: Rizzoli, 1992*; History Portraits*. New York: Rizzoli, 1991; *Untitled Film Stills*. New York: Rizzoli, 1990; *Cindy Sherman*. New York: Pantheon, 1984.

Exhibition Catalogs: *Cindy Sherman*. London: Thames & Hudson; Chicago: Museum of Contemporary Art; Los Angeles: Museum of Contemporary Art, 1997; *CS*. Rotterdam: Museum Boijmans Van Beuningen, 1996; *Becher, Mapplethorpe, Sherman*. Monterrey, N.L.: Museo de Monterrey, 1992; *CS*. New York: Whitney Museum of American Art, 1987; *CS*. Munster, Germany: Der Kunstverein, 1985; *CS*. Saint-Etienne, France: Le Musée, 1983.

SHERMAN, Stuart

(9 November 1945).

In the mid-1970s, Sherman developed a sort of chamber Theater, or miniature Theater, which he called *Spectacles*, in which, working solo, he presents for only a few minutes, through mime and the manipulation of objects, his responses to specific subjects, such as people or places he has known. A typical Sherman evening thus consists of several sketches in sequence. As such theater can be set up quickly, Sherman has worked in a variety of nonstandard venues, including street corners and public plazas, on all the continents. Especially in mixing props not normally seen together (e.g., taking a telephone receiver from a flower pot, unscrewing the receiver's cap to release rose petals, etc.), his works reflect COLLAGE. Sherman has also made films and created extraordinary visual fictions that I have seen, even though they have not yet been published. In 1992, he founded *The Quotidian Review*, a "monthly magazine" to be wholly devoted to "new and recent artwork (verbal and visual) and articles by Stuart Sherman." Such a personal periodical is not something every artist can expect to produce monthly.

Plays: *Spectacles*, 1975–1990; *Hamlet*, 1981; *Faust*, 1982; *Oedipus*, 1984; *The Second Trilogy: Chekov, Strindberg, Brecht*. 1985–86; *The Man in Room 2538*, 1986; *It is Against the Law to Shout "Fire!" in a Crowded Theater*, 1986; *Endless Meadow and So Forth*, 1986; *This House is Mine Because I Live in It*, 1986; *Slant*, 1987; *Crime and Punishment, or the Book and the Word*, 1987; *An Evening of One-Act Plays*, 1987; *"A" is for "Actor,"* 1987; *One Acts and Two Trilogies*, 1987; *The Yellow Chair,*, 1987; *But What is the Word for "Bicycle"?*, 1988; *The Play of Tea, or Pinkies Up!*, 1989; *Objects of Desire*, 1989; *Knock, Knock, Knock, Knock*, 1989; *Taal Eulenspiegal*, 1990; *Solaris*, 1992.

Writings: Sherman, Stuart. *The Quotidian Review*. New York: Privately published (P.O. Box 209, Old Chelsea Station, New York, NY 10011), 1992–ongoing.

SIMPSON, N. F.

(29 January 1919; b. Norman Frederick S.).

Among the most original playwrights of his English-speaking generation, Simpson has released remarkably few works, beginning in 1957 with *A Resounding Tinkle*. The play opens with Mr. and Mrs. Paradock purchasing for their suburban house an elephant that, since it is too large, they exchange for a snake, very much as suburbanites purchase and exchange new furniture. They invite to their home two comedians who learnedly discuss Henri Bergson's theory of laughter. The Paradocks seem unperturbed that their son has returned home as a woman. The author himself appears to apologize for the play, which he says came to him in Portuguese, which is alien to him, while I apologize for a summary that hardly equals the wild, fundamental absurdity of *Tinkle*.

In another Simpson play, *The Hole* (1957), literally about a hole in the street, a crowd gathers around a "visionary" whose specialty is double-talk: "I make a practice of eating far more than I need. And for that reason food is of no interest to me. I eat merely to put food out of my mind. I eat all the time so that I shall not be preoccupied with supplying my bodily needs so far as food is concerned. It leaves my mind free." As more people arrive, projecting their preoccupations upon the hole, their talk becomes a survey of suburban fantasies, beginning with sports, continuing through nature to crime and then political fantasies. All the metaphysical aura collapses when a laborer emerges to say the hole contains a junction box serving the electrical supply. This prompts incredible pseudo-philosophical discussion. After everyone else departs, the self-styled visionary is still waiting for a revelation.

One-Way Pendulum, subtitled *An Evening of High Drung and Slarrit*, portrays a family, the Groomkirbys, whose individuals are so self-preoccupied they barely make contact with one another. The climax of absurd events is their son's confession that he has murdered forty-three people simply because he enjoys mourning for them. In addition to satirizing the idealized family and the legal system, the play mocks conventional playwriting in its ridiculous twists and turns.

Plays: *One-Way Pendulum*. New York: Grove, 1961; *The Hole and Other Plays and Sketches*. (Includes *A Resounding Tinkle, The Form, Gladly Otherwise, Oh, One Blast and Have Done*.) London: Faber, 1964; *Some Tall Tinkles: Television Plays*. (Includes *We're Due in Eastborn in Ten Minutes, The Best I Can Do by Way of a Gate-Leg Table is a Hundredweight of Coal, At Least It's a Precaution Against Fire*.) London: Faber, 1968.

Bibliography: Esslin, Martin. *The Theatre of the Absurd* (1961). Rev. ed. Garden City, NY: Doubleday, 1969.

SITE

(1969).

The taken name of an architectural collaborative formed by the sometime sculptor James Wines (1932), who remains its principal contributor, SITE became noted in the early 1970s for spectacular contextual humor. In the parking lot of a Connecticut shopping center, they buried automobiles to various depths, their upper parts encased in cement that visually echoes their original shapes, creating the image of a car cemetery. For the front wall of a Houston discount showroom, they composed a wall with falling bricks, suggesting the striking image of a collapsing building. In another showroom, the corner wall cuts away from the building to provide an entranceway, only to close up at night. Not only are the architectural images different, they are strong, giving SITE's buildings a definition far more memorable than that offered not only by familiar post-BAUHAUS boxes but also radical alternatives to rigorous geometry.

Interpretation: Jencks, Charles. *Bizarre Architectures*. New York: Rizzoli, 1978; Wines, James. "De-Architecturization." In *Esthetics Contemporary* (1978), ed. Richard Kostelanetz. 2d ed. Buffalo, New York: Prometheus, 1989; *De-Architecture*. New York: Rizzoli, 1987.

Exhibition Catalogs: *The Ghost Parking Lot Project by SITE*. Rye, NY: National Shopping Centers, 1978; *SITE: Architecture as Art*. Texts Pierre Restany, Bruno Zevi, & SITE. London: Academy, 1980.

SITE-SPECIFIC ART

See **INSTALLATION**.

SITUATIONIST INTERNATIONAL

See **LETTRISM**.

SKLANDOWSKY, Max

(30 April 1863–1939).

The son of a magic lantern showman, he worked in collaboration with his brother Emil (1859–1945) in constructing a double projection machine that was patented in 1895 under the name of "Bioskop." (It had two sets of film strips, each running at a speed of eight frames per second, which is to say that it projected a series of picture sequences but not continuous imagery.) Some historians credit Sklandowsky with the first public presentation of moving pictures in Germany at the Berlin Wintergarten on 1 November 1895, six weeks ahead of the Lumière brothers' first public screening (though defenders of the Frenchmen respond that they had private presentions for nonpaying audiences before 1 November). According to the *Encyclopedia of European Cinema* (1995), "Apart from this opening programme, which consisted of nine short sketches, Skladanowsky put together a second series of Berlin city views for touring through Germany in 1896–97 (*Berlin Alexanderplatz*)." However, since other projection systems were more successful, Sklandowsky retired the Bioskop and later had some modest success with the retrograde format of photograph flip books.

Books: Vincendeau, Ginette, ed. *Encyclopedia of European Cinema*. London: Cassell/British Film Institute, 1995.

S

SLONIMSKY, Nicolas

(27 April 1894–25 December 1995).

More famous as a pioneering conductor of American avant-garde music (whose 1931 premieres included EDGARD VARÈSE'S *Ionisation* and CHARLES IVES'S *Three Places in New England*) and as the most prodigious musical lexicographer—not only the author of such celebrated, stylish reference books as *Music Since 1900* (1938; 5th ed., 1993) and *Lectionary of Music* (1989), but from 1958 to his death the sole editor of *Baker's Biographical Dictionary of Musicians* (8th ed., 1992)—Slonimsky was also a composer of works that are innovative and yet modest in ways that his books are not. His compositions are short, none being more than seven minutes in length, and are all scored for limited instrumentation (for, not unlike other avant-garde composers, he tends to write for himself and his immediate friends). They fall into three groups: songs, piano miniatures, and others. *Five Advertising Songs* (1924) is a suite composed to jingles that a recent immigrant found in the slick magazines of the time. The opening phrases become their subtitles: "Make this a day of Pepsodent!"; "And then her doctor told her. . ."; "Snowy-white"; "No more shiny nose!"; and "Children cry for Castoria! " The wit comes from setting distinctly American words to post-Rimsky-Korsakov harmonies that make such doggerel sound even more ridiculous. To my mind, these songs resemble DADA, especially in putting together conventional elements not normally found together, and by that technique deflating all sides.

For "Bach Dislocated," the music of J. S. Bach's C-minor Fugue starts in the correct key, only to shift down a semitone, and then continues similar shifting for the remainder of the piece. For "Czerny, Schmerny," exercises from the most famous piano pedagogue of Beethoven's time are played with one hand, while the other hand pounds chords in a deviant key. Other instrumental pieces begin with a radical structural premise. For "Studies in Black and White" (1928), Slonimsky posited a complex experiment in mutually exclusive counterpoint. Essentially, the right hand plays the white keys one note at a time in consonant intervals, and the left hand plays only on the black keys. Though pieces with two hands playing in different keys should sound dissonant, the structure of alternate monodies permits the illusion of aural consonance. Just as *Five Advertising Songs* resembles Dada, "Studies" extends into music the esthetics of another European visual art development——CONSTRUCTIVISM, which de-emphasized emotion and representation in favor of both pure abstraction and the fairly rigorous deployment of structural ideas.

In the meantime, Slonimsky developed a theoretical interest in musical scales other than major, minor, or chromatic. More than two thousand of them were published as a book, *Thesaurus of Scales and Melodic Patterns* (1947), which is a collection of "every possible succession of notes arranged by intervals as counted in semitones." In his preface to this book, he compares his collection to language "phrase books and dictionaries of idiomatic expressions. But while phrase books are limited to locutions consecrated to usage, this *Thesaurus* includes a great number of melodically plausible patterns that are new," which is to say hypothetical structures. My own opinion is that such a gathering represents Slonimsky's most extraordinary conceptual composition—a "big piece" for scales (or materials for extended composition) that epitomize his systematic intelligence and radical musical interests. It is not surprising that this *Thesaurus* is his most perfect book, the only one that has never been revised in fifty years, notwithstanding numerous reprintings.

Selected Compositions: *Five Advertising Songs*, 1924; *Studies in Black and White*, 1928; *My Toy Balloon*, 1942; *Gravestones*, 1945; *Minitudes*, 50 quaquaversal piano pieces, 1971–77.

Writings: *Music in Latin America* (1945). New York: Da Capo, 1972; *The Road to Music* (1947). New York: Da Capo, 1979; *Thesaurus of Scales and Melodic Patterns* (1947). New York: Schirmer Books, 1975; *Music since 1900* (1937). 5th ed. New York: Schirmer Books, 1994; *Perfect Pitch*. New York: Oxford University Press, 1988; *Slonimsky's Book of Musical Anecdotes* (1948). New York: Schirmer Books, 1997; as ed. *International Cyclopedia of Music and Musicians*, 4th to 8th editions, 1946–58; as ed. *Bakers Biographical Dictionary of Musicians,* 5th through 8th editions. New York: Schirmer Books, 1958, 1978, 1984, 1992.

Anthologies: *Nicolas Slonimsky: The First 100 Years*. Ed. Richard Kostelanetz. New York: Schirmer Books, 1994.

Web Site: http://www.otherminds.org/Slonimsky.html

Interpretation: Kostelanetz, Richard. *More On Innovative Music(ian)s*. Berkeley, CA: Fallen Leaf, 2000.

SMALL PRESS

(c. 1970).

This has become the accepted term for modestly financed book publishers that issue the sorts of titles that commercial publishers will not publish. Customarily printing less than 100 copies of any title (in contrast to the commercial publishers' minimum of 10,000), they tend to base their editorial selections not upon financial prospects but love, which may be literary love, political love, esthetic love, personal love, or even self-love. Thus, compared to commercial publishers, Small Presses have been particularly open to those who are generally excluded—political or sexual radicals, avant-garde writers, black writers, or religious writers, to name a few. In contrast to "general publishers," Small Presses tend to specialize in one kind of book. Many Small Presses are one-person operations wherein the "publisher" functions as editor, designer, secretary, and delivery person, if not the printer as well. As loans for this kind of venture are not easy to come by, most alternative publishers are self-financed, their founders scarcely compensating themselves for their working time. Too many are excessively dependent upon a single individual's health and energy. Only a scant few, unlike little magazines, are currently subsidized by universities or other cultural institutions. As I wrote a quarter-century ago, "The best of them print serious writing that would otherwise be lost."

Sources: Kostelanetz, Richard. "Alternative Book Publishers." In *The End of Intelligent Writing*. New York: Sheed & Ward, 1974; Swallow, Alan. *An Editor's Essays of Two Decades*. Seattle, WA, and Denver, CO: Experiment, 1962.

Web Site: www.smallpress.org (Association of small presses.)

SMITH, David

(9 March 1906–23 May 1965).

On the one hand drawing upon his training as a painter who had assimilated CUBIST lessons of diverse planes and

David Smith. *Voltri XIX*, 1962. Welded Metal. CORBIS/Burstein Collection. © Estate of David Smith/Licensed by VAGA, New York, NY.

ABSTRACT imagery and, on the other, upon his experience on the assembly line of an automobile plant, Smith produced sculpture that measured its distance from the past by rejecting the traditions of modeling (carving the semblance of an extrinsic image out of a block of material) and representational space and proportion. The innovative equal of ALEXANDER CALDER, Smith assembled sculpture (which was generally welded) from contemporary industrial materials that were displayed for their own properties and identities—steel looked like steel, etc. As early as the middle 1930s, he established artistic signatures that he sustained for the remainder of his career: first, skeletal images in iron that he forged himself and, then, large metal abstractions with faintly representational semblances, such as *Hudson River Landscape* (1951). So inappropriate as a setting for his tall pieces was the enclosed space of traditional galleries that Smith himself would "house" his largest works on his own front lawn, exposed to the elements; and museums would tend to display them in their gardens. He spoke frequently of his disdain for architects and the limits their buildings imposed upon sculptors. By the 1950s, Smith had progressed beyond the Cubistic form of overlapping planes into favoring a flat and spineless sculptural field, usually circular in overall shape, populated with sparsely constructed images. This lifetime consistency distinguished him from other major artists of his generation, most of whom were metaphorically reborn into their most successful styles.

Selected Sculptures: *Agricola Head*, 1933; *Head*, 1938; *Interior for Exterior*, 1939; *Spectre Riding the Golden Ass*, 1945; *Hudson River Landscape*, 1951; *Tanktotem II* (sounding), 1952; *Lectern Sentinel,*, 1961; *Circles I, II, III*, 1962.

Anthology: Gray, Cleve, ed. *David Smith by David Smith*. New York: Holt, 1968.

Exhibition Catalogs: Greenberg, David. *David Smith's New Sculpture*. Philadelphia: Institute of Contemporary Art, University of Pennsylvania, 1964; *David Smith*. Los Angeles: County Museum of Art, 1965; *David Smith*. London: Tate Gallery, 1966; Cone, Jane Harrison. *David Smith: A Retrospective Exhibition*. Cambridge, MA: Fogg Art Museum, 1966; Fry, Edward. *David Smith*. New York: Guggenheim Museum, 1969; *Painted Steel: the Late Work of David Smith*. Text William Rubin. New York: Gagosian Gallery, 1998; *David Smith: Photographs 1931–65*. New York: Matthew Marks Gallery, 1998.

Interpretation: McCoy, Garnett, ed. *David Smith*. New York: Praeger, 1973. Krauss, Rosalind E. *The Terminal Iron Works of David Smith*. Cambridge: MIT Press, 1971; *David Smith: A Catalogue Raisonné of the Sculpture*. New York: Garland, 1977; Witkin, Karen. *David Smith*. New York: Abbeville, 1984.

SMITH, HARRY

(29 May 1923–11 November 1991; b. H. Everett S.).
A minor independent filmmaker, sometime street person, friend-of-ALLEN-GINSBERG and DOWNTOWN New York personality, Harry Smith's most lasting creation was the *Anthology of American Folk Music*, a six-LP set, first issued in 1952. When the major record labels were busily throwing away thousands of old 78s, Smith—and a few others—were happily buying up the discarded discs, creating personal archives of previously ignored musical genres, including Southern Appalachian music and blues recordings. Smith envisioned a community of songsters, and grouped his selections topically in three 2 LP sets (Ballads; Social Music; Songs), regardless of the race of the original performers. This "invisible republic" (as critic Greil Marcus calls it) was Smith's unique vision; that across ethnic and class lines, American music makers had created a virtual community, where songs and musical styles were freely shared, to create a new musical form. Smith annotated each of his selections, using newspaper headline style in a humorous fashion to describe the contents of each song. The most famous example is his description of the traditional playparty song, "King Kong Kitchie" (better known as "Froggie Went A-Courtin'"), in which a frog successfully woos a mouse to be his bride. As Smith paraphrased the story: "Zoologic miscegeny achieved in Mouse Frog nuptials, Relatives approve."

Smith took his collection to Moses Asch, owner of a tiny alternative music label, Folkways Records. Asch viewed the copyright laws as mere annoyances, figuring that record companies had no right to keep the "people's music" away from the people. So, he happily issued Smith's collection, and even won a lawsuit against the major labels—establishing the LP-reissue industry. Many of the artists Smith featured on his set—including DOCK BOGGS, Mississippi John Hurt, and The Carolina Tar Heels—were subsequently tracked down and "rediscovered" during the folk revival of the '50s and '60s. Smith won a Grammy late in life for his pioneering work, and made a famously semi-coherent acceptance speech . (Years of living on the margins of New York life—plus heavy alcohol and drug use—gave him the shaggy-haired aura of a Bowery denizen.) Besides his interest in traditional music, Smith also studied the Indians of the Northwest, recording an entire Peyote ritual, and also was said to have amassed the world's largest private paper airplane collection (now part of the Smithsonian Air and Space Museum). He was also "employed" as a "Shaman-in-Residence" at Ginsberg's Naropa Institute in the late '80s.

In 1997, the original *Anthology* was reissued with much fanfare by Smithsonian-Folkways (now the holders of the "Folkways archive"), and Smith's name was celebrated anew. The enhanced CD included some of Smith's famously out-of-focus, double-exposed "avant-garde" films.

—Richard Carlin

The Record: *The Anthology of American Folk Music* (1952). Washington, DC: Smithsonian Folkways 40090, 1997.

Interviews: Singh, Rami, ed. *Think of the Self Speaking: Harry Smith, Selected Interviews*. Seattle, WA: Elbow/Cityful Press (POB 4477, 98104–0477).

Website: www.harrysmitharchives.com

Interpretation: Marcus, Greil. *Invisible Republic Bob Dylan and the Basement Tapes*. New York: Holt, 1996; Cantwell, Robert. *When We Were Good: The Folk Revival*. Cambridge: Harvard University Press, 1996.

S

SMITH, Jack

(14 November 1932–16 September 1989).

A film so shocking in its content that it was legally proscribed soon after its birth, Smith's *Flaming Creatures* (1963) has become the mythic avant-garde American film, known by all film students who think themselves sophisticated, in part because of its portrayal of the aftermath of a polymorphous orgy with a few females and several males, some of whom are dressed as women. Yet precisely because of its stylistic character, with sharp visual contrasts (such as quick shifts between close-ups and long-range shots), dizzying spins of a hand-held camera, and passages of overexposed footage, the effect is finally less pornographic than hallucinatory to an extraordinary degree. This impression depends as well upon a soundtrack full of harsh juxtapositions, ranging from non-sequitur Chinese music to a mixture of rock music with church bells. Smith also had a truly underground reputation for theatrical performances that depended upon his own strong presence for their success. Ephemeral at their beginnings, witnessed only by a few, some of them are described by Stefan Brecht. The New York alternative space PS 1 reopened in 1997, after years closed for renovation, with a mammoth Smith retrospective.

Films: *Buzzards over Bagdad*, 1951; *Scotch Tape*, 1963; *Normal Love*, 1963; *The Yellow Sequence*, 1963; *Flaming Creatures*, 1963; *No President*, 1967.

Exhibition Catalog: *Flaming Creative Jack Smith: His Amazing Life and Times*. Ed. Edward Leffingwell, et al. New York: The Institute for Contemporary Art, P.S. 1-Serpent's Tail, 1997.

Interpretation: Brecht, Stefan. *Queer Theatre*. Munich, Germany: Suhrkamp, 1978; Marranca, Bonnie, and Gautam Dasgupta, eds. *Theatre of the Ridiculous*. Baltimore: Johns Hopkins University Press, 1999.

SMITH, Tony

(23 September 1912–26 December 1980).

After apprenticing himself to FRANK LLOYD WRIGHT and practicing architecture for twenty years, this Smith emerged in the 1960s as an extremely MINIMAL sculptor, making large cubes, as tall as a man is tall, sometimes in steel, usually in wood, which were sometimes painted black to give them the illusion of density and weight. Some sculptures were composed of modular cubes that could be tastefully distributed, much as rocks in Japanese gardens. Smith's rise in status from a friend of artists to an influential sculptor was meteoric; he was even featured on the cover of *Time* magazine. As a teacher, he could devote a sculpture course to the close reading of *FINNEGANS WAKE*.

Sculptures: *Gracehoper*, 1961–72; *Cigarette*, 1961–68; *Black Box*, 1962; *The Snake is Out*, 1962; *Smoke*, 1967; *Smug*, 1973.

Exhibition Catalogs: *Tony Smith: Two Exhibitions of Sculpture*. Hartford, CT: Wadsworth Atheneum, 1966; *Tony Smith: Recent Sculpture*. New York: Knoedler, 1961; *Tony Smith: Painting and Sculpture*. College Park: University of Maryland Art Gallery, 1974; *Tony Smith Selected Sculptures 1961–1973*. New York: Xavier Fourcade, 1985; *Tony Smith: A Drawing Retrospective*. Eds. Klaus Kertress and Joan Pachner. New York: Matthew Marks Gallery, 1995; Storr, Robert. *Tony Smith: Architect, Painter, Sculptor*. New York: MoMA, 1998.

Interpretation: Lippard, Lucy R. *Tony Smith*. London: Thames & Hudson, 1971.

Tony Smith, *Smug*. Installation in St. James Rotary, NY, October 1988–October 1989. Photograph © Fred W. McDarrah.

SMITHSON, Robert

(2 January 1938–20 July 1973).

A brilliant theoretician at a time receptive to radical esthetic theories, Smithson gained considerable influence in his short life, mostly for advocating earth as a material valid for sculpture. Because many of Smithson's major sculptures no longer exist, perhaps the principal achievement of his career was making works that successfully survive in secondary literature, beginning with his own writings. To my mind, the paradigmatic Smithson masterpiece is "Incidents of Mirror Travel in the Yucatan" (1968), which tells in elaborate prose of him placing mirrors in a sequence of Mexican places. Even though the placements were temporary, the essay becomes so rich with insight and reference, with esthetic observations and stylistic flourishes, that a reader comes away believing that the activities may not have happened at all—that even the accompanying photographs (in color in the original periodical publication) may have been faked. The *Spiral Jetty*, the principal open-air project of Smithson's short life, now exists only in a film. Smithson's essay "A Tour of the Monuments of Passaic" is a classic of alternative American autobiography. Precisely because his writings reflect both advanced literature and advanced art, they come to epitomize what I have elsewhere called the literature of SoHo.

Writings: Holt, Nancy, ed. *The Writings of Robert Smithson*. New York: New York University Press, 1979. Expanded and revised as *The Collected Writings*. Ed. Jack Flam. Berkeley: University of California Press, 1996.

Exhibition Catalog: *Robert Smithson: Drawings*. New York: N.Y. Cultural Center, 1974; Sobieszek, Robert A.

Robert Smithson: Photo Works. Los Angeles: L.A. County Museum of Art/University of New Mexico, 1993.

Bibliography: Hobbs, Robert. *Robert Smithson: Sculpture*. Ithaca, NY: Cornell University Press, 1981; Kostelanetz, Richard, ed. *The Literature of SoHo*. New York: Shantih, 1983; Shapiro, Gary. *Earthwards: Robert Smithson and Art After Babel*. Berkeley: University of California Press, 1995; Tsai, Eugenie. *Robert Smithson Unearthed: Drawings, Collages, Writings*. New York: Columbia University Press, 1991.

S

SNELSON, Kenneth

(29 June 1927).

If some visual art students at BLACK MOUNTAIN COLLEGE took from Albers, and others learned from DE KOONING, Snelson followed yet another teacher who has passed through its western North Carolina campus, BUCKMINSTER FULLER, who gave him the concept of "tensegrity." Snelson's most familiar sculptures are polished aluminum tubes suspended in space by taut steel cables, so that if the viewer moves sufficiently far away, the cable disappears from the unaided eye, leaving the illusion of shiny objects suspended geometrically in space, in apparent defiance of gravity. (They are one of the few examples of sculpture designed to be seen from a distance, and thus represent a position contrary to that of CARL ANDRE and GEORGE RHOADS, among others, whose sculptures depend upon the principle of *revealing* gravity.) Also a photographer, Snelson has made highly detailed 360-degree photographs of cityscapes around the world: Paris, Venice, Rome, Siena, and Kyoto. More recently, he has been using a computer to make pictures of otherwise invisible atoms.

Works: *Sun River,* 1967; *Needle Tower*, 1968; *Easy-K II*, 1970–92; *Stereoscopic Atom Landscapes New Dimensions (Easy Landing)*, 1977; *Mozart I*, 1982; *I, II, III*, computer images, 1987.

Books: *Full Circle: Panoramas*. New York: Aperture, 1990.

Exhibition Catalogs: Fox, Howard N. *Kenneth Snelson*. Buffalo, NY: Fine Arts Academy, 1981; *Kenneth Snelson, The Nature of Structure*. New York: Academy of Sciences, 1989; *Kenneth Snelson Sculptures*. New York: Maxwell Davidson Gallery, 1994.

SNOW, Michael

(10 December 1929).

A pre-eminent Canadian POLYARTIST, Snow has produced major films, exhibited memorable paintings and sculpture, played JAZZ (with less distinction), and authored first-rank book-art. Though I admire individual works of his, I find it hard to discern what principles, other than cool cleverness, animate Snow's entire *oeuvre*. Of his films, I was especially awed by *Le Région Centrale* (1970–71) for which he mounted a camera on a supple revolving tripod in a barren but beautiful area of northern Quebec. As the camera spins around at various angles for three full hours, we witness the changing colors of a terribly barren and starkly beautiful landscape. *Wavelength* (1966–67) is a single, slow, forty-five minute long zoom shot down the length of Snow's loft.

For the new baseball stadium in Toronto, Snow made a collection of striking gargoyles. *Cover to Cover* (1975) is a two-front book, composed entirely of photographs that bleed to the edges of 360 pages, that can be read in either direction, also requiring the reader to flip the book over somewhere in the middle. Some find significance in his cutout paintings, done throughout the 1960s, collectively titled *Walking Woman* because they portray a striding female. Though honored as a Canadian genius (in a country very respectful of its geniuses), Snow has not had a comprehensive retrospective in his home country since 1970; and, though he lived for several years in New York, his work is rarely exhibited in the United States.

Paintings: *Walking Woman*, 1960s.

Films: *Wavelength*, 1966–67; *Le Région Centrale*, 1970–71.

Books: *Cover to Cover*. Halifax, Canada: Nova Scotia College of Art & Design, 1975; *The Collected Writings of Michael Snow*. Waterloo, Ont.: Wilfrid Laurier University, 1994.

Exhibition Catalogs: Fulford, Robert, et al. *Michael Snow/A Survey*. Toronto, Canada: Art Gallery of Ontario, 1970; *Michael Snow: Works 1969–1978, Films 1964–1976*. Luzern, Switzerland: Kunstmuseum, 1979; *Michael Snow: Selected Photographic Works*. Los Angeles: Frederick S. Wight Art Gallery, UCLA, 1983; *Presence and Absence: the Films of Michael Snow 1956–1991*. Ed Jim Shedden. Toronto: Art Gallery of Ontario, 1995.

SOHO

(c. 1967).

Called SoHo because it lies south of Houston Street in lower Manhattan, it became, especially in the 1970s, a center for avant-garde activities in American visual art, PERFORMANCE ART, music, MIXED-MEANS THEATER, CONCEPTUAL ART, and literature, much as MONTMARTRE was to Parisian art nearly a century before. Though previously an industrial slum with empty lofts, SoHo—bounded by West Broadway to the west, Broadway to the east, and Canal Street to the south—in the late 1960s attracted artists looking for working space in empty industrial spaces. At first they rented from landlords, later purchasing whole buildings that would then be divided among "co-op" owners, most of whom lived in their studios. Because this area was zoned for industrial activities, New York City required that artists who need a lot of space to do their work (e.g., painters, sculptors, musicians, dancers, playwrights, but *not* writers) obtain a city-certified "variance" to also reside there. Precisely because no one had resided there before and nonartists could not do so legally, SoHo became a one-industry town, so to speak, within a larger city, perhaps the first exclusive artists' enclave in the history of U.S. culture. The art galleries came in the 1970s, followed by the boutiques that exploited the neighborhood's growing reputation for advanced taste. By 1979 or so, the real estate prices suddenly escalated, forbidding entrance to newcomers unless they were considerably wealthier than the previous inhabitants. It is said that 25 percent of all the applicants for individual grants from the Visual Arts Program at the National Endowment for the Arts reside in zip codes 10012 (which is SoHo proper) and 10013 (the contiguous, architecturally similar neighborhood of Tribeca), both of which are considerably different from Greenwich Village to the north, the Lower East Side to the east, and the financial district to the south.

By the late 1990s, the galleries mostly moved to Chelsea, on Manhattan's lower West Side, which, as SoHo was three decades before, is an industrial slum undergoing renovation. In their wake, the spaces of SoHo get not pizza parlors, which can't afford the street-level rents, but yet more high-end retailers exploiting its reputation for advanced taste.

Bibliography: *Soho—Downtown Manhattan: Theater, Musik, Performance, Video, Film*. Ed. René Block. Berlin: Akademie der Kunste & Berliner Festwochen, 1976; Simpson, Charles R. *SoHo: The Artist in the City*. Chicago: University of Chicago Press, 1981.

SOLT, Mary Ellen

(8 July 1920).

Solt was, for a moment in the mid-1960s, the most impressive VISUAL POET in America, the author of a portfolio of prints, *Flowers in Concrete* (1966), whose images were widely reproduced at the time. Ostensibly poems about flowers, realized in collaboration with professional designers, they used large typeset letters and incorporated various visual devices to enhance their subjects, such as circles of letters within circles of letters for "Zinnia" and both letters for the flowers and Morse code symbols for the stems of "Forsythia." Solt also compiled the first compendious anthology of CONCRETE POETRY, with almost as many pages devoted to critical introductions, notes, and manifestos as poems. This initially appeared as a special issue of *Artes Hispanics/Hispanic Arts* (I/3–4, Winter–Spring 1968) and then as a book (1969). Once she became a professor of Polish Studies at the University of Indiana, her creative work dissipated.

Visual Poetry: *Flowers in Concrete*. Bloomington, IN: Privately published, 1966; *The Peoplemover 1968: A Demonstration Poem*. Reno, NV: West Coast Poetry Review, 1978.

Anthologies: ——, ed. *Concrete Poetry: A World View*. Bloomington: Indiana University Press, 1969.

SOMETHING ELSE PRESS

(1964–1974).

Though its efforts were taken too much for granted during its short lifetime, it is now clear that this SMALL PRESS was not only the most distinguished small publisher ever in America, it was the bookish equivalent of BLACK MOUNTAIN COLLEGE in the education of avant-garde intelligence. Quite simply, SEP issued, in well-produced editions, the more experimental works of GERTRUDE STEIN, which were not available before in the United States and have not been wholly available since; BOOK-ART books by CLAES OLDENBURG, EMMETT WILLIAMS, JOHN GIORNO, BERN PORTER, MERCE CUNNINGHAM, JACKSON MAC LOW, BRION GYSIN, EUGEN GOMRINGER, Ruth Krauss (1910), Geoff Hendricks (1931), and Daniel Spoerri (1930), among others, including its founder and principal editor, DICK HIGGINS; and anthologies of CONCRETE POETRY and radically alternative fiction. In its initial years, SEP also published major pamphlets, really among the best of their kind, by GEORGE BRECHT, DAVID ANTIN JOHN CAGE, and ALLAN KAPROW, among others. It would be disingenuous for me not to acknowledge SEP's impact on my own education. Perhaps the simplest measure of the void caused by SEP's demise is that most of what it did, even by individuals of the first rank, is no longer in print anywhere. PETER FRANK produced an annotated bibliography with an intelligence reflecting that of his subject.

Annotation: Frank, Peter. *Something Else Press*. N.p.: McPherson & Co., 1983.

SONDHEIM, Alan

(3 February 1943).

"A slmpla lp$f pf bra$d/ I survive by Windows into Your Late-Night Soul" is the way writer/teacher/videomaker/cyberspace-theorist Sondheim's "Tha Hermit" begins. Nothing earth-shakingly meta-Joycean about these words "pushed towards a kind of exploratory psychosis," as their author says he tries for in his poetry—except that (1) they are a result of continuously rewritten creative computer programming, and (2) they later go through all sorts of transformations that make "Tha Hermit" (and other, often ambitiously lengthy, similar pieces) far more theme-and-variation than anything Joyce did. Sondheim has been aesthetically active in computers since the sixties, in 1971 creating a piece called "Typed Glossolalia: Computer Analysis of Determinism in Man," which used punch-card entries done by Gregert Johnson. Seven years later his and Geralyn Donahue's *Texts* appeared with a sampling of his computer-generated work (done on a Terak minicomputer using both the TF59 calculator and UCSD Pascal programming languages, two of the six or more computer languages Sondheim has "modified, denied, and confused" texts with, as he puts it). In short, Sondheim is one of our pathfinders from the page onto the screen and beyond.

—Bob Grumman

Books: *The Case of the Real*. Elmwood, CT: Potes & Poets Press (181 Edgemont Ave., 06110), 1998; and Geralyn Donahue. *Texts*. Irvine: University of California Press, Irvine, 1978.

SONIC YOUTH

(1981).

Born against the dawn of the age of Ronald Reagan, Sonic Youth lived in New York City and created a sound that pushed rock music through the avant-garde wringer. Their sound was post-Beat, POST-WARHOL, post-PUNK ROCK, post-hardcore ("Black Flag growing their hair out"), post-No Wave. Their music was different because they were different; schooled in the aesthetics of pop music and art, Sonic Youth combined their punk education with an intense experimentation that changed everything from the instruments they played to the people who heard them. In the liner notes to the reissue of their first album, *Confusion Is Sex*, the critic Greil Marcus recalled: "In 1983, Sonic Youth was going to extremes most other bands didn't know existed; in a certain way, they were issuing a challenge to the rest of pop music. As things turned out, they pretty much had to answer it themselves." And these "extremes" continue.

In many ways, the story of Sonic Youth begins with a man who made JOHN CAGE shake in his boots. His name was GLENN BRANCA. After hearing a piece Branca composed for ten guitars, Cage remarked: "I found myself responding in ways that brought me back to my ego. My feelings were disturbed. . . . I found in myself the willingness to connect the music with evil—with power. I don't want such a power in my life." Such an invocation of frightening power was Branca's aim. Influenced by KRZYSZTOF PENDERECKI, OLIVIER MESSIAEN, and the rumor of war that had been New York punk, Branca came to Manhattan in 1976. He borrowed instruments and formed a band called Theoretical Girls, who almost immediately tied themselves into the SoHo art scene by "playing" before a performance piece by DAN GRAHAM. Theoretical Girls became the basis for the SoHo side of No Wave, the short lived ('78–'79) but intensely influential post-punk movement that combined the punk ethos with a vibrant and often disturbing energy. (BRIAN ENO is credited with killing the scene by attempting to capture it on the infamous compilation *No New York* [1978].) After No Wave dissolved, Branca began forming revolving "bands" or "guitar armies" with himself as composer and conductor. The guitars used were modified junk set to odd tunings.

It was this mix of art and rock, No Wave and performance art, punk and Cage, Branca and Graham that was the background for the emergence of Sonic Youth. Art school graduate Kim Gordon worked with Graham and met Branca through him. She played bass in Sonic Youth but, more importantly, she brought her interest in the avant-garde to the music. Lee Ranaldo played with Branca before bringing his guitar to Sonic Youth and Thurston Moore, the band's other guitarist, brought to the new music an extensive knowledge of the punk subculture. The band went through several drummers before Steve Shelley permanently kept the polyphonic beat: they came upon him in a hardcore band called the Crucifucks during the Dead Kennedys' Rock against Reagan tour in 1985.

Sonic Youth's first recordings were stunning affairs combining energy, inventiveness, an interest in dark Americana, and subtle humor. But the most striking feature of the music was the sound of their guitars. Extending Branca's fascination with the power of the electric guitar, Sonic Youth compiled an arsenal of junk-shop guitars and set them to bizarre tunings. These "prepared guitars" opened a whole new world of noise, and breaking with the traditional sound and, more importantly, the traditional limits of rock. Like good Dadaists, bad children, and SUN RA, Sonic Youth broke their toys to make new toys. Not since JIMI HENDRIX repositioned the guitar in relation to his amplifiers and his audience—not since Hendrix *reinvented* the electric guitar—has there been such a revolution in the approach to the standard tool of rock.

This revaluation of the guitar was, however, just the beginning of Sonic Youth experiments. They played their instruments *hard* and invoked HENRY COWELL's banging, shattering tone clusters. (Moore and Ranaldo often use egg beaters, screw drivers, and other hardware against their strings.) Their later albums and performances are marked by improvisation inspired by free jazz. (Moore has played with CECIL TAYLOR and Milford Graves.) In 1997, Sonic Youth played a night of music at Avery Fisher Hall under the title "Guitar Futurism." The title and their performance that night was a gesture toward their avant-garde background, implicitly recalling this adage from LUIGI RUSSOLO's *The Art of Noise* (1913): "It is necessary to break this restricted circle of pure sounds and conquer the infinite variety of noise-sounds." But before Avery Fisher Hall, Sonic Youth followed Warhol into pop.

After a trilogy of extraordinary albums—*EVOL* (1986), *Sister* (1987), *Daydream Nation* (1988)—on the influential independent label SST, Sonic Youth signed with a major label, Geffen/DGC, in 1990. Since that time they have released six albums that have stretched and redefined popular music. (They were also instrumental in having Geffen sign Nirvana, the band that conquered the mainstream and effectively ended punk.) Redefinition has always been Sonic Youth's goal and their ability to achieve this has always come from their knowledge of the avant-garde tradition. Their 1998 album *A Thousand Leaves* includes a song called "Hits of Sunshine." Dedicated to ALLEN GINSBERG, it extends Sonic Youth's experiments in noise and song structure. It is also an acknowledgment of the Beat influence on their music. To quote Allen Ginsberg: "The person lives in us and then we perish. What perishes is an embodiment of the person, who never dies. He is like time—the present dies, becomes past, but Time never dies in the continuum." "Hits of Sunshine" is Sonic Youth's *Lycidas*: it is an elegy pointing to pastures new.

—John Rocco

Web Site: http://www.geffen.com/sonic-youth/ (official page; there are many "unofficial" ones).

Interpretation: Foege, Alec. *Confusion is Next: The Sonic Youth Story*. New York: St. Martin's Press, 1994; Gordon, Kim. "American Prayers." *Artforum* 23, no. 8 (April 1985): 73–77; "I'm Really Scared When I Kill in My Dreams." *Artforum* 21, no. 5 (January 1983): 54–57; Heylin, Clinton. *From the Velvets to the Voidoids: A Pre-Punk History for a Post-Punk World*. New York: Penguin, 1993; Marcus, Greil. *Ranters and Crowd Pleasers: Punk in Pop Music, 1977–1992*. New York: Doubleday, 1993; Moore, Thurston. "Stabb's Hand Touched Me and I Slept." In *The Penguin Book of Rock 'n' Roll Writing*, ed. Clinton Heylin. New York: Penguin, 1992.

SOUND POETRY

See **TEXT-SOUND**.

SPECTOR, Phil

(26 December 1940).

One of the most important, influential, and downright strange figures in the history of rock, Spector enjoyed a short period of genius, followed by a long period of eccentric behavior—the perfect life for a rock icon. Spector's family moved to California when he was 13, and as a Jew-out-of-water he felt alienated from the blond, blue-eyed culture he discovered there. At about the same time, Spector's father died—a fact immortalized in Spector's first hit, "To Know Him Is to Love Him" which he recorded with his first group, The Teddy Bears, in 1958. (The song's title was taken from his father's tombstone.) Uncomfortable as a performer, Spector soon moved behind the microphone. Working with a series of groups over whom he had almost total control, Spector created what he called "teenage symphonies to God." Doubling, tripling, and even quadrupling the normal instrumental lineup, Spector created a "wall of sound" behind the perky voices of the singers he used. Between 1962 and 1966, he was the mastermind behind dozens of hits by interchangeable groups like the Crystals and the Ronettes. Spector considerably broadened the sound palette of rock and roll, and his productions were incredibly well-crafted, designed to be heard and enjoyed over the monophonic turntables and transistor radios that were at the time cutting-edge listening technology. His streak ended with the 1966 single "River Deep—Mountain High" that he produced for Ike and Tina Turner; a commercial flop, it sent him into a period of seclusion. Spector briefly came out of retirement to work with ex-BEATLES George Harrison and JOHN LENNON in the early seventies, but his eccentric behavior in the studio made him a less-than-reliable collaborator. In 1991, the CD box set *Back to Mono* reintroduced the glories of Spector's early heyday, and brought renewed interest to his work.

—Richard Carlin

Recordings: *Back to Mono*. ABKCO 7118, 1991; *A Christmas Gift for You*. Los Angeles: Rhino 70235, 1989.

SPIEGEL, Laurie

(20 September 1945).

Drawing upon her various experience as a string musician, Spiegel began in 1973 to compose with COMPUTERS at Bell Laboratories, the source of the GROOVE program that was prominent at the time. In contrast to those composers who employed the computer to realize a SERIAL complexity impossible with live musicians, she initially favored modal and dramatic pieces. Using the computer to control SYNTHESIZERS, Spiegel was able to perform with them live (in "real time") well before the development of the computer as a live performing instrument. She also designed and wrote the computer program *Music Mouse* (1986), a floppy disc "intelligent instrument," which, because it "requires no previous musical training" is conducive to improvisation and thus popular with users of Amiga, Atari, and Macintosh computers.

Compositions: *Introit*, 1973; *Water Music*, 1974; *Drums*, 1975.

Computer Program: *Music Mouse*. New York: Aesthetic Engineering (175 Duane St., New York, NY 10013), 1986.

Recordings: *Unseen Worlds*, with *Three Sonic Spaces, From a Harmonic Algorithm*, et. al. Wilton, CT: Scarlet, 1990; ——, et. al. *The Virtuoso in the Computer Age III*. Baton Rouge, LA: Centaur, 1993; ——, et. al. *New Music for Electronic and Recorded*. Media Composers, 1997.

STANKIEWICZ, Richard

(18 October 1922–27 March 1983).

Stankiewicz is generally reputed to be the first sculptor to weld works together out of the lost junk of the industrial environment, preceding JOHN CHAMBERLAIN's assemblies of wrecked automobiles by ten years. Through his use of industrial materials and techniques beginning in the mid-1950s, Stankiewicz is a direct descendant of ALEXANDER CALDER and DAVID SMITH. But, unlike them both, he did not polish and refine the look of his metal forms. His rusted and ruined pieces of broken machinery, pots, pulleys, scrap iron, gears, and chains retain their rude appearance; they brandish their corrosion. Even so, Stankiewicz's completion of a mere 300 or so sculptures does more than reflect back to us the degradation and decimation of the world of the machine, or imply a critique of consumerism, as do the sculptures of Chamberlain. Stankiewicz's creations animate the mechanical world. Playing with it and making it play, they conjure the discarded garbage of the machine era so that it may prance, posture, and loom—as if the industrial landscape were a fairyland, and the discarded materials of mechanization had collected together as goblins, trolls, mythical kings, and queens.

—Mark Daniel Cohen

Works: *Tribal Diagram*, 1953–55; *Soldier*, 1955; *Machine People*, 1958; *Assault*, 1959; *Railroad Urchin*, 1959; *Chain People*, 1960; *Dark Mother*, 1961; *Untitled (Double Tank)*, 1963.

Exhibition Catalogs: *Richard Stankiewicz, Welded Sculptures*. Melbourne: National Gallery of Victoria, 1969; *The Sculpture of Richard Stankiewicz: A Selection of Works from the Years, 1953–1979*. Albany: University Art

S

Gallery, SUNY at Albany, 1979; *Richard Stankiewicz: Thirty Years of Sculpture 1952–1982*. New York: Zabriskie Gallery, 1983; *Richard Stankiewicz: Sculpture from the 1950s and 1960s: December 8, 1987–January 16, 1988*. New York: Zabriskie Gallery, 1987; Donadio, Emmie. *Richard Stankiewicz: Sculpture in Steel*. Middlebury, VT: Middlebury College, 1994.

S

STEIN, Gertrude

(3 February 1874–27 July 1946).

Stein was, simply, the Great American Person-of-Avant-Garde Letters in that she produced distinguished work in poetry as well as prose, theater as well as criticism, nearly all of it unconventional, if not decidedly avant-garde. Stein could not write an ordinary sentence if she tried, for, though her diction is mundane and her vocabulary nearly always accessible, her sentence structures are not. One early development, evident in *Three Lives* (drafted around 1904), was the shifting of syntax, so that parts of a sentence appear in unusual places. These shifts not only repudiate the conventions of syntactical causality, but also introduce dimensions of subtlety and accuracy. Instead of saying "someone is alive," Stein writes, "Anyone can be a living one," the present participle indicating the process of living.

It is clear that there are two Gertrude Steins in American literature's canon. Those who prefer *Three Lives* and the *Autobiography of Alice B. Toklas* tend to dismiss as "incomprehensible junk" an *oeuvre* that I find the richest experimental writing ever done by an American. More than a half-century after Stein's death, even generations after it was written, much of this writing is not understood, is not taught in the universities, and, for the most part, is not even in print. In the unabridged, 925-page *The Making of Americans* (1926; first drafted around 1906–08, well before the innovative novels of James Joyce and William Faulkner), Stein developed what subsequently became her most notorious device—linguistic repetition. To be precise, she repeats certain key words or phrases within otherwise different clauses and sentences, so that even though the repetitions are never exact, this repeated material comes to dominate the entire paragraph or section, often becoming the primary cohesive force within an otherwise diffuse passage. As Stein neglected subject, setting, anecdote, conflict, analysis, and many other conventional elements, *style* became the dominant factor in her writing, more important than "theme" or "character."

Freed from conventional syntax (and the Aristotelian principles informing it), Stein was able to explore the possibilities of not just one but several kinds of alternative English. Having worked with accretion and explicitness, as well as syntactical transpositions, she then experimented with ellipses and economy; having written about experience with many more words than usual, she tried to write with far, far fewer. In *Tender Buttons* (1914), for instance, her aim was the creation of texts that described a thing without mentioning it by name. Other prose pieces by Stein have as their real theme, their major concern, kinds of coherence established within language itself: "Able there to ball bawl able to call and seat a tin a tin whip with a collar"; or, "Appeal, a peal, laugh, hurry merry, good in night, rest stole." The unifying forces in such sentences are stressed sounds, rhythms, alliterations, rhymes, textures, and consistencies in diction—linguistic qualities other than subject and syntax; and, even when divorced from semantics, these dimensions of prose can affect readers.

After experimenting with prolix paragraphs, Stein then made fictions out of abbreviated notations, such as these from "The King of Something" in *Geography and Plays* (1922):

> PAGE XVI.
> Did you say it did.
> PAGE XVIII.
> Very likely I missed it.
> PAGE XIX
> Turn turn.

Not only does such compression (along with the omission of page XVII) represent a radical revision of narrative scale, but writings like these also realize the French Symbolists' theoretical ideal of a completely autonomous language—creating a verbal reality apart from extrinsic reality. However, whereas the Symbolists regarded language as the top of the iceberg, revealing only part of the underlying meaning, Stein was primarily concerned with literature's surfaces, asking her readers to pay particular attention to words, rather than to the content and the motives that might lie behind them. What you read is most of what there is.

Stein's plays consist primarily of prose passages that are sometimes connected to characters (and other times are not). Only occasionally are characters identified at the beginning of the text, while the customarily concise texts rarely include stage directions of any kind. Stein was not adverse to having "Act II" follow "Act III," which had followed a previous "Act II." There is typically nothing in her theatrical scenarios about tone, pace, costumes, decor, or any other specifics—all of which are thus necessarily left to the interpretation of the plays' directors. Because scripts like these are simply not conducive to conventional realistic staging, most directors have favored highly spectacular, sensorily abundant productions that incorporate music and dance, in sum exemplifying Stein's idea of theater as an art of sight and sound.

Stein's essays were also unlike anything written before in that vein. In discussing a particular subject, she avoided the conventions of exposition, such as example and elaboration, in favor of accumulated disconnected details and miscellaneous insights, often frustrating those readers requiring accessible enlightenment. Stein's reputation for distinguished prose has obscured her poetry, which was likewise concerned with alternative forms, beginning with acoherence, especially in her monumental "Stanzas in Meditation," and including the horizontal MINIMALISM of one-word lines:

There
Why
There
Why
There
Able
Idle

Stein frequently boasted that in writing she was "telling what she knew," but most of her knowledge concerned alternative writing. It is indicative that the principal theme of her essays, reiterated as much by example as by explanation, is the inventions possible to an author accepting the esthetic autonomy of language.

Selected Writings: *Tender Buttons: Objects, Food, Rooms* (1914). New York: Dover, 1997; *Geography and Plays (1922)*. New York: Something Else, 1968; *The Making of Americans* (1925). Normal, IL: Dalkey Archive, 1995.

Anthologies: Dydo, Ulla, ed., with an intro. *A Stein Reader*. Evanston, IL: Northwestern University Press, 1993; Kostelanetz, Richard, ed. with an intro. *The Yale Gertrude Stein*. New Haven: Yale University Press, 1980.

Correspondence: *The Letters of Gertrude Stein & Carl Van Vechten*. Ed. Edward Burns. 2 vols. New York: Columbia University Press, 1986; *The Letters of Gertrude Stein & Thornton Wilder*. Ed. Edward Burns, et al. New Haven: Yale University Press, 1996; *A History of Having a Great Many Times Not Continued To be Friends: Correspondence Between Mabel Doge & Gertrude Stein, 1911–1934*. Ed. Patricia R. Everett. Albuquerque, NM: University of New Mexico Press, 1996.

Biography: Mellow, James. *Charmed Circle: Gertrude Stein and Company*. New York: Praeger, 1974.

Web Site: http://www.sappho.com/poetry/g_stein.htm

Interpretation: Bowers, Jane Palatini. *They Watch Me As They Watch Me*. Philadelphia: University of Pennsylvania Press, 1991; Kostelanetz, Richard, ed.

Gertrude Stein Advanced. Jefferson, NC: McFarland, 1990; Sutherland, Donald. *Gertrude Stein*. New Haven: Yale University Press, 1951.

STERN, Gerd

See **USCO**.

STELLA, Frank

(12 May 1936).

Hailed before he turned twenty-five, Stella's early canvases consist of regularly patterned geometric shapes painted with evenly applied strokes out to the canvas's edge, so that the viewer cannot distinguish any one figure from the background, or form from content, or one image from any larger shape. These faintly mechanical paintings depend upon the appreciation of such strictly visual virtues as the relation of one color to another, the solidity of the geometric shapes, and the potential complexity of elemental simplicity, as well as Stella's decidedly cerebral deductive solution to certain problems in painting's recent history. In 1960, the twenty-four-year-old artist told an undergraduate art-school audience:

> I had to do something about relational painting, i.e., the balancing of the various parts of the painting with and against one another. The obvious answer was

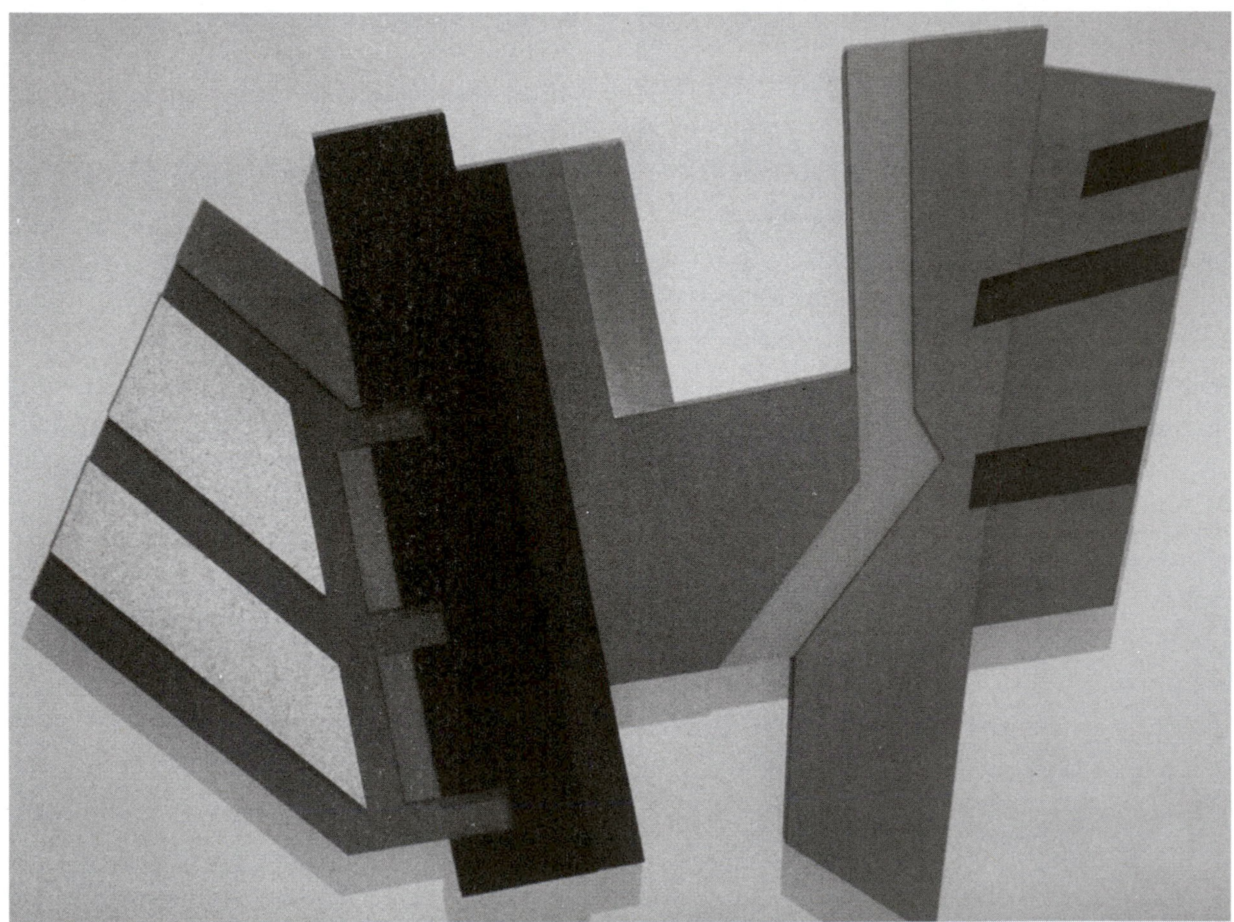

Frank Stella, *Rozdol II*, 1973. Mixed media collage. CORBIS/Seattle Art Museum. © Frank Stella/Artists Rights Society (ARS), New York.

> symmetry—make it the same all over. The question still remained, though, of how to do this in depth. A symmetrical image or configuration placed on an open ground is not balanced out in the illusionistic space. The solution I arrived at—and there are probably quite a few, although I know of only one other, color density—forces illusionistic space out of the painting at a constant rate by a regulated pattern.

Even though Stella's initial innovation succeeded rather quickly, nothing he has done since is comparably pioneering.

Selected Paintings: *Black Paintings*, 1958–1960; *Aluminum Paintings*, 1960; *Copper Paintings*, 1960–61; *Purple Paintings*, 1963; *Notched V Paintings*, 1964–65; *Running V Paintings*, 1964–65; *Moroccan Paintings*, 1964–65.

Writings: *Working Space*. Cambridge: Harvard University Press, 1986.

Exhibition Catalogs: *Three American Painters: Kenneth Noland, Jules Olitski, Frank Stella*. Cambridge, MA: Fogg Art Museum, 1965; Fried, Michael. *Frank Stella*. Pasadena, CA: Pasadena Art Museum, 1966; *Frank Stella*. London: Arts Council of Great Britain, 1970; Rubin, William. *Frank Stella*. New York: MOMA, 1970; *Frank Stella: 1970–1987*. New York: Musuem of Modern Art, 1990; *Frank Stella since 1970*. Ft. Worth, TX: Art Museum, 1978; *Frank Stella: Black Paintings, 1958–60; Cones and Pillars, 1984–87*. Germany: Staatsgalerie Stuttgart, 1988.

Catalogues Raisonnés: Axsom, Richard H. *The Prints of Frank Stella: A Catalogue Raisonee 1967–82*. New York: Hudson Hills, 1983; Rubin, Lawrence. *Frank Stella: Paintings 1958–1965, A Catalogue Raisonné*. New York: Stewart, Tabori and Chang, 1986.

Biography: Guberman, Sidney. *Frank Stella: An Illustrated Biography*. New York: Rizzoli, 1995.

Interpretation: Rosenblum, Robert. *Frank Stella*. With an appendix reprinting Stella's 1960 short lecture. Baltimore: Penguin, 1971.

STETSER, Carol

(11 April 1948).

Because VISUAL POETRY, like other avant-garde art, is forever being pronounced "dead" by those opposed to or ignorant of it, one is always gratified to see the emergence of new talents, even in the 1990s. The principal virtue of Carol Stetser's *Currents* (1992) is demonstrating other ways to do it, in her case by mixing black-and-white images with words, which are handwritten as well as typeset, which may be drawn from newsprint or originate in her own head, all with a unique signature style that is always the measure of a mature artist. In the afterword to that book she writes:

> The role of today's visual poetry is to carry on in the tradition of the Indian vedic poets, the Zen Buddhists, poets Chuang Tzu and William Blake, and the philosopher Ludwig Wittgenstein who each attempted to explode our familiar language patterns so we can see clearly and directly. . . . Visual poetry can provide the jolt necessary for us to cut through the conceptualizations of language and to experience the transcendence of The Word.

True.

Writings: *Black and White*. Oatman, AZ: Padma, 1977; *Chopping Wood, Carrying Water*. Village of Oak Creek, AZ: Padma, 1978; *Continuum An Autobio at 30*. Village of Oak Creek, AZ: Padma, 1979; *Hierograms*. Village of Oak Creek, AZ: Padma, 1992; *Positive Negatives*. Village of Oak Creek, AZ: Padma, 1992; *Persistence of Memory*. Village of Oak Creek, AZ: Padma, 1992; *Currents*. Village of Oak Creek, AZ: Padma, 1992; *Geophaphia Poetica*. Sedona, AZ: Padma (P.O.Box 20081, 86341), 1999.

STEWART, Ellen

See **LA MAMA EXPERIMENTAL THEATER CLUB**

STIEGLITZ, Alfred

(1 January 1864–13 July 1946).

Had Stieglitz not existed, the development of more than one American art would have been retarded. As an art

Alfred Stieglitz. *The Sweeper*, c. 1902. CORBIS.

S

dealer at 291 Fifth Avenue in New York during the first two decades of this century, he exhibited first photographs and then other avant-garde visual art, initially European, eventually American, incidentally elevating the esthetic status of fine photography. His gallery presented the first American exhibitions of Henri Matisse (1869–1954), FRANCIS PICABIA, and CONSTANTIN BRANCUSI, in addition to introducing GEORGIA O'KEEFFE, before she became his wife, and Marsden Hartley (1887–1943), among many others. From his gallery Steiglitz published the periodical *Camera Work* (1903–17), which included not only photography and reviews of the visual arts but advanced American writing, such as one of the first appearances of GERTRUDE STEIN in print. Stieglitz also edited *291* (1915–916), which represented NEW YORK DADA. After the building at 291 Fifth was torn down in 1917, Steiglitz's work as cultural impresario continued in other galleries to his death. As a practicing photographer, Stieglitz imitated various painterly styles, including Hudson River Impressionism (in a famous photograph of lower Manhattan behind the East River) and several kinds of abstraction. It is scarcely surprising that the "The Complete Illustrations 1903–1917" from *Camera Work* should come from a publisher based in Germany.

Books: *Picturesque Bits of New York and Other Studies*. New York: R. H. Russell, 1897; *Poetics of Place: Selected Essays and Notes* New York: Aperture, forthcoming.

Anthologies: Geesaman, Lynn, ed. *Alfred Stieglitz: Photographs and Writings*. New York: Bulfinch, 1999; Green, Jonathan, ed. *"Camera Work": A Critical Anthology*. Millerton, NY: Aperture, 1974; Greenough, Sarah, and Juan Hamilton, eds. *Alfred Stieglitz: Photographs and Writings*. Washington, DC: National Gallery of Art/Callaway, 1983; Norman, Dorothy, ed. *Stieglitz Memorial Portfolio*. New York: Twice a Year, 1947; Stieglitz, Alfred. *Camera Work: The Complete Illustrations 1903–1917*. Köln: Taschen, 1997.

Exhibition Catalogs: Zigrosser, Carl. *Alfred Stieglitz: His Photographs and His Collection*. New York: MoMA, 1947;

——, and Henry Clifford. *History of an America, Alfred Steiglitz: 291 and After*. Philadelphia: Museum of Art, 1944; Bry, Doris. *Alfred Steiglitz: Photography.* Washington, DC: National Gallery of Art, 1958; *Alfred Steiglitz: Photographer*. Boston & Greenwich, CT: Boston Museum of Fine Arts & New York Graphic Society, 1965; Naef, Weston J. *The Collection of Alfred Stieglitz: Fifty Pioneers of Modern Photography*. New York: Metropolitan Museum & Viking, 1978; *Alfred Stieglitz: Photographs from the J. Paul Getty Museum*. Malibu, CA: Getty Museum, 1995.

Biography: Frank, Waldo. ed. *America and Alfred Stieglitz* (1934). New York: Octagon, 1975; Lowe, Sue Davidson. *Stieglitz: A Memoir/Biography*. New York: Farrar, Straus, 1983; Norman, Dorothy. *Alfred Stieglitz: An American Seer*. New York: Random House, 1973; Seligmann, Herbert J. *Alfred Stieglitz Talking*. New Haven: Yale University Library, 1966; Whelen, Richard. *Alfred Stieglitz* (1995). New York: Da Capo, 1997.

Web Site: http://www.masters-of-photography.com/S/stieglitz/stieglitz.html

Interpretation: Arrowsmith, Alexandra, and Thomas West, eds. *Two Lives. Georgia O'Keeffe and Alfred Stieglitz*. New York: HarperCollins/Callaway, 1992; Dijkstra, Bram. *The Hieroglyphics of a New Speech: Cubism, Stieglitz, and the Early Poetry of William Carlos Williams*. Princeton: Princeton University Press, 1969; Homer, William Innes. *Alfred Stieglitz and the American Avant-Garde*. Boston: New York Graphic Society, 1977; Newhall, Beaumont and Nancy. "Alfred Stieglitz," *Masters of Photography*. New York: Braziller, 1958; Norman, Dorothy. *Alfred Stieglitz: Introduction to an American Seer*. New York: Duell, Sloan, & Pearce, 1960.

STOCKHAUSEN, Karlheinz

(22 August 1928).

Stockhausen is at once the most successful and thus powerful of contemporary composers and, not surprisingly, the most problematic. His success is easy to measure—decades of support from the strongest European music publisher and the strongest German record label, not to mention the incomparably high-minded German radio stations. He has received commissions from orchestras and opera houses all over the world; he has been a visiting professor in America and, as NICOLAS SLONIMSKY put it, "a lecturer and master of ceremonies at avant-garde meetings all over the world." No composer younger than IGOR STRAVINSKY has been as successful at getting the world's major music institutions to invest in him. As a performer, he plays only his own work, which is to say that sponsors inviting him know in advance they won't get music by anyone else. If only to keep his patrons happy, Stockhausen has produced a huge amount of stuff, often accompanied by willful declarations of embarrassing pretension. He is accustomed to charging fees that are high, if not ridiculously extravagant, and is continually on the verge of pricing himself out of a career. The history of Stockhausen-envy and Stockhausen-mockery is nearly as long as his career. I remember hearing, as early as 1962, the joke that "When Karlheinz gets up in the morning, he thinks he invented the light bulb."

The problems are harder to define: Egregiously uneven, his works often fall short of Stockhausen's announced intentions, because they are not as inventive or pioneering as he claims. Indeed, they are often patently derivative, of old ideas as well as new, and sometimes opportunistic in combining contrary esthetics. Paul Griffiths writes that "Stockhausen increasingly found ways of mediating between polar extremes, [in] his pursuit of unity in diversity," which may be a rationale for what strikes others as opportunism.

Stockhausen has composed in various distinctive ways, with a succession of governing ideas. He was initially a SERIAL composer concerned with extending Schoenberg's compositional innovation beyond pitch to duration, timbre, and dynamics, to which Stockhausen added stage directions, serially distributing his performers over different parts of the concert hall. *Gruppen* (1959), for instance, requires three chamber orchestras and three conductors beating different tempi.

Stockhausen meanwhile became involved with ELECTRONIC MUSIC producing in *Der Gesang der Jünglinge* (1956) an early classic of vocal processing that succeeded on disc, even though two-track stereo recording compromised its initial form of having five synchronized monophonic tapes resound through five loudspeakers surrounding the audience. By the 1960s, Stockhausen was incorporating various radical live human sounds (including screaming, stamping, whispering, whistling) that perhaps reflected new electronic possibilities.

Later, with *Stimmung* (1967), Stockhausen appropriated ALEATORY esthetics by having dancers activate eggshells placed on the floor or piano wires strung across the stage. *Kurzwellen* (1969) depends upon sounds inadvertently discovered on shortwave radios at the time of the performance; in the current age of digital radio tuners, which are designed to exclude acoustic fuzz coming from unfocused reception and the static between stations, *Kurzwellen* must necessarily be performed "on original instruments."

With *Hymnen* (1967–1969), Stockhausen adopted COLLAGE, producing a spectacular pastiche of national anthems that is, depending upon one's taste and experience, either the last great musical assemblage ever or an example of how collage, the great early twentieth-century innovation, has degenerated into an expired form. (I used to hold the second position on *Hymnen* until moving closer to the first.) By the late 1970s, the composer had appropriated Wagnerian operatic conceptions with *Light: The 7 Days of the Week* (1981–88), which is a cycle of seven operas, one for each day of the week (with no sabbatical).

I could go on; he goes on, in both 1998 and 1999, for instance, sending around the world fliers offering a week-long summer school, so to speak, on his own turf in Kürtin, outside Köln, with both performances and "courses" about his various works for 495 DM (or $330) payable to Stockhausen Stiftung für Musik. Though several books of Stockhausen's miscellaneous writings have appeared in German, only one has been translated into English, curiously demonstrating that even lives of great success contain dimensions of minor failure.

Selected Compositions: *Kurzspiel*, for oboe, bass clarinet, piano, and 3 percussion, 1951; *Klavierstücke I–IV*, 1952–53; *Kontra-Puntke*, for 10 instruments, 1953; *Zeitmasse*, for 5 woodwinds, 1955–56; *Gesang der Jünglinge*, 1956; *Gruppen*, for 3 orchestras, 1959; *Carre*, for 4 orchestras and chorus, 1960; *Originale*, music theater, 1961; *Mikrophonie II*, for 12 singers, Hammond organ, 4 ring modulators, and tape, 1965; *Spiral*, for soloist and short-wave transmitter, 1968; *Hymnen*, 1969; *Mantra*, for two pianos, 1970; *Musik im Brauch*, for percussion and musical clocks, 1975; *Light: The 7 Days of the Week*, 1981–88.

Books: *Texte*. 6 vols. Köln: Dumont, 1963–88; *Texts on Music*. Vols. 7–10. Kürten, Germany: Stockhausen Verlag (Kettenberg 15, D-51515), n.d.; *Stockhausen on Music: Lectures and Interviews*. Ed. R. Maconie. London & New York: Marion Boyars, 1989; *Towards a Cosmic Music*. Trans. Tim Nevill. Longmead Shaftsbury, Forest: Element, 1989.

Interviews: Cott, Jonathan. *Stockhausen: Conversations with the Composer*. New York: Simon & Schuster, 1973.

Recordings: *Aus den sieben Tagen*. France: Musique D'Abord, 1989; *Aus den sieben Tagen*. Aloys Kontarsky, Harald Boje et. al., prfs. Kürten, Germany: Stockhausen Verlag, 1993; *Klavierstücke*. Mainz, Germany: Wergo, 1996; *Kontakte*. David Tudor, Karlheinz Stockhausen et al. Mainz, Germany: Wergo, 1992; *Michael's Reise*. Markus Stockhausen prf. München: ECM, 1993; *Mantra*, with Ole Orsted, Rosalind Bevan, and Yvar Mikashoff, prfs. San Francisco: New Albion, 1990; *Mantra*. Mainz, Germany:

Wergo, 1995; *Stimmung*. Cond. Gregory Rose. London: Hyperion, 1986; *Tierkreis*. Ivan Zenaty et al. Prague, Czech Republic: Arta, 1992.

Biography: Kurtz, Michael. *Stockhausen: A Biography*. Trans. Richard Toop. London & Boston: Faber & Faber, 1992; Worner, Karl H. *Stockhausen: Life and Work*. London: Faber & Faber, 1973.

Web Page: http://www.stockhausen.org/

Interpretation: Griffiths, Paul. *The Thames and Hudson Encyclopedia of 20th-Century Music*. London: Thames & Hudson, 1986; Maconie, Robin. *The Works of Karlheinz Stockhausen* (1976). Oxford: Oxford University Press, 1990.

STOKOWSKI, Leopold

(18 April 1882–13 September 1977).

Of all the famous twentieth-century orchestral conductors, Stokowski, more than any other, was predisposed not only to new music but new technologies for both the production and reproduction of music. From his earliest years, initially with the Philadelphia Orchestra, Stokowski presented avant-garde compositions, often addressing the audience about them in advance, including both ALEXANDER SCRIABIN'S *Divine Poem* and ARNOLD SCHOENBERG'S Chamber Symphony No. 1 in 1915–16 and Alban Berg's *Wozzeck* (1917–1921) in 1931. Stokowski premiered EDGARD VARÈSE'S *Amériques* in 1926 and Alan Hovhaness's (1911) *Mysterious Mountain* in 1955, among many others. One astounding figure attributed to him is nearly 100 American or world premieres during his twenty-three years at the helm of the Philadelphians.

Extravagant by nature, Stokowski once engaged 950 singers, 110 orchestral musicians, and eight soloists to play Gustav Mahler's Eighth Symphony ("of a Thousand"). He scheduled over 500 performances of Schoenberg's *Gurrelieder*. For the American premiere of Alban Berg's *Wozzeck*, he required 80 preparatory rehearsals and 60 stage rehearsals. When audience noises disturbed his performance of ANTON VON WEBERN'S sole symphony, Stokowski stopped conducting, walked off the stage, and then returned to repeat the work from its beginning. He embarrassed potential coughers by having his orchestra cough on cue and mocked latecomers by having some of his musicians arrive late on stage in breathless haste. Stokowski was the first conductor to use a THEREMIN to boost the orchestra's bass section. He starred in Walt Disney's FANTASIA (1941). The only current American conductor to do as well by contemporary music is Dennis Russell Davis (1944), who works mostly, to no surprise, in Germany.

Recordings: Countless, for decades.

Biography: Chasins, Abram. *Leopold Stokowski, A Profile*. New York: Hawthorn, 1979; Opperby, Preben. *Leopold Stokowski*. New York: Hippocrene, 1982.

Web Page: http://www.stokowski.mcmail.com/

Interpretation: Daniel, Oliver. *Stokowski: A Counterpoint of View*. New York: Dodd, Mead, 1982; Smith, William A. *The Mystery of Leopold Stokowski*. Rutherford, NJ: Fairleigh Dickinson University Press, 1990.

STRAMM, August

(1874–1 September 1915).

A civil servant with a family to support, Stramm wrote short plays and poems that formally surpass what self-conscious bohemians were doing at his time. The story is that in November 1913 he heard F. T. MARINETTI lecture in Berlin. Prompted to destroy all his earlier work, he began anew, initially by befriending HERWARTH WALDEN, who edited *Der Sturm*. Stramm's literary esthetic comprised three principles: use the fewest words, express as concisely as possible, and avoid all clichés. Thus, "In the Fire" (1915) puts eight words into six lines: "Death drags/Dying rattles/Lonely/Immures/Worlddeep/Loneliness." Many years later we can recognize such poetry as PROTO-MINIMALISM. Stramm died on 1 September 1915, fighting for Germany in World War I.

Books: *Twenty-Two Poems*. Trans. Patrick Bridgewater. Wymandham, England: Brewhouse, 1969.

STRATOS, Demetrio

(22 April 1945–13 June 1979).

An extraordinary vocalist whose brief career bridged rock and the experimental avant-garde, Demetrio Stratos was born to Greek parents in Alexandria, Egypt. In 1962, after studying piano and accordion at the Athens National Consevatory, Stratos moved to Milan. There, in 1967, he joined the Italian rock group Ribelli, as a keyboard player; he soon dropped out, however, to focus on voice. In 1972 he cofounded the progressive rock band Area, which blended rock, jazz and Middle-Eastern music, and featured Stratos as lead vocalist. He had by that time developed a unique style, partly operatic, partly Middle-Eastern, and influenced as well by the vocal experiments of contemporary classical singers like Cathy Berberian. The group's music, though, was of uneven quality—forceful and original at times, at its worst, it was merely uninspired jazz rock. Area's two best albums are, perhaps, *Arbeit Macht Frei* (1973) and the live recording *Event '76* (1979), the latter featuring improvisers Steve Lacy and Paul Lytton.

Parallel to his activities with Area—who became quite popular in Italy—Stratos pursued a solo career focused on vocal experimentation, even as he explored various non-Western vocal traditions. He worked for years on an unfinished study of Eastern and Near-Eastern vocal traditions, and had encounters with musicians from various cultures—on one odd occasion he met with a delegation of Mongolians in Cuba! At the same time, in Milan, he collaborated with Juan Hidalgo and Walter Marchetti, founders of the avant-garde group Zaj. He studied phonetic and experimental poetry, and developed an interest in FLUXUS; this led him to the work of JOHN CAGE, whose *Mesostics re. Merce Cunningham* he adapted for solo voice, and recorded in 1974. His version was apparently greatly appreciated by Cage, and the piece became a staple of Stratos's subsequent live performances.

In 1976 and 1978, respectively, Stratos released his two most important solo works: *Metrodora* and *Cantare la Voce*. Both display an amazing array of extended vocal techniques, including overtone singing, an odd kind of yodeling, wheezing, gulping, and many effects that seem almost inexplicable, and are as yet nameless; through overdubbing, polyphonies of two, three, and four voices are created. Impressive formally and technically, these two works are also very striking for their conviction and naturalness. With them, Stratos succeeded in creating an unselfconscious, nonacademic experimental vocal music, which is simultaneously innovative and directly emotional.

In 1978 Stratos was invited by John Cage to come to New York to take part in a series of events at the Roundabout Theatre, in collaboration with MERCE CUNNINGHAM, JASPER JOHNS and Cage himself; these were well-received and brought Stratos a greater degree of international recognition. Tragically, however, Stratos succumbed to chronic leukemia the following year; he died in New York on 13 June 1979, at the age of 34. The day after, in Italy, a memorial concert was attended by over 60,000 people.

—Tony Coulter

Discography: A) As soloist: *Cantata Rossa per Tall al Zaatar*. VPA, 1976; *Metrodora*. Milan: Cramps Records, 1976; *O Tzitziras o Mitziras*. Milan: Cramps Records, 1978; *Cantare la Voce*. Milan: Cramps Records, 1978; *Rock and Roll Exhibition*. Milan: Cramps Records, 1979; *Recitarcantando*. Milan: Cramps Records, 1980; *Le Milleuna*. Milan: Cramps Records, 1990; *Concerto all' Elfo*. Milan: Cramps/EMI, 1998; B) with Area: *Arbeit Macht Frei*. Milan: Cramps Records, 1973; *Caution Radiation Area Milan*. Milan: Cramps Records, 1974; *Crac*. Milan: Cramps

Records, 1974; *Are(A)zione*. Milan: Cramps Records, 1975; *Maledetti*. Milan: Cramps Records, 1976; *1978, Gli dei Se Ne Vanno Gli Arrabbiati Restano*. Ascolto, 1978; *Event '76*. Milan: Cramps Records, 1979; *Concerto Teatro Uomo* [recorded 1976]. Milan: Cramps Records, n.d.; *Parigi - Lisbona*. Milan: Cramps, 1996.

STRAVINSKY, Igor

(17 June 1882–6 April 1971).

Like the New York ARMORY SHOW of 1913, the Paris premiere of *Le Sacre du Printemps (The Rite of Spring; Vesna svyashchennaya* in Russian) in the same year, with music by Igor Stravinsky and choreography by Vaslav Nijinsky (c. 1889–1950), became a turning point in the development of the modernist arts. Outraged public reaction at the premiere—including catcalls, hissing, and a near riot in the audience—helped rally an audience predisposed toward the avant-garde, the occasion also becoming, for critics sympathetic to the new, a standard against which subsequent avant-garde art could be measured.

Fortunate to be part of SERGE DIAGHILEV'S Ballets Russes, newly established in Paris in 1910, Stravinsky scored three of the dance company's first important works: *L'Oiseau de Feu (The Firebird*, 1910), *Petrouchka* (1911), and, of course, *Sacre*. Two hallmarks of Stravinsky's ballet scores were a reliance on folk melodies and harmonies, often sounding remarkably dissonant and strange to Western ears unfamiliar with Slavic traditions, and heavy, shifting rhythmic patterns.

After working sporadically with Diaghilev through the early twenties, Stravinsky turned his back on innovation, forging a "neo-classical" style that seems in retrospect a proto-POSTMODERNISM, paralleling the return of balletic choreography in the works of George Balanchine (1904–83) and classical literary ideals in the poetry of T. S. ELIOT. Making another radical shift in the 1950s, after the death of his archcompetitor ARNOLD SCHOENBERG, Stravinsky appropriated SERIAL MUSIC, always for pieces short in duration, although never accepting its rigorous theoretical assumptions. A smugly Olympian artist, he began in his late seventies to publish in collaboration with his American acolyte, Robert Craft (1923), a series of "conversations" books from supposedly reputable publishers, in which the master is portrayed as suspiciously speaking better, wittier English than anyone else ever heard from him. (Whereas some older elderly artists have younger female muses to reinvigorate their work, Stravinsky, securely married, had Craft.) Late in his long life, Stravinsky, like his near-contemporary Picasso, lived off his reputation as a sometime innovator, rather than continuing to produce avant-garde work.

—with Richard Carlin

Select Compositions: *L'Oiseau de feu/The Firebird*, ballet, 1909–10; *Pétrouchka,* ballet, 1910–11; *Le Sacre du Printemps/The Rite of Spring*, ballet, 1911–13; rev. 1947; *Four Russian Peasant Songs*, for equal voices unaccompanied, 1914–17; *Renard*, burlesque in song and dance, 1915–16; *Le Chant du rossignol/The Song of the Nightingale*, 1917; *L'Histoire du soldat/The Soldier's Tale*, 1918; *Ragtime*, for eleven instruments, 1918; *Quatre Chants russes*, 1918; *Pulcinella*, ballet, 1920; *Les Noces/The Wedding*, ballet, 1921–23; *Octet for Wind Instruments*, 1923; rev. 1952; *Oedipus Rex*, opera-oratorio, 1926–27; rev. 1948; *Symphony of Psalms*, for chorus and orchestra, 1930; rev. 1948; *Credo*, mixed chorus unaccompanied, 1932; *Duo concertant*, 1932; *Jeu de cartes/Card Game*, 1935–37; *Star-Spangled Banner*, 1941; *Ebony Concerto*, for dance band, 1945; *Mass*, choral, 1948; *Orpheus,* ballet, 1946–47; *The Rake's Progress*, opera, 1948–51; *Three Songs from William Shakespeare*, 1953; *In Memoriam Dylan Thomas*, 1954; *Four Russian Songs,* 1954; *Canticum sacrum*, 1956; *A Sermon, A Narrative, and A Prayer*, 1960–62; *The Flood*, for narrator, vocal soloists, chorus, orchestra, and dancers, 1962.

Writings: *Poetics of Music*. Cambridge: Harvard University Press, 1942; *An Autobiography* (1936). New York: Norton, 1962.

S

Simulated Conversations: Stravinsky, Igor, and Robert Craft. *Conversations with Igor Stravinsky*. Garden City, NY: Doubleday, 1959; ——. *Memories and Commentaries*. Garden City, NY: Doubleday, 1960; ——. *Expositions and Developments*. Garden City, NY: Doubleday, 1962; ——. *Themes and Episodes*. New York: Knopf, 1972.

Correspondence: Craft, Robert Ed. *Stravinsky: Selected Correspondence*, 3 vols. New York: Knopf, 1982, 1984, 1985; ——. *Dearest Babushkin: Selected Letters and Diaries of Vera and Igor Stravinsky*. London: Thames & Hudson, 1985.

Biography: Craft, Robert. *Stravinsky: Chronicle of a Friendship 1948–1971*. New York: Vintage, 1973; ——. *Igor and Vera Stravinsky: A Photograph Album*. London: Thames & Hudson, 1982; ——. *A Stravinsky Scrapbook*. London: Thames & Hudson, 1983; ——. *Stravinsky*. New York: St. Martin's Press, 1993; ——, and Arnold Newman. *Bravo Stravinsky*. Cleveland, OH: World, 1967; ——, and Vera Stravinsky. *Stravinsky in Pictures and Documents*. New York: Simon & Schuster, 1978; Libman, Lillian. *And Music at the Close: Stravinsky's Last Years*. New York: Norton, 1972; Stravinsky, Theodore. *Catherine & Igor Stravinsky: A Family Album*. London: Boosey & Hawkes, 1973; Vlad, Roman. *Stravinsky* (1958). London: Oxford University Press, 1960. 3d ed., 1979; White, Eric Walter. *Stravinsky: The Composer and His Works* (1966). Berkeley: University of California Press, 1979.

Web Page: http://www.island-of-freedom.com/STRAV.HTM

Interpretation: Asafev, Boris. *A Book about Stravinsky*. Trans. Richard F. French. Ann Arbor, MI: UMI Research, 1982; Boretz, Benjamin, and Edward T. Cone, eds. *Perspectives on Schoenberg and Stravinsky*. Princeton: Princeton University Press, 1968; Corle, Edwin, ed. *Igor Stravinsky*. New York: Duell, Sloan-Merle Armitage, 1949; Druskin, Mikhail. *Igor Stravinsky: His Life and Work*. Trans. Michael Cooper. Cambridge, England, & New York: Cambridge University Press, 1983; Forte, Allen. *The Harmonic Orgaization of "The Rite of Spring."* New Haven: Yale University Press, 1978; Griffiths, Paul. *Igor Stravinsky: The Rake's Progress*. Cambridge, England: Cambridge University Press, 1982; *Stravinsky*. New York: Schirmer, 1992; Lang, Paul Henry. *Stravinsky: A New Appraisal of His Work (*1962). New York: Norton, 1963; Lederman, Minna, ed. *Stravinsky in the Theatre*. New York: Pellegrini & Cudahy, 1949; Meyers, Rollo. *Introduction to the Music of Stravinsky*. London: Dobson, 1950; Oliver, Michael. *Igor Stravinsky*. London: Phaidon, 1995; Pasler, Jann, ed. *Confronting Stravinsky*. Berkeley: University of California Press, 1986; Read, George, and Selma Jeanne Cohen. *Stravinsky and the Dance*. New York: New York Public Library, 1962; Riviere, Jacques. "Le Sacre du Printemps." In *What Is Dance?* Ed. Roger Copeland and Marshall Cohen. New York: Oxford University Press, 1983; Strobel, Heinrich. *Stravinsky: Classic Humanist*. Trans. Hans Rosenwald. New York: Merlin, 1955; Strawinsky, Théodore. *The Message of Igor Strawinsky*. Trans. Robert Craft and Andre Marion. New York: Boosey & Hawkes, 1953; Tansman, Alexandre. *Igor Stravinsky: The Man and His Music*. Trans. Therese and Charles Bleefield. New York: Putnam, 1949; van der Toorn, Pieter C. *The Music of Igor Stravinsky*. New Haven: Yale University Press, 1983; Walsh, Steven. *The Music of Stravinsky*. NY: Routledge, 1988; Vlad, Roman. *Stravinsky*. Trans. Frederick and Ann Fuller. London: Oxford University Press, 1960; White, Eric W. *Stravinsky: A Critical Survey* (1948). Westport, CT: Greenwood, 1979.

STREB, Elizabeth

(23 February 1950).

The central, radical idea of Streb's choreography is the use of props not as extensions of one's body, as Alwin Nikolais used them, but as resistances. So her dancers collide with walls, fall face down onto mats, perform inside boxes in which they can't stand up, and rebound off trampolines. Streb's dance is very physical, to be sure, but it's also inventive and engaging. Her company has performed at such venues as the Coney Island boardwalk and the mall outside the Smithsonian as well as theaters and museums.

The classic Streb piece is *Surface* (1993), in which two 100-pound, door-sized planks of wood lay on a padded floor. Two dancers raise the planks up to be be near-vertical, so that two other dancers can hurl their bodies at the planks that then fall backwards to be picked up again, while the second pair of performers scamper off the mats. The process is repeated with other dancers. The piece's accompanying music, the entire background sound, is the amplified noise of performers and boards; Matthew Ostrovsky's sound design, here and elsewhere, enhances the impression of violence. This piece customarily runs seven minutes. In *Look Up* (1993), three harnessed dancers are suspended by ropes from the ceiling against a wall whose surface they bounce across. Another Streb classic, *Breakthru* (1997), is very brief, as a dancer propels himself through a pane of suspended glass, falling to the floor milliseconds before the shards do. "Don't blink," Streb advises. "It happens in a split-second." *Breakthru* especially must be seen to be believed.

Up (1995) is performed on a large, world-class trampoline between high ledges on the two short sides. The dancers jump onto the apparatus in various configurations, from various angles, and then leap into the air, sometimes repeatedly, before exiting onto side mats. The ways in which they fall onto the trampoline, often in pairs or trios (which is contrary to solo trampoline technique), is continually inventive and kinetically striking. All the action takes place in the air, illustrating Streb's radical contention that "returning to the floor is the biggest obstacle to the advancement of action. I like to break Newton's laws a lot."

Up and *Breakthru*, even more than *Surface*, are about trajectories, which is the ultimate theme of Streb's dance—not movements, not poses, not couplings, not elegance, not stories, not even steps to accompany preexisting music. Nearly all her dance (and all the sound) results from executing a physical task, such as falling, tumbling, or colliding; key terms are velocity and impact.

In this emphasis on trajectories, Streb's dance resembles the circus—not only the three-ring Barnum but the more sophisticated Cirque du Soleil. Two differences between the touring circus and Ringside is that Streb's performances are more austere, especially in costuming and lighting, and Streb doesn't mind revealing, initially through sound, that her performers strain and sweat. Her pieces are more inventive than gymnastics, which typically comprise a limited set of moves performed ad nauseam.

Works: *Springboard*, 1979; *Fall Line*, 1981; *Little Ease*, 1985; *Airwork (Airlines, Midair, Freeflight, Airwaves)*, 1987; *Wall*, 1991; *Impact*, 1991; *Look-Up!* 1993; *Freeflight*, 1993; *Surface*, 1993; *Bounce*, 1994; *Up*, 1995; *Rise*, 1995; *Breakthru*, 1996; *Fly*, 1997; *Across*, 1997; *Intro Action*, 1997; *All/Wall*, 1997.

Web Site: http://www.shaganarts.com/html/streb.html

Interpretation: Kostelanetz, Richard. "Elizabeth Streb, Extraordinary Choreographer," *Brooklyn Bridge*, III/1 (September 1997).

STROBE LIGHT

The strobe, as it is commonly called, is an intensely bright, rapidly flashing light that, when directed at a moving object, appears to freeze its movement, often in a succession of postures. Invented by Harold Edgerton (1903–1990), originally for the industrial purpose of examining the movement of machine parts, the strobe has since the 1930s enabled photographers to represent within a single image a movement as a sequence of moments. A classic Edgerton photograph, *Golf Drive by Denmore Shute* (1938), portrays within one photograph over four dozen different positions of a single golf swing. The strobe also became popular in the 1960s in some MIXED-MEANS theatrical performances and even social dance palaces (aka discos). The first strobes featured a revolving disc that passed in front of the light source; one advance in strobe design came from the development of electronic switching, which enabled the strobe user to adjust the flicker to speeds as quick as one-millionth of a second. While artists as various as USCO and WEN-YING TSAI incorporated strobes into their work, Edgerton himself, though nominally an electrical engineering professor at Massachusetts Institute of Technology, from time to time exhibited and published his extraordinary photographs.

Books: Edgerton, Harold. *Stopping Time*. New York: Abrams, 1987; ——. *Electronic Strobe*. Cambridge: MIT Press, 1987; C. with James R. Killian, Jr. *Moments of Vision*. Cambridge: MIT Press.

S

STROHEIM, Erich von

(22 September 1885–12 May 1957; b. Erich Oswald S., not Erich Hans Carl Maria Stroheim von Nordenwall, as was sometimes claimed).

Born in Vienna, the son of a Jewish hatter from Prussian Silesia who had settled in Vienna (and was not aristocratic), Stroheim emigrated to America sometime between 1906 and 1909 and took odd jobs before arriving around 1914 in Hollywood, where he soon began to work for and with D. W. GRIFFITH as an actor and assistant director. Stroheim soon starred as a prototypical Prussian with a monocle highlighting his autocratic manner. Once World War I ended, as Stroheim's acting opportunities declined, he turned to directing, beginning with *Blind Husbands* (1919), for which he also served as writer, art director, cinematographer, and actor.

Stroheim's great innovation as a director was the very long film. Extending D. W. GRIFFITH, whose *Intolerance* (1918) ran over three hours, Stroheim produced in *Greed* (1923–25) a film whose original version ran for several hours. Adapting Frank Norris's brutally realistic novel *McTeague* (1899), he wrote at the time, "I felt that after the last war [WWI], the motion picture going public had tired of the cinematographic 'chocolate eclairs' which had been stuffed down their throats, and which had in a large degree figuratively ruined their stomachs with this overdose of saccharosein pictures. Now, I felt, they were ready for a large bowl of plebeian but honest 'corned beef and cabbage.'" As an avatar of epic-length films, Stroheim precedented LENI RIEFENSTAHL, HANS JÜRGEN SYBERBERG, ABEL GANCE, ULRIKE OTTINGER, and ANDY WARHOL, among others.

My hunch is that Stroheim learned from such literary examples as Leo Tolstoy's *War and Peace*, the esthetic advantages to be gained from making a book bigger (in this case, longer) than normal. Needless to say, perhaps, the film's backers demanded that Stroheim reduce 42 reels to 24, which they felt was still too long for commercial release. When Stroheim refused to make additional cuts, the moneymen hired some hacks to reduce the footage first to 18 reels and then to ten reels, which got mixed notices. Ephraim Katz writes that those "who had seen Stroheim's 42-reel original version acclaimed it one of the great masterpieces of cinema art. The complete version is said to be preserved in the MGM vaults, but it hasn't been seen by anyone in several decades." From time to time, a three-hour version of *Greed* appears on American television, its stark imagery, especially of people in the desert, suggesting still what must have been a much greater work.

Whereas a later Stroheim film, *Queen Kelly* (1928), was never finished, a sequel, *Walking Down Broadway* (1932–33), was never released. He returned to his earlier career as an on-screen Teutonic "You-Love-to-Hate." Given the discriminatory mechanisms of critical art history, it is scarcely surprising that his bosses are forgotten while Stroheim is remembered. More importantly, the complete shooting script of *Greed* survives as a book that is a kind of CONCEPTUAL ART suggesting through words alone an esthetic experience that is otherwise unavailable.

Filmography: (as director): *Blind Husbands*, 1919; *The Devil's Pass Key*, 1920; *Foolish Wives*, 1922; *Merry-Go-Round*, 1923; *Greed*, 1923–25; *The Wedding March*, 1928.

Script: Stroheim, Erich von. *Greed* (1972). With contributions from Herman G. Weinberg, Jean Hersholt, and William Daniels. London: Faber, 1989.

Biography: Noble, Peter. *Hollywood Scapegoat: The Biography of Erich von Stroheim*. London: Fortune, 1951.

Web Site: http://www.mdle.com/ClassicFilms/BTC/direct28.htm

Interpretation: Finler, Joel W. *Stroheim*. Berkeley: University of California Press, 1968; Katz, Ephraim. *The Film Encyclopedia*. 2d ed. New York: HarperCollins, 1994.

STRZEMINSKI, Wladyslaw

(21 November 1893–26 December 1952).

Influenced by Kasimir Malevich, in 1924 Strzeminski formed a group of several Abstract Polish artists who published the periodical *Blok*. Other members included Henryk Stazewski (1894–1988) and Henryk Berlewi (1884–1967), both of whom had experienced Western European Abstraction at first hand, and Strzeminski's Russian-born wife the sculptor Katarzyna Kobro (1898–1950). Strzeminski preceded later geometric artists in making the canvas a nonhierarchical field in which imagery was continuously present, from end to end. The esthetic behind seeing paintings as a single entity he called Unism. He recognized that this forced the painter to renounce divisions within a painting and thus compositional rhythms and contrasts. Strzeminski claimed he transcended Malevich by abolishing any image as distinct as the latter's squares.

Paintings: *Architectural Composition 1*, 1926; *Architectural Composition 13c*, 1929; *Unistic Composition 7*, 1929; *Unistic Composition 8*, 1931; *Unistic Composition 11*, 1931; *Abstract Composition 21 VI*, 1933; *Unistic Composition 13*, 1934.

Writings: Strzeminski, Wladislaw. *Unizm w malarstwie,*, 1928.

Exhibition Catalogs: *Constructivism in Poland*. New York: MOMA, 1976; *Lót'z/Lyon: Mzeum Sztuki w Lodzi: Collection-Documentation-Actualité*. Lyon, France: Museee d'Art Contemporain, 1992; *Wladislaw Strzeminski on the 100th Anniversary of his Birth*. Lódz, Poland: Muzeum Sztuki, 1993; *Wladislaw Strzeminski*. Valencia, Spain: IVAM Centre Julio González, 1994.

STURTEVANT, Elaine

(23 August 1930).

From the beginning of her remarkable career, Sturtevant has made fairly exact replicas (and only replicas) of works by famous, mostly living artists. Among the modern masters whose work she has replicated are Marcel Duchamp, Roy Lichtenstein, Frank Stella, Robert Morris, Jasper Johns, and James Rosenquist (1933), sometimes with their cooperation (which is to say that they lent her work to be copied). Sturtevant customarily signs her replicas and insists they differ from the originals, although in ways not immediately discernible. In a New York City exhibition in the mid-1980s, she showed one and only one replica of several contemporaries—one Stella, one Duchampian urinal—as though she were a collector proud of her masterpieces. While each was technically a forgery, a room full of such replicas represented an esthetic vision. Few exhibitions ever raised so many substantial questions about esthetic/financial value, authorship, professional integrity, and, yes, originality. (The obvious paradox is that such a meticulous duplicator can be so innovative.) Not unlike other work so strong, Sturtevant's has had its imitators, such as Sherrie Levine (1947), who works mostly with photographs (a medium in which imitation is easier to do), and Mike Bidlo (1953), of whom Peter Frank writes, "Bidlo's work transforms the fetish of originality into the fetish of replication—the oxymoronic 'original copy' made flesh. He has refabricated Warhols, Pollocks, Brancusis, Légers, Matisses, Kleins, Cézannes, and numerous other modern museum pieces and auction-house goodies," with less technical accuracy than Sturtevant.

Exhibition Catalog: *Sturtevant*. Stuttgart, Germany: Württembergischer Kunstverein, 1992.

Interpretation: Frank, Peter. *New, Used and Improved*. New York: Abbeville, 1987.

SUBOTNICK, Morton

(14 April 1933).

After studying conventional music composition at Mills College, Subotnick became an electronic pioneer, initially among the first Americans to produce MUSIQUE CONCRÈTE by taping the sounds of an electric piano along with junkyard percussion, and occasionally running the tape backwards. He gathered machinery into early mixed-media installations. In the mid-1960s, Subotnick obtained an early synthesizer, producing in *Silver Apples of the Moon* (1967), the first synthesizer composition made for recording rather than performance. Subotnick later produced one of the first totally composed CD-ROMs. One recurring disappointment with his work comes from an excessive dependence upon repetition, or at least the illusion of repetition. Since his late marriage to JOAN LA BARBARA, his music has come, as noted before, to resemble hers.

Compositions: Viola Sonata, 1959; String Quartet, 1960; *Serenade No. 1*, for flute, clarinet, vibraphone, mandolin, cello, and piano, 1960; *Sound Blocks*, for narrator, violin, cello, xylophone, marimba, tape, and lights, 1961; *Mandolin*, for viola, tape, and film, 1963; *Play! No. 1*, for wind quintet, tape, and film, 1963; *No. 2,* for orchestra and tape, 1964; *No. 3*, for piano, tape, and film, 1964, *No. 4*, for 4 actors, performers, piano, vibraphone, cello, and 2 films, 1965; *10*, for 10 instruments, 1963–76; *Play! No.2*, for orchestra and tape, 1964; *The Tarot*, for chamber ensemble, 1965; *Silver Apples of the Moon*, 1967; *Lamentations No.1*, for orchestraand tape (1968), *No. 2*, for chamber ensemble and electronics, 1969; *Sidewinder*, 1971; *Before the Butterfly*, for 7 solo instruments and orchestra, 1975; *2 Butterflies*, for amplified orchestra, 1975; *Liquid Strata*, for piano and electronics, 1977; *Place*, 1978; *The Wild Beasts*, for trombone, piano, and electronics, 1978; *The 1st Dream of Light*, for tuba, piano, and electronics, 1979; *Ice Floe*, 1978; *Sky with Clouds*, 1978; *An Arsenal of Defense*, for viola, and electronics, 1982; *Axolotl*, for cello, chamber orchestra, and electronics, 1982; *Jacob's Room*, for voice and string quartet, 1984; *The Key to Songs*, for chamber orchestra and synthesizer, 1985; *And the Butterflies Began to Sing*, for YCAMS and chamber ensemble, 1988; *All My Hummingbirds Have Alibis,* for flute, cello, Midi piano, Midi mallets, and electronics, 1991.

Recordings: *Silver Apples of the Moon* (1967). New York: Nonesuch, 1967; *The Key to Songs/Return*. California E.A.R. Unit. Albany, CA: New Albion, 1986; *Touch, Jacob's Room*. Mainz, Germany: Wergo, 1994; *And the Butterflies Began to Sing*. New York: New World, 1997.

CD ROM: *All My Hummingbirds Have Alibis*. New York: Voyager, 1997.

Web Site: http://www.mala.bc.ca/~mcneil/subotnic.htm (Links)

SUMNER CARNAHAN, Melody

(5 January 1951).

A veteran small-press writer and publisher, she ranks among the keenest prose writers in America, particularly appreciated by composers who write music less for traditional settings of poetry than to accompany her texts imaginatively. Her masterwork, a compact disc *The Time Is Now*, has work by fifteen composers, including ROBERT ASHLEY and JOAN LA BARBARA, many of them doubling as their own performers, between 1983 and 1996. The disc comes with an 80-page booklet, CD-sized, with the words heard on the disc. For example:

> I seek thy say. In the name now not of. In the name of brought he and within our feet to stand. I was gladdened when no further spoke he of it. Let go us then. Further and father. I died of no evil did only in thy palaces love becoming more than that I could conceive. Only he that may love never me having been to believe so of it. Loving always then and all.

Whereas many contemporary "songs" require such booklets for the words to be recognized, most of Carnahan's prose is comprehensible to the ear. (Do not confuse this booklet + CD with a *book* of the same title published under the name Melody Sumner over a dozen years before.) No other writer since E. E. CUMMINGS has inspired such a wealth of innovative music. As the publisher of Burning Books, Carnahan has produced large, well-designed volumes that resemble commercial publications in their initial appearance, but differ radically in their contents.

Recordings: Polansky, Larry, et al. *The Time Is Now*. Lebanon, NH: Frog Peak (Box 1052, 03766), 1998. (Other composers represented on this CD include Elodie Lauten, Laetitia Sonami, Susan Stone, and Maggi Payne.)

Books: *The Time Is Now*. San Francisco: Burning Books (P.O. Box 2638, Santa Fe, NM 87504), 1983; *Thirteen Stories*. Santa Fe, NM: Burning Books, 1995; Co-ed. *The Guests Go into Supper*, with contributions by John Cage, Robert Ashley, Yoko Ono, Laurie Anderson, Charles Amirkhanian, et al. San Francisco: Burning Books, 1986.

Interpretation: Kostelanez, Richard. Preface to "Texts Set to Music." In *AnOther E. E. Cummings*. New York: Liveright, 1998.

SUN RA

(12 May 1914–30 May 1993, b. Herman Poole "Sonny" Blount).

Sun Ra began his avant-garde assault upon the music of planet Earth by not being born here. He claimed that he was from Saturn and that he brought with him his Solar Arkestra, a big band/commune/experimental art collective/invading force. Their weapons were instruments called the "space gong," the "space harp," and the "intergalactic space organ," among many others. The Arkestra lived together in a big house and worked together under the leadership of Sun Ra, who produced the most experimental music ever made by a "big band." (The Arkestra's version of Duke Ellington's [1899–1974] "Take the 'A' Train" on *Live at Montreux* [1976] is a famous example of the big-band sound pushed to its limits.) As one of the pioneers of FREE JAZZ, Sun Ra's music provided one of the earliest examples of that form on a large scale.

At his early earthly professional beginnings, in the '40s, Sun Ra worked with Fletcher Henderson (1897–1952) as pianist and arranger. He also choreographed shows for Henderson, and this experience carried over into his compositions for his Arkestra, where a performance became a multimedia event combining music, dance, singing, lights shows, and film, along with African ritual and sci-fi theatrics. Before Ken Kesey's (1935) Acid Tests and before ANDY WARHOL opened the Exploding Plastic Inevitable, Sun Ra's "theater" was "psychedelic" without drugs. On stage the band wore robes and "space" hats. Their instruments were often modified Earth tools dug up in junk shops.

Sun Ra himself was an influential force in new keyboards technology, and as early as the mid-50s he was using an electric organ. Notorious for pounding across keyboard registers with his fists, Sun Ra was also a very controlling force in his playing; his ideas and sound set the Arkestra off, as his keyboard sculpted its "compositions" and brought the other musicians back to Earth when the piece ended.

The music of Sun Ra could be characterized as FREE JAZZ pushed through a sort-of orchestra: driving riffs, wild soloing, and free movement among musicians. (Pharaoh Sanders [1940], the most influential member of the band, went on to contribute to the late work of John Coltrane [1926–67].) Free jazz always had its "spiritual" side, its concentration on music as meaningful expression beyond its sound, as in Coltrane's late spiritual search and CECIL TAYLOR's exploration of black consciousness. Sun Ra's music was tied up in his visionary poetry, as he included many of his own texts on his album covers. An example: "Music rushing forth like a fiery law/ Loosening the chains that bind,/ Ennobling the mind/ With all the many greater dimensions/ Of a living tomorrow."

Sun Ra's otherworldliness wasn't an act; as he described it, it was an *action*:

> I'm not human. . . . I've separated myself from everything that in general you call life. I've concentrated entirely on the music, and I'm preoccupied with the planet. In my music I create experiences that are difficult to express, especially in words. I've abandoned the habitual, and my previous life is of no significance anymore.

S

As Sun Ra's music was his action, his space talk was not figurative language. He was being *literal* and his example created a dimension to free jazz that influenced his fellow practitioners as well as providing an example for later experiments in rock by the MC5, the Grateful Dead, and SONIC YOUTH. In his essential biography of Sun Ra, John F. Szwed describes the Arkestra's place in modern music: "Black music represented for Western music a kind of pre-electronic distortion, an irruption into the system, a breaking of the rules of musical order; later electronic distortion itself became a technological emblem of the black component of Western art." Sun Ra was an "irruption," a sun gone nova through jazz.

—John Rocco

Selected Recordings: *Comments and Poetry by Sun Ra*. Chicago: Saturn Research, n.d.; *Super-Sonic Jazz*. Chicago: Saturn H70P0216, 1956; *We Travel the Spaceways*. Chicago: Saturn HK 5445, 1956; *Sound Sun Pleasure!!* Chicago: Saturn SR 512, 1958; *Rocket Number Nine Take Off for the Planet Venus*. Chicago: Saturn SR 9956–2-M/N, 1960; *The Futuristic Sounds of Sun Ra*. Newark: Savoy MG 12169, 1961; *Art Forms of Dimensions Tomorrow*. Chicago: Saturn 9956, 1962; *Cosmic Tones for Mental Therapy*. Chicago: Saturn 408, 1963; *The Heliocentric Worlds of Sun Ra, Volume 1*. New York: ESP-Disk 1014, 1965; *The Heliocentric Worlds of Sun Ra, Volume 2*. New York: ESP-Disk 1017, 1965; *The Magic City*. Chicago: Saturn LPB 711, 1965; *Atlantis*. Chicago: Saturn ESR 507, 1967; *Soundtrack to the Film Space Is the Place*. New York: Evidence 22070, 1972; *Pathways to Unknown Worlds*. New York: Impulse, ASD-9298, 1973; *Live at Montreux*. Chicago: Saturn, MS 87976, 1976; *Ra to the Rescue*. Chicago: Saturn IX, 1983–220, 1982.

Biography: Szwed, John. *Space is the Place: The Lives and Times of Sun Ra*. New York: Pantheon, 1997.

Web Site: http://www.fusebox.com/~jimr/

Interpretation: Baraka, Amiri. *Eulogies*. New York: Marsilio, 1996; Campbell, Robert L. *The Earthly Recordings of Sun Ra*. Redwood, NY: Cadence Jazz, 1994; Zwerin, Michael. *Close Enough For Jazz*. London: Quartet, 1983.

SUPREMATISM

See **MALAVICH, Kasimir**.

SURREALISM

(c. 1920).

I would be remiss if I did not confess my reluctance to write this entry, from a lack of sympathy for the esthetics, the art politics, and even the practitioners of organized Surrealism. Consider the authoritarian structure that placed ANDRÉ BRETON as a kind of pope who was forever excommunicating those with whom he disagreed or those who disputed his authority. (Would such "grotesque parodies of Stalinist purges," in Paul Mann's phrase, have been as feasible in a Protestant culture?)

The epithet "Surrealism" comes from GUILLAUME APOLLINAIRE, who used it in passing in the preface to *Les Mamelles de Tirésias* (implicitly raising the question, whose answer is not obvious, of whether someone of his anti-authoritarian temper would have survived as a Surrealist had he lived into the 1920s). Surrealist art and writing purportedly depended upon the unconscious as the source of images not otherwise available—and by extension upon deranged mentality—on the assumption that surreality offered more truth and insight than social reality.

Within the corpus of Surrealist art can be found the revelation of unconscious imagery analogous to automatic writing, extending from the amoeba forms of Joan Miró (1893–1983) to the EXPRESSIONISTIC calligraphy of MARK TOBEY and JACKSON POLLOCK; neatly rendered representations of hallucinations, in Giorgio de Chirico (1888–1978) and RENÉ MAGRITTE (1898–1967); and COLLAGES and ASSEMBLAGES of unrelated objects supposedly making a surreality apart from the quotidian norm. Perhaps the principal index of Surrealism's general deficiencies as a POLYARTISTIC movement is the absence of Surrealist music.

After 1925, the Parisian Surrealists were forever arguing over politics, and it is perhaps an index of their general stupidity that, from 1927 through the mid-1930s, they officially supported the French Communist party. The Surrealists always got a lot more attention in the press than other artists, even of comparable presence. As the critic HENRY MCBRIDE wrote in his newspaper column in 1936, "Whatever else you may say about surrealism it sure is a great incentive to conversation, and the choice bits you overhear are always illuminating."

Another problem is that artists unaffiliated with the group accomplished its esthetic aims better—the American Theodore Roethke (1908–1962), for instance, writing dream poems far superior to those by any Surrealist, and the Greek-American LUCAS SAMARAS epitomizing Surrealist sculpture. Though some current artists and writers profess an allegiance to Surrealism, they are rarely, if ever, of the first rank. Sexist beyond belief, they barely acknowledged women, not only among themselves but those doing similar work elsewhere, so that Penelope Rosement could long afterwards compile an anthology with 97 women from 28 countries.

Enough already?

Anthology: Breton, André. *Manifestoes of Surrealism*. Trans. Richard and Jeanette Seaver. Ann Arbor, MI: University of Michigan Press, 1969; *What Is Surrealism? Selected Writings*. Intro. Franklin Rosemont. New York: MoMA, 1978; *Anthology of Black Humor*. Trans. Mark Polizzotti. San Francisco: City Lights, 1997; ——, et al. *The Automatic Message/The Magnetic Fields/The Immaculate Conception*. London: Atlas (BCM, WCIN 3 XXX), 1997; Hammond, Paul. *The Shadow and its Shadow: Surrealist Writings on Cinema*. London: British Film Institute, 1978; Matthews, J. H., ed. *Anthology of French Surrealist Poetry*. London: University of London, 1966; Read, Herbert, ed. *Surrealism*. New York: Harcourt, Brace, 1936; Rosemont, Penelope, ed. *Surrealist Women*. Austin: University of Texas Press, 1998.

Web Site: http://pharmdec.wustl.edu/juju/surr/surrealism.html

Interpretation: Balakian, Anna. *The Literary Origins of Surrealism*. New York: King's Crown, 1947; *Surrealism: The Road to the Absolute* (1950). Bloomington: Indiana University Press, 1960; Fowlie, Wallace. *The Age of Surrealism* (1950). Bloomington: Indiana University Press, 1960; Gascoyne, David. *A Short Survey of Surrealism*. London: Cobden-Sanderson, 1935; Gershman, Herbert S. *The Surrealist Revolution in France*. Ann Arbor: University of Michigan Press, 1969; Jean, Marcel. *The Autobiography of Surrealism*. New York: Viking, 1987; Krauss, Rosalind; Jane Livingston, and Dawn Ades. *L'Amour Fou: Photography and Surrealism*. New York: Abbeville, 1983; Lemaire, Geroes E. *From Cubism to Surrealism in French Literature*. Cambridge: Harvard University Press, 1941; Martin, Richard. *Fashion and Surrealism*. New York: Rizzoli, 1987; Matthews, J. H. *An Introduction to Surrealism*. State College: Penn State University Press, 1965; *Theatre in Dada and Surrealism*. Syracuse, NY: Syracuse University Press, 1974; *Imagery of Surrealism*. Syracuse, NY: Syracuse University Press, 1977; *Surrealism, Insanity, and Poetry*. Syracuse, NY: Syracuse University Press, 1982; *Languages of Surrealism*. Columbia, MO: University of Missouri Press, 1986; Nadeau, Maurice. *The History of Surrealism* (1964). Trans. Richard Howard. New

S

York: Macmillan, 1965; Raymond, Marcel. *From Baudelaire to Surrealism* (1933, 1950). London: Metheun, 1970; Rubin, William S. *Dada and Surrealist Art*. New York: Abrams, 1968; Sawin, Martica. *Surrealism in Exile and the Beginning of the New York School*. Cambridge: MIT Press, 1995; Sitney, P. Adams. "The Instant of Love: Image and Title in Surrealist Cinema," *Modernist Montage*. New York: Columbia University Press, 1990; Spector, Jack J. *Surrealist Art & Writing 1919/39*. Cambridge, England: Cambridge University Press, 1997; Waldberg, Patrick. *Surrealism*. New York: McGraw-Hill, 1966.

Bibliography: Gershman, Herbert S. *A Bibliography of the Surrealist Revolution in France*. Ann Arbor: University of Michigan Press, 1969.

S

SURVEILLANCE CAMERA PLAYERS

(1996).

This New York City activist-performance group, founded by Bill Brown (1959), stages plays before the surveillance cameras abundantly located in city subways and parks. Following in the art/political tradition of the LIVING THEATER and the Situationists, the Surveillance Camera Players aim to draw awareness to the State's authoritarian use of technology, as well as to how acceptant society has become of being watched.

The group creates an intriguing scenario because, within their single performances, are two structurally different plays with varied casts and audiences. First there is the silent performance, at times George Orwell's *1984*, acted out before the surveillance cameras. Since these cameras do not record sound, the performers use large posters in place of spoken dialogue. The cast consists solely of S.C.P. actors and actresses. The primary audience are the station attendants watching on their monitors, but may also include anyone viewing on an overhead monitor.

The second play is not the actual silent performance, which is difficult to follow from many perspectives, but simply the theatre created by the players performing before a manned surveillance camera. Structurally it is closer to a staged happening. The field becomes the entire subway station. The cast now includes the unknowing attendants, whose observing becomes part of the performance, and upon whose act(-ions) depend whether additional cast members, such as the N.Y.P.D., will be involved. The audience includes intrigued passersby and sometimes invited guests.

The actions of one become theatre for another, who—simply observing—creates theater for a third. The suggestion is that at times one can simultaneously be both audience and performer, or, in this case, surveillant and surveilled.

—Douglas Puchowski

Sources: Bill Brown's presentation at the Libertarian Book Club/Anarchist Forum New York, February, 1999; Surveillance Camera Players' performance of *1984* in Washington Square Park, New York, April 15, 1999.

Website: www.panix.com/~notbored/the-scp.html.

SUVERO, Mark di

See **DI SUVERO, Mark**.

SVOBODA, Josef

(10 May 1920).

At the 1967 Montreal World's Fair, I saw Svoboda's Diapolyscreen, which was a wall of 112 adjacent screens, each roughly two-feet square, distributed evenly in rows 8 screens high and 14 screens across (making the grand image roughly thirty feet across and twenty feet high). Each of these screens could be moved slightly forward and back from its moorings in the wall, and each received its own image from projectors behind it. That meant that the entire field could cohere into a larger image, or that the field could be split up into several different images, if not 112 disconnected fragments. Though the fifteen-minute show in Montreal, which depended upon 15,000 slides, was disappointingly linear and obvious, I'd wager dollars to donuts that Svoboda's medium was used more imaginatively elsewhere. My assumption is that his presentations before a more self-selective audience, such as those in a traditional theater, are more sophisticated. I heard of simultaneous projections in his spectacular designs the year before for a London theatrical production of Aleksandr Ostrovsky's *The Storm*, but, alas, did not see it.

Exhibition Catalog: *Josef Svoboda: Bühenbilder und Szenographien*. Berlin: Academie der Kunst, 1969.

Books: Burian, Jarka. *Josef Svoboda's Scenography for Richard Wagner's Operas*. Middletown: Wesleyan University Press, 1983; *The Secret of Theatrical Space: The Memoirs of Josef Svoboda*. Ed. J. M. Burian. New York: Applause, 1995; Siskind, Jacob. *Expo 67: Films*. Montreal, Canada: Tundra Books, 1967.

Web Site: http://www.laterna.cz/svoboda_a.html

SYNAESTHESIA

(1900s).

Color associations with certain sounds or tonalities are common subjective phenomena. It is said that Newton chose to divide the visible spectrum into seven distinct colors by analogy with the seven degrees of the diatonic scale. Individual musicians differ greatly in associating a sound with a certain color. The most ambitious attempt to incorporate light into a musical composition was the inclusion of a projected color organ in ALEXANDER SCRIABIN'S score *Prometheus*, in which the changes of instrumental coloration were to be accompanied by changing lighting in the concert hall. The most common association between tonality and color is that of C major and whiteness. It is particularly strong for pianists, for the obvious reason that the C major scale is played on white keys. However, Scriabin, who had a very strong feeling for color associations, correlated C major with red. By all conjecture, F-sharp major should be associated with black, for it comprises all five different black keys of the piano keyboard, but Scriabin associated it with bright blue and Rimsky-Korsakov with dull green. Any attempt to objectivize color associations is doomed to failure, if for no other reason than the arbitrary assignment of a certain frequency to a given note. The height of pitch rose nearly a semitone in the last century, so that the color of C would now be associated with C-sharp in relation to the old standards. Some artists have dreamed of a total synaesthesia in which not only audio-visual but tactile, gustatory, and olfactory associations would be brought into a sensual synthesis. Charles Baudelaire said: "Les parfums, les couleurs et les sons se répondent." J. K. Huysmans conjured up an organ of liqueurs. He describes it in Chapter IV of his book *À Rebours*:

> Interior symphonies were played as one drank a drop of this or that liqueur creating the sensations in the throat analogous to those that music pours into the ear. In this organ of liqueurs, Curaçao sec corresponded to the clarinet with its somewhat astringent but velvety sound; Kümmel suggested the oboe with its nasal quality; menthe and anisette were like the flute, with its combination of sugar and pepper, petulance and sweetness; kirsch recalled the fury of the trumpet; gin and whiskey struck the palate with the strident explosions of cornets and trombones; vodka fulminated with deafening noise of tubas, while raki and mastic hurled thunderclaps of the cymbal and of the bass drum with full force.

Huysmans continued by suggesting a string ensemble functioning in the mouth cavity, with the violin representing vodka, the viola tasting like rum, the cello caressing the gustatory rods with exotic liqueurs, and the double-bass contributing its share of bitters.

Composers in MIXED MEDIA, anxious to embrace an entire universe of the senses, are seeking ultimate synaesthesia by intuitive approximation, subjective objectivization, and mystical adumbrations. ARNOLD SCHOENBERG was extremely sensitive to the correspondences between light

S

and sound. In the score of his monodrama *Die glückliche Hand* he indicates a "crescendo of illumination" with the dark violet light in one of the two grottos quickly turning to brownish red, blue green, and then to orange yellow.

—Nicolas Slonimsky

SYNTHESIZER

(c. 1955).

This has become the standard name for pre-COMPUTER electronic machines that produce musical sound by assembling specifications of its elements into a synthesis that, thanks to ANALOG CONVERSION, can be heard as sound. The first synthesizers were, like the first computers, mammoth machines that cost hundreds of thousands of dollars and could fill a room. However, once transistors replaced vacuum tubes, multiple production became feasible; once integrated circuits superseded transistors, portability became possible. ROBERT MOOG was a pioneering entrepreneur. Synthesizers can create sounds wholecloth or process sounds fed into them. Video synthesizers also exist, if less popularly, and have been used by STEPHEN BECK and NAM JUNE PAIK, among others. The David Dunn book listed below, originally an exhibition catalog, includes detailed histories of both audio and video synthesizers.

History: Dunn, David, ed. *Eigenwelt der Apparatewelt/Pioneers of Electronic Art*. Linz, Austria, and Santa Fe, NM: Ars Electronica and the Vasulkas (Rte. 6, Box 100, 87501), 1992; Vail, Mark. *Vintage Synthesizers*. San Francisco: Miller Freeman, 1993.

S

TAKIS, Vassilakis

(29 October 1925).

Takis, a Greek sculptor who was born in Athens and lives and works in London and Paris, has made an impressive contribution to KINETIC ART, a contribution that has amounted to a reconceiving of its principal subject matter: the nature and dynamism of vacant space. Whereas ALEXANDER CALDER'S mobiles and, later, GEORGE RICKEY'S sculptures were designed to respond to the subtlest of air currents, Takis's sculptures since 1959 have employed, reacted to, and marked out the forms of magnetic currents. In works such as *Magnetic Ballets* (1961) and *Electro Magnetic* (1960–67), Takis suspends magnets on threads from the ceiling so that they hang near an electromagnet on a platform. As the electromagnet switches on and off in a regular rhythm, the hovering magnets, frequently embedded in metal spheres, move in complex orbital patterns around it. The magnets dance a delicate ballet following the shapes inherent in the flow of the electromagnetic energy that fills space. What Takis is sculpting is not matter, nor even the felt movements of air, but immaterial energy. His use of spheres adds a cosmic suggestion, making his sculptures look like models of planetary motion. As ALLEN GINSBERG once observed, Takis "explained to me that the stars were all pulled together with myriad thin invisible wires of magnetism radiating from every star to every other star—so we imagined, if you pulled out any one star the whole thrumming mechanism would slip a cosmic inch like a quavering mobile 601magnetic tracks, *thunk*."

—Mark Daniel Cohen

Works: *Electro Magnetic*, 1960–67; *Magnetic Ballets*, 1961; *Télélumière*, 1963; *Electromagnetic Sculpture II*, 1965; *Signal*, 1966.

Exhibition Catalogs: Calas, Nicolas. *Takis*. Milano: Galleria Schwarz, 1962; Andersen, Wayne V. *Takis, Evidence of the Unseen*. Cambridge: MIT Press, 1968; *Takis, Magnetic Fields*. New York: Howard Wise Gallery, 1970.

Criticism: Vieville, Dominique. *Takis*. Paris: Editions du regard, 1993.

TALBOT, William Henry Fox

(11 February 1800–17 September 1877).

Talbot is generally regarded as the father of photography. He invented the negative-positive process that enabled the production of multiple prints on paper from a single negative, which continues to be the basis of photography today.

A brilliant student at Harrow and Trinity College in Cambridge, Talbot was graduated in 1825. A scientist at heart, he was elected to the Royal Society in 1831. Like earlier inventors, he experimented with salt and silver nitrate and the camera obscura (Latin for "dark chamber"), and the possibilities of fixing the reverse image it projected. In August 1835 he produced what has become the first surviving negative, a one-square-inch image of a latticed window, taken with an exposure time of about 30 minutes.

A scholar of many pursuits, Talbot left photography after those experiments, but in early January 1839, when he heard of Daguerre's work, he became disturbed that he would not receive credit for his findings, so he presented his "photogenic drawings" on 25 January and described his experiments in a paper presented to the Royal Society on 31 January.

In 1843 he produced a book, *The Pencil of Nature*, with twenty-four photographs and text detailing the scope and potential of his calotype process. He would go on to take many images of insects, leaves, and other botanical specimens.

In June 1844 Talbot made a walking tour of Scotland and published a portfolio—the world's first photo book without text—*Sun Pictures of Scotland*. Talbot went on to discover in 1851 a method for taking instantaneous pictures, invented a new photoengraving process the next year, and in 1854 created a traveler's camera. It combined a camera and two tanks, one for sensitizing wet plates and one for developing prints.

Much of Talbot's work was of scenes in and around his home, Lacock Abbey (now a photography museum) and its environs. He usually created simple documents of nineteenth-century life. Other especially notable photos are his chess players and the construction of Nelson's Column in Trafalgar Square.

In 1855 Talbot won the Grand Medal of Honor in the Paris Exposition for his contributions to photography and another major prize in Berlin in 1865. By then, however, he had essentially retired from photography to concentrate on mathematical theory. He was made an honorary member of the Royal Photographic Society in 1873.

—Gloria S. and Fred W. McDarrah

Works: Talbot, William Henry Fox, *The Fruit Sellers*, 1842.

Books: Talbot, William Henry Fox. *The Pencil of Nature* (1843). New York: Da Capo, 1969; *Sun Pictures of Scotland*. (1844). Ann Arbor: University of Michigan Museum of Art, 1989.

Web Site: http://www.r-cube.co.uk/fox-talbot/

Interpretation: Newhall, Beaumont. *Latent Image: The Discovery of Photography*. Garden City, NY: Doubleday, 1967; Thomas, D. B. *The First Negatives*. London: H.M.S.O., 1964.

TANERAIC

(August 1968).

Over the centuries, people have invented languages for many purposes. These planned languages often had one main purpose: to de-Babelize the globe, enabling people to live and function more comfortably and peacefully together. Other languagewrights had as their goal the development of a perfect language, a language that was logical, or a language that hearkened back to a pre-Babelian time when language was pure and singular, or a language without exceptions or ambiguity. All these languages failed, and the new ones invented continue to fail. But the planned language that succeeds the most in my mind is the hermetic language Taneraic. Devised by the Australian Javant Biarujia (8 August 1955), when the creator was only 13, Taneraic is a beautifully systematic language built not—as most planned languages are—on the roots of other languages, but out of the thin air of human imagination. The language developed from the modest cryptographic notations of a teenager into a language with inflections and set grammatical rules. Within two years of the inception of this language, Biarujia was using Taneraic to write a diary (quite Pepysian for a teenager), having studied English, French, Russian, Esperanto, and the national creole of Indonesia on the way. By 1978, Javant Biarujia (both of whose names are Taneraic inventions) drifted away from the language, gave up writing a diary in Taneraic, and eventually began to forget his language. Having burned all the holographic Taneraic-English dictionaries, Biarujia discovered that the language was no longer open even to the inventor and had to rebuild and rediscover the vocabulary word by word. This act of invention (not of a play or a story or a painting, but of a language) so detailed, so exact, so real, to produce a language for the creator's personal use alone, is the ultimate hermetic art: art for the artist's sake. Occasionally, the lessons of learning the language are "poetic" in themselves: "Ava vayole esnula. Beqa an vayole esnula./We are friends. All of us are friends." But what makes this language-making an art is the wonder the process creates, even as we can't begin to fathom it all.

—Geof Huth

Bibliography: Biarujia, Javant. *This Is a Table*. Seattle, WA: emPO (1002 E. Denny Way, # 202, 98122), 1989; *Abaq Tanerai ilouggi Nanougacyou Tanerai Sasescya Sepou*. Melbourne, Australia: Nosukumo GPO Box 994-H, 3001), 1992–94.

TARNMAN, Ian

(1949–1978).

This is the taken name of a rather conventional Nevada writer and arts executive who, as sometimes happens, discovered that the use of a PSEUDONYM gave him the *freedom* to create extraordinary VISUAL POETRY. Some of Tarnman's poems integrate language with astral projections in a variety of ways; others are composed of just words or just numbers in evocative arrays. Many of them appear as white images on deep black paper, reminding us of a printing option that is still rarely used. Unfortunately, soon after his book *First Principles* (1978) appeared, Tarnman disappeared—though the sometime owner of his name reportedly survives.

Book: *First Principles*. New York: Future (P.O. Box 444, 10012–0008), 1978.

TATI, Jacques

(9 October 1908–5 November 1982, b. Jacques Tatischeff, reportedly of Russian-Dutch-Italian-French descent).

The most sophisticated of the modern comedy directors, Tati resembled Chaplin in both directing his films and playing the protagonist. Tati's self-star is tall, gangling, clumsy, self-absorbed (if not oblivious)—a childlike innocent whose ignorance of social rules causes chaos around him. Because his second major film, *Les Vacances de Monsier Hulot/Mister Hulot's Holiday* (1953) did not depend upon speech, it was an international success. Indeed, the soundtrack is a brilliant mixture of noises, human grunts, snatches of distant conversation in different languages, and much else that would be dismissed as aural garbage did it not enhance the ambience of chaos. Tati's first film, *Jour de Fête* (1949), portrays a provincial postman inspired by an American film about increasing efficiency. *Mon Oncle* (1958) was likewise an international success. Tati's later films become more serious, their satire heavier (particularly in ridiculing moderization/Americanization), and less popular. Financing for subsequent projects became more problematic. "Confusion," announced in 1977, never materialized, though it would have been only his seventh film in a career spanning three decades. Their classic qualities notwithstanding, Tati's films have had remarkably little influence, perhaps because one-person shows are increasingly rare in feature-length filmmaking.

Other Films: *Play-Time/Playtime*, 1964 (but not released until 1967); *Trafic/Traffic*, 1971; *Parade*, 1974.

Videotapes: *Jour de Fête* (1949), Public Media Home VI, 1993; *Mr. Hulot's Holiday* (1953), Home Vision Cinema, 1993; *Mon Oncle* (1958), Home Vision Cinema, 1994; *Play-Time/Playtime* (1964 but not released until 1967), Home Vision Cinema, 1996; *Trafic/Traffic* (1971), Home Vision Cinema, 1996; *Parade* (1974), Home Vision Cinema, 1993.

Web Site: www.ensam.inra.fr/~fontaine/tati (in French and English).

Interpretation: Chion, Michel. *The Films of Jacques Tati*. Trans. Monique Vinas et al. Toronto & New York: Guernica, 1997; Fischer, Lucy. *Jacques Tati: A Guide to References and Resources*. Boston: G. K. Hall, 1983; Harding, James. *Jacques Tati: Frame by Frame*. London: Secker & Warburg, 1984; Maddock, Brent. *The Films of Jacques Tati*. Metuchen, NJ: Scarecrow, 1997.

TATLIN, Vladimir

(16 December 1885–31 May 1953).

Commonly regarded as a founder and principal figure in Soviet CONSTRUCTIVISM, Tatlin returned to Russia from a 1913 visit to PABLO PICASSO'S Paris studio to make innovative abstract reliefs composed of sub-art materials such as tin, glass, and wood. Always rivaling KAZIMIR MALEVICH, Tatlin called his art Productivist (and later Constructivist), in contrast to Malevich's Suprematism. Nonetheless, their purposes were complementary. As Andrei B. Nakov put it, "Tatlin's sculpture is really free of any connection to extra-artistic reality in the same way as Malevich's suprematist forms are purely non-illusionistic."

Once the Soviet Revolution succeeded, the government's Department of Fine Arts commissioned Tatlin to design a *Monument to the Third International* (1919), which he exhibited as a model. With a continuous sloping line resembling that of a roller coaster, this was intended to be 2,000 feet high and to contain assembly halls, smaller spaces for executive committee meetings, all within a central lucite cylinder that would revolve mechanically. Though the proposal was never executed, the architectural historian Kenneth Frampton, for one, has testified, "Few projects in the history of contemporary architecture can compare in impact or influence to Vladimir Tatlin's 1920 design." After the Stalinist crackdown on vanguard art, Tatlin worked mostly on applied projects, such as furniture design, workers' clothing, and the like. Beginning in the late 1920s, he spent several years designing a glider plane which he called *Latatlin*. Though he died in Moscow in relative obscurity, an exhibition was mounted there in 1977 that included paintings, book illustrations, and stage designs. By the mammoth Paris-Moscow traveling show, which I saw in Moscow in 1981, Tatlin was clearly portrayed as a lost star, the exhibition there featuring his *Letatlin*, for instance.

Sculpture: *Monument to the Third International* (aka Tatlin's Tower), 1919–20, eventually destroyed.

Paintings: *Fish Monger*, 1911; *Sailor*, 1912.

Exhibition Catalogs: Anderson, Troels. *Vladimir Tatlin*. Stockholm: Moderna Museet, 1968; Frampton, Kenneth, et al. *Art in Revolution*. London, England: Arts Council of Great Britain, 1971; *Tatlin's Dream: Russian Suprematist & Constructivist Art 1910–1923*. London: Fischer Fine Art, 1974; Nakov, Andréi. *Russian Pioneers of Non-Objective Art*. London: Annely Juda, 1976; *V. E. Tatlin*. Moscow: Sovetskii knudozhnik, 1977; *Paris-Moscow, 1900–1930*. Paris: Centre Georges Pompidou, 1979.

Interpretation: Milner, John. *Vladimir Tatlin and the Russian Avant-Garde*. New Haven: Yale University Press, 1983; Strigalev, Anatolij, & Jürgen Harten, eds. *Vladimir Tatlin, Retrospective*. Köln: DuMont, 1993; Zhadova, Larissa Alekseevna, ed. *Tatlin*. Trans. Paul Filotas, et.al. New York: Rizzoli, 1988.

TATTOOING

(forever).

This is the modern name of a body art that comes from making permanent designs and drawings on human skin. In certain cultures, appropriate design can represent status. In others, such as modern America prior to 1980, tattoos generally refleted declassé living. They have since become more acceptable among the bourgeois, or at least their children, though it is indicative that most tattoos are put on body parts customarily covered by clothing, at least in Western cultures nowadays. This may change, as face painting could become the last frontier of social challenge. (Would you hire a receptionist who had indelibly emblazoned on his or her forehead a barnyard expletive?) The most ingenious tattoos exploit the peculiar luminescnce of human skin, or perhaps body movement, so that an image changes shape when a body part moves, etc. For some, the next step was piercing the body, not just in the ears, as women had done for decades, but elsewhere—nose, tongue, private parts of both men and women, often prompting questions, if not conversation, in otherwise icy social circumstances. Scholars appreciative of artistic tattooing, such as Mark Taylor, have traced it back to the Edo period of Japan at the beginning of the seventeenth century.

This entry, requested by my publisher as the book was going to press, is probably too POSTMODERN for my taste.

Exhibition Catalog: Rubin, Arnold, ed. *Masks of Civilization*. Los Angeles: Museum of Cultural History, 1988.

Interpretation: Carswell, John. *Coptic Tattoo Designs*. Beruit, Lebanon: American University of Beirut, 1958; Hardy, D. E., ed. *Tattoo Time*. 5 vols. Honolulu: Hardy Marks, 1988–91; Thévoz, Michel. *The Painted Body*. New York: Rizzoli, 1984; Taylor, Mark C. *Hiding*. Chicago: University of Chicago Press, 1997.

TAVENER, John

(28 January 1944).

Many people whose taste I respect consider Tavener the strongest composer of his generation, now in late middle age. Whether his music is avant-garde is an open question. On the one hand, he assimilated serial music and electronics; on the other hand, after his conversion to Greek Orthodoxy in 1976, his compositions often sound quasi-medieval in conventional forms, with standard instrumentation. Perhaps this contemporary kind of neoclassicism accounts for why his music is frequently recorded in his native Britain. Tavener is the sort of eccentric composer I'd like to say belongs in this book. His name is often confused with that of John Taverner (c. 1490–1545), whose music is authentically medieval.

Compositions: *3 Holy Sonnets*, for baritone, 2 horns, 2 trombones, strings, and tape, 1962; Piano Concerto, 1962–63; *The Whale*, for mezzo-soprano, baritone, chorus, children's chorus, speakers, 6 actors, organ, orchestra, and tape, 1965–66; *3 Surrealist Songs*, for mezzo-soprano, tape, and piano, 1967–68; *Grandma's Footsteps*, for oboe, bassoon, horn, 5 music boxes, and double string quartet, 1967–68; *Canticle of the Mother of God*, for soprano and chorus, 1976; *Russian Folksongs*, for soprano and 8 instruments, 1977; *Lamentation, Last Prayer and Exaltation*, for soprano and handbells or piano, 1977; *Palintropes*, for piano and orchestra, 1978–79; *He Hath Entered the Heaven*, for trebles and optional handbells, 1982; *Threnos*, for cello, 1990; *Eternal Memory*, for cello and ensemble, 1992.

Recordings: *The Whale*. London: Ring O'Records, 1970; *Music of Tavener*, with several pieces. Collins; *Music of Tavener* (different selection). S. Kringelhorn, soprano; Winchester Cathedral Choir, cond. David Hill. Virgin Classics; *Akathist of Thanksgiving*, for 2 countertenors, orchestra, chorus, and organ. BBC Symphony Orch, cond. Martin Neary. London: Virgin Classics, 1994; *The Protecting Veil*, for cello and orchestra. Stephen Isserlis, cello; London Symphony Orchestra, cond. Gennadii Rozhdestvensky. Virgin Classics, 1992; Quartets No. 1 & 2 for strings. Chilingarian SQ. Virgin Classics; *The Repentant Thief* (1990). Andrew Marriner, clarinet; London Symphony Orchestra, cond. Michael Tilson Thomas, Collins Classics, 1992.

Web Site: http://www.schirmer.com/composers/tavener/bio.html

Interpretation: Haydon, Geoffrey. *John Tavener: Glimpses of Paradise*. London: Gollancz, 1995.

TAYLOR, Cecil

(15 March 1933).

A reclusive musician who rarely performs and whose few available recordings are reportedly not always authoritative, Taylor is one of those rare artists whose reputation gains from personal absence. Active as a JAZZ pianist, poet, composer, and bandleader since the late fifties, Taylor derived compositional ideas from European Impressionism, relying more on tone and texture than rhythm and melody. His group improvisations often featured highly energetic articulations, jagged starts and stops, abrupt changes in mood, and evershifting structures often devoid of melody or beat. Eschewing harmonic landmarks, he refused to use a bassist; and when he played piano behind a soloist, Taylor's improvisations were less complementary than independent. When I heard his *Black Goat* performed at New York's Metropolitan Museum in 1972, I found his favorite structure to be a succession of sounds, quickly articulated and followed by a pause, so that individual instrumentalists played vertical clusters at varying speeds.

Recordings: *Conquistador*. New York: Blue Note B11 E-84260, n.d. (c. 1960); *Silent Tongues*. London: Freedom, 1975; *One Too Many Salty Swift and Not Goodbye* (1978). Therwil, Switzerland: Hat Hut, 1991; *Unit Structures*. New York: Blue Note, 1987; *Looking Ahead*. Fantasy/Original Jazz Classics, 1990; *Jazz Advance*. Hollywood, CA: Blue Note, 1991; *The Cecil Taylor Unit*. New York: New World, 1992; *Air Above Mountains*. Burbank, CA: Enja, 1992; *3 Phasis*. New York: New World, 1992; *Oluiwa*. Milano: Soul Note, 1994; *Dark to Themselves*. Santa Monica, CA: Enja, 1996; *Trance*. Diepholz, Germany: Black Lin, 1997; ——, and Rudd, Rowell. *Mixed*, 1998.

TEITELBAUM, Richard

(19 May 1939).

One of the first virtuosos of the Moog synthesizer, Teitelbaum joined his fellow Americans abroad, Frederic Rzewski and Alvin Curran in the collaboration that would become known as Music Elettronica Viva (MEV). Long committed to live electronic music, Teitelbaum typically used a computer to activitate traditional instruments during concerts. Given his interest in musical robots, along with his Jewish background, it is scarcely surprising that Teitelbaum's most ambitious work should be devoted to the mythical Jewish Golem, a sort of anthropomorphic robot imagined in the Middle Ages to save the Jewish people, only to need to be destoyed because of the damage it created. The result was a kind of opera, *Golem* (1989), for two vocalists along with video projectors and slide projectors. Also familiar with Japanese culture, Teitelbaum was in 1988 the only non-Asian composer commissioned to write a piece in ancient Japanese notation for twenty Buddhist monks.

Compositions: *In the Accumulte Mode*, 1982; *Concerto Grosso*, 1985; *Iro Wa Nioedo/Colors Will Fade*, 1988; *Golem*, 1989.

Recordings: *Golem: An Interactive Opera*. New York: Tzadik, 1995; *Concerto Grosso* (1985) for human concertino and robotic ripieno, with Anthony Braxton, winds, and George Lewis, trombone. Therwil, Switzerland: Hat Art, 1988.

TELEVISION

(c. 1930s).

As an alternative to radio, television should have been hospitable to an avant-garde art, but precisely because it became a medium of universal dissemination, that opportunity rapidly gave way to the American genius for mass-merchandising a new technology that Europeans thought would belong exclusively to the elite (whether automobiles, motion pictures, or portable computers).

However, some early performers used television in ways radically different from the common run, exploiting capabilities unavailable in film and live performance. Before the age of videotape and thus in live time, the comedian Ernie Kovacs (1919–62) tilted the camera to create the illusion that coffee was being poured at a diagonal impossible in life; he used two cameras to situate himself inside a milk bottle; he used smoke from a Sterno can to blur focus; he put two separate images in a split screen (echoing collage); he composed live video accompaniments to the warhorses of classical music; and he used an electronic switch to make half the screen mirror the other, enabling him to stage interviews and even sword fights with himself, etc. Because of the small scale of the TV monitor (compared to the much larger movie screen), Kovacs was able to stage close-up sight gags: His

Television: Ernie Kovacs. Courtesy WhiteStar, Kulture/Video.

femme fatale would, in David G. Walley's words, "slowly turn her head to an admiring camera and then catch a pie in the face," in an image that would not work as well on a big screen (and not at all on radio).

Once videotape was invented, producers could use such devices as instant replay for essentially MODERNIST techniques such as scrambling continuous time; most innovations in broadcast television in the past quarter-century have come less from tinkering with the medium itself than from ingenuity with videotape. A further implication of the dissemination of the portable video camera and the home VCR was the possibility of circumventing television stations in the creation and distribution of VIDEO ART.

Interpretation: Walley, David G. *The Ernie Kovacs Phile* (1975). Rev. ed. New York: Fireside, 1987.

TENNEY, James

(10 August 1934).

An American now teaching in Toronto, Tenney as a musician (pianist and conductor) was part of the Tone Roads ensemble that performed post-Cagean avant-garde music in the early 1960s. As a composer, he worked with industrial engineers at Bell (AT&T) Laboratories in the development of computer-synthesized music and, in 1961–1963, produced early examples. His other compositions have employed a variety of instruments and tape-instrumental configurations. *Ergodos I* (1963) consists of two computer-generated tapes that may be played separately or together, backwards as well as forwards, to be performed with or without certain other Tenney instrumental compositions. As a writer, Tenney authored *Meta + Hodos: A Phenomenology of 20th Century Music and an Approach to the Study of Form* (1964), as well as highly thoughtful essays on JOHN CAGE and CONLON NANCARROW, among others.

Compositions: *Seeds*, for flute, clarinet, bassoon, horn, violin, and cello, 1956; *Essay*, for chamber orchestra, 1957; *13 Ways of Looking at a Blackbird*, for tenor, 2 flutes, violin, viola, and cello or for bass, alto, flute, oboe, viola, cello, and double bass, 1958; *Collage No. 1: Blue Suede*, for Tape, 1961; *Analog No. 1: Noise Study*, for computer, 1961; *Ergodos I*, 1963; *Dialog*, for computer, 1963; *String Complement*, for strings, 1964; *Ergodos II*, for computer, 1964; *Fabric for Che*, for computer, 1967; *Quiet Fan for Erik Satie*, 1970; *Quintext*, for string quartet and double bass, 1972; *In the Aeolian Mode*, for prepared piano and variable ensemble, 1973; *3 Pieces*, for drum quartet 1974–5; *Chorales*, 1974; *Harmonia Nos. 1 to 6*, for various ensembles, 1976–81; *Saxony*, for saxophones and tape delay, 1978; *Glissade*, for viola, cello, double bass, and tape delay, 1982; *Voice(s)*, for women's voice(s) instrumental ensemble, and multiple tape delay, 1982; *Koan*, for string quartet, 1984; *Rune*, for percussion ensemble, 1988; *Critical Band*, for ensemble, 1988; *Cognate Canons*, for string quartet and 2 percussionists, 1995.

Writings: *Meta+Hodos* (1961). Oakland, CA: Frog Peak, 1988; *A History of Consonance and Dissonance.* New York: Gordon & Breach, 1988; "John Cage and the Theory of Harmony (1983)." In *Writings about John Cage*, ed. Richard Kostelanetz. Ann Arbor: University of Michigan Press, 1993.

Recordings: *Selected Works 1961–69*. Berkeley, CA: Artifact, 1992; *Bridge & Flocking*. Therwil, Switzerland: Hat Hut, 1996.

Web Site: http://www.yorku.ca/faculty/finearts/faculty/profs/tenney.htm

TER BRAAK, Menno

(26 January 1902–14 May 1940).

Ter Braak and Edgar Du Perron (1899–1940) were the principal Dutch literary critics of their era, very much predisposed to the avant-garde developments introduced by PAUL VAN OSTAIJEN, among others. They collaborated in starting the periodical *Forum* (1932–1935), which made the radical move of renouncing the division between Dutch and Flemish (Belgian) literature, and thus acknowledged the importance of the Belgian-born van Ostaijen to Holland. They also introduced polemics into a smug cultural scene, beginning with a critique of pretentious and verbose language. The more artistic Du Perron influenced the more intellectual Ter Braak. "What *Forum* stood for, and what its creators practiced," writes E. M. Beekman, "left a lasting impression on Dutch literary and intellectual life. It prepared the Dutch artist for the rapid changes of the contemporary world and dispelled from Holland's intellectual life a smothering nationalism." When the Nazis conquered Holland on 14 May 1940, Ter Braak committed suicide and Du Perron coincidentally died of a heart attack.

Interpretation: Beekman, E. M. "Menno Ter Braak." In *Criticism*, ed. L. S. Dembo. Madison: University of Wisconsin Press, 1968.

TEXT-SOUND

(forever).

As distinct from text-print and text-seen, text-sound refers to texts that must be sounded and thus heard to be "read," in contrast to those that must be printed and thus seen. The term "text-sound" is preferable to "sound-text," if only to acknowledge the initial presence of a text, which is subject to aural enhancements more typical of music. To be precise, it is by nonmelodic auditory structures that language or verbal sounds are poetically charged with meanings or resonances they would not otherwise have. An elementary example is the tongue twister, which is literally about variations on a particular consonant. This term is also preferable to "sound poetry" because several writers working in this area, including GERTRUDE STEIN and W. BLIEM KERN, produced works that, even in their emphasis on sound, are closer to prose than poetry. Only in recent times have we become aware of text-sound as an INTERMEDIUM between language arts on the one side and musical arts on the other, drawing upon each but lying between both, and thus, as a measure of its newness, often unacceptable to purists based in each.

Anthology: Kostelanetz, Richard, ed. *Text-Sound Texts*. New York: Morrow, 1980.

Recordings: Amirkhanian, Charles. *Lexical Music*. Berkeley, CA: 1750 Arch, 1979; ——, ed. *10 + 2 American Text-Sound*. Berkeley, CA: 1750 Arch, 1974; Kern, W. Bliem. *Meditationsmeditationsmeditations-meditations: Selected Poems 1964–73*. New York: New Rivers, 1973; *Text-Sound Festivals: 10 Years, 1967–1977*. Stockholm, Sweden: Fylkingen, 1977; Scholz, Christian, ed. *Lautpoesie: Eine Anthologie*. Obermichelbach, Germany: Gertrud Scholz (Rothenberg, Weinbergstr. 11, D-8501), 1989.

Exhibition Catalog: *Sound Texts: Concrete Poetry Visual Texts*. Amsterdam: Stediljk Museum, 1969.

Interpretation: Hultberg, Teddy, ed. *Literally Speaking: Sound Poetry & Text-Sound Composition*. Göteberg, Sweden: Bo Ejeby (Box 19076, S-400 12), 1993; Kostelanetz, Richard, ed. *Aural Literature Criticism*. New York: Precisely-Archae, 1981; Scholz, Christian. *Untersuchungen zur Geschichte und Typologie der Lautpoesie*. 3 vols. Obermichelbach, Germany: Gertrud Scholz (Rothenberg, Weinbergstr. 11, D-8501), 1989.

THARP, Twyla

(1 July 1941).

Those familiar with Tharp's current choreography, so popular in larger theaters, can hardly believe, or remember, that her dance was once avant-garde. At the beginning of her choreographic career, in the late 1960s, Tharp created a series of rigorously CONSTRUCTIVIST pieces that, in their constrained style, were never exceeded. Using a company composed entirely of female dancers (and thus excluding any of the customary themes dependent upon sexual difference), she choreographed pieces such as *Group Activities* (1968), in which ten dancers, including herself, perform individualized instructions, themselves derived from a numerical system, on two sets of checkerboard-like floor spaces, creating an asymmetrical field of animate patterns, all to the accompaniment of only a ticking metronome. Performed totally without sound accompaniment on an unadorned stage, *Disperse* (1967) depends upon the ratio of 2:3, which requires the stage lighting to turn ever darker as the dancers move progressively into the right rear corner. In *The One Hundreds* (1970), Tharp recruited members of the audience to execute 100 phrases. Her credo at the time: "Dance belonged to everyone, and everyone could be a dancer if the material was appropriate to them."

Tharp around that time also choreographed dances for previously unexploited spaces, such as a playing field in New York's Central Park in the late afternoon. (I remember a rugby game beginning on an adjacent field.) *Dance in the Streets of London and Paris, Continued in Stockholm and Sometimes Madrid* had its premiere on two floors of the Wadsworth Athenæum in Hartford, Connecticut. As Don McDonagh remembers it, "The audience flowed in and around the performers at all levels and at times trailed them from one floor to another. There was no set position from which to view the dance . . . the nine dancers kept in touch with one another by means of verbal time checks called up the stairwell and by the use of video monitors connected to a closed-circuit television hookup between the various galleries." Composed in sections, this Tharp dance could be re-created to suit different venues.

Select Choreography: *Disperse*, 1967; *Group Activities,*, 1968; *Medley*, 1969; *Dancing in the Streets of London and Paris, Continued in Stockholm and Sometimes Madrid,*, 1969; *The Fugue*, 1970; *Push Comes to Shove*, 1976; *Nine Sinatra Songs*, 1982; *The Little Ballet*, 1983; *Bach Partita*, 1983; *In the Upper Room*, 1986; *Quartet*, 1989; *Everlast*, 1989; *Bum's Rush*, 1989; *Brief Fling*, 1990; *Jump Start*, 1995; *How Near Heaven*, 1995; *Americans We*, 1995; *The Elements*, 1996.

Writings: Tharp, Twyla. *Push Comes to Shove*. New York: Bantam, 1992.

Web Site: http://www.abt.org/no_javascript/archives/choreographers/tharp_t.html

Bibliography: McDonagh, Don. "Twyla Tharp." In *The Rise and Fall and Rise of Modern Dance* (1970). Pennington, NJ: A Cappella, 1990.

THEATRE OF CRUELTY

See **ARTAUD, ANTONIN**.

THEATRE OF THE ABSURD

See **ABSURD, THEATRE OF THE**.

THEMERSON, Stefan

(5 January 1910–6 September 1988).

Born in Poland, Themerson was initially a Warsaw painter who also made an avant-garde film, *Europa* (1931), that subsequently disappeared. Working with his wife Franciszka (1907–88), according to the *Encyclopedia of European Cinema* (1995), "They invented an apparatus for making photograms in motion, scratched and painted on film, and fused animation and photomontage with live action." After serving in the Polish army in France during

World War II, Stefan Themerson escaped to England, where he resided until his death, publishing poetry, fiction, and unclassifiable experimental writings almost exclusively in English, mostly with the marvelously titled Gaberbocchus Press (1948): among them, the novels *Bayamus* (1949, which includes typographic poetry), *The Adventures of Peddy Bottom* (1951), *Cardinal Polatuo* (1961), and *Tom Harris* (1967); philosophical essays with titles such as *factor T* (1972); and *St. Francis and the Wolf of Gubbio or Brother Francis' Lamb Chops* (1972), "an opera in two acts," complete with a musical score, handwritten plot summaries, and sketches for stage designs (which is, of course, how operas should be published). Respectful of avant-garde traditions, Themerson also produced a memoir of *Kurt Schwitters in England* (1958) and, in a large-page format, the richest edition of *Apollinaire's Lyrical Ideograms* (1968). It is unfortunate that Themerson's work isn't often mentioned in histories of contemporary British literature, perhaps because like most authors of avant-garde English literature written in Britain, he was born outside of the British Isles. His wife, once settled in London, worked mostly as a painter.

Writings: *Bayamus*. London, England: Editions Poetry, 1949; *Wooff Wooff or Who Killed Richard Wagner?* London: Gaberbocchus, 1951; *The Adventures of Peddy Bottom* (1950). Rev. ed. London: Gaberbocchus, 1954; *Factor T*. London: Gaberbocchus, 1956; *Kurt Schwitters in England*. London: Gaberbocchus, 1958; *Cardinal Pölatuo*. London: Gaberbocchus, 1961; *Tom Harris*. London: Gaberbocchus, 1967; *Apollinaire's Lyrical Ideograms*. London: Gaberbocchus, 1968; *St. Francis and the Wolf of Gubbio or Brother Francis' Lamb Chops*. London: Gaberbocchus, 1972; *The Urge to Create Visions*. Amsterdam: Gabberbocchus & De Harmonie, 1983; *Professor Mmaa's Lecture* (1953). New York: Viking, 1984; *Collected Poems*. New York: Overlook, 1998.

Interpretation: Woods, Gerald, et al. *Art Without Boundaries*. New York: Praeger, 1972.

THEREMIN

(c. 1920).

One of the earliest ELECTRONIC instruments, named after its creator Leon Theremin (1896–1992, b. Lev Sergeyevich Termen), who invented it just after the First World War, this consists of two poles that come out perpendicularly from a metal cabinet. Both poles respond not to touch, like traditional instruments, but to hand movements in the electrified air immediately around them. (Roberta Reeder and Claas Cordes write, "He created his instrument while working on an alarm system to protect the diamond collection at the Kremlin," which seems obvious in retrospect.) One pole controls the instrument's pitch, the other its volume, together producing sustained, tremulous sounds that, needless to say perhaps, were particularly popular in horror films in the 1930s and 1940s. The principal Thereminist in America, if not the world, was Clara Rockmore (1911–98). One of Rockmore's records was produced by ROBERT MOOG, who, before he made the SYNTHESIZER bearing his name, manufactured Theremins. More familiarly, the Theremin was also used with a cello to produce the "Good Vibrations" in a 1966 Beach Boys recording of the same name.

During his eleven years in America (1927–1938), Theremin, according to his countryman NICOLAS SLONIMSKY, "on April 29, 1930, presented a concert with an ensemble of ten of his instruments, also introducing a space-controlled synthesis of color and music. On 1 April 1932, in the same hall, he introduced the first electrical symphony orchestra, conducted by Stoessel, including Theremin fingerboard and keyboard instruments. He also invented the Rhythmicon [with HENRY COWELL], for playing different rhythms simultaneously." Theremin disappeared from New York in 1938 and was thought dead until he emerged from post-Gorbachev Russia in 1991 to attend European music festivals, by then well into his nineties. Recent information indicates that Theremin worked for the KGB on his return to Russia, perfecting electronics for eavesdropping. In the 1990s, in his own nineties, after more than five decades back in Russia, Theremin returned to New York for a visit that is memorialized in an excellent documentary film by Stephen Martin (1993).

Recordings: Rockmore, Clara. *Theremin*. N.p.: Delos 25437,1975; The Beach Boys, "Good Vibrations." Hollywood, CA: Capitol Records, 1966.

History: Reeder, Roberta, and Claas Cordes. "Light Music in the Soviet Union." In *Eigenwelt der Apparatewelt/ Pioneers of Electronic Art*, ed. David Dunn. Linz, Austria, and Santa Fe, NM: Ars Electronica and the Vasulkas, 1992.

Documentary: Martin, Stephen, *Theremin*. Orion Home Video, 1995.

Web Site: http://www.nashville.net/~theremin/

THOMAS, Dylan

(27 October 1914–9 November 1953).

Dylan Thomas was the first modern poet whose work was best "published," best made public, not on the printed page or in the public auditorium but through electronic media, beginning with live radio, eventually including records and audiotape. So strongly did Thomas establish how his words should sound that it is hard not to hear his voice as you read his poetry; his interpretations put at a disadvantage anyone else who has tried to declaim his words since. It is not surprising that he also became the first prominent English-speaking poet to earn much of his income initially not from writing or teaching but from radio recitals, mostly for the British Broadcasting Corporation. (Given the American media's lack of interest in poetry, it is indicative that Thomas's sole peer as a reader of his own verse, Carl Sandburg [1878–1967], a quarter-century older, made his living mostly as a traveling performer of considerably less difficult poetry.) In 1946, Edward Sackville-West gushed: "A verbal steeplejack, Mr. Thomas scales the dizziest heights of romantic eloquence. Joycean portmanteau words, toppling castles of alliteration, a virtuoso delivery which shirked no risk—this was radio at its purest and a superb justification of its right to be considered as an art in itself." Indeed, it could be said that the principal recurring deficiency of Thomas's prose is the pointless garrulousness, filling space with verbiage, that we associate with broadcasting at its least consequential.

So popular did Thomas become that his *Collected Poems* (1952) reportedly sold 30,000 copies within a year after its publication—a number no less spectacular then than now—so popular did brilliant declamation make a difficult poet.

Writings: *The Collected Poems* (1956). Ed. Walford Davies and Ralph Maud. New York: New Directions, 1988; *Selected Poems of Dylan Thomas*. London: Dent, 1975; *Portrait of the Artist as a Young Dog*. New York: New Directions, 1940; *Quite Early One Morning*. New York: New Directions, 1954; *Under Milk Wood*. New York: New Directions, 1954; *Adventures in the Skin Trade and Other Stories*. New York: New Directions, 1955; *The Collected Stories*. New York: New Directions, 1986.

Recordings: *An Evening with Dylan Thomas Reading His Own and Other Poems*. New Rochelle, NY: Caedmon, 1963; *Selections from the Writings of Dylan Thomas*. New Rochelle, NY: Caedmon 1952–60; *More Dylan Thomas Reads: Adventures in the Skin Trade, Quite Early One Morning*. New York: Caedmon Audio, 1993; *Dylan Thomas Reads And Death Shall Have No Dominion and Other Selections*. New York: Caedmon Audio, 1992.

Anthologies: Fitzgibbon, Constantine, ed. *Selected Letters of Dylan Thomas*. New York: New Directions, 1966; Ferris, Paul, ed. *Collected Letters*. New York: Macmillan, 1985; Maud, Ralph, ed. *On the Air with Dylan Thomas*. New York: New Directions, 1991; Thomas, Dylan. *Miscellany: Poems Stories Broadcasts*. London: J. M. Dent, 1963.

Biography: Ackerman, John. *Dylan Thomas: His Life and Work*. New York: Oxford University Press, 1964; Fitzgibbon, Constantine. *The Life of Dylan Thomas*. Boston: Little, Brown, 1965; Sinclair, Andrew. *Dylan Thomas: Poet of His People*. London: M. Joseph, 1975.

Web Page: http://pcug.org.au/~wwhatman/dylan_thomas.html

Interpretation: Cleverdon, Douglas. *The Growth of Milk Wood*. New York: New Directions, 1969; Davies, Aneirin Talfan. *Dylan: Druid of the Broken Body*. London: Dent, 1964; Holbrook, David. *Llareggub Revisited: Dylan Thomas and the State of Modern Poetry*. London: Bowes & Bowes, 1962; Pratt, Annis. *Dylan Thomas' Early Prose: A Study in Creative Mythology*. Pittsburgh: University of Pittsburgh Press, 1970; Tedlock, E. W., ed. *Dylan Thomas: The Legend and the Poet, a Collection of Biographical and Critical Essays*. London: Heineman, 1960; Tindall, William York. *A Reader's Guide to Dylan Thomas*. New York: Farrar, Straus, 1962.

THOMPSON, Francis

(3 January 1908).

Initially a painter, Thompson made several masterpieces of experimental short film that are generally omitted from histories and encyclopedias of the medium. The first short, *New York, New York* (1958, 18 min.), views the city through distorting prisms that function to exaggerate through visual abstraction its distance from nature. The second, *To Be Alive* (1962, also 18 min.), made with Alexander Hammid (1907) for the Johnson Wax Pavilion at the 1964 New York World's Fair, used three screens, of standard ratios, but with fifteen inches between each one to distinguish them from the *continuous* horizontal screens of CinemaScope and Cinerama, which had been developed in the decade before. *To Be Alive* opens with high-speed shots of New York City simultaneously on three screens and subsequently depicts the maturation of people around the world. In one sequence, a prepubescent American boy is learning to ride a bicycle on one screen, a young Italian is learning to paddle a boat, and a similarly young African is learning to ride a mule. Disaster hits each simultaneously, prompting them to cry in unison. For many years after, *To Be Alive* was screened continuously at the Johnson Wax Factory in Racine, Wisconsin. For Hemisfair (San Antonio, 1968), Thompson and Hammid made *US*, which begins with the audience divided into three parts of a circle. When the walls between them are taken up, they are watching a circle surrounded by three screens, each 145-feet wide.

For the Canadian Pacific pavilion at Expo '67 in Montreal, Thompson and Hammid made *We Are Young* (1967, 18 mins.) for six separate screens. The three screens in the lower row were roughly thirty feet square; the three in the upper row were a little wider, much lower, and pushed forward about a foot in front of those below. As in *To Be Alive*, each screen is clearly separated from the others. Sometimes all six screens present the same image synchronously; at other times only one screen is used (while the others are blank). One particularly stunning sequence has the audience moving down six railway tracks simultaneously, each one turned to be perpendicular to the top of the bottom middle screen, the sound of six trains emerging from the amplification system. It seems inappropriate to write about this film as though it may still be available, because once the original venue was dismantled it was never seen again and, according to the filmmaker, may not even exist any longer.

Having established a unique competence with expanded image films, Thompson produced several films in 70 mm. IMAX technology, including *To Fly* (1976), which, at eighteen minutes, is an aerial tour of America from balloon ascent in the 1890s to space flight; *American Years* (1976, 45 mins.), which celebrates Philadelphia's bicentennial as the first historic film show in IMAX. In 1998, Thompson at the age of ninety received from the LFCA (Large Format Cinema Assocation) the Abel Gance Lifetime

Achievement Award, its name recalling the man whose films Thompson saw in Paris in the early 1930s, as his first exposure to the fertile possibility of multiple projection.

Films: *Evolution of the Skyscraper*, 1938–39; *New York, New York*, 1951; *To the Fair*, 1963; *Us*, 1968; *Moonwalk One*, 1971; *City Out of Wilderness*, 1974; *To Fly*, 1976; *American Years*, 1976; *Livng Planet*, 1979; *Energy Energy*, 1982; *On the Wing*, 1986; —— and Hammid, Alexander. *To Be Alive*, 1964; —— and Alexander Hammid. *We Are Young*, 1967.

Interpretation: Krantz, Stewart. *Science and Technology in the Arts*. New York: Van Nostrand, 1974; Youngblood, Gene. *Expanded Cinema*. New York: Dutton, 1970.

THOMSON, Virgil

(25 November 1896–30 September 1989).

A conservative tonal composer of rather simple works, Thomson had the good fortune to get involved in the mid-1920s with Gertrude Stein, his fellow American in Paris. Out of their collaboration came first "Capital Capitals" (1927), a uniquely brilliant (if under-recognized) art song for four male voices, and then *Four Saints in Three Acts* (1927–29), more famous, which was probably the most impressive deviant modern opera of its time. The plot was incomprehensible; so, at first, was much of the language. The sets by the New York painter Florine Stettheimer (1871–1948) featured cellophane. All the performers were African-Americans, which Thomson favored not only for the theatrical value of skin color but for their superior competence at clearly singing English words. (Some identify this as the first prominent twentieth-century appearance of blacks in roles that could have been given to whites.) The excellence of *Four Saints* depended on Thomson's inventive settings of Stein's fanciful, often repeated lyrics:

Pigeons on the grass alas
Shorter long grass short longer longer shorter yellow grass
Pigeons large pigeons on the shorter longer yellow grass also
Pigeons on the grass

To measure the difference, just compare *Four Saints* on the one hand with the colloquial slickness of George Gershwin's *Porgy and Bess* (1935) and, on another hand, the forgotten pseudo-traditional operas produced in the 1920s and 30s. Though Thomson and Stein had to wait several years for the *Four Saints* premiere, which occurred in 1934, not in New York but in Hartford, it received enough acclaim to have a Broadway run. A later Thomson-Stein collaboration, *The Mother of Us All* (1947), was less successful.

As chief music critic at the *New York Herald-Tribune* from 1940 to 1954, Thomson also wrote some of the strongest music criticism, measured sentence by sentence, paragraph by paragraph, though his neglect of younger avant-garde composers makes him appear conservative in retrospect. The problem, in short, was that Thomson didn't learn enough from Stein to advance his musical taste.

Writings: *The State of Music* (1939). 2d ed., revised. New York: Vintage, 1962; *The Art of Judging Music*. New York: Knopf, 1948; *Music Reviewed 1940–54*. New York: Vintage, 1967; *American Music since 1910*. New York: Holt, Rinehart & Winston, 1971.

Autobiography: Thomson, Virgil. *Virgil Thomson*. New York: Knopf, 1966.

Anthology: *A Virgil Thomson Reader*. Intro. John Rockwell. New York: Dutton, 1984.

Recordings: *Capital Capitals*, with Paul Kirby, et al. (Classical Arts); *Four Saints in Three Acts*, cond. Joel Thome (Nonesuch/Elektra, 2–79035–2); *The Mother of Us All*, rec. 1977, Santa Fe Opera, cond. Raymond Leopard (New World 288/289), 1982.

Biography: Cage, John, and Kathleen O'Donnell. *Virgil Thomson: His Life and Music* (1959). Freeport, NY: Books for Libraries, 1970; Watson, Steven. *Prepare for Saints*. New York: Random House, 1998.

Web Page: http://www.schirmer.com/composers/thomson_bio.html

TIERNEY, Hanne

(22 February 1940).

German-born, American-educated, Tierney initially developed the traditional idea of the puppet theater to include modernist texts, such as those by GERTRUDE STEIN. While always manipulating strings, she has used such substitutes for traditional puppets as strikingly colored cloths that, hanging from the ceiling, are made to swirl through the air in her imaginative adaptation of Oscar Wilde's *Salomé* (1986). In *Drama for Strings* (1988), Tierney used geometric formations of suspended plumbing pipes that make their own sounds in a spectacular abstract theater. Even in pieces fifty minutes long, as hers customarily are, she reclaims the ideal of a "theater without actors" made by one person working mostly alone.

Installations and Performances: *Rosie's Compromise*. Flushing, NY: Queens Museum, 1981; *McFarley's Floozie*. New York: Rosa Esman Gallery, 1981; *Salome* (Oscar Wilde). New York: Art Galaxy, 1984; *Stories*. Amsterdam: Mickery Theatre, 1985.

Interpretations: Bass, Ruth. "Hanne Tierney" *Art News* vol. XX, no. 8, April, 1982; Marinelli, Donald. *"Drama for Strings* in Three Movements." *High Performance*, XI/3 (4, 1988).

TIFFANY, Louis Comfort

(18 February 1848–17 January 1933).

Tiffany belongs here, no joke, because he repudiated ornate complexity fashionable in the mid-nineteenth century to design glass lamp fixtures and window screens with uncommon geometries. Commonly classified as Art Nouveau, many Tiffany designs resemble Islamic art in their scrupulous avoidance of representation and thus suggest geometric ABSTRACT ART done decades later. Beginning as an Impressionist painter, Tiffany studied glassmaking in the 1870s and, at the end of that decade, opened a business devoted to interior decoration. In 1880, he parented "favrile" glass that had an iridescent finish. Quickly recognized for excellence, his firm was invited to redecorate the White House in 1883–84. Tiffany persuaded churchmen to accept stained-glass windows with secular subjects. One of the most exquisite permanent exhibitions in Manhattan is that devoted to Tiffany's art in, of all places, the New York Historical Society. He was the son of Charles L. Tiffany, who founded a New York jewelry firm, whose name is synonymous with superfluous luxury, which was a misfortune for the son, whose art realized elegant purity.

Exhibition Catalog: Frelinghuysen, Alice Cooney. *Louis Comfort Tiffany: At the Metropolitan Museum*. New York: Abrams, 1995.

Biography: Koch, Robert. *Louis C. Tiffany: Rebel in Glass*. New York: Crown, 1964.

Web Site: http://www.tiffany.com/intro/lcttifbibli.htm

Interpretation: Duncan, Alastair. *Louis C. Tiffany*. New York: Abrams, 1992; *The Art Work of Louis Comfort Tiffany*. Poughkeepsie, New York: Apollo, 1987.

TINGUELY, Jean

(22 May 1925–30 August 1991).

Born in Germany, educated in Switzerland, Tinguely became the epitome of the inefficient KINETIC ARTIST, which is to say that his flimsily constructed machines were meant to run down. Instead of being a technological artist, he was actually antitechnological, albeit with a sense of humor. His drawing machines of the late 1950s have moving, jointed arms attached to crayons that draw jerky, artistically trivial lines on rolls of paper mechanically fed

Jean Tinguely in front of one of his sculptures, 28 November 1962. Photograph © Fred W. McDarrah.

across them, satirizing the theoretical automatism of EXPRESSIONIST painting fashionable at the time. *Metamatic 17* (1959) could reportedly produce a thousand drawings in an hour, before the age of photocopying and laser printers. Perhaps the climax of Tinguely's career, certainly from a journalistic viewpoint, was his *Hommage à New York* (1960), a sculptural agglomeration that self-destructed in the garden of the Museum of Modern Art, before a distinguished group of invitees, of course, including the writer Calvin Tomkins (1925), who memorialized the pseudo-monumental event first in *The New Yorker* and then in a popular book.

Sculpture: *Metamatic 17*, 1959; *Meta-mechanical Automatic Sculpture*, 1954; *Hommage à New York*, 1960; *Lotus*, 1960; *Baluba Bleu*, 1962; *Fontaine b5*, 1966; *Radio Stockholm*, 1966; *Spirale A III*, 1967; *Char No. 8*, 1968.

Exhibition Catalogs: *Two Kinetic Sculptors, Nicolas Schöffer and Jean Tinguely*. New York: Jewish Museum, 1965; *Tinguely at the Tate Gallery*. London: Tate, 1982.

Catalogue Raisonné: *Jean Tinguely Catalogue Raisonné*. Compiled Christina Bischofberger, Küsnacht/Zurich: Galerie Bruno Bischofberger, 1982.

Bibliography: Tomkins, Calvin. "Jean Tinguely." In *The Bride and the Bachelors*. New York: Viking, 1965; Violand-Hobi, Heidi E. *Jean Tinguely: Life and Work*. Munich & New York: Prestel, 1995.

Web Site: http://www2.tingley.ch/ (in French, German, and English).

TOBEY, Mark

(11 December 1890–24 April 1976).

Before becoming a profoundly original American painter, Tobey joined the Bahai religious movement and then studied calligraphy both in Seattle and in Shanghai. He was well into his forties before discovering his innovative calligraphic "white writing," in which an unmodulated collection of lines, roughly equal in width, run to the edges of the canvas, at times creating a shimmering surface. As in the careers of KAZIMIR MALEVICH and PIET MONDRIAN before him, the turn to ABSTRACTION reflected his religious faith, the Bahai believing in a common humanity and accessibility to all, notwithstanding cultural differences. Such painting presaged the all-over paintings of a later generation and both the OPTICAL ART and monochromic painting of subsequent periods. In the late 1950s, Tobey began to use broader strokes, as well as other colors, including black. Not unlike other spiritual Abstractionists, Tobey had a taste for strong statements: "At a time when experimentation expresses itself in all forms of life, search becomes the only valid expression of the spirit."

Paintings: *Mountains*, 1952; *Edge of August*, 1953; *Canticle*, 1954; *White Journey*, 1956; *Prophetic Light—Dawn*, 1958; *Sagittarius Red*; 1963; *Silverspace*, 1967; *Drift*, 1969.

Exhibition Catalogs: *Mark Tobey, Paintings (1920–1960)*. New York: Yoshii, 1944; *Mark Tobey*. New York: Whitney Museum, 1957; Seitz, William C. *Mark Tobey*. New York: MoMA, 1962; *Tribute to Mark Tobey*. Washington, DC: Smithsonian Institution, 1974; Cummings, Paul. "Lines, Memories, Celebrations." In *Mark Tobey: Works on Paper*. Stanford, CA: Stanford University Museum of Art, 1990.

Interpretation: Dahl, Arthur L. et al. *Mark Tobey: Art and Belief*. Oxford, England: G. Ronald, 1984.

TOCH, Ernst

(7 December 1887–1 October 1964).

As a brilliant young Viennese, Toch composed string quartets while a teenager, studied medicine at the University of Vienna from 1906 to 1909, and then received prizes to study piano and composition at the Frankfurt Conservatory. After service in World War I, he completed a doctorate and became prominent as a musical modernist who both composed and performed. Thanks to an American tour in 1932, he was prepared to emigrate here in 1935, moving the following year to Hollywood, where he composed for films. Though Toch produced a wealth of music in conventional forms, he should be remembered for his innovative masterpiece, *Geographical Fugue* (1930), a SOUND POEM really, for a chorus, not of singers, but speakers who pronounce the acoustically eccentric names of geographical places (e.g., Mississippi, Lake Titicaca, Yokohama, etc.) to a score that emphasizes rhythm. Rarely played or recorded, *Geographical Fugue* include moves that presage electronic SAMPLING. For better or worse, Toch, unlike many other immigrants to the United States from Teutonic countries, never Anglicized the spelling of his first name.

Selected Compositions: *Divertissement for Strings*, for Violin and Cello, Op. 37, No. 1 for Violin and Viola, Op. 37, No. 2 (1925); 13 string quartets: nos. 1–5 (1902–03), no. 6 (1905), no. 7 (1908), no. 8 (1910), no. 9 (1919), no. 10, on "BASS" (1921), no. 11 (1924), no. 12 (1946), no. 13 (1953); *Geographical Fugue*, 1930; 7 Symphonies: no. 1 (1949–50), no. 2 (1950–51), no. 3 (prf. 1955), no. 4 (prf. 1957), no. 5, *Jephtha, Rhapsodic Poem* (1961–62), no. 6 (1963), no. 7 (1964); *Sinfonietta*, for winds and percussion, 1964.

Writings: *The Shaping Forces of Music* (1948). 2d ed., ed. Lawrence Wechler. New York: Dover, 1977; *Placed as a Link in this Chain: A Medley of Observations*. Ed. Mantel Hood. Los Angeles: UCLA Press, 1971.

Biography: Jezic, Diana Peacock. *The Musical Migration and Ernst Toch*. Ames: Iowa State University Press, 1989.

Web Site: http://www.library.ucla.edu/libraries/music/mlsc/toch/

TOLSON, Melvin

(6 February 1898–29 August 1967).

A professor who spent his entire adult life teaching at black colleges and coaching consistently successful varsity debate teams, Tolson was also a poet who raised nonsensical parody to high literary levels. He was a great American DADA poet, though scarcely recognized as such, who could ridicule the allusive techniques of the great moderns, beginning with self-conscious obscurity, in the same breath as certain African-American myths about Africa and much, much else:

> The *Höhere* of God's stepchildren is beyond the
> sabotaged world, is beyond *das Diktat der*
> *Menschenverachtung,*
> *la muerte sobre el esqueleto de la nada,*
> the pelican's breast rent red to feed the young,
> summer's third-class ticket, the *Revue des morts*, the
> skulls trepanned to hold ideas plucked from dung,
> Dives' crumbs in the church of the unchurched,
> absurd life shaking its ass's ears among
> the colors of vowels and Harrar blacks
> with Nessus shirts from Europe on their backs.

Perhaps because such lines offended as they honored (and were easily misunderstood as well), they were not easily published. Though his books appeared from general publishers, it is unfortunate that most recognition of Tolson's innovative work has appeared in special situations reserved for African-American writers.

Books: *Harlem Gallery: Book One, The Curator*. New York: Twayne, 1965; *Rendezvouz with America*. New York: Dodd, 1944; *Libretto for the Republic of Africa*. New York: Twayne, 1953; *Caviar and Cabbage: Selected Columns by Melvin Tolson from the Washington Tribune*. Ed. and intro. Robert M. Farnsworth. Columbia: University of Missouri Press, 1982.

Biography: Farnsworth, Robert M. *Melvin B. Tolson, 1898–1966: Plain Talk and Poetic Prophecy*. Columbia: University of Missouri Press, 1984.

Interpretation: Bérubé, Michael. *Marginal Forces/Cultural Centers: Tolson, Pynchon, and the Politics of the Canon*. Ithaca, NY: Cornell University Press, 1992; Flasch, Joy. *Melvin B. Tolson*. New York: Twayne, 1972. Russel, Mariann. *Melvin B. Tolson's Harlem Gallery*. Columbus, MO: University of Missouri Press, 1980.

TONE CLUSTERS

(1912).

The technique of tone clusters was demonstrated for the first time in public by HENRY COWELL at the San Francisco Music Club on 12 March 1912, on the day after his fifteenth birthday. It consists of striking a pandiatonic complex of two octaves on white keys, using one's forearm, or a panpentatonic set of black keys, as well as groups of 3 or 4 notes struck with the fists or the elbow. Cowell notated the tone clusters by a thick black line on a stem for rapid notes or a white-note rod attached to a stem for half-notes. By a remarkable coincidence, the Russian composer Vladimir Rebikov made use of the same device, with an identical notation, at about the same time, in a piano piece entitled *Hymn to Inca*. Still earlier, CHARLES IVES made use of tone clusters in his *Concord Sonata*, to be played with a wood plank to depress the keys. Béla Bartók used tone clusters to be played by the palm of the hand in his Second Piano Concerto, a device that he borrowed expressly from Cowell, by permission.

—Nicolas Slonimsky

Discography: Bartók, Béla. *Second Piano Concerto*; Cowell, Henry. *Piano Music*, played and introduced by the composer (1963). Washington, DC: Folkways, 1993; *The Piano Music of Henry Cowell*, played by Sorrel Doris Hays. Frederick, MD: Town Hall, 1997; Ives, Charles. *Concord Sonata*. Many other recordings.

TONE ROADS

See **TENNEY, James**.

TORRES-GARCíA, Joaquín

(28 July 1874–8 August 1949).

Born in Montevideo of a Catalan father and a Uruguayan mother, Torres-García studied and worked in Spain before coming in 1920 to New York, where he shared a studio with the painter STUART DAVIS at the Whitney Studio Club, making wooden toys that presaged his later CONSTRUCTIVIST painting. Returning to Europe in 1922, he lived in Paris, where he befriended THEO VAN DOESBURG, PIET MONDRIAN, and MICHEL SEUPHOR, among others. Then in his forties, Torres-García collaborated with Seuphor in founding the periodical *Cercle et Carré* and in organizing the first major ABSTRACT ART exhibition, including over eighty artists. Mindful of his origins, he also organized the first exhibition in Paris of such Latin American artists as the Mexican muralists JOSÉ CLEMENTE OROZCO and DIEGO RIVERA. Returning to his native Uruguay in 1933, Torres-García published manifestos, organized the *Asociación Arte Constructivo*, and founded both an art school and two magazines, in addition to writing a thousand-page book, *Constructive Universalism* (1944). His idiosyncratic paintings favored ideographic images within a grid. Though his name may be forgotten in Europe and North America, Torres-García was one of those modernists who redirected the course of Latin American culture.

Paintings: *Estructura Abstracta Tubular*, 1937; *Construction in Black and White*, 1938; *Rhythm with Obliques with Black & White*, 1938; *Three Figures*, 1946; *Composition with Fish and Sun*, 1948.

Sculpture: *Cosmic Monument*, 1938; *Pachamama*, 1944.

Exhibition Catalogs: Robbins, Daniel. *Joaquín Torres-García*. Providence, RI: Rhode Island School of Design, 1970; Fletcher, Valerie. *Crosscurrents of Modernism: Four Latin American Pioneers*. Washington, DC: Hirshhorn-Smithsonian, 1992.

Interpretation: Castillo, Jorge et al. *The Antagonistic Link: Joaquin Torres-García, Theo van Doesburg*. Amsterdam: Institute of Cont. Art, 1991.

TRANSFUTURISTS

The only Russian group in the post-Stalin period to have a close relationship to the RUSSIAN FUTURISTS consists of a husband and wife team, SERGE SEGAY and REA NIKONOVA and Nikonova's brother-in-law, BORIS KONSTRIKTOR, plus a number of other, less constant associates. Their orientation toward the original avant-garde began in the 1960s in Sverdlovsk (now, again, Yekaterinburg) under the name of the Uktus School (1964–74), after a local ski jump, and from the beginning included experimental activities in the visual and verbal arts simultaneously. While some of their works were not innovative when compared with developments in the West, they were created independently, since access to Western sources of information was very limited at the time. Nikonova and Segay published a journal, *Nomer* (1965–75, 35 issues) in one copy; and the group was one of the first to produce works of a minimalist or conceptualist sort. After the couple returned to Nikonova's birthplace of Yeisk on the Azov Sea in 1974, and the existing issues of *Nomer* were confiscated by the police, they began to issue a new journal, *Transponans* (1979–86, 36 issues), this time in only five copies (the legal limit at the time) that gradually grew in size and elaborateness of means. Since the issues were all handmade, it was possible to vary and combine materials, use elaborate original collages, hand coloring, original sketches, unusually shaped and cutout pages, to spectacular effect. Contributors to the journal included a wide range of contemporary avant-gardists, such as Dmitry Prigov, Genrikh Sapgir, A. Nik, Igor Bakhterev (the last surviving member of the OBERIU group), Yuri Lederman, Anna Alchuk, and many others. Toward the end of its existence, the journal took on the unique shape of what Nikonova dubbed a "rea-structure," in which groups of pages were cut in a variety of shapes, such as triangles, M's, and squares within one issue. While a certain genetic link to the primitivism and ZAUM of Cubo-Futurism is evident in many of their products, the group has nevertheless also created a large body of fresh and unprecedently inventive poetry, visual art, theater pieces, handmade bookworks, mixed media, and intermedia works under rather difficult circumstances.

—Gerald Janecek

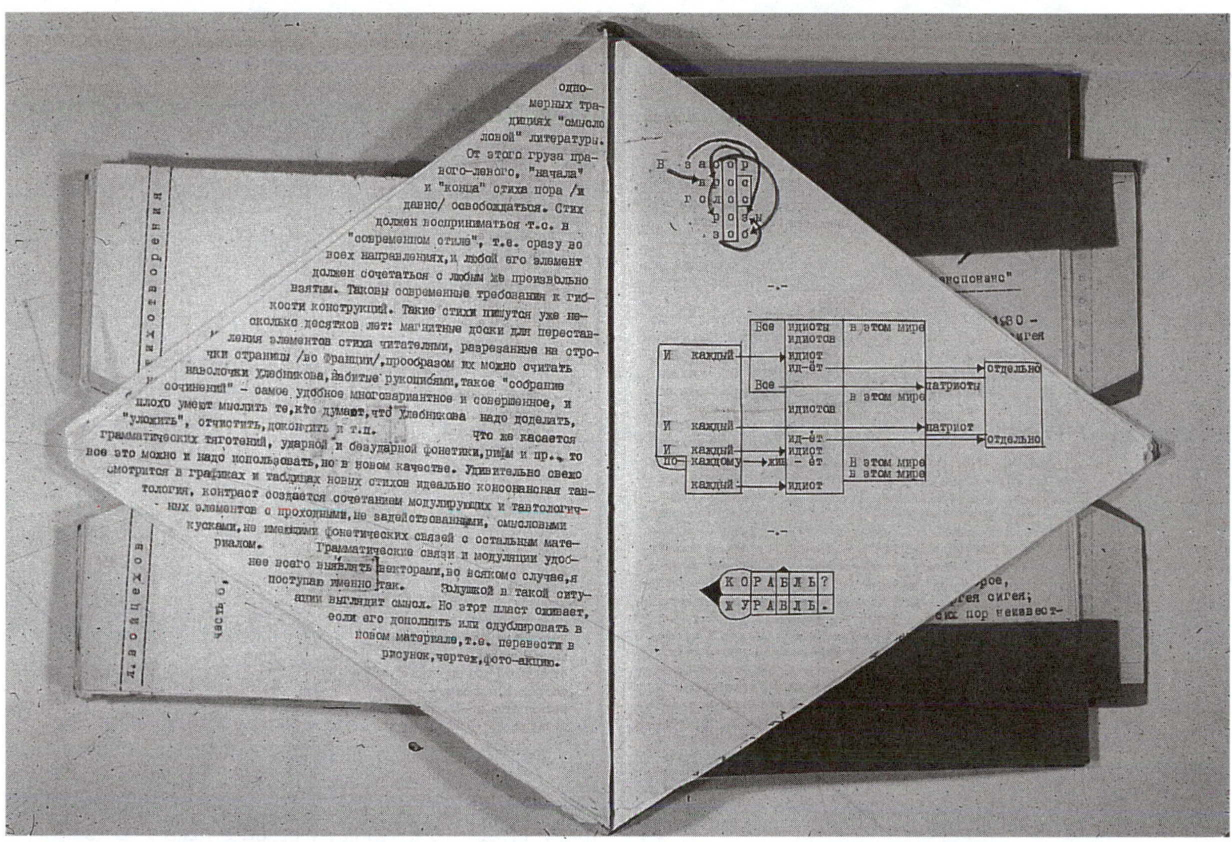

Transfuturists. *Transponans*. Courtesy Gerard Janacek.

Writings: Segay, Serge, and Rea Nikonova. *Transponance Transfuturismus, oder kaaba der abstraktion*. Seigen: experimentelle texte, 1989; *Zaum*. Vienna: Das Fröhliche Wohnzimmer-Edition, 1990; ——, et al. *Transpoetry*. Trento: Centro Arti Visivi, 1989.

Interpretation: Janecek, Gerald. "A Report on the Transfuturists," *Wiener Slawistischer Almanach*, Band 19 (1987), p. 123–42.

TRANSITION

(1927–38).

The most distinguished avant-garde magazine of its time, it was founded by Eugene Jolas, a polylingual American long resident in Paris. In its pages appeared early texts by Samuel Beckett, Bob Brown, and Gertrude Stein; reproductions or pictures of art by Alexander Calder, Man Ray, Constantin Brancusi, L. Moholy-Nagy, and Pablo Picasso; and even musical scores by Aaron Copland and Henry Cowell (in a departure distinguishing it from other literary-art magazines before or since). *Transition* also sponsored symposia on such questions as "Why Do Americans Live in Europe," "Inquiry on the Malady of Language," "Inquiry into the Spirit and Language of Night," or the puzzling early versions of James Joyce's *Work in Progress* (later published as *Finnegans Wake*). So strong has the aura of *transition* been that other literary and art magazines founded by Americans in Paris have tried to recapture it, with less ambition and, alas, less success. Complete tables of contents of all 27 issues appear in 44 pages of the Dugald

McMillan history cited below. Simply looking through them whets one's appetite.

History: McMillan, Dougald. *Transition 1927–38: The History of a Literary Era*. New York: Braziller, 1976.

Anthologies: Jolas, Eugene, and Robert Sage. *Transition Stories*. New York: Walter McKee, 1929; Jolas, Eugene, ed. *Transition Workshop*. New York: Vanguard, 1949; *In Transition: A Paris Anthology*. Intro. Noel Riley Fitch. New York: Doubleday Anchor, 1990.

t

TRNKA, Jiří

(24 February 1912–30 December 1969).

Having created a puppet theater before World War II, Trnka set up in 1945 a film studio in Prague that specialized in puppet animation, which depends not upon drawings in sequence but on the movement of three-dimensional figures on a field. Unlike American animators, who were restricted to short films, Trnka founded his reputation on a feature, *Špalíček/The Czeck Year* (1947). His principal achievement is an adaptation of William Shakespeare's *A Midsummer Night's Dream (Sen noci svatojánské)* (1959). *Ruka/The Hand* (1965) is a parable about the role of the artist under Communist totalitarianism.

Other Films: *Staré pověsti české/Old Czech Legends*, 1953; *Osudy dobrého vojáka Švejka/The Good Soldier Švejk*, 1954; *Kybernetická babička/Cybernetic Grandmother*, 1963; *Archandêl Gabriel a paní Husa/Archangel Gabriel and Mother Goose*, 1964.

Videotapes: *Two Little Frosts*. New York: Phoenix Films, 1973; *A Midsummer Night's Dream*. New Jersey: Laserdisk Corp. of America, 1986.

Book: Bocek, Jaroslav. *Jiri Trnka, Artist and Puppet Master*. Prague: Artia, 1965.

TRUCK, Fred

(6 September 1946).

Born in Iowa, where he still lives, Truck produced a chapbook of hieroglyphic VISUAL POETRY, *Tangerine Universe in 3 Refrains* (1975), in addition to *Loops!!* (1978), an edition of fifteen jars, each containing a Mobius strip, among other unusual literary objects. An early user of desktop computers, Truck began publishing his *Catalog of the Des Moines Festival of the Avant-Garde Invites You to Show (without really being there)* (1979, 1982, 1984) out of his house. *George Maciunas, Fluxus, and the Face of Time* (1984) he describes as "a graphically indexed study of Maciunas's work," which he printed on two long, continuous sheets of computer paper.

In 1985 Truck cofounded the *Art Com Electronic Network*, an early "electronic publishing medium uniting menu-driven magazines, a bulletin board service for performances and discussion of art," for computer-modem-assisted artists hooked into the WELL, a national arts network. In continual contact with other artists similarly advanced, Truck from 1986 through 1991 worked on "an artificially intelligent art work, *ArtEngine*, which applies heuristics to graphics and text analysis." His book *Archaeopteryx* (1992) has "designs for an artist's flight simulator based on Leonardo da Vinci's flying machine, which flies in visual reality."

Bottega (1995) was probably the first CD-ROM produced by an artist in America. Designed for a Macintosh computer with "8 megabytes of RAM and a 640 x 480 x 256 color monitor," it became inoperable when Apple upgraded the Macintosh operating system from 7.0x to System 8. "Unfortunately, nothing can be done about this except a complete rewrite," Truck wrote me at the end of 1998, "and I have since moved on to other things, motivated in no small part by the fact that digital art has a life expectancy of about 6 weeks due to the constant shifting of operating standards. My new work is focused on output that cannot be affected by changes in the hardware or operating system software. Try http://www.fredtruck.com/frontend.html." Truck has become, in short, the epitome of the advanced literary-computer artist, more experienced and better prepared than most to work in the twenty-first century.

Publications: *Tangerine Universe in 3 Refrains*. Des Moines, IA: Privately published (4225 University, 50311), 1975; *The Development of Signs in Space* (the book). Des Moines, IA: Privately published, 1981; *The Biennial Report of the Performance Bank*. Des Moines, IA: Privately published, 1982; *George Maciunas, Fluxus and the Face of Time*. 2 vols. Des Moines, IA: Privately published, 1984; *The Memory Bank*. Des Moines, IA: Privately published, 1986; *ArtEngine Texts: Manual and Essays on ArtEngine Software*. Des Moines, IA: Privately published, 1991; *Archaeopteryx*. Des Moines, IA: Privately published, 1992; *Bottega*. CD-ROM. Des Moines, IA: Privately published, 1995; *The Monitor*. CD-ROM. Des Moines, IA: Privately published, 1996; Double Reflecting Pool. Computer Game. CD-ROM. Des Moines, IA: Privately published, 1997.

Services: *The Electric Bank*, a database of performance art, including text and images (currently in progress), 1983; *The Art Com Electronic Network*, and a database implemented, 1985.

Sculpture: *loops*, 1978; *Mr. Milk Bottle Gets Into Advertising,* 1998; *Mr. Milk Bottle after his Adventure with the Steamroller,* 1998; *The Marching Watertowers,* 1998; *Mr. Milk Bottle Action Figure Waiting for Godot (He Does Not Move),* 1998; *The Badge of Quality Collection,* 1999.

Web Site: http://www.fredtruck.com/frontend.html

TSAI, Wen-Ying

(13 October 1928).

Tsai calls his innovative work Tsaibernetic Sculptures (a play on "CYBERNETIC"), which is his generic term for nearly 100 unique objects that are similar in their operations but different in measurements and details. Born in China, trained at American colleges in engineering, which qualified him for years of work as a project manager in the construction industry, Tsai deduced in the 1960s that he could combine engineering with his painterly interests, producing sterling examples of avant-garde technological art. Influenced by an USCO exhibition in 1966, he used a flickering STROBE LIGHT that was aimed at shiny flexible rods with tops the size of bottle caps. Thanks to a motorized base, these rods could shake at variable speeds. The strobe light, flickering at a slightly different frequency, caught these vibrating rods in a succession of striking postures. Because the result was the anthropomorphic illusion of dancing, he transformed a firm material, steel, to look as though it had lost its rigidity

One improvement in the evolution of this genre was the ability to change the flickering speed of the strobe in response to either sounds in the surrounding space or the spectator's proximity to a sensing device in the sculptures themselves, making them a pioneering example of responsive or cybernetic art (which I take to be technically more advanced than artistic machines that move autonomously). Another later development was making the upright rods out of fiberglass, rather than stainless steel. Though no two of these Tsai sculptures are identical, they resemble one another much like siblings in a family that, at last count, is still growing.

Of Tsai's other KINETIC sculptures, *Upwards-Falling Fountain* (1979) is particularly impressive, creating an illusion that must be seen to be believed. As the water falling from a vibrating showerhead is illuminated by a strobe, the droplets are caught dancing in response to sound; at certain strobe speeds, the droplets appear to be moving upwards, violating all rules of gravity. *Living Fountain* (1980–88) is a yet larger water sculpture, incorporating a showerhead three feet in diameter, plus three concentric circles of water jets, all installed above a basin twelve by sixteen feet. Here the strobe is designed to respond to combinations of changes in audible music, random sensors, audio-feedback controls, and a computer program.

Painting: *Random Field,*, 1963.

Sculpture: *Multi-Kinetic Wall*, 1965; *Multi-chromics*, 1971; *Upwards-Falling Fountain*, 1979; *Computer*

Column, 1980; *Sun Dial*, 1988; *Living Fountain*, 1980–88.

Exhibition Catalogs: *Cybernetic Art of Tsai Wen-Ying*. Taipei, Republic of China: National Museum of History, n.d. [1990]; *Cybernetic Sculptures: The World of Tsai Wen-Ying*. Beijing, China: Center Art and Science Foundation, 1997.

Interpreation: Kostelanetz, Richard. "Artistic Machines." In *Metamorphosis in the Arts*. New York: Assembling, 1981; —— "Tsaibernetics." In *On Innovative Art(ist)s*. Jefferson, NC: McFarland, 1992.

t

TUCKER, William

(28 February 1935).

One of the New Generation British sculptors of the early 1960s, Tucker presented sculptures not much different from those of his contemporaries, but he accompanied them with an intellectual program of surprising rigor. In his writings, Tucker located the significance of sculpture in its condition of being an object—in its stable and unchanging nature. In essence, sculpture is the fixed point in a turning world. Despite the cogency of Tucker's thinking, his early works added little to the ground that was already being covered by PHILIP KING. In the middle of the 1980s, Tucker turned to a style completely different from that of his previous efforts, and far more his own. Tucker began modeling by hand large and ponderous masses that look half like nearly formless lava boulders and half like human figures committing heroic gestures. In their craggy appearance, they harken back to the rough surfaces of Alberto Giacometti (1901–66) and GERMAINE RICHIER. But unlike his predecessors, Tucker walks the line between the formed and the formless, creating shapes that seem as much the byproducts of geological forces as human images produced by a human being.

—Mark Daniel Cohen

Works: *Persephone*, 1964; *Memphis*, 1965–66; *Series A (Number 1)*, 1968–69; *Cybele*, 1994; *Vishnu*, 1995.

Exhibition Catalogs: *William Tucker: Sculpture: 4–26 July, 1963*. London: Rowan Gallery, 1963; *William Tucker, Sculpture 1970–73*. London: Arts Council of Great Britain, 1973; David McKee Gallery. *William Tucker: September 9 to October 3, 1987*. New York: David McKee Gallery, 1987; *William Tucker, Recent Sculptures and Monotypes: 10 July–5 September 1987*. London: Annely Juda Fine Art, 1987; *William Tucker: Gods, Five Recent Sculptures*. London: Tate Gallery, 1987; Ashton, Dore, and Dahlia Morgan. *William Tucker*. Miami, FL: Art Museum at Florida International University, 1988.

TUDOR, David

(20 January 1926–13 August 1996).

Trained in piano and organ, as well as music composition, Tudor established himself in the 1950s as the premier pianist for avant-garde music by giving first performances of major pieces by PIERRE BOULEZ, EARLE BROWN, JOHN CAGE, KARLHEINZ STOCKHAUSEN, and CHRISTIAN WOLFF, among others. Indeed, before long, pieces were written especially for him, one composer reportedly joking that Tudor "could play the raisins in a slice of fruitcake." By the late 1960s, however, he gave up piano performing to become a composer, alas with less distinction, specializing in "live ELECTRONIC MUSIC", in contrast to that composed in a tape studio. In live Electronic Music, the composer has at his or her disposal a variety of sound-generators and processors, some of his or her own invention, customarily performing in collaboration with others. Among those younger musicians who later performed themselves in this genre are Linda Fisher (1949) and John Driscoll. Kyle Gann writes, "Tudor's magnum opus was a series of works begun in 1968 under the collective title *Rainforest*. In these works, assemblages of suspended cast-off objects—lawn sprinklers, car windshields, bicycle rims—were made to vibrate with transducers, bringing the detritus of civilization to acoustic life." Tudor was for many years one of the few musicians performing regularly with the MERCE CUNNINGHAM Dance Company.

Works: *Flourescent Sound*. Stockholm, 1964, *Bandoneon!* for Factorial Bandoneon, 1966; *Rainforest*, 1968; *Pepsi Bird, Pepscillator*, and *Anima Pepsi*, 1970; *Untitled*, 1972; *Melodics*, 1972; *Microphone (1–9)*, 1973; *Laser Bird* and *Laser Rock*, 1973; *Photocell Action*, 1974; —— with Nakaya, F. *Island Eye and Island Ear* sound and fog environment, 1974–78; *Pulsars* 1976; *Pulsars II*, 1978; *Sea Tails*, 1983; *9 Lines Reflected*, 1986; *Web for J.C., Web for J.C. II*, and *Electronic Web*, 1987; *Lines and Reflections*, installation, 1987; *Neural Synthesis (No. 2)*, 1993.

Recordings: *Rain Forest; Pulsars/Untitled*. New York: Lovely LML 1601, n.d.

Web Site: http://wolfpack.bard.edu/tudor/

Interpretation: Gann, Kyle. *American Music in the Twentieth Century*. New York: Schirmer, 1997.

TURRELL, James

(6 May 1943).

The most remarkable thing about James Turrell's career, when you look back on three decades of it, was that he knew from the beginning that his medium would be light. He didn't discover light after a career of exhibiting objects or a period of theorizing. His first exhibition, in 1967, just two years after his graduation from college, consisted entirely of projections within a museum space. He then created, in his own Southern California studio, a series of light-based installations by cutting slits into the walls and ceiling to let sunlight sweep through his space in various experimental ways; he used lenses to refract it strategically.

The first Turrell work I saw was *Laar* (1980). On the other side of a darkened room appeared to be a large, grey monochromic painting. As you moved closer, it retained that identity, its surface shimmering, much as good monochromic painting sometimes does. Only when you are literally on top of the work, close enough to bump your head into it, do you discover that, surprise, the monochromic rectangle is really a hole in the wall—or, to be more precise, an open window into a three-dimensional space painted gray. If only to accentuate the illusion of entering a palpably different world, you could feel that the air behind the aperture had a perceptually different weight—heavier to my extended hand. In a later variation, *Daygo* (1990), shown at the Gladstone Gallery in New York in 1990, I stuck my head through the rectangle and noticed purplish light fixtures. In either case, the effect was magical, the illusion inexplicable.

For nearly two decades now, Turrell has been working in remote Arizona on transforming a volcanic crater into a celestial observatory. The "Roden Crater Project," as he calls it, should be a masterpiece; but until it is complete, as well as more popularly accessible, my Turrell nomination for the contemporary canon would be *Meeting*, as installed in 1986 at P.S. 1 in Long Island City. You are asked to come no earlier than an hour before sunset and to stay no later than an hour after sunset. You're ushered into a former classroom, perhaps twenty feet square; most of the ceiling has been cut away into a smaller rectangle, leaving the sky exposed. (It looked like clear glass to me until I felt the temperature change.) Benches are run along the walls, but it is perhaps more comfortable to lie on the floor rug, looking skyward. Along the top of the benches runs a track, behind which is a low level of orange light, emerging from tungsten filaments of thin, clear, meter-long, 150 watt Osram bulbs. (Having no visible function before sunset, these lamps make a crucial contribution to an illusion.)

What Turrell has done is frame the sunsetting sky, making its slow metamorphosis visible, in an unprecedented kind of theater that proceeds apart from human intervention. The sky looks familiar until it begins to turn dark. Lying in the middle of the floor, I saw the sky pass through a deep blue reminiscent of YVES KLEIN. Above me developed, literally out of nowhere, the shape of a pyramid, extending into the sky; and as the sky got darker, the apex of the navy blue pyramid slowly descended down into the space. Eventually it vanished, as the square became a flat, dark grey expanse, looking like nothing else as much as a James Turrell wall "painting," before turning a deep uninflected black that looked less like the open sky than a solid ceiling. Now, I know as well as the next New Yorker that the sky here is never black; there is too much ambient light. What made it appear black was the low level of internal illumination mentioned before. (You can see the same illusion at an open-air baseball night game where, because of all the lights shining down onto the field, the sky likewise looks black.) I returned on another day that was cloudier than before, to see textures different from those I remembered. On the simplest level, what Turrell does is manipulate the natural changing colors of the sky, first through the frame that requires you to look only upwards, and then with thoughtful internal illumination that redefines its hues.

What is also remarkable is how much intellectual resonance the work carries to a wealth of contemporary esthetic issues, such as illusion/anti-illusion, painting/theater, unprecedentedly subtle perception, the use of "found objects" (in this case, natural light), and conceptualism (bestowing meaning on apparent nothing), all the while transcending all of them. I personally thought of JOHN CAGE'S 4′ 33″, his "noise piece," in which he puts a frame around all the miscellaneous inadvertent sounds that happen to be in the concert hall for that duration, much as Turrell frames unintentional developments in the sky. *Meeting* is essentially *theatrical* in that it must be experienced over a requisite amount of time; no passing glance, as well as no single photograph, would be appropriate. Indeed, though *Meeting* could have been realized technically prior to the 1950s, there was no esthetic foundation for it prior to then.

Works *Afrum*, 1967; *Laar*, 1980; *Meeting*. New York: PS 1, 1986; *Daygo*. New York: SteinGladstone, 1990; *Roden Crator Project* (forthcoming).

Exhibition Catalogs: Adcock, Craig. *James Turrell*. Tallahassee: Florida State University Gallery and Museum, 1979; *James Turrell, Light & Space*. New York: Whitney, 1980; *Occluded Front*. Ed. Julia Brown. Los Angeles: Museum of Contemporary Art—Lapis, 1985. Herbert, Lynn, et. al. *James Turrell: Spirit and Light*. Houston, TX: Contemporary Arts Museum, 1998; Rothschild, Deborah Menaker, ed. *James Turrell*. Williamstown, MA: Williams College Museum of Art, 1991; Andrews, Richard, and Chris Bruce. *James Turrell: Sensing Space*. Seattle, WA: Henry Art Gallery, 1992; *Air Mass, James Turrell*. Ed. Mark Holborn. London: South Bank Centre, 1993.

Interpretation: Adcock, Craig. *James Turrell: The Art of Light and Space*. Berkeley: University of California Press, 1990.

TUTUOLA, Amos

(June 1920–8 June 1997).

Tutuola is Nigeria's most original novelist, a thinly educated war veteran who wrote English as only a Nigerian could. "I was a palm-wine drinkard since I was a boy of ten years of age," Tutuola's first book begins. "I had no other work more than to drink palm-wine in my life. In those days we did not know other money, except COWRIES, so that everything was very cheap, and my father was the richest man in our town." And it gets only more original. Because Tutuola reportedly grew up speaking Yoruba, he makes authentic errors of English grammar and spelling on every page; yet his several novels have clear plots, usually about a protagonist with (or with access to) supernatural powers, who suffers awesome hardships before accomplishing his mission. One scholar reports that educated Nigerians "were extremely angry that such an unschooled author should receive so much praise and publicity abroad, for they recognized his borrowings, disapproved of his bad grammar, and suspected he was being lionized by condescending racists who had a clear political motive for choosing to continue to regard Africans as backward and childlike primitives." Even with modest success, authentically original artists will always be attacked for some purported deficiency or another.

Writings: *The Palm-Wine Drinkard and His Dead Palm-Wine Tapster in the Dead's Town* (1952). New York: Grove, 1994; *My Life in the Bush of Ghosts* (1954). New York: Grove, 1994; *Simbi and the Satyr of the Dark Jungle* (1955). San Francisco: City Lights, 1988; *The Brave African Hunters*. New York: Grove, 1958; *Ajaiyi and His Inherited Poverty*. London: Faber, 1967; *The Witch-Herbalist of the Remote Town*. London: Faber, 1981; *Pauper, Brawler, and Slanderer*. London: Faber, 1987; *Feather Woman of the Jungle*. San Francisco: City Lights, 1988; *The Village Witch Doctor and Other Stories*. London: Faber, 1990.

Interpretation: Lindfors, Bernth, ed. *Critical Perspectives on Amos Tutuola*. Washington: Three Continents, 1975.

TWELVE-TONE MUSIC

See **SERIAL MUSIC**.

2001

(1968).

Stanley Kubrick (1927–99) was a good, intelligent, morally sensitive filmmaker who, in the heady wake of the success of his second-best early film, *Dr. Strangelove* (1964), made this classic for CinemaScope projection. Because *2001* was not publicly available in that form for many years, we tend to forget how it filled wide, encompassing screens with memorable moving images, all of which had an otherworldly quality: the wholly abstract, richly textured, and incomparably spectacular eight-minute "Jupiter and Beyond the Infinite" (as the clumsy subtitle announces the sequence); the stewardess performing her routine duties in the gravity-less spaceship; and the opening scenes in the space vehicle (which are filled with more arresting details than the eye can comfortably assimilate). Rather than focusing our attention, the movie consistently drives our eyes to the very edges of the screen (much like another CinemaScope masterpiece, David Lean's *Lawrence of Arabia*, 1962), in the course of emphasizing the visual over the aural.

Over two hours long, *2001* has only forty-six minutes of dialogue, making it in large part, paradoxically, a mostly silent film for the age of wide-screen color, incidentally placing it in the great avant-garde tradition of mixing the archaic with the new as a way of eschewing expected conventions. Indicatively, *2001* ends with several minutes of images-without-words, rather than, say, an exchange of lines. The central image of the monolith, whose initial mysteriousness is reminiscent of the whale in Melville's *Moby Dick*, becomes a symbol whose final meaning is revealed as literally the sum of the movie itself, putting a seal of accumulated perception upon the preceding action.

One is surprised to recall how many intelligent people, including prominent reviewers, disliked *2001* at the beginning, and how many parents were less enthusiastic than their children. "I ought not to have found this surprising," wrote the physicist Freeman Dyson (1923), "for I am myself of the generation that was bowled over by Disney's Fantasia thirty years ago, while our sophisticated elders complained in vain about our shocking bad taste." Even though *2001* alludes to Georges Melies's *Trip to the Moon* (1902), there has not been anything like it since, whether for small screens or large; it's too bad that the large-screen motion-picture theaters capable of showing it best are by now nearly extinct.

Videotapes: *2001: A Space Odyssey*. Los Angeles: Rhino Video, 1998.

Web Site: http://www.palantir.net/2001/

Interpretation: Agel, Jerome, ed. *The Making of Kubrick's 2001*. New York: New American Library, 1970.

TYPEWRITER LITERATURE

(c. 1940s).

Composing literature directly on the typewriter enables authors to exploit its capacity for regularizing inscriptions and, better yet, for giving publishers camera-ready pages to print, rather than allowing typesetters to falsify the spacing and other design dimensions. Though certain typewriters presaged computers in permitting closer spacing of lines and/or letters, the creation of expressive shapes was possible on all typewriters. Among those making poems in this way were two older poets of conservative tastes, William Jay Smith (1914) and May Swenson (1919–89), in both cases briefly, and then younger poets, among them DOM SYLVESTER HOUÉDARD and KARL KEMPTON. Robert Caldwell (1946) founded his periodical *Typewriter* (1971) on the reasonable assumption that such writing deserved an outlet of its own. More interesting, to my mind, were the novels composed on the typewriter and printed directly from a typescript: the original edition of RAYMOND FEDERMAN'S *Double or Nothing* (1971), Willard Bain's *Informed Sources* (1969), and especially Guy Gravenson's brilliant *The Sweetmeat Saga* (1971), in which fragments are splayed rectilinearly across the manuscript page. Since the early 1980s, authors have used home computers to produce camera-ready pages that approach (but don't quite equal, especially in the lack of subtle kerning) the appearance of professional typesetting.

Books: Gravenson, Guy. *The Sweetmeat Saga*. New York: Outerbridge & Dienstfrey, 1971; Riddell, Alan. *Typewriter Poems*. London, England: London Magazine, 1975.

TZARA, Tristan

(4 April 1896–24 December 1963; b. Samuel or Sami Rosenstock).

A Rumanian Jew who left his native country at nineteen, Tzara almost always wrote in French, initially as a cofounder of ZURICH DADA in 1917 and then as a SURREALIST in Paris from 1920–34, when ANDRÉ BRETON ousted him from the club for his deviant radicalism. He remains the only poet to make substantial contributions to both movements. The critic Marc Dachy credits Tzara with giving "French poetry a new impetus, a sudden acceleration. He took unpunctuated free verse, inherited in part from GUILLAUME APOLLINAIRE and BLAISE CENDRARS, and transformed it into an extraordinarily powerful instrument. By exciting the latent energies in language he created an extreme poetry filled with vertiginously polysemic meanings and the novel rhythms of substantives flashing by like telephone poles seen from a speeding car." Apart from this achievement, Tzara wrote a great long poem, *L'Homme approximatif* (1931, *The Approximate Man)*, and a classic protoCONCEPTUAL manifesto in the form of a poem:

> "To make a Dadaist poem/ Take a newspaper./Take a pair of scissors./ Choose an article as long as you are planning to make your poem./ Cut out the article./ Then cut out each of the words that make up this article & put them in a bag./ Shake it gently./ Then take out the scraps one after the other in the order in which they left the bag./ Copy conscientiously./ The poem will be like you."

The image of the Jewish emigré avant-garde literary activist, working in a country and language both not his own, has inspired later poets.

Works: *Approximate Man, and Other Writings*. Trans. Mary Ann Caws. Detroit, MI: Wayne State University Press, 1973; *Seven Dada Manifestoes and Lampisteries* (1924). Trans. Barbara Wright. London: Calder, 1971; *Selected Poems*. Trans. Lee Harwood. Toronto, Canada: Coach House-Underwhich, 1987.

Bibliography: Caws, Mary Ann. *The Poetry of Dada and Surrealism*. Princeton: Princeton University Press, 1970; Dachy, Marc. *Tristan Tzara: Dompteur des Acrobates*. Paris, France: L'Échoppe, 1992; Peterson, E. *Tristan Tzara*. New Brunswick: Rutgers University Press, 1971.

Web Site: http://dept.english.upenn.edu/~jenglish/English104/tzara.html (essay on Dadaism by Tzara).

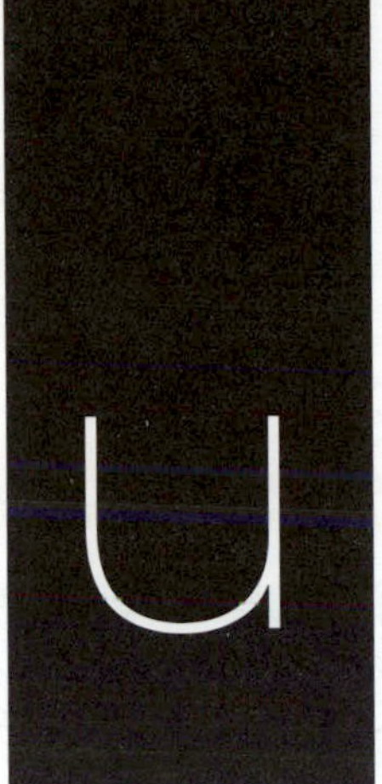

UITTI, Frances-Marie

(c. 1950).

An American who has spent most of her life in Europe, she now lives mainly in the Netherlands. Initially an accomplished cellist, Uitti has worked closely with a number of major figures—including JOHN CAGE, GIACINTO SCELSI, and the Dutch composer Louis Andriessen (1939). Her most distinctive contribution is the development of a method of playing the cello with two bows (in one hand) simultaneously. This enables her to create three- and four-part polyphony, giving the instrument the potential for unprecedented harmonic richness. Luigi Nono (1924–90), Scelsi, Sylvano Bussotti (1931), György Kurtàg (1926), and Vinko Globokar (1934) have all written works for her utilizing this technique. It figures in her own compositions and improvisations, along with other novelties, including six-string cello, prepared cello, viola da gamba, and various electronic modifications. Uitti's own compositions, which seem most influenced by Scelsi, have a brooding, meditative quality that is perhaps best represented on the LP *The Second Bow* (1980). More active in recent years as an improvisor than as a composer, Uitti has collaborated frequently with British composer Jonathan Harvey (1939), and has recorded an album with the American avant rock guitarist Elliott Sharp (1951).

—Tony Coulter

Discography: A) as composer and improvisor: *The Second Bow*. Milan: Cramps Records, 1980; *Museum Cello Tour*. The Hague: Haags Gemeentenmuseum, 1983; *2 Bows*. Amsterdam: BvHaast, 1995; *Imaginings* (with Jonathan Harvey). London: Planet Blue Records, 1994; *Improvisations* (with Elliott Sharp). Amsterdam: Jdk Productions, 1997. B) as performer [selected]: Cage, John. *Works for Cello*. Amsterdam: Etcetera Records, 1991; Harvey, Jonathan. *Music for Cello*. Amsterdam: Etcetera Records, 1991; Scelsi, Giacinto. *Music for Cello*. Amsterdam: Etcetera Records, 1992.

Web Site: http://htdocs.com/Uitti/

UKELES, Mierle Laderman

(25 September 1939).

A courageously unfashionable artist who has pursued the implications of her chosen subject, Ukeles has focused on the business of garbage in New York City since publishing her 1969 *Manifesto for Maintenance Art*. For one of her pieces, *Touch Sanitation Performance* (1978), she endeavored to shake hands individually with all of the city's sanitation workers; for the multi-part *Sanitation Celebrations* (1983), she made *The Social Mirror*, "a mobile public sculpture" that was actually a sanitation truck "clad in hand-fitted tempered glass mirror with Plexiglas trim," and instructed six other three-wheeled sweepers to perform a five-part "Futurist Ballet" on Madison Avenue. For the World Financial Center, she made *Ceremonial Arch Honoring Service Workers in the New Service Economy* (1988). Though Ronald Reagan's head of the NEA once ridiculed awarding her work a government grant, he lacked sufficient religious sophistication to notice that, as an observant orthodox Jew, Ukeles was basing her art upon rituals of cleansing. It is not for nothing that she has also proposed *MIKVA* (1986), or a ritual bath of female purification. "Her vision unfolds in her artistic decisions," the Jewish Museum's exhibition catalog tells us, "which derive from a personal interpretation of rabbinical injunctions relating to the specifications for constructing a *mikveh*." She has been artist-in-residence at New York City's Sanitation Department for nearly three decades.

Writings: *Manifesto for Maintenance Art* (1969). In *Idea Art*, ed. Gregory Battcock. New York: Dutton, 1973.

Works: *Touch Sanitation Performance*, 1978; *Sanitation Celebrations*, 1983.

Web Site: http://longman.awl.com/artforms/profiles/meirle.asp (interview and photos of works).

Interpretation: Morgan, Robert C. "Mierle Laderman Ukeles: Shaking off the Material Art." In *Art into Ideas: Essays on Conceptual Art*. New York: Cambridge University Press, 1996; "Mierle Laderman Ukeles." In *Jewish Themes/Contemporary American Artists II*. New York: The Jewish Museum, 1986.

ULRICHS, Timm

(31 March 1940).

A distinguished German POLYARTIST, Ulrichs has worked with various ideas in VISUAL POETRY, PERFORMANCE ART, graphics, and sculpture, in a bewildering variety of formats. For himself, he has taken the banners of *total Kunst* and *Totalkünstler* ("total artist"). His work is very popular with German *Künsthallen*, which are city-sponsored exhibition spaces more predisposed to avant-garde shows than, say, the comparable American venue of university galleries. Even though Ulrichs speaks English fluently and has even exhibited English-language visual poetry:

roseroseros erose
* * *
roseroseroseroserose
eros

his work is rarely seen in the United States.

Works: *Unten links: Ich drücke der Welt meinen Stempel auf!*, 1965; *Bild-Bild*, 1966; *Tür-Winkelmesser*, 1968–69; *Scharnier-Raum*, 1968; *Strasse*, 1969; *Baum-Plomben und-Prothesen (Baumchirurgische Operationen)*, 1970–71; *Vom Sockel-in-Sockel*, 1981–1990.

Artist's Book: *Ich Mache (Diese) Schlagzeilen!* [10 posters in a box.] Hannover, Germany: Privately published, 1980.

Exhibition Catalogs: *Timm Ulrichs: übersetzung translation traduction*. Hannover, Germany: Privately published, 1974; *Timm Ulrichs: Retrospektive 1960–1975*. Braunschweig, Germany: Kunstverein, 1975; *Timm Ulrichs, Totalkunst*. Lüdenscheid, Germany: Städtische Gallery, 1980.

ULYSSES

(2 February 1922).

Born on James Joyce's fortieth birthday, *Ulysses* is the center of his *oeuvre*. The experiments in realism and language in *Dubliners* (1914) and *A Portrait of the Artist as a Young Man* (1916) are the basis of the day given in *Ulysses*. Beginning in Dublin at 8:00 AM on the morning of 16 June 1904, the book ends early the next day, as Molly Bloom fades into sleep. Many of the characters who appear in Joyce's early books show up during this day in *Ulysses*: it is a continuation of the adventures of the autobiographical Stephen Dedalus in the Dublin of Joyce's earlier fiction. However, if this modern epic is a continuation of Joyce's writing, it is also a radical break with his own work and that of early modernism. Thus it lies at the very heart of what we now call high modernism.

At the end of the novel, after Molly puts the book to sleep, there is this tag:

Trieste-Zurich-Paris
1914–1921

Three cities and seven years are the geographical and temporal markers of a literary revolution. From the experiments of *Ulysses*—especially its later chapters—spring Joyce's "nightbook" called *FINNEGANS WAKE* (1939). But, as with everything to do with Joyce, we must begin with a city not named here—a city "named" throughout his writing. Joyce maintained that if the entire city of Dublin were burned down—a real possibility after the events of 1916—it could have been rebuilt, brick by brick, from the pages of *Ulysses*.

HUGH KENNER, one of the more famous of modernist critics to take on the mantle of "Joycean," has stated that Joyce is the greatest writer of the metropolis since Milton raised the infernal city in *Paradise Lost*. "Dear Dirty Dublin," as Joyce calls it repeatedly throughout the *Wake*, was always his subject. Even after his self-imposed exile from his homeland at the age of twenty-two, Joyce always went back to Dublin in his writing. The parochialism of Irish culture, the overall colonial position of Ireland, and the power of the Roman Catholic Church were forces that repelled Joyce because he saw them as threats to his art. But Dublin itself always remained in his imagination; he felt that it was part of his artistic mission to give the city on the Liffey to the world.

Important for Joyce for many reasons, Dublin was most important for producing *him*. Deep in *A Portrait of the Artist as a Young Man*, Stephen tells an Irish nationalist friend: "—This race and this country and this life produced me . . . I shall express myself as I am." Also Joyce's sentiment, this lies behind all of his work. In 1904—the same year in which *Ulysses* takes place—Joyce, then twenty-one, wrote a self-portrait called "A Portrait of the Artist as a Young Man" for the Dublin magazine *Dana*. Combining autobiographical elements with stylistic flourishes that place the piece somewhere between essay and short story, this Paterian attempt to give some account of his evolution as an artist became the seed for the early version of *A Portrait* called *Stephen Hero*. The piece met with a reaction that would almost always accompany Joyce's work; the "essay-story" was rejected by the magazine's editor, who told Joyce: "I can't print what I can't understand." What is fascinating about this early piece is that it demonstrates how Joyce's views about experience and consciousness were already challenging traditional views of both. And this led into what he called the "looking-glass" of *Dubliners*.

A collection of fifteen stories about the lives of people living in Dublin, *Dubliners* is commonly taken to exhibit the realist Joyce of epiphanies and resolutions, the Joyce whose characters come to some kind of revelation about their lives and struggles. However, the stories in the collection consistently resist any kind of "solution." They actually pose problems that are not resolved for their characters—or readers. It is thus fitting that the seed of what would become *Ulysses* was planted with Joyce's first assault upon the realist tradition.

When Joyce started to write his novel *Ulysses*, it was late 1914 (or, by some accounts, early 1915), and Europe had plunged into the Great War. The Joyces moved from Trieste to neutral Zurich to wait out the conflict, incidentally marking a major stage in Joyce's writing career. *Dubliners* finally appeared in June 1914 after a seven-year struggle. Joyce's publisher objected to many passages he found either libelous or otherwise objectionable; and Joyce, characteristically, refused to alter a single word. Joyce's only play, *Exiles*, was completed in 1915. *A Portrait of the Artist* was published in New York in 1916, and

Joyce wrote the collection of erotic sketches known as *Giacomo Joyce* (first published in 1968). The infamous trouble with his eyes also began around this time, and he had the first of a series of painful eye operations in August 1917.

What is fascinating about Joyce's composition of *Ulysses* is that his conception of the entire book changed as he wrote it. These changes did not occur on the level of plot but in the novel's "styles" and experiments. Through the help of EZRA POUND, who aided Joyce with almost everything during this time, including advice about good eye doctors, chapters of the novel were serialized in the pages of *The Little Review* in New York and, in London, in *The Egoist*. The serialization in *The Egoist* ended after only three chapters because the magazine could not find an English printer who would agree to set type for it.

The Little Review had more success, as fourteen installments of the novel appeared in its pages between 1918 and 1920. But in 1920 four issues of the magazine containing excerpts from the novel were seized and burned by the U.S. Post Office. *The Little Review's* editors, Jane Heap and Margaret Anderson, were put on trial for publishing obscenity. The lawyer who defended them was John Quinn, a New York based Irish-American attorney who collected modernist manuscripts (including a famous early manuscript of *Ulysses*, later known as the Rosenbach Manuscript) and modern art. Quinn's defense of the novel centered on the premise that, since it was "incomprehensible," it could not also be obscene. Joyce did not think this defense had merit, and neither did the judges. Heap and Anderson were found guilty of publishing obscenity and prohibited from printing any more of *Ulysses*. Only in 1933 was the novel cleared of obscenity charges in the United States by Judge John M. Woolsey, who wrote: "But my considered opinion . . . is that whilst in many places the effect of *Ulysses* on the reader is undoubtedly emetic, nowhere does it tend to be an aphrodisiac."

Joyce feared that the novel would never see the light of day. And for good reason—it had been declared obscene even before he had finished it. But this respite from meeting publication deadlines also gave him the opportunity to expand his vision of the latter part of *Ulysses*. At the nadir of his feelings over the fate of his novel, help came in the form of an American expatriate bookseller named SYLVIA BEACH, who owned Shakespeare and Company, a Paris bookstore and meeting place for writers and readers, primarily of English and American literature. Beach offered to print the novel under the imprint of her bookstore. It was a courageous decision. Without her support the book might never have been completed.

Faced with the loss of *The Little Review* as an outlet for his writing, Joyce spent more time revising earlier parts of the book and expanding later ones. The opening chapters of *Ulysses* are marked by Joyce's development of the interior monologue, a technique he said he first appreciated in a late-Symbolist work by Edouard Dujardin. In the second half of the book, Joyce's experiments in technique and form are intensified. The tenth episode, called "Wandering Rocks," depicts a simultaneous moment with many different characters moving through the streets, homes, shops, and pubs of the city (this chapter stands behind Dos Passos's development of his "Camera Eye" technique in *Manhattan Transfer* [1925] and *The USA Trilogy* [1930–1936]). The eleventh episode, "Sirens," is in the form of a *fuga per canone* ("A fugue according to rule"), while the twelfth episode, "Cyclops," analyzes the violence inherent in colonialism and the Irish nationalist response to it by injecting seemingly dissociated stylistic parodies into the "realist" setting of a pub.

Joyce's experiments reach a climax in the fifteenth episode of the novel called "Circe." Here the very form of the novel breaks apart to reveal what the French critic Hélène Cixous (1937) calls an "opera-out-of-gear," or a play "out of control" because everything that has happened in the novel up to this point recurs and impossible things happen (objects speak, ghosts emerge, Shakespeare himself appears in a mirror wearing horns, Leopold Bloom gives birth to multiple children, and Dublin itself is burned down after a Black Mass).

From this point onward, the novel slows down; the remaining chapters take up the theme of being tired (episode sixteen using exhausted metaphors and clichés), as well as the desire to understand everything about the Bloom household and the world around it. Episode seventeen is written in the form of a catechism, with things such as the flow of water into the Bloom sink described in intricate detail—a technique sure to have had effect on those who would later practice the *nouveau roman*. The last, "infamous" chapter of the book is Molly Bloom's interior monologue in eight long sentences unencumbered by the rules of punctuation.

The place of *Ulysses* in modernism may be judged by its immediate effect on those writers and artists associated with the avant-garde at the time. Pound claimed the book ended the realist tradition: "He has done what Flaubert set out to do in *Bouvard and Pécuchet*, done it better, more succinct. An epitome." Pound's reading of the early parts of the novel seems to have had an important effect on his revisions of the *Cantos*. Virginia Woolf was at first put off by Joyce's subject matter: she wrote that *Ulysses* was "a book of a self-taught working man, and we all know how distressing they are, how egotistic, insistent, raw, striking, and ultimately nauseating." Ultimately, however, Joyce's work forced her to her most extreme experiments, including *Mrs. Dalloway* (1925), a novel reflecting a great debt to the "Wandering Rocks" chapter of *Ulysses*. The Soviet filmmaker SERGEI EISENSTEIN called Joyce the single great influence on his work and went so far as to credit the Irish novelist with shaping his vision of film: "The year that gave birth to the idea of intellectual cinema was the year I became acquainted with Joyce's *Ulysses*." (The two met in Paris in the thirties, and Joyce showed interest in having Eisenstein bring *Ulysses* to the screen.)

In a famous review of the novel, T. S. ELIOT pointed to the "mythical method" in *Ulysses* as a technique "of controlling, of ordering, of giving a shape and a significance to the immense panorama of futility and anarchy which is contemporary history." The description of this "method" seems to have even more relevance for that other key text of 1922, *The Waste Land*. As an editor at *The Egoist*, Eliot had been exposed to the early installments of the novel, and it exerted a great influence on his composition and "controlling" of contemporary history in *The Waste Land*. But if Eliot's review said more about his poem than it did about Joyce's novel, something he said to Woolf says more about *Ulysses* than many were able to admit when the first book appeared. For Eliot, *Ulysses* "destroyed the whole of the 19th century. It left Joyce with nothing to write another book on. It showed up the futility of all the English styles." It left nothing for Joyce to write except *Finnegans Wake*, a text that first emerged from some of the notes he had made while working on his modernist epic.

The battles over *Ulysses* that still rage are concerned not with the novel's subject matter but with the establishment of a definitive text. Since the first (Paris) edition was filled with errors, there have since been ten other editions that have likewise been contested by textual scholars. In 1986, Hans Walter Gabler, a professor in Germany, issued with the original American publisher what was called "the Corrected Text." However, his "corrections," along with several additions, were quickly questioned, most notably by John Kidd of Boston University. This dispute placed Random House in the odd position of keeping in print two different editions of *Ulysses* (Gabler's and a 1961 text it was intended to supersede). As a high modernist text, *Ulysses* remains a fluid odyssey that denies "meanings" and interpretative theories at the same time that it resists textual standardization.

—John Rocco

Text: Joyce, James. *Ulysses*. Ed. Hans Walter Gabler with Wolfhard Steppe and Claus Melchior. New York: Vintage, 1986.

Recordings: *Ulysses* (BBC, 1993, 6 hrs.). New York: Bantam Doubleday Dell Audio, n.d.

Web Site: http://home.att.net/%7Ejoycewars/build.html (Discusses the controversy over the publication of Ulysses.)

Interpretation: Arnold, Bruce. *The Scandal of "Ulysses."* New York: St. Martin's Press, 1991; Barrow, Craig Wallace. *Montage in James Joyce's "Ulysses."* Madrid: Jose Porrua Turanzas, 1980; Budgen, Frank. *James Joyce and the Making of "Ulysses" and Other Writings*. Oxford & New York: Oxford University Press, 1960; Cixous, Hélène. "At Circe's, or the Self-Opener." Trans. Carol Bove. *Boundary* 2, 3 (1979); Davison, Neil R. *James Joyce, "Ulysses," and the Construction of Jewish Identity*. Cambridge & New York: Cambridge University Press, 1996; Eliot, T. S. "*Ulysses*, Order, and Myth." In *Selected Prose of T. S. Eliot*. Ed. Frank Kermode. New York: Harcourt Brace, 1975; Ellmann, Richard. *The Consciousness of Joyce*. New York: Oxford University, 1977; ——. *"Ulysses" on the Liffey*. New York: Oxford University Press, 1972; French, Marilyn. *The Book as World: James Joyce's Ulysses*. New York: Marlowe 1994; Gilbert, Stuart. *James Joyce's "Ulysses."* New York: Vintage, 1955; Gottfried, Roy. *Joyce's Iritis and the Irritated Text: The Dis-Lexic "Ulysses."* Gainesville: University of Florida Press, 1995; Groden, Michael. *"Ulysses" in Progress*. Princeton: Princeton University Press, 1977; Hart, Clive, and David Hayman, eds. *James Joyce's "Ulysses": Critical Essays*. Berkeley: University of California Press, 1977; Hayman, David. *"Ulysses": The Mechanics of Meaning*. Englewood Cliffs, NJ: Prentice–Hall, 1970; Herring, Philip F., ed. *Joyce's Notes and Early Drafts for "Ulysses": Selections from the Buffalo Collection*. Charlottesville: University of Virginia Press, 1977; ——, ed. *Joyce's "Ulysses" Notesheets in the British Museum*. Charlottesville: University of Virginia Press, 1972; Kenner, Hugh. *Dublin's Joyce*. Bloomington: Indiana University Press, 1956; ——. *Ulysses*. Baltimore and London: Johns Hopkins University Press, 1987; Lawrence, Karen. *The Odyssey of Style in "Ulysses."* Princeton: Princeton University Press, 1981; Pound, Ezra. *Pound/Joyce: The Letters of Ezra Pound to James Joyce*. Ed. Forrest Read. New York: New Directions, 1967; Segal, Jeffrey. *Joyce in America: Cultural Politics and the Trails of "Ulysses."* Berkeley: University of California Press, 1993; Weldon, Thorton. *Allusions in "Ulysses": An Annotated List*. Chapel Hill: University of North Carolina, 1982.

UNDERGROUND COMIX

(1968–)

The first question that comes to mind about underground comix (the x in the last word being the preferred spelling) is "Why are these avant-garde?" Often seen as nothing more than a grandchild of the Tijuana bibles of the 1930s through 1950s, underground comix showed their vanguard colors by their disdain for conservative mores, their frenetic devolution of the narrative form, and sometimes by their style of drawing, which could erupt in a flow of interconnected images of sex, violence, and drug use, blowing apart in a single page the safe and easy reliability of the middle-class life most of the artists had come from. This artform may appear mainstream because of its mode of publication, but at heart underground comix presented a serious break with the traditions of the past and were an examination of the possibilities of the medium. That is what the avant-garde is about.

—Geof Huth

Bibliography: Estren, Mark J. *A History of Underground Comics*. 4th ed. Berkeley: Ronin, 1993; *The New Comics: Interiews from the Pages of Comics Journal*. Ed. Gary Groth & Robert Fiore. New York: Berkeley, 1988.

UNEMPLOYMENT INSURANCE

(1935)

The hidden truth, which should not be forgotten, is that this economic safety net has done more for American artists, both avant-garde and traditional, in times of genuine economic need than all of the Arts Councils combined. Only when the latter become as effective as the former at fundamental support will they have earned genuine respect from the art community.

UNITED STATES

(1776).

America has historically been a country hospitable to avant-garde art, in spite of an oppressively commercial civilization and an uneven history of patronage by individuals and the state. The United States was founded on the ideals of freedom and independence, no less for art than for enterprise, and so artistic possibility becomes entwined in financial opportunity. The archetypal American creative artist has been the "pathfinder" who leaves, often with naive motives, the confines of "civilization," a metaphor for conventional, historically European notions of artistic possibility, to explore the uncharted frontier, sometimes achieving a "breakthrough" into esthetic territory unknown before. What particularly characterizes American explorations is a willingness to pursue esthetic ideas literally, wholeheartedly, and unself-consciously to ultimate and unprecedented ends. In a culture in which politics and, alas, arts patronage even at its best have been limited by the art of the possible, art exemplifies the politics of the impossible. America became the Western world's artistic virgin land, as many of the compositional ideas that have strongly influenced the organized European avant-gardes—from Edgar Allan Poe's Symbolist poetic theory through Henry James's and WILLIAM FAULKNER'S fictional techniques to JOHN CAGE'S notions of aleatory music—have been American in origin. This tradition accounts for why America's greatest representational arts—fiction as well as painting—tend, in contrast to European, to be more visionary and mythic (penetrating to the hidden essences of life), rather than concrete and realistic (encompassing a wealth of verifiable experience).

Bibliography: Kostelanetz, Richard, ed. *The New American Arts* (1965). New York: Collier, 1967, Lynes, Russell. *The Lively Audience: A Social History of the Visual and Performing Arts in America, 1890–1950*. New York: Harper & Row, 1985.

Web Site: http://www.fedworld.gov/

UNITED STATES OF AMERICA

(1967–1970).

A sort of rock band formed in 1967 by Joseph Byrd (1937), an avant-garde composer who had worked with LA MONTE YOUNG and TERRY RILEY, this group featured Byrd on pre-SYNTHESIZER electronic sound generators, Dorothy Moskowitz on vocals, and others playing electronic percussion, an electric violin, and a fretless guitar-like bass. Not unlike FRANK ZAPPA, they tried to incorporate avant-garde ideas into rock music, such as using a ring modulator to alter singers' voices in live time. In spite of initial support from a large record company, they lacked the popular appeal of, say, Zappa's Mothers of Invention. They performed with a three-foot by four-foot neon American flag whose red and white stripes flashed alternately, and sometimes dressed as businessmen in suits, priests with Roman collars, or Japanese World War II soldiers with rifles and bayonets. "We were a Left Wing band (for ex: 'Love Song for the Dead Che')," Byrd wrote me a while ago, "but one which had no constituency among the political Left." Once the group disbanded, Byrd produced under his own name *The American Metaphysical Circus* (1969). Many other pop musicians have nonetheless followed the group's precedent of using electronic instruments in live time.

Recordings: *United States of America* (1968). Brentford, Middlesex, England: Edsel, 1997; Byrd, Joe, and the Field Hippies. *The American Metaphysical Circus*. New York: Columbia, 1969.

USCO

(c. 1965–1970).

In the era of "hippie" collaboration, USCO was the epitome of a POLYARTISTIC commune—literally meaning Us Company, or Company of Us. The three principals were Michael Callahan (1944, initially a technician), Steve Durkee (1938, originally a painter), and Gerd Stern (1928, historically a poet). Collectively USCO produced striking posters, KINETIC sculptures, a mixed-media discotheque, kinetic information displays, and MIXED-MEANS theatrical events. Their masterworks were kinetic ENVIRONMENTS filled with paintings, objects, audio, slides, films (sometimes looped), colored lamps, and a pulsing STROBE LIGHT. The one I remember best, and which incidentally influenced many artists who saw it, was at the Riverside Museum in Manhattan in May 1966. The space was filled with elemental symbols and materials: male and female, heartbeats, and seven spheres representing seven planets. "We also had five elements," Durkee told me. "We had sand in the box in the middle; fire in the candles; we had air; we had water in the fountain around the periphery of the column, which was also the lingam inside the yoni—a psychosexual situation. There was an 'om' tape playing on a stereo tape recorder. 'Om' was the original sound of the universe. What we had in that room, in short, was everything that is."

USCO disbanded in the 1970s. The last time I checked, Callahan was working as a technician at Harvard University's Carpenter Center, Stern in a family food business, and Durkee in architecture.

Bibliography: Kostelanetz, Richard. "USCO." In *The Theatre of Mixed Means* (1968). New York: Archae, 1980.

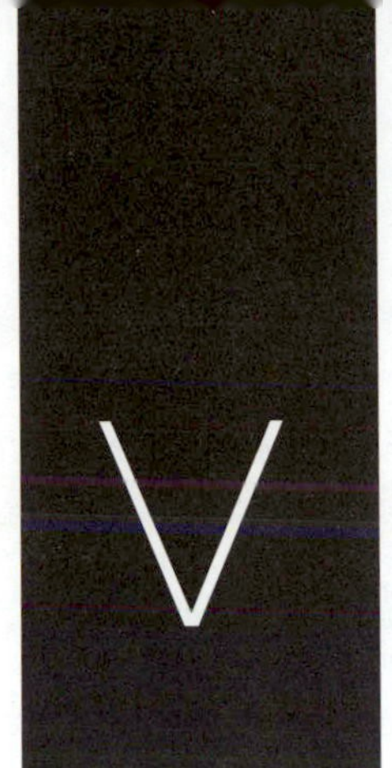

VALDEZ, Luis

See **EL TEATRO CAMPENSINO**.

VAN DOESBURG, Theo

(30 August 1883–7 March 1931).

Van Doesburg was, like his near-contemporary MOHOLY-NAGY, essentially a POLYARTIST, excelling at two or more non-adjacent arts—painting, architectural design, criticism, and creative literature. In the first respect, he was famous for rigorously geometric, CONSTRUCTIVIST paintings, such as *Composition XI* (1918) and *Counter-Composition XIII* (1924), and then for deviating from his fellow Dutchman PIET MONDRIAN by introducing diagonals into his art. For the second art, consider particularly his CONCEPTUAL ARCHITECTURE in the form of spectacular models, only one of which was ever realized—his designs for the interiors of the Aubette Café in Strasbourg, France.

Van Doesburg's critical essays are filled with incisive distinctions and stunning prophecies, for he had mastered the manifesto writer's art of resonant sentences: "We are painters who think and measure"; "in the name of humanism one has tried to justify quite a lot of nonsense in art"; and "the best handicraft is the one which displays no human touch."

Van Doesburg's contributions to creative writing began with his second *DE STIJL* manifesto (1920), which was devoted to "literature." If only to distinguish the DADA side of his activity from the Constructivist, he coined not one but two PSEUDONYMS, I. K. Bonset and Aldo Camini (the former echoing a Dutch phrase for "I am crazy"), and then labored to preserve their secrecy. Whereas Bonset published poetry (reproduced in facsimile in *Nieume Woordbeeldingen* [1975]), Camini wrote essays. My favorite Bonset text is "VoorbijtrekkendeTroep" (Marching Infantry, 1916), a sound poem reprinted in Carola

Theo van Doesburg, *Geometrical Composition*, 1916. Oil on canvas. CORBIS/Francis G. Meyer.

Giedion-Welcker's extraordinary *Anthologie der Abseitigen/Poètes à l'Icart* (1965), which has never been translated, alas. In part because Van Doesburg's work was so various, his achievement remains incompletely understood, even decades after his death.

Paintings: *Composition IX, The Card Players*, 1917; *Composition VIII*, 1917; *Composition X*, 1918; *Composition XI*, 1918; *Composition XIII*, 1918; *Variation*, 1918; *Composition in Disorders*, 1918; *Rhythms of a Russian Dance*, 1918; *Composition XIII, Still Life*,1918; *Composition XII, Composition in Black and White*, 1918; *Composition of Three Paintings XVIII*, 1920; *Counter-Composition XII*, 1924; *Counter-Composition XIII*, 1924; *Counter-Composition XV*, 1925; *Counter-Composition XVI*, 1925; *Simultaneous Counter-Composition XXI*, 1929; *Simultaneous Counter Composition XXIV*, 1929; *Arithmetic Composition*, 1930.

Writings: Van Doesburg, Theo. *Die nieuwe Beweging in de Schilderkunst* (The New Movement in Painting) (1917). Amsterdam: Meulenhoff/Landshoff, 1983; *Principles of Neo-Plastic Art*. London: Lund, Humphries, 1968; *On European Architecture: Complete Essays from Het Bouwbedrijf 1924–31*. Basel, Switzerland, & Boston: Birkhauser, 1990.

Correspondence: *The Antagonistic Link: Theo Van Doesburg and Joaquin Torres-Garcia*. Amsterdam: Institute of Contemporary Art, 1993.

Exhibition Catalogs: *Theo van Doesburg*. New York: Art of This Century, 1947; *Theo van Doesburg*. Eindhoven, Netherlands: Stedelijk van Abbe Museum, 1968; Van Straaten, Evert. *Theo Van Doesburg, Constructor of a New Life*. Otterlo, Netherlands: Kröller-Müller Museum, 1994.

Interpretation: Baljeu, Joost. *Theo van Doesburg*. New York: Macmillan, 1974; Doig, Allan. *Theo Van Doesburg: Painting into Architecture, Theory into Practice*. Cambridge, England & New York: Cambridge University Press, 1986; Hedrick, Hannah L. *Theo Van Doesburg: Propagandist and Practitioner of the Avant-Garde, 1909–1923*. Ann Arbor, MI: UMI Research, 1980; Mansbach, Steven. *Visions of Totality: Lazslo Moholy-Nagy, Theo van Doesburg, and El Lissitzky*. Ann Arbor, MI: UMI Research, 1978.

VAN MEEGEREN, Hans

(1889–30 December 1947).

He was the preeminent forger of modern times, specializing in the production of fake Vermeers that initially survived detection. van Meegeren used canvases from Jan Vermeer's time (1632–1675), removing the previous paint before duplicating style and signature down to the finest details. A disappointed classical painter, van Meegeren initially fantasized that, if his paintings could pass for a master's, in turn he would be regarded as Vermeer's equal. Once successful with one semblance of Vermeer, he made more, selling them for increasingly higher prices. His downfall came after the Nazi Herman Goering purchased a Vermeer that originated with van Meegeren, making the living Dutchman appear after the war to be a collaborator with the enemy. Forced to stand trial, van Meegeren had, in an unexpected twist, to prove himself a forger, which, given his own ambitions and pride, he did to an excessive degree.

van Meegeren's fraud incidentally has undermined the business of art certification to this day, while his career makes most subsequent "appropriation" artists look like superficial duffers. van Meegeren subsequently became, to philosophers like Nelson Goodman (1906–98), the most useful example in any discussion of whether esthetic value wholly depends upon authentic authorship. Though not what the artist intended, such immortality constitutes an avant-garde kind of inadvertent surprise; don't dismiss it.

Paintings (i.e., classic forgeries): *Woman Drinking*, 1935 or 1936; *Portrait of a Man*, 1935 or 1936; *Woman Reading Music*, 1935 or 1936; *Woman Playing Music*, 1935 or 1936; *Christ at Emmaus*, 1937; *Interior with Drinkers*, 1938; *Interior with Cardplayers*, 1939; *Last Supper*, 1939; *Head of Christ*, 1940; *Last Supper*, 1941; *Isaac Blessing Jacob*, 1942; *Christ and the Adultress*, 1942; *The Washing of Christ's Feet*, 1943; *Young Christ*, 1945.

Biography: Godley, John. *The Master Forger: The Story of Hans van Meegeren*. New York: Funk & Wagnalls, 1951; Kilbracken, Lord. *van Meegeren: Master Forger*. New York: Scribner's, 1967.

Interpretation: Goodman, Nelson. "Art and Authenticity." In *Problems and Projects*. Indianapolis, IN: Hackett, 1972; Jones, Mark, ed. *Fake? The Art of Deception*. Berkeley: University of California Press, 1990.

VAN OSTAIJEN, Paul

(22 February 1896–18 March 1928).

Though born in Belgium, van Ostaijen was by common consent the most advanced Dutch-language writer of his time. Residing in Berlin in the early twenties, van Ostaijen assimilated DADA and wrote satires he called "grotesques" that often depended upon ironically contrasting the present with the past and the sublime with the disgusting. Back in Belgium, he started an art gallery that failed and worked as a journalist before succumbing to tuberculosis at the age of thirty-two. The single English-language collection of his work contains a richly envisioned film script that survives brilliantly, even though the film was never made. Van Ostaijen also wrote VISUAL POEMS that are mostly unavailable in English.

Writing: *Patriotism, Inc*. Trans. and ed. E. M. Beekman. Amherst: University of Massachusetts Press, 1971; *Feasts of Fear and Agony* (1918–20). New York: New Directions, 1976; *First Book of Schmoll: A Major Collection of Poetry by the Great Dutch Experimentalist*. Los Angeles: Sun & Moon, 1999.

Interpretation: Beekman, E. M. *Homeopathy of the Absurd: The Grotesque in Paul Van Ostaijen's Creative Prose*. The Hague, Nijhoff, 1970.

VAN VECHTEN, Carl

(17 June 1880–21 December 1964).

One of the great early publicists for the avant-garde in literature, dance, and music, Van Vechten began as a reporter and then joined in 1906 the *New York Times* as a music critic and later a Paris correspondent, collecting his better pieces into books: *Interpreters and Interpretations* (1917, 1920) and *Excavation: A Book of Advocacies* (1926). Van Vechten gave his loyal publisher, young Alfred A. Knopf, a reputation for avant-garde intelligence that might have otherwise been unavailable. Prior to GERTRUDE STEIN'S celebrity in the mid-1930s, Van Vechten was Stein's most effective advocate in America, remembering this relationship, along with others similarly enthusiastic, in *Sacred and Profane Memories* (1932). It was appropriate that he was invited to edit *Selected Writings of Gertrude Stein* (Modern Library, 1946), which succeeded for decades in presenting the most accessible Stein texts (while barely acknowledging her more experimental, more extraordinary work) and thus became a totem to be tumbled for those, like myself, favoring the more avant-garde Stein.

An esthetic pioneer, Van Vechten published one of the first American books exclusively devoted to dance criticism. His most important book of fiction, *Nigger Heaven* (1926), is remembered for sympathetic portrayal of Harlem life and its emerging cultural activity. As a literary patron, Van Vechten established the James Weldon Johnson Memorial Collection of Negro Arts and Letters at Yale University. His photographs, particularly of prominent artists and witers in the 1930s and 1940s, became the foundation of important documentary collections at the Museum of Modern Art and elsewhere. He wore more than one finger-ring and wrist bracelets long before other men did and publicized art by fellow homosexuals without, as was standard then, acknowledging their difference. Enthusiasms that seem acceptable today were radical then; for, if Van Vechten is forgotten today, a principal reason is that he was too far ahead of his time." He published little in the last two decades of his life.

Fiction: *The Tiger in the House*. New York: Knopf, 1920; *The Tattooed Countess*. New York: Knopf, 1924; *Nigger Heaven*. New York: Knopf, 1926; *Spider Boy*. New York:

Knopf, 1928; *Parties: Scenes from Contemporary New York Life*. New York: Knopf, 1930.

Criticism: *Music After the Great War*. New York: G. Schirmer, 1915; *Music and Bad Manners*. New York: Knopf, 1916; *Interpreters and Interpretations*. New York: Knopf, 1917; *The Music of Spain*. New York: Knopf, 1918; *Interpreters*. New York: Knopf, 1920; *Keep A-Inchin' Along: Selected Writings of Carl Van Vechten about Black Art and Letters*. Westport, CT: Greenwood, 1979.

V

Correspondence: Kellner, Bruce. *Letters of Carl Van Vechten*. New Haven: Yale University Press, 1987; *The Letters of Gertrude Stein & Carl Van Vechten*. Ed. Edward Burns. 2 vols. New York: Columbia University Press, 1986.

Autobiography: *Sacred and Profane Memories*. New York: Knopf, 1932; *Fragments from an Unwritten Autobiography*. 2 vols. New Haven: Yale University Library, 1955.

Exhibition Catalog: Padgette, Paul. *Carl Van Vechten*. San Francisco: Blindweed, 1965.

Interpretation: Lueders, Edward. *Carl Van Vechten and the Twenties*. Albuquerque, University of New Mexico Press, 1955; ——. *Carl Van Vechten*. New York: Twayne, 1964; Kellner, Bruce. *Carl Van Vechten and the Irreverent Decades*. Norman: University of Oklahoma Press, 1968.

Bibliography: Cunningham, Scott. *A Bibliography of the Writings of Carl Van Vechten*. Philadelphia: Centaur Book Shop, 1924.

VANDERBEEK, Stan

(6 January 1927–19 September 1984).

His earliest distinguished work was animation that depended upon collaging images found in popular magazines, sometimes abetted by his own drawings, all reminiscent of outrageous SURREALISM. VanDerBeek also made ink drawings directly on an animation stand, documenting their progress on film. Possessed of a restless, forward-looking imagination, VanDerBeek was using television imagery in film as early as *One* (1958–59) and computer graphics in the mid-1960s, collaborating with Ken Knowlton at Bell Labs in producing nine computer-generated films between 1964 and 1970, some of which he called *Poem Fields*, because they combine words with rapidly moving abstractions. In the late 1960s, next to his own house in Stony Point, New York, VanDerBeek erected a small hemispheric (dome-shaped) building that he envisioned as a prototype for multiprojection spaces, which he called the "movie-drome." Audiences were instructed to lie down at the outer edge, with their feet toward the center of the dome, looking up at an abundance of moving images. Unfortunately, VanDerBeek was more adept at envisioning than finishing; and once he became a full-time college professor, beginning in the 1960s, his propensity for procrastination increased. Another tragedy was that, not unlike other forward-looking artists, he died too soon to exploit subsequent technologies.

Interpretation: Russett, Robert, and Cecile Starr. *Experimental Animation*. New York: Van Nostrand, 1976; Woods, Gerald, et al. *Art Without Boundaries*. New York: Praeger, 1972.

Films: *What Who How*, 1957; *Mankinda*, 1957; *Astral Man*, 1957; *Ala Mode*, 1958; *Wheeeeels No. 1*, 1958; *One*, 1958–59; *Science Fiction*, 1959; *Skullduggery*, 1960; *Blacks and Whites in Days and Nights*, 1960; *Snapshots of the City*, 1961; *Breathdeath Phenomenon No. 1*, 1964; *See, Saw, Seems*, 1970; *Spherical Space No. 1*, 1967; *Computer Generation*, 1973; *Color Fields*, 1977; *Mirrored Reason*, 1980; *After Laughter*, 1981.

Documentary: Havinga, Nick, prod. & dir. *Stan Vanderbeekiana*. Kent, CT: Creative Arts Television, 1997.

VANTONGERLOO, Georges

(24 November 1886–5 October 1965).

One of the youngest members of the group founding *DE STIJL*, this Belgian rejected MONDRIAN'S strict insistence upon only horizontal and vertical lines. In addition to introducing diagonals and then curves, Vantongerloo favored mathematics, thinking that his works would thus reveal universal truths unavailable to artists unfamiliar with math. To him the measure of beauty is ∞ + 1. What resulted was, first, geometric constructions in the early 1930s—paintings and sculptures with curves and spirals set against straight lines; wire constructions in the 1940s; and colored Plexiglas objects in the 1950s. About his *Composition Green-Blue-Violet-Black* (1937), in the Guggenheim Museum's permanent collection, the curator Vivian Endicott Barnett writes, "The artist has arranged the five rectangles of decreasing width in a counterclockwise spiral beginning at the lower right and ending at the center. This spiral progression is, in turn, a variation of the Golden Section." Vantongerloo's principal protegé was the Swiss MAX BILL, who organized several Vantongerloo exhibitions. Though his paintings pale beside Mondrian's, Vantongerloo remains a hero to those respecting the recurring aspirations for a rational art.

Sculptures: *Construction in the Sphere*, c. 1918; *Interrelation of Volumes*, 1919.

Writings: Vantongerloo, Georges. *Paintings, Sculptures, Reflections*. New York: Wittenborn, 1948.

Exhibition Catalogs: Bill, Max, ed. *Georges Vantongerloo*. London: Malborough Gallery, 1962; *Georges Vantongerloo*. Zürich: Gallery Lopes, 1977.

Bibliography: Barnett, V. E. *Handbook: The Guggenheim Museum Collection*. New York: Guggenheim Museum, 1980.

Interpretation: Blotkamp, Carel. *De Stijl: The Formative Years*, 1982. Cambridge: MIT Press, 1986; Hill, Anthony, ed. *DATA: Directions in Art, Theory and Aesthetics*. London: Faber, 1968.

VARÈSE, Edgard

(22 December 1883–6 November 1965).

A Frenchman who studied in Italy and lived in Berlin before emigrating to America in 1915, Varèse developed the concept of "organized sound" that eschewed precise pitch and other traditional musical structures for alternative kinds of musical coherence. His monumental departure *Ionisation* (1931) is a wholly percussive piece that employs such nonmusical sound generators as sirens, sleigh bells, and brake drums that, incidentally, have indefinite pitch. To say that this short work, only several minutes in length, sounded like nothing done before it would be an understatement. Writing in 1967, only a few years after I first heard *Ionisation*, I was still awed by it, observing: "The interaction of such large blocks of unusual percussive material produced a chaotic sound so distinctly unlike any previous musical experience that laymen and critics condemned the piece as merely noise (that was 'not music') and even professional composers feared that the apocalypse—the end of music—had come." What happened, however, was that the acceptance of *Ionisation*, along with Varèse's idea of "organized sound," created a precedent for further music with imprecise pitch and alternative acoustic structuring. One measure of this change in thinking is that *Ionisation*, a work requiring many rehearsals for its premiere, is by now frequently performed by amateurs. (Misspelling it in the American way, Ionization, is an illiteracy comparable to adding an apostrophe to *Finnegans Wake*—something that most readers would miss and, alas, copyeditors would "fix.")

Varèse was neglected for most of his professional life; not until 1955, for instance, when he was over seventy, was he elected to the National Institute of Arts and Letters. Long alienated here (but faithful to his American wife, the translator Louise Norton), he continued to use French titles for his compositions and for a while spelled his first name as Edgar. He frequently left New York for the American southwest, where HENRY MILLER found him in the early 1940s and wrote a memorable appreciation, "With Edgar Varèse in the Gobi Desert." Indeed, because Varèse's innovations were initially unacceptable, they remain so incompletely understood that debate over them continues among a curious diversity of admirers. John Cage always honored Varèse as a precursor of the chaotic tradition of modernist music; the sophisticated rock musician Frank Zappa staged in New York at his own expense an evening-length concert of Varèse's music in 1981; and Milton Babbitt, as a serial theorist, has found complex structures in Varèse's work more typical of his own, post-Schoenbergian kind of music. Varèse's close friend Nicolas Slonimsky reports: "On the centennial of his birth, in 1983, festivals of his music were staged in Strasbourg, Paris, Rome, Washington, DC, New York, and Los Angeles."

Not unlike his near-contemporary Anton Webern, Varèse finished few pieces, each being remarkably different from the others; each can be admired for various reasons. My own choice for his second innovative monument would be *Poème électronique* (1958), which ranks among the early masterpieces of music wholly for the medium new to the post-Second World War period—magnetic tape. Commissioned for Philips Radio's three-peaked pavilion designed by Le Corbusier at the Brussels World Exposition, this eight-minute example of organized sound was densely composed, from sound sources both human and mechanical, to emerge through four hundred separate loudspeakers, sweeping through the space as "continuous arcs of sound." To quote from the liner notes to the first recording:

> The sound itself was accompanied by a series of projected images chosen by Le Corbusier, some of them photographs, others montages, paintings, printed or written script. No synchronization between sight and sound was attempted by the two artists; part of the effect achieved was the result of a discordance between aural and visual impressions. . . . The audience, some fifteen or sixteen thousand people daily for six months, evinced reactions almost as kaleidoscopic as the sounds and images they encountered.

Were this complete *Poème* redone today, as it should be, I sense it would still be awesome and innovative, and I'd like to experience it. Until then I know only a stereophonic audiotape once available on a long-playing record (remember them?). Varèse's widow, also known for her literary translations, published only the first voume of a biography.

Compositions: *Un Grand Sommeil noir*, for voice and piano, 1906; *Offrandes*, for soprano and chamber orchestra, 1921; *Amériques*, for orchestra, 1918-21; *Hyperprism*, for 9 wind instruments and 18 percussion devices, 1923; *Octandre*, for septet,1924; *Intègrales*, for 11 instruments and 4 percussionists, 1925; *Arcana*, for orchestra, 1925–27; *Ionisation*, for percussion enemble (using instruments of indefinite pitch), piano, and 2 sirens, 1929–31; *Equatorial*, for bass, 4 trumpets, 4 trombones, piano, organ, percussion, and thereminovox, 1932–34; *Density 21.5*, for flute, 1936; *Etude pour Espace*, for chorus, 2 pianos, and percussion, 1947; *Dance for Burgess*, for chamber ensemble 1949; *Déserts*, for winds, percussion, and electronics, 1954; *Poème électronique*, for electronic tape and more than 400 spatially distributed loudspeakers, 1957–58; *Nocturnal*, for soprano, bass chorus, and chamber orchestra, 1961.

Recordings: *Music of: Ionisation, Density 21.5, Intègrales, Octandre, Hyperprism, Poème électronique*. New York: Columbia 6146, n.d.; *The Complete Works*. Cond. Riccardo Chailly. New York: London Classics, 1998.

Biography: Ouellette, Fernand. *Edgar Varèse* (1968). Trans. Derek Coltman. New York: Da Capo, 1973; Varèse, Louise (Norton). *Varèse: A Looking-Glass Diary*. Vol. I: 1883–1928. New York: Norton, 1972.

Web Site: http://picasso.cslab.wesleyan.edu/~jfei/varese/

Interpretation: Babbitt, Milton. "Edgard Varèse: A Few Observations on His Music." In *Perspectives of New Music IV/2* (Spring–Summer 1966); Bernard, Jonathan W. *The Music of Edgar Varèse*. New Haven: Yale University Press, 1987; Kostelanetz, Richard. "Contemporary Music (1967)." In *On Innovative Music(ian)s*. New York: Limelight, 1989; Miller, Henry. "With Edgar Varèse in the Gobi Desert." In *The Air-Conditioned Nightmare*. New York: New Directions, 1945; Trieb, Marc. *Space Articulation in*

Victor Vasarely. *Ilava*, 1956. CORBIS/Burstein Collection/© 2000 Artists Rights Society (ARS), New York/ADGAP, Paris.

Seconds: The Philips Pavilion, Le Corbusier Edgard Varèse. Princeton: Princeton University Press, 1996; Van Solkema, Sherman, ed. *New Worlds of Edgar Varèse: Papers and Discussion from a Varèse Symposium at the City University of N.Y.* Brooklyn, NY: Institute for Studies in American Music 1979; Zappa, Frank. "Edgard Varese: Idol of My Youth." In *Stereo Review* (June 1971), 61–62.

VASARELY, Victor

(9 April 1908–15 March 1997).

Vasarely has so popularized his work, mostly through the medium of prints, that it is hard to remember that he was once a genuinely innovative Optical artist. Born in Hungary, Vasarely moved to France as a young man. His generative idea was to use an array of simple geometric forms to create, on a two-dimensional static canvas, the illusion of movement. At times the illusory activities are so contrary and intense that the painting cannot be stared at without inducing dizziness. Vasarely customarily fills a good structural idea with a wide variety of unmodulated colors. His son Jean-Pierre Vasarely (1934), professionally known as Yvaral, is also a distinguished geometric artist who was a founding member of GRAV *(Groupe de recherche d'art visuel).*

Painting: *Chessboard*, 1935; *Harlequin*, 1935; *Movement Study*, 1939; *Ujjain*, 1951; *Homage to Malevich*, 1952–58; *Altai*, 1955; *Socotora*, 1955; *Monast Ir II*, 1955; *Horn*, 1955–56; *Afa*, 1955; *Ob II*, 1955; *Riukiu*, 1956; *Anadyr*, 1956; *Lucon*, 1956; *Ilava*, 1956; *Elbrouz*, 1956; *Sorata*, 1956; *Kara*, 1956; *Betelgeusel*, 1957; *Beta*, 1958–64; *Tyneu*, 1959; *Planetary Folklore*, 1960–64; *Capella I*, 1964.

Exhibition Catalog: Seitz, William C. *The Responsive Eye*. New York: Museum of Modern Art, 1965; Compton, Michael. *Optical and Kinetic Art*. London: Tate, 1967.

Vasarely in Retrospect. Stratford, Canada: Rothmans Art Gallery, 1971.

Anthology: *Vasarely: Erfinder der Op-Art*. Ed. Richard W. Gassen. Ostfildern-Ruit, Germany: G. Hatje, 1997.

Interpretation: Hill, Anthony, ed. *DATA: Directions in Art, Theory and Aesthetics*. London: Faber, 1968; Parola, Rene. *Optical Art: Theory and Practice*. New York: Reinhold, 1969; Spies, Werner. *Victor Vasarely*. New York: Abrams, 1971.

Documentation: *Vasarely*. 4 vols. Trans. Haakon Chevalier. Neuchatel: Griffon, 1967, 1970, 1974.

V

VASSILAKIS, Nico

(13 February 1963).

Small, home-made, undated, privately circulated pamphlet-like booklets are Vassilakis's main output. In one of the best of these, *Aggregate*, in which Vassilakis performs all sorts of "multi-junctive" experiments with texts, graphics, and the two together, he places "BL," "UR" and "RED," respectively, one above the other in the three sections of a quasi-scientific diagram, with "blue," "purple" and "red" inscribed at strategic locations to speak of, among other things, the blur from some Ur-like (and pURple) beginning to blue and its opposite. Part of another page lists the following names: "gertrude/ kerouac/ dh lawrence/ lorca/ kandinsky/ fenollosa/ pound/ zukofsky/ klee/ olson/ malevich/ schwitters/ max ernst" and, after a big gap, "euclid." The last (*delayed*) name makes a poem of the list; the list as a whole perfectly expresses the primary direction of Vassilakis's still-developing art.

—Bob Grumman

Booklets: *Vowel*. Seattle: meemaw & pawpaw (124 1/2 Broadway East, Box 16, 98102), 1989; *A Name For Radio*. Seattle: Elbow (Box 21671, 98111–3671), 1993; *Orange: A Manual*. Seattle: Sub Rosa Press (2127 2nd Avenue, #103, 98121), 1997.

VAUGHN-JAMES, Martin

See **GROSS, Milt; VISUAL POETRY**.

VAUTIER, Ben

(18 July 1935).

Born in Naples of a Swiss-French father and an Irish mother, Vautier gravitated in the mid-1950s to Nice, France, where he has worked ever since. One mark of his art is ironic audacity, which begins with his signing his works only "Ben," with large, open letters whose calligraphy reeks of egotism. Vautier's essential move is to give esthetic value to common things, such as his lying face down on a busy sidewalk or by entitling and signing familiar objects. His Nice store, initially called *Laboratorie* and then renamed *Galeries Ben Doute de Tour*, is now owned by the National Museum of Modern Art at the Centre Pompidou. Vautier also likes to write in large letters conundrums that are considerably wittier than similar to later pseudoaphorisms by JENNY HOLZER. Among other clever Vautier is "Postman's Choice" (1965), which is classic MAIL ART because it must travel through the public post. As each side of the standard card bears its own stamp and address, it is up to the unwitting postman to decide who its recipient will be.

Books: *Réédition des bag'arts de Ben, 1978–1988*. 2 vols. Milan, Italy: Mudima, 1991; *Fluxus and Friends Going Out for a Drive*. Berlin: Rainer, 1983; *A Letter from Berlin*. Nice: Privately published, 1979; *Textes Théorques, Tracts, 1960–1974*. Milano: C. Politi, 1975.

Exhibition Catalogs: *La Vérité de A à Z/Ben*. Toulouse: Arpap, 1987. *Ben, pour ou contre: un rétrospective*. Marseille: Musées de Marseille, 1995.

VELVET UNDERGROUND

(c. 1966–1972).

As one of the first DOWNTOWN Manhattan rock bands, initially championed by ANDY WARHOL, the Velvet Underground participated in the Exploding Plastic Inevitable, Warhol's multimedia discotheque on St. Marks Place in 1966. Their leaders were the singer/songwriter Lou Reed

Edie Sedgwick dancing with Gerard Malanga on stage at Filmmakers Cinematheque to the music of the Velvet Underground, 8 February 1966. Photograph © Fred W. McDarrah.

(1942) and the string player John Cale (1940), who had previously performed with La Monte Young. Their choice of subject matter (drug addiction, street life, tortured sexuality) and their contemptuous attitude toward their audience placed them squarely against the more listener-friendly groups like The Beatles. Their songs were longer than standard pop/rock fare, and they made no attempt to polish the rough edges off their performances. Not unlike many other avant-garde combines, the Velvets had a greater impact after they dissolved, incidentally influencing the punk-rock movement of the 1970s.

—Richard Carlin

Selected Recordings: *With Nico*. New York: Verve 5008,1967; *White Light/White Heat*. New York: Verve 5046, 1967.

Interpretation: Zak, Alban *Velvet Underground Companion*. New York: Schirmer, 1997.

Web Site: http://www.angelfire.com/ny/vu1/

VERCOE, Barry

(24 July 1937).

Born in New Zealand, Vercoe came to the Massachusetts Institute of Technology in the 1960s and created the MUSIC 360 program for synthesizing on IBM/360 computers. About his composition *Synthesism* (1970) he writes, "Much of its material is either derived from or modified by the totally patternless output of a random-number generator. The structural base of the work is an ordered set of sixteen numbers that comprise a geometric series from 1 to 2. This set is projected into various domains as a compositional determinant—for example, onto the octave to form an equal-tempered sixteen-note series and into the time domain to determine durations or to control successions of varying attack rates." Especially with its base in a sixteen-note scale, Vercoe's music was inevitably original. He has recently been working on questions of perception. His wife, Elizabeth Vercoe (23 April 1941), is a composer especially known for three song cycles for voice and instrumental accompaniment, *Herstory I–III* (1975, 1979, 1986), to texts written by, not surprisingly, women.

Compositions: *Digressions*, for band, 2 choruses, computer, and orchestra, 1968; *Synthesism*, for computer 1970; *Synapse I*, for viola and computer, 1976; *Synapse II*, for flute and 4X processor, 1984.

Recordings: Vercoe, Barry. *Synthesism* (1976). New York: Nonesuch H71245, n.d.; Vercoe, Elizabeth. *Herstory II*. Boston, MA: Northeastern Records NR 221, 1985.

VIDEO ART

(c. 1960).

The pioneer here is NAM JUNE PAIK, who realized early in the 1960s that magnets applied to points outside a live TV screen could distort its kinetic image. Paik later placed an electrified wire across a reel of recorded videotape, thereby causing erasure every few seconds; he was among the first to assemble several monitors into unified objects called video sculptures.

Once the portable video camera became commercially available, artists were among the first to purchase it. I remember ROBERT WHITMAN using one to tape his outdoor MIXED-MEANS piece in 1967, no doubt discovering on the small screen an image considerably different from that available on black-and-white film. Two years later, I saw FRANK GILLETTE and Ira Schneider's *Wipe Cycle*, which exploited the new medium's capability to produce a picture of the scene before it, making video different from film, which needs to be photographically developed before being shown.

Technically, video depended upon advances in the technology of magnetic tape that was previously used for sound recording (in contrast, say, to HOLOGRAPHY, which depended upon film technology). Though video producers could use switchers and other devices to combine images in live time (such as splitting the screen image into discrete parts or setting foreground images against a different background), one audio technique that at last count could not be reproduced was MULTITRACKING, which is the layering at equal strength on a single tape of separately generated video material.

Once the cost of portable cameras decreased, video became a popular art medium, much like photography before it, so that one measure of artistry became the creation of work different from the very common run. Some used video to document live performances; others, such as AMY GREENFIELD, exploited its different scale to "film" performances that were never meant to be seen live. STEPHEN BECK eschewed the camera completely for synthesizers that could create images never seen before; Bill Viola (1951) and Bucky Schwartz (1932), among others, realized perceptual incongruities unique to the new medium, while Davidson Gigliotti (1939) and Mary Lucier (1944) used several monitors to portray a continuous image that ran from screen to screen.

It was perhaps unfortunate that video art developed in the 1970s and 1980s, when content-based fads became more acceptable in critical discourse than before. By the 1990s, many of the prominent video artists have done work that will date, not for technical reasons (the best early photography is still exhibited), but because of transiently fashionable attitudes. It is indicative that the esthetics of COLLAGE, long passé in all other arts, should have currency in video art, along with literal representationalism, journalistic commentary disguised as Leftish agitprop, and a limited sense of what the new medium can do.

Videotapes: *Bill Viola: Selected Works*. Los Angeles, CA: Voyager, 1986.

Books: Birnbaum, Dara. *Rough Edits: Popular Image Video Works 1977–1980*. Halifax: Nova Scotia College of Art & Design, 1987; Hall, Douglas. *Illuminating Video: An Essential Guide to Video Art*. New York: Aperture, 1991; Quasha, George, and Charles Stein. *Gary Hill's Projective Installations*. 3 vols. Barrytown, NY: Station Hill Arts, 1996–97.

Interpretation: Battcock, Gregory, ed. *New Artists Video*. New York: Dutton, 1978; Kostelanetz, Richard. "Waiting for Revisionism" (1991). In *On Innovative Art(ist)s*. Jefferson, NC: McFarland, 1992; Ryan, Paul. *Cybernetics of the Sacred*. Garden City, NY: Doubleday Anchor, 1974; Schneider, Ira, and Beryl Korot. *Video Art: An Anthology*. New York: Harcourt, Brace, 1976; Schwartz, Bucky. *Videoconstructions*. Ed. Bill Judson. Pittsburgh, PA: The Carnegie Museum of Art, 1992; Viola, Bill. *Reasons for Knocking on an Empty House: Writings 1973–94*. Ed. Robert Violette. Cambridge: MIT Press, 1995.

Exhibition Catalogs: Connor, Russell. *Vision and Television*. Waltham, MA: Rose Art Museum, Brandeis University, 1970; Ross, David A. *Work from the Experimental Televison Center, Binghamton, New York*. Syracuse, NY: Everson Museum, 1972; Livingston, Jane. *William Wegman*. Los Angeles: L.A. County Museum, 1973; *Video Art*. Philadelphia: Institute of Contemporary Art, University of Pennsylvania, 1975; *Bill Viola*. New York: Whitney Museum, 1997.

VIEIRA, John

(24 December 1949).

As one might expect of a man who has been trained and serves as an Adidam (Ruchira Buddhist) priest, Vieira is a master of the simple/serene—as, for example, when in his 1994 chapbook, *A Songbird in Igor's Yard*, he splits a square into two rectangles of equal size, the left one containing l's, the right o's—and swings a triangular section of the o's on top of some l's to make d's of them, and finish a spelling of "old." What makes the poem is the adventurously strange window through the o's, and "old," into nothingness, that results. Active in a number of verbo-visual and related arts since 1970, Vieira is noteworthy, too, for (among other things) pioneering in the use of musical notation structures in visual poetry.

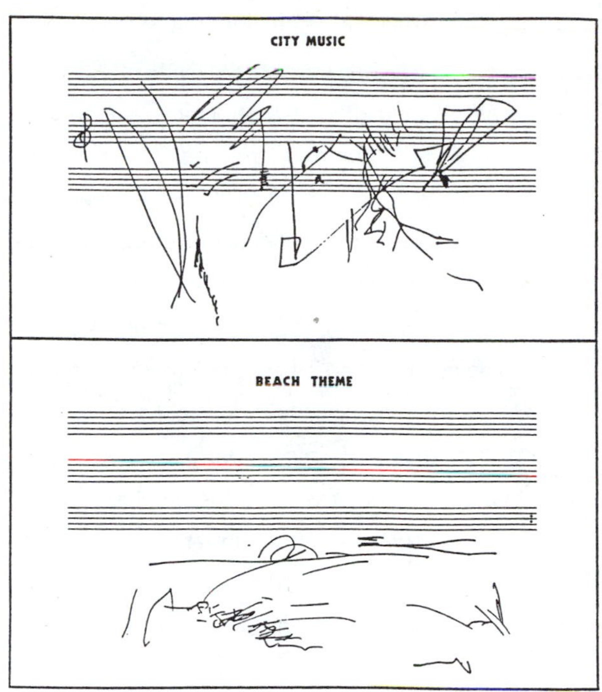

John Vieira. From *Reality Slices*. Courtesy Runaway Spoon Press.

—Bob Grumman

Book: Vieira, John. *Slow Moving Pictures*. Pullman, WA: Score (1015 NW Clifford St., 99163), 1993; *A Songbird in Igor's Yard*. Charleston, IL: tel-let (1818 Phillips Pl., 61920–3145), 1994; *Reality Slices*. Port Charlotte, FL: Runaway Spoon (Box 3621, 33949–3621), 1996.

VIENNA GROUP

(late 1950s).

Several of the most experimental German-language poets gathered in Vienna in the late 1950s, and, in the manner of ambitious Europeans (but not comparably ambitious Americans), declared themselves a group: Friedrich

Achleitner (1930), H. C. (Hans Carl) Artmann (1921), Konrad Bayer (1932–64), Gerhard Rühm (1930), and Oswald Wiener (1935). They worked with VISUAL POETRY, language games, and alternative structures, among other innovations. Gerhard Rühm's *Mann und Frau* (1972), for instance, is a book approximately 8 1/2 inches square with pages composed of lines, large alphabet letters drawn the hand, pages cut horizontally in half, and a few German words. The importance of the Vienna Group in Europe notwithstanding, few English translations of their work exist, none of them particularly complete. Many German-speaking colleagues of mine consider Wiener's *Die Verbesserung von Mitteleuropa* (The Improvement of Middle Europe, 1969) the most substantial experimental novel after ARNO SCHMIDT'S works. The standard German anthology of the Vienna Group suffers from the omission of another Viennese poet, Ernst Jandl (1925), who in many ways seems more interesting (if only for his poems originally in English).

V

Books: Artmann, Hans Carl. *The Quest for Dr. U.* (1977). London: Atlas (BCM, England WC1N 3XX), 1993; Jandl, Ernst. *Der kunstliche Baum*. Neuwied, Germany: Luchterhand, 1970; Rühm, Gerhard. *Mann und Frau*. Darmstadt: Luchterhand, 1972.

Anthology: Ruhm, Gerhard, ed. *Die Wiener Gruppe*. Hamburg, Germany: Rowohlt, 1967; Mayrocker, Fridericka, et. al. *The Vienna Group*. Barrytown, NY: Station Hill, 1985.

VIEW

(1940–1947).

Founded and edited in New York by CHARLES HENRI FORD, a young American who had lived in Paris in the 1930s, *View* was meant initially to publish European artists and writers who had fled here at the beginning of World War II. Indeed, in its pages appeared ANDRÉ BRETON, MAX ERNST, MAN RAY, and the poet Edouard Roditi (1910–1992). It served a more important function in publishing, amongst the famous Europeans and American writers and artists who were young at the time—JOSEPH CORNELL, Paul Goodman (1911–72), Paul Bowles (1910), Parker Tyler (1907–1974), many of whom would become more prominent in later decades. (Breton, partly out of priggish distaste for the homosexuality he found in *View*, founded his own magazine, *VVV* [1942–44], which he typically claimed was the only true Surrealist publication here.) A recent anthology of selections from *View*'s pages is subtitled "Parade of the Avant-Garde," which is true. I wonder how many literary/art magazines published today will look as percipient when a selection from their pages is published a half-century from now?

Books: *Parade of the Avant-Garde*. Compiled & introduced by Catrina Neiman. New York: Thunder's Mouth, 1991.

VILLA, Jose Garcia

(5 August 1908–7 February 1996).

Born in the Philippines, educated at the universities of New Mexico and Columbia, Villa became an English poet in the tradition of E.E. CUMMINGS, focusing upon expression through typographic inventions. His "Sonnet in Polka Dots," for instance, consists of fourteen lines of just the letter O, distributed horizontally as though the letters stand for words. Another poem has syntactically normal sequences of words, punctuated, however, with commas that give them a different rhythm and meaning: "Moonlight's, melody, alone, has, secrecy,/ To, make, watermelons, sweet, and, juicy." Whereas most experimental poets in America suffer neglect at their professional beginnings, Villa was formerly far more prominent, commercial publishers issuing his work, than he later became.

Writings: *Selected Poems and New*. New York: McDowell, 1958; *Poems 55: The Best Poems of Jose*

García-Villa as chosen by himself. Manila: A. S. Florentino, 1962; *Selected Stories*. Manila: A. S. Florentino, 1962; *Appasionata*. Teaneck, NJ: Bravo (1801 Trafalgar St., 07666), 1993; *Parlement of Giraffes: Poems for the World's Children*. Teaneck, NJ: Bravo, 1993.

VILLA-LOBOS, Heitor

(5 March 1887–17 November 1959).

The most prominent Brazilian composer of his generation, Villa-Lobos had an illustrious career that began with the collecting of folk songs in his native country. The pianist Artur Rubinstein (1887–1982), meeting him in Brazil, asked for a composition, which Villa-Lobos produced as *Rudepoema* (1921–26), a work for solo piano that was technically so hazardous only the greatest virtuosos could play it. (The last time I looked in a thick catalog of recordings in print, none were available of this piece for piano alone, though someone had recorded the orchestral arrangement that Villa-Lobos made in the early 1940s.) In 1923, Villa-Lobos went to Europe, where he stayed for several years establishing his reputation as a Brazilian abroad, which is to say an exotic. Returning home in 1930, he became active in music education, eventually founding a conservatory. Essentially self-taught as a composer, he developed graphic notation, using the shapes in drawings and photographs as outlines for his melodies. For instance, *The New York Skyline* (1939) reportedly depended upon a photograph for initial guidance. Prolific, he produced over 2,000 discrete compositions.

Villa-Lobos's principal compositional departure, which had considerable influence, was combining Brazilian folk rhythms with J. S. Bachian counterpoint, producing nine numbered pieces for various instrumental and vocal ensembles. The most famous is probably *Bachianas brasileiras* # 5 for the unusual combination of voice and eight cellos. Apart from everything else Villa-Lobos did, these "re-Bachs" have survived, initially for establishing one way of adapting the eighteenth-century German master to the twentieth century.

Compositions: *Confidencia*, 1908; *Valsa Romantica*, 1908; *Primeira suite infantil* 5 pieces, 1912; *Izaht*, 1912–14; *Mal secreto*, 1913; *Il nome di Maria*, 1915; *Dansas africanas*, 1914; 17 String Quartets 1915–1958; *Uirapuru*, 1917; *Hinos aos artistas*, for chorus and orchestra, 1919; *Sertão no Estio*, 1919; *4 Sonatas-Fantasia*, for violin and piano (1912, 1914, 1915, 1918); *Lenda do Caboclo*, 1920; 15 *Chŏros*, 1920–29; *3 Poemas indìgenas*, 1926; *9 Bachianas brasileiras*, 1932–44; *Pedra Bonita*, 1933; *The New York Skyline*, 1939; *Madona*, tone poem 1945; *Duo*, for violin and viola, 1946; *Magdalena*, 1947; *Rudá*, 1951; *Dawn in a Tropical Forest*, 1953; *Yerma*, 1953–56; *Gênesis*, 1954; Harmonica concerto, 1955; *Izi*, symphonic poem, 1957; *Duo*, for oboe and bassoon, 1957; *Bendita sabedoria* (Blessed Wisdom), for chorus, 1958.

Recordings: *Bachianas Brasileiras* (Nos. 1–9, complete), with soprano Victoria de los Angeles. New York: Angel, 1958 (For #5 alone, perhaps a dozen recordings were recently available, including one with a harmonica taking the solos and another arr. for saxophonist Branford Marsalis.); *Piano Music of Villa-Lobos*. Alma Petchersky, piano. 2 vols. London: ASV, 1995–96.

Biography: Tarasti, Eero. *Hector Villa-Lobos: The Life and Works, 1887–1959*. Jefferson, NC: McFarland, 1995.

Web Site: http://www.alternex.com.br/~mvillalobos/ (in Spanish).

Interpretation: Peppercorn, Lisa Margaret. *Villa-Lobos: The Music, An Analysis of His Style*. Trans. Stefan de Haan. London: Kahn & Averill, 1991; Slonimsky, Nicolas. *Music of Latin America* (1945, 1949). New York: Da Capo, 1972; Wright, Simon. *Villa-Lobos*. New York: Oxford University, 1992.

VIOLA, Bill

See **VIDEO ART**.

V

VIRTUAL REALITY

(c. 1990).

This is a technology whose artistic possibilities have scarcely been discovered. Thanks to glasses over your eyes and earphones over your ears, your eyes and ears can be programmed with materials that transport your head into other realms. The visual element in particular generally comes from a computer. Because firsthand experience of virtual reality is scarce, the idea of virtual reality has probably had more imaginative impact. In this last respect, it resembles HYPERTEXT. Not untypically, the book *Virtualities* (1998) is less about virtual reality as such than short video installations as "undoubtedly the most complex art form in contemporary culture."

Resources: Harrison, David J. *Experiments in Virtual Reality*. Oxford: Butterworth/Heinemann, 1996; Morse, Margaret. *Virtualities: Television, Media Art, and Cyberculture*. Bloomington: Indiana University Press, 1998; Moser, Mary Ann. *Immersed in Technology: Art and Virtual Environments*. Cambridge: MIT Press, 1996.

VISUAL FICTION

See **VISUAL POETRY**.

VISUAL POETRY

(c. 325 BC).

This is my preferred term for minimal, customarily nonsyntactical language that is visually enhanced to a significant degree. It differs from PATTERN POETRY, where the ends of conventionally syntactical lines define a perceptible shape; from CONCRETE POETRY, which at its purest identifies a materialist attitude toward language, wholly apart from syntax and semantics; and from whatever it was that WILLIAM BLAKE did (consider, word + image). Thus, the term "visual poetry" is applicable to the word-signs of ROBERT INDIANA, "eyeye" of ARAM SAROYAN (with its hint of eyeglasses), "Forsythia" of MARY ELLEN SOLT, PAUL VAN OSTAIJEN'S "Zeppelin," and the door-high towers of JOHN FURNIVAL, among many others. It differs as well from Poesia Vivisa, which was an Italian term, popular in the 1970s, for visual art that incorporates words, usually handwritten, along with pictures, usually photographs, largely for political content, and thus formally updates the genre of William Blake.

An extension is Visual Fiction, which is the preferred term for narrative that depends upon changes in roughly continuous pictures; among this art's major practitioners are DUANE MICHALS, MILT GROSS, Martin Vaughn-James (1943), and LYND WARD.

Anthologies: Bory, Jean-François, ed. *Once Again*. New York: New Directions, 1968; Kostelanetz, Richard, ed. *Imaged Words and Worded Images*. New York: Outerbridge & Dienstfrey, 1970.

Exhibition Catalogs: *Sound Texts ? Concrete Poetry Visual Texts*. Amsterdam: Stediljk Museum, 1969; *Visuelle Poesie*. Curated Klaus Peter Dencker. Saarbrücken, Germany: Saarländischen Rundfunk, 1984.

Interpretation: Bohn, William. *The Aesthetics of Visual Poetry, 1914–1928*. Cambridge, England: Cambridge University Press, 1980; Kostelanetz, Richard, ed. *Visual Literature Criticism*. Carbondale: S. Illinois University Press, 1981; Sackner, Marvin & Ruth, eds. *The Ruth & Marvin Sackner Archive of Concrete and Visual Poetry 1984*. Miami Beach, FL: Privately published, 1986; Weiss, Irving. *Visual Voices: The Poem as Print Object*. Pt. Charlotte, FL: Runaway Spoon, 1994.

VKHUTEMAS

(1920–1925 or 1931).

The Soviet term for Higher Technical-Artistic Studios, established first in Moscow in 1920 and then in both Petrograd and Vetebsk the following year. Independent of one another, they nonetheless became important for teaching and theoretical discussions, especially of CONSTRUCTIVISM. Among the artists on the faculties were KAZIMIR MALEVICH, WASSILY KANDINSKY, ALEXANDR RODCHENKO,and VLADIMIR TATLIN. A sort of visiting lecturer, NAUM GABO remembered "seven departments. Painting, Sculpture, Architecture, Ceramics, Metalwork and Woodwork, Textile, and Typography, but general discussions were held and seminars conducted among the students on diverse problems where the public could participate, and artists not officially on the faculty could speak and give lessons." Gabo continues, "During these seminars, as well as during the general meetings, many ideological questions between opposing artists in our abstract group were thrashed out. These gatherings had a much greater influence on the later development of constructive art than all the teaching." Qualitatively, the Vkhutemas academies represent the Soviet equivalent of the BAUHAUS, though, like so many other independent movements in Russia at the time, they fell by the early 1930s under central party control.

Bibliography: Gray, Camilla. *The Russian Experiment in Art 1863–1922*. London, England: Thames & Hudson, 1962; Barron, Stephanie and Maurice Tuchman. *The Avant-Garde in Russia 1910–1936*. L.A. County Museum of Art, 1980; Lodder, Christina. *Russian Constructivism*. New Haven: Yale University Press, 1983.

VORTICISM

(1913–1918).

Perhaps the most avant-garde movement in the history of British visual art, Vorticism began over a quarrel between the London critic Roger Fry (1866–1934) and the writer-painter WYNDHAM LEWIS. The latter declared an allegiance to ITALIAN FUTURISM, which had just emerged on the continent. Reflecting Italian influence, the Vorticists produced visual art filled with angular lines and poetry filled with hysterical declamations, some of which appeared in Lewis's two-shot magazine *BLAST*. Vorticism is sometimes characterized as the most advanced version of British ABSTRACT ART. Among those joining Lewis were younger artists such as David Bomberg (1890–1957) and HENRI GAUDIER-BRZESKA, and emerging writers, such as EZRA POUND, who coined the term "Vorticism," and T. E. Hulme (1883–1917) who wrote the "Vortex" manifesto in 1913. Hulme's 1914 lecture on "Modern Art and Its Philosophy" is said to be the best introduction to Vorticist esthetics. Perhaps for the same reasons that British culture ignored DADA and hardly acknowledged SURREALISM, Vorticism did not survive the end of World War I.

Exhibition Catalogs: *Wyndham Lewis and Vorticism*. London: Tate, 1956. *Vorticism and its Allies*. London: Arts Council of Great Britain, 1974.

Interpretation: Hulme, T. E. *Speculations*. Ed. Herbert Read. New York: Harcourt, Brace, 1936; Cork, Richard. *Vorticism and Abstract Art in the First Machine Age*. 2 vols. London, England: Gordon Fraser, 1976; Wees, William C. *Vorticism and the English Avant-Garde*. Toronto: University of Toronto Press, 1972.

VOULKOS, Peter

(29 January 1924).

Voulkos is broadly recognized as being single-handedly responsible for the emergence of ceramics as a serious art form in the mid-twentieth century. After studying in 1953 at BLACK MOUNTAIN COLLEGE, where he met WILLEM DE KOONING, JOSEF ALBERS, ROBERT RAUSCHENBERG, JOHN CAGE, and MERCE CUNNINGHAM, Voulkos went to New York and became infused with the artistic ferment of ABSTRACT EXPRESSIONISM. Although Voulkos has practiced in many sculptural forms over the course of his career, most of his work has been in ceramics that display a number of affinities with the Abstract Expressionist movement. His sculptures are purely self-referential, executed as variations on traditional ceramic forms. Voulkos models and throws clay bottles, bowls, plates, and large vessels (some of which stand over four feet tall), which he breaks apart and reassembles, leaving holes and internal edges, and incises with seemingly random lines and markings. After firing, he generally leaves his works unglazed. They are filled with a compulsive, nervous energy, similar to the paintings of JACKSON POLLOCK and de Kooning. And they are, at least presumably, expressive of his subjective state at the time of their making. It is easy to argue that Voulkos's ceramics are lacking in any perceptible message or intellectual content, and that they remain, like many ordinary ceramics works, merely decorative objects. However, except for the difference in medium, the same objection can be made to many Pollock paintings.

—Mark Daniel Cohen

Works: *Rocking Pot*, 1956; *Black Bulerias*, 1958; *5000 Feet*, 1958; *Little Big Horn*, 1959; *Firestone*, 1965; *Hall of Justice*, 1967–71; *Zoroaster*, 1981; *Asturias*, 1990; *Tsunami*, 1994.

Exhibition Catalogs: *Peter Voulkos: Sculpture, Painting, Ceramics*. Los Angeles: Felix Landau Gallery, 1959; Selz, Peter. *Sculpture and Painting by Peter Voulkos*. New York: Museum of Modern Art, 1960; *Peter Voulkos*. San Francisco: Braunstein/Quay Gallery, 1991.

Criticism: Slivka, Rose. *Peter Voulkos: A Dialogue with Clay*. Boston: New York Graphic Society, 1978; Slivka, Rose, and Tsujimoto, Karen. *The Art of Peter Voulkos*. New York: Kodansha International, in collaboration with the Oakland Museum, 1995.

VVEDENSKY, Aleksandr

(6 December 1904–20 December 1941?).

The Russian poet Aleksandr Ivanovich Vvedensky studied in the Institute of Artistic Culture, a St. Petersburg art school dominated in the 1920s by the FUTURISTS and headed by KAZIMIR MALEVICH. In his early work, Vvedensky quickly moved from following ideas of poetry radical in its phonetics (ZAUM) to poetry radical in its semantics. His creative breakthrough pointed the way out of the post-Zaum gridlock. A group of young poets including DANIIL KHARMS joined him and formed a group called OBERIU (1926–31).

As Stalin's regime was suspicious of any writing of a "difficult" or "coded" nature, all of the OBERIU members were detained in 1931 and the group dissolved. Vvedensky' writing grew much darker in the '30s and became more sophisticated, evolving from the direct attack on the "rational/meaningful," to the synthesis of different semantic/poetic devices (defamiliarization, substitution, etc.) and from his philosophic views into a highly original literal style. The long poem "God Possibly Surrounds" (1931) is a key to understanding the coherent poetic universe developed in his later work.

In 1941, at the start of World War II, Vvedensky was arrested and during a forced evacuation. None of his major works were published in his lifetime. Only about a quarter of his writing has survived. As far as the Russian-born author of this entry is aware, the only Vvedensky works available to American readers are the unsatisfying George Gibian translations and the much better 1998 New York Off-Broadway production of the Vvedensky play *Chrismas at Ivanov's* (1938).

—Igor Satanovsky

Bibliography: Gibian, George, ed. and trans. *Russia's Lost Literature of the Absurd, A Literary Discovery: Selected Works of Daniil Kharms and Alexander Vvedensky*. Ithaca & London: Cornell University Press,1971; Meylakh, M., and V. I. Erl', eds. *Alesksandr Vvedensky. Polnoe Sobranie Sochineniy*. Ann Arbor, MI: Ardis, 1984 (in Russian).

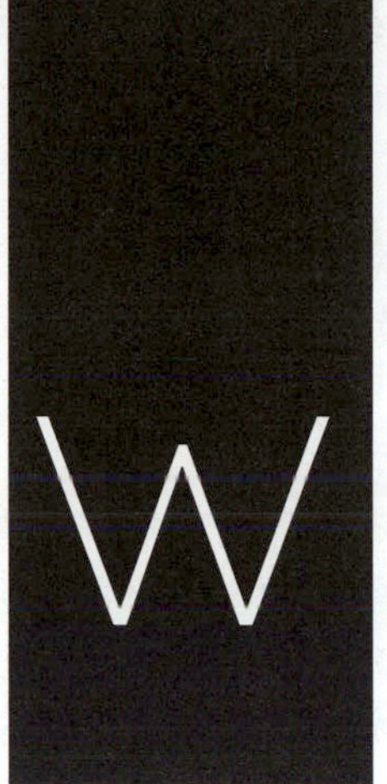

WALDEN, Herwarth

(16 September 1879–31 October 1941; b. Georg Levine).

After writing music reminiscent of Claude Debussy (1862–1918) and poetry reflecting the influence of his first wife, Else Lasker Schüler (1869–1945), Walden founded the important Berlin-based periodical *Der Sturm* (1910–32, The Storm), publishing FUTURISTS along with EXPRESSIONISTS in addition to poets such as AUGUST STRAMM and painters. In 1912, Walden opened an art gallery named after his magazine and was the first to exhibit several artists who later taught at the BAUHAUS; his gallery survived for a dozen years. Reacting to the rise of Fascism in Germany, Walden allied with the Communist party in 1929, emigrating to the Soviet Union in 1932. He disappeared around 1941, probably in a Russian prison camp. Perhaps because he was so much more than just an art dealer, Walden is among the few members of his trade to be honored, let alone remembered, decades later.

Exhibition Catalog: *Herwarth Walden and Der Sturm: Artists and Publications*. New York: La Boetie Gallery, 1981.

Interpretation: Roters, Eberhard, et al. *Berlin 1910–1933*. Trans. Marguerite Mounier. New York: Rizzoli, 1982.

WARD, Lynd

(26 June 1905–28 June 1985).

An American visual fictioneer, needlessly forgotten, Ward credited FRANS MASEREEL as the "first to go beyond the idea of a short sequence of pictures" in making extended visual narratives that differ from comic strips, say, but resemble certain silent films in completely eschewing words. Ward's medium, the woodcut, ideally suited his taste for heavy shading, which in turn reflected a penchant for melodramatic moralizing. Ward's first visual narrative, *God's Man* (1929), starkly portrays a young artist in a hostile world, while a later work, *Wild Pilgrimage* (1932), turns upon the clever device of changing color when the narrative portrays the protagonist's inner thoughts. Ward's career as a book-artist ended late in the 1930s, which is unfortunate, because he had a sure sense for making pictures that gather meanings as the reader turns the page, becoming a precursor to EDWARD GOREY and DUANE MICHALS, among other first-rank visual storytellers, as well as Eric Drooker (1957), whose *Flood! A Novel in Pictures* (1992) likewise opens by portraying a young artist in a hostile city.

Books: *God's Man*. New York: Cape & Smith, 1929; *Mad Man's Drum*. New York: Cape & Smith, 1930; *Wild Pilgrimage*. New York: Smith & Haas, 1932; *Prelude to A Million Years*. New York: Equinox, 1933; Drooker, Eric. *Flood! A Novel in Pictures*. New York: 4 Walls 8 Windows, 1992.

Self-Anthology: Ward, Lynd. *Storyteller Without Words*. New York: Abrams, 1974.

WARHOL, Andy

(6 August 1928–22 February 1987; b. Andrew Warhola).

Surely the most audacious of those artists initially classified as POP, Warhol created in the early 1960s representational

paintings that, in retrospect, seem thoroughly designed to violate several earlier rules for "high art." Originally a commercial artist with a reputation for drawing shoes, Warhol used silkscreening processes to transfer photographs and advertising imagery to fine-art canvas. (The other Pop artists created their images from scratch.) In these Warhol paintings, "found" images, mostly familiar, are transformed—enlarged, recolored, reshaded—to emphasize pictorial qualities partly reflective of the silkscreening process, and partly reflective of Warhol's tasteless, campy use of flat coloring. Essentially a graphic artist, Warhol repeated images interminably in a grid previously unknown in representational art, audaciously drawing upon popular iconography, as in *210 Coca-Cola Bottles* (1962); horrifying public events, as in *Atomic Bomb* (1963), *Car Crash* (1963), and *Race Riot* (1964); and the faces of either celebrities (Jacqueline Kennedy, Elizabeth Taylor) or art collectors, who were flattered by being subjected to the same style of repetitive portraiture as that accorded celebrities.

Around this time Warhol also made radically underedited films that depended upon the casual performances of eccentric, moderately compelling people and then upon projection at speeds slower than the customary twenty-four frames per second, sometimes for hours at a stretch. Of the latter, none rivaled *Chelsea Girls* (1966), which became less boring when Warhol projected two images simultaneously, side by side. In *Outer and Inner Space* (1966), he made ingenious use of a video recorder, in this case to film a handsome young woman named Edie Sedgwick, responding to her video image in live time. The film critic J. Hoberman writes, "Becoming in a sense her own audience, the 'live' Sedgwick often seems startled, distracted, even sometimes distressed by the effect of having her own voice whispering in her ear." Though *Andy Warhol's Index (Book)* (1967) remains a model of inventive book-art, his other books, mostly of transcribed prose, did not survive as well as his most famous aphorism: "In the future everyone will be famous for fifteen minutes."

Warhol was also one of several nouveau celebrities, the poet Allen Ginsberg being another, who made unashamed homosexuality more acceptable, at least to the mass media, if not to sophisticated society in general. No other major modern painter learned to capitalize so well upon what was once called "selling out" (his only rival for this superlative being Salvador Dali), and none ever earned so much money, selling nearly all of the thousands of images he manufactured. Though the subversive point of Warhol's esthetic strategy was obliterating the distinction between high art and graphics, the distinction survived, while many patrons-come-lately who thought they were commissioning or purchasing high art are stuck with decoration. Indeed, Warhol's subversive achievement, whose full measure is not yet apparent, is getting a large number of rich people to overpay, not only for his art and the bric-a-brac of his estate but for the publication of books by and even about him, making him, without doubt, the most successful "ripoff artist" of all time.

Why Warhol gave up experimental art remains a mystery; perhaps he thought he could do nothing else new and so feared becoming, say, another Willem de Kooning, who would spend half of his adult life haunted by an inability to produce work equal to his acclaimed earlier masterpieces. Perhaps Warhol lost heart after being seriously wounded in 1968. He sought stardom because he thought it would increase the monetary value of everything he produced (and at times should have discarded), as indeed it did. Because Warhol was no longer making consequential art, it was no small achievement for him to remain a pseudo-cultural celebrity for over a quarter-century in this fickle country, surviving the predictions of those who thought him strictly a fifteen-minute man, but also becoming an unfortunate model for aspiring younger

Andy Warhol at George Segal's Chicken Farm, 19 May 1963. Photograph © Fred W. McDarrah.

artists who con themselves into believing that publicity—any publicity—can be more important than peer or critical respect, let alone esthetic achievement.

Selected Paintings: *Water Heater*, 1960; *Saturday's Popeye*, 1960; *210 Coca-Cola Bottles*, 1962; *Atomic Bomb*, 1963; *Car Crash*, 1963; *Race Riot*, 1964.

Selected Films: *Sleep*, 1963; *Eat*, 1963; *Blow-Job*, 1963; *The Thirteen Most Beautiful Women*, 1964; *The Life of Juanita Castro*, 1965; *Vinyl*, 1965; *Outer and Inner Space*, 1965; *My Hustler*, 1965; *The Velvet Underground and Nico*, 1966; *Chelsea Girls*, 1966; **** (aka *The Twenty-Four Hour Movie*), 1966; *Nude Restaurant*, 1967; *Lonesome Cowboys*,1967. (Note that films made afterwards were customarily produced with Paul Morrissey, with the latter receiving most of the directorial credit.)

Books: Warhol, Andy. *Andy Warhol's Index (Book)*. New York: Random House, 1967; *a, a novel*. New York: Grove, 1968; *The Philosophy of Andy Warhol (From A to B and Back Again)*. San Diego, CA: Harcourt, Brace, 1975; *America*. New York: Harper Row, 1985; *The Warhol Diaries*. Ed. Pat Hackett. New York: Harcourt, Brace, 1989; ——, and Pat Hackett. *Andy Warhol's Party Book*. New York: Crown, 1988; *POPism: The Warhol Sixties*. New York: Harcourt, Brace, 1980.

Exhibition Catalogs: Green, Samuel Adams. *Andy Warhol*. Philadelphia: Institute of Contemporary Art, University of Pennsylvania, 1965; Solomon, Alan. *Andy Warhol*. Boston: Institute of Contemporary Art, 1966; *Andy Warhol*. Stockholm: Modern Museet, 1968; *Andy Warhol: His Early Works, 1947–1959*. New York: Gotham Book Mart, 1971; Rosenblum, Robert, and David Whitney, eds. *Andy Warhol: A Retrospective*. New York: MoMA, 1989; Hanhardt, John, and Jon Gartenberg. *The Films of Andy Warhol: An Introduction*. New York: Whitney Museum, 1988; *Catalogues of the Andy Warhol Collection*. 6 vols. New York: Sotheby's, 1988; *Andy Warhol: A Retrospective*. Ed. Kynaston McShine. New York: MoMA, 1989; *After the Party: Andy Warhol Works 1956–86*. Dublin: Irish Museum of Modern Art, 1997.

Biography: Bockris, Victor. *The Life and Death of Andy Warhol*. New York: Bantam, 1989; Colacello, Bob. *Holy Terror: Andy Warhol Close Up*. New York: HarperCollins, 1990; Guiles, Fred Lawrence. *Loner at the Ball: The Life of Andy Warhol*. New York: Bantam Doubleday, 1989; Wilcock, John. *The Autobiography and Sex Life of Andy Warhol*. New York: Other Scenes, 1971.

Web Site: www.warhol.org

Interpretation: Bourdon, David. *Andy Warhol*. New York: Abrams, 1989; Coplans, John, with Jonas Mekas and Calvin Tomkins. *Andy Warhol*. Greenwich, CT: New York Graphic Society, 1970; Crone, Rainer. *Andy Warhol*. New York: Praeger, 1970; ——. *A Picture Show by the Artist*. New York: Rizzoli, 1987; Gidal, Peter. *Andy Warhol:*

Films and Paintings. New York: Dutton, 1971; Hoberman, J. "A Pioneering Dialogue Between Actress and Image," *New York Times*, November 22, 1998; Koch, Stephen. *Stargaze; The Life, World, and Films of Andy Warhol* (1973). New York: Boyars, 1985; Pratt, Allan R., ed. *The Critical Response to Andy Warhol*. Westport, CT: Greenwood, 1997; Ratcliff, Carter. *Andy Warhol*. New York: Abbeville, 1983; Smith, Patrick. *Andy Warhol's Art and Films*. Ann Arbor, MI: UMI Research, 1986; Wolf, Reva. *Andy Warhol: Poetry and Gossip in the 1960s*. Chicago: University of Chicago Press, 1997; Yau, John. *In the Realm of Appearance: The Art of Andy Warhol*. Hopewell, NJ: Ecco, 1993.

W

Documentation: Feldman, Frayda, and Jorg Schellman, eds. *Andy Warhol Prints: A Catalogue Raisonné 1962–1987*. New York: Abbeville, 1985.

WARNER BROTHERS CARTOONS

(1930–1968; 1990–).

Collectively, they were the best; only the FLEISCHERS' studio came close. (Disney was more skilled at monopolizing publicity.) The artists working at Termite Terrace, as the Warner cartoon production studio was called, had a rich collection of mature characters (including Bugs Bunny, Daffy Duck, Yosemite Sam, Speedy Gonzales, Porky Pig, Sylvester & Tweety, the Road Runner and his pal Wile E. Coyote), the most virtuostic vocal stylist of all in MEL BLANC; and the strongest music director in Carl Stallings (1888–1972), whose most memorable compositions were released in the 1990s on audio-only compact discs (*sans* images). Since their fare was six-minute films that were meant to be screened before the feature, the Hollywood studio chiefs didn't much care about content, let alone form. Nor did the censors of the 1940s and 1950s care, enabling Warner cartoon directors to slip through certain images that would have been unacceptable in feature films. Some of the spiky quality of Warner toons comes from working for a unit boss who reportedly opened screenings with "Roll the trash." They might have been forgotten when Warner ceased producing them (1969), were their handiwork not revived on television, initially for children on Saturday mornings, eventally for adults with the establishment of a cable channel that broadcast them around the clock. (One truth that should not be forgotten is that Warner toons, unlike Disney's, were originally made as much for adults as for children.)

What continually impresses me esthetically about the best Warner cartoons is how much action and characterization is compressed into their standard six-minute form. Nearly all the Warner toons were made by four directors—Robert McKimson, Fritz Freleng (1905–1995), Robert Clampett (1913–84), and Chuck (aka Charles M.) Jones (1912) who has recently been giving remarkably intelligent and percipient interviews about their work. TEX (AKA FRED) AVERY collaborated with them at the beginning, in the 1930s, but left around 1940 to create havoc elsewhere, fortunately leaving behind his most successful creation—Bugs Bunny. A second truth is that two characters—Bugs and Daffy Duck, different though they are—inspired the best work.

My own sense is that the very best Warner toons involve music, usually classical music: *What's Opera, Doc*, 1957, dir. Chuck Jones), *The Corny Concerto* (1943, dir. Robert Clampett), *The Rabbit of Seville* (1950, Charles M. Jones), all of which I've seen many times, and would gladly see again anytime. Though I've been watching Warner toons with enthusiasm for over a decade, I cannot tell for sure, unless I know in advance, which of the four directors is responsible for which films, so dominant is the studio style (and why this entry appears under W, rather than C, F, J, and/or M). Thanks to my preference for these six-minute gems, I find it almost impossible to sit through feature-length films and rarely do.

In 1985, Warner's, not Disney's, became the first animation studio to have a full-scale retrospective at the

Museum of Modern Art in New York, which, in addition to screening the films regularly for a few months, put drawings on its walls. Reviewers of this exhibition dubbed the Warner masters "among the century's great humorists," as indeed they are," who have made an invaluable contribution to the culture that only in recent years has begun to receive the outpourings of appreciation it deserves."

In the 1990s, a much larger corporation still partly named Warner sponsored first Tiny Toon Adventures, their first animated series produced expressly for television, and then Animaniacs, a new television series that seems better than other recent toons, if only for attempting with sporadic success to capture the quality of the classic Warner films.

Memoirs: Jones, Chuck. *Chuck Amuck* (1989). New York: Avon, 1990; Blanc, Mel. *That's Not All Folks! My Life in the Golden Age of Cartoons and Radio*. New York: Warner, 1988.

Videotape: *A Salute to Chuck Jones*. Burbank, CA: Warner Home Video, 1985. (Video stores carry many compilations of the classic Warner cartoons.)

Recordings: *The Carl Stallings Project Music from Warner Brothers Cartoons 1936–58*, Warner Brothers 1990; *The Carl Stallings Project, Volume 2: Motion Picture Music*, Warner Brothers, 1995.

Anthology: Friedwald, Will, and Jerry Beck. *Warner Bros. Animation Art: The Characters, the Creators, the Limited Editions*. New York: WB Worldwide Publishing-Hugh Lauter Levin Assocs., 1997.

Interpretation: Kenner, Hugh. *Chuck Jones: A Flurry of Drawings*. Berkeley: University of California Press, 1994; Schneider, Steve. *That's All, Folks!: The Art of Warner Bros. Animation*. New York: Holt, 1988.

Documentary: Canemaker, John. *The Boys from Termite Terrace*. New York: CBS, 1975.

Filmography: Friedwald, Will, and Jerry Beck. *The Warner Brothers Cartoons*. Metuchen, NJ: Scarecrow, 1981.

Web Site: http://www.geocities.com/Hollywood/Location/2135/webring.html (Web ring)

WATSON, James Sibley, Jr.

(10 August 1894–31 March 1982).

One of the forgotten figures in the history of American culture, Watson was, in the 1920s, the publisher of the monthly *The Dial*, the most prestigious literary magazine of its time. He earned a medical degree in his spare time. In the 1930s, he collaborated with others in making experimental films that are still shown (and available on videotape): *The Fall of the House of Usher* (1933, produced with Melville Webber) and *Lot in Sodom* (1935, with Webber, Ransom Wood, and Alec Wilder). While the former, which Watson photographed, uses prisms, mirrors, and distorting lenses to EXPRESSIONISTIC ends, the latter, with the addition of sound, has a richer plot. Telling of sensual corruption, this film depends less upon plot than upon the rhythmical presentation of symbolic scenes. The film historian Lewis Jacobs (1906–97) writes:

> Its brilliant array of diaphanous shots and scenes—smoking plains, undulating curtains, waving candle flames, glistening flowers, voluptuous faces, sensual bodies, frenzied orgies—were so smoothly synthesized on the screen that the elements of each composition seemed to melt and flow into one another with extraordinary iridescence.

Watson was among the first to call himself "an independent film producer," the term declaring proudly that he worked apart from the commercial studios, much as avant-garde writers ignored commercial publishing.

As a doctor, on the faculty of the medical school at the University of Rochester from the 1940s to the 1960s, Watson did pioneering research in cineradiography, following the gastrointestinal track with X-ray motion picture film (as a rare example of an avant-garde artist becoming an advanced scientist, similar to the Russian composer

Alexander Borodin [1833–1887], who was also a distinguished chemist).

Films: *The Eyes of Science*, 1931; *Highlights and Shadows*, 1937; Many studies in cineradiography, 1946–60; ——, and Melville Webber. *It Never Happened* (aka *What May Happen* & *Tomatoes Another Day*), 1930; ——, and Melville Webber. *The Fall of the House of Usher*, 1933; ——, with Webber, Ransom Wood, and Alec Wilder, *Lot in Sodom*, 1935.

Bibliography: Brown, Gaye. *The Dial: Arts and Letters in the 1920's*. Amherst: University of Massachusetts Press, 1983; Cartwright, Lisa. "U.S. Modernism and the Emergence of 'The Right Wing of Film Art': The Films of James Sibley Watson, Jr., and Melville Webber." In *Lovers of Cinema: The First American Film Avant-Garde, 1919–1945*, ed. Jan-Christopher Horak. Madison: University of Wisconsin Press, 1995; Jacobs, Lewis. *The Rise of the American Film* (1939). Expanded ed. New York: Teachers College, 1968; Wasserstrom, William. *A Dial Miscellany*. Syracuse, New York: Syracuse University Press, 1963.

W

WATTS TOWERS (OR LOS ANGELES WATTS TOWERS)

See **RODIA, Simon**.

WEBERN, Anton

(3 December 1883–15 September 1945; b. A. von W.). It was Webern, more than any other composer born in the nineteenth century, who explored the possibility of less becoming more, which is to say the esthetics of MINIMALISM. Indicatively, the initial Columbia Masterworks edition of his *The Complete Music* fits on only four long-playing discs, with eight sides, containing less than three dozen works.

Raised in Vienna, taking a doctorate in musicology (and thus perhaps becoming the first trained musicologist to become a distinguished composer), Webern became ARNOLD SCHOENBERG'S initial pupil, and he wrote the first critical study on his master's music. Along with Alban Berg (1875–1935), a less avant-garde composer, Webern was in almost daily contact with Schoenberg from 1906 to 1912. Meanwhile Webern earned his living as a conductor, mostly of provincial and radio orchestras (before the latter became more prestigious). Though subsequent composers admire Webern's strict observance of SERIAL rules, the layperson tends to hear his works as spare, intricate, and nonrepresentational. Webern's compositions are typically for small ensembles; several of them incorporate poetic (German) texts. At the premiere of his *Six Pieces for Orchestra*, Opus 6, on 31 March 1913, "Hissing, laughter, and applause vie[d] for prominence during and immediately after the new Webern pieces [were] performed," according to Richard Burbank.

> A group of composers and musicians, mostly unknown and conservative, attend[ed] this concert intent on causing a disturbance. Webern shout[ed] from his seat that the human baggage must be removed from the concert hall. The police arrive[ed] and [were] ineffective in securing order.

I remember a week-long Webern festival at Juilliard in early 1995, when a piece played on various instruments by three students was followed by another played by say five different students and then yet another with four more students, and so on, apparently drawing upon an endless supply of accomplished young performers. I realized that perhaps the most appropriate performance medium for Webern is not an orchestra or even a single chamber group but a populous, first-rank conservatory.

Not until Opus 17 (1924), *Drei geistliche Volkslieder* (Three Spiritual Folksongs, sometimes translated as Three Traditional Rhymes), does Webern fully adopt the Schoenberg formulation of the SERIAL row. Of Opus 21 (1928) and Opus 22 (1930), the conductor Robert Craft (1923) writes, "Here is Webern writing small sonata-breadth pieces with expositions, developments, recapitulations, codas, and with his only material the purest of contrapuntal forms, the canon." Opus 21, in particular, broaches subsequent multiple serialization, allowing the particular tone-row to influence other musical dimensions. Paul Griffiths contends that only in his Symphony (1928) does Webern realize "the potential of the new technique for creating densely patterned music." Everything he composed thereafter was strictly serial. Unlike his mentor Schoenberg, Webern did not double back. In the early 1930s, he incidentally produced a brilliant orchestration of the Recercar from J. S. Bach's *A Musical Offering*.

Though his music was proscribed by the Nazis, Webern continued to live in Austria during World War II, working as a music publisher's proofreader. While taking a pre-bedtime smoke outside at his son-in-law's rural house, he was accidentally shot dead by an American soldier. To certain prominent younger European composers immediately after World War II, Webern was a greater figure than his teacher Schoenberg.

Compositions: *Im Sommerwind*, idyll for large orchestra, 1904; *Passacaglia*, Op. 1, 1908; *Entflieht auf leichten Kähnen*, for chorus, Op. 2, 1908; 2 sets of 5 songs for voice and piano after Stefan George, Op. 3 & 4, 1908–09; *5 Movements*, for string quartet, Op. 5, 1909/ arr. for string orchestra, 1928–29; *Six Orchestral pieces,* Op. 6, 1909; 4 pieces for violin and piano, Op. 7, 1910; 2 songs for voice and instrumental ensemble, after Rilke, Op. 8, 1910; Six bagatelles for string quartet, Op. 9, 1911–13; *5 Orchestral Pieces,* Op.10, 1911–13; *3 Little Pieces* for cello and piano, Op. 11, 1914; 4 songs for voice and piano, Op. 12, 1915–17; 4 songs for voice and orchestra, Op. 13, 1914–1918. 6 songs for voice and instruments, after Georg Trakl, Op. 14, 1919–1921; *5 Sacred Songs*, for voice and instruments, Op. 15, 1917–22; *5 Canons* on Latin texts for voice, clarinet, and bass clarinet, Op.16, 1923–24; *3 Traditional Rhymes*, for voice and instruments, Op. 17, 1924–25; 3 songs for voice, clarinet, and guitar, Op. 18, 1925. String Trio, Op. 20, 1926–27; Symphony for chamber ensemble, Op. 21, 1928; Quartet for violin, clarinet, tenor saxophone,and piano, Op. 22, 1930; 3 songs for voice and piano, Op. 23, 1933–34. Concerto for 9 instruments, Op. 24, 1934; 3 songs for voice and piano, Op. 25, 1934; *Das Augenlicht*, for chorus and orchestra, Op. 26, 1935; String Quartet, Op. 28, 1938; 1st Cantata for soprano, orchestra, & chorus, 1938–39; *Variations*, Op. 30, 1940; *2nd Cantata* for soprano, bass, orchestra, & chorus, Op. 31, 1941–43.

Recordings: Webern, Anton. *The Complete Works*. Cond. Robert Craft. New York: Columbia, n.d. (c. 1956); *Complete Works*. Cond. Pierre Boulez. New York: Sony Classical, 1991; *Complete String Trios & String Quartets*. Arditi Quartet. Los Angeles: Montaigne; *Works for String Quartet*. Emerson String Quartet Hamburg, Germany: DG, 1995.

Writings: *The Path to the New Music* (1960). Bryn Mawr, PA: 1963; *Sketches*. Commentary by Ernst Krenek; foreword by H. Moldenhauer. New York: C. Fischer, 1968.

Biography: Bailey, Kathryn. *The Life of Webern*. New York: Cambridge University Press, 1998; Moldenhauer, Hans and Rosaleen. *Anton von Webern: A Chronicle of His Life and Work*. New York: Knopf, 1978.

Interpretation: Bailey Kathryn, ed. *Webern Studies*. New York: Cambridge University Press, 1996; Forte, Allen. *The Atonal Music of Anton Webern*. New Haven: Yale University Press, 1998; Griffith, Paul. *The Thames and Hudson Encyclopedia of 20th-Century Music*. New York: Thames & Hudson, 1986; Hayes, Malcolm. *Anton von Webern*. London: Phaidon, 1995; Kolneder, Walter. *Anton Weber: An Introduction to His Work*. Trans. Humphrey Searle. Berkeley: University of California Press, 1968; Leibowitz, René. *Schoenberg and His School* (1949). New York: Da Capo, 1975; Moldenhauer, Hans. *The Death of Anton Webern: A Drama in Documents*. New York: Philosophical Library, 1961; ——, ed. *Anton Webern Perspectives* (1966). Seattle: University of Washington Press, 1978; Perle, George. *Serial Composition and Atonality: An Introduction to the Music of Schoenberg, Berg, and Webern* (1962). 6th ed. Berkeley: University of California Press, 1991; Bailey, Kathryn B. *The Twelve-Note*

Music of Anton Webern; Old Forms in a New Language. Cambridge, England & New York: Cambridge University Press, 1991.

WEEGEE

(12 June 1899– 26 December 1968; b. Usher/ Arthur H. Felig).

A naturalized New Yorker of Polish birth, he adopted the name Weegee by Americanizing the orthography of the "Ouija" board and liked to call himself "Weegee the Famous." Essentially self-taught in photography, he worked at various times as an assistant to commercial photographers, a darkroom assistant, and as a street free-lance before becoming a professional employed mostly by newspapers. A serious crime photographer, Weegee lived for many years across the street from Manhattan's police headquarters, obtained a special radio that received emergency signals initially destined for firemen and the police, and finally installed a portable darkroom in his car. Sleeping fully dressed, he was early to every scene, eventually claiming to have photographed more than 5,000 crimes in 10 years (or more than one every day).

As a photographer, Weegee's forte was distinctively realistic pictures, customarily of shocking nighttime urban scenes. Depending upon a Speed Graphic camera and a brighly intrusive flashbulb, his best pictures emphasize black and white, to the neglect of gray, which was traditionally thought to be the most subtle color in black-and-white photography. In the 1950s, more conscious of himself as an artist, Weegee adopted mirrors and kaleidoscopic effects, among other distortions, but even photographs produced with these means depend upon familiar subjects: in Italian critic Daniela Palazzoli's (1942) summary: "Marilyn Monroe with her mouth stretched out in a grotesque kiss, Elizabeth Taylor with exaggerated elongated eyelashes. . . . And Charles de Gaulle, too, all nose and ears, Dwight D. Eisenhower with a smile stretching from eye to ear, Khrushchev like a Roman emperor as seen by Walt Disney."

For a 1948 film usually screened as *Weegee's New York*, he drew upon primitive color film to shoot Manhattan at a very slow speed early in the morning, so that moving lights become a blur, the colors of flashing signs superimpose, and the sunrise becomes a momentous event. The background music is Leonard Bernstein's *Fancy Free* (1944), which never sounded so good. In the film's second half, depicting a crowded Coney Island on a sunny summer's day, Weegee's camera is insultingly nosy, watching people dress and undress, fat girls sunbathing, and so forth. Because of his cheap color stock, the sand often looks like snow and the eroticism of the beach is washed out. Its eccentricities notwithstanding, this ranks among the great New York City films. Incidentally, a Hollywood producer purchased the film rights to Weegee's *Naked City* book, but had the final film directed by Jules Dassin (1948). A 1997 *Weegee* retrospective at New York's International Center of Photography was a rich first-rate exhibition.

Books: *Naked City* (1945). New York: Da Capo, 1975; *Weegee's People* (1946). New York: Da Capo, 1975; —— and Mel Harris. *Naked Hollywood* (1953). New York: Da Capo, 1975; *Weegee's New York: 335 Photographs 1935–1960* (1948). Munchen: Schirmer/Mosel 1982; *Weegee by Weegee: An Autobiography* (1961). New York: Da Capo, 1975.

Films: *Weegee's New York*, 1948; *Cocktail Party*, 1950; *The Idiot Box*, 1965.

Exhibition Catalogs: *Weegee the Famous*. Texts by Cornell Capa and John Coplans. New York: MoMA, 1977; *Weegee*. Text by Louis Stettner. New York: Knopf, 1977; Barth, Miles, ed. *Weegee's World*. New York: Bullfinch, 1997.

Interpretation: Palazzol, Daniela, "Weegee." In *Contemporary Photographers*. 2d ed. Colin Naylor. Chicago & London: St. James's Press, 1988.

Documentaries: Jourdan, Erven, and Esther McCoy. *Weegee in Hollywood*, 1950; Stoumen, Lou, *The Naked Eye*, 1957.

WEIDENAAR, Reynold

(25 September 1945).

A trained ELECTRONIC MUSIC composer who became a major video artist, Weidenaar has brought to the new medium a technical sophistication rare among his colleagues. His video, more than most, depends upon KINETIC visual synthesis and optimal picture processing to realize imagery unique to the medium and yet painterly (he is the son of a noted Michigan painter of the same name). He also composes his soundtracks, producing audiovideotapes that are best seen on projection televisions and heard through hi-fi stereo audio systems, rather than the tiny speakers customary with television monitors. Whereas other prominent video artists established themselves through exhibitions in art galleries, Weidenaar has favored festivals of video, film, and electronic music, often winning prizes. His very best work, *Love of Line, of Light and Shadow: The Brooklyn Bridge* (1982), a masterpiece that I have seen many times without decreasing pleasure, which indicatively won an international prize, scarcely resembles the VIDEO ART more prominent in the 1980s and 1990s. A professor with a doctorate, Weidenaar also produced both a book and a video on the Telharmonium, the first music-making machine.

Audiovideotapes: *Wavelines I: Four Visual-Musical Compositions*, 1978; *Wavelines II/ Three Visual-Musical Compositions*, 1979; *Pathways III; Visual-Musical Variations*, 1980; *Pentimento*, 1981; *Twilight Flight*, 1981; *Between the Motion and the Act Falls the Shadow*, 1981; *Love of Line, of Light, and Shadow: The Brooklyn Bridge*, 1982; *Night Flame Ritual*, 1983; *The Stillness*, 1985; *The Thundering Scream of the Seraphim's Delight*, 1987; *Bass Bars*, 1988; *Long River*, 1993; *Long into the Night, Heavenly Electrical Music Flowed Out of the Street*, 1995; *Swing Bridge*, 1997; *Magic Music from the Telharmonium*, 1998.

Audiovideotape Anthology: Weidenaar, Reynold. *Concert Videos*. Minneapolis, MN: Intermedia Arts, n.d. (c. 1989); *Concert Videos 1981–1995*. New York: Magnetic Music, 1996.

Books: *Magic Music from the Telharmonium*. Metuchen, NJ: Scarecrow, 1995.

WEISS, Irvin

(11 September 1921)

Perhaps what is most interesting about Weiss as an avant-garde figure is the extent of his roots in tradition. His *Visual Voices*, for instance, weds the most up-to-date visual poetry techniques to poems dating back to the Elizabethans and earlier—as when he shows us Robert Herricks seventeenth-century poem, "Delight in Disorder," from the side (so that a line beginning with "K" is rendered with a capital I, and one beginning with an "A," as several do, is rendered with the same letter, but with its top horizontal missing, to make an amusing light joke, but also heightening the wantonness of Herrick's picture of the "sweet disorder" in a woman's dress by depicting it stealthily peeped-at, as well as suggesting something of its rhythm with the dance of full and partial I's); or when Weiss entirely fills a page with sometimes overlapping, repeating, floating, colliding lines from several relatedly romantic classic poems, including the one about Campaspe playing at cards for kisses, in "Reverberations: Night Mind Anthology." Weiss and his wife, Anne D. W., were the authors of the *Thesaurus of Book Digests: 1950–1980* (1981), which, though mostly mainstream in its coverage, included entries on such avant-garde works as Richard Kostelanetz's *Assemblings* (1967) and *Possibilities of Poetry* (1970). Always interested in intermedia, Weiss taught courses like The Avant Garde and Mass Culture, Literature and Print, Words and Images before retiring from SUNY-New Paltz. Aside from his visual poetry, his most notable achievement in literature has been his ongoing translations of Malcolm de Chazal.

—Bob Grumman

Interpretation: *Visual Voices: The Poem as a Print Object*. Port Charlotte, FL: Runaway Spoon, 1994; and Anne D. *Thesaurus of Book Digests 1950–1980*. New York: Crown, 1981.

Poetry: *Number Poems*. Ft. Charlotte, FL: Runaway Spoon (P.O. Box 3621, 11949), 1997.

Translations: *Sens-plastique/Plastic Sense* (1948). New York: Herder & Herder, 1971. 2d enlarged ed. New York: Sun, 1979.

WEISSHAUS, I.

(22 October 1904–28 November 1987).

On page 356 of my edition of Béla Bartók's essays is this evocative passage about a composer I'd like to know more about, if only because this book should have a full entry on him: "He wrote a song for solo voice, without any accompaniment, of course, in which vowels replace words as the text. Moreover, this song is based on a single tone continuously repeated in various values, with alternating crescendos, etc." Bartok continues:

> He wrote a piece in which one theme eight or ten bars in length is repeated without change throughout the work. The orchestra is divided into twelve groups of instruments, each group playing the theme in unison. The groups, simultaneously playing the same theme, in the twelve possible keys.

Though Bartók concluded his acknowledgement of Weisshaus with the judgment "these ideas have no future," I thought of Weisshaus as a proto modular composer, and so looked for his name in encyclopedias and histories.

It happened that I was looking in the wrong place. In 1930, Weisshaus moved to Paris and adopted the pseudonym Paul Arma, which scarcely resembled his birth names (perhaps accounting for why his former teacher a dozen years later didn't know the new name). Not unlike other Hungarian refugees, Weisshaus became an adept writer in a second language, even publishing what Nicolas Slonimsky calls "a modernistically planned *Nouveau dictionnaire de musique*." Weisshaus-cum-Arma also composed experimental pieces with French titles that I for one would like to hear sometime, which won't be easy, because none are listed in American record catalogs.

Compositions: Arma, Paul. Concerto for string quartet and orchestra, 1947; Violin Sonata, 1949; *31 instantanés* for woodwind, percussion, celesta, xylophone, and piano, 1951; *Polydiaphonie* for orchestra, 1962; *Structures variées* for orchestra, 1964; *Prismes sonores* for orchestra, 1966; *6 transparencies* for oboe and string orchestra, 1968; *Résonances* for orchestra, 1971.

Interpretation: Bartók, Béla. *Essays* (1976). Lincoln, NE: University of Nebraska Press, 1992; Slonimsky, Nicolas. *Baker's Biographical Dictionary of Twentieth-Century Classical Musicians*. Ed. Laura Kuhn. New York: Schirmer, 1997.

WELLES, Orson

(6 May 1915–9 October 1985).

By most measures, Welles was the most inspired and courageous creator of live theater ever in America; incidentally, he directed at least two great movies and was a masterful radio artist. Running away from Kenosha, Wisconsin, his birthplace, Welles made his way to Dublin, Ireland where, at the precocious age of sixteen, he joined the famed Abbey Theatre; within five years, he was back in the States directing audacious adaptations of Shakespeare, in addition to new plays, initially for the Federal Theatre Project and then for his own Mercury Theatre. Invited to work in radio, Welles made it a medium for the adaptation of classic literary narratives, including Victor Hugo's *Les Misèrables*, Joseph Conrad's *Heart of Darkness*, and both *Seventeen* and *The Magnificent Ambersons* by

Orson Welles. Scene from *Citizen Kane*, 1941. CORBIS/Bettmann.

Booth Tarkington. His 1938 production of H. G. Wells's novel *Invasion from Mars* (popularly known as *War of the Worlds*) was so acoustically realistic that it created a panic across the nation.

Welles's first feature-length film, *Citizen Kane* (1941), weaves a complex story through the memories of several narrators, using wide-angle photography that enabled him to shoot continuous scenes by moving his camera and his actors, instead of by using conventional cutting. Drawing upon his radio experience, in only the second decade of sound films, Welles made feature films based on sound, not only of speech but of silence, as in the great scene where Kane surveys his collections. (It was not for nothing that the complete soundtrack of *Kane* was once available on two long-playing records.)

My own opinion is that *The Magnificent Ambersons* (1942) is the greater film, if only for its soundtrack, drawing as it did upon Welles's radio production, made only a few years before, of the Booth Tarkington text. Using such radio conventions as a spoken introduction and spoken closing credits (including Welles's identifying himself under the image of a fat microphone), the film incorporates sensitive acoustic shifts between foreground and background and overlapping conversations. As his biographer Charles Higham (1931) put it, "Just as we constantly see people framed in uprights, half-glimpsed through doorways, or reflected in mirrors and windows, so we hear their muffled voices through doorways or in the far distance of rooms, floating down a stairway or mingled with the measures of a dance or the hiss and clang of a factory."

The tragedy of Welles's life was that he wanted most to make films and that, for various reasons, not entirely his fault, his later films never equaled the first two. It is easy to say in retrospect that his last forty years could have been better spent working in those two media whose production costs are generally lower, in which his genius was already established: live theater and radio. Incidentally, though most colorized versions of black-and-white classics are embarrassingly bad, the brown-tinged *Ambersons*, most frequently seen on Turner Network Television, is not.

Selected Films: *Citizen Kane*, 1941; *The Magnificent Ambersons*, 1942; *The Stranger*, 1946; *Macbeth*, 1948; *Othello*, 1952; *Touch of Evil*, 1958; *The Trial*, 1962; *Chimes at Midnight*, 1966; *The Immortal Story*, 1968.

Videotapes: *The Magnificent Ambersons*. New York: RKO, 1985; *A Touch of Evil* (1958). Universal City, CA: MCA, 1991; *Citizen Kane*. Turner Home Video, 1996.

Recordings: *Theatre of the Imagination: Radio Stories by Orson Welles & The Mercury Theatre*. Prod. Frank Beacham & Richard Wilson. Santa Monica, CA: Voyager, 1988.

Conversations: Welles, Orson, & Peter Bogdanovich. *This Is Orson Welles*. Ed. Jonathan Rosenbaum. New York: HarperCollins, 1992.

Biography: Callow, Simon. *Orson Welles: The Road to Xanadu*. New York: Viking, 1996; Higham, Charles. *Orson Welles*. New York: St. Martin's Press, 1985; Leaming, Barbara. *Orson Welles: A Biography* (1985). New York: Limelight, 1995.

Web Site: http://film.tierranet.com/directors/o.wells/

Interpretation: Bazin, André. *Orson Welles: A Critical View* (1958, 1978). Los Angeles: Acrobat, 1991; Carringer, Robert L. *The Making of Citizen Kane*. Berkeley: University of California Press, 1985; Cowie, Peter. *Ribbon of Dreams: The Cinema of Orson Welles* (1973). New York: Da Capo, 1988; Howard, James. *The Complete Films of Orson Welles*. New York: Citadel Press, 1991; Kael, Pauline, et al. *The Citizen Kane Book*. Boston: Atlantic Monthly/Little Brown, 1971; Kostelanetz, Richard. "Orson Welles as a Wunderkindhörspielmacher." In *Alternative Film and Video* (forthcoming).

WEST, Nathanael

(17 September 1903–22 December 1940, b. Nathan Wallenstein Weinstein).

The essential move in radical thinking, especially about art, is considering the opposite of any opinion entrenched in established taste. If the standard judgment holds that the writings of Nathanael West steadily improved to *The Day of the Locust* (1939), which appeared just before his premature death in a Southern California car crash, let me propose a contrary judgment more appropriate for this book. West's most original, certainly most audacious book was his first one, *The Dream Life of Balso Snell* (1931), a novella reprinted only in collections of West's complete work, most recently in that produced by the Library of America. Begun in Paris in 1927 and finished in New York by 1929, *Balso Snell* is implicitly SURREALIST at a time when realism was becoming the norm for American writing, while forecasting later West in its satirical bites. Indeed, as a perverted fantasy about a trip through the anus of the Trojan Horse, it has scant connection to anyone's experience. Consider the following passage which incidentally acknowledges a SURREALIST claim about dreams as a source for art:

> Balso dreamt that he was a young man again, lurking in a corner of the Carnegie Hall lobby among the assembled friends and relatives of music. The lobby was crowded with the many beautiful girl-cripples who congregate there because Art is their only solace, most men looking upon their strange forms with distaste. But it was otherwise with Balso Snell. He likened their disarranged hips, their short legs, their limps, their splay feet, their wall-eyes, to ornament. These strange fore-shortenings, hanging heads, bulging spinesacks, were a delight, for he had ever preferred the imperfect, knowing well the plainness, the niceness of perfection.

Knowing that he is moving into offensive territory (that would nowadays be consigned to a Politically Incorrect trashcan), West continued:

> Spying a beautiful hunchback, he suddenly became sick with passion. The cripple of his choice looked like some creature from the depths of the sea. She was tall and extraordinarily hunched. She was tall in spite of her enormous hump; but for her dog-leg spine she would have been seven feet high. Moreover, he could be certain that, like all hunchbacks, she was intelligent.

If any of the self-conscious Parisian Surrealists could have read English in the early 1930s, they would have been lucky to write as well in French. Whereas DADA's nonsequitur's attracted West's brother-in-law S. J. PERELMAN, West began as the truest American Surrealist, only to become something else, to our loss.

Acknowledging the concerns of his more established literary friends, West's next books had progressively more social relevance. As *Miss Lonelyhearts* (1933) portrays the life of a lovelorn newspaper columnist; *A Cool Million* (1937) is a needlessly forgotten satire of fascism, and *The Day of the Locust* (1939) satirizes Hollywood in a far slicker style and structure than West had used before. Though the last has always been his most popular book, what this decline also reflected, in my judgment, was West's going to Hollywood in 1933 to earn a living (whereas he had previously been a night clerk in a New York hotel).

My own opinion is that *Balso Snell* should be reprinted as a single volume with very large type, so that its unique qualities not be missed or lost.

Writings: *The Dream Life of Balso Snell*. New York: Contact, 1931; *Miss Lonelyhearts*. New York: Liveright, 1933; *A Cool Million*. New York: Covici-Friede, 1934; *The Day of the Locust*. New York: Random House, 1939; *The Complete Works of Nathanael West*. Intro. Alan Ross. New York: Farrar, Straus, 1957; *Nathanael West*. New York: Library of America, 1997. [This last contains not only the four novels but previously uncollected shorter pieces and selected literary correspondence.]

Biography: Martin, Jay. *Nathanael West: The Art of His Life*. New York: Farrar, Straus, 1970.

Interpretation: Comerchero, Victor. *Nathanael West: The Ironic Prophet*. Syracuse, NY: Syracuse University Press, 1964; Hamilton, Ian. *Writers in Hollywood, 1915–1951* (1990). New York: Carroll & Graf, 1991; Hyman, Stanley Edgar. *Nathanael West*. Minneapolis: University of Minnesota Press, 1962. [Reprinted in William Van O'Connor, ed. *Seven Modern American Novelists: An*

Introduction. Minneapolis: University of Minnesota Press, 1964; Madden, David, ed. *Nathanael West: The Cheaters and the Cheated, A Collection of Critical Essays*. Deland, FL: Everett/Edwards, 1973; Malin, Irving. *Nathanael West's Novels*. Carbondale: S. Illinois University Press, 1972; Light, James F. *Nathanael West: An Interpretive Study*. Evanston: Northwestern University, 1961; Martin, Jay, ed. *Nathanael West: A Collection of Critical Essays*. Englewood Cliffs, NJ: Prentice-Hall, 1971; Ried, Randall. *The Fiction of Nathanael West: No Redeemer, No Promised Land*. Chicago: University of Chicago Press, 1967; Scott, Nathan A., Jr. *Nathanael West: A Critical Essay*. Grand Rapids, MI: Eerdmans,1971.

Bibliography: White, William. *Nathanael West: A Comprehensive Bibliography*. Kent, OH: Kent State University Press, 1975.

WHITEREAD, Rachel

(1963–).

The British sculptor Whiteread has managed to become one of the few contemporary artists with a unique subject, which she achieved by inverting a traditional principle of visual art. She has transformed negative space into positive, by the process of casting the spaces that objects occupy, the spaces that separate them, the spaces they enclose. She has cast mattresses leaning against walls, the areas below bathroom sinks, bathtubs, and in one instance, an entire house. The fact that she generally selects domestic articles adds a human dimension to Whiteread's works, and their staid, lifeless, usually white appearance gives them the look and air of cenotaphs. There is a touch of the morbid about them, as if they were the death masks of the kind of articles we use daily. The impression is confirmed by the title of one of her best known sculptures: *Ghost* (1990), a cast of the interior of a room, with the outer surfaces of the enormous block bearing the impressions in reverse of the door, door knob, molding, even cracks in the plaster. Despite the touching quality of many of her sculptures, in sum they come across as gimmicky, as a single mechanical process, repeated over and over, that has little to do with the application of skill or talent.

—Mark Daniel Cohen

Works: *Closet*, 1988; *Ghost*, 1990; *Untitled (Amber Bed)*, 1991; *House*, 1993; BBC. *Untitled (Five Shelves)*, 1995–96.

Exhibition Catalogs: Kellein, Thomas. *Rachel Whiteread*. Basel: Kunsthalle Basel; Philadelphia: Institute of Contemporary Art, University of Pennsylvania; Boston: Institute of Contemporary Art, 1994; Lingwood, James, ed. *House*. London: Phaidon Press, in association with Artangel, 1995; Bradley, Fiona, ed. *Rachel Whiteread: Shedding Life*. London: Tate Gallery, 1996; Weitman, Wendy. *Rachel Whiteread: Demolished*. New York: Museum of Modern Art, Dept. of Prints and Illustrated Books, 1997.

WHITMAN, Robert

(1935).

It looks as though, more than three decades after the fact, Whitman's reputation remains based upon a single innovative work of visual theater, *Prune. Flat*. (1965—sometimes spelled without the periods), which will always be, for those who have seen it during infrequent revivals, a masterpiece of alternative theater. It opens with a film whose image is a movie projector, implicitly announcing that one theme is cinematic images. The film then shows a grapefruit (whose image nearly fills the screen) being cut by a knife. After other images, a tomato appears, which is also cut, small black egg-like objects pouring out of it. When the tomato-cutting sequence is repeated, two young women dressed in white smocks and white kerchiefs walk in front of the film screen, the film blade appearing to cut through them as well. As the film shows the two women walking down the street, one slightly behind the other, the same two women walk live across

Bob Whitman's *Prune Flat*, performed 21 August 1966.

the stage, at an angle perpendicular to their images on the screen, but in a similar formation. Later in the piece, the image of a woman undressing and showering is projected directly on a full-length body of one of the women performers; but once the film shuts off, the woman who appears to be undressed is suddenly revealed to be clothed. The subject of *Prune. Flat.* is the perceptual discrepancies between filmed image and theatrical presence, and it differs from other MIXED-MEANS THEATER not only in its precise control but in its visual plenitude.

Theater: *American Moon*, 1960; *Flower*, 1963; *Prune. Flat*, 1965; *Nighttime Sky*, 1965; *Two Holes of the Water*, 1966; *Salad PN*, 1974; *Light Touch*, 1976.

Bibliography: Kostelanetz, Richard. "Robert Whitman." In *The Theatre of Mixed Means*. New York: Dial, 1968.

Exhibition Catalog: Marter, Joan, ed. *Off Limits: Rutgers University and the Avant-Garde, 1957–1963*. Newark, NJ: The Newark Museum & Rutgers University Press, 1999.

WICKHAM-SMITH, Simon

(2 February 1968).

In the mail, early in 1992, as I was drafting the first edition of this book, came two chapbooks of visual literature that were so original that their author deserves mention here. The shorter, *indic plaid poem* (1992), sixteen pages long, has on each page several lines of a hieroglyphic language that changes beneath a continuous horizontal line that unites all the signs. The other, *The Rotations* (1992), subtitled "a novel," has hundreds of small squares, set twenty-five to a page, each square divided by a jagged channel, some of them having parts that are fully shaded in. The author, born in England, tells me that he is also a musician. Stay tuned.

Books: Wickham-Smith, Simon. *The Rotations*. Davis, CA: Fuzzy Blue Books (P.O. Box 73463, Davis, CA), 1992; *Few*. Port Charlotte, FL: Runaway Spoon, 1994.

WIGMAN, Mary

(13 November 1886–18 September 1973).

A pioneer of German Expressionist dance, Wigman began her training with the music theoretician Emile Jaques-Dalcroze (1865–1950), who created "Eurhythmics," in Hellarau near Dresden. She later collaborated with the movement analyst Rudolf van Laban (1879–1958), who developed a movement notation system called Labanotation. Dancing barefoot, exploring primitive rhythms and motifs, experimenting with costumes, props, and masks, Wigman created numerous distinguished solos and group works. Largely abstract, frequently dark or angst-ridden, these pieces focused on fundamental forms and essential emotions. Wigman also incorporated improvisation into her framing system. Many important German modern dancers attended her school, as did Hanya Holm (1898–1992), who was her assistant and later came to America, sponsored by the impressario Sol Hurok (1888–1974), to open a Wigman school. Holm became a modern American dance pioneer and influential choreographer, and she taught Alwin Nikolais, influencing his technique along with that of his associate, Murray Louis.

—Katy Matheson

Dances: Wigman, Mary. *Dances of Night* includes the cycles *Four Hungarian Dances, Dance Songs, and Ecstatic Dances*, 1919; *The Seven Dances of Life*, 1921; *Scenes from a Dance Drama*, 1923–24; *Dance of Death*, 1926; *Witch Dance*, 1926; *Monotony Whirl*, 1926; *Celebration*, 1927–28; *Shifting Landscape*, 1929; *Totenmal*, 1930; *Sacrifice*, 1931; *Women Dances*, 1934; *Autumnal Dances*, 1937; *Rite of Spring*, 1957.

Writings: Wigman, Mary. *The Language of Dance*. Trans. Walter Sorell. Middletown: Wesleyan University Press, 1966; Sorell, Walter, ed. *The Mary Wigman Book: Her Writings*. Middletown: Wesleyan University Press, 1975.

Interpretation: Manning, Susan A. *Ecstasy and the Demon: Feminism and Nationalism in the Dances of Mary Wigman*. Berkeley: University of California Press, 1993.

WILDE, Oscar

(16 October 1854–30 November 1900; b. Fingal O'Flahertie Wills W.).

The avant-garde Wilde is less the dramatist, who worked safely within Victorian conventions, than the essayist, particularly as an aphorist whose prinicipal proto-modernist theme was that art is primarily about materials and experience indigenous to art. Few writers in any language could create so many memorable knockout lines, whether in speech or in print, especially about art, artists' lives, and the artistic process. Among them:

> The artist is the creator of beautiful things.
>
> Art never expresses anything except itself.
>
> To reveal art and conceal the artist is art's aim.
>
> The critic is he who can translate into another manner or a new material his impression of beautiful things.
>
> Diversity of opinion about a work of art shows that the work is new, complex, and vital.
>
> A work of art is the unique result of a unique temperament. Its beauty comes from the fact that its author is what he is. It has nothing to do with the fact that other people want what they want. Indeed, the moment that an artist takes notice of what other people want, and tries to supply the demand, he ceases to be an artist, and becomes a dull or an amusing craftsman, an honest or dishonest tradesman. He has no further claim to be considered as an artist.

If you are an artist at all, you will be not the mouthpiece of a century, but the master of eternity.

No great artist ever sees things as they really are. If he did, he would cease to be an artist.

There is only one thing in the world worse than being talked about, and that is not being talked about.

There seems to be some curious connection between piety and poor rhymes.

Good artists give everything to their art and consequently are perfectly uninteresting themselves.

He [Bernard Shaw] hasn't an enemy in the world, and none of his friends like him.

[Upon arriving at New York City customs immigration] I have nothing to declare except my genius.

In his tragically short life, Wilde was also a successful playwright; a father whose sexual tastes were primarily homoerotic; a litigant in a monumental libel case; a jailbird; and a bankrupt. About the last his monumental quip was, "I'm dying beyond my means." It is scarcely surprising that plays, films, and other literary works have been based on his life.

My admittedly alternative opinion is that none of Wilde's other work is finally quite as strong as his aphorisms, which is to say that their excellence establishes a measure not equaled elsewhere in his work, perhaps because, to quote Wilde against himself, his life was not "perfectly uninteresting."

Books: *Complete Works of Oscar Wilde: Stories, Plays, Poems, & Essays*. New York: HarperCollins, 1989; *The Artist as Critic: Critical Writings of Oscar Wilde*. Ed. Richard Ellmann. New York: Random House, 1969; *Selected Writings of Oscar Wilde*. Ed. Russell Fraser. Boston: Houghton, 1969; *The Letters of Oscar Wilde*. Ed. Rupert Hart-Davis. London: Rupert Hart-Davis, 1962; *More Letters of Oscar Wilde*. Ed. Rupert Hart-Davis. New York: Vanguard, 1985; *Witticisms of Oscar Wilde*. Ed. Derek Stanford. London: John Baker, 1971; *I Can Resist Everything Except Temptation: And Other Quotations from Oscar Wilde*. Ed. Karl. E. Beckson. Columbia University Press, 1996. *The Importance of Being a Wit: The Insults of Oscar Wilde*. Ed. Maria Leach, New York: Carroll & Graf, 1997.

Biography: Harris, Frank. *Oscar Wilde: His Life and Confessions* (1930), together with G. B. Shaw's "My Memories of O.W." & Robert Ross's "O.W.'s Last Days." New York: Dell, 1960; Ellmann, Richard. *Oscar Wilde*. New York: Random House, 1988.

Web Site: http://www.jonno.com/oscariana/

Interpretation: Freedman, Jonathan, ed. *Oscar Wilde: A Collection of Critical Essays*. Upper Saddle River, NJ: Prentice–Hall, 1996; Hoare, Philip. *Oscar Wilde's Last Stand: Decades, Conspiracy, and the Most Outspoken Trial of the Century*. New York: Arcade, 1999; Nicholls, Mark.*The Importance of Being Oscar: The Wit and Wisdom of Oscar Wilde Set Against His Times*. New York: St. Martin's Press, 1980; Roditi, Eduard. *Oscar Wilde: A Critical Guidebook*. New York: New Directions, 1947.

WILFRED, Thomas

(18 June 1889–15 August 1968; b. Richard Edgar Løvstrøm).

Wilfred is commonly credited as the first modern artist to use electric light not for illumination but as an autonomous artistic medium. Wilfred called this art "Lumia," which might have become more important than his own name had other artists been able to do it as well. He began in 1905, he wrote, "with a cigar box, a small incandescent lamp, and some pieces of colored glass." By the 1920s he had developed the *clavilux*, a keyboard controller for light projectors and optical amplifiers, such as lenses and filters, which could endlessly vary the forms and colors of projected light. As the critic Donna M. Stein writes, "The simplest clavilux consists of at least four projection units, each regulating a different function. Registers permit the coupling of one or more of the projection units to any of the manuals." While several Wilfred claviluxes were permanently installed, he made portable models for recital tours. He also accompanied classical music concerts on his clavilux and designed stage backdrops. Wilfred had his own theater, Grand Central Palace, until it became an induction center during World War II. His last successful innovation was the free-standing light box whose screen would present, thanks to cleverly complementary color wheels, a continuously original visual stream whose afterimage would be not one or another picture but a constant, ingratiating flow. I remember one on exhibition through the 1960s in the basement of the Museum of Modern Art, *Lumia Suite* (Opus 158). Six feet high and eight feet across, it kept the eyes of the queues occupied while they waited to enter the adjacent movie theater. This light machine seemed at the time an image-model for the rear-projected JOSHUA LIGHT SHOW behind rock-music performances at the legendary Fillmore East (1967–72) around that time. So forgotten is Wilfred's pioneering work that it isn't at all acknowledged in Jan Butterfield's otherwise informative survey, *The Art of Light and Space* (1993).

Books: Wilfred, Thomas. *On Lumia, The Art of Light: Selected Articles, Criticisms, and Information*. New York: Art Institute of Light, 1940(?); *Projected Scenery: A Technical Manual*. New York: Drama Book Specialists, 1965.

Exhibition Catalog: Stein, Donna M. *Thomas Wilfred: Lumia, A Retrospective*. Washington, DC: Corcoran Gallery, 1971.

Bibliography: Butterfield, Jan. *The Art of Light and Space*. New York: Abbeville, 1993; Krantz, Stewart. *Science and Technology in the Arts*. New York: Reinhold, 1974.

WILLIAMS, Emmett

(4 April 1925).

Williams was perhaps the only American writer of his generation to become intimately involved, in the 1950s, with the European intermedia avant-garde. By the 1960s, he was an initiator of FLUXUS. As an American who has found more acceptance for his work abroad, Williams has produced straight poetry, VISUAL POETRY, VISUAL FICTION, prints, ARTIST'S BOOKS, paintings, TEXT-SOUND, and performance, working with a variety of radical ideas that he tends to use sparingly. As a poet, he has favored such severe constraints as repetition, permutation, and lingustic MINIMALISM. In *Sweethearts* (1967), his BOOK-ART masterpiece, the eleven letters of the title word are visually distributed over 150 or so sequentially expressive pages. The work as a whole, when read from right to left (much like a Hebrew book), wittily relates, solely by typographical rearrangement, the evolution of a man-woman relationship. Williams spent several years in America in the 1970s, trying without success to secure an academic position such as his affable personality merited. His wife, Ann Noel (1944; b. Ann Stevenson) became in the 1980s the author/artist of exquisite book-art.

Poetry: *Konkretionen*. Darmstadt, Germany: Material, 1958; *13 Variations on 6 Words by Gertrude Stein* (1958). Cologne: Galerie der Spiegel, 1965; *Rotapoems*. Stuttgart, Hansjörg Mayer, 1966; *The Last French-Fried Potato and Other Poems*. New York: Something Else, 1967; *Sweethearts*. Stuttgart: Hansjörg Mayer, 1967; New York: Something Else, 1968; *The Book of Thorn and Eth*. Stuttgart, Hansjörg Mayer, 1968; *The Boy and the Bird*. Stuttgart: Hansjörg Mayer, 1969; *A Valentine for Nöel*. Stuttgart: Hanjörg Mayer, 1973; *Selected Shorter Poems*. New York: New Directions, 1975; *The Voyage*. Stuttgart: Hansjörg Mayer, 1975; *Deutsche Gedichte und Lichtskulpturen*. Berlin, Germany: Rainer, 1988; *Aleph, Alpha, and Alfalfa*. Berlin, Germany: Haus am Lutzowplatz, 1993; Noel, Ann. *You*. Berlin, Germany: Daadgalerie, 1982.

Plays: *Ja, es war noch da*. Darmstadt, Germany, 1960; trans. as *Yes It Was Still There*. New York: 1965; *Cellar Song for 5 Voices*. New York, 1962; *A Directional Song for Doubt for 5 Voices*. Wiesbaden, 1962; *The Ultimate Poem*. Arras, France, 1964.

Autobiography: *Themes and Variations*. Stuttgart: Hansjörg Mayer, 1981; *My Life in Flux and Vice Versa*. London: Thames & Hudson, 1992.

Anthologies: Ed. *Poésie et cetera américaine*. Paris: Biennale, 1963; Ed. *An Anthology of Concrete Poetry*. New York: Something Else, 1967; Ed. *Store Days*, by Claes Oldenburg. New York: Something Else, 1967.

Translations: *An Anecdoted Typography of Chance*, by Daniel Spoerri. New York: Something Else, 1966; *The Mythological Travels of a Modern Sir John Mandeville*, by Daniel Spoerri. New York: Something Else, 1970; *Mythology and Meatballs: A Great Island Diary-Bookbook*, by Daniel Spoerri. Berkeley, CA: Aris, 1982.

WILLIAMS, Jonathan

(8 March 1929).

This Williams calls himself "a poet" above all, but he is really an old-fashioned person-of-letters advancing literature in a variety of ways. He is a SMALL PRESS person, whose Jargon Society (1951) probably stands second to SOMETHING ELSE PRESS in publishing the people mentioned in this book (e.g. KENNETH PATCHEN, BOB BROWN, and BUCKMINSTER FULLER, among others). Second, Williams is a critic whose speciality is the affectionate portrait of undervalued artists and writers, including some of those mentioned in this book. Third, he is a poet working in a wide variety of modes, only some of them avant-garde, who has issued books and chapbooks with a greater number of alternative publishers than anyone else in America. (In this respect, he is the American equivalent of BOB COBBING, likewise an uncalculating nonacademic.)

Books: *Red/Gray*. Black Mountain, North Carolina: Jargon, 1952; *An Ear in Bartram's Tree: Selected Poems, 1957–67* (1969). New York: New Directions, 1972; *Blues & Roots Rue & Blues: A Garland for the Appalachians*. Photographs by Nicholas Dean. New York: Grossman, 1971; *The Loco Logodaedalist in Situ: Selected Poems 1968–70*. New York: Grossman, 1972; *Gists from a Presidential Report on Hardcornponeography*. Highlands, NC: Jargon, 1975; *Imaginary Postcards*. London: Trigram, 1975; *Elite/Elate Poems: Poems 1971–1975*. Highlands, NC: Jargon, 1979; *Get Hot or Get Out: A Selection of Poems, 1957–1981*. Metuchen, NJ: Scarecrow, 1982.

Essays: Williams, Jonathan. *The Magpie's Bagpipe*. San Francisco: North Point, 1982.

WILLIAMS, William Carlos

(17 September 1883–4 March 1963).

The most avant-garde W. C. Williams was less the poet-playwright-fictioneer than the essayist who, out of his broad and generous sympathies, coupled with his professional independence as a family doctor in New Jersey, was able to appreciate many of the most radical developments of his time. (This stands in contrast to T. S. ELIOT, who ignored them, for instance keeping Williams unpublished in England during their almost common lifetimes.) In this respect, consider not only Williams's early appreciation of GERTRUDE STEIN and JAMES JOYCE'S *Work in Progress* (aka *FINNEGANS WAKE*), but the essays and notes posthumously published as *The Embodiment of Knowledge* (1974). "Pure writing is represented by all whose interest is primarily in writing as an art, of far more interest to them than what it conveys," Williams states there. "Writing as an art is of course completely inundated by journalism, which is meant to 'put something over.' But all other writing is more or less in the same class with journalism."

Vehemently opposed to Eliot's high-literary bent, deriding his *The Waste Land* at a time when it was almost universally regarded as the greatest achievement of American literature, Williams emphasized the search for American language and imagery. In his rewriting of American

William Carlos Williams, c. 1930, photograph by Charles Sheeler. Courtesy New Directions Publishing Corporation.

history (in *In the American Grain* [1925]), Williams was perhaps the first to question the white/European bias of most other accounts.

Williams's more avant-garde creative work was largely forgotten in his lifetime. In the early 1920s, he published a series of books, including *Kora in Hell: Improvisations* (1920) and *Spring and All* (1923), which were inspired by his friendship with the DADA artists in New York. *Kora in Hell* has examples of automatic writing, followed by brief explications (the scientist in Williams could not let these little pieces of SURREALISM go unexplained). *Spring and All* features a mock critical introduction, upside-down chapter heads, and other typographical abnormalities. The unnamed poems often comment ironically on the texts that precede or follow them. (Predictably, when these poems were reprinted during Williams's lifetime, the experimental prose sections were removed and the poems given conventional titles.) At this time, Williams also wrote his first extended work of prose, *The Great American Novel* (1923), which makes fun of sentimental fiction by portraying a romance between a little Ford roadster and a truck. Williams's later, long poem, *Paterson* (1946–1962), incorporates historical FOUND TEXTS, overheard conversations, short lyric fragments, letters from friends, including young ALLEN GINSBERG asking for advice and Williams's sometime college buddy EZRA POUND giving it, all on the theme of one American's search for his roots.

WCW the poet is not to be confused with the fusion-rock band of the same name from Atlanta, Georgia.

—with Richard Carlin

Selected Books: *In the American Grain*. New York: New Directions, 1956; *The Embodiment of Knowledge*. Ed. Ron Loewinsohn. New York: New Directions, 1974; *Imaginations: Kora in Hell, Spring and All, The Great American Novel, The Descent of Winter, A Novelette and Other Prose* (1920–1932). Ed. Webster Schott. New York: New Directions, 1970; *The Collected Poems 1909–1962*. 2 vols. Ed. A. Walton Litz and Christopher MacGowan. New York: New Directions, 1986, 1988; *Paterson (1946–1962)*. Rev. ed. Ed. Christopher MacGowan. New York: New Directions, 1992.

Autobiography: *Autobiography of William Carlos Williams*. New York: New Directions, 1967.

Anthology: *Selected Poems*. Ed. Charles Tomlinson. New York: New Directions, 1985; *The William Carlos Williams Reader*. Ed. M. L. Rosenthal. New York: New Directions, 1966.

Biography: Mariani, Paul. *William Carlos Williams: A New World Naked*. New York: McGraw-Hill, 1981; Whittemore, Reed. *William Carlos Williams: A Poet from New Jersey*. Boston: Houghton Mifflin, 1975.

Bibliography: Wallace, Emily Mitchell. *A Bibliography of William Carlos Williams*. Middletown: Wesleyan University Press, 1968.

Web Site: http://endeavor.med.nyu.edu/lit-med/lit-med-db/webdocs/webauthors/williams90-au-.html

WILOCH, Thomas

(3 February 1953).

Wiloch writes short prose pieces, poems to some and stories to others, that reflect the influence of both SURREALISM and science fiction, which is a combination so complementary that you wonder why it is not more popular. Speaking of "revelatory moments of cynical gnosis or divine terror, drawing upon Zen, Sufi, and Christian mystical sources for inspiration but rendering the insights through the dark filter of twentieth-century realities," Wiloch has published many chapbooks with small publishers, those of COLLAGES being less original than those mostly of prose. For both *Decoded Factories of the Heart* (1991) and *Narcotic Signature* (1992), short syntactical statements, like that of the first title, customarily divided into three lines (to resemble haiku), are followed by a counter-statement typeset underneath in parentheses, in the case of the title poem " (tiny sculptures)."

Writings: *Stigmata Junction*. Crewe, Cheshire, England: Stride, 1985; *Paper Mask*. Exeter, Devon, England: Stride, 1988; *The Mannikin Cypher*. Seattle: Bomb Shelter Props, 1989; *Takes of Lord Shantih*. Greensboro, NC: Unicorn, 1989; *Decoded Factories of the Heart* (1991). 2d ed. Port Charlotte, FL: Runaway Spoon (P.O. Box 3621, 33952), 1995; *Narcotic Signature*. Lakewood, OH: Burning Press 1992; *Mr. Templeton's Toyshop*. La Grande, OR: Jazz Police (P.O. Box 3235, 97850), 1995; *Neon Trance*. Port Charlotte, FL: Runaway Spoon, 1997.

WILSON, Brian

(20 June 1942).

Eccentric, visionary "boy wonder" who led the Beach Boys and created a new style of vocal harmony and pop production. The group began as just another "fun-in-the-sun" California-style ensemble, but from the first their music was tinged with a melancholy that was unusual for the surf-and-sand sound. Wilson, ironically, was afraid of the water and never surfed, so his sunny lyrics hid a more troubling interior. He first began to show his individuality in songs like "In My Room," a classic teenage boy's admission that his private world—the world of his room—is the place where he feels most at ease. Wilson began to show his unusual ear for production in early songs like "When I Grow Up (To Be a Man)," with its insistent harpsichord figure and the vocal backup featuring the chanted years (16-17-18 etc.) indicating the passage of time. Despite its dopey lyrics, "California Girls" is one of the most wonderfully produced pop singles of all times, with its mini-orchestral introduction, carnival-like organ figure, and sweeping/swooping high harmonies. In fact, many of the band's mid-sixties singles were miniature classics, such as "Help Me, Rhonda" and "Fun, Fun, Fun," in which not a note is out of place, not an instrument wasted.

Wilson's pop masterpiece in many critics' eyes is the album *Pet Sounds*, which he recorded mostly while the Beach Boys' band was touring. He viewed it as a solo effort, and many of the tracks feature only his vocals. For once, his lyricist—Tony Asher, a former advertising writer—was well-suited to capturing Brian's moods, and the resulting songs are classics of pop music—although none were hits except the cover of the folk song classic, "Sloop John B." For its unusual harmonic progression, exquisite harmonies, and colorful instrumentation, "God Only Knows" is one of the greatest pop recordings of all time.

Wilson followed *Pet Sounds* with the greatest pop single of its day: "Good Vibrations." Pieced together from months of sessions, the over three-minute song has several distinct "movements," making it almost a miniature symphony—or perhaps, more accurately, a chorale.

The use of the THEREMIN is an interesting novelty, but the song's real power comes from its contrasting moods and the strong melodic hooks. Sadly, it would be Wilson's last great creation.

Always a troubled person, Wilson's manic-depressive personality was exacerbated by the continued pressure from his band mates and record company to produce hits—along with his use of drugs. Working with lyricist Van Dyke Parks (1941), he began his most ambitious album project yet, to be titled *Smile*. Sadly, the sessions were aborted—some claim due to the disapproval of the Beach Boys for the innovative material, others say that Wilson simply fell apart and was unable to complete the complicated work. In any case, like the fragmentary "Kubla Khan," *Smile* has become the great lost work of rock music, attracting more praise than albums that actually exist!

Wilson spent much of the seventies, eighties, and nineties in "recovery." Although he has made many publicized "comebacks," he has never really returned to his full powers. Nonetheless, he has occasionally produced music of charm and beauty that reflects on his original creations.

—Richard Carlin

Recordings: The Beach Boys. *Pet Sounds*. Hollywood: Capitol Records, 1966. (Reissued many times; there is also a *Pet Sounds* box set with session outtakes.)

Autobiography: *Wouldn't It Be Nice?* New York: HarperCollins, 1991.

Interpretation: Leaf, David. *The Beach Boys and the Southern California Myth*. New York: Dutton, 1979; White, Timothy. *The Nearest Far Away Place*. New York: Holt, 1996.

WILSON, Edmund

(8 May 1895–12 June 1972).

As a reviewer seriously engaged with new developments in the 1920s, he concluded the decade by writing *Axel's Castle* (1931), an influential introduction to T. S. ELIOT, MARCEL PROUST, JAMES JOYCE, GERTRUDE STEIN, and developments around and before them. Wilson was particularly important at legitimizing *Finnegans Wake*, then still called *Work in Progress*. By the end of the 1930s, he was more interested in Marxism, so that by the time literature became his central interest again in the 1940s and 1950s, he barely confronted new works, except in passing remarks that reflected retrograde taste. Wilson also produced poems and other creative texts, a scant few of which were legitimately innovative. Because these last are rarely acknowledged, let alone reprinted, let me cite the ballet "Cronkhite's Clocks" that first appeared in *Discordant Encounters* (1926) but was omitted from Wilson's *Five Plays* (1954), or "The Three Limperary Cripples" that appeared in *Note-Books of Night* (1942), which includes this passage: "I would ravver read *This Side of Paralyzed* by F. Scotch Fitzgerald, or *Is*(!) by hee-hee cummings, or a transformation by Ezra Penaloosa of the lyrics of Bertran van Boren. . . ." As Wilson was repackaged for more conservative readers, these more experimental texts disappeared.

Books: *Axel's Castle* (1931). New York: Modern Library, 1996; *Note-Books of Night*. San Francisco: Colt Press, 1942.

Anthology: *The Edmund Wilson Reader* (1983). Ed. Lewis Dabney. Rev. and expanded ed. New York: Da Capo, 1997.

Correspondence: *Letters on Literature and Politics*. New York: Farrar, Straus, 1977.

Biography: Meyers, Jeffrey. *Edmund Wilson: A Biography*. Boston: Houghton Mifflin, 1995.

Interpretation: Castronovo, David. Edmund Wilson. New York: Ungar, 1984. Dabney, Lewis M., ed. *Edmund Wilson: Cenennial Reflections*. Princeton: Princeton University Press, 1997; Groth, Janet. *Edmund Wilson: A Critic for Our Time*. Athens: Ohio University Press, 1989; Wain, John, ed. *Edmund Wilson: The Man and His Work*. New York: New York University Press, 1978.

WILSON, Robert

(4 October 1941).

An American theatrical artist trained in visual art, Wilson knew from the beginning that his theater would emphasize image and movement over scripts. His early works also revealed a predisposition toward thinking big—using larger theaters, more performers, and larger props (requiring greater funding) than his predecessors in nonliterary theater did. Much more abundant in some respects, Wilson's theater broached unprecedented slowness in the movements of the principal performers. Wilson also used amateurs who were clearly amateur, as well as freaks who had never before appeared on stage, let alone much in public; some of his images, such as a chorus of "black mammies," could be audacious beyond belief. He would tuck portions of earlier pieces into new ones that had completely different names.

Wilson's masterpiece, of those I have seen, was *The Life and Times of Joseph Stalin* (1973), which ran for some twelve hours, filling the stage of the Brooklyn Academy of Music with several score performers and many props. Its first three acts incorporated much of an earlier Wilson piece, *The Life and Times of Sigmund Freud* (1969), while the fourth act included much of *Deafman Glance* (1971). In the first act, as dancers move about the stage, one performer obliquely refers to Stalin by giving an effectively concise summary of dialectical materialism, itself spoken against background music drawn from various sections of Gabriel Fauré's *Messe de Requiem* (1886–87). In the last act, a chorus of ostriches dances in unison. What did not make sense as intellectual exposition or as a theatrical script seemed reasonably coherent as a MIXED-MEANS performance experience. I'd see it again any time.

Wilson's more recent theatrical work, mostly operas in collaboration with composers as various as Richard Wagner (1813–83) and PHILIP GLASS, is not as original as his earlier theater was, though, because he works primarily in Europe, few of his American admirers have seen enough of it to make any definitive generalizations. He seems to be particularly receptive to accepting European commissions to produce "interpretations" of historical personages or events (much like the American playwright Paul Green [1893–1981], who made commissioned pageants for some Southern states a few decades ago). Wilson also has generously exhibited videotapes, drawings, furniture, costumes, and theater props in museums both prominent and obscure around the world. Stefan Brecht's 1978 monograph on Wilson gives elaborately detailed summaries, really a model of their kind, of theatrical events in Wilson's early productions.

Selected Major Theatrical Productions: *Dance Event*, New York, 1965; *Solo Performance*, New York, 1966; *ByrdwoMAN*, New York, 1968; *The King of Spain*, New York, 1969; *The Life and Times of Sigmund Freud*. New York: 1969. *Deafman Glance* (1970). Iowa City; New York; Nancy, France; Rome; Paris: Amsterdam; *KA MOUNTAIN AND GUARDenia TERRACE a story about a family and some people changing*. Shiraz, Iran, 1972; *The Life and Times of Joseph Stalin* (1973). Copenhagen; New York: Sao Paulo; *The CIVIL warS* (1984). With various parts, variously in collaboration with Heiner Móller, Maita di Niscemi, David Byrne, in Minneapolis, MN; Frankfurt; Paris; Madrid; Venice; Bologne; Cologne; Los Angeles; Tokyo; Brisbane, Australia; Houston, TX; etc.; *A Letter for Queen Victoria*, Spoleto, Italy; New York, 1974–75; *The $ Value of Man*, New York, 1975; *Einstein on the Beach*, New York, 1976; *I Was Sitting on My Patio This guy Appeared I Thought I Was Hallucinating*, Austin, TX; Yipsilanti, MI; & New York, 1977; *Dialogue/Curious George*, Brussels & New York, 1979–80; *Medea*, with Gavin Bryars, Washington, DC, 1981; *The Golden Windows*, 1982; *King Lear*, 1985; *Death, Destruction, and Detroit II*, 1987; *Orlando*, 1989; *The Black Rider: The Casting of Magic Bullets*, 1990; *Doctor Faustus Lights the Lights*. Berlin: Hebbel Theater, 1992; *Madame Butterfly*. Paris: Opéra Bastille, 1993; *The Meek Girl*. Bobigny, France, 1994; *Hamlet: A Monologue*. Houston, TX;

Venice; New York; Paris, etc, 1995; *Four Saints in Three Acts*. Houston, TX & New York, 1996.

Books: ——, and Philip Glass. *Einstein on the Beach: An Opera in Four Acts*. Ed. Vicky Alliata. New York: Eos Enterprises, n.d.

Videotapes: *Spaceman*, with Ralf Hilton, 1976; *Video 50*, 1978; *Deafman Glance*, 1981; *Stations*, 1982; *La Femme à la Cafetière*, 1989; *The Death of King Lear*, 1989.

Exhibition Catalogs: *Robert Wilson's Civil Wars Drawings, Models, and Documentation*. Los Angeles: Otis Art Institute, 1984; *Robert Wilson, from a Theater of Images*. Cincinnati, OH: Contemporary Art Center, 1980; *Mr. Bojangles' Memory: og son of fire*. Paris: Centre Pompidou, 1991; *Portrait, Still Life, Landscape*. Rotterdam, Holland: Boymans-van Beuningen Museum, 1993.

Interpretation: *Robert Wilson: Steel Velvet*. Munich: Prestel, 1997; Brecht, Stefan. *The Theatre of Visions: Robert Wilson*. Frankfurt, Germany: Suhrkamp, 1978; Fairbrother, Trevor. *Robert Wilson's Vision*. New York: Abrams, 1991; Nelson, Craig, ed. *Robert Wilson: The Theater of Images* (1980). New York: Harper & Row, 1984; Shyer, Laurence. *Robert Wilson and His Collaborators*. New York: Theater Communications Group, 1990; Quadri, Franco, Franco Bertoni, and Robert Stearns. *Robert Wilson*. New York: Rizzoli, 1997 [This contains a complete listing of Wilson's theatrical productions, solo exhibitions and museum installations, films and videos, and Wilson's miscellaneous publications to 1996, but neglects his critical literature.]

WINES, James (27 June 1932)

See **SITE**.

WINTERS, Yvor

(17 October 1900–25 January 1968).

It was Kenneth Rexroth who often reminded readers that before Yvor Winters became an apostle of classicism (and a Stanford professor) he was an experimental poet whose forte was Minimalism, especially in the appreciation of nature. Thus Winters's poem "The Magpie's Shadow" (1922) has sections such as "The Aspen's Song," which reads in its entirety:

> The summer holds me here.

Or "Sleep," which reads:

> Like winds my eyelids close.

Or "A Deer":

> The trees rose in the dawn.

These sentences are, to my mind, poetic, rather than fictional or expository, if only for their conciseness and lyricism. Other examples of early Winters can be found, along with his later, far more traditional work, in the latest edition of his complete poetry. Winters's mature criticism was based upon the unfashionable premises that the best poetry is morally edifying and that criticism, as well as poetry, should favor rational, paraphrasable statements about human life. His wife was the novelist Janet Lewis (1899–1998), whose intelligent historical novels are remembered, especially for their elegant and evocative prose.

Poetry: *The Immobile Wind*. Evanston, IL: Monroe Wheeler, 1921; *The Magpie's Shadow*. Chicago: Muster Bookhouse, 1922; *The Bare Hills*. Boston: Four Seas, 1927; *The Proof*. New York: Coward-McCann, 1930; *The Brink of Darkness*. Denver, CO: Swallow, 1947; *The Collected Poems*. Denver, CO: Swallow, 1952, 1960; *The Poetry of Yvor Winters*. Intro. Donald Davie. Chicago, IL: Swallow, 1978; *The Selected Poems of Yvor Winters*. Athens: Ohio University, 1999.

Works of Criticism: *The Function of Criticism: Problems and Exercises*. Denver, CO: Swallow, 1957; *In Defense of Reason* [incorporating *Primitivism and Decadence: A Study of American Experimental Poetry* (1937), *Maule's Curse: Seven Studies in the History of American Obscurantism* (1938), *The Anatomy of Nonsense* (1943), & *The Significance of* The Bridge *by Hart Crane*]. Denver, CO: Alan Swallow, 1947.

Interpretation: Isaacs, Elizabeth. *An Introduction to the Poetry of Ivor Winters*. Athens: Swallow—Ohio University Press, 1981.

WITTENBORN, George

(1908–October 1974).

The proprietor of a prominent Manhattan bookstore specializing in art books, he also became a small publisher, reissuing in English translations many important avant-garde books by GUILLAUME APOLLINAIRE, VASSILY KANDINSKY, L. MOHOLY-NAGY, and the American architect Louis Sullivan, in addition to commissioning the painter Robert Motherwell (1915–1991) to edit the monumentally significant anthology *The Dada Painters and Poets* (1951) and hiring the literary designer Paul Rand (1914–97) to do covers and typography. Between the complementary activities of publishing and retailing, Wittenborn made available thoughts and images that would have otherwise been hidden and, as a result, had an immense, if implicit, influence on the literacy of visual artists, first in New York and, by extension, all over America from the 1940s into the 1970s. One of his sometime employees, Jaap Reitman (1942) established a similar store in the 1970s; but whereas Wittenborn was located uptown, at 1018 Madison Avenue, near the final stop of the Whitney Museum, Reitman situated his bookshop downtown in SoHo. Because Reitman was a sensitive retailer who knew the interests of his art-world customers, he had a similar influence upon the literacy of consequential artists in the 1970s and 1980s, before closing his bookshop in the wake of the neighborhood's decline as an artistic center.

Books: Motherwell, Robert, ed. *The Dada Painters and Poets,* 1951. Boston: G. K. Hall; Apollinaire, Guillaume. *The Cubist Painters (Aesthetic Meditations)* (1913). Trans. Lionel Abel. New York: Wittenborn, 1949; Sullivan, Louis H. *Kindergarten Chats and Other Writings* (1918). New York: Wittenborn, 1949; Kandinsky, Wassily. *Concerning the Spiritual in Art* (1912). New York: Wittenborn, 1947; Moholy-Nagy, Laszlo. *The New Vision* (1928) and *Abstract of an Artist*. New York: Wittenborn, 1947.

WOJNAROWICZ, David

(14 September 1956–22 July 1992).

An openly gay POLYARTIST who left home early and lived on the streets as a teenager, Wojnarowicz made paintings and sculptures, graphics and photographs, films and videos, in addition to contributing prolifically to literary journals during the 1980s. His style at its best echoes F.-L. Céline:

> I am all emptiness and futility. I am an empty stranger, a carbon copy of my form. I can no longer find what I'm looking for ourside of myself. It doesn't exist out there. Maybe it's only in here, inside my head. But my head is glass and my eyes have stopped being cameras, the tape has run out and nobody's words can touch me. No gesture can touch me. I've been dropped into all this from another world and I can't speak your language any longer.

Wojnarowicz's work was finally about a kind of homosexual life, from promiscuity to AIDS, with which he was diagnosed in the late 1980s and which contributed to his early death. Especially in the late 1990s, he became, like the photographer ROBERT MAPPLETHORPE, someone whom his advocates wanted to make more acceptable to a larger American public. One hesitates to remind them that there is a difference between asking that homosexuality be regarded as acceptable, which it should be, and that the work produced by someone like Wojnarowicz is necessarily superior, which isn't true. To someone not part of this push, Wojnarowicz's work seems splenetic, as individual moves seem opportunistic (his paintings, for instance, taking too much from comic books)—for the tragedy was that he did not live long enough to make his variousness cohere around themes greater than his own disintegrating life.

Books: *Close to the Knives: A Memoir of Disintegration*. New York: Vintage, 1991; *Brush Fires in the Social Landscape*. New York: Aperture, 1994; *Fever: The Art of David Wojnarowicz*. Ed. Amy Scholder. New York: Rizzoli,

1998; *In The Shadow of the American Dream: The Diaries of David Wojnarowicz*. Ed. and intro. Amy Scholder. New York: Grove, 1999.

Photography: *Ant Series*, 1988–89; *Arthur Rimbaud in New York (peep show)*, 1978–79.

Paintings: *Fuck You Faggot Fucker*, 1984; *Crash: The Birth of Language/The Invention of Lies*, 1986; *Something from Sleep IV (dream)*, 1988–89.

Sculpture: *Dollar Totem*, 1983; *Untitled (shark)*, 1984.

Exhibition Catalogs: *David Wojnarowicz: Tongues of Flame*. Normal: University Gallery of Illinois State, 1990; *David Wojnarowicz*. New York: New Museum, 1999.

WOLFF, Christian

(8 March 1934).

As a teenager in the early 1950s, Wolff joined the circle that included John Cage, Earle Brown, and Morton Feldman, with whom he continued to be associated while pursuing academic degrees in the classics, which he has taught at Harvard and teaches lately at Dartmouth. The mark of Wolff's early music was a limited number of pitches—three for his *Duo for Violin and Piano*, four for *Trio for Flute, Cello, and Trumpet* (1951), tending, in David Revill's words, "to encourage concentration on individual sounds and their combinations rather than progressions." The result was static, if not pointillistic, like some Webernian compositions, though proceding from different nonserial premises.

Wolff later pioneered in the use of "scores" whose instructions were words or charts (or both) and in offering variable directions on how one performer could respond to the moves of another, as though the musicians were playing a game. (This kind of restricted improvisatory music influenced John Zorn, among others in his universe, in the 1980s.) In the 1970s, Wolff incorporated Leftist political criticism into his work, at times drawing upon traditional radical texts and songs. "Wolff began writing works less as experiences for the audiences than as models for social interaction," according to Kyle Gann. "One of the most ambitious of these works is *Changing the System* (1972–73), in which the performers must collaborate on group decisions about when and what to play. One premise of Wolff's middle-period music, like that of many of the political composers, is that it is performable by nonmusicians as well as by professionals."

Compositions: Trio for Flute, Cello, and Trumpet, 1951; *Summer*, for string quartet, 1961; *For 5 or 10 Players*, for any instruments, 1962; *For 1, 2 or 3 People*, for any sound-producing means, 1964; *Pairs* for any 2, 4, 6, or 8 players, 1968; *Prose Collection*, for variable number of players, found and constructed materials, instruments, and voices, 1968–71; *Lines*, for string quartet, 1972; *Changing the System*, for 8 or more instruments, voices, and percussion, 1972–73; *Wobbly Music*, for chorus, keyboard, guitars, and at least 2 melody instruments, 1975–76; *Braverman Music*, for chamber ensemble, 1978; *Isn't This a Time?* for any saxophone or multiple reeds, 1982; *Peace March 1*, for flute, 1983–84; *2*, for flute, clarinet, cello, percussion, and piano, 1984; *3*, for flute, cello, and percussion, 1984; *Emma*, for viola, cello, and piano, 1989.

Recordings: *Bread & Roses for Piano*, 1976; *Hay Una Mujer Desapareida for Piano*, 1979; *Piano Song "I Am a Dangerous Woman,"* 1983; *Preludes for Piano*, 1981. New York: Mode; *Pairs for any 2, 4, 6 or 8 Players*, 1968. Therwil, Switzerland: Hat Hut; *For Ruth Crawford*, 1993; *Ruth for Trombone & Piano*, 1991; *Snowdrop for Trombone, Piano & Violin*, 1970. Roland Dahinden, trombone; Hildegard Kleeb, piano. Therwil, Switzerland: Hat Hut, 1994; *Duo for Pianists I* (1957), *Duo for Pianists 1/2nd version* (1957). David Tudor, piano. Therwil, Switzerland: Hat Hut; *Exercises*. Eberhard Blum, flute; Roland Danded, trombone; et al. Therwil, Switzerland: Hat Hut, 1995.

Interpretation: Nyman, Michael. *Experimental Music*. New York: Schirmer, 1974; DeLio, Thomas. *Circumscribing*

Frank Lloyd Wright, Avery Coonley House, 1908. CORBIS/Bettmann.

the Open Universe. Lanham, MD: University Press of America, 1984; Gann, Kyle. *American Music in the Twentieth Century*. New York: Schirmer, 1997.

WOOSTER GROUP

See **PERFORMANCE GROUP**.

WRIGHT, Frank Lloyd

(8 June 1869–9 April 1959).

The ideal of Wright's architectural philosophy was organicism, which he defined as successfully relating a building both to its intrinsic purposes and its surrounding environment, so that "inside" and "outside" blend into each other. "Thus environment and building are one," he wrote in *A Testament* (1957). "Planning the grounds around the building on the site as well as adorning the building take on a new importance as they become features harmonious with the space-within-to-be lived-in. Site, structure, furnishing—decoration too, planting as well—all these become one in organic architecture." That accounts for why, in his private homes, such as the legendary *Falling Water* (1936), Wright's architecture melts into its landscape and looks as though it belongs precisely where it is set. On the other hand, like other megalomaniacs, Wright didn't always follow his own rules, creating in the original Guggenheim Museum in New York City (1959) an awkward showcase for both works of painting and sculpture that nonetheless conquered ventilation problems, which typically plague other museums. Wright's Guggenheim, as it is commonly called, attained sculptural qualities by climaxing earlier Wright penchants for spirals and inverted ziggurats, in addition to constantly impressing its peculiarities upon everyone entering it. Not unlike other architects with few buildings to construct, Wright produced a wealth of essays and books.

Selected Architecture: *Willits House*. Highland Park, IL, 1902; *Larkin Building*. Buffalo, NY, 1902–1906, destroyed 1950; *Unity Temple*. Oak Park, IL, 1905–08; Imperial Hotel. Tokyo, 1916; Falling Water. Bear Run, PA, 1935; *Usonia House,* Madison, WI, 1936; *Johnson Wax Administration Building*. Racine, WI, 1936–1938; Johnson Wax Research Tower, Racine, 1944; *First Unitarian Church*. Shorewood Hills, WI, 1947–51; *Harold Price Tower*. Bartlesville, OK, 1956; *Beth Shalom Synagogue*. Elkins Park, PA, 1954–57; *Friedman House*. Pleasantville, NY, 1948; *Greek Orthodox Church*. Wauwatosa, WI, 1959; *Guggenheim Museum*. New York, 1959.

Proposals: Broadacre City, 1934.

Writings: Wright, Frank Lloyd. *The Disappearing City*. New York: W. F. Payson, 1932. Rev. as *When Democracy Builds Chicago* (1945). Portions appear in *The Living City*. New York: Horizon, 1958; *An Organic Architecture* 1939. Cambridge: MIT Press, 1970; An *Autobiography* (1932, 1943). New York: Horizon, 1962; *The Future of Architecture*. New York: Horizon, 1953; *The Natural House*. New York: Horizon, 1954; *An American Architecture*. Ed. Edgar Kauffman. New York: Horizon, 1955; *The Living City*. New York: Horizon, 1958; *Genius and Mobocracy*. New York: Horizon, 1971; *An Autobiography* (1932). New York: Horizon, 1977; *Collected Writings 1894–1959*. 5 vols. Ed. Bruce Brooks Pfeiffer. New York: Rizzoli, 1992–95.

Anthology: Wasmuth, Ernst, ed. *Drawings and Plays of Frank Lloyd Wright: The Early Period (1893–1909)* (1910). New York: Dover, 1983; *Frank Lloyd Wright: Early Visions* Trans. Brigitte Goldstein. New York: Gramercy, 1995; De Long, David, ed. *Frank Lloyd Wright and the Living City*. New York: Abbeville, 1999; Kaufmann, Edgar, and Ben Raeburn, eds. *Frank Lloyd Wright: Writings and Buildings*. New York: Horizon, 1960; Izzo, Alberto, and Camillo Gubitosi. *Frank Lloyd Wright: Three Quarters of a Century of Drawings*. Trans. Stella Cragie. New York: Horizon, 1981; Pfeiffer, Bruce Brooks. *Frank Lloyd Wright Drawings: Masterworks from the Frank Lloyd Wright Archives*. New York: Abrams, 1990; Storer, William Allen. *The Architecture of Frank Lloyd Wright: A Complete Catalog*. Cambridge: MIT Press, 1978.

Exhibition Catalog: *Frank Lloyd Wright and Madison: Eight Decades of Artistic and Social Interaction*. Ed. Paul E. Sprague. Madison, WI: Elvehjem Museum of Art, University of Wisconsin, 1990.

Biography: Gill, Brendan. *Many Masks: A Life of Frank Lloyd Wright*. New York: Putnam, 1987; Kaufmann, Edgar J., Jr. *Fallingwater: A Frank Lloyd Wright Country House*. New York: Abbeville, 1986; Secrest, Meryle. *Frank Lloyd Wright: A Biography*. New York: Knopf, 1992; Twombley, Robert C. *Frank Lloyd Wright: His Life and Architecture*. New York: Harper & Row, 1974; Wright, John Lloyd. *My Father Who Is on Earth*. New York: Penguin, 1946.

Web Site: http://members.aol.com/ddukesf/index.html

Interpretation: Blake, Peter. *Frank Lloyd Wright: Architecture and Space*. New York: Penguin, 1964; Bolen, Carol R., et al., eds. *The Nature of Frank Lloyd Wright*. Chicago: University of Chicago Press, 1988; Hanna, Paul R., and Jean S. Hanna. *Frank Lloyd Wright's Hanna House: The Client's Report*. 2d ed. Carbondale: Southern Illinois University Press, 1987; Hertz, David Michael. *Angels of Reality: Emersonian Unfoldings in Wright, Stevens, and Ives*. Carbondale: Southern Illinois University Press, 1993; Hoffmann, Donald. *Frank Lloyd Wright: Architecture and Nature*. New York: Dover, 1986; ——. *Frank Lloyd Wright's Fallingwater*. New York: Dover, 1978; ——. *Frank Lloyd Wright's Robie House*. New York: Dover, 1984; Jacobs, Herbert, and Catherine Jacobs. *Building with Frank Lloyd Wright*. San Francisco: Chronicle, 1978; ——.

Frank Lloyd Wright: America's Greatest Architect. New York: Harcourt, Brace, 1965; Lipman, Jonathan. *Frank Lloyd Wright and the Johnson Wax Building*. New York: Rizzoli, 1986; Manson, Grant Carpenter. *Frank Lloyd Wright to 1910: The First Golden Age*. New York: Van Nostrand Reinhold, 1958; Pfeiffer, Bruce Brooks. *Frank Lloyd Wright: His Living Voice*. Fresno: California State University Press, 1987; Quinan, Jack. *Frank Lloyd Wright's Larkin Building: Myth and Fact*. Cambridge: MIT Press, 1987; Scully, Vincent, Jr. *Frank Lloyd Wright*. New York: Braziller, 1960; Storrer, William Allen. *The Architecture of Frank Lloyd Wright*. Cambridge: MIT Press, 1986; ——. *A Frank Lloyd Wright Companion*. Chicago: University of Chicago Press, 1994.

Documentary Video: Burns, Ken, and Lynn Novick, *Frank Lloyd Wright*, 1998.

Bibliography: Sweeney, Robert L. *Frank Lloyd Wright: An Annotated Bibliography*. Los Angeles: Hennessey & Ingalls, 1978.

WRITERS FORUM (England)

See **COBBING, Bob**.

XENAKIS, Iannis

(29 May 1922).

Born Greek in Rumania, Xenakis was trained in architecture in Athens; between 1947 and 1959, he worked with LE CORBUSIER, reportedly contributing to the spatial installation of EDGARD VARÈSE'S *Poème électronique* at the 1958 Brussels World's Fair. While working in architecture, he studied music with OLIVIER MESSIAEN (1908–92) and Darius Milhaud (1892–1974). Using various kinds of mathematics, Xenakis has advocated what NICOLAS SLONIMSKY calls "the stochastic method which is teleologically directed and deterministic, as distinct from a purely aleatory [i.e., JOHN CAGEAN] handling of data." Xenakis also founded and directed the Centre d'Études Mathematiques et Automatiques Musicales in Paris (and for a while a comparable Center for Mathematical and Automated Music in the U.S.), purportedly in competition with PIERRE BOULEZ'S IRCAM. All the theory notwithstanding, much of Xenakis's music has thickly atonal textures, which sound like bands of frequencies in the tradition of tone clusters, often distributed among many loudspeakers. For the French pavilion at Montreal's Expo '67, Xenakis also created, as an accompaniment to his audiotape, a spatially extended flickering light show.

Compositions: Countless.

Books in English: *Arts/Sciences: Alloys*. Stuyvesant, NY: Pendragon, 1985; *Formalized Music: Thought and Mathmatics in Composition* (1971). Stuyvesant, NY: Pendragon, 1992; Varga, Balint-Andras. *Conversations with Iannis Xenakis*. London: Faber, 1996.

Recordings: *AVs*, for amplified baritone, solo percussionist, and large orch. (1980); *Gendy 3*, for computer generated sound (1991); *Mycenae-Alpha* (1978); *Tauriphanie*, for computer generated sound (1987–88). Acton, MA: Neuma, 1994; *Chamber Music*: *Akea*, Quintet for piano & strings (1986); *À R. (Hommage to Ravel)*, for piano (1987); *Dikhthas*, for violin & piano (1979); *Embellie*, for viola (1981); *Evryali* for piano (1973); *Herma*, for piano (1960–61); *Ikhoor* for string trio (1978); *Kottos*, for cello (1977); *Mikka*, for violin (1971); *Mikka "S"*, for violin (1976); *Mists*, for piano (1980); *Nomos Alpha*, for cello (1966); *ST/4*, for string quartet (1955–62); *Tetora*, for string quaret (1990); *Tetras*, for string quartet (1983), etc. Claude Helffer, piano; Arditti Quartet. Paris: Montaigne, 1992 (Most of the recent recordings with Xenakis's work include works by other composers as well.); *Electronic Music/ Xenakis*, with *Diamorphoses*, *Concert PH*, *Bohor*, et. al. Albany, NY: Electronic Music Foundation, 1997; *Iannnisimo! Xenakis Complete Vol. 2*. Cond. Charles Zachary Bernstein. New York: Vandenburg, 1997.

Interpretation: Bois, Mario. *Iannis Xenakis: The Man and His Music*. Westport, CT: Greenwood, 1980; Matossian, Nouritza. Xenakis. London: Kahn & Averill, 1986.

XEROGRAPHIC ART

(c. 1970).

This mode of art began to flourish in the 1980s with the improvement and the nascent omnipresence of the cleanly effective photocopier. (It is hard for us to remember now the poor quality of photocopies in the 1960s.) Although xerographic art can take many shapes (including simple image degradation and serial imagery), its major form is the method of collaging sometimes called xerage or xerolage. While some xerages are merely photocopied COLLAGES, constrained by the somewhat limited reproductive capabilities of available photocopy machines, the most expressive examples bring together elements in new and interesting ways: by actually copying (rather than pasting) one image over another; by combining different colors of monochromic xerography; by degrading individual images, and by distorting images after computer scanning. While xerage has become an important genre of avant-garde art, some of its tendencies (including overprinting and image degradation) have been appropriated by Madison Avenue in recent years, illustrating how the avant-garde in the visual arts always becomes more acceptable than its counterpart in literature.

—Geof Huth

YAHOO!

(1994).

The Internet would be one vast morass without Web browsers to dig through the undergrowth. Yahoo! was among the first and the best of the lot; without it, most of the Web sites mentioned in this text would have been unfindable. Here's the official company history (from their Web site):

> Like many other aspects of the computer age, Yahoo! began as an idea, grew into a hobby and lately has turned into a full-time passion. The two developers of Yahoo!, David Filo and Jerry Yang, Ph.D. candidates in electrical engineering at Stanford University, started their guide in April 1994 as a way to keep track of their personal interests on the Internet. Before long they found that their home-brewed lists were becoming too long and unwieldy. Gradually they began to spend more and more time on Yahoo!

During 1994 they converted Yahoo! into a customized database designed to serve the needs of the thousands of users who began to use the service through the closely bound Internet community. They developed customized software to help them efficiently locate, identify, and edit material stored on the Internet. The name Yahoo! is supposed to stand for "Yet Another Hierarchical Officious Oracle," but Filo and Yang insist they selected the name because they considered themselves yahoos. Yahoo! itself first resided on Yang's student workstation, "akebono" while the search engine was lodged on Filo's computer, "konishiki." (These machines were named after legendary Hawaiian sumo wrestlers.)

In early 1995 Marc Andreessen, cofounder of Netscape Communications in Mountain View, California, invited Filo and Yang to move their files over to larger computers housed at Netscape. As a result Stanford's computer network returned to normal, and both parties benefited. Today, Yahoo! contains organized information on tens of thousands of computers linked to the Web. The *San Jose Mercury* news recently noted that "Yahoo is closest in spirit to the work of Linnaeus, the 18th-century botanist whose classification system organized the natural world."

—Richard Carlin

Web Site: www.yahoo.com

YOUNG, Karl

(7 October 1947).

One of the great eccentric recluses of contemporary American literature, Young has published since 1966, out of his homes in Milwaukee and Kenosha, Wisconsin, a series of remarkable books, as distinguished for their formal inventions as for his literary intelligence. A printer as well as a poet, Young has used a variety of alternative formats, including poems printed on both sides of a sheet of paper folded in the shape of a folding screen (and thus requiring considerable turning to be read). One masterpiece of book-art is a perfect-bound volume of used, colored blotting papers, nearly three inches thick, otherwise devoid of markings, whose multiple title establishes a variety of inferential contexts: *A Book of Hours/ A Day Book/ A Log Book/ A Thesaurus/ A Wordbook/A Book of Etiquette/A Cumulative Record/ A Hymnal/ A Dictionary/ An Album/ A Missal/ An Illuminated Book/ A Crib/ A Testament*, none of which characterizes its blotted pages, unless you take those titles, as I do, to be ironically true. As an associate editor of *Margins* (1973–77), the most eclectic and serious review of alternative publishing ever in America, Young initiated critical symposia on CLARK COOLIDGE and *ASSEMBLING*. The publisher of Membrane Press and Open Meeting Books, Young has also written some of the most penetrating extended critical essays on avant-garde literature and founded the most informative Web site so far for experimental literature and criticism, LIGHT & DUST at http://www/thing.net/~l&d/lighthom.htm. About the last Young wrote me in 1999: "The web site has had successes that I couldn't have anticipated—that come as a great relief after thirty years of print. Perhaps the biggest is averaging 1,400 hits a day. That may not mean that all readers are intelligent or ideal, but this sure beats producing maybe seven titles a year in editions of 500, of which perhaps 400 actually get read over a period of ten years. It's also great getting feedback from readers." In southeastern Wisconsin, Young connects as well to this worldwide literary universe as he could living anywhere else.

Writings: *Letters*. Milwaukee, WI: Homebrew, 1968; *Membranes*. Milwaukee, WI: Membrane, 1970; *Prayer Through Saturn's Rings*. Milwaukee, WI: Monday Morning, 1973; *First Book of Omens (from Middle American Dialogues)*. Milwaukee, WI: Membrane, 1976; *Cried an Measured*. Berkeley, CA: Tree, 1977; *To Dream Kalapuya*. St. Paul, MN: Truck, 1977; *Questions and Goddesses (from Middle American Dialogues)*. Milwaukee, WI: Membrane, 1984; *Five Kwaiden in Sleeve Pages*. Tucson, AZ: Chax, 1986; *Days and Years*. Milwaukee, WI: Membrane, 1987; *Milestones, Set 1*. Madison, WI: Landlocked, 1987; *Seafarer*, with carpet pages by Nancy Leavitt. Bangor, ME: Tatlin, 1990; *Orange Gold*. Kenosha, WI: Light and Dust, 1992; *a few short lines*, with Sherry Reniker. Japan & Kenosha, WI: Word Press & Light and Dust, 1993; *Solar Dreams*. Bangor, ME: Tatlin, 1997.

YOUNG, La Monte

(14 October 1935).

The truest MINIMAL composer, this Young has devoted most of his professional life to exploring the possibilities of a severely limited palette. After beginning as an audacious post-Cagean composer who, among other stunts, released butterflies into a performance space as a piece of "music," he hit upon *The Tortoise, His Dreams and Journeys*, in which Young along with a few colleagues produce a continuous, barely changing, harmonic (consonant)

Y

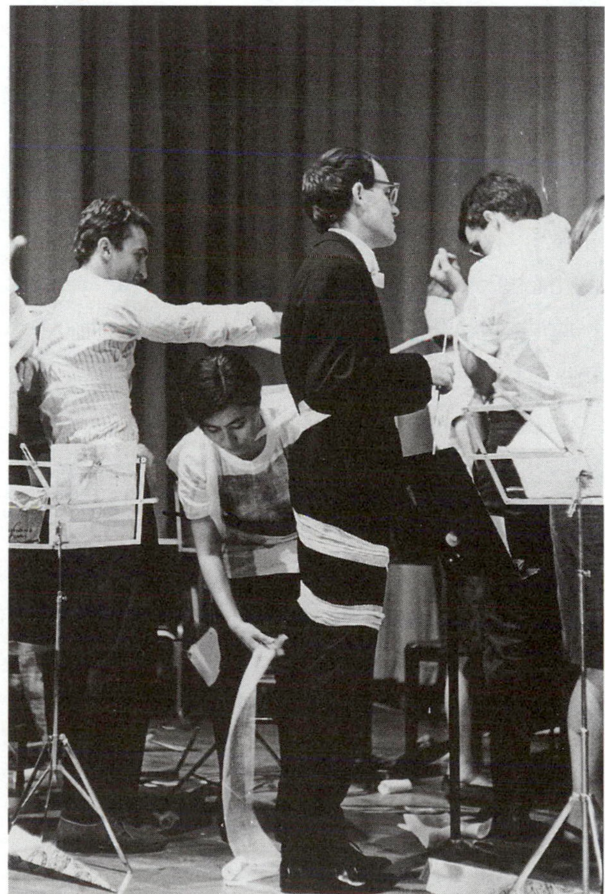

LaMonte Young being wrapped by Yoko Ono, 22 September 1965. Photograph © Fred W. McDarrah.

sound that is amplified through a prodigious system to the threshold of aural pain. Designed to last several hours, filled with dancing overtones, the piece is usually performed in a darkened, enclosed space that contains the odor of incense and projected wistful, abstract images made by his wife Marian Zazeela (1940). (Sometimes called The Theater of Eternal Music, the resulting concert could be accurately classified as an ENVIRONMENT, which is to say an artistically defined space.) Though audiotape recordings of this work exist, in my experience *The Tortoise* works best as a theatrical experience that depends upon multisensory overload to move its listeners. Young's other major composition is *The Well-Tuned Piano* (1964), a five-hour piano work (in the great tradition of comparably exhaustive keyboard pieces by J. S. Bach, Dmitri Shostakovich [1906–75], Paul Hindemith [1895–1963], JOHN CAGE, and WILLIAM DUCKWORTH), in which Young plays a Boisendorfer piano that has been retuned to just intonation. To the charge, heard often, that Young's music represents a "dead end," consider *From Ancient World* (1992), a composition by his sometime piano tuner Michael Harrison (1958), who developed a harmonic piano that realizes a different form of just intonation with twenty-four different notes within an octave.

Works: *Composition 1960*, 1960; *Arabic Numeral* (any Integer) for Gong or Piano, 1960; *Studies in the Bowed, Disc for Gong*, 1963; *The Well-Tuned Piano*, 1964; *The Tortoise Droning Selected Pitches from the Holy Numbers of the 2 Black Tigers, the Green Tiger, and the Hermit*, 1964; *The Tortoise Recalling the Drone of the Holy Numbers as They Were Revealed in the Dreams of the Whirlwind and the Obsidian Gong, Illuminated by the Sawmill, the Green Sawtooth Ocelot, and the High-Tension Line Stepdown Transformer*, 1964; *Map of 49's Dream of Two Systems of 11 Sets of Galactic Intervals Ornamental Lightyears Tracery*, for voices, various instruments, and sine wave drones, 1968; *The Subsequent Dreams of China*, 1980.

Writings: Young, La Monte/Marian Zazeela. *Selected Writings*. Munich, Germany: Heiner Friedrich, 1969.

Recordings: Young, La Monte. *The Well-Tuned Piano* (1964–81). New York: Grammavision; ——. *The Second Dream of the High-Tension Line Stepdown Transformer for Trumpet Ensemble* (1985). New York: Grammavision; Harrison, Michael. *From Ancient World*. San Francisco, CA: New Albion 22SS1-0042–2, 1992.

Extended Interviews: Kostelanetz, Richard. "La Monte Young." In *The Theatre of Mixed Means* (1968). New York: Archae, 1980; Strickland, Edward. "La Monte Young." In *American Composers*. Bloomington: Indiana University Press, 1991.

Interpretation: Duckworth, William, & Richard Fleming. eds. *Sound and Light: La Monte Young and Marian Zazeela*. Lewisburg, PA: Bucknell University Press, 1996.

ZAPPA, Frank

(21 December 1940–4 December 1993.

b. Francis Vincent Z., Jr.).

Familiar from his youth with avant-garde composers such as Edgard Varèse, and thus musically more sophisticated than others involved with 1960s rock, Zappa tried at various times and in various ways to introduce avant-garde elements into the formally expansive popular music of the late 1960s. Because successful pop musicians were allowed to transcend the short time limits of the 45 rpm disc to create long-playing 33 rpm records, Zappa's group, the Mothers of Invention, produced music in twenty-five-minute stretches; the result were "concept albums" that he released on a label appropriately named Bizarre. Some of the stronger works mocked California fads and popular music itself. *Freak Out* (1966) includes "Return of the Son of Monster Magnet," subtitled "An Unfinished Ballet in Two Tableaux," which appropriates the techniques of MUSIQUE CONCRÈTE. I saw Zappa in performance when he instructed various sections of the Fillmore East audience to perform preassigned sounds in response to his hand-signals from the front of the stage. Once we got going, he said to himself, audibly and with proud irony, "wouldn't PIERRE BOULEZ like that?" Here and elsewhere, Zappa's conceited sense of humor is refreshing to some and disaffecting to others. He has produced, with less success, not only orchestral scores but eccentric motion pictures, such as *200 Motels* (1971) and *Baby Snakes* (1980). He was to his death perhaps the only alumnus of 1960s rock still capable of generating an esthetic surprise. Zappa also released synthesizer arrangements of an eighteenth-century composer authentically named Francesco Zappa.

Selected Recordings: —— and the Mothers of Invention. *Freak Out* (1966). Pickering Wharf, MA: Rykodisc RCD40062, 1988; *Absolutely Free* (1967). Hollywood, CA: Barking Pumpkin/Capitol D41G-74214, 1988; *We're Only in It for the Money/Lumpy Gravy* (1967). Pickering Wharf, MA: Rykodisc RCD40024, 1986; Countless packagings and repackagings.

Writings: Zappa, Frank. *The Real Frank Zappa Book*, with Peter Occhiogrosso. New York: Poseidon, 1989.

Biography: Colbeck, Julian. *Zappa, A Biography*. London: W.H. Allen, 1987; Miles. *Zappa: A Visual Documentary*. London: Omnibus, 1993 [This includes an extended chronology and track-by-track discography.]; Walley, David. *No Commercial Potential* (1972, 1980). 3d ed. New York: Da Capo, 1996.

Web Site: www.zappa.com

Interpretation: Kostelanetz, Richard, ed. *A Frank Zappa Companion*. New York: Schirmer, 1997; Watson, Ben. *Frank Zappa: The Negative Dialectics of Poodle Play*. New York: St. Martin's Press, 1995.

ZAUM

(1912).

Coined by a Russian FUTURIST, probably ALEKSEI KRUCHONYKH, to indicate language that was indefinite or indeterminate in meaning (and phonetically translated as zaum', to indicate the palatalized m'), this term literally means something "beyond or outside of reason or intelligibility"; common English translations are "transrational," "trans-sense," or "beyond-sense" language. The idea of writing poetry in invented words was suggested to Kruchonykh by David Burliuk (1882–1967) in December 1912. By March 1913, the former published his notorious poem "Dyr bul shchyl," which is generally considered to be the first work of Zaum, though VELIMIR KHLEBNIKOV had for several years before this been producing poetry with obscure coinages. The principal difference is that Khlebnikov apparently intended that his experiments be eventually understood, and thus that they be conceptual demonstrations of language's creative potential to renew itself with ancient Slavic linguistic resources, whereas Kruchonykh intended, at least in the initial stages, that his Zaum be indeterminate in meaning, though not meaningless. Such indeterminate meaning was based on the suggestiveness of sound articulations and roots.

By dislocating language units ranging from phonemes to syntactic structures, Kruchonykh created a whole range of types of Zaum, often combined within a single work. One measure of true Zaum is that it should not be able to be motivated or decoded by such factors as onomatopoeia or psychopathological states. In 1917–19, he created a series of "autographic" works in which the verbal elements were sometimes reduced to a minimum of letters and lines. Thereafter, however, as Kruchonykh moved closer to the mainstream, Zaum appeared only as spice in otherwise non-Zaum works, sometimes arguing for the psychological motivation of such effects. By 1923, Kruchonykh had ceased experimenting with the use of Zaum, though he continued to theorize about its importance.

Other major Zaumniks were ILIAZD, Igor Terentev (1892–1937), and Aleksandr Tufanov (1887–1942). Some avant-garde painters, such as KAZIMIR MALEVICH, Olga Rozanova (1886–1918), and Varvara Stepanova (1894–1958), also experimented with Zaum as an analog to abstraction.

Because Zaum is usually considered the most radical product of RUSSIAN FUTURISM, its value is still, decades later, the subject of fierce dispute.

—Gerald Janecek

Bibliography: Beaujour, Elizabeth Klosty. "Zaum," *Dada/Surrealism 2* (1972); Janecek, Gerald. AA Zaum' Classification." *Canadian/American Slavic Studies XXX/1–2* (1986); ——. *Zaum: The Transrational Poetry of Russian Futurism*. San Diego: San Diego State University Press, 1996; Mickiewicz, Denis. "Semantic Functions in Zaum'." *Russian Literature XV* (1984).

ZEKOWSKI, Arlene

See **BERNE, Stanley**.

ZELEVANSKY, Paul

(10 September 1946).

Trained in painting, Zelevansky developed in his twenties a unique and precociously mature style of VISUAL POETRY that mixed texts of his own authorship, set with various typefaces (including rubber-stamped), with graphic drawings. Zelevansky makes each medium of communication as important as the others, so that his works take their rightful place in a tradition that includes both WILLIAM BLAKE and Hebrew illuminated manuscripts. This style informs not only the modest *Sweep* (1979), but a highly ambitious epic about a historical culture, *The Hegemonians*, filled with both literary and visual references. Issued as a trilogy, *The Case for the Burial of Ancestors* (1981, 1986, 1991), for depth and scope, ranks among the strongest book-art. Zelevansky has exhibited pages from it along with sculptures and other artifacts relating to the project. After working briefly with theater music, he authored one of the first narratives exclusively for computer interaction, *Swallows* (1986), only to encounter the principal difficulty in distributing literature on computer disc—the systems that can read *Swallows* (Apple IIe, II+) aren't universally popular. Later, Zelevansky created computer-assisted response displays for the Queens Museum in New York.

Books: *The Crossroad Novelty Corp. Spring Catalog Fall 1982*. New York: Crossroad Novelty Corp., 1982; *The Case for the Burial of Ancestors*. 3 vols. New York: Zartscorp (1455 Clairidge Dr., Beverly Hills, CA 90210–2214), 1981, 1986, 1991; *Monkey & Man*. New York: Old Neighborhood, 1992.

ZEND, Robert

(2 December 1929–1985).

"I lost everything but my accent," Robert Zend once noted, with reference to escaping from his native Hungary during the 1956 Revolution and arriving in Toronto. What he gained in the process was a fresh start in life, art, outlook, and language. In Budapest, he had worked as a humorist and columnist; in Toronto, employed as an arts producer for CBC Radio's "Ideas," he wrote reams of imaginative and fanciful poems—some in English (mostly in print) and some in Hungarian (currently being collected). He incessantly doodled and drew in pen and ink on all surfaces, from scraps of paper to toilet rolls, often incorporating found objects (like automobile gaskets) into his compositions. Three features of Zend's fanciful poems and surreal prose are noteworthy: individuality, language, and humor. Independent of prior work by EUGEN GOMRINGER and others, he "invented" CONCRETE POETRY; ignorant of the stories and poems of JORGE LUIS BORGES, he intuitively produced Borgesian "fictions"—and continued to do so in his own inimitable fashion long after his encounter with the "originals." Regarding the use of language, he wrote with the simplicity and clarity of a nonnative English speaker. So there is an odd "translated" quality about his poems and stories; they were written in the international, unidiomatic style of a George Steiner rather than in the idiosyncratic manner of a VLADIMIR NABOKOV. *Oab* (1983, 1985) is an extended visual fiction.

—John Robert Colombo

Works: *From Zero to One*. Victoria, Canada: Sono Nis, 1973; *Ariel and Caliban: Selected Poems*. Aya Press, 1980; *My Friend, Jeronimo*. Omni Books, 1982; *Arbormundi: Sixteen Selected Typescapes*. blewointment press, 1982; *Beyond Labels*. Toronto: Hounslow, 1982; *Oab*. 2 vols. Toronto: Exile, 1983, 1985; *Daymares: Selected Fiction on Dreams and Time*. Vancouver, BC: Ronsdale (3350 W. 21st Ave.; V65 1G7), 1990; *Nicolette: A Novel Novel* Vancouver, B.C.: Ronsdale, 1994.

ZINES

See **MICROPRESS**.

ZORN, John

(2 September 1953).

Born and bred in New York, where he lives most of the year, trained in classical music, self-educated in JAZZ, avowedly fond of motion-picture composers, Zorn has developed highly idiosyncratic, modestly original improvisations that tend to be very dissonant and disjunctive and thus aggressive, if not abrasively hideous, in acoustic quality. It is not for nothing that he speaks of himself as descending from a tradition that includes CHARLES IVES, EDGARD VARÈSE, and ORNETTE COLEMAN. In the course of an interview with Zorn, the writer Edward Strickland compares his music to the experience of "being in a New York subway station: the same diversity of different influences you suggested, but also there's a lot of mechanical sound in your music, as if the train pulls in once in a while. In the station you've got all these different types of musicians playing jazz sax or classical violins or Peruvian flutes. Part of the mix there is that you're blending a lot of 'high art' and 'low art.'" Zorn has collaborated with many other musicians, most less prominent than he, who are likewise active in DOWNTOWN Manhattan.

Works: *Archery*, 1981; *Cobra* (group improvisation), 1986; *The Big Gundown*, 1986; *Roadrunner*, for Accordian, 1986; *A Classic Guide to Strategy*, Vol. I (solo with tape), 1987; *Cat O'Nine Tails*, for String Quartet 1988; *The Deadman*, for String Quartet, 1990.

Recordings: *Naked City*. New York: Elektra Nonesuch, 1990; *Cobra*. Therwil, Switzerland: Hat Hut, 1990; *Torture*

Garden. Tokyo: Toy Factory, 1991; *The Book of Heads*. New York: Tzadik, 1995; *Kristallnacht*. Tokyo: Eva, 1993; *Red Bird*. New York: Tzadik, 1995; *Classic Guide to Strategy*. 2 vols. New York: Tzadik, 1996; *New Traditions in East Asian Bar Bands*. New York: Tzadik, 1997; *Duras: 69 Paroxyms for Marcel Duchamp*. New York: Tzadik, 1997; *Angelus Novus*. New York: Tzadik, 1998.

Extended Interview: Strickland, Edward. "Meredith Monk." In *American Composers*. Bloomington: Indiana University Press, 1991; Duckworth, William. *Talking Music*. New York: Schirmer, 1995.

Website: mars.superlink.net/marko/jz.html

ZUKOFSKY, Louis

(23 January 1904–12 May 1978).

There is no doubt that Zukofsky did something unprecedented in literature, particularly in poetry, but exactly what is hard to say, even two decades after his death. To point out that he was obscure or that his work remains mostly incomprehensible is merely to avoid the issue of whether greater understanding is possible. Zukofsky worked with unusual forms, including a numerical counterpoint in his early classic "Poem Beginning 'The'"; he produced a musical *Autobiography* in collaboration with his wife, Celia. He began in 1927 a "poem of a life," *A*, that conceptually echoes the *Cantos* of Ezra Pound, whose closest Jewish friend he was. It differs from other extended contemporary poems in revealing little about its author. Hugh Kenner called it "the most hermetic poem in English, which they will still be elucidating in the 22nd century." His son Paul Z. (1943) has been for many years a distinguished interpreter of avant-garde American music, initially as a violinist, more recently as a conductor.

Books: *A*. Berkeley: University of California Press, 1978; *Autobiography/Louis Zukovsky*. New York: Grossman, 1970; *All: The Collected Short Poems, 1923–58*. London: Cape, 1966; *All: The Collected Short Poems, 1956–64* London: Cape, 1967; *Collected Fiction* (1961, 1970). Elmwood Park, IL: Dalkey Archive, 1990; *Complete Short Poetry*. Baltimore: Johns Hopkins University Press, 1991; *Prepositions: The Collected Critical Essays*. Expanded ed. Berkeley: University of California Press, 1981; *Bottom: On Shakespeare* (1963). Berkeley: University of California Press, 1986.

Correspondence: Ahearn, Barry, ed. *Pound/Zukofsky: Selected Letters*. New York: New Directions, 1987.

Web Site: http://www.lib.ksu.edu/depts/spec/findaids/pc94-07.html

Interpretation: Ahearn, Barry. *Zukofsky's "A": An Introduction*. Berkeley: University of California Press, 1983; Heller, Michael. *Conviction's Net of Branches: Essays on the Objectivist Poets and Poetry*. Carbondale: Southern Illinois University Press, 1985; Scroggins, Mark. *Upper Limit Music: The Writing of Louis Zukofsky*. Tuscaloosa, AL: University of Alabama Press, 1997; ——. *Louis Zukofsky and the Poetry of Knowledge*. Tuscaloosa, AL: University of Alabama Press, 1998; Stanley, Sandra Kumamoto. *Louis Zukovsky and the Transformation of Modern American Poetics*. Berkeley: University of California Press, 1994; Terrell, Carroll F., ed. *Louis Zukofsky: Man and Poet*. Orono: National Poetry Foundation, University of Maine, 1979.

Bibliography: Booth, Marcella. *A Catalogue of the Louis Zukofsky Manuscript Collection*. Austin, TX: Humanities Research Center, University of Texas Press, 1975.

POSTFACE

I mentioned in the preface my love of cultural dictionaries/encyclopedias and so would be remiss if I did not mention several that I consulted more than once, initially for facts such as dates, sometimes to discover an interpretative idea (usually acknowledged), at other times to knock them for failing to include individuals featured here.

Baigell, Matthew. *Dictionary of American Art*. New York: Harper & Row, 1979.

Bullock, Alan, and R. B. Woodings, eds. *20th Century Culture: A Biographical Companion*. New York: Harper & Row, 1983.

Burbank, Richard. *Twentieth Century Music*. New York: Facts on File, 1984.

Bureaud, Annick. *Guide International des Arts Electroniques/International Directory of Electronic Arts*. Paris, France: Chaos, 1992.

Evans, Martin M. *Contemporary Photographers*. 3d ed. Chicago & London: St. James's Press, 1995.

Greenhill, Eleanor S. *Dictionary of Art*. New York: Dell, 1974.

Griffiths, Paul. *The Thames and Hudson Encyclopedia of 20th-Century Music*. New York: Thames & Hudson, 1986.

Hamilton, Ian, ed. *The Oxford Companion to Twentieth-Century Poetry*. New York: Oxford University Press, 1994.

Hatje, Gerd, ed. *Encyclopedia of Modern Architecture*. London: Thames & Hudson, 1963.

Katz, Ephraim. *The Film Encyclopedia*. New York: Crowell, 1979. 2d ed. New York: HarperCollins, 1994.

Morgan, Ann Lee, and Colin Naylor, eds. *Contemporary Architects*. Chicago & London: St. James's Press, 1977.

Morton, Brian, and Pamela Collins, eds. *Contemporary Composers*. Chicago & London: St. James's Press, 1992.

Naylor, Colin, ed. *Contemporary Artists*. Chicago & London: St. James's Press, 1977, 1989.

———. *Contemporary Masterworks*. Chicago & London: St. James's Press, 1991.

Osborne, Harold, ed. *The Oxford Companion to Twentieth-Century Art*. New York: Oxford University Press, 1984.

Read, Herbert, consulting ed. *Encyclopedia of the Arts*. New York: Meredith, 1966.

Richard, Lionel. *Phaidon Encyclopedia of Expressionism*. London: Phaidon, 1978.

Runes, Dagobert D., and Harry G. Schrickel, eds. *Encyclopedia of the Arts*. New York: Philosophical Library, 1946.

Seymour-Smith, Martin. *Who's Who in Twentieth Century Literature*. London: Weidenfeld & Nicolson, 1976.

Slonimsky, Nicolas. *Bakers' Biographical Dictionary of Musicians*. 8th ed. New York: Schirmer, 1992.

Vinson, James, ed. *Contemporary Dramatists*. Chicago & London: St. James's Press, 1973, 1977, 1982 (ed. D. L. Kirkpatrick), 1987, (ed. K. A. Birney), 1993, (ed. Thomas Riggs), 1999.

———. *Contemporary Novelists*. London-New York: St. James-St. Martin's Press, 1972, 1976, 1981, 1986 (ed. Lesley Henderson), 1991, (ed. Susan Windisch Brown), 1996.

———. *Contemporary Poets*. London-New York: St. James-St. Martin's Press, 1970, 1975, 1980, 1985 (ed. Tracy Chevalier), 1990, (ed. Thomas Riggs, 1996).

Vinton, John, ed. *Dictionary of Contemporary Music*. New York: Dutton, 1974.

CONTRIBUTORS

H. R. BRITTAIN completed an undergraduate degree at the University of Wisconsin at Madison in the early 1990s, and has recently worked as an actor.

RICHARD CARLIN commissioned the first edition of this *Dictionary* as the founding publisher of a cappella books and then the second edition as the editor of Schirmer Books. He is the author of *Classical Music* (1992) and his own "biographical encyclopedia," *The Big Book of Country Music* (1995), among other texts on music.

MARK DANIEL COHEN is a New York-based art critic, sculptor, and graphic designer.

JOHN ROBERT COLOMBO is a Canadian poet, writer, and editor.

TONY COULTER is a Brooklyn writer who also produces radio programs featuring avant-garde music on WKCR in New York and WFMU in New Jersey.

ULRIKE MICHAL DORDA is a German-born historian who works as a two-way translator in New York.

CHARLES DORIA is a poet and translator who specializes in the classical and romance languages.

BOB GRUMMAN is a poet, literary critic, and the publisher of Runaway Spoon Press.

ROBERT HALLER administers the Anthology Film Archives in New York.

GEOF HUTH is a poet and micro-publisher living in Schenectady, NY, whose primary interest is linguistic invention.

GERALD JANECEK is a scholar specializing in the most avant-garde Russian artists and authors.

KATY MATHESON is an independent dance critic and former editor of *Dance Magazine* living in New York and outside Washington, DC.

FRED AND GLORIA McDARRAH produced *Photography Encyclopedia* (1999). He was for many years the photo editor at *The Village Voice*; she has written many travel guides with and without her husband.

MICHAEL PETERS is a poet, fiction-writer, and rock musician in the band Poem Rocket. Residing in New York, he founded his own press Aseidad.

DOUGLAS PUCHOWSKI edited and designed Richard Kostelanetz's *Political Essays* (1999). Living in Jersey City, NJ, he has recently been working as a freelance editor.

JOHN ROCCO completed a doctorate on James Joyce, in addition to editing books on the Grateful Dead, Nirvana, the Doors, and The Beastie Boys.

IGOR SATANOVSKY is a Russian-American poet/translator/visual artist. He currently resides in Florida where he leads The RUSH-INS Poetry project.

NICOLAS SLONIMSKY (1984–1995) was for decades the author of Baker's *Biographical Dictionary of Musicians* and *Music Since 1900* (1938; 5th ed., 1993), which are incomparable guides. Born in Russia, he didn't write in English until his thirties and, before long, became a master of American prose.

THE PRINCIPAL AUTHOR

RICHARD KOSTELANETZ, born in 1940 in New York City, has been an unaffiliated writer and artist for the past four decades, publishing numerous books of his fiction, poetry, experimental prose, criticism, and cultural history, as well as editing over three dozen anthologies of literature, esthetics, and social thought. He has received grants from private foundations, including Guggenheim, Pulitzer, Fulbright, Woodrow Wilson, Vogelstein, CCLM, ASCAP, and the DAAD Berliner Kunstlerprogramm, in addition to several individual fellowships from the National Endowment for the Arts. He has covered the artistic avant-garde since *The New American Arts* (1965), which he edited and coauthored, and has at one time or another published extended criticism of all the arts.

Wordsand, a retrospective of his art with words, numbers, and lines, in several media, toured several universities, while his texts for theater and music have been performed both live and on tape. A film he coproduced and codirected, *A Berlin Lost* (1984), received an award from the Ann Arbor Film Festival and subsequently toured with other award-winners. Portions of another film of his, the four-hour *Epiphanies* (1981–1993), were broadcast over the North German Television Network; the whole has been screened at the Anthology Film Achives in New York and other venues. His videotapes, most of them based on language and produced cameraless, have been exhibited in both one-person and group shows since 1975. German radio has broadcast not only his electro-acoustic compositions but his extended critical features about the art of radio in North America. For one semester in 1977, he was a Visiting Professor of American Studies and English at the University of Texas at Austin. Since his works fall into several fields, entries on him appear in various editions of *A Readers Guide to Twentieth-Century Writers* (ed. Peter Parker, Oxford), the *Merriam-Webster Encyclopedia of Literature*, *Contemporary Poets*, *Contemporary Novelists*, *Postmodern Fiction*, *Baker's Biographical Dictionary of Musicians*, *Directory of American Scholars*, and *Who's Who in American Art*, among other selective directories. He lives in lower Manhattan among thousands of books, hundreds of discs and audiotapes, and dozens of videotapes, as well as book-length projects in various stages of (in)completion.

INDEX OF NAMES

SUBJECT INDEX